D0787614

AMPHIBIAN SPECIES
OF THE WORLD

Compiled for the
Parties to the Convention on International Trade in Endangered Species
of Wild Fauna and Flora to serve as a
standard reference to amphibian nomenclature

under the auspices of the
World Congress of Herpetology
and its Checklist Committee

William E. Duellman, Chairman
Robert C. Drewes
Carl Gans
Alice G. C. Grandison
Marinus S. Hoogmoed

AMPHIBIAN
SPECIES OF
THE WORLD

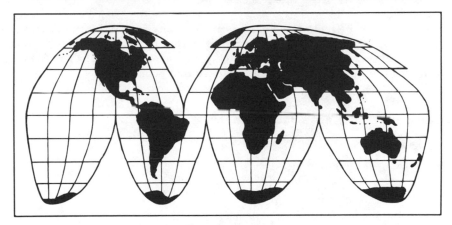

A TAXONOMIC AND GEOGRAPHICAL REFERENCE

Edited by

Darrel R. Frost

Published as a Joint Venture of
Allen Press, Inc.
and
The Association of Systematics Collections
Lawrence, Kansas, U.S.A.

AMPHIBIAN SPECIES OF THE WORLD
A TAXONOMIC AND GEOGRAPHIC REFERENCE

Published August 23, 1985

Library of Congress Cataloging in Publication Data

Frost, Darrel R.
  Amphibian species of the world.

  Bibliography: p.
  Includes index.
    1. Amphibians—Classification. 2. Amphibians—
Geographical distribution. I. Association of
Systematics Collections. II. Title.
QL645.F76   1985   597.6′012   85-9220

ISBN 0-942924-11-8

Copies of **Amphibian Species of the World: A Taxonomic and Geographic Reference** can be ordered from:

Amphibian Species of the World
P.O. Box 368
Lawrence, Kansas 66044
U.S.A.
(913) 864-4867

Foreword

Systematics is the study of diversity and relationships of organisms. Besides furnishing basic descriptions of organisms, systematics provides classifications designed to reflect the evolutionary relationships of organisms. As a consequence of progress in understanding these relationships, scientific names change and the higher taxonomy (i.e., the classification) of species is altered.

In practice, "new species" are described one at a time or in small groups. Interpretation of evolutionary relationships of species is usually addressed within the context of a study of a limited number of taxa, such as a species-group or genus. The literature of systematics is therefore dispersed, and much of it is not readily available to most workers. A comprehensive checklist of a large taxonomic group, such as the Amphibia, not only provides insights into higher-level taxonomic relationships, but makes the systematics literature available to herpetologists, biologists, and others for research or more immediate applications.

Today, public issues like environmental conservation, species preservation, maintenance of biotic diversity, and genetic engineering are placing greater demands on the systematics community to provide information on organisms and their relationships. The Convention on International Trade in Endangered Species of Wild Fauna and Flora (CITES) has particular need for authoritative, up-to-date checklists of species. The Management and Scientific Authorities in the Party-Nations need these checklists to effectively implement the terms of the treaty. Common usage of species names and an understanding of organismal relationships are essential for accurate communications of experimental results among researchers in other fields of biology. Curators find comprehensive checklists essential for managing museum collections and cataloging specimens.

In response to these fundamental needs, the Association of Systematics Collections (ASC) initiated its taxonomic checklist series. Funding to develop the initial data bases for the checklists was provided by the United Nations Environment Programme through the CITES Secretariat. Publication of these checklists is made possible under a Joint Venture Agreement between the Association of Systematics Collections and Allen Press, Inc., both of Lawrence, Kansas, USA.

ASC's goal has been to publish checklists that are comprised of contributions from large numbers of professionals. Development of these checklists in a relatively short time has been possible by employing computer technology and data base management techniques. The information provided reflects the current taxonomic status of species. There has been no attempt to use the published checklists to redefine taxonomic relationships. And, the checklists have been subject to extensive review within the professional communities involved. Our intent has been to provide reference volumes that would serve as "dictionaries" of species names and as standard references to taxonomic relationships for the professional and layman.

In 1982, with contributions from 189 mammalogists from throughout the world, the ASC and Allen Press, Inc., published *Mammal Species of the World: A Taxonomic and Geographic Reference* (Honacki *et al.*, 694 pages) as the first in the vertebrate checklist series. Editorial responsibility for updating the mammal checklist rests with the Checklist Committee of the American Society of Mammalogists.

Amphibian Species of the World is the second volume in the vertebrate checklist series. This volume represents a synthesis of the present systematic knowledge on amphibians based on contributions from 59 professional herpetologists from 21 countries, who cooperated over the past three years in its development. The World Congress of Herpetology has appointed an editorial committee to assure long-term maintenance of this checklist. Based on what was learned in the development of the mammal checklist, we have incorporated into this checklist additional information categories, such as "Type Species", "Original Name", and "Type(s)", the latter noting the institution where type material is deposited. In addition to the complete cross-index to scientific names used in the list, two appendices are provided. One lists all periodical and book titles abbreviated in the text. The other provides a translation of the abbreviations used to identify the institutions where type material is stored.

It is impossible to estimate the rate at which this list will change. However, of the 4014 species referenced in this volume, nearly one-third were described in the last twenty-five years. Therefore, this edition should not be viewed as the final or definitive statement on amphibian species nomenclature. Rather, it represents a consensus view of amphibian taxonomy today.

The data presented in this volume will be revised and updated in collaboration with the World Congress of Herpetology. You can assist by informing us of errors in the present text and providing references or copies of pertinent taxonomic literature. Moreover, if you have expertise in a particular taxonomic group, we encourage you to serve as a reviewer for subsequent editions. We welcome your comments as well as any references to pertinent literature that may have been overlooked. Direct correspondence to: The Association of Systematics Collections, % Museum of Natural History, The University of Kansas, Lawrence, Kansas 66045, USA.

STEPHEN R. EDWARDS
Executive Director
Association of Systematics Collections

Preface

The classification of organisms and lists of species in various groups and/or in different parts of the world have been major contributions of taxonomists since Linnaeus. Throughout the history of systematic biology these kinds of compilations have provided basic data for various kinds of investigations, principally systematic and biogeographic studies. Non-taxonomists commonly view a checklist as the last word on the taxonomy and distribution of a group of organisms; however, systematists familiar with the group of organisms are fully aware that a checklist represents a basis for further refinement. The present checklist of amphibians of the world is no exception.

The last comprehensive coverage of the amphibians of the world consisted of Boulenger's catalogues of the amphibians in the British Museum in 1882. Detailed checklists of various families of frogs were included in Das Tierreich (e.g., Nieden, 1923; Ahl, 1931; Gorham, 1966; Duellman, 1977), and an account of the caecilians of the world was prepared by Taylor (1968). Gorham (1974) published a list of species of amphibians but provided no citations, type localities, or distributions.

The present *Amphibian Species of the World* is the first list of its kind in this century. The preparation of an accurate taxonomic synopsis of this kind is beyond the scope of expertise of any one individual or small group. Therefore, the members of the editorial committee for this volume were chosen not necessarily for their expertise within given families or groups of amphibians, but rather for their knowledge of, and acquaintance with, specialists the world over. *Amphibian Species of the World* is truly an international endeavor representing the efforts of 59 contributors and reviewers in 21 countries.

Originally it was hoped that the list would contain synonyms and subspecies. However, it soon became obvious that the inclusion of synonyms (and their citations and type localities) would not only increase the size of the volume beyond the reasonable limitations that had been set for it, but would require much more effort by the contributors and reviewers.

Any checklist is out of date before it is published. The data base for this checklist is being maintained on computer files; these files will be updated so that a new up-to-date version of the list can be produced at any time in the future. This will be a continuing project under the editorial sponsorship of the World Congress of Herpetology in collaboration with ASC, which will be responsible for maintaining and publishing the lists.

The editorial committee extends its deep gratitude and appreciation to the amphibian systematists from throughout the world (see *List of Contributors and Reviewers*) whose combined efforts have made this checklist possible. We are especially indebted to Darrel R. Frost, who dedicated the better part of four years of his life to this checklist, and whose diligence has resulted in a carefully researched document.

WORLD CONGRESS OF HERPETOLOGY AMPHIBIAN CHECKLIST COMMITTEE

ROBERT C. DREWES
CARL GANS
ALICE G. C. GRANDISON

MARINUS S. HOOGMOED
WILLIAM E. DUELLMAN (CHAIRMAN)

Table of Contents

Introduction

Amphibian Species of the World, an annotated checklist of the 4014 nominal species of amphibians, is the culmination of an international cooperative effort of 59 amphibian biologists and does not represent the views of any one person. Although we have tried to bring amphibian nomenclature into compliance with the International Code of Zoological Nomenclature, this checklist is an attempt to report the state of the literature of amphibian systematics and is in no way intended to standardize or institutionalize amphibian taxonomy. Systematics is currently undergoing great progress in both theory and application; for this reason the taxonomy of amphibians should be expected to change considerably in the next few years. Do not be discouraged by the apparent lack of consensus in systematic herpetology appearing within this volume. Controversies and lacunae of information have been highlighted in the hope that these problem areas will receive the attention that they deserve.

For ease of use this introduction is divided into four sections: (1) historical background; (2) review of the rules of list-compilation; (3) description of the process of compilation; and (4) an explanation of the organization of the taxonomic accounts. To avoid any misunderstandings when using this volume the reader should at least read the sections that explain the taxonomic accounts.

Historical Background

As the result of a resolution by the Parties to the Convention on International Trade in Endangered Species of Wild Fauna and Flora (CITES) to create a superior secondary source of taxonomic information on vertebrates, the Association of Systematics Collections (ASC) began in the spring of 1981 to pursue the objective of constructing a checklist of amphibians, along the lines of *Mammal Species of the World* (1982), which was reaching completion at that time. First contacted was William E. Duellman, who agreed to act as coordinator and chairman of the editorial/steering committee that would set policy. Subsequently, Darrel R. Frost was hired as editor/compiler and Robert C. Drewes, Carl Gans, Alice G. C. Grandison, and Marinus S. Hoogmoed were recruited to complete the committee. The editorial/steering committee (with the exception of Hoogmoed) and the editor met in June of 1981 to set the standards for the projected amphibian volume and to identify potential contributors for various geographic and taxonomic sections. Policies set at this meeting (and in subsequent correspondence) were followed by the editor. From 1982 to mid-1984 the volume was compiled. In 1984 an agreement was reached with the World Congress of Herpetology, through its Secretary General, Kraig Adler, to transfer editorial sponsorship (through the existing committee) to the World Congress of Herpetology and for the World Congress of Herpetology to accept responsibility for future updating and editions in cooperation with ASC.

Rules of Compilation

Amphibian Species of the World has been compiled as a summary of the state of the literature of amphibian taxonomy. Except for suprageneric taxonomy and a very few exceptional cases, a rule of following the most recent revisions has been arbitrarily applied. To ameliorate problems created by this arbitrary rule we have allowed virtually unlimited comment by contributors and reviewers. Users of this volume should pay close attention to the content of these comments. Although *contributors* had primary responsibility for the construction of sections of the checklist, they could not exercise editorial control over the comments included by *reviewers,* although they could provide rebuttal comments. No attempt was made to limit the number of reviewers or the scope of their reviews. Where seemingly intractable problems presented themselves the editorial/steering committee was polled by the editor and a resolution was reached.

To the best of our knowledge, the nomenclature used in *Amphibian Species of the World* complies with the requirements of the International Code of Zoological Nomenclature (Ed. 3). Although at the time of this writing the third edition of the Code had not been published (scheduled to appear in 1985) it is necessary to follow the Code that will be in force for the useful life of this volume. The new Code has stricter rules on what constitutes a justified emendation, and a number of spellings had to be revised to meet this new standard. Unjustified emendations of spellings because of the confounding of Scandinavian and German umlauts have also required a number of corrections.

Process of Compilation

The editorial/steering committee decided that the best way to accomplish the task of developing the checklist was to recruit, where possible, *contributors* to construct sections of the list and for the editor to submit these sections to *reviewers* for augmentation, comment, and correction. In reality, many of the sections had substantial improvements made by workers only attributed as *reviewers.* Other sections did not have contributors, either because the sections were too small or because they required more work than most workers could afford to spend. These sections were completed in cooperation between the editor and the reviewers.

To facilitate construction of the list a skeleton checklist was compiled by the editor. Various sections were then sent to contributors for completion. Corrected/completed sections were then returned to the editor for addition to the computerized data base. A corrected section, as well as the earlier working copy, was then sent back to the contributor, either for additional work or to assure that the changes had, in fact, been made in the data base. Sections completed to the satisfaction of the editor and contributor were then sent to one or more reviewers for augmentation and correction. As with the contributors, this became an iterative procedure.

The process of compilation was continued until June of 1984 when 'final' (except for literature standardization and style editing) copies were sent to the contributors and editorial/checklist committee for perusal, final corrections, and approval. Upon return of these corrected copies, the data-gathering process was finished and editing and standardization of literature citations (see *Appendix I: Literature Abbreviations*) began in earnest. The checklist, therefore, can be regarded as being complete to 1 June 1984.

Organization of the Accounts

Higher taxonomy—The higher taxonomy employed represents a consensus reasonably close to the taxonomy used by most workers. This taxonomy should be considered an index to the names of taxa rather than a set of formal statements of phylogenetic relationship. Comments under the headings of higher taxa illustrate some of the contention currently at work in the systematic herpetological commmunity. Each higher taxon (Class, Order, Family, and Subfamily) has an account, arranged alphabetically within the taxonomic hierarchy. That is, Orders are alphabetical within the Class, Families within Orders, Subfamilies within Families, Genera within Subfamilies, and Species within Genera. Putative phylogenetic order has been rejected in favor of alphabetical organization to increase the usefulness of this volume for non-taxonomists.

Scientific name, authority, year of publication, and citation—In each account the taxon name, as well as the author of the name and the literature citation of the published description, is given. When the author and year of publication of the name appear in parentheses (only in species accounts) that means that the species was described in a genus other than the one in which it now resides. In these cases an additional line of information, "ORIGINAL NAME", appears. In this line the original spelling of the specific epithet as well as the genus of its original combination appears. The literature citation notes only the first nomenclaturally valid use of the name and not the entire paper or book in which it appeared. Complete serial and book titles may be found in *Appendix I: Literature Abbreviations*. In cases where the actual date of publication is known to differ from the printed publication date a second date in quotations follows the actual date; this quoted date is the date stated in the original paper. In a few Family accounts a date appears in parentheses after the regular date of publication. This parenthetical date is the date to be used for reasons of priority under the provisions of Article 40 of the International Code of Zoological Nomenclature (Ed. 3).

Type species—In generic accounts the type species (generic name bearer) appears. In most cases it is stated how that species was designated (e.g., by monotypy or tautonomy). In addition, comments regarding some aspect of the nomenclature of the type species may appear in this line of information.

Type specimen(s)—In species accounts the known status of primary types is stated. The information ranges from a simple 'not traced' or 'unknown' to museum abbreviations and registry number(s) of types (see *Appendix II: Museum Abbreviations*). In cases where changes in type status (lectotype or neotype designations) have been made, a comment noting such appears. Further comments noting disagreements and other pertinent information may also appear.

Type locality—In each species account a type locality, the locality at which the type specimen was collected, is stated. When this locality is enclosed within quotation marks, this means that the stated locality was taken as a direct quotation from the original publication. If the stated locality is not enclosed in quotation marks, the locality was taken either from some secondary source or it is a translation of the original statement. Checking original publications has resulted in the detection of a number of errors that have been perpetuated by careless use of literature. To reduce further error, information added for clarity by the editor was placed in brackets, and non-quoted type localities have been reproduced exactly as received from contributors, reviewers, and secondary literature. Type locality corrections and restrictions have been noted also in this line. However, restrictions have no status under the International Code of Zoological Nomenclature except when associated with lectotype or neotype designations (but see Recommendations 72H and 74A).

Distribution—Distributions are stated as accurately as possible under format restrictions. Contributors and reviewers were not restricted to basing their statements of distributions on published information. That objective was considered impossible to achieve and probably not desirable in many cases. Spellings of place names follow *Webster's New Geographical Dictionary* (1980) (G. & C. Merriam Company, Springfield, Massachusetts) as a standard, except that Pinyin transliterations of Chinese place names were used whenever possible.

Comments—A general comment section has been appended to accounts where necessary. Comments dealing with taxonomic controversy, distributional uncertainty, citations to recent revisions, and synonymies have been included in this section. Comments by contributors or reviewers without citation to published literature have been noted with the initials of the person supplying the comment. These comments form one of the most important parts of this checklist in that they supply the user with more depth and access to corollary literature than would a simple checklist.

Attribution—Contributors and reviewers are attributed by name with the sections on which they worked. Contributors and reviewers who worked on sections larger than families are attributed at the level of constituent families as well as at the highest taxonomic category of their work. Those who worked on geographic subsets of taxa have the geographic region of their contribution or review noted in parentheses. This information is also available under *List of Contributors and Reviewers*.

Protected status—Amphibian species governed by the USA Endangered Species Act (USA ESA) and those listed in the Appendices of the Convention on International Trade in Endangered Species of Wild Flora and Fauna (CITES) have been noted where appropriate. Dates of listing are also included within parentheses in this line of information. The Federal Register (U.S. Govt. Printing Office), for USA ESA, and the CITES Appendices should be consulted for details. This information was current as of 31 December 1984.

Acknowledgments

To acknowledge all of the people whose efforts furthered the development of this volume would take more pages than space allows. A list of contributors and reviewers is included separately; these contributors and reviewers have consistently placed the development of this volume over any proprietary view of taxonomy that they may have had. Their altruism and good scientific attitudes have set a high standard for future cooperation in herpetology. Glancing through the pages of this checklist it is easy to underestimate the number of hours spent by these workers checking details and searching out necessary literature. Even the smallest contribution or review required considerable time and effort.

It is appropriate, however, that a few individuals be recognized here whose efforts far exceeded expectations. Among the contributors a number stand out for the quality of their efforts (see *List of Contributors and Reviewers* for more complete information): Leo J. Borkin, David C. Cannatella, William E. Duellman, Sushil Dutta, Alice G. C. Grandison, Marinus S. Hoogmoed, Shuqin Hu, Raymond Laurent, Masafumi Matsui, Jean-Luc Perret, J. C. Tinsley, and Richard G. Zweifel. These workers produced very useful, informative sections for poorly known taxa and/or regions.

I thank particularly the World Congress of Herpetology Checklist Committee. The efforts of this committee to set policy, make initial contacts, and cajole reluctant workers did much to improve the degree of involvement of herpetologists in this project. William E. Duellman, beyond his role as chairman of the committee and contributor of a large section of the list, allowed his personal library to suffer constant heavy use. He also read the entire manuscript in detail. Without his encyclopedic knowledge of frog systematics and systematists, this volume would have suffered. Robert C. Drewes' personal acquaintance with African herpetologists had more positive effects on the project than he is probably aware. The personal contacts of Carl Gans in Eastern Europe and Asia were of great assistance, as were his pragmatism and common sense throughout the development of this project. Alice G. C. Grandison came to the rescue on several occasions; her willingness to take on *Phrynobatrachus* at a late date, after already preparing the section on African bufonids, will not soon be forgotten. Her frankness in correspondence and honest appraisals saved a great deal of time. Marinus S. Hoogmoed, in addition to preparing the extensive section on Neotropical bufonids, read closely the entire manuscript and made extensive corrections and additions. His help in chasing down obscure literature was also appreciated.

Richard G. Zweifel graciously supplied his unpublished list of current frog names without which this checklist would probably still be incomplete. Jay M. Savage and John D. Lynch were unparalleled sources of nomenclatural wisdom. Savage supplied a preprint of the new International Code of Zoological Nomenclature (Ed. 3) and was always available for questions. Lynch took a particular interest in nomenclature of family-group taxa. Paulo E. Vanzolini was of help in locating old literature and in providing the benefit of his extensive experience in Brazil.

Finally, I thank the United Nations Environment Programme (UNEP) through the Convention on International Trade in Endangered Species of Wild

Fauna and Flora (CITES) for continued financial support of this project. The willingness of these organizations to support construction of taxonomic compendia by systematists should be applauded. The wisdom of this choice will become more obvious with time as the need for access to systematic literature by conservationists and governmental agencies becomes more pressing.

DARREL R. FROST

List of Contributors and Reviewers

Angel Alcala
REVIEWED: Philippine species.
ADDRESS: Department of Biology, Silliman University, Dumaguete City, Philippines.

J.-L. Amiet
CONTRIBUTED: *Cardioglossa* (Arthroleptinae) and Astylosterninae (Arthroleptidae), *Petropedetes* and *Phrynodon* (Petropedetinae, Ranidae).
REVIEWED: Anuran species of Cameroon (except for Arthroleptinae).
ADDRESS: Laboratoire de Zoologie, Université de Yaoundé, B.P. 812, Yaoundé, Cameroon.

Steven C. Anderson
REVIEWED: Species of southwestern Asia (Turkey to Arabian Peninsula, east through Caucasus region to Pakistan, Afghanistan, and adjacent USSR).
ADDRESS: Department of Biological Sciences, College of the Pacific, Stockton, California 95211, USA.

Rose M. A. Blommers-Schlösser
CONTRIBUTED: Cophylinae, *Dyscophus* (Dyscophinae), and Scaphiophryninae (Microhylidae), Mantellinae (Ranidae), and Madagascan Rhacophoridae.
REVIEWED: Madagascan species of Hyperoliidae, *Microhyla* (Microhylinae), and Raninae.
ADDRESS: Herenstraat 102, 3911 JH Rhenen, Netherlands.

Werner C. A. Bokermann
REVIEWED: Brazilian species.
ADDRESS: Parque Zoologico de São Paulo, C.P. 12954, 01000 São Paulo, S.P., Brazil.

Leo J. Borkin
CONTRIBUTED: Palearctic Raninae (Ranidae) (with some overlap with S. Hu and M. Matsui).
REVIEWED: Raninae and species of Palearctic Region, including all of China.
ADDRESS: Department of Herpetology, Zoological Institute, USSR Academy of Sciences, Leningrad 199034, USSR.

Arden H. Brame, Jr. II
CONTRIBUTED: Caudata.
ADDRESS: 9545 E. Guess Street, Rosemead, California 91770, USA.

Edmund D. Brodie
REVIEWED: Caudata.
ADDRESS: Department of Biology, UTA Box 19489, University of Texas at Arlington, Arlington, Texas 76019, USA.

Walter C. Brown
CONTRIBUTED: *Batrachylodes, Ceratobatrachus, Discodeles, Palmatorappia,* and *Platymantis* (Raninae, Ranidae).
REVIEWED: Philippine species.
ADDRESS: Department of Herpetology, California Academy of Sciences, Golden Gate Park, San Francisco, California 94118, USA.

Jonathan A. Campbell
REVIEWED: Mexican and Central American species.
ADDRESS: Department of Biology, UTA Box 19489, University of Texas at Arlington, Arlington, Texas 76019, USA.

David C. Cannatella
CONTRIBUTED: Centrolenidae (with W. E. Duellman), Leptodactylidae (excluding *Eleutherodactylus*), and Heleophrynidae.
REVIEWED: New World Bufonidae, Phyllomedusinae (Hylidae), and higher classification.
ADDRESS: Museum of Natural History, The University of Kansas, Lawrence, Kansas 66045, USA.

Ulisses Caramaschi
REVIEWED: Brazilian species.
ADDRESS: Departamento de Zoologia, Instituto Básico de Biologia Médica e Agrícola, Universidade Estadual Paulista, Rubião Junior, 18.610 Botucatu, S.P., Brazil. [Current address: Sector de Herpetologia—Departamento Vertebrados, Museu Nacional do Rio de Janeiro/UFRJ, Quinta da Boa Vista, s/no., 20.942 Rio de Janeiro, R.J., Brazil.]

Gustavo Casas-Andreu
REVIEWED: Mexican species.
ADDRESS: Instituto de Biología, Universidad Nacional Autónoma de México, Apartado Postal 70-153, México 20, D.F., Mexico.

Alan Channing
CONTRIBUTED: *Strongylopus* and African *Tomopterna* (Raninae, Ranidae).
REVIEWED: South African species.
ADDRESS: Biochemistry Department, University of the Western Cape, Private Bag X17, Bellville 7530, Rep. South Africa.

Barry T. Clarke
CONTRIBUTED: Discoglossidae and Leiopelmatidae.
ADDRESS: Department of Zoology, British Museum (Natural History), Cromwell Road, London SW7 5BD, United Kingdom.

Ronald I. Crombie
REVIEWED: New World Anura.
ADDRESS: Division of Amphibians and Reptiles, National Museum of Natural History, Smithsonian Institution, Washington, D.C. 20560, USA.

J. C. Daniel
REVIEWED: Species of India and Sri Lanka.
ADDRESS: Bombay Natural History Society, Hornbill House, Shahid Bhagat Singh Road, Bombay 400 023, India.

Margaret Davies
REVIEWED: Species of Australia and New Guinea.
ADDRESS: Department of Zoology, University of Adelaide, G.P.O. Box 498, Adelaide, South Australia 5001, Australia.

Robert C. Drewes
REVIEWED: Hyperoliidae.
ADDRESS: Department of Herpetology, California Academy of Sciences, Golden Gate Park, San Francisco, California 94118, USA.

William E. Duellman
CONTRIBUTED: Centrolenidae (with D. C. Cannatella), Hylidae, and Pseudidae.
REVIEWED: All Amphibia.
ADDRESS: Museum of Natural History, The University of Kansas, Lawrence, Kansas 66045, USA.

Sushil Dutta
CONTRIBUTED: Raninae (Ranidae) of southern Asia (with some overlap with S. Hu and M. Matsui).
REVIEWED: Species of India and Sri Lanka.
ADDRESS: Museum of Natural History, The University of Kansas, Lawrence, Kansas 66045, USA.

Oscar Flores-Villela
REVIEWED: Species of Mexico.
ADDRESS: Instituto de Biología and Museo de Zoología, Facultad de Ciencias, Universidad Nacional Autónoma de México, Apartado Postal 70-399, México, D.F. 04510, Mexico.

Linda S. Ford
REVIEWED: Dendrobatidae and Central American *Eleutherodactylus* (Leptodactylidae).
ADDRESS: Museum of Natural History, The University of Kansas, Lawrence, Kansas 66045, USA.

Ramón Formas
CONTRIBUTED: Rhinodermatidae.
REVIEWED: *Alsodes, Batrachyla, Caudiverbera, Eupsophus, Hylorhina, Insuetophrynus,* and *Telmatobufo* (Leptodactylidae).
ADDRESS: Instituto de Zoología, Universidad Austral de Chile, Casilla de Correo 567, Valdivia, Chile.

Alice G. C. Grandison
CONTRIBUTED: African Bufonidae and *Phrynobatrachus* (Petropedetinae, Ranidae).
ADDRESS: Department of Zoology, British Museum (Natural History), Cromwell Road, London SW7 5BD, United Kingdom.

Eduardo Gudynas
CONTRIBUTED: *Pseudopaludicola* (Leptodactylinae, Leptodactylidae).
REVIEWED: Species of Uruguay, northeastern Argentina, and southern Brazil.
ADDRESS: Centro Educativo Don Orione, Departamento de Biología, Casilla de Correo 13125, Montevideo, Uruguay.

Keith A. Harding
REVIEWED: *Ascaphus* (Leiopelmatidae), New World Bufonidae, Centrolenidae, Dendrobatidae, New World Microhylinae (Microhylidae), Pipinae (Pipidae), Pseudidae, Ambystomatidae, Amphiumidae, Plethodontidae, Proteidae, and Sirenidae.
ADDRESS: 5 Drakewalls Place, Gunnislake, Cornwall PL18 9EJ, United Kingdom.

W. Ronald Heyer
REVIEWED: Leptodactylidae.
ADDRESS: Division of Amphibians and Reptiles, National Museum of Natural History, Smithsonian Institution, Washington, D.C. 20560, USA.

Richard Highton
REVIEWED: Caudata of USA.
ADDRESS: Department of Zoology, University of Maryland, College Park, Maryland 20742, USA.

David M. Hillis
CONTRIBUTED: Nearctic *Bufo* (Bufonidae) and New World *Rana* (Ranidae).
ADDRESS: Museum of Natural History, The University of Kansas, Lawrence, Kansas 66045, USA.

Marinus S. Hoogmoed
CONTRIBUTED: South and Central American Bufonidae and *Adelophryne* and *Phyzelaphryne* (Telmatobiinae, Leptodactylidae).
REVIEWED: All Amphibia.
ADDRESS: Rijksmuseum van Natuurlijke Historie, Postbus 9517, 2300 RA Leiden, Netherlands.

Kim M. Howell
REVIEWED: Species of East Africa.
ADDRESS: Department of Zoology, Box 35064, University of Dar es Salaam, Dar es Salaam, Tanzania.

Shuqin Hu
CONTRIBUTED: Chinese Raninae (with L. J. Borkin and M. Matsui).
REVIEWED: Chinese species.
ADDRESS: Chengdu Institute of Biology, Academia Sinica, P.O. Box 416, Chengdu, Sichuan, P. R. China.

Robert F. Inger
CONTRIBUTED: Asian Bufonidae, Old World Microhylinae (Microhylidae), and non-Madagascan Rhacophoridae.
REVIEWED: Megophryinae (Pelobatidae).
ADDRESS: Division of Amphibians and Reptiles, Field Museum of Natural History, Roosevelt Road at Lake Shore Drive, Chicago, Illinois 60605, USA.

Rafael Joglar
REVIEWED: West Indian *Eleutherodactylus* (Telmatobiinae, Leptodactylidae).
ADDRESS: Museum of Natural History, The University of Kansas, Lawrence, Kansas 66045, USA.

Enrique La Marca
REVIEWED: Dendrobatidae and Venezuelan species of Anura.
ADDRESS: School of Life Sciences, University of Nebraska, Lincoln, Nebraska 68508, USA. [Current address: Calle 15 con Carrera 7ma, Edificio La Marca, Apdo. 1, Guanare, Portuguesa 3310, Venezuela.]

Raymond Laurent
CONTRIBUTED: Arthroleptinae (excluding *Cardioglossa*) (Arthroleptidae), Hemisidae, and Hyperoliidae.
REVIEWED: Species of Africa and higher classification.
ADDRESS: Fundación Miguel Lillo, Director of PRHERP (CONICET), Miguel Lillo 205, Tucumán 4000, Argentina.

Esteban O. Lavilla
REVIEWED: *Alsodes* and *Telmatobius* (Telmatobiinae, Leptodactylidae).
ADDRESS: Fundación Miguel Lillo, Miguel Lillo 205, Tucumán 4000, Argentina.

John D. Lynch
CONTRIBUTED: *Eleutherodactylus* (excluding West Indian species) (Telmatobiinae, Leptodactylidae).
REVIEWED: Higher taxonomy.
ADDRESS: School of Life Sciences, University of Nebraska, Lincoln, Nebraska 68508, USA.

Masafumi Matsui
CONTRIBUTED: Megophryinae (Pelobatidae) and East Asian Raninae (overlapping with L. J. Borkin, S. Dutta, and S. Hu) (Ranidae).
REVIEWED: East Asian species.
ADDRESS: Biological Laboratory, Yoshida College, Kyoto University, Sakyo, Kyoto 606, Japan.

Roy W. McDiarmid
REVIEWED: Brachycephalidae and Neotropical Bufonidae.
ADDRESS: U.S. Fish and Wildlife Service, National Museum of Natural History, Washington, D.C. 20560, USA.

Craig E. Nelson
CONTRIBUTED: New World Microhylinae (Microhylidae).
ADDRESS: Department of Biology, Jordan Hall 138, University of Indiana, Bloomington, Indiana 47405, USA.

Ronald A. Nussbaum
CONTRIBUTED: Sooglossidae.
REVIEWED: Gymnophiona.
ADDRESS: Museum of Zoology, The University of Michigan, Ann Arbor, Michigan 48104, USA.

Jean-Luc Perret
CONTRIBUTED: African Raninae (excluding *Strongylopus* and *Tomopterna*) (Ranidae).
REVIEWED: Hyperoliidae and *Petropedetes* (Petropedetinae, Ranidae).
ADDRESS: Museum d'Histoire Naturelle, Route de Malagnou, C.P. 434, 1211 Geneve 6, Switzerland.

John C. Poynton
REVIEWED: African species.
ADDRESS: Department of Biological Sciences, University of Natal, King George V Avenue, Durban, Natal 4001, Rep. South Africa.

William F. Pyburn
REVIEWED: Centrolenidae, New World Hylidae, and New World Microhylinae (Microhylidae).
ADDRESS: Department of Biology, UTA Box 19489, University of Texas at Arlington, Arlington, Texas 76019, USA.

Juan A. Rivero
REVIEWED: *Atelopus* (Bufonidae), Dendrobatidae, and South American *Eleutherodactylus* (Telmatobiinae, Leptodactylidae).
ADDRESS: Departamento de Biología, Universidad de Puerto Rico, Mayagüez, Puerto Rico 00708, USA.

Jay M. Savage
REVIEWED: Centrolenidae, Dendrobatidae, nomenclature, higher taxonomy, and Central American species.
ADDRESS: Department of Biology, University of Miami, P.O. Box 249118, Coral Gables, Florida 33124, USA.

Arne Schiøtz
REVIEWED: Hyperoliidae and *Chiromantis* (Rhacophoridae).
ADDRESS: Danmarks Akvarium, 2920 Charlottenlund, Denmark.

Albert Schwartz
CONTRIBUTED: *Peltophryne* (Bufonidae) and West Indian *Eleutherodactylus* (Leptodactylidae).
REVIEWED: West Indian species.
ADDRESS: Miami-Dade Community College, North Campus, Miami, Florida 33167, USA.

Norman J. Scott, Jr.
REVIEWED: Central and South American species.
ADDRESS: Denver Wildlife Research Center, U.S. Fish and Wildlife Service, Museum of Southwestern Biology, University of New Mexico, Albuquerque, New Mexico 87131, USA.

Richard Thomas
REVIEWED: West Indian species.
ADDRESS: Departamento de Biología, Universidad de Puerto Rico, Río Piedras, Puerto Rico 00931, USA.

R. C. Tinsley
CONTRIBUTED: Xenopodinae (Pipidae).
ADDRESS: School of Biological Sciences, Queen Mary College (University of London), London E1 4NS, United Kingdom.

Michael J. Tyler
CONTRIBUTED: Myobatrachidae.
REVIEWED: Species of Australia and New Guinea.
ADDRESS: Department of Zoology, University of Adelaide, G.P.O. Box 498, Adelaide, South Australia 5001, Australia.

Paulo E. Vanzolini
REVIEWED: Brazilian species and nomenclature of higher taxa.
ADDRESS: Museu de Zoologia/USP, C.P. 7172, 01.051 São Paulo, S.P., Brazil.

David B. Wake
REVIEWED: Caudata.
ADDRESS: Museum of Vertebrate Zoology, University of California, Berkeley, California 94720, USA.

Marvalee H. Wake
CONTRIBUTED: Gymnophiona.
ADDRESS: Department of Zoology and Museum of Vertebrate Zoology, University of California, Berkeley, California 94720, USA.

Ermi Zhao

REVIEWED: Species of China.

ADDRESS: Chengdu Institute of Biology, Academia Sinica, P.O. Box 416, Chengdu, Sichuan, P. R. China.

Richard G. Zweifel

CONTRIBUTED: Asterophryinae and Genyophryninae (Microhylidae).

REVIEWED: Species of New Guinea.

ADDRESS: Department of Herpetology, American Museum of Natural History, Central Park West at 79th Street, New York, New York 10024, USA.

CHECKLIST OF
AMPHIBIAN SPECIES OF THE WORLD
CLASS AMPHIBIA

CLASS: **Amphibia** Linnaeus, 1758.

CITATION: Syst. Nat., Ed. 10, 1:194.

DISTRIBUTION: Cosmopolitan except for extreme northern latitudes, Antarctica, and most oceanic islands.

COMMENT: The phylogenetic relationships of the groups within the Class are problematical. Jarvik, 1968, In Ørvig (ed.), Current Problems of Lower Vertebrate Phylogeny, Nobel Symp. 4:497–527; Schmalhausen, 1968, The Origin of Terrestrial Vertebrates, Academic Press; Wake, 1970, Forma et Functio, 3:33–60; and Shishkin, 1973, The Morphology of the Early Amphibia and Some Problems of Tetrapod Evolution, Publ. House 'Nauka', Moscow, considered the Recent Amphibia to be polyphyletic while Eaton, 1959, Univ. Kansas Publ. Mus. Nat. Hist., 12:155–180; Szarski, 1962, Q. Rev. Biol., 37:189–241; Parsons and Williams, 1963, Q. Rev. Biol., 38:26–53; Estes and Reig, 1973, In Vial (ed.), Evol. Biol. Anurans:11–63; Rage and Janvier, 1982, Geobios, Lyon, Mém. Spec., 6:65–83; Lebedkina, 1979, Evolution of the Skull in Amphibians, Publ. House 'Nauka', Moscow; and Gardiner, 1983, Zool. J. Linn. Soc., 74:207–232, considered the modern groups of Amphibia to form a monophyletic group. Lombard, 1979, Biol. J. Linn. Soc., 11:19–76, discussed alternative views, but suggested, on the basis of ear anatomy, that the modern amphibian groups formed a monophyletic group. An increasing number of systematists (e.g., Gaffney, 1979, Bull. Carnegie Mus. Nat. Hist., 13:92–105, and Wiley, 1979, Zool. J. Linn. Soc., 67:149–179) reject the Amphibia as a valid taxon for those tetrapods (fossil and living) that are not amniotes. Gaffney, in particular, noted groups of extinct "Amphibia" that may be more closely related to amniotes than to the modern amphibians, the Lissamphibia.

REVIEWERS: David C. Cannatella (DCC) (Higher taxonomic accounts); William E. Duellman (WED); Marinus S. Hoogmoed (MSH); Raymond Laurent (RL) (Higher taxonomic accounts); John D. Lynch (JDL) (Higher taxonomic accounts); Jay M. Savage (JMS) (Higher taxonomic accounts).

ORDER ANURA

ORDER: **Anura** Rafinesque, 1815.
  CITATION: Analyse Nat.:78.
  DISTRIBUTION: Cosmopolitan except for extreme northern latitudes, Antarctica, and most
    oceanic islands.
  COMMENT: As first formed, the group name was Anuria, an explicit suborder. Kluge and
    Farris, 1969, Syst. Zool., 18:1–32; Inger, 1967, Evolution, 21:369–384; Lynch, 1973, *In*
    Vial (ed.), Evol. Biol. Anurans:133–183; and Duellman, 1975, Occas. Pap. Mus. Nat.
    Hist. Univ. Kansas, 42:1–14, discussed anuran phylogeny. Starrett, 1973, *In* Vial (ed.),
    Evol. Biol. Anurans:252–271, provided a classification based on larval morphology but
    this was contested by Sokol, 1975, Copeia, 1975:1–23. See also Laurent, 1979, Bull. Soc.
    Zool. France, 104:397–422. Savage, 1973, *In* Vial (ed.), Evol. Biol. Anurans:351–445,
    provided a biogeography and an extended classification based on Starrett's
    arrangement.
  REVIEWERS: William E. Duellman (WED); Marinus S. Hoogmoed (MSH).

FAMILY: **Arthroleptidae** Mivart, 1869.
  CITATION: Proc. Zool. Soc. London, 1869:294.
  DISTRIBUTION: Subsaharan Africa.
  COMMENT: As originally formed, the group name was Arthroleptina; the first use of the
    group name Arthroleptidae was by Dubois, 1981, Monit. Zool. Ital., N.S., Suppl., 15:
    259. Before Dubois (1981), the Arthroleptinae and Astylosterninae were included
    either in the Ranidae or Hyperoliidae. The recognition of this family is premature
    given that no phylogenetic justification or diagnosis has been presented (JDL).
  REVIEWERS: William E. Duellman (WED); Marinus S. Hoogmoed (MSH); Raymond
    Laurent (RL); John C. Poynton (JCP).

SUBFAMILY: **Arthroleptinae** Mivart, 1869.
  CITATION: Proc. Zool. Soc. London, 1869:294.
  DISTRIBUTION: Subsaharan Africa.
  COMMENT: The original spelling of the group name was Arthroleptina; the first use of
    the justified emendation Arthroleptinae was by Noble, 1931, Biol. Amph.:515.
    Savage, 1973, *In* Vial (ed.), Evol. Biol. Anurans:356, following Griffiths, 1959, Ann.
    Mag. Nat. Hist., (13)2:626–640, posited that this group had affinities with the
    Sooglossidae. Laurent, 1951, Rev. Zool. Bot. Afr., 45:119, included this subfamily
    in the Hyperoliidae. Poynton, 1964, Ann. Natal Mus., 17:159, kept this group in
    the Ranidae. Dubois, 1981, Monit. Zool. Ital., N.S., Suppl., 15:259, included this
    group with the Astylosterninae in his Arthroleptidae.
  REVIEWER: Alice G. C. Grandison (AGCG).

Arthroleptis Smith, 1849. Illustr. Zool. S. Afr., Rept., App.:24.
  TYPE SPECIES: *Arthroleptis wahlbergii* Smith, 1849, by monotypy.
  DISTRIBUTION: Africa south of the Sahara.
  COMMENT: The content of this genus is controversial; see comment under
    Schoutedenella.
  CONTRIBUTOR: Raymond Laurent (RL).

Arthroleptis adelphus Perret, 1966. Zool. Jahrb., Abt. Syst., 93:397.
  TYPE(S): Holotype: MHNG 1040.12.
  TYPE LOCALITY: "Foulassi", Cameroon.
  DISTRIBUTION: Forests of South Cameroon.
  COMMENT: See Amiet, 1973, Ann. Fac. Sci. Cameroun, 13:150–151.

Arthroleptis adolfifriderici Nieden, 1910. Sitzungsber. Ges. Naturforsch. Freunde
    Berlin, 1910:440.
  ORIGINAL NAME: *Arthroleptis adolfi-friderici.*
  TYPE(S): Syntypes: (2 specimens) ZMB 21787, 21789.
  TYPE LOCALITY: "Rugegewald" and "Bugoiewald", Rwanda.
  DISTRIBUTION: Montane forests from eastern Zaire, Rwanda, Burundi, Uganda,
    Kenya, Tanzania, and Malawi.

COMMENT: Grandison, 1983, Bull. Brit. Mus. (Nat. Hist.), Zool., 45:77–84, discussed this and other large-sized species.

Arthroleptis affinis Ahl, 1939. Sitzungsber. Ges. Naturforsch. Freunde Berlin, 1939:303.
TYPE(S): Holotype: ZMB 23093.
TYPE LOCALITY: Amani (Deutsch-Ost-Afrika) [East Usambara Mountains, Tanzania].
DISTRIBUTION: Usambara and Uzungwe mountains, Tanzania.
COMMENT: Discussed by Grandison, 1983, Bull. Brit. Mus. (Nat. Hist.), Zool., 45: 77–84.

Arthroleptis brevipes Ahl, 1923. Arch. Naturgesch., (A)90:252.
TYPE(S): Holotype: ZMB.
TYPE LOCALITY: "Bismarckburg, Togo".
DISTRIBUTION: Known only from the type locality.

Arthroleptis carquejai Ferreira, 1906. J. Sci. Math. Phys. Nat., Lisboa, (2)17:165.
TYPE(S): Holotype: MUP.
TYPE LOCALITY: "Cambondo", Angola.
DISTRIBUTION: Known only from the type locality.

Arthroleptis poecilonotus Peters, 1863. Monatsber. Preuss. Akad. Wiss. Berlin, 1863:446.
TYPE(S): Holotype: ZMB 3345.
TYPE LOCALITY: "Hollandischen Besitzungen (Boutry) an der Kuste von Guinea" (Ghana).
DISTRIBUTION: Southern Sudan to Guinea and south to Zaire and Uganda.

Arthroleptis reichei Nieden, 1910. Sitzungsber. Ges. Naturforsch. Freunde Berlin, 1910:437.
TYPE(S): Syntypes: ZMB 21772, 21780.
TYPE LOCALITY: "Kratersee des Ngosi Vulcans", Poroto Mountains, Tanzania.
DISTRIBUTION: Poroto, Rungwe, Uzungwe, and Uluguru mountains of Tanzania and Malawi.

Arthroleptis stenodactylus Pfeffer, 1893. Jahrb. Hamburg. Wiss. Anst., 10:93.
TYPE(S): Holotype: ZMH; destroyed in World War II.
TYPE LOCALITY: "Kihengo", Tanzania.
DISTRIBUTION: Southern and eastern Zaire to Kenya and south to northern Natal (Rep. South Africa), Zimbabwe, and Mozambique.
COMMENT: Laurent, 1960, Rev. Zool. Bot. Afr., 34:85, proposed the subgenus *Coracodichus* for this species. Subsequent authors have retained *Coracodichus* as a synonym of *Arthroleptis*.

Arthroleptis tanneri Grandison, 1983. Bull. Brit. Mus. (Nat. Hist.), Zool., 45:78.
TYPE(S): Holotype: BM 1974.59.
TYPE LOCALITY: "Mazumbai, 4° 48' S 38° 29' E, West Usambara Mountains, ca. 1530 m elevation", Tanzania.
DISTRIBUTION: West Usambara Mountains, Tanzania.

Arthroleptis tuberosus Andersson, 1905. Ark. Zool., (2)20:14.
ORIGINAL NAME: *Arthroleptis variabilis* var. *tuberosus*.
TYPE(S): NHMG.
TYPE LOCALITY: Cameroon.
DISTRIBUTION: Rainforest from Cameroon to eastern Zaire.

Arthroleptis variabilis Matschie, 1893. Sitzungsber. Ges. Naturforsch. Freunde Berlin, 1893:173.
TYPE(S): ZMB.
TYPE LOCALITY: Buea, Cameroon.
DISTRIBUTION: Rainforest from Guinea to lower and eastern Zaire.

Arthroleptis wahlbergii Smith, 1849. Illustr. Zool. S. Afr., Rept., App.:24.
TYPE(S): Holotype: BM 55.11.25.17.
TYPE LOCALITY: "interior of Southern Africa".
DISTRIBUTION: Transkei and Natal, Rep. South Africa.

Cardioglossa Boulenger, 1900. Proc. Zool. Soc. London, 1900:445.
TYPE SPECIES: *Cardioglossa gracilis* Boulenger, 1900, by monotypy.
DISTRIBUTION: Forested areas of western and central Africa.
COMMENT: Amiet, 1981, Ann. Fac. Sci. Yaoundé, 28:117–131, presented a dendrogram
of the Cameroonian species in this genus. Amiet, 1972, Biol. Gabonica, 8:201–
231, described five new species.
CONTRIBUTOR: J.-L. Amiet (JLA).

Cardioglossa aureoli Schiøtz, 1964. Vidensk. Medd. Dansk Naturhist. Foren., 127:26.
TYPE(S): Holotype: ZMUC R.075881.
TYPE LOCALITY: "Fourah Bay College, Freetown, Sierra Leone".
DISTRIBUTION: ". . . connected with the hilly forested part of the Freetown
peninsula", Sierra Leone.
COMMENT: Perhaps allied to *Cardioglossa nigromaculata* Nieden, with which it was
compared by Schiøtz in his description (JLA).

Cardioglossa cyaneospila Laurent, 1950. Rev. Zool. Bot. Afr., 44:4.
ORIGINAL NAME: *Cardioglossa nigromaculata cyaneospila*.
TYPE(S): Holotype: RGMC.
TYPE LOCALITY: "rivière Mukuzira, à 5 km de Bururi, Urundi", Zaire.
DISTRIBUTION: Rwanda, Urundi, and Kivu, eastern Zaire, in highlands.
COMMENT: Elevated to specific status by Laurent, 1956, Nat. Belges, 1956:286.

Cardioglossa dorsalis (Peters, 1875). Monatsber. Preuss. Akad. Wiss. Berlin, 1875:209.
ORIGINAL NAME: *Hylambates dorsalis*.
TYPE(S): Holotype: ZMB.
TYPE LOCALITY: "Yoruba, Lagos", Nigeria (in error, see comment).
DISTRIBUTION: Unknown.
COMMENT: According to A. Dubois (pers. comm. to JLA), this species, never found
in Africa after its description, is not a *Cardioglossa*; rather, it is an Asiatic
member of the Rhacophoridae (JLA).

Cardioglossa elegans Boulenger, 1906. Ann. Mag. Nat. Hist., (7)17:324.
TYPE(S): Syntypes: BM (4 specimens) 1947.2.30.34–37 (formerly 1903.7.28.21–23).
TYPE LOCALITY: "Efulen", Cameroon.
DISTRIBUTION: Southwestern Cameroon in hilly, forested areas below 1000 m elev.

Cardioglossa escalerae Boulenger, 1903. Mem. Soc. Esp. Hist. Nat., 1:64.
TYPE(S): Holotype: BM.
TYPE LOCALITY: "Cap Saint Jean, Guinée espagnole [=Equatorial Guinea]".
DISTRIBUTION: Southern Cameroon, east and south of the Sanaga River, and
probably also in Gabon, Central African Rep., Rep. Congo, and Zaire, in low
elevation forest.

Cardioglossa gracilis Boulenger, 1900. Proc. Zool. Soc. London, 1900:446.
TYPE(S): Syntypes: BM 1947.2.30.39.43 (formerly 1900.2.17.77–81), MRHN (1
specimen).
TYPE LOCALITY: "Rio Benito, Guinee espagnole [=Equatorial Guinea]".
DISTRIBUTION: Eastern Nigeria to Zaire through southern Cameroon and Gabon, in
forested areas under 1200 m elev.

Cardioglossa gratiosa Amiet, 1972. Biol. Gabonica, 8:221.
TYPE(S): Holotype: MHNG 1253.85 (formerly JLA 71.070).
TYPE LOCALITY: "Ongot, env. 750 m", Cameroon.
DISTRIBUTION: Widely distributed in Cameroon south of 7° 5′ N, except in the
littoral plain and mountains.

COMMENT: Closely related to *Cardioglossa nigromaculata* (JLA).

Cardioglossa leucomystax (Boulenger, 1903). Mem. Soc. Esp. Hist. Nat., 1:62.
ORIGINAL NAME: *Arthroleptis leucomystax*.
TYPE(S): Holotype: BM.
TYPE LOCALITY: "Cap Saint Jean, Guinée espagnole [=Equatorial Guinea]".
DISTRIBUTION: Rainforest from Guinea to Zaire.
COMMENT: Boulenger, 1906, Ann. Mag. Nat. Hist., (7)17:322, transferred this
   species to *Cardioglossa*. In the original description Boulenger mentioned other
   specimens from Rio Benito and Kribi; two of them are figured, but they are
   not conspecific: one (Figure 2) agrees with the description of *Cardioglossa
   leucomystax*, while the other (Figure 1) agrees with *Cardioglossa gratiosa* Amiet;
   see Amiet, 1972, Biol. Gabonica, 8:225.

Cardioglossa liberiensis Barbour and Loveridge, 1927. Proc. New England Zool. Club,
   10:16.
TYPE(S): Holotype: MCZ 12034.
TYPE LOCALITY: "Peahtah, St. Paul's River", Liberia.
DISTRIBUTION: Known only from the type locality.
COMMENT: According to J.-J. Morère (pers. comm. to JLA), not a *Cardioglossa*, but
   rather a *Phrynobatrachus* (JLA).

Cardioglossa melanogaster Amiet, 1972. Biol. Gabonica, 8:212.
TYPE(S): Holotype: MHNG 1253.86 (formerly JLA 71.765).
TYPE LOCALITY: "Mwakoumel, env. 1250 m", Cameroon.
DISTRIBUTION: Southern and western slopes of the Cameroon Range (except Mt.
   Cameroon), 1100–1200 m elev.

Cardioglossa nigromaculata Nieden, 1908. Mitt. Zool. Mus. Berlin, 3:506.
TYPE(S): Syntypes: ZMB (2 specimens).
TYPE LOCALITY: "Johann-Albrechtshöhe [=Kumba]", Cameroon.
DISTRIBUTION: Southern Nigeria and southwestern Cameroon, at low elevations.
COMMENT: Description completed by Amiet, 1972, Ann. Fac. Sci. Cameroun, 9:137–
   160. The subspecies *Cardioglossa nigromaculata inornata* Laurent, 1951, Rev.
   Zool. Bot. Afr., 46:30, is probably a distinct species (JLA).

Cardioglossa oreas Amiet, 1972. Biol. Gabonica, 8:217.
TYPE(S): Holotype: MHNG 1253.87 (formerly JLA 71.123).
TYPE LOCALITY: "Mts. Bamboutos, env. 2650 m", Cameroon.
DISTRIBUTION: Central Cameroon Range, from Mt. Manengouba to Mt. Okou,
   above 2000 m, Cameroon.

Cardioglossa pulchra Schiøtz, 1963. Vidensk. Medd. Dansk Naturhist. Foren., 125:33.
TYPE(S): Holotype: ZMUC R.072173.
TYPE LOCALITY: "Obudu Plateau, Ogoja Province, Eastern Nigeria, where the road
   from Obudu Cattle Ranch to Ogoja passes a stream, a few hundred yards
   from the Ranch, about 5500 feet above the sea".
DISTRIBUTION: Cameroon Range, except Mt. Cameroon, 900–1800 m elev.

Cardioglossa schioetzi Amiet, 1981. Ann. Fac. Sci. Yaoundé, 28:117.
TYPE(S): Holotype: J.-L. Amiet 79.090.
TYPE LOCALITY: "Acha Tugi (monts d'Oshié), 1640 m", Cameroon.
DISTRIBUTION: Oshie-Obudu Range (Cameroon and Nigeria).
COMMENT: Affinities of this species with the very similar *Cardioglossa melanogaster*
   are commented on in the original description.

Cardioglossa trifasciata Amiet, 1972. Biol. Gabonica, 8:204.
TYPE(S): Holotype: MHNG 1253.88 (formerly JLA 70.599).
TYPE LOCALITY: "Nsoung, 1750–1800 m", Cameroon.
DISTRIBUTION: Southern slope of Mt. Manengouba, in afro-montane forest,
   Cameroon.

COMMENT: Closely related to *Cardioglossa pulchra* and *Cardioglossa venusta* (JLA).

Cardioglossa venusta Amiet, 1972. Biol. Gabonica, 8:209.
TYPE(S): Holotype: MHNG 1253.89 (formerly JLA 71.872).
TYPE LOCALITY: "Fotabong, 950–1000 m", Cameroon.
DISTRIBUTION: Southern and western slopes of the Cameroon Highlands, except Mt. Cameroon, 1000–1300 m elev.
COMMENT: See comment under *Cardioglossa trifasciata*.

Schoutedenella Witte, 1921. Rev. Zool. Afr., 9:19.
TYPE SPECIES: *Schoutedenella globosa* Witte, 1921, by monotypy.
DISTRIBUTION: Subsaharan Africa.
COMMENT: Laurent, 1954, Ann. Mus. R. Congo Belge, Tervuren, N.S. Quarto, Sci. Zool., 1:34, expanded the genus to accommodate all small species previously included in *Arthroleptis*. Subsequent authors, e.g., Loveridge, 1957, Bull. Mus. Comp. Zool., 117:350; Schmidt and Inger, 1959, Explor. Parc Natl. Upemba, 56: 123; and Poynton, 1964, Ann. Natal Mus., 17:159, rejected this view. Laurent, 1961, Publ. Univ. État, Elisabethville, 1:200, and Laurent, 1973, Rev. Zool. Bot. Afr., 87:666–678, maintained that *Schoutedenella* was valid, noting that to merge *Schoutedenella* with *Arthroleptis* would make *Arthroleptis* diphyletic, since *Schoutedenella* is more closely related to *Cardioglossa* than to *Arthroleptis*. Poynton, 1976, Rev. Zool. Afr., 90:215–220, held that a sufficiently wide-ranging synthesis was still needed to justify generic separation, i.e., the small-sized *Schoutedenella xenodactyloides* possesses maxillary teeth, yet absence of teeth was Witte's sole diagnostic feature. Size seems arbitrary; see comment under *Schoutedenella troglodytes* (JCP). Size is correlated with several osteological features overlooked by JCP (RL).
CONTRIBUTOR: Raymond Laurent (RL).

Schoutedenella bivittata (F. Müller, 1885). Verh. Naturforsch. Ges. Basel, 7:67.
ORIGINAL NAME: *Arthroleptis bivittatus*.
TYPE(S): Holotype: NHMB 1257.
TYPE LOCALITY: "Tumbo-Insel", Sierra Leone.
DISTRIBUTION: Sierra Leone to lower Zaire.
COMMENT: Synonymy includes *Arthroleptis taeniatus* Boulenger, 1906, and *Arthroleptis variabilis* var. *pica* Andersson, 1907.

Schoutedenella crusculum (Angel, 1950). Bull. Mus. Natl. Hist. Nat., Paris, (2)22:559.
ORIGINAL NAME: *Arthroleptis* (*Arthroleptulus*) *crusculum*.
TYPE(S): MNHNP.
TYPE LOCALITY: "le piste de Bie (altitude 1000 metres) region du mont Nimba", Guinea-Bissau.
DISTRIBUTION: Known only from the type locality.
COMMENT: Laurent, 1954, Ann. Mus. R. Congo Belge, Tervuren, N.S. Quarto, Sci. Zool., 1:37, included this species in *Schoutedenella*.

Schoutedenella globosa Witte, 1921. Rev. Zool. Afr., 9:18.
TYPE(S): Syntypes: RGMC (8 specimens).
TYPE LOCALITY: "Lofoi, Katanga [=Shaba]", southeastern Zaire.
DISTRIBUTION: Southeastern Zaire.
COMMENT: Two subspecies (RL). See comments under *Schoutedenella xenochirus* and *Schoutedenella lameerei*.

Schoutedenella hematogaster Laurent, 1954. Ann. Mus. R. Congo Belge, Tervuren, N.S. Quarto, Sci. Zool., 1:37.
TYPE(S): RGMC.
TYPE LOCALITY: "May ya Moto, riv. May ya Moto, Alt. 2350–2400 m, Terr. de Mwenga, Kivu sud", Zaire.
DISTRIBUTION: Montane forests of the Itombwe and Kabobo highlands, Kivu and Shaba provinces, eastern Zaire.

Schoutedenella lameerei (Witte, 1921). Rev. Zool. Afr., 9:12.
ORIGINAL NAME: *Arthroleptis lameerei.*
TYPE(S): Syntypes: RGMC (5 specimens).
TYPE LOCALITY: "Lofoi (Katanga)", Shaba, southeastern Zaire.
DISTRIBUTION: Northeastern Angola to western Burundi, through southeastern Zaire.
COMMENT: Synonymy includes *Schoutedenella muta* Witte, 1921, according to Schmidt and Inger, 1959, Explor. Parc Natl. Upemba, 56:127, who also considered *Schoutedenella lameerei* a synonym of *Schoutedenella globosa,* an arrangement doubted by Laurent, 1964, Publ. Cult. Companhia Diamantes Angola, 67:146.

Schoutedenella loveridgei (Witte, 1933). Rev. Zool. Bot. Afr., 24:99.
ORIGINAL NAME: *Arthroleptis loveridgei.*
TYPE(S): Syntypes: RGMC 2624–25 (2 specimens).
TYPE LOCALITY: Arebi, Ituri, northeastern Zaire.
DISTRIBUTION: Known only from the type locality.

Schoutedenella milletihorsini (Angel, 1922). Bull. Mus. Natl. Hist. Nat., Paris, 28:41.
ORIGINAL NAME: *Arthroleptis milleti-horsini.*
TYPE(S): ?MNHNP; not mentioned by Guibé, 1950 "1948", Cat. Types Amph. Mus. Natl. Hist. Nat.
TYPE LOCALITY: "la region caillouteuse de Beledougou à Kati (12 kilometres au nord de Bamakko)", Mali.
DISTRIBUTION. Known only from the type locality
COMMENT: Laurent, 1954, Ann. Mus. R. Congo Belge, Tervuren, N.S. Quarto, Sci. Zool., 1:40, discussed affinities.

Schoutedenella mossoensis Laurent, 1954. Ann. Mus. R. Congo Belge, Tervuren, N.S. Quarto, Sci. Zool., 1:36.
TYPE(S): RGMC.
TYPE LOCALITY: "Murugaragara, Mosso, Terr. de Rutana Urundi, alt. 1200 m", southeastern Burundi.
DISTRIBUTION: Known only from the type locality.

Schoutedenella nimbaensis (Angel, 1950). Bull. Mus. Natl. Hist. Nat., Paris, (2)22:560.
ORIGINAL NAME: *Arthroleptis (Arthroleptis) nimbaense.*
TYPE(S): Syntypes: MNHNP (3 specimens).
TYPE LOCALITY: "Mont Nimba, fôret Ga, altitude 1100 a 1200 metres", Guinea.
DISTRIBUTION: Known only from the type locality.

Schoutedenella phrynoides Laurent, 1976. Rev. Zool. Afr., 90:540.
TYPE(S): Holotype: RGMC 75.43.B.23.
TYPE LOCALITY: "Lomami, terr. de Lomela, Sankuru, Zaire".
DISTRIBUTION: Known only from the type locality.

Schoutedenella pyrrhoscelis (Laurent, 1952). Rev. Zool. Bot. Afr., 46:28.
ORIGINAL NAME: *Arthroleptis pyrrhoscelis.*
TYPE(S): Holotype: RGMC.
TYPE LOCALITY: "Haute Lubitshako, 1900–2000 m., Terr. de Fizi Kivu", eastern Zaire.
DISTRIBUTION: Montane grasslands in southern Kivu (Itombwe and Kabobo highlands), Zaire.

Schoutedenella schubotzi (Nieden, 1910). Sitzungsber. Ges. Naturforsch. Freunde Berlin, 1910:440.
ORIGINAL NAME: *Arthroleptis schubotzi.*
TYPE(S): Holotype: ZMB 21774.
TYPE LOCALITY: Usumbura, Belgian Ruanda-Urundi [Burundi].
DISTRIBUTION: Western African Rift Valley from the northern shores of Lake Tanganyika to northern Kivu (Zaire), western Rwanda, and Burundi.

Schoutedenella spinalis (Boulenger, 1919). Rev. Zool. Afr., 7:187.
ORIGINAL NAME: *Arthroleptis spinalis.*
TYPE(S): RGMC.
TYPE LOCALITY: "la plaine Saint-Louis, au [Lake] Tanganyika", eastern Zaire.
DISTRIBUTION: Known only from the type locality.

Schoutedenella sylvatica Laurent, 1954. Ann. Mus. R. Congo Belge, Tervuren, N.S.
    Quarto, Sci. Zool., 1:38.
TYPE(S): RGMC.
TYPE LOCALITY: "Buta", Uele, Zaire.
DISTRIBUTION: Rainforest from Cameroon to eastern Zaire.

Schoutedenella troglodytes (Poynton, 1963). Ann. Natal Mus., 15:327.
ORIGINAL NAME: *Arthroleptis troglodytes.*
TYPE(S): Holotype: NMZB (formerly UM) 3730.
TYPE LOCALITY: Western Chimanimani Mountains, South Rhodesia [=Zimbabwe].
DISTRIBUTION: Western range, Chimanimani Mountains, Zimbabwe.
COMMENT: The large size (to 26 mm) of some specimens of this species makes
    Laurent's diagnosis of *Schoutedenella* unclear (JCP). RL disagrees with JCP.

Schoutedenella vercammeni Laurent, 1954. Ann. Mus. R. Congo Belge, Tervuren, N.S.
    Quarto, Sci. Zool., 1:39.
TYPE(S): RGMC.
TYPE LOCALITY: "Mwana, Alt. 1650 m., Terr. de Mwenga, Kivu-sud", Zaire.
DISTRIBUTION: Known only from the type locality.

Schoutedenella xenochirus (Boulenger, 1905). Ann. Mag. Nat. Hist., (7)16:108.
ORIGINAL NAME: *Arthroleptis xenochirus.*
TYPE(S): Holotype: BM 1947.2.30.54 (formerly 1904.5.2.101).
TYPE LOCALITY: "Marimba", Angola.
DISTRIBUTION: Northern Angola, northern Malawi, and southeastern Zaire.
COMMENT: Laurent, 1964, Publ. Cult. Companhia Diamantes Angola, 67:146, noted
    that this form is possibly a subspecies of *Schoutedenella globosa.* JCP agrees and
    notes that material assigned to *Schoutedenella xenodactyloides nyikae* by
    Poynton, 1964, Senckenb. Biol., 45:213, should be assigned to this species.

Schoutedenella xenodactyla (Boulenger, 1909). Ann. Mag. Nat. Hist., (8)4:496.
ORIGINAL NAME: *Arthroleptis xenodactylus.*
TYPE(S): Holotype: BM 1909.10.19.16.
TYPE LOCALITY: "Amani", Usambara Mountains, Tanzania.
DISTRIBUTION: Montane forest in eastern Tanzania.
COMMENT: Attribution of a wide range for this species by some authors is based on
    apparent misidentifications (JCP).

Schoutedenella xenodactyloides (Hewitt, 1933). Occas. Pap. Natl. Mus. S. Rhodesia, 2:49.
ORIGINAL NAME: *Arthroleptis xenodactyloides.*
TYPE(S): Syntypes: NMZB (formerly UM) NM/M 2758–61 (5 specimens).
TYPE LOCALITY: "Chirinda Forest, about 150 miles south of Umtali, S. Rhodesia,
    close to the border of Portuguese East Africa", Zimbabwe.
DISTRIBUTION: Eastern highlands of Zimbabwe, central Mozambique, to southern
    Tanzania.
COMMENT: Two subspecies recognized (RL). This species is sympatric with
    Schoutedenella xenochirus; see comment under *Schoutedenella xenochirus.*
    Subspecies are difficult to distinguish against the known variation within the
    species (JCP).

Schoutedenella zimmeri (Ahl, 1923). Sitzungsber. Ges. Naturforsch. Freunde Berlin,
    1923:104.
ORIGINAL NAME: *Pararthroleptis zimmeri.*
TYPE(S): Syntypes: ZMB (2 specimens).
TYPE LOCALITY: "Accra", Ghana.
DISTRIBUTION: Known only from the type locality.

SUBFAMILY: **Astylosterninae** Noble, 1927.
CITATION: Ann. New York Acad. Sci., 30:110.
DISTRIBUTION: Tropical west and west-central Africa.
COMMENT: See comment under Hyperoliidae. Amiet, 1977, Ann. Fac. Sci. Yaoundé, 23–24:101–103, compared the genera.
CONTRIBUTOR: J.-L. Amiet (JLA).

Astylosternus Werner, 1898. Verh. Zool. Bot. Ges. Wien, 48:191.
TYPE SPECIES: *Astylosternus diadematus* Werner, 1898, by monotypy.
DISTRIBUTION: Sierra Leone to Central African Republic and Mayombe Hills, Zaire.
COMMENT: Amiet, 1977, Ann. Fac. Sci. Yaoundé, 23–24:99–227, reviewed the Cameroon species, and defined species groups noted in the species accounts.

Astylosternus batesi (Boulenger, 1900). Proc. Zool. Soc. London, 1900:442.
ORIGINAL NAME: *Gampsosteonyx batesi*.
TYPE(S): Holotype: BM.
TYPE LOCALITY: "Benito River", Equatorial Guinea.
DISTRIBUTION: Cameroon south of Sanaga River, Equatorial Guinea, Gabon, Central African Republic, and Mayombe Hills of extreme western Zaire.
COMMENT: In the *Astylosternus diadematus* group. Synonymy includes *Dilobates platycephalus* Boulenger, 1900, according to Boulenger, 1903, Mem. Soc. Esp. Hist. Nat., 1:61–64.

Astylosternus diadematus Werner, 1898. Verh. Zool. Bot. Ges. Wien, 48:200.
TYPE(S): Holotype: ZMB 13920.
TYPE LOCALITY: "Victoria" (now Limbé), Cameroon.
DISTRIBUTION: Western and southwestern Cameroon, and probably extreme eastern Nigeria, at low elevations.
COMMENT: In the *Astylosternus diadematus* group.

Astylosternus fallax Amiet, 1977. Ann. Fac. Sci. Yaoundé, 23–24:133.
TYPE(S): Holotype: MHNG 1562.73 (formerly JLA 76.091).
TYPE LOCALITY: "Fopouanga", Cameroon.
DISTRIBUTION: A small part of southwestern Cameroon, between Yabassi and Nkongsamba, at low elevations.
COMMENT: In the *Astylosternus perreti* group.

Astylosternus laurenti Amiet, 1977. Ann. Fac. Sci. Yaoundé, 23–24:125.
TYPE(S): Holotype: MHNG 1562.76 (formerly JLA 74.234).
TYPE LOCALITY: "Ekomtolo", Cameroon.
DISTRIBUTION: A small part of southwestern Cameroon, at low elevations.
COMMENT: In the *Astylosternus perreti* group.

Astylosternus montanus Amiet, 1977. Ann. Fac. Sci. Yaoundé, 23–24:162.
TYPE(S): Holotype: MHNG 1562.76 (formerly JLA 74.279).
TYPE LOCALITY: "Djan", Cameroon.
DISTRIBUTION: Cameroon Range and along the northern and southern edges of the Adamaoua Plateau, in the submontane zone.
COMMENT: In the *Astylosternus diadematus* group.

Astylosternus nganhanus Amiet, 1977. Ann. Fac. Sci. Yaoundé, 23–24:211.
TYPE(S): Holotype: MHNG 1562.71 (formerly JLA 73.226).
TYPE LOCALITY: "Montagne de Nganha", Cameroon.
DISTRIBUTION: Montagne de Nganha, Cameroon.
COMMENT: In the *Astylosternus nganhanus* group.

Astylosternus occidentalis Parker, 1931. Ann. Mag. Nat. Hist., (10)7:432.
TYPE(S): BM.
TYPE LOCALITY: "Sandaru", Sierra Leone.
DISTRIBUTION: West Africa: Sierra Leone, Guinea, Ivory Coast.

COMMENT: Not assigned to a species group.

Astylosternus perreti Amiet, 1977. Ann. Fac. Sci. Yaoundé, 23–24:117.
   TYPE(S): Holotype: MHNG 1562.72 (formerly JLA 73.029).
   TYPE LOCALITY: "Mouandong, env. 1350 m", Cameroon.
   DISTRIBUTION: Southern slopes of the Cameroon Range, Cameroon.
   COMMENT: In the *Astylosternus perreti* group.

Astylosternus ranoides Amiet, 1977. Ann. Fac. Sci. Yaoundé, 23–24:200.
   TYPE(S): Holotype: MHNG 1562.78 (formerly JLA 71.039).
   TYPE LOCALITY: "Mont Mélétan (massif des Bamboutos), env. 2600 m", Cameroon.
   DISTRIBUTION: Central Cameroon Range, in the afro-subalpine zone.
   COMMENT: In the *Astylosternus rheophilus* group.

Astylosternus rheophilus Amiet, 1977. Ann. Fac. Sci. Yaoundé, 23–24:189.
   TYPE(S): Holotype: MHNG 1562.74 (formerly JLA 70.282).
   TYPE LOCALITY: "Bafut-Ngemba, 1800 m environ", Cameroon.
   DISTRIBUTION: Cameroon Range (except Mt. Cameroon), Cameroon.
   COMMENT: In the *Astylosternus rheophilus* group.

Astylosternus schioetzi Amiet, 1977. Ann. Fac. Sci. Yaoundé, 23–24:143.
   TYPE(S): Holotype: MHNG 1562.79 (formerly JLA 73.528).
   TYPE LOCALITY: "Apouh, 20 km au Sud d'Edéa", Cameroon.
   DISTRIBUTION: Known only from two localities near Edéa, southern Cameroon.
   COMMENT: In the *Astylosternus schioetzi* group.

Leptodactylodon Andersson, 1903. Verh. Zool. Bot. Ges. Wien, 53:141.
   TYPE SPECIES: *Leptodactylodon ovatus* Andersson, 1903, by monotypy.
   DISTRIBUTION: Eastern Nigeria and western and southwestern Cameroon.
   COMMENT: Revised by Amiet, 1980, Ann. Fac. Sci. Yaoundé, 27:69–224, who supplied
      information on life history and relationships. Synonymy includes *Bulua*
      according to Andersson, 1905, Ark. Zool., (2)2:22.

Leptodactylodon albiventris (Boulenger, 1905). Ann. Mag. Nat. Hist., (7)15:283.
   ORIGINAL NAME: *Bulua albiventris*.
   TYPE(S): Syntypes: BM (3 specimens).
   TYPE LOCALITY: "Efulen", Cameroon.
   DISTRIBUTION: Western edge of the southern Cameroon Plateau and periphery of
      Mt. Cameroon.

Leptodactylodon axillaris Amiet, 1971. Ann. Fac. Sci. Cameroun, 7–8:164.
   TYPE(S): Holotype: MHNG 2031.08 (formerly JLA 71.622).
   TYPE LOCALITY: Monts Bamboutos, env. 2300 m [Cameroon].
   DISTRIBUTION: Bamboutos Mts., and probably Mt. Okou, in the Cameroon Range,
      Cameroon.

Leptodactylodon bicolor Amiet, 1971. Ann. Fac. Sci. Cameroun, 7–8:156–160.
   TYPE(S): Holotype: MHNG 2031.07 (formerly JLA 71.595).
   TYPE LOCALITY: Foto [Cameroon].
   DISTRIBUTION: Southern and western edge of the Cameroon Range, except Mt.
      Cameroon, Cameroon.

Leptodactylodon boulengeri Nieden, 1910. Arch. Naturgesch., 76:242.
   TYPE(S): Holotype: ZMB.
   TYPE LOCALITY: Region of Banyo, Cameroon.
   DISTRIBUTION: Cameroon Range, in the submontane zone, Cameroon.
   COMMENT: Synonymy includes *Astylosternus bamilekianus* Amiet, 1971, according to
      Amiet, 1980, Ann. Fac. Sci. Yaoundé, 27:105.

Leptodactylodon erythrogaster Amiet, 1971. Ann. Fac. Sci. Cameroun, 5:67.
TYPE(S): Holotype: MHNG 2031.11 (formerly JLA 70.920).
TYPE LOCALITY: "Nsoung, versant sud du Mont Manengouba, 1700 m d'altitude",
Cameroon.
DISTRIBUTION: Mt. Manengouba, Cameroon.

Leptodactylodon mertensi Perret, 1959. Bull. Soc. Neuchâtel. Sci. Nat., 82:247.
TYPE(S): Holotype: MHNG 951.39.
TYPE LOCALITY: Nsoung, on the southern slope of Mont Manengouba, 1400 m
[Cameroon].
DISTRIBUTION: Southern slopes of the Bamileke Plateau and Mt. Manengouba,
between 1200-1850 m, Cameroon.

Leptodactylodon ornatus Amiet, 1971. Ann. Fac. Sci. Cameroun, 5:59.
TYPE(S): Holotype: MHNG 2031.10.
TYPE LOCALITY: "Mont Nlonako, ESE de Nkongsamba, 800-1000 m d'altitude",
Cameroon.
DISTRIBUTION: Hilly country near the southern and western slopes of the Bamileke
Plateau and Mt. Manengouba, Cameroon.

Leptodactylodon ovatus Andersson, 1903. Verh. Zool. Bot. Ges. Wien, 53:141.
TYPE(S): Syntypes: NHMG (10 specimens).
TYPE LOCALITY: "Kamerun".
DISTRIBUTION: Eastern Nigeria and part of western Cameroon, at low elevations.

Leptodactylodon perreti Amiet, 1971. Ann. Fac. Sci. Cameroun, 7-8:160.
TYPE(S): Holotype: MHNG 2031.05 (formerly JLA 69.261).
TYPE LOCALITY: "Mont Mbam", Cameroon.
DISTRIBUTION: Central Cameroon Range, Cameroon.

Leptodactylodon polyacanthus Amiet, 1971. Ann. Fac. Sci. Cameroun, 5:76.
TYPE(S): Holotype: MHNG 2031.09 (formerly JLA 70.939).
TYPE LOCALITY: "Bafut-Ngemba", Cameroon.
DISTRIBUTION: Cameroon Range, except Mt. Cameroon, Cameroon.

Leptodactylodon ventrimarmoratus (Boulenger, 1904). Ann. Mag. Nat. Hist., (7)13:262.
ORIGINAL NAME: *Bulua ventrimarmorata.*
TYPE(S): Holotype: BM.
TYPE LOCALITY: "Efulen", Cameroon.
DISTRIBUTION: Cameroon: western edge of the southern Cameroon Plateau, and
littoral plain south of the Sanaga River.

Nyctibates Boulenger, 1904. Ann. Mag. Nat. Hist., (7)13:261.
TYPE SPECIES: *Nyctibates corrugatus* Boulenger, 1904, by monotypy.
DISTRIBUTION: As for the single species.

Nyctibates corrugatus Boulenger, 1904. Ann. Mag. Nat. Hist., (7)13:261.
TYPE(S): Syntypes: BM (2 specimens).
TYPE LOCALITY: "Efulen, Bulu Country, Southern Cameroon".
DISTRIBUTION: Southwestern Cameroon, at low elevations.
COMMENT: The species figured as *Astylosternus corrugatus* by Perret, 1966, Zool.
Jahrb., Abt. Syst., 93:380, is *Astylosternus perreti;* see Amiet, 1973, Ann. Fac. Sci.
Cameroun, 13:140.

Scotobleps Boulenger, 1900. Proc. Zool. Soc. London, 1900:438.
TYPE SPECIES: *Scotobleps gabonicus* Boulenger, 1900, by monotypy.
DISTRIBUTION: As for the single species.

Scotobleps gabonicus Boulenger, 1900. Proc. Zool. Soc. London, 1900:439.
TYPE(S): Syntypes: BM (3 specimens).
TYPE LOCALITY: "Benito River", Equatorial Guinea.
DISTRIBUTION: Eastern Nigeria to Mayombe Hills (Zaire), through western and southwestern Cameroon, Equatorial Guinea, and western Gabon.
COMMENT: Synonymy includes *Astylosternus oxyrhynchus* Nieden, 1908, and *Scotobleps camerunensis* Ahl, 1927, according to Perret, 1966, Zool. Jahrb., Abt. Syst., 93:380.

Trichobatrachus Boulenger, 1900. Proc. Zool. Soc. London, 1900:443.
TYPE SPECIES: *Trichobatrachus robustus* Boulenger, 1900, by monotypy.
DISTRIBUTION: As for the single species.

Trichobatrachus robustus Boulenger, 1900. Proc. Zool. Soc. London, 1900:443.
TYPE(S): Syntypes: BM (2 specimens).
TYPE LOCALITY: "Benito River", Equatorial Guinea.
DISTRIBUTION: Osomba Hills (eastern Nigeria) to Mayombe Hills (Zaire) through western and southwestern Cameroon and Equatorial Guinea.

FAMILY: **Brachycephalidae** Günther, 1859 "1858".
CITATION: Cat. Batr. Sal. Coll. Brit. Mus.:45.
DISTRIBUTION: Atlantic forests of southeastern Brazil, up to 1500 m.
COMMENT: Formerly included in the family Atelopodidae (which is now included in the Bufonidae). McDiarmid, 1971, Sci. Bull. Nat. Hist. Mus. Los Angeles Co., 12:1–66, and Izecksohn, 1971, Bol. Mus. Nac., Rio de Janeiro, N.S., Zool., 280:1–12, considered these two genera to be members of a distinct family of problematic relationships.
REVIEWERS: Werner C. A. Bokermann (WCAB); David C. Cannatella (DCC); Ulisses Caramaschi (UC); Ronald I. Crombie (RIC); William E. Duellman (WED); Eduardo Gudynas (EG); Marinus S. Hoogmoed (MSH); Roy W. McDiarmid (RWM); Norman J. Scott, Jr. (NJS); Paulo E. Vanzolini (PEV).

Brachycephalus Fitzinger, 1826. Neue Classif. Rept.:39.
TYPE SPECIES: *Bufo ephippium* Spix, 1824.
DISTRIBUTION: As for the single species.

Brachycephalus ephippium (Spix, 1824). Spec. Nov. Testud. Ran. Brasil.:48.
ORIGINAL NAME: *Bufo ephippium.*
TYPE(S): Holotype: ZSM 1021/0, according to Hoogmoed and Gruber, 1983, Spixiana, Suppl., 9:374.
TYPE LOCALITY: "Provincia Bahiae"; "provàvelmente região de Ilhéus", Bahia, Brazil, according to Bokermann, 1966, Lista Anot. Local. Tipo Anf. Brasil.:201.
DISTRIBUTION: Eastern and southeastern Brazil (Bahia, Rio de Janeiro, São Paulo, Paraná).
COMMENT: See Cochran, 1955, Bull. U.S. Natl. Mus., 206:5–7, and Hoogmoed and Gruber, 1983, Spixiana, Suppl., 9:374, for synonymy. Synonymy of the varieties of Miranda-Ribeiro, 1920, Rev. Mus. Paulista, São Paulo, 12:313–314, was premature (RWM).

Psyllophryne Izecksohn, 1971. Bol. Mus. Nac., Rio de Janeiro, N.S., Zool., 280:2.
TYPE SPECIES: *Psyllophryne didactyla* Izecksohn, 1971, by original designation.
DISTRIBUTION: As for the single species.

Psyllophryne didactyla Izecksohn, 1971. Bol. Mus. Nac., Rio de Janeiro, N.S., Zool., 280:2.
TYPE(S): Holotype: EI 4950.
TYPE LOCALITY: "Sacra Família do Tinguá, Município de Paulo de Frontin, Estado do Rio de Janeiro", Brazil.
DISTRIBUTION: Forests in the state of Rio de Janeiro, Brazil.

FAMILY: **Bufonidae** Gray, 1825.
  CITATION: Ann. Philos., (2)10:214.
  DISTRIBUTION: Cosmopolitan except for the Australian, Madagascan, and Oceanic regions.
  COMMENT: As first formed the group name was Bufonina, a subfamily by implication; the justified emendation Bufonidae first appeared in Bell, 1839, Hist. Brit. Rept.:105. Includes the Atelopodidae of other authors, according to Duellman and Lynch, 1969, Herpetologica, 25:239; McDiarmid, 1971, Sci. Bull. Nat. Hist. Mus. Los Angeles Co., 12:1–66; and Trueb, 1971, Contrib. Sci. Nat. Hist. Mus. Los Angeles Co., 216:1– 40. Reig, 1972, In Blair (ed.), Evol. Genus *Bufo*:14–36, derived the Bufonidae directly from his Ceratophryidae (here considered the Ceratophryinae of the Leptodactylidae), an arrangement questioned by Lynch, 1973, In Vial (ed.), Evol. Biol. Anurans:133–182. Cei, Erspamer, and Roseghini, 1968, Syst. Zool., 17:232–245, discussed species groups and phylogeny of bufonids. McDiarmid, 1971, Sci. Bull. Nat. Hist. Mus. Los Angeles Co., 12:1–66, discussed the relationships of the genera *Atelopus*, *Dendrophryniscus*, *Melanophryniscus*, and *Oreophrynella* and redefined the family. Ruíz-Carranza and Hernández-Camacho, 1976, Caldasia, 11:93–148, discussed the relationships of the genera *Atelopus*, *Crepidophryne*, *Dendrophryniscus*, *Melanophryniscus*, *Oreophrynella*, *Osornophryne*, and *Rhamphophryne*. Cruz and Peixoto, 1982, Rev. Brasil. Biol., 42:627–629, discussed the relationships between *Atelopus pernambucensis*, *Atelopus*, and *Dendrophryniscus*. Tihen, 1960, Copeia, 1960:225–233; Grandison, 1978, Monit. Zool. Ital., N.S., Suppl., 11:119–172; and Grandison, 1981, Monit. Zool. Ital., N.S., Suppl., 15:187–215, discussed the phylogenetic relationships of the African genera. Cei, 1980, Monit. Zool. Ital., N.S., Monogr., 2:157–213, discussed the species found in Argentina. Liu and Hu, 1961, Tailless Amph. China: 113–126, discussed the Chinese species.
  CONTRIBUTORS: Alice G. C. Grandison (AGCG) (Africa); David M. Hillis (DMH) (North America); Marinus S. Hoogmoed (MSH) (Central and South America); Robert F. Inger (RFI) (Asia).
  REVIEWERS: Angel Alcala (AA) (Philippines); J.-L. Amiet (JLA) (Cameroon); Steven C. Anderson (SCA) (southwestern Asia); Werner C. A. Bokermann (WCAB) (Brazil); Leo J. Borkin (LJB) (Europe and Palearctic Asia); Walter C. Brown (WCB) (Philippines); Jonathan A. Campbell (JAC) (Mexico and Central America); David C. Cannatella (South America); Ulisses Caramaschi (UC) (Brazil); Gustavo Casas-Andreu (GCA) (Mexico); Alan Channing (AC) (southern Africa); Ronald I. Crombie (RIC) (New World); J. C. Daniel (JCD) (India and Sri Lanka); William E. Duellman (WED); Sushil Dutta (SD) (India and Sri Lanka); Eduardo Gudynas (EG) (southeastern South America); Keith A. Harding (KAH) (New World); Kim M. Howell (KMH) (East Africa); Shuqin Hu (SH) (China); Raymond Laurent (RL) (Africa); Masafumi Matsui (MM) (East Asia); Roy W. McDiarmid (RWM) (South America); John C. Poynton (JCP) (Africa); Jay M. Savage (JMS) (Central America); Norman J. Scott, Jr. (NJS) (Central and South America); Paulo E. Vanzolini (PEV) (Brazil); Ermi Zhao (EZ) (China).

Ansonia Stoliczka, 1870. J. Asiat. Soc. Bengal, 39:152.
  TYPE SPECIES: *Ansonia penangensis* Stoliczka, 1870.
  DISTRIBUTION: South India; Malay Peninsula; Tioman Is.; Borneo; Mindanao (Philippines).
  COMMENT: See Inger, 1960, Fieldiana: Zool., 39:473–503, for discussion and review. See Dring, 1979, Bull. Brit. Mus. (Nat. Hist.), Zool., 34:181–244, for discussion of Malayan populations. See Daniel, 1963, J. Bombay Nat. Hist. Soc., 60:430–431, for characterizations of, and key to, species of India.

Ansonia albomaculata Inger, 1960. Fieldiana: Zool., 39:489.
  TYPE(S): Holotype: FMNH 81975.
  TYPE LOCALITY: "1,400–2,000 feet above sea level, in the headwaters of the Baleh River, Third Division, Sarawak", Malaysia (Borneo).
  DISTRIBUTION: Sarawak (Malaysia) and western Kalimantan (Indonesia), Borneo.
  COMMENT: See Inger, 1966, Fieldiana: Zool., 52:1–402, for distribution.

Ansonia fuliginea (Mocquard, 1890). Nouv. Arch. Mus. Natl. Hist. Nat., Paris, (3)2:158.
ORIGINAL NAME: *Bufo fuliginea.*
TYPE(S): Holotype: MNHNP 130.89.330.
TYPE LOCALITY: North Borneo [Malaysia].
DISTRIBUTION: Sabah, Malaysia (Borneo).

Ansonia guibei Inger, 1966. Fieldiana: Zool., 52:104.
TYPE(S): Holotype: FMNH 152159.
TYPE LOCALITY: "Mesilau Cave, 1800 m, Mount Kina Balu, Sabah", Malaysia
    (Borneo).
DISTRIBUTION: Western Sabah, Malaysia (Borneo).

Ansonia hanitschi Inger, 1960. Fieldiana: Zool., 39:484.
TYPE(S): Holotype: BM 99.8.19.13.
TYPE LOCALITY: "Kadamaian River at 4,200 feet on Mount Kina Balu, North
    Borneo", Malaysia (Borneo).
DISTRIBUTION: Northern Sarawak and western Sabah, Malaysia (Borneo).

Ansonia latidisca Inger, 1966. Fieldiana: Zool., 52:108.
TYPE(S): Holotype: RMNH 10677.
TYPE LOCALITY: "Mount Damus, Sambas, Kalimantan", Indonesia (Borneo).
DISTRIBUTION: Western Kalimantan (Borneo), Indonesia.

Ansonia leptopus (Günther, 1872). Proc. Zool. Soc. London, 1872:598.
ORIGINAL NAME: *Bufo leptopus.*
TYPE(S): Holotype: BM 1947.2.20.51 (formerly 73.4.25.3).
TYPE LOCALITY: Matang, Sarawak [Malaysia (Borneo)].
DISTRIBUTION: Northern, western, and central Borneo.

Ansonia longidigita Inger, 1960. Fieldiana: Zool., 39:480.
TYPE(S): Holotype: BM 99.8.19.12.
TYPE LOCALITY: "4,200 feet on Mount Kina Balu, North Borneo", Malaysia (Borneo).
DISTRIBUTION: Northern and western Borneo.

Ansonia malayana Inger, 1960. Fieldiana: Zool., 39:477.
TYPE(S): Holotype: BM 1900.9.26.16.
TYPE LOCALITY: "4,000 feet in the Larut Hills, Perak, Malaya", Malaysia.
DISTRIBUTION: Malay Peninsula from the Isthmus of Kra southward.
COMMENT: See Dring, 1979, Bull. Brit. Mus. (Nat. Hist.), Zool., 34:181–244, for
    discussion of populations; see also Berry, 1975, Amph. Fauna Peninsular
    Malaysia:43.

Ansonia mcgregori (Taylor, 1922). Philippine J. Sci., 21:182.
ORIGINAL NAME: *Bufo mcgregori.*
TYPE(S): Holotype: EHT 1468A; now lost.
TYPE LOCALITY: Pasonanca, Zamboanga, Mindanao [Philippines].
DISTRIBUTION: Zamboanga Province, Mindanao, Philippines.

Ansonia minuta Inger, 1960. Fieldiana: Zool., 39:493.
TYPE(S): Holotype: FMNH 77424.
TYPE LOCALITY: "450 feet above sea level at Matang, First Division, Sarawak",
    Malaysia (Borneo).
DISTRIBUTION: Western Sarawak (Malaysia) and western Kalimantan (Indonesia),
    Borneo.

Ansonia muelleri (Boulenger, 1887). Ann. Mag. Nat. Hist., (5)20:52.
ORIGINAL NAME: *Bufo muelleri.*
TYPE(S): Holotype: BM 1947.2.20.57 (formerly 87.4.12.18).
TYPE LOCALITY: "Mindanao, Philippine Islands".
DISTRIBUTION: Mindanao, Philippines.

Ansonia ornata Günther, 1875. Proc. Zool. Soc. London, 1875:568.
TYPE(S): Syntypes: BM 74.4.29.944–953.
TYPE LOCALITY: Brahmagiri Hills, Coorg, [Mysore,] India.
DISTRIBUTION: Southwestern peninsular India.

Ansonia penangensis Stoliczka, 1870. J. Asiat. Soc. Bengal, 39:152.
TYPE(S): Syntypes: BM (?) (4 specimens).
TYPE LOCALITY: "on Penang, two near the great water-fall (above Alexandra bath), and two in a narrow gorge about half way up the Penang hill", Malaysia.
DISTRIBUTION: Southern Thailand through Malaya; Borneo.
COMMENT: See Bourret, 1942, Batr. Indochine:165–167, for synonymy and review; see also Berry, 1975, Amph. Fauna Peninsular Malaysia:44

Ansonia platysoma Inger, 1960. Fieldiana: Zool., 39:487.
TYPE(S): Holotype: FMNH 28213.
TYPE LOCALITY: "Luidan River near Bundu Tuhan at 3,300 feet on Mount Kina Balu, North Borneo", Sarawak, Malaysia.
DISTRIBUTION: Northern Sarawak and western Sabah, Malaysia (Borneo).

Ansonia rubrigina Pillai and Pattabiraman, 1981. Proc. Indian Acad. Sci., (B)90:203.
TYPE(S): Holotype: ZSIM, no number given.
TYPE LOCALITY: "Kummattan Thodu, a tributary of River Kunthi, Silent Valley, S. India, Altitude 1005 metres", Kerala, India.
DISTRIBUTION: Southwestern India.

Ansonia tiomanica Hendrickson, 1966. Bull. Natl. Mus., Singapore, 34:74.
TYPE(S): Holotype: BPBM (formerly J. R. Hendrickson 5129).
TYPE LOCALITY: Ulu Lalang, Pulo Tioman, West Malaysia [Malaya].
DISTRIBUTION: Known only from the type locality.
COMMENT: See Berry, 1975, Amph. Fauna Peninsular Malaysia:44–45, for account.

Ansonia torrentis Dring, 1984 "1983". Amphibia-Reptilia, 4:103.
TYPE(S): Holotype: BM 1978.69.
TYPE LOCALITY: "camp four 1800 m, Gunung Mulu, Fourth Division, Sarawak", Malaysia (Borneo).
DISTRIBUTION: Known only from the type locality.

Atelopus Duméril and Bibron, 1841. Erp. Gén., 8:660.
TYPE SPECIES: *Atelopus flavescens*, Duméril and Bibron, 1841, by monotypy.
DISTRIBUTION: Costa Rica to Bolivia, with disjunct areas in Guyana and coastal eastern Brazil (Recife).
COMMENT: McDiarmid, 1971, Sci. Bull. Nat. Hist. Mus. Los Angeles Co., 12:49, considered *Atelopus* to be the sister-taxon of *Dendrophryniscus* plus *Melanophryniscus*. Peters, 1973, Smithson. Contrib. Zool., 145:1–49, reviewed the species of Ecuador and defined species groups.
REVIEWERS: Enrique La Marca (ELM); Juan A. Rivero (JAR).

Atelopus arthuri Peters, 1973. Smithson. Contrib. Zool., 145:10.
TYPE(S): Holotype: USNM 193470.
TYPE LOCALITY: "15 km N of Pallatanga, Chimborazo Province, Ecuador, at an altitude between 2800 and 2860 m".
DISTRIBUTION: Known only from the type locality.
COMMENT: In the *Atelopus ignescens* group.

Atelopus balios Peters, 1973. Smithson. Contrib. Zool., 145:12.
TYPE(S): Holotype: AMNH 17638.
TYPE LOCALITY: "Rio Pescado, Guayas Province, Ecuador".
DISTRIBUTION: Guayas Province, Ecuador.

COMMENT: In the *Atelopus longirostris* group.

Atelopus bomolochos Peters, 1973. Smithson. Contrib. Zool., 145:14.
TYPE(S): Holotype: CAS 93910.
TYPE LOCALITY: "Ecuador, Azuay Province, Sevilla de Oro, approximately 2800 m".
DISTRIBUTION: Azuay Province, Ecuador, between 2500 and 2800 m.
COMMENT: In the *Atelopus ignescens* group.

Atelopus boulengeri Peracca, 1904. Boll. Mus. Zool. Anat. Comp. Univ. Torino, 19:20.
TYPE(S): Syntypes: MSNT 559–560 (17 specimens).
TYPE LOCALITY: "Gualaquiza", Santiago-Zamora Province, Ecuador, and "parecchi
    di S. Josè, Ecuador orientale" (San José = San José de Cuchipamba, about 5
    mi. above Gualaquiza on the Río Blanco at 1000 m, according to Peters, 1955,
    Rev. Ecuat. Entomol. Parasitol., 2:348).
DISTRIBUTION: Eastern Andean ranges in southeastern Ecuador, between 950 and
    1560 m.
COMMENT: For discussion and synonymy see Peters, 1973, Smithson. Contrib.
    Zool., 145:16–18, who noted that this species was intermediate between the
    Atelopus longirostris and the *Atelopus ignescens* groups.

Atelopus carauta Ruíz-Carranza and Hernández-Camacho, 1978. Caldasia, 12:183.
TYPE(S): Holotype: ICN 603.
TYPE LOCALITY: "Río Carauta, Parque Nacional Natural de las Orquídeas, Municipio
    de Frontino, vertiente occidental de la Cordillera Occidental, Departamento
    de Antioquia, Colombia; 1300 m alt."
DISTRIBUTION: Known only from the type locality.
COMMENT: In the *Atelopus longirostris* group; see Cannatella, 1981, J. Herpetol., 15:
    135–137, for discussion.

Atelopus carbonerensis Rivero, 1972. Bol. Soc. Venezolana Cienc. Nat., 29:603.
ORIGINAL NAME: *Atelopus oxyrhynchus carbonerensis*.
TYPE(S): Holotype: BM 1968.940.
TYPE LOCALITY: "La Carbonera (San Eusebio), 2330 m, Estado Mérida, Venezuela".
DISTRIBUTION: Known only from the vicinity of the type locality.
COMMENT: Elevated from subspecies status under *Atelopus oxyrhynchus* by La
    Marca, 1983, Milwaukee Public Mus. Contrib. Biol. Geol., 54:1–12. In the
    Atelopus ignescens group.

Atelopus carrikeri Ruthven, 1916. Occas. Pap. Mus. Zool. Univ. Michigan, 28:1.
TYPE(S): Holotype: UMMZ 48271.
TYPE LOCALITY: Paramo de Macostama, Santa Marta Mts. [Magdalena, Colombia];
    emended to "Department Guajira, Páramo de Macotama (E. Arahuaco Indian
    village Macotama)", Colombia, by Kluge, 1983, Misc. Publ. Mus. Zool. Univ.
    Michigan, 166:22.
DISTRIBUTION: Sierra Santa Marta, Colombia, between 2353 and 4412 m.
COMMENT: See Cochran and Goin, 1970, Bull. U.S. Natl. Mus., 288:139–140, for
    account.

Atelopus certus Barbour, 1923. Occas. Pap. Mus. Zool. Univ. Michigan, 129:12.
ORIGINAL NAME: *Atelopus spurrelli certus*.
TYPE(S): Holotype: MCZ 8538; the listing of syntypes by Kluge, 1983, Misc. Publ.
    Mus. Zool. Univ. Michigan, 166:23, is in error.
TYPE LOCALITY: "from a stream on Mt. Sapo, eastern Panama".
DISTRIBUTION: Darién, Panama.
COMMENT: Savage, 1972, Herpetologica, 28:91, recognized this taxon as a species
    and denied any close relation to *Atelopus spurrelli*; Cochran and Goin, 1970,
    Bull. U.S. Natl. Mus., 288:131, considered it a synonym of *Atelopus spurrelli*.

Atelopus chiriquiensis Shreve, 1936. Occas. Pap. Boston Soc. Nat. Hist., 8:269.
TYPE(S): Holotype: MCZ 19966.
TYPE LOCALITY: "'from Mr. Lewis' place [4 km NE El Hato del Volcán, 1500 m],' Rio
Chiriqui, Viejo, and branches, Panama Republica".
DISTRIBUTION: Western Panama (Chiriquí and Bocas del Toro-Cerro Pando) and
Cordillera de Talamanca of Costa Rica.
COMMENT: See Savage, 1972, Herpetologica, 28:79-81, for review.

Atelopus coynei Miyata, 1980. Breviora, 458:1.
TYPE(S): Holotype: MCZ 91444.
TYPE LOCALITY: "Banks of Río Faisanes where it crosses Ecuador Hwy 28 (the road
from La Palma to Quito via Chiriboga), 14.4 km from the junction with Hwy
30 (the Aloag to Santo Domingo de los Colorados road) at La Palma,
Pichincha Province, Ecuador, 1380 m".
DISTRIBUTION: Provinces Pichincha, Imbabura, and Carchi in northwestern
Ecuador.
COMMENT: In the *Atelopus longirostris* group; see Cannatella, 1981, J. Herpetol., 15:
137, for discussion.

Atelopus cruciger (Lichtenstein and Martens, 1856). Nomencl. Rept. Amph. Mus.
Zool. Berolin.:41.
ORIGINAL NAME: *Phrynidium crucigerum*.
TYPE(S): Syntypes: ZMB 3387 (3 specimens) and (?) MNIINP 5020 (3 specimens);
see comment.
TYPE LOCALITY: Veragua, Panama; corrected to coastal range of Venezuela by
Rivero, 1961, Bull. Mus. Comp. Zool., 126:173.
DISTRIBUTION: The coastal range of Venezuela from Yaracuy to Sucre.
COMMENT: For synonymy, review, and subspecies, see Rivero, 1961, Bull. Mus.
Comp. Zool., 126:171-174. The suggestion by La Marca, 1983, Milwaukee
Publ. Mus. Contrib. Biol. Geol., 54:5, that the correct epithet is *crucigerum* is in
error (ELM). Although Guibé, 1950 "1948", Cat. Types Amph. Mus. Natl. Hist.
Nat.:32, reported MNHNP 5020 as syntypes, these specimens are not from the
stated type locality, rather they are from Caracas, Venezuela; their status as
types is therefore suspect.

Atelopus ebenoides Rivero, 1963. Caribb. J. Sci., 3:120.
TYPE(S): Holotype: FMNH 69746.
TYPE LOCALITY: "Páramo de las Papas, 3600 m, San Agustín, Huila, Colombia".
DISTRIBUTION: Huila, Boyacá, and Tolima, Colombia.
COMMENT: See Cochran and Goin, 1970, Bull. U.S. Natl. Mus., 288:122-125, for
subspecies and account.

Atelopus elegans (Boulenger, 1882). Cat. Batr. Sal. Brit. Mus.:155.
ORIGINAL NAME: *Phryniscus elegans*.
TYPE(S): Holotype: BM 82.7.13.2.
TYPE LOCALITY: "Ecuador, Tanti, 2000 feet [=588 m]".
DISTRIBUTION: Northwestern Ecuador; Gorgona I., Colombia.
COMMENT: Synonymy includes *Atelopus gracilis* Barbour, 1905, according to Rivero,
1963, Caribb. J. Sci., 3:109. Treated as a subspecies of *Atelopus varius* by
Cochran and Goin, 1970, Bull. U.S. Natl. Mus., 288:133-135.

Atelopus erythropus Boulenger, 1903. Ann. Mag. Nat. Hist., (7)12:555.
TYPE(S): Holotype: BM 1903.6.30.7.
TYPE LOCALITY: "Santo Domingo, Carabaya, S. E. Peru, 6000 feet [=1800 m]".
DISTRIBUTION: Known only from the type locality.

Atelopus flavescens Duméril and Bibron, 1841. Erp. Gén., 8:661.
  TYPE(S): Syntypes: MNHNP 803, 256 (2 specimens), RMNH 2208 (2 specimens);
    MNHNP 803 designated lectotype by Lescure, 1976, Bull. Mus. Natl. Hist.
    Nat., Paris, (3)377(Zool.)265:478.
  TYPE LOCALITY: "sur les bords d'un ruisseau, dans une montagne près Cayenne",
    French Guiana.
  DISTRIBUTION: French Guiana, northeastern coastal region and adjacent Brazil
    (Amapá).
  COMMENT: In the *Atelopus flavescens* group. Lescure, 1973, Vie Milieu, 23(C):125–
    141, discussed the status of this species and the former confusion about this
    name. Synonymy includes *Atelopus vermiculatus* McDiarmid, 1973, according
    to Lescure, 1976, Bull. Mus. Natl. Hist. Nat., Paris, (3)377(Zool.)265:478.

Atelopus franciscus Lescure, 1974. Vie Milieu, 23(C):131.
  TYPE(S): Holotype: MNHNP 1975–1502 (formerly LG 192).
  TYPE LOCALITY: Crique Gregoire (Kerenroch), [Guyane Francaise] près de la Station
    ORSTOM, sur le fleuve Sinnamary (lat. 5° 5' N, long. 53° 2' W).
  DISTRIBUTION: French Guiana, central coastal region.
  COMMENT: In the *Atelopus flavescens* group.

Atelopus glyphus Dunn, 1931. Occas. Pap. Boston Soc. Nat. Hist., 5:396.
  ORIGINAL NAME: *Atelopus varius glyphus*.
  TYPE(S): Holotype: USNM 50230.
  TYPE LOCALITY: Pirri Range, near head of Río Limón, Darién, Panama.
  DISTRIBUTION: Eastern Panama and Chocó of Colombia.

Atelopus halihelos Peters, 1973. Smithson. Contrib. Zool., 145:22.
  TYPE(S): Holotype: AMNH 16716.
  TYPE LOCALITY: "Ecuador: Morona-Santiago Province, Cordillera Cutucú".
  DISTRIBUTION: Known only from the type locality.
  COMMENT: In the *Atelopus ignescens* group.

Atelopus ignescens (Cornalia, 1849). Vert. Syn. Mus. Mediolanense Extant.:316.
  ORIGINAL NAME: *Phryniscus ignescens*.
  TYPE(S): Formerly MSNM, but now lost, according to Conci, 1967, Atti Soc. Ital.
    Sci. Nat. Mus. Civ. Stor. Nat. Milano, 106:94.
  TYPE LOCALITY: "in locis humidus circa Latacunga prope Quito"; restated as
    Latacunga (2771 m), Cotopaxi Province, Ecuador, by Peters, 1955, Rev. Ecuat.
    Entomol. Parasitol., 2:338.
  DISTRIBUTION: Inter-Andean hoyas and higher parts of major Andean Cordilleras in
    Ecuador and southern Colombia.
  COMMENT: In the *Atelopus ignescens* group. See Rivero, 1963, Caribb. J. Sci., 3:110–
    112, for review, and Cochran and Goin, 1970, Bull. U.S. Natl. Mus., 288:125–
    127, and Peters, 1973, Smithson. Contrib. Zool., 145:2427, for synonymy,
    review, and discussion.

Atelopus longibrachius Rivero, 1963. Caribb. J. Sci., 3:112.
  TYPE(S): Holotype: FMNH 54283.
  TYPE LOCALITY: "El Tambo, Guisitó, Cauca, Colombia, 300 m, Pacific side of
    Colombia".
  DISTRIBUTION: Known only from the type locality (Cauca, Colombia) and from
    Chocó (Colombia) according to Cochran and Goin, 1970, Bull. U.S. Natl. Mus.,
    288:137.

Atelopus longirostris Cope, 1868. Proc. Acad. Nat. Sci. Philadelphia, 20:116.
  TYPE(S): Apparently lost; not located in ANSP or USNM.
  TYPE LOCALITY: "Valley of Quito", Ecuador.
  DISTRIBUTION: Western Ecuador; Colombia (exact range unknown).

COMMENT: In the *Atelopus longirostris* group; see Cannatella, 1981, J. Herpetol., 15: 135–137, for discussion, and Peters, 1973, Smithson. Contrib. Zool., 145:27–30, for discussion and review.

Atelopus lynchi Cannatella, 1981. J. Herpetol., 15:133.
TYPE(S): Holotype: KU 178412.
TYPE LOCALITY: "Maldonado, Provincia Carchi, Ecuador, 1410 m, 01° 00' N, 78° 11' W".
DISTRIBUTION: Pacific slopes of northern Ecuador (Maldonado) and southern Colombia, north to Cisneros, between 800 and 1410 m.
COMMENT: In the *Atelopus longirostris* group.

Atelopus mindoensis J. Peters, 1973. Smithson. Contrib. Zool., 145:30.
TYPE(S): Holotype: USNM 193554.
TYPE LOCALITY: "Mindo, Pichincha Province, Ecuador, 1200 m."
DISTRIBUTION: Western Ecuador between 700 and 1200 m.
COMMENT: Intermediate between the *Atelopus longirostris* group and the *Atelopus ignescens* group, according to Peters, 1973, Smithson. Contrib. Zool., 145:2.

Atelopus mucubajiensis Rivero, 1972. Bol. Soc. Venezolana Cienc. Nat., 29:606.
TYPE(S): Holotype: BM 1971.763.
TYPE LOCALITY: "Mucubají Region, Santo Domingo, 3100 m, Estado Mérida, Venezuela".
DISTRIBUTION: Vicinity of the type locality, 2900–3100 m.
COMMENT: See La Marca, 1983, Milwaukee Public Mus. Contrib. Biol. Geol., 54:5. See comment under *Atelopus pinangoi*.

Atelopus nepiozomus Peters, 1973. Smithson. Contrib. Zool., 145:32.
TYPE(S): Holotype: USNM 193543.
TYPE LOCALITY: "slightly above Suro Rancho (also called Gualecenita), a single house on the trail between Limón and Gualeceo, approximately 16 kilometers airline west of Limón (which is now known as General Plaza), Morona Santiago Province, Ecuador, approximately 3000 meters".
DISTRIBUTION: Eastern flanks of Andes in Morona-Santiago Province, Ecuador, between 2000 and 3500 m.
COMMENT: In the *Atelopus ignescens* group.

Atelopus nicefori Rivero, 1963. Caribb. J. Sci., 3:115.
TYPE(S): Holotype: FMNH 69748.
TYPE LOCALITY: "Caicedo, Antioquia, Colombia, 1800 m".
DISTRIBUTION: Antioquia Province, Colombia.
COMMENT: See Cochran and Goin, 1970, Bull. U.S. Natl. Mus., 288:130–131.

Atelopus oxyrhynchus Boulenger, 1903. Ann. Mag. Nat. Hist., (7)12:554.
TYPE(S): BM 1947.2.14.66 (formerly 1903.10.30.15) designated lectotype by Rivero, 1972, Bol. Soc. Venezolana Cienc. Nat., 29:601.
TYPE LOCALITY: "Rio Albirregas [=Albarregas], [La] Culata, Sierra Nevada de Merida, Venezuela [3000–3330 m]".
DISTRIBUTION: Subtropical zone and above (2010–3500 m) in the Mérida Andes, Venezuela.
COMMENT: In the *Atelopus ignescens* group. See comment under *Atelopus sorianoi*. See Rivero, 1972, Bol. Soc. Venezolana Cienc. Nat., 29:600–612.

Atelopus pachydermus (Schmidt, 1857). Sitzungsber. Akad. Wiss. Wien, Math. Naturwiss. Kl., 24:15.
ORIGINAL NAME: *Phirix pachydermus*.
TYPE(S): KM.
TYPE LOCALITY: "Neu Grenada"; later expanded to "Westen von Neu Grenada, bei Bonaventura, in einen Höhe 5000' sehr salten" by Schmidt, 1857, Denkschr. Akad. Wiss. Wien, Math. Naturwiss. Kl., 14:257; see Rivero, 1968, Caribb. J. Sci., 8:23, for discussion.
DISTRIBUTION: Colombia (Buenaventura region); Ecuador (Napo Province).

COMMENT: See Rivero, 1965, Caribb. J. Sci., 5:138, and Peters, 1973, Smithson. Contrib. Zool., 145:34–37, for review.

Atelopus palmatus Andersson, 1945. Ark. Zool., (2)37A:12.
TYPE(S): Syntypes: NHRM 1908 (5 specimens).
TYPE LOCALITY: "Rio Pastaza, 1000 m", Ecuador.
DISTRIBUTION: Napo and Pastaza provinces, eastern Ecuador, between 1150 and 1740 m.
COMMENT: For review and discussion see Peters, 1973, Smithson. Contrib. Zool., 145:38–39, and Rivero, 1969, Mem. Soc. Cienc. Nat. La Salle, 29:142–145.

Atelopus pedimarmoratus Rivero, 1963. Caribb. J. Sci., 3:121.
TYPE(S): Holotype: FMNH 81872.
TYPE LOCALITY: "San Isidro, Cundinamarca, Colombia".
DISTRIBUTION: Cundinamarca, Colombia, and doubtfully from Caucá; in Cordilleras Central and Oriental between 2600 and 3100 m according to Cochran and Goin, 1970, Bull. U.S. Natl. Mus., 288:130.
COMMENT: See Cochran and Goin, 1970, Bull. U.S. Natl. Mus., 288:128–130.

Atelopus pernambucensis Bokermann, 1962. Neotropica, 8:42.
TYPE(S): Holotype: WCAB 3511.
TYPE LOCALITY: "Dois Irmãos, alrededores de Recife, Pernambuco, Brasil".
DISTRIBUTION: Known only from the type locality.
COMMENT: Not closely related to any of the other known species of *Atelopus* and showing a distribution disjunct from the other species of the genus. On the basis of data on larval biology and morphology, Cruz and Peixoto, 1982, Rev. Brasil. Biol., 42:627–629, arrived at the conclusion that this species probably represents a taxon generically distinct from *Atelopus* and *Dendrophryniscus*.

Atelopus pinangoi Rivero, 1980. Mem. Soc. Cienc. Nat. La Salle, 40:130.
TYPE(S): Holotype: UPRM 05354.
TYPE LOCALITY: "Piñango, 2920 m, Edo. Mérida, Venezuela".
DISTRIBUTION: Known only from the type locality.
COMMENT: Related to *Atelopus mucubajiensis*, according to the original description.

Atelopus planispina Jiménez de la Espada, 1875. Vert. Viaj. Pacif., Batr.:148.
TYPE(S): Syntypes: MNCN 212 (28 specimens).
TYPE LOCALITY: "San José de Moti, Ecuador"; corrected to San José Nuevo, Mount Sumaco, Napo Province, Ecuador, by Peters, 1973, Smithson. Contrib. Zool., 145:40.
DISTRIBUTION: Known only from Mt. Sumaco (Napo Province, Ecuador) at about 2000 m.
COMMENT: For discussion see Rivero, 1969, Mem. Soc. Cienc. Nat. La Salle, 29:142–145.

Atelopus rugulosus Noble, 1921. Am. Mus. Novit., 29:3.
TYPE(S): Holotype: AMNH 6097.
TYPE LOCALITY: "Vicinity of Juliaca, Peru".
DISTRIBUTION: Cordillera Oriental, Peru, between 2100 and 2500 m.
COMMENT: Very similar (and presumably closely related) to *Atelopus tricolor* according to the original description.

Atelopus seminiferus Cope, 1874. Proc. Acad. Nat. Sci. Philadelphia, 26:130.
TYPE(S): Holotype: ANSP 11383.
TYPE LOCALITY: "From between Balsa Puerto and Moyabamba, Peru".
DISTRIBUTION: Peru (Upper Amazon).

Atelopus senex Taylor, 1952. Univ. Kansas Sci. Bull., 35:630.
TYPE(S): Holotype: R. C. Taylor 766 (now FMNH?).
TYPE LOCALITY: "near pass between Volcán Poás and Volcán Barba, western slope Volcán Poás, Pacific drainage, elev. app. 6800 ft.", Costa Rica.
DISTRIBUTION: Cordilleras Volcánica and Talamanca in Costa Rica.

Atelopus sorianoi La Marca, 1983. Milwaukee Public Mus. Contrib. Biol. Geol., 54:1.
TYPE(S): Holotype: UAM 2783.
TYPE LOCALITY: "cloud forest 10 km SSE Tovar, 2718 m, Estado Mérida, Venezuela".
DISTRIBUTION: Known only from the type locality.
COMMENT: In the *Atelopus ignescens* group; closest to *Atelopus oxyrhynchus* and *Atelopus carbonerensis*, according to the original description.

Atelopus spumarius Cope, 1871. Proc. Acad. Nat. Sci. Philadelphia, 23:222.
TYPE(S): ANSP, lost; MNHNP 1979-8382 designated neotype by Lescure, 1981, Bull. Mus. Natl. Hist. Nat., Paris, (4)3:894.
TYPE LOCALITY: "Ambyiacu River"; =Ampiyacu River, Pebas, Departamento Loreto, Peru, according to Lescure, 1981, Bull. Mus. Natl. Hist. Nat., Paris, (4)3:894.
DISTRIBUTION: Amazon lowlands of Ecuador and eastern Peru, to Amazonas, Pará, Amapá (Brazil), and the Guianas.
COMMENT: In the *Atelopus flavescens* group. *Atelopus pulcher* Boulenger, 1882, is a junior synonym according to Rivero, 1968, Caribb. J. Sci., 8:19–21, and Lescure, 1981, Bull. Mus. Natl. Hist. Nat., Paris, (4)3:894. For a discussion of the *Atelopus spumarius–Atelopus pulcher* controversy and subspecies see Rivero, 1968, Caribb. J. Sci., 8:19–21; Peters, 1973, Smithson. Contrib. Zool., 145:41–43; Lescure, 1973, Vie Milieu, 23:125–127; Lescure, 1973, Bull. Mus. Natl. Hist. Nat., Paris, (3)108:144; Lescure, 1976, Bull. Mus. Natl. Hist. Nat., Paris, (3)265: 478–479; and Lescure, 1981, Bull. Mus. Natl. Hist. Nat., Paris, (4)3:893–910.

Atelopus spurrelli Boulenger, 1914. Proc. Zool. Soc. London, 1914:813.
TYPE(S): Holotype: BM 1914.5.21.81.
TYPE LOCALITY: "Peña Lisa, Condoto", Colombia.
DISTRIBUTION: Chocó and Caldas provinces in western Colombia.
COMMENT: See comment under *Atelopus certus*.

Atelopus tricolor Boulenger, 1902. Ann. Mag. Nat. Hist., (7)10:397.
TYPE(S): Syntypes: BM 1902.5.29.192–195, ZFMK 28103.
TYPE LOCALITY: "Marcapata Valley, E. Peru".
DISTRIBUTION: Peru (Marcapata Valley), between 1700 and 2100 m in Cordillera Oriental according to Duellman, 1979, *In* Duellman (ed.), Monogr. Mus. Nat. Hist. Univ. Kansas, 7:449.
COMMENT: See comment under *Atelopus rugulosus*.

Atelopus varius (Lichtenstein and Martens, 1856). Nomencl. Rept. Amph. Mus. Zool. Berolin.:40.
ORIGINAL NAME: *Phrynidium varium.*
TYPE(S): ZMB 3377 designated neotype by Savage, 1972, Herpetologica, 28:84.
TYPE LOCALITY: "Veragoa"; discussed by Savage, 1972, Herpetologica, 28:89.
DISTRIBUTION: Lower Costa Rica and Panama to Colombia.
COMMENT: For review, discussion, and synonymy see Cochran and Goin, 1970, Bull. U.S. Natl. Mus., 288:118–145, and Savage, 1972, Herpetologica, 28:77–94. Evidence provided by Mosher et al., 1975, Science, Washington, D.C., 189: 151–152, suggested that *Atelopus varius zeteki* Dunn, 1933 (of the Cerro Campana-Valle de Antón area of western Panama) is a distinct species (JMS).
PROTECTED STATUS: CITES—Appendix I (1 Jul. 1975) and USA ESA—Endangered (14 Jun. 1976); as *Atelopus varius zeteki* subspecies only.

Atelopus walkeri Rivero, 1963. Caribb. J. Sci., 3:117.
TYPE(S): Holotype: UMMZ 48077.
TYPE LOCALITY: "Don Diego (Santa Marta Region), Colombia".
DISTRIBUTION: Sierra Santa Marta region of northern Colombia, between 1500 and 1800 m.

Atelopus willimani Donoso-Barros, 1969. Physis, Buenos Aires, 28:327.
TYPE(S): Holotype: IZUC (formerly D. Barros 660).
TYPE LOCALITY: "Río Beni, Runerrabaque [=Rurrenabaque], Bolivia".
DISTRIBUTION: Known only from the type locality.
COMMENT: Generic placement doubtful (RIC).

Bufo Laurenti, 1768. Synops. Rept.:25.
TYPE SPECIES: *Bufo vulgaris* Laurenti, 1768 (=*Rana bufo* Linnaeus, 1758), by subsequent designation of Tschudi, 1838, Classif. Batr.:88.
DISTRIBUTION: Cosmopolitan except for Arctic regions; also absent from New Guinea, Australia, and adjacent islands.
COMMENT: Literature and recent work were summarized in Blair (ed.), 1972, Evol. Genus *Bufo*. Unless otherwise noted the species group assignments in the species accounts follow that work. Zweifel, 1970, Am. Mus. Novit., 2407:1–10, discussed the *Bufo debilis* group. Martin, 1972, Am. Midl. Nat., 88:300–317, studied relationships of neotropical species. Morescalchi and Gargiulo, 1969, Arch. Soc. Biol. Montevideo, 27:88–91, discussed cytotaxonomy. See Mertens and Wermuth, 1960, Amph. Rept. Europas:45–48, for synonymies of European species.
REVIEWER: Leo J. Borkin (LJB) (USSR and China).

Bufo abatus Ahl, 1925. Zool. Anz., 63:110.
TYPE(S): Holotype: ZMB 28016; now lost (RFI).
TYPE LOCALITY: Darjeeling, [West Bengal,] northern India.
DISTRIBUTION: Known only from the type locality.

Bufo achalensis Cei, 1972. Acta Zool. Lilloana, 29:237.
TYPE(S): Holotype: IBMUNC 1284-3.
TYPE LOCALITY: "Pampa de Achala, Sierra Grande, Córdoba, 2200 m", Argentina.
DISTRIBUTION: Sierra Grande, Córdoba Province, Argentina, between 1600 and 2200 m.
COMMENT: Tentatively assigned to the *Bufo spinulosus* group.

Bufo alvarius Girard, 1859. *In* Baird, *In* Emory, Rep. U.S.–Mex. Bound. Surv., Zool., 2:26.
TYPE(S): Syntypes: USNM 2571-72; USNM 2572 designated lectotype by Fouquette, 1970, Cat. Am. Amph. Rept., 93.1.
TYPE LOCALITY: "Valley of the Gila and Colorado"; restricted to "Colorado River bottomlands below Yuma, Arizona", USA, by Schmidt, 1953, Check List N. Am. Amph. Rept., Ed. 6:61; modified to "Fort Yuma, Imperial County, California", USA, by Fouquette, 1968, Great Basin Nat., 28:70–72.
DISTRIBUTION: Extreme southeastern California, southern Arizona, and extreme southwestern New Mexico (USA) south through Sonora and extreme southwestern Chihuahua to northern Sinaloa (Mexico).
COMMENT: Reviewed by Fouquette, 1970, Cat. Am. Amph. Rept., 93.1–4. In the *Bufo alvarius* group.

Bufo amatolicus Hewitt, 1925. Rec. Albany Mus., 3:360.
ORIGINAL NAME: *Bufo angusticeps amatolica.*
TYPE(S): Syntypes: 13 specimens including AMG 4044, 4922.
TYPE LOCALITY: "Amatola Range, near Hogsback on summit at about 5500 feet", Cape Province, Rep. South Africa.
DISTRIBUTION: The Winterberg-Amatola Escarpment, eastern Cape Province, Rep. South Africa.

COMMENT: In the *Bufo angusticeps* group.

Bufo americanus Holbrook, 1836. N. Am. Herpetol., Ed. 1, 1:75.
  TYPE(S): Holotype: ?ANSP 2474.
  TYPE LOCALITY: " . . . mountains of Maine through all the Atlantic states . . .
    common in the upper districts of [South Carolina] . . . along the western side
    of the Alleghenies, and in the Valley of the Mississippi"; restricted to
    "vicinity of Philadelphia", Pennsylvania, USA, by Schmidt, 1953, Check List
    N. Am. Amph. Rept., Ed. 6:65.
  DISTRIBUTION: Southeastern Canada and eastern USA.
  COMMENT: In the *Bufo americanus* group.

Bufo anderssoni Melin, 1941. Göteborgs K. Vetensk. Vitterh. Samh. Handl., (6)1B,
  4:14.
  TYPE(S): Holotype: NHMG 6.
  TYPE LOCALITY: "Taracuá, Rio Uaupés, Brazil".
  DISTRIBUTION: Known only from the type locality.
  COMMENT: In the *Bufo guttatus* group. Andersson, 1945, Ark. Zool., 37A:62,
    proposed the name *Bufo melini* for this taxon as a replacement name because,
    according to him, *Bufo anderssoni* was preoccupied by *Bufo andersonii*
    Boulenger, 1883 (a junior synonym of *Bufo stomaticus*). However, the one
    letter difference (s rather than ss) suffices to prevent homonymy according to
    the International Code for Zoological Nomenclature (Art. 57d). Lutz, 1971, *In*
    Bücherl and Buckly (eds.), Venomous Animals and Their Venoms, vol. 2:423–
    473, was apparently unaware of the relation between *Bufo anderssoni* and *Bufo
    melini* and listed both names as different taxa. According to Melin, 1941,
    Göteborgs K. Vetensk. Vitterh. Samh. Handl., (6), 1B, 4:16, this taxon is
    related to *Bufo guttatus* and to *Bufo glaberrimus*. Andersson, 1945, Ark. Zool.,
    37A(2):63, thought it closely allied to *Bufo glaberrimus*. Rivero, 1961, Bull. Mus.
    Comp. Zool., 126:22, thought that it was probably identical to *Bufo guttatus*.

Bufo angusticeps Smith, 1848. Illustr. Zool. S. Afr., Rept.:pl. 69.
  TYPE(S): Syntypes: BM 58.11.25.160–163.
  TYPE LOCALITY: "interior of South Africa".
  DISTRIBUTION: Southwestern Cape Province, Rep. South Africa.
  COMMENT: In the *Bufo angusticeps* group.

Bufo arenarum Hensel, 1867. Arch. Naturgesch., 33:143.
  TYPE(S): ZMB.
  TYPE LOCALITY: "bei der Stadt Rio-Grande do Sul" (=near the city of Rio Grande
    do Sul, Brazil); stated as "Rio Grande, Rio Grande do Sul", Brazil, by
    Bokermann, 1966, Lista Anot. Local. Tipo Anf. Brasil.:18.
  DISTRIBUTION: Southern Brazil, Argentina, Uruguay, Bolivia, 2600 m.
  COMMENT: In the *Bufo marinus* group. Laurent, 1969, Acta Zool. Lilloana, 25:67–80,
    demonstrated that most subspecies could not be maintained; this arrangement
    was followed by Cei, 1980, Monit. Zool. Ital., N.S., Monogr., 2:173–178, but
    Braun, 1978, Iheringia, Zool., 52:77, still recognized four subspecies.

Bufo arequipensis Vellard, 1959. Mem. Mus. Hist. Nat. Javier Prado, 8:17.
  ORIGINAL NAME: *Bufo spinulosus arequipensis*.
  TYPE(S): Syntypes: MHNJP 812.
  TYPE LOCALITY: "Rio Chili, Arequipa", Peru.
  DISTRIBUTION: Arequipa region and upper parts of western valleys, between Tacna
    and Camaná, southern Pacific Peru.
  COMMENT: In the *Bufo spinulosus* group. Considered a distinct species by Cei, 1972,
    Acta Zool. Lilloana, 29:233–246, and Cei, 1980, Monit. Zool. Ital., N.S.,
    Monogr., 2:170–171; still treated as a subspecies of *Bufo spinulosus* by Gorham,
    1974, Checklist World Amph.:84.

Bufo asmarae Tandy, Bogart, Largen, and Feener, 1982. Monit. Zool. Ital., N.S.,
    Suppl., 17:5.
    TYPE(S): Holotype: TNHC 39397.
    TYPE LOCALITY: Asmara, Eritrea, Ethiopia (15° 20' N—38° 55' E), Sta. 39, altitude
    2340 m.
    DISTRIBUTION: Ethiopia between latitudes 7° 2' and 15° 35' N and longitudes 38° 45'
    and 42° 07' E.
    COMMENT: A tetraploid species of the *Bufo regularis* complex most similar to *Bufo
    kerinyagae* and *Bufo regularis*, according to the original description.

Bufo asper Gravenhorst, 1829. Delic. Mus. Zool. Vratislav., 1:58.
    TYPE(S): Largest specimen of RMNH 2172 (4 specimens originally, paralectotypes
    now 10681) designated lectotype by Inger, 1966, Fieldiana: Zool., 52:66. MSH
    doubts the validity of this, because Gravenhorst's specimens, although sent
    from the RMNH, are probably in Breslau.
    TYPE LOCALITY: Java [Indonesia].
    DISTRIBUTION: Southern Burma through western and peninsular Thailand to
    Sumatra, Borneo, and Java.
    COMMENT: See Taylor, 1962, Univ. Kansas Sci. Bull., 43:326–329, and Bourret, 1942,
    Batr. Indochine:176–178, for synonymy and discussion; also see Berry, 1975,
    Amph. Fauna Peninsular Malaysia:46–47, for account. In the *Bufo asper* group;
    see Inger, 1972, *In* Blair (ed.), Evol. Genus *Bufo*:102–118.

Bufo atacamensis Cei, 1961. Invest. Zool. Chilen., 7:77.
    ORIGINAL NAME: *Bufo spinulosus atacamensis*.
    TYPE(S): Syntypes: IBMUNC 0421–0422.
    TYPE LOCALITY: "Río Huasco, Vallenar", Chile.
    DISTRIBUTION: Atacama desert, south of Antofagasta, Chile.
    COMMENT: In the *Bufo spinulosus* group. Considered a distinct species by Cei, 1972,
    In Blair (ed.), Evol. Genus *Bufo*:82–92; still treated as a subspecies of *Bufo
    spinulosus* by Gorham, 1974, Checklist World Amph.:84.

Bufo atelopoides Lynch and Ruíz-Carranza, 1981. Lozania, 33:4.
    TYPE(S): Holotype: ICN 06373.
    TYPE LOCALITY: "Quebrada Sopladero, Parque Nacional Natural de Munchique,
    road from Uribe to La Gallera (*ca.* Km. 54), western slope on the Cordillera
    Occidental, Departamento del Cauca, Colombia; 2190 m alt."
    DISTRIBUTION: Known only from the type locality.
    COMMENT: A possible member of the *Bufo typhonius* group, according to the
    original description.

Bufo atukoralei Bogert and Senanayake, 1966. Am. Mus. Novit., 2264:2.
    TYPE(S): Holotype: AMNH 74290.
    TYPE LOCALITY: "near the Buttuwa Circuit Bungalow at Yala, Southern Province,
    Ceylon [=Sri Lanka]".
    DISTRIBUTION: Southern Sri Lanka.
    COMMENT: In the *Bufo stomaticus* group. Related to *Bufo fergusonii*, according to the
    original description.

Bufo beddomii Günther, 1875. Proc. Zool. Soc. London, 1875:569.
    TYPE(S): Holotype: BM 1947.2.20.55 (formerly 74.4.29.1145).
    TYPE LOCALITY: "Malabar", Kerala, India.
    DISTRIBUTION: Kerala, India.
    COMMENT: Questionably referred to the *Bufo stomaticus* group by Inger, 1972, *In*
    Blair (ed.), Evol. Genus *Bufo*:102–118. See Daniel, 1963, J. Bombay Nat. Hist.
    Soc., 60:432–433.

Bufo beiranus Loveridge, 1932. Occas. Pap. Boston Soc. Nat. Hist., 8:45.
ORIGINAL NAME: *Bufo taitanus beiranus.*
TYPE(S): Holotype: BM 1947.2.21.10 (formerly 1907.4.29.124).
TYPE LOCALITY: Beira, Mozambique.
DISTRIBUTION: Coastal Mozambique and Zambia.
COMMENT: Grandison, 1972, Zool. Meded., Leiden, 47:41, considered *Bufo beiranus* distinct from *Bufo taitanus.* In the *Bufo taitanus* group.

Bufo berghei Laurent, 1950. Rev. Zool. Bot. Afr., 44:1.
TYPE(S): Not traced.
TYPE LOCALITY: Makamba (Alt. 1500 m.), Terr. de Bururi, Urundi, Afrique Centrale [Burundi].
DISTRIBUTION: Burundi and Rwanda.
COMMENT: Tandy and Keith, 1972, *In* Blair (ed.), Evol. Genus *Bufo*:158, suggested that *Bufo berghei* is a junior synonym of *Bufo funereus.* Tandy, 1972, Univ. Texas Diss.:164, regarded *Bufo berghei* and *Bufo funereus* as conspecific.

Bufo biporcatus Gravenhorst, 1829. Delic. Mus. Zool. Vratislav., 1:53.
TYPE(S): Not traced.
TYPE LOCALITY: Java [Indonesia].
DISTRIBUTION: Philippines, Sumatra, Java, Borneo, Malaya, and southern Thailand.
COMMENT: Synonymy and review in Bourret, 1942, Batr. Indochine:183–184.

Bufo bisidanae Hulselmans, 1977. Rev. Zool. Afr., 91:407.
TYPE(S): Holotype: BM 1969.101.
TYPE LOCALITY: River Bisidana, East of Harrar [Ethiopia], 1500 m.
DISTRIBUTION: Ethiopia.
COMMENT: Not assigned to species group.

Bufo blanfordii Boulenger, 1882. Cat. Batr. Sal. Brit. Mus.:301.
TYPE(S): Syntypes: BM 69.11.4.22, 69.11.4.30–31.
TYPE LOCALITY: "Ain Samhar" and "Sooroo", Ethiopia.
DISTRIBUTION: Ethiopia and northern Somalia.
COMMENT: In the *Bufo blanfordii* group. Synonymy includes *Bufo somalicus* Calabresi, 1927, according to Lanza, 1981, Monit. Zool. Ital., N.S., Suppl., 15: 152. See also comment under *Bufo sibiliai.*

Bufo blombergi Myers and Funkhouser, 1951. Zoologica, New York, 36:279.
TYPE(S): Holotype: CAS-SU 10419.
TYPE LOCALITY: "Nachao, Nariño Province, southwestern Colombia, at an altitude of about 550 meters".
DISTRIBUTION: Northern Ecuador to southwestern Colombia.
COMMENT: In the *Bufo guttatus* group. See Cochran and Goin, 1970, Bull. U.S. Natl. Mus., 288:107, for synonymy. A junior synonym of *Bufo hypomelas* (JDL).

Bufo bocourti Brocchi, 1877. Bull. Soc. Philomath. Paris, (7)1:186.
TYPE(S): Syntypes: MNHNP 6343–44, 6471 (9 syntypes).
TYPE LOCALITY: Totonicapan, Guatemala.
DISTRIBUTION: Intermediate and high elevations of southwestern Guatemala and adjacent Chiapas, Mexico.
COMMENT: In the *Bufo bocourti* group.

Bufo boreas Baird and Girard, 1852. Proc. Acad. Nat. Sci. Philadelphia, 6:174.
TYPE(S): Syntypes: USNM 15467–70.
TYPE LOCALITY: Columbia River, Puget Sound, Washington; restricted to "vicinity of Puget Sound", Washington, USA, by Schmidt, 1953, Check List N. Am. Amph. Rept., Ed. 6:61.
DISTRIBUTION: Western North America from southern Alaska, USA, through western Canada and western USA to southern Colorado, Utah, Nevada, and northern Baja California, Mexico.

COMMENT: In the *Bufo boreas* group. Synonymy includes *Bufo politus* according to Savage, 1967, Copeia, 1967:225–226. See comment under *Bufo exsul*.

Bufo brauni Nieden, 1910. Sitzungsber. Ges. Naturforsch. Freunde Berlin, 10:450.
TYPE(S): Not traced.
TYPE LOCALITY: "Amani in Deutschostafrika" (=Usambara Mountains, northeastern Tanzania).
DISTRIBUTION: Usambara and Uluguru mountains, Tanzania.
COMMENT: In the *Bufo regularis* group.

Bufo brevirostris Rao, 1937. Proc. Indian Acad. Sci., (B)6:403.
TYPE(S): Holotype: CCB (no number given); now lost (SD).
TYPE LOCALITY: "Kempholey, Hassan District, Mysore State", India.
DISTRIBUTION: Southwest India.

Bufo brongersmai Hoogmoed, 1972. Zool. Meded., Leiden, 47:50.
TYPE(S): Holotype: RMNH 16782.
TYPE LOCALITY: "10 km SW of Tiznit, along road Tiznit-Mirhleft, Morocco".
DISTRIBUTION: Sous valley, southern Morocco to Cape Bojador, former Spanish Sahara.
COMMENT: In the *Bufo viridis* group, according to the original description.

Bufo buchneri Peters, 1882. Sitzungsber. Ges. Naturforsch. Freunde Berlin, 10:147.
TYPE(S): Not traced; probably ZMB.
TYPE LOCALITY: "Lunda (W. Africa)", Angola.
DISTRIBUTION: Known only from the type locality.
COMMENT: Tandy and Keith, 1972, *In* Blair (ed.), Evol. Genus *Bufo*:158, tentatively referred *Bufo buchneri* to the synonym of *Bufo funereus*. Tandy, 1972, Univ. Texas Diss.:164, considered *Bufo buchneri* to be a junior synonym of *Bufo funereus*.

Bufo bufo (Linnaeus, 1758). Syst. Nat., Ed. 10, 1:210.
ORIGINAL NAME: *Rana bufo*.
TYPE(S): Not traced; see Andersson, 1900, Bih. K. Svenska Vetensk. Akad. Handl., 26:20.
TYPE LOCALITY: In Europae . . . imprimus Ucraniae; restricted to Sweden by Mertens and Müller, 1928, Abh. Senckenb. Naturforsch. Ges., 41:18.
DISTRIBUTION: Europe, except Ireland and some Mediterranean islands, east to Lake Baikal in southern Siberia; the Caucasus; northern Asia Minor and northern Iran; northwestern Africa.
COMMENT: In the *Bufo bufo* group. Relationships of forms usually treated as subspecies is uncertain (RFI). See comments under *Bufo gargarizans, Bufo minshanicus,* and *Bufo japonicus*. Synonymy includes *Bufo vulgaris* Laurenti, 1768.

Bufo burmanus Andersson, 1939. Ark. Zool., 30A(23):6.
TYPE(S): Syntypes: ZIUS (5 specimens).
TYPE LOCALITY: "Kambaiti", northeastern Burma; elsewhere in the description noted as "surrounding of the little village of Kambaiti, situated in N. East Burma near the border of China in a highland 2,000 m above the sea level".
DISTRIBUTION: Northern Burma and Yunnan, China.
COMMENT: In the *Bufo melanostictus* group. Poorly known.

Bufo caeruleocellatus Fowler, 1913. Proc. Acad. Nat. Sci. Philadelphia, 65:154.
TYPE(S): Holotype: ANSP 21092 (formerly 18069).
TYPE LOCALITY: "Bucay, province of Guayas, western Ecuador".
DISTRIBUTION: Pacific lowlands of Ecuador.
COMMENT: Compared with *Bufo haematiticus, Bufo caeruleopunctatus,* and *Bufo*

glaberrimus in the original description, which leads to the assumption that this species is in the *Bufo guttatus* group. Considered a synonym of *Bufo haematiticus* by Gorham, 1974, Checklist World Amph.:80, but recognized as a distinct species by Miyata, 1982, Smithson. Herpetol. Inform. Serv., 54:3.

Bufo caeruleostictus Günther, 1859. Proc. Zool. Soc. London, 1859:415.
TYPE(S): Syntypes: BM 1947.2.20.48–49 (formerly 60.6.16.93–94).
TYPE LOCALITY: "Andes of western Ecuador".
DISTRIBUTION: Western Ecuador.
COMMENT: In the *Bufo typhonius* group.

Bufo calamita Laurenti, 1768. Synops. Rept.:27.
TYPE(S): Not traced.
TYPE LOCALITY: "in variis latebris terrae rimis"; restricted to "Mitteldeutschland" (=central Germany) by Mertens and Müller, 1928, Abh. Senckenb. Naturforsch. Ges., 41:18; restricted to "Nürnberg", F.R. Germany by Mertens and Müller, 1940, Abh. Senckenb. Naturforsch. Ges., 451:17.
DISTRIBUTION: Western and northern Europe as far east as western USSR and including parts of England and Ireland.
COMMENT: In the *Bufo viridis* group.

Bufo camerunensis Parker, 1936. Proc. Zool. Soc. London, 1936:153.
TYPE(S): Holotype: BM 1947.2.21.33 (formerly 1910.2.23.5).
TYPE LOCALITY: Oban, Calabar [Nigeria].
DISTRIBUTION: Nigeria to eastern Zaire; Fernando Po.
COMMENT: In the *Bufo latifrons* group.

Bufo camortensis Mansukhani and Sarkar, 1980. Bull. Zool. Surv. India, 3:97.
TYPE(S): Holotype: ZSI A6955.
TYPE LOCALITY: "compound of Camorta Guest House, Camorta, Andaman and Nicobar Islands, India".
DISTRIBUTION: Camorta and Nancowry Is., Nicobar Is., India.
COMMENT: Closely related to *Bufo melanostictus*, according to the original description.

Bufo canaliferus Cope, 1877. Proc. Am. Philos. Soc., 17:85.
TYPE(S): Syntypes: USNM 30315–24.
TYPE LOCALITY: "West Tehuantepec", Oaxaca, Mexico.
DISTRIBUTION: Pacific slopes of Oaxaca and Chiapas, Mexico, into Guatemala; possibly to El Salvador.
COMMENT: In the *Bufo valliceps* group. Reviewed by Porter, 1963, Herpetologica, 19: 229–247.

Bufo canorus Camp, 1916. Univ. California Publ. Zool., 17:59.
TYPE(S): Holotype: MVZ 2129.
TYPE LOCALITY: "Porcupine Flat, 8100 feet, Yosemite National Park, Mariposa Co., California", USA.
DISTRIBUTION: High elevations of the Sierra Nevada of California, USA, from Alpine County to Fresno County.
COMMENT: Reviewed by Karlstrom, 1973, Cat. Am. Amph. Rept., 132.1–2. In the *Bufo boreas* group.

Bufo cavifrons Firschein, 1950. Copeia, 1950:84.
TYPE(S): Holotype: UIMNH 8741.
TYPE LOCALITY: "500 feet below peak of Volcán San Martín, San Andrés Tuxtla, Veracruz", Mexico.
DISTRIBUTION: Scattered higher elevations in the Gulf of Mexico drainage from central Veracruz, Oaxaca, and Chiapas, Mexico.

COMMENT: In the *Bufo valliceps* group. Reviewed by Porter, 1963, Herpetologica, 19: 229–247.

Bufo celebensis Günther, 1859 "1858". Cat. Batr. Sal. Coll. Brit. Mus.:60.
TYPE(S): Syntypes: BM.
TYPE LOCALITY: "Celebes" and "India".
DISTRIBUTION: Celebes, Indonesia.

Bufo ceratophrys Boulenger, 1882. Cat. Batr. Sal. Brit. Mus.:319.
TYPE(S): Holotype: BM 80.12.5.151.
TYPE LOCALITY: "Ecuador".
DISTRIBUTION: Eastern Ecuador, eastern Colombia, and Marahuaca, Venezuela, up to 1234 m.
COMMENT: In the *Bufo typhonius* group. See Hoogmoed, 1977, Zool. Meded., Leiden, 51:265–275, for discussion.

Bufo chanchanensis Fowler, 1913. Proc. Acad. Nat. Sci. Philadelphia, 65:155.
TYPE(S): Holotype: ANSP 21095 (formerly 18181).
TYPE LOCALITY: "Camp Chiguancay, in Chanchan River valley, western Ecuador".
DISTRIBUTION: Western Ecuador.
COMMENT: Not mentioned in Blair (ed.), 1972, Evol. Genus *Bufo*, but has been treated as a relative of *Bufo typhonius* and is therefore assumed to be a member of the *Bufo typhonius* group. Gorham, 1974, Checklist World Amph.: 85, considered this a synonym of *Bufo typhonius*, but still recognized as a valid species by Miyata, 1982, Smithson. Herpetol. Inform. Serv., 54:3.

Bufo chappuisi Roux, 1936. Mém. Mus. Natl. Hist. Nat., Paris, (2)4:182.
TYPE(S): Holotype: NHMB 4824.
TYPE LOCALITY: "Delta de l'Omo, st. 27, 570 m.", W. Suk, Turkana, Ethiopia.
DISTRIBUTION: Known only from the type locality.
COMMENT: Species based on a 10 mm specimen. Tentatively considered a synonym of *Bufo lonnbergi* (in the *Bufo taitanus* group) by Tandy and Keith, 1972, *In* Blair (ed.), Evol. Genus *Bufo*:156.

Bufo chilensis Duméril and Bibron, 1841. Erp. Gén., 8:678.
TYPE(S): Syntypes: MNHNP 4932–4935 (five specimens) and 15 others not traced.
TYPE LOCALITY: "au Pérou et au Chili".
DISTRIBUTION: Central Chilean arid steppe from Coquimbo to Concepción, Chile.
COMMENT: In the *Bufo spinulosus* group. Considered a synonym of *Bufo spinulosus* by Cei, 1961, Invest. Zool. Chilen., 7:59–81, and Cei, 1962, Batr. Chile, but recognized as a distinct species by Cei, 1972, *In* Blair (ed.), Evol. Genus *Bufo*: 82–92. Considered a subspecies of *Bufo spinulosus* by Gorham, 1974, Checklist World Amph.:84.

Bufo chlorogaster Daudin, 1802. Hist. Nat. Rain. Gren. Crap.:49.
TYPE(S): MNHNP?; not mentioned by Guibé, 1950 "1948", Cat. Types Amph. Mus. Natl. Hist. Nat.
TYPE LOCALITY: "sur une montagne de l'île Java", Indonesia.
DISTRIBUTION: Java.
COMMENT: A doubtful species according to van Kampen, 1923, Amph. Indo-Aust. Arch.:92.

Bufo chudeaui Chabanaud, 1919. Bull. Mus. Natl. Hist. Nat., Paris, 25:454.
TYPE(S): Syntypes: MNHNP 19-80 (4 specimens).
TYPE LOCALITY: Sénégal: mare de Bata [Sahel de Nioro].
DISTRIBUTION: Known only from the type locality.
COMMENT: Very questionably referred to the *Bufo blanfordii* group by Tandy, 1972, Univ. Texas Diss.:196–197.

Bufo claviger Peters, 1863. Monatsber. Preuss. Akad. Wiss. Berlin, 1863:405.
TYPE(S): Not traced, probably ZMB.
TYPE LOCALITY: Benkulen, Sumatra [Indonesia].
DISTRIBUTION: Nias I. and Sumatra, Indonesia.

Bufo coccifer Cope, 1866. Proc. Acad. Nat. Sci. Philadelphia, 18:130.
TYPE(S): Holotype: USNM 6490.
TYPE LOCALITY: "Arriba" (=? highlands of) Costa Rica.
DISTRIBUTION: Michoacán east and south though Guerrero, Oaxaca, and Chiapas (Mexico) and south to western Panama on the Pacific versant.
COMMENT: Stuart, 1963, Misc. Publ. Mus. Zool. Univ. Michigan, 122:25, doubted that the Mexican and Central American populations were conspecific. Reviewed by Porter, 1963, Herpetologica, 19:229–247. See comments under *Bufo cycladen* and *Bufo ibarrai*.

Bufo cognatus Say, 1823. *In* Long, Account Exped. Pittsburgh–Rocky Mts., 2:190.
TYPE(S): Lost.
TYPE LOCALITY: Arkansas River, Prowers County, Colorado [USA].
DISTRIBUTION: Great Plains in southern Manitoba and Saskatchewan (Canada) and south through Texas (USA) to San Luis Potosí (Mexico), west to southeastern California (USA), and then south to Sinaloa (Mexico).
COMMENT: In the *Bufo cognatus* group. Rogers, 1972, Copeia, 1972:381–383, compared phenetically *Bufo cognatus*, *Bufo compactilis*, and *Bufo speciosus*.

Bufo compactilis Wiegmann, 1833. Isis von Oken, 26:661.
TYPE(S): Holotype: ZMB 3528.
TYPE LOCALITY: Mexico; restricted to "vicinity of city of Mexico", Mexico, by Schmidt, 1953, Check List N. Am. Amph. Rept., Ed. 6:62.
DISTRIBUTION: Central highlands of Mexico.
COMMENT: In the *Bufo cognatus* group. See comment under *Bufo cognatus*.

Bufo coniferus Cope, 1862. Proc. Acad. Nat. Sci. Philadelphia, 14:158.
TYPE(S): Holotype: USNM 4335.
TYPE LOCALITY: "Turbo region, New Grenada" = Chocó, Colombia, according to Cochran and Goin, 1970, Bull. U.S. Natl. Mus., 288:109.
DISTRIBUTION: Costa Rica and Panama on both Atlantic and Pacific slopes, extending to Pacific parts of Colombia and northern Ecuador.
COMMENT: In the *Bufo valliceps* group. See Cochran and Goin, 1970, Bull. U.S. Natl. Mus., 288:109, for synonymy. See comment under *Bufo gabbi*.

Bufo cophotis Boulenger, 1900. Ann. Mag. Nat. Hist., (7)6:181.
TYPE(S): Syntypes: BM 1947.2.20.86 (formerly 1900.3.30.24) and 1947.2.20.87–90 (formerly 1900.6.20.35–38).
TYPE LOCALITY: Paramo, Cajamarca, 9000 feet, and Carao, 7000 feet [Peru].
DISTRIBUTION: Atlantic and Amazonian Andes (2000 to 3500 m), northern Peru.
COMMENT: In the *Bufo spinulosus* group.

Bufo cristatus Wiegmann, 1833. Isis von Oken, 26:660.
TYPE(S): Syntypes: ZMB 3523–24; ZMB 3524 designated lectotype by Porter, 1963, Herpetologica, 19:233.
TYPE LOCALITY: Jalapa, Veracruz, Mexico.
DISTRIBUTION: Central-western Veracruz and adjacent part of Puebla, Mexico.
COMMENT: In the *Bufo valliceps* group. Reviewed by Porter, 1963, Herpetologica, 19: 229–247.

Bufo cristiglans Inger and Menzies, 1961. Fieldiana: Zool., 39:589.
TYPE(S): Holotype: FMNH 109741.
TYPE LOCALITY: "Tingi Hills, Sierra Leone", West Africa.
DISTRIBUTION: Known only from the type locality.

COMMENT: In the *Bufo latifrons* group. Uncertain status; tentatively referred to both *Bufo latifrons* and *Bufo camerunensis* by Tandy, 1972, Univ. Texas Diss.:181, 187.

Bufo crucifer Wied-Neuwied, 1821. Reise Brasil., 2:132.
TYPE(S): Not traced; AMNH?
TYPE LOCALITY: Between São Pedro de Alcantara [Santa Catarina] and Barra da Vereda [Bahia], Brazil; from the text it is clear that the actual type locality can be narrowed down to between Córrego da Paibanha and Ribeirao Issar [=Jissara = upper Rio Ilhéus, Bahia, Brazil] (PEV); stated as Córrego Piabanda, Itabuna, Bahia, Brazil, by Bokermann, 1966, Lista Anot. Local. Tipos Anf. Brasil.:19.
DISTRIBUTION: Misiones, Argentina; northeastern, eastern, and southeastern Brazil; Uruguay and eastern Paraguay.
COMMENT: In the *Bufo crucifer* group according to Cei, 1980, Monit. Zool. Ital., N.S., Monogr., 2:200.

Bufo cryptotympanicus Liu and Hu, 1962. Acta Zool. Sinica, 14(Suppl.):87.
TYPE(S): Holotype: CIB (formerly SWIBASC) 603507.
TYPE LOCALITY: "San-men of Hua-ping, Lung-shen-hsien, altitude 870 m, Kwangsi [=Guangxi]", China.
DISTRIBUTION: Known only from the type locality.
COMMENT: Related to *Bufo burmanus* according to the original description. Presumably in the *Bufo melanostictus* group.

Bufo cycladen Lynch and Smith, 1966. Southwest. Nat., 11:19.
TYPE(S): Holotype: UIMNH 57142.
TYPE LOCALITY: "3 mi. S Putla de Guerrero, Oaxaca, Mexico".
DISTRIBUTION: Guerrero and Oaxaca, Mexico.
COMMENT: In the *Bufo coccifer* group and possibly conspecific with *Bufo coccifer* according to Blair, 1972, *In* Blair (ed.), Evol. Genus *Bufo*:93–101. Considered a *nomen dubium* by Porter, 1967, Southwest. Nat., 12:200–201. For additional comments see McDiarmid and Foster, 1981, Southwest. Nat., 26:337.

Bufo cyphosus Ye, 1977. Acta Zool. Sinica, 23:55.
TYPE(S): Holotype: CIB (formerly SWIBASC) 73I0559.
TYPE LOCALITY: "Chayü, Xizang [=Tibet], altitude 1540 m", Tibet, China.
DISTRIBUTION: Eastern Tibet (1430–2100 m) and Hengduanshan Mountains of Yunnan, China.
COMMENT: Similar to *Bufo biporcatus*, according to the original description.

Bufo danatensis Pisanets, 1978. Doklady Akad. Nauk Ukr. S.S.R., Ser. B, 1978:282.
TYPE(S): Holotype: ZIK AN1.
TYPE LOCALITY: Neighborhood of the Danata village, Kyuren-Dagh mountain ridge, southwestern Turkmenia, USSR.
DISTRIBUTION: Mountains of Turkmenia, Tadjikistan, Kirghizia (Tien-Shan in the Issyk-kul Lake region) and Zaisan Depression in southeastern Kazakhstan, USSR.
COMMENT: In the *Bufo viridis* group. Relationships with other members of the groups are uncertain (LJB). See comments under *Bufo latastii* and *Bufo viridis*.

Bufo danielae Perret, 1977. Rev. Suisse Zool., 84:238.
TYPE(S): Holotype: MHNG 1519.90.
TYPE LOCALITY: Monogaga, en forêt dense cotière de Sassandra, Côte d'Ivoire occidentale.
DISTRIBUTION: Known only from the type locality (Ivory Coast).
COMMENT: Bachmann, Hemmer, Konrad, and Maxson, 1980, Amphibia-Reptilia, 1: 173–183, discussed phylogenetic relationships and considered this species closely related to *Bufo maculatus*.

Bufo dapsilis Myers and Carvalho, 1945. Bol. Mus. Nac., Rio de Janeiro, N.S., Zool., 35:10.
TYPE(S): Holotype: MN A840.
TYPE LOCALITY: "Bom Jardim, near Benjamin Constant, at the mouth of the Rio Javary, on the Peruvian border of the state of Amazonas, Brazil".
DISTRIBUTION: Amazonian Brazil, Peru, and Ecuador.
COMMENT: In the *Bufo typhonius* group. See Dixon, 1976, Herpetol. Rev., 7:172, for discussion. Miyata, 1982, Smithson. Herpetol. Inform. Serv., 54:3, reported this species for Ecuador without mentioning material.

Bufo debilis Girard, 1854. Proc. Acad. Nat. Sci. Philadelphia, 7:87.
TYPE(S): Syntypes: USNM 2621 (8 specimens).
TYPE LOCALITY: Lower part of the Río Grande del Norte and in the Province [state] of Tamaulipas, Mexico; restricted to vicinity of Brownsville, Texas, USA, by Sanders and Smith, 1951, Field and Laboratory, 19:142.
DISTRIBUTION: Southeastern Arizona to southwestern Kansas (USA) and south to Tamaulipas, San Luis Potosí, Durango, and Zacatecas (Mexico).
COMMENT: In the *Bufo punctatus* group. See comment under *Bufo punctatus*.

Bufo dhufarensis Parker, 1931. Ann. Mag. Nat. Hist., (10)8:518.
TYPE(S): Holotype: BM 1947.2.21.66 (formerly 1931.7.16.1).
TYPE LOCALITY: "Milwah Alaud (220 ft.)", Oman.
DISTRIBUTION: Western mountains and coastal hinterland of the Arabian Peninsula, including the United Arab Emirates, Oman, and Masirah I.
COMMENT: In the *Bufo stomaticus* group. Arnold, 1980, J. Oman Stud., Spec. Rep.: 273–332, discussed this and other Arabian species.

Bufo diptychus Cope, 1862. Proc. Acad. Nat. Sci. Philadelphia, 14:353.
TYPE(S): USNM 5841 (apparently lost); not mentioned in USNM type list by Cochran, 1961, Bull. U.S. Natl. Mus., 220, or for ANSP by Malnate, 1971, Proc. Acad. Nat. Sci. Philadelphia, 123:345–375.
TYPE LOCALITY: Not stated (but taken on the Page La Plata–Paraguay expedition—RIC).
DISTRIBUTION: Peru and Paraguay.
COMMENT: Of uncertain relationships.

Bufo dodsoni Boulenger, 1895. Proc. Zool. Soc. London, 1895:540.
TYPE(S): Holotype: BM 1947.2.21.19 (formerly 95.6.11.9).
TYPE LOCALITY: Rassa Alla, Galla or Western Somaliland.
DISTRIBUTION: Eastern Africa from southeastern Egypt to Somalia.
COMMENT: In the *Bufo orientalis* group. Synonymy includes *Bufo brevipalmata* Ahl, 1924, according to Lanza, 1981, Monit. Zool. Ital., N.S., Suppl., 15:155.

Bufo dombensis Bocage, 1895. J. Sci. Math. Phys. Nat., Lisboa, (2)13:152.
TYPE(S): Syntypes: BM 1947.2.21.3–4 (formerly 96.2.28.3–4) and MBL T.4-366 and T.4-367 (presumed destroyed in the 1978 fire), 14 syntypes not traced.
TYPE LOCALITY: Dombé, sur le littoral, au sud de Benguella, Angola.
DISTRIBUTION: Angola and northwestern Namibia.
COMMENT: In the *Bufo vertebralis* group. Synonymy includes *Bufo damaranus* Mertens, 1954, according to Tandy and Keith, 1972, *In* Blair (ed.), Evol. Genus *Bufo*:159.

Bufo dorbignyi Duméril and Bibron, 1841. Erp. Gén., 8:697.
TYPE(S): Holotype: MNHNP 4960.
TYPE LOCALITY: "Montévidéo", Uruguay.
DISTRIBUTION: Northern Argentina, Uruguay, and southeastern Brazil.
COMMENT: In the *Bufo granulosus* group. Until recently considered a subspecies of *Bufo granulosus*, but considered a distinct species by Blair (ed.), 1972, Evol. Genus *Bufo*, and Cei, 1980, Monit. Zool. Ital., N.S., Monogr., 2:195.

Bufo exsul Myers, 1942. Occas. Pap. Mus. Zool. Univ. Michigan, 460:3.
  TYPE(S): Holotype: UMMZ 83357 (formerly SU 2191).
  TYPE LOCALITY: Deep Springs, Inyo County, California [USA].
  DISTRIBUTION: Known only from the type locality.
  COMMENT: In the *Bufo boreas* group. Considered by some authors to be a subspecies
    of *Bufo boreas*.

Bufo fastidiosus (Cope, 1875). J. Acad. Nat. Sci. Philadelphia, (2)8:96.
  ORIGINAL NAME: *Cranopsis fastidiosus*.
  TYPE(S): USNM 32585 designated lectotype (and neotype of *Ollotis coerulescens*) by
    Savage, 1972, J. Herpetol., 6:25.
  TYPE LOCALITY: "2500 feet elevation on the slope of the Pico Blanco, in the district
    of Uren", Costa Rica.
  DISTRIBUTION: Atlantic slopes of the Cordillera de Talamanca-Chiriquí of
    southeastern Costa Rica and western Panama.
  COMMENT: Savage, 1972, J. Herpetol., 6:25, grouped this species, together with *Bufo
    holdridgei* and *Bufo peripatetes* in an assemblage related to the lowland *Bufo
    valliceps* group. He also synonymized *Ollotis coerulescens* Cope, 1875.

Bufo fenoulheti Hewitt and Methuen, 1913. Trans. R. Soc. S. Afr., 3:108.
  TYPE(S): Syntypes: TM 10877–78, AMG 1520.
  TYPE LOCALITY: Newington, N. E. Transvaal and the Woodbush (Zoutpansberg
    District), Rep. South Africa.
  DISTRIBUTION: Southeastern and southern Africa.
  COMMENT: Considered by Tandy and Keith, 1972, *In* Blair (ed.), Evol. Genus *Bufo*:
    159, and Tandy, 1972, Univ. Texas Diss.:157, to be a member of the *Bufo
    vertebralis* complex, and who variously described status as that of a distinct
    species or as a junior synonym of *Bufo dombensis*.

Bufo fergusonii Boulenger, 1892. J. Bombay Nat. Hist. Soc., 7:317.
  TYPE(S): Holotype: BM 1947.2.21.17 (formerly 92.6.9.3).
  TYPE LOCALITY: "Trivandrum on the Cavalry Parade Ground", Travancore, India.
  DISTRIBUTION: Sri Lanka and peninsular India.
  COMMENT: In the *Bufo stomaticus* group. See Bogert and Senanayake, 1966, Am.
    Mus. Novit., 2269:1–18, and Kirtisinghe, 1957, Amph. Ceylon:22–24. See
    comment under *Bufo atukoralei*. See Donahue and Daniel, 1967, J. Bombay Nat.
    Hist. Soc., 63:447, for northeastern India record.

Bufo fernandezae Gallardo, 1957. Rev. Mus. Argent. Cienc. Nat. Bernardino Rivadavia,
    Cienc. Zool., 3:347.
  ORIGINAL NAME: *Bufo granulosus fernandezae*.
  TYPE(S): Holotype: MACN 2389.
  TYPE LOCALITY: "Bella Vista (Prov. de Buenos Aires, Argentina)".
  DISTRIBUTION: Northeastern Argentina, southern Paraguay, Uruguay, and
    southeastern Brazil.
  COMMENT: In the *Bufo granulosus* group. Until recently this taxon was considered a
    subspecies of *Bufo granulosus*, but Cei, 1972, *In* Blair (ed.), Evol. Genus *Bufo*,
    and Cei, 1980, Monit. Zool. Ital., N.S., Monogr., 2:193, considered it a distinct
    species.

Bufo fissipes Boulenger, 1903. Ann. Mag. Nat. Hist., (7)12:552.
  TYPE(S): Holotype: BM 1947.2.20.64 (formerly 1903.6.30.12).
  TYPE LOCALITY: "Santo Domingo, Carabaya, S. E. Peru, 6000 feet".
  DISTRIBUTION: Departamento de Cochabamba (Bolivia) and Puno (Peru), to about
    1900 m.
  COMMENT: In the *Bufo typhonius* group.

Bufo flavolineatus Vellard, 1959. Mem. Mus. Hist. Nat. Javier Prado, 8:25.
  ORIGINAL NAME: *Bufo spinulosus flavolineatus*.
  TYPE(S): Syntypes: MHNJP 279.
  TYPE LOCALITY: "Capillacocha, 30 kms del lago de Junín, Estado de Junín", Peru.
  DISTRIBUTION: Altiplanicie of Junín, between Junín and Callejon de Huaylas,
    between 4000 and 4600 m.
  COMMENT: In the *Bufo spinulosus* group. Considered a distinct species by Cei, 1972,
    In Blair (ed.), Evol. Genus *Bufo*:82–92, but still considered a subspecies of *Bufo
    spinulosus* by Gorham, 1974, Checklist World Amph.:94.

Bufo fuliginatus Witte, 1932. Rev. Zool. Bot. Afr., 22:1.
  TYPE(S): Holotype: RGMC 1200.
  TYPE LOCALITY: Lukafu, Katanga [=Shaba], Zaire.
  DISTRIBUTION: Montane gallery forest of Shaba Province, Zaire.
  COMMENT: Considered a synonym of *Bufo funereus* by Laurent, 1969, Publ. Cult.
    Companhia Diamantes Angola, 67:131, but retained as a distinct species by
    Tandy and Keith, 1972, *In* Blair (ed.), Evol. Genus *Bufo*.

Bufo funereus Bocage, 1866. J. Sci. Math. Phys. Nat., Lisboa, 1:77.
  TYPE(S): Holotype: MBL T.5-363; presumably destroyed in 1978 fire.
  TYPE LOCALITY: Duque de Bragança, Angola.
  DISTRIBUTION: West-central Africa from Benin to Uganda, southward to Zaire and
    Angola in rainforest.
  COMMENT: In the *Bufo funereus* group. See comment under *Bufo fuliginatus*.

Bufo gabbi Taylor, 1952. Univ. Kansas Sci. Bull., 35:619.
  TYPE(S): Syntypes: including USNM 30676; other not traced.
  TYPE LOCALITY: "East coast region" (=Talamanca), Costa Rica.
  DISTRIBUTION: Presumably confined to Talamanca Range, eastern Costa Rica.
  COMMENT: Replacement name for *Bufo auritus* Cope, 1876, which is preoccupied by
    Bufo auritus Raddi, 1821. A junior synonym of *Bufo coniferus*, based on
    examination of type (JMS).

Bufo galeatus Günther, 1864. Rept. Brit. India:421.
  TYPE(S): Holotype: BM 1947.2.21.13 (formerly 60.8.28.25).
  TYPE LOCALITY: "Gamboja" (=Cambodia).
  DISTRIBUTION: Indochina and Hainan I. (China).
  COMMENT: Reviewed by Bourret, 1942, Batr. Indochine:179–180.

Bufo gargarizans Cantor, 1842. Ann. Mag. Nat. Hist., (1)9:483.
  TYPE(S): BM.
  TYPE LOCALITY: Chusan Island [East China Sea, off northeast coast of Zhejiang,
    China].
  DISTRIBUTION: Amur River basin and Sakhalin I., USSR; Korea; China, except for
    southern and western areas; Miyakojima, Ryukyu Is., Japan.
  COMMENT: In the *Bufo bufo* group; usually treated as a subspecies of *Bufo bufo*, but
    considered a valid species by Gumilevskij, 1936, Trudy Zool. Inst. Akad. Nauk
    SSSR, Leningrad, 4:167–171. See Matsui, 1980, Annot. Zool. Japon., 53:56–68,
    for discussion. See also Matsui, 1984, Contrib. Biol. Lab. Kyoto Univ., 26:209–
    428, for discussion of variation and relationships of the Japanese population.
    Synonymy includes *Bufo sachalinensis* (originally *Bufo vulgaris* var. *sachalinensis*
    Nikolsky, 1905, Mém. Acad. Sci. Imp. St. Petersbourg, (8)17:389 [Syntypes:
    ZIL 1934–1936; Type locality: Sakhalin I.]), according to Borkin and Roshchin,
    1981, Zool. Zh., 60:1802–1812.

Bufo gariepensis Smith, 1848. Illustr. Zool. S. Afr., Rept.:pl. 69.
  TYPE(S): Syntypes: BM 58.11.25.157, 58.11.25.160–163.
  TYPE LOCALITY: Orange (Gariep) river [Rep. South Africa].
  DISTRIBUTION: Southern Namibia east to the Transvaal Natal Drakensberg and
    south to the uplands of Cape Province, Rep. South Africa.

COMMENT: In the *Bufo angusticeps* group.

Bufo garmani Meek, 1897. Field Mus. Nat. Hist. Publ., Zool. Ser., 1:176.
TYPE(S): Syntypes: FMNH 415, MCZ 19082.
TYPE LOCALITY: "Haili" [foot of Gobis range about 30 mi. southeast of Berbera]
   Somaliland; corrected to Halleh, Somalia, by Poyton, 1964, Ann. Natal Mus.,
   17:55.
DISTRIBUTION: In disjunct populations in East Africa to northern parts of the Rep.
   South Africa, also Angola.
COMMENT: In the *Bufo regularis* group. Synonymy includes *Bufo bisidanae*
   Hulselmans, according to Tandy, Bogart, Largen, and Feener, 1982, Monit.
   Zool. Ital., N.S., Suppl., 17:3.

Bufo gemmifer Taylor, 1940 "1939". Univ. Kansas Sci. Bull., 26:490.
TYPE(S): Holotype: FMNH 100026 (formerly EHT-HMS 18509).
TYPE LOCALITY: El Limoncito, near La Venta, Guerrero, Mexico.
DISTRIBUTION: Coastal region near Acapulco, Guerrero, Mexico.
COMMENT: In the *Bufo valliceps* group. Reviewed by Porter, 1963, Herpetologica, 19:
   229–247, who noted the close, possibly conspecific, relationship with *Bufo
   mazatlanensis*.

Bufo glaberrimus Günther, 1868. Proc. Zool. Soc. London, 1868:483.
TYPE(S): Holotype: BM 1947.2.20.56 (formerly 68.3.4.9).
TYPE LOCALITY: "Bogota", Cundinamarca, Colombia; considered doubtful by
   Schlüter, 1981, Stud. Neotrop. Fauna Environ., 16:222.
DISTRIBUTION: Amazonian and Pacific Colombia; Amazonian Ecuador and Peru.
COMMENT: In the *Bufo guttatus* group. Considered a subspecies of *Bufo guttatus* by
   Stebbins and Hendrickson, 1959, Univ. California Publ. Zool., 56:497–540,
   and Rivero, 1961, Bull. Mus. Comp. Zool., 126:20, but considered a distinct
   species by Cochran and Goin, 1970, Bull. U.S. Natl. Mus., 288:113, and
   Schlüter, 1981, Stud. Neotrop. Fauna Env., 16:221–223.

Bufo gnustae Gallardo, 1967. Neotropica, 13:54.
TYPE(S): Holotype: MACN 4775.
TYPE LOCALITY: "Rio Grande, Provincia de Jujuy, Argentina".
DISTRIBUTION: Known only from the type locality.
COMMENT: In the *Bufo typhonius* group and of uncertain validity according to Cei,
   1972, *In* Blair (ed.), Evol. Genus *Bufo*:82–91. Recognized as a poorly known
   species by Cei, 1980, Monit. Zool. Ital., N.S., Monogr., 2:203, and belonging to
   the *Bufo veraguensis* (formerly *Bufo ockendeni*) group.

Bufo gracilipes Boulenger, 1899. Ann. Mag. Nat. Hist., (7)3:276.
TYPE(S): Holotype: BM 99.4.27.9.
TYPE LOCALITY: Benito River, French Congo [Gabon].
DISTRIBUTION: Nigeria eastward to Cameroon, Gabon, and Zaire; Fernando Po.

Bufo granulosus Spix, 1824. Spec. Nov. Testud. Ran. Brasil.:51.
TYPE(S): Formerly ZSM 40/0, now lost.
TYPE LOCALITY: "Habitat in Provincia Bahiae", Brazil.
DISTRIBUTION: Panama to the Guianas, south through the Amazon Basin to
   northeastern Peru, non-Andean Bolivia, northwestern Paraguay, northeastern
   Argentina, and southern Brazil.
COMMENT: In the *Bufo granulosus* group. Gallardo, 1965, Bull. Mus. Comp. Zool.,
   134:107–138, revised the species and reported on geographic variation.
   Bokermann, 1967, *In* Lent (ed.), Atas Simp. Biota Amaz. Zool., 5:103–109,
   provided additional data. Considerable evidence suggests that this nominal
   species is composed of several biological species. A number of former
   subspecies have been elevated to specific rank (see comments under *Bufo*

dorbignyi, Bufo fernandezae, and *Bufo pygmaeus*) and more should be expected to follow. *Bufo granulosus humboldti* (of Panama, Colombia, and Venezuela) geographically overlaps *Bufo granulosus beebei* (of Trinidad, coastal Colombia, and Venezuela) in northern Colombia and western Venezuela; *Bufo granulosus merianae* (of the Guiana Shield of northeastern South America) overlaps *Bufo granulosus nattereri* (Roraima Massif, Brazil-Guyana border); *Bufo granulosus mini* (formerly *Bufo granulosus minor*) (of the Río Beni drainage) overlaps *Bufo granulosus major* (of the Chaco of Bolivia). In addition, a number of subspecies approach each other without evidence of intergradation: *Bufo granulosus azarai* (of Paraguay and Mato Grosso, Brazil) and *Bufo granulosus* in southwestern Brazil; *Bufo granulosus beebei* and *Bufo granulosus merianae* in eastern Venezuela and western Guyana; *Bufo granulosus nattereri* and *Bufo granulosus goeldii* (of Amazonian Brazil to eastern Amazonian Brazil); *Bufo granulosus granulosus, Bufo granulosus lutzi,* and *Bufo granulosus mirandaribeiroi* (of Pará, Goiás, and Mato Grosso, Brazil); *Bufo granulosus lutzi* (of Minas Gerais and Bahia, Brazil) and *Bufo granulosus goeldii; Bufo granulosus mini* and *Bufo granulosus goeldii* in the Mamoré/Beni area of Brazil and Bolivia (RIC).

Bufo guttatus Schneider, 1799. Hist. Amph., 1:218.
 TYPE(S): Holotype: ZMB 3517.
 TYPE LOCALITY: "India Orientali"; stated to be Surinam by Rivero, 1961, Bull. Mus. Comp. Zool., 126:21.
 DISTRIBUTION: Ecuador, Colombia, Guianas, and Venezuela; Amazonian and central Brazil.
 COMMENT: In the *Bufo guttatus* group. Formerly included *Bufo glaberrimus* as a subspecies; see comment under *Bufo glaberrimus.*

Bufo gutturalis Power, 1927. Trans. R. Soc. S. Afr., 14:416.
 TYPE(S): Syntypes: MMK.
 TYPE LOCALITY: Lobatsi and Kuruman [Botswana-Transvaal border].
 DISTRIBUTION: Western Uganda eastward to coastal Kenya, south to Transkei and Natal (Rep. South Africa) and Botswana.
 COMMENT: In the *Bufo regularis* group.

Bufo hadramautinus Cherchi, 1964. Boll. Mus. Ist. Biol. Univ. Genova, 32:5.
 TYPE(S): Holotype: "N. 5" to be deposited in MSNG.
 TYPE LOCALITY: Suia Hadramaut (S. Arabia).
 DISTRIBUTION: Mountains of southern Arabian peninsula.

Bufo haematiticus Cope, 1862. Proc. Acad. Nat. Sci. Philadelphia, 14:157.
 TYPE(S): Syntypes: USNM 48448–49.
 TYPE LOCALITY: "Region of the Truando [Chocó], New Grenada [Colombia]".
 DISTRIBUTION: From eastern Honduras (Caribbean slopes) and from southern Costa Rica (Pacific versant) south to northern Colombia (Pacific and Atlantic slopes) to western Ecuador.
 COMMENT: In the *Bufo guttatus* group. For a recent range extension see Díaz and Wilson, 1983, Herpetol. Rev., 14:31. Also see comment under *Bufo caeruleocellatus.*

Bufo hemiophrys Cope, 1886. Proc. Am. Philos. Soc., 23:515.
 TYPE(S): Syntypes: USNM 11927 (7 specimens), MCZ 3728.
 TYPE LOCALITY: "Northern boundary of Montana", USA; corrected to "Pembina, Pembina County, North Dakota", USA, by Cochran, 1961, Bull. U.S. Natl. Mus., 220:34; Barbour and Loveridge, 1929, Bull. Mus. Comp. Zool., 69:232, gave "Pembina and Turtle Mts., N. Dakota, U.S.A." for the MCZ syntype; see comment.
 DISTRIBUTION: Eastern South Dakota and western Minnesota (USA) to western Ontario, eastern Alberta, and extreme southern Northwest Territories (Canada); isolated population in southeastern Wyoming (USA).

COMMENT: In the *Bufo americanus* group. Cope mentioned only 6 specimens in his type series but Cochran, 1961, Bull. U.S. Natl. Mus., 220:34, noted 7, of which 1 had been exchanged to the MCZ.

PROTECTED STATUS: USA ESA—Endangered (*Bufo hemiophrys baxteri* subspecies only) (17 Jan. 1984).

Bufo himalayanus Günther, 1864. Rept. Brit. India:422.
ORIGINAL NAME: *Bufo melanostictus* var. *himalayanus*.
TYPE(S): Syntypes: BM 53.8.12.31, 58.6.24.1.
TYPE LOCALITY: "in the Himalayas (in Sikkim and Nepal)".
DISTRIBUTION: Southern slopes of the Himalayas in Tibet (China), Nepal, and Sikkim.
COMMENT: In the *Bufo melanostictus* group.

Bufo hoeschi Ahl, 1934. Zool. Anz., 107:335.
TYPE(S): Not designated although 4 examples were mentioned in the original description; Mertens, 1955, Abh. Senckenb. Naturforsch. Ges., 490:26, listed ZMB 35128 as 'Typus'.
TYPE LOCALITY: Okahandja, Deutsch-Sudwestafrika [Namibia].
DISTRIBUTION: Central highlands of Namibia.
COMMENT: In the *Bufo vertebralis* group according to Poynton, 1964, Ann. Natal Mus., 17:65. Considered a synonym of *Bufo dombensis* by Tandy and Keith, 1972, *In* Blair (ed.), Evol. Genus *Bufo*:159, without discussion.

Bufo holdridgei Taylor, 1952. Univ. Kansas Sci. Bull., 35:607.
TYPE(S): Holotype: KU 30885.
TYPE LOCALITY: "at an elevation of approximately 7500 ft [2272 m] on Volcán Barba, western slope", Heredia Province, Costa Rica.
DISTRIBUTION: Cordillera Central, Costa Rica.
COMMENT: Placed in the *Bufo guttatus* group by Blair (ed.), 1972, Evol. Genus *Bufo*. According to Savage, 1972, J. Herpetol., 6:25, this species, together with *Bufo fastidiosus* and *Bufo peripatetes*, forms a group related to the lowland *Bufo valliceps*.

Bufo hololius Günther, 1875. Proc. Zool. Soc. London, 1875:569.
TYPE(S): Holotype: BM 1947.2.20.50 (formerly 74.4.29.1297).
TYPE LOCALITY: "Malabar", Kerala, India.
DISTRIBUTION: Kerala, India.
COMMENT: See Daniel, 1963, J. Bombay Nat. Hist. Soc., 60:432.

Bufo houstonensis Sanders, 1953. Herpetologica, 9:27.
TYPE(S): Holotype: UIMNH 33687.
TYPE LOCALITY: "Fairbanks, Harris Co., Texas", USA.
DISTRIBUTION: Bastrop to Liberty counties in east-central Texas, USA.
COMMENT: Reviewed by Brown, 1973, Cat. Am. Amph. Rept., 133.1–2. In the *Bufo americanus* group.
PROTECTED STATUS: USA ESA—Endangered (13 Oct. 1970).

Bufo hypomelas Boulenger, 1913. Proc. Zool. Soc. London, 1913:1022.
TYPE(S): Holotype: BM 1947.2.20.85 (formerly 1913.11.12.102).
TYPE LOCALITY: "upper waters of the Condo, altitude 1200 feet", Chocó, Colombia.
DISTRIBUTION: Chocó and Antioquia, western Colombia.
COMMENT: Placed in the *Bufo guttatus* group by Cochran and Goin, 1970, Bull. U.S. Natl. Mus., 288:117. See comment under *Bufo blombergi*.

Bufo ibarrai Stuart, 1954. Proc. Biol. Soc. Washington, 67:162.
TYPE(S): Holotype: UMMZ 10800.
TYPE LOCALITY: Oak-pine zone at Aserradero San Lorenzo (about 12 airline km slightly east of north of Jalapa), Jalapa, Guatemala.
DISTRIBUTION: Moderate and intermediate elevations of central and southeastern Guatemala; Sierra de las Minas, eastern Guatemala.

COMMENT: In the *Bufo valliceps* group. Possibly conspecific with *Bufo coccifer* (JAC).

Bufo ictericus Spix, 1824. Spec. Nov. Testud. Ran. Brasil.:44.
TYPE(S): Syntypes: including RMNH 2182, the other in ZSM is lost; RMNH 2182 designated lectotype by Hoogmoed and Gruber, 1983, Spixiana, Suppl., 9:372.
TYPE LOCALITY: "Provincia Rio de Janeiro", Brazil.
DISTRIBUTION: Southern Brazil; eastern Paraguay.
COMMENT: In the *Bufo marinus* group. For review and discussion see P. Müller, 1969, Aquar. Terr. Z., 22:340–342. Long considered a subspecies of *Bufo marinus* but L. Müller, 1927, Abh. Senckenb. Naturforsch. Ges., 40:261, showed consistent differences between the two taxa.

Bufo inca Stejneger, 1913. Proc. U.S. Natl. Mus., 45:541.
TYPE(S): Holotype: USNM 49557.
TYPE LOCALITY: "Huadquinia, Peru, about 5000 feet altitude".
DISTRIBUTION: Southeastern Peru; Departments of Ayacucho and Cuzco (1500 to 2000 m).
COMMENT: In the *Bufo typhonius* group. Formerly considered a subspecies of *Bufo ockendeni* (=*Bufo veraguensis*) but considered a distinct species by Cei, 1968, Pearce-Sellards Ser., Texas Mem. Mus., 13:12, and other recent authors.

Bufo intermedius Günther, 1859 "1858". Cat. Batr. Sal. Coll. Brit. Mus.:140.
TYPE(S): Syntypes: BM 1947.3.6.43–46 (formerly 58.9.20.3–6).
TYPE LOCALITY: "Andes of Ecuador".
DISTRIBUTION: Andes of Ecuador.
COMMENT: In the *Bufo typhonius* group.

Bufo inyangae Poynton, 1963. Ann. Natal Mus., 15:319.
ORIGINAL NAME: *Bufo gariepensis inyangae.*
TYPE(S): Holotype: NMZB (formerly UM) 1289.
TYPE LOCALITY: Inyangani Mountain (8,400 ft, 2560 m), Inyanga, Southern Rhodesia [=Zimbabwe].
DISTRIBUTION: Inyanga Mountains, Zimbabwe.
COMMENT: Martin, 1972, *In* Blair (ed.), Evol. Genus *Bufo*:62, treated *Bufo inyangae* as distinct from *Bufo gariepensis* and discussed osteological differences.

Bufo iserni (Jiménez de la Espada, 1875). Vert. Viaje Pacif., Batr.:185.
ORIGINAL NAME: *Oxyrhynchus iserni.*
TYPE(S): Holotype: MNCN 3057.
TYPE LOCALITY: "en los andes de Chanchamayo, al N.E. de Tarma (Perú)".
DISTRIBUTION: Upper reaches of valleys of Río Chanchamayo and Río Perene, Peru.
COMMENT: Soon after its description this taxon was synonymized with *Bufo typhonius*. Savage, 1978, Intr. Vert. Viaje Pacif.:xiii, however, recognized it as valid. Examination of the holotype corroborates Savage's opinion (MSH).

Bufo japonicus Temminck and Schlegel, 1838. *In* Von Siebold, Fauna Japon., Rept.: 106.
ORIGINAL NAME: *Bufo vulgaris* var. *japonicus.*
TYPE(S): Syntypes: RMNH 2109, 2115–17, 2119; RMNH 2119A designated lectotype by Matsui, 1984, Contrib. Biol. Lab. Kyoto Univ., 26:407.
TYPE LOCALITY: Japan.
DISTRIBUTION: Southern Hokkaido, Honshu, Shikoku, and Kyushu (Japan).
COMMENT: In the *Bufo bufo* group; usually considered a subspecies of *Bufo bufo*, but considered a distinct species by Kawamura, Nishioka, and Ueda, 1980, Sci. Rep. Lab. Amph. Biol. Hiroshima Univ., 4:1–125. See also Matsui, 1980, Annot. Zool. Japon., 53:56–68, and Matsui, 1976, Japan. J. Herpetol., 6:80–92. Matsui, 1984, Contrib. Biol. Lab. Kyoto Univ., 26:210–428, revised the species, reported on morphometrics and geographic variation.

Bufo jordani Parker, 1936. Novit. Zool., 40:145.
TYPE(S): Holotype: BM 1947.2.20.94 (formerly 1936.8.1.227).
TYPE LOCALITY: Satansplatz, circa 1,300 m., South West Africa [=Namibia].
DISTRIBUTION: Southern highlands of Namibia.
COMMENT: In the *Bufo vertebralis* group according to Poynton, 1964, Ann. Natal
Mus., 17:66. Considered a synonym of *Mertensophryne micranotis* by Tandy and
Keith, 1972, *In* Blair (ed.), Evol. Genus *Bufo*:156, without discussion.

Bufo juxtasper Inger, 1964. Fieldiana: Zool., 44:154.
TYPE(S): Holotype: FMNH 77472.
TYPE LOCALITY: "on the banks of the Sungei Tawan, Kalabakan, Tawau District,
Sabah", Malaysia (Borneo).
DISTRIBUTION: Borneo and Sumatra.
COMMENT: In the *Bufo asper* group. See Inger, 1966, Fieldiana: Zool., 52:69–70, for
review.

Bufo kavirensis Andrén and Nilson, 1979. J. Herpetol., 13:93.
TYPE(S): Holotype: NHMG Ba.ex 1276.
TYPE LOCALITY: "Chechmeh-ye Sefied Ab (34° 21' N, 52° 14' E), situated 10 km
southwest of Kuh-e Ghal'e-ye Sard mountains and about 30 km south of Siah
Kuh mountains in the southern part of the Kavir Protected Region about 200
km south of Teheran, Iran".
DISTRIBUTION: Known only from the type locality in central Iran.
COMMENT: In the *Bufo viridis* group, according to the original description.

Bufo kelaartii Günther, 1859 "1858". Cat. Batr. Sal. Coll. Brit. Mus.:140.
TYPE(S): Syntypes: BM 1947.2.20.58–62 (formerly 55.2.12.10, 56.7.9.4, 58.10.15.9,
58.11.25.168).
TYPE LOCALITY: "Ceylon" (=Sri Lanka).
DISTRIBUTION: Sri Lanka.
COMMENT: See Kirtisinghe, 1957, Amph. Ceylon:16–17.

Bufo kelloggi Taylor, 1938 "1936". Univ. Kansas Sci. Bull., 24:510.
TYPE(S): Holotype: FMNH 100088 (formerly EHT-HMS 21).
TYPE LOCALITY: "Two miles east of Mazatlán, Sinaloa", Mexico.
DISTRIBUTION: North-central Sonora through Sinaloa to Nayarit, Mexico.
COMMENT: Reviewed by Hulse, 1977, Cat. Am. Amph. Rept., 200.1–2. In the *Bufo
punctatus* group. See comment under *Bufo punctatus*.

Bufo kerinyagae Keith, 1968. Am. Mus. Novit., 2345:4.
TYPE(S): Holotype: AMNH 75165.
TYPE LOCALITY: "On the Nanyuki-Isiola road, 5 miles east-northeast of Nanyuki, at
an elevation of 6400 feet on the north west slope of Mt. Kenya, Kenya".
DISTRIBUTION: Ethiopia to Kenya, Uganda, and Tanzania.
COMMENT: In the *Bufo latifrons* complex. See comment under *Bufo asmarae*.

Bufo kisoloensis Loveridge, 1932. Occas. Pap. Boston Soc. Nat. Hist., 8:52.
ORIGINAL NAME: *Bufo regularis kisoloensis*.
TYPE(S): Holotype: FMNH 12005.
TYPE LOCALITY: "Kisolo, Kigezi district, southwestern Uganda".
DISTRIBUTION: Rep. Congo eastwards through Kivu (Zaire) and Rwanda to Uganda,
Kenya, and possibly northern Malawi.
COMMENT: In the *Bufo regularis* group.

Bufo koynayensis Soman, 1963. J. Biol. Sci., Bombay, 6:73.
TYPE(S): Not stated but in ZSI (SD).
TYPE LOCALITY: Humbali Village, Shivaji Sagar lake at Koyna, Satara District,
Maharashtra [India], about 4000 feet.
DISTRIBUTION: Known only from the type locality.

COMMENT: See comment under *Bufo sulphureus*.

Bufo langanoensis Largen, Tandy, and Tandy, 1978. Monit. Zool. Ital., N.S., Suppl., 10:4.
    TYPE(S): Holotype: BM 1975.1192.
    TYPE LOCALITY: "Northwest shore of Lake Langano, Shoa Province, Ethiopia (07° 38' N 38° 42' E, altitude 1585 m)".
    DISTRIBUTION: Ethiopian Rift Valley at Lake Langano and mouth of River Horocallo.

Bufo latastii Boulenger, 1882. Cat. Batr. Sal. Brit. Mus.:294.
    TYPE(S): Syntypes: BM 1947.2.21.28–31 (formerly 72.4.17.223–226, 72.4.17.371).
    TYPE LOCALITY: "Ladak" (=Ladakh), India and Pakistan.
    DISTRIBUTION: Mountains of Central Asia, Iran, Afghanistan, Pakistan, and adjacent India (see comment).
    COMMENT: In the *Bufo viridis* group. Although Hemmer, Schmidtler, and Böhme, 1978, Zool. Abh. Staatl. Mus. Tierkd., Dresden, 34:349–384, gave an extensive distribution for this species, the allocation of the tetraploid populations in the USSR to *Bufo danatensis* by Pisanets and Ščerbak, 1979, Vestn. Zool., Kiev, 1979(4):11–16, has rendered previous distributional statements provisional. See Dubois and Martens, 1977, Bull. Soc. Zool. France, 102:459–465, for discussion of distribution in Ladakh and Kashmir.

Bufo latifrons Boulenger, 1900. Proc. Zool. Soc. London, 1900:435.
    TYPE(S): Syntypes: BM 1900.2.17.114–116.
    TYPE LOCALITY: "Benito River, north of the Gaboon River between 20 and 30 miles inland from the coast, Gaboon" (Gabon).
    DISTRIBUTION: Sierra Leone to Zaire in high tropical forest.
    COMMENT: Tandy, 1972, Univ. Texas Diss.:170–171, discussed the affinities of this species.

Bufo lemairii Boulenger, 1901. Ann. Mus. R. Congo Belge, Tervuren, C-Zool., 2:1.
    TYPE(S): Not traced.
    TYPE LOCALITY: "Pweto, Lake Moero", southeastern Zaire.
    DISTRIBUTION: Southern Rep. Congo, southeastern Zaire, northern Botswana, northern western Zambia, and northeastern and eastern Angola.
    COMMENT: In the *Bufo lemairii* group. Haacke, 1982, J. Herpetol. Assoc. Afr., 27:11–12, discussed distribution records. See Schmidt and Inger, 1959, Explor. Parc Natl. Upemba, 56:21–23.

Bufo leptoscelis Boulenger, 1912. Ann. Mag. Nat. Hist., (8)10:186.
    TYPE(S): Holotype: BM 1907.5.7.32.
    TYPE LOCALITY: "Santo Domingo, Carabaya, S. E. Peru, 6500 feet".
    DISTRIBUTION: Departmento de Puno, Peru.
    COMMENT: In the *Bufo typhonius* group.

Bufo limensis Werner, 1901. Abh. Ber. K. Zool. Anthro. Ethno. Mus. Dresden, 9:14.
    TYPE(S): Holotype: MTKD D1795.
    TYPE LOCALITY: "Umgebung von Lima", Peru.
    DISTRIBUTION: Arid Peruvian coast from Pisco north to Sechura desert.
    COMMENT: In the *Bufo spinulosus* group. Possibly conspecific with *Bufo vellardi* (as *Bufo orientalis* Vellard, 1959) according to Cei, 1972, *In* Blair (ed.), Evol. Genus *Bufo*:82–91. See comment under *Bufo vellardi*. Considered a subspecies of *Bufo spinulosus* by Gorham, 1974, Checklist World Amph.:84.

Bufo lindneri Mertens, 1955. Jahr. Vereins Vaterl. Naturkd. Württemberg, 110:48.
    TYPE(S): Holotype: SMNS.
    TYPE LOCALITY: "Dar-es-Salaam", Tanzania.
    DISTRIBUTION: Type locality and 20 km WSW Dar es Salaam, Tanzania.

COMMENT: Howell, 1979, Herpetol. Rev., 10:101, commented on a range extension. Without discussion considered a synonym of *Bufo taitanus* by Tandy and Keith, 1972, *In* Blair (ed.), Evol. Genus *Bufo*:156.

Bufo lonnbergi Andersson, 1911. K. Svenska Vetensk. Akad. Handl., 47:35.
ORIGINAL NAME: *Bufo lönnbergi.*
TYPE(S): Syntypes: BM 1911.7.7.4–5, MCZ 17804, 17830–31, NHRM (3 unnumbered specimens).
TYPE LOCALITY: "Mount Kenya, 2500 m", Kenya.
DISTRIBUTION: Kenya southwards to Malawi and Zambia above 2000 m.
COMMENT: In the *Bufo taitanus* group. See Grandison, 1972, Zool. Meded., Leiden, 47:31–35, for synonymy and review. The spelling *loennbergi* is incorrect; under the International Code of Zoological Nomenclature (1985), only German umlauts (not Scandinavian umlauts) are to be corrected by the addition of an 'e'. See comment under *Bufo chappuisi.*

Bufo luetkenii Boulenger, 1891. Ann. Mag. Nat. Hist., (6)8:455.
TYPE(S): Syntypes: BM 1947.2.21.67 (formerly 91.6.17.2) + 2 lost.
TYPE LOCALITY: "Cartago, Costa Rica".
DISTRIBUTION: Low elevations along the Pacific versant from Costa Rica to southeastern Guatemala; dry interior valleys of Guatemala.
COMMENT: In the *Bufo valliceps* group. Erroneously included with *Bufo valliceps* by Porter, 1970, Cat. Am. Amph. Rept., 94.1. All of Porter's records for southeastern Guatemala, El Salvador, western Nicaragua, and northwestern Costa Rica are based on this species (JMS).

Bufo lughensis Loveridge, 1932. Occas. Pap. Boston Soc. Nat. Hist., 8:49.
TYPE(S): Holotype: BM 1947.2.21.9 (formerly 96.2.24.38).
TYPE LOCALITY: "Between Matagoi and Lugh, Italian Somaliland" (Somalia).
DISTRIBUTION: Ethiopia, Somalia, and Kenya.
COMMENT: In the *Bufo vertebralis* group. Synonymy includes *Bufo gardoensis* Scortecci, 1933, according to Balletto, Cherchi, and Lanza, 1978, Monit. Zool. Ital., N.S., Suppl., 11:223.

Bufo macrotis Boulenger, 1887. Ann. Mus. Civ. Stor. Nat. Genova, (2)5:422.
TYPE(S): Syntypes: BM 1947.2.21.15–16 (formerly 89.3.25.52–53), NHMW 16555, MSNG (10 specimens); MSNG 29616 designated lectotype by Capocaccia, 1957, Ann. Mus. Civ. Stor. Nat. Genova, 69:212.
TYPE LOCALITY: "Bhamò, Teinzò and Me-tan-jà in the Kakhien Hills [Burma]"; restricted to Teinzò, Burma, by lectotype designation.
DISTRIBUTION: Burma through western and southern Thailand, to northern Malaya.
COMMENT: See Taylor, 1962, Univ. Kansas Sci. Bull., 43:324–326, and Bourret, 1942, Batr. Indochine:169–170, for synonymy and discussion.

Bufo maculatus Hallowell, 1855 "1854". Proc. Acad. Nat. Sci. Philadelphia, 7:101.
TYPE(S): Unknown; probably lost.
TYPE LOCALITY: "Liberia West coast of Africa".
DISTRIBUTION: West and East Africa southward to northeastern Rep. South Africa in moist savanna.
COMMENT: *Bufo maculatus* is a replacement name for *Bufo cinereus* Hallowell, 1846, Proc. Acad. Nat. Sci. Philadelphia, 2:169, which is preoccupied by *Bufo cinereus* Schneider, 1799. In the *Bufo maculatus* group (Tandy, 1972, Univ. Texas Diss.:187–195, discussed this possibly monotypic group). Removed from the synonymy of *Bufo regularis* by Laurent, 1972, Explor. Parc Natl. Virunga, (2)22:1–125. See comment under *Bufo danielae.*

Bufo manicorensis Gallardo, 1961. Breviora, 141:1.
TYPE(S): Holotype: BM 1898.3.10.1.
TYPE LOCALITY: "Manicoré, Rio Madeira, State of Amazonas, Brasil".
DISTRIBUTION: Known only from the type locality.

COMMENT: In the *Bufo typhonius* group.

Bufo marinus (Linnaeus, 1758). Syst. Nat., Ed. 10, 1:211.
ORIGINAL NAME: *Rana marina.*
TYPE(S): Originally in Seba collection.
TYPE LOCALITY: America; restricted by Müller and Hellmich, 1936, Wiss. Ergebn.
Deutsch. Gran Chaco-Exped., Amph. Rept.:4, to Surinam.
DISTRIBUTION: Extreme southern Texas (USA) through tropical Mexico and Central
America to northern South America (central Brazil and Peru); introduced
widely (Antilles, Hawaii, Fiji, Philippines, Taiwan, Ryukyu Is., New Guinea,
Australia, and many Pacific islands) (see comment).
COMMENT: In the *Bufo marinus* group. See Schwartz and Thomas, 1975, Carnegie
Mus. Nat. Hist. Spec. Publ., 1:12, for list of Antilles on which this species has
been introduced. See Easteal, 1981, Biol. J. Linn. Soc., 16:93–113, for a detailed
history of introductions. For discussion of natural range in neotropics see
Zug and Zug, 1979, Smithson. Contrib. Zool., 284:1–58. Also see comment
under *Bufo poeppigii.*

Bufo marmoreus Wiegmann, 1833. Isis von Oken, 26:66.
TYPE(S): Syntypes: ZMB 3529–31.
TYPE LOCALITY: Veracruz, Veracruz, Mexico.
DISTRIBUTION: Southern Sonora to Chiapas on the Pacific versant and Veracruz to
the Isthmus of Tehuantepec on the Atlantic versant, Mexico.
COMMENT: In the *Bufo marmoreus* group.

Bufo mauritanicus Schlegel, 1841. *In* Wagner, Reisen Algier, 3:134.
TYPE(S): Holotype: RMNH 2122.
TYPE LOCALITY: " . . . in den Umgebungen der Stadt Algier. Sumpfen der Ebene
Metidscha; . . . . Bona", Algeria.
DISTRIBUTION: Morocco to Algeria.
COMMENT: In the *Bufo mauritanicus* group.

Bufo mazatlanensis Taylor, 1940 "1939". Univ. Kansas Sci. Bull., 26:492.
TYPE(S): Holotype: FMNH 100027 (formerly EHT-HMS 374).
TYPE LOCALITY: Two miles east of Mazatlán, Sinaloa, Mexico.
DISTRIBUTION: Northern Sonora to Colima, Pacific coastal area, Mexico.
COMMENT: In the *Bufo valliceps* group. Reviewed by Porter, 1963, Herpetologica, 29:
229–247. See comment under *Bufo gemmifer.*

Bufo melanochloris Cope, 1878. Proc. Am. Philos. Soc., 17:85.
TYPE(S): Holotype: USNM 30592.
TYPE LOCALITY: Eastern Costa Rica.
DISTRIBUTION: Eastern central Costa Rica.
COMMENT: In the *Bufo valliceps* group. See Taylor, 1952, Univ. Kansas Sci. Bull., 35:
616, for synonymy. Records from Nicaragua are based on misidentified
specimens of *Bufo luetkenii* or *Bufo valliceps* according to Villa, 1972, Anf.
Nicaragua.

Bufo melanogaster Hallowell, 1861 "1860". Proc. Acad. Nat. Sci. Philadelphia, 12:486.
TYPE(S): Not traced, not in ANSP or USNM.
TYPE LOCALITY: "Nicaragua".
DISTRIBUTION: Nicaragua.
COMMENT: Villa, 1972, Anf. Nicaragua, doubted the validity of this species and
supposed it might be a synonym of *Bufo haematiticus.*

Bufo melanopleura Schmidt and Inger, 1959. Explor. Parc. Natl. Upemba, 56:23.
TYPE(S): Holotype: Inst. Parc. Nat. Congo Belge 807 (now RGMC or MRHN).
TYPE LOCALITY: "Kankunde (rivière affluent gauche de la Lupiala et sous-affluent
droit de la Lufirá) Parc National de l'Upemba, Belgian Congo [=Zaire], . . .
elevation 1300 m."
DISTRIBUTION: Upemba National Park, Zaire, 695–1300 m.

COMMENT: Considered a synonym of *Mertensophryne micranotis* by Tandy and Keith, 1972, *In* Blair (ed.), Evol. Genus *Bufo*:156, without discussion.

Bufo melanostictus Schneider, 1799. Hist. Amph., 1:216.
TYPE(S): Not traced.
TYPE LOCALITY: "Ex India orientalis".
DISTRIBUTION: Southwestern and southern China (including Taiwan) throughout southern Asia to Sri Lanka and Sumatra, Java, Borneo, and Bali.
COMMENT: See Bourret, 1942, Batr. Indochine:172–175; Okada, 1931, Tailless Batr. Japan. Emp.:50–53; Liu, 1950, Fieldiana: Zool. Mem., 2:203; and Taylor, 1962, Univ. Kansas Sci. Bull., 43:332–335, for discussion and synonymy. See Inger, 1966, Fieldiana: Zool, 52:70–74, for a review of the Bornean population. Ceylonese population discussed by Kirtisinghe, 1957, Amph. Ceylon:20–22. See Pope, 1931, Bull. Am. Mus. Nat. Hist., 61:454–456, for discussion of Chinese population. In the *Bufo melanostictus* group. See comment under *Bufo camortensis*.

Bufo microscaphus Cope, 1867 "1866". Proc. Acad. Nat. Sci. Philadelphia, 18:301.
TYPE(S): Syntypes: USNM 4106 (now lost), 4184, 132901; USNM 4184 designated lectotype by Shannon, 1949, Bull. Chicago Acad. Sci., 8:307.
TYPE LOCALITY: Arizona and the upper Colorado region; restricted to "Fort Mohave, Mohave County, Arizona", USA, by Shannon, 1949, Bull. Chicago Acad. Sci., 8:307.
DISTRIBUTION: Coastal southern California (USA) and northern Baja California (Mexico); scattered populations from southern Nevada, southern Utah, and montane Arizona (USA) and south along the Sierra Madre Occidental to Durango (Mexico).
COMMENT: In the *Bufo americanus* group. Shannon, 1949, Bull. Chicago Acad. Sci., 8: 307, redescribed the lectotype.

Bufo microtympanum Boulenger, 1882. Cat. Batr. Sal. Brit. Mus.:307.
TYPE(S): Syntypes: BM 74.4.29.1146–1157.
TYPE LOCALITY: "Malabar", Kerala, India.
DISTRIBUTION: Southern India and Sri Lanka.
COMMENT: Reviewed by Kirtisinghe, 1957, Amph. Ceylon:19–20. See also Daniel, 1963, J. Bombay Nat. Hist. Soc., 60:438.

Bufo minshanicus Stejneger, 1926. J. Washington Acad. Sci., 16:446.
TYPE(S): Holotype: USNM 68567.
TYPE LOCALITY: "Choni on Tao River, Kansu [=Gansu] China".
DISTRIBUTION: Gansu and Sichuan, China.
COMMENT: In the *Bufo bufo* group. Usually treated as a subspecies of *Bufo bufo*, but regarded by Yang, 1983, Acta Herpetol. Sinica, 2(2):1–9, as a distinct species. Reviewed (as *Bufo bufo*) by Liu, 1950, Fieldiana: Zool. Mem., 2:212–214.

Bufo nasicus Werner, 1903. Zool. Anz., 26:252.
TYPE(S): Holotype: MRHN I.G. 9422 reg. 1015 (formerly 4792).
TYPE LOCALITY: "ohne irgend welche Fundortsangabe" (=without locality data).
DISTRIBUTION: Northeastern South America in eastern Venezuela and northwestern Guyana.
COMMENT: In the *Bufo typhonius* group. Hoogmoed, 1977, Zool. Meded., Leiden, 51: 265–275, reported recent material of this species, provided a synonymy, and discussed its relationships.

Bufo nesiotes Duellman and Toft, 1979. Herpetologica, 35:62.
TYPE(S): Holotype: KU 154920.
TYPE LOCALITY: "Laguna, west slope of Serranía de Sira, 1280 m, Departamento Huanuco, Peru".
DISTRIBUTION: Known only from the type locality.

COMMENT: Presumably in the *Bufo veraguensis* group (MSH).

Bufo ngamiensis FitzSimons, 1932. Ann. Transvaal Mus., 15:40.
ORIGINAL NAME: *Bufo regularis ngamiensis.*
TYPE(S): TM.
TYPE LOCALITY: Motlhatlogo, Ngamiland [northern Botswana].
DISTRIBUTION: Known only from the type locality.
COMMENT: In the *Bufo regularis* group. Provisionally regarded as a distinct species; possibly synonymous with *Bufo garmani* or *Bufo gutturalis* according to Tandy, 1972, Univ. Texas Diss.

Bufo occidentalis Camerano, 1879. Atti Accad. Sci. Torino, Cl. Sci. Fis. Mat. Nat., 14: 887.
TYPE(S): MSNT.
TYPE LOCALITY: Mexico.
DISTRIBUTION: Eastern Sonora and Veracruz to the Isthmus of Tehuantepec, Mexico.
COMMENT: Confused with *Bufo simus* in early literature. In the *Bufo valliceps* group.

Bufo ocellatus Günther, 1859 "1858". Cat. Batr. Sal. Coll. Brit. Mus.:64.
TYPE(S): Holotype: BM 1947.2.21.86 (formerly 57.10.28.57).
TYPE LOCALITY: "Brazil".
DISTRIBUTION: Brazil: Minas Gerais (Januária), Mato Grosso (Posto Pimentel Barbosa), Goiás (Ilha do Bananal), and Pará (Cachimbo).
COMMENT: In the *Bufo typhonius* group. Discussed and redescribed by Leão and Cochran, 1952, Mem. Inst. Butantan, São Paulo, 24:271–280.

Bufo olivaceus Blanford, 1874. Ann. Mag. Nat. Hist., (4)14:35.
TYPE(S): Syntypes: BM 1947.2.20.93 (formerly 74.11.23.122), 3 others not traced.
TYPE LOCALITY: "in Gedrosia", Iran.
DISTRIBUTION: Southeastern Iran and Baluchistan (Pakistan).
COMMENT: In the *Bufo stomaticus* group.

Bufo orientalis Werner, 1895. Verh. Zool. Bot. Ges. Wien, 45:20.
ORIGINAL NAME: *Bufo viridis orientalis.*
TYPE(S): Syntypes: BM 1947.2.20.45–46 (formerly 95.11.1.2–3).
TYPE LOCALITY: "Maskat (Arabien)", Oman.
DISTRIBUTION: Western highlands of Arabia, P.D.R. Yemen, United Arab Emirates, and Oman.
COMMENT: In the *Bufo orientalis* group. Tandy and Keith, 1972, *In* Blair (ed.), Evol. Genus *Bufo*:160, provisionally regarded *Bufo arabicus* Heyden, 1827, *In* Rüppel, Atlas Reise N. Afr., Rept.:20 (of the Arabian peninsula), as a distinct species. Subsequent authors (e.g., Inger, 1972, *In* Blair (ed.), Evol. Genus *Bufo*:115, and Eiselt and Schmidtler, 1973, Ann. Naturhist. Mus. Wien, 77:181–243), have not.

Bufo pageoti Bourret, 1937. Annexe Bull. Gén. Instr. Publique, Hanoi, 1937(4):9.
TYPE(S): Holotype: MNHNP 48-125 (formerly Lab. Sci. Nat. Univ. Hanoi B-145).
TYPE LOCALITY: Tonkin: Fan-Si-Pan, 2500 m., (près Chapa, province de Laokay) [Vietnam].
DISTRIBUTION: Tonkin, Vietnam.
COMMENT: Reviewed by Bourret, 1942, Batr. Indochine:170–172.

Bufo paracnemis Lutz, 1925. C. R. Séances Soc. Biol., Paris, 93:213.
TYPE(S): Syntypes: USNM 97238–39.
TYPE LOCALITY: Belo Horizonte, Minas Gerais, Brazil.
DISTRIBUTION: Brazil, from the Atlantic coast inland to central Bolivia; and southwest to northern and central Argentina and Uruguay.
COMMENT: In the *Bufo marinus* group. Formerly confused with *Bufo marinus.*

Possibly a synonym of *Bufo schneideri* according to Gallardo, 1962, Physis, Buenos Aires, 23:96. See comment under *Bufo schneideri*.

Bufo pardalis Hewitt, 1935. Rec. Albany Mus., 4:288.
ORIGINAL NAME: *Bufo regularis pardalis*.
TYPE(S): Syntypes: AMG.
TYPE LOCALITY: "Gleniffer, Kei Road, C[ape]. P[rovince].", Rep. South Africa.
DISTRIBUTION: Southern coastal Cape Province, Rep. South Africa.
COMMENT: In the *Bufo latifrons* group.

Bufo parietalis Boulenger, 1882. Cat. Batr. Sal. Brit. Mus.:312.
TYPE(S): Syntypes: BM 74.4.9.1156–57, 82.2.10.60.
TYPE LOCALITY: "Malabar", Kerala, India.
DISTRIBUTION: Kerala, India.
COMMENT: In the *Bufo melanostictus* group. See Daniel, 1963, J. Bombay Nat. Hist. Soc., 60:434.

Bufo parkeri Loveridge, 1932. Bull. Mus. Comp. Zool., 72:382.
TYPE(S): Holotype: MCZ 16330.
TYPE LOCALITY: "Swamped flats below Mangasini Village, Usandawi, Tanganyika Territory [Tanzania]".
DISTRIBUTION: Known only from the type locality (Tanzania) and southern Rift Valley of Kenya.
COMMENT: In the *Bufo vertebralis* group.

Bufo parvus Boulenger, 1887. Ann. Mag. Nat. Hist., (5)19:346.
TYPE(S): Syntypes: BM 1947.2.21.72–82 (formerly 86.12.28.42–51), MCZ 2208 (3 specimens), MSNG; MSNG 29413 designated lectotype by Capocaccia, 1957, Ann. Mus. Civ. Stor. Nat. Genova, 69:212.
TYPE LOCALITY: "Malacca", Malaysia (Malaya).
DISTRIBUTION: Southern Burma and southern Thailand to Malaya and Sumatra.
COMMENT: See Taylor, 1962, Univ. Kansas Sci. Bull., 43:329–332, and Bourret, 1942, Batr. Indochine:181–183, for synonymy and discussion. See also Berry, 1975, Amph. Fauna Peninsular Malaysia:50. In the *Bufo biporcatus* group.

Bufo pentoni Andersson, 1893. Ann. Mag. Nat. Hist., (6)12:440.
TYPE(S): Syntypes: BM 1947.2.21.90–92 (formerly 97.10.28.661–63).
TYPE LOCALITY: Shaata gardens, about one mile outside Suakin, Egypt.
DISTRIBUTION: Mauritania eastward to the Red Sea coast of Sudan, Ethiopia, and the Arabian Peninsula.
COMMENT: In the *Bufo pentoni* group. See Balletto and Cherchi, 1973, Boll. Mus. Ist. Biol. Univ. Genova, 41:105–119, for analysis of characters.

Bufo periglenes Savage, 1967. Rev. Biol. Tropical, 14:153.
TYPE(S): Holotype: LACM 1893.
TYPE LOCALITY: "Costa Rica: Provincia de Alajuela: Cantón de San Carlos: Cordillera de Tilarán, 2 miles ENE of Monteverde, Provincia de Puntarenas; 1590 meters".
DISTRIBUTION: Cordillera de Tilarán on the divide between Puntarenas and Alajuela provinces (Costa Rica), at 1600 m.
COMMENT: In the *Bufo periglenes* group.
PROTECTED STATUS: CITES—Appendix I (1 Jul. 1975) and USA ESA—Endangered (14 Jun. 1976).

Bufo peripatetes Savage, 1972. J. Herpetol., 6:26.
TYPE(S): Holotype: UMMZ 58430.
TYPE LOCALITY: "Panama: Provincia de Chiriqui: above Boquete on Almirante trail, 1500 m."
DISTRIBUTION: Known only from the type locality.

COMMENT: Most closely related to *Bufo fastidiosus* and *Bufo holdridgei*, according to the original description. Not formally assigned to any species group but in the original description said to be related to the *Bufo valliceps* group.

Bufo perplexus Taylor, 1943. Univ. Kansas Sci. Bull., 29:347.
TYPE(S): Formerly EHT-HMS 707 (now FMNH?).
TYPE LOCALITY: "near the edge of the Balsas River, near the town of Mexcala, Guerrero, México".
DISTRIBUTION: Balsas Basin of southern Mexico.
COMMENT: In the *Bufo marmoreus* group.

Bufo perreti Schiøtz, 1963. Vidensk. Medd. Dansk Naturhist. Foren., 125:17.
TYPE(S): Holotype: ZMUC 13549.
TYPE LOCALITY: "Idanre Hills near Idanre Resthouse, Ondo Province, 7° 06' N 5° 06' E, W. Nigeria".
DISTRIBUTION: Known only from the type locality.
COMMENT: In the *Bufo perreti* group.

Bufo poeppigii Tschudi, 1845. Arch. Naturgesch., 11:169.
TYPE(S): Not designated.
TYPE LOCALITY: "Republica Peruana".
DISTRIBUTION: Cloud forests on the Andean slopes of Colombia, Ecuador, Peru, and Bolivia, 800–1670 m; reported from the Serranía de Sira in Amazonian Peru by Duellman and Toft, 1979, Herpetologica, 35:64.
COMMENT: In the *Bufo marinus* group. Considered a subspecies of *Bufo marinus* by Gorham, 1974, Checklist World Amph.:81.

Bufo poweri Hewitt, 1935. Rec. Albany Mus., 4:293.
ORIGINAL NAME: *Bufo regularis poweri*.
TYPE(S): Syntypes: AMG.
TYPE LOCALITY: Kimberley [Rep. South Africa].
DISTRIBUTION: Namibia and Botswana southward to Cape Province, Rep. South Africa.
COMMENT: In the *Bufo regularis* group. Without comment, considered a synonym of *Bufo garmani* by Tandy and Keith, 1972, *In* Blair (ed.), Evol. Genus *Bufo*:159.

Bufo punctatus Baird and Girard, 1852. Proc. Acad. Nat. Sci. Philadelphia, 6:173.
TYPE(S): Syntypes: USNM 2618 (3 specimens); apparently lost.
TYPE LOCALITY: Rio San Pedro [Devil's River], Val Verde County, Texas [USA].
DISTRIBUTION: Southeastern California, Utah and western Kansas (USA) south to southern Baja California, Sinaloa, Guanajuato, San Luis Potosí, and Tamaulipas (Mexico).
COMMENT: In the *Bufo punctatus* group. See Ferguson and Lowe, 1969, Am. Midl. Nat., 81:435–466, for a discussion of relationships with *Bufo kelloggi*, *Bufo debilis*, and *Bufo retiformis*.

Bufo pygmaeus Myers and Carvalho, 1952. Zoologica, New York, 37:1.
TYPE(S): MN.
TYPE LOCALITY: "São João da Barra, at the mouth of the Rio Parahyba (right bank), state of Rio de Janeiro, Brazil".
DISTRIBUTION: Southeastern coastal Brazil, northeastern Argentina, and central Paraguay.
COMMENT: In the *Bufo granulosus* group. Repeatedly considered a subspecies of *Bufo granulosus* (e.g., Gallardo, 1965, Bull. Mus. Comp. Zool., 134:121), but see comment under *Bufo fernandezae* and *Bufo granulosus*.

Bufo quadriporcatus Boulenger, 1887. Ann. Mag. Nat. Hist., (5)19:347.
TYPE(S): Holotype: BM 1947.2.21.94 (formerly 86.12.28.41).
TYPE LOCALITY: "Malacca", Malaysia (Malaya).
DISTRIBUTION: Malaya; Sumatra; Borneo.

COMMENT: In the *Bufo biporcatus* group. See Bourret, 1942, Batr. Indochine:180–181, and Inger, 1966, Fieldiana: Zool., 52:63–66, for review. See also Berry, 1975, Amph. Fauna Peninsular Malaysia:52.

Bufo quechua Gallardo, 1961. Breviora, 141:4.
  TYPE(S): Holotype: CM 4225.
  TYPE LOCALITY: "Incachaca, 2500 m, Department of Cochabamba, Bolivia".
  DISTRIBUTION: Yungas of Departamento de Cochabamba, Bolivia, 2200–2600 m.
  COMMENT: In the *Bufo typhonius* group according to Blair (ed.), 1972, Evol. Genus *Bufo*, but considered a member of the *Bufo ockendeni* (=*Bufo veraguensis*) group in the original description, a group recognized by Cei, 1980, Monit. Zool. Ital., N.S., Monogr., 2:203.

Bufo quercicus Holbrook, 1840. N. Am. Herpetol., Ed. 1, 4:109.
  TYPE(S): Not designated.
  TYPE LOCALITY: "near Charleston in South Carolina, and at Smithville in North Carolina"; restricted to "Charleston, South Carolina", USA, by Schmidt, 1953, Check List N. Am. Amph. Rept., Ed. 6:109.
  DISTRIBUTION: Southeastern Louisiana and southeastern Virginia along the coastal plain to peninsular Florida, USA.
  COMMENT: Reviewed by Ashton and Franz, 1979, Cat. Am. Amph. Rept., 222.1–2. In the *Bufo quercicus* group.

Bufo raddei Strauch, 1876. *In* Przewalski, Mongholiya i Strana Tanghutov, 2(3):53.
  TYPE(S): Syntypes: ZIL 921–925, MCZ 1958.
  TYPE LOCALITY: Ordos and Alashan Desert [China].
  DISTRIBUTION: Northern and western China, Korea, Mongolia, and north to Lake Baikal and Amur River in USSR.
  COMMENT: See Liu, 1950, Fieldiana: Zool. Mem., 2:203–206, for synonymy and discussion. Also see Pope, 1931, Bull. Am. Mus. Nat. Hist., 61:459–462. See also Hemmer, Schmidtler, and Böhme, 1978, Zool. Abh. Staatl. Mus. Tierkd., Dresden, 34:349–384. In the *Bufo viridis* group.

Bufo rangeri Hewitt, 1935. Rec. Albany Mus., 4:285.
  ORIGINAL NAME: *Bufo regularis rangeri.*
  TYPE(S): Syntypes: AMG (2 specimens).
  TYPE LOCALITY: "Gleniffer, near Kei Road, C[ape]. P[rovince].", Rep. South Africa.
  DISTRIBUTION: Lesotho; eastern and southern parts of the Rep. South Africa.
  COMMENT: In the *Bufo regularis* group.

Bufo reesi Poynton, 1977. Ann. Natal Mus., 23:37.
  TYPE(S): Holotype: BM 1969.1520.
  TYPE LOCALITY: Merera, Tanzania 36° 02' E 8° 33' S, Kihanzi-Kilombero floodplain, 200–500 m.
  DISTRIBUTION: Kihanzi-Kilombero floodplain, Mahenge District, southern Tanzania.

Bufo regularis Reuss, 1833. Mus. Senckenb., 1:60.
  TYPE(S): SMF 3429 designated lectotype by Mertens, 1967, Senckenb. Biol., 48:40.
  TYPE LOCALITY: "Aegypten".
  DISTRIBUTION: West Africa to Egypt and southwestern Ethiopia southwards to East Africa in savanna and farmbush.
  COMMENT: In the *Bufo regularis* group. See Schmidt and Inger, 1959, Explor. Parc Natl. Upemba, 56:27–33. See Stean, 1938, J. Soc. Bibliogr. Nat. Hist., 1:155, for discussion of the publication data of the description.

Bufo retiformis Sanders and Smith, 1951. Field and Laboratory, 19:153.
  ORIGINAL NAME: *Bufo debilis retiformis.*
  TYPE(S): Holotype: UIMNH 5847.
  TYPE LOCALITY: "14.4 miles south of Ajo, Pima County, Arizona", USA.
  DISTRIBUTION: Central-western Sonora (Mexico) to south-central Arizona (USA).

COMMENT: Reviewed by Hulse, 1978, Cat. Am. Amph. Rept., 207.1–2. In the *Bufo punctatus* group. See comment under *Bufo punctatus*.
PROTECTED STATUS: CITES—Appendix II (1 Jul. 1975).

Bufo rubropunctatus Guichenot, 1843. *In* Gay, Hist. Fis. Polit. Chile, 2:128.
TYPE(S): Not designated.
TYPE LOCALITY: " . . . Bosques humedos de la Provincia de Valdivia" (=wet forests of Valdivia Province), Chile.
DISTRIBUTION: Southern Chile (Valdivia, Llanquihué, Arauco and Cautin provinces); Argentina, in the vicinity of Esquel (Chubut Province) and El Bolsón (Río Negro Province).
COMMENT: In the *Bufo spinulosus* group. At times considered a subspecies of *Bufo spinulosus* (e.g., Cei, 1962, Batr. Chile), but currently considered a distinct species (see Cei, 1980, Monit. Zool. Ital., N.S., Monogr., 2:171).

Bufo rufus Garman, 1877. Proc. Boston Soc. Nat. Hist., 18:413.
TYPE(S): Syntypes: MCZ 367–68 (2 specimens).
TYPE LOCALITY: "near Goyaz [=city of Goiás], on the highlands of east Brazil" (actually in central Brazil).
DISTRIBUTION: Brazil (Goiás, Minas Gerais) and extreme northeastern Argentina (Misiones).
COMMENT: In the *Bufo marinus* group of Blair (ed.), 1972, Evol. Genus *Bufo*, but in the *Bufo arenarum* group of Cei, 1980, Monit. Zool. Ital., N.S., Monogr., 2:173. *Bufo missionum* Berg, 1896, was synonymized by Gallardo, 1961, Neotropica, 7: 24, though still treated as a distinct species by Gorham, 1974, Checklist World Amph.:82.

Bufo schneideri Werner, 1894. Zool. Anz., 17:411.
TYPE(S): Holotype: NHMB 1916.
TYPE LOCALITY: "Paraguay".
DISTRIBUTION: Paraguay.
COMMENT: According to the original description most closely related to *Bufo sternosignatus*. Gallardo, 1962, Physis, Buenos Aires, 23:96, apparently studied the holotype and in a note concluded that *Bufo paracnemis* appeared to be a synonym. *Bufo schneideri* has priority over *Bufo paracnemis*, which would involve a name change for the taxon widely known as *Bufo paracnemis*. In order to not upset current nomenclature and because Gallardo's statement was not definite both names are retained here (MSH).

Bufo scortecci Balletto and Cherchi, 1970. Boll. Mus. Ist. Biol. Univ. Genova, 38:34.
TYPE(S): Holotype: IZUG 4.
TYPE LOCALITY: "Mafhaq, [P.D.R.] Yemen".
DISTRIBUTION: Known only from the type locality.

Bufo sibiliai Scortecci, 1929. Atti. Soc. Ital. Sci. Nat. Mus. Civ. Stor. Nat. Milano, 68: 186.
TYPE(S): Holotype: MSNM 589.
TYPE LOCALITY: Regione Fil-Fil, presso Ghinda Eritrea [Ethiopia].
DISTRIBUTION: Known only from the type locality.
COMMENT: Tentatively referred to *Bufo blanfordii* by Tandy and Keith, 1972, *In* Blair (ed.), Evol. Genus *Bufo*:158. Regarded by Tandy, 1972, Univ. Texas Diss.:197, to be synonymous with *Bufo blanfordii*.

Bufo silentvalleyensis Pillai, 1981. Bull. Zool. Surv. India, 3:156.
TYPE(S): Not stated but in ZSIM (SD).
TYPE LOCALITY: Valaiparai Thodu, Silent Valley, Kerala, India.
DISTRIBUTION: South India.

Bufo simus Schmidt, 1857. Sitzungsber. Akad. Wiss. Wien, Math. Naturwiss. Kl.,
      24:10.
   TYPE(S): Syntypes: BM 1947.2.21.18 (formerly 98.9.14.6), ZMH 1527, KM 1029/1351
      (5 specimens), ZSM 593-20, and NHMW 16521; BM 1947.2.21.18 designated
      lectotype by Savage, 1972, J. Herpetol., 6:32.
   TYPE LOCALITY: Rio Chiriqui near Boca del Toro [Panama]; doubted by Savage,
      1972, J. Herpetol., 6:25-33, who suggested that the true type locality was in
      South America, possibly Peru or Bolivia.
   DISTRIBUTION: Unknown, probably South America.
   COMMENT: The taxonomic confusion regarding this species was reviewed by
      Savage, 1972, J. Herpetol., 6:25-33. Confused with *Bufo occidentalis* and *Bufo
      peripatetes* in the literature.

Bufo speciosus Girard, 1854. Proc. Acad. Nat. Sci. Philadelphia, 7:85.
   TYPE(S): Syntypes: USNM 2608 (Ringgold Barracks = Rio Grande City, Starr
      County, Texas, USA), 2610 (Brownsville, Cameron County, Texas, USA), 2611,
      and 131559 (Pesquiería Grande, Nuevo León, Mexico).
   TYPE LOCALITY: Valley of the Río Bravo [=Río Grande] and not uncommon in the
      province [state] of New Leon [Nuevo León, Mexico].
   DISTRIBUTION: Eastern New Mexico and southern Oklahoma (USA) south to central
      Tamaulipas, northern Nuevo León, and Chihuahua (Mexico).
   COMMENT: In the *Bufo cognatus* group. See comment under *Bufo cognatus*. Older
      literature confused this species with *Bufo compactilis*.

Bufo spinulosus Wiegmann, 1834. Nova Acta Acad. Caesar. Leop. Carol., Halle, 17:265.
   TYPE(S): Not traced (ZMB?).
   TYPE LOCALITY: "Peru".
   DISTRIBUTION: Andean Argentina, Chile, Bolivia, Peru, and southern Ecuador.
   COMMENT: In the *Bufo spinulosus* group. Cei, 1961, Invest. Zool. Chilen., 7:59-81,
      showed that *Bufo arunco* Molina, 1775, has priority over *Bufo spinulosus*, but
      refrained from reintroducing this name because of the widespread
      consequences of such an act. Cei, 1962, Batr. Chile:38, and Cei, 1980, Monit.
      Zool. Ital., N.S., Monogr., 2:164, considered *Phryniscus nigricans* Wiegmann a
      synonym. Also see comments under *Bufo arequipensis*, *Bufo atacamensis*, *Bufo
      flavolineatus*, *Bufo chilensis*, *Bufo limensis*, *Bufo trifolium*, and *Bufo vellardi*.

Bufo steindachneri Pfeffer, 1893. Jahrb. Hamburg. Wiss. Anst., 10:103.
   TYPE(S): Probably lost.
   TYPE LOCALITY: "Kihengo", Tanzania.
   DISTRIBUTION: Nigeria eastward to Kenya, Ethiopia, Somalia, Kenya, Uganda, and
      Tanzania.
   COMMENT: In the *Bufo funereus* group.

Bufo stejnegeri Schmidt, 1931. Copeia, 1931:94.
   TYPE(S): Holotype: FMNH 11417.
   TYPE LOCALITY: "Songdo, Korea (Chosen)".
   DISTRIBUTION: Korea; northeastern China.
   COMMENT: Redescribed by Matsui, 1980, Herpetologica, 36:37-41 (who included
      Bufo kangi Yoon, 1975, in synonymy); see also Zhao, 1983, Acta Herpetol.
      Sinica, 2(3):72 (who included *Bufo cycloparotidos* Zhao and Huang, 1983, in
      synonymy), for discussion.

Bufo sternosignatus Günther, 1859 "1858". Cat. Batr. Sal. Coll. Brit. Mus.:68.
   TYPE(S): Syntypes: BM 1947.2.21.68-69 (formerly 47.6.22.58-59), 1947.2.21.70
      (formerly 49.11.7.38), 1947.2.21.87 (formerly 56.3.17.25), 1947.2.21.88 (formerly
      57.7.31.29) (total of 5 specimens).
   TYPE LOCALITY: "Venezuela"; "Puerto Cabello"; "Cordova"; "Mexico".
   DISTRIBUTION: Coastal Range and Falcón region, Venezuela, to 1800 m.

COMMENT: In the *Bufo typhonius* group. Specimens from Mexico proved to be *Bufo valliceps*. The presence in Colombia was denied by Rivero, 1961, Bull. Mus. Comp. Zool., 126:29, but accepted for Bogotá by Cochran and Goin, 1970, Bull. U.S. Natl. Mus., 288:112.

Bufo stomaticus Lütken, 1862. Vidensk. Medd. Dansk Naturhist. Foren., 1862:305.
   TYPE(S): Syntypes: Not traced (?ZMUC).
   TYPE LOCALITY: "Assam", India.
   DISTRIBUTION: Eastern Iran and southern Afghanistan to Sind and Rajasthan areas of India and Pakistan; Nepal; Sri Lanka; southeastern corner of the Arabian Peninsula.
   COMMENT: In the *Bufo stomaticus* group. See comment under *Bufo stuarti*. See Kirtisinghe, 1957, Amph. Ceylon:17–19, and Daniel, 1963, J. Bombay Nat. Hist. Soc., 60:433–434. Synonymy includes *Bufo andersonii* Boulenger, 1883, Ann. Mag. Nat. Hist., (5)12:163 (Syntypes: BM 1947.2.20.47, 1947.2.20.50–53; Type localities: "Agra district", "Ajmere", and "Tatta"), according to Mertens, 1969, Stuttgart. Beitr. Naturkd., 197:4, and Schmidtler and Schmidtler, 1969, Salamandra, 5:122.

Bufo stuarti Smith, 1929. Rec. Indian Mus., 31:77.
   TYPE(S): Not traced.
   TYPE LOCALITY: "Putao plain, N.E. Burma, near the Tibetan frontier".
   DISTRIBUTION: Extreme northeastern India and upper Burma.
   COMMENT: In the *Bufo melanostictus* group. Closely related to *Bufo stomaticus*, according to the original description.

Bufo sulphureus Grandison and Daniel, 1964. J. Bombay Nat. Hist. Soc., 61:192.
   TYPE(S): Holotype: BNHM 377.
   TYPE LOCALITY: "approximately 4000 ft. near Humbelevi village Koyna, Satara District, Maharashtra", India.
   DISTRIBUTION: Known only from the type locality.
   COMMENT: A junior synonym of *Bufo koynayensis* (AGCG).

Bufo sumatranus Peters, 1871. Monatsber. Preuss. Akad. Wiss. Berlin, 1871:648.
   TYPE(S): Holotype: ZMB 6292.
   TYPE LOCALITY: Central Sumatra [Indonesia].
   DISTRIBUTION: Sumatra.

Bufo superciliaris Boulenger, 1887. Proc. Zool. Soc. London, 1887:565.
   TYPE(S): Syntypes: BM 1947.2.21.41–49 (formerly 87.12.21.10–18).
   TYPE LOCALITY: "Rio del Rey, Cameroons", Africa.
   DISTRIBUTION: Ivory Coast eastward to northern Zaire.
   PROTECTED STATUS: CITES—Appendix I (1 Jul. 1975) and USA ESA—Endangered (14 Jun. 1976).

Bufo surdus Boulenger, 1891. Ann. Mag. Nat. Hist., (6)7:282.
   TYPE(S): Holotype: BM 1947.2.21.20 (formerly 90.12.17.1).
   TYPE LOCALITY: "Baluchistan", Pakistan.
   DISTRIBUTION: Mountains of southern Iran and western Pakistan.
   COMMENT: In the *Bufo viridis* group. See Schmidtler and Schmidtler, 1969, Salamandra, 5:113–123, for taxonomy, distribution, and ecology, and inclusion of *Bufo viridis* var. *persica* Nikolsky, 1899, in synonymy. See Eiselt and Schmidtler, 1973, Ann. Naturhist. Mus. Wien, 77:181–243, for synonymy of *Bufo luristanica* Schmidt, 1959.

Bufo tacanensis Smith, 1952. Copeia, 1952:176.
   TYPE(S): Holotype: UMMZ 88359.
   TYPE LOCALITY: "at 1500 meters on Volcán de Tacaná, Unión Juárez, Chiapas, México".
   DISTRIBUTION: Intermediate elevations along the Pacific versant of eastern Chiapas (Mexico) and western Guatemala.

Bufo taitanus Peters, 1878. Monatsber. Preuss. Akad. Wiss. Berlin, 1878:208.
TYPE(S): Syntypes: ZMB 9298, MCZ 22327.
TYPE LOCALITY: "Taita", Kenya.
DISTRIBUTION: Kenya southward to Malawi and Zambia.
COMMENT: In the *Bufo taitanus* group. See Grandison, 1972, Zool. Meded., Leiden, 47:38–42, for synonymy and review.

Bufo terrestris (Bonnaterre, 1789). Tabl. Encycl. Méth. Trois Règ. Nat., Erp.:8.
ORIGINAL NAME: *Rana terrestris*.
TYPE(S): Unknown.
TYPE LOCALITY: "La Caroline"; restricted to "Charleston, South Carolina", USA, by Schmidt, 1953, Check List N. Am. Amph. Rept., Ed. 6:65.
DISTRIBUTION: Extreme southeastern Virginia and southeastern Louisiana along the coastal plain to peninsular Florida, USA.
COMMENT: Reviewed by Blem, 1979, Cat. Am. Amph. Rept., 223.1–4. In the *Bufo americanus* group.

Bufo tibetanus Zarevsky, 1926 "1925". Ann. Mus. Zool. Acad. Sci., Petrograd, 26:74.
TYPE(S): Syntypes: ZIL 1970–71, 2633, 2637–38.
TYPE LOCALITY: Kham Plateau, Tibet [Tatsienlo (=Kangting), Sichuan and Qinghai, China].
DISTRIBUTION: High elevations of western China (Sichuan, Qinghai, and Tibet).
COMMENT: A derivative of *Bufo bufo* according to Liu, 1950, Fieldiana: Zool. Mem., 2:207–212, who reviewed this species and supplied a synonymy. In the *Bufo bufo* group.

Bufo tienhoensis Bourret, 1937. Annexe Bull. Gén. Instr. Publique, Hanoi, 1937(4):11.
TYPE(S): Syntypes: MNHNP 48–123, 48–124 (formerly Lab. Sci. Nat. Univ. Hanoi B-126 and B-127).
TYPE LOCALITY: Tonkin: Col de Tien-Ho, sur la route de Hanoi à Langson [Vietnam].
DISTRIBUTION: Known only from the type locality.
COMMENT: Reviewed by Bourret, 1942, Batr. Indochine:175–176.

Bufo togoensis Ahl, 1924. Arch. Naturgesch., (A)90:253.
TYPE(S): Syntypes: including MCZ 19576.
TYPE LOCALITY: "Bismarkburg [=Adele], Togo".
DISTRIBUTION: Togo eastward to southwestern Cameroon and Congo.
COMMENT: In the *Bufo latifrons* group. The status of this form is doubtful; possibly a synonym of *Bufo latifrons*, according to Tandy, 1972, Univ. Texas Diss.:181.

Bufo torrenticola M. Matsui, 1976. Contrib. Biol. Lab. Kyoto Univ., 25:1.
TYPE(S): Holotype: OMNH Am4202.
TYPE LOCALITY: Shiokara-dani Valley, Mt. Hidegatake, Ohdaigahara, Nara Prefecture, Honshu, Japan.
DISTRIBUTION: Southeastern Honshu, Japan.
COMMENT: In the *Bufo bufo* group; related to *Bufo japonicus*, according to the original description. Kawamura, Nishioka, and Ueda, 1980, Sci. Rep. Lab. Amph. Biol. Hiroshima Univ., 4:12, found no genetic isolation in laboratory hybridization between *Bufo japonicus* and *Bufo torrenticola* and considered *Bufo torrenticola* to be a subspecies of *Bufo japonicus*. However, both forms remain distinct in sympatry according to M. Matsui, 1976, Contrib. Biol. Lab. Kyoto Univ., 25:7. See M. Matsui, 1984, Contrib. Biol. Lab. Kyoto Univ., 26:209:428, for morphometric variation analysis and revision.

Bufo trifolium Tschudi, 1845. Arch. Naturgesch., 11:169.
TYPE(S): Not designated.
TYPE LOCALITY: "Republica Peruana".
DISTRIBUTION: Peru; Amazonian head of Huallaga-Marañón basin, in the subtropical range of Huánuco to the Andean tops of Junín, Tarma, Ayacucho, Andahuaylas, and eastern borders of Cajamarca, between 2800 and 4600 m.

COMMENT: In the *Bufo spinulosus* group. Formerly considered a subspecies of *Bufo spinulosus*, but considered a distinct species by Cei, 1972, *In* Blair (ed.), Evol. Genus *Bufo*:82–92.

Bufo tuberosus Günther, 1859 "1858". Cat. Batr. Sal. Coll. Brit. Mus.:60.
TYPE(S): Holotype: BM 1947.2.21.14 (formerly 51.10.25.7).
TYPE LOCALITY: "Fernando Po".
DISTRIBUTION: High tropical forest of the Gabon-Cameroon-Congo-Zaire region and Fernando Po.
COMMENT: In the *Bufo tuberosus* group.

Bufo typhonius (Linnaeus, 1758). Syst. Nat., Ed. 10, 1:211.
ORIGINAL NAME: *Rana typhonia*.
TYPE(S): Not traced.
TYPE LOCALITY: "Americas".
DISTRIBUTION: Throughout South America.
COMMENT: In the *Bufo typhonius* group. See Cochran and Goin, 1970, Bull. U.S. Natl. Mus., 288:101–102, for synonymy. Hoogmoed, 1977, Zool. Meded., Leiden, 51:274, indicated that there are at least four sibling species confused under this name. Also see comments under *Bufo iserni* and *Bufo chanchanensis*.

Bufo urunguensis Loveridge, 1932. Bull. Mus. Comp. Zool., 72:383.
TYPE(S): Holotype: MCZ 16376.
TYPE LOCALITY: "Kitungulu, Urungu, [Namanyere District,] Tanganyika Territory [=Tanzania]".
DISTRIBUTION: Tanzania and Zambia near southeastern corner of Lake Tanganyika.

Bufo uzunguensis Loveridge, 1932. Occas. Pap. Boston Soc. Nat. Hist., 8:44.
ORIGINAL NAME: *Bufo taitanus uzunguensis*.
TYPE(S): Holotype: MCZ 16383.
TYPE LOCALITY: Kigogo, Uzungwe Mountains, southern Tanganyika Territory [Tanzania].
DISTRIBUTION: Southwestern Tanzania above 1800 m.
COMMENT: Grandison, 1972, Zool. Meded., Leiden, 47:35, considered *Bufo uzunguensis* distinct from *Bufo taitanus*.

Bufo valhallae Meade-Waldo, 1908. Proc. Zool. Soc. London, 1908:786.
TYPE(S): Syntypes: BM 1909.9.6.1 plus 1 not traced.
TYPE LOCALITY: "Pulo Weh Island, off N. Sumatra", Indonesia.
DISTRIBUTION: Known only from the type locality.

Bufo valliceps Wiegmann, 1833. Isis von Oken, 26:657–659.
TYPE(S): Syntypes: ZMB 3525–27, 3532 (8 specimens).
TYPE LOCALITY: "Mexico" and "Vera Cruz, Mexico"; restricted to "Vera Cruz, Vera Cruz", Mexico, by Schmidt, 1953, Check List N. Am. Amph. Rept., Ed. 6:66.
DISTRIBUTION: Louisiana, southern Arkansas, and eastern and southern Texas (USA) south through eastern Mexico to northern Costa Rica on the Atlantic versant; from the Isthmus of Tehuantepec to south-central Guatemala on the Pacific slope; one specimen from Atlantic versant of Costa Rica near Río San Juan.
COMMENT: Reviewed by Porter, 1970, Cat. Am. Amph. Rept., 94.1–4. See comments under *Bufo luetkenii* and *Bufo melanochloris*, with which this species has been confused. In the *Bufo valliceps* group.

Bufo variegatus (Günther, 1870). Proc. Zool. Soc. London, 1870:402.
ORIGINAL NAME: *Nannophryne variegata*.
TYPE(S): Syntypes: BM 69.5.3.50–51, 69.5.3.59, 1947.2.21.96 (formerly 68.9.22.3), and 2 not traced.
TYPE LOCALITY: "Puerto Bueno, Port Grappler, and in Eden Harbour", Magallanes, Chile.
DISTRIBUTION: Southern Peru to Patagonia and southern Chile.

COMMENT: For discussion and synonymy see Gallardo, 1962, Physis, Buenos Aires, 23:93–102. For review see Cei, 1962, Batr. Chile:51–52, and Cei, 1980, Monit. Zool. Ital., N.S., Monogr., 2:160–164. Cei, 1980, declined to place this species in any of the species groups.

Bufo vellardi Leviton and Duellman, 1978. J. Herpetol., 12:246.
TYPE(S): Syntypes: MHNJP 815 (2 specimens).
TYPE LOCALITY: "Hacienda Yanasona (Alto Marañón)", Peru.
DISTRIBUTION: Northern Peru in the upper Marañón area.
COMMENT: In the *Bufo typhonius* group. *Bufo vellardi* is a replacement name for *Bufo spinulosus orientalis* Vellard, 1959, Mem. Mus. Hist. Nat. Javier Prado, 8:1–48, which is preoccupied by *Bufo viridis orientalis* Werner, 1895. Elevated to species status by Cei, 1972, In Blair (ed.), Evol. Genus *Bufo*:82–91. Considered a subspecies of *Bufo limensis* by Leviton and Duellman, 1978; see comment under *Bufo limensis*.

Bufo veraguensis Schmidt, 1857. Sitzungsber. Akad. Wiss. Wien, Math. Naturwiss. Kl., 24:10.
TYPE(S): Holotype: KM 1032/1350.
TYPE LOCALITY: "Neu Granada, Provinz Veragua" (in error); Savage, 1969, Copeia, 1969:178–179, showed this type locality to be wrong and assumed that the type came from Bolivia or Peru.
DISTRIBUTION: Southeastern Peru and adjacent Bolivia, between 1300 and 1900 m.
COMMENT: Savage, 1969, Copeia, 1969:178–179, showed that *Bufo veraguensis* is identical with *Bufo ockendeni* Boulenger, 1902, over which it takes priority.

Bufo vertebralis Smith, 1848. Illustr. Zool. S. Afr., Rept.:pl. 68, fig. 2.
TYPE(S): Syntypes: BM 1947.2.20.96–99, 1947.2.21.1–2 (formerly 58.11.25.11).
TYPE LOCALITY: Interior districts of Southern Africa northeast of the Cape Colony.
DISTRIBUTION: Orange Free State and to Cape Province (Rep. South Africa); southeastern highlands of Zimbabwe.
COMMENT: In the *Bufo vertebralis* group. *Bufo vertebralis grindleyi* Poynton, 1963, Ann. Natal Mus., 15:320 (Type: NMZB [formerly UM]; Type locality: Chimanimani Mountains, Zimbabwe), is now regarded by JCP as a distinct species.

Bufo villiersi Angel, 1940. Bull. Mus. Natl. Hist. Nat., Paris, (2)12:238.
TYPE(S): Holotype: MNHNP 39–130.
TYPE LOCALITY: "Djuttitsa (Monts Bamboutos); alt. 2000 m., Cameroun".
DISTRIBUTION: Western Cameroon, 1200–2500 m.
COMMENT: Tentatively referred to the *Bufo funereus–Bufo steindachneri–Bufo vittatus* complex by Tandy, 1972, Univ. Texas Diss.:161.

Bufo viridis Laurenti, 1768. Synop. Rept.:27.
TYPE(S): Not designated.
TYPE LOCALITY: "Viennae", Austria.
DISTRIBUTION: Europe (including southern tip of Sweden, but excluding the rest of Fenno-Skandia and the British Isles and western Europe west of the Rhine River) east to Kazakhstan and Altai mountains in USSR, Mongolia, and extreme western China; northern coast of Africa.
COMMENT: In the *Bufo viridis* group. See Hemmer, Schmidtler, and Böhme, 1978, Zool. Abh. Staatl. Mus. Tierkd., Dresden, 34:349–384, for discussion. See comment under *Bufo danatensis*.

Bufo vittatus Boulenger, 1906. Proc. Zool. Soc. London, 1906:573.
TYPE(S): Holotype: BM 1947.2.21.12 (formerly 1906.5.30.56).
TYPE LOCALITY: "Entebbe", Uganda.
DISTRIBUTION: Egypt and Uganda.

COMMENT: Closely related to *Bufo steindachneri* and considered to be closely related to the *Bufo funereus–Bufo steindachneri–Bufo vittatus* complex by Tandy, 1972, Univ. Texas Diss.:161–165. Redescribed by Perret, 1971, Rev. Zool. Bot. Afr., 84:130–139.

Bufo wazae Hulselmans, 1977. Rev. Zool. Afr., 91:512.
TYPE(S): Holotype: Missions Zoologiques Belges au Cameroun 2-99.
TYPE LOCALITY: Waza (Cameroon).
DISTRIBUTION: Senegal eastward through Mali, Guinea, Niger, Algeria to Cameroon.
COMMENT: Hulselmans, in addendum, suggested that *Bufo wazae* may be a junior synonym of *Bufo xeros*.

Bufo woodhousii Girard, 1854. Proc. Acad. Nat. Sci. Philadelphia, 7:86.
TYPE(S): Holotype: USNM 2531.
TYPE LOCALITY: "[Territory of] New Mexico, having so far been found in the province of Sonora, and in the San Francisco Mts."; restricted to "San Francisco Mountain, Coconino County," Arizona, USA, by Smith and Taylor, 1948, Bull. U.S. Natl. Mus., 194:40.
DISTRIBUTION: Southern Ontario (Canada), USA (excluding Great Basin and Pacific Coast), and northern Mexico south to Durango.
COMMENT: In the *Bufo americanus* group. The status of *Bufo fowleri* (here considered a junior synonym) is controversial. The unjustified emendation of the specific epithet to *woodhousei* has been used widely.

Bufo xeros Tandy, Tandy, Keith, and Duff-Mackay, 1976. Pearce-Sellards Ser., Texas Mem. Mus., 24:3.
TYPE(S): Holotype: TNHC 39376.
TYPE LOCALITY: "Ghinda, Eritrea, Ethiopia, station 32, 15° 26' N 39° 05' E, altitude 940 m."
DISTRIBUTION: Subsaharan Africa southwards to Tanzania.
COMMENT: See comment under *Bufo wazae*.

Bufoides Pillai and Yazdani, 1973. J. Zool. Soc. India, 25:65.
TYPE SPECIES: *Ansonia meghalayana* Yazdani and Chanda, 1971, by original designation.
DISTRIBUTION: As for the single species.

Bufoides meghalayanus (Yazdani and Chanda, 1971). J. Assam Sci. Soc., 14:76.
ORIGINAL NAME: *Ansonia meghalayana*.
TYPE(S): Holotype: ZSI.
TYPE LOCALITY: Plateau of a large hill at Mawblang, about 5 kms by road from Cherrapunji town [Assam, India].
DISTRIBUTION: Known only from the type locality.

Capensibufo Grandison, 1980. Bull. Brit. Mus. (Nat. Hist.), Zool., 39:294.
TYPE SPECIES: *Bufo tradouwi* Hewitt, 1926, by original designation.
DISTRIBUTION: Cape Province, Rep. South Africa.
COMMENT: See Grandison, 1981, Monit. Zool. Ital., N.S., Suppl., 15:187–215, and Grandison, 1980, Bull. Brit. Mus. (Nat. Hist.), Zool., 39:293–298, for a discussion of the phylogenetic relationships of this genus.

Capensibufo rosei (Hewitt, 1926). Ann. S. Afr. Mus., 20:417.
ORIGINAL NAME: *Bufo rosei*.
TYPE(S): Syntypes: AMG.
TYPE LOCALITY: "Muizenberg Mountain", Cape Peninsula, Rep. South Africa.
DISTRIBUTION: Southwestern Cape Folded Belt west of Breede River and south of Worcester, Cape Province, Rep. South Africa.

COMMENT: Poynton, 1964, Ann. Natal Mus., 17:45, reported this and *Capensibufo tradouwi* from one locality.

Capensibufo tradouwi (Hewitt, 1926). Ann. S. Afr. Mus., 20:486.
ORIGINAL NAME: *Bufo tradouwi.*
TYPE(S): Syntypes: SAM.
TYPE LOCALITY: "Swellendam Mountains and in Tradouw Pass at 3500–5500 feet altitude", Rep. South Africa.
DISTRIBUTION: Cape Folded Belt east of Breede River and north of Worcester, Cape Province, Rep. South Africa.
COMMENT: See comment under *Capensibufo rosei.*

Crepidophryne Cope, 1889. Bull. U.S. Natl. Mus., 34:260.
TYPE SPECIES: *Crepidius epioticus* Cope, 1876, by monotypy.
DISTRIBUTION: As for the single species.
COMMENT: *Crepidophryne* is a replacement name for *Crepidius* Cope, 1876, preoccupied by *Crepidius* Candeze, 1859 (Coleoptera).

Crepidophryne epiotica (Cope, 1876). J. Acad. Nat. Sci. Philadelphia, (2)8:97.
ORIGINAL NAME: *Crepidius epioticus.*
TYPE(S): USNM, apparently lost.
TYPE LOCALITY: "from 5000 feet elevation on Pico Blanco [=Cerro Kámuk, Provincia Limón]", Costa Rica.
DISTRIBUTION: Atlantic slopes of the Cordillera de Talamanca of Costa Rica and western Panama.
COMMENT: For review and redescription see Savage and Kluge, 1961, Rev. Biol. Tropical, 9:39–51.

Dendrophryniscus Jiménez de la Espada, 1871. J. Sci. Math. Phys. Nat., Lisboa, 3:65.
TYPE SPECIES: *Dendrophryniscus brevipollicatus* Jiménez de la Espada, 1871, by monotypy.
DISTRIBUTION: Atlantic forests of Brazil; Amazonian Ecuador, Peru, and Brazil; Guianas.
COMMENT: McDiarmid, 1971, Sci. Bull. Nat. Hist. Mus. Los Angeles Co., 12:49, considered *Dendrophryniscus* to be most closely related to *Melanophryniscus.*

Dendrophryniscus brevipollicatus Jiménez de la Espada, 1871. J. Sci. Math. Phys. Nat., Lisboa, 3:65.
TYPE(S): Not traced; MNCN?
TYPE LOCALITY: In Brasil; prope Rio de Janeiro, in Monte Corcovado. Rendered as "Corcovado, Rio de Janeiro", Rio de Janeiro, Brazil, by Bokermann, 1966, Lista Anot. Local. Tipo Anf. Brasil.:65.
DISTRIBUTION: Coastal ranges of from Espírito Santo to Rio Grande do Sul, Brazil.
COMMENT: See comment under *Dendrophryniscus leucomystax.* For discussion of distribution see Braun and Braun, 1979, Iheringia, Zool., 54:47–54.

Dendrophryniscus leucomystax Izecksohn, 1968. Rev. Brasil. Biol., 28:357.
TYPE(S): Holotype: EI 4069.
TYPE LOCALITY: "Tinguá, município de Nova Iguaçu, Estado do Rio de Janeiro", Brazil.
DISTRIBUTION: Lowland coastal forests of Rio de Janeiro and São Paulo, Brazil.
COMMENT: Related to *Dendrophryniscus brevipollicatus* according to the original description.

Dendrophryniscus minutus (Melin, 1941). Göteborgs K. Vetensk. Vitterh. Samh. Handl., 4:18.
ORIGINAL NAME: *Atelopus minutus.*
TYPE(S): Syntypes: NHMG (5 specimens).
TYPE LOCALITY: "Taracúa, Rio Uaupés, [State of Amazonas,] Brazil".
DISTRIBUTION: Amazonian Ecuador, Peru, Brazil, and southern Guianas.

COMMENT: Transferred to *Dendrophryniscus* from *Atelopus* by McDiarmid, 1971, Sci. Bull. Nat. Hist. Mus. Los Angeles Co., 12:40. Reviewed by Duellman, 1978, Misc. Publ. Mus. Nat. Hist. Univ. Kansas, 65:120–121, who reported geographic variation in belly pattern. DCC and MSH believe that this variation is due to two species being confounded.

Didynamipus Andersson, 1903. Verh. Zool. Bot. Ges. Wien, 1903:143.
TYPE SPECIES: *Didynamipus sjöstedti* Andersson, 1903, by monotypy.
DISTRIBUTION: As for the single species.
COMMENT: The phylogenetic relationships of this genus were discussed by Grandison, 1981, Monit. Zool. Ital., N.S., Suppl., 15:187–215.

Didynamipus sjostedti Andersson, 1903. Verh. Zool. Bot. Ges. Wien, 1903:143.
ORIGINAL NAME: *Didynamipus sjöstedti*.
TYPE(S): Syntypes: Zool. Inst. Göteborgs Univ. (NHMG?) 221 (2 specimens).
TYPE LOCALITY: "Kamerun".
DISTRIBUTION: Fernando Po and extreme southwestern Cameroon.
COMMENT: Synonymy includes *Didynamipus minutus* (Boulenger, 1906), according to Noble, 1924, Bull. Am. Mus. Nat. Hist., 49:147–347. The incorrect spelling *sjoestedti* has been used; under the International Code of Zoological Nomenclature (1985) only German umlauts, not Scandinavian umlauts, are corrected by the addition of an 'e'.

Laurentophryne Tihen, 1960. Copeia, 1960:226.
TYPE SPECIES: *Wolterstorffina parkeri* Laurent, 1950, by original designation.
DISTRIBUTION: As for the single species.
COMMENT: Grandison, 1981, Monit. Zool. Ital., N.S., Suppl., 15:187–215, discussed the phylogenetic relationships of this genus and considered it close to *Nectophryne*.

Laurentophryne parkeri (Laurent, 1950). Rev. Zool. Bot. Afr., 44:3.
ORIGINAL NAME: *Wolterstorffina parkeri*.
TYPE(S): Not traced.
TYPE LOCALITY: "Kiandjo (Alt. 1850–1950 m.), Territoire de Mwenga, Kivu", Zaire.
DISTRIBUTION: Known only from the type locality.

Leptophryne Fitzinger, 1843. Syst. Rept.:32.
TYPE SPECIES: *Bufo cruentatus* Tschudi, 1838.
DISTRIBUTION: Malay Peninsula and Greater Sunda Is.
COMMENT: *Cacophryne* Davis, 1935, is a junior synonym of *Leptophryne*. See Laurent, 1979, Bull. Soc. Zool. France, 104:406, and Dubois, 1982, J. Herpetol., 16:173, for discussion.

Leptophryne borbonica (Kuhl and van Hasselt, 1827). *In* Schlegel, Isis von Oken, 20: 294.
ORIGINAL NAME: *Hylaplesia borbonica*.
TYPE(S): Syntypes: RMNH 1739 (2 specimens).
TYPE LOCALITY: East Indies; restricted to "Java", Indonesia, by Inger, 1966, Fieldiana: Zool., 52:75.
DISTRIBUTION: Southern Thailand to Java and Borneo.
COMMENT: See Taylor, 1962, Univ. Kansas Sci. Bull., 43:342–344, and Inger, 1966, Fieldiana: Zool., 52:75–78, for discussion and synonymy of this species (as *Cacophryne borbonica*); see also Berry, 1975, Amph. Fauna Peninsular Malaysia: 52–54.

Leptophryne cruentata (Tschudi, 1838). Classif. Batr.:52.
ORIGINAL NAME: *Bufo cruentatus*.
TYPE(S): Syntypes: RMNH 2130 (2 specimens).
TYPE LOCALITY: Java [Indonesia].
DISTRIBUTION: Java.

Melanophryniscus Gallardo, 1961. Neotropica, 7:72.
TYPE SPECIES: *Hyla stelzneri* Weyenbergh, 1876, by monotypy.
DISTRIBUTION: Argentina (northern half including Misiones, Salta, and Jujuy); Brazil
(coastal lowlands of southern Brazil and Rio Grande do Sul); Paraguay;
Uruguay.
COMMENT: McDiarmid, 1971, Sci. Bull. Nat. Hist. Mus. Los Angeles Co., 12:49,
considered *Melanophryniscus* to be most closely related to *Dendrophryniscus*.

Melanophryniscus cambaraensis Braun and Braun, 1979. Iheringia, Zool., 54:7.
TYPE(S): Holotype: MRGS 9797.
TYPE LOCALITY: "Fortaleza dos Aparados, Município de Cambará do Sul, Rio
Grande do Sul (RS), Brasil, 900 m".
DISTRIBUTION: Known only from the type locality.
COMMENT: In the *Melanophryniscus tumifrons* group.

Melanophryniscus devincenzii Klappenbach, 1968. Comun. Zool. Mus. Hist. Nat.
Montevideo, 9 (118):7.
TYPE(S): Holotype: MHNM 1675.
TYPE LOCALITY: "La Palma, Rubio Chico, próximo a Subida de Pena, Cuchilla
Negra, departamento de Rivera, República del Uruguay".
DISTRIBUTION: Known only from the type locality.
COMMENT: In the *Melanophryniscus tumifrons* group. See Braun, 1973, Iheringia,
Zool., 44:3–13, for discussion.

Melanophryniscus macrogranulosus Braun, 1973. Iheringia, Zool., 44:4.
TYPE(S): Holotype: MRGS 01694.
TYPE LOCALITY: "Torres, RS [Rio Grande do Sul], Brasil".
DISTRIBUTION: Known only from the type locality.
COMMENT: In the *Melanophryniscus tumifrons* group. For discussion see Braun, 1973,
Iheringia, Zool., 44:3–13.

Melanophryniscus moreirae (Miranda-Ribeiro, 1920). Rev. Mus. Paulista, São Paulo, 12:
307.
ORIGINAL NAME: *Atelopus moreirae*.
TYPE(S): Syntypes: MN and MZUSP 718.
TYPE LOCALITY: Itatiaia, Rio de Janeiro, Brazil.
DISTRIBUTION: Coastal mountains of southern Brazil (1800–2400 m) and (?)
Castanhal Grande, Óbidos, Pará, Brazil.
COMMENT: In the *Melanophryniscus moreirae* group. A strangely disjunct population
from Óbidos, Pará, Brazil, was described as a subspecies by Cochran, 1948,
Bull. Mus. R. Hist. Nat. Belg., 24(24):1–4. Bokermann, 1967, An. Acad. Brasil.
Cienc., 39:301–306, doubted the correctness of this locality and assumed that
the specimens came from Itatiaia.

Melanophryniscus rubriventris (Vellard, 1947). Acta Zool. Lilloana, 4:115.
ORIGINAL NAME: *Atelopus rubriventris*.
TYPE(S): Holotype: FML 173/1.
TYPE LOCALITY: "San Andrés, Dpto. Orán, province de Salta", Argentina.
DISTRIBUTION: Salta and Jujuy provinces, northern Argentina.
COMMENT: Transferred to *Melanophryniscus* from *Atelopus* by McDiarmid, 1972,
Physis, Buenos Aires, 31:15–21. For discussion and subspecies see Laurent,
1973, Acta Zool. Lilloana, 26:319–334, and Cei, 1980, Monit. Zool. Ital., N.S.,
Monogr., 2:205–207.

Melanophryniscus sanmartini Klappenbach, 1968. Comun. Zool. Mus. Hist. Nat.
Montevideo, 9(118):3.
TYPE(S): Holotype: MHNM 1676.
TYPE LOCALITY: "Villa Serrana, próximo a la represa del arroyo Aiguá,
departamento de Lavalleja, República del Uruguay".
DISTRIBUTION: Known only from the type locality.

COMMENT: In the *Melanophryniscus moreirae* group. For discussion see Klappenbach, 1968, Comun. Zool. Mus. Hist. Nat. Montevideo, 9(118):1–12.

Melanophryniscus stelzneri (Weyenbergh, 1875). Periód. Zool., 1:331.
ORIGINAL NAME: *Phryniscus stelzneri.*
TYPE(S): Not traced.
TYPE LOCALITY: Sierra de Córdoba, Argentina.
DISTRIBUTION: Argentina (northern half); Brazil (Rio Grande do Sul and Santa Catarina); Paraguay; Uruguay.
COMMENT: For comments on subspecies and synonymies see Cei, 1980, Monit. Zool. Ital., N.S., Monogr., 2:207–212; Braun, 1978, Iheringia, Zool., 51:39–41; and Klappenbach, 1968, Comun. Zool. Mus. Hist. Nat. Montevideo, 9(118): 1–12.

Melanophryniscus tumifrons (Boulenger, 1905). Ann. Mag. Nat. Hist., (7)16:181.
ORIGINAL NAME: *Atelopus tumifrons.*
TYPE(S): Holotype: BM 1902.12.8.5.
TYPE LOCALITY: "Pernambuco", Brazil; Bokermann, 1966, Lista Anot. Local. Tipo Anf. Brasil.:5, doubted the type locality and supposed the type came from Rio Grande do Sul.
DISTRIBUTION: Santa Catarina and Rio Grande do Sul, Brazil; Misiones, Argentina.
COMMENT: In the *Melanophryniscus tumifrons* group.

Mertensophryne Tihen, 1960. Copeia, 1960:226.
TYPE SPECIES: *Bufo micranotis rondoensis* Loveridge, 1942, by original designation.
DISTRIBUTION: Zaire eastward to Tanzania (including Zanzibar) and Kenya.
COMMENT: Grandison, 1981, Monit. Zool. Ital., N.S., Suppl., 15:208, discussed the phylogenetic relationships of *Mertensophryne.*

Mertensophryne micranotis (Loveridge, 1925). Proc. Zool. Soc. London, 1925:770.
ORIGINAL NAME: *Bufo micranotis.*
TYPE(S): Holotype: MCZ 10333.
TYPE LOCALITY: "Kilosa, Morogoro District, Tanganyika Territory [=Tanzania]".
DISTRIBUTION: Kenya, Tanzania (including Zanzibar).

Mertensophryne schmidti Grandison, 1972. Zool. Meded., Leiden, 47:44.
TYPE(S): Holotype: BM 1968.642.
TYPE LOCALITY: "Republic of the Congo [=Zaire]:—Kateke affluent of the Muovwe, right subaffluent of the Lufira, 960 m, Upemba National Park".
DISTRIBUTION: Upemba National Park, Zaire.

Nectophryne Buchholz and Peters, 1875. Monatsber. Preuss. Akad. Wiss. Berlin, 1875: 202.
TYPE SPECIES: *Nectophryne afra* Buchholz and Peters, 1875, by monotypy.
DISTRIBUTION: Nigeria, Cameroon, Gabon, northeastern Zaire; Fernando Po.
COMMENT: See comment under *Laurentophryne.*

Nectophryne afra Buchholz and Peters, 1875. Monatsber. Preuss. Akad. Wiss. Berlin, 1875:202.
TYPE(S): Holotype: ZMB, according to Roux, 1906, Proc. Zool. Soc. London, 1906:59.
TYPE LOCALITY: "Cameruns".
DISTRIBUTION: West Africa from southern Nigeria to Gabon, also Fernando Po and northeastern Zaire.

Nectophryne batesii Boulenger, 1913. Ann. Mag. Nat. Hist., (8)12:71.
TYPE(S): Syntypes: BM 1907.5.22.148–150, 1908.5.30.112–117, 1911.5.30.15, 1913.10.27.45–48.
TYPE LOCALITY: "Neighbourhood of Bitye, on the Ja River (Congo System), Cameroon".
DISTRIBUTION: South Cameroon and northeastern Zaire, West Africa.

Nectophrynoides Noble, 1926. Am. Mus. Novit., 212:15.
TYPE SPECIES: *Nectophryne tornieri* Roux, 1906.
DISTRIBUTION: Montane environments in Liberia, Guinea, Ethiopia, and Tanzania.
COMMENT: Grandison, 1978, Monit. Zool. Ital., N.S., Suppl., 11:119–172, and
Grandison, 1981, Monit. Zool. Ital., N.S., Suppl., 15:187–215, discussed
characters and relationships of this genus.
PROTECTED STATUS: CITES—Appendix I (1 Jul. 1975) and USA ESA—Endangered (14
Jun. 1976); as *Nectophrynoides* spp.

Nectophrynoides cryptus Perret, 1971. Ann. Fac. Sci. Cameroun, 6:104.
TYPE(S): Holotype: MCZ 12480.
TYPE LOCALITY: "Nyingwa, Monts Uluguru, 7 10′ S: 37 40′ E, Tanzanie, 2,200 m".
DISTRIBUTION: East-central Tanzania in forested basement hills.
PROTECTED STATUS: CITES—Appendix I (1 Jul. 1975) and USA ESA—Endangered
(14 Jun. 1976); as *Nectophrynoides* spp.

Nectophrynoides liberiensis Xavier, 1979. Bull. Soc. Zool. France, 103:432.
TYPE(S): Holotype: MNHNP 1978.3088.
TYPE LOCALITY: "au plateau de la mine à 1290 m d'altitude, Monts Nimba, Liberia".
DISTRIBUTION: Mt. Nimba region of Liberia.
PROTECTED STATUS: CITES—Appendix I (1 Jul. 1975) and USA ESA—Endangered
(14 Jun. 1976); as *Nectophrynoides* spp.

Nectophrynoides malcolmi Grandison, 1978. Monit. Zool. Ital., N.S., Suppl., 11:124.
TYPE(S): Holotype: BM 1975.1961.
TYPE LOCALITY: 6–8 km SE Goba, road to Maslo, Balé Province, Ethiopia, 06° 59′ N,
40° 01′ E, elevation 3200 m.
DISTRIBUTION: Balé Province, Ethiopia.
PROTECTED STATUS: CITES—Appendix I (1 Jul. 1975) and USA ESA—Endangered
(14 Jun. 1976); as *Nectophrynoides* spp.

Nectophrynoides minutus Perret, 1972. Ann. Fac. Sci. Cameroun, 11:106.
TYPE(S): Holotype: MCZ 12463.
TYPE LOCALITY: "Bagilo, Monts Uluguru, 2200 m d'altitude, 7-10 S, 37-40 E,
Tanzanie".
DISTRIBUTION: Known only from the type locality.
PROTECTED STATUS: CITES—Appendix I (1 Jul. 1975) and USA ESA—Endangered
(14 Jun. 1976); as *Nectophrynoides* spp.

Nectophrynoides occidentalis Angel, 1943. Bull. Mus. Natl. Hist. Nat., Paris, (2)15:167.
TYPE(S): Holotype: MNHNP 44-149.
TYPE LOCALITY: "Serengbara (forêt primaire) près du Mont Nimba, Haute Guinée
Française".
DISTRIBUTION: Mt. Nimba region of the Ivory Coast and Guinea.
PROTECTED STATUS: CITES—Appendix I (1 Jul. 1975) and USA ESA—Endangered
(14 Jun. 1976); as *Nectophrynoides* spp.

Nectophrynoides osgoodi (Loveridge, 1932). Occas. Pap. Boston Soc. Nat. Hist., 8:47.
ORIGINAL NAME: *Bufo osgoodi*.
TYPE(S): Holotype: FMNH 12529.
TYPE LOCALITY: "Ethiopia probably from Gedeb Mountains of Bali, just south of the
western branch of the Webi Shebili River, 8–10,000 ft."
DISTRIBUTION: South-central Ethiopia (Balé and Sidamo provinces).
PROTECTED STATUS: CITES—Appendix I (1 Jul. 1975) and USA ESA—Endangered
(14 Jun. 1976); as *Nectophrynoides* spp.

Nectophrynoides tornieri (Roux, 1906). Proc. Zool. Soc. London, 1906:63.
ORIGINAL NAME: *Nectophryne tornieri*.
TYPE(S): Holotype: NHMB 2384.
TYPE LOCALITY: Ukami, German East Africa [Uluguru Mountains, Tanzania].
DISTRIBUTION: Forested basement hills of Tanzania (Usambara, Uluguru, and
Uzungwe mountains).

PROTECTED STATUS: CITES—Appendix I (1 Jul. 1975) and USA ESA—Endangered (14 Jun. 1976); as *Nectophrynoides* spp.

Nectophrynoides viviparus (Tornier, 1905). Sitzungsber. Preuss. Akad. Wiss. Berlin, 39: 855.
ORIGINAL NAME: *Pseudophryne vivipara*.
TYPE(S): Syntypes: ZMB (lost?); MHNG 1221.55 designated neotype by Perret, 1972, Ann. Fac. Sci. Cameroun, 11:112.
TYPE LOCALITY: "Daressalam, Rungwe und im Kingagebirge Deutsch-Ostafrika"; neotype not selected from original type locality but "Morogoro, Mt Uluguru, Tanzanie".
DISTRIBUTION: Mountains of central to southwestern Tanzania.
PROTECTED STATUS: CITES—Appendix I (1 Jul. 1975) and USA ESA—Endangered (14 Jun. 1976); as *Nectophrynoides* spp.

Oreophrynella Boulenger, 1895. Ann. Mag. Nat. Hist., (6)16:125.
TYPE SPECIES: *Oreophryne quelchii* Boulenger, 1895, by monotypy.
DISTRIBUTION: On sandstone mountains (tepuis) in south-central Venezuela and adjacent Guyana.
COMMENT: *Oreophrynella* is a replacement name for *Oreophryne* Boulenger, 1895, Ann. Mag. Nat. Hist., (6)15:521, which is preoccupied by *Oreophryne* Boettger, 1895. McDiarmid, 1971, Sci. Bull. Nat. Hist. Mus. Los Angeles Co., 12:49, placed *Oreophrynella* as the sister-taxon of *Atelopus* plus *Dendrophryniscus* plus *Melanophryniscus*. Several undescribed species are known from tepuis (sandstone mountains) in Venezuela (MSH).

Oreophrynella macconnelli Boulenger, 1900. Trans. Linn. Soc. London, Zool., (2)7:55.
TYPE(S): Holotype: BM 1947.2.14.49 (formerly 99.3.25.17).
TYPE LOCALITY: "Base of Mount Roraima, 3500 feet [=1060 m]", Guyana.
DISTRIBUTION: Known only from the type locality.
COMMENT: Rivero, 1961, Bull. Mus. Comp. Zool., 126:175, considered this form to be a subspecies of *Oreophrynella quelchii*, but McDiarmid, 1971, Sci. Bull. Nat. Hist. Mus. Los Angeles Co., 12:41, treated it as a distinct species.

Oreophrynella quelchii (Boulenger, 1895). Ann. Mag. Nat. Hist., (6)15:521.
ORIGINAL NAME: *Oreophryne quelchii*.
TYPE(S): Syntypes: BM 95.4.19.1–5, 99.3.25.7–13, KU 126081–82 (formerly BM 99.3.25.14–15), ZFMK, MCZ 3500–02.
TYPE LOCALITY: "Summit of Mt. Roraima, between British Guiana [=Guyana] and Venezuela, at an altitude of 8500 feet".
DISTRIBUTION: Mt. Roraima, Venezuela and Guyana.

Osornophryne Ruíz-Carranza and Hernández-Camacho, 1976. Caldasia, 11:97.
TYPE SPECIES: *Osornophryne percrassa* Ruíz-Carranza and Hernández-Camacho, 1976, by original designation.
DISTRIBUTION: Cordillera Central in Colombia to extreme northern Cordilleras Occidental and Oriental in Ecuador, between 2700 and 3700 m.
COMMENT: For discussion and review see Ruíz-Carranza and Hernández-Camacho, 1976, Caldasia, 11:93–148.

Osornophryne bufoniformis (Peracca, 1904). Boll. Mus. Zool. Anat. Comp. Univ. Torino, 19:20.
ORIGINAL NAME: *Atelopus bufoniformis*.
TYPE(S): Syntypes: MSNT 561 (2 specimens).
TYPE LOCALITY: Puno, Carchi Province, Ecuador.
DISTRIBUTION: Northern Ecuador (Carchi) to southern Colombia (Cauca), between 2700 and 3700 m.

Osornophryne percrassa Ruíz-Carranza and Hernández-Camacho, 1976. Caldasia, 11: 126.
TYPE(S): Holotype: ICN 319.
TYPE LOCALITY: "Páramo de Herveo, eastern flank of Cordillera Central, Munícipio de Herveo, Departamento del Tolima, Colombia".
DISTRIBUTION: Known only from the type locality.

Pedostibes Günther, 1875. Proc. Zool. Soc. London, 1875:576.
TYPE SPECIES: *Pedostibes tuberculosus* Günther, 1875.
DISTRIBUTION: South India, Malay Peninsula to Borneo and Sumatra; one doubtful species from northeastern India.
COMMENT: Barbour, 1938, Proc. Biol. Soc. Washington, 51:191–195, supplied synonymies and distributions.

Pedostibes everetti (Boulenger, 1896). Ann. Mag. Nat. Hist., (6)17:450.
ORIGINAL NAME: *Nectophryne everetti.*
TYPE(S): Holotype: BM 1947.2.18.27 (formerly 96.4.29.13).
TYPE LOCALITY: Mount Kina Balu, Sabah [Malaysia (Borneo)].
DISTRIBUTION: Mt. Kina Balu, Sabah, Malaysia (Borneo).
COMMENT: Reviewed by Inger, 1966, Fieldiana: Zool., 52:92.

Pedostibes hosii (Boulenger, 1892). Proc. Zool., Soc. London, 1892:508.
ORIGINAL NAME: *Nectophryne hosii.*
TYPE(S): Holotype: BM 92.6.3.19.
TYPE LOCALITY: Mt. Dulit, Sarawak [Malaysia (Borneo)].
DISTRIBUTION: Extreme southern Thailand, Malaya, Borneo, and Sumatra.
COMMENT: See Taylor, 1962, Univ. Kansas Sci. Bull., 43:336–339, for synonymy and discussion as well as Inger, 1966, Fieldiana: Zool., 52:93–96. See Berry, 1975, Amph. Fauna Peninsular Malaysia:54–55, for account.

Pedostibes kempi (Boulenger, 1919). Rec. Indian Mus., 16:207.
ORIGINAL NAME: *Nectophryne kempi.*
TYPE(S): Syntypes: 2 specimens (not traced, BM or ZSI?).
TYPE LOCALITY: Tura, 2,500 ft., Garo Hills, Assam [India].
DISTRIBUTION: Known only from the type locality.

Pedostibes maculatus (Mocquard, 1890). Nouv. Arch. Mus. Natl. Hist. Nat., Paris, (3)2: 162.
ORIGINAL NAME: *Nectophryne maculatus.*
TYPE(S): Syntypes: MNHNP 89-266 to -288.
TYPE LOCALITY: Mount Kina Balu, Sabah [Malaysia (Borneo)].
DISTRIBUTION: Northern part of Borneo.

Pedostibes rugosus Inger, 1958. Sarawak Mus. J., 8:476.
TYPE(S): Holotype: FMNH 81297.
TYPE LOCALITY: "Menuang, headwaters of the Baleh River", Third Division, Sarawak, Malaysia (Borneo).
DISTRIBUTION: Central and western Borneo.
COMMENT: See Inger, 1966, Fieldiana: Zool., 52:96–97.

Pedostibes tuberculosus Günther, 1875. Proc. Zool. Soc. London, 1875:576.
TYPE(S): Syntypes: BM 1947.2.22.70–71 (formerly 74.4.29.1375–1376).
TYPE LOCALITY: Malabar, South India.
DISTRIBUTION: South India.
COMMENT: See Daniel, 1963, J. Bombay Nat. Hist. Soc., 60:431–432 (as *Nectophryne tuberculosa*).

Pelophryne Barbour, 1938. Proc. Biol. Soc. Washington, 51:192.
TYPE SPECIES: *Pelophryne albotaeniata* Barbour, 1938, by original designation.
DISTRIBUTION: Philippines; Borneo; Malaya; Hainan I., China.

COMMENT: Inger, 1966, Fieldiana: Zool., 52:78–90, reviewed the Bornean species and Inger, 1954, Fieldiana: Zool., 33:233–239, reviewed the Philippine forms.

Pelophryne albotaeniata Barbour, 1938. Proc. Biol. Soc. Washington, 51:194.
TYPE(S): Holotype: MCZ 23291.
TYPE LOCALITY: Thumb Peak, Palawan [Philippines].
DISTRIBUTION: Thumb Peak, Palawan, Philippines.

Pelophryne api Dring, 1984 "1983". Amphibia-Reptilia, 4:107.
TYPE(S): Holotype: BM 1978.1575.
TYPE LOCALITY: "camp five 150 m, base of Gunung Api, Gunung Mulu N[ational]. P[ark]., Fourth Division, Sarawak", Malaysia (Borneo).
DISTRIBUTION: Melinau Limestone area of Gunung Api, Sarawak, Malaysia (Borneo).

Pelophryne brevipes (Peters, 1867). Monatsber. Preuss. Akad. Wiss. Berlin, 1867:34.
ORIGINAL NAME: *Hylaplesia brevipes*.
TYPE(S): Syntypes: NHMW 16554.
TYPE LOCALITY: Zamboanga, Mindanao [Philippines].
DISTRIBUTION: Malaya; Mindanao (Philippines); Sumatra, Borneo, and adjacent islands.
COMMENT: See Inger, 1966, Fieldiana: Zool., 52:85, for synonymy and distribution; see also Berry, 1975, Amph. Fauna Peninsular Malaysia:55–56, for account.

Pelophryne guentheri (Boulenger, 1882). Cat. Batr. Sal. Brit. Mus.:280.
ORIGINAL NAME: *Nectophryne guentheri*.
TYPE(S): Holotype: BM 1947.2.19.28 (formerly 72.2.19.27).
TYPE LOCALITY: "Matang", Sarawak, Malaysia (Borneo).
DISTRIBUTION: Sarawak (Borneo), Malaysia.

Pelophryne lighti (Taylor, 1920). Philippine J. Sci., 16:338.
ORIGINAL NAME: *Nectophryne lighti*.
TYPE(S): Holotype: EHT (lost).
TYPE LOCALITY: Bunawan, Agusan Province, Mindanao [Philippines].
DISTRIBUTION: Mindanao and Bohol Is., Philippines.

Pelophryne macrotis (Boulenger, 1895). Ann. Mag. Nat. Hist., (6)16:171.
ORIGINAL NAME: *Nectophryne macrotis*.
TYPE(S): Holotype: BM 1947.2.19.43 (formerly 95.7.2.36).
TYPE LOCALITY: Akar River, Sarawak [Malaysia (Borneo)].
DISTRIBUTION: Sarawak (Borneo), Malaysia.

Pelophryne misera (Mocquard, 1890). Nouv. Arch. Mus. Natl. Hist. Nat., Paris, (3)2: 161.
ORIGINAL NAME: *Nectophryne misera*.
TYPE(S): Syntypes: MNHNP 89-331, 89-332.
TYPE LOCALITY: North Borneo [Malaysia].
DISTRIBUTION: Sabah and northern Sarawak (Malaysia), Borneo.

Pelophryne scalpta (Liu and Hu, 1973). Acta Zool. Sinica, 19:389.
ORIGINAL NAME: *Nectophryne scalptus*.
TYPE(S): Holotype: CIB (formerly SWIBASC) 64III0604.
TYPE LOCALITY: Xin-min Ziang, Wuzhi Shan, Hainan, altitude 750 m [China].
DISTRIBUTION: Known only from the type locality.

Peltophryne Fitzinger, 1843. Syst. Rept.:32.
TYPE SPECIES: *Bufo peltocephalus* Tschudi, 1838.
DISTRIBUTION: Greater Antilles.

COMMENT: Removed from *Bufo* by Pregill, 1978, Copeia, 1981:273–285. Synonymies (under *Bufo*) are available in Schwartz and Thomas, 1975, Carnegie Mus. Nat. Hist. Spec. Publ., 1:11–13, and in Schwartz, Thomas, and Ober, 1978, Carnegie Mus. Nat. Hist. Spec. Publ., 5:3. Closely tied to the *Bufo granulosus* group according to Cei, 1972, *In* Blair (ed.), Evol. Genus *Bufo*:87.

CONTRIBUTOR: Albert Schwartz (AS).

REVIEWER: Richard Thomas (RT).

Peltophryne cataulaciceps (Schwartz, 1959). Proc. Biol. Soc. Washington, 72:110.
ORIGINAL NAME: *Bufo cataulaciceps*.
TYPE(S): Holotype: AMNH 61982.
TYPE LOCALITY: 7.9 mi. N Santa Fé, Habana Province, Isla de Pinos [=Isla de Juventud], Cuba.
DISTRIBUTION: Isla de Pinos (=Isla de Juventud) and extreme western Cuba in Pinar del Río Province.

Peltophryne empusa Cope, 1863. Proc. Acad. Nat. Sci. Philadelphia, 14:344.
ORIGINAL NAME: *Peltaphryne empusa*.
TYPE(S): Holotype: ANSP 2721.
TYPE LOCALITY: Cuba.
DISTRIBUTION: Cuba and Isla de Pinos (=Isla de Juventud), island-wide at low elevations.

Peltophryne fluviatica (Schwartz, 1972). J. Herpetol., 6:226.
ORIGINAL NAME: *Bufo fluviaticus*.
TYPE(S): Holotype: CM 54074.
TYPE LOCALITY: 1.8 mi. (2.9 km) W Los Quemados, Santiago Rodríguez Province, República Dominicana.
DISTRIBUTION: Northwestern Domincan Republic, elev. near 500 ft.

Peltophryne guentheri (Cochran, 1941). Bull. U.S. Natl. Mus., 177:8.
ORIGINAL NAME: *Bufo güntheri*.
TYPE(S): Holotype: USNM 59081.
TYPE LOCALITY: Port-au-Prince, Département de l'Ouest, Haiti.
DISTRIBUTION: Hispaniola, West Indies.

Peltophryne gundlachi (Ruibal, 1959). Breviora, 105:2.
ORIGINAL NAME: *Bufo gundlachi*.
TYPE(S): Holotype: MCZ 30551.
TYPE LOCALITY: About 14 km NE Camagüey, Camagüey Province, Cuba.
DISTRIBUTION: Cuba; known from all provinces but in Oriente apparently only in the extreme southwest (now Granma Province), Isla de Pinos (=Isla de Juventud).

Peltophryne lemur Cope, 1869 "1868". Proc. Acad. Nat. Sci. Philadelphia, 20:311.
ORIGINAL NAME: *Peltaphryne lemur*.
TYPE(S): Not traced.
TYPE LOCALITY: Puerto Rico.
DISTRIBUTION: Puerto Rico, where known from a few, widely scattered, lowland localities, including both the northern and southern coastal areas; Virgin Gorda I.
COMMENT: See Rivero, Mayorga, Estremera, and Izquierdo, 1980, Caribb. J. Sci., 15: 33–40.

Peltophryne longinasus (Stejneger, 1905). Proc. U.S. Natl. Mus., 28:765.
ORIGINAL NAME: *Bufo longinasus*.
TYPE(S): Holotype: USNM 27419.
TYPE LOCALITY: El Guamá, Pinar del Río Province, Cuba.
DISTRIBUTION: Cuba.

COMMENT: See Valdés de la Osa and Ruiz García, 1980, Poeyana, 206:1–34, for review.

Peltophryne peltocephala (Tschudi, 1838). Classif. Batr.:52.
ORIGINAL NAME: *Bufo peltocephalus.*
TYPE(S): Holotype: MNHNP 4989.
TYPE LOCALITY: Cuba; restricted to vicinity of Santiago de Cuba, Oriente Province [now Santiago de Cuba Province] by Schwartz, 1960, Proc. Biol. Soc. Washington, 73:47.
DISTRIBUTION: Cuba.
COMMENT: According to Schwartz and Thomas, 1975, Carnegie Mus. Nat. Hist. Spec. Publ., 1:13, there is a possibility that the two subspecies of *Peltophryne peltocephala* may be distinct species, *Peltophryne peltocephala* and *Peltophryne fustiger.*

Peltophryne taladai (Schwartz, 1960). Proc. Biol. Soc. Washington 73:51.
ORIGINAL NAME: *Bufo taladai.*
TYPE(S): Holotype: AMNH 63485.
TYPE LOCALITY: 2 mi. S Taco Bay (Bahía de Taco), Oriente Province [now Guantánamo Province], Cuba.
DISTRIBUTION: Central and eastern Cuba, from Soledad and Cumanayagua, Las Villas Province (now Sancti Spíritus Province), east to the type locality.
COMMENT: *Peltophryne taladai* hybridizes with *Peltophryne peltocephala* in Oriente Province (now Holguin Province), Cuba, according to Schwartz, 1960, Proc. Biol. Soc. Washington 73:54.

Pseudobufo Tschudi, 1838. Classif. Batr.:87.
TYPE SPECIES: *Pseudobufo subasper* Tschudi, 1838, by monotypy.
DISTRIBUTION: As for the single species.

Pseudobufo subasper Tschudi, 1838. Classif. Batr.:87.
TYPE(S): Syntypes: RMNH 2200, 2216.
TYPE LOCALITY: Borneo.
DISTRIBUTION: Malay Peninsula, Sumatra, and Borneo.
COMMENT: Reviewed by Bourret, 1942, Batr. Indochine:186–187. See also Berry, 1975, Amph. Fauna Peninsular Malaysia:57.

Rhamphophryne Trueb, 1971. Contrib. Sci. Nat. Hist. Mus. Los Angeles Co., 216:6.
TYPE(S): *Rhamphophryne acrolopha* Trueb, 1971, by original designation.
DISTRIBUTION: Moderate elevations in the mountains of northern Colombia and eastern Panama; Andean slopes of the upper Amazon Basin in Ecuador; eastern Brazil (Bahia).
COMMENT: See Trueb, 1971, Contrib. Sci. Nat. Hist. Mus. Los Angeles Co., 216:6, for discussion and review, as well as synonymies for all of the species, except for *Rhamphophryne proboscidea.*

Rhamphophryne acrolopha Trueb, 1971. Contrib. Sci. Nat. Hist. Mus. Los Angeles Co., 216:18.
TYPE(S): Holotype: KU 76965.
TYPE LOCALITY: "Cerro Malí, Darién Province, Panamá, elevation 1410 m".
DISTRIBUTION: Serranía del Darién in Panama and adjacent Colombia.

Rhamphophryne festae (Peracca, 1904). Boll. Mus. Zool. Anat. Comp. Univ. Torino, 19:18.
ORIGINAL NAME: *Atelopus festae.*
TYPE(S): Syntypes: MSNT 2903 (Gualaquiza) and 2904 (Valle Santiago).
TYPE LOCALITY: "Valle Santiago" (=lower Río Zamora, according to Peters, 1955, Rev. Ecuat. Entomol. Parasitol., 2:348) and "Gualaquiza", Morona-Santiago Province, Ecuador.
DISTRIBUTION: Moderate and low elevations (100–700 m) on the Atlantic Andean slopes and upper Amazon Basin of Ecuador.

Rhamphophryne macrorhina Trueb, 1971. Contrib. Sci. Nat. Hist. Mus. Los Angeles Co., 216:25.
TYPE(S): Holotype: LACM 44394.
TYPE LOCALITY: "Santa Rita, Departamento de Antioquia, Colombia, between elevations of 1890 and 1910 m".
DISTRIBUTION: Departamento Antioquia, Colombia.

Rhamphophryne nicefori (Cochran and Goin, 1970). Bull. U.S. Natl. Mus., 288:95.
ORIGINAL NAME: *Bufo rostratus nicefori.*
TYPE(S): Holotype: USNM 163476.
TYPE LOCALITY: Hacienda Palmas, El Chaquiro, Departamento de Antioquia, Colombia, 2670 m.
DISTRIBUTION: Known only from the type locality.

Rhamphophryne proboscidea (Boulenger, 1882). Cat. Batr. Sal. Brit. Mus.:150.
ORIGINAL NAME: *Phryniscus proboscideus.*
TYPE(S): Syntypes: BM 69.2.22.8, 69.11.3.24, 69.11.3.28.
TYPE LOCALITY: "Bahia", Brazil.
DISTRIBUTION: Known only from the type locality.
COMMENT: Transferred to *Rhamphophryne* from *Atelopus* by Izecksohn, 1976, Rev. Brasil. Biol., 36:341–345, who also supplied a synonymy and review.

Rhamphophryne rostrata (Noble, 1920). Bull. Am. Mus. Nat. Hist., 42:445.
ORIGINAL NAME: *Bufo rostratus.*
TYPE(S): Holotype: AMNH 1359.
TYPE LOCALITY: Santa Rita Creek, 14 miles north of the village of Mesopotamia in the Department of Antioquia, Colombia.
DISTRIBUTION: Known only from the type locality.

Schismaderma Smith, 1849. Illustr. Zool. S. Afr. Rept., App.:28.
TYPE SPECIES: *Schismaderma lateralis* Smith, 1849 (substitute name for *Bufo carens* Smith, 1848), by monotypy.
DISTRIBUTION: As for the single species.

Schismaderma carens (Smith, 1848). Illustr. Zool. S. Afr., Rept.:pl. 68, fig. 1 and facing page.
ORIGINAL NAME: *Bufo carens.*
TYPE(S): Syntypes: BM 65.5.11.124–126, 58.11.25.91–93.
TYPE LOCALITY: "Interior of Southern Africa".
DISTRIBUTION: Tanzania and southeastern Zaire to northeastern Cape Province (Rep. South Africa).
COMMENT: Reviewed by Poynton, 1964, Ann. Natal Mus., 17:60–62, as *Bufo carens.*

Stephopaedes Channing, 1978. Herpetologica, 34:394.
TYPE SPECIES: *Bufo anotis* Boulenger, 1907, by monotypy.
DISTRIBUTION: As for the single species.

Stephopaedes anotis (Boulenger, 1907). Ann. Mag. Nat. Hist., (7)20:48.
ORIGINAL NAME: *Bufo anotis.*
TYPE(S): Syntypes: BM 1947.2.20.91–92 (formerly 1907.7.2.17–18).
TYPE LOCALITY: "S. E. Mashonaland", Zimbabwe.
DISTRIBUTION: Southern Tanzania, western Mozambique, and Zimbabwe.
COMMENT: Reviewed by Poynton, 1964, Ann. Natal Mus., 17:68, as *Bufo anotis.*

Werneria Poche, 1903. Zool. Anz., 26:701.
TYPE SPECIES: *Stenoglossa fulva* Andersson, 1903 (=*Werneria preussi*), by monotypy.
DISTRIBUTION: Togo and Cameroon, West Africa.
COMMENT: *Werneria* is a replacement name for *Stenoglossa* Andersson, 1903, Verh.

Zool. Bot. Ges. Wien, 53:144, which is preoccupied by *Stenoglossa* Chaudoir, 1848, Bull. Soc. Imp. Nat. Moscou, 21:116, a beetle. Reviewed by Amiet, 1972, Ann. Fac. Sci. Cameroun, 11:121–140, and Amiet, 1976, Rev. Zool. Afr., 90:33–45. Grandison, 1981, Monit. Zool. Ital., N.S., Suppl., 15:187–215, discussed the phylogenetic relationships of the genus.

Werneria bambutensis (Amiet, 1972). Ann. Fac. Sci. Cameroun, 11:132.
ORIGINAL NAME: *Bufo bambutensis.*
TYPE(S): Holotype: MHNG 1253.92.
TYPE LOCALITY: Mts. Bamboutos, env. 2600 m [Cameroon].
DISTRIBUTION: Cameroon, between Mts. Manengouba and Okou, West Africa.

Werneria mertensiana (Amiet, 1976). Rev. Zool. Bot. Afr., 90:43.
ORIGINAL NAME: *Bufo mertensiana.*
TYPE(S): Holotype: MHNG 1253.91.
TYPE LOCALITY: Mt. Nlonako, env. de N'Kongsamba, 1000 m., Cameroon.
DISTRIBUTION: Submontane Cameroon, West Africa.
COMMENT: *Bufo mertensiana* is a replacement name for *Bufo mertensi* Amiet, 1972, Ann. Fac. Sci. Cameroun, 11:125, which is preoccupied by *Bufo ictericus mertensi* Cochran, 1950.

Werneria preussi (Matschie, 1893). Sitzungsber. Ges. Naturforsch. Freunde Berlin, 1893:175.
ORIGINAL NAME: *Bufo preussi.*
TYPE(S): Syntypes: BM 1935.2.8.3, MCZ 10296.
TYPE LOCALITY: "Buea, Kamerun".
DISTRIBUTION: Togo and southwestern Cameroon, West Africa.
COMMENT: Grandison, 1981, Monit. Zool. Ital., N.S., Suppl., 15:187–215, discussed characters and relationships of this species.

Werneria tandyi (Amiet, 1972). Ann. Fac. Sci. Cameroun, 11:129.
ORIGINAL NAME: *Bufo tandyi.*
TYPE(S): Holotype: MHNG 1253.93.
TYPE LOCALITY: "Nsoung, env. 1400 m.", Cameroon.
DISTRIBUTION: Mont Manengouba, western Cameroon, West Africa.

Wolterstorffina Mertens, 1939. Abh. Ber. Mus. Nat. Heimatkd. Magdeburg, 7:122.
TYPE SPECIES: *Nectophryne parvipalmata* Werner, 1898, by monotypy.
DISTRIBUTION: Cameroon and Nigeria, West Africa.
COMMENT: Grandison, 1981, Monit. Zool. Ital., N.S., Suppl., 15:187–215, discussed characters and relationships of this genus.

Wolterstorffina mirei (Perret, 1971). Ann. Fac. Sci. Cameroun, 6:100.
ORIGINAL NAME: *Nectophrynoides mirei.*
TYPE(S): Holotype: MHNG 1182.77.
TYPE LOCALITY: "Mont Okou, 6 14 N; 10 26 E, Cameroun, 2,500 m".
DISTRIBUTION: Mt. Okou and Mt. Bamboutos, 2400–2700 m, Cameroon.

Wolterstorffina parvipalmata (Werner, 1898). Verh. Zool. Bot. Ges. Wien, 48:201.
ORIGINAL NAME: *Nectophryne parvipalmata.*
TYPE(S): Not traced; probably in ZIUW.
TYPE LOCALITY: "Kamerun?".
DISTRIBUTION: Eastern Nigeria on the Obudu Plateau, western and southern slopes of Cameroon Range (including Mt. Cameroon) and Yaoundé Hills, Cameroon.

FAMILY: **Centrolenidae** Taylor, 1951.
CITATION: Proc. Biol. Soc. Washington, 64:36.
DISTRIBUTION: Southern Mexico to Bolivia, northeastern Argentina, and southeastern Brazil.

COMMENT: According to Lynch, 1973, *In* Vial (ed.), Evol. Biol. Anurans:133–182, the
Centrolenidae is phylogenetically close to the Pseudidae and the Hylidae.
Cannatella and Duellman, 1982, Herpetologica, 38:380–388, reviewed the species
from Bolivia and Peru. Lynch and Duellman, 1973, Occas. Pap. Mus. Nat. Hist.
Univ. Kansas, 16:1–66, reviewed the Ecuadorian species. See Hayes and Starrett,
1980, Bull. S. California Acad. Sci., 79:89–96, for additional records. Synonymies of
most of the species can be found in Duellman, 1977, Das Tierreich, 95:1–225.
CONTRIBUTORS: William E. Duellman (WED) and David C. Cannatella (DCC).
REVIEWERS: Werner C. A. Bokermann (WCAB) (Brazil); Jonathan A. Campbell (JAC)
(Mexico and Central America); Ulisses Caramaschi (UC) (Brazil); Ronald I. Crombie
(RIC); Eduardo Gudynas (EG) (Brazil); Keith A. Harding (KAH); Marinus S.
Hoogmoed (MSH); Enrique La Marca (ELM) (South America); Roy W. McDiarmid
(RWM); William F. Pyburn (WFP); Jay M. Savage (JMS); Norman J. Scott, Jr. (NJS);
Paulo E. Vanzolini (PEV) (Brazil).

Centrolene Jiménez de la Espada, 1872. An. Soc. Esp. Hist. Nat., 1:87.
TYPE SPECIES: *Centrolene geckoideum* Jiménez de la Espada, 1872.
DISTRIBUTION: As for the single species.
COMMENT: Recognition of this monotypic genus is based on the extreme size
difference compared to other members of the family, and not on a concept of
relationships (see Goin, 1964, Herpetologica, 20:1–8) (DCC).

Centrolene geckoideum Jiménez de la Espada, 1872. An. Soc. Esp. Hist. Nat., 1:88.
TYPE(S): Formerly in MNCN; now lost.
TYPE LOCALITY: "Rio Napo", Ecuador (apparently in error; see comment).
DISTRIBUTION: Pacific Andean slopes of Colombia and Ecuador.
COMMENT: For discussion see Goin, 1964, Herpetologica, 20:1–8, and Lynch, Ruíz,
and Rueda, 1983, Stud. Neotrop. Fauna Environ., 18:239–243. In spite of the
Amazonian type locality, the species is known only from the Pacific slopes of
the Andes.

Centrolenella Noble, 1920. Bull. Am. Mus. Nat. Hist., 42:441.
TYPE SPECIES: *Centrolenella antioquiensis* Noble, 1920, by original designation.
DISTRIBUTION: Tropical America from Guerrero and Veracruz in Mexico, to Bolivia,
southeastern Brazil and northeastern Argentina, with a hiatus in the lower
Amazon Basin.
COMMENT: For synonymies and discussion of relationships, see Goin, 1964,
Herpetologica, 20:1–8; Savage, 1967, Copeia, 1967:325–331; Lynch and
Duellman, 1973, Occas. Pap. Mus. Nat. Hist. Univ. Kansas, 16:1–66; and Heyer,
1978, Pap. Avulsos Zool., São Paulo, 32:15–33. Lynch, 1981, J. Herpetol., 15:283–
291, suggested that *Hylopsis* Werner, 1894, is a senior synonym. McDiarmid and
Savage, 1984, J. Herpetol., 18:213, argued for the suppression of *Hylopsis* and
conservation of *Centrolenella*. Pending some resolution of the problem we retain
Centrolenella.

Centrolenella albomaculata Taylor, 1949. Univ. Kansas Sci. Bull., 33:267.
TYPE(S): Holotype: KU 23814.
TYPE LOCALITY: "Los Diamantes, one mile south of Guápiles, [Provincia Limón,]
Costa Rica".
DISTRIBUTION: Caribbean slopes of Costa Rica and Pacific slopes of Costa Rica and
Panama to western Colombia.

Centrolenella albotunica (Taylor and Cochran, 1953). Univ. Kansas Sci. Bull., 35:1648.
ORIGINAL NAME: *Cochranella albotunica*.
TYPE(S): Holotype: USNM 96559.
TYPE LOCALITY: "Serra da Bocaina, boundary of Rio de Janeiro and São Paulo,
Brasil".
DISTRIBUTION: Highlands of southeastern Brazil from Rio de Janeiro to São Paulo.

Centrolenella altitudinalis Rivero, 1968. Mem. Soc. Cienc. Nat. La Salle, 28:319.
TYPE(S): Holotype: MCZ 72500.
TYPE LOCALITY: "Quebrada cerca de Río Albarregas, 2.400 m., Estado Mérida, Venezuela".
DISTRIBUTION: Known only from the type locality.

Centrolenella andina Rivero, 1968. Mem. Soc. Cienc. Nat. La Salle, 28:317.
TYPE(S): Holotype: MCZ 72502.
TYPE LOCALITY: "La Azulita, 1050 m, Estado Mérida, Venezuela".
DISTRIBUTION: Northern slopes of Mérida Andes, western Venezuela.

Centrolenella anomala Lynch and Duellman, 1973. Occas. Pap. Mus. Nat. Hist. Univ. Kansas, 16:14.
TYPE(S): Holotype: KU 143299.
TYPE LOCALITY: "Río Azuela, 1740 m, Quito–Lago Agrio road, Provincia Napo, Ecuador".
DISTRIBUTION: Known only from the type locality.

Centrolenella antioquiensis Noble, 1920. Bull. Am. Mus. Nat. Hist., 42:444.
TYPE(S): Holotype: AMNH 1354.
TYPE LOCALITY: "Santa Rita Creek, fourteen miles north of village of Mesopotamia, in the southern part of the Department of Antioquia, Colombia".
DISTRIBUTION: North-central Colombia.

Centrolenella antisthenesi Goin, 1963. Acta Biol. Venezuelica, 3:283.
TYPE(S): Holotype: MBUCV 4033.
TYPE LOCALITY: "Parque Nacional de Rancho Grande, Aragua, Venezuela".
DISTRIBUTION: Cordillera de la Costa, northern Venezuela.

Centrolenella audax Lynch and Duellman, 1973. Occas. Pap. Mus. Nat. Hist. Univ. Kansas, 16:16.
TYPE(S): Holotype: KU 146624.
TYPE LOCALITY: "Salto de Agua, 2.5 km NNE Río Reventador on Quito–Lago Agrio road, 1660 m, Provincia Napo, Ecuador".
DISTRIBUTION: Amazonian slopes of Andes in Napo Province, Ecuador.

Centrolenella balionota Duellman, 1981. Occas. Pap. Mus. Nat. Hist. Univ. Kansas, 88:1.
TYPE(S): Holotype: KU 164702.
TYPE LOCALITY: "3.5 km (by road) northeast of Mindo, 1540 m, Provincia de Pichincha, Ecuador (00° 01' S, 78° 44' W)".
DISTRIBUTION: Known only from type locality (Pichincha, Ecuador) and La Costa, 800 m, Departamento Cauca, Colombia.

Centrolenella bejaranoi Cannatella, 1980. Proc. Biol. Soc. Washington, 93:715.
TYPE(S): Holotype: KU 182369.
TYPE LOCALITY: "58.1 km SW Villa Tunari (by road), 1980 m, Departamento Cochabamba, Bolivia (65° 50' W, 17° 11' S)".
DISTRIBUTION: Known only from the type locality.

Centrolenella bergeri Cannatella, 1980. Proc. Biol. Soc. Washington, 93:719.
TYPE(S): Holotype: KU 182363.
TYPE LOCALITY: "58.1 km SW Villa Tunari (by road), 1980 m, Departamento Cochabamba, Bolivia (65° 50' W, 17° 11' S)".
DISTRIBUTION: Amazonian slopes of Andes from west-central Bolivia to extreme southeastern Peru.

Centrolenella buckleyi (Boulenger, 1882). Cat. Batr. Sal. Brit. Mus.:420.
ORIGINAL NAME: *Hylella buckleyi*.
TYPE(S): Syntypes: BM 78.1.25.16 (Intac), 80.12.5.201. (Pallatanga) [lost]; see comment.
TYPE LOCALITY: "Intac" and "Paitanga" (=Pallatanga), Ecuador.
DISTRIBUTION: Andes from western Venezuela to southern Ecuador.
COMMENT: The Venezuelan form was named as a subspecies by Rivero, 1968, Mem. Soc. Cienc. Nat. La Salle, 28:323. Goin, 1961, Zool. Anz., 166:101, noted that the Pallatanga type specimen had distintegrated and the Intac type specimen could not be found.

Centrolenella chirripoi (Taylor, 1958). Univ. Kansas Sci. Bull., 39:59.
ORIGINAL NAME: *Cochranella chirripoi*.
TYPE(S): Holotype: KU 36865.
TYPE LOCALITY: "Cocales Creek, Suretka, Limón Province", Costa Rica.
DISTRIBUTION: Costa Rica to western Colombia.

Centrolenella cochranae (Goin, 1961). Zool. Anz., 166:97.
ORIGINAL NAME: *Cochranella cochranae*.
TYPE(S): Holotype: BM 1912.11.1.68.
TYPE LOCALITY: "El Topo, Rio Pastaza, Eastern Ecuador, 4200 feet".
DISTRIBUTION: Lower Amazonian slopes of Andes in Ecuador.

Centrolenella colymbiphyllum Taylor, 1949. Univ. Kansas Sci. Bull., 33:262.
TYPE(S): Holotype: KU 23812.
TYPE LOCALITY: "American Cinchona Plantation, elev. 5,600 ft., Caribbean drainage of Volcán Poás, Costa Rica".
DISTRIBUTION: Central and southeastern Costa Rica.

Centrolenella dubia (Taylor and Cochran, 1953). Univ. Kansas Sci. Bull., 35:1644.
ORIGINAL NAME: *Cochranella dubia*.
TYPE(S): Holotype: USNM 96722.
TYPE LOCALITY: "Serra da Bocaina, boundary of Rio de Janeiro and São Paulo", Brazil.
DISTRIBUTION: Known only from the type locality.

Centrolenella estevesi Rivero, 1968. Mem. Soc. Cienc. Nat. La Salle, 28:314.
TYPE(S): Holotype: MCZ 72498.
TYPE LOCALITY: "Quebrada cerca de Río Albarregas, 2400 m, Estado Mérida, Venezuela".
DISTRIBUTION: Mérida Andes, western Venezuela.
COMMENT: A hylid (pers. comm., Priscilla Starrett to JMS).

Centrolenella euknemos Savage and Starrett, 1967. Copeia, 1967:604.
TYPE(S): Holotype: LACM 26764.
TYPE LOCALITY: "Costa Rica: Provincia de San José: Canton de Coronado: 1.5 km S Alto La Palma, 1500 m."
DISTRIBUTION: Costa Rica and Panama to northern Colombia.

Centrolenella eurygnatha (A. Lutz, 1925). C. R. Séances Soc. Biol., Paris, 93:138.
ORIGINAL NAME: *Hyla (Hylella) eurygnatha*.
TYPE(S): Syntypes: AL-MN 973–975.
TYPE LOCALITY: "Serra da Bocaina", Rio de Janeiro, Brazil.
DISTRIBUTION: Highlands of southeastern Brazil.
COMMENT: Synonymy includes four species named by Taylor and Cochran, 1953 (*Cochranella bokermanni, Cochranella delicatissima, Cochranella divaricans,* and *Cochranella surda*), synonymized with *Centrolenella eurygnatha* by Heyer, 1978, Pap. Avulsos Zool., São Paulo, 32:15–33.

Centrolenella flavopunctata Lynch and Duellman, 1973. Occas. Pap. Mus. Nat. Hist. Univ. Kansas, 16:25.
TYPE(S): Holotype: KU 121048.
TYPE LOCALITY: "Mera, Provincia Pastaza, Ecuador".
DISTRIBUTION: Lower Amazonian slopes of Andes in Ecuador.

Centrolenella fleischmanni (Boettger, 1893). Ber. Senckenb. Naturforsch. Ges., 1892–1893(1893):251.
ORIGINAL NAME: *Hylella fleischmanni*.
TYPE(S): SMF 3760 designated lectotype by Mertens, 1967, Senckenb. Biol., 48:42.
TYPE LOCALITY: "San José, [Provincia San José,] Costa Rica".
DISTRIBUTION: Guerrero and Veracruz, Mexico, to Surinam and Ecuador.
COMMENT: For discussion see Lynch and Duellman, 1973, Occas. Pap. Mus. Nat. Hist. Univ. Kansas, 16:1–66; Goin, 1964, Herpetologica, 20:1–8; and Starrett and Savage, 1973, Bull. S. California Acad. Sci., 72:57–78.
REVIEWERS: Gustavo Casas-Andreu (GCA); Oscar Flores-Villela (OFV).

Centrolenella geijskesi Goin, 1966. Stud. Fauna Suriname and other Guyanas, 8:77.
TYPE(S): Holotype: RMNH 11041.
TYPE LOCALITY: "at about 200 meters altitude on the south slope of the Wilhelmina Mountains, District Nickerie, Suriname".
DISTRIBUTION: Known only from the type locality.

Centrolenella grandisonae Cochran and Goin, 1970. Bull. U.S. Natl. Mus., 288:513.
TYPE(S): Holotype: BM 1910.7.11.68.
TYPE LOCALITY: "Pueblo Rico, [Departamento] Caldas, southwestern Colombia, 5000 feet altitude".
DISTRIBUTION: Pacific slopes of Andes in southern Colombia and Ecuador.
COMMENT: As used by Lynch and Duellman, 1973, Occas. Pap. Mus. Nat. Hist. Univ. Kansas, 16:1–66, this name applies to the species currently recognized as *Centrolenella lynchi*; see Duellman, 1980, Trans. Kansas Acad. Sci., 83:26–32.

Centrolenella granulosa Taylor, 1949. Univ. Kansas Sci. Bull., 33:265.
TYPE(S): Holotype: FMNH 178269 (formerly R. C. Taylor 2463).
TYPE LOCALITY: "Los Diamantes, one mile south of Guápiles, [Provincia Limón,] Costa Rica".
DISTRIBUTION: Caribbean slopes of Nicaragua and Costa Rica; Pacific lowlands of southwestern Costa Rica.

Centrolenella griffithsi (Goin, 1961). Zool. Anz., 166:97.
ORIGINAL NAME: *Cochranella griffithsi*.
TYPE(S): Holotype: BM 1940.2.20.4.
TYPE LOCALITY: "Río Saloya, [Provincia Pichincha,] Ecuador, 4000 feet".
DISTRIBUTION: Pacific slopes of Andes in southern Colombia and Ecuador.

Centrolenella heloderma Duellman, 1981. Occas. Pap. Mus. Nat. Hist. Univ. Kansas, 88:4.
TYPE(S): Holotype: KU 164715.
TYPE LOCALITY: "Quebrada Zapadores, 5 km east-southeast of Chiriboga, 2010 m, Provincia de Pichincha, Ecuador (00° 17' S, 78° 47' W)".
DISTRIBUTION: Cloud forest (1960–2150 m) on the Pacific slopes of the western Andes in Pichincha Province, Ecuador.

Centrolenella ilex Savage, 1967. Copeia, 1967:326.
TYPE(S): Holotype: LACM 25205.
TYPE LOCALITY: "Costa Rica: Provincia de Limón: Canton de Limón: Alta Talamanca: 16 km SW Amubri, on Río Lari, 300 m."
DISTRIBUTION: Caribbean slopes of Nicaragua, Costa Rica, and Panama, to western Colombia.

Centrolenella johnelsi Cochran and Goin, 1970. Bull. U.S. Natl. Mus., 288:515.
  TYPE(S): Holotype: MLS 432.
  TYPE LOCALITY: "San Pedro, north of Medellín, [Departamento] Antioquia,
    Colombia".
  DISTRIBUTION: Known only from the type locality.

Centrolenella lutzorum (Taylor and Cochran, 1953). Univ. Kansas Sci. Bull., 35:1638.
  ORIGINAL NAME: *Cochranella lutzorum.*
  TYPE(S): Holotype: USNM 101134.
  TYPE LOCALITY: "Petrópolis, Rio de Janeiro", Brazil.
  DISTRIBUTION: Mountains of Rio de Janeiro, Brazil.

Centrolenella lynchi Duellman, 1980. Trans. Kansas Acad. Sci., 83:29.
  TYPE(S): Holotype: KU 164691.
  TYPE LOCALITY: "a stream 4 km northeast (by road) of Dos Ríos, Provincia
    Pichincha, Ecuador, 1140 m (00° 21' S, 78° 54' W)".
  DISTRIBUTION: Elevations of 1140–1500 m on the Pacific slopes of the western
    Andes in Ecuador.
  COMMENT: See comment under *Centrolenella grandisonae.*

Centrolenella mariae Duellman and Toft, 1979. Herpetologica, 35:66.
  TYPE(S): Holotype: KU 174713.
  TYPE LOCALITY: "Serranía de Sira, ± 1550 m, Departamento Huánuco, Peru".
  DISTRIBUTION: Known only from the type locality.

Centrolenella medemi Cochran and Goin, 1970. Bull. U.S. Natl. Mus., 288:511.
  TYPE(S): Holotype: USNM 152277.
  TYPE LOCALITY: "Puerto Asís, upper Río Putumayo, [Comisaria] Putumayo,
    Colombia".
  DISTRIBUTION: Lower Amazonian slopes of southern Colombia and Ecuador.

Centrolenella megacheira Lynch and Duellman, 1973. Occas. Pap. Mus. Nat. Hist.
  Univ. Kansas, 16:36.
  TYPE(S): Holotype: KU 143245.
  TYPE LOCALITY: "16.5 km NNE of Santa Rosa, 1700 m. on Quito–Lago Agrio road,
    Provincia Napo, Ecuador".
  DISTRIBUTION: Amazonian slopes of Andes in Napo Province, Ecuador, and
    Departamento Putumayo, Colombia.

Centrolenella midas Lynch and Duellman, 1973. Occas. Pap. Mus. Nat. Hist. Univ.
  Kansas, 16:38.
  TYPE(S): Holotype: KU 123219.
  TYPE LOCALITY: "Santa Cecilia, 340 m, Provincia Napo, Ecuador".
  DISTRIBUTION: Amazon Basin in Ecuador and northeastern Peru.

Centrolenella munozorum Lynch and Duellman, 1973. Occas. Pap. Mus. Nat. Hist.
  Univ. Kansas, 16:40.
  TYPE(S): Holotype: KU 118054.
  TYPE LOCALITY: "Santa Cecilia, 340 m, Provincia Napo, Ecuador".
  DISTRIBUTION: Upper Amazon Basin in Ecuador and Peru (see comment).
  COMMENT: Previous records from Colombia are in error (WED).

Centrolenella ocellata (Boulenger, 1918). Ann. Mag. Nat. Hist., (9)2:433.
  ORIGINAL NAME: *Hylella ocellata.*
  TYPE(S): Holotype: BM 1912.11.1.19.
  TYPE LOCALITY: "Huancabamba, [Departamento Pasco,] E. Peru, above 3000 feet".
  DISTRIBUTION: Amazonian slopes of Andes in central and southern Peru.

Centrolenella ocellifera (Boulenger, 1899). Ann. Mag. Nat. Hist., (7)3:277.
ORIGINAL NAME: *Hyla ocellifera*.
TYPE(S): Holotype: BM 98.5.19.3.
TYPE LOCALITY: "Paramba, [Provincia Imbabura,] N. W. Ecuador".
DISTRIBUTION: Pacific slopes of Andes in Ecuador.

Centrolenella orientalis Rivero, 1968. Mem. Soc. Cienc. Nat. La Salle, 28:308.
TYPE(S): Holotype: MCZ 72497.
TYPE LOCALITY: "Cerro Turumiquire, 1200 m, Estados Sucre-Monagas, Venezuela".
DISTRIBUTION: Mountains of northeastern Venezuela and Tobago I.

Centrolenella orocostalis Rivero, 1968. Mem. Soc. Cienc. Nat. La Salle, 28:305.
TYPE(S): Holotype: MCZ 47501.
TYPE LOCALITY: "Cerro Platillón (Hacienda Picachitos), Cordillera del Interior, 1200 m., Estado Guárico, Venezuela".
DISTRIBUTION: Cordillera del Interior and Cordillera de la Costa, north-central Venezuela.

Centrolenella oyampiensis Lescure, 1975. Bull. Soc. Zool. France, 100:386.
TYPE(S): Holotype: MNHNP 1973-1673.
TYPE LOCALITY: "village Zidok (Haut-Oyapock), Guyane française".
DISTRIBUTION: Southern French Guiana and Surinam.

Centrolenella parvula (Boulenger, 1894). Proc. Zool. Soc. London, 1894:646.
ORIGINAL NAME: *Hylella parvula*.
TYPE(S): Syntypes: BM 88.2.7.32 (Lages), 93.12.22.16 (Theresopolis).
TYPE LOCALITY: "Lages, Santa Catharina" and "Theresopolis" (now Queçaba, Santa Catarina, according to Bokermann, 1966, Lista Anot. Local. Tipo Anf. Brasil.: 116), Brazil.
DISTRIBUTION: Santa Catarina, southeastern Brazil.

Centrolenella pellucida Lynch and Duellman, 1973. Occas. Pap. Mus. Nat. Hist. Univ. Kansas, 16:43.
TYPE(S): Holotype: KU 143298.
TYPE LOCALITY: "Río Azuela, 1740 m, Quito–Lago Agrio road, Provincia Napo, Ecuador".
DISTRIBUTION: Known only from the type locality.

Centrolenella peristicta Lynch and Duellman, 1973. Occas. Pap. Mus. Nat. Hist. Univ. Kansas, 16:45.
TYPE(S): Holotype: KU 118051.
TYPE LOCALITY: "Tandapi, 1460 m, Provincia Pichincha, Ecuador".
DISTRIBUTION: Pacific slopes of Andes in Ecuador.

Centrolenella petropolitana (Taylor and Cochran, 1953). Univ. Kansas Sci. Bull., 35: 1637.
ORIGINAL NAME: *Cochranella petropolitana*.
TYPE(S): Holotype: USNM 101135.
TYPE LOCALITY: "Petrópolis, Rio de Janeiro, Brazil".
DISTRIBUTION: Mountains of Rio de Janeiro, Brazil.

Centrolenella phenax Cannatella and Duellman, 1982. Herpetologica, 38:382.
TYPE(S): Holotype: KU 162263.
TYPE LOCALITY: "Tutumbaro, Río Piene, 1840 m, Departmento Ayacucho, Peru (73° 55' W, 12° 42' S)".
DISTRIBUTION: Known only from the type locality.

Centrolenella pipilata Lynch and Duellman, 1973. Occas. Pap. Mus. Nat. Hist. Univ. Kansas, 16:46.
TYPE(S): Holotype: KU 143278.
TYPE LOCALITY: "a stream 16.5 km NNE of Santa Rosa, 1700 m on Quito–Lago Agrio road, Provincia Napo, Ecuador".
DISTRIBUTION: Amazonian slopes of Andes in Napo Province, Ecuador.

Centrolenella pluvialis Cannatella and Duellman, 1982. Herpetologica, 38:380.
TYPE(S): Holotype: KU 173224.
TYPE LOCALITY: "Pistipata, Río Umasbamba (=Río Santa María), 12 km SE Huyro, 1820 m, Departamento Cuzco, Peru (72° 30′ W, 13° 03′ S)".
DISTRIBUTION: Known only from the type locality.

Centrolenella prasina Duellman, 1981. Occas. Pap. Mus. Nat. Hist. Univ. Kansas, 88:6.
TYPE(S): Holotype: KU 169693.
TYPE LOCALITY: "Río Calima, 1.5 km (by road) west of Lago Calima, 1230 m, Departamento de Valle, Colombia. (4° 00′ N, 76° 35′ W)".
DISTRIBUTION: Known only from the type locality.

Centrolenella prosoblepon (Boettger, 1892). Kat. Batr. Samml. Mus. Senckenb. Naturforsch. Ges.:45.
ORIGINAL NAME: *Hyla prosoblepon.*
TYPE(S): Syntypes: SMF 3756, ZMB 28019; SMF 3756 designated lectotype by Mertens, 1967, Senckenb. Biol., 48:42.
TYPE LOCALITY: "Plantage Cairo (La Junta) bei Limon, atlantische Seite von Costa Rica".
DISTRIBUTION: Nicaragua, Costa Rica, Panama, and Pacific slopes of Colombia and Ecuador.
COMMENT: Lynch and Duellman, 1973, Occas. Pap. Mus. Nat. Hist. Univ. Kansas, 16:49, discussed variation and synonyms.

Centrolenella pulidoi Rivero, 1968. Mem. Soc. Cienc. Nat. La Salle, 28:312.
TYPE(S): Holotype: MCZ 72499.
TYPE LOCALITY: "Monte Duida, 2,000 pies, Territorio Amazonas, Venezuela".
DISTRIBUTION: Known only from the type locality.
COMMENT: A hylid (pers. comm., Priscilla Starrett to JMS).

Centrolenella pulverata (Peters, 1873). Monatsber. Preuss. Akad. Wiss. Berlin, 1873:614.
ORIGINAL NAME: *Hyla pulverata.*
TYPE(S): Holotype: ZMB 7842.
TYPE LOCALITY: "Chiriqui", Panama; see comment with type locality in *Dendrobates maculatus* account.
DISTRIBUTION: Caribbean versant of Nicaragua and Pacific slopes and lowlands in Costa Rica and Panama.

Centrolenella resplendens Lynch and Duellman, 1973. Occas. Pap. Mus. Nat. Hist. Univ. Kansas, 16:51.
TYPE(S): Holotype: KU 118053.
TYPE LOCALITY: "Santa Cecilia, 340 m, Provincia Napo, Ecuador".
DISTRIBUTION: Upper Amazon Basin in Ecuador and southern Colombia.

Centrolenella ritae (B. Lutz, 1952). *In* B. Lutz and Kloss, Mem. Inst. Oswaldo Cruz, Rio de Janeiro, 50:658.
ORIGINAL NAME: *Centrolene ritae.*
TYPE(S): Formerly in MN; destroyed.
TYPE LOCALITY: "Benjamin Constant, Alto Solimões", Estado do Amazonas, Brazil.
DISTRIBUTION: Known only from the type locality.

Centrolenella siren Lynch and Duellman, 1973. Occas. Pap. Mus. Nat. Hist. Univ. Kansas, 16:54.
TYPE(S): Holotype: KU 146610.
TYPE LOCALITY: "small tributary of the Río Salado, about 1 km upstream from the Río Coca, 1410 m, Provincia Napo, Ecuador".
DISTRIBUTION: Amazonian slopes of Andes in Napo Province, Ecuador, and Departamento Putumayo, Colombia, to southern Peru.

Centrolenella spiculata Duellman, 1976. Occas. Pap. Mus. Nat. Hist. Univ. Kansas, 52:5.
TYPE(S): Holotype: KU 162284.
TYPE LOCALITY: "Río Cosñipata, 4 kilometers southwest of Santa Isabel, Departamento Cuzco, Perú, 1700 m".
DISTRIBUTION: Eastern slopes of Andes in central and southern Peru.

Centrolenella spinosa Taylor, 1949. Univ. Kansas Sci. Bull., 33:259.
TYPE(S): Holotype: KU 23809.
TYPE LOCALITY: "Los Diamantes, one mile south of Guápiles, [Provincia Limón,] Costa Rica".
DISTRIBUTION: Caribbean slopes of Costa Rica and Pacific slopes from Costa Rica to Ecuador.
COMMENT: Included as the sole member of the genus *Teratohyla* by Taylor, 1951, Proc. Biol. Soc. Washington, 64:35.

Centrolenella talamancae (Taylor, 1952). Univ. Kansas Sci. Bull., 35:781.
ORIGINAL NAME: *Cochranella talamancae.*
TYPE(S): Holotype: KU 30887 (not KU 4143 as originally stated; 4143 is the R. C. Taylor field number).
TYPE LOCALITY: "Moravia [de Chirripó, Provincia Cartago], Costa Rica, Caribbean drainage".
DISTRIBUTION: Known only from the type locality.

Centrolenella taylori Goin, 1968. Q. J. Florida Acad. Sci., 30:115.
TYPE(S): Holotype: BM 1939.1.1.65.
TYPE LOCALITY: "elevation of 750 ft. along the New River, Guyana" (locality actually in southwestern Surinam—MSH).
DISTRIBUTION: Guianan Shield in southern Surinam, Guyana, and southeastern Venezuela.

Centrolenella truebae Duellman, 1976. Occas. Pap. Mus. Nat. Hist. Univ. Kansas, 52:6.
TYPE(S): Holotype: KU 162268.
TYPE LOCALITY: "Río Cosñipata, 4 kilometers southwest of Santa Isabel, Departamento Cuzco, Perú, 1700 m".
DISTRIBUTION: Known only from the type locality.

Centrolenella uranoscopa (Müller, 1924). Zool. Anz., 59:234.
ORIGINAL NAME: *Hyla (Hylella) uranoscopa.*
TYPE(S): Holotype: ZSM 81/1921.
TYPE LOCALITY: "Humboldt (Flussgebiet des Rio Novo), Staat Santa Catharina", Brazil.
DISTRIBUTION: Eastern Brazil from Minas Gerais to Santa Catarina.

Centrolenella valerioi (Dunn, 1931). Occas. Pap. Boston Soc. Nat. Hist., 5:397.
ORIGINAL NAME: *Centrolene valerioi.*
TYPE(S): Holotype: MCZ 16003.
TYPE LOCALITY: "La Palma, [Provincia San José,] Costa Rica, 4500 feet".
DISTRIBUTION: Central Costa Rica to Pacific slope of Ecuador.

Centrolenella vanzolinii (Taylor and Cochran, 1953). Univ. Kansas Sci. Bull., 35:1646.
ORIGINAL NAME: *Cochranella vanzolinii*.
TYPE(S): Holotype: MZUSP 2952.
TYPE LOCALITY: "Boracea, São Paulo" (=Estação Biológica de Boracéia, Salesópolis, São Paulo, Brazil, according to Bokermann, 1966, Lista Anot. Local. Tipo Anf. Brasil.:28).
DISTRIBUTION: Highlands of southeastern Brazil from Rio de Janeiro to São Paulo; northeastern Argentina.
COMMENT: See Cei, 1982, Monit. Zool. Ital., N.S., Monogr., 2:499–501.

Centrolenella vireovittata Starrett and Savage, 1973. Bull. S. California Acad. Sci., 72:66.
TYPE(S): Holotype: LACM 75141.
TYPE LOCALITY: "Costa Rica: Provincia de San Jose: Canton Perez Zeledon: 0.5 km NE Alfombra: a place 16 km SW San Isidro de El General on the road to Dominical, 880 m".
DISTRIBUTION: Known only from the type locality.

FAMILY: **Dendrobatidae** Cope, 1865.
CITATION: Nat. Hist. Rev., N.S., 5:103.
DISTRIBUTION: Nicaragua to the Amazon Basin of Bolivia and to the Guianas and southeastern Brazil.
COMMENT: Dubois, 1982, Bull. Zool. Nomencl., 39:267–278, noted that the family-group name Phyllobatae Fitzinger, 1843, Syst. Rept.:32, has priority over Dendrobatidae. He petitioned the Commission of Zoological Nomenclature to give Dendrobatidae Cope, 1865, nomenclatural precedence over Phyllobatidae. See Holthius, 1983, Bull. Zool. Nomencl., 40:197–198, for a dissent. Griffiths, 1959, Proc. Zool. Soc. London, 132:457–487, considered the Dendrobatidae to be a subfamily of the Ranidae, derived from the Petropedetinae (Ranidae). Noble, 1922, Bull. Am. Mus. Nat. Hist., 46:1–87, and Lynch, 1971, Misc. Publ. Mus. Nat. Hist. Univ. Kansas, 53:1–238, provided evidence that the Dendrobatidae was derived from the Hylodinae of the Leptodactylidae. Savage, 1982, Ann. Missouri Bot. Garden, 69:464–547, discussed some aspects of biogeography, and Rivero, 1980, *In* Salinas (ed.), Actas VIII Congr. Latino Am. Zool., 1:91–123, discussed briefly possible origin and relationships in South America. Lynch and Ruíz, 1981, Proc. Biol. Soc. Washington, 95:557–567, criticized and discussed the current generic classification.
REVIEWERS: Werner C. A. Bokermann (WCAB) (Brazil); Ulisses Caramaschi (UC) (Brazil); Ronald I. Crombie (RIC); William E. Duellman (WED); Linda S. Ford (LSF); Eduardo Gudynas (EG) (Brazil); Keith A. Harding (KAH); Marinus S. Hoogmoed (MSH); Enrique La Marca (ELM); Juan A. Rivero (JAR); Jay M. Savage (JMS); Norman J. Scott, Jr. (NJS); Paulo E. Vanzolini (PEV) (Brazil).

Atopophrynus Lynch and Ruíz-Carranza, 1982. Proc. Biol. Soc. Washington, 95:557.
TYPE SPECIES: *Atopophrynus syntomopus* Lynch and Ruíz-Carranza, 1982, by original designation.
DISTRIBUTION: As for the single species.
COMMENT: Of uncertain relationship to the other genera in the family according to Lynch and Ruíz-Carranza, 1982, Proc. Biol. Soc. Washington, 95:557–562.

Atopophrynus syntomopus Lynch and Ruíz-Carranza, 1982. Proc. Biol. Soc. Washington, 95:557.
TYPE(S): Holotype: ICN 8611.
TYPE LOCALITY: "crest of the Cordillera Central [2780 m], 8 km by road E Sonsón, Municipio Sonsón, Departamento Antioquia, Colombia".
DISTRIBUTION: Known only from the type locality.

Colostethus Cope, 1866. Proc. Acad. Nat. Sci. Philadelphia, 18:130.
TYPE SPECIES: *Phyllobates latinasus* Cope, 1863, by monotypy.
DISTRIBUTION: Central Costa Rica to northern Peru and the Guianas and through the Amazon Basin to southeastern Brazil.

COMMENT: See Savage, 1968, Copeia, 1968:745–776, for synonymy, nomenclatural history, and definition of the genus. Edwards, 1971, Proc. Biol. Soc. Washington, 84:147–162, expanded on Savage's arrangement and provided a tentative list of species referred to *Colostethus*. Lynch, 1982, Herpetologica, 38: 366, pointed out that *Colostethus* is defined solely on features primitive for the family. Rivero, 1979, *In* Salgado-Labouriau (ed.), El Medio Ambiente Páramo, discussed biogeography of some of the Venezuelan species. Edwards, 1974, Occas. Pap. Mus. Nat. Hist. Univ. Kansas, 30:1–14, provided a basic schema for identification. The species taxonomy of this likely paraphyletic group is poorly known. More than 20 species await description; see Edwards, 1974, Univ. Kansas Diss.:1–499.

Colostethus abditaurantius Silverstone, 1975. Contrib. Sci. Nat. Hist. Mus. Los Angeles Co., 268:1.
TYPE(S): Holotype: LACM 72000.
TYPE LOCALITY: "Quebrada Altagracia, Bello, Departamento de Antioquia, Colombia, about 1450 m elevation".
DISTRIBUTION: Known only from the type locality.

Colostethus alagoanus (Bokermann, 1967). Rev. Brasil. Biol., 27:351.
ORIGINAL NAME: *Phyllobates alagoanus*.
TYPE(S): Holotype: WCAB 2801.
TYPE LOCALITY: "Mangabeiras, Estado de Alagoas, Brasil".
DISTRIBUTION: State of Alagoas in northeastern Brazil.
COMMENT: Related to *Colostethus olfersioides*, according to Bokermann, 1967, Rev. Brasil. Biol., 27:352.

Colostethus alboguttatus (Boulenger, 1903). Ann. Mag. Nat. Hist., (7)11:482.
ORIGINAL NAME: *Phyllobates alboguttatus*.
TYPE(S): Holotype: BM 1947.2.13.88.
TYPE LOCALITY: "Merida, [Estado Mérida,] Venezuela, at an altitude of 1600 metres".
DISTRIBUTION: Páramos and immediate subpáramos of the Mérida and Táchira Andes of Venezuela, 2000–3000 m.
COMMENT: Reviewed by Rivero, 1961, Bull. Mus. Comp. Zool., 126:163–164. The published descriptions of specimens allocated to this name vary suspiciously; Edwards, 1974, Occas. Pap. Mus. Nat. Hist. Univ. Kansas, 30:2, listed the species as webless and Rivero, 1976, Mem. Soc. Cienc. Nat. La Salle, 105:328–344, considered the species to have a short basal web and lateral fringes. See comment under *Colostethus inflexus*.

Colostethus anthracinus Edwards, 1971. Proc. Biol. Soc. Washington, 84:155.
TYPE(S): Holotype: KU 120639.
TYPE LOCALITY: "Páramo de Raranga, 12 km S Cutchil, Morona-Santiago Province, Ecuador, 3400 m".
DISTRIBUTION: Andes of southern Ecuador, 2500–3500 m.

Colostethus beebei (Noble, 1923). Zoologica, New York, 3:289.
ORIGINAL NAME: *Hyloxalus beebei*.
TYPE(S): Holotype: AMNH 18683.
TYPE LOCALITY: "near Kaeiteur Falls, British Guiana [=Guyana]".
DISTRIBUTION: Known only from the type locality.
COMMENT: Considered a synonym of *Colostethus brunneus* by Cochran, 1955, Bull. U.S. Natl. Mus., 206:44, and Cochran and Goin, 1970, Bull. U.S. Natl. Mus., 288:48, but considered distinct by Edwards, 1974, Occas. Pap. Mus. Nat. Hist. Univ. Kansas, 30:2.

Colostethus bocagei (Jiménez de la Espada, 1871). J. Sci. Math. Phys. Nat., Lisboa, 3:59.
ORIGINAL NAME: *Hyloxalus Bocagei.*
TYPE(S): Syntypes: MNCN.
TYPE LOCALITY: "in Ecuador; ad sylvas pagi S. Jose de Moti", Cantón de Quijos, Napo Province, Ecuador.
DISTRIBUTION: Known only from the type locality.
COMMENT: Lescure, 1975, Bull. Mus. Natl. Hist. Nat., Paris, (3)293(Zool.)203:418, cited a personal communication from S. R. Edwards indicating that *Colostethus bocagei* is a synonym of *Colostethus fuliginosus.*

Colostethus bromelicola (Test, 1956). Occas. Pap. Mus. Zool. Univ. Michigan, 577:6.
ORIGINAL NAME: *Phyllobates bromelicola.*
TYPE(S): Holotype: UMMZ 113027.
TYPE LOCALITY: "1310 m on Pico Periquito, Rancho Grande, Estado Aragua, Venezuela".
DISTRIBUTION: Coastal Range of Venezuela, above 1000 m.
COMMENT: See Rivero, 1961, Bull. Mus. Comp. Zool., 126:164–166. Related to *Colostethus brunneus*, according to the original description.

Colostethus brunneus (Cope, 1887). Proc. Am. Philos. Soc., 24:54.
ORIGINAL NAME: *Prostherapis brunneus.*
TYPE(S): Syntypes: ANSP 11241–61.
TYPE LOCALITY: "Chupada" (=Chapada dos Guimaraẽs), 30 miles north-east of Cuiabá and near the headwater of the Xingu, Estado do Mato Grosso, Brazil.
DISTRIBUTION: Mato Grosso, Brazil, to Surinam and Peru.
COMMENT: See comment under *Colostethus marchesianus.*

Colostethus capixaba (Bokermann, 1967). Rev. Brasil. Biol., 27:349.
ORIGINAL NAME: *Phyllobates capixaba.*
TYPE(S): Holotype: WCAB 1952.
TYPE LOCALITY: "próximo à Lagoa Macuco, Refúgio Sooretama, Linhares, Espírito Santo, Brasil".
DISTRIBUTION: Eastern Brazil.
COMMENT: Related to *Colostethus olfersioides* according to Bokermann, 1967, Rev. Brasil. Biol., 27:350.

Colostethus carioca (Bokermann, 1967). Rev. Brasil. Biol., 27:352.
ORIGINAL NAME: *Phyllobates carioca.*
TYPE(S): Holotype: WCAB 38601.
TYPE LOCALITY: "Represa Rio Grande, Rio de Janeiro, Guanabara [now Rio de Janeiro], Brasil".
DISTRIBUTION: Espírito Santo and Rio de Janeiro, Brazil.
COMMENT: Related to *Colostethus olfersioides* according to Bokermann, 1967, Rev. Brasil. Biol., 27:353.

Colostethus chocoensis (Boulenger, 1912). Ann. Mag. Nat. Hist., (8)10:190.
ORIGINAL NAME: *Hylixalus chocoensis.*
TYPE(S): BM.
TYPE LOCALITY: "Noananoa, Rio San Juan, [Departamento] Choco, S. W. Colombia, about 100 feet".
DISTRIBUTION: San Juan and Atrato drainages in the Departments of Chocó and Antioquia, Colombia.

Colostethus collaris (Boulenger, 1912). Ann. Mag. Nat. Hist., (8)10:190.
ORIGINAL NAME: *Hylixalus collaris.*
TYPE(S): Syntypes: BM 1947.2.14.29–39.
TYPE LOCALITY: "Merida, 5200 feet [1585 m] and Rio Albireggas [=Albarregas], 11300 feet [3444 m], [Estado Mérida,] Venezuela".
DISTRIBUTION: Mérida Andes, Venezuela, 1500–3600 m.

COMMENT: Reviewed by Rivero, 1961, Bull. Mus. Comp. Zool., 126:154–155. See also Rivero, 1976, Mem. Soc. Cienc. Nat. La Salle, 105:332–334.

Colostethus degranvillei Lescure, 1975. Bull. Mus. Natl. Hist. Nat., Paris, (3)293(Zool.)203:413.
TYPE(S): Holotype: MNHNP 1973-1655.
TYPE LOCALITY: "monts Atachi-Bacca, (Guyane française) près du camp III (3° 34' N, 53° 55' W; 360 m)", French Guiana.
DISTRIBUTION: French Guiana and Surinam.

Colostethus dunni (Rivero, 1961). Bull. Mus. Comp. Zool., 126:157.
ORIGINAL NAME: *Prostherapis dunni*.
TYPE(S): Holotype: FMNH 35987.
TYPE LOCALITY: "above Caracas", Distrito Federal, Venezuela.
DISTRIBUTION: Central portion of the Coastal Range of Venezuela, 500–1520 m.
COMMENT: The specimens considered by Hardy, 1983, Bull. Maryland Herpetol. Soc., 19:47–51, to be *Colostethus dunni* do not represent this species, but are closely allied with or conspecific with *Colostethus herminae* (=*Colostethus trinitatis* of this list) (ELM).

Colostethus edwardsi Lynch, 1982. Herpetologica, 38:367.
TYPE(S): Holotype: ICN 6376.
TYPE LOCALITY: "Cueva de Las Moyas, 0.7 km SW Los Patios, vereda Las Mollas (=Moyas?), municipio La Calera, Departamento Cundinamarca, Colombia, 3030 m".
DISTRIBUTION: Mountains immediately east of Bogotá, Colombia, at elevations of 3030–3300 m in subterranean sites.
COMMENT: Most closely related to *Colostethus ruizi*, according to the original description.

Colostethus elachyhistus Edwards, 1971. Proc. Biol. Soc. Washington, 84:149.
TYPE(S): Holotype: KU 120540.
TYPE LOCALITY: "Loja, Loja Province, Ecuador, 2150 m".
DISTRIBUTION: Pacific slopes of the Andes in southern Ecuador (800–1300 m); Amazonian slopes of the Andes in southern Ecuador and in northern Peru in the Huancabamba Depression (1800–2000 m).

Colostethus festae (Peracca, 1904). Boll. Mus. Zool. Anat. Comp. Univ. Torino, 19:16.
ORIGINAL NAME: *Prostherapis festae*.
TYPE(S): Holotype: ?MSNT.
TYPE LOCALITY: "Valle Santiago", eastern Ecuador.
DISTRIBUTION: Known only from the type locality.

Colostethus fraterdanieli Silverstone, 1971. Contrib. Sci. Nat. Hist. Mus. Los Angeles Co., 215:4.
TYPE(S): Holotype: LACM 44164.
TYPE LOCALITY: "Colombia: Antioquia: Santa Rita (near Río Nare), 1890–1910 m".
DISTRIBUTION: Cordillera Central of Colombia in Caldas and Antioquia, 1800–2500 m elev.

Colostethus fuliginosus (Jiménez de la Espada, 1871). J. Sci. Math. Phys. Nat., Lisboa, 3:59.
ORIGINAL NAME: *Hyloxalus fuliginosus*.
TYPE(S): Syntypes: MNCN 276 (2 specimens).
TYPE LOCALITY: "in Ecuador; ad nemores pagi S. Jose de Moti", Cantón de Quijos, Napo Province, Ecuador.
DISTRIBUTION: Amazonian slopes of the Andes of Ecuador and Colombia.
COMMENT: See comment under *Colostethus bocagei*.

Colostethus goianus Bokermann, 1975. Iheringia, Zool., 46:13.
TYPE(S): Holotype: WCAB 47779.
TYPE LOCALITY: "Chapada dos Veadeiros, 1700 m, cerca de 30 km de Alto Paraíso, Goiás, Brasil".
DISTRIBUTION: Known only from the type locality.

Colostethus haydeeae Rivero, 1976. Mem. Soc. Cienc. Nat. La Salle, 105:334.
TYPE(S): Holotype: UPRM 4706.
TYPE LOCALITY: "El Vivero, entre Páramo El Zumbador y Mesa del Aura, 2570 m, Edo. Táchira, Venezuela".
DISTRIBUTION: Páramo El Zumbador, Táchira, Venezuela.
COMMENT: Related to *Colostethus orostoma*, according to the original description.

Colostethus humilis Rivero, 1978. Mem. Soc. Cienc. Nat. La Salle, 109:105.
TYPE(S): Holotype: UPRM 3526.
TYPE LOCALITY: "Boconó (Laguneta artificial del Ministerio de Agricultura), Edo. Trujillo, Venezuela, 1470 m".
DISTRIBUTION: Known only from the type locality.
COMMENT: Related to *Colostethus brunneus* and *Colostethus marchesianus*, according to the original description.

Colostethus imbricolus Silverstone, 1975. Contrib. Sci. Nat. Hist. Mus. Los Angeles Co., 268:6.
TYPE(S): Holotype: LACM 71998.
TYPE LOCALITY: "upper Quebrada Mutata, Alto de Buey, Departamento del Chocó, Colombia, about 200 to 300 m elevation".
DISTRIBUTION: Known only from the type locality.

Colostethus inflexus Rivero, 1978. Mem. Soc. Cienc. Nat. La Salle, 109:97.
TYPE(S): Holotype: UPRM 4696.
TYPE LOCALITY: "El Almogral, entre Boca del Monte y el cruce La Grita–Bailadores, Carr. de Pregonero, Edo. Táchira, Venezuela, 3075 m".
DISTRIBUTION: Known only from the type locality.
COMMENT: A synonym of *Colostethus alboguttatus* (JAR), with which it was stated to be closely related in the original description.

Colostethus infraguttatus (Boulenger, 1898). Proc. Zool. Soc. London, 1898:118.
ORIGINAL NAME: *Phyllobates infraguttatus*.
TYPE(S): Syntypes: BM 1947.2.14.7-8.
TYPE LOCALITY: "Chimbo"; also noted in the original description as "Puente del Chimbo, the railway terminus about 70 miles from Guayaquil, at an elevation of about 1000 feet", Provincia Chimborazo, Ecuador.
DISTRIBUTION: Pacific slopes of Ecuador Andes, 500–1000 m.

Colostethus inguinalis (Cope, 1868). Proc. Acad. Nat. Sci. Philadelphia, 20:137.
ORIGINAL NAME: *Prostherapis inguinalis*.
TYPE(S): Holotype: USNM 4349.
TYPE LOCALITY: "From the river Truando, [Departamento Chocó,] New Grenada [=Colombia]".
DISTRIBUTION: Northern Departamento Chocó (Colombia) and eastern and west-central Panama.
COMMENT: Reviewed by Savage, 1968, Copeia, 1968:751–754.

Colostethus intermedius (Andersson, 1945). Ark. Zool., 37A:5.
ORIGINAL NAME: *Phyllobates intermedius*.
TYPE(S): Holotype: NHRM 1903.
TYPE LOCALITY: "Rio Pastaza", Provincia Pastaza, Ecuador.
DISTRIBUTION: Known only from the type locality.

COMMENT: Reviewed by Edwards, 1974, Occas. Pap. Mus. Nat. Hist. Univ. Kansas, 30:5–7. Considered a synonym of *Colostethus kingsburyi* by Edwards, 1974, Univ. Kansas Diss.:202.

Colostethus kingsburyi (Boulenger, 1918). Ann. Mag. Nat. Hist., (9)2:427.
ORIGINAL NAME: *Phyllobates kingsburyi.*
TYPE(S): Syntypes: BM 1947.2.14.3–6; BM 1947.2.14.5 designated lectotype by Silverstone, 1971, Contrib. Sci. Nat. Hist. Mus. Los Angeles Co., 215:7.
TYPE LOCALITY: "El Topo, Rio Pastaza, [Provincia Pastaza,] Eastern Ecuador, altitude 4200 feet".
DISTRIBUTION: Amazonian slopes of Ecuador Andes, 1000–2000 m.
COMMENT: See comment under *Colostethus intermedius.*

Colostethus latinasus (Cope, 1863). Proc. Acad. Nat. Sci. Philadelphia, 15:48.
ORIGINAL NAME: *Phyllobates latinasus.*
TYPE(S): ANSP; lost, according to Barbour and Noble, 1920, Bull. Mus. Comp. Zool., 63:399; USNM 50198 designated neotype by Savage, 1968, Copeia, 1968: 755.
TYPE LOCALITY: "Truando region, [Departamento Chocó,] New Granada [= Colombia]"; neotype from "Panamá: Provincia de Darién, Cana".
DISTRIBUTION: Darién (Panama) and Departamento Chocó (Colombia).
COMMENT: Peracca, 1904, Boll. Mus. Zool. Anat. Comp. Univ. Torino, 19:17, considered this a junior synonym of *Colostethus pulchellus.*

Colostethus lehmanni Silverstone, 1971. Contrib. Sci. Nat. Hist. Mus. Los Angeles Co., 215:3.
TYPE(S): Holotype: LACM 44156.
TYPE LOCALITY: "Colombia: Antioquia: Santa Rita (near Río Nare), 1890–1910 m".
DISTRIBUTION: Known only from the type locality.

Colostethus leopardalis Rivero, 1976. Mem. Soc. Cienc. Nat. La Salle, 105:327.
TYPE(S): Holotype: UPRM 5157.
TYPE LOCALITY: "Mucubají, 3300 m, Edo. Mérida, Venezuela".
DISTRIBUTION: Known only from the type locality.
COMMENT: Related to *Colostethus alboguttatus*, according to the original description.

Colostethus littoralis Péfaur, 1984. J. Herpetol., 18:492.
TYPE(S): Holotype: UAM IV-2505.
TYPE LOCALITY: "Chorillos, Lima, Perú, 5 m".
DISTRIBUTION: Known only from the type locality.

Colostethus mandelorum (Schmidt, 1932). Field Mus. Nat. Hist. Publ., Zool. Ser., 18: 160.
ORIGINAL NAME: *Phyllobates mandelorum.*
TYPE(S): Holotype: FMNH 17788.
TYPE LOCALITY: "camp at altitude of 8,000 feet [2630 m] on Mount Turumiquire, [Estados Sucre and Monagas,] Venezuela".
DISTRIBUTION: Known only from the type locality.
COMMENT: Considered by Rivero, 1961, Bull. Mus. Comp. Zool., 126:160, to be a subspecies of *Colostethus trinitatis.* Resurrected by Edwards, 1974, Occas. Pap. Mus. Nat. Hist. Univ. Kansas, 30:2.

Colostethus marchesianus (Melin, 1941). Göteborgs K. Vetensk. Vitterh. Samh. Handl., (B)1:64.
ORIGINAL NAME: *Phyllobates marchesianus.*
TYPE(S): Syntypes: NHMG 509.
TYPE LOCALITY: "Taracuá, Rio Uaupés, [Estado do Amazonas,] Brazil".
DISTRIBUTION: Upper Amazon Basin of Brazil and lower Amazonian slopes of the Andes in Colombia, Ecuador, and Peru.

COMMENT: Reviewed by Edwards, 1974, Occas. Pap. Mus. Nat. Hist. Univ. Kansas, 30:7–10. Without discussion, considered a synonym of *Colostethus brunneus* by Silverstone, 1976, Sci. Bull. Nat. Hist. Mus. Los Angeles Co., 27:6.

Colostethus mayorgai Rivero, 1978. Mem. Soc. Cienc. Nat. La Salle, 109:100.
TYPE(S): Holotype: UPRM 5160.
TYPE LOCALITY: "El Chorotal (El Sineral), Carr. Mérida a La Azulita, 1800 m, Edo. Mérida, Venezuela".
DISTRIBUTION: Known only from the type locality.

Colostethus meridensis Dole and Durant, 1972. Caribb. J. Sci. 12:191.
TYPE(S): Holotype: MBUCV 6168.
TYPE LOCALITY: "Chorotal", 15 km southeast of La Azulita, 1880 m, Estado Mérida, Venezuela.
DISTRIBUTION: Southwestern slopes of the Mérida Andes, in the vicinity of Mérida, Venezuela, 1600–1700 m.
COMMENT: The allocation of this species to the "black chest-bar" group by Edwards, 1974, Occas. Pap. Mus. Nat. Hist. Univ. Kansas, 30:2, is based on misidentified specimens of *Colostethus collaris* (JAR).

Colostethus mertensi (Cochran and Goin, 1964). Senckenb. Biol., 45:255.
ORIGINAL NAME: *Phyllobates mertensi*.
TYPE(S): Holotype: FMNH 54456.
TYPE LOCALITY: Quintana, near Popayán, Departamento Cauca, Colombia.
DISTRIBUTION: Cauca Valley in the vicinity of Popayán, Cauca, Colombia, 2100–2350 m.

Colostethus neblina (Test, 1956). Occas. Pap. Mus. Zool. Univ. Michigan, 577:2.
ORIGINAL NAME: *Prostherapis neblina*.
TYPE(S): Holotype: UMMZ 113001.
TYPE LOCALITY: "Portachuelo Pass [900–1100 m], Estado Aragua, Venezuela".
DISTRIBUTION: Known only from the type locality.
COMMENT: Reviewed by Rivero, 1961, Bull. Mus. Comp. Zool., 126:161–162. Considered a synonym of *Colostethus herminae* (=*Colostethus trinitatis* of this list) by Edwards, 1974, Univ. Kansas Diss.:182.

Colostethus nubicola (Dunn, 1924). Occas. Pap. Mus. Zool. Univ. Michigan, 151:7.
ORIGINAL NAME: *Phyllobates nubicola*.
TYPE(S): Holotype: UMMZ 58292.
TYPE LOCALITY: "rain forest above Boquete on the trail to Chiriquí Grande, 4500 feet [1372 m]", Provincia Chiriquí, Panama.
DISTRIBUTION: Costa Rica to Colombia (Chocó), 0–1800 m.
COMMENT: Reviewed by Savage, 1968, Copeia, 1968:755–759.

Colostethus olfersioides (Lutz, 1925). C. R. Séances Soc. Biol., Paris, 93:138.
ORIGINAL NAME: *Eupemphix olfersioides*.
TYPE(S): Holotype: MN 783.
TYPE LOCALITY: Littoral of the state of Rio de Janeiro, Brazil; restricted to "Angra dos Reis, Estado do Rio de Janeiro", Brazil, by Bokermann, 1966, Lista Anot. Local. Tipo Anf. Brasil.:40.
DISTRIBUTION: Minas Gerais and Rio de Janiero, Brazil.

Colostethus olmonae Hardy, 1983. Bull. Maryland Herpetol. Soc., 19:47.
TYPE(S): Holotype: USNM 198505.
TYPE LOCALITY: "Bloody Bay, St. John Parish, Tobago, West Indies".
DISTRIBUTION: Mountainous areas of Tobago I., West Indies.
COMMENT: Closely related to *Colostethus dunni*, according to the original description; but see comment under *Colostethus dunni*.

Colostethus orostoma Rivero, 1976. Mem. Soc. Cienc. Nat. La Salle, 105:337.
TYPE(S): Holotype: UPRM 4509.
TYPE LOCALITY: "Boca de Monte, Camino de Pregonero, 2615 m, Edo. Táchira, Venezuela".
DISTRIBUTION: Known only from the type locality.
COMMENT: Related to *Colostethus haydeeae* and *Colostethus alboguttatus*, according to the original description.

Colostethus palmatus (Werner, 1899). Verh. Zool. Bot. Ges. Wien, 49:479.
ORIGINAL NAME: *Phyllobates* (*Hypodictyon*) *palmatus*.
TYPE(S): Holotype: ZFMK 28134.
TYPE LOCALITY: Fusagasuga, 1700 m, near Bogotá, Departamento Cundinamarca, Colombia.
DISTRIBUTION: Cordillera Oriental and Serranía de La Macarena, Colombia.
COMMENT: Synonymy includes *Hylixalus granuliventris* Boulenger, 1919, according to Cochran and Goin, 1970, Bull. U.S. Natl. Mus., 288:52.

Colostethus peruvianus (Melin, 1941). Göteborgs K. Vetensk. Vitterh. Samh. Handl., (B)1:61.
ORIGINAL NAME: *Phyllobates peruvianus*.
TYPE(S): Holotype: NHMG 510.
TYPE LOCALITY: "Roque, [Provincia San Martín,] Perú".
DISTRIBUTION: Lower Amazonian slopes of the Andes in Peru, 400–1500 m.

Colostethus pratti (Boulenger, 1899). Ann. Mag. Nat. Hist., (7)3:274.
ORIGINAL NAME: *Phyllobates Pratti*.
TYPE(S): Syntypes: BM 1947.2.13.94–95; BM 1947.2.13.94 designated lectotype by Silverstone, 1971, Contrib. Sci. Nat. Hist. Mus. Los Angeles Co., 215:6.
TYPE LOCALITY: "Santa Ines, N. of Medellin, [Departamento Antioquia,] Republic of Colombia, altitude 3800 feet".
DISTRIBUTION: Western Panama to Chocó and Antioquia, Colombia.
COMMENT: Reviewed by Savage, 1968, Copeia, 1968:757–758.

Colostethus pulchellus (Jiménez de la Espada, 1871). Vert. Viaje Pacif., Batr.: Lam. 3.
ORIGINAL NAME: *Phyllodromus pulchellum*.
TYPE(S): Not designated.
TYPE LOCALITY: Not designated.
DISTRIBUTION: Unknown.
COMMENT: Probably an older name for *Colostethus taeniatus* (pers. comm., S. R. Edwards to DRF). See comment under *Colostethus latinasus*.

Colostethus ramosi Silverstone, 1971. Contrib. Sci. Nat. Hist. Mus. Los Angeles Co., 215:1.
TYPE(S): Holotype: LACM 44147.
TYPE LOCALITY: "Colombia: Antioquia: Alto de la Honda (hill near San Rafael), 1240 m".
DISTRIBUTION: Known only from the type locality.

Colostethus ranoides (Boulenger, 1918). Ann. Mag. Nat. Hist., (9)2:428.
ORIGINAL NAME: *Dendrobates ranoides*.
TYPE(S): Holotype: BM 1947.2.15.35.
TYPE LOCALITY: "Villavicencio, Quatiquía River, [Departamento Meta,] Colombia, altitude 400 feet".
DISTRIBUTION: Lower slopes of the Cordillera Oriental and the llanos of Colombia, 100–400 m.
COMMENT: Removed from the synonymy of *Colostethus brunneus* by Silverstone, 1971, Contrib. Sci. Nat. Hist. Mus. Los Angeles Co., 215:7.

Colostethus riveroi (Donoso-Barros, 1964). Caribb. J. Sci., 4:485.
ORIGINAL NAME: *Prostherapis riveroi.*
TYPE(S): Holotype: Donoso-Barros 307 (now IZUC?).
TYPE LOCALITY: "Cerro Azul, Macuro", Estado Sucre, Venezuela.
DISTRIBUTION: Cerro Azul on the Península de Paria, Sucre, Venezuela, above
    500 m.

Colostethus ruizi Lynch, 1982. Herpetologica, 38:371.
TYPE(S): Holotype: ICN 5419.
TYPE LOCALITY: "on the border of a stream, [along] the road to Fusagasuga,
    between [Alto de] San Miguel and La Aguadita", Departamento
    Cundinamarca, Colombia.
DISTRIBUTION: Vicinity of the Alto de San Miguel in cloud forests on the western
    slopes of the Cordillera Oriental, Departamento Cundinamarca, Colombia,
    2410–2469 m.

Colostethus saltuensis Rivero, 1978. Mem. Soc. Cienc. Nat. La Salle, 109:108.
TYPE(S): Holotype: UPRM 5147.
TYPE LOCALITY: "de La Fría a Michelena, Edo. Táchira, Venezuela, 830 m".
DISTRIBUTION: Known only from the type locality.

Colostethus sauli Edwards, 1974. Occas. Pap. Mus. Nat. Hist. Univ. Kansas, 30:10.
TYPE(S): Holotype: KU 122217.
TYPE LOCALITY: "Santa Cecilia, 340 m, Provincia Napo, Ecuador".
DISTRIBUTION: Amazonian lowlands of eastern Ecuador.

Colostethus shrevei (Rivero, 1961). Bull. Mus. Comp. Zool., 126:155.
ORIGINAL NAME: *Prostherapis shrevei.*
TYPE(S): Holotype: MCZ 28567.
TYPE LOCALITY: "Mt. Marahuaca, 5000–6000 ft. [1524–1829 m]", Territorio
    Amazonas, Venezuela.
DISTRIBUTION: Known only from the type locality.
COMMENT: Considered a synonym of *Colostethus fuliginosus* by Edwards, 1974, Univ.
    Kansas Diss.:171.

Colostethus subpunctatus (Cope, 1899). Philadelphia Mus. Sci. Bull., 1:5.
ORIGINAL NAME: *Prostherapis subpunctatus.*
TYPE(S): Syntypes: ANSP 77 (8 specimens).
TYPE LOCALITY: Near Bogota, [Departamento Cundinamarca,] Colombia.
DISTRIBUTION: Interandean slopes of the Eastern Andes in northern Colombia
    (Boyacá and Cundinamarca), 2100–3300 m.
COMMENT: See Cochran and Goin, 1970, Bull. U.S. Natl. Mus., 288:65, for
    subspecies (2). Synonymy includes *Prostherapis variabilis* Werner, 1899.

Colostethus sylvaticus (Barbour and Noble, 1920). Bull. Mus. Comp. Zool., 63:396.
ORIGINAL NAME: *Phyllobates sylvatica.*
TYPE(S): Holotype: MCZ 5344.
TYPE LOCALITY: "from stream-bed at Tabacónas (near Huancabamba) [Provincia
    Cajamarca,] northwestern Peru".
DISTRIBUTION: Amazonian slopes of the Eastern Andes and in the Huancabamba
    Depression in northern Peru, 2000–3250 m.

Colostethus taeniatus (Andersson, 1945). Ark. Zool., 37A:8.
ORIGINAL NAME: *Phyllobates taeniatus.*
TYPE(S): Holotype: NHRM 1904.
TYPE LOCALITY: "Rio Cosanga near Archidona, 800 m", Provincia Pastaza, Ecuador.
DISTRIBUTION: Amazonian slopes of the Andes in southern Colombia and northern
    Ecuador, 2000–3000 m.

COMMENT: Synonymy includes *Phyllobates riocosangae* Andersson, 1945, according to Edwards, 1974, Occas. Pap. Mus. Nat. Hist., 30:1–5. See comment under *Colostethus pulchellus*.

Colostethus talamancae (Cope, 1875). J. Acad. Nat. Sci. Philadelphia, (2)8:102.
ORIGINAL NAME: *Dendrobates talamancae*.
TYPE(S): ANSP; lost, according to Dunn, 1931, Occas. Pap. Boston Soc. Nat. Hist., 5: 390.
TYPE LOCALITY: near Old Harbour [=Puerto Viejo], on the East Coast, [Cantón de Limón, Provincia Limón,] Costa Rica.
DISTRIBUTION: Costa Rica to western Colombia, 0–750 m.
COMMENT: Reviewed by Savage, 1968, Copeia, 1968:758–759.

Colostethus thorntoni (Cochran and Goin, 1970). Bull. U.S. Natl. Mus., 288:67.
ORIGINAL NAME: *Phyllobates thorntoni*.
TYPE(S): Holotype: AMNH 1347.
TYPE LOCALITY: "Medellín, Antioquia, Colombia".
DISTRIBUTION: Known only from the region of the type locality.

Colostethus trilineatus (Boulenger, 1883). Proc. Zool. Soc. London, 1883:636.
ORIGINAL NAME: *Phyllobates trilineatus*.
TYPE(S): Holotype: BM.
TYPE LOCALITY: "Yurimaguas, Huallaga River, [Departamento Loreto,] Northern Peru".
DISTRIBUTION: Known only from the type locality.

Colostethus trinitatis (Garman, 1887). Bull. Essex Inst., 19:13.
ORIGINAL NAME: *Phyllobates trinitatis*.
TYPE(S): Syntypes: including BM 1947.2.14.23–24, UMMZ 47218 (formerly MCZ 2181), MCZ 2181 (9 specimens) + 8 others not traced.
TYPE LOCALITY: "Trinidad".
DISTRIBUTION: Trinidad; coastal range of Venezuela, 150–1300 m.
COMMENT: *Prostherapis herminae* Boettger, 1893, Ber. Senckenb. Naturforsch. Ges., 1893:37 (of Venezuela), was considered a species distinct from *Colostethus trinitatis* by Edwards, 1974, Occas. Pap. Mus. Nat. Hist. Univ. Kansas, 30:1–14, but he provided no evidence or discussion for this taxonomic change. See Edwards, 1974, Univ. Kansas Diss.:182–186. Discussed by Rivero, 1961, Bull. Mus. Comp. Zool., 126:159. Origin and relationships discussed by Rivero, 1979, *In* Salgado-Labouriau (ed.), El Medio Ambiente Páramo:169–174.

Colostethus vergeli (Hellmich, 1940). Zool. Anz., 131:122.
ORIGINAL NAME: *Hyloxalus vergeli*.
TYPE(S): Holotype: ZSM 110/1937.
TYPE LOCALITY: Finca El Vergel, 1800 m, near Fusagasuga, Departamento Cundinamarca, Colombia.
DISTRIBUTION: Known only from the type locality.
COMMENT: Reviewed by Cochran and Goin, 1970, Bull. U.S. Natl. Mus., 288:68. Considered a synonym of *Colostethus fuliginosus* by Edwards, 1974, Univ. Kansas Diss.:171.

Colostethus vertebralis (Boulenger, 1899). Ann. Mag. Nat. Hist., (7)4:456.
ORIGINAL NAME: *Phyllodromus vertebralis*.
TYPE(S): Syntypes: BM.
TYPE LOCALITY: "Cañar, 8400 feet altitude", Cañar, Ecuador.
DISTRIBUTION: High Amazonian and Pacific slopes of the Andes in Ecuador, 2500–3200 m.
COMMENT: Reviewed by Edwards, 1971, Proc. Biol. Soc. Washington, 84:158–162.

Colostethus whymperi (Boulenger, 1882). Ann. Mag. Nat. Hist., (5)9:462.
ORIGINAL NAME: *Prostherapis Whymperi*.
TYPE(S): Holotype: BM 1947.2.14.25.
TYPE LOCALITY: "Tanti, 2000 ft [607 m]", Provincia Pichincha, Ecuador.
DISTRIBUTION: Pacific slopes of the western Andes in northern Ecuador, 1400–2200 m.

Dendrobates Wagler, 1830. Nat. Syst. Amph.:202.
TYPE SPECIES: *Calamita tinctorius* Schneider, 1799, by subsequent designation of Duméril and Bibron, 1841, Erp. Gén., 8:651 (see comment).
DISTRIBUTION: Southern Nicaragua to Bolivia, Brazil, and the Guianas.
COMMENT: See Silverstone, 1975, Sci. Bull. Nat. Hist. Mus. Los Angeles Co., 21:1–55, for review and revision. Myers and Daly, 1976, Bull. Am. Mus. Nat. Hist., 157: 173–262, transferred all but the *Phyllobates bicolor* group of Silverstone's *Phyllobates* into *Dendrobates*, so the earlier revision of *Phyllobates* by Silverstone, 1976, Sci. Bull. Nat. Hist. Mus. Los Angeles Co., 27:1–53, is a prime source for synonymies and reviews of many of the species formerly in *Phyllobates*. While *Phyllobates* (in the strict sense) is a monophyletic group, *Dendrobates* as utilized here is probably composite and may represent as many as three genera (JMS). Species groups noted in the species accounts follow Silverstone's reviews (Silverstone, 1975, 1976); Myers and Daly, 1980, Am. Mus. Novit., 2692:20; Myers, 1982, Am. Mus. Novit., 2721:1; and Myers, Daly, and Martínez, 1984, Am. Mus. Novit., 2783:19. Savage, 1968, Copeia, 1968:747, and Silverstone (1975) followed earlier authors in regarding the type species of *Dendrobates* to be *Hyla nigerrima* Spix, 1824, Spec. Nov. Testud. Ran. Brasil.:36, by the subsequent designation of Fitzinger, 1843, Syst. Rept.:52. Lescure, 1982, Bull. Zool. Nomencl., 39:264–272, demonstrated the priority of Duméril and Bibron's 1841 designation of *Calamita tinctorius* as the logotype (JMS). See Dubois, 1981, Bull. Zool. Nomencl., 39:267–277, for nomenclatural discussion.

Dendrobates abditus Myers and Daly, 1976. Occas. Pap. Mus. Nat. Hist. Univ. Kansas, 59:1.
TYPE(S): Holotype: AMNH 89603.
TYPE LOCALITY: "lower montane rain forest at 1700 meters elevation, south-west of the Río Azuela bridge on the Quito–Lago Agrio road, eastern base of Volcán Reventador, Napo Province, Ecuador (latitude 0° 05′ S, longitude 77° 37′ W)".
DISTRIBUTION: Known only from the type locality.
COMMENT: In the *Dendrobates minutus* group.

Dendrobates altobueyensis Silverstone, 1975. Sci. Bull. Nat. Hist. Mus. Los Angeles Co., 21:27.
TYPE(S): Holotype: LACM 71972.
TYPE LOCALITY: "summit marker of Alto del Buey, Departamento del Chocó, Colombia, 1070 m."
DISTRIBUTION: 985–1070 m elev. on the Alto del Buey, a mountain in the Serranía de Baudó, Chocó, Colombia.
COMMENT: In the *Dendrobates minutus* group.

Dendrobates anthonyi (Noble, 1921). Am. Mus. Novit., 29:5.
ORIGINAL NAME: *Phyllobates anthonyi*.
TYPE(S): Holotype: AMNH 13739.
TYPE LOCALITY: "small stream at Salvias, Prov. del Oro, Ecuador".
DISTRIBUTION: Southwestern Ecuador and northwestern Peru, west of the Andes, 153–1387 m elev.
COMMENT: In the *Dendrobates femoralis* group.

Dendrobates arboreus Myers, Daly, and Martínez, 1984. Am. Mus. Novit., 2783:5.
TYPE(S): Holotype: AMNH 116724.
TYPE LOCALITY: "in cloud forest at 1120 m. elevation on the continental divide above the upper Quebrada de Arena, at longitude 82° 12′ 31″ W, on the border between the provinces of Chiriquí and Bocas del Toro, Panama".
DISTRIBUTION: Region of the type locality.
COMMENT: In the *Dendrobates histrionicus* group, according to the original description.

Dendrobates auratus (Girard, 1855). Proc. Acad. Nat. Sci. Philadelphia, 7:226.
ORIGINAL NAME: *Phyllobates auratus.*
TYPE(S): Holotype: USNM 10307.
TYPE LOCALITY: Taboga Island, Panama.
DISTRIBUTION: Southern Nicaragua to the Golfo de Urabá in Colombia on the Caribbean and from Costa Rica through Panama to the lower Atrato River drainage of Colombia, 0–800 m elev.; introduced in Oahu, Hawaii, USA.
COMMENT: In the *Dendrobates tinctorius* group. According to Silverstone, 1975, Sci. Bull. Nat. Hist. Mus. Los Angeles Co., 21:41, this species is possibly conspecific with *Dendrobates truncatus.* Reviewed by Savage, 1968, Copeia, 1968:759–760.

Dendrobates azureus Hoogmoed, 1969. Zool. Meded., Leiden, 44:134.
TYPE(S): Holotype: RMNH 13837A.
TYPE LOCALITY: "Sipaliwini, forest island on western slope Vier Gebroeders Mountain, 2° N 55° 58′ W, Surinam".
DISTRIBUTION: Known only from the vicinity of the type locality.
COMMENT: In the *Dendrobates tinctorius* group. Possibly derived from *Dendrobates tinctorius,* according to Silverstone, 1975, Sci. Bull. Nat. Hist. Mus. Los Angeles Co., 21:43.

Dendrobates bassleri Melin, 1941. Göteborgs K. Vetensk. Vitterh. Samh. Handl., (B)1:65.
TYPE(S): Holotype: NHMG 511.
TYPE LOCALITY: "Roque, [San Martín,] Peru [1097 m]".
DISTRIBUTION: Amazon drainage of Peru, from the eastern foothills of the Andes east to the Río Huallaga, 274–1097 m elev.
COMMENT: In the *Dendrobates trivittatus* group.

Dendrobates bolivianus (Boulenger, 1902). Ann. Mag. Nat. Hist., (7)10:397.
ORIGINAL NAME: *Prostherapis bolivianus.*
TYPE(S): Syntypes: BM 1947.2.13.89–90 (San Carlos), 1947.2.13.91 (San Ernesto); BM 1947.2.13.89 designated lectotype by Silverstone, 1976, Sci. Bull. Nat. Hist. Mus. Los Angeles Co., 27:35.
TYPE LOCALITY: "San Carlos, [La Paz,] Bolivia, 1200 m. and . . . S. Ernesto, [La Paz,] Bolivia, 800 m."; restricted to San Carlos, La Paz, Bolivia, by lectotype designation.
DISTRIBUTION: Amazon drainage of Bolivia, 800–1200 m elev.
COMMENT: In the *Dendrobates pictus* group.

Dendrobates bombetes Myers and Daly, 1980. Am. Mus. Novit., 2692:2.
TYPE(S): Holotype: AMNH 102601.
TYPE LOCALITY: "mountains above south side of Lago de Calima, 1580–1600 meters elevation, about 2 km airline southwest of Puente Tierra (village), Department of Valle del Cauca, Colombia. The locality is roughly 50 km north of Cali, on the mountain above kilometer post 23 on the present Loboguerrero–Buga road (about 3° 52′ N, 76° 25′ W)".
DISTRIBUTION: Known only from the region of the type locality.
COMMENT: In the *Dendrobates minutus* group.

Dendrobates boulengeri (Barbour, 1909). Proc. Biol. Soc. Washington, 22:89.
ORIGINAL NAME: *Prostherapis boulengeri.*
TYPE(S): Syntypes: MCZ 2422, USNM 52406, USNM 118232–33, BM 1947.2.13.92–
93, UMMZ 48070; BM 1947.2.13.93 designated lectotype by Silverstone, 1976,
Sci. Bull. Nat. Hist. Mus. Los Angeles Co., 27:29.
TYPE LOCALITY: "Gorgona Island", Departamento Nariño, Colombia.
DISTRIBUTION: Dense, wet forests of Gorgona I. and the wet southern Chocoan
region from the lower San Juan drainage of Colombia south to northwestern
Ecuador.
COMMENT: *Prostherapis boulengeri* is a replacement name for *Prostherapis femoralis*
Barbour, 1905, Bull. Mus. Comp. Zool., 46:101, which is preoccupied by
Prostherapis femoralis Boulenger, 1883. In the *Dendrobates femoralis* group.

Dendrobates captivus Myers, 1982. Am. Mus. Novit., 2721:14.
TYPE(S): Holotype: AMNH 42963.
TYPE LOCALITY: "mouth of the Río Santiago, 580 feet (177 m.) elevation,
Department of Amazonas, Peru. The Río Santiago flows into the Río Marañón
at about 4° 26′ S, 77° 38′ W".
DISTRIBUTION: Known only from the type locality.
COMMENT: Not assigned to species group. Myers, 1982, Am. Mus. Novit., 2721:22,
suggested that *Dendrobates mysteriosus* and *Dendrobates captivus* are sister-
species.

Dendrobates erythromos Vigle and Miyata, 1980. Breviora, 459:2.
TYPE(S): Holotype: MCZ 96384.
TYPE LOCALITY: "Centro Científico, Río Palenque, 47 km S of Santo Domingo de los
Colorados, Provincia Pichincha, Ecuador, 170 m".
DISTRIBUTION: Known only from the type locality.
COMMENT: In the *Dendrobates pictus* group.

Dendrobates espinosai (Funkhouser, 1956). Zoologica, New York, 41:76.
ORIGINAL NAME: *Phyllobates espinosai.*
TYPE(S): Holotype: CAS-SU 10577.
TYPE LOCALITY: "Hacienda Espinosa, elevation about 1,000 ft., 9 km. west of Santo
Domingo de los Colorados, Province of Pichincha, northwestern Ecuador".
DISTRIBUTION: Wet Chocoan region of the Andes in northwestern Ecuador.
COMMENT: In the *Dendrobates femoralis* group.

Dendrobates fantasticus Boulenger, 1884 "1883". Proc. Zool. Soc. London, 1883:636.
TYPE(S): Syntypes: BM 1947.2.15.1–4; BM 1947.2.15.4 designated lectotype by
Silverstone, 1975, Sci. Bull. Nat. Hist. Mus. Los Angeles Co., 21:35.
TYPE LOCALITY: "Yurimaguas, Huallaga River, [Loreto,] Northern Peru".
DISTRIBUTION: Known only from the type locality.
COMMENT: Forms a monophyletic group with *Dendrobates quinquevittatus,*
Dendrobates reticulatus, and *Dendrobates vanzolinii* according to Myers, 1982,
Am. Mus. Novit., 2721:17, who also removed *Dendrobates fantasticus* from the
synonymy of *Dendrobates quinquevittatus.* In the *Dendrobates minutus* group of
Silverstone. In the *Dendrobates quinquevittatus* group of Myers, 1982, Am. Mus.
Novit., 2721:2.

Dendrobates femoralis (Boulenger, 1884 "1883"). Proc. Zool. Soc. London, 1883:635.
ORIGINAL NAME: *Prostherapis femoralis.*
TYPE(S): Syntypes: BM 1947.2.14.21–22; BM 1947.2.14.21 designated lectotype by
Silverstone, 1976, Sci. Bull. Nat. Hist. Mus. Los Angeles Co., 27:31.
TYPE LOCALITY: "Yurimaguas, Huallaga River, [Loreto,] Northern Peru".
DISTRIBUTION: Lowland forests of Guyana, Surinam, and French Guiana, and of the
Amazon drainage of Colombia, Ecuador, Peru, and Brazil.
COMMENT: In the *Dendrobates femoralis* group.

Dendrobates fulguritus Silverstone, 1975. Sci. Bull. Nat. Hist. Mus. Los Angeles Co., 21:28.
TYPE(S): Holotype: LACM 42319.
TYPE LOCALITY: "Playa de Oro, Departamento del Chocó, Colombia, 160 m."
DISTRIBUTION: Lowland forests of the Chocoan region of Colombia, in the Atrato and San Juan drainages, west of the Andes, 160–800 m.
COMMENT: In the *Dendrobates minutus* group.

Dendrobates galactonotus Steindachner, 1864. Verh. Zool. Bot. Ges. Wien, 14:260.
TYPE(S): Holotype: NHMW 19189.
TYPE LOCALITY: "Rio do Muría bei Sitio do S'Pedro Gurção, nördlich von Virgia zur F. reguezia [=Frequenza]", Pará, Brazil.
DISTRIBUTION: Lowland forests of southern tributaries of the Amazon, from the Rio Tapajós east to the mouth of the Amazon, Brazil.
COMMENT: In the *Dendrobates tinctorius* group.

Dendrobates granuliferus Taylor, 1958. Univ. Kansas Sci. Bull., 39:10.
TYPE(S): Holotype: KU 43874.
TYPE LOCALITY: "on low mountains, north of the Río Diquis, about 3 miles north of Palmar, Puntarenas Province, Costa Rica".
DISTRIBUTION: Lowland forests of the Golfo Dulce region of the Pacific coast of Costa Rica.
COMMENT: In the *Dendrobates histrionicus* group of Myers, Daly, and Martínez, 1984, Am. Mus. Novit., 2783:19. Reviewed by Savage, 1968, Copeia, 1968:760.

Dendrobates histrionicus Berthold, 1846 "1845". Nachr. Ges. Wiss. Göttingen, 1845:43.
TYPE(S): Syntypes: ZFMK 28119–25.
TYPE LOCALITY: "Provinz Popayan", Colombia.
DISTRIBUTION: Chocoan region of western Colombia and northwestern Ecuador, 18–1070 m.
COMMENT: In the *Dendrobates histrionicus* group.

Dendrobates ingeri Cochran and Goin, 1970. Bull. U.S. Natl. Mus., 288:16.
TYPE(S): Holotype: USNM 146846.
TYPE LOCALITY: "Aserrío, near Río Pescado, Caquetá, Colombia".
DISTRIBUTION: Known only from the type locality.
COMMENT: In the *Dendrobates pictus* group.

Dendrobates labialis Cope, 1874. Proc. Acad. Nat. Sci. Philadelphia, 26:129.
TYPE(S): Not stated; not in ANSP or USNM.
TYPE LOCALITY: "Nauta", Loreto, Peru.
DISTRIBUTION: Known only from the type locality.
COMMENT: Status uncertain; Silverstone did not review this species in either of his revisions, listing it only as "*Phyllobates*?; status uncertain".

Dendrobates lehmanni Myers and Daly, 1976. Bull. Am. Mus. Nat. Hist., 157:240.
TYPE(S): Holotype: AMNH 88153.
TYPE LOCALITY: "in montane forest approximately 13 km west of Dagua (town), 850–1200 meters elevation on south-facing versant of upper Río Anchicayá drainage, Department of Valle, Colombia".
DISTRIBUTION: Known only from the type locality.
COMMENT: In the *Dendrobates histrionicus* group of Myers, Daly, and Martínez, 1984, Am. Mus. Novit., 2783:19.

Dendrobates leucomelas Steindachner, 1864. Verh. Zool. Bot. Ges. Wien, 14:260.
TYPE(S): Holotype: NHMW 19188.
TYPE LOCALITY: "Columbien" (=Colombia).
DISTRIBUTION: Guianan Orinoco drainage of Venezuela north to the Río Orinoco, east into Guyana to the Essequibo River, south into extreme northern Brazil, and west into Amazonian Colombia.

COMMENT: In the *Dendrobates histrionicus* group of Silverstone (1975); species not addressed or listed by Myers, Daly, and Martínez, 1984, Am. Mus. Novit., 2783:19, as part of their *Dendrobates histrionicus* group. Reviewed by Rivero, 1961, Bull. Mus. Comp. Zool., 126:168–169, and Hoogmoed and Gorzula, 1979, Zool. Meded., Leiden, 54:188–189.

Dendrobates maculatus Peters, 1873. Monatsber. Preuss. Akad. Wiss. Berlin, 1873:617.
ORIGINAL NAME: *Dendrobates trivittatus* var. *maculata*.
TYPE(S): Holotype: ZMB 7815.
TYPE LOCALITY: "Chiriqui", Panama; at the time of the description "Chiriqui" included both Atlantic and Pacific versants of extreme western Panama, according to Myers, 1982, Am. Mus. Novit., 2721:5.
DISTRIBUTION: Known only from the holotype.
COMMENT: Of uncertain relationship to other *Dendrobates*. See Myers, 1982, Am. Mus. Novit., 2721:5–9, for discussion.

Dendrobates minutus Shreve, 1935. Occas. Pap. Boston Soc. Nat. Hist., 8:212–213.
TYPE(S): Holotype: MCZ 15288.
TYPE LOCALITY: "Barro Colorado Island, Panama Canal Zone".
DISTRIBUTION: Central Panama to midway down the Pacific coast of Colombia.
COMMENT: In the *Dendrobates minutus* group. Reviewed by Savage, 1968, Copeia, 1968:760–761.

Dendrobates myersi Pyburn, 1981. Proc. Biol. Soc. Washington, 94:67.
TYPE(S): Holotype: UTA A-3989.
TYPE LOCALITY: "near Wacará (elev. 216 m, long. 69° 53' W, lat. 1° 08' N), Comisaria de Vaupés, Colombia".
DISTRIBUTION: Known only from the region of the type locality.
COMMENT: In the *Dendrobates femoralis* group.

Dendrobates mysteriosus Myers, 1982. Am. Mus. Novit., 2721:18.
TYPE(S): Holotype: AMNH 55349.
TYPE LOCALITY: "vicinity of Santa Rosa, 3000 feet (*ca.* 900 m.) elevation, upper Río Marañón drainage, Department of Cajamarca, Peru. The type locality lies in the hills northwest of the confluence of the Río Chinchipe with the Río Marañón, at about 5° 22' S, 78° 41' W".
DISTRIBUTION: Known only from the holotype.
COMMENT: Not assigned to species group. See comment under *Dendrobates captivus*.

Dendrobates occultator Myers and Daly, 1976. Bull. Am. Mus. Nat. Hist., 157:244.
TYPE(S): Holotype: AMNH 88143.
TYPE LOCALITY: "La Brea, 50 meters elevation, on the Río Patia (=upper tributary Río Saija), at an estimated 15 km by river below mouth of Quebrada Guanguí, Department of Cauca, Colombia".
DISTRIBUTION: Known only from the region of the type locality.
COMMENT: Considered to be a derivative of *Dendrobates histrionicus* in the original description; in the *Dendrobates histrionicus* group of Myers, Daly, and Martínez, 1984, Am. Mus. Novit., 2783:19.

Dendrobates opisthomelas Boulenger, 1899. Ann. Mag. Nat. Hist., (7)3:275.
TYPE(S): Syntypes: BM 1947.2.15.21–34; BM 1947.2.15.29 designated lectotype by Silverstone, 1975, Sci. Bull. Nat. Hist. Mus. Los Angeles Co., 21:32.
TYPE LOCALITY: "Santa Inés, N. of Medellin, [Departamento Antioquia,] Republic of Colombia; altitude 3800 feet [1160 m]".
DISTRIBUTION: Cordillera Occidental and Central of Colombia, 1160–3813 m.
COMMENT: In the *Dendrobates minutus* group.

Dendrobates parvulus Boulenger, 1882. Cat. Batr. Sal. Brit. Mus.:145.
TYPE(S): Syntypes: BM 1947.2.30.89–90; BM 1947.2.30.89 designated lectotype by Silverstone, 1976, Sci. Bull. Nat. Hist. Mus. Los Angeles Co., 27:36.
TYPE LOCALITY: "Sarayacu", Pastaza, Ecuador and "Canelos", Pastaza, Ecuador; restricted to Sarayacu, Pastaza, Ecuador, by lectotype designation.
DISTRIBUTION: Forests of the Amazon drainage of Colombia, Ecuador, and Peru, 300–1000 m.
COMMENT: In the *Dendrobates pictus* group.

Dendrobates petersi (Silverstone, 1976). Sci. Bull. Nat. Hist. Mus. Los Angeles Co., 27:37.
ORIGINAL NAME: *Phyllobates petersi.*
TYPE(S): Holotype: USNM 166763.
TYPE LOCALITY: "Santa Isabel (a village on the Río Nevati, a tributary of the Río Pichis, Pachitea drainage, 35 km SE Puerto Bermúdez, 80 km ENE Oxapampa . . . slightly upriver from the village . . .), Departamento de Pasco, Perú, 458 m".
DISTRIBUTION: Amazon drainage of Peru, west to the eastern foothills of the Andes, 274–800 m.
COMMENT: In the *Dendrobates pictus* group.

Dendrobates pictus (Tschudi, 1838). Classif. Batr.:28.
ORIGINAL NAME: *Hylaplesia picta.*
TYPE(S): Syntypes: MNHNP 4910 (2 specimens); male designated lectotype by Silverstone, 1976, Sci. Bull. Nat. Hist. Mus. Los Angeles Co., 27:42.
TYPE LOCALITY: "Santa Cruz", Santa Cruz, Bolivia.
DISTRIBUTION: South America, east of the Andes, north of 20° S latitude.
COMMENT: In the *Dendrobates pictus* group. Reviewed as *Phyllobates pictus* by Lescure, 1976, Bull. Mus. Natl. Hist. Nat., (3)377(Zool.)265:487–488.

Dendrobates pulchripectus (Silverstone, 1976). Sci. Bull. Nat. Hist. Mus. Los Angeles Co., 27:43.
ORIGINAL NAME: *Phyllobates pulchripectus.*
TYPE(S): Holotype: LACM 42297.
TYPE LOCALITY: "Serra do Navio, Territorio do Amapá, Brasil, about 120 m".
DISTRIBUTION: Known only from the type locality in the Guiana region of northern Brazil, near the Rio Amapari (tributary of the Rio Araguari), 100–310 m.
COMMENT: In the *Dendrobates pictus* group.

Dendrobates pumilio O. Schmidt, 1857. Sitzungsber. Akad. Wiss. Wien, Math. Naturwiss. Kl., 24:12.
TYPE(S): Holotype: KM 1018/1346; lost.
TYPE LOCALITY: "Neugranada"; restricted to "der Weg zwischen Bocca del toro und dem Vulcan Chiriqui [Panama] . . . zwischen 5000' und 7000' Höhe" by Schmidt, 1857, Denkschr. Akad. Wiss. Wien, Math. Naturwiss. Kl., 14:249.
DISTRIBUTION: Lowland forests of the Caribbean drainage of Central America, from northern Nicaragua to western Panama.
COMMENT: In the *Dendrobates pumilio* group of Silverstone (1975); in the *Dendrobates histrionicus* group by Myers, Daly, and Martínez, 1984, Am. Mus. Novit., 2783: 19. Reviewed by Savage, 1968, Copeia, 1968:761–762.

Dendrobates quinquevittatus Steindachner, 1864. Verh. Zool. Bot. Ges. Wien, 14:260.
TYPE(S): Holotype: NHMW 16517.
TYPE LOCALITY: "Salto do Girao", upper Rio Madeiro, Brazil.
DISTRIBUTION: Amazon drainage of Colombia, Ecuador, Peru, and Brazil, from the foothills of the Andes east to the mouth of the Amazon and north into French Guiana.
COMMENT: In the *Dendrobates minutus* group of Silverstone; in the less inclusive

Dendrobates quinquevittatus group of Myers, 1982, Am. Mus. Novit., 2721:2. Synonymy and review available in Lescure, 1976, Bull. Mus. Natl. Hist. Nat., Paris, (3)377(Zool.)265:483. See comment under *Dendrobates fantasticus*.

Dendrobates reticulatus Boulenger, 1884 "1883". Proc. Zool. Soc. London, 1883:635.
TYPE(S): Syntypes: BM; BM 1947.2.5.10 designated lectotype by Silverstone, 1975, Sci. Bull. Nat. Hist. Mus. Los Angeles Co., 21:35.
TYPE LOCALITY: "Yurimaguas, Huallaga River, [Loreto,] Northern Peru".
DISTRIBUTION: Type locality and possibly a locality in northwestern Loreto, Peru (see comment).
COMMENT: In the *Dendrobates minutus* group of Silverstone; in the less inclusive *Dendrobates quinquevittatus* group of Myers, 1982, Am. Mus. Novit., 2721:1–23, who removed this species from the synonymy of *Dendrobates quinquevittatus*. See comment under *Dendrobates fantasticus*. Zimmermann and Zimmermann, 1984, Aquar. Mag., 1984(1):41, mapped an unstated locality other than the type locality.

Dendrobates silverstonei Myers and Daly, 1979. Am. Mus. Novit., 2674:2.
TYPE(S): Holotype: AMNH 91844.
TYPE LOCALITY: "montane forest of Cordillera Azul, 1330 meters elevation, approximately 30 km airline northeast of Tingo María, Department of Huánuco, Peru. This locality lies alongside the gravel road from Tingo María to Pucallpa, about 5 km by road southwest of the road's crest at 1640 m elevation."
DISTRIBUTION: Cordillera Azul, Huánuco, Peru.
COMMENT: In the *Dendrobates trivittatus* group.

Dendrobates smaragdinus (Silverstone, 1976). Sci. Bull. Nat. Hist. Mus. Los Angeles Co., 27:44.
ORIGINAL NAME: *Phyllobates smaragdinus*.
TYPE(S): Holotype: LACM 64435.
TYPE LOCALITY: "Pan de Azúcar, 39 km NNE Oxapampa, 10° 15' S, 75° 14' W, in the Iscozazin Valley (the Río Iscozazin is a tributary of the Río Palcazú, in the Pachitea drainage), Departamento de Pasco, Perú, 380 m".
DISTRIBUTION: Region of the type locality.
COMMENT: In the *Dendrobates pictus* group.

Dendrobates speciosus O. Schmidt, 1857. Sitzungsber. Akad. Wiss. Wien, Math. Naturwiss. Kl., 24:12.
TYPE(S): Syntypes: KM 1017/1345 (now lost); Häupl and Tiedemann, 1978, Kat. Wiss. Samml. Naturhist. Mus. Wien, 2(Vert. 1):16, recorded NHMW 16518 and 16513 as syntypes.
TYPE LOCALITY: "Neugranada"; restricted to "der Weg zwischen Bocca del toro und dem Vulcan Chiriqui [Panama] . . . zwischen 5000' und 7000' Höhe" by Schmidt, 1857, Denkschr. Akad. Wiss. Wien, Math. Naturwiss. Kl., 14:249.
DISTRIBUTION: Lower montane forest of western Panama.
COMMENT: In the *Dendrobates pumilio* group of Silverstone (1975); in the *Dendrobates histrionicus* group of Myers, Daly, and Martínez, 1984, Am. Mus. Novit., 2783: 19. Reviewed by Savage, 1968, Copeia, 1968:763.

Dendrobates steyermarki Rivero, 1971. Kasmera, 3:390.
TYPE(S): Holotype: UPRM 3399.
TYPE LOCALITY: "Cerro Yapacana, 1200 m., Territorio Federal Amazonas, Venezuela".
DISTRIBUTION: Cerro Yapacana, Amazonas, Venezuela.
COMMENT: In the *Dendrobates minutus* group.

Dendrobates tinctorius (Schneider, 1799). Hist. Amph., 1:175.
ORIGINAL NAME: *Calamita tinctorius.*
TYPE(S): Not designated; LACM 43927 designated neotype by Silverstone, 1975, Sci. Bull. Nat. Hist. Mus. Los Angeles Co., 21:47.
TYPE LOCALITY: "Americae meridionalis"; neotype from "lower Rivière Matarony (Approuague drainage), Bruynzeel lumber camp, French Guiana, 35 m." (see comment).
DISTRIBUTION: Lowland forests of the Guianas and adjacent Brazil.
COMMENT: In the *Dendrobates tinctorius* group. The nomenclatural history of this species was reviewed by Lescure, 1976, Bull. Mus. Natl. Hist. Nat., Paris, (3)377(Zool.)265:484–486. Hoogmoed, 1971, Aquar. Terr. Z. 24:1–7, discussed distribution in Surinam. Problems associated with the neotype designation were discussed by Lescure, 1982, Bull. Zool. Nomencl., 39:267.

Dendrobates tricolor (Boulenger, 1899). Ann. Mag. Nat. Hist., (7)4:455.
ORIGINAL NAME: *Prostherapis tricolor.*
TYPE(S): Syntypes: BM 1947.2.14.16–19; BM 1947.2.14.18 designated lectotype by Silverstone, 1976, Sci. Bull. Nat. Hist. Mus. Los Angeles Co., 27:33.
TYPE LOCALITY: "Porvenir, Bolivar, western slope, about 5800 feet [1769 m]", Ecuador.
DISTRIBUTION: Pacific slope of the Andes in southwestern Ecuador, 1250–1769 m.
COMMENT: In the *Dendrobates femoralis* group.

Dendrobates trivittatus (Spix, 1824). Spec. Nov. Testud. Ran. Brasil :35.
ORIGINAL NAME: *Hyla trivittata.*
TYPE(S): Syntypes: ZSM 43/0 and RMNH 1836; RMNH 1836 designated lectotype by Hoogmoed and Gruber, 1983, Spixiana, Suppl., 9:367.
TYPE LOCALITY: "juxta flumen Teffé" (=Rio Tefé, Brazil).
DISTRIBUTION: Guianas and the Amazon drainage of Brazil, Peru, Ecuador, and Colombia.
COMMENT: In the *Dendrobates trivittatus* group. Synonymy includes *Dendrobates obscurus* Duméril and Bibron, 1841, and *Hyla nigerrima* Spix, 1824, according to Hoogmoed and Gruber, 1983, Spixiana, Suppl., 9:367.

Dendrobates truncatus (Cope, 1861 "1860"). Proc. Acad. Nat. Sci. Philadelphia, 12:372.
ORIGINAL NAME: *Phyllobates truncatus.*
TYPE(S): Syntypes: ANSP 2251–52.
TYPE LOCALITY: "New Grenada" (=Colombia).
DISTRIBUTION: Río Magdalena drainage from Chaparral north to the Caribbean coast, and in the lowlands around the northern ends of the central and western Andes, west to the Golfo de Urabá, Colombia.
COMMENT: In the *Dendrobates tinctorius* group. See comment under *Dendrobates auratus.*

Dendrobates vanzolinii Myers, 1982. Am. Mus. Novit., 2721:9.
TYPE(S): Holotype: MZUSP 51597.
TYPE LOCALITY: "at Pôrto Walter on the Rio Juruá, Territory [state] of Acre, Brazil (8° 16' S, 72° 46' W)".
DISTRIBUTION: East-central Peru and adjacent Brazil.
COMMENT: In the *Dendrobates minutus* group of Silverstone; in the less inclusive *Dendrobates quinquevittatus* group of Myers, 1982, Am. Mus. Novit., 2721:2. See comment under *Dendrobates fantasticus.*

Dendrobates viridis Myers and Daly, 1976. Bull. Am. Mus. Nat. Hist., 157:247.
TYPE(S): Holotype: AMNH 88133.
TYPE LOCALITY: "in montane forest approximately 13 km west of Dagua (town), 850–1200 meters elevation on south-facing versant of upper Río Anchicayá drainage, Department of Valle, Colombia".
DISTRIBUTION: Western slope of the Cordillera Occidental of Colombia, 100–1200 m elev.

COMMENT: In the *Dendrobates minutus* group. See Myers and Daly, 1976, Bull. Am. Mus. Nat. Hist., 157:249, for speculation on distribution.

Dendrobates zaparo Silverstone, 1976. Sci. Bull. Nat. Hist. Mus. Los Angeles Co., 27:33.
ORIGINAL NAME: *Phyllobates zaparo.*
TYPE(S): Holotype: KU 120669.
TYPE LOCALITY: "2 km west of Canelos, Provincia de Pastaza, Ecuador, 580 m."
DISTRIBUTION: Dense forests of the Napo and Pastaza drainages of Ecuador, east of the Andes.
COMMENT: In the *Dendrobates femoralis* group.

Phyllobates Bibron, 1841. *In* Sagra, Hist. Phys. Polit. Nat. Cuba, Rept.:pl. 29.
TYPE SPECIES: *Phyllobates bicolor* Bibron, 1841.
DISTRIBUTION: Costa Rica to Colombia.
COMMENT: Even though most of the species formerly included in this genus, except for the former *Phyllobates bicolor* group, have been transferred to *Dendrobates* by Myers, Daly, and Malkin, 1978, Bull. Am. Mus. Nat. Hist., 161:307–366, the most comprehensive review of this genus is that by Silverstone, 1976, Sci. Bull. Nat. Hist. Mus. Los Angeles Co., 27:1–53. See comment under *Dendrobates.*

Phyllobates aurotaenia (Boulenger, 1913). Proc. Zool. Soc. London, 1913:1029.
ORIGINAL NAME: *Dendrobates aurotaenia.*
TYPE(S): Holotype: BM 1947.2.15.13.
TYPE LOCALITY: "Peña Lisa, Condoto, 300 feet", Departamento Chocó, Colombia.
DISTRIBUTION: Wet forests of the Chocoan region of Colombia in the Atrato and San Juan drainages.

Phyllobates bicolor Bibron, 1841. *In* Sagra, Hist. Phys. Polit. Nat. Cuba, Rept.:pl. 29.
TYPE(S): Holotype: MNHNP 838.
TYPE LOCALITY: Cuba; corrected to Colombia by Silverstone, 1976, Sci. Bull. Nat. Hist. Mus. Los Angeles Co., 27:23.
DISTRIBUTION: Western foothills of the western Andes of Colombia.

Phyllobates lugubris (O. Schmidt, 1857). Sitzungsber. Akad. Wiss. Wien, Math. Naturwiss. Kl., 24:12.
ORIGINAL NAME: *Dendrobates lugubris.*
TYPE(S): Holotype: KM 1016/1347; lost.
TYPE LOCALITY: "Neugranada"; restricted to "der Weg zwischen Bocca del toro und dem Vulcan Chiriqui [Panama] . . . zwischen 5000' und 7000' Höhe" by Schmidt, 1857, Denkschr. Akad. Wiss. Wien, Math. Naturwiss. Kl., 14:249.
DISTRIBUTION: Atlantic lowlands of Costa Rica and northwestern Panama.
COMMENT: Reviewed by Savage, 1968, Copeia, 1968:763–766; Pacific versant populations reviewed now regarded as a distinct species, *Phyllobates vittatus.*

Phyllobates terribilis Myers, Daly, and Malkin, 1978. Bull. Am. Mus. Nat. Hist., 161: 313.
TYPE(S): Holotype: AMNH 88876.
TYPE LOCALITY: "lowland rain forest at Quebrada Guanguí, about 0.5 km above its junction with Río Patia, 100–200 m elevation, in upper Río Saija drainage, Department of Cauca, Colombia".
DISTRIBUTION: Region of the type locality.

Phyllobates vittatus (Cope, 1893). Proc. Am. Philos. Soc., 31:340.
ORIGINAL NAME: *Dendrobates tinctorius vittatus.*
TYPE(S): Not traced.
TYPE LOCALITY: "Buenos Ayres", (=Buenos Aires, Puntarenas Province,) Costa Rica.
DISTRIBUTION: Wet forests of the Golfo Dulce region of the Pacific coast of Costa Rica.

COMMENT: See comment under *Phyllobates lugubris*.

FAMILY: **Discoglossidae** Günther, 1859 "1858".

CITATION: Cat. Batr. Sal. Coll. Brit. Mus.:34.

DISTRIBUTION: Europe, North Africa, Israel, Syria (?), Turkey, western and eastern USSR (disjunct), China, Korea, Vietnam, Borneo (western Kalimantan, Indonesia), and the Philippines.

COMMENT: Alytidae Fitzinger, 1843, Syst. Rept.:32 (originally Alytae, an explicit family) is the name with priority for this group as noted by Dubois, 1983, Bull. Mens. Soc. Linn. Lyon, 52:271. Both of the names Discoglossidae and Alytidae were used by Günther, 1859 "1858", Cat. Batr. Sal. Coll. Brit. Mus.:37, and Lataste, 1878, Rev. Int. Sci., Paris, 2:448, as separate families. Cope, 1865, Nat. Hist. Rev., N.S., 5:104–107, combined the families, but failed to use the family-group name with priority, Alytidae. Subsequent authors who considered Alytidae and Discoglossidae synonymous have perpetuated Cope's error to the present (JDL). The use of Discoglossidae is continued here in order to not disturb nearly universal usage (DRF). The association of this family with the Leiopelmatidae is based on shared primitive features; most authors draw attention to the relatively few similarities rather than to the many differences (BTC); see Lynch, 1973, *In* Vial (ed.), Evol. Biol. Anurans:133–182. Comment on the distribution of the Discoglossidae was given in Savage, 1973, *In* Vial (ed.), Evol. Biol. Anurans:351–445. Lanza, Cei, and Crespo, 1975, Monit. Zool. Ital., N.S., Suppl., 9:153–162, and Lanza, Cei, and Crespo, 1976, Monit. Zool. Ital., N.S., Suppl., 10:311–314, considered, on the basis of immunological evidence, that *Discoglossus* should be maintained in the Discoglossidae while *Alytes* and *Bombina* should be placed in a distinct family, the Bombinidae; *Barbourula* was not assigned to family. Osteology of this family was discussed by Friant, 1960, Acta Zool., Stockholm, 41:113–139. Estes and Sanchíz, 1982, J. Vert. Paleontol., 2:18, discussed relationships within the family. Mertens and Wermuth, 1960, Amph. Rept. Europas:38–42, supplied synonymies for the European species, as did Liu and Hu, 1961, Tailless Amph. China:35–44, for the Chinese species.

CONTRIBUTOR: Barry T. Clarke (BTC).

REVIEWERS: Leo J. Borkin (LJB); William E. Duellman (WED); Marinus S. Hoogmoed (MSH).

Alytes Wagler, 1830. Nat. Syst. Amph.:206.

TYPE SPECIES: *Bufo obstetricans* Laurenti, 1768.

DISTRIBUTION: Europe, with the exception of the northern and eastern part; northwestern Africa.

COMMENT: See comment under *Baleaphryne*. Boulenger, 1897, Tailless Batr. Europe, vol. 1, provided what is still probably the best general account of the genus and species. See also Crespo, 1979, Tese (Thesis), Fac. Cienc. Univ. Lisboa, 399 pp.

Alytes cisternasii Boscá, 1870. An. Soc. Esp. Hist. Nat., 8:217.

TYPE(S): Not traced.

TYPE LOCALITY: Restricted to "Mérida, Prov. Badajoz, Spanien" by Mertens and Müller, 1928, Abh. Senckenb. Naturforsch. Ges., 41:17.

DISTRIBUTION: Portugal and western and central Spain.

Alytes obstetricans (Laurenti, 1768). Synops. Rept.:28.

ORIGINAL NAME: *Bufo obstetricans*.

TYPE(S): Not traced.

TYPE LOCALITY: Restricted to "Frankreich" (=France) by Mertens and Müller, 1928, Abh. Senckenb. Naturforsch. Ges., 41:17.

DISTRIBUTION: Western Europe: northern limit in southern Holland (Netherlands), eastern limit in Germany, Switzerland, and southeastern France; also Morocco.

Baleaphryne Sanchíz and Adrover, 1979 "1977". Doñana, Acta Vert., 4:6.

TYPE SPECIES: *Baleaphryne muletensis* Sanchíz and Adrover, 1977.

DISTRIBUTION: As for the single species.

Baleaphryne muletensis Sanchíz and Adrover, 1979 "1977". Doñana, Acta Vert., 4:6.
   TYPE(S): Holotype: "Museo Arqueologica de Deya (Mallorca) (MAD) . . . Ilion izquierdo". No registration number given.
   TYPE LOCALITY: Cueva Muleta, sector X, nivel 200–300 cm (Mallorca, España).
   DISTRIBUTION: Majorca, Balearic Is., Spain.
   COMMENT: Described as a fossil species from Middle and Upper Pleistocene. See Mayol and Alcovez, 1981, Amphibia-Reptilia, 1:343–345, for data on living population.

Barbourula Taylor and Noble, 1924. Am. Mus. Novit., 121:1.
   TYPE SPECIES: *Barbourula busangensis* Taylor and Noble, 1924.
   DISTRIBUTION: Philippines and Borneo (Kalimantan, Indonesia).
   COMMENT: Inger, 1954, Fieldiana: Zool., 33:209, considered *Barbourula* to be intermediate between *Bombina* and *Discoglossus*. Savage, 1973, *In* Vial (ed.), Evol. Biol. Anurans:351–445, commented on the distribution of *Barbourula*. Unique among the discoglossids in being associated with tropical conditions.
   REVIEWERS: Angel Alcala (AA); Walter C. Brown (WCB); Masafumi Matsui (MM).

Barbourula busangensis Taylor and Noble, 1924. Am. Mus. Novit., 121:1.
   TYPE(S): Holotype: MCZ 14004.
   TYPE LOCALITY: Busuanga I., Philippines.
   DISTRIBUTION: Busuanga and Palawan Is., Philippines.
   COMMENT: See Inger, 1954, Fieldiana: Zool., 33:209.

Barbourula kalimantanensis Iskandar, 1978. Copeia, 1978:565.
   TYPE(S): Holotype: MZB Amph. 2330.
   TYPE LOCALITY: Nanga Sayan (0° 44' S; 111° 40' E), 33 km south of Nanga Pinoh, West Kalimantan, Indonesia [Borneo].
   DISTRIBUTION: Known only from the type locality.
   COMMENT: The only discoglossid south of the equator (BTC).

Bombina Oken, 1816. Lehrb. Naturgesch., 3(Zool.):207.
   TYPE SPECIES: *Rana bombina* Linnaeus, 1761.
   DISTRIBUTION: Europe, Turkey, western USSR, eastern USSR (disjunct), China, Korea, and Vietnam.
   COMMENT: Maxson and Szymura, 1979, Comp. Biochem. Physiol., 63B:517–519, compared immunologically and discussed relationships of *Bombina bombina*, *Bombina orientalis*, and *Bombina variegata*.
   REVIEWERS: Steven C. Anderson (SCA) (Southwestern Asia); Shuqin Hu (SH) (China); Masafumi Matsui (MM) (East Asia); Ermi Zhao (EZ) (China).

Bombina bombina (Linnaeus, 1761). Fauna. Svec., Ed. 2:101.
   ORIGINAL NAME: *Rana bombina*.
   TYPE(S): Possibly syntypes: Holm, 1957, Acta Univ. Upsaliensis, 6:5–68, stated that there are two specimens in the Alströmer collection, which now belongs to the ZIUU. The status of these specimens is questionable; see comment below.
   TYPE LOCALITY: "Scaniae compestris fossis australibus".
   DISTRIBUTION: Central and eastern Europe from Denmark and western Germany east to the Ural Mountains and south to the Caucasus Mountains; in the north to the Gulf of Finland; Turkey; specimens from Sweden are probably introduced.
   COMMENT: Lönnberg, 1896, Bih. K. Svenska Vetensk. Akad. Handl., 22:3–45, divided Linnaean collections into two classes, the Alströmer collection belongs to the group that had been in Linnaeus' care, had been seen by him and therefore are considered to have "a certain value in dubious cases", and some of the specimens have been considered possible types. Holm, 1957, Acta Univ. Upsaliensis, 6:5–68, noted that the greater part of the Alströmer collection was deposited in the Linnaean Museum of the Swedish Linnaean

Society in 1939. This species maintains stable hybrid zones in Poland with *Bombina variegata* according to Szymura, 1976, Bull. Acad. Pol. Sci., Sér. Sci. Biol., 24:355–368, and Gollman, 1984, Z. Zool. Syst. Evolutionsforsch., 22: 51–64.

Bombina fortinuptialis Tian and Wu, 1981. Acta Herpetol. Sinica, 5(17):111.
  TYPE(S): Holotype: CIB 601750.
  TYPE LOCALITY: "Yangliuchong, Jinxiu, Yaoshan, Guangxi, altitude 1350 m", China.
  DISTRIBUTION: Yaoshan and Longsheng, Guangxi, China, 1200–1640 m.
  COMMENT: Related to *Bombina microdeladigitora*, according to the original description.

Bombina maxima (Boulenger, 1905). Ann. Mag. Nat. Hist., (7)15:188.
  ORIGINAL NAME: *Bombinator maximus.*
  TYPE(S): Syntypes: BM 1947.2.25.66–68 (formerly 1905.1.30.69–71).
  TYPE LOCALITY: near Ton Chuan Fu in Yunnan (altitude about 6000 feet) [China].
  DISTRIBUTION: Yunnan, ?Guizhou, and Sichuan (Yunkwei Plateau) China; northern Vietnam.
  COMMENT: Reviewed by Bourret, 1942, Batr. Indochine:154–155. See also Pope, 1931, Bull. Am. Mus. Nat. Hist., 61:435–436; Liu, 1950, Fieldiana: Zool. Mem., 2:110–117; and Liu and Hu, 1961, Tailless Amph. China:38–41.

Bombina microdeladigitora Liu, Hu, and Yang, 1960. Acta Zool. Sinica, 12(2):157.
  TYPE(S): Holotype: CIB 583158.
  TYPE LOCALITY: "Huang-tsiao-ling, Ching-tung, Yunnan, altitude 2240 m", China.
  DISTRIBUTION: Yunnan and Hubei, China.
  COMMENT: Related to *Bombina maxima*, according to the original description. See also Liu and Hu, 1961, Tailless Amph. China:42. Record for Guangxi, China, is incorrect (SH).

Bombina orientalis (Boulenger, 1890). Ann. Mag. Nat. Hist., (6)5:143.
  ORIGINAL NAME: *Bombinator orientalis.*
  TYPE(S): Syntypes: BM 1947.2.25.53–64, 1947.2.25.69, 1947.2.25.70–72, and 1947.2.25.73–76 (formerly 74.1.16.90, 83.3.26.11, 89.12.16.198–200, and 72.1.29.16–17).
  TYPE LOCALITY: Chefoo [=Yantai, Shandong] . . . N. China . . . S.E. coast of Corea . . . Chabarowka; restricted to "Chefoo" (=Yantai), Shandong, China, by Pope, 1931, Bull. Am. Mus. Nat. Hist., 61:435.
  DISTRIBUTION: Southern part of Soviet Far East (Primorsky Kraj [=Maritime Territory]); northeastern China (south to Jiangsu) and Korea.
  COMMENT: Reviewed by Liu and Hu, 1961, Chinese Tailless Amph.:36–38.

Bombina variegata (Linnaeus, 1758). Syst. Nat., Ed. 10, 1:211.
  ORIGINAL NAME: *Rana variegata.*
  TYPE(S): Not traced; probably lost.
  TYPE LOCALITY: Restricted to "Schweiz" (=Switzerland) by Mertens and Müller, 1928, Abh. Senckenb. Naturforsch. Ges., 41:16.
  DISTRIBUTION: Central and southern Europe (excluding the Iberian Peninsula, adjacent France, and Britain) southeast to the Carpathian Mountains in the USSR.
  COMMENT: See Arntzen, 1978, J. Biogeogr., 5:335–345, for detailed distribution.

Discoglossus Otth, 1837. Neue Denkschr. Allgem. Schweiz. Ges. Naturwiss., 1:6.
  TYPE SPECIES: *Discoglossus pictus* Otth, 1837.
  DISTRIBUTION: Southern Europe, northwestern Africa, Israel, and Syria (?).
  COMMENT: See Lanza, Cei, and Crespo, 1975, Monit. Zool. Ital., N.S., Suppl., 9:153–162, for history of taxonomy and relationships of species.
  REVIEWER: Steven C. Anderson (SCA).

Discoglossus nigriventer Mendelssohn and Steinitz, 1943. Copeia, 1943:231.
TYPE(S): Holotype: HUJ ("Amphib. Discogl., No. 1, Collection of the Dept. of Zool., Hebrew University, Jerusalem").
TYPE LOCALITY: "East shore of Lake Huleh (Northern District, Safed Subdistrict)", Palestine (now Israel).
DISTRIBUTION: Lake Huleh region, Israel; possibly adjacent parts of Syria.
COMMENT: Known only from five specimens, four mentioned in the original description (a female, a juvenile, and two tadpoles); an adult was collected in 1955 and reported by Steinitz, 1955, Bull. Res. Counc. Israel, Sect. B, 5:192–193. Possibly extinct due to swamp drainage and agricultural development; see Honegger, 1981, Biol. Conserv., 19:142 and 157.
PROTECTED STATUS: USA ESA—Endangered (2 Dec. 1970).

Discoglossus pictus Otth, 1837. Neue Denkschr. Allgem. Schweiz. Ges. Naturwiss., 1:6.
TYPE(S): MSNT.
TYPE LOCALITY: Restricted to "Sizilien" (=Sicily) by Mertens and Müller, 1928, Abh. Senckenb. Naturforsch. Ges., 41:15.
DISTRIBUTION: Iberian Peninsula (except the northeast) and eastern Pyrenees; north of the Sahara in Tunisia, Algeria, and Morocco; Sicily and Malta.

Discoglossus sardus Tschudi, 1837. *In* Otth, Neue Denkschr. Allgem. Schweiz. Ges. Naturwiss., 1:8.
TYPE(S): Not traced.
TYPE LOCALITY: Sardinien, wahrescheinlich auch die übrigen mediterranischen Länder.
DISTRIBUTION: Sardinia, Corsica, Giglio, and Monte Cristo (Italy); Iles d'Hyeres (France).

FAMILY: **Heleophrynidae** Noble, 1931.
CITATION: Biol. Amph.:498.
DISTRIBUTION: As for the single genus.
COMMENT: As originally formed the group name was Heleophryninae (a subfamily of the Leptodactylidae). The view that the Heleophrynidae is a distinct family was developed by Heyer and Liem, 1976, Smithson. Contrib. Zool., 233:1–29. Lynch, 1973, *In* Vial (ed.), Evol. Biol. Anurans:139, considered the Heleophrynidae to be a subfamily of the Myobatrachidae and the sister-taxon of the Limnodynastinae. Some workers still consider the Heleophrynidae, along with the Myobatrachidae, to be part of the Leptodactylidae. For synonymies see Gorham, 1966, Das Tierreich, 85:32–222, who considered this family to be part of the Leptodactylidae as did Lynch, 1971, Misc. Publ. Mus. Nat. Hist. Univ. Kansas, 53:1–238, who reviewed the taxonomy and evolutionary relationships of the group.
CONTRIBUTOR: David C. Cannatella (DCC).
REVIEWERS: Alan Channing (AC); William E. Duellman (WED); Marinus S. Hoogmoed (MSH); Raymond Laurent (RL); John C. Poynton (JCP).

Heleophryne Sclater, 1899. Ann. S. Afr. Mus., 1:110.
TYPE SPECIES: *Heleophryne purcelli* Sclater, 1899.
DISTRIBUTION: Mountainous areas of the Cape and Transvaal regions of Rep. South Africa.
COMMENT: Poynton, 1964, Ann. Natal Mus., 17:36–41, and Passmore and Carruthers, 1979, S. Afr. Frogs:50–57, summarized the biology of these frogs. The Cape species were reviewed by Boycott, 1982, Ann. Cape Prov. Mus. (Nat. Hist.), 14: 89–108.

Heleophryne natalensis Hewitt, 1913. Ann. Natal Mus., 2:477.
TYPE(S): Holotype: in the Marianhill Monastery Mus.
TYPE LOCALITY: "a tributary of the Krantz Kloof River"; probably in the Krantzkloof Nature Reserve, 12 miles north-west of Durban, Natal, Rep. South Africa, according to Poynton, 1964, Ann. Natal Mus., 17:40.
DISTRIBUTION: In the vicinity of fast-flowing streams in Natal and on the eastern Transvaal escarpment, Rep. South Africa.

Heleophryne purcelli Sclater, 1899. Ann. S. Afr. Mus., 1:95.
  TYPE(S): Holotype: SAM 1313.
  TYPE LOCALITY: Jonkershoek, Stellenbosch [Cape Province, Rep. South Africa].
  DISTRIBUTION: Western part of southern Cape fold mountains, Rep. South Africa.
  COMMENT: Three subspecies recognized; see Boycott, 1982, Ann. Cape Prov. Mus.
    (Nat. Hist.), 14:89–108.

Heleophryne regis Hewitt, 1909. Ann. Transvaal Mus., 2:45.
  TYPE(S): Holotype: TM 10093.
  TYPE LOCALITY: Knysna [Cape Province, Rep. South Africa].
  DISTRIBUTION: Eastern part of southern Cape fold mountains, Rep. South Africa.
  COMMENT: Elevated from subspecies status under *Heleophryne purcelli* by Boycott,
    1982, Ann. Cape Prov. Mus. (Nat. Hist.), 14:89–108.

Heleophryne rosei Hewitt, 1925. Rec. Albany Mus., 3:363.
  TYPE(S): Syntypes: AMG (2 adults and 10 tadpoles).
  TYPE LOCALITY: Skeleton Gorge, Table Mountain [Cape Province, Rep. South
    Africa].
  DISTRIBUTION: Eastern slopes of Table Mountain, Cape Province, Rep. South Africa.

FAMILY: **Hemisidae** Cope, 1867.
  CITATION: J. Acad. Nat. Sci. Philadelphia, (2)6:198.
  DISTRIBUTION: Africa south of the Sahara.
  COMMENT: Savage, 1973, *In* Vial (ed.), Evol. Biol. Anurans:355–356, posited an affinity of
    this group with the Sooglossidae, and by implication, with the Arthroleptinae, but
    presented no evidence to support this conjecture. Lynch, 1973, *In* Vial (ed.), Evol.
    Biol. Anurans:133–210, regarded the Hemisidae as forming an unresolved polytomy
    with the Hyperoliidae and Ranidae (including the Arthroleptidae of this list).
    Laurent, 1979, Bull. Soc. Zool. France, 104:417, raised this group from subfamily
    status within his Hyperoliidae (from within the Ranidae of other authors) to family
    status.
  CONTRIBUTOR: Raymond Laurent (RL).
  REVIEWERS: Alan Channing (AC); William E. Duellman (WED); Marinus S. Hoogmoed
    (MSH); Kim M. Howell (KMH) (East Africa); John C. Poynton (JCP).

Hemisus Günther, 1859 "1858". Cat. Batr. Sal. Coll. Brit. Mus.:47.
  TYPE SPECIES: *Engystoma guttatum* Rapp, 1842, by monotypy.
  DISTRIBUTION: Tropical and subtropical Africa south of the Sahara.
  COMMENT: See Laurent, 1972, Ann. Mus. R. Afr. Cent., Tervuren, Ser. Octavo, Sci.
    Zool., 194:1–67, for the most recent revision of this genus. Confusion about the
    gender (neuter) of this name has given rise to incorrect spellings of specific
    epithets; see Poynton, 1978, J. Herpetol. Assoc. Afr., 19:8.

Hemisus brachydactylum Laurent, 1963. Copeia, 1963:396.
  ORIGINAL NAME: *Hemisus brachydactylus.*
  TYPE(S): Holotype: MCZ 16469.
  TYPE LOCALITY: "Masiliwa, Tanganyika [=Tanzania]".
  DISTRIBUTION: Central Tanzania.

Hemisus guineense Cope, 1865. Nat. Hist. Rev., N.S., 5:100.
  ORIGINAL NAME: *Hemisus guineensis.*
  TYPE(S): Holotype: NHMW 1095.
  TYPE LOCALITY: Guinea [by inference].
  DISTRIBUTION: From Senegal to Angola and Mozambique, around the rainforest.
  COMMENT: Laurent, 1972, Ann. Mus. R. Afr. Cent., Tervuren, Ser. Octavo, Sci.
    Zool., 194:50–59, described five subspecies.

Hemisus guttatum (Rapp, 1842). Arch. Naturgesch., 8:290.
  ORIGINAL NAME: *Engystoma guttatum.*
  TYPE(S): Not traced.
  TYPE LOCALITY: Natal [Rep. South Africa].
  DISTRIBUTION: Natal, Rep. South Africa.

Hemisus marmoratum (Peters, 1854). Monatsber. Preuss. Akad. Wiss. Berlin, 1854:628.
ORIGINAL NAME: *Engystoma marmoratum.*
TYPE(S): ZMB.
TYPE LOCALITY: Cabaceira, Mozambique.
DISTRIBUTION: Subsaharan Africa, excluding rainforest, Somalia, and northern and
   northeastern part of Rep. South Africa.
COMMENT: Laurent, 1972, Ann. Mus. R. Afr. Cent., Tervuren, Ser. Octavo, Sci.
   Zool., 194:33–38, recognized three subspecies.

Hemisus microscaphus Laurent, 1972. Ann. Mus. R. Afr. Cent., Tervuren, Ser. Octavo,
   Sci. Zool., 194:38.
TYPE(S): Holotype: MCZ 19396.
TYPE LOCALITY: "lake Zwai, Ethiopia".
DISTRIBUTION: Known only from the type locality.

Hemisus olivaceum Laurent, 1963. Copeia, 1963:398.
ORIGINAL NAME: *Hemisus olivaceus.*
TYPE(S): Holotype: RGMC 40061.
TYPE LOCALITY: "Mongbwalu, Ituri, northeastern Congo [=Zaire]".
DISTRIBUTION: Northeastern Zaire.

Hemisus perreti Laurent, 1972. Ann. Mus. R. Afr. Cent., Tervuren, Ser. Octavo, Sci.
   Zool., 194:44.
TYPE(S): Holotype: RGMC 197a.
TYPE LOCALITY: "Lukula, Lower-Congo", Zaire.
DISTRIBUTION: Lower Zaire, north of the estuary.

Hemisus wittei Laurent, 1963. Copeia, 1963:397.
TYPE(S): Holotype: RGMC 100840.
TYPE LOCALITY: "Mabwe, Katanga [=Shaba], southeastern Congo [=Zaire]".
DISTRIBUTION: Lower Shaba Province, Zaire, and northwestern Zambia.

FAMILY: **Hylidae** Gray, 1825 (1815).
CITATION: Ann. Philos., (2)10:213.
DISTRIBUTION: North and South America, the West Indies, and the Australo-Papuan
   Region; one species group of *Hyla* in temperate Eurasia, including extreme northern
   Africa and the Japanese Archipelago.
COMMENT: As first formed, the group name was Hylina, by implication a subfamily.
   Hylidae is a conserved name in zoology (under provisions of Article 40 of the
   International Code of Zoological Nomenclature, 1985) and for purposes of priority
   derives its date from Hylarinia Rafinesque, 1815, Analyse Nat.:78. Duellman, 1970,
   Monogr. Mus. Nat. Hist. Univ. Kansas, 1:1–753, arranged the family into four
   subfamilies: Amphignathodontinae, Hemiphractinae, Hylinae, and
   Phyllomedusinae. Trueb, 1974, Occas. Pap. Mus. Nat. Hist. Univ. Kansas, 29:1–60,
   demonstrated the close relationship of the amphignathodontines and
   hemiphractines and suggested that the hemiphractines be included with the
   amphignathodontines, an arrangement followed here. On the basis of work done by
   Tyler, 1971, Univ. Kansas Publ. Mus. Nat. Hist., 19:319–360, and Savage, 1973, *In*
   Vial (ed.), Evol. Biol. Anurans:351–445, Dowling and Duellman, 1978, Syst.
   Herpetol., 37.1, placed the Australian hylids in the subfamily Pelodryadinae. Lynch,
   1971, Misc. Publ. Mus. Nat. Hist. Univ. Kansas, 53:1–238, suggested that the
   Australian hylids were independently derived from the Myobatrachidae, an
   hypothesis, if true, that would make the Hylidae polyphyletic. The taxonomy of this
   family was summarized by Duellman, 1977, Das Tierreich, 95:1–225. The Middle
   American taxa were treated in detail by Duellman, 1970, Monogr. Mus. Nat. Hist.
   Univ. Kansas, 1:1–752.
CONTRIBUTOR: William E. Duellman (WED).
REVIEWERS: Werner C. A. Bokermann (WCAB) (Brazil); Ulisses Caramaschi (UC) (Brazil);
   Ronald I. Crombie (RIC) (New World); Eduardo Gudynas (EG) (Uruguay and

adjacent Brazil and Argentina); Marinus S. Hoogmoed (MSH); Enrique La Marca (ELM) (Northern South America); William F. Pyburn (WFP) (New World); Jay M. Savage (JMS) (Central America); Norman J. Scott, Jr. (NJS) (Central and South America); Paulo E. Vanzolini (PEV) (Brazil).

SUBFAMILY: **Hemiphractinae** Peters, 1862.
CITATION: Monatsber. Preuss. Akad. Wiss. Berlin, 1862:146.
DISTRIBUTION: Tropical and Andean South America; Panama.
COMMENT: The original spelling of the group name was Hemiphractidae; first use as a subfamily was by Gadow, 1901, Amphibia and Reptiles:210. Duellman, 1970, Monogr. Mus. Nat. Hist. Univ. Kansas, 1:18, included eight genera. Subsequent workers, i.e., Duellman and Trueb, 1976, Occas. Pap. Mus. Nat. Hist. Univ. Kansas, 58:12, and Maxson, 1977, Syst. Zool., 26:72, placed two of these genera, *Anotheca* and *Nyctimantis*, in the Hylinae. Includes the Amphignathodontinae (of Boulenger, 1882, Cat. Batr. Sal. Brit. Mus.:449); see comment under Hylidae. Duellman and Gray, 1983, Herpetologica, 39:333–358, provided a cladogram of the genera, as did Duellman and Hoogmoed, 1984, Misc. Publ. Mus. Nat. Hist. Univ. Kansas, 75:33.

Amphignathodon Boulenger, 1882. Cat. Batr. Sal. Brit. Mus.:450.
TYPE SPECIES: *Amphignathodon guentheri* Boulenger, 1882, by monotypy.
DISTRIBUTION: As for the single species.

Amphignathodon guentheri Boulenger, 1882. Cat. Batr. Sal. Brit. Mus.:450.
TYPE(S): Holotype: BM 1946.9.7.28.
TYPE LOCALITY: "Intac", Imbabura Province, Ecuador.
DISTRIBUTION: Pacific slopes of Andes in Ecuador and southern Colombia.
COMMENT: This species resembles structurally *Gastrotheca angustifrons, Gastrotheca cornuta,* and *Gastrotheca dendronastes,* from which it differs in the usual 'specific level' characters, plus the unique (for anurans) feature of having true teeth on the dentary (WED). Probably a member of the *Gastrotheca cornuta* group (DCC).

Cryptobatrachus Ruthven, 1916. Occas. Pap. Mus. Zool. Univ. Michigan, 33:1.
TYPE SPECIES: *Cryptobatrachus boulengeri* Ruthven, 1916.
DISTRIBUTION: Northern Andes and Sierra Santa Marta, Colombia.
COMMENT: For an account see Cochran and Goin, 1970, Bull. U.S. Natl. Mus., 288: 155–162.

Cryptobatrachus boulengeri Ruthven, 1916. Occas. Pap. Mus. Zool. Univ. Michigan, 33:2.
TYPE(S): Holotype: UMMZ 48530.
TYPE LOCALITY: San Lorenzo, Departamento Magdalena, Colombia.
DISTRIBUTION: Sierra Santa Marta, northern Colombia.

Cryptobatrachus fuhrmanni (Peracca, 1914). Mém. Soc. Neuchâtel. Sci. Nat., 5:108.
ORIGINAL NAME: *Hyla fuhrmanni.*
TYPE(S): Unknown.
TYPE LOCALITY: Gauca (=Heliconia), Departamento Antioquia, Colombia.
DISTRIBUTION: Northern parts of the Cordillera Central and Cordillera Oriental of the Andes in Colombia.

Cryptobatrachus nicefori Cochran and Goin, 1970. Bull. U.S. Natl. Mus., 288:156.
TYPE(S): Holotype: MLS 138.
TYPE LOCALITY: La Salina, Departamento Boyacá, Colombia.
DISTRIBUTION: Type locality on eastern slopes of Andes in Colombia.

Flectonotus Miranda-Ribeiro, 1920. Rev. Mus. Paulista, São Paulo, 12:327.
TYPE SPECIES: *Nototrema pygmaeum* Boettger, 1893.
DISTRIBUTION: Andes and Cordillera de la Costa of northern Venezuela; Tobago and Trinidad.

COMMENT: Genus redefined and reviewed by Duellman and Gray, 1983, Herpetologica, 39:333–358. See comment under *Fritziana*.

Flectonotus fitzgeraldi (Parker, 1933). Trop. Agric., Trinidad, 11:123.
ORIGINAL NAME: *Gastrotheca fitzgeraldi*.
TYPE(S): Holotype: BM 1947.2.22.41.
TYPE LOCALITY: Mt. Tucutche, Trinidad.
DISTRIBUTION: Trinidad, Tobago, and Península de Paria, Venezuela.
COMMENT: The taxonomic status of mainland and insular populations needs to be verified (WED).

Flectonotus pygmaeus (Boettger, 1893). Ber. Senckenb. Naturforsch. Ges., 1893:40.
ORIGINAL NAME: *Nototrema pygmaeum*.
TYPE(S): SMF 2679 designated lectotype by Mertens, 1967, Senckenb. Biol., 48:43.
TYPE LOCALITY: Puerto Cabello, Estado Carabobo, Venezuela.
DISTRIBUTION: Northern Cordillera Oriental, Colombia; Mérida Andes, and Cordillera de la Costa, Venezuela.

Fritziana Mello-Leitão, 1920. Rev. Mus. Paulista, São Paulo, 12:321.
TYPE SPECIES: *Hyla goeldii* Boulenger, 1895.
DISTRIBUTION: Mountains of southeastern Brazil from Espírito Santo to São Paulo; adjacent coastal islands.
COMMENT: See Duellman and Gray, 1983, Herpetologica, 39:333–358, who redefined *Fritziana* as the stem-group of *Flectonotus*.

Fritziana fissilis (Miranda-Ribeiro, 1920). Rev. Mus. Paulista, São Paulo, 12:324.
ORIGINAL NAME: *Coelonotus fissilis*.
TYPE(S): MZUSP 30A designated lectotype by Bokermann, 1950, Pap. Avulsos Dep. Zool., São Paulo, 9:218.
TYPE LOCALITY: Serra de Macaé, Rio de Janeiro, Brazil.
DISTRIBUTION: Mountains of southeastern Brazil (Rio de Janeiro, São Paulo), 500–1800 m.
COMMENT: This species was transferred from *Flectonotus* to *Fritziana* by Duellman and Gray, 1983, Herpetologica, 39:348, on the basis of patristic similarity.

Fritziana goeldii (Boulenger, 1895). Proc. Zool. Soc. London, 1894:645.
ORIGINAL NAME: *Hyla goeldii*.
TYPE(S): Syntypes: BM 1947.2.12.69–70.
TYPE LOCALITY: Colônia Alpina, Teresópolis, Rio de Janeiro, Brazil.
DISTRIBUTION: Mountains of southeastern Brazil.

Fritziana ohausi (Wandolleck, 1907). Abh. Ber. K. Zool. Anthro. Ethno. Mus. Dresden, 11:14.
ORIGINAL NAME: *Hyla ohausi*.
TYPE(S): Holotype: MTKD D2033, destroyed.
TYPE LOCALITY: Petrópolis, Rio de Janeiro, Brazil.
DISTRIBUTION: Mountains of central Rio de Janeiro and São Paulo, Brazil.

Gastrotheca Fitzinger, 1843. Syst. Rept.:30.
TYPE SPECIES: *Hyla marsupiata* Duméril and Bibron, 1841, by monotypy.
DISTRIBUTION: Panama, northern and western South America southward to northern Argentina; eastern and southeastern Brazil.
COMMENT: Various taxa were named and species groups defined by Duellman and Fritts, 1972, Occas. Pap. Mus. Nat. Hist. Univ. Kansas, 9:1–37; Duellman, 1974, Occas. Pap. Mus. Nat. Hist. Univ. Kansas, 22:1–27; Duellman, 1974, Occas. Pap. Mus. Nat. Hist. Univ. Kansas, 27:1–27; and Duellman, 1983, Copeia, 1983:868–874. See Scanlon, Maxson, and Duellman, 1980, Evolution, 34:222–229, for discussion of albumin evolution in the genus.

Gastrotheca andaquiensis Ruíz and Hernández, 1976. Caldasia, 11:151.
TYPE(S): Holotype: ICN 401.
TYPE LOCALITY: Cueva de los Guachoros, Valle del Río Sauza, ca. 2000 m,
Departamento Huila, Colombia.
DISTRIBUTION: Cordillera Oriental of the Andes in Ecuador and southern Colombia.
COMMENT: In the *Gastrotheca longipes* group.

Gastrotheca angustifrons (Boulenger, 1898). Proc. Zool. Soc. London, 1898:124.
ORIGINAL NAME: *Nototrema angustifrons*.
TYPE(S): Syntypes: BM 1947.2.22.38–39.
TYPE LOCALITY: "Cachabé" (=Cachabí), Provincia Esmeraldas, Ecuador.
DISTRIBUTION: Pacific lowlands of northwestern Ecuador and southwestern
Colombia.
COMMENT: In the *Gastrotheca cornuta* group.

Gastrotheca argenteovirens (Boettger, 1892). Ber. Senckenb. Naturforsch. Ges., 1892:46.
ORIGINAL NAME: *Hyla argenteovirens*.
TYPE(S): SMF 2676 designated lectotype by Mertens, 1967, Senckenb. Biol., 48:41.
TYPE LOCALITY: Popayán, Departamento Cauca, Colombia.
DISTRIBUTION: Southern part of Cordillera Occidental and central and southern
part of Cordillera Central in Colombia.
COMMENT: In the *Gastrotheca plumbea* group; B. Lutz, 1977, Bol. Mus. Nac., Rio de
Janeiro, N.S., Zool., 190:6, recognized a subspecies, *Gastrotheca argenteovirens
dunni*, from the northern part of the Cordillera Central.

Gastrotheca aureomaculata Cochran and Goin, 1970. Bull. U.S. Natl. Mus., 288:177.
TYPE(S): Holotype: FMNH 69701.
TYPE LOCALITY: "in [Departamento] Huila, Colombia, at San Antonio, a small
village 25 kilometers west of San Agustín, at 2,300 meters".
DISTRIBUTION: Eastern slopes Cordillera Central in south-central Colombia.
COMMENT: In the *Gastrotheca plumbea* group. Includes *Gastrotheca mertensi* Cochran
and Goin, 1970, according to Duellman, 1983, Herpetologica, 39:105–110.

Gastrotheca bufona Cochran and Goin, 1970. Bull. U.S. Natl. Mus., 288:164.
TYPE(S): Holotype: MLS 344.
TYPE LOCALITY: "Ventanas (about 50 kilometers [by road] northwest of Yarumal),
[Departamento] Antioquia, Colombia".
DISTRIBUTION: Known only from the type locality.
COMMENT: In the *Gastrotheca cornuta* group. This species was incorrectly associated
with *Gastrotheca weinlandii* by Duellman, 1974, Occas. Pap. Mus. Nat. Hist.
Univ. Kansas, 27:5, according to Duellman, 1983, Copeia, 1983:872.

Gastrotheca cavia Duellman, 1974. Occas. Pap. Mus. Nat. Hist. Univ. Kansas, 22:5.
TYPE(S): Holotype: KU 148532.
TYPE LOCALITY: Isla Pequeña, Laguna Cuicocha, 2390 m, Provincia Imbabura,
Ecuador.
DISTRIBUTION: Cordillera Occidental in northern Ecuador.
COMMENT: In the *Gastrotheca plumbea* group.

Gastrotheca christiani Laurent, 1967. Acta Zool. Lilloana, 22:354.
TYPE(S): Holotype: FML 1369.
TYPE LOCALITY: Monumento Ruta Valle Grande, 50 km northwest of Calilegua,
Provincia Jujuy, Argentina.
DISTRIBUTION: Vicinity of type locality on mid-elevational slopes of Andes in
northern Argentina.
COMMENT: In the *Gastrotheca marsupiata* group. See Cei, 1980, Monit. Zool. Ital.,
N.S., Monogr., 2:439–442.

Gastrotheca chrysosticta Laurent, 1976. Acta Zool. Lilloana, 32:58.
TYPE(S): Holotype: FML 2098.
TYPE LOCALITY: Palca de San Martín, Serranía de Porongal, Departamento Santa Victoria, Provincia Salta, Argentina.
DISTRIBUTION: Vicinity of type locality on lower Andean slopes in northern Argentina.
COMMENT: In the *Gastrotheca marsupiata* group.

Gastrotheca cornuta (Boulenger, 1898). Proc. Zool. Soc. London, 1898:124.
ORIGINAL NAME: *Nototrema cornutum.*
TYPE(S): Holotype: BM 1947.2.22.49.
TYPE LOCALITY: "Cachabé" (=Cachabí), Provincia Esmeraldas, Ecuador.
DISTRIBUTION: Pacific lowlands of Ecuador amd Colombia; eastern Panama and the Caribbean slopes of western Panama.
COMMENT: In the *Gastrotheca cornuta* group. Includes *Gastrotheca ceratophrys* (Stejneger, 1911) according to Duellman, 1983, Copeia, 1983:872.

Gastrotheca dendronastes Duellman, 1983. Copeia, 1983:868.
TYPE(S): Holotype: KU 169381.
TYPE LOCALITY: Río Calima, 1.5 km (by road) west of Lago Calima, 1230 m, Departamento de Valle, Colombia.
DISTRIBUTION: Pacific slopes of Andes in southern Colombia and northern Ecuador.
COMMENT: In the *Gastrotheca cornuta* group.

Gastrotheca ernestoi Miranda-Ribeiro, 1920. Rev. Mus. Paulista, São Paulo, 12:323.
TYPE(S): Holotype: MZUSP 238.
TYPE LOCALITY: Macahí [=Macaé], Rio de Janeiro, Brazil.
DISTRIBUTION: Known only from the type locality.
COMMENT: Probably conspecific with *Gastrotheca microdiscus* (WED).

Gastrotheca excubitor Duellman and Fritts, 1972. Occas. Pap. Mus. Nat. Hist. Univ. Kansas, 9:23.
TYPE(S): Holotype: KU 139194.
TYPE LOCALITY: "northern slope of Abra Acanacu, 31 kilometers (by road) north-northeast of Paucartambo, Departamento Cuzco, Perú, 3370 m".
DISTRIBUTION: Amazonian slopes of Andes in central and southern Peru.
COMMENT: In the *Gastrotheca marsupiata* group.

Gastrotheca fissipes (Boulenger, 1888). Ann. Mag. Nat. Hist., (6)2:42.
ORIGINAL NAME: *Nototrema fissipes.*
TYPE(S): Holotype: BM 1947.2.22.40.
TYPE LOCALITY: "Iguarasse" (=Igaraçu), Pernambuco, Brazil.
DISTRIBUTION: Coastal lowlands from Pernambuco to Espírito Santo, Brazil.
COMMENT: In the *Gastrotheca ovifera* group.

Gastrotheca galeata Trueb and Duellman, 1978. Copeia, 1978:498.
TYPE(S): Holotype: LSUMZ 32058.
TYPE LOCALITY: "15 km (by road) east of Canchaque, Departamento Piura, Perú, 1740 m elevation (05° 22' S, 79° 33' W)".
DISTRIBUTION: Vicinity of type locality in northern Peru.
COMMENT: In the *Gastrotheca marsupiata* group.

Gastrotheca gracilis Laurent, 1969. Acta Zool. Lilloana, 25:146.
TYPE(S): Holotype: FML 1389.
TYPE LOCALITY: La Banderita, kilometer 51, Ruta Concepción–Andalgalá, Provincia de Catamarca, Argentina.
DISTRIBUTION: Eastern slopes of Sierra del Aconquija and Taficillo (near Tucumán), northwestern Argentina.

COMMENT: In the *Gastrotheca marsupiata* group. See Cei, 1980, Monit. Zool. Ital., N.S., Monogr., 2:443–444.

Gastrotheca griswoldi Shreve, 1941. Proc. New England Zool. Club, 18:83.
ORIGINAL NAME: *Gastrotheca boliviana griswoldi.*
TYPE(S): Holotype: MCZ 24102.
TYPE LOCALITY: Marainyoc, Departamento Junín, Peru.
DISTRIBUTION: Andes of central Peru.
COMMENT: In the *Gastrotheca marsupiata* group.

Gastrotheca helenae Dunn, 1944. Caldasia, 2:404.
TYPE(S): Holotype: MLS 268.
TYPE LOCALITY: Páramo de Tamá, Departamento Norte de Santander, Colombia.
DISTRIBUTION: Cerro Tamá, Colombia and Venezuela.
COMMENT: In the *Gastrotheca longipes* group.

Gastrotheca humbertoi Lutz, 1977. Bol. Mus. Nac., Rio de Janeiro, N.S., Zool., 290:1.
TYPE(S): Formerly in MLS; now lost.
TYPE LOCALITY: El Mirador, 57 km from Mocoa on road from that town to Sibundoy, Departamento Putumayo, Colombia.
DISTRIBUTION: Amazonian slopes of Andes in southern Colombia and Ecuador.
COMMENT: In the *Gastrotheca longipes* group.

Gastrotheca lojana Parker, 1932. Ann. Mag. Nat. Hist., (10)9.25.
ORIGINAL NAME: *Gastrotheca marsupiata lojana.*
TYPE(S): Holotype: BM 1947.2.31.13.
TYPE LOCALITY: Loja, Provincia Loja, Ecuador.
DISTRIBUTION: Inter-Andean valleys in southern Ecuador and northern Peru.
COMMENT: In the *Gastrotheca plumbea* group.

Gastrotheca longipes (Boulenger, 1882). Cat. Batr. Sal. Brit. Mus.:418.
ORIGINAL NAME: *Nototrema longipes.*
TYPE(S): Syntypes: BM 1947.2.31.4–5.
TYPE LOCALITY: "Canelos" and "Sarayacu", Provincia Pastaza, Ecuador.
DISTRIBUTION: Upper Amazon Basin in Ecuador and northern Peru.
COMMENT: In the *Gastrotheca longipes* group.

Gastrotheca marsupiata (Duméril and Bibron, 1841). Erp. Gén., 8:598.
ORIGINAL NAME: *Hyla marsupiata.*
TYPE(S): Holotype: MNHNP 4877.
TYPE LOCALITY: "Cuzco, [Departamento Cuzco,] au Pérou [=Peru]".
DISTRIBUTION: Amazonian drainage systems of Andes from central Peru to southern Bolivia.
COMMENT: In the *Gastrotheca marsupiata* group.

Gastrotheca medemi Cochran and Goin, 1970. Bull. U.S. Natl. Mus., 288:172.
TYPE(S): Holotype: UMMZ 123068.
TYPE LOCALITY: "Caño Guapáyita, 400 meters, Serranía de La Macarena, [Departamento] Meta, Colombia".
DISTRIBUTION: Serranía de la Macarena, Colombia.
COMMENT: In the *Gastrotheca ovifera* group. Probably conspecific with *Gastrotheca nicefori* (WED).

Gastrotheca microdiscus (Andersson, 1910). Ark. Zool., 6(9):9.
ORIGINAL NAME: *Nototrema microdiscus.*
TYPE(S): Syntypes: NHRM 1480 (2 specimens).
TYPE LOCALITY: Desvio Ribas, Paraná, Brazil.
DISTRIBUTION: Coastal regions and mountains of southeastern Brazil from Rio de Janeiro to Santa Catarina.

COMMENT: In the *Gastrotheca longipes* group. See comments under *Gastrotheca ernestoi* and *Gastrotheca viridis*.

Gastrotheca monticola Barbour and Noble, 1920. Bull. Mus. Comp. Zool., 63:426.
TYPE(S): Holotype: MCZ 5290.
TYPE LOCALITY: Huancabamba, Departamento Piura, Peru.
DISTRIBUTION: Andean slopes in Huancabamba Depression of southern Ecuador and northern Peru.
COMMENT: In the *Gastrotheca plumbea* group.

Gastrotheca nicefori Gaige, 1933. Occas. Pap. Mus. Zool. Univ. Michigan, 263:1.
TYPE(S): Holotype: UMMZ 73242.
TYPE LOCALITY: Pensilvania, Departamento Caldas, Colombia.
DISTRIBUTION: Andean slopes of northern Venezuela and northern and central Colombia; highlands of eastern and central Panama.
COMMENT: In the *Gastrotheca ovifera* group. B. Lutz and Ruíz-C., 1977, Bol. Mus. Nac., Rio de Janeiro, N.S., Zool., 289:12, recognized *Gastrotheca nicefori descampi* from the Amazonian slopes of the Cordillera Oriental of the Andes in southern Colombia. See comment under *Gastrotheca medemi* and *Gastrotheca yacambuensis*.

Gastrotheca ochoai Duellman and Fritts, 1972. Occas. Pap. Mus. Nat. Hist. Univ. Kansas, 9:27.
TYPE(S): Holotype: KU 139202.
TYPE LOCALITY: "southwest base of Cordillera de Vilcanota, west of Río Runtumayo, about 3 kilometers north of Chilca, 10 kilometers (by road) northwest of Ollantaytambo, Departamento Cuzco, Perú, 2760 m".
DISTRIBUTION: Amazonian slopes of Andes in southern Peru.
COMMENT: In the *Gastrotheca marsupiata* group.

Gastrotheca orophylax Duellman and Pyles, 1980. Occas. Pap. Mus. Nat. Hist. Univ. Kansas, 84:5.
TYPE(S): Holotype: KU 164243.
TYPE LOCALITY: "11 km (by road) east-south-east of Papallacta, 2660 m, Provincia Napo, Ecuador".
DISTRIBUTION: Upper Amazonian slopes of Andes in Ecuador.
COMMENT: In the *Gastrotheca plumbea* group.

Gastrotheca ovifera (Lichtenstein and Weinland, 1854). Monatsber. Preuss. Akad. Wiss. Berlin, 1854:373.
ORIGINAL NAME: *Notodelphys ovifera*.
TYPE(S): Holotype: ZMB 3073.
TYPE LOCALITY: Puerto Cabello, Carabobo, Venezuela.
DISTRIBUTION: Cordillera de la Costa, northern Venezuela.
COMMENT: In the *Gastrotheca ovifera* group.

Gastrotheca peruana (Boulenger, 1900). Ann. Mag. Nat. Hist., (7)6:181.
ORIGINAL NAME: *Nototrema peruanum*.
TYPE(S): Syntypes: BM 1947.2.22.42–46.
TYPE LOCALITY: Caraz, Departamento Ancash, Peru.
DISTRIBUTION: Andes and inter-Andean valleys of northern and central Peru.
COMMENT: In the *Gastrotheca marsupiata* group.

Gastrotheca plumbea (Boulenger, 1882). Cat. Sal. Batr. Brit. Mus.:417.
ORIGINAL NAME: *Nototrema plumbeum*.
TYPE(S): Holotype: BM 1947.2.31.19.
TYPE LOCALITY: "Intac", Provincia Imbabura, Ecuador.
DISTRIBUTION: Pacific slopes of Andes in northern and central Ecuador.

COMMENT: In the *Gastrotheca plumbea* group.

Gastrotheca psychrophila Duellman, 1974. Occas. Pap. Mus. Nat. Hist. Univ. Kansas, 22:15.
TYPE(S): Holotype: KU 120760.
TYPE LOCALITY: "ridge between Loja and Zamora, 2850 m, 13–14 km E (by road) of Loja, Provincia Zamora-Chinchipe, Ecuador".
DISTRIBUTION: Cordillera Oriental of Andes east of Loja, southern Ecuador.
COMMENT: In the *Gastrotheca plumbea* group.

Gastrotheca riobambae (Fowler, 1913). Proc. Acad. Nat. Sci. Philadelphia, 65:157.
ORIGINAL NAME: *Hyla riobambae*.
TYPE(S): Holotype: ANSP 16161.
TYPE LOCALITY: Riobamba, Provincia Chimborazo, Ecuador.
DISTRIBUTION: Andes and inter-Andean valleys in northern and central Ecuador and southern Colombia.
COMMENT: In the *Gastrotheca plumbea* group. Biochemical and karyological evidence shows that this taxon is a composite of two or more cryptic species (WED).

Gastrotheca splendens (Schmidt, 1857). Sitzungsber. Akad. Wiss. Wien, Math. Naturwiss. Kl., 34:11.
ORIGINAL NAME: *Hyla splendens*.
TYPE(S): Holotype: KM 1008/1340.
TYPE LOCALITY: "Chiriqui-flusse unweit Bocca del toro", Panama; in error according to Savage and Heyer, 1969, Rev. Biol. Tropical, 16:63, who suggested that the type may have come from Colombia, Peru, or Bolivia.
DISTRIBUTION: ?Bolivia, ?Peru, ?Colombia.
COMMENT: Name provisionally applied to *Gastrotheca*; known only from poorly preserved type specimen (Duellman, 1970, Monogr. Mus. Nat. Hist. Univ. Kansas, 1:651).

Gastrotheca testudinea (Jiménez de la Espada, 1871). J. Sci. Math. Phys. Nat., Lisboa, 3:62.
ORIGINAL NAME: *Nototrema testudineum*.
TYPE(S): Holotype: MNCN 155.
TYPE LOCALITY: San José de Moti, Provincia Napo, Ecuador.
DISTRIBUTION: Amazonian slopes of Andes in Colombia, Ecuador, and Peru.
COMMENT: In the *Gastrotheca ovifera* group.

Gastrotheca viridis A. Lutz and B. Lutz, 1939. An. Acad. Brasil. Cienc., 11(1):81.
TYPE(S): Holotype: AL-MN 969.
TYPE LOCALITY: Bonito, Serra da Bocaina, border of São Paulo and Rio de Janeiro, Brazil.
DISTRIBUTION: Serra do Mar, Rio de Janeiro and São Paulo, southeastern Brazil.
COMMENT: In the *Gastrotheca longipes* group. Probably conspecific with *Gastrotheca microdiscus* (WED).

Gastrotheca walkeri Duellman, 1980. Occas. Pap. Mus. Zool. Univ. Michigan, 690:1.
TYPE(S): Holotype: UMMZ 117177.
TYPE LOCALITY: "between Estación Biológica Rancho Grande and Paso Portachuelo, Estado Aragua, Venezuela, 1100 m".
DISTRIBUTION: Central part of Cordillera de la Costa, Venezuela.
COMMENT: In the *Gastrotheca longipes* group.

Gastrotheca weinlandii (Steindachner, 1892). Sitzungsber. Akad. Wiss. Wien, Math. Naturwiss. Kl., 101:837.
ORIGINAL NAME: *Nototrema weinlandii*.
TYPE(S): Holotype: NHMW 16481.
TYPE LOCALITY: "Ecuador".
DISTRIBUTION: Amazonian slopes of Andes in Colombia, Ecuador, and northern Peru.

COMMENT: In the *Gastrotheca ovifera* group.

Gastrotheca williamsoni Gaige, 1922. Occas. Pap. Mus. Zool. Univ. Michigan, 107:1.
TYPE(S): Holotype: UMMZ 55559.
TYPE LOCALITY: San Esteban, Carabobo, Venezuela.
DISTRIBUTION: Known only from the type locality on the north-central coastal lowlands of Venezuela.
COMMENT: In the *Gastrotheca longipes* group.

Gastrotheca yacambuensis Yuztis, 1976. Rev. Univ. Centroccid. Lisandro Alvarado, Tarea Común, 1978:87.
TYPE(S): Holotype: MBUCV 6015.
TYPE LOCALITY: Quebrada El Cedral, Parque Nacional Yacambu, south slope Sierra de Portuguesa, Estado Lara, Venezuela, 1700 m.
DISTRIBUTION: Known only from the vicinity of type locality.
COMMENT: In the *Gastrotheca ovifera* group. Probably conspecific with *Gastrotheca nicefori* (WED).

Hemiphractus Wagler, 1828. Isis von Oken, 21:743.
TYPE SPECIES: *Hemiphractus spixii* Wagler, 1828 (=*Rana scutata* Spix, 1824), by subsequent designation of Peters, 1862, Monatsber. Preuss. Akad. Wiss. Berlin, 1862:146.
DISTRIBUTION: Panama; Pacific slopes of Colombia and northwestern Ecuador; upper Amazon Basin and Amazonian slopes and Andes in Brazil, Ecuador, Peru, and Bolivia.
COMMENT: For review of the genus see Trueb, 1974, Occas. Pap. Mus. Nat. Hist. Univ. Kansas, 29:1–60.

Hemiphractus bubalus (Jiménez de la Espada, 1871). J. Sci. Math. Phys. Nat., Lisboa, 3:64.
ORIGINAL NAME: *Cerathyla bubalus.*
TYPE(S): Holotype: MNCN 176.
TYPE LOCALITY: Archidona, Provincia Pastaza, Ecuador.
DISTRIBUTION: Upper Amazon Basin and lower Amazonian slopes of Andes in Ecuador and Colombia.

Hemiphractus fasciatus Peters, 1862. Monatsber. Preuss. Akad. Wiss. Berlin, 1862:149.
TYPE(S): Holotype: ZSM 36/0.
TYPE LOCALITY: "Pastassa-Thal, an der Ostseite der Anden in Ecuador" (in error).
DISTRIBUTION: Panama, northern Colombia, and Pacific slopes of Colombia and northwestern Ecuador.

Hemiphractus johnsoni (Noble, 1917). Bull. Am. Mus. Nat. Hist., 37:798.
ORIGINAL NAME: *Cerathyla johnsoni.*
TYPE(S): Holotype: AMNH 1341.
TYPE LOCALITY: Santa Rita Creek, 14 mi. north of Mesopotamia, Departamento Antioquia, Colombia.
DISTRIBUTION: Northern Andean slopes of Colombia; upper Amazon Basin and lower Amazonian slopes of Andes from Ecuador to northern Bolivia.

Hemiphractus proboscideus (Jiménez de la Espada, 1871). J. Sci. Math. Phys. Nat., Lisboa, 3:64.
ORIGINAL NAME: *Cerathyla proboscidea.*
TYPE(S): Holotype: MNCN 173.
TYPE LOCALITY: Sumaco, Provincia Napo, Ecuador.
DISTRIBUTION: Upper Amazon Basin in Ecuador.
COMMENT: See Duellman, 1978, Misc. Publ. Mus. Nat. Hist. Univ. Kansas, 65:127, for comment on identification.

Hemiphractus scutatus (Spix, 1824). Spec. Nov. Testud. Ran. Brasil.:28.
ORIGINAL NAME: *Rana scutata.*
TYPE(S): Formerly ZSM 37/0, now lost; see Hoogmoed and Gruber, 1983, Spixiana, Suppl., 9:358–359, for discussion.
TYPE LOCALITY: Rio Solimões, Amazonas, Brazil.
DISTRIBUTION: Upper Amazon Basin in Ecuador, Peru, and western Brazil.

Stefania Rivero, 1968 "1966". Caribb. J. Sci., 6:142.
TYPE SPECIES: *Hyla evansi* Boulenger, 1904.
DISTRIBUTION: Highlands of the Guiana Shield in Venezuela and Guyana.
COMMENT: Duellman and Hoogmoed, 1984, Misc. Publ. Mus. Nat. Hist. Univ. Kansas, 75:1–39, revised the genus, provided a cladogram of the species, and defined two species groups on the basis of overall similarity.

Stefania evansi (Boulenger, 1904). Proc. Zool. Soc. London, 1904:106.
ORIGINAL NAME: *Hyla evansi.*
TYPE(S): Holotype: BM 1947.2.13.11.
TYPE LOCALITY: Groete Creek, Essequibo, Guyana.
DISTRIBUTION: Guyana and southeastern Venezuela.
COMMENT: In the *Stefania evansi* group. Synonymy includes *Stefania scalae* Rivero, according to Duellman and Hoogmoed, 1984, Misc. Publ. Mus. Nat. Hist. Univ. Kansas, 75:9.

Stefania ginesi Rivero, 1968 "1966". Caribb. J. Sci., 6:145.
TYPE(S): Holotype: FMNH 74041.
TYPE LOCALITY: "Chimanta-Tepui, Estado Bolívar, Venezuela, rock outcrops near E. branch of headwater Río Tirica, 7300 ft."
DISTRIBUTION: Tepuis (sandstone mountains) in southeastern Venezuela.
COMMENT: In the *Stefania ginesi* group.

Stefania goini Rivero, 1968 "1966". Caribb. J. Sci., 6:145.
TYPE(S): Holotype: AMNH 23193.
TYPE LOCALITY: Vegas Falls, Cerro Duida, Territorio Federal Amazonas, Venezuela, 4600 ft.
DISTRIBUTION: Known only from the type locality.
COMMENT: In the *Stefania ginesi* group.

Stefania marahuaquensis (Rivero, 1961). Bull. Mus. Comp. Zool., 126:118.
ORIGINAL NAME: *Hyla marahuaquensis.*
TYPE(S): Holotype: MCZ 28566.
TYPE LOCALITY: Caño Caju, Cerro Marahuaca, Territorio Federal Amazónas, Venezuela, about 1200 m.
DISTRIBUTION: Cerro Duida and Cerro Marahuaca, southern Venezuela.
COMMENT: In the *Stefania evansi* group.

Stefania riae Duellman and Hoogmoed, 1984. Misc. Publ. Mus. Nat. Hist. Univ. Kansas, 75:23.
TYPE(S): Holotype: KU 174688.
TYPE LOCALITY: "Cerro Sarisariñama, 1400 m, Estado Bolívar, Venezuela".
DISTRIBUTION: Known only from the type locality.
COMMENT: In the *Stefania evansi* group.

Stefania roraima Duellman and Hoogmoed, 1984. Misc. Publ. Mus. Nat. Hist. Univ. Kansas, 75:24.
TYPE(S): Holotype: Univ. Georgetown (Guyana) 10.
TYPE LOCALITY: "Roraima, Guyana, 1410 m".
DISTRIBUTION: Known only from the type locality.
COMMENT: In the *Stefania evansi* group.

Stefania woodleyi Rivero, 1968. Caribb. J. Sci., 6:147.
   TYPE(S): Holotype: BM 1967.654 (formerly OUM 3056).
   TYPE LOCALITY: Mt. Kanaima, near the Potaro River, Guyana.
   DISTRIBUTION: Known only from the type locality.
   COMMENT: In the *Stefania evansi* group.

SUBFAMILY: **Hylinae** Gray, 1825 (1815).
   CITATION: Ann. Philos., (2)10:213.
   DISTRIBUTION: North and South America; West Indies; temperate Eurasia, including
      extreme northern Africa and the Japanese Archipelago.
   COMMENT: This subfamily probably is an unnatural group containing all those genera
      that have not been split off into the other subfamilies, as noted by Duellman,
      1970, Monogr. Mus. Nat. Hist. Univ. Kansas, 1:18–20.

Acris Duméril and Bibron, 1841. Erp. Gén., 8:506.
   TYPE SPECIES: *Rana gryllus* LeConte, 1825, by fiat; see Duellman, 1970, Monogr. Mus.
      Nat. Hist. Univ. Kansas, 1:645–46, for discussion.
   DISTRIBUTION: USA east of the Rocky Mountains; southern Ontario (Pt. Pelee),
      Canada; northern Coahuila, Mexico.

Acris crepitans Baird, 1854. Proc. Acad. Nat. Sci. Philadelphia, 7:59.
   TYPE(S): Not designated.
   TYPE LOCALITY: "Northern states generally"; restricted to Albany, Albany County,
      New York, USA, by Smith and Taylor, 1950, Univ. Kansas Sci. Bull., 33:35 (in
      error—a locality outside of the known range, according to Duellman, 1970,
      Monogr. Mus. Nat. Hist. Univ. Kansas, 1:647); restricted to "Potomac River at
      Harper's Ferry, West Virginia", USA, by Schmidt, 1953, Check List N. Am.
      Amph. Rept., Ed. 6:68.
   DISTRIBUTION: USA east of Rocky Mountains, except extreme southeastern part;
      southern Ontario (Pt. Pelee), Canada; northern Coahuila, Mexico.

Acris gryllus (LeConte, 1825). Ann. Lyc. Nat. Hist. New York, 1:282.
   ORIGINAL NAME: *Rana gryllus.*
   TYPE(S): Syntypes: USNM 3564 (7 specimens), 5909 (7 specimens).
   TYPE LOCALITY: Riceboro, Liberty County, Georgia, USA, according to Schmidt,
      1953, Check List N. Am. Amph. Rept., Ed. 6:67.
   DISTRIBUTION: Southeastern USA.

Allophryne Gaige, 1926. Occas. Pap. Mus. Zool. Univ. Michigan, 176:1.
   TYPE SPECIES: *Allophryne ruthveni* Gaige, 1926, by original designation.
   DISTRIBUTION: Guyana, Surinam, and northeastern Brazil.
   COMMENT: Relationship to other frogs is problematical. Included tentatively in the
      Hylidae by Lynch and Freeman, 1966, Univ. Kansas Publ. Mus. Nat. Hist., 17:
      493–502, and Duellman, 1975, Occas. Pap. Mus. Nat. Hist. Univ. Kansas, 42:10.
      Dubois, 1983, Bull. Mens. Soc. Linn. Lyon, 52:272, considered *Allophryne* to be a
      member of the Bufonidae, following Laurent, 1979, Bull. Soc. Zool. France, 104:
      406, but neither presented any evidence to support this conjecture. Noble, 1931,
      Biol. Amph.:510, considered *Allophryne* to be a "toothless *Centrolenella*". Savage,
      1973, *In* Vial (ed.), Evol. Biol. Anurans:354, considered this species to form a
      monotypic family, the Allophrynidae. Unfortunately the name Allophrynidae
      does not meet the requirements of Article 13.a (statement of diagnosis or
      reference to a diagnosis for new names proposed after 1930) of the 1985
      International Code of Zoological Nomenclature, and as such is not a valid
      taxonomic name. Although *Allophryne* is here replaced in the Hylidae, this is
      not because we think it belongs there. See Lynch, 1984, Herpetol. Rev., 15:46–
      47, for a summary of the nomenclatural problem.
   DISTRIBUTION: As for the single species.

Allophryne ruthveni Gaige, 1926. Occas. Pap. Mus. Zool. Univ. Michigan, 176:2.
TYPE(S): Holotype: UMMZ 63419.
TYPE LOCALITY: "Tukeit Hill, below Kaiteur Falls, British Guiana [=Guyana]".
DISTRIBUTION: The Guianan region from Venezuela, through French Guiana, Guyana, and Surinam to northeastern Brazil.
COMMENT: For discussion see Hoogmoed, 1969, Zool. Meded., Leiden, 44:75–81.

Anotheca Smith, 1939. Proc. Biol. Soc. Washington, 52:190.
TYPE SPECIES: *Gastrotheca coronata* Stejneger, 1911 (=*Hyla spinosa* Steindachner, 1864), by original designation.
DISTRIBUTION: Central America and southern Mexico.
COMMENT: Erroneously placed in the Amphignathodontinae (included in the Hemiphractinae of this list) by Duellman, 1970, Monogr. Mus. Nat. Hist. Univ. Kansas, 1:18; see Duellman and Trueb, 1976, Occas. Pap. Mus. Nat. Hist. Univ. Kansas, 58:12, and Maxson, 1977, Syst. Zool., 26:72.

Anotheca spinosa (Steindachner, 1864). Verh. Zool. Bot. Ges. Wien, 14:239.
ORIGINAL NAME: *Hyla spinosa*.
TYPE(S): Holotype: NHMW 16101.
TYPE LOCALITY: "Brazil".
DISTRIBUTION: Southeastern Mexico (Atlantic slopes of Oaxaca and Veracruz), Costa Rica, and western Panama.
COMMENT: For discussion see Duellman, 1970, Monogr. Mus. Nat. Hist. Univ. Kansas, 1:145–150.

Aparasphenodon Miranda-Ribeiro, 1920. Rev. Mus. Paulista, São Paulo, 12:87.
TYPE SPECIES: *Aparasphenodon brunoi* Miranda-Ribeiro, 1920.
DISTRIBUTION: Coastal region of southeastern Brazil; upper Orinoco Basin, Venezuela.
COMMENT: For discussion see Carvalho, 1941, Pap. Avulsos Dep. Zool., São Paulo, 1: 101–110, and Trueb, 1970, Univ. Kansas Publ. Mus. Nat. Hist., 18:547–716.

Aparasphenodon brunoi Miranda-Ribeiro, 1920. Rev. Mus. Paulista, São Paulo, 12:87.
TYPE(S): Holotype: MN 2475.
TYPE LOCALITY: "S. E. brasileiro"; stated as Rio de Janeiro, Brazil, by Bokermann, 1966, Lista Anot. Local. Tipo Anf. Brasil.:13.
DISTRIBUTION: Coastal lowlands of southeastern Brazil from Espírito Santo to São Paulo.
COMMENT: See Sazima and Cardoso, 1980, Iheringia, Zool., 55:3–7.

Aparasphenodon venezolanus (Mertens, 1950). Senckenb. Biol., 31:1.
ORIGINAL NAME: *Corythomantis venezolana*.
TYPE(S): Holotype: SMF 22168.
TYPE LOCALITY: San Fernando de Atabapo, Territorio Federal Amazonas, Venezuela.
DISTRIBUTION: Southwestern Amazonian Venezuela.
COMMENT: For generic assignment see Trueb, 1970, Univ. Kansas Publ. Mus. Nat. Hist., 18:599. For recent discussion see Paolillo and Cerda, 1983 "1981", Mem. Soc. Cienc. Nat. La Salle, 41(115):77–95.

Aplastodiscus A. Lutz, 1950. *In* B. Lutz, Mem. Inst. Oswaldo Cruz, Rio de Janeiro, 46: 612.
TYPE SPECIES: *Aplastodiscus perviridis* A. Lutz, 1950.
DISTRIBUTION: As for the single species.
COMMENT: Discussed by Cei, 1980, Monit. Zool. Ital., N.S., Monogr., 2:450–452. Caramaschi, 1983, Resumos X Congreso Brasil. Zool.:306–307, presented summary information on *Aplastodiscus* as a synonym of *Hyla*. Resolution of this must await publication of the complete paper.

Aplastodiscus perviridis A. Lutz, 1950. *In* B. Lutz, Mem. Inst. Oswaldo Cruz, Rio de Janeiro, 46:612.
    TYPE(S): Holotype: AL-MN 2132.
    TYPE LOCALITY: Fazenda do Bonito, Serra de Bocaina, São José do Barreiro, São Paulo, Brazil.
    DISTRIBUTION: Central and southeastern Brazil from Brasília and Serra da Mantiqueira and coastal ranges south to Rio Grande do Sul and northeastern Argentina.

Argenteohyla Trueb, 1970. Herpetologica, 26:255.
    TYPE SPECIES: *Hyla siemersi* Mertens, 1937, by original designation.
    DISTRIBUTION: Drainages and mouth of the Río Paraná and the Delta La Plata in Argentina and southern coast of Uruguay; south-central Paraguay; questionably Amazon Basin in Peru.
    COMMENT: For discussion see Trueb, 1970, Herpetologica 26:254–267, and Cei, 1980, Monit. Zool. Ital., N.S., Monogr., 2:452–453. See comment under *Argenteohyla altamazonica*.

Argenteohyla altamazonica Henle, 1981. Amphibia-Reptilia, 2:134.
    TYPE(S): Holotype: ZFMK 29993.
    TYPE LOCALITY: "Peru; Pucallpa, ca. 200 m NN".
    DISTRIBUTION: Known only from the type locality.
    COMMENT: Probably a junior synonym of *Phrynohyas venulosa* (WED).

Argenteohyla siemersi (Mertens, 1937). Senckenb. Biol., 19:12.
    ORIGINAL NAME: *Hyla siemersi*.
    TYPE(S): Holotype: SMF 22249.
    TYPE LOCALITY: Río La Plata, Provincia Buenos Aires, Argentina.
    DISTRIBUTION: Drainages and mouth of the Río Paraná (Corrientes, Entre Ríos, and Buenos Aires provinces) in Argentina and southern coast of Uruguay; south-central Paraguay.

Calyptahyla Trueb and Tyler, 1974. Occas. Pap. Mus. Nat. Hist. Univ. Kansas, 24:41.
    TYPE SPECIES: *Trachycephalus lichenatus* Gosse, 1851 (=*Hyla crucialis* Harlan, 1826).
    DISTRIBUTION: Jamaica, West Indies.
    REVIEWERS: Albert Schwartz (AS); Richard Thomas (RT).

Calyptahyla crucialis (Harlan, 1826). Am. J. Sci. Arts, 10:64.
    ORIGINAL NAME: *Hyla crucialis*.
    TYPE(S): Holotype: ANSP 2180; see Crombie, 1973, Bull. Zool. Nomencl., 30:4–6.
    TYPE LOCALITY: "Jamaica".
    DISTRIBUTION: Jamaica, West Indies.

Corythomantis Boulenger, 1896. Ann. Mag. Nat. Hist., (5)10:405.
    TYPE SPECIES: *Corythomantis greeningi* Boulenger, 1896.
    DISTRIBUTION: Northeastern Brazil.

Corythomantis greeningi Boulenger, 1896. Ann. Mag. Nat. Hist., (5)10:405.
    TYPE(S): Holotype: BM 1947.2.25.97.
    TYPE LOCALITY: "Brazil (exact locality unknown)"; catalogue in BM has locality recorded as "Espirito Santo, Brazil" (WED).
    DISTRIBUTION: Xeric and subhumid regions of northeastern Brazil.
    COMMENT: For discussion see Carvalho, 1941, Pap. Avulsos Dep. Zool., São Paulo, 1:101–110, and Trueb, 1970, Univ. Kansas Publ. Mus. Nat. Hist., 18:546–716. See Sazima and Cardoso, 1980, Iheringia, Zool., 55:3–7.

Hyla Laurenti, 1768. Synops. Rept.:32.
    TYPE SPECIES: *Hyla viridis* Laurenti, 1768 (=*Rana arborea* Linnaeus, 1758), by subsequent designation of Stejneger, 1907, Bull. U.S. Natl. Mus., 58:75.
    DISTRIBUTION: Central and southern Europe; eastern Asia; northwestern Africa; North, Central, and South America; Greater Antilles in West Indies.

COMMENT: Duellman, 1970, Monogr. Mus. Nat. Hist. Univ. Kansas, 1:173–518, reviewed the Mexican and Central American species and discussed species groups. B. Lutz, 1973, Brazil. Spec. *Hyla*, discussed the Brazilian species. Duellman, 1972, Occas. Pap. Mus. Nat. Hist. Univ. Kansas, 11:1–31, reviewed the *Hyla bogotensis* group. Duellman, 1973, Copeia, 1973:515–533, reviewed the *Hyla geographica* group. Duellman, 1974, Occas. Pap. Mus. Nat. Hist., 23:1–40, reviewed the *Hyla parviceps* group. Duellman and Trueb, 1983, *In* Rhodin and Miyata (eds.), Adv. Herpetol. Evol. Biol.:33–51, reviewed the *Hyla columbiana* group, and discussed the phylogenetic relationships of groups of *Hyla* characterized by 30 chromosomes and reduced larval mouthparts (*Hyla labialis*, *Hyla columbiana*, *Hyla minuta*, *Hyla marmorata*, *Hyla parviceps*, *Hyla leucophyllata*, and *Hyla microcephala* groups). Pyburn and Hall, 1984, Herpetologica, 40:366–372, supplied a key to the species of the *Hyla geographica* group.

REVIEWERS: Jonathan A. Campbell (JAC) (Mexico and Central America); Gustavo Casas-Andreu (GCA) (Mexico); Oscar Flores-Villela (OFV) (Mexico).

Hyla acreana Bokermann, 1964. Senckenb. Biol., 45:244.
TYPE(S): Holotype: WCAB 1363.
TYPE LOCALITY: "Tarauacá, Acre, Brazil".
DISTRIBUTION: Western Brazil (Acre and Amazonas), northeastern Bolivia, and southeastern Peru.
COMMENT: In the *Hyla marmorata* group; see Heyer, 1977, Pap. Avulsos Zool., São Paulo, 31:142. See comment under *Hyla senicula*.

Hyla albicans Bokermann, 1967. Neotropica, 13:64.
TYPE(S): Holotype: WCAB 19519.
TYPE LOCALITY: Teresópolis, Rio de Janeiro, Brazil.
DISTRIBUTION: Known only from the type locality.

Hyla albofrenata A. Lutz, 1924. C. R. Séances Soc. Biol. Paris, 90:241.
TYPE(S): Syntypes: AL-MN 577 (2 specimens, Tijuca), USNM 96478 (Angra dos Reis), 96319 (Sumare), 96339–45 (Paineiras).
TYPE LOCALITY: "Environs of Rio de Janeiro", Brazil.
DISTRIBUTION: Mountain slopes of southeastern Brazil (Minas Gerais, Espírito Santo, Rio de Janeiro, São Paulo).
COMMENT: In the *Hyla albomarginata* group, according to Duellman, 1970, Monogr. Mus. Nat. Hist. Univ. Kansas, 1:240.

Hyla alboguttata Boulenger, 1882. Cat. Batr. Sal. Brit. Mus.:356.
TYPE(S): Syntypes: BM 1947.2.13.47–48 (Sarayacu), 1947.2.3.49 (Canelos).
TYPE LOCALITY: "Sarayacu" and "Canelos", Provincia Pastaza, Ecuador.
DISTRIBUTION: Amazonian Ecuador.

Hyla albolineata A. Lutz and B. Lutz, 1939. An. Acad. Brasil. Cienc., 11:69.
TYPE(S): Holotype: AL-MN 1778.
TYPE LOCALITY: Teresópolis, Rio de Janeiro, Brazil.
DISTRIBUTION: Known only from the type locality.
COMMENT: In the *Hyla albomarginata* group, according to Duellman, 1970, Monogr. Mus. Nat. Hist. Univ. Kansas, 1:240.

Hyla albomarginata Spix, 1824. Spec. Nov. Testud. Ran. Brasil.:33.
TYPE(S): Holotype: formerly ZSM 2370/0; destroyed.
TYPE LOCALITY: Bahia, Brazil.
DISTRIBUTION: Caribbean lowlands of Colombia to Guianas, lower Amazon Basin, and Atlantic forests of eastern Brazil from Pernambuco to Santa Catarina.
COMMENT: In the *Hyla albomarginata* group. It is highly likely that the populations along the Caribbean lowlands are specifically distinct (WED).

Hyla albonigra Nieden, 1923. Das Tierreich, 46:278.
  TYPE(S): Syntypes: MNHNP 4817 (2 specimens).
  TYPE LOCALITY: "Buenos-Ayrés", Argentina.
  DISTRIBUTION: ? Bolivia (according to Nieden, 1923, Das Tierreich, 46:278).
  COMMENT: *Hyla albonigra* is a replacement name for *Hyla zebra* Duméril and Bibron,
    1841, Erp. Gén., 8:575.

Hyla albopunctata Spix, 1824. Spec. Nov. Testud. Ran. Brasil.:33.
  TYPE(S): Formerly in ZSM, now lost; KU 100000 designated neotype by Duellman,
    1971, Herpetologica, 27:402.
  TYPE LOCALITY: Unknown; neotype from Belo Horizonte, Minas Gerais, Brazil.
  DISTRIBUTION: Central and southeastern Brazil; northeastern Argentina (Provincia
    Corrientes); eastern Paraguay.
  COMMENT: In the *Hyla albopunctata* group. See Cei, 1980, Monit. Zool. Ital., N.S.,
    Monogr., 2:462–463.

Hyla albopunctulata Boulenger, 1882. Cat. Batr. Sal. Brit. Mus.:385.
  TYPE(S): Syntypes: including BM 80.12.5.159–162.
  TYPE LOCALITY: "Sarayacu", Provincia Pastaza, Ecuador (in error ?) and "Ecuador".
  DISTRIBUTION: Known only from the type locality.
  COMMENT: Questionably in the *Hyla bogotensis* group.

Hyla albosignata A. Lutz and B. Lutz, 1938. An. Acad. Brasil. Cienc., 10:185.
  TYPE(S): Holotype: AL-MN 722.
  TYPE LOCALITY: Alto da Serra, Paranapiacaba, São Paulo, Brazil.
  DISTRIBUTION: Serra do Mar and Serra da Mantiqueira in southeastern Brazil.
  COMMENT: In the *Hyla albomarginata* group, according to Duellman, 1970, Monogr.
    Mus. Nat. Hist. Univ. Kansas, 1:240.

Hyla albovittata Lichtenstein and Martens, 1856. Nomencl. Rept. Amph. Mus. Zool.
    Berolin.:37.
  TYPE(S): Not traced (in ZMB if still extant).
  TYPE LOCALITY: Brazil.
  DISTRIBUTION: Unknown.

Hyla alemani Rivero, 1964. Caribb. J. Sci., 4:302.
  TYPE(S): Holotype: SCN 238.
  TYPE LOCALITY: Cagua, Estado Aragua, Venezuela.
  DISTRIBUTION: Known only from the type locality.
  COMMENT: Closely allied to *Hyla granosa*, according to the original description, or a
    possible synonym, according to Rivero, 1967, Mem. Soc. Cienc. Nat. La Salle,
    27:7–8.

Hyla altipotens Duellman, 1968. Univ. Kansas Publ. Mus. Nat. Hist., 17:572.
  TYPE(S): Holotype: KU 101001.
  TYPE LOCALITY: "37 kilometers (by road) north of San Gabriel Mixtepec (kilometer
    post 183 on road from Oaxaca to Puerto Escondido), Oaxaca, Mexico,
    elevation 1860 meters".
  DISTRIBUTION: Pacific slopes of Sierra Madre del Sur in Oaxaca, Mexico.
  COMMENT: In the *Hyla taeniopus* group. See Duellman, 1970, Monogr. Mus. Nat.
    Hist. Univ. Kansas, 1:450–453.

Hyla alvarengai Bokermann, 1956. Pap. Avulsos Dep. Zool., São Paulo, 12:357.
  TYPE(S): Holotype: MZUSP 1680.
  TYPE LOCALITY: "Santa Barbara, próximo a Belo Horizonte, Estado de Minas Gerais,
    Brasil".
  DISTRIBUTION: Serra do Espinhaço in Bahia and Minas Gerais, Brazil.

Hyla alytolylax Duellman, 1972. Occas. Pap. Mus. Nat. Hist. Univ. Kansas, 11:15.
TYPE(S): Holotype: KU 111903.
TYPE LOCALITY: "Tandapi, Provincia Pichincha, Ecuador, 1460 m".
DISTRIBUTION: Pacific slopes of Andes in southern Colombia and Ecuador.
COMMENT: In the *Hyla bogotensis* group.

Hyla americana (Duméril and Bibron, 1841). Erp. Gén., 8:506.
ORIGINAL NAME: *Litoria americana.*
TYPE(S): Holotype: MNHNP 756.
TYPE LOCALITY: "Nouvelle-Orléans" (=New Orleans), Orleans Parish, Louisiana,
    USA.
DISTRIBUTION: Unknown.
COMMENT: This name has never been associated with a population of anurans
    (WED).

Hyla anataliasiasi Bokermann, 1973. Rev. Brasil. Biol., 34:593.
TYPE(S): Holotype: WCAB 45272.
TYPE LOCALITY: 80 km north of Paraíso do Norte, Município de Brejinho do
    Nazaré, Goiás, Brazil.
DISTRIBUTION: Central Brazil (upper Rios Araguaia, Tocantins, and Xingu).

Hyla anceps A. Lutz, 1929. C. R. Séances Soc. Biol. Paris, 101:943.
TYPE(S): Syntypes: AL-MN 1776–77, USNM 96441–42.
TYPE LOCALITY: Estrela, Magé, Rio de Janeiro, Brazil.
DISTRIBUTION: Lowlands of Rio de Janeiro in southeastern Brazil.
COMMENT: For discussion see Cochran, 1955, Bull. U.S. Natl. Mus., 206:188.

Hyla andersonii Baird, 1854. Proc. Acad. Nat. Sci. Philadelphia, 7:60.
TYPE(S): Holotype: USNM 3600.
TYPE LOCALITY: "Anderson, S[outh]. C[arolina].", USA, in error; designated as
    "Aiken County, South Carolina", USA, by Schmidt, 1953, Check List N. Am.
    Amph. Rept., Ed. 6:69; see Gosner and Black, 1967, Cat. Am. Amph. Rept.,
    54.1, who regarded the type locality as unknown.
DISTRIBUTION: Atlantic Coastal Plain from central New Jersey to northern Florida,
    USA, in scattered populations.
COMMENT: Reviewed by Gosner and Black, 1967, Cat. Am. Amph. Rept., 54.1–2.
PROTECTED STATUS: USA ESA—Endangered (11 Nov. 1977); Florida population only.

Hyla angustilineata Taylor, 1952. Univ. Kansas Sci. Bull., 35:850.
TYPE(S): Holotype: USNM 75060.
TYPE LOCALITY: "La Palma, [Provincia San José,] Costa Rica".
DISTRIBUTION: Cordillera of Costa Rica.
COMMENT: In the *Hyla pseudopuma* group; see Duellman, 1970, Monogr. Mus. Nat.
    Hist. Univ. Kansas, 1:273.

Hyla anisitzi (Méhelÿ, 1904). Ann. Hist. Nat. Mus. Natl. Hungarici, 2:229.
ORIGINAL NAME: *Hylella anisitzi.*
TYPE(S): MNH.
TYPE LOCALITY: ? Asuncion or Villa Sana, Paraguay.
DISTRIBUTION: Known only from the type locality.

Hyla annectans (Jerdon, 1870). Proc. Asiat. Soc. Bengal, 1870:84.
ORIGINAL NAME: *Polypedates annectans.*
TYPE(S): Holotype: ZMB 3500.
TYPE LOCALITY: Khasi Hills, Assam, India.
DISTRIBUTION: Southern Asia (south of Himalayas) from Assam (India) through
    northern Burma, Thailand, and Vietnam to western China.
COMMENT: In the *Hyla arborea* group; reviewed by Bourret, 1942, Batr. Indochine:

222–223; Pope, 1931, Bull. Am. Mus. Nat. Hist., 61:474–477; Liu, 1950, Fieldiana: Zool. Mem., 2:224–231; and Liu and Hu, 1961, Tailless Amph. China:130–1323.
REVIEWERS: Leo J. Borkin (LJB); J. C. Daniel (JCD); Sushil Dutta (SD); Shuqin Hu (SH); Masafumi Matsui (MM); Ermi Zhao (EZ).

Hyla aperomea Duellman, 1982. Amphibia-Reptilia, 3:153.
TYPE(S): Holotype: KU 181812.
TYPE LOCALITY: 8 km NNE of Balzapata, 1850 m, Departamento Amazonas, Peru.
DISTRIBUTION: Amazonian slopes of Andes in northern and central Peru.
COMMENT: In the *Hyla minima* group.

Hyla arborea (Linnaeus, 1758). Syst. Nat., Ed. 10, 1:213.
ORIGINAL NAME: *Rana arborea*.
TYPE(S): Unknown (see comment).
TYPE LOCALITY: "Sub foliis arborum Europae, Americae".
DISTRIBUTION: Central and southern Europe east to Caucasus, northwestern coast of Africa, and Turkey.
COMMENT: Two of Linnaeus' type specimens (NHRM 155) are syntypes of *Hyla punctata* (Schneider). Andersson, 1900, Bih. K. Svenska Vetensk. Akad. Handl., 26:17, noted a third specimen in the same jar which "seems to me to be *Hyla inframaculata*". He noted further "All three specimens thus are from America, and Linnaeus says also that his type come from this part of the world". The third specimen was not found by Duellman when he was in the NHRM in 1969. Thus, it seems no European specimen is now listed as a type specimen (Duellman, 1977, Das Tierreich, 95:31). In the *Hyla arborea* group. Four subspecies (*arborea, kretensis, molleri,* and *schelkownikowi*) presently recognized; other subspecies listed by Duellman, 1977, Das Tierreich, 95:31–33, have been elevated to specific status.
REVIEWERS: Steven C. Anderson (SCA); Leo J. Borkin (LJB); Kim M. Howell (KMH); Shuqin Hu (SH); Masafumi Matsui (MM); Ermi Zhao (EZ).

Hyla arborescandens Taylor, 1939. Univ. Kansas Sci. Bull., 25:388.
TYPE(S): Holotype: UIMNH 25045 (formerly EHT 3135).
TYPE LOCALITY: "on a mountain side about 3 km. southwest of Acultzingo, Veracruz", Mexico.
DISTRIBUTION: Sierra Madre Oriental in eastern Mexico (Puebla, Oaxaca, and Veracruz).
COMMENT: In the *Hyla miotympanum* group; see Duellman, 1970, Monogr. Mus. Nat. Hist. Univ. Kansas, 1:380–384.

Hyla arenicolor Cope, 1886. J. Acad. Nat. Sci. Philadelphia, (2)6:84.
TYPE(S): Syntypes: USNM 11410 (five specimens); USNM 11410a designated lectotype by Gorman, 1960, Herpetologica, 16:218.
TYPE LOCALITY: "Northern Sonora", Mexico, or what is now southern Arizona, USA; restricted to Santa Rita Mountains, Arizona, USA, by Smith and Taylor, 1950, Univ. Kansas Sci. Bull., 33:354; restricted to Peña Blanca Springs, 10 miles northwest of Nogales, Santa Cruz County, Arizona, USA, by Gorman, 1960, Herpetologica, 16:218.
DISTRIBUTION: Mountains and plateau areas of USA (southern Utah and western Colorado southward through eastern Arizona, western New Mexico, and western Texas) southward in Mexico to Michoacán, Guerrero, and Oaxaca.
COMMENT: *Hyla arenicolor* is a replacement name for *Hyla affinis* Baird, 1854, Proc. Acad. Nat. Sci. Philadelphia, 7:61, which is preoccupied by *Hyla affinis* Spix, 1824. In the *Hyla versicolor* group; for discussion see Duellman, 1970, Monogr. Mus. Nat. Hist. Univ. Kansas, 1:514.

Hyla ariadne Bokermann, 1967. Neotropica, 13:61.
TYPE(S): Holotype: WCAB 29492.
TYPE LOCALITY: Campo de Fruticultura da Serra da Bocaina, São José do Barreiro, São Paulo, Brazil.
DISTRIBUTION: Serra da Bocaina, São Paulo, southeastern Brazil.

Hyla armata Boulenger, 1902. Ann. Mag. Nat. Hist., (7)10:394.
TYPE(S): Syntypes: BM 1947.2.13.59-60.
TYPE LOCALITY: "La Paz, Bolivia, 4000 m."
DISTRIBUTION: Eastern slopes of Andes in Peru and Bolivia.

Hyla astartea Bokermann, 1967. Rev. Brasil. Biol., 27:157.
TYPE(S): Holotype: WCAB 1019.
TYPE LOCALITY: Paranapiacaba, São Paulo, Brazil.
DISTRIBUTION: Serra do Mar, southeastern Brazil.
COMMENT: In the *Hyla circumdata* group according to the original description.

Hyla auraria Peters, 1873. Monatsber. Preuss. Akad. Wiss. Berlin, 1873:615.
TYPE(S): Formerly in ZSM; now lost.
TYPE LOCALITY: "South America".
DISTRIBUTION: Unknown.
COMMENT: This name has not been associated with a population of anurans (WED).

Hyla avivoca Viosca, 1928. Proc. Biol. Soc. Washington, 41:89.
TYPE(S): Holotype: USNM 75017.
TYPE LOCALITY: "outskirts of Mandeville, [St. Tammany Parish,] Louisiana", USA.
DISTRIBUTION: Southeastern USA (Mississippi River drainage from southern Illinois southward; eastern Georgia and adjacent South Carolina); isolated records in southeastern Oklahoma and central Arkansas.
COMMENT: In the *Hyla versicolor* group; for discussion see Smith, 1966, Cat. Am. Rept. Amph., 28.1-2.

Hyla baileyi Cochran, 1953. Herpetologica, 8:114.
ORIGINAL NAME: *Hyla goughi baileyi.*
TYPE(S): Holotype: UMMZ 106737.
TYPE LOCALITY: Fazenda Poço Grande, 8 km north of Juquia, São Paulo, Brazil.
DISTRIBUTION: Atlantic forests of São Paulo, Brazil.

Hyla balzani Boulenger, 1898. Ann. Mus. Civ. Stor. Nat. Genova, (2)19:132.
TYPE(S): Holotype: MSNG 28872.
TYPE LOCALITY: "Prov. Yungas, at 1600 metres altitude", Bolivia.
DISTRIBUTION: Amazonian slopes of Bolivia and Peru.

Hyla battersbyi Rivero, 1961. Bull. Mus. Comp. Zool., 126:138.
TYPE(S): Holotype: BM 53.2.4.165.
TYPE LOCALITY: Caracas, Venezuela.
DISTRIBUTION: Known only from the type locality.

Hyla benitezi Rivero, 1961. Bull. Mus. Comp. Zool., 126:116.
TYPE(S): Holotype: MCZ 28564.
TYPE LOCALITY: Cano Wanadi, Cerro Marahuaca, Territorio Amazonas, Venezuela.
DISTRIBUTION: Western part of Guyana Highlands in Amazonas, Venezuela.
COMMENT: See Rivero, 1971, Caribb. J. Sci., 11:181-193.

Hyla berthalutzae Bokermann, 1962. Neotropica, 8:84.
TYPE(S): Holotype: WCAB 6597.
TYPE LOCALITY: "Paranapiacaba, Estado de São Paulo, Brasil".
DISTRIBUTION: Coastal lowlands from Espírito Santo to São Paulo, and Serra do Mar, São Paulo, Brazil.

COMMENT: Related to *Hyla misera* and *Hyla nana*, according to the original description.

Hyla bifurca Andersson, 1954. Ark. Zool., 37A(2):79.
ORIGINAL NAME: *Hyla* (*Hylella*) *bifurca*.
TYPE(S): Holotype: NHRM 1962.
TYPE LOCALITY: Río Pastaza, Provincia Pastaza, Ecuador.
DISTRIBUTION: Upper Amazon Basin in Colombia, Ecuador, Peru, and Acre, Brazil.
COMMENT: In the *Hyla leucophyllata* group; see Duellman, 1974, Occas. Pap. Mus. Nat. Hist. Univ. Kansas, 27:15.

Hyla biobeba Bokermann and Sazima, 1974. Rev. Brasil. Biol., 33:329.
TYPE(S): Holotype: WCAB 46249.
TYPE LOCALITY: Usina, Serra do Cipo, Jaboticatubas, Minas Gerais, Brazil.
DISTRIBUTION: Serra do Espinhaço in Minas Gerais, Brazil.
COMMENT: In the *Hyla martinsi–Hyla langei* group, according to the original description. UC regards this statement as in error and considers this species to be either closely related to or a junior synonym of *Hyla pardalis*.

Hyla bipunctata Spix, 1824. Spec. Nov. Testud. Ran. Brasil.:36.
TYPE(S): Syntypes: ZSM 2497/0 (4 specimens) (destroyed); Hoogmoed and Gruber, 1983, Spixiana, Suppl., 9:368, noted that Spix based his description on two syntypes only.
TYPE LOCALITY: "Bahia", Brazil.
DISTRIBUTION: Coastal region of eastern Brazil from Bahia to Rio de Janeiro

Hyla bischoffi Boulenger, 1887. Ann. Mag. Nat. Hist., (5)20:298.
TYPE(S): Syntypes: BM 1947.2.12.81–82.
TYPE LOCALITY: "Mundo Novo, [Taquara,] Rio Grande do Sul", Brazil.
DISTRIBUTION: Southeastern Brazil from Rio de Janeiro to Rio Grande do Sul.

Hyla bistincta Cope, 1877. Proc. Am. Philos. Soc., 17:87.
TYPE(S): Holotype: USNM 32261.
TYPE LOCALITY: "Vera Cruz most probably", Mexico.
DISTRIBUTION: Mountains of Mexico from Durango and Veracruz to Oaxaca.
COMMENT: In the *Hyla bistincta* group; for discussion see Duellman, 1970, Monogr. Mus. Nat. Hist. Univ. Kansas, 1:457–462.

Hyla boans (Linnaeus, 1758). Syst. Nat., Ed. 10, 1:213.
ORIGINAL NAME: *Rana boans*.
TYPE(S): Holotype: ZIUU 27; designation of RMNH 16603 as neotype by Duellman, 1971, Herpetologica, 27:399, is invalid. See comment under *Hyla leucophyllata*.
TYPE LOCALITY: "America".
DISTRIBUTION: Amazon Basin, upper Orinoco Basin, Guianas, and Pacific lowlands of Colombia in South America; eastern Panama; Trinidad.
COMMENT: In the *Hyla boans* group; for discussion see Duellman, 1971, Herpetologica, 27:398, and Mertens, 1972, Senckenb. Biol., 53:197–198.

Hyla bogertae Straughan and Wright, 1969. Contrib. Sci. Nat. Hist. Mus. Los Angeles Co., 169:1.
TYPE(S): Holotype: LACM 44400.
TYPE LOCALITY: Tributary of Río Atoyac, below Vivero El Tapanal, 1.6 km south of La Cofradia, Distrito Sola de Vega, Oaxaca, Mexico.
DISTRIBUTION: Known only from the type locality.
COMMENT: In the *Hyla bistincta* group; for discussion see Duellman, 1970, Monogr. Mus. Nat. Hist. Univ. Kansas, 1:479–482.

Hyla bogotensis (Peters, 1882). Sitzungsber. Ges. Naturforsch. Freunde Berlin, 1882: 107.
ORIGINAL NAME: *Hylonomus bogotensis*.
TYPE(S): Holotype: ZMB 10209.
TYPE LOCALITY: Bogotá, Departamento Cundinamarca, Colombia.
DISTRIBUTION: Central and southern part of Cordillera Oriental of Andes and ? southern part of Cordillera Central in Colombia.
COMMENT: In the *Hyla bogotensis* group; for discussion see Duellman, 1972, Occas. Pap. Mus. Nat. Hist. Univ. Kansas, 11:1–31, and Ruíz-C. and Lynch, 1982, Caldasia, 13:647, who considered *Hyloscirtus vermiculatus* B. Lutz and Ruíz-C., 1977, to be a synonym.

Hyla bokermanni Goin, 1960. Ann. Mag. Nat. Hist., (13)2:721.
TYPE(S): Holotype: WCAB 2881.
TYPE LOCALITY: Tarauaca, Acre, Brazil.
DISTRIBUTION: Upper Amazon Basin in Colombia, Ecuador, Peru, and western Brazil.
COMMENT: In the *Hyla parviceps* group; see Duellman and Crump, 1974, Occas. Pap. Mus. Nat. Hist. Univ. Kansas, 23:14.

Hyla brevifrons Duellman and Crump, 1974. Occas. Pap. Mus. Nat. Hist. Univ. Kansas, 23:15.
TYPE(S): Holotype: KU 126370.
TYPE LOCALITY: "Santa Cecilia, Provincia Napo, Ecuador".
DISTRIBUTION: Amazon Basin and French Guiana.
COMMENT: In the *Hyla parviceps* group.

Hyla bromeliacia Schmidt, 1933. Field Mus. Nat. Hist. Publ., Zool. Ser., 20:19.
TYPE(S): Holotype: FMNH 4718.
TYPE LOCALITY: "Mountains west of San Pedro Sula", Cortés, Honduras.
DISTRIBUTION: Atlantic slopes of Guatemala and Honduras.
COMMENT: In the *Hyla bromeliacia* group; for discussion see Duellman, 1970, Monogr. Mus. Nat. Hist. Univ. Kansas, 1:429–434.

Hyla cadaverina Cope, 1866. Proc. Acad. Nat. Sci. Philadelphia, 18:84.
TYPE(S): Syntypes: ANSP 1987–88.
TYPE LOCALITY: "Tejon Pass", Los Angeles County, California, USA.
DISTRIBUTION: Southern California, USA, and northern Baja California, Mexico.
COMMENT: *Hyla cadaverina* is a replacement name for *Hyla nebulosa* Hallowell, 1854, Proc. Acad. Nat. Sci. Philadelphia, 7:96. In the *Hyla eximia* group; for discussion of this species see Gaudin, 1979, Cat. Am. Amph. Rept., 225.1–2.

Hyla calcarata Troschel, 1848. Amph. *In* Schomburgk, Reisen Brit. Guiana:660.
TYPE(S): Unknown.
TYPE LOCALITY: "Britisch-Guiana" (=Guyana).
DISTRIBUTION: Guianas, Amazon Basin, and upper Orinoco Basin in Venezuela and Brazil.
COMMENT: In the *Hyla geographica* group; for discussion see Duellman, 1973, Copeia, 1973:522–523.

Hyla callipleura Boulenger, 1902. Ann. Mag. Nat. Hist., (7)10:394.
TYPE(S): Syntypes: BM 1947.2.13.64–73 (Charuplaya), 1947.2.13.74 (San Ernesto).
TYPE LOCALITY: "Bolivia at Charuplaya (1350 m.) and at San Ernesto, Mapiri district (500 m.)".
DISTRIBUTION: Amazon slopes of Andes in southern Peru and Bolivia.

Hyla carinata Andersson, 1938. Ark. Zool., 30A(23):22.
TYPE(S): Syntypes: NHRM 1874 (3 specimens).
TYPE LOCALITY: San José, Tarraco, Bolivia.
DISTRIBUTION: Known only from the type locality.

Hyla carnifex Duellman, 1969. Herpetologica, 25:242.
TYPE(S): Holotype: KU 117993.
TYPE LOCALITY: "Tandapi (formerly known as Corneja Astorga, 0° 24' S, 78° 51' W),
Provincia Pichincha, Ecuador, 1460 m".
DISTRIBUTION: Pacific slopes of Andes in Colombia and Ecuador.
COMMENT: In the *Hyla columbiana* group.

Hyla carvalhoi Peixoto, 1981. Rev. Brasil. Biol., 41:515.
TYPE(S): Holotype: EI 6501.
TYPE LOCALITY: Parque Nacional da Serra dos Órgãos, Teresópolis, Rio de Janeiro,
Brazil.
DISTRIBUTION: Known only from the type locality.
COMMENT: In the *Hyla circumdata* group, according to the original description.

Hyla cembra Caldwell, 1974. Occas. Pap. Mus. Nat. Hist. Univ. Kansas, 23:16.
TYPE(S): Holotype: KU 137035.
TYPE LOCALITY: Campamento Río Molino, 2160 m, Oaxaca, Mexico.
DISTRIBUTION: Known only from the type locality.
COMMENT: In the *Hyla bistincta* group according to the original description.

Hyla chaneque Duellman, 1961. Herpetologica, 17:1.
TYPE(S): Holotype: KU 58439.
TYPE LOCALITY: "stream above (6.2 kilometers by road south of) Rayón Mescalapa,
Chiapas, Mexico, (elevation 1690 meters)".
DISTRIBUTION: Atlantic slopes in Oaxaca and Chiapas and Pacific slopes in Chiapas
in southern Mexico.
COMMENT: In the *Hyla taeniopus* group; see Duellman, 1970, Monogr. Mus. Nat.
Hist. Univ. Kansas, 1:440–445.

Hyla charadricola Duellman, 1964. Univ. Kansas Publ. Mus. Nat. Hist., 15:478.
TYPE(S): Holotype: KU 58414.
TYPE LOCALITY: "Río Totolapa, 14.4 kilometers by road west of Huachinango,
Puebla, Mexico, elevation 2280 meters".
DISTRIBUTION: High mountains of Hidalgo and Puebla in eastern Mexico.
COMMENT: In the *Hyla bistincta* group; see Duellman, 1970, Monogr. Mus. Nat.
Hist. Univ. Kansas, 1:466–468.

Hyla charazani Vellard, 1970. Rev. Mus. Argent. Cienc. Nat. Bernardino Rivadavia,
10:16.
TYPE(S): MACN.
TYPE LOCALITY: Charazani, Departamento Munecas, Bolivia.
DISTRIBUTION: Known only from the type locality.

Hyla chinensis Günther, 1859 "1858". Cat. Batr. Sal. Coll. Brit. Mus.:108.
ORIGINAL NAME: *Hyla arborea* var. *chinensis*.
TYPE(S): Syntypes: including BM 1947.2.23.93 (+ several not traced); Duellman,
1977, Das Tierreich, 95:45, considered BM 1947.2.23.93 to be the holotype.
TYPE LOCALITY: "China"; given by Boulenger, 1882, Cat. Batr. Sal. Brit. Mus.:382, as
"China", "Formosa", and "Chusan?".
DISTRIBUTION: Central and southeastern China (including Taiwan) to northern
Vietnam.
COMMENT: In the *Hyla arborea* group; see Pope, 1931, Bull. Am. Mus. Nat. Hist., 61:
466; Liu, 1950, Fieldiana: Zool. Mem., 2:225; Okada, 1931, Tailless Batr. Japan.
Emp.:64–66; Bourret, 1942, Batr. Indochine:223–226; and Liu and Hu, 1961,
Tailless Amph. China:132–134, for discussion.
REVIEWERS: Leo J. Borkin (LJB); Shuqin Hu (SH); Masafumi Matsui (MM); Ermi
Zhao (EZ).

Hyla chryses Adler, 1965. Occas. Pap. Mus. Zool. Univ. Michigan, 642:1.
  TYPE(S): Holotype: UMMZ 125374.
  TYPE LOCALITY: "between 'Puerto Chico' and 'Asoleadero' (about 45 km airline
    west-northwest of Chilpancingo), Guerrero, Mexico, 2540–2600 m."
  DISTRIBUTION: Sierra Madre del Sur in Guerrero, Mexico.
  COMMENT: In the *Hyla bistincta* group; for discussion see Duellman, 1970, Monogr.
    Mus. Nat. Hist. Univ. Kansas, 1:468–470.

Hyla chrysoscelis Cope, 1880. Bull. U.S. Natl. Mus., 17:29.
  ORIGINAL NAME: *Hyla femoralis chrysoscelis*.
  TYPE(S): Holotype: ANSP 13672.
  TYPE LOCALITY: Dallas, Texas, USA.
  DISTRIBUTION: Southeastern North America from eastern North Dakota and
    Delaware to southern Texas and northern Florida, USA.
  COMMENT: In the *Hyla versicolor* group. *Hyla chrysoscelis* is one of a pair of cryptic
    species with *Hyla versicolor*. See Maxson, Pepper, and Maxson, 1977, Science,
    Washington D.C., 197:1012–13, and Johnson, 1966, Texas J. Sci., 18:361.

Hyla cinerea (Schneider, 1792). Hist. Amph., 1:174.
  ORIGINAL NAME: *Calamita cinereus*.
  TYPE(S): Unknown.
  TYPE LOCALITY: "Carolina"; restricted to "Charleston, South Carolina", USA, by
    Schmidt, 1953, Check List N. Am. Amph. Rept., Ed. 6:69.
  DISTRIBUTION: Southeastern USA; introduced into northwestern Puerto Rico.
  COMMENT: See Duellman and Schwartz, 1958, Bull. Florida State Mus., Biol. Sci., 3:
    241, for discussion. The frequent citation of *Calamita carolinensis* Pennant,
    1792, as an older name for this species is based on a bibliographic error by
    Schneider; *Calamita carolinensis* has never been proposed (DRF).

Hyla circumdata (Cope, 1867). Proc. Am. Philos. Soc., 11:555.
  ORIGINAL NAME: *Hypsiboas circumdatus*.
  TYPE(S): Syntypes: including MCZ 1508, other syntype not traced.
  TYPE LOCALITY: Rio de Janeiro, Brazil.
  DISTRIBUTION: Mountains of Espírito Santo, Rio de Janeiro, São Paulo, and Santa
    Catarina in southeastern Brazil.
  COMMENT: In the *Hyla circumdata* group.

Hyla claresignata A. Lutz and B. Lutz, 1939. An. Acad. Brasil. Cienc., 11:67.
  TYPE(S): Holotype: AL-MN 1971.
  TYPE LOCALITY: Teresópolis, Rio de Janeiro, Brazil.
  DISTRIBUTION: Serra do Mar in Rio de Janeiro, São Paulo, and Paraná, southeastern
    Brazil to Misiones Plateau, Argentina.
  COMMENT: See Cochran, 1955, Bull. U.S. Natl. Mus., 206:86, and Cei, 1980, Monit.
    Zool. Ital., N.S., Monogr., 2:467–469, for discussion.

Hyla clepsydra A. Lutz, 1925. C. R. Séances Soc. Biol., Paris, 93:211.
  TYPE(S): Holotype: AL-MN 976.
  TYPE LOCALITY: Serra da Bocaina, São Paulo, Brazil.
  DISTRIBUTION: Known only from the type locality.

Hyla columbiana Boettger, 1892. Kat. Batr. Samml. Mus. Senckenb. Naturforsch.
  Ges.:41.
  TYPE(S): SMF 2365 designated lectotype by Mertens, 1967, Senckenb. Biol., 48:41.
  TYPE LOCALITY: Popayán, Departamento Cauca, Colombia.
  DISTRIBUTION: Highlands of southern Colombia.
  COMMENT: In the *Hyla columbiana* group; synonymy includes *Hyla variabilis*
    according to Duellman and Trueb, 1983, *In* Rhodin and Miyata (eds.), Adv.
    Herpetol. Evol. Biol.:33–51.

Hyla colymba Dunn, 1931. Occas. Pap. Boston Soc. Nat. Hist., 5:400.
  TYPE(S): Holotype: MCZ 10234.
  TYPE LOCALITY: La Loma, Provincia Bocas del Toro, Panama.
  DISTRIBUTION: Caribbean slopes of Costa Rica and western Panama and Pacific
    slopes of central and eastern Panama.
  COMMENT: In the *Hyla bogotensis* group; see Duellman, 1972, Occas. Pap. Mus. Nat.
    Hist. Univ. Kansas, 11:21-22.

Hyla crassa (Brocchi, 1877). Bull. Soc. Philomath. Paris, (7)1:130.
  ORIGINAL NAME: *Cauphias crassus.*
  TYPE(S): Holotype: MNHNP 6331.
  TYPE LOCALITY: Mexico.
  DISTRIBUTION: Cerro San Felipe and Sierra Mixe, Oaxaca, Mexico.
  COMMENT: In the *Hyla bistincta* group; see Caldwell, 1974, Occas. Pap. Mus. Nat.
    Hist. Univ. Kansas, 28:1-37.

Hyla crepitans Wied-Neuwied, 1824. Abbild. Naturgesch. Brasil.:pl. 47, fig. 1.
  TYPE(S): Syntypes: including AMNH 785, other syntypes not traced.
  TYPE LOCALITY: Tamburil, Jiboya, and Areal da Conquista, Bahia, Brazil.
  DISTRIBUTION: Central and northeastern Brazil, Guianas, northern Colombia and
    Venezuela, eastern Panama, northern Honduras.
  COMMENT: In the *Hyla boans* group. This taxon apparently is a composite of several
    species; see Kluge, 1979, Occas. Pap. Mus. Zool. Univ. Michigan, 688:1-24.

Hyla crucifer Wied-Neuwied, 1838. Reise N. Am., 1:249.
  TYPE(S): Unknown.
  TYPE LOCALITY: "Cantonment Leavenworth" (=Fort Leavenworth), Leavenworth
    County, Kansas, USA.
  DISTRIBUTION: Eastern North America; introduced at Marianao and Canasí, Cuba.
  REVIEWERS: Albert Schwartz (AS); Richard Thomas (RT).

Hyla cyanomma Caldwell, 1974. Occas. Pap. Mus. Nat. Hist. Univ. Kansas, 28:8.
  TYPE(S): Holotype: KU 137014.
  TYPE LOCALITY: 1.2 km north of Cerro Pelón, 1650 m, Oaxaca, Mexico.
  DISTRIBUTION: Sierra Juárez, Oaxaca, Mexico.
  COMMENT: In the *Hyla bistincta* group according to the original description.

Hyla cymbalum Bokermann, 1963. Neotropica, 9:27.
  TYPE(S): Holotype: WCAB 9153.
  TYPE LOCALITY: "Campo Grande, Santo André, São Paulo, Brasil".
  DISTRIBUTION: Known only from the type locality.
  COMMENT: In the *Hyla raddiana* (=*Hyla pulchella*) group, according to the original
    description. Probably conspecific with *Hyla pulchella* (UC).

Hyla debilis Taylor, 1952. Univ. Kansas Sci. Bull., 35:880.
  TYPE(S): Holotype: KU 28184.
  TYPE LOCALITY: "Isla Bonita, (American Cinchona Plantation) eastern slope of
    Vólcan Póas, [Provincia Heredia,] Costa Rica, 5600 ft."
  DISTRIBUTION: Caribbean slopes of Costa Rica and Pacific slopes of southwestern
    Panama.
  COMMENT: In the *Hyla rivularis* group; see Duellman, 1970, Monogr. Mus. Nat.
    Hist. Univ. Kansas, 1:289-292.

Hyla decipiens A. Lutz, 1925. C. R. Séances Soc. Biol., Paris, 93:212.
  TYPE(S): Syntypes: AL-MN 90-91, USNM 96194.
  TYPE LOCALITY: Rio de Janeiro, Rio de Janeiro, Brazil.
  DISTRIBUTION: Coastal region of eastern Brazil from Pernambuco to Rio de Janeiro.
  COMMENT: See B. Lutz, 1973, Brazil. Spec. *Hyla*:208.

Hyla dendroscarta Taylor, 1940. Proc. U.S. Natl. Mus., 89:45.
TYPE(S): Holotype: USNM 103679.
TYPE LOCALITY: "Cuautlapa, Veracruz", Mexico.
DISTRIBUTION: Mountains of central Veracruz and northern Oaxaca, Mexico.
COMMENT: In the *Hyla bromeliacia* group; see Duellman, 1970, Monogr. Mus. Nat.
Hist. Univ. Kansas, 1:434–437.

Hyla dentei Bokermann, 1967. Rev. Brasil. Biol., 27:109.
TYPE(S): Holotype: WCAB 35880.
TYPE LOCALITY: Serra do Navio, Amapá, Brazil.
DISTRIBUTION: Known only from the type locality.
COMMENT: In the *Hyla albopunctata* group or *Hyla geographica* group, according to
the original description.

Hyla denticulenta Duellman, 1972. Occas. Pap. Mus. Nat. Hist. Univ. Kansas, 11:22.
TYPE(S): Holotype: KU 133451.
TYPE LOCALITY: "Charta, Departamento Santander, Colombia, 2400 m".
DISTRIBUTION: Andes of northern Colombia.
COMMENT: In the *Hyla bogotensis* group.

Hyla dolloi Werner, 1903. Zool. Anz., 26:253.
TYPE(S): Syntypes: MRHN 6481 (2 specimens).
TYPE LOCALITY: "Brasil".
DISTRIBUTION: Unknown.
COMMENT: Name not associated with any known species (WED).

Hyla ebraccata Cope, 1874. Proc. Acad. Nat. Sci. Philadelphia, 26:69.
TYPE(S): Holotype: ANSP 2079.
TYPE LOCALITY: "region of Nicaragua".
DISTRIBUTION: Lowlands of southern Mexico and Central America to northwestern
Colombia.
COMMENT: In the *Hyla leucophyllata* group; see Duellman, 1970, Monogr. Mus. Nat.
Hist. Univ. Kansas, 1:227.

Hyla echinata Duellman, 1962. Trans. Kansas Acad. Sci., 64:349.
TYPE(S): Holotype: UIMNH 49339.
TYPE LOCALITY: Campamento Vista Hermosa, 1500 m, Oaxaca, Mexico.
DISTRIBUTION: Sierra Juárez in northern Oaxaca, Mexico.
COMMENT: In the *Hyla miliaria* group; see Duellman, 1970, Monogr. Mus. Nat. Hist.
Univ. Kansas, 1:346–348.

Hyla elegans Wied-Neuwied, 1824. Isis von Oken, 6:671.
TYPE(S): Not traced (?AMNH).
TYPE LOCALITY: Ponte do Gentio, Rio Alcobaça, Daravelas, Bahia, Brazil, according
to Bokermann, 1966, Lista Anot. Local. Tipo Anf. Brasil.:49.
DISTRIBUTION: Atlantic forests from Bahia to São Paulo, Brazil.
COMMENT: In the *Hyla leucophyllata* group. Removed from the synonymy of *Hyla
leucophyllata* by Caramaschi and Jim, 1982, Cienc. Cult., Supl., 7:848.

Hyla elkejungingerae Henle, 1981. Amphibia-Reptilia, 2:123.
TYPE(S): Holotype: ZFMK 33352.
TYPE LOCALITY: "Peru: El Boqueron, ca. 1000 m NN".
DISTRIBUTION: Vicinity of the type locality.
COMMENT: Most likely a synonym of *Osteocephalus taurinus* (MSH).

Hyla erythromma Taylor, 1937. Proc. Biol. Soc. Washington, 50:48.
TYPE(S): Holotype: FMNH 100083 (formerly EHT-HMS 5976).
TYPE LOCALITY: "in pines along Mexico–Acapulco highway at km. 350, near a
spring known as Agua del Obispo, between Rincon and Cajones", Guerrero,
Mexico.
DISTRIBUTION: Mountains of southern Mexico (Sierra Madre del Sur in Guerrero;
Sierra Juárez in Oaxaca).

COMMENT: Sole member of the *Hyla erythromma* group; see Duellman, 1970, Monogr. Mus. Nat. Hist. Univ. Kansas, 1:392–395.

Hyla euphorbiacea Günther, 1859 "1858". Cat. Batr. Sal. Coll. Brit. Mus.:109.
TYPE(S): Syntypes: BM 1947.2.24.15–16 (Mexico), 1947.2.24.17 (Cordova), 1947.2.24.18–19 (Cordilleras).
TYPE LOCALITY: "Cordova" (=Córdoba, Veracruz, Mexico); "Cordilleras"; "Mexico".
DISTRIBUTION: Highlands of southern Mexico (central Veracruz to Oaxaca) and Alta Verapaz, Guatemala.
COMMENT: In the *Hyla eximia* group; *Hyla bocourti* (Mocquard, 1899), synonymized with *Hyla euphorbiacea* by Duellman, 1970, Monogr. Mus. Nat. Hist. Univ. Kansas, 1:505–510, is probably a distinct species in the highlands of Alta Verapaz and Baja Verapaz, Guatemala (WED and JAC).

Hyla eximia Baird, 1854. Proc. Acad. Nat. Sci. Philadelphia, 7:61.
TYPE(S): Syntypes: USNM 3248 (2 specimens).
TYPE LOCALITY: "Valley of Mexico", Mexico.
DISTRIBUTION: Highlands of southwestern USA (Arizona and New Mexico) and Mexico southward to Guerrero, Morelos, and Puebla.
COMMENT: In the *Hyla eximia* group; includes as a synonym *Hyla wrightorum* Taylor, 1939, Univ. Kansas Sci. Bull., 25:436. For discussion see Duellman, 1970, Monogr. Mus. Nat. Hist. Univ. Kansas, 1:499–505, and Blair, 1960, Southwest. Nat., 5:129–135.

Hyla faber Wied-Neuwied, 1821. Reise Brasil., 2:249.
TYPE(S): Unknown (?AMNH).
TYPE LOCALITY: Santa Inês ("Fazenda St. Agnes"), Bahia, Brazil.
DISTRIBUTION: Eastern to southern Brazil; southeastern Paraguay; Misiones, Argentina.
COMMENT: In the *Hyla boans* group; for discussion see B. Lutz, 1973, Brazil. Spec. *Hyla*:11. See also Cei, 1980, Monit. Zool. Ital., N.S., Monogr., 2:454–459.

Hyla fasciata Günther, 1859 "1858". Cat. Batr. Sal. Coll. Brit. Mus.:100.
TYPE(S): Holotype: BM 58.4.25.22.
TYPE LOCALITY: "Andes of Ecuador".
DISTRIBUTION: Guianas and upper Amazon Basin from Ecuador to Bolivia.
COMMENT: In the *Hyla geographica* group; see Duellman, 1973, Copeia, 1973:523–526.

Hyla favosa Cope, 1886. Proc. Am. Philos. Soc., 23:95.
TYPE(S): Holotype: ANSP 11398.
TYPE LOCALITY: Pebas, Departamento Loreto, Peru.
DISTRIBUTION: Upper Amazon Basin in Ecuador, Peru, Bolivia, and western Brazil; French Guiana.
COMMENT: In the *Hyla leucophyllata* group; see Duellman, 1974, Occas. Pap. Mus. Nat. Hist. Univ. Kansas, 27:17.

Hyla femoralis Bosc, 1800. *In* Daudin, Hist. Nat. Quadrup. Ovip., Livr. 1:10.
TYPE(S): Unknown.
TYPE LOCALITY: "La Caroline"; restricted to "Charleston, South Carolina", USA, by Schmidt, 1953, Check List N. Am. Amph. Rept., Ed. 6:71.
DISTRIBUTION: Southeastern USA (Atlantic Coastal Plain from Virginia to Louisiana).
COMMENT: In the *Hyla versicolor* group.

Hyla fimbrimembra Taylor, 1948. Copeia, 1948:233.
TYPE(S): Holotype: R. C. Taylor 761 (now FMNH?).
TYPE LOCALITY: Isla Bonita, Provincia Heredia, Costa Rica.
DISTRIBUTION: Caribbean slopes of north-central Costa Rica, from Monteverde to Volcán Barba.

COMMENT: In the *Hyla miliaria* group; see Duellman, 1970, Monogr. Mus. Nat. Hist. Univ. Kansas, 1:348.

Hyla fuentei C. Goin and O. Goin, 1968. Copeia, 1968:581.
TYPE(S): Holotype: CM 44218.
TYPE LOCALITY: Powakka, Suriname District, Surinam.
DISTRIBUTION: Known only from the type locality.

Hyla fusca Laurenti, 1768. Synops. Rept.:34.
TYPE(S): Unknown.
TYPE LOCALITY: Unknown.
DISTRIBUTION: Unknown.
COMMENT: Name not associated with any known species (WED).

Hyla geographica Spix, 1824. Spec. Nov. Testud. Ran. Brasil.:39.
TYPE(S): Formerly ZSM 35/0 (lost); see Hoogmoed and Gruber, 1983, Spixiana, Suppl., 9:370, for discussion.
TYPE LOCALITY: Rio Tefé, Amazonas, Brazil.
DISTRIBUTION: Tropical South America east of the Andes; Trinidad.
COMMENT: In the *Hyla geographica* group; see Duellman, 1973, Copeia, 1973:526–530, and Lutz, 1973, Brazil. Spec. *Hyla*:34–37.

Hyla giesleri Mertens, 1950. Wochenschr. Aquar. Terrarienkd., 44:185.
TYPE(S): Holotype: SMF 41217.
TYPE LOCALITY: Barro Branco, Rio de Janeiro [Brazil].
DISTRIBUTION: Lowlands of Espírito Santo and Rio de Janeiro, Brazil.
COMMENT: In the *Hyla parviceps* group; see Heyer, 1980, Proc. Biol. Soc. Washington, 93:655, for taxonomic status.

Hyla godmani Günther, 1901. Biol. Cent. Am., Rept. Batr.:275.
TYPE(S): Syntypes: BM 1901.12.19.88–95 (Jalapa), and 1901.12.19.96 (Misantla); BM 1901.12.19.96 designated lectotype by Duellman, 1964, Copeia, 1964:455.
TYPE LOCALITY: Restricted to Misantla, Veracruz, Mexico, by lectotype designation.
DISTRIBUTION: Lowlands of Veracruz, Mexico.
COMMENT: In the *Hyla godmani* group; see Duellman, 1970, Monogr. Mus. Nat. Hist. Univ. Kansas, 1:356–359.

Hyla graceae Myers and Duellman, 1982. Am. Mus. Novit., 2752:5.
TYPE(S): Holotype: AMNH 107966.
TYPE LOCALITY: Continental Divide southeast of Cerro Colorado, 1650 m, Provincia Chiriquí, Panama.
DISTRIBUTION: Mountains of eastern Panama.
COMMENT: In the *Hyla pseudopuma* group.

Hyla grandisonae Goin, 1966. Q. J. Florida Acad. Sci., 29:39.
TYPE(S): Holotype: BM 1938.10.3.25.
TYPE LOCALITY: Mazaruni, Guyana.
DISTRIBUTION: Known only from the type locality.

Hyla granosa Boulenger, 1882. Cat. Batr. Sal. Brit. Mus.:358.
TYPE(S): Syntypes: BM 1947.2.12.93 (Demerara Falls), 1947.2.12.94–96 (Santarém), 1947.2.12.97–98 (Interior of Brazil), 1947.2.12.99 (Canelos); BM 1947.2.12.99 designated lectotype by Duellman, 1974, Occas. Pap. Mus. Nat. Hist. Univ. Kansas, 27:8.
TYPE LOCALITY: "Demerara Falls", Guyana; "Santarem", Pará, Brazil; "Interior of Brasil"; "Canelos, [Provincia Pastaza,] Ecuador". Restricted to Canelos by lectotype designation.
DISTRIBUTION: Guianas and Amazon Basin in Brazil, Colombia, Venezuela, Ecuador, and Peru.

COMMENT: In the *Hyla granosa* group; see Hoogmoed, 1979, Zool. Verh., Leiden, 172:1–45.

Hyla gratiosa LeConte, 1856. Proc. Acad. Nat. Sci. Philadelphia, 8:146.
TYPE(S): Holotype: ANSP 2089; the status of type(s) is confusing, see Caldwell, 1982, Cat. Am. Amph. Rept., 298.1, for discussion.
TYPE LOCALITY: "Lower part of Georgia"; restricted to "Liberty County, Georgia", USA, by Schmidt, 1953, Check List N. Am. Amph. Rept., Ed. 6:71.
DISTRIBUTION: Southeastern USA (North Carolina to eastern Louisiana); isolated records from southern Kentucky, Tennessee, and northern Alabama.
COMMENT: Reviewed by Caldwell, 1982, Cat. Am. Amph. Rept., 298.1–2.

Hyla gryllata Duellman, 1973. Herpetologica, 29:219.
TYPE(S): Holotype: KU 146452.
TYPE LOCALITY: "Estación Biológica Río Palenque, 56 km north of Quevedo, Provincia Los Ríos [Pichincha], Ecuador, 220 m".
DISTRIBUTION: Pacific lowlands of northwestern Ecuador.
COMMENT: In the *Hyla microcephala* group.

Hyla guentheri Boulenger, 1886. Ann. Mag. Nat. Hist., (5)18:445.
TYPE(S): Holotype: BM 62.5.8.9.
TYPE LOCALITY: "Rio Grande do Sul", Brazil.
DISTRIBUTION: Southeastern Brazil (Rio Grande do Sul and Santa Catarina) and northeastern Argentina.
COMMENT: *Hyla guentheri* is a replacement name for *Hyla leucotaenia* Günther, 1868, Proc. Zool. Soc. London, 1868:489. See Lutz, 1973, Brazil. Spec. *Hyla*:120.

Hyla hallowellii Thompson, 1912. Herpetol. Not., 2:2.
TYPE(S): Holotype: CAS 23808.
TYPE LOCALITY: "Kikaigashima, Loo Choo [=Ryukyu] Islands, Japan".
DISTRIBUTION: Ryukyu Is., Japan.
COMMENT: In the *Hyla arborea* group; for discussion see Nakamura and Ueno, 1963, Japan. Rept. Amph. Color:35, and Okada, 1931, Tailless Batr. Japan. Emp.:67–70. See also Matsui and Matsui, 1982, Japan. J. Herpetol., 9:79–86.
REVIEWERS: Leo J. Borkin (LJB); Shuqin Hu (SH); Masafumi Matsui (MM); Ermi Zhao (EZ).

Hyla haraldschultzi Bokermann, 1962. Neotropica, 8:88.
TYPE(S): Holotype: WCAB 2896.
TYPE LOCALITY: "Santa Rita do Weill, São Paulo de Olivença, Estado de Amazonas, Brasil".
DISTRIBUTION: Eastern Peru and Rio Solimões, Brazil.

Hyla hazelae Taylor, 1940. Univ. Kansas Sci. Bull., 26:385.
TYPE(S): Holotype: FMNH 100047 (formerly EHT-HMS 16262).
TYPE LOCALITY: "Cerro San Felipe, about 10 miles north of Oaxaca, Oaxaca", Mexico.
DISTRIBUTION: Mountains of central Oaxaca, Mexico.
COMMENT: In the *Hyla hazelae* group; see Duellman, 1970, Monogr. Mus. Nat. Hist. Univ. Kansas, 1:385.

Hyla heilprini Noble, 1923. Am. Mus. Novit., 61:1.
TYPE(S): Holotype: AMNH 11401.
TYPE LOCALITY: Lo Bracito [=Los Bracitos], Provincia Pacificador [now Duarte], Dominican Republic.
DISTRIBUTION: Hispaniola, West Indies.
COMMENT: Questionably in the *Hyla albomarginata* group; see Trueb and Tyler, 1974, Occas. Pap. Mus. Nat. Hist. Univ. Kansas, 24:1–60.

REVIEWERS: Albert Schwartz (AS); Richard Thomas (RT).

Hyla helenae Ruthven, 1919. Occas. Pap. Mus. Zool. Univ. Michigan, 69:10.
TYPE(S): Holotype: UMMZ 52681.
TYPE LOCALITY: Valley of the Demerara River, Guyana.
DISTRIBUTION: Known only from the type locality.

Hyla hobbsi Cochran and Goin, 1970. Bull. U.S. Natl. Mus., 288:311.
TYPE(S): Holotype: MCZ 28052.
TYPE LOCALITY: "Caño Goacayá, a tributary of the Río Apoporis, in Amazonas, Colombia".
DISTRIBUTION: Region of Río Apoporis, Amazonas, Colombia.
COMMENT: In the *Hyla punctata* group; see Pyburn, 1978, Proc. Biol. Soc. Washington, 91:123, for taxonomic status.

Hyla hutchinsi Pyburn and Hall, 1984. Herpetologica, 40:366.
TYPE(S): Holotype: Estación de Biología Tropical Roberto Franco 3000.
TYPE LOCALITY: "about 2 km SW Umuñapíto (0° 34' N, 70° 05' W), Comisaria de Vaupés, Colombia".
DISTRIBUTION: Known only from the type locality.
COMMENT: In the *Hyla geographica* group, according to the original description. See comment under *Hyla*.

Hyla hypselops (Cope, 1870). Proc. Am. Philos. Soc., 11:554.
ORIGINAL NAME: *Hypsiboas hypselops*.
TYPE(S): Unknown.
TYPE LOCALITY: "Pebas", Departamento Loreto, Peru.
DISTRIBUTION: Known only from the type locality.
COMMENT: Name not associated with any known species (WED).

Hyla ibitiguara Cardoso, 1983. Iheringia, Zool., 62:38.
TYPE(S): Holotype: MN 4152.
TYPE LOCALITY: "Fazenda Salto (20° 40' S—46° 16' W; 900 m), Alpinópolis, Minas Gerais, Brasil".
DISTRIBUTION: Known only from the type locality.
COMMENT: In the *Hyla circumdata* group, according to the original description.

Hyla imitator (Barbour and Dunn, 1921). Proc. Biol. Soc. Washington, 34:160.
ORIGINAL NAME: *Paludicola imitator*.
TYPE(S): Holotype: MCZ 345.
TYPE LOCALITY: Lake Cudajaz (=Lago Codajás), Amazonas, Brazil.
DISTRIBUTION: Known only from the type locality.

Hyla inframaculata Boulenger, 1882. Cat. Batr. Sal. Brit. Mus.:354.
TYPE(S): Holotype: BM 1947.2.13.10.
TYPE LOCALITY: "Santarem", Pará, Brazil.
DISTRIBUTION: Known only from the type locality.

Hyla intermixta Daudin, 1802. Hist. Nat. Rain. Gren. Crap.:23.
TYPE(S): Formerly in MNHNP; now lost.
TYPE LOCALITY: Unknown.
DISTRIBUTION: Unknown.
COMMENT: This name is not assignable to any known species (WED).

Hyla izecksohni Jim and Caramaschi, 1979. Rev. Brasil. Biol., 39:717.
TYPE(S): Holotype: MZUSP 50178.
TYPE LOCALITY: "Rubião Júnior, Botucatu, São Paulo, Brasil (aprox. 22° 53' S e 48° 30' W)".
DISTRIBUTION: Known only from the type locality.

COMMENT: In the *Hyla circumdata* group according to the original description.

Hyla japonica Günther, 1859 "1858". Cat. Batr. Sal. Coll. Brit. Mus.:109.
   ORIGINAL NAME: *Hyla arborea* var. *japonica*.
   TYPE(S): Syntypes: BM 44.2.22.107 (3 specimens).
   TYPE LOCALITY: Japan.
   DISTRIBUTION: Japan, Korea, Mongolia, central (south to Guizhou) and northeastern
      China, and USSR from Lake Baikal through the Amur and Ussuri river basins
      southeast to the coast, Sakhalin I. and Kunashir I.
   COMMENT: In the *Hyla arborea* group; see Kuramoto, 1980, Copeia, 1980:106.
      Chinese population reviewed by Liu and Hu, 1961, Tailless Amph. China:
      127–128 (as *Hyla arborea*). Genetically isolated from European *Hyla arborea*,
      according to Daito, 1968, Zool. Mag., Tokyo, 77:117–127, and Kawamura and
      Nishioka, 1977, In Taylor and Guttman (eds.), The Reproductive Biology of
      Amphibians:132.
   REVIEWERS: Leo J. Borkin (LJB); Shuqin Hu (SH); Masafumi Matsui (MM); Ermi
      Zhao (EZ).

Hyla juanitae Snyder, 1972. J. Herpetol., 6:5.
   TYPE(S): Holotype: KU 128736.
   TYPE LOCALITY: 15 km (by road) northeast of San Vicente de Benítez, 1070 m,
      Guerrero, Mexico.
   DISTRIBUTION: Pacific slopes of Sierra Madre del Sur in Guerrero and Oaxaca,
      Mexico.
   COMMENT: In the *Hyla melanomma* group.

Hyla kanaima Goin and Woodley, 1965. Zool. J. Linn. Soc., 48:135.
   TYPE(S): Holotype: BM 1965.230.
   TYPE LOCALITY: Mt. Kanaima, Potaro District, Guyana.
   DISTRIBUTION: Mt. Kanaima and Mt. Roraima, southern Guyana.
   COMMENT: In the *Hyla geographica* group.

Hyla labialis Peters, 1863. Monatsber. Preuss. Akad. Wiss. Berlin, 1863:463.
   TYPE(S): Holotype: ZMB 4913.
   TYPE LOCALITY: Mountains surrounding Bogota, Departamento Cundinamarca,
      Colombia.
   DISTRIBUTION: Andes of central and northeastern Colombia and western
      Venezuela.
   COMMENT: In the *Hyla labialis* group; see Cochran and Goin, 1970, Bull. U.S. Natl.
      Mus., 288:251. *Hyla labialis meridensis* Rivero, 1961, Bull. Mus. Comp. Zool.,
      126:131, is probably a distinct species (WED).

Hyla lancasteri Barbour, 1928. Proc. New England Zool. Club, 10:31.
   TYPE(S): Holotype: MCZ 13062.
   TYPE LOCALITY: Peralta, Provincia Cartago, Costa Rica.
   DISTRIBUTION: Caribbean slopes of Costa Rica and Panama.
   COMMENT: In the *Hyla lancasteri* group; see Myers and Duellman, 1982, Am. Mus.
      Novit., 2752:15.

Hyla lanciformis (Cope, 1870). Proc. Am. Philos. Soc., 11:556.
   ORIGINAL NAME: *Hypsiboas lanciformis*.
   TYPE(S): Unknown.
   TYPE LOCALITY: "Ecuador".
   DISTRIBUTION: Middle and upper Amazon Basin and north-central Venezuela.
   COMMENT: In the *Hyla albopunctata* group. Population in north-central Venezuela
      recognized as *Hyla lanciformis guerreroi* Rivero, 1971, Caribb. J. Sci., 11:4.

Hyla langei Bokermann, 1965. J. Ohio Herpetol. Soc., 5:49.
   TYPE(S): Holotype: WCAB 30428.
   TYPE LOCALITY: Marumbi, Morretes, Paraná, Brazil.
   DISTRIBUTION: Known only from the type locality.

COMMENT: In the *Hyla martinsi* group according to original description.

Hyla larinopygion Duellman, 1973. Herpetologica, 29:224.
TYPE(S): Holotype: KU 144127.
TYPE LOCALITY: "Quebrada Santa Tereza, between Popayán and Quintana, Departamento Cauca, Colombia, 2200 m".
DISTRIBUTION: Cordillera Central, Colombia; Cordillera Oriental in southern Colombia and northern Ecuador.
COMMENT: In the *Hyla larinopygion* group.

Hyla lascinia Rivero, 1969. Caribb. J. Sci., 9:145.
TYPE(S): Holotype: MCZ 65901.
TYPE LOCALITY: Tabor, above Delicias (opposite Herran, Colombia), Páramo de Tamá, Táchira, Venezuela.
DISTRIBUTION: Eastern slopes of northern part of Cordillera Oriental of Andes in extreme western Venezuela.
COMMENT: In the *Hyla bogotensis* group.

Hyla leali Bokermann, 1964. Neotropica, 10:3.
TYPE(S): Holotype: WCAB 10397.
TYPE LOCALITY: "Forte Príncipe [da Beira], Território Federal de Rondônia, Brasil".
DISTRIBUTION: Upper Amazon Basin in Brazil and Peru.
COMMENT: In the *Hyla minima* group; for discussion of taxonomic status see Heyer, 1977, Pap. Avulsos Zool., São Paulo, 31:144.

Hyla legleri Taylor, 1958. Univ. Kansas Sci. Bull., 39:33.
TYPE(S): Holotype: KU 32932.
TYPE LOCALITY: "15 km WSW San Isidro del General, San José Province", Costa Rica.
DISTRIBUTION: Pacific slopes of southern Costa Rica and western Panama.
COMMENT: In the *Hyla salvadorensis* group; see Duellman, 1970, Monogr. Mus. Nat. Hist. Univ. Kansas, 1:333–337.

Hyla lemai Rivero, 1971. Caribb. J. Sci., 11:183.
TYPE(S): Holotype: UPRM 3179.
TYPE LOCALITY: Paso del Danto, La Escalera, between El Dorado and Santa Elena de Uairen, 1300–1400 m, Serranía de Lema, Estado Bolívar, Venezuela.
DISTRIBUTION: La Escalera region (Bolívar, Venezuela) and Mount Roraima, Guyana (MSH).

Hyla leptolineata P. Braun and C. Braun, 1977. Rev. Brasil. Biol., 37:853.
TYPE(S): Holotype: MRGS 8086.
TYPE LOCALITY: "Fortaleza dos Aparados, Município de Cambará do Sul, Rio Grande do Sul, Brasil".
DISTRIBUTION: Rio Grande do Sul, Brazil.
COMMENT: In the *Hyla polytaenia* group and most closely related to *Hyla guentheri*, according to the original description.

Hyla leucophyllata (Beireis, 1783). Schr. Ges. Naturforsch. Freunde Berlin, 4:182.
ORIGINAL NAME: *Rana leucophyllata*.
TYPE(S): NHRM 157 (now lost) was regarded as the holotype by Duellman, 1977, Das Tierreich, 95:69; this was disputed by Böhme, 1981, Bonn. Zool. Beitr., 32:283–295, who suggested that the holotype was lost and that NHRM 157 was one of the original Linnaean syntypes of *Hyla boans*.
TYPE LOCALITY: "Surinam".
DISTRIBUTION: The Amazon Basin and the Guianas.
COMMENT: In the *Hyla leucophyllata* group; for discussion of geographic variation and synonyms, see Duellman, 1974, Occas. Pap. Mus. Nat. Hist. Univ. Kansas, 27:18. See comment under *Hyla elegans*.

Hyla limai Bokermann, 1962. Neotropica, 8:81.
TYPE(S): Holotype: WCAB 4.
TYPE LOCALITY: "São Vicente, Estado de São Paulo, Brasil".
DISTRIBUTION: Known only from the type locality.
COMMENT: Related to *Hyla minuta* and *Hyla werneri,* according to the original description.

Hyla lindae Duellman and Altig, 1978. Herpetologica, 34:177.
TYPE(S): Holotype: KU 164402.
TYPE LOCALITY: "11 km east-southeast (by road) of Papallacta, Provincia Napo, Ecuador, 2660 m".
DISTRIBUTION: Amazonian slopes of Andes in southern Colombia and northern Ecuador.
COMMENT: In the *Hyla larinopygion* group.

Hyla loquax Gaige and Stuart, 1934. Occas. Pap. Mus. Zool. Univ. Michigan, 281:1.
TYPE(S): Holotype: UMMZ 75446.
TYPE LOCALITY: Ixpuc Aguada, north of La Libertad, Departamento El Petén, Guatemala.
DISTRIBUTION: Atlantic lowlands from southern Veracruz, Mexico, to Costa Rica.
COMMENT: In the *Hyla godmani* group; see Duellman, 1970, Monogr. Mus. Nat. Hist. Univ. Kansas, 1:359–363.

Hyla loveridgei Rivero, 1961. Bull. Mus. Comp. Zool., 126:108.
TYPE(S): Holotype: MCZ 28565.
TYPE LOCALITY: Pico Culebra, Cerro Duida, Territorio Amazonas, Venezuela.
DISTRIBUTION: Known only from the type locality.
COMMENT: See La Marca and Smith, 1982, Caribb. J. Sci., 18:21, for discussion of the use of this name rather than *Hyla ginesi.*

Hyla luteoocellata Roux, 1927. Verh. Naturforsch. Ges. Basel, 38:260.
ORIGINAL NAME: *Hyla luteo-ocellata.*
TYPE(S): NHMB 3900 designated lectotype by Forcart, 1946, Verh. Naturforsch. Ges. Basel, 56:124.
TYPE LOCALITY: "El Mene, Prov. Falcon, Vénézuéla".
DISTRIBUTION: Northern Venezuela (Lake Maracaibo to Unare Depression).
COMMENT: In the *Hyla parviceps* group; see Duellman and Crump, 1974, Occas. Pap. Mus. Nat. Hist. Univ. Kansas, 23:1–40.

Hyla lythrodes Savage, 1968. Bull. S. California Acad. Sci., 67:1.
TYPE(S): Holotype: LACM 26766.
TYPE LOCALITY: 21 km SW Amburi at confluence of Río Lari and Río Dipnari, Limón, Costa Rica.
DISTRIBUTION: Caribbean slopes of southern Costa Rica and western Panama.
COMMENT: In the *Hyla uranochroa* group; see Myers and Duellman, 1982, Am. Mus. Novit., 2752:21.

Hyla marginata Boulenger, 1887. Ann. Mag. Nat. Hist., (5)20:298.
TYPE(S): Holotype: BM 1947.2.12.80.
TYPE LOCALITY: "Mundo Novo, [Taquara,] Rio Grande do Sul", Brazil.
DISTRIBUTION: Southeastern Brazil (northern Rio Grande do Sul and southern Santa Catarina).

Hyla marianae Dunn, 1926. Proc. Boston Soc. Nat. Hist., 38:129.
TYPE(S): Holotype: MCZ 11122.
TYPE LOCALITY: "Spaldings, Clarendon Parish (altitude 2900 feet)", Jamaica.
DISTRIBUTION: Jamaica, West Indies.
COMMENT: In the *Hyla wilderi* group; see Trueb and Tyler, 1974, Occas. Pap. Mus. Nat. Hist. Univ. Kansas, 24:1–60.

REVIEWERS: Albert Schwartz (AS); Richard Thomas (RT).

Hyla marmorata (Laurenti, 1768). Synops. Rept.:29.
ORIGINAL NAME: *Bufo marmoratus.*
TYPE(S): Unknown.
TYPE LOCALITY: "Surinam".
DISTRIBUTION: Amazon Basin in Brazil, Colombia, Ecuador, and Peru; southern
Venezuela; Guianas.
COMMENT: In the *Hyla marmorata* group; see Bokermann, 1964, Senckenb. Biol., 45:
243–254.

Hyla martinsi Bokermann, 1964. Neotropica, 10:67.
TYPE(S): Holotype: WCAB 14759.
TYPE LOCALITY: "región del Colegio de Caraça, Serra do Caraça, Santa Barbara,
Minas Gerais, Brasil".
DISTRIBUTION: Mountains of central Minas Gerais, Brazil.
COMMENT: In the *Hyla martinsi* group.

Hyla mathiassoni Cochran and Goin, 1970. Bull. U.S. Natl. Mus., 288:286.
TYPE(S): Holotype: FMNH 81779.
TYPE LOCALITY: "Villavicencio, [Departamento] Meta, Colombia".
DISTRIBUTION: Llanos of central Colombia.
COMMENT: In the *Hyla microcephala* group.

Hyla melanargyrea Cope, 1887. Proc. Am. Philos. Soc., 24:45.
TYPE(S): Syntypes: ANSP 11216–18.
TYPE LOCALITY: Chapada dos Guimarães, Mato Grosso, Brazil.
DISTRIBUTION: Interior basins of Mato Grosso to northeastern Brazil; Surinam
(MSH).
COMMENT: In the *Hyla marmorata* group; see comment under *Hyla senicula.*

Hyla melanomma Taylor, 1940. Univ. Kansas Sci. Bull., 26:508.
TYPE(S): Holotype: FMNH 100074 (formerly EHT-HMS 21578).
TYPE LOCALITY: "7 miles east of Chilpancingo (Ciudad Bravo), Guerrero, Mexico".
DISTRIBUTION: Pacific slopes of Sierra Madre del Sur in Guerrero and Oaxaca;
Atlantic slopes of Chiapas in southern Mexico.
COMMENT: In the *Hyla melanomma* group; see Duellman, 1970, Monogr. Mus. Nat.
Hist. Univ. Kansas, 1:397–403, who recognized two subspecies.

Hyla melanopleura Boulenger, 1912. Ann. Mag. Nat. Hist., (8)10:185.
TYPE(S): Syntypes: BM 1947.2.13.54–58.
TYPE LOCALITY: "Huancabamba, [Departamento Pasco,] E. Peru".
DISTRIBUTION: Lower Andean slopes in central Peru.

Hyla melanorhabdota (Schneider, 1799). Hist. Amph., 1:173.
ORIGINAL NAME: *Calamita melanorhabdotus.*
TYPE(S): Unknown.
TYPE LOCALITY: Brazil.
DISTRIBUTION: ? Brazil.
COMMENT: Name not assignable to any known species (WED).

Hyla meridionalis Boettger, 1874. Abh. Senckenb. Naturforsch. Ges., 9:186.
ORIGINAL NAME: *Hyla arborea* var. *meridionalis.*
TYPE(S): SMF 1872 designated lectotype by Mertens, 1967, Senckenb. Biol., 48:41.
TYPE LOCALITY: Orotava Valley Tenerife, Canary Islands [Spain].
DISTRIBUTION: Northwestern Africa and southwestern Europe, including Portugal
(Madeira), southern and eastern Spain, southern France, northwestern Italy,
and Balearic and Canary Is.

COMMENT: In the *Hyla arborea* group; see Crespo, 1973, Arq. Mus. Bocage, (2)3:613–632.

REVIEWER: Leo J. Borkin (LJB).

Hyla microcephala Cope, 1886. Proc. Am. Philos. Soc., 23:281.
TYPE(S): Syntypes: USNM 13473 (2 specimens); now lost.
TYPE LOCALITY: "Chiriqui", Panama (see comment under *Dendrobates maculatus*).
DISTRIBUTION: Southeastern Mexico, Central America, northern and eastern South America to southeastern Brazil.
COMMENT: In the *Hyla microcephala* group; see Duellman, 1970, Monogr. Mus. Nat. Hist. Univ. Kansas, 1:211; B. Lutz, 1973, Brazil. Species *Hyla*:214; and Duellman, 1974, Occas. Pap. Mus. Nat. Hist. Univ. Kansas, 27:9, who recognized five subspecies. *Hyla cherrei* Cope, 1894, Proc. Acad. Nat. Sci. Philadelphia, 46:195, was placed in the synonymy of *Hyla microcephala* by Savage and Heyer, 1970, Rev. Biol. Tropical, 16:17.

Hyla microderma Pyburn, 1977. J. Herpetol., 11:405.
TYPE(S): Holotype: UTA A-5012.
TYPE LOCALITY: "about 2 km S. Yapima (long. 69° 28' W, lat. 1° 03' N), Comisaria de Vaupés, Colombia".
DISTRIBUTION: Upper Amazon Basin in southeastern Colombia and Brazil.
COMMENT: In the *Hyla geographica* group.

Hyla microps Peters, 1872. Monatsber. Preuss. Akad. Wiss. Berlin, 1872:682.
TYPE(S): Holotype: ZMB 7472.
TYPE LOCALITY: Nova Friburgo, Rio de Janeiro, Brazil.
DISTRIBUTION: Atlantic forests of southeastern Brazil.
COMMENT: In the *Hyla parviceps* group; see Duellman and Crump, 1974, Occas. Pap. Mus. Nat. Hist. Univ. Kansas, 23:1–40, and Heyer, 1977, Proc. Biol. Soc. Washington, 93:365.

Hyla miliaria (Cope, 1886). Proc. Am. Philos. Soc., 23:272.
ORIGINAL NAME: *Hypsiboas miliarius*.
TYPE(S): Holotype: USNM 14193.
TYPE LOCALITY: "Nicaragua".
DISTRIBUTION: Nicaragua through Costa Rica and Panama to north-central Colombia.
COMMENT: In the *Hyla miliaria* group; see Duellman, 1970, Monogr. Mus. Nat. Hist. Univ. Kansas, 1:352–355. Specimens from Honduras previously allocated to this species are being described by Larry David Wilson (WED).

Hyla minima Ahl, 1933. Zool. Anz., 104:28.
TYPE(S): Holotype: NHMW 19436.
TYPE LOCALITY: Taperinha, near Santarém, Pará, Brazil.
DISTRIBUTION: Central Amazon Basin.
COMMENT: In the *Hyla minima* group; see Duellman, 1982, Amphibia-Reptilia, 3:159.

Hyla minuscula Rivero, 1971. Caribb. J. Sci., 11:1.
TYPE(S): Holotype: UPRM 3377.
TYPE LOCALITY: Nirgua, Estado Yaracay, Venezuela.
DISTRIBUTION: Interior llanos of Venezuela eastward through Guianas to Belém, Brazil.

Hyla minuta Peters, 1872. Monatsber. Preuss. Akad. Wiss. Berlin, 1872:680.
TYPE(S): Syntypes: ZMB 7456 (5 specimens).
TYPE LOCALITY: Nova Friburgo, Rio de Janeiro, Brazil.
DISTRIBUTION: Lowlands east of Andes from Colombia, Venezuela, and Trinidad southward to Bolivia, Argentina, and Uruguay.

COMMENT: For discussion see Cochran and Goin, 1970, Bull. U.S. Natl. Mus., 288: 277–280, and Cei, 1980, Monit. Zool. Ital., N.S., Monogr., 2:492–495.

Hyla miotympanum Cope, 1863. Proc. Acad. Nat. Sci. Philadelphia, 15:47.
TYPE(S): Syntypes: USNM 6311 and one with no number; now lost.
TYPE LOCALITY: Jalapa and Mirador, Veracruz, Mexico.
DISTRIBUTION: Highlands from Nuevo León to Oaxaca and central Chiapas in eastern Mexico.
COMMENT: In the *Hyla miotympanum* group; see Duellman, 1970, Monogr. Mus. Nat. Hist. Univ. Kansas, 1:372.

Hyla mixe Duellman, 1965. Herpetologica, 21:32.
TYPE(S): Holotype: KU 87110.
TYPE LOCALITY: "a stream 4.2 kilometers by road south of Campamento Vista Hermosa, (near latitude 17° 50' N and longitude 96° 20' W), at an elevation of 1,800 meters on the northern slope of Sierra de Juárez, Distrito de Ixtlán, Oaxaca, México".
DISTRIBUTION: Sierra Juárez and Sierra Madre del Sur in Oaxaca, Mexico.
COMMENT: In the *Hyla mixomaculata* group; see Duellman, 1970, Monogr. Mus. Nat. Hist. Univ. Kansas, 1:425.

Hyla mixomaculata Taylor, 1950. Copeia, 1950:274.
TYPE(S): Holotype: KU 26777.
TYPE LOCALITY: Coscomatepec, Veracruz, Mexico.
DISTRIBUTION: Central Veracruz in eastern Mexico.
COMMENT: In the *Hyla mixomaculata* group; see Duellman, 1970, Monogr. Mus. Nat. Hist. Univ. Kansas, 1:417–421.

Hyla molitor Schmidt, 1857. Sitzungsber. Akad. Wiss. Wien, Math. Naturwiss. Kl., 24:11.
TYPE(S): Syntypes: NHMW 16494; other syntypes unknown.
TYPE LOCALITY: "Chiriqui-Flusse unweit Bocca del toro", Panama; in error, according to Duellman, 1970, Monogr. Mus. Nat. Hist. Univ. Kansas, 1:650.
DISTRIBUTION: ? Bolivia (see comment).
COMMENT: Name not assigned to any known species; see Duellman, 1970, Monogr. Mus. Nat. Hist. Univ. Kansas, 1:650.

Hyla multifasciata Günther, 1859 "1858". Cat. Batr. Sal. Coll. Brit. Mus.:101.
TYPE(S): Holotype: BM 1947.2.23.6.
TYPE LOCALITY "Para", Brazil; stated as Belém, Pará, Brazil, by Duellman, 1977, Das Tierreich, 95:78.
DISTRIBUTION: Lowlands of eastern Venezuela, Guianas, and Amazon Basin, Brazil.
COMMENT: In the *Hyla albopunctata* group.

Hyla musica B. Lutz, 1949. Mem. Inst. Oswaldo Cruz, Rio de Janeiro, 46:576.
TYPE(S): Syntypes: MN 3203–19.
TYPE LOCALITY: Parque Nacional Serra dos Órgãos, Teresópolis, Rio de Janeiro, Brazil.
DISTRIBUTION: Serra dos Órgãos, southeastern Brazil.
COMMENT: See Cochran, 1955, Bull. U.S. Natl. Mus., 206:170. In the *Hyla albomarginata* group, according to Duellman, 1970, Monogr. Mus. Nat. Hist. Univ. Kansas, 1:240.

Hyla mykter Adler and Dennis, 1972. Occas. Pap. Mus. Nat. Hist. Univ. Kansas, 7:8.
TYPE(S): Holotype: KU 137553.
TYPE LOCALITY: "11.4 km (by road) southwest of Puerto del Gallo, Guerrero, México (about 35 km airline northeast of Atoyác de Álvarez, elevation 1985 meters".
DISTRIBUTION: Vicinity of Cerro Teótepec, Sierra Madre del Sur, Guerrero, Mexico.

COMMENT: In the *Hyla bistincta* group, according to the original description.

Hyla nahdereri B. Lutz and Bokermann, 1963. Copeia, 1963:559.
  TYPE(S): Syntypes: MN 3294–96.
  TYPE LOCALITY: "at Estrada Saraiva, outside and slightly below São Bento do Sul, a small town in northern Santa Catarina, Brazil (26° 14' 55" S, 49° 22' 50" W, 800 m alt.)".
  DISTRIBUTION: Serra do Mar in Santa Catarina, Brazil.
  COMMENT: In the *Hyla marmorata* group, according to the original description.

Hyla nana Boulenger, 1889. Ann. Mus. Civ. Stor. Nat. Genova, (2)7:249.
  TYPE(S): Syntypes: BM 1947.2.12.83–85 and MSNG 29721A; MSNG 29721A designated lectotype by Capocaccia, 1957, Ann. Mus. Civ. Stor. Nat. Genova, 69:213.
  TYPE LOCALITY: "Colonia Resistencia, South Chaco, Argentine Republic".
  DISTRIBUTION: Northeastern Brazil southward through central Paraguay, northern Argentina, eastern Bolivia; extreme southern Brazil, Uruguay, and La Plata Basin in Argentina.
  COMMENT: In the *Hyla nana* group. See Cei, 1980, Monit. Zool. Ital., N.S., Monogr., 2:495–498. *Hyla sanborni* Schmidt, 1944, Field Mus. Nat. Hist. Publ., Zool. Ser., 29:153 (Holotype: FMNH 9581; Type locality: Hacienda Alvarez, 15 km NE San Carlos, Uruguay; Distribution: Southern Paraguay, central and eastern Argentina, and Uruguay) is probably a distinct species (NJS). See Barrio, 1967, Physis, Buenos Aires, 26:521–524, for subspecies.

Hyla nanuzae Bokermann and Sazima, 1974. Rev. Brasil. Biol., 33:333.
  TYPE(S): Holotype: WCAB 45808.
  TYPE LOCALITY: Kilometer 126, Serra do Cipó, Jaboticatubas, Minas Gerais, Brazil.
  DISTRIBUTION: Known only from the type locality.
  COMMENT: In the *Hyla circumdata* group, according to the original description.

Hyla novaisi Bokermann, 1968. J. Herpetol., 1:26.
  TYPE(S): Holotype: WCAB 31743.
  TYPE LOCALITY: "'Fazenda Santo Onofre,' 10 km east of Maracás, Bahia, Brazil".
  DISTRIBUTION: Bahia, Brazil.
  COMMENT: In the *Hyla marmorata* group; see comment under *Hyla senicula*.

Hyla nubicola Duellman, 1964. Herpetologica, 19:225.
  TYPE(S): Holotype: UMMZ 118160.
  TYPE LOCALITY: "stream 3 kilometers southwest of Huatusco, Veracruz, Mexico (elevation 1,325 meters)".
  DISTRIBUTION: Mountains of central Veracruz in eastern Mexico.
  COMMENT: In the *Hyla mixomaculata* group; see Duellman, 1970, Monogr. Mus. Nat. Hist. Univ. Kansas, 1:423–425.

Hyla ocapia Andersson, 1938. Ark. Zool., 30A(23):19.
  TYPE(S): Syntypes: NHRM 1873 (7 specimens).
  TYPE LOCALITY: Puka Khara, Bolivia.
  DISTRIBUTION: Eastern slopes of Andes in Bolivia.
  COMMENT: In the *Hyla ocapia* group.

Hyla oliveirai Bokermann, 1963. Atas Soc. Biol. Rio de Janeiro, 7(2):6.
  TYPE(S): Holotype: WCAB 12306.
  TYPE LOCALITY: "Maracás, Bahia, Brasil".
  DISTRIBUTION: Xeric areas of Bahia, Brazil.
  COMMENT: Related to *Hyla decipiens*, according to the original description.

Hyla ornatissima Noble, 1923. Zoologica, New York, 3:291.
  TYPE(S): Holotype: AMNH 13491.
  TYPE LOCALITY: Meamu, Mazaruni River, Guyana.
  DISTRIBUTION: Guianas and Amapá, Brazil.

COMMENT: In the *Hyla granosa* group; see Hoogmoed, 1979, Zool. Verh., Leiden, 172:15.

Hyla pachyderma Taylor, 1942. Univ. Kansas Sci. Bull., 28:308.
TYPE(S): Holotype: USNM 115029.
TYPE LOCALITY: "Pan de Olla [in Puebla], south of Tezuitlán, Veracruz", Mexico.
DISTRIBUTION: Known only from the type locality.
COMMENT: In the *Hyla bistincta* group; see Duellman, 1970, Monogr. Mus. Nat. Hist. Univ. Kansas, 1:473–475.

Hyla palliata Cope, 1863. Proc. Acad. Nat. Sci. Philadelphia, 15:47.
TYPE(S): Formerly Smithsonian Museum (USNM) 6225; now lost.
TYPE LOCALITY: "Paraguay".
DISTRIBUTION: Known only from the type locality.
COMMENT: This name has not been assigned to any known species (WED).

Hyla palmeri Boulenger, 1908. Ann. Mag. Nat. Hist., (8)2:515.
TYPE(S): Syntypes: BM 1907.2.13.32–33.
TYPE LOCALITY: Jiménez, Departamento Valle, Colombia.
DISTRIBUTION: Central Panama and Pacific slopes of Colombia and Ecuador.
COMMENT: In the *Hyla bogotensis* group; see Myers and Duellman, 1982, Am. Mus. Novit., 2752:23.

Hyla pantosticta Duellman and Berger, 1982. Herpetologica, 38:456.
TYPE(S): Holotype: KU 190000.
TYPE LOCALITY: 0.5 km S Santa Barbara on road to La Bonita, 2650 m, Provincia Carchi, Ecuador.
DISTRIBUTION: Upper Río Chingual Valley on eastern slopes of Andes in Colombia and Ecuador.
COMMENT: In the *Hyla larinopygion* group.

Hyla pardalis Spix, 1824. Spec. Nov. Testud. Ran. Brasil.:34.
TYPE(S): Syntypes: ZSM 2499 (2 specimens), now lost; see Hoogmoed and Gruber, 1983, Spixiana, Suppl., 9:366, for discussion.
TYPE LOCALITY: "Rio de Janeiro", Brazil.
DISTRIBUTION: Central and eastern Brazil to São Paulo; to Misiones, Argentina.
COMMENT: In the *Hyla boans* group; see Lutz, 1973, Brazil. Spec. *Hyla*:26–29, and Cei, 1980, Monit. Zool. Ital., N.S., Monogr., 2:459–462. See comment under *Hyla biobeba*.

Hyla parviceps Boulenger, 1882. Cat. Batr. Sal. Brit. Mus.:393.
TYPE(S): Holotype: BM 1947.2.13.5.
TYPE LOCALITY: "Sarayacu", Provincia Pastaza, Ecuador.
DISTRIBUTION: Upper Amazon Basin in Brazil, Colombia, Ecuador, and Peru.
COMMENT: In the *Hyla parviceps* group; see Duellman and Crump, 1974, Occas. Pap. Mus. Nat. Hist. Univ. Kansas, 23:1–40.

Hyla pauiniensis Heyer, 1977. Pap. Avulsos Zool., São Paulo, 31:145.
TYPE(S): Holotype: MZUSP 49892.
TYPE LOCALITY: Boca do Pauini, Amazonas, Brazil.
DISTRIBUTION: Known only from the type locality in central Amazon Basin.
COMMENT: In the *Hyla parviceps* group according to the original description.

Hyla pellita Duellman, 1968. Univ. Kansas Publ. Mus. Nat. Hist., 17:568.
TYPE(S): Holotype: KU 100970.
TYPE LOCALITY: "33 kilometers north of San Gabriel Mixtepec, Oaxaca, México, elevation 1675 meters".
DISTRIBUTION: Pacific slopes of the Sierra Madre del Sur in Oaxaca, Mexico.

COMMENT: In the *Hyla mixomaculata* group; see Duellman, 1970, Monogr. Mus. Nat. Hist. Univ. Kansas, 1:421–423.

Hyla pellucens Werner, 1901. Verh. Zool. Bot. Ges. Wien, 50:600.
   TYPE(S): Holotype: ZMB 16590.
   TYPE LOCALITY: "Palmar (100 m., westliche der Anden", Ecuador; Duellman, 1977, Das Tierreich, 95:82, thought this might be Palmar on Río Chila, Provincia Manabí, Ecuador.
   DISTRIBUTION: Pacific lowlands of Colombia and Ecuador.
   COMMENT: See Duellman, 1971, Herpetologica, 27:212–227, and Duellman, 1974, Occas. Pap. Mus. Nat. Hist. Univ. Kansas, 27:1–27.

Hyla pentheter Adler, 1965. Occas. Pap. Mus. Zool. Univ. Michigan, 642:5.
   TYPE(S): Holotype: UMMZ 125381.
   TYPE LOCALITY: "37 km N of San Gabriel Mixtepec (about 100 km airline SSW of Oaxaca de Juárez), 1700 m", Oaxaca, Mexico.
   DISTRIBUTION: Pacific slopes of the Sierra Madre del Sur in Oaxaca and Guerrero, Mexico.
   COMMENT: In the *Hyla bistincta* group. See Duellman, 1970, Monogr. Mus. Nat. Hist. Univ. Kansas, 1:462–466.

Hyla phlebodes Stejneger, 1906. Proc. U.S. Natl. Mus., 30:817.
   TYPE(S): Holotype: USNM 2997.
   TYPE LOCALITY: "San Carlos" (Llanuras de San Carlos), Provincia Alajuela, Costa Rica.
   DISTRIBUTION: Caribbean lowlands from southern Nicaragua to Panama and Pacific lowlands of eastern Panama and northwestern Colombia.
   COMMENT: In the *Hyla microcephala* group; see Duellman, 1970, Monogr. Mus. Nat. Hist. Univ. Kansas, 1:220.

Hyla phyllognatha Melin, 1941. Göteborgs K. Vetensk. Vitterh. Samh. Handl., (B)1(4):30.
   TYPE(S): Holotype: NHMG 474.
   TYPE LOCALITY: Roque, Departamento San Martín, Peru.
   DISTRIBUTION: Amazonian slopes of Andes in Colombia, Ecuador, and Peru.
   COMMENT: In the *Hyla bogotensis* group; see Duellman, 1972, Occas. Pap. Mus. Nat. Hist. Univ. Kansas, 11:1–31.

Hyla picadoi Dunn, 1937. Copeia, 1937:164.
   TYPE(S): Holotype: MCZ 16002.
   TYPE LOCALITY: Volcán Barba, Provincia Heredia, Costa Rica.
   DISTRIBUTION: Mountains of Costa Rica and western Panama.
   COMMENT: In the *Hyla zeteki* group; see Duellman, 1970, Monogr. Mus. Nat. Hist. Univ. Kansas, 1:319–323.

Hyla piceigularis Ruíz-C. and Lynch, 1982. Caldasia, 13:659.
   TYPE(S): Holotype: ICN 5180.
   TYPE LOCALITY: "Cabeceras del río Luisito (tributary del río Oibita), Municipio El Encino, Departamento Santander, vertiente oriental de la Cordillera, Colombia: altura 1.750 m.s.n.m., Long. 73° 17' 17" W de Greenwich, Lat. 6° 5' 54" N".
   DISTRIBUTION: Known only from the type locality in Cordillera Oriental of Andes.
   COMMENT: In the *Hyla bogotensis* group according to the original description.

Hyla picta (Günther, 1901). Biol. Cent. Am., Rept. Batr.:286.
   ORIGINAL NAME: *Hylella picta*.
   TYPE(S): Holotype: BM 1947.2.22.62.
   TYPE LOCALITY: Jalapa, Veracruz, Mexico.
   DISTRIBUTION: Atlantic lowlands of Mexico, Guatemala, and Honduras.

COMMENT: In the *Hyla picta* group; see Duellman, 1970, Monogr. Mus. Nat. Hist. Univ. Kansas, 1:365–367.

Hyla pictipes Cope, 1876. J. Acad. Nat. Sci. Philadelphia, (2)8:106.
ORIGINAL NAME: *Hyla punctariola pictipes*.
TYPE(S): Syntypes: USNM 30631, 30652.
TYPE LOCALITY: Pico Blanco, Provincia Limón, Costa Rica.
DISTRIBUTION: Mountains of Costa Rica and western Panama.
COMMENT: Sole member of the *Hyla pictipes* group; see Duellman, 1970, Monogr. Mus. Nat. Hist. Univ. Kansas, 1:295.

Hyla picturata Boulenger, 1882. Ann. Mag. Nat. Hist., (7)3:276.
TYPE(S): Holotype: BM 1947.2.13.35.
TYPE LOCALITY: "Paramba, [Province Imbabura,] N. W. Ecuador".
DISTRIBUTION: Pacific lowlands of southwestern Colombia and northwestern Ecuador.
COMMENT: Questionably in the *Hyla geographica* group (WED).

Hyla pinima Bokermann and Sazima, 1974 "1973". Rev. Brasil. Biol., 33:525.
TYPE(S): Holotype: WCAB 46238.
TYPE LOCALITY: Kilometer 132, Serra do Cipó, Jaboticatubas, Minas Gerais, Brazil.
DISTRIBUTION: Minas Gerais and Rio Grande do Sul, Brazil.
COMMENT: Without known affinities, according to the original description.

Hyla pinorum Taylor, 1937. Proc. Biol. Soc. Washington, 50:46.
TYPE(S): Holotype: UIMNH 25049 (formerly EHT-HMS 5972).
TYPE LOCALITY: "in pines on Mexico–Acapulco highway between kilometers 350 and 351, near a spring known as Agua del Obispo, between the towns of Rincon and Cajones", Guerrero, Mexico.
DISTRIBUTION: Pacific slopes of Sierra Madre del Sur in southern Mexico.
COMMENT: In the *Hyla melanomma* group; see Duellman, 1970, Monogr. Mus. Nat. Hist. Univ. Kansas, 1:403–408.

Hyla platydactyla Boulenger, 1905. Ann. Mag. Nat. Hist., (7)16:183.
TYPE(S): Holotype: BM 1947.2.13.14.
TYPE LOCALITY: "Merida, Andes of Venezuela".
DISTRIBUTION: Mérida Andes in western Venezuela.
COMMENT: In the *Hyla bogotensis* group; see Duellman, 1972, Occas. Pap. Mus. Nat. Hist. Univ. Kansas, 11:1–31. Differences in calls, morphology, and larval features in various parts of the Mérida Andes suggest that more than one species may be recognizable and that the nominal taxa *Hyla jahni* and *Hyla paramica* Rivero, 1961, Bull. Mus. Comp. Zool., 126:112–113, may be recognizable species in the *Hyla bogotensis* group (WED); these names were synonymized with *Hyla platydactyla* by Duellman, 1972, Occas. Pap. Mus. Nat. Hist. Univ. Kansas, 11:1–31. This synonymy was discussed and supported by Ruíz and Lynch, 1982, Caldasia, 13:655–657.

Hyla plicata Brocchi, 1877. Bull. Soc. Philomath. Paris, (7)1:126.
TYPE(S): Holotype: MNHNP 6317.
TYPE LOCALITY: "Mexique".
DISTRIBUTION: High mountains of Sierra Madre Oriental and Cordillera Volcánica in southern Mexico.
COMMENT: In the *Hyla eximia* group; see Duellman, 1970, Monogr. Mus. Nat. Hist. Univ. Kansas, 1:496–497.

Hyla polytaenia Cope, 1869. Proc. Am. Philos. Soc., 11:164.
TYPE(S): Syntypes: MCZ 1544 (2 specimens).
TYPF LOCALITY: "Brasil".
DISTRIBUTION: Southeastern Brazil from Minas Gerais to Santa Catarina; eastern Paraguay and northhestern Argentina.

COMMENT: In the *Hyla polytaenia* group. See Cei, 1980, Monit. Zool. Ital., N.S., Monogr., 2:479–480.

Hyla praestans Duellman and Trueb, 1983. *In* Rhodin and Miyata (eds.), Adv. Herpetol. Evol. Biol.:43.
TYPE(S): Holotype: KU 169575.
TYPE LOCALITY: "Parque Arqueológica San Agustín, 3 km southwest of the village of San Agustín, Departamento de Huila, Colombia (1° 53' N, 76° 16' W), 1750 m".
DISTRIBUTION: Eastern slopes of Cordillera Central and upper Río Magdalena Valley, Colombia.
COMMENT: In the *Hyla columbiana* group.

Hyla prasina Burmeister, 1856. Erläut. Fauna Brasil.:106.
TYPE(S): Holotype: ZMB 4675.
TYPE LOCALITY: Nova Friburgo, Rio de Janeiro, Brazil.
DISTRIBUTION: Moderate elevations in southeastern Brazil (Minas Gerais, Rio de Janeiro, and São Paulo).
COMMENT: In the *Hyla pulchella* group, according to Lutz, 1973, Brazil. Spec. *Hyla*: 83.

Hyla pseudopseudis Miranda-Ribeiro, 1937. Campo, Rio de Janeiro, 1937:68.
TYPE(S): Holotype: MN 579.
TYPE LOCALITY: Veadeiros, Goiás, Brazil.
DISTRIBUTION: Interior highlands of Brazil.

Hyla pseudopuma Günther, 1901. Biol. Cent. Am., Rept. Batr.:274.
TYPE(S): Syntypes: BM 96.10.8.61–67, 1902.1.28.25–26.
TYPE LOCALITY: La Palma, Provincia San José, Costa Rica.
DISTRIBUTION: Mountains of Costa Rica and western Panama.
COMMENT: In the *Hyla pseudopuma* group; two subspecies were recognized by Duellman, 1970, Monogr. Mus. Nat. Hist. Univ. Kansas, 1:263.

Hyla pugnax Schmidt, 1857. Sitzungsber. Akad. Wiss. Wien, Math. Naturwiss. Kl., 24:11.
TYPE(S): Holotype: KM 1009.
TYPE LOCALITY: "Chiriqui-Flusse unweit Bocca del toro", Panama.
DISTRIBUTION: Central Panama, Caribbean lowlands and valleys of the Río Cauca and Río Magdalena in Colombia.
COMMENT: In the *Hyla boans* group; this species was shown to be distinct from *Hyla crepitans* by Kluge, 1979, Occas. Pap. Mus. Zool. Univ. Michigan, 688: 1–24.

Hyla pulchella Duméril and Bibron, 1841. Erp. Gén., 8:588.
TYPE(S): Syntypes: MNHNP 163 and 4836.
TYPE LOCALITY: "Montévidéo", Uruguay.
DISTRIBUTION: Southeastern Brazil, Uruguay, Bolivia, southern Paraguay, and northern Argentina.
COMMENT: In the *Hyla pulchella* group. Some of the five recognized subspecies may be specifically distinct; see Barrio, 1965, Physis, Buenos Aires, 25:115–128, and Lutz, 1973, Brazil. Spec. *Hyla*:74–81. See also Cei, 1980, Monit. Zool. Ital., N.S., Monogr., 2:469–476. See comment under *Hyla cymbalum*.

Hyla pulchrilineata Cope, 1869. Proc. Acad. Nat. Sci. Philadelphia, 11:163.
TYPE(S): Holotype: ANSP 14495.
TYPE LOCALITY: "East St. Domingo", Hispaniola, West Indies.
DISTRIBUTION: Hispaniola, West Indies.
COMMENT: In the *Hyla pulchrilineata* group; see Trueb and Tyler, 1974, Occas. Pap. Mus. Nat. Hist. Univ. Kansas, 24:1–60.

REVIEWERS: Albert Schwartz (AS); Richard Thomas (RT).

Hyla punctata (Schneider, 1799). Hist. Amph., 1:170.
ORIGINAL NAME: *Calamita punctatus*.
TYPE(S): Syntypes: NHRM 155 (2 specimens).
TYPE LOCALITY: "Surinam".
DISTRIBUTION: The Amazon Basin; upper Orinoco Basin; central Brazil; Chaco of
  Paraguay, and Argentina; Guianas, northern Colombia and Trinidad.
COMMENT: *Hyla punctata rubrolineata* Lutz, 1951, Mem. Inst. Oswaldo Cruz, Rio de
  Janeiro, 47:307 (reviewed by Cei, 1980, Monit. Zool. Ital., N.S., Monogr., 2:
  482–484) may be a recognizable species (WED), as is *Hyla hobbsi* (see Pyburn,
  1978, Proc. Biol. Soc. Washington, 91:123); both of these were considered to
  be synonyms of *Hyla punctata* by Duellman, 1974, Occas. Pap. Mus. Nat. Hist.
  Univ. Kansas, 27:1–27. See Hoogmoed and Gruber, 1983, Spixiana, Suppl., 9:
  365, for discussion of some of the synonyms.

Hyla quadrilineata (Schneider, 1799). Hist. Amph., 1:169.
ORIGINAL NAME: *Calamita quadrilineatus*.
TYPE(S): Unknown.
TYPE LOCALITY: Unknown.
DISTRIBUTION: Unknown.
COMMENT: This name has not been assigned to any known population (WED).

Hyla raniceps (Cope, 1862). Proc. Acad. Nat. Sci. Philadelphia, 14:353.
ORIGINAL NAME: *Hypsiboas raniceps*.
TYPE(S): Syntypes: USNM 5403 (3 specimens), 5408, 12160, 12172 (2 specimens).
TYPE LOCALITY: "Paraguay".
DISTRIBUTION: French Guiana, eastern Brazil, Paraguay, northern Argentina, and
  eastern Bolivia.
COMMENT: In the *Hyla albopunctata* group. See Cei, 1980, Monit. Zool. Ital., N.S.,
  Monogr., 2:463–466.

Hyla regilla Baird and Girard, 1852. Proc. Acad. Nat. Sci. Philadelphia, 6:174.
TYPE(S): Syntypes: USNM 9182 (Puget Sound), USNM 15409 (Sacramento River);
  USNM 9182 designated lectotype by Jameson, Mackey, and Richmond, 1966,
  Proc. California Acad. Sci., 33:553.
TYPE LOCALITY: Puget Sound, Washington, and Sacramento River, California, USA;
  restricted to "Sacramento County, California", USA, by Schmidt, 1953, Cat.
  Am. Amph. Rept., Ed. 6:72; restricted to Fort Vancouver, Washington, USA,
  by lectotype designation of Jameson, Mackey, and Richmond, 1966, Proc.
  California Acad. Sci., 33:553.
DISTRIBUTION: Western North America from southern British Columbia (Canada)
  and western Montana (USA) to southern Baja California (Mexico).
COMMENT: In the *Hyla eximia* group; see Jameson, Mackey, and Richmond, 1966,
  Proc. California Acad. Sci. 33:551–620, and Duellman, 1970, Monogr. Mus.
  Nat. Hist. Univ. Kansas, 1:484–493; seven subspecies are recognized.

Hyla rhodopepla Günther, 1859 "1858". Cat. Batr. Sal. Coll. Brit. Mus.:112.
TYPE(S): Holotype: BM 1947.2.23.53.
TYPE LOCALITY: "Andes of Ecuador".
DISTRIBUTION: Upper Amazon Basin from southern Colombia to Bolivia.
COMMENT: In the *Hyla microcephala* group; see Duellman, 1972, Herpetologica, 28:
  369–375.

Hyla riveroi Cochran and Goin, 1970. Bull. U.S. Natl. Mus., 288:284.
TYPE(S): Holotype: CM 37433.
TYPE LOCALITY: "Leticia, Amazonas, Colombia."
DISTRIBUTION: Upper Amazon Basin in Colombia, Ecuador, and western Brazil;
  probably in adjacent Peru.

COMMENT: In the *Hyla minima* group; see Duellman, 1982, Amphibia-Reptilia, 3: 159.

Hyla rivularis Taylor, 1952. Univ. Kansas Sci. Bull., 35:847.
TYPE(S): Holotype: KU 28197.
TYPE LOCALITY: "American Cinchona Plantation (Isla Bonita), eastern slope of Volcán Poás, [Provincia Heredia,] Costa Rica, elevation 5,500 ft."
DISTRIBUTION: Mountains of Costa Rica and western Panama.
COMMENT: In the *Hyla rivularis* group; see Duellman, 1970, Monogr. Mus. Nat. Hist. Univ. Kansas, 1:284–289.

Hyla robertmertensi Taylor, 1937. Proc. Biol. Soc. Washington, 50:43.
TYPE(S): Holotype: FMNH 100096 (formerly EHT-HMS 2270).
TYPE LOCALITY: "near Tapachula, Chiapas", Mexico.
DISTRIBUTION: Pacific lowlands from eastern Oaxaca, Mexico, to El Salvador; Cintalapa Valley in Chiapas, Mexico.
COMMENT: In the *Hyla microcephala* group; see Duellman, 1970, Monogr. Mus. Nat. Hist. Univ. Kansas, 1:217.

Hyla robertsorum Taylor, 1940. Univ. Kansas Sci. Bull., 26:393.
TYPE(S): Holotype: FMNH 100124 (formerly EHT-HMS 16264).
TYPE LOCALITY: "El Chico National Park, Hidalgo", Mexico.
DISTRIBUTION: Sierra Madre Oriental in eastern Mexico (Puebla and Hidalgo).
COMMENT: In the *Hyla bistincta* group; see Duellman, 1970, Monogr. Mus. Nat. Hist. Univ. Kansas, 1:470–473.

Hyla rodriguezi Rivero, 1968. Breviora, 307:1.
TYPE(S): Holotype: MCZ 64740.
TYPE LOCALITY: Paso del Danto, Region de La Escalera, 1400 meters, road from El Dorado to Santa Elena de Uairén, Estado Bolívar, Venezuela.
DISTRIBUTION: La Escalera region and Gran Sabana, Bolívar, Venezuela.
COMMENT: This species probably belongs in *Osteocephalus* (WED and MSH).

Hyla roeschmanni DeGrys, 1938. Zool. Anz., 124:315.
TYPE(S): Formerly in ZMH; destroyed.
TYPE LOCALITY: Beni, Bolivia.
DISTRIBUTION: Known only from the type locality.
COMMENT: This name has not been associated with any known population (WED).

Hyla rosenbergi Boulenger, 1898. Proc. Zool. Soc. London, 1898:123.
TYPE(S): Syntypes: BM 1947.2.12.71–75.
TYPE LOCALITY: "Cachabé" (=Cachabí), Provincia Esmeraldas, Ecuador.
DISTRIBUTION: Pacific lowlands from southern Costa Rica to northwestern Ecuador.
COMMENT: In the *Hyla boans* group; see Kluge, 1979, Occas. Pap. Mus. Zool. Univ. Michigan, 688:1–24.

Hyla rossalleni Goin, 1959. Copeia, 1959:340.
TYPE(S): Holotype: FSM 8501.
TYPE LOCALITY: Leticia, Comisaria Amazonas, Colombia.
DISTRIBUTION: Upper Amazon Basin in Ecuador, Peru, southeastern Colombia, and northeastern Bolivia; Brazilian Amazonia.
COMMENT: *Hyla rossalleni* is a replacement name for *Hyla alleni* Goin, 1957, J. Washington Acad. Sci., 47:60. In the *Hyla minima* group; see Duellman, 1982, Amphibia-Reptilia, 3:159.

Hyla rubicundula Reinhardt and Lütken, 1862. Vidensk. Medd. Dansk Naturhist. Foren., 3:197.
TYPE(S): Syntypes: NHMW 16511, ZMUC 1440–41.
TYPE LOCALITY: Lagoa Santa, Minas Gerais, Brazil.
DISTRIBUTION: Southern Pará to central Minas Gerais and São Paulo, Brazil, and eastern Paraguay.

COMMENT: In the *Hyla rubicundula* group.

Hyla rubracyla Cochran and Goin, 1970. Bull. U.S. Natl. Mus., 288:229.
TYPE(S): Holotype: USNM 157820.
TYPE LOCALITY: "Río Calima, near Córdoba, [Departamento] Valle, Colombia".
DISTRIBUTION: Pacific lowlands of Colombia.
COMMENT: In the *Hyla albomarginata* group; see Duellman, 1974, Occas. Pap. Mus. Nat. Hist. Univ. Kansas, 27:13.

Hyla rufioculis Taylor, 1952. Univ. Kansas Sci. Bull., 35:827.
TYPE(S): Holotype: KU 28216.
TYPE LOCALITY: "Isla Bonita (American Cinchona Plantation), eastern slope of Volcán Poás, [Provincia Heredia,] Costa Rica".
DISTRIBUTION: Mountains of Costa Rica.
COMMENT: In the *Hyla uranochroa* group; see Duellman, 1970, Monogr. Mus. Nat. Hist. Univ. Kansas, 1:307-311.

Hyla rufitela Fouquette, 1961. Fieldiana: Zool., 39:595.
TYPE(S): Holotype: FMNH 13053.
TYPE LOCALITY: Barro Colorado Island, Canal Zone, Panama.
DISTRIBUTION: Caribbean lowlands from Nicaragua to Panama; Golfo Dulce region of Costa Rica.
COMMENT: In the *Hyla albomarginata* group; see Duellman, 1970, Monogr. Mus. Nat. Hist. Univ. Kansas, 1:240-245.

Hyla sabrina Caldwell, 1974. Occas. Pap. Mus. Nat. Hist. Univ. Kansas, 23:12.
TYPE(S): Holotype: KU 137086.
TYPE LOCALITY: 16.6 km south of Vista Hermosa, 2020 m, Oaxaca, Mexico.
DISTRIBUTION: Moderate elevations on north slopes of Sierra de Juárez, Oaxaca, Mexico.
COMMENT: In the *Hyla bistincta* group according to the original description.

Hyla salvadorensis Mertens, 1952. Senckenb. Biol., 33:169.
TYPE(S): Holotype: SMF 43045.
TYPE LOCALITY: Hacienda San José, Sierra Metapán, Departamento Santa Ana, El Salvador.
DISTRIBUTION: Pacific slopes of El Salvador and Honduras.
COMMENT: In the *Hyla salvadorensis* group; see Duellman, 1970, Monogr. Mus. Nat. Hist. Univ. Kansas, 1:337-341.

Hyla sanchiangensis Pope, 1929. Am. Mus. Novit., 352:2.
TYPE(S): Holotype: AMNH 30198.
TYPE LOCALITY: "San Chiang, Chungan Hsien, northwestern Fukien [=Fujian] Province, China, 3000-3500 feet altitude".
DISTRIBUTION: Northwestern Fujian, Guangxi, Guizhou, Anhui, Zhejiang, Hunan, and Jiangxi, China.
COMMENT: In the *Hyla arborea* group; closely allied to *Hyla chinensis*, according to the original description. See Liu and Hu, 1961, Tailless Amph. China:135, and Ma et al., 1982, Nat. Hist., Shanghai, 1:37.
REVIEWERS: Leo J. Borkin (LJB); Shuqin Hu (SH); Masafumi Matsui (MM); Ermi Zhao (EZ).

Hyla sarampiona Ruíz-C. and Lynch, 1982. Caldasia, 13:664.
TYPE(S): Holotype: ICN 7440.
TYPE LOCALITY: "Quebrada Sopladero, Parque Nacional Natural de Munchique, 33 km NNE of La Uribe, flanco occidental de la Cordillera Occidental, 2.190 m. s. n. m., Departamento del Cauca, Colombia".
DISTRIBUTION: Known only from the type locality on the western slopes of Cordillera Occidental of Andes.

COMMENT: In the *Hyla larinopygion* group according to original description.

Hyla sarayacuensis Shreve, 1935. Occas. Pap. Boston Soc. Nat. Hist., 8:215.
ORIGINAL NAME: *Hyla leucophyllata sarayacuensis.*
TYPE(S): Holotype: MCZ 19729.
TYPE LOCALITY: Sarayacu, Provincia Pastaza, Ecuador.
DISTRIBUTION: Upper Amazon Basin in Colombia, Ecuador, Peru, and Brazil.
COMMENT: In the *Hyla leucophyllata* group; see Duellman, 1974, Occas. Pap. Mus. Nat. Hist. Univ. Kansas, 27:18.

Hyla sarda De Betta, 1853. Mem. Accad. Agric. Commerc. Arti, Verona, 35:284.
TYPE(S): Unknown.
TYPE LOCALITY: Sardinia [Italy].
DISTRIBUTION: Sardinia (Italy), Corsica (France), and nearby islands in the Tyrrhenian Sea.
COMMENT: In the *Hyla arborea* group. Elevated from status as a subspecies of *Hyla arborea* by Lanza, 1983, Lav. Soc. Ital. Biogeogr., N.S., 8:730.

Hyla sartori Smith, 1951. Herpetologica, 7:186.
ORIGINAL NAME: *Hyla microcephala sartori.*
TYPE(S): Holotype: UIMNH 20934.
TYPE LOCALITY: 1 mi. north of Organos, south of El Treinta, Guerrero, Mexico.
DISTRIBUTION: Pacific slopes of southwestern Mexico (Jalisco to Oaxaca).
COMMENT: In the *Hyla microcephala* group; see Duellman, 1970, Monogr. Mus. Nat. Hist. Univ. Kansas, 1:223.

Hyla savignyi Audouin, 1827. Descr. Égypte, 1:183.
TYPE(S): Unknown.
TYPE LOCALITY: Western Syria.
DISTRIBUTION: Syria and southern Turkey to northern and western Iran, and southern Armenia and Azerbaijan in USSR; southern Arabian Peninsula.
COMMENT: In the *Hyla arborea* group. This species was regarded as distinct from *Hyla arborea* by Schneider, 1974, Oecologia, Berlin, 14:99–110.
REVIEWERS: Steven C. Anderson (SCA); Leo J. Borkin (LJB).

Hyla sazimai Cardoso and Andrade, 1983 "1982". Rev. Brasil. Biol., 42:589.
TYPE(S): Holotype: MN 4149.
TYPE LOCALITY: "Chapadão da Zagaia, Parque Nacional Serra da Canastra, São Roque de Minas, Minas Gerais, Brasil (46° 50′ W 20° 10′ S; approx. 1350 m alt.)".
DISTRIBUTION: Known only from the type locality.
COMMENT: In the *Hyla circumdata* group, according to the original description.

Hyla schubarti Bokermann, 1963. Rev. Brasil. Biol., 23:249.
TYPE(S): Holotype: WCAB 7848.
TYPE LOCALITY: "Rondônia, Território [now Estado] de Rondônia", Brazil.
DISTRIBUTION: Brazilian Amazonia.

Hyla secedens B. Lutz, 1963. Copeia, 1963:561.
TYPE(S): Holotype: MN 3591.
TYPE LOCALITY: Barro Branco, Rio de Janeiro, Brazil.
DISTRIBUTION: Serra dos Órgãos, southeastern Brazil.

Hyla semiguttata A. Lutz, 1925. C. R. Séances Soc. Biol., Paris, 93:211.
TYPE(S): Holotype: MN 68.
TYPE LOCALITY: São Bento do Sul, Santa Catarina, Brazil.
DISTRIBUTION: Highlands of extreme southeastern Brazil (Rio Grande do Sul and Santa Catarina) and extreme northeastern Argentina (Misiones).

COMMENT: See Cei, 1980, Monit. Zool. Ital., N.S., Monogr., 2:477.

Hyla senicula Cope, 1868. Proc. Acad. Nat. Sci. Philadelphia, 20:111.
TYPE(S): Unknown.
TYPE LOCALITY: Corcovado, Rio de Janeiro, Brazil; Lutz, 1973, Brazil. Spec. *Hyla*:88,
    rendered the type locality as "Laranjeiras, a residential part of Rio de Janeiro,
    below Corcovado Mountain".
DISTRIBUTION: Coastal region of southeastern Brazil (Espírito Santo and Rio de
    Janeiro).
COMMENT: In the *Hyla marmorata* group. *Hyla senicula* is a replacement name for
    Hyla marmorata Burmeister, 1856, Erläut. Fauna Brasil.:93. See Bokermann,
    1964, Senckenb. Biol., 45:252. Lutz, 1977, Brazil. Spec. *Hyla*:88–93, regarded
    Hyla acreana, *Hyla melanargyrea*, and *Hyla novaisi* as subspecies of *Hyla senicula*.
    Heyer, 1977, Pap. Avulsos Zool., São Paulo, 31:141–162, re-elevated *Hyla*
    acreana to species status. Caramaschi and Jim, 1983, Rev. Brasil. Biol., 43:198,
    disputed the subspecific status of *Hyla melanargyrea* and *Hyla novaisi*, and
    elevated them to species status.

Hyla sibleszi Rivero, 1971. Caribb. J. Sci., 11:182.
TYPE(S): Holotype: UPRM 3177.
TYPE LOCALITY: Paso del Danto, La Escalera, between El Dorado and Santa Elena de
    Uairén, 1300–1400 m., Serranía de Lema, Estado Bolívar, Venezuela.
DISTRIBUTION: Moderate elevations in the southwestern Venezuela and adjacent
    Guyana.
COMMENT: In the *Hyla granosa* group; see Hoogmoed, 1978, Zool. Verh., Leiden,
    172:23.

Hyla simplex Boettger, 1901. Ber. Senckenb. Naturforsch. Ges., 1901:53.
ORIGINAL NAME: *Hyla chinensis* var. *simplex*.
TYPE(S): Holotype: SMF 2626.
TYPE LOCALITY: Phuc-Son, Annam, Vietnam.
DISTRIBUTION: Vietnam (Annam and Tonkin) and southern China (Guangxi,
    Zhejiang, Guangdong and Hainan I.).
COMMENT: In the *Hyla arborea* group; see Pope, 1931, Bull. Am. Mus. Nat. Hist., 61:
    477–480, and Liu and Hu, 1961, Tailless Amph. China:128–130.
REVIEWERS: Shuqin Hu (SH); Masafumi Matsui (MM); Ermi Zhao (EZ).

Hyla siopela Duellman, 1968. Univ. Kansas Publ. Mus. Nat. Hist., 17:570.
TYPE(S): Holotype: KU 100981.
TYPE LOCALITY: "a small stream on west slope of Cofre de Perote, Veracruz,
    México, elevation 2500–2550 meters".
DISTRIBUTION: Sierra Madre Oriental in eastern Mexico (Oaxaca and Veracruz).
COMMENT: In the *Hyla bistincta* group; see Duellman, 1970, Monogr. Mus. Nat.
    Hist. Univ. Kansas, 1:475–477.

Hyla smaragdina Taylor, 1940. Copeia, 1940:18.
TYPE(S): Holotype: FMNH 100009 (formerly EHT-HMS 17534).
TYPE LOCALITY: "on a mountain side rising from eastern end of Lake Chapala, 6
    km. east of Cojumatlán, Michoacán", Mexico.
DISTRIBUTION: Pacific slopes of western Mexico from Sinaloa to Morelos.
COMMENT: In the *Hyla sumichrasti* group; see Duellman, 1970, Monogr. Mus. Nat.
    Hist. Univ. Kansas, 1:413–416.

Hyla smithii Boulenger, 1901. Zool. Rec., 38:33.
TYPE(S): Syntypes: BM 1947.2.12.76–82.
TYPE LOCALITY: Cuernavaca, Morelos, Mexico.
DISTRIBUTION: Pacific lowlands of Mexico from northern Sinaloa to southern
    Oaxaca and in the Balsas Depression from Michoacán to Puebla.

COMMENT: *Hyla smithii* is a replacement name for *Hyla nana* Günther, 1901, Biol.
Cent. Am., Rept. Batr.:263. In the *Hyla picta* group; see Duellman, 1970,
Monogr. Mus. Nat. Hist. Univ. Kansas, 1:368–370.

Hyla soaresi Caramaschi and Jim, 1983. Rev. Brasil. Biol., 43:195.
TYPE(S): Holotype: J. Jim 5740.
TYPE LOCALITY: Picos (approx. 07° 05′ S—41° 30′ W), Piauí, Brazil.
DISTRIBUTION: Known only from the type locality.
COMMENT: In the *Hyla marmorata* group, according to the original description, and
related to *Hyla senicula*, *Hyla melanargyrea*, and *Hyla novaisi*.

Hyla squirella Bosc, 1800. *In* Daudin, Hist. Nat. Quadrup. Ovip., Livr. 1:9.
TYPE(S): Unknown.
TYPE LOCALITY: "La Caroline"; restricted to Charleston, South Carolina, USA, by
Harper, 1940, Am. Midl. Nat., 23:692–723.
DISTRIBUTION: Coastal Plain and Mississippi Valley of southeastern North America;
introduced on Grand Bahama I., Bahama Is.
COMMENT: Reviewed by Martof, 1975, Cat. Am. Amph. Rept., 168.1–2.

Hyla steinbachi Boulenger, 1905. Ann. Mag. Nat. Hist., (7)16:182.
TYPE(S): Syntypes: BM 1947.2.13.61–63.
TYPE LOCALITY: "Province Sara, Departament Santa Cruz de la Sierra, Bolivia".
DISTRIBUTION: Known only from the type locality.

Hyla subocularis Dunn, 1934. Am. Mus. Novit., 747:2.
TYPE(S): Holotype: AMNH 41117.
TYPE LOCALITY: Río Chucunaque at the first creek above the Río Tuquesa, Provincia
Darién, Panama.
DISTRIBUTION: Eastern Panama and northern Colombia.
COMMENT: In the *Hyla parviceps* group; see Duellman and Crump, 1974, Occas. Pap.
Mus. Nat. Hist. Univ. Kansas, 23:1–40.

Hyla sumichrasti (Brocchi, 1879). Bull. Soc. Philomath. Paris, (7)3:20.
ORIGINAL NAME: *Exerodonta sumichrasti*.
TYPE(S): Formerly in MNHNP; now lost.
TYPE LOCALITY: Santa Efigenia, Oaxaca, Mexico.
DISTRIBUTION: Pacific slopes of southern Mexico (Chiapas and Oaxaca) and Chiapan
highlands, Mexico.
COMMENT: In the *Hyla sumichrasti* group; see Duellman, 1970, Monogr. Mus. Nat.
Hist. Univ. Kansas, 1:409–413.

Hyla surinamensis Daudin, 1802. Hist. Nat. Rain. Gren. Crap.:44.
TYPE(S): None designated; based on Seba, 1734, Loc. Nat. Thes. Desc. Icon. Exp.:pl.
70, fig. 4.
TYPE LOCALITY: "Surinam."
DISTRIBUTION: ? Surinam.
COMMENT: This name has not been assigned to any known taxon (WED).

Hyla suweonensis Kuramoto, 1980. Copeia, 1980:102.
TYPE(S): Holotype: OMNH 6035.
TYPE LOCALITY: Office of Rural Development, Suweon, Korea.
DISTRIBUTION: South Korea.
COMMENT: In the *Hyla arborea* group according to the original description.
REVIEWERS: Leo J. Borkin (LJB); Shuqin Hu (SH); Masafumi Matsui (MM); Ermi
Zhao (EZ).

Hyla taeniopus Günther, 1901. Biol. Cent. Am., Rept. Batr.:269.
TYPE(S): Syntypes: BM 1947.2.23.32–33.
TYPE LOCALITY: Jalapa, Veracruz, Mexico.
DISTRIBUTION: Atlantic slopes of Sierra Madre Oriental, Mexico.

COMMENT: In the *Hyla taeniopus* group; see Duellman, 1970, Monogr. Mus. Nat. Hist. Univ. Kansas, 1:445–450.

Hyla thorectes Adler, 1965. Occas. Pap. Mus. Zool. Univ. Michigan, 642:10.
TYPE(S): Holotype: UMMZ 125390.
TYPE LOCALITY: "about 37 km N of San Gabriel Mixtepec (about 100 km airline SSW of Oaxaca de Juárez), Oaxaca, 1700 m", Mexico.
DISTRIBUTION: Pacific slopes of Sierra Madre del Sur, Oaxaca, Mexico.
COMMENT: In the *Hyla hazelae* group; see Duellman, 1970, Monogr. Mus. Nat. Hist. Univ. Kansas, 1:388–391.

Hyla thysanota Duellman, 1966. Univ. Kansas Publ. Mus. Nat. Hist., 17:259.
TYPE(S): Holotype: USNM 151080.
TYPE LOCALITY: "Cerro Malí, Darien Province, Panamá, (elevation 1265 meters)".
DISTRIBUTION: Type locality in the eastern part of the Serranía de Darién, Panama.
COMMENT: In the *Hyla miliaria* group; see Duellman, 1970, Monogr. Mus. Nat. Hist. Univ. Kansas, 1:350–352.

Hyla tica Starrett, 1966. Bull. S. California Acad. Sci., 65:23.
TYPE(S): Holotype: UMMZ 122482.
TYPE LOCALITY: Stream at 4500 feet on Volcán Turrialba, Provincia Cartago, Costa Rica.
DISTRIBUTION: Mountains of Costa Rica and western Panama.
COMMENT: In the *Hyla tica* group; see Duellman, 1970, Monogr. Mus. Nat. Hist. Univ. Kansas, 1:278–284.

Hyla tintinnabulum Melin, 1941. Göteborgs K. Vetensk. Vitterh. Samh. Handl., (B)1(4):29.
TYPE(S): Syntypes: NHMG 473 (2 specimens).
TYPE LOCALITY: "Rio Uaupés (some days' journey north of Ipanoré), [Amazonas,] Brazil".
DISTRIBUTION: Known only from the type locality.

Hyla torrenticola Duellman and Altig, 1978. Herpetologica, 34:181.
TYPE(S): Holotype: KU 169571.
TYPE LOCALITY: "10.3 km west (by road) of El Pepino, Departamento Putumayo, Colombia, 1,440 m, 01° 11' N, 76° 41' W".
DISTRIBUTION: Eastern slopes of Andes in southern Colombia and northern Ecuador.
COMMENT: In the *Hyla bogotensis* group according to the original description.

Hyla triangulum Günther, 1869 "1868". Proc. Zool. Soc. London, 1868:489.
TYPE(S): Holotype: BM 1947.2.23.88.
TYPE LOCALITY: "Brazil".
DISTRIBUTION: Upper Amazon Basin in Colombia, Ecuador, Peru, and western Brazil.
COMMENT: In the *Hyla leucophyllata* group; see Duellman, 1974, Occas. Pap. Mus. Nat. Hist. Univ. Kansas, 27:19. Many color morphs of this species have been recognized taxonomically (WED).

Hyla tritaeniata Bokermann, 1965. Rev. Brasil. Biol., 25:259.
TYPE(S): Holotype: WCAB 16211.
TYPE LOCALITY: São Vicente, Cuiabá, Mato Grosso, Brazil.
DISTRIBUTION: Southern Mato Grosso, Brazil.
COMMENT: In the *Hyla rubicundula* group.

Hyla truncata Izecksohn, 1959. Rev. Brasil. Biol., 19:259.
TYPE(S): Holotype: EI 107.
TYPE LOCALITY: Itaguaí, Rio de Janeiro, Brazil.
DISTRIBUTION: Coastal lowlands of Rio de Janeiro, Brazil.

COMMENT: In the *Hyla truncata* group, according to the original description.

Hyla trux Adler and Dennis, 1972. Occas. Pap. Mus. Nat. Hist. Univ. Kansas, 7:1.
TYPE(S): Holotype: KU 137551.
TYPE LOCALITY: "11.4 km. (by road) southwest of Puerto del Gallo, Guerrero,
    México (about 35 km airline northeast of Atoyác de Álvarez), elevation 1985
    meters".
DISTRIBUTION: Vicinity of Cerro Teótepec, Sierra Madre del Sur, Guerrero, Mexico,
    1760–2120 m.
COMMENT: In the *Hyla taeniopus* group according to the original description.

Hyla tsinlingensis Liu and Hu, 1966. *In* Hu, Djao, and Liu, Acta Zool. Sinica, 18(1):74.
TYPE(S): Holotype: CIB (formerly SIB-AC) 623149.
TYPE LOCALITY: "Hou-tseng-tze, Couchih Hsien, Shensi [=Shaanxi], alt. 1341 m.",
    China.
DISTRIBUTION: Gansu, Sichuan, Shaanzi, and Hubei, China.
COMMENT: In the *Hyla arborea* group and related to *Hyla annectans*, according to the
    original description.
REVIEWERS: Leo J. Borkin (LJB); Shuqin Hu (SH); Masafumi Matsui (MM); Ermi
    Zhao (EZ).

Hyla tuberculosa Boulenger, 1882. Cat. Batr. Sal. Brit. Mus.:355.
TYPE(S): Holotype: BM 1947.2.13.34.
TYPE LOCALITY: "Canelos", Provincia Pastaza, Ecuador.
DISTRIBUTION: Upper Amazon Basin in western Brazil, Colombia, Ecuador, and
    Peru.
COMMENT: In the *Hyla miliaria* group; see Duellman, 1974, Occas. Pap. Mus. Nat.
    Hist. Univ. Kansas, 27:1–27.

Hyla uranochroa Cope, 1876. J. Acad. Nat. Sci. Philadelphia, (2)8:103.
TYPE(S): Holotype: USNM 20651.
TYPE LOCALITY: Near Sipurio, Provincia Limón, Costa Rica.
DISTRIBUTION: Mountains of Costa Rica and western Panama.
COMMENT: In the *Hyla uranochroa* group; see Duellman, 1970, Monogr. Mus. Nat.
    Hist. Univ. Kansas, 1:302–306.

Hyla valancifer Firschein and Smith, 1956. Herpetologica, 12:18.
TYPE(S): Holotype: UIMNH 35398.
TYPE LOCALITY: "Volcán San Martín, 4500 ft., Veracruz, Mexico".
DISTRIBUTION: Cloud forests of the Sierra de los Tuxtlas, southern Veracruz,
    Mexico.
COMMENT: In the *Hyla miliaria* group; see Duellman, 1970, Monogr. Mus. Nat. Hist.
    Univ. Kansas, 1:342–346. Specimens previously allocated to this species from
    the Sierra de las Minas, Guatemala, are being described by Larry David
    Wilson (WED).

Hyla vasta Cope, 1871. Proc. Acad. Nat. Sci. Philadelphia, 23:219.
TYPE(S): Holotype: ANSP 2097.
TYPE LOCALITY: "Near the city of Santo Domingo [República Dominicana,] W. I."
DISTRIBUTION: Hispaniola, West Indies.
COMMENT: In the *Hyla boans* group; see Trueb and Tyler, 1974, Occas. Pap. Mus.
    Nat. Hist. Univ. Kansas, 24:1–60.
REVIEWERS: Albert Schwartz (AS); Richard Thomas (RT).

Hyla versicolor LeConte, 1825. Ann. Lyc. Nat. Hist. New York, 1:281.
TYPE(S): Unknown.
TYPE LOCALITY: "Northern States"; restricted to "vicinity of New York, New York",
    USA, by Schmidt, 1953, Check List N. Am. Amph. Rept., Ed. 6:73.
DISTRIBUTION: Northeastern USA and extreme southern Canada from eastern
    North Dakota and eastern Missouri to southern Maine and Delaware; south-
    central USA (eastern Oklahoma, Texas, and southwestern Louisiana).

COMMENT: In the *Hyla versicolor* group. *Hyla versicolor* and *Hyla chrysoscelis* are sibling species which can only be distinguished by call, karyotypes, or cell volume. The actual range of each species is poorly understood.

Hyla vigilans Solano, 1971. Acta Biol. Venezuelica, 7:212.
TYPE(S): Holotype: MBUCV IV-6163.
TYPE LOCALITY: Km 20 on road between Coloncito and El Vigia, Estado Zulia, Venezuela.
DISTRIBUTION: Maracaibo Basin, Venezuela.
COMMENT: This species is a member of *Ololygon* (ELM).

Hyla viridifusca Laurenti, 1768. Synops. Rept.:34.
ORIGINAL NAME: *Hyla viridi-fusca*.
TYPE(S): Unknown.
TYPE LOCALITY: "Surinam".
DISTRIBUTION: Unknown.
COMMENT: This name has not been assigned to any known species (WED).

Hyla walkeri Stuart, 1954. Proc. Biol. Soc. Washington, 67:165.
TYPE(S): Holotype: UMMZ 106817.
TYPE LOCALITY: Aserradero San Lorenzo, 12 km (airline) slightly east of north of Jalapa, Jalapa, Guatemala.
DISTRIBUTION: Mountains of Chiapas, Mexico, and western and southeastern Guatemala.
COMMENT: In the *Hyla eximia* group; see Duellman, 1970, Monogr. Mus. Nat. Hist. Univ. Kansas, 1:510–513.

Hyla wilderi Dunn, 1925. Occas. Pap. Boston Soc. Nat. Hist., 5:161.
TYPE(S): Holotype: MCZ 10500.
TYPE LOCALITY: "Moneague, Saint Ann Parish, Jamaica; altitude 1200 feet".
DISTRIBUTION: Jamaica, West Indies.
COMMENT: In the *Hyla wilderi* group; see Trueb and Tyler, 1974, Occas. Pap. Mus. Nat. Hist. Univ. Kansas, 24:1–60.
REVIEWERS: Albert Schwartz (AS); Richard Thomas (RT).

Hyla xanthosticta Duellman, 1968. Univ. Kansas Publ. Mus. Nat. Hist., 17:562.
TYPE(S): Holotype: KU 103772.
TYPE LOCALITY: "south Fork of the Río Las Vueltas on the south slope of Volcán Barba, near the northwest base of Cerro Chompipe, Heredia Province, Costa Rica, elevation 2100 meters".
DISTRIBUTION: Known only from the type locality in the central cordillera of Costa Rica.
COMMENT: In the *Hyla rivularis* group; see Duellman, 1970, Monogr. Mus. Nat. Hist. Univ. Kansas, 1:292–294.

Hyla zeteki Gaige, 1929. Occas. Pap. Mus. Zool. Univ. Michigan, 207:4.
TYPE(S): Holotype: UMMZ 63875.
TYPE LOCALITY: Caldera Valley above Boquete, Provincia Chiriquí, Panama.
DISTRIBUTION: Mountains of Costa Rica and western Panama.
COMMENT: In the *Hyla zeteki* group; see Duellman, 1970, Monogr. Mus. Nat. Hist. Univ. Kansas, 1:323–327.

Limnaoedus Mittleman and List, 1953. Copeia, 1953:83.
TYPE SPECIES: *Hyla ocularis* Bosc and Daudin, 1801.
DISTRIBUTION: As for the single species.
COMMENT: A monotypic genus distinguished by paedomorphic osteological features; posited by various authors to be related to *Hyla*, *Acris*, or *Pseudacris*; see Franz and Chantell, 1978, Cat. Am. Amph. Rept., 209.1, for discussion.

Limnaoedus ocularis (Bosc and Daudin, 1801). *In* Sonnini and Latreille, Hist. Nat. Rept., 2:187.
ORIGINAL NAME: *Hyla ocularis.*
TYPE(S): Unknown.
TYPE LOCALITY: "Carolina"; restricted to "vicinity of Charleston", South Carolina, USA, by Harper, 1939, Am. Midl. Nat., 22:139–144.
DISTRIBUTION: Coastal plain of southeastern Virginia to western and peninsular Florida, USA.
COMMENT: Reviewed by Franz and Chantell, 1978, Cat. Am. Amph. Rept., 209.1–2.

Nyctimantis Boulenger, 1882. Cat. Batr. Sal. Brit. Mus.:421.
TYPE SPECIES: *Nyctimantis rugiceps* Boulenger, 1882, by monotypy.
DISTRIBUTION: Amazonian Ecuador.
COMMENT: A monotypic genus of uncertain relationships; see Duellman and Trueb, 1976, Occas. Pap. Mus. Nat. Hist. Univ. Kansas, 58:1–14.

Nyctimantis rugiceps Boulenger, 1882. Cat. Batr. Sal. Brit. Mus.:422.
ORIGINAL NAME: *Nyctimantis rugiceps.*
TYPE(S): Syntypes: BM 80.12.5.152 (Ecuador), 80.12.5.163–164 (3 specimens) (Canelos).
TYPE LOCALITY: "Ecuador" and "Canelos", Pastaza, Ecuador.
DISTRIBUTION: Amazonian Ecuador.
COMMENT: For discussion see Duellman and Trueb, 1976, Occas. Pap. Mus. Nat. Hist. Univ. Kansas, 58:1–14.

Ololygon Fitzinger, 1843. Syst. Rept.:31.
TYPE SPECIES: *Hyla strigilata* Spix, 1824, by monotypy.
DISTRIBUTION: Southern Mexico to Argentina and Uruguay.
COMMENT: Fouquette and Delahoussaye, 1977, J. Herpetol., 11:387–396, removed the former *Hyla rubra* group to this genus, discussed species groups (noted in the individual species accounts) within *Ololygon*, and discussed intergeneric relationships, all on the basis of sperm morphology. Osteological characters of the adults and morphology of larvae support the recognition of *Ololygon* as a monophyletic group (WED). A number of species currently placed in *Hyla* probably belong in this genus; see comment under *Hyla vigilans*. See León, 1969, Univ. Kansas Publ. Mus. Nat. Hist. Univ. Kansas, 18:505–545, for a review of the Mexican and Central American species (as *Hyla*).

Ololygon acuminata Cope, 1862. Proc. Acad. Nat. Sci. Philadelphia, 14:354.
ORIGINAL NAME: *Hyla acuminata.*
TYPE(S): Syntypes: USNM 5843, 102700.
TYPE LOCALITY: "Paraguay".
DISTRIBUTION: Southern Mato Grosso and Mato Grosso do Sul (Brazil), Paraguay, and northern Argentina.
COMMENT: In the *Ololygon x-signata* group. See Cei, 1980, Monit. Zool. Ital., N.S., Monogr., 2:484–487.

Ololygon agilis (Cruz and Peixoto, 1983). Rev. Brasil. Biol., 42:721.
ORIGINAL NAME: *Hyla agilis.*
TYPE(S): Holotype: EI 7123.
TYPE LOCALITY: "Ibiriba (19° 14' S, 39° 55' W, alt. aprox. 20 m.), Município de Linhares, Estado do Espírito Santo", Brazil.
DISTRIBUTION: Known only from the region of the type locality.
COMMENT: Related to *Ololygon berthae*, according to the original description, and in the *Ololygon staufferi* group by implication.

Ololygon alleni (Cope, 1870). Proc. Am. Philos. Soc., 11:162.
ORIGINAL NAME: *Scytopis alleni.*
TYPE(S): Syntypes: ANSP 2159 (Pebas), MCZ 1519 (Pará).
TYPE LOCALITY: "Pebas", Loreto, Peru, and "Pará" (=Belém, Pará), Brazil.
DISTRIBUTION: At least the Amazon Basin; range undefined at the present time.

COMMENT: In the *Ololygon catharinae* group.

Ololygon argyreornata (Miranda-Ribeiro, 1926). Arq. Mus. Nac., Rio de Janeiro, 27:57.
ORIGINAL NAME: *Hylodes argyreornatus*.
TYPE(S): Syntypes: MN 114 (2 specimens).
TYPE LOCALITY: Rio Mutum, Colatina, Espírito Santo, Brazil.
DISTRIBUTION: Coastal region from Espírito Santo to São Paulo, Brazil.
COMMENT: Not assigned to species group.

Ololygon aurata (Wied-Neuwied, 1821). Reise Brasil., 2:249.
ORIGINAL NAME: *Hyla aurata*.
TYPE(S): Unknown.
TYPE LOCALITY: Santa Inês, Bahia, Brazil.
DISTRIBUTION: Eastern Bahia, Brazil.
COMMENT: Not assigned to species group.

Ololygon baumgardneri (Rivero, 1961). Bull. Mus. Comp. Zool., 126:123.
ORIGINAL NAME: *Hyla baumgardneri*.
TYPE(S): Holotype: MCZ 28563.
TYPE LOCALITY: Casa de Julian, between Tabana and Caño Chana, 609 m., Territorio Amazonas, Venezuela.
DISTRIBUTION: Amazonas, Venezuela.
COMMENT: In the *Ololygon stauffcri* group.

Ololygon berthae (Barrio, 1962). Physis, Buenos Aires, 23:137.
ORIGINAL NAME: *Hyla berthae*.
TYPE(S): Holotype: LIHUBA 1080.
TYPE LOCALITY: Punta Lara, Departamento Buenos Aires, Argentina.
DISTRIBUTION: Northeastern Argentina, southern Paraguay, Uruguay, and southern Brazil.
COMMENT: In the *Ololygon staufferi* group. See Cei, 1980, Monit. Zool. Ital., N.S., Monogr., 2:491–492.

Ololygon blairi (Fouquette and Pyburn, 1972). Herpetologica, 28:176.
ORIGINAL NAME: *Hyla blairi*.
TYPE(S): Holotype: AMNH 84585.
TYPE LOCALITY: Near junction of Río Guaviare and Río Ariari, Comisaria Vaupés, Colombia.
DISTRIBUTION: Llanos of central Colombia.
COMMENT: In the *Ololygon rubra* group.

Ololygon boesemani (Goin, 1966). Zool. Meded., Leiden, 41:229.
ORIGINAL NAME: *Hyla boesemani*.
TYPE(S): Holotype: RMNH 12601.
TYPE LOCALITY: Zanderij, Suriname District, Surinam.
DISTRIBUTION: Northern Guyana and Surinam and Amazonas, Venezuela, to Amazonas and Pará, Brazil.
COMMENT: In the *Ololygon x-signata* group.

Ololygon boulengeri (Cope, 1887). Bull. U.S. Natl. Mus., 32:12.
ORIGINAL NAME: *Scytopis boulengeri*.
TYPE(S): Holotype: USNM 13974.
TYPE LOCALITY: "Nicaragua".
DISTRIBUTION: Caribbean lowlands of Central America from Nicaragua to Panama; Pacific lowlands of Costa Rica and eastern Panama.
COMMENT: For discussion (as *Hyla boulengeri*) see Duellman, 1970, Monogr. Mus. Nat. Hist. Univ. Kansas, 1:200, and Duellman, 1972, Zool. Meded., Leiden, 47: 180–181. In the *Ololygon rostrata* group.

Ololygon canastrensis (Cardoso and Haddad, 1982). Rev. Brasil. Biol., 42:499.
ORIGINAL NAME: *Hyla canastrensis.*
TYPE(S): Holotype: MN 4147.
TYPE LOCALITY: Parque Nacional da Serra da Canastra, 1.300 m, São Roque de Minas (approx. 20° 15'—46° 30' W), Minas Gerais, Brazil.
DISTRIBUTION: Known only from the type locality.
COMMENT: Related to *Ololygon rubra* and *Ololygon catharinae* groups, according to the original description.

Ololygon catharinae (Boulenger, 1888). Ann. Mag. Nat. Hist., (6)1:417.
ORIGINAL NAME: *Hyla catharinae.*
TYPE(S): Syntypes: BM 1947.2.12.65–66.
TYPE LOCALITY: "Serra do Catharina", Santa Catarina, Brazil.
DISTRIBUTION: Mountains of eastern and southeastern Brazil.
COMMENT: For discussion see (as *Hyla catharinae*) B. Lutz, 1973, Brazil. Spec. *Hyla*: 183. In the *Ololygon catharinae* group. Many of the subspecies cited by B. Lutz, 1973, Brazil. Spec. *Hyla*:183–189, and by Duellman, 1977, Das Tierreich, 95:43–44, are recognizable species (UC).

Ololygon crospedospila (A. Lutz, 1925). C. R. Séances Soc. Biol., Paris, 93:211.
ORIGINAL NAME: *Hyla crospedospila.*
TYPE(S): AL-MN 655 designated lectotype by Bokermann, 1966, Lista Anot. Local. Tipo Anf. Brasil.:48.
TYPE LOCALITY: "Estado do Rio e Sao Paulo"; restricted to Campo Belo, Itatiaia, Rio de Janeiro, by Bokermann, 1966, Lista Anot. Local. Tipo Anf. Brasil.:48.
DISTRIBUTION: Coastal mountains of Rio de Janeiro and São Paulo in southeastern Brazil.
COMMENT: In the *Ololygon x-signata* group.

Ololygon cruentomma (Duellman, 1972). Copeia, 1972:266.
ORIGINAL NAME: *Hyla cruentomma.*
TYPE(S): Holotype: KU 126587.
TYPE LOCALITY: "Santa Cecilia on the Río Aguarico, Provincia Napo, Ecuador (0° 02' N—76° 58' W), elevation 340 m".
DISTRIBUTION: Upper Amazon Basin in Ecuador and Peru.
COMMENT: In the *Ololygon x-signata* group.

Ololygon cuspidata (A. Lutz, 1925). C. R. Séances Soc. Biol., Paris, 93:211.
ORIGINAL NAME: *Hyla cuspidata.*
TYPE(S): Syntypes: AL-MN 299–302.
TYPE LOCALITY: Rio de Janeiro, Brazil.
DISTRIBUTION: Coastal lowlands of Espírito Santo and Rio de Janeiro in southeastern Brazil.
COMMENT: In the *Ololygon x-signata* group.

Ololygon cynocephala (Duméril and Bibron, 1841). Erp. Gén., 8:558.
ORIGINAL NAME: *Hyla cynocephala.*
TYPE(S): Holotype: MNHNP 765.
TYPE LOCALITY: "Guyane".
DISTRIBUTION: Northern French Guiana.
COMMENT: Recognized as distinct from *Ololygon rubra* by Lescure, 1976, Bull. Mus. Natl. Hist. Nat., Paris, (3)377(Zool.)265:492. In the *Ololygon rubra* group. The incorrect spelling *Hyla cyanocephala* has been used by some authors.

Ololygon duartei (B. Lutz, 1951). Hospital, Rio de Janeiro, 39:705.
ORIGINAL NAME: *Hyla rubra duartei.*
TYPE(S): Holotype: MN 3257.
TYPE LOCALITY: Itatiaia, Rio de Janeiro, Brazil.
DISTRIBUTION: Mountains of southeastern Brazil; Serra do Espinhaço in Minas Gerais, Brazil.

COMMENT: See B. Lutz, 1973, Brazil. Spec. *Hyla*:161. Not assigned to species group.

Ololygon ehrhardti (Müller, 1924). Zool. Anz., 59:233.
ORIGINAL NAME: *Hyla ehrhardti.*
TYPE(S): Holotype: formerly ZSM 80/1921; destroyed.
TYPE LOCALITY: Humboldt, Santa Catarina, Brasil; stated as "Corupá (=Humboldt), Santa Catarina", Brazil, by Bokermann, 1966, Lista Anot. Local. Tipo Anf. Brasil.:49.
DISTRIBUTION: Known only from the type locality.
COMMENT: Not assigned to species group. Occasionally misspelled as *Ololygon erhardti.*

Ololygon elaeochroa (Cope, 1876). J. Acad. Nat. Sci. Philadelphia, (2)8:105.
ORIGINAL NAME: *Hyla elaeochroa.*
TYPE(S): USNM 30689 designated lectotype by Cochran, 1961, Bull. U.S. Natl. Mus., 220:53.
TYPE LOCALITY: East foot of mountains near Sipurio, Provincia Limón, Costa Rica.
DISTRIBUTION: Caribbean lowlands from Nicaragua to western Panama; Pacific lowlands of Golfo Dulce region in Costa Rica and Panama.
COMMENT: For discussion see Duellman, 1970, Monogr. Mus. Nat. Hist. Univ. Kansas, 1:188–193. In the *Ololygon rubra* group.

Ololygon epacrorhina (Duellman, 1972). Zool. Meded., Leiden, 47:182.
ORIGINAL NAME: *Hyla epacrorhina.*
TYPE(S): Holotype: KU 139247.
TYPE LOCALITY: "Pilcopata, Departamento Cuzco, Perú, 13° 05' S, 71° 12' W, elevation 750 m."
DISTRIBUTION: Amazonian lowlands of southeastern Peru and northeastern Bolivia.
COMMENT: In the *Ololygon rostrata* group.

Ololygon eurydice (Bokermann, 1968). J. Herpetol., 1:29.
ORIGINAL NAME: *Hyla eurydice.*
TYPE(S): Holotype: WCAB 31795.
TYPE LOCALITY: Fazenda Santo Onofre, 10 km east of Maracás, Brazil.
DISTRIBUTION: Southern Bahia to Rio de Janeiro, Brazil.
COMMENT: Not assigned to species group.

Ololygon flavoguttata (A. Lutz and B. Lutz, 1939). An. Acad. Brasil. Cienc., 11:75.
ORIGINAL NAME: *Hyla flavoguttata.*
TYPE(S): Holotype: AL-MN 2090.
TYPE LOCALITY: Fazenda do Bonito, Serra da Bocaina, São José do Barreiro, São Paulo, Brazil.
DISTRIBUTION: Coastal range in Brazil from Espírito Santo to Rio Grande do Sul, Brazil.
COMMENT: In the *Ololygon catharinae* group.

Ololygon funerea (Cope, 1874). Proc. Acad. Nat. Sci. Philadelphia, 25:123.
ORIGINAL NAME: *Hyla funerea.*
TYPE(S): Syntypes: ANSP 11396–97.
TYPE LOCALITY: Moyobamba, Departamento San Martín, Peru.
DISTRIBUTION: Upper Amazon Basin in Ecuador and northern Peru.
COMMENT: In the *Ololygon rubra* group.

Ololygon fuscomarginata (A. Lutz, 1925). C. R. Séances Soc. Biol., Paris, 93:138.
ORIGINAL NAME: *Hyla fuscomarginata.*
TYPE(S): Syntypes: AL-MN 845–846, USNM 96964.
TYPE LOCALITY: "São Paulo and Belo Horizonte", Brazil; restricted to Belo Horizonte, Minas Gerais, Brazil, by B. Lutz, 1973, Brazil. Spec. *Hyla*:165.
DISTRIBUTION: Southern, central, and eastern Brazil, eastern Bolivia, Paraguay and northwestern Argentina.

COMMENT: For discussion see B. Lutz, 1973, Brazil. Spec. *Hyla*:164. In the *Ololygon staufferi* group.

Ololygon fuscovaria (A. Lutz, 1925). C. R. Séances Soc. Biol., Paris, 93:212.
ORIGINAL NAME: *Hyla fuscovaria*.
TYPE(S): Syntypes: AL-MN 76, MCZ 15851.
TYPE LOCALITY: Água Branca (=Agua Limpa), Juiz de Fora, Minas Gerais, Brazil.
DISTRIBUTION: Southern and southeastern Brazil, northern Argentina, Paraguay and eastern Bolivia.
COMMENT: See B. Lutz, 1973, Brazil. Spec. *Hyla*:127, for discussion. See also Cei, 1980, Monit. Zool. Ital., N.S., Monogr., 2:487–488. In the *Ololygon rubra* group.

Ololygon garbei (Miranda-Ribeiro, 1926). Arq. Mus. Nac., Rio de Janeiro, 27:96.
ORIGINAL NAME: *Garbeana garbei*.
TYPE(S): Holotype: MZUSP 277.
TYPE LOCALITY: Eirunepé, Rio Juruá, Amazonas, Brazil.
DISTRIBUTION: Middle and upper Amazon Basin in Colombia, Ecuador, northern Peru, and Brazil.
COMMENT: See Duellman, 1972, Zool. Meded., Leiden, 47:185–186, for discussion. In the *Ololygon rostrata* group.

Ololygon goinorum (Bokermann, 1962). Neotropica, 8:86.
ORIGINAL NAME: *Hyla goinorum*.
TYPE(S): Holotype: WCAB 1401.
TYPE LOCALITY: "Tarauacá, Estado de Acre, Brasil".
DISTRIBUTION: Acre, Brazil.
COMMENT: In the *Ololygon staufferi* group.

Ololygon hayii (Barbour, 1909). Proc. New England Zool. Club, 4:51.
ORIGINAL NAME: *Hyla hayii*.
TYPE(S): Holotype: MCZ 2513.
TYPE LOCALITY: Petrópolis, Rio de Janeiro, Brazil.
DISTRIBUTION: Serra do Mar from Espírito Santo to Santa Catarina in southeastern Brazil.
COMMENT: In the *Ololygon rubra* group.

Ololygon humilis (B. Lutz, 1954). Mem. Inst. Oswaldo Cruz, Rio de Janeiro, 52:160.
ORIGINAL NAME: *Hyla humilis*.
TYPE(S): Holotype: MN 2248.
TYPE LOCALITY: Rio Babi, Nova Iguaçu, Rio de Janeiro, Brazil.
DISTRIBUTION: Coastal lowlands of Rio de Janeiro in southeastern Brazil.
COMMENT: In the *Ololygon catharinae* group.

Ololygon kennedyi (Pyburn, 1973). J. Herpetol., 7:297.
ORIGINAL NAME: *Hyla kennedyi*.
TYPE(S): Holotype: UTA A-3697.
TYPE LOCALITY: About 110 mi. east-southeast of Puerto Gaitan, Departamento Meta, Colombia.
DISTRIBUTION: Llanos of eastern Colombia.
COMMENT: In the *Ololygon rostrata* group.

Ololygon longilinea (B. Lutz, 1968). Pearce-Sellards Ser., Texas Mem. Mus., 10:5.
ORIGINAL NAME: *Hyla longilinea*.
TYPE(S): Holotype: MN 4060.
TYPE LOCALITY: Morro de São Domingos, Poços de Caldas, Minas Gerais, Brazil.
DISTRIBUTION: Southeastern mountains of Minas Gerais, Brazil.
COMMENT: Not assigned to species group.

Ololygon machadoi (Bokermann and Sazima, 1973). Rev. Brasil. Biol., 33:521.
ORIGINAL NAME: *Hyla machadoi.*
TYPE(S): Holotype: WCAB 46847.
TYPE LOCALITY: Kilometer 121, Serra do Cipó, Jaboticatubas, Minas Gerais, Brazil.
DISTRIBUTION: Serra do Espinhaço, Minas Gerais, Brazil.
COMMENT: Related to small species in the *Ololygon catharinae* group, according to
the original description.

Ololygon maracaya (Cardoso and Sazima, 1980). Rev. Brasil. Biol., 40:75.
ORIGINAL NAME: *Hyla maracaya.*
TYPE(S): Holotype: MN 4119.
TYPE LOCALITY: Fazenda Salto, Alpinópolis, Minas Gerais, Brazil.
DISTRIBUTION: Mountains of southwestern Minas Gerais, Brazil.
COMMENT: Although named as a species of *Hyla* by Cardoso and Sazima, the
authors stated that the species was a member of *Ololygon* as recognized by
Fouquette and Delahoussaye, 1977, J. Herpetol., 11:387–396.

Ololygon mirim (B. Lutz, 1973). Bol. Mus. Nac., Rio de Janeiro, N.S., Zool., 288:3.
ORIGINAL NAME: *Hyla mirim.*
TYPE(S): Syntypes: MN 3626–34.
TYPE LOCALITY: Rio Vermelho, São Bento do Sul, Santa Catarina, Brazil.
DISTRIBUTION: Known only from the type locality.
COMMENT: Not assigned to species group.

Ololygon nasica (Cope, 1862). Proc. Acad. Nat. Sci. Philadelphia, 14:354.
ORIGINAL NAME: *Hyla nasica.*
TYPE(S): Syntypes: USNM 5835, 32371.
TYPE LOCALITY: "Paraguay".
DISTRIBUTION: Paraguay, northern Argentina, Uruguay, eastern Bolivia, and
southern Brazil.
COMMENT: In the *Ololygon staufferi* group. Placement of *Ololygon nasica* as a
subspecies of *Ololygon x-signata* as done by B. Lutz, 1973, Brazil. Spec. *Hyla*:
143, seems to be unwarranted (see Fouquette and Delahoussaye, 1977, J.
Herpetol., 11:393).

Ololygon nebulosa (Spix, 1824). Spec. Nov. Testud. Ran. Brasil.:39.
ORIGINAL NAME: *Hyla nebulosa.*
TYPE(S): Syntypes: probably ZSM 2531/0, now lost; MN 4055 (holotype of *Hyla
egleri* Lutz, 1968) designated neotype by Hoogmoed and Gruber, 1983,
Spixiana, Suppl., 9:369.
TYPE LOCALITY: "in sylvis prope flumen Teffé", Amazonas, Brazil.
DISTRIBUTION: Southeastern Venezuela, through the Guianas and the lower
Amazon region to Alagoas in northeastern Brazil.
COMMENT: In the *Ololygon rostrata* group. Until recently this species was known as
Ololygon egleri (Lutz, 1968, Pearce-Sellards Ser., Texas Mem. Mus., 10:8), but
Hoogmoed and Gruber, 1983, Spixiana, Suppl., 9:371, pointed out that *Hyla
nebulosa* Spix, 1824, is the oldest name for this species.

Ololygon obtriangulata (B. Lutz, 1973). Brazil. Spec. *Hyla*:190.
ORIGINAL NAME: *Hyla obtriangulata.*
TYPE(S): Holotype: MN 4035.
TYPE LOCALITY: Brejo da Lapa, Alto Itatiaia, Rio de Janeiro, Brazil.
DISTRIBUTION: Serra da Mantiqueira and Serra do Mar; city of São Paulo, Brazil.
COMMENT: *Hyla obtriangulata* is a replacement name for *Hyla catharinae simplex* B.
Lutz, 1968, Pearce-Sellards Ser., Texas Mem. Mus., 12:5. Not assigned to
species group.

Ololygon opalina (B. Lutz, 1968). Pearce-Sellards Ser., Texas Mem. Mus., 12:6.
ORIGINAL NAME: *Hyla catharinae opalina.*
TYPE(S): Syntypes: MN 4037–38.
TYPE LOCALITY: Serra dos Órgãos, Teresópolis, Rio de Janeiro, Brazil.
DISTRIBUTION: Serra do Mar in Rio de Janeiro, Brazil.
COMMENT: For discussion of species status, see Heyer, 1980, Proc. Biol. Soc.
	Washington, 93:657. Presumably in the *Ololygon catharinae* group.

Ololygon pachychrus (Miranda-Ribeiro, 1937). Campo, Rio de Janeiro, 1937:55.
ORIGINAL NAME: *Hyla pachychrus.*
TYPE(S): Syntypes: MN 237 (4 specimens).
TYPE LOCALITY: Poção, Pernambuco, Brazil.
DISTRIBUTION: Northeastern Brazil.
COMMENT: Not assigned to species group.

Ololygon perpusilla (A. Lutz and B. Lutz, 1939). An. Acad. Brasil. Cienc., 11:78.
ORIGINAL NAME: *Hyla perpusilla.*
TYPE(S): Holotype: AL-MN 2622.
TYPE LOCALITY: Recreio dos Bandeirantes, Rio de Janeiro, Brazil.
DISTRIBUTION: Southeastern Brazil (Rio de Janeiro and São Paulo).
COMMENT: In the *Ololygon rubra* group.

Ololygon proboscidea (Brongersma, 1933). Zool. Anz., 103:267.
ORIGINAL NAME: *Hyla proboscidea.*
TYPE(S): Holotype: ZMA 5710.
TYPE LOCALITY: Upper Gran Rio, Surinam.
DISTRIBUTION: Interior of the Guianas.
COMMENT: In the *Ololygon rostrata* group; see Duellman, 1972, Zool. Meded.,
	Leiden, 47:186–187, and Duellman, 1972, Occas. Pap. Mus. Nat. Hist. Univ.
	Kansas, 11:1–31.

Ololygon quinquefasciata (Fowler, 1913). Proc. Acad. Nat. Sci. Philadelphia, 55:160.
ORIGINAL NAME: *Hyla quinquefasciata.*
TYPE(S): Holotype: ANSP 18115.
TYPE LOCALITY: "Mountains above Chimbo"; corrected to Durán, Provincia Guayas,
	Ecuador, by Duellman, 1971, Herpetologica 27:212–227.
DISTRIBUTION: Pacific lowlands of Colombia and Ecuador.
COMMENT: In the *Ololygon rubra* group.

Ololygon rizibilis (Bokermann, 1964). Rev. Brasil. Biol., 24:430.
ORIGINAL NAME: *Hyla rizibilis.*
TYPE(S): Holotype: WCAB 13947.
TYPE LOCALITY: "Campo Grande, Santo André, São Paulo, Brasil".
DISTRIBUTION: Known only from the type locality.
COMMENT: Not assigned to species group.

Ololygon rostrata (Peters, 1863). Monatsber. Preuss. Akad. Wiss. Berlin, 1863:466.
ORIGINAL NAME: *Hyla rostrata.*
TYPE(S): Holotype: ZMB 3175.
TYPE LOCALITY: Caracas, Venezuela.
DISTRIBUTION: Central Panama eastward on coastal lowlands to French Guiana;
	valleys of Río Cauca and Río Magdalena in Colombia; llanos of Colombia and
	Venezuela.
COMMENT: For discussion see Duellman, 1970, Monogr. Mus. Nat. Hist. Univ.
	Kansas, 1:204, and Duellman, 1972, Zool. Meded., Leiden, 47:187–190. In the
	Ololygon rostrata group.

Ololygon rubra (Laurenti, 1768). Synops. Rept.:5.
ORIGINAL NAME: *Hyla rubra*.
TYPE(S): None designated; RMNH 15292B considered neotype (pending designation by Fouquette) by Duellman, 1977, Das Tierreich, 95:96.
TYPE LOCALITY: "America"; potential neotype from Paramaribo, Surinam.
DISTRIBUTION: Amazon Basin; coastal Brazil (southward to Espírito Santo); Guianas; coastal northern South America; eastern Panama; Tobago, Trinidad, and St. Lucia (Lesser Antilles).
COMMENT: There is disagreement whether Laurenti, 1768, or Daudin, 1802, is the proper authority for the name *Ololygon rubra*; the earliest name is used herein pending a decision by the International Commission of Zoological Nomenclature (WED). In the *Ololygon rubra* group. *Ololygon rubra* as currently recognized is a composite of several species (WED).

Ololygon similis (Cochran, 1952). J. Washington Acad. Sci., 42:50.
ORIGINAL NAME: *Hyla similis*.
TYPE(S): Holotype: USNM 97317.
TYPE LOCALITY: Manguinhos, Rio de Janeiro, Brazil.
DISTRIBUTION: Coastal region of Rio de Janeiro, Brazil.
COMMENT: In the *Ololygon rubra* group. The placement of *Ololygon similis* in the *Ololygon rubra* group by Fouquette and Delahoussaye, 1977, J. Herpetol., 11: 392, is contrary to the recognition of *Ololygon similis* as a subspecies of *Ololygon x-signata* by B. Lutz, 1973, Brazil. Spec. *Hyla*:145.

Ololygon squalirostris (A. Lutz, 1925). C. R. Séances Soc. Biol., Paris, 93:212.
ORIGINAL NAME: *Hyla squalirostris*.
TYPE(S): Syntypes: AL-MN 954–955, USNM 96719.
TYPE LOCALITY: Fazenda do Bonito, Serra da Bocaina, São Paulo, Brazil.
DISTRIBUTION: Southeastern Brazil, southern Paraguay, Uruguay, and northeastern Argentina.
COMMENT: In the *Ololygon staufferi* group.

Ololygon staufferi (Cope, 1865). Proc. Acad. Nat. Sci. Philadelphia, 17:195.
ORIGINAL NAME: *Hyla staufferi*.
TYPE(S): Holotype: USNM 15317.
TYPE LOCALITY: Orizaba, Veracruz, Mexico.
DISTRIBUTION: Mexico (Tamaulipas and Guerrero southward) through Central America to central Panama.
COMMENT: For discussion of two subspecies see Duellman, 1970, Monogr. Mus. Nat. Hist. Univ. Kansas, 1:193–203. In the *Ololygon staufferi* group.

Ololygon strigilata (Spix, 1824). Spec. Nov. Testud. Ran. Brasil.:38.
ORIGINAL NAME: *Hyla strigilata*.
TYPE(S): Formerly ZSM 2369/0 (destroyed); see Hoogmoed and Gruber, 1983, Spixiana, Suppl., 9:368–369, for discussion.
TYPE LOCALITY: Bahia, Brazil.
DISTRIBUTION: Northeastern Brazil.
COMMENT: In the *Ololygon catharinae* group.

Ololygon sugillata (Duellman, 1973). Herpetologica, 29:223.
ORIGINAL NAME: *Hyla sugillata*.
TYPE(S): Holotype: KU 146444.
TYPE LOCALITY: "Estación Biológica Río Palenque, 56 km north of Quevedo, Provincia Los Ríos [Pichincha], Ecuador".
DISTRIBUTION: Pacific lowlands of Colombia and northwestern Ecuador.
COMMENT: In the *Ololygon rostrata* group.

Ololygon trachythorax (Müller and Hellmich, 1936). Wiss. Ergebn. Deutsch. Gran Chaco-Exped., Amph. Rept., 1:73.
ORIGINAL NAME: *Hyla trachythorax*.
TYPE(S): Syntypes: ZSM 156 (2 specimens).
TYPE LOCALITY: "Apa-Bergland (San Luis)", Paraguay.
DISTRIBUTION: Known only from the type locality.
COMMENT: The unjustified emended spelling *Ololygon trachytorax* has been used. Although considered a synonym of *Ololygon fuscovaria* by Lutz, 1973, Brazil. Spec. *Hyla*:127, and subsequently by Cei, 1980, Monit. Zool. Ital., N.S., Monogr., 2:487, Fouquette and Delahoussaye, 1977, J. Herpetol., 11:387–396, not only considered *Ololygon trachythorax* to be a distinct species, but placed it in a different species group (the *Ololygon catharinae* group) from *Ololygon fuscovaria* (in the *Ololygon rubra* group). Cei did not mention the earlier paper by Fouquette and Delahoussaye so we presume that he did not see it prior to his monograph going to press.

Ololygon trilineata Hoogmoed and Gorzula, 1979. Zool. Meded., Leiden, 54:193.
TYPE(S): Holotype: RMNH 18357.
TYPE LOCALITY: 12 km SE El Manteco, Bolívar, Venezuela.
DISTRIBUTION: Llanos of eastern Venezuela and savannas of Guyana and Surinam.
COMMENT: Not assigned to species group.

Ololygon wandae (Pyburn and Fouquette, 1971). J. Herpetol., 5:97.
ORIGINAL NAME: *Hyla wandae*.
TYPE(S): Holotype: USNM 192305.
TYPE LOCALITY: 12 km north-northeast of Villavicencio, Departamento Meta, Colombia.
DISTRIBUTION: Ecotone of forest and llanos in central Colombia.
COMMENT: In the *Ololygon staufferi* group.

Ololygon x-signata (Spix, 1824). Spec. Nov. Testud. Ran. Brasil.:40.
ORIGINAL NAME: *Hyla x-signata*.
TYPE(S): Formerly ZSM 2494/0 (now destroyed).
TYPE LOCALITY: Bahia, Brazil.
DISTRIBUTION: Northern Venezuela to Surinam; eastern, southern, and southeastern Brazil.
COMMENT: In the *Ololygon x-signata* group. See Cei, 1980, Monit. Zool. Ital., N.S., Monogr., 2:488–491. Hoogmoed and Gruber, 1983, Spixiana, Suppl., 9:364, included *Hyla affinis* Spix and *Hyla coerulea* Spix in synonymy.

Osteocephalus Steindachner, 1862. Arch. Zool. Anat. Physiol. Wiss. Med., 2:77.
TYPE SPECIES: *Osteocephalus taurinus* Steindachner, 1862, by original designation.
DISTRIBUTION: Guianas, Amazon Basin, upper Orinoco and Magdalena drainages in Venezuela and Colombia, southeastern Brazil, and northeastern Argentina.
COMMENT: See Trueb and Duellman, 1971, Occas. Pap. Mus. Nat. Hist. Univ. Kansas, 1:1–47, for a review of this genus. See comment under *Hyla rodriguezi*.

Osteocephalus buckleyi (Boulenger, 1882). Cat. Batr. Sal. Brit. Mus.:362.
ORIGINAL NAME: *Hyla buckleyi*.
TYPE(S): Syntypes: BM 1947.2.13.36–39 (Sarayacu), 1947.2.13.40–41, 1947.2.13.43–45 (Canelos), 1947.2.13.46 (Pallatanga); BM 1947.2.13.44 designated lectotype by Trueb and Duellman, 1971, Occas. Pap. Mus. Nat. Hist. Univ. Kansas, 1:19.
TYPE LOCALITY: "Sarayacu" and "Canelos", Provincia Pastaza, and "Paitanga" (=Pallatanga), Provincia Chimborazo (in error), Ecuador; type locality restricted to Canelos by Cochran and Goin, 1970, Bull. U.S. Natl. Mus., 288: 213, and by lectotype designation.
DISTRIBUTION: Amazon Basin from Amapá, Brazil, through the Guianas to Colombia, Ecuador, Peru, and Bolivia.

Osteocephalus langsdorffii (Duméril and Bibron, 1841). Erp. Gén., 8:557.
ORIGINAL NAME: *Hyla Langsdorffii.*
TYPE(S): Holotype: MNHNP 4634.
TYPE LOCALITY: "Brésil".
DISTRIBUTION: Atlantic forests from Bahia, Brazil, to northeastern Argentina.
COMMENT: See Duellman, 1974, Occas. Pap. Mus. Nat. Hist. Univ. Kansas, 24:20, for generic allocation.

Osteocephalus leprieurii (Duméril and Bibron, 1841). Erp. Gén., 8:553.
ORIGINAL NAME: *Hyla Leprieurii.*
TYPE(S): Holotype: MNHNP 4629.
TYPE LOCALITY: "Cayenne", French Guiana.
DISTRIBUTION: Amazon Basin, in the Guianas and the upper Amazon Basin in Colombia, Ecuador, Peru, and western Brazil.

Osteocephalus pearsoni (Gaige, 1929). Occas. Pap. Mus. Zool. Univ. Michigan, 207:3.
ORIGINAL NAME: *Hyla pearsoni.*
TYPE(S): Holotype: UMMZ 57548.
TYPE LOCALITY: Upper Río Beni, below mouth of Río Mapiri, Departamento El Beni, Bolivia.
DISTRIBUTION: Upper Amazon Basin and lower Andean slopes from central Peru to northern Bolivia.

Osteocephalus taurinus Steindachner, 1862. Arch. Zool. Anat. Physiol. Wiss. Med., 2:77.
TYPE(S): Holotype: NHMW 16492.
TYPE LOCALITY: Barra do Rio Negro, Manáus, Amazonas, Brazil.
DISTRIBUTION: Amazon Basin, upper Orinoco Basin, and the Guianas.
COMMENT: As presently recognized, this taxon consists of two species that differ in size and advertisement call (WED). See comment under *Hyla elkejungingerae.*

Osteocephalus verruciger (Werner, 1901). Verh. Zool. Bot. Ges. Wien, 50:601.
ORIGINAL NAME: *Hyla verrucigera.*
TYPE(S): Holotype: ZMB 16589.
TYPE LOCALITY: "Ecuador".
DISTRIBUTION: Lower Amazonian slopes of Andes from Colombia to central Peru.
COMMENT: The incorrect epithet *verrucigerus* has had widespread use.

Osteopilus Fitzinger, 1843. Syst. Rept.:30.
TYPE SPECIES: *Trachycephalus marmoratus* Duméril and Bibron, 1841 (=*Hyla septentrionalis* Duméril and Bibron, 1841).
DISTRIBUTION: The Greater Antilles, Bahama Is., and southern Florida (USA).
COMMENT: For a review of the genus see Trueb and Tyler, 1974, Occas. Pap. Mus. Nat. Hist. Univ. Kansas, 24:1–60.
REVIEWERS: Albert Schwartz (AS); Richard Thomas (RT).

Osteopilus brunneus (Gosse, 1851). Naturalist's Sojourn in Jamaica:361.
ORIGINAL NAME: *Hyla brunnea.*
TYPE(S): Unknown.
TYPE LOCALITY: Savanna-la-Mar, [Westmoreland Parish,] Jamaica.
DISTRIBUTION: Jamaica, West Indies.

Osteopilus dominicensis (Tschudi, 1838). Classif. Batr.:30.
ORIGINAL NAME: *Hypsiboas dominicensis.*
TYPE(S): Syntypes: MNHNP 4614 (4 specimens).
TYPE LOCALITY: "Saint-Domingue".
DISTRIBUTION: Hispaniola, including Ile de la Gonâve, Ile-à-Vache, Ile Grande Cayemite, Ile de la Tortue, and Isla Saona (West Indies).
COMMENT: Peters, 1974, Mitt. Zool. Mus. Berlin, 50:299–322, regarded this as a subspecies of *Osteopilus septentrionalis.*

Osteopilus septentrionalis (Duméril and Bibron, 1841). Erp. Gén., 8:538.
ORIGINAL NAME: *Hyla septentrionalis.*
TYPE(S): Holotype: MNHNP 4612.
TYPE LOCALITY: "Cuba".
DISTRIBUTION: West Indies: Cuba, Isla de Pinos (now Isla de Juventud), Cayman Is.,
   Bahama Is.; introduced on northwestern Puerto Rico, Virgin Is., and southern
   Florida (USA).
COMMENT: Reviewed by Duellman and Crombie, 1970, Cat. Am. Amph. Rept.,
   92.1–4 (as *Hyla septentrionalis*). *Hyla septentrionalis* is a replacement name for
   Trachycephalus marmoratus Duméril and Bibron, 1841, Erp. Gén., 8:538. See
   comment under *Osteopilus dominicensis.*

Phrynohyas Fitzinger, 1843. Syst. Rept.:30.
TYPE SPECIES: *Hyla zonata* Spix, 1824 (=*Rana venulosa* Laurenti, 1768), by monotypy
   and subsequent designation of the Int. Comm. Zool. Nomencl., 1958, Opin. 520.
DISTRIBUTION: Lowlands of Mexico, Central and South America east of the Andes,
   south to northern Argentina.
COMMENT: For a review of the genus see Duellman, 1971, Occas. Pap. Mus. Nat. Hist.
   Univ. Kansas, 4:1–21.

Phrynohyas coriacea (Peters, 1867). Monatsber. Preuss. Akad. Wiss. Berlin, 1867:711.
ORIGINAL NAME: *Hyla coriacea.*
TYPE(S): Syntypes: ZMB 5807 (3 specimens).
TYPE LOCALITY: "Surinam".
DISTRIBUTION: Surinam and upper Amazon Basin in Ecuador and Peru.

Phrynohyas imitatrix (Miranda-Ribeiro, 1926). Arq. Mus. Nac., Rio de Janeiro, 27:77.
ORIGINAL NAME: *Hyla imitatrix.*
TYPE(S): Syntypes: MN 154 (2 specimens).
TYPE LOCALITY: Teresópolis, Rio de Janeiro, Brazil.
DISTRIBUTION: States of São Paulo and Rio de Janeiro, Brazil.

Phrynohyas mesophaea (Hensel, 1867). Arch. Naturgesch., 33:154.
ORIGINAL NAME: *Hyla mesophaea.*
TYPE(S): Holotype: ZMB 6810.
TYPE LOCALITY: Porto Alegre, Rio Grande do Sul, Brazil.
DISTRIBUTION: Atlantic forests of southeastern Brazil.

Phrynohyas resinifictrix (Goeldi, 1907). Proc. Zool. Soc. London, 1907:135.
ORIGINAL NAME: *Hyla resinifictrix.*
TYPE(S): Holotype: BM 1947.2.23.24.
TYPE LOCALITY: "Mission of San Antonio do Prata, at the River Maracanã", Brazil.
DISTRIBUTION: Surinam, French Guiana and Amazonian Brazil.
COMMENT: Recognized as distinct from *Phrynohyas venulosa* by Lescure, 1976, Bull.
   Mus. Natl. Hist. Nat., Paris, (3)377(Zool.)265:503.

Phrynohyas venulosa (Laurenti, 1768). Synops. Rept.:31.
ORIGINAL NAME: *Rana venulosa.*
TYPE(S): Unknown; based on pl. 72 in Seba, 1734, Loc. Nat. Thes. Desc. Icon.
   Exp., 1.
TYPE LOCALITY: "America".
DISTRIBUTION: Lowlands of Mexico, Central America (to 2500 m in Guatemala), to
   Amazon Basin of Brazil, Guianas, and south to Paraná (Brazil), Paraguay,
   northern Argentina; Trinidad and Tobago.
COMMENT: See Cei, 1980, Monit. Zool. Ital., N.S., Monogr., 2:444–450, and
   Duellman, 1970, Monogr. Mus. Nat. Hist. Univ. Kansas, 1:163–172. See
   comment under *Argenteohyla altamazonica.*

Phyllodytes Wagler, 1830. Nat. Syst. Amph.:202.
TYPE SPECIES: *Hyla luteola* Wied-Neuwied, 1824.
DISTRIBUTION: Eastern Brazil; Trinidad.
COMMENT: The most recent review of the genus was by Bokermann, 1966, An. Acad.
Brasil. Cienc., 38:335–344.

Phyllodytes acuminatus Bokermann, 1966. An. Acad. Brasil. Cienc., 38:342.
TYPE(S): Holotype: WCAB 2701.
TYPE LOCALITY: Mangabeiras, Alagoas, Brazil.
DISTRIBUTION: Known only from the type locality.

Phyllodytes auratus (Boulenger, 1917). Ann. Mag. Nat. Hist., (8)20:185.
ORIGINAL NAME: *Amphodus auratus.*
TYPE(S): Syntypes: BM 1917.9.27.39–41.
TYPE LOCALITY: Mt. Tucutche, Trinidad.
DISTRIBUTION: Known only from the type locality.
COMMENT: See Kenny, 1969, Stud. Fauna Curaçao and other Caribb. Is., 29:1–78.

Phyllodytes luteolus (Wied-Neuwied, 1824). Abbild. Naturgesch. Brasil.:pl. 41, fig. 2.
ORIGINAL NAME: *Hyla luteola.*
TYPE(S): Unknown (?AMNH).
TYPE LOCALITY: Rêgencia, Espírito Santo, Brazil (by subsequent designation of
Bokermann, 1966, An. Acad. Brasil. Cienc., 38:336).
DISTRIBUTION: Coastal region of eastern Brazil from Paraíba to southern Espírito
Santo.

Phyllodytes tuberculosus Bokermann, 1966. An. Acad. Brasil. Cienc., 38:339.
TYPE(S): Holotype: WCAB 31922.
TYPE LOCALITY: Maracás, Bahia, Brazil.
DISTRIBUTION: Sergipe to Bahia, Brazil.

Plectrohyla Brocchi, 1877. Bull. Soc. Philomath. Paris, (7)1:92.
TYPE SPECIES: *Plectrohyla guatemalensis* Brocchi, 1877, by original designation.
DISTRIBUTION: Highlands of southeastern Mexico and northern Central America.
COMMENT: For review of genus and definition of species groups see Duellman, 1970,
Monogr. Mus. Nat. Hist. Univ. Kansas, 1:547–584.

Plectrohyla avia Stuart, 1952. Proc. Biol. Soc. Washington, 65:6.
TYPE(S): Holotype: UMMZ 102280.
TYPE LOCALITY: Granja Lorena, 10 km airline northwest of Colombia, Departamento
Quetzaltenango [now Quezaltenango], Guatemala.
DISTRIBUTION: Pacific slopes of Chiapas, Mexico, and southwestern Guatemala.
COMMENT: In the *Plectrohyla guatemalensis* group.

Plectrohyla dasypus McCranie and Wilson, 1981. Occas. Pap. Mus. Nat. Hist. Univ.
Kansas, 92:1.
TYPE(S): Holotype: KU 186025.
TYPE LOCALITY: Quebrada Cusuco at El Cusuco, 6.5 km WSW Buenos Aires,
Departamento Cortes, Honduras.
DISTRIBUTION: Sierra Omoa, Honduras.
COMMENT: In the *Plectrohyla sagorum* group.

Plectrohyla glandulosa (Boulenger, 1883). Ann. Mag. Nat. Hist., (5)12:164.
ORIGINAL NAME: *Hyla glandulosa.*
TYPE(S): Syntypes: BM 1947.2.20.40–41.
TYPE LOCALITY: "Guatemala".
DISTRIBUTION: Highlands of Guatemala and El Salvador.
COMMENT: In the *Plectrohyla guatemalensis* group.

Plectrohyla guatemalensis Brocchi, 1877. Bull. Soc. Philomath. Paris, (7)1:92.
TYPE(S): Syntypes: MNHNP 6332 (2 specimens).
TYPE LOCALITY: "Pacicilla" (=Patzicia), Departamento Chimaltenango, Guatemala.
DISTRIBUTION: Highlands of Chiapas, Mexico, southeastward to El Salvador and
north-central Honduras.
COMMENT: In the *Plectrohyla guatemalensis* group. This taxon consists of at least
three distinct species (WED).

Plectrohyla hartwegi Duellman, 1968. Univ. Kansas Publ. Mus. Nat. Hist., 17:576.
TYPE(S): Holotype: UMMZ 94428.
TYPE LOCALITY: "Barrejonel (9 kilometers west of Chicomuselo), Chiapas, México,
elevation 1000 meters".
DISTRIBUTION: Pacific slopes of Chiapas and eastern Oaxaca, Mexico; Sierra de las
Minas, Guatemala.
COMMENT: In the *Plectrohyla guatemalensis* group.

Plectrohyla ixil Stuart, 1942. Occas. Pap. Mus. Zool. Univ. Michigan, 455:4.
TYPE(S): Holotype: UMMZ 89092.
TYPE LOCALITY: Finca San Francisco, 25 km N of Nebaj, 1175 m, Departamento el
Quiche, Guatemala.
DISTRIBUTION: Atlantic slopes of the highlands in western Guatemala and Chiapas,
Mexico.
COMMENT: In the *Plectrohyla sagorum* group.

Plectrohyla lacertosa Bumzahem and Smith, 1954. Herpetologica, 10:64.
TYPE(S): Holotype: UIMNH 33693.
TYPE LOCALITY: "Region del Soconusco", Chiapas, Mexico.
DISTRIBUTION: Unknown from any precise locality.
COMMENT: Known only from the holotype; relationships and status of the species
are unknown (WED).

Plectrohyla matudai Hartweg, 1941. Occas. Pap. Mus. Zool. Univ. Michigan, 437:5.
TYPE(S): Holotype: UMMZ 88863.
TYPE LOCALITY: Cerro Ovando, Distrito Soconusco, Chiapas, Mexico.
DISTRIBUTION: Pacific slopes of southeastern Mexico (Oaxaca and Chiapas) and
Guatemala.
COMMENT: In the *Plectrohyla sagorum* group.

Plectrohyla pokomchi Duellman and Campbell, 1984. Copeia, 1984:394.
TYPE(S): Holotype: KU 190231.
TYPE LOCALITY: "Río Sananjá, 3.5 km E of La Unión Barrios, Departamento Baja
Verapaz, Guatemala, 1,585–1,707 m (15° 11' N, 90° 10' W)".
DISTRIBUTION: Cloud forest above 1400 m in the Sierra de las Minas and the
contiguous Sierra de Xucaneb in eastern Guatemala.
COMMENT: In the *Plectrohyla guatemalensis* group.

Plectrohyla pycnochila Rabb, 1959. Herpetologica, 15:45.
TYPE(S): Holotype: AMNH 62667.
TYPE LOCALITY: "Coyame, Veracruz, Mexico" (in error).
DISTRIBUTION: Highlands of central Chiapas, Mexico.
COMMENT: In the *Plectrohyla guatemalensis* group.

Plectrohyla quecchi Stuart, 1942. Occas. Pap. Mus. Zool. Univ. Michigan, 455:1.
TYPE(S): Holotype: UMMZ 89086.
TYPE LOCALITY: Barranca Las Palmas, 2 km north of Finca Los Alpes, Alta Verapaz,
Guatemala, elevation 1015 m.
DISTRIBUTION: Atlantic slopes of central Guatemala.
COMMENT: In the *Plectrohyla sagorum* group.

Plectrohyla sagorum Hartweg, 1941. Occas. Pap. Mus. Zool. Univ. Michigan, 437:2.
TYPE(S): Holotype: UMMZ 88862.
TYPE LOCALITY: Cerro Ovando, 1800 m, Distrito Soconusco, Chiapas, Mexico.
DISTRIBUTION: Pacific slopes of southeastern Mexico (Chiapas) to El Salvador.
COMMENT: In the *Plectrohyla sagorum* group.

Plectrohyla tecunumani Duellman and Campbell, 1984. Copeia, 1984:391.
TYPE(S): Holotype: KU 39956.
TYPE LOCALITY: "a cave 1 km east of Chemal, Departamento Huehuetenango,
    Guatemala, 3,395 m (15° 27' N, 91° 31' W)".
DISTRIBUTION: Two localities in the Sierra de Cuchumatanes (type locality and 2.6
    km N Huehuetenango), Guatemala.

Pseudacris Fitzinger, 1843. Syst. Rept.:31.
TYPE SPECIES: *Rana nigrita* Le Conte, 1825, by monotypy.
DISTRIBUTION: North America east of the Rocky Mountains from Hudson Bay to the
    Gulf of Mexico.

Pseudacris brachyphona (Cope, 1889). Bull. U.S. Natl. Mus., 34:341.
ORIGINAL NAME: *Chorophilus feriarum brachyphonus*.
TYPE(S): Unknown.
TYPE LOCALITY: "in west Pennsylvania, near the Kiskiminitas River",
    Westmoreland County, Pennsylvania, USA.
DISTRIBUTION: Appalachian Mountains from Pennsylvania to Alabama, USA.
COMMENT: Reviewed by Hoffmann, 1980, Cat. Am. Amph. Rept., 234.1–2.

Pseudacris brimleyi Brandt and Walker, 1933. Occas. Pap. Mus. Zool. Univ. Michigan,
    262:2.
TYPE(S): Holotype: UMMZ 74316.
TYPE LOCALITY: "near Washington, [Beaufort County,] North Carolina", USA.
DISTRIBUTION: Atlantic Coastal Plain from Virginia to Georgia, USA.
COMMENT: Reviewed by Hoffmann, 1983, Cat. Am. Amph. Rept., 311.1–2.

Pseudacris clarkii (Baird, 1854). Proc. Acad. Nat. Sci. Philadelphia, 7:60.
ORIGINAL NAME: *Helocaetes clarkii*.
TYPE(S): Syntypes: USNM 3313, 3315, 3317.
TYPE LOCALITY: Galveston and Indianola, Texas, USA; restricted to "Galveston",
    Galveston County, Texas, USA, by Schmidt, 1953, Check List N. Am. Amph.
    Rept., Ed. 6:74.
DISTRIBUTION: Central USA from Kansas to the Gulf of Mexico; lower Rio Grande
    Valley (Texas, USA, and Tamaulipas, Mexico).
COMMENT: See Duellman, 1970, Monogr. Mus. Nat. Hist. Univ. Kansas, 1:642–645.

Pseudacris nigrita (Le Conte, 1825). Ann. Lyc. Nat. Hist. New York, 1:282.
ORIGINAL NAME: *Rana nigrita*.
TYPE(S): Unknown.
TYPE LOCALITY: None given; designated as "Liberty County, Georgia", USA, by
    Schmidt, 1953, Check List N. Am. Amph. Rept., Ed. 6:74.
DISTRIBUTION: Atlantic Coastal Plain from North Carolina to Mississippi, USA.
COMMENT: Two subspecies recognized; for discussion see Smith and Smith, 1952,
    Am. Midl. Nat., 48:165–180, and Schwartz, 1957, Am. Mus. Novit., 1838:1–12.

Pseudacris ornata (Holbrook, 1836). N. Am. Herpetol., Ed. 1, 1:97.
ORIGINAL NAME: *Rana ornata*.
TYPE(S): Unknown.
TYPE LOCALITY: " . . . only in South Carolina . . . about four miles from Charleston,
    between the Cooper and Ashley rivers . . . ", Charleston County, South
    Carolina, USA.
DISTRIBUTION: Atlantic Coastal Plain from North Carolina to central Florida and
    southeastern Louisiana, USA.

COMMENT: For discussion see Harper, 1937, Am. Midl. Nat., 22:134–149.

Pseudacris streckeri A. H. Wright and A. A. Wright, 1923. Handbook Frogs Toads, Ed. 1:26.
TYPE(S): Syntypes: CU 2485 (5 specimens), now lost according to Smith, 1966, Cat. Am. Amph. Rept., 27.1.
TYPE LOCALITY: Not stated; designated (in error) as "Waco, McLennan County, Texas", USA by Schmidt, 1953, Check List N. Am. Amph. Rept., Ed. 6:76; revised to "Somerset, Bexar County, Texas", USA, by Smith, 1966, Cat. Am. Amph. Rept., 27.1.
DISTRIBUTION: Discontinuous in south-central USA: west-central Illinois; southeastern Missouri and adjoining areas; Oklahoma south to the Gulf of Mexico.
COMMENT: Reviewed by Smith, 1966, Cat. Am. Amph. Rept., 27.1–2.

Pseudacris triseriata (Wied-Neuwied, 1838). Reise N. Am., 1:249.
ORIGINAL NAME: *Hyla triseriata*.
TYPE(S): Lost.
TYPE LOCALITY: "Mount Vernon, Ohio River, Indiana", USA; restricted to between Rush Creek and Big Creek along route from New Harmony to Mt. Vernon, Posey County, Indiana, USA, by Harper 1955, Proc. Biol. Soc. Washington, 68: 155.
DISTRIBUTION: North America east of Rocky Mountains from Great Bear Lake and southeastern Quebec, Canada, southward to northern Florida and Texas, USA.
COMMENT: Four subspecies recognized; for discussion see Smith and Smith, 1952, Am. Midl. Nat., 48:165–180, and Schwartz, 1957, Am. Mus. Novit., 1838:1–12.

Pternohyla Boulenger, 1882. Ann. Mag. Nat. Hist., (5)10:326.
TYPE SPECIES: *Pternohyla fodiens* Boulenger, 1882, by monotypy.
DISTRIBUTION: Southern Arizona (USA) southward to Michoacán and Aguascalientes, Mexico.
COMMENT: See Trueb, 1970, Univ. Kansas Publ. Mus. Nat. Hist., 18:546–716, and Duellman, 1970, Monogr. Mus. Nat. Hist. Univ. Kansas, 1:618–628. Reviewed by Trueb, 1969, Cat. Am. Amph. Rept., 77.1.

Pternohyla dentata Smith, 1957. Herpetologica, 13:1.
TYPE(S): Holotype: UIMNH 40551.
TYPE LOCALITY: "8 mi. NE Lagos de Moreno, Jalisco, Mexico".
DISTRIBUTION: Central Mexico (Aguascalientes and adjacent Jalisco).
COMMENT: Reviewed by Trueb, 1969, Cat. Am. Amph. Rept., 77.1–2.

Pternohyla fodiens Boulenger, 1882. Ann. Mag. Nat. Hist., (5)10:326.
TYPE(S): Holotype: BM 1947.2.24.26.
TYPE LOCALITY: "Presidio, [Sinaloa,] W. Mexico".
DISTRIBUTION: Southern Arizona, USA, southward to Michoacán, Mexico.
COMMENT: Reviewed by Trueb, 1969, Cat. Am. Amph. Rept., 77.3–4.

Ptychohyla Taylor, 1944. Univ. Kansas Sci. Bull., 30:41.
TYPE SPECIES: *Ptychohyla adipoventris* Taylor, 1944 (=*Hyla leonhardschultzei* Ahl, 1934), by original designation.
DISTRIBUTION: Moderate elevations of southern Mexico (Chiapas, Guerrero, Oaxaca) southeastward in Central America to northern Nicaragua.
COMMENT: For review of genus see Duellman, 1970, Monogr. Mus. Nat. Hist. Univ. Kansas 1:518–547.

Ptychohyla euthysanota (Kellogg, 1923). Proc. Biol. Soc. Washington, 41:123.
ORIGINAL NAME: *Hyla euthysanota*.
TYPE(S): Holotype: USNM 73296.
TYPE LOCALITY: Los Esemiles, Departamento Chalatenango, El Salvador.
DISTRIBUTION: Southeastern Mexico (Chiapas, Oaxaca) and Pacific slopes of Guatemala and El Salvador.

COMMENT: The two subspecies recognized by Duellman, 1970, Monogr. Mus. Nat. Hist. Univ. Kansas, 1:518–547, are possibly specifically distinct (WED).

Ptychohyla ignicolor Duellman, 1961. Univ. Kansas Publ. Mus. Nat. Hist., 13:352.
  TYPE(S): Holotype: UMMZ 119603.
  TYPE LOCALITY: "a stream 6 kilometers (by road) south of Vista Hermosa, Oaxaca, México (1865 meters)".
  DISTRIBUTION: Northern slopes of Sierra Juárez, Oaxaca, Mexico.

Ptychohyla leonhardschultzei (Ahl, 1934). Zool. Anz., 106:185.
  ORIGINAL NAME: *Hyla leonhard-schultzei.*
  TYPE(S): Holotype: ZMB 34353.
  TYPE LOCALITY: Malinaltepec, Guerrero, Mexico.
  DISTRIBUTION: Atlantic and Pacific slopes of Oaxaca and Guerrero, Mexico.

Ptychohyla panchoi Duellman and Campbell, 1982. Herpetologica, 38:374.
  TYPE(S): Holotype: KU 190333.
  TYPE LOCALITY: "Aldea Vista Hermosa, Municipio Los Amates, Departamento de Izabal, Guatemala . . . . Vista Hermosa is situated on the northern escarpment of the Sierra de las Minas at approximately 15° 17' N, 89° 13' W, at an elevation of 600 m."
  DISTRIBUTION: Sierra de las Minas, Guatemala.

Ptychohyla schmidtorum Stuart, 1954. Proc. Biol. Soc. Washington, 67:169.
  TYPE(S): Holotype: FMNH 27055.
  TYPE LOCALITY: El Porvenir, 17 km airline west of San Marcos, Departamento San Marcos, Guatemala.
  DISTRIBUTION: Atlantic slopes of Chiapas, Mexico, and Pacific slopes of southeastern Mexico and Guatemala.
  COMMENT: The two subspecies recognized by Duellman, 1970, Monogr. Mus. Nat. Hist. Univ. Kansas, 1:518–547, are probably distinct species (WED).

Ptychohyla spinipollex (Schmidt, 1936). Proc. Biol. Soc. Washington, 49:45.
  ORIGINAL NAME: *Hyla spinipollex.*
  TYPE(S): Holotype: MCZ 21300.
  TYPE LOCALITY: "Mountains behind Ceiba", Departamento Atlantidad, Honduras.
  DISTRIBUTION: Atlantic slopes of Central American highlands from Guatemala to northern Nicaragua.

Smilisca Cope, 1865. Proc. Acad. Nat. Sci. Philadelphia, 17:194.
  TYPE SPECIES: *Smilisca daulinia* Cope, 1865 (=*Hyla baudinii* Duméril and Bibron, 1841).
  DISTRIBUTION: Lowlands of Mexico, extreme southern Texas (USA), Central America and northwestern South America (exclusive of Amazon Basin).
  COMMENT: For review see Duellman and Trueb, 1966, Univ. Kansas Publ. Mus. Nat. Hist., 17:281–375, and Duellman, 1970, Monogr. Mus. Nat. Hist. Univ. Kansas, 1: 585–618. Generic synonymy and key in Duellman, 1968, Cat. Am. Amph. Rept., 58.1–2.

Smilisca baudinii (Duméril and Bibron, 1841). Erp. Gén., 8:564.
  ORIGINAL NAME: *Hyla Baudinii.*
  TYPE(S): Holotype: MNHNP 4798.
  TYPE LOCALITY: "Mexique"; restricted to Córdoba, Veracruz, Mexico, by Smith and Taylor, 1950, Univ. Kansas Sci. Bull., 33:347; restricted (in error) to "Mexico City" by Schmidt, 1953, Check List N. Am. Amph. Rept., Ed. 6:69.
  DISTRIBUTION: Extreme southern Texas (USA) and southern Sonora (Mexico) south in tropical lowlands to Costa Rica.
  COMMENT: Reviewed by Duellman, 1968, Cat. Am. Amph. Rept., 59.1–2.

Smilisca cyanosticta (Smith, 1953). Herpetologica, 8:150.
ORIGINAL NAME: *Hyla phaeota cyanosticta.*
TYPE(S): Holotype: USNM 111147.
TYPE LOCALITY: "Piedras Negras, Petén, Guatemala".
DISTRIBUTION: Atlantic slopes of southeastern Mexico and Guatemala from Jalapa
    de Díaz (Mexico) to the Montañas del Mico (Guatemala).
COMMENT: Reviewed by Duellman, 1968, Cat. Am. Amph. Rept., 60.1–2.

Smilisca phaeota (Cope, 1862). Proc. Acad. Nat. Sci. Philadelphia, 14:358.
ORIGINAL NAME: *Hyla phaeota.*
TYPE(S): Holotype: USNM 4347.
TYPE LOCALITY: "Turbo, [Intendencia de Chocó, Colombia,] New Granada".
DISTRIBUTION: Caribbean lowlands of Central America from Nicaragua to
    northwestern Colombia; Pacific lowlands of southeastern Costa Rica, eastern
    Panama, Colombia, and northwestern Ecuador; valleys of the Río Cauca and
    Río Magdalena, Colombia.
COMMENT: Reviewed by Duellman, 1968, Cat. Am. Amph. Rept., 61.1–2.

Smilisca puma (Cope, 1885). Proc. Am. Philos. Soc., 22:183.
ORIGINAL NAME: *Hyla puma.*
TYPE(S): Holotype: USNM 13735.
TYPE LOCALITY: "Nicaragua".
DISTRIBUTION: Caribbean lowlands of Costa Rica and adjacent Nicaragua.
COMMENT: Reviewed by Duellman, 1968, Cat. Am. Amph. Rept., 62.1–2.

Smilisca sila Duellman and Trueb, 1966. Univ. Kansas Publ. Mus. Nat. Hist., 17:318.
TYPE(S): Holotype: KU 91852.
TYPE LOCALITY: "a small stream at north edge of the village of El Volcán, Chiriquí,
    elevation 1280 meters", Panama.
DISTRIBUTION: Pacific lowlands of Costa Rica and Panama; Caribbean lowlands of
    Panama and Colombia.
COMMENT: Reviewed by Duellman, 1968, Cat. Am. Amph. Rept., 63.1–2.

Smilisca sordida (Peters, 1863). Monatsber. Preuss. Akad. Wiss. Berlin, 1863:460.
ORIGINAL NAME: *Hyla sordida.*
TYPE(S): Syntypes: ZMB 3141 (2 specimens).
TYPE LOCALITY: "Veragua", Panama.
DISTRIBUTION: Costa Rica and western Panama.
COMMENT: Reviewed by Duellman, 1968, Cat. Am. Amph. Rept., 64.1–2.

Sphaenorhynchus Tschudi, 1838. Classif. Batr.:71.
TYPE SPECIES: *Hyla lactea* Daudin, 1802, by monotypy.
DISTRIBUTION: Amazon and Orinoco basins of South America; Guianas; eastern
    Brazil; Trinidad.

Sphaenorhynchus bromelicola Bokermann, 1966. Rev. Brasil. Biol., 26:18.
TYPE(S): Holotype: WCAB 31941.
TYPE LOCALITY: Fazenda Santo Onofre, 10 km east of Maracás, Bahia, Brazil.
DISTRIBUTION: Known only from the type locality.

Sphaenorhynchus carneus (Cope, 1868). Proc. Acad. Nat. Sci. Philadelphia, 20:111.
ORIGINAL NAME: *Hylella carnea.*
TYPE(S): Lost.
TYPE LOCALITY: "Napo or upper Maranon", Peru.
DISTRIBUTION: Upper Amazon Basin in southern Colombia, Peru, and Ecuador;
    central Amazonia in Brazil.
COMMENT: See Duellman, 1974, Occas. Pap. Mus. Nat. Hist Univ. Kansas, 27:22.

Sphaenorhynchus dorisae (Goin, 1957). Caldasia, 8(36):16.
ORIGINAL NAME: *Sphoenohyla dorisae*.
TYPE(S): Holotype: FSM 3506.
TYPE LOCALITY: Leticia, Comisaria Amazonas, Colombia.
DISTRIBUTION: Upper Amazon Basin in southeastern Colombia, Ecuador, and
  Brazilian Amazonia.

Sphaenorhynchus lacteus (Daudin, 1802). Hist. Nat. Rain. Gren. Crap.:20.
ORIGINAL NAME: *Hyla lactea*.
TYPE(S): Holotype: MNHNP 4871.
TYPE LOCALITY: "Brasil".
DISTRIBUTION: Amazon and Orinoco basins, Guianas, and Trinidad.
COMMENT: See Duellman and Lynch, 1981, J. Herpetol., 15:237–239, for discussion
  of nomenclature and synonymy of *Sphaenorhynchus eurhostus* Rivero, 1969,
  Copeia, 1969:701. For discussion (as *Sphaenorhynchus eurhostus*) see Rivero,
  1969, Copeia, 1969:700–703.

Sphaenorhynchus orophilus (A. Lutz and B. Lutz, 1938). An. Acad. Brasil. Cienc., 10:
  178.
ORIGINAL NAME: *Hyla (Sphoenohyla) orophila*.
TYPE(S): Holotype: AL-MN 3309.
TYPE LOCALITY: Quitandinha, Petrópolis, Rio de Janeiro, Brazil.
DISTRIBUTION: Serra do Mar in Rio de Janeiro and São Paulo, Brazil.

Sphaenorhynchus palustris Bokermann, 1966. Rev. Brasil. Biol., 26:16.
TYPE(S): Holotype: WCAB 19235.
TYPE LOCALITY: Sooretama, Linhares, Espírito Santo, Brazil.
DISTRIBUTION: Known only from the type locality.

Sphaenorhynchus pauloalvini Bokermann, 1973. Rev. Brasil. Biol., 33:592.
TYPE(S): Holotype: WCAB 46453.
TYPE LOCALITY: Centro de Pesquisas do Cacau, Ilhéus, Bahia, Brazil.
DISTRIBUTION: Known only from the type locality.

Sphaenorhynchus planicola (A. Lutz and B. Lutz, 1938). An. Acad. Brasil. Cienc., 10:182.
ORIGINAL NAME: *Hyla (Sphoenohyla) planicola*.
TYPE(S): Holotype: AL-MN 2658.
TYPE LOCALITY: Recreio dos Bandeirantes, Rio de Janeiro, Brazil.
DISTRIBUTION: Coastal lowlands of Rio de Janeiro, southeastern Brazil.

Sphaenorhynchus prasinus Bokermann, 1973. Rev. Brasil. Biol., 33:589.
TYPE(S): Holotype: WCAB 46499.
TYPE LOCALITY: Centro de Pesquisas do Cacau, Ilhéus, Bahia, Brazil.
DISTRIBUTION: Known only from the type locality.

Sphaenorhynchus surdus (Cochran, 1953). Herpetologica, 8:112.
ORIGINAL NAME: *Hyla aurantiaca surda*.
TYPE(S): Holotype: UMMZ 106736.
TYPE LOCALITY: Curitiba, Paraná, Brazil.
DISTRIBUTION: Known only from the type locality.

Trachycephalus Tschudi, 1838. Classif. Batr.:74.
TYPE SPECIES: *Trachycephalus nigromaculatus* Tschudi, 1838, by monotypy.
DISTRIBUTION: Eastern Brazil and Pacific lowlands from southern Colombia to
  northern Peru.
COMMENT: See Trueb, 1970, Univ. Kansas Publ. Mus. Nat. Hist., 18:546–716.

Trachycephalus atlas Bokermann, 1966. Neotropica, 12:120.
TYPE(S): Holotype: WCAB 33669.
TYPE LOCALITY: Fazenda Santo Onofre, 10 km east of Maracás, Bahia, Brazil.
DISTRIBUTION: Northeastern Brazil.

Trachycephalus jordani (Stejneger and Test, 1891). Proc. U.S. Natl. Mus., 14:167.
ORIGINAL NAME: *Tetraprion jordani.*
TYPE(S): Holotype: USNM 12274.
TYPE LOCALITY: Guayaquil, Provincia Guayas, Ecuador.
DISTRIBUTION: Pacific lowlands of South America from southern Colombia to northern Peru.

Trachycephalus nigromaculatus Tschudi, 1838. Classif. Batr.:74.
TYPE(S): Syntypes: MNHNP 4608–9.
TYPE LOCALITY: "America meridionalis".
DISTRIBUTION: Coastal regions of southern Brazil from Espírito Santo to São Paulo; interior in Minas Gerais and Goiás.

Triprion Cope, 1866. Proc. Acad. Nat. Sci. Philadelphia, 18:127.
TYPE SPECIES: *Pharyngodon petasatus* Cope, 1865, by monotypy.
DISTRIBUTION: Pacific lowlands of Mexico; Yucatan Peninsula of Mexico and Guatemala.
COMMENT: For discussion see Duellman, 1970, Monogr. Mus. Nat. Hist. Univ. Kansas, 1:628–640. *Triprion* is a replacement name for *Pharyngodon* Cope, 1865, Proc. Acad. Nat. Sci. Philadelphia, 17:193, which is preoccupied.

Triprion petasatus (Cope, 1865). Proc. Acad. Nat. Sci. Philadelphia, 17:193.
ORIGINAL NAME: *Pharyngodon petasatus.*
TYPE(S): Holotype: USNM 12287.
TYPE LOCALITY: Cenote Tamaché, 17 km north of Mérida, Yucatán, Mexico.
DISTRIBUTION: Yucatan Peninsula, Mexico, through El Petén, Guatemala, to northern Honduras.

Triprion spatulatus Günther, 1882. Ann. Mag. Nat. Hist., (5)10:279.
TYPE(S): Syntypes: BM 1947.2.25.79–81.
TYPE LOCALITY: Presidio de Mazatlán, Sinaloa, Mexico.
DISTRIBUTION: Pacific lowlands of western Mexico (Sinaloa to Oaxaca).
COMMENT: Two subspecies were recognized by Duellman, 1970, Monogr. Mus. Nat. Hist. Univ. Kansas, 1:629–637.

SUBFAMILY: **Pelodryadinae** Günther, 1859 "1858".
CITATION: Cat. Batr. Sal. Coll. Brit. Mus.:119.
DISTRIBUTION: The Australo-Papuan region.
COMMENT: As originally formed the group name was Pelodryadidae. On the basis of work by Tyler, 1971, Univ. Kansas Publ. Mus. Nat. Hist., 19:319–360, Savage, 1973, *In* Vial (ed.), Evol. Biol. Anurans:351–445, considered this group independently derived from a "leptodactylid" stock in Australia (convergent with the Hylidae) and placed it in a distinct family, the Pelodryadidae. This arrangement was followed by Fouquette and Delahoussaye, 1977, J. Herpetol., 11:387–396, and Goin, Goin, and Zug, 1978, Intr. Herpetol., Ed. 3. The Pelodryadidae was considered a subfamily of the Hylidae by Duellman, 1977, Das Tierreich, 95:1–225, an arrangement followed by most subsequent authors who recognize this group. Cogger, Cameron, and Cogger, 1983, Zool. Cat. Aust., 1(Amph. Rept.):35–51, supplied synonymies and literature reviews for the Australian species.
REVIEWERS: Margaret Davies (MD); Michael J. Tyler (MJT); Richard G. Zweifel (RGZ) (New Guinea).

Cyclorana Steindachner, 1867. Reise Freg. Novara, Amph.:29.
TYPE SPECIES: *Cyclorana novaehollandiae* Steindachner, 1867, by monotypy.
DISTRIBUTION: Australia, except extreme southeastern and southwestern parts.
COMMENT: Australian frogs of the *Cyclorana australis* group were reviewed by Tyler and Martin, 1975, Trans. R. Soc. S. Aust., 99:93–99, and other species by Tyler and Martin, 1977, Rec. S. Aust. Mus., 17:261–276. Tyler, Davies, and King, 1979,

Aust. J. Zool., 27:699–708, reported on karyology. *Cyclorana* was omitted from
the Myobatrachidae by Heyer and Liem, 1976, Smithson. Contrib. Zool., 233:11,
thereby implying transfer to the Hylidae. Transferred formally by Tyler, 1978,
Amph. S. Aust.

Cyclorana australis (Gray, 1842). Zool. Misc., 2:56.
ORIGINAL NAME: *Alytes australis.*
TYPE(S): Syntypes: BM 1947.2.18.43–44.
TYPE LOCALITY: "North coast of Australia"; restricted to Port Essington, Northern
Territory, Australia, by Tyler and Martin, 1975, Trans. R. Soc. S. Aust., 99:94.
DISTRIBUTION: Kimberley Division (Western Australia) through northern Australia
as far as the Gulf District of Queensland, Australia.

Cyclorana brevipes (Peters, 1871). Monatsber. Preuss. Akad. Wiss. Berlin, 1871:648.
ORIGINAL NAME: *Chiroleptes brevipes.*
TYPE(S): Holotype: ZMB 7063 (not located).
TYPE LOCALITY: Port Bowen [=Port Clinton] Queensland [Australia].
DISTRIBUTION: Northeastern and Gulf region of Queensland, Australia.
COMMENT: Redefined by Tyler and Martin, 1977, Rec. S. Aust. Mus., 17:263.

Cyclorana cryptotis Tyler and Martin, 1977. Rec. S. Aust. Mus., 17:271.
TYPE(S): Holotype: SAMA R14716.
TYPE LOCALITY: Daly Waters, Northern Territory, Australia.
DISTRIBUTION: Western Australia and Northern Territory, between latitudes 17° 20'
and 14° 30' S.
COMMENT: Redefined by Tyler, Davies, and Martin, 1982, Copeia, 1982:260.

Cyclorana cultripes Parker, 1940. Novit. Zool., 42:22.
TYPE(S): Holotype: BM 1947.2.18.45.
TYPE LOCALITY: Alexandria Station, Northern Territory [Australia].
DISTRIBUTION: Lower eastern half of Northern Territory to southwestern
Queensland and possibly northern South Australia, Australia.
COMMENT: See Tyler and Martin, 1977, Rec. S. Aust. Mus., 17:261–276.

Cyclorana longipes Tyler and Martin, 1977. Rec. S. Aust. Mus., 17:271.
TYPE(S): Holotype: WAM R43258.
TYPE LOCALITY: Mitchell Plateau (14° 52' S, 125° 50' E), Kimberley Division,
Western Australia.
DISTRIBUTION: Kimberley region of Western Australia and adjacent Northern
Territory to northern Queensland, Australia.

Cyclorana maculosa Tyler and Martin, 1977. Rec. S. Aust. Mus., 17:269.
ORIGINAL NAME: *Cyclorana maculosus.*
TYPE(S): Holotype: SAMA R14719.
TYPE LOCALITY: Daly Waters, Northern Territory, Australia.
DISTRIBUTION: Northeastern Northern Territory to northwestern Queensland,
Australia.

Cyclorana maini Tyler and Martin, 1977. Rec. S. Aust. Mus., 17:273.
TYPE(S): Holotype: SAMA R15191.
TYPE LOCALITY: Barrow Creek, Northern Territory, Australia.
DISTRIBUTION: Southern half of Northern Territory through central Western
Australia to the western coastal region, Australia.

Cyclorana manya van Beurden and McDonald, 1980. Trans. R. Soc. S. Aust., 104:193.
TYPE(S): Holotype: QM J34886.
TYPE LOCALITY: Between Coen airport and Deep Creek crossing, 25 km N of Coen
township (13° 52' S, 143° 12' E), Queensland, Australia.
DISTRIBUTION: Cape York Peninsula, Queensland, Australia.

Cyclorana novaehollandiae Steindachner, 1867. Reise Freg. Novara, Amph.:29.
  TYPE(S): Syntypes: NHMW 4716–17 (probable).
  TYPE LOCALITY: Rockhampton, Queensland [Australia].
  DISTRIBUTION: Cape York Peninsula (Queensland) to the New South Wales border
    and interiors of Queensland and New South Wales, Australia.
  COMMENT: In the *Cyclorana australis* complex; see Tyler and Martin, 1975, Trans. R.
    Soc. Aust., 99:93–99.

Cyclorana platycephala (Günther, 1873). Ann. Mag. Nat. Hist., (4)11:350.
  ORIGINAL NAME: *Chiroleptes platycephalus.*
  TYPE(S): Holotype: BM 1947.2.18.42.
  TYPE LOCALITY: Fort Bourke [New South Wales, Australia].
  DISTRIBUTION: Drier inland regions of Australia, except Victoria.
  COMMENT: See comment under *Cyclorana slevini.*

Cyclorana slevini Loveridge, 1950. Proc. Biol. Soc. Washington, 63:131.
  TYPE(S): Holotype: CAS 82052.
  TYPE LOCALITY: Noondoo, southeastern Queensland, Australia.
  DISTRIBUTION: Known only from the type locality.
  COMMENT: *Cyclorana slevini* was included as a synonym of *Cyclorana platycephala* by
    Cogger, Cameron, and Cogger, 1983, Zool. Cat. Aust., 1(Amph. Rept.):37,
    with no discussion.

Cyclorana vagitus Tyler, Davies, and Martin, 1981. Rec. W. Aust. Mus., 9:148.
  TYPE(S): Holotype: WAM R71037.
  TYPE LOCALITY: "junction of the Great Northern Highway and the road to Derby,
    41 km S of Derby, 124° 38′ E, 17° 44′ S, Kimberley Division", Western
    Australia.
  DISTRIBUTION: Kimberley Division, Western Australia, and northwestern Northern
    Territory, Australia. The grammatically incorrect epithet *vagita* has
    been used.

Cyclorana verrucosa Tyler and Martin, 1977. Rec. S. Aust. Mus., 17:267.
  ORIGINAL NAME: *Cyclorana verrucosus*
  TYPE(S): Holotype: QM J18105.
  TYPE LOCALITY: 18 km W of Dalby, Queensland, Australia.
  DISTRIBUTION: Interior basins of Queensland and New South Wales, Australia.

Litoria Tschudi, 1838. Classif. Batr.:36.
  TYPE SPECIES: *Litoria freycineti* Tschudi, 1838, by monotypy.
  DISTRIBUTION: New Guinea, Moluccan Is., Lesser Sunda Is., Timor, Bismarck
    Archipelago, Solomon Is., and Australia, including Tasmania; introduced into
    New Caledonia, New Hebrides, Guam, and New Zealand.
  COMMENT: Species groups noted in the species accounts were defined by Tyler and
    Davies, 1978, Aust. J. Zool., Suppl. Ser., 63:1–47. Papuan species were reviewed
    (as *Hyla*) by Tyler, 1968, Zool. Verh., Leiden, 96:1–203; Australian state
    checklists provided by Tyler, 1982, Frogs, Ed. 2.

Litoria adelaidensis (Gray, 1841). Ann. Mag. Nat. Hist., (2)7:90.
  ORIGINAL NAME: *Hyla adelaidensis.*
  TYPE(S): Holotype: BM 1947.2.22.80.
  TYPE LOCALITY: "western Australia".
  DISTRIBUTION: Southwestern Western Australia.
  COMMENT: Discussed by Tyler, Smith, and Johnstone, 1984, Frogs W. Aust. In the
    Litoria adelaidensis group.

Litoria alboguttata (Günther, 1867). Ann. Mag. Nat. Hist., (3)20:54.
  ORIGINAL NAME: *Chiroleptes alboguttatus.*
  TYPE(S): Syntypes: BM 1947.2.20.6–7 (formerly 67.5.6.78–79) (Cape York),
    1947.2.18.50–51 (formerly 1936.12.3.125–126) (Port Denison).
  TYPE LOCALITY: Port Denison and Cape York, Queensland, Australia.
  DISTRIBUTION: Queensland and New South Wales, Australia.

COMMENT: In the *Litoria aurea* group. Transferred to *Litoria* from *Cyclorana* by Tyler, 1974, Proc. R. Soc. Queensland, 85:27. Maxson, Tyler, and Maxson, 1982, Aust. J. Zool., 30:643, discussed relationships with *Cyclorana*.

Litoria albolabris (Wandolleck, 1911). Abh. Ber. K. Zool. Anthro. Ethno. Mus. Dresden, 13:12.
ORIGINAL NAME: *Hyla albolabris*.
TYPE(S): NHMW 16976 and SAMA R4947 considered syntypes by Duellman, 1977, Das Tierreich, 95:114; Obst, 1977, Zool. Abh. Staatl. Mus. Tierkd. Dresden, 34:173, listed MTKD D2220 as holotype (destroyed) and a paratype in NHMW.
TYPE LOCALITY: "Eitapé" (=Aitape), West Sepik Province, Papua New Guinea.
DISTRIBUTION: Known only from the type locality.
COMMENT: In the *Litoria albolabris* group.

Litoria amboinensis (Horst, 1883). Notes Leyden Mus., 5:239.
ORIGINAL NAME: *Hyla amboinensis*.
TYPE(S): Syntypes: RMNH 4418 (Amboina, 2 specimens), 4419 (Misool).
TYPE LOCALITY: "Amboina" and "Misool", Moluccas, Indonesia.
DISTRIBUTION: New Guinea (southern lowlands, Huon and Vogelkop peninsulas) and Moluccan Is. (Amboina, Ceram, Misool).
COMMENT: For discussion see Tyler, 1968, Zool. Verh., Leiden, 96:27. In the *Litoria peronii* group.

Litoria angiana (Boulenger, 1915). Ann. Mag. Nat. Hist., (8)16:402.
ORIGINAL NAME: *Hyla angiana*.
TYPE(S): Syntypes: BM 1947.2.24.6 and 1947.2.30.95–98.
TYPE LOCALITY: "Angi Lakes (6000 feet) in the Arfak Mountains, . . . Mt. Koebré (8000 feet) in the same mountains", Vogelkop Peninsula, Irian Jaya (New Guinea), Indonesia.
DISTRIBUTION: Mountains of New Guinea.
COMMENT: For discussion see Tyler, 1968, Zool. Verh., Leiden, 96:33. In the *Litoria angiana* group.

Litoria arfakiana (Peters and Doria, 1878). Ann. Mus. Civ. Stor. Nat. Genova, 13:421.
ORIGINAL NAME: *Hyla (Litoria) arfakiana*.
TYPE(S): MSNG 29723A designated lectotype by Capocaccia, 1957, Ann. Mus. Civ. Stor. Nat. Genova, 69:213.
TYPE LOCALITY: "Hatam", Arfak Mountains, Vogelkop Peninsula, Irian Jaya, Indonesia (New Guinea).
DISTRIBUTION: Highlands of New Guinea.
COMMENT: In the *Litoria arfakiana* group. See Menzies and Zweifel, 1974, Am. Mus. Novit., 2558:1–16.

Litoria aruensis (Horst, 1883). Notes Leyden Mus., 5:242.
ORIGINAL NAME: *Hyla aruensis*.
TYPE(S): Syntypes: RMNH 4416 (Aru, 2 specimens), 4417 (Misool).
TYPE LOCALITY: "Aroe-Islands" (=Aru) and "Misool", Irian Jaya (New Guinea) and Moluccas, New Guinea.
DISTRIBUTION: New Guinea, Moluccan Is. (Waigeo, Misool), Aru Is., and Louisiade Archipelago.
COMMENT: For discussion see Tyler, 1968, Zool. Verh., Leiden, 96:43. In the *Litoria aruensis* group.

Litoria aurea (Lesson, 1830). Voy. Coquille, Zool., 2:60.
ORIGINAL NAME: *Rana aurea*.
TYPE(S): MNHNP 4857 listed as lectotype by Roux-Estève, 1979, Bull. Trim. Soc. Géol. Normandie et Amies Mus. Harve, 66:26.
TYPE LOCALITY: Macquarie River, Bathurst, New South Wales, Australia; lectotype from Port Jackson (=Sydney), New South Wales, Australia.
DISTRIBUTION: Eastern New South Wales, south of the Richmond River, Australia.

COMMENT: In the *Litoria aurea* group. See Courtice and Grigg, 1975, Aust. Zool., 18: 149–163, and Maxson, Tyler, and Maxson, 1982, Aust. J. Zool., 30:643. Cogger, Cameron, and Cogger, 1983, Zool. Cat. Aust., 1(Amph. Rept.):39, discussed types and citation of the description.

Litoria becki (Loveridge, 1945). Proc. Biol. Soc. Washington, 58:53.
ORIGINAL NAME: *Hyla becki.*
TYPE(S): Holotype: MCZ 25900.
TYPE LOCALITY: "Mt. Wilhelm, 5000–8000 feet, Bismarck Range, Madang Division", Chimbu Province, Papua New Guinea.
DISTRIBUTION: Known only from the type locality.
COMMENT: For discussion see Tyler, 1968, Zool. Verh., Leiden, 96:47. In the *Litoria becki* group.

Litoria bicolor (Gray, 1842). Zool. Misc., 3:57.
ORIGINAL NAME: *Eucnemis bicolor.*
TYPE(S): Holotype: BM 1947.2.22.59.
TYPE LOCALITY: Port Essington, Northern Territory, Australia.
DISTRIBUTION: Coastal Australia from Western Australia to northeastern Queensland; southern lowlands of New Guinea; Aru Is.
COMMENT: For discussion see Straughan, 1969, Proc. R. Soc. Queensland, 80:43.

Litoria booroolongensis (Moore, 1961). Bull. Am. Mus. Nat. Hist., 121:292.
ORIGINAL NAME: *Hyla booroolongensis.*
TYPE(S): Holotype: AM R16006.
TYPE LOCALITY: Guy Fawkes Creek, Ebor, New South Wales, Australia.
DISTRIBUTION: Eastern New South Wales, Australia.
COMMENT: In the *Litoria booroolongensis* group.

Litoria brevipalmata Tyler, Martin, and Watson, 1972. Proc. Linn. Soc. New South Wales, 97:82.
TYPE(S): Holotype: SAMA R11236.
TYPE LOCALITY: Ourimbah Creek, 5 mi. northwest of Gosford, New South Wales, Australia.
DISTRIBUTION: Eastern New South Wales, Australia.
COMMENT: In the *Litoria brevipalmata* group.

Litoria brongersmai (Loveridge, 1945). Proc. Biol. Soc. Washington, 58:56.
ORIGINAL NAME: *Hyla brongersmai.*
TYPE(S): Holotype: MCZ 15203.
TYPE LOCALITY: "Parana [=Panara] Valley, central Dutch New Guinea", near Doorman Top, Snow Mountains, Irian Jaya (New Guinea), Indonesia.
DISTRIBUTION: Known only from the type locality.
COMMENT: See Tyler, 1968, Zool. Verh., Leiden, 96:54. Questionably in the *Litoria becki* group.

Litoria bulmeri (Tyler, 1968). Zool. Verh., Leiden, 96:56.
ORIGINAL NAME: *Hyla bulmeri.*
TYPE(S): Holotype: SAMA R5625.
TYPE LOCALITY: " . . . at an altitude of approximately 7300 ft at Glkm, upper Aunjung Valley, Schrader Mountains, Eastern Mountains, [Madang Province, Papua] New Guinea".
DISTRIBUTION: Known only from the type locality.
COMMENT: In the *Litoria bulmeri* group.

Litoria burrowsi (Scott, 1942). Rec. Queen Victoria Mus., 1:5.
ORIGINAL NAME: *Hyla burrowsi.*
TYPE(S): Holotype: QVM 1941.41.
TYPE LOCALITY: Cradle Valley, Tasmania [Australia].
DISTRIBUTION: Southwestern and western Tasmania, Australia.

COMMENT: In the *Litoria maculata* group. See Martin and Littlejohn, 1982, Tasman. Amph.:30, for discussion.

Litoria caerulea (White, 1790). J. Voy. New South Wales:248.
ORIGINAL NAME: *Rana caerulea*.
TYPE(S): Formerly in Hunterian Mus. (presumed lost); see Tyler and Dobson, 1973, Herpetologica, 29:373–375.
TYPE LOCALITY: New South Wales, Australia.
DISTRIBUTION: Northern and eastern Australia; islands in the Torres Straits; New Guinea (northern lowlands, southern lowlands, and Vogelkop Peninsula); New Zealand (introduced).
COMMENT: See Tyler, 1968, Zool. Verh., Leiden, 96:60, and Tyler, Crook, and Davies, 1983, Rec. S. Aust. Mus., 18:424. In the *Litoria caerulea* group. Without discussion, Cogger, Cameron, and Cogger, 1983, Zool. Cat. Aust., 1(Amph. Rept.):43, recognized *Litoria gilleni* (=*Hyla gilleni* Spencer, 1896, Rep. Horn Exp. Cent. Aust., 2:173; Holotype: NMM D9827; Type locality: Alice Springs, Northern Territory, Australia), usually considered a subspecies or synonym of *Litoria caerulea*, as a distinct species.

Litoria capitula (Tyler, 1968). Zool. Verh., Leiden, 96:64.
ORIGINAL NAME: *Hyla capitula*.
TYPE(S): Holotype: RMNH 5317.
TYPE LOCALITY: "Samlakki, Tenimber Island", Moluccan Is., Indonesia.
DISTRIBUTION: Tenimber I., Moluccan Is., Indonesia.
COMMENT: In the *Litoria rubella* group.

Litoria cavernicola Tyler and Davies, 1979. Trans. R. Soc. S. Aust., 103:149.
TYPE(S): Holotype: WAM R43228.
TYPE LOCALITY: 3 km west of Surveyor's Pool, Mitchell Plateau, Kimberley Division, Western Australia, Australia.
DISTRIBUTION: Gorges bordering the Mitchell Plateau, northern Western Australia.
COMMENT: In the *Litoria caerulea* group. See Tyler, Smith, and Johnstone, 1984, Frogs W. Aust.

Litoria chloris (Boulenger, 1893). Proc. Linn. Soc. New South Wales, (2)7:403.
ORIGINAL NAME: *Hyla chloris*.
TYPE(S): Holotype: BM 1947.2.23.86.
TYPE LOCALITY: Dunoon, Richmond River, New South Wales, Australia.
DISTRIBUTION: Eastern Australia (Queensland and New South Wales).
COMMENT: In the *Litoria aruensis* group.

Litoria chloronota (Boulenger, 1911). Ann. Mag. Nat. Hist., (8)8:55.
ORIGINAL NAME: *Hylella chloronota*.
TYPE(S): Syntypes: BM 1947.2.31.20–21.
TYPE LOCALITY: "Arfak Mountains at an altitude of 8000 feet", Vogelkop Peninsula, Irian Jaya (New Guinea), Indonesia.
DISTRIBUTION: Known only from the type locality.
COMMENT: See Tyler, 1968, Zool. Verh., Leiden, 96:66. In the *Litoria bicolor* group.

Litoria citropa (Duméril and Bibron, 1841). Erp. Gén., 8:600.
ORIGINAL NAME: *Hyla citropa*.
TYPE(S): Holotype: MNHNP 4854.
TYPE LOCALITY: "Nouvelle-Hollande . . . au Port Jackson [=Sydney]", New South Wales, Australia.
DISTRIBUTION: Mountains and coastal areas of New South Wales and mountains of Victoria in southeastern Australia.
COMMENT: In the *Litoria citropa* group. See comment under *Litoria jenolanensis*. See also Tyler and Anstis, 1975, Rec. S. Aust. Mus., 17:41. *Dendrohyas citropa*

Tschudi, 1838, Classif. Batr.:75, is a *nomen nudum* according to Cogger, Cameron, and Cogger, 1983, Zool. Cat. Aust., 1(Amph. Rept.):41.

Litoria congenita (Peters and Doria, 1878). Ann. Mus. Civ. Stor. Nat. Genova, 13:427.
ORIGINAL NAME: *Hyla* (*Litoria*) *congenita*.
TYPE(S): MSNG 9722A designated lectotype by Capocaccia, 1957, Ann. Mus. Civ. Stor. Nat. Genova, 69:213.
TYPE LOCALITY: "Yule Island", Central Province, Papua New Guinea.
DISTRIBUTION: Southern coastal lowlands of New Guinea; Aru Is.
COMMENT: See Tyler, 1968, Zool. Verh., Leiden, 96:68. In the *Litoria rubella* group.

Litoria contrastens (Tyler, 1968). Zool. Verh., Leiden, 96:72.
ORIGINAL NAME: *Hyla contrastens*.
TYPE(S): Holotype: SAMA R5845.
TYPE LOCALITY: "Barabuna", near Kundiawa, eastern mountains, Chimbu Province, Papua New Guinea.
DISTRIBUTION: Eastern mountains, Papua New Guinea.
COMMENT: In the *Litoria bicolor* group.

Litoria cooloolensis Liem, 1974. Mem. Queensland Mus., 17:169.
TYPE(S): Holotype: QM J22646.
TYPE LOCALITY: Lake Coolamera, Cooloola, southeast Queensland, Australia.
DISTRIBUTION: Southeastern Queensland, Australia.
COMMENT: In the *Litoria bicolor* group.

Litoria coplandi (Tyler, 1968). Rec. S. Aust. Mus., 15:416.
ORIGINAL NAME: *Hyla coplandi*.
TYPE(S): Holotype: WAM R13722G
TYPE LOCALITY: Inverway Station, Northern Territory, Australia.
DISTRIBUTION: Northwestern Western Australia and Northern Territory, Australia.
COMMENT: In the *Litoria coplandi* group.

Litoria cyclorhynchus (Boulenger, 1882). Cat. Batr. Sal. Brit. Mus.:411.
ORIGINAL NAME: *Hyla aurea* var. *cyclorhynchus*.
TYPE(S): Syntypes: AMNH 62493, BM 69.7.22.3–7.
TYPE LOCALITY: "W. Australia".
DISTRIBUTION: Southern coastal Western Australia.
COMMENT: In the *Litoria aurea* group. Discussed by Tyler, Smith, and Johnstone, 1984, Frogs W. Aust.

Litoria dahlii (Boulenger, 1896). Proc. Zool. Soc. London, 1895:867.
ORIGINAL NAME: *Chiroleptes dahlii*.
TYPE(S): Syntypes: BM 1947.2.18.49 (formerly 95.11.14.25), UZMO K2002.
TYPE LOCALITY: Daly River, Northern Territory, Australia.
DISTRIBUTION: Northeastern Western Australia, Northern Territory, and northwestern Queensland, Australia.
COMMENT: In the *Litoria aurea* group. For discussion see Tyler, Davies, and King, 1978, Trans. R. Soc. S. Aust., 102:17–24.

Litoria darlingtoni (Loveridge, 1945). Proc. Biol. Soc. Washington, 58:53.
ORIGINAL NAME: *Hyla darlingtoni*.
TYPE(S): Holotype: MCZ 25890.
TYPE LOCALITY: "Mount Wilhelm, 5000–8000 feet, Bismarck Range, Madang Division, [Chimbu Province, Papua] New Guinea ".
DISTRIBUTION: Eastern mountains of New Guinea.
COMMENT: See Tyler, 1968, Zool. Verh., Leiden, 96:76. In the *Litoria peronii* group.

Litoria dentata (Keferstein, 1868). Arch. Naturgesch., 34:284.
ORIGINAL NAME: *Hyla dentata*.
TYPE(S): Holotype: probably ZFMK (formerly Zool. Mus. Göttingen 123a),
according to Cogger, Cameron, and Cogger, 1983, Zool. Cat. Aust., 1(Amph.
Rept.):42.
TYPE LOCALITY: New South Wales, Australia.
DISTRIBUTION: Eastern New South Wales and southeastern Queensland, Australia.
COMMENT: See Moore, 1961, Bull. Am. Mus. Nat. Hist., 12:275. In the *Litoria rubella*
group.

Litoria dorsalis Macleay, 1877. Proc. Linn. Soc. New South Wales, 2:138.
TYPE(S): Unknown.
TYPE LOCALITY: "Katow", near mouth of Binaturi River, Western Province, Papua
New Guinea; stated as "Mawatta, Binaturi River (as Katow), Papua New
Guinea", by Cogger, Cameron, and Cogger, 1983, Zool. Cat. Aust., 1(Amph.
Rept.):42.
DISTRIBUTION: Southern lowlands, New Guinea.
COMMENT: In the *Litoria dorsalis* group; see Tyler, 1968, Zool. Verh., Leiden, 96:80.
See comment under *Litoria microbelos*.

Litoria dorsivena (Tyler, 1968). Zool. Verh., Leiden, 96:83.
ORIGINAL NAME: *Hyla dorsivena*.
TYPE(S): Holotype: SAMA R7901.
TYPE LOCALITY: "Telefomin, Eastern Mountains, [West Sepik Province, Papua] New
Guinea".
DISTRIBUTION: Eastern and Arfak mountains, New Guinea.
COMMENT: In the *Litoria dorsivena* group.

Litoria eucnemis (Lönnberg, 1900). Ann. Mag. Nat. Hist., (7)6:579.
ORIGINAL NAME: *Hyla eucnemis*.
TYPE(S): Syntypes: BM 1947.2.23.87, ZIUU (no number).
TYPE LOCALITY: Sattelberg, Huon Peninsula, New Guinea.
DISTRIBUTION: Southern lowlands and Huon Peninsula, New Guinea; northeastern
coastal Queensland, Australia.
COMMENT: In the *Litoria eucnemis* group; see Tyler, 1968, Zool. Verh., Leiden, 96:86.
With no discussion, Australian populations were recognized as a distinct
species, *Litoria serrata*, by Cogger, Cameron, and Cogger, 1983, Zool. Cat.
Aust., 1(Amph. Rept.):49. See Tyler, 1965, Proc. Zool. Soc. London, 145:91–
106. See comment under *Litoria genimaculata*.

Litoria everetti (Boulenger, 1897). Ann. Mag. Nat. Hist., (6)19:509.
ORIGINAL NAME: *Hyla everetti*.
TYPE(S): Syntypes: BM 1947.2.23.60–65 (Savu), 1947.2.23.66–67 (Sumba).
TYPE LOCALITY: Savu and Sumba Is., Indonesia.
DISTRIBUTION: Timor and adjacent Lesser Sunda Is., Indonesia.
COMMENT: See Tyler, 1968, Zool. Verh., Leiden, 96:90. In the *Litoria peronii* group.

Litoria ewingii (Duméril and Bibron, 1841). Erp. Gén., 8:597.
ORIGINAL NAME: *Hyla Ewingii*.
TYPE(S): Holotype: MNHNP 4851.
TYPE LOCALITY: "la terre de Van Diéman" (=Tasmania), Australia.
DISTRIBUTION: Southeastern Australia and Tasmania; introduced into New Zealand.
COMMENT: See Moore, 1961, Bull. Am. Mus. Nat. Hist., 12:278. In the *Litoria ewingii*
group.

Litoria fallax (Peters, 1881). Monatsber. Preuss. Akad. Wiss. Berlin, 1881:224.
ORIGINAL NAME: *Hylomantis fallax*.
TYPE(S): Syntypes: ZMB 5887 (2 specimens), 5925 (2 specimens), 6633 (2 specimens), 9650.
TYPE LOCALITY: Port Bowen [=Port Clinton], MacKay, and Rockhampton, Queensland, Australia.
DISTRIBUTION: East coast of Australia and New South Wales.
COMMENT: In the *Litoria bicolor* group. For discussion (as *Litoria glauerti*) see Straughan, 1969, Proc. R. Soc. Queensland, 80:43–54.

Litoria flavipunctata Courtice and Grigg, 1975. Aust. Zool., 18:159.
TYPE(S): Holotype: AM R40676.
TYPE LOCALITY: Booralong Creek Road, 12.8 km W of Guyra, New South Wales, Australia, 30° 16′ S, 151° 33′ E.
DISTRIBUTION: New England Tableland, New South Wales, Australia.
COMMENT: In the *Litoria aurea* group. Cogger, Cameron, and Cogger, 1983, Zool. Cat. Aust., 1(Amph. Rept.):40, resurrected the name *Litoria castanea* (=*Hyla castanea* Steindachner, 1867, Reise Freg. Novara, Amph.:67; Types: unknown; Type locality: unknown) and regarded *Litoria flavipunctata* as a junior synonym. We here retain *Litoria flavipunctata* for this taxon because none of the collecting localities of the 'Novara' expedition (Gans, 1955, Ann. Carnegie Mus., 33:280) are within the known range of *Litoria flavipunctata* (MJT and MD).

Litoria freycineti Tschudi, 1838. Classif. Batr.:77.
TYPE(S): Syntypes: MNHNP 246 (2 specimens).
TYPE LOCALITY: "Australia".
DISTRIBUTION: East coast of southern Queensland and New South Wales, Australia.
COMMENT: See Moore, 1961, Bull. Am. Mus. Nat. Hist., 12:302. In the *Litoria freycineti* group.

Litoria genimaculata (Horst, 1883). Notes Leyden Mus., 5:240.
ORIGINAL NAME: *Hyla genimaculata*.
TYPE(S): Holotype: RMNH 4420.
TYPE LOCALITY: "Gebeh" (=Gagie?) I., west of Waigeo I., Indonesia.
DISTRIBUTION: Lowlands of southern New Guinea and adjacent islands.
COMMENT: See Tyler, 1968, Zool. Verh., Leiden, 96:94. In the *Litoria eucnemis* group. Ingram and Covacevich, 1981, Mem. Queensland Mus., 20:291–396, without discussion, regarded Australian specimens of *Litoria eucnemis* as representing this species.

Litoria gracilenta (Peters, 1869). Monatsber. Preuss. Akad. Wiss. Berlin, 1869:789.
ORIGINAL NAME: *Hyla gracilenta*.
TYPE(S): Holotype: ZMB 6618.
TYPE LOCALITY: Port Mackay, Queensland, Australia.
DISTRIBUTION: East coast of Australia from the Cape York Peninsula to New South Wales; eastern mountains and southern lowlands of New Guinea.
COMMENT: See Moore, 1961, Bull. Am. Mus. Nat. Hist., 12:265, and Tyler, 1968, Zool. Verh., Leiden, 96:97. In the *Litoria aruensis* group.

Litoria graminea (Boulenger, 1905). Ann. Mag. Nat. Hist., (7)16:183.
ORIGINAL NAME: *Hyla graminea*.
TYPE(S): Holotype: BM 1947.2.23.31.
TYPE LOCALITY: "Northern British New Guinea, altitude 900 feet".
DISTRIBUTION: New Guinea.
COMMENT: See Tyler, 1968, Zool. Verh., Leiden, 96:100.

Litoria impura (Peters and Doria, 1878). Ann. Mus. Civ. Stor. Nat. Genova, 13:426.
ORIGINAL NAME: *Hyla* (*Litoria*) *impura*.
TYPE(S): MSNG designated lectotype by Capocaccia, 1957, Ann. Mus. Civ. Stor.
   Nat. Genova, 69:218.
TYPE LOCALITY: "Yule Island in Nova Guinea australi".
DISTRIBUTION: Southeastern New Guinea.
COMMENT: In the *Litoria thesaurensis* group. See Menzies and Zug, 1979,
   Micronesica, 15:325–333.

Litoria inermis (Peters, 1867). Monatsber. Preuss. Akad. Wiss. Berlin, 1867:30.
ORIGINAL NAME: *Chiroleptes inermis*.
TYPE(S): Syntypes: RMNH 1888, AMNH 23582, NHMW 18384 (2 specimens), ZMB
   5589; Cogger, Cameron, and Cogger, 1983, Zool. Cat. Aust., 1(Amph. Rept.):
   44, regarded ZMB 5589 as the holotype and regarded the putative syntype
   status of other specimens as in error.
TYPE LOCALITY: Rockhampton, Queensland, Australia.
DISTRIBUTION: Northern and northeastern Australia.
COMMENT: See Straughan, 1969, Proc. R. Soc. Queensland, 80:207. In the *Litoria
   latopalmata* group. Davies, Martin, and Watson, 1983, Trans. R. Soc. S. Aust.,
   107:87, redefined the species.

Litoria infrafrenata (Günther, 1867). Ann. Mag. Nat. Hist., (3)20:56.
ORIGINAL NAME: *Hyla infrafrenata*.
TYPE(S): Holotype: BM 1947.2.24.11.
TYPE LOCALITY: Cape York Peninsula, Queensland, Australia.
DISTRIBUTION: Cape York Peninsula, Queensland, Australia, and New Guinea; New
   Ireland, Bismarck Archipelago; introduced into Java.
COMMENT: See Tyler, 1968, Zool. Verh., Leiden, 96:104. In the *Litoria infrafrenata*
   group.

Litoria iris (Tyler, 1962). Rec. S. Aust. Mus., 14:253.
ORIGINAL NAME: *Hyla iris*.
TYPE(S): Holotype: BM 1961.1206.
TYPE LOCALITY: "Bamna, near Nondugl (Lat. 5° 49' S; Long. 144° 44' E) at 6,500
   feet", Western Highlands Province, Papua New Guinea.
DISTRIBUTION: Snow and Eastern mountains, New Guinea.
COMMENT: See Tyler, 1968, Zool. Verh., Leiden, 96:111. In the *Litoria nigropunctata*
   group.

Litoria jenolanensis (Copland, 1957). Proc. Linn. Soc. New South Wales, 82:97.
ORIGINAL NAME: *Hyla jenolanensis*.
TYPE(S): Holotype: AM R14412.
TYPE LOCALITY: Bottomless Pit, Jenolan Caves, New South Wales, Australia.
DISTRIBUTION: New South Wales, Australia.
COMMENT: With no discussion, considered a synonym of *Litoria citropa* by Cogger,
   Cameron, and Cogger, 1983, Zool. Cat. Aust., 1(Amph. Rept.):41.

Litoria jervisiensis (Duméril and Bibron, 1841). Erp. Gén., 8:580.
ORIGINAL NAME: *Hyla jervisiensis*.
TYPE(S): Holotype: MNHNP 4826.
TYPE LOCALITY: "la baie de Jervis" (=Jervis Bay), New South Wales, Australia.
DISTRIBUTION: Southeastern New South Wales, Australia.
COMMENT: In the *Litoria ewingii* group. See White, Whitford, and Watson, 1980,
   Aust. Zool., 20:375–390, for discussion of identity of this species.

Litoria jeudii (Werner, 1901). Zool. Anz., 24:99.
ORIGINAL NAME: *Hyla jeudii*.
TYPE(S): Holotype: ZMB 16498.
TYPE LOCALITY: "German New Guinea" (=northern part of Papua New Guinea).
DISTRIBUTION: Known only from the type locality.

COMMENT: See Tyler, 1968, Zool. Verh., Leiden, 96:116. In the *Litoria jeudii* group.

Litoria kinghorni (Loveridge, 1950). Proc. Biol. Soc. Washington, 63:132.
  ORIGINAL NAME: *Hyla kinghorni*.
  TYPE(S): Holotype: AM R13818.
  TYPE LOCALITY: Ulong, New South Wales, Australia.
  DISTRIBUTION: Known only from the type locality.
  COMMENT: In the *Litoria lesueurii* group. With no discussion, considered a synonym
    of *Litoria lesueurii* by Cogger, Cameron, and Cogger, 1983, Zool. Cat. Aust.,
    1(Amph. Rept.):46.

Litoria latopalmata Günther, 1867. Ann. Mag. Nat. Hist., (3)20:55.
  TYPE(S): Syntypes: BM 1947.2.24.27–28.
  TYPE LOCALITY: Port Denison [=Bowen], Queensland, Australia.
  DISTRIBUTION: Eastern Australia to the interior of Queensland and northeastern
    South Australia.
  COMMENT: See Davies, Martin, and Watson, 1983, Trans. R. Soc. S. Aust., 107:87–
    108, for definition of species. In the *Litoria latopalmata* group.

Litoria lesueurii (Duméril and Bibron, 1841). Erp. Gén., 8:595.
  ORIGINAL NAME: *Hyla Lesueurii*.
  TYPE(S): Syntypes: MNHNP 4845–46.
  TYPE LOCALITY: "port Jackson" (=Sydney), New South Wales, Australia.
  DISTRIBUTION: Eastern Australia from northern Queensland to southern Victoria.
  COMMENT: In the *Litoria lesueurii* group. See comments under *Litoria kinghorni* and
    Litoria vinosa.

Litoria leucova (Tyler, 1968). Zool. Verh., Leiden, 96:119.
  ORIGINAL NAME: *Hyla leucova*.
  TYPE(S): Holotype: SAMA R6461.
  TYPE LOCALITY: "Busilmin, Eastern Mountains, [West Sepik Province, Papua] New
    Guinea".
  DISTRIBUTION: Known only from the type locality.
  COMMENT: In the monotypic *Litoria leucova* group.

Litoria longicrus (Boulenger, 1911). Ann. Mag. Nat. Hist., (8)8:55.
  ORIGINAL NAME: *Hylella longicrus*.
  TYPE(S): Syntypes: BM 1947.2.22.60–61.
  TYPE LOCALITY: "one from Fakfak and the other from Wendessi", Vogelkop
    Peninsula, Irian Jaya (New Guinea), Indonesia.
  DISTRIBUTION: Eastern mountains and Vogelkop Peninsula, New Guinea.
  COMMENT: See Tyler, 1968, Zool. Verh., Leiden, 96:122. In the *Litoria bicolor* group.

Litoria longirostris Tyler and Davies, 1977. Copeia, 1977:620.
  TYPE(S): Holotype: QM J26930.
  TYPE LOCALITY: Rocky River, McIlwraith Ranges, Cape York Peninsula,
    Queensland, Australia.
  DISTRIBUTION: McIlwraith Range, Cape York Peninsula, Queensland, Australia.
  COMMENT: In the *Litoria dorsalis* group.

Litoria lorica Davies and McDonald, 1979. Trans. R. Soc. S. Aust., 103:170.
  TYPE(S): Holotype: QM J36090.
  TYPE LOCALITY: Alexandra Creek near Thornton Peak (16° 07′ S, 145° 20′ E),
    Queensland, Australia.
  DISTRIBUTION: Known only from the type locality.
  COMMENT: In the *Litoria nannotis* group.

Litoria louisiadensis (Tyler, 1968). Zool. Verh., Leiden, 96:124.
ORIGINAL NAME: *Hyla louisiadensis*.
TYPE(S): Holotype: AMNH 60133.
TYPE LOCALITY: "Mount Rossell, Rossell Island, Louisiade Archipelago, [Milne Bay Province, Papua] New Guinea".
DISTRIBUTION: Rossell and Sudest Is., Louisiade Archipelago, Papua New Guinea.
COMMENT: In the monotypic *Litoria louisiadensis* group.

Litoria lutea (Boulenger, 1887). Proc. Zool. Soc. London, 1887:337.
ORIGINAL NAME: *Hyla lutea*.
TYPE(S): Syntypes: BM 1947.2.23.50–52.
TYPE LOCALITY: Faro Island, Solomon Islands.
DISTRIBUTION: Northwestern islands of the Solomon Is.
COMMENT: See Tyler, 1968, Zool. Verh., Leiden, 96:127. In the *Litoria thesaurensis* group.

Litoria maculata (Spencer, 1901). Proc. R. Soc. New South Wales, (2)13:177.
ORIGINAL NAME: *Hyla maculata*.
TYPE(S): Holotype: NMM D8498.
TYPE LOCALITY: Poowong, Victoria, Australia.
DISTRIBUTION: Eastern New South Wales and Victoria, Australia.
COMMENT: In the *Litoria maculata* group.

Litoria meiriana (Tyler, 1969). Rec. S. Aust. Mus., 16:2.
ORIGINAL NAME: *Hyla meiriana*.
TYPE(S): Holotype: SAMA R9082.
TYPE LOCALITY: 98 miles north of Mainoru, Northern Territory, Australia.
DISTRIBUTION: Northern Territory and northern Western Australia.
COMMENT: In the monotypic *Litoria meiriana* group.

Litoria microbelos (Cogger, 1966). Aust. Zool., 13:223.
ORIGINAL NAME: *Hyla dorsalis microbelos*.
TYPE(S): Holotype: AM R25836.
TYPE LOCALITY: Cairns, Queensland [Australia].
DISTRIBUTION: Northern Queensland to coastal northern Western Australia, Australia.
COMMENT: Considered a synonym of *Litoria dorsalis* by Cogger, Cameron, and Cogger, 1983, Zool. Cat. Aust., 1(Amph. Rept.):42, without discussion. Cogger and Lindner, 1974, In Frith and Calaby (eds.), Aust. CSIRO Div. Wildl. Res. Tech. Pap., 28:63–107, also questioned the distinctiveness of this species. See Tyler and Parker, 1972, Trans. R. Soc. S. Aust., 96:161.

Litoria micromembrana (Tyler, 1963). Trans. R. Soc. S. Aust., 86:121.
ORIGINAL NAME: *Hyla micromembrana*.
TYPE(S): Holotype: SAMA R4150.
TYPE LOCALITY: "at an elevation of 7,500 ft. on Mt. Podamp, Wahgi–Sepik Divide, near Nondugl", Western Highlands Province, Papua New Guinea.
DISTRIBUTION: Snow Mountains in eastern Irian Jaya (Indonesia) to Huon Peninsula (Papua New Guinea), New Guinea.
COMMENT: For discussion see Tyler, 1968, Zool. Verh., Leiden, 96:131. In the *Litoria becki* group.

Litoria modica (Tyler, 1968). Zool. Verh., Leiden, 96:135.
ORIGINAL NAME: *Hyla modica*.
TYPE(S): Holotype: MCZ 52856.
TYPE LOCALITY: "Oruge, Eastern Mountains, [Papua] New Guinea".
DISTRIBUTION: Central ranges of Papua New Guinea.
COMMENT: In the *Litoria becki* group.

Litoria moorei (Copland, 1957). Proc. Linn. Soc. New South Wales, 82:83.
ORIGINAL NAME: *Hyla moorei.*
TYPE(S): Holotype: WAM R5981.
TYPE LOCALITY: Pemberton, Western Australia.
DISTRIBUTION: Southwest Western Australia.
COMMENT: In the *Litoria aurea* group. See Maxson, Tyler, and Maxson, 1982, Aust. J.
   Zool., 30:643, and Tyler, Smith, and Johnstone, 1984, Frogs W. Aust.

Litoria multiplica (Tyler, 1964). Am. Mus. Novit., 2187:2.
ORIGINAL NAME: *Hyla multiplica.*
TYPE(S): Holotype: AMNH 66854.
TYPE LOCALITY: "Kassam, elevation 4500 feet, Kratke Mountains, Eastern Highlands
   [Province], Australian Trusteeship Territory of New Guinea [now Papua New
   Guinea]".
DISTRIBUTION: Eastern mountains, New Guinea.
COMMENT: For discussion see Tyler, 1968, Zool. Verh., Leiden, 96:139. In the *Litoria
   aruensis* group.

Litoria mystax (van Kampen, 1906). Nova Guinea, 5:173.
ORIGINAL NAME: *Hyla mystax.*
TYPE(S): Holotype: RMNH 4632.
TYPE LOCALITY: "Moaif", northern lowlands, Irian Jaya (New Guinea), Indonesia.
DISTRIBUTION: Known only from the type locality.
COMMENT: For discussion see Tyler, 1968, Zool. Verh., Leiden, 96:142. In the *Litoria
   bicolor* group.

Litoria nannotis (Andersson, 1916). K. Svenska Vetensk. Akad. Handl., (4)52:16.
ORIGINAL NAME: *Hyla nannotis.*
TYPE(S): Holotype: NHRM 1645.
TYPE LOCALITY: Tully River, Queensland, Australia.
DISTRIBUTION: Northeastern Queensland, Australia.
COMMENT: For discussion see Liem, 1974, Mem. Queensland Mus., 17:151, and
   Davies and MacDonald, 1979, Trans. R. Soc. S. Aust., 103:169. In the *Litoria
   nannotis* group.

Litoria napaea (Tyler, 1968). Zool. Verh., Leiden, 96:145.
ORIGINAL NAME: *Hyla napaea.*
TYPE(S): Holotype: AMNH 49659.
TYPE LOCALITY: "at an altitude of 2830 ft at Camp 2, 3–4 miles south-west of
   Bernhard Camp, Idenburg River, Snow Mountains, New Guinea", Irian Jaya,
   Indonesia.
DISTRIBUTION: Known only from the type locality.
COMMENT: In the monotypic *Litoria napaea* group.

Litoria nasuta (Gray, 1842). Zool. Misc., 3:56.
ORIGINAL NAME: *Pelodytes nasutus.*
TYPE(S): Holotype: BM 1947.2.22.81.
TYPE LOCALITY: Port Essington, Northern Territory, Australia.
DISTRIBUTION: Coastal Australia from northern Western Australia to southern New
   South Wales; southern lowlands and southeast peninsula of New Guinea.
COMMENT: See Moore, 1961, Bull. Am. Mus. Nat. Hist. 121:305, and Tyler, 1968,
   Zool. Verh., Leiden, 96:148. In the *Litoria freycineti* group.

Litoria nigrofrenata (Günther, 1867). Ann. Mag. Nat. Hist., (3)20:56.
ORIGINAL NAME: *Hyla nigrofrenata.*
TYPE(S): Syntypes: BM 1947.2.23.46–47.
TYPE LOCALITY: Cape York Peninsula, Queensland, Australia.
DISTRIBUTION: East coast of Cape York Peninsula, northern Australia, and southern
   New Guinea.

COMMENT: For discusssion see Tyler, 1968, Zool. Verh., Leiden, 96:724. In the *Litoria nigrofrenata* group.

Litoria nigropunctata (Meyer, 1875). Monatsber. Preuss. Akad. Wiss. Berlin, 1874:139.
ORIGINAL NAME: *Hyperolius nigropunctatus.*
TYPE(S): Formerly in MTKD; destroyed in World War II.
TYPE LOCALITY: "Jobi" (=Japen) I., Geelvink Bay, Irian Jaya (New Guinea), Indonesia (see comment).
DISTRIBUTION: Northern New Guinea and Gebe and Jobi Is.
COMMENT: In the *Litoria nigropunctata* group. See Menzies, 1972, Herpetologica, 28: 291–300. Obst, 1977, Zool. Abh. Staatl. Mus. Tierkd., Dresden, 34:174, mentioned "Ansus, Jobi", as the locality for the destroyed holotype.

Litoria nyakalensis Liem, 1974. Mem. Queensland Mus., 17:157.
TYPE(S): Holotype: QM J22624.
TYPE LOCALITY: Henrietta Creek, Palmerston Nat. Pk., 800 m., Queensland, Australia.
DISTRIBUTION: Northern Queensland, Australia.
COMMENT: In the *Litoria nannotis* group. See Davies and MacDonald, 1979, Trans. R. Soc. S. Aust., 103:169, for discussion.

Litoria obtusirostris Meyer, 1875. Monatsber. Preuss. Akad. Wiss. Berlin, 1874:139.
TYPE(S): Formerly in MTKD; destroyed in World War II.
TYPE LOCALITY: "Jobi" (=Japen) I., Geelvink Bay, Irian Jaya (New Guinea), Indonesia (see comment).
DISTRIBUTION: Known only from the type locality.
COMMENT: For discussion see Tyler, 1968, Zool. Verh., Leiden, 96:155. Obst, 1977, Zool. Abh. Staatl. Mus. Tierkd., Dresden, 34:174, mentioned "Ansus, Jobi", as the locality for the destroyed holotype.

Litoria oenicolen Menzies and Zweifel, 1974. Am. Mus. Novit., 2558:10.
TYPE(S): Holotype: AMNH 37922.
TYPE LOCALITY: "beside the Trauna River (a tributary of the Baiyer River) at the Baiyer River Wildlife Sanctuary (141° 11' E, 5° 29' S), Western Highlands District [now Province], Papua New Guinea, elevation 1200 m."
DISTRIBUTION: Known only from the type locality.
COMMENT: In the *Litoria arfakiana* group.

Litoria olongburensis Liem and Ingram, 1977. Victorian Nat., 94:259.
TYPE(S): Holotype: QM J22652.
TYPE LOCALITY: Coomboo Lake, Fraser Island, Queensland, Australia.
DISTRIBUTION: Southeastern Queensland and northeastern New South Wales, Australia.
COMMENT: In the *Litoria dorsalis* group.

Litoria pallida Davies, Martin, and Watson, 1983. Trans. R. Soc. S. Aust., 107:101.
TYPE(S): Holotype: SAMA R19555.
TYPE LOCALITY: Gulungul Creek Crossing, Arnhem Highway, Northern Territory, Australia.
DISTRIBUTION: Northern Australia from Broome in Western Australia to Cape York in Queensland.

Litoria paraewingi Watson, Loftus-Hills, and Littlejohn, 1971. Aust. J. Zool., 19:414.
TYPE(S): Holotype: NMM D27601.
TYPE LOCALITY: O'Connors Flat, 8.3 km south-southeast of Yea, Victoria, Australia.
DISTRIBUTION: Eastern Victoria, Australia.
COMMENT: In the *Litoria ewingii* group.

Litoria pearsoniana (Copland, 1961). Proc. Linn. Soc. New South Wales, 86:168.
ORIGINAL NAME: *Hyla pearsoniana.*
TYPE(S): Holotype: AM R18588.
TYPE LOCALITY: Cedar Creek, E of Mt. Glorious, about 20 mi. NW of Brisbane,
    Queensland, Australia.
DISTRIBUTION: Elevated areas of northeastern New South Wales, Australia.
COMMENT: In the *Litoria citropa* group. *Hyla pearsoniana* is a replacement name for
    Hyla pearsoni Copland, 1960, Proc. Linn. Soc. New South Wales, 85:154, which
    is preoccupied by *Hyla pearsoni* Gaige, 1929. Cogger, Cameron, and Cogger,
    1983, Zool. Cat. Aust., 1(Amph. Rept.):48, considered *Litoria pearsoniana* to be a
    junior synonym of *Litoria phyllochroa* but provided no evidence to contradict
    evidence of dispecificity provided by Barker and Grigg, 1977, Field Guide
    Aust. Frogs:54–56 (call differences), or King, 1981, Proc. Melbourne Herpetol.
    Symp., R. Melbourne Zool. Gardens, Melbourne:172 (chromosomal
    differences).

Litoria peronii (Tschudi, 1838). Classif. Batr.:75.
ORIGINAL NAME: *Dendrohyas peronii.*
TYPE(S): Holotype: MNHNP 4809.
TYPE LOCALITY: "Nov. Holl." (=Australia).
DISTRIBUTION: Eastern Australia, south from Mary River (Queensland).
COMMENT: For discussion see Martin, Gartside, Littlejohn, and Loftus-Hills, 1979,
    Proc. Linn. Soc. New South Wales, 103:23. In the *Litoria peronii* group.

Litoria personata Tyler, Davies, and Watson, 1978. Trans. R. Soc. S. Aust., 102:151.
TYPE(S): Holotype: SAMA R16773.
TYPE LOCALITY: Birndu (12° 32' S, 132° 08' E), southeast of Cannon Hill Station, East
    Alligator River Region, Northern Territory, Australia.
DISTRIBUTION: Known only from the type locality.
COMMENT: In the *Litoria nigrofrenata* group.

Litoria phyllochroa (Günther, 1863). Proc. Zool. Soc. London, 1863:251.
ORIGINAL NAME: *Hyla phyllochroa.*
TYPE(S): Syntypes: BM 1947.2.24.3–5, ZMB 4929.
TYPE LOCALITY: Sydney and Errumanga, New South Wales, Australia.
DISTRIBUTION: Eastern part of New South Wales and adjacent Queensland and
    Victoria, Australia.
COMMENT: In the *Litoria citropa* group; see Moore, 1961, Bull. Am. Mus. Nat. Hist.,
    121:255. See comment under *Litoria pearsoniana.*

Litoria pratti (Boulenger, 1911). Ann. Mag. Nat. Hist., (8)8:56.
ORIGINAL NAME: *Hyla pratti.*
TYPE(S): Syntypes: BM 1947.2.23.54–56 (Wendessi), 1947.2.23.57–58 (Arfak
    Mountains).
TYPE LOCALITY: "Wendessi . . . [and] Arfak Mountains at an altitude of 8000 feet",
    Vogelkop Peninsula, Irian Jaya (New Guinea), Indonesia.
DISTRIBUTION: Known only from the type localities.
COMMENT: For discussion see Tyler, 1968, Zool. Verh., Leiden, 96:157. In the *Litoria
    becki* group.

Litoria prora (Menzies, 1969). Trans. R. Soc. S. Aust., 93:165.
ORIGINAL NAME: *Hyla prora.*
TYPE(S): Holotype: UP 1015.
TYPE LOCALITY: ". . . near Efogi . . . at an altitude 3,800'; location 147° 38' E.; 9° 9' S.
    and approximately 37 miles northeast of Port Moresby", Central Province,
    Papua New Guinea.
DISTRIBUTION: Known only from the type locality.
COMMENT: In the monotypic *Litoria prora* group.

Litoria pygmaea (Meyer, 1875). Monatsber. Preuss. Akad. Wiss. Berlin, 1874:139.
ORIGINAL NAME: *Hyperolius pygmaeus.*
TYPE(S): Formerly in MTDK; destroyed in World War II.
TYPE LOCALITY: "Jobi" (=Japen) I., Geelvink Bay, Irian Jaya (New Guinea),
Indonesia (see comment).
DISTRIBUTION: Lowlands of New Guinea.
COMMENT: For discussion see Tyler, 1968, Zool. Verh., 96:159. In the *Litoria rubella*
group. Obst, 1977, Zool. Abh. Staatl. Mus. Tierkd., Dresden, 34:174,
mentioned "Ansus, Jobi" as the locality for the destroyed holotype.

Litoria quadrilineata Tyler and Parker, 1974. Trans. R. Soc. S. Aust., 98:71.
TYPE(S): Holotype: SAMA R13489.
TYPE LOCALITY: "Jalan Trikora [=Tridora Road], Merauke, Irian Jaya, New Guinea",
Indonesia.
DISTRIBUTION: Known only from the type locality.
COMMENT: In the monotypic *Litoria quadrilineata* group.

Litoria raniformis (Keferstein, 1867). Nachr. Ges. Wiss. Göttingen, 18:358.
ORIGINAL NAME: *Chirodryas raniformis.*
TYPE(S): Holotype: formerly Zool. Mus. Göttingen (now in ZFMK) 93h; presumed
lost.
TYPE LOCALITY: "New South Wales?", Australia.
DISTRIBUTION: Southeastern Australia (exclusive of coastal New South Wales);
Tasmania.
COMMENT: In the *Litoria aurea* group. See Courtice and Grigg, 1975, Aust. Zool., 18:
149–163, and Maxson, Tyler, and Maxson, 1982, Aust. J. Zool., 30:643.

Litoria revelata Ingram, Corben, and Hosmer, 1982. Mem. Queensland Mus., 20:635.
TYPE(S): Holotype: QM J28233.
TYPE LOCALITY: O'Reilly's (28° 14' S, 153° 08' E), Lamington Plateau, SE
Queensland, Australia.
DISTRIBUTION: Southeastern Queensland and northeastern New South Wales,
Australia.
COMMENT: In the *Litoria ewingii* group.

Litoria rheocola Liem, 1974. Mem. Queensland Mus., 17:152.
TYPE(S): Holotype: QM J22631.
TYPE LOCALITY: Kuranda, 50 km west [actually ca. 33 km by road NW—RGZ] of
Cairns, Queensland, Australia.
DISTRIBUTION: Northern Queensland, Australia.
COMMENT: In the *Litoria nannotis* group. See Davies and McDonald, 1979, Trans. R.
Soc. S. Aust., 103:169, for discussion.

Litoria rothii (De Vis, 1884). Proc. Linn. Soc. New South Wales, 9:66.
ORIGINAL NAME: *Hyla rothii.*
TYPE(S): Syntypes: formerly in QM; now lost.
TYPE LOCALITY: Mackay, Queensland, Australia.
DISTRIBUTION: Northern Australia from northeastern Western Australia to
Queensland north of Mary River; southern New Guinea.
COMMENT: In the *Litoria peronii* group.

Litoria rubella (Gray, 1842). Zool. Misc., 2:56.
ORIGINAL NAME: *Hyla rubella.*
TYPE(S): Syntypes: BM 1947.2.24.7–9.
TYPE LOCALITY: Port Essington, Northern Territory, Australia.
DISTRIBUTION: Northern two thirds of Australia and southern New Guinea.
COMMENT: For discussion see Copland, 1957, Proc. Linn. Soc. New South Wales,
82:46. In the *Litoria rubella* group.

Litoria sanguinolenta (van Kampen, 1909). Nova Guinea, 9:33.
ORIGINAL NAME: *Hyla sanguinolenta*.
TYPE(S): ZMA 5676 designated lectotype by Daan and Hillenius, 1966, Beaufortia, 158:121.
TYPE LOCALITY: "Sabang, Lorentz River, West New Guinea" (Irian Jaya, Indonesia).
DISTRIBUTION: Southern lowlands in western New Guinea.
COMMENT: For discussion see Tyler, 1968, Zool. Verh., Leiden, 96:164. In the *Litoria infrafrenata* group.

Litoria spinifera (Tyler, 1968). Zool. Verh., Leiden, 96:167.
ORIGINAL NAME: *Hyla spinifera*.
TYPE(S): Holotype: MCZ 54510.
TYPE LOCALITY: "at an altitude of approximately 5000 ft at Oruge, Eastern Mountains, [Papua] New Guinea".
DISTRIBUTION: Eastern mountains, New Guinea.
COMMENT: In the *Litoria becki* group.

Litoria splendida Tyler, Davies, and Martin, 1977. Trans. R. Soc. S. Aust., 101:133.
TYPE(S): Holotype: WAM R56840.
TYPE LOCALITY: Lake Argyle Tourist Village, Kimberley Division, Western Australia.
DISTRIBUTION: Northern Western Australia.
COMMENT: In the *Litoria caerulea* group.

Litoria subglandulosa Tyler and Anstis, 1983. Trans. R. Soc. S. Aust., 107:130.
TYPE(S): Holotype: SAMA R13504.
TYPE LOCALITY: Barwick Creek, Point Lookout, near Ebor, New South Wales, Australia.
DISTRIBUTION: Mountains of northeastern New South Wales and southeastern Queensland, Australia.
COMMENT: In the *Litoria citropa* group. *Litoria subglandulosa* is a replacement name for *Litoria glandulosa* Tyler and Anstis, 1975, Rec. S. Aust. Mus., 17:46, which is preoccupied by *Litoria glandulosa* Bell, 1843.

Litoria thesaurensis (Peters, 1877). Monatsber. Preuss. Akad. Wiss. Berlin, 1877:421.
ORIGINAL NAME: *Hyla thesaurensis*.
TYPE(S): Syntypes: ZMB 9121 (2 specimens).
TYPE LOCALITY: Treasury Island, Solomon Islands.
DISTRIBUTION: New Guinea, New Britain, New Ireland, and Solomon Is.
COMMENT: In the *Litoria thesaurensis* group. See Menzies and Zug, 1979, Micronesica, 15:325–333.

Litoria timida Tyler and Parker, 1972. Trans. R. Soc. S. Aust., 96:157.
TYPE(S): Holotype: SAMA R11658.
TYPE LOCALITY: "Menemsorae, Western District [Province], Papua New Guinea".
DISTRIBUTION: Eastern and central New Guinea.
COMMENT: In the *Litoria dorsalis* group.

Litoria tornieri (Nieden, 1923). Das Tierreich, 46:228.
ORIGINAL NAME: *Hyla tornieri*.
TYPE(S): Holotype: BM 1947.2.22.79.
TYPE LOCALITY: North coast of Australia; corrected to Port Essington, Northern Territory, Australia, by Boulenger, 1882, Cat. Batr. Sal. Brit. Mus.:413.
DISTRIBUTION: Northern and eastern Australia.
COMMENT: In the *Litoria latopalmata* group. *Hyla tornieri* Nieden, 1923, is a substitute name for *Pelodytes affinis* Gray, 1842, Zool. Misc., 3:56. Davies, Martin, and Watson, 1983, Trans. R. Soc. S. Aust., 107:87, reviewed the species.

Litoria tyleri Martin, Watson, Gartside, Littlejohn, and Loftus-Hills, 1979. Proc. Linn. Soc. New South Wales, 103:25.
TYPE(S): Holotype: AM R64754.
TYPE LOCALITY: Ryan's Swamp, Caves Beach Reserve, 14 km S Huskisson, New South Wales, Australia.
DISTRIBUTION: Coastal southeastern Queensland and northeastern New South Wales, Australia.
COMMENT: In the *Litoria peronii* group.

Litoria umbonata Tyler and Davies, 1983. Copeia, 1983:803.
TYPE(S): Holotype: AMNH 43766.
TYPE LOCALITY: "Baliem River Valley, 1600 m . . . Irian Jaya, . . . New Guinea", Indonesia.
DISTRIBUTION: Vicinity of type locality.
COMMENT: In the *Litoria wisselensis* group.

Litoria vagabunda (Peters and Doria, 1878). Ann. Mus. Civ. Stor. Nat. Genova, 13:424.
ORIGINAL NAME: *Hyla (Litoria) vagabunda.*
TYPE(S): MSNG 29704A designated lectotype by Capocaccia, 1957, Ann. Mus. Civ. Stor. Nat., Genova, 69:214.
TYPE LOCALITY: "Wahai, Seram Island (Moluccas)".
DISTRIBUTION: Vogelkop Peninsula, Irian Jaya (New Guinea) and Ceram I., Moluccan Is., Indonesia.
COMMENT: For discussion see Tyler, 1968, Zool. Verh., Leiden, 96:177. In the monotypic *Litoria vagabunda* group.

Litoria verreauxii (Duméril, 1853). Ann. Sci. Nat., Paris, (3)19:171.
ORIGINAL NAME: *Hyla verreauxii.*
TYPE(S): Syntypes: MNHNP 4849 (5 specimens), 4850 (9 specimens).
TYPE LOCALITY: Australia.
DISTRIBUTION: Eastern Australia.
COMMENT: For discussion see Littlejohn, 1965, Evolution, 19:234. In the *Litoria ewingii* group.

Litoria vinosa (Lamb, 1911). Ann. Queensland Mus., 10:27.
ORIGINAL NAME: *Hyla vinosa.*
TYPE(S): Holotype: QM J74.
TYPE LOCALITY: Ithaca Creek, Brisbane, Queensland, Australia.
DISTRIBUTION: Northern Queensland, Australia.
COMMENT: For discussion see Moore, 1961, Bull. Am. Mus. Nat. Hist., 96:212. Without discussion, considered a synonym of *Litoria lesueurii* by Cogger, Cameron, and Cogger, 1983, Zool. Cat. Aust., 1(Amph. Rept.):46.

Litoria vocivincens Menzies, 1972. Herpetologica, 28:296.
TYPE(S): Holotype: UP 1957.
TYPE LOCALITY: "Brown River forestry station, . . . 147° 14' E; 10° 48' S, sea level, about 25 miles NW Port Moresby", Central Province, Papua New Guinea.
DISTRIBUTION: Coastal lowlands of southeastern New Guinea.
COMMENT: In the *Litoria rubella* group.

Litoria watjulumensis (Copland, 1957). Proc. Linn. Soc. New South Wales, 82:96.
ORIGINAL NAME: *Hyla latopalmata watjulumensis.*
TYPE(S): Syntypes: WAM R11196, 11198–99, 11633–35, 11896–107, 11932–38.
TYPE LOCALITY: Watjulum [=Wotjulum] Mission, Western Australia.
DISTRIBUTION: Northern Western Australia and Northern Territory, Australia.
COMMENT: In the *Litoria nigrofrenata* group. The unjustified emendation of the specific epithet to *wotjulumensis* was by Tyler, 1968, Rec. S. Aust. Mus., 15:713. MJT disputes DRF's interpretation of the International Code of Zoological Nomenclature.

Litoria wisselensis (Tyler, 1968). Zool. Verh., Leiden, 96:180.
ORIGINAL NAME: *Hyla wisselensis.*
TYPE(S): Holotype: RMNH 12295.
TYPE LOCALITY: "Enarotali, Lake Paniai, Wissel Lakes, Snow Mountains, [Irian Jaya,] New Guinea", Indonesia.
DISTRIBUTION: Montane lakes in Snow Mountains, New Guinea.
COMMENT: In the *Litoria wisselensis* group; see Tyler and Davies, 1983, Copeia, 1983: 803–808.

Litoria wollastoni (Boulenger, 1914). Trans. Zool. Soc. London, 20:248.
ORIGINAL NAME: *Hyla wollastoni.*
TYPE(S): Holotype: BM 1947.2.23.59.
TYPE LOCALITY: "Camp VI, Utakwa [=Octakwa] R., 2100 ft.", Irian Jaya (New Guinea), Indonesia.
DISTRIBUTION: Highlands of New Guinea.
COMMENT: In the *Litoria arfakiana* group. See Menzies and Zweifel, 1974, Am. Mus. Novit., 2558:1–16.

Nyctimystes Stejneger, 1916. Proc. Biol. Soc. Washington, 29:85.
TYPE SPECIES: *Nyctimantis papua* Boulenger, 1897, by original designation.
DISTRIBUTION: New Guinea, eastern islands in Moluccas, and northern Queensland, Australia.
COMMENT: Genus defined and species listed by Tyler and Davies, 1979, Aust. J. Zool., 27:755–772. See also Zweifel, 1983, Am. Mus. Novit., 2759:1–21.

Nyctimystes avocalis Zweifel, 1958. Am. Mus. Novit., 1896:6.
TYPE(S): Holotype: AMNH 56886.
TYPE LOCALITY: "east side of Goodenough Island, D'Entrecasteaux Group, [Milne Bay Province,] Territory of Papua [=Papua New Guinea], New Guinea".
DISTRIBUTION: Known only from the type locality.

Nyctimystes cheesmani Tyler, 1964. Zool. Abh. Staatl. Mus. Tierkd., Dresden, 27:268.
TYPE(S): Holotype: BM 1947.2.24.31.
TYPE LOCALITY: "Mondo, Papua (5000 ft.)", Central Province, Papua New Guinea.
DISTRIBUTION: Eastern New Guinea and D'Entecasteaux Is.
COMMENT: For discussion see Zweifel, 1958, Am. Mus. Novit., 1896:21. *Nyctimystes cheesmani* is a replacement name for *Hyla montana* Parker, 1936, Ann. Mag. Nat. Hist., (10)17:80.

Nyctimystes dayi (Günther, 1897). Novit. Zool., 4:406.
ORIGINAL NAME: *Hyla dayi.*
TYPE(S): Unknown.
TYPE LOCALITY: Bartle Frere Mountains, Queensland, Australia.
DISTRIBUTION: Known only from the type locality.
COMMENT: For discussion see Liem, 1974, Mem. Queensland Mus., 17:156. Regarded as a *species inquirenda* by Cogger, Cameron, and Cogger, 1983, Zool. Cat. Aust., 1(Amph. Rept.):260. See comments under *Nyctimystes hosmeri*, *Nyctimystes tympanocryptis*, and *Nyctimystes vestigia*.

Nyctimystes daymani Zweifel, 1958. Am. Mus. Novit., 1896:8.
TYPE(S): Holotype: AMNH 57070.
TYPE LOCALITY: "North slope of Mt. Dayman, Territory of Papua, [Milne Bay Province, Papua] New Guinea".
DISTRIBUTION: Mountains of eastern New Guinea.

Nyctimystes disrupta Tyler, 1963. Rec. Aust. Mus., 26:118.
TYPE(S): Holotype: AM R15923.
TYPE LOCALITY: "at an elevation of 6,000 feet in the Kaironk Valley, Schrader Mountains, Australian Trusteeships Territory of New Guinea" (Madang Province, Papua New Guinea).
DISTRIBUTION: Highlands of Huon Peninsula and central Papua New Guinea.

COMMENT: See Zweifel, 1983, Am. Mus. Novit., 2759:8–12.

Nyctimystes fluviatilis Zweifel, 1958. Am. Mus. Novit., 1896:11.
TYPE(S): Holotype: AMNH 49567.
TYPE LOCALITY: "Bernhard Camp, Idenburg River, Netherlands New Guinea" (Irian Jaya, Indonesia).
DISTRIBUTION: Known only from the type locality.

Nyctimystes foricula Tyler, 1963. Rec. Aust. Mus., 26:120.
TYPE(S): Holotype: AM R15904.
TYPE LOCALITY: "between 5,000 feet and 6,000 feet in the Kaironk Valley, Schrader Mountains, Australian Trusteeships Territory of New Guinea" (Madang Province, Papua New Guinea).
DISTRIBUTION: Mountains of eastern New Guinea.

Nyctimystes granti (Boulenger, 1914). Trans. Zool. Soc. London, 20:249.
ORIGINAL NAME: *Nyctimantis granti.*
TYPE(S): Holotype: BM 1947.2.24.47.
TYPE LOCALITY: "Camp VIa, Utakwa [=Octakwa] R., 3000 ft.", Irian Jaya (New Guinea), Indonesia.
DISTRIBUTION: Mountains of New Guinea.
COMMENT: For discussion see Zweifel, 1958, Am. Mus. Novit., 1896:13.

Nyctimystes gularis Parker, 1936. Ann. Mag. Nat. Hist., (10)17:78.
TYPE(S): Holotype: BM 1947.2.24.29.
TYPE LOCALITY: "Mondo, Papua (5000 ft.)", Central Province, Papua New Guinea.
DISTRIBUTION: Mountains of southeastern New Guinea.
COMMENT: For discussion see Zweifel, 1958, Am. Mus. Novit., 1896:14, and Tyler, 1962, Copeia, 1962:435–436.

Nyctimystes hosmeri Tyler, 1964. Trans. R. Soc. S. Aust., 88:111.
TYPE(S): Holotype: AMNH 65538.
TYPE LOCALITY: Tully Falls, Cape York Peninsula, Queensland, Australia.
DISTRIBUTION: Atherton Tableland and adjacent mountains, Queensland, Australia.
COMMENT: Ingram and Covacevich, 1981, Mem. Queensland Mus., 20:298, implied that this form is synonymous with *Nyctimystes dayi.*

Nyctimystes humeralis (Boulenger, 1912). Zool. Jahrb., 1(Suppl. 15):216.
ORIGINAL NAME: *Hyla humeralis.*
TYPE(S): Holotype: BM 1947.2.23.48.
TYPE LOCALITY: "Madew [=Madiu], St. Joseph [Angabunga] River, British New Guinea, between 2000 and 3000 feet", Central Province, Papua New Guinea.
DISTRIBUTION: Mountains of eastern New Guinea.
COMMENT: For discussion see Zweifel, 1958, Am. Mus. Novit., 1896:16.

Nyctimystes kubori Zweifel, 1958. Am. Mus. Novit., 1896:18.
TYPE(S): Holotype: AMNH 55913.
TYPE LOCALITY: "Kubor Mountains near Kup . . . between 5000 and 8000 feet, north-eastern New Guinea" (Chimbu Province, Papua New Guinea).
DISTRIBUTION: Mountains of eastern New Guinea.
COMMENT: For discussion see Tyler, 1963, Rec. Aust. Mus., 26:123.

Nyctimystes montana (Peters and Doria, 1878). Ann. Mus. Civ. Stor. Nat. Genova, 13: 423.
ORIGINAL NAME: *Hyla (Litoria) montana.*
TYPE(S): Holotype: MSNG 29720.
TYPE LOCALITY: "Hatam", Arfak Mountains, Vogelkop Peninsula, Irian Jaya (New Guinea), Indonesia.
DISTRIBUTION: Known only from the type locality.

COMMENT: For discussion see Tyler, 1964, Zool. Abh. Staatl. Mus. Tierkd., Dresden, 27:265.

Nyctimystes narinosa Zweifel, 1958. Am. Mus. Novit., 1896:26.
TYPE(S): Holotype: AMNH 60372.
TYPE LOCALITY: "Mt. Hagen in the Wahgi Valley region of north-east New Guinea at an elevation of over 8000 feet", Western Highlands Province, Papua New Guinea.
DISTRIBUTION: Mountains of central New Guinea.

Nyctimystes obsoleta (Lönnberg, 1900). Ann. Mag. Nat. Hist., (7)6:580.
ORIGINAL NAME: *Hyla obsoleta*.
TYPE(S): ZIUU (no number).
TYPE LOCALITY: "Simbang", Huon Peninsula, Morobe Province, Papua New Guinea.
DISTRIBUTION: Known only from the type locality.
COMMENT: For discussion see Tyler, 1965, Proc. Zool. Soc. London, 145:92.

Nyctimystes papua (Boulenger, 1897). Ann. Mag. Nat. Hist., (6)19:12.
ORIGINAL NAME: *Nyctimantis papua*.
TYPE(S): BM 96.10.31.50 designated lectotype by Zweifel, 1983, Am. Mus. Novit., 2759:4.
TYPE LOCALITY: "Mount Victoria, Owen Stanley Range, [Papua] New Guinea".
DISTRIBUTION: Type locality on the western slope of Mt. Victoria, Papua New Guinea.
COMMENT: For discussion see Zweifel, 1983, Am. Mus. Novit., 2759:4–8.

Nyctimystes perimetri Zweifel, 1958. Am. Mus. Novit., 1896:31.
TYPE(S): Holotype: AMNH 60081.
TYPE LOCALITY: "at an elevation of 250–350 meters . . . on the west slope of Mt. Riu, Sudest (Tagula) Island, Louisiade Archipelago, Territory of Papua New Guinea" (Milne Bay Province, Papua New Guinea).
DISTRIBUTION: Sudest and Rossel Is., Louisiade Archipelago, New Guinea.

Nyctimystes persimilis Zweifel, 1958. Am. Mus. Novit., 1896:34.
TYPE(S): Holotype: AMNH 56838.
TYPE LOCALITY: "north slope of Mt. Dayman, Territory of Papua, New Guinea, at an elevation of 1570 meters" (Milne Bay Province, Papua New Guinea).
DISTRIBUTION: Known only from the type locality.

Nyctimystes pulchra (Wandolleck, 1911). Abh. Ber. K. Zool. Anthro. Ethno. Mus. Dresden, 13(6):12.
ORIGINAL NAME: *Hyla pulchra*.
TYPE(S): Syntypes: MTKD D2219 (4 specimens), destroyed.
TYPE LOCALITY: "Sacksackhütte", Torricelli Mountains, West Sepik Province, Papua New Guinea.
DISTRIBUTION: Mountains of New Guinea.
COMMENT: For discussion see Tyler, 1964, Zool. Abh. Staatl. Mus. Tierkd., Dresden, 27:267, and Zweifel, 1980, Bull. Am. Mus. Nat. Hist., 165:400.

Nyctimystes rueppelli (Boettger, 1895). Zool. Anz., 18:137.
ORIGINAL NAME: *Hyla rueppelli*.
TYPE(S): SMF 2614 designated lectotype by Mertens, 1967, Senckenb. Biol., 48:42.
TYPE LOCALITY: "Kau, N-Halmaheira, Moluccas", Indonesia.
DISTRIBUTION: Halmahera and Morotai Is., Moluccan Is., Indonesia.
COMMENT: For discussion see Zweifel, 1958, Am. Mus. Novit., 1896:34.

Nyctimystes semipalmata Parker, 1936. Ann. Mag. Nat. Hist., (10)17:83.
TYPE(S): Holotype: BM 1947.2.24.25.
TYPE LOCALITY: "Kokoda (1200 ft.)", Northern Province, Papua New Guinea.
DISTRIBUTION: Papua New Guinea.

COMMENT: See Zweifel, 1958, Am. Mus. Novit., 1896:38, and Zweifel, 1980, Bull. Am. Mus. Nat. Hist., 165:400.

Nyctimystes trachydermis Zweifel, 1983. Am. Mus. Novit., 2759:12.
   TYPE(S): Holotype: AMNH 82866.
   TYPE LOCALITY: "at an elevation of about 1250 m. at Gapaia Creek, trail between Garaina and Saureli, Morobe Province, Papua New Guinea".
   DISTRIBUTION: Mountains of eastern New Guinea.

Nyctimystes tyleri Zweifel, 1983. Am. Mus. Novit., 2759:16.
   TYPE(S): Holotype: AMNH 82878 (erroneously given as 82867 in the original publication—RGZ).
   TYPE LOCALITY: "elevation of about 1280 m. at Gapaia Creek, between Garaina and Saureli, Morobe Province, Papua New Guinea".
   DISTRIBUTION: Type locality in the highlands of eastern New Guinea.

Nyctimystes tympanocryptis (Andersson, 1916). K. Svenska Vetensk. Akad. Handl., (4)52:19.
   ORIGINAL NAME: *Hyla tympanocryptis.*
   TYPE(S): Holotype: NHRM 1649.
   TYPE LOCALITY: Malanda, Queensland, Australia.
   DISTRIBUTION: Cape York Peninsula, Queensland, Australia.
   COMMENT: See Tyler, 1968, Ark. Zool., (2)20:501. Ingram and Covacevich, 1981, Mem. Queensland Mus., 20:298, implied that this form is synonymous with *Nyctimystes dayi.*

Nyctimystes vestigia Tyler, 1964. Trans. R. Soc. S. Aust., 88:113.
   TYPE(S): Holotype: NHMW 17187.
   TYPE LOCALITY: Mount Bartle Frere, Cape York Peninsula, Queensland, Australia.
   DISTRIBUTION: Northeastern Queensland, Australia.
   COMMENT: Ingram and Covacevich, 1981, Mem. Queensland Mus., 20:298, implied that this form is synonymous with *Nyctimystes dayi.*

Nyctimystes zweifeli Tyler, 1967. Trans. R. Soc. S. Aust., 91:191.
   TYPE(S): Holotype: SAMA R5426.
   TYPE LOCALITY: "Telefomen [=Telefomin], Western Highlands, New Guinea" (West Sepik Province, Papua New Guinea).
   DISTRIBUTION: Known only from the vicinity of the type locality.

SUBFAMILY: **Phyllomedusinae** Günther, 1859 "1858".
   CITATION: Cat. Batr. Sal. Coll. Brit. Mus.:120.
   DISTRIBUTION: Mexico to Argentina.
   COMMENT: As originally formed, the group name was Phyllomedusidae. Frogs referred to this subfamily possess distinctive morphological, biochemical, behavioral, and reproductive features (Duellman, 1968, Univ. Kansas Publ. Mus. Nat. Hist., 18:3–10). Bagnara and Ferris, 1973, J. Exp. Zool., 190:367–372, suggested that similar melanosomes in some *Phyllomedusa* and some *Litoria* might be indicative of a close relationship between the Phyllomedusinae and the Pelodryadinae. The immunological evidence of Maxson, 1976, Experientia, 32:1149–1150, does not refute such a relationship, but suggests that the divergence has not been recent. Osteological and myological evidence of Tyler and Davies, 1978, Herpetologica, 34:219–224, does not refute such a hypothesized relationship (DCC).
   REVIEWER: David C. Cannatella (DCC).

Agalychnis Cope, 1864. Proc. Acad. Nat. Sci. Philadelphia, 16:181.
   TYPE SPECIES: *Hyla callidryas* Cope, 1862 (see comment).
   DISTRIBUTION: Southern Mexico, Central America, Pacific lowlands of Colombia and northwestern Ecuador, and Amazonian Ecuador.

COMMENT: For discussion see Duellman, 1970, Monogr. Mus. Nat. Hist. Univ.
  Kansas, 1:87–130. The designation of *Agalychnis moreletii* as the type species of
  Agalychnis by Taylor, 1952, Univ. Kansas Sci. Bull., 35:801, and the comments by
  Duellman, 1970, Monogr. Mus. Nat. Hist. Univ. Kansas, 1:87–88, are in error;
  see Cope, 1864, Proc. Acad. Nat. Sci. Philadelphia, 16:181.

Agalychnis annae (Duellman, 1963). Rev. Biol. Tropical, 11:1.
  ORIGINAL NAME: *Phyllomedusa annae.*
  TYPE(S): Holotype: KU 64020.
  TYPE LOCALITY: "Tapantí, Cartago Province, Costa Rica, 1200 meters".
  DISTRIBUTION: Caribbean slopes and Meseta Central of Costa Rica.

Agalychnis calcarifer Boulenger, 1902. Ann. Mag. Nat. Hist., (7)9:52.
  TYPE(S): Holotype: BM 1947.2.24.22.
  TYPE LOCALITY: "Rio Durango, 350 feet", Provincia Esmeraldas, Ecuador.
  DISTRIBUTION: Caribbean slopes of Costa Rica and Panama and Pacific lowlands of
    Colombia and northwestern Ecuador.
  COMMENT: See Myers and Duellman, 1982, Am. Mus. Novit., 2752:25–26.

Agalychnis callidryas (Cope, 1862). Proc. Acad. Nat. Sci. Philadelphia, 14:359.
  ORIGINAL NAME: *Hyla callidryas.*
  TYPE(S): Holotype: ANSP 2091.
  TYPE LOCALITY: "Darien" (Provincia), Panama; corrected to Córdoba, Veracruz,
    Mexico, by Smith and Taylor, 1950, Univ. Kansas Sci. Bull., 33:347; correction
    considered unjustified by Duellman, 1970, Monogr. Mus. Nat. Hist. Univ.
    Kansas, 1:102.
  DISTRIBUTION: Atlantic lowlands of Veracruz and Oaxaca, Mexico, southeastward on
    the Caribbean lowlands to central Panama; Pacific lowlands of southern Costa
    Rica and eastern Panama.
  COMMENT: Savage and Heyer, 1967, Beitr. Neotrop. Fauna, 50:111–131, analyzed
    intraspecific variation.

Agalychnis craspedopus (Funkhouser, 1957). Occas. Pap. Nat. Hist. Mus. Stanford
  Univ., 5:23.
  ORIGINAL NAME: *Phyllomedusa craspedopus.*
  TYPE(S): Holotype: CAS-SU 10310.
  TYPE LOCALITY: "Chicherota, Rio Bobonaza, Napo-Pastaza [now Pastaza] Province,
    eastern Ecuador (Lat. 2° 22' S., Long. 76° 38' W.), at an altitude of about 250
    meters".
  DISTRIBUTION: Known only from the type series and RMNH material from
    Montalvo (MSH), in Amazonian Ecuador.

Agalychnis litodryas (Duellman and Trueb, 1967). Copeia, 1967:125.
  ORIGINAL NAME: *Phyllomedusa litodryas.*
  TYPE(S): Holotype: KU 96149.
  TYPE LOCALITY: "1 km west-southwest of the junction of the Río Mono and the Río
    Tuira, Darién Province, Panamá, elevation 130 m".
  DISTRIBUTION: Eastern Panama to northwestern Ecuador.

Agalychnis moreletii (Duméril, 1853). Ann. Sci. Nat., Paris, (3)19:169.
  ORIGINAL NAME: *Hyla moreletii.*
  TYPE(S): Syntypes: MNHNP 428 (parchment label 767) (2 specimens).
  TYPE LOCALITY: "Verapaz", Guatemala; restricted to "Cobán, [Departamento] Alta
    Verapaz", Guatemala, by Smith and Taylor, 1950, Univ. Kansas Sci. Bull., 33:
    317.
  DISTRIBUTION: Atlantic and Pacific slopes from Veracruz and Guerrero, Mexico, to
    Guatemala and El Salvador.

Agalychnis saltator Taylor, 1955. Univ. Kansas Sci. Bull., 37:527.
TYPE(S): Holotype: KU 35615.
TYPE LOCALITY: "4 km NNE of Tilarán [=Finca San Bosco], [Provincia] Guanacaste, Costa Rica".
DISTRIBUTION: Caribbean lowlands of Nicaragua and Costa Rica.

Agalychnis spurrelli Boulenger, 1913. Proc. Zool. Soc. London, 1913:1024.
TYPE(S): Syntypes: BM 1947.2.24.24–25.
TYPE LOCALITY: "Peña Lisa, Condoto, altitude 300 feet", Provincia Chocó, Colombia.
DISTRIBUTION: Southeastern Costa Rica to the Pacific lowlands of Colombia.

Pachymedusa Duellman, 1968. Univ. Kansas Publ. Mus. Nat. Hist., 18:5.
TYPE SPECIES: *Phyllomedusa dacnicolor* Cope, 1864, by original designation.
DISTRIBUTION: As for the single species.
COMMENT: See Pyburn, 1970, Copeia, 1970:209–218, for arguments against recognition at generic level. *Pachymedusa* is the sister-taxon of other phyllomedusines (DCC).

Pachymedusa dacnicolor (Cope, 1864). Proc. Acad. Nat. Sci. Philadelphia, 16:181.
ORIGINAL NAME: *Phyllomedusa dacnicolor.*
TYPE(S): Formerly in USNM; now lost.
TYPE LOCALITY: "near Colima", Mexico.
DISTRIBUTION: Pacific lowlands of Mexico from southern Sonora to the Isthmus of Tehuantepec.
COMMENT: See Duellman, 1970, Monogr. Mus. Nat. Hist. Univ. Kansas, 1:81, for review.

Phyllomedusa Wagler, 1830. Nat. Syst. Amph.:201.
TYPE SPECIES: *Rana bicolor* Boddaert, 1772.
DISTRIBUTION: Costa Rica, Panama, Pacific slopes of Colombia, and South America east of the Andes, including Trinidad, southward to northern Argentina.
COMMENT: Although species groups have not been defined for all species, Cannatella, 1982, Copeia, 1982:501–513, has discussed and defined the *Phyllomedusa perinesos* group, and Cannatella, 1980, Occas. Pap. Mus. Nat. Hist. Univ. Kansas, 87:1–40, has discussed and defined the *Phyllomedusa buckleyi* group.

Phyllomedusa aspera (Peters, 1872). Monatsber. Preuss. Akad. Wiss. Berlin, 1872:772.
ORIGINAL NAME: *Hylomantis aspera.*
TYPE(S): Syntypes: ZMB 7507 (4 specimens).
TYPE LOCALITY: Bahia, Brazil; probably Caravelas, Bahia, Brazil, according to Bokermann, 1966, Lista Anot. Local. Tipo Anf. Brasil.:68.
DISTRIBUTION: Known only from the type locality.

Phyllomedusa ayeaye (B. Lutz, 1966). Copeia, 1966:236.
ORIGINAL NAME: *Pithecopus ayeaye.*
TYPE(S): Holotype: AL-MN 3722.
TYPE LOCALITY: "Morro do Ferro, a hill inside an ancient volcanic crater, at Poços de Caldas, Minas Gerais", Brazil.
DISTRIBUTION: Mountains of Minas Gerais, Brazil.
COMMENT: In the *Phyllomedusa hypocondrialis* group.

Phyllomedusa bahiana A. Lutz, 1925. C. R. Séances Soc. Biol., Paris, 93:139.
TYPE(S): Holotype: AL-MN 768.
TYPE LOCALITY: "Bahia", Brazil; probably Salvador, Bahia, Brazil, according to Bokermann, 1966, Lista Anot. Local. Tipo Anf. Brasil.:82.
DISTRIBUTION: Central and eastern Brazil in the states of Bahia and Minas Gerais.

COMMENT: In the *Phyllomedusa burmeisteri* group.

Phyllomedusa baltea Duellman and Toft, 1979. Herpetologica, 35:64.
  TYPE(S): Holotype: KU 154746.
  TYPE LOCALITY: "Laguna, on the west slope of Serranía de Sira, 1280 m,
    Departamento Huánuco, Perú".
  DISTRIBUTION: Serranía de Sira, Peru.
  COMMENT: In the *Phyllomedusa perinesos* group.

Phyllomedusa bicolor (Boddaert, 1772). Epistola . . . de Rana bicolore:19.
  ORIGINAL NAME: *Rana bicolor*.
  TYPE(S): Unknown (originally in collection of Johann Albert Schlosser).
  TYPE LOCALITY: Restricted to "Surinam" by Funkhouser, 1957, Occas. Pap. Nat.
    Hist. Mus. Stanford Univ., 5:38.
  DISTRIBUTION: Amazon Basin in Brazil, Colombia, and Peru; the Guianan region of
    Venezuela and the Guianas.
  COMMENT: Reviewed by Duellman, 1974, Herpetologica, 30:105–112.

Phyllomedusa boliviana Boulenger, 1902. Ann. Mag. Nat. Hist., (7)10:395.
  TYPE(S): Syntypes: BM 1947.2.22.32–33.
  TYPE LOCALITY: "Chulumani, Bolivia, 2000 metres".
  DISTRIBUTION: Amazonian slopes of Andes and lowlands in Bolivia, northern
    Argentina, and western Mato Grosso and Rôndonia, Brazil.
  COMMENT: See Cannatella, 1983, Proc. Biol. Soc. Washington, 96:59–66.

Phyllomedusa buckleyi Boulenger, 1882. Cat. Batr. Sal. Brit. Mus.:425.
  TYPE(S): Holotype: BM 1947.2.22.35.
  TYPE LOCALITY: "Sarayacu, [Provincia Pastaza,] Ecuador".
  DISTRIBUTION: Upper Amazon Basin and lower Amazonian slopes of the Andes in
    Ecuador.
  COMMENT: In the *Phyllomedusa buckleyi* group.

Phyllomedusa burmeisteri Boulenger, 1882. Cat. Batr. Sal. Brit. Mus.:428.
  TYPE(S): BM 1947.2.22.22 designated lectotype by Funkhouser, 1957, Occas. Pap.
    Nat. Hist. Mus. Stanford Univ., 5:56.
  TYPE LOCALITY: "Rio Janeiro", "Brazil", and "Oran Salta, Buenos Ayres"; restricted
    to "the city of Rio de Janeiro, specifically the Tijuca", Brazil, by Funkhouser,
    1957, Occas. Pap. Nat. Hist. Mus. Stanford Univ., 5:56.
  DISTRIBUTION: Central and southeastern Brazil.
  COMMENT: In the *Phyllomedusa burmeisteri* group.

Phyllomedusa centralis Bokermann, 1965. Rev. Brasil. Biol., 25:258.
  TYPE(S): Holotype: WCAB 15380.
  TYPE LOCALITY: "Chapada dos Guimarães, Mato Grosso, Brasil".
  DISTRIBUTION: Known only from the type locality.
  COMMENT: In the *Phyllomedusa hypocondrialis* group.

Phyllomedusa cochranae Bokermann, 1966. Herpetologica, 22:293.
  TYPE(S): Holotype: WCAB 31184.
  TYPE LOCALITY: "Campo de Fruticultura da Bocaina, Serra da Bocaina, São Jose do
    Barreiro, state of São Paulo, Brazil, collected at 1,600 m."
  DISTRIBUTION: Coastal mountains, São Paulo, Brazil.
  COMMENT: In the *Phyllomedusa guttata* group; see Cannatella, 1980, Occas. Pap.
    Mus. Nat. Hist. Univ. Kansas, 87:1–40.

Phyllomedusa coelestis (Cope, 1874). Proc. Acad. Nat. Sci. Philadelphia, 26:121.
  ORIGINAL NAME: *Pithecopus coelestis*.
  TYPE(S): Holotype: ANSP 11384; incorrectly reported as lost by Duellman, 1974,
    Herpetologica, 30:105–112 (DCC).
  TYPE LOCALITY: "Moyabamba [=Moyobamba], [Departamento San Martín,] Peru".
  DISTRIBUTION: Known only from the type locality.

Phyllomedusa distincta B. Lutz, 1950. Mem. Inst. Oswaldo Cruz, Rio de Janeiro, 48:608.
ORIGINAL NAME: *Phyllomedusa (Pithecopus) burmeisteri distincta.*
TYPE(S): Holotype: AL-MN 775.
TYPE LOCALITY: "Rio Vermelho", Santa Catarina, Brazil.
DISTRIBUTION: Southeastern Brazil (São Paulo and Santa Catarina).
COMMENT: In the *Phyllomedusa burmeisteri* group.

Phyllomedusa duellmani Cannatella, 1982. Copeia, 1982:502.
TYPE(S): Holotype: KU 181813.
TYPE LOCALITY: "8 km NNE (by road) Balzapata, Depto. Amazonas, Perú, 1,850 m, 05° 47' S, 77° 48' W".
DISTRIBUTION: Known only from the type locality on Amazonian slopes of Andes.
COMMENT: In the *Phyllomedusa perinesos* group.

Phyllomedusa ecuatoriana Cannatella, 1982. Copeia, 1982:507.
TYPE(S): Holotype: USNM 215750.
TYPE LOCALITY: "Agua Rica, a one-house posada on the trail between Limón and Gualeceo, slightly south and west of Limón, Provincia de Morona-Santiago, Ecuador, 1,890 m, 03° 02' S, 78° 27' W".
DISTRIBUTION: Known only from the type locality on the Amazonian slopes of the Andes.
COMMENT: In the *Phyllomedusa perinesos* group.

Phyllomedusa exilis Cruz, 1980. Rev. Brasil. Biol., 40(4):683.
TYPE(S): Holotype: EI 5584.
TYPE LOCALITY: "Santa Tereza, Espírito Santo, Brasil".
DISTRIBUTION: Known only from the type locality.
COMMENT: In the *Phyllomedusa guttata* group, according to the original description.

Phyllomedusa fimbriata (Miranda-Ribeiro, 1923). Bol. Mus. Nac., Rio de Janeiro, 1:4.
ORIGINAL NAME: *Phrynomedusa fimbriata.*
TYPE(S): Holotype: MZUSP 316.
TYPE LOCALITY: "Alto da Serra", Paranapiacaba, São Paulo, Brazil.
DISTRIBUTION: Serra do Mar from Rio de Janeiro to Santa Catarina, southeastern Brazil.
COMMENT: In the *Phyllomedusa fimbriata* group. See Cannatella, 1980, Occas. Pap. Mus. Nat. Hist. Univ. Kansas, 87:1–40.

Phyllomedusa guttata A. Lutz, 1925 "1924". C. R. Séances Soc. Biol., Paris, 90:241.
TYPE(S): Syntypes: AL-MN 297, USNM 96244–46 (Tijuca); AL-MN 449, USNM 96317–18 (Sumaré); USNM 96338 (Paineiras).
TYPE LOCALITY: "dans les montagnes, près de Rio"; implicitly restricted to "the Carioca mountain at Tijuca, Rio de Janeiro", Brazil, by Lutz and Lutz, 1939, An. Acad. Brasil. Cienc., 11:219–263.
DISTRIBUTION: Coastal mountains from Rio de Janeiro to São Paulo, Brazil.
COMMENT: In the *Phyllomedusa guttata* group; see Cannatella, 1980, Occas. Pap. Mus. Nat. Hist. Univ. Kansas, 87:1–40.

Phyllomedusa hypocondrialis (Daudin, 1802). Hist. Nat. Rain. Gren. Crap.:29.
ORIGINAL NAME: *Hyla hypocondrialis.*
TYPE(S): Unknown.
TYPE LOCALITY: "Surinam".
DISTRIBUTION: South America east of the Andes from Bolivia, Colombia, and the Guianas southward to Argentina, Paraguay, and southeastern Brazil.
COMMENT: See Cei, 1980, Monit. Zool. Ital., N.S., Monogr., 2:437–439. In the *Phyllomedusa hypocondrialis* group. The unjustified emendation *hypochondrialis* has been widely used.

Phyllomedusa iheringii Boulenger, 1885. Ann. Mag. Nat. Hist., (5)16:88.
   TYPE(S): Syntypes: BM 1947.2.22.26–31, ZFMK 28560.
   TYPE LOCALITY: "S. Lorenzo, on the southern border of the Lagoa dos Patos", Rio
   Grande do Sul, Brazil.
   DISTRIBUTION: Extreme southern Brazil (Rio Grande do Sul), Uruguay, and
   Argentina (Misiones).
   COMMENT: Reviewed by Cei, 1980, Monit. Zool. Ital., N.S., Monogr., 2:435–436. In
   the *Phyllomedusa burmeisteri* group.

Phyllomedusa jandaia Bokermann and Sazima, 1978. Rev. Brasil. Biol., 38:927.
   TYPE(S): Holotype: WCAB 48131.
   TYPE LOCALITY: "Km 126 da estrada de Vespasiano a Conceição do Mato Dentro,
   1500 m, Jaboticatubas, Minas Gerais, Brasil".
   DISTRIBUTION: Type locality in the Serra do Espinhaço, Minas Gerais, Brazil.
   COMMENT: In the *Phyllomedusa guttata* group, according to the original description.

Phyllomedusa lemur Boulenger, 1882. Cat. Batr. Sal. Brit. Mus.:425.
   TYPE(S): Holotype: BM 1947.2.22.37.
   TYPE LOCALITY: "Costa Rica".
   DISTRIBUTION: Moderate elevations in Costa Rica and Panama.
   COMMENT: In the *Phyllomedusa buckleyi* group.

Phyllomedusa marginata Izecksohn and Cruz, 1976. Rev. Brasil. Biol., 36:257.
   TYPE(S): Holotype: EI 5177.
   TYPE LOCALITY: "Santa Tereza, Estado do Espírito Santo, Brasil".
   DISTRIBUTION: Known only from the type locality.
   COMMENT: In the *Phyllomedusa fimbriata* group, according to the original
   description; see Cannatella, 1980, Occas. Pap. Mus. Nat. Hist. Univ. Kansas,
   87:1–40.

Phyllomedusa medinae Funkhouser, 1962. Copeia, 1962:588.
   TYPE(S): Holotype: EBRG (no number).
   TYPE LOCALITY: "the biological station 'Henry Pittier'", Estado Aragua, Venezuela.
   DISTRIBUTION: Known only from the type locality.
   COMMENT: In the *Phyllomedusa buckleyi* group.

Phyllomedusa palliata Peters, 1872. Monatsber. Preuss. Akad. Wiss. Berlin 1872:773.
   TYPE(S): Holotype: ZMB 7181.
   TYPE LOCALITY: "Ucayali", Peru.
   DISTRIBUTION: Upper Amazon Basin in Ecuador and Peru.
   COMMENT: Reviewed by Duellman, 1974, Herpetologica, 30:105–112.

Phyllomedusa perinesos Duellman, 1973. Herpetologica, 29:226.
   TYPE(S): Holotype: KU 146562.
   TYPE LOCALITY: "Río Salado, about 1 km upstream from the Río Coca, Provincia
   Napo, Ecuador, 1410 m".
   DISTRIBUTION: Amazonian slopes of Andes in Napo Province, Ecuador.
   COMMENT: In the *Phyllomedusa perinesos* group. See Cannatella, 1982, Copeia, 1982:
   501–513.

Phyllomedusa psilopygion Cannatella, 1980. Occas. Pap. Mus. Nat. Hist. Univ. Kansas,
   87:32.
   TYPE(S): Holotype: KU 169608.
   TYPE LOCALITY: "8 km W Danubio, Río Anchicayá, Departamento de Valle,
   Colombia, 300 m, (03° 37' N, 76° 47' W)".
   DISTRIBUTION: Pacific lowlands of southern Colombia.
   COMMENT: In the *Phyllomedusa buckleyi* group.

Phyllomedusa rohdei Mertens, 1926. Senckenb. Biol., 8:140.
TYPE(S): Holotype: SMF 2061.
TYPE LOCALITY: "Rio de Janeiro, Brasilien".
DISTRIBUTION: Lowlands of southeastern Brazil (Rio de Janeiro and São Paulo).
COMMENT: In the *Phyllomedusa hypocondrialis* group.

Phyllomedusa sauvagii Boulenger, 1882. Cat. Batr. Sal. Brit. Mus.:429.
TYPE(S): Syntypes: BM 1947.2.25.83–84.
TYPE LOCALITY: "Oran Salta" and "Buenos Ayres", Argentina.
DISTRIBUTION: The Chacoan region of eastern Bolivia, northern Paraguay, Mato
    Grosso do Sul (Brazil), and northern Argentina.
COMMENT: See Cei, 1980, Monit. Zool. Ital., N.S., Monogr., 2:426–434.

Phyllomedusa tarsius (Cope, 1868). Proc. Acad. Nat. Sci. Philadelphia, 20:113.
ORIGINAL NAME: *Pithecopus tarsius.*
TYPE(S): Formerly Smithsonian Museum (USNM) 6652; now lost.
TYPE LOCALITY: "Río Napo, or Upper Amazon, below the mouth of the former",
    Departamento Loreto, Peru.
DISTRIBUTION: Amazon Basin in southern Colombia, Ecuador, and Peru.
COMMENT: Closely related to *Phyllomedusa trinitatis* and *Phyllomedusa venusta*,
    according to Duellman, 1974, Herpetologica, 30:105–112.

Phyllomedusa tomopterna (Cope, 1868). Proc. Acad. Nat. Sci. Philadelphia, 20:112.
ORIGINAL NAME: *Pithecopus tomopternus.*
TYPE(S): Syntypes: Smithsonian Museum (USNM) 6651 (2 specimens), now lost.
TYPE LOCALITY: "Río Napo, or Upper Amazon, below the mouth of the former",
    Departamento Loreto, Peru.
DISTRIBUTION: Upper Amazon Basin in Ecuador and Peru; Guianan region from
    southeastern Venezuela to French Guiana; Brazilian Amazonia.
COMMENT: Reviewed by Duellman, 1974, Herpetologica, 30:105–114.

Phyllomedusa trinitatis Mertens, 1926. Senckenb. Biol., 8:145.
TYPE(S): Holotype: SMF 2633.
TYPE LOCALITY: "Port of Spain", Trinidad.
DISTRIBUTION: Trinidad and the coastal mountains in northern Venezuela.

Phyllomedusa vaillanti Boulenger, 1882. Cat. Batr. Sal. Brit. Mus.:427.
TYPE(S): Holotype: BM 1947.2.22.34.
TYPE LOCALITY: "Santarem, [Pará,] Brazil".
DISTRIBUTION: Guianas and Amazon Basin from northeastern Brazil to Colombia,
    Ecuador, Peru, and northern Bolivia.
COMMENT: See Duellman, 1974, Herpetologica, 30:105–112.

Phyllomedusa venusta Duellman and Trueb, 1967. Copeia, 1967:128.
TYPE(S): Holotype: KU 96150.
TYPE LOCALITY: "1 km west-southwest of the junction of the Río Mono and the Río
    Tuira, Darién Province, Panamá, elevation 130 m".
DISTRIBUTION: Known only from the type locality.

FAMILY: **Hyperoliidae** Laurent, 1943.
CITATION: Bull. Mus. R. Hist. Nat. Belg., 19(28):16.
DISTRIBUTION: Africa and nearby islands south of the Sahara; Madagascar; Seychelles Is.
    in the Indian Ocean.
COMMENT: As first formed, the group name was Hyperoliinae. Laurent, 1951, Rev. Zool.
    Bot. Afr., 45:119, was the first to consider this group a distinct family, including the
    Arthroleptinae and Astylosterninae in the Hyperoliidae, an arrangement considered

to be monophyletic. See comment under Arthroleptidae. Liem, 1970, Fieldiana: Zool., 57:1–145, suggested that the Hyperoliidae was derived from an ancestor in the Astylosterninae but retained that group (as well as the Arthroleptinae) in the Ranidae. Drewes, 1984, Occas. Pap. California Acad. Sci., 139:1–70, found the hyperoliids to be monophyletic but could not support a phylogenetic relationship with the astylosternines or arthroleptines (a relationship that RL still supports). Until the revision by Liem the Hyperoliidae was included by most authors as a subfamily in the family Rhacophoridae. For synonymies and reviews of most of the species in this family see Schiøtz, 1967, Spolia Zool. Mus. Haun., 25:1–346 (for West Africa), and Schiøtz, 1975, Treefrogs E. Afr.:1–232. The subfamilial classification employed here is that of Dubois, 1981, Monit. Zool. Ital., N.S., Suppl., 15:225–284. Drewes, 1984, Occas. Pap. California Acad. Sci., 139:1–70, did not agree with that subfamilial classification on phylogenetic grounds; he considered *Afrixalus* (here in the Kassininae) to be closely related to *Hyperolius* (here in the Hyperoliinae), *Acanthixalus* (here in the Leptopelinae) to be close to the Hyperoliinae, and *Nesionixalus* (formerly in the Leptopelinae; see comment under *Hyperolius*) to be a synonym of *Hyperolius* (Hyperoliinae). Drewes also supplied generic synonymies and diagnoses.

CONTRIBUTOR: Raymond Laurent (RL).

REVIEWERS: J.-L. Amiet (JLA) (Cameroon); Alan Channing (AC) (Southern Africa); Robert C. Drewes (RCD); William E. Duellman (WED); Marinus S. Hoogmoed (MSH); Kim M. Howell (KMH) (East Africa); Jean-Luc Perret (JLP); John C. Poynton (JCP); Arne Schiøtz (AS).

SUBFAMILY: **Hyperoliinae** Laurent, 1943.
   CITATION: Bull. Mus. R. Hist. Nat. Belg., 19(28):16.
   DISTRIBUTION: Coextensive with the family.
   COMMENT: The subfamily *sensu* Dubois, 1981, Monit. Zool. Ital., N.S., Suppl., 15:263, corresponds in content to the tribe Hyperoliini as defined by Laurent, 1972, Copeia, 1972:201. See comments under *Afrixalus* (Kassininae) and *Acanthixalus* (Leptopelinae).

Callixalus Laurent, 1950. Rev. Zool. Bot. Afr., 44:5.
   TYPE SPECIES: *Callixalus pictus* Laurent, 1950, by original designation.
   DISTRIBUTION: As for the single species.

   Callixalus pictus Laurent, 1950. Rev. Zool. Bot. Afr., 44:5.
      TYPE(S): Holotype: RGMC 105745.
      TYPE LOCALITY: Lutsiro, Rwanda.
      DISTRIBUTION: Itombwe and Kabobo highlands of eastern Zaire, and in mountains of western Rwanda.

Chrysobatrachus Laurent, 1951. Rev. Zool. Bot. Afr., 44:376.
   TYPE SPECIES: *Chrysobatrachus cupreonitens* Laurent, 1951, by original designation.
   DISTRIBUTION: As for the single species.
   COMMENT: Laurent, 1964, Evolution, 18:458–467, suggested a close relationship with *Hyperolius*. Drewes, 1984, Occas. Pap. California Acad. Sci., 139:39, concluded that *Chrysobatrachus* was the sister-taxon of *Acanthixalus* + *Callixalus*.

   Chrysobatrachus cupreonitens Laurent, 1951. Rev. Zool. Bot. Afr., 44:376.
      TYPE(S): Holotype: RGMC 109970.
      TYPE LOCALITY: Kitadjabukwe River, in Itombwe highlands, eastern Zaire.
      DISTRIBUTION: Grasslands above 2400 m in the Itombwe highlands of eastern Zaire.

Cryptothylax Laurent and Combaz, 1950. Rev. Zool. Bot. Afr., 43:276.
   TYPE SPECIES: *Hylambates greshoffii* Schilthuis, 1889, by original designation.
   DISTRIBUTION: Forest swamps and waterways of the Congo Basin, north to Uele Province (Zaire) and west to Cameroon.

Cryptothylax greshoffii (Schilthuis, 1889). Tijdschr. Nederl. Dierkd. Ver., (2)2:286.
ORIGINAL NAME: *Hylambates greshoffii.*
TYPE(S): Not traced; formerly in the Zoological Museum of the University of
   Utrecht, now possibly in the RMNH (MSH).
TYPE LOCALITY: Boma, lower Zaire.
DISTRIBUTION: Rainforest from south-central Cameroon to Zaire.

Cryptothylax minutus Laurent, 1976. Ann. Mus. R. Afr. Cent., Tervuren, Ser. Octavo,
   Sci. Zool., 213:13.
TYPE(S): Holotype: RGMC 117082.
TYPE LOCALITY: Mabali, western Zaire.
DISTRIBUTION: Region of Lake Tumba, Zaire.

Heterixalus Laurent, 1944. Rev. Zool. Bot. Afr., 38:111.
TYPE SPECIES: *Eucnemis madagascariensis* Duméril and Bibron, 1841, by original
   designation.
DISTRIBUTION: Madagascar.
COMMENT: See comment under *Hyperolius.* See Blommers-Schlösser, 1978, Genetica,
   48:23–40, for karyotypes.
REVIEWER: Rose M. A. Blommers-Schlösser (RMABS).

Heterixalus alboguttatus (Boulenger, 1882). Cat. Batr. Sal. Brit. Mus.:129.
ORIGINAL NAME: *Megalixalus madagascariensis* var. *alboguttata.*
TYPE(S): Syntypes: BM 80.7.15.13–14 and 74.4.25.2–3.
TYPE LOCALITY: "S. E. Betsileo", and "Madagascar (?)".
DISTRIBUTION: Betsileo Province and east coast of Madagascar.
COMMENT: Synonymy includes *Megalixalus variabilis* Ahl, 1930, according to
   Blommers-Schlösser, 1982, Beaufortia, 32:9.

Heterixalus betsileo (Grandidier, 1872). Ann. Sci. Nat., Paris, (15)20:10.
ORIGINAL NAME: *Eucnemis betsileo.*
TYPE(S): Syntypes: MNHNP 1895-267 (2 specimens).
TYPE LOCALITY: Betsileo, Madagascar.
DISTRIBUTION: Central and western Madagascar.
COMMENT: Synonymy includes *Heterixalus renifer* (Boettger, 1881), according to
   Blommers-Schlösser, 1982, Beaufortia, 32:2.

Heterixalus boettgeri (Mocquard, 1902). Bull. Soc. Philomath. Paris, (9)4:21.
ORIGINAL NAME: *Megalixalus boettgeri.*
TYPE(S): Syntypes: MNHNP 1901-205 and 1901-206.
TYPE LOCALITY: Isaka, Madagascar.
DISTRIBUTION: Known only from the type locality.
COMMENT: Blommers-Schlösser, 1982, Beaufortia, 32:7, removed this species from
   the synonymy of *Heterixalus tricolor.*

Heterixalus madagascariensis (Duméril and Bibron, 1841). Erp. Gén., 8:528.
ORIGINAL NAME: *Eucnemis madagascariensis.*
TYPE(S): Syntypes: MNHNP 4596 (3 specimens), NHMW 22914.
TYPE LOCALITY: "Madagascar".
DISTRIBUTION: Known only from the type locality.

Heterixalus mocquardi (Boettger, 1913). *In* Voeltzkow, Reise Ost-Afr., 3:280.
ORIGINAL NAME: *Megalixalus mocquardi.*
TYPE(S): Holotype: SMF 7270.
TYPE LOCALITY: Fort Dauphin, Madagascar.
DISTRIBUTION: Known only from the type locality.

Heterixalus nossibeensis (Ahl, 1930). Zool. Anz., 90:66.
ORIGINAL NAME: *Hyperolius nossibeensis.*
TYPE(S): ZMB.
TYPE LOCALITY: Nosy Bé [Madagascar].
DISTRIBUTION: Nossi Bé I., Madagascar.
COMMENT: Provisionally transferred from *Hyperolius* to *Heterixalus* by Drewes,
    1984, Occas. Pap. California Acad. Sci., 139:50.

Heterixalus rutenbergi (Boettger, 1881). Zool. Anz., 4:47.
ORIGINAL NAME: *Hyperolius rutenbergi.*
TYPE(S): Bremen Mus.
TYPE LOCALITY: Imerina, central Madagascar.
DISTRIBUTION: Central Madagascar.
COMMENT: Transferred from *Hyperolius* to *Heterixalus* by Blommers-Schlösser, 1982,
    Beaufortia, 32:10.

Heterixalus tricolor (Boettger, 1881). Zool. Anz., 4:650.
ORIGINAL NAME: *Megalixalus tricolor.*
TYPE(S): SMF 7268 designated lectotype by Mertens, 1967, Senckenb. Biol., 48:48.
TYPE LOCALITY: Nosy Bé [Madagascar].
DISTRIBUTION: Nossi Bé and eastern coast of Madagascar.

Hyperolius Rapp, 1842. Arch. Naturgesch., 8:289.
TYPE SPECIES: *Hyla horstockii* Schlegel, 1837, by monotypy; see Dubois, 1981, Monit.
    Zool. Ital., N.S., Suppl., 13:264, for a discussion of the type species.
DISTRIBUTION: Savanna, farmbush, and forests of Africa, south of the Sahara.
COMMENT: Blommers-Schlösser, 1982, Beaufortia, 32:1, discovered that all so-called
    Hyperolius species from Madagascar that she examined were either *Boophis* or
    Heterixalus. Synonymy includes *Nesionixalus* Perret, 1976, Arq. Mus. Bocage, (2)6:
    29, according to Drewes, 1984, Occas. Pap. California Acad. Sci., 139:52. See
    comment under *Hyperolius thomensis.*

Hyperolius acutirostris Peters, 1875. Monatsber. Preuss. Akad. Wiss. Berlin, 1875:207.
TYPE(S): ZMB, lost; MHNG 965.12 (holotype of *Hyperolius mosaicus*) designated
    neotype by Perret, 1966, Zool. Jahrb., Abt. Syst., 93:408; neotype designation
    invalidated by Perret, 1975, Rev. Suisse Zool., 82:191.
TYPE LOCALITY: Cameroon; restricted to Ngam, Cameroon, by Perret, 1966, Zool.
    Jahrb., Abt. Syst., 93:408; restriction rejected by Perret, 1975, Rev. Suisse
    Zool., 82:191.
DISTRIBUTION: South Cameroon, in rainforest.
COMMENT: See comment under *Hyperolius mosaicus.*

Hyperolius adametzi Ahl, 1931. Das Tierreich, 55:295.
TYPE(S): ZMB 10794a designated lectotype by Perret, 1962, Rev. Zool. Bot. Afr., 45:
    244.
TYPE LOCALITY: "Bamenda, Kamerun [=Cameroon]".
DISTRIBUTION: Highlands of western Cameroon.
COMMENT: Amiet, 1978, Ann. Fac. Sci. Yaoundé, 25:250, compared this species with
    Hyperolius kuligae.

Hyperolius albifrons Ahl, 1931. Das Tierreich, 55:354.
TYPE(S): Holotype: ZMB 36095.
TYPE LOCALITY: "Afrika (ohne genaueren Fundort)".
DISTRIBUTION: Unknown.

Hyperolius albofrenatus Ahl, 1931. Das Tierreich, 55:315.
TYPE(S): ZMB.
TYPE LOCALITY: "Deutsch-OstAfrika [=Tanzania] (genauerer Fundort unbekkant)".
DISTRIBUTION: Known only from the type locality.

COMMENT: Probably a synonym of *Hyperolius pusillus* (RL).

Hyperolius albolabris Ahl, 1931. Das Tierreich, 55:287.
TYPE(S): Holotype: ZMB unnumbered.
TYPE LOCALITY: "Kwa Buosch oder [or] Bnorch, (Deutsch-Ostafrika [=Tanzania])".
DISTRIBUTION: Known only from the type locality.

Hyperolius alticola Ahl, 1931. Das Tierreich, 55:379.
TYPE(S): ZMB, lost.
TYPE LOCALITY: "Ruwenzori, 1800 m.", Zaire.
DISTRIBUTION: Western Uganda and eastern Zaire.
COMMENT: Schiøtz, 1975, Treefrogs E. Afr.:143, noted that this species may be conspecific with *Hyperolius frontalis*. Laurent, 1972, Explor. Parc Natl. Virunga, (2)22:72, stated that *Hyperolius alticola* is a synonym or a subspecies of *Hyperolius discodactylus*.

Hyperolius angolanus Ahl, 1931. Das Tierreich, 55:271.
TYPE(S): MUP.
TYPE LOCALITY: N'Golla Bumba, Angola.
DISTRIBUTION: Northern Angola.
COMMENT: A replacement name for *Rappia platyceps* var. *angolensis* Ferreira, 1906, J. Sci. Math. Phys. Nat., Lisboa, (2)7:161. Probably a synonym of *Hyperolius platyceps* (RL).

Hyperolius argus Peters, 1854. Monatsber. Preuss. Akad. Wiss. Berlin, 1854:628.
TYPE(S): ZMB, lost.
TYPE LOCALITY: Boror, Mozambique.
DISTRIBUTION: Southern Somalia to Natal (Rep. South Africa) in the low-lying eastern parts of the savanna.

Hyperolius atrigularis Laurent, 1941. Rev. Zool. Bot. Afr., 34:159.
TYPE(S): Holotype: RGMC 18408.
TYPE LOCALITY: Kasiki, southeastern Zaire.
DISTRIBUTION: Marungu highlands, southeastern Zaire.

Hyperolius balfouri (Werner, 1907). Sitzungsber. Akad. Wiss. Wien, Math. Naturwiss. Kl., 116:1904.
ORIGINAL NAME: *Rappia balfouri*.
TYPE(S): Syntypes: NHMW 22894.
TYPE LOCALITY: Gondokoro, Uganda.
DISTRIBUTION: Cameroon to Uganda.
COMMENT: In the *Hyperolius concolor* superspecies and including *Hyperolius viridistriatus*, according to Schiøtz, 1975, Treefrogs E. Afr.:112.

Hyperolius baumanni Ahl, 1931. Das Tierreich, 55:291.
TYPE(S): Syntypes: ZMB, MCZ 17627.
TYPE LOCALITY: "Misahöhe, Togo".
DISTRIBUTION: Southwestern Ghana to northern Togo.
COMMENT: Possibly a subspecies of *Hyperolius picturatus* according to Schiøtz, 1967, Spolia Zool. Mus. Haun., 25:203.

Hyperolius benguellensis (Bocage, 1893). J. Sci. Math. Phys. Nat., Lisboa, 3:119.
ORIGINAL NAME: *Rappia benguellensis*.
TYPE(S): Syntypes: MBL 17-220 to 17-223; destroyed in 1978 fire.
TYPE LOCALITY: Caota, Benguella, Angola.
DISTRIBUTION: African savannas from Angola to Uganda, through Zambia, Zimbabwe, southeastern Zaire, and presumably Tanzania; possibly eastern Nigeria.

COMMENT: Synonymy includes *Rappia granulata* Boulenger, 1901, and *Hyperolius oxyrhynchus*, according to Perret, 1976, Arq. Mus. Bocage, (2)6:26. JCP has examined the types of these and believes that they are not conspecific. Which (if either) is conspecific with *Hyperolius benguellensis* remains unsettled owing to the loss of the types of *Hyperolius benguellensis*.

Hyperolius bicolor Ahl, 1931. Das Tierreich, 55:414.
TYPE(S): ZMB; lost.
TYPE LOCALITY: "Farenda Bango, Loanda", Angola.
DISTRIBUTION: Known only from the type locality.
COMMENT: Probably a synonym of *Hyperolius marmoratus insignis* Bocage (RL).

Hyperolius bobirensis Schiøtz, 1967. Spolia Zool. Mus. Haun., 25:236.
TYPE(S): Holotype: ZMUC R074633.
TYPE LOCALITY: "a small temporary pond near the forestry resthouse in Bobiri Forest Reserve, Ghana".
DISTRIBUTION: Known only from the type locality.

Hyperolius bocagei Steindachner, 1867. Reise Freg. Novara, Amph., 1:51.
TYPE(S): Holotype: NHMW 14846.
TYPE LOCALITY: "Angola".
DISTRIBUTION: Angola and western Zambia to southeastern Zaire.
COMMENT: See comment under *Hyperolius seabrai*.

Hyperolius bolifambae Mertens, 1938. Abh. Senckenb. Naturforsch. Ges., 442:28.
TYPE(S): Holotype: SMF 22457.
TYPE LOCALITY: Bolifamba, Mt. Kamerun [Cameroon].
DISTRIBUTION: Southeastern Nigeria to northern Zaire.
COMMENT: See comment under *Hyperolius erythropus*.

Hyperolius bopeleti Amiet, 1979. Ann. Fac. Sci. Yaoundé, 26:113.
TYPE(S): Holotype: MHNG 2031.02.
TYPE LOCALITY: Near Dizangué, Cameroun.
DISTRIBUTION: Coastal region of Cameroon.

Hyperolius brachiofasciatus Ahl, 1931. Das Tierreich, 55:361.
TYPE(S): ZMB, lost.
TYPE LOCALITY: "Ngoto, Lobajegebiet, Westafrika [Congo]".
DISTRIBUTION: Congo and western Zaire.

Hyperolius castaneus Ahl, 1931. Das Tierreich, 55:286.
TYPE(S): ZMB, lost.
TYPE LOCALITY: "Vulkangebiet nordöstlich des Kivu-Sees" (volcanoes northeast of Lake Kivu).
DISTRIBUTION: Mountains of eastern Zaire, western Rwanda, Burundi, and Uganda.
COMMENT: Synonymy includes *Hyperolius latifrons* Ahl, 1931, and *Hyperolius ventrimaculatus* Ahl, 1931, according to Laurent, 1950, Explor. Parc Natl. Albert, 64:26.

Hyperolius chabanaudi Ahl, 1931. Das Tierreich, 55:407.
TYPE(S): ZMB; lost.
TYPE LOCALITY: "Beniló [=Benito], Französischer Kongo [=Gabon]".
DISTRIBUTION: Known only from the type locality.
COMMENT: Probably a synonym of *Hyperolius phantasticus* (RL).

Hyperolius chlorosteus (Boulenger, 1915). Proc. Zool. Soc. London, 1915:243.
ORIGINAL NAME: *Rappia chlorostea*.
TYPE(S): BM.
TYPE LOCALITY: Sierra Leone.
DISTRIBUTION: Rainforest of Sierra Leone to southern Ivory Coast.

Hyperolius chrysogaster Laurent, 1950. Rev. Zool. Bot. Afr., 44:13.
TYPE(S): Holotype: RGMC.
TYPE LOCALITY: Bitale, west of the Kahusi, Kivu, Zaire.
DISTRIBUTION: Transition forests in Kivu from the Ruwenzori latitude to the
northern slopes of the Itombwe highlands.

Hyperolius cinereus Monard, 1937. Bull. Soc. Neuchâtel. Sci. Nat., 62:32.
TYPE(S): Syntypes: LCFM (2 specimens).
TYPE LOCALITY: "Kalukembé", Angola.
DISTRIBUTION: Angola.

Hyperolius cinnamomeoventris Bocage, 1866. J. Sci. Math. Phys. Nat., Lisboa, 1:75.
TYPE(S): Holotype: MBL, lost.
TYPE LOCALITY: Duque de Bragança, Angola.
DISTRIBUTION: Cameroon and Angola to Kenya.
COMMENT: Two savanna and forest forms from Cameroon described by Perret,
1966, Zool. Jahrb., Abt. Syst., 93:406–407.

Hyperolius concolor (Hallowell, 1844). Proc. Acad. Nat. Sci. Philadelphia, 2:60.
ORIGINAL NAME: *Ixalus concolor*.
TYPE(S): Holotype: ANSP 3216.
TYPE LOCALITY: Liberia.
DISTRIBUTION: Eastern Sierra Leone to western Cameroon.
COMMENT: In the *Hyperolius concolor* superspecies according to Schiøtz, 1975,
Treefrogs E. Afr.:113. See comment under *Hyperolius stenodactylus*.

Hyperolius cystocandicans Richards and Schiøtz, 1977. Copeia, 1977:285.
TYPE(S): Holotype: UMMZ 135194.
TYPE LOCALITY: "Tigoni, 2200 m above sea level", Kenya.
DISTRIBUTION: Highlands of Kenya.
COMMENT: Related to *Hyperolius montanus*, *Hyperolius alticola*, *Hyperolius frontalis*,
Hyperolius castaneus, and *Hyperolius discodactylus*, according to the original
description.

Hyperolius dermatus Ahl, 1931. Das Tierreich, 55:382.
TYPE(S): ZMB; lost.
TYPE LOCALITY: "Cabayra, (Port. Ost-Afrika [=Mozambique])".
DISTRIBUTION: Known only from the type locality.
COMMENT: Probably a synonym of *Hyperolius marmoratus taeniatus* Peters (RL).

Hyperolius destefanii Scortecci, 1943. Miss. Biol. Sagan-Omo, 7(Zool.):312.
TYPE(S): Unknown.
TYPE LOCALITY: Hargi, Ethiopia.
DISTRIBUTION: Known only from the type locality.
COMMENT: Probably a synonym of *Hyperolius viridiflavus* (RL).

Hyperolius diaphanus Laurent, 1972. Explor. Parc Natl. Virunga, (2)22:67.
TYPE(S): RGMC.
TYPE LOCALITY: Kigulube, Kivu, eastern Zaire.
DISTRIBUTION: Rainforest in eastern Zaire.

Hyperolius discodactylus Ahl, 1931. Das Tierreich, 55:363.
TYPE(S): Syntypes: ZMB 36089, MCZ 17634.
TYPE LOCALITY: "Rugege-Wald und westlich des Albert-Edward-Sees".
DISTRIBUTION: Montane forest in Rwanda, Burundi, Uganda, and eastern Zaire.
COMMENT: See comment under *Hyperolius alticola*.

Hyperolius endjami Amiet, 1980. Rev. Suisse Zool., 87:445.
TYPE(S): Holotype: MHNG 2006.77.
TYPE LOCALITY: Kala, 20 km west of Yaoundé, Cameroon.
DISTRIBUTION: Rainforest of southwestern Cameroon.

Hyperolius erythromelanus Monard, 1937. Bull. Soc. Neuchâtel. Sci. Nat., 62:36.
  TYPE(S): Syntypes: LCFM (?) (2 specimens).
  TYPE LOCALITY: "Sangevé", Angola.
  DISTRIBUTION: Known only from the type locality.

Hyperolius erythropus Laurent, 1943. Ann. Mus. R. Congo Belge, Tervuren, Zool., (1)4:
    102.
  TYPE(S): Holotype: RGMC 315.
  TYPE LOCALITY: Medje, northern Zaire.
  DISTRIBUTION: Northern Zaire.
  COMMENT: A synonym of *Hyperolius bolifambae*; Laurent did not see the description
    of *Hyperolius bolifambae* until after World War II (RL).

Hyperolius fasciatus (Ferreira, 1906). J. Sci. Math. Phys. Nat., Lisboa, (2)7:64.
  ORIGINAL NAME: *Rappia fasciata*.
  TYPE(S): MUP.
  TYPE LOCALITY: Quilombo, Angola.
  DISTRIBUTION: Known only from the type locality.
  COMMENT: Probably a synonym of *Hyperolius platyceps* (RL).

Hyperolius ferreirai Noble, 1924. Bull. Am. Mus. Nat. Hist., 49:324.
  TYPE(S): MUP.
  TYPE LOCALITY: Rio Luinha, Quilombo, N'golla Bumba, Angola.
  DISTRIBUTION: Known only from the type localities.
  COMMENT: Probably a synonym of *Hyperolius platyceps* (RL). *Hyperolius ferreirai* is a
    replacement name for *Rappia bivittatus* Ferreira, 1906, J. Sci. Math. Phys. Nat.,
    Lisboa, (2)7:161, which is preoccupied by *Hyperolius bivittatus* Peters, 1855.

Hyperolius ferrugineus Laurent, 1943. Ann. Mus. R. Congo Belge, Tervuren, Zool.,
    (1)4:100.
  TYPE(S): Holotype: RGMC 40224.
  TYPE LOCALITY: Lodjo on the River Mongbwalu, Ituri, Zaire.
  DISTRIBUTION: Known only from the type locality.

Hyperolius fimbriolatus Peters, 1876. Monatsber. Preuss. Akad. Wiss. Berlin, 1876:121.
  TYPE(S): ZMB, lost.
  TYPE LOCALITY: Lambarene, Gabon.
  DISTRIBUTION: Known only from the type locality.
  COMMENT: Probably a synonym of *Hyperolius cinnamomeoventris* (RL).

Hyperolius frontalis Laurent, 1950. Rev. Zool. Bot. Afr., 44:11.
  TYPE(S): RGMC.
  TYPE LOCALITY: Bushoho, Kivu, Zaire.
  DISTRIBUTION: Transition forest of eastern Zaire, 700–2000 m elev.
  COMMENT: Schiøtz, 1975, Treefrogs E. Afr.:143–145, noted that this species may be
    conspecific with *Hyperolius alticola*; RL disagrees with this view.

Hyperolius fusciventris Peters, 1876. Monatsber. Preuss. Akad. Wiss. Berlin, 1876:122.
  TYPE(S): ZMB.
  TYPE LOCALITY: Liberia.
  DISTRIBUTION: Sierra Leone to western Cameroon.

Hyperolius ghesquieri Laurent, Ann. Mus. R. Congo Belge, Tervuren, Zool.,
    (1)4:98.
  TYPE(S): Holotype: RGMC 1159.
  TYPE LOCALITY: Befale, central Zaire.
  DISTRIBUTION: Known only from the type locality.

Hyperolius gularis Ahl, 1931. Das Tierreich, 55:408.
TYPE(S): ZMB; lost.
TYPE LOCALITY: "Loanda", Angola.
DISTRIBUTION: Known only from the type locality.
COMMENT: Probably a synonym of *Hyperolius marmoratus* (RL).

Hyperolius guttulatus Günther, 1859 "1858". Cat. Batr. Sal. Coll. Brit. Mus.:86.
TYPE(S): Syntypes: BM (3 specimens).
TYPE LOCALITY: "Africa".
DISTRIBUTION: Sierra Leone to western Cameroon.

Hyperolius horstockii (Schlegel, 1837). Abbild. Amph.:24.
ORIGINAL NAME: *Hyla horstockii*.
TYPE(S): Syntypes: RMNH 1775, 10770 (2 specimens).
TYPE LOCALITY: Cape of Good Hope [Cape Province, Rep. South Africa].
DISTRIBUTION: Southern seaboard of South Africa, from Cape Town to Knysna.

Hyperolius houyi Ahl, 1931. Das Tierreich, 55:374.
TYPE(S): ZMB; lost.
TYPE LOCALITY: "Ussagara (Neue Kamerun [=Cameroon])".
DISTRIBUTION: Known only from the type locality.
COMMENT: Probably a synonym of *Hyperolius viridiflavus* (RL).

Hyperolius inornatus Laurent, 1943. Ann. Mus. R. Congo Belge, Tervuren, Zool., (1)4:
136.
TYPE(S): Holotype: RGMC 261.
TYPE LOCALITY: Congo da Lemba, lower Zaire.
DISTRIBUTION: Known only from the type locality.

Hyperolius kachalolae Schiøtz, 1975. Treefrogs E. Afr.:162.
TYPE(S): Holotype: ZMUC R078722.
TYPE LOCALITY: "near Kachalola, Zambia".
DISTRIBUTION: Known only from the type locality.

Hyperolius kibarae Laurent, 1957. Explor. Parc Natl. Upemba, 42:8.
TYPE(S): RGMC.
TYPE LOCALITY: Lusinga, Upemba National Park, Shaba, southeastern Zaire.
DISTRIBUTION: Highlands of lower Shaba, southeastern Zaire.

Hyperolius kivuensis Ahl, 1931. Das Tierreich, 55:280.
TYPE(S): Holotype: ZMB 36098.
TYPE LOCALITY: "Kivu-See" (=Lake Kivu), Zaire.
DISTRIBUTION: Eastern Zaire and western Kenya to southern Malawi and Zambia.
COMMENT: In the *Hyperolius concolor* superspecies according to Schiøtz, 1975,
Treefrogs E. Afr.:113. Easily confused with *Hyperolius quinquevittatus*, to which
Schiøtz's Malawi record should be referred. See comment under *Hyperolius
raveni* and *Hyperolius pustulifer*.

Hyperolius koehleri Mertens, 1940. Senckenb. Biol., 22:121.
ORIGINAL NAME: *Hyperolius köhleri*.
TYPE(S): Holotype: SMF 28291.
TYPE LOCALITY: "Musake-Quelle, oberhalb Buëa, 1800 m. H., Kamerun-Berg",
Cameroon.
DISTRIBUTION: South Cameroon to Gabon in forest.
COMMENT: Discussed by Amiet, 1976, Ann. Fac. Sci. Cameroun, 21–22:159–169,
who described the tadpoles.

Hyperolius krebsi Mertens, 1938. Abh. Senckenb. Naturforsch. Ges., 442:30.
TYPE(S): Holotype: SMF 22459.
TYPE LOCALITY: Mubengue, Cameroon.
DISTRIBUTION: Southwestern Cameroon.

COMMENT: Perret, 1976, Arq. Mus. Bocage, (2)6:28–32, stated that this species belongs to an undescribed genus related to *Acanthixalus*. See also Amiet, 1976, Ann. Fac. Sci. Cameroun, 21–22:160, who described the tadpoles.

Hyperolius kuligae Mertens, 1940. Senckenb. Biol., 22:124.
TYPE(S): Holotype: SMF 28300.
TYPE LOCALITY: "'Camp II': 920 m über Mubenge, Kamerun-Berg", Cameroon.
DISTRIBUTION: From southwestern Cameroon to western Uganda.
COMMENT: Revised by Amiet, 1978, Ann. Fac. Sci. Yaoundé, 25:234–243, and compared to *Hyperolius platyceps* and *Hyperolius adametzi*.

Hyperolius lamottei Laurent, 1958. Mém. Inst. Franç. Afr. Noire, 53:292.
TYPE(S): MNHNP.
TYPE LOCALITY: Entre Zouguépo et Sérenbara [Liberia].
DISTRIBUTION: Savannas of Sierra Leone to southern Ivory Coast.

Hyperolius lateralis Laurent, 1940. Rev. Zool. Bot. Afr., 34:1.
TYPE(S): Holotype: RGMC 38902.
TYPE LOCALITY: N'Gesho, Zaire.
DISTRIBUTION: Northwestern Tanzania to eastern Zaire to western Kenya.
COMMENT: Ten subspecies (RL).

Hyperolius laticeps Ahl, 1931. Mitt. Zool. Mus. Berlin, 17:69.
TYPE(S): Not traced.
TYPE LOCALITY: "Togo".
DISTRIBUTION: Known only from the type locality.

Hyperolius laurenti Schiøtz, 1967. Spolia Zool. Mus. Haun., 25:209.
TYPE(S): Holotype: ZMUC R073284.
TYPE LOCALITY: "near the forestry resthouse in Bobiri Forest Reserve, Ghana".
DISTRIBUTION: Rainforests of southeastern Ivory Coast to southern Ghana.
COMMENT: Possibly a subspecies of *Hyperolius chlorosteus* according to Schiøtz, 1967, Spolia Zool. Mus. Haun., 25:212.

Hyperolius leleupi Laurent, 1951. Rev. Zool. Bot. Afr., 44:371.
TYPE(S): RGMC.
TYPE LOCALITY: Upper Luvubu, Itombwe highlands, Kivu, eastern Zaire.
DISTRIBUTION: Itombwe highlands, Kivu, eastern Zaire.

Hyperolius leucotaenius Laurent, 1950. Rev. Zool. Bot. Afr., 44:14.
TYPE(S): RGMC.
TYPE LOCALITY: Kinadjo, western slope of Itombwe highlands, Kivu, eastern Zaire.
DISTRIBUTION: Transition forest west of the southern part of the Itombwe highlands and northern slopes of the Kabobo highlands, Zaire.
COMMENT: A vicariant of *Hyperolius chrysogaster* (RL).

Hyperolius lucani Rochebrune, 1885. Bull. Soc. Philomath. Paris, (2)9:91.
TYPE(S): Unknown.
TYPE LOCALITY: Landana, Cabinda enclave [Angola].
DISTRIBUTION: Known only from the type locality.
COMMENT: Probably a synonym of *Hyperolius ocellatus* (RL).

Hyperolius maestus Rochebrune, 1885. Bull. Soc. Philomath. Paris, (2)9:91.
TYPE(S): Not traced.
TYPE LOCALITY: Landana, Cabinda enclave [Angola].
DISTRIBUTION: Known only from the type locality.
COMMENT: Probably a synonym of *Hyperolius marmoratus* (RL).

Hyperolius marginatus Peters, 1854. Monatsber. Preuss. Akad. Wiss. Berlin, 1854:627.
TYPE(S): ZMB.
TYPE LOCALITY: Macanga, Mozambique [not located with certainty—JCP].
DISTRIBUTION: Upland area north and south of the middle Zambesi River, Central Africa.
COMMENT: Considered a subspecies of *Hyperolius marmoratus* by RL. See comment under *Hyperolius marmoratus.*

Hyperolius marmoratus Rapp, 1842. Arch. Naturgesch., 8:289.
TYPE(S): Not traced.
TYPE LOCALITY: Natal [Rep. South Africa].
DISTRIBUTION: African savannas south of the rainforest, embracing much of Tanzania and southern Kenya in East Africa.
COMMENT: Synonymy includes *Hyperolius bergeri* Ahl, 1931, according to Schiøtz, 1975, Treefrogs E. Afr.:198, and *Hyperolius guttolineatus* Ahl, 1931, according to Laurent, 1951, Ann. Soc. R. Zool. Belg., 82:389. The status of *Hyperolius parallelus* Günther, 1859 "1858", Cat. Batr. Sal. Coll. Brit. Mus.:86 (Type: BM; Type locality: "South Africa", in error; Distribution: Angola east to western Tanzania, Malawi, and eastern Zambia), is controversial (RCD). Laurent, 1950, Explor. Parc Natl. Albert, 64:81, considered it a synonym of *Hyperolius marmoratus.* Schiøtz, 1971, Vidensk. Medd. Dansk Naturhist. Foren., 134:28, considered *Hyperolius parallelus* to be a distinct species, and *Hyperolius marmoratus* to be a subspecies of *Hyperolius viridiflavus.* Laurent, 1976, Ann. Mus. R. Afr. Cent., Tervuren, Ser. Octavo, Sci. Zool., 213:90, considered *Hyperolius parallelus* to be a subspecies of *Hyperolius marginatus.* Drewes, 1984, Occas. Pap. California Acad. Sci., 189:52, regarded *Hyperolius parallelus* as a distinct species, without discussion. JCP regards all southern African forms treated variously in the literature as subspecies of *Hyperolius marmoratus*, *Hyperolius viridiflavus*, *Hyperolius marginatus*, and *Hyperolius parallelus*, to be subspecies of *Hyperolius marmoratus.* Laurent, 1983, Monit. Zool. Ital., N.S., Suppl., 18:4, recognized three species in the *Hyperolius viridiflavus* superspecies: *Hyperolius viridiflavus* (in northern savannas), *Hyperolius marmoratus* (in southern savannas), and *Hyperolius tuberculatus* (in the rainforest). See comments under *Hyperolius protchei* and *Hyperolius maestus.*

Hyperolius minutissimus Schiøtz, 1975. Treefrogs E. Afr.:167.
TYPE(S): Holotype: ZMUC R079213.
TYPE LOCALITY: "10 miles west of Njombe, Tanzania".
DISTRIBUTION: Southern Tanzania; possibly in northern Malawi.

Hyperolius mitchelli Loveridge, 1953. Bull. Mus. Comp. Zool., 110:360.
ORIGINAL NAME: *Hyperolius puncticulatus mitchelli.*
TYPE(S): Holotype: MCZ 27272.
TYPE LOCALITY: Mtimbuka, Malawi.
DISTRIBUTION: Northeastern Tanzania to Mozambique; possibly in Zimbabwe and Rep. South Africa (not confirmed—JCP).
COMMENT: See comment under *Hyperolius rubrovermiculatus.*

Hyperolius molleri (Bedriaga, 1892). Instituto, Coimbra, (2)39:642.
ORIGINAL NAME: *Rappia molleri.*
TYPE(S): Not traced.
TYPE LOCALITY: São Thomé Island.
DISTRIBUTION: São Tomé I., Gulf of Guinea.

Hyperolius montanus (Angel, 1924). Bull. Mus. Natl. Hist. Nat., Paris, 30:269.
ORIGINAL NAME: *Rappia montana.*
TYPE(S): Syntypes: MNHNP 24-30 to 24-34.
TYPE LOCALITY: Mt. Kinangop, Kenya.
DISTRIBUTION: Central Kenya.

Hyperolius mosaicus Perret, 1959. Rev. Suisse Zool., 66:716.
  TYPE(S): Holotype: MHNG 965.12.
  TYPE LOCALITY: "Ngam, Sangmelina, Cameroun".
  DISTRIBUTION: South Cameroon.
  COMMENT: Considered a synonym of *Hyperolius acutirostris* by Perret, 1966, Zool.
    Jahrb., Abt. Syst., 93:408, but subsequently considered a distinct species by
    Perret, 1975, Rev. Suisse Zool., 82(1):191. Amiet, 1980, Ann. Fac. Sci. Yaoundé,
    27(2):458, compared this species to *Hyperolius acutirostris* and *Hyperolius
    endjami*.

Hyperolius nasutus Günther, 1864. Proc. Zool. Soc. London, 1864:482.
  TYPE(S): Holotype: BM.
  TYPE LOCALITY: Duque de Bragança, Angola.
  DISTRIBUTION: Savannas of Ivory Coast east to Uganda, thence to southern Zambia,
    Natal (Rep. South Africa), Malawi, and coastal Kenya to Natal (Rep. South
    Africa) and across to northern Namibia.
  COMMENT: Synonymy includes *Hyperolius acuticeps* Ahl, 1931, according to Laurent,
    1961, Rev. Zool. Bot. Afr., 64:93.

Hyperolius obscurus Laurent, 1943. Ann. Mus. R. Congo Belge, Tervuren, Zool., (1)4:
    135.
  TYPE(S): Holotype: RGMC 11107.
  TYPE LOCALITY: Sandoa, Kasai, Zaire.
  DISTRIBUTION: Known only from the type locality.

Hyperolius obstetricans Ahl, 1931. Das Tierreich, 55:364.
  TYPE(S): ZMB, lost; MHNG 995.48 designated neotype by Perret, 1966, Zool. Jahrb.,
    Abt. Syst., 93:410.
  TYPE LOCALITY: "Bipindi, Kamerun [=Cameroon]"; neotype from "Foulassi, rivière
    Lobô".
  DISTRIBUTION: Southern and southwestern Cameroon.
  COMMENT: Amiet, 1974, Bull. Inst. Fondam. Afr. Noire, (A)36:981, suggested that
    Hyperolius obstetricans might best be placed in a separate genus because of its
    unique larval morphology.

Hyperolius occidentalis Schiøtz, 1967. Spolia Zool. Mus. Haun., 25:193.
  TYPE(S): Holotype: ZMUC R076225.
  TYPE LOCALITY: "near the forestry resthouse in Kassewe Forest Reserve, Sierra
    Leone".
  DISTRIBUTION: Western Sierra Leone and possibly in adjacent Guinea.

Hyperolius ocellatus Günther, 1859 "1858". Cat. Batr. Sal. Coll. Brit. Mus.:88.
  TYPE(S): Syntypes: including BM 1947.2.9.22.
  TYPE LOCALITY: "Fernando Po" and "Angola" (apparently in error).
  DISTRIBUTION: Forests of southeastern Nigeria to Zaire and Uganda.
  COMMENT: See Perret, 1975, Ann. Fac. Sci. Yaoundé, 20:23–31, for discussion of
    subspecific variation. Includes *Hyperolius purpurescens* Laurent, 1943, as a
    subspecies, according to Perret, 1975, Ann. Fac. Sci. Yaoundé, 20:27. See
    comment under *Hyperolius lucani*.

Hyperolius pardalis Laurent, 1947. Ann. Mag. Nat. Hist., (11)14:294.
  ORIGINAL NAME: *Hyperolius steindachneri pardalis*.
  TYPE(S): Holotype: BM 1913.10.29.29.
  TYPE LOCALITY: Bitye, Cameroon.
  DISTRIBUTION: Forests of Cameroon to Congo and lower Zaire.
  COMMENT: Elevated to species status and discussed by Perret, 1976, Arq. Mus.
    Bocage, (2)6:25.

Hyperolius parkeri Loveridge, 1933. Bull. Mus. Comp. Zool., 74:410.
TYPE(S): Holotype: MCZ 13365.
TYPE LOCALITY: "Mogoni swamp, south of Dar-es-Salaam, Usaramo, Tanganyika [=Tanzania]".
DISTRIBUTION: Coastal Kenya, Tanzania, and Mozambique.
COMMENT: Schiøtz, 1975, Treefrogs E. Afr.:175, suggested that this species might best be placed in a separate genus.

Hyperolius phantasticus (Boulenger, 1899). Proc. Zool. Soc. London, 1899:274.
ORIGINAL NAME: *Rappia phantasticus*.
TYPE(S): BM.
TYPE LOCALITY: Benito River, Gabon.
DISTRIBUTION: Forests of Gabon and southern Cameroon to central Zaire.
COMMENT: Synonymy includes *Hyperolius boulengeri* Laurent, 1943, according to Laurent, 1961, Rev. Zool. Bot. Afr., 64:73, and *Hyperolius nigropalmatus* Ahl, 1931, according to Perret, 1966, Zool. Jahrb., Abt. Syst., 93:408. See comment under *Hyperolius chabanaudi*.

Hyperolius pickersgilli Raw, 1982. Durban Mus. Novit., 8:118.
TYPE(S): Holotype: NMP 6658.
TYPE LOCALITY: Avoca, North of Durban, Natal [Rep. South Africa].
DISTRIBUTION: Natal coastal lowlands, Rep. South Africa.

Hyperolius picturatus Peters, 1875. Monatsber. Preuss. Akad. Wiss. Berlin, 1875:206.
TYPE(S): Holotype: ZMB 3063.
TYPE LOCALITY: Boutry [=mouth of River Butre], Ghana.
DISTRIBUTION: Eastern Sierra Leone and southern Guinea to southern Ghana.
COMMENT: Probably composed of two cryptic species, according to Schiøtz, 1967, Spolia Zool. Mus. Haun., 25:192.

Hyperolius pictus Ahl, 1931. Das Tierreich, 55:301.
TYPE(S): ZMB; lost.
TYPE LOCALITY: "Ost-Afrika [=Tanzania] (Uhehe, Ngori-See, Rugwe am Nyassa-See, Nairobi)".
DISTRIBUTION: Highlands of southwestern Tanzania, northern Malawi, and northeastern Zambia.

Hyperolius platyceps (Boulenger, 1900). Proc. Zool. Soc. London, 1900:444.
ORIGINAL NAME: *Rappia platyceps*.
TYPE(S): BM.
TYPE LOCALITY: Benito River, Gabon.
DISTRIBUTION: Cameroon to northwestern Zambia.
COMMENT: Possibly composed of several cryptic species (RL). Revised by Amiet, 1978, Ann. Fac. Sci. Yaoundé, 25:224–254, who discussed relationships.

Hyperolius polli Laurent, 1943. Ann. Mus. R. Congo Belge, Tervuren, Zool., (1)4:96.
TYPE(S): Holotype: RGMC 656.
TYPE LOCALITY: Tshimbulu on Luebi, Kasai, Zaire.
DISTRIBUTION: Kasai, Zaire.

Hyperolius polystictus Laurent, 1943. Ann. Mus. R. Congo Belge, Tervuren, Zool., (1)4:133.
TYPE(S): Holotype: RGMC 181o.
TYPE LOCALITY: Lofoi, Upper Shaba, Zaire (falls of the Lofoi River).
DISTRIBUTION: Known only from the type locality.

Hyperolius protchei Rochebrune, 1885. Bull. Soc. Philomath. Paris, (3)9:92.
TYPE(S): Not traced.
TYPE LOCALITY: Landana, Cabinda enclave [Angola].
DISTRIBUTION: Known only from the type locality.

COMMENT: Probably a synonym of *Hyperolius marmoratus* (RL).

Hyperolius puncticulatus (Pfeffer, 1893). Jahrb. Hamburg. Wiss. Anst., 10:99.
ORIGINAL NAME: *Rappia puncticulata.*
TYPE(S): ZMH; lost.
TYPE LOCALITY: Zanzibar [Tanzania].
DISTRIBUTION: Coastal Kenya to Malawi.
COMMENT: Synonymy includes *Hyperolius scriptus* Ahl, 1931, according to Schiøtz, 1975, Treefrogs E. Afr.:146. Records south of Malawi are referable to *Hyperolius argus* (JCP).

Hyperolius punctulatus (Bocage, 1895). Herpetol. Angola Congo:168.
ORIGINAL NAME: *Rappia punctulata.*
TYPE(S): Holotype: MBL T.23-227; destroyed in 1978 fire.
TYPE LOCALITY: "sur les bords du Quanza", Angola.
DISTRIBUTION: Known only from the type locality.
COMMENT: Discussed by Perret, 1976, Arq. Mus. Bocage, (2)6:27.

Hyperolius pusillus (Cope, 1862). Proc. Acad. Nat. Sci. Philadelphia, 14:343.
ORIGINAL NAME: *Crumenifera pusilla.*
TYPE(S): Holotype: ANSP 11323.
TYPE LOCALITY: Umvoti, Natal [Rep. South Africa].
DISTRIBUTION: Southern Somalia south along coastal lowlands of Africa to Transkei, Rep. South Africa.

Hyperolius pustulifer Laurent, 1940. Rev. Zool. Bot. Afr., 34:6.
TYPE(S): Holotype: RGMC 37025.
TYPE LOCALITY: Luvungi, Kivu, eastern Zaire.
DISTRIBUTION: Known only from the type locality.
COMMENT: Probably a synonym of *Hyperolius kivuensis* (RL).

Hyperolius quadratomaculatus Ahl, 1931. Das Tierreich, 55:412.
TYPE(S): Holotype: ZMB 36108.
TYPE LOCALITY: "Mohorro, Deutsch-Ostafrika [=Tanzania]".
DISTRIBUTION: Known only from the type locality.

Hyperolius quinquevittatus Bocage, 1866. J. Sci. Math. Phys. Nat., Lisboa, 1:56.
TYPE(S): Syntypes: MBL 24-214 and 24-215; destroyed by 1978 fire.
TYPE LOCALITY: Duque de Bragança, Angola.
DISTRIBUTION: Angola, Zaire, southern Tanzania, Malawi, and northern Zambia.
COMMENT: Includes *Hyperolius mertensi* Poynton, 1964, as a subspecies, according to Schiøtz, 1975, Treefrogs E. Afr.:105.

Hyperolius raveni Ahl, 1931. Das Tierreich, 55:291.
TYPE(S): ZMB; lost.
TYPE LOCALITY: "Vulkangebiet nordöstlich des Kivu-Sees" (volcano region northeast of Lake Kivu, boundary between Zaire and Rwanda).
DISTRIBUTION: Known only from the type locality.
COMMENT: Probably a synonym of *Hyperolius kivuensis* (RL).

Hyperolius rhizophilus Rochebrune, 1885. Bull. Soc. Philomath. Paris, (7)9:92.
TYPE(S): Not traced.
TYPE LOCALITY: Landana, Cabinda [Angola].
DISTRIBUTION: Known only from the type locality.

Hyperolius riggenbachi (Nieden, 1910). Arch. Naturgesch., 76:244.
ORIGINAL NAME: *Rappia riggenbachi.*
TYPE(S): ZMB.
TYPE LOCALITY: Banjo [Nigeria].
DISTRIBUTION: Mambilla Plateau of eastern Nigeria; Cameroon Range (except Mount Cameroon) and Adamaoua Plateau, Cameroon.

COMMENT: Synonymy includes *Hyperolius hieroglyphicus* according to Amiet, 1973, Ann. Fac. Sci. Cameroun, 13:157.

Hyperolius robustus Laurent, 1979. Rev. Zool. Afr., 43:783.
TYPE(S): Holotype: RGMC 79.24.B.4.
TYPE LOCALITY: Gembe, Lodja Terr., Sankuru, Zaire.
DISTRIBUTION: Northern Sankuru, central Zaire.

Hyperolius rubrovermiculatus Schiøtz, 1975. Treefrogs E. Afr.:154.
TYPE(S): Holotype: ZMUC R073854.
TYPE LOCALITY: "Shimba Hills, Kenya".
DISTRIBUTION: Southern Kenya.
COMMENT: Possibly a subspecies of *Hyperolius mitchelli*, according to Schiøtz, 1975, Treefrogs E. Afr.:156.

Hyperolius salinae (Bianconi, 1848). Nuovi Ann. Sci. Nat., Bologna, (2)10:107.
ORIGINAL NAME: *Euchnemis salinae.*
TYPE(S): Not traced.
TYPE LOCALITY: Inhambane, Mozambique.
DISTRIBUTION: Known only from the type locality.
COMMENT: Probably a synonym of *Hyperolius tuberilinguis* (RL).

Hyperolius sankuruensis Laurent, 1979. Rev. Zool. Afr., 93:779.
TYPE(S): Holotype: RGMC 79.24.B.1.
TYPE LOCALITY: Omaniundu, Lodja Terr. Sankuru, Zaire.
DISTRIBUTION: Known only from the type locality.

Hyperolius schoutedeni Laurent, 1943. Ann. Mus. R. Congo Belge, Tervuren, Zool., (1)4:86.
TYPE(S): Holotype: RGMC 39837.
TYPE LOCALITY: Kunungu, western Zaire.
DISTRIBUTION: Roughly the northern half of Zaire.

Hyperolius seabrai (Ferreira, 1906). J. Sci. Math. Phys. Nat., Lisboa, (2)7:163.
ORIGINAL NAME: *Rappia seabrai.*
TYPE(S): Syntypes: MUP.
TYPE LOCALITY: Quilombo, Angola.
DISTRIBUTION: Known only from the type locality.
COMMENT: Probably a synonym of *Hyperolius bocagei* (RL).

Hyperolius semidiscus Hewitt, 1927. Rec. Albany Mus., 3:410.
TYPE(S): AMG.
TYPE LOCALITY: Marianhill, Natal [Rep. South Africa].
DISTRIBUTION: Southeastern midlands and lowlands of Rep. South Africa.

Hyperolius sheldricki Duff-MacKay and Schiøtz, 1971. J. E. Afr. Nat. Hist. Soc. Natl. Mus., 29:1.
TYPE(S): Holotype: NMK A/366/3.
TYPE LOCALITY: North of Aruba Dam, Tsavo National Park, Kenya.
DISTRIBUTION: Type locality and '15 miles west of Kakoneni', Kenya.
COMMENT: In the *Hyperolius viridiflavus* superspecies, according to Schiøtz, 1975, Treefrogs E. Afr.:218. Considered a subspecies of *Hyperolius viridiflavus* by Laurent, 1976, Ann. Mus. R. Afr. Cent., Tervuren, Ser. Octavo, Sci. Zool., 213:90.

Hyperolius soror (Chabanaud, 1921). Bull. Com. Études Hist. Scient. Afr. Occid. Franç., 1921:458.
ORIGINAL NAME: *Rappia soror.*
TYPE(S): Not traced.
TYPE LOCALITY: N'Zerekoré, Guinea.
DISTRIBUTION: Southern Guinea, Liberia, and western Ivory Coast.

COMMENT: See comment under *Hyperolius wermuthi*.

Hyperolius spinigularis Stevens, 1971. Zool. Afr., 6:313.
   TYPE(S): Holotype: NMZB (formerly UM).
   TYPE LOCALITY: Chisambo Estate, Mulanje, Malawi.
   DISTRIBUTION: Usambara Mountains, Tanzania, and Mt. Mulanje, Malawi.

Hyperolius steindachneri Bocage, 1866. J. Sci. Math. Phys. Nat., Lisboa, 1:75.
   TYPE(S): Holotype: MBL T.25-226; destroyed by 1978 fire.
   TYPE LOCALITY: Duque de Bragança, Angola.
   DISTRIBUTION: Northern Angola and southwestern Zaire.
   COMMENT: Synonymy includes *Hyperolius machadoi* Laurent, 1954, according to
      Laurent, 1964, Publ. Cult. Companhia Diamantes Angola, 67:157. See
      comment under *Hyperolius pardalis*.

Hyperolius stenodactylus Ahl, 1931. Das Tierreich, 55:271.
   TYPE(S): ZMB; lost.
   TYPE LOCALITY: "Bipindi, Kamerun [=Cameroon]".
   DISTRIBUTION: Known only from the type locality.
   COMMENT: Probably a synonym of *Hyperolius concolor*; see Perret, 1966, Zool.
      Jahrb., Abt. Syst., 93:411.

Hyperolius sylvaticus Schiøtz, 1967. Spolia Zool. Mus. Haun., 25:165.
   TYPE(S): Holotype: ZMUC R074497.
   TYPE LOCALITY: Bobiri Forest Reserve, Ghana.
   DISTRIBUTION: Forests in southern Ivory Coast to western Cameroon.

Hyperolius tanneri Schiøtz, 1982. Steenstrupia, 8:269.
   TYPE(S): Holotype: ZMUC R77372.
   TYPE LOCALITY: "Forest swamp at 1410 m above sea level in Mazumbai Forest
      Reserve, Western Usambaras, Tanzania".
   DISTRIBUTION: Known only from the type locality.

Hyperolius thomensis Bocage, 1886. J. Sci. Math. Phys. Nat., Lisboa, (2)3:74.
   TYPE(S): Syntypes: MBL T.26-216 (2 specimens) and 26-219; destroyed by 1978
      fire.
   TYPE LOCALITY: Roça Saudade, São Thomé Island.
   DISTRIBUTION: São Tomé I., Gulf of Guinea.
   COMMENT: Transferred from *Nesionixalus* Perret, 1976, Arq. Mus. Bocage, (2)6:29, to
      Hyperolius by Drewes, 1984, Occas. Pap. California Acad. Sci., 139:1–70. Perret
      erected *Nesionixalus* to include the type series of this species which was later
      destroyed by fire. Drewes examined what appear to be the only 4 remaining
      representatives of the taxon (BM 1951.1.1.91, 98.3.30.39, and NHMW 3695–96).
      JLA and JLP disagree with the synonymy of *Nesionixalus*, noting that this
      species does not fit the diagnosis of *Hyperolius* in several features. RCD
      disagrees with JLA and JLP.

Hyperolius thoracotuberculatus Ahl, 1931. Das Tierreich, 55:371.
   TYPE(S): Holotype: ZMB 36097.
   TYPE LOCALITY: "Afrika (ohne genauen Fundort)" (=Africa, without precise locality
      data).
   DISTRIBUTION: Unknown.

Hyperolius tornieri Ahl, 1931. Das Tierreich, 55:304.
   TYPE(S): ZMB; lost.
   TYPE LOCALITY: "Ukami, [Uluguru Mountains,] Deutsch-Ost-Afrika [=Tanzania]".
   DISTRIBUTION: Known only from the type locality.

Hyperolius torrentis Schiøtz, 1967. Spolia Zool. Mus. Haun., 25:218.
TYPE(S): Holotype: ZMUC R074376.
TYPE LOCALITY: "at a small stream near the village Biakpa, Ghana".
DISTRIBUTION: Southeastern Ghana and adjacent Togo.

Hyperolius tuberculatus (Mocquard, 1897). Bull. Soc. Philomath. Paris, (8)9:18.
ORIGINAL NAME: *Rappia tuberculata*.
TYPE(S): Holotype: MNHNP 96-570.
TYPE LOCALITY: Lambarene, Gabon.
DISTRIBUTION: Southern Guinea; rainforests from southeastern Nigeria to eastern
    Zaire.
COMMENT: In the *Hyperolius viridiflavus* superspecies according to Schiøtz, 1975,
    Treefrogs E. Afr.:172. Synonymy includes *Hyperolius nimbae* Laurent, 1958,
    according to Schiøtz, 1975, Vidensk. Medd. Dansk Naturhist. Foren., 134:28.
    See Laurent, 1983, Monit. Zool. Ital., N.S., Suppl., 18:1–93, for discussion.

Hyperolius tuberilinguis Smith, 1849. Illustr. Zool. S. Afr., Rept., App.:26.
TYPE(S): Not traced.
TYPE LOCALITY: Country to the eastward of the Cape Colony [Rep. South Africa].
DISTRIBUTION: Coastal region from Kenya to Natal (Rep. South Africa).
COMMENT: In the *Hyperolius concolor* superspecies, according to Schiøtz, 1975,
    Treefrogs E. Afr.:112. See comment under *Hyperolius salinae*.

Hyperolius vilhenai Laurent, 1964. Publ. Cult. Companhia Diamantes Angola, 67:155.
TYPE(S): MD.
TYPE LOCALITY: Cuilo, forest gallery along the Luita River, Angola.
DISTRIBUTION: Known only from the type locality.

Hyperolius viridiflavus (Duméril and Bibron, 1841). Erp. Gén., 8:528.
ORIGINAL NAME: *Eucnemis viridiflavus*.
TYPE(S): Syntypes: MNHNP 412, 4599, and NHMW 22896.
TYPE LOCALITY: "Abyssinie".
DISTRIBUTION: Savannas of West, Central, and East Africa (occurrence south of
    Tanzania is controversial—JCP).
COMMENT: In the *Hyperolius viridiflavus* superspecies according to Schiøtz, 1975,
    Treefrogs E. Afr.:172. See also Schiøtz, 1971, Vidensk. Medd. Dansk Naturhist.
    Foren., 134:21–76; Laurent, 1976, Ann. Mus. R. Afr. Cent., Tervuren, Ser.
    Octavo, Sci. Zool., 213:84–90; and Laurent, 1983, Monit. Zool. Ital., N.S.,
    Suppl., 18:1–93. Synonymy includes *Hyperolius nitidulus* Peters, 1875,
    according to Schiøtz, 1971, Vidensk. Medd. Dansk Naturhist. Foren., 134:49.
    Hyperolius nitidulus considered a distinct species by Drewes, 1984, Occas. Pap.
    California Acad. Sci., 139:52, without discussion. JCP and RL do not consider
    this species to occur in southern Africa. See comments under *Hyperolius
    marmoratus* and *Hyperolius sheldricki*.

Hyperolius viridigulosus Schiøtz, 1967. Spolia Zool. Mus. Haun., 25:213.
TYPE(S): Holotype: ZMUC R073439.
TYPE LOCALITY: "in Bobiri Forest Reserve, Ghana, at a small stream near the
    forestry resthouse".
DISTRIBUTION: Rainforests of central Ghana to southern Ivory Coast.

Hyperolius viridis Schiøtz, 1975. Treefrogs E. Afr.:110.
TYPE(S): Holotype: ZMUC R079491.
TYPE LOCALITY: "30 miles southwest of Mbeya, Tanzania".
DISTRIBUTION: Savannas of southern Tanzania and northeastern Zambia.

Hyperolius wermuthi Laurent, 1961. Rev. Zool. Bot. Afr., 64:71.
TYPE(S): MNHNP.
TYPE LOCALITY: Nimba [Ivory Coast].
DISTRIBUTION: Liberia and Ivory Coast and possibly adjacent Guinea.

COMMENT: Probably a synonym of *Hyperolius soror* (RL).

Hyperolius xenorhinus Laurent, 1972. Explor. Parc Natl. Virunga, (2)22:73.
  TYPE(S): RGMC.
  TYPE LOCALITY: Mount Teye, Virunga National Park, Kivu, Zaire.
  DISTRIBUTION: Known only from the type locality.

Hyperolius zavattarii Scortecci, 1943. Miss. Biol. Sagan-Omo, 7(Zool.):319.
  TYPE(S): Not traced.
  TYPE LOCALITY: Pozzi di Gondaraba, Ethiopia.
  DISTRIBUTION: Known only from the type locality.

Hyperolius zonatus Laurent, 1958. Mém. Inst. Franç. Afr. Noire, 53:276.
  TYPE(S): MNHNP.
  TYPE LOCALITY: Yanlé, Nimba, Ivory Coast.
  DISTRIBUTION: Rainforests of eastern Sierra Leone to southern Ivory Coast, through
    extreme southern Guinea.

Opisthothylax Perret, 1966. Zool. Jahrb., Abt. Syst., 93:445.
  TYPE SPECIES: *Megalixalus immaculatus* Boulenger, 1903, by monotypy.
  DISTRIBUTION: As for the single species.

Opisthothylax immaculatus (Boulenger, 1903). Mem. Soc. Esp. Hist. Nat., 1:63.
  ORIGINAL NAME: *Megalixalus immaculatus.*
  TYPE(S): BM.
  TYPE LOCALITY: Cap Saint-Jean, Gabon.
  DISTRIBUTION: Southern Nigeria through southern Cameroon, to Gabon and
    southwestern Zaire.

Tachycnemis Fitzinger, 1843. Syst. Rept.:31.
  TYPE SPECIES: *Eucnemis seychellensis* Duméril and Bibron, 1841, by original
    designation.
  DISTRIBUTION: Seychelles Is., Indian Ocean.
  COMMENT: Dubois, 1981, Monit. Zool. Ital., N.S., Suppl., 15:265, noted that
    Tachycnemis Fitzinger, 1843, has priority over *Megalixalus* Günther, 1868.

Tachycnemis seychellensis (Duméril and Bibron, 1841). Erp. Gén., 8:526.
  ORIGINAL NAME: *Eucnemis seychellensis.*
  TYPE(S): Syntypes: MNHNP 4592, 4593.
  TYPE LOCALITY: "îles Seychelles".
  DISTRIBUTION: Central granitic Seychelles Is.

SUBFAMILY: **Kassininae** Laurent, 1972.
  CITATION: Copeia, 1972:201.
  DISTRIBUTION: Subsaharan Africa.
  COMMENT: The group name was originally proposed as Kassinini, a tribe within a more
    extensively constructed Hyperoliidae. See comment under Hyperoliidae.

Afrixalus Laurent, 1944. Rev. Zool. Bot. Afr., 38:113.
  TYPE SPECIES: *Megalixalus fornasinii congicus* Laurent, 1941 (=*Rappia osorioi* Ferreira,
    1906).
  DISTRIBUTION: Subsaharan Africa.
  COMMENT: See Schiøtz, 1974, Vidensk. Medd. Dansk Naturhist. Foren., 137:9–18, for a
    revision and review of the East African forms, and Laurent, 1982, Ann. Mus. R.
    Afr. Cent., Tervuren, Ser. Octavo, Sci. Zool., 235:1–58, for a revision of the
    Central African forms. See Perret, 1976, Bull. Soc. Neuchâtel. Sci. Nat., 99:19–28,
    for revision of some West and Central African forms. See comment under
    Hyperoliidae.

Afrixalus brachycnemis (Boulenger, 1896). Ann. Mag. Nat. Hist., (6)17:403.
ORIGINAL NAME: *Megalixalus brachycnemis.*
TYPE(S): Syntypes: BM (3 specimens).
TYPE LOCALITY: "Chiradzulu, British Central Africa [=Malawi]".
DISTRIBUTION: Southern Somalia to eastern Zambia and eastern Rep. South Africa.
COMMENT: Two subspecies (RL). Mozambique and South African records believed
to be based on undescribed cryptic species (JCP). JCP currently believes that
Hyperolius knysnae Loveridge, 1954, Ann. Natal Mus., 13:95 (Holotype: MCZ
10884; Type locality: Knysna, Cape Province, Rep. South Africa; Distribution:
Natal midlands to southeastern Cape Province, Rep. South Africa), which is
currently considered a subspecies of *Afrixalus brachycnemis*, is a distinct
species, *Afrixalus knysnae.*

Afrixalus clarkei Largen, 1974. Monit. Zool. Ital., N.S., Suppl., 5:116.
TYPE(S): Holotype: BM 1973.2852.
TYPE LOCALITY: "West of Bonga, Kaffa Province, 1800 m. a.s.l. (07° 14' N—35° 58'
E)", Ethiopia.
DISTRIBUTION: Edge of tropical deciduous forest in southwestern Ethiopia.

Afrixalus dorsalis (Peters, 1875). Monatsber. Preuss. Akad. Wiss. Berlin, 1875:206.
ORIGINAL NAME: *Hyperolius dorsalis.*
TYPE(S): ZMB.
TYPE LOCALITY: Boutry [mouth of River Butre, Ghana].
DISTRIBUTION: Sierra Leone to central coastal Angola.
COMMENT: Two subspecies recognized (RL). Synonymy includes *Afrixalus
leptosomus* (Peters), according to Schiøtz, 1975, Treefrogs E. Afr.:78.

Afrixalus enseticola Largen, 1974. Monit. Zool. Ital., N.S., Suppl., 5:121.
TYPE(S): Holotype: BM 1973.2882.
TYPE LOCALITY: "West of Bonga, Kaffa Province, 1800 m. a.s.l. (07° 14' N—35° 58'
E)", Ethiopia.
DISTRIBUTION: Cleared tropical deciduous forest in southwestern Ethiopia.

Afrixalus equatorialis (Laurent, 1941). Rev. Zool. Bot. Afr., 35:122.
ORIGINAL NAME: *Megalixalus equatorialis.*
TYPE(S): Holotype: RGMC 36169.
TYPE LOCALITY: Flandria, Zaire.
DISTRIBUTION: Rainforests of central Zaire.
COMMENT: Sympatric with *Afrixalus osorioi* in central Zaire, according to Schiøtz,
1982, Steenstrupia, 8:261, and Laurent, 1982, Ann. Mus. R. Afr. Cent.,
Tervuren, Ser. Octavo, Sci. Zool., 235:18.

Afrixalus fornasinii (Bianconi, 1849). Nuovi Ann. Sci. Nat., Bologna, (2)10:107.
ORIGINAL NAME: *Euchnemis fornasinii.*
TYPE(S): Not traced.
TYPE LOCALITY: Mozambique.
DISTRIBUTION: Savannas of coastal Kenya southward through eastern and southern
Tanzania, Malawi, Mozambique to coastal Natal, Rep. South Africa.

Afrixalus fulvovittatus (Cope, 1861 "1860"). Proc. Acad. Nat. Sci. Philadelphia, 1860:
517.
ORIGINAL NAME: *Hyperolius fulvovittatus.*
TYPE(S): Holotype: ANSP 3219.
TYPE LOCALITY: Liberia.
DISTRIBUTION: Savanna regions of tropical Africa.
COMMENT: This species name has been wrongly applied to a number of different
forms, most notably *Afrixalus vittiger*; see Perret, 1976, Bull. Soc. Neuchâtel.
Sci. Nat., 99:20–23. Two subspecies (RL). Synonymy includes *Megalixalus*

leptosomus quadrivittatus Werner, 1907, according to Laurent, 1982, Ann. Mus. R. Afr. Cent., Tervuren, Ser. Octavo, Sci. Zool., 235:45.

Afrixalus lacteus Perret, 1976. Bull. Soc. Neuchâtel. Sci. Nat., 99:25.
TYPE(S): Holotype: MHNG 1506.58.
TYPE LOCALITY: Nsoung, Mt. Manengouba, Cameroun.
DISTRIBUTION: Western and southern parts of the Cameroon Range, Cameroon.
COMMENT: Confused with *Afrixalus lindholmi* by Amiet, 1972, Ann. Fac. Sci. Cameroun, 9:148 (JLP).

Afrixalus laevis (Ahl, 1930). Sitzungsber. Naturforsch. Ges. Freunde Berlin, 1930:93.
ORIGINAL NAME: *Megalixalus laevis*.
TYPE(S): ZMB.
TYPE LOCALITY: Cameroon.
DISTRIBUTION: Rainforests of Liberia to eastern Zaire.
COMMENT: One subspecies from Nigeria (*Afrixalus laevis vibekensis*) described by Schiøtz, 1967, Spolia Zool. Mus. Haun., 25:125, is probably a distinct species (JLP). See comment under *Afrixalus uluguruensis*.

Afrixalus leucostictus Laurent, 1950. Rev. Zool. Bot. Afr., 44:7.
TYPE(S): Holotype: RGMC 75-19-B-8.
TYPE LOCALITY: Makese, Kivu, Zaire.
DISTRIBUTION: Rainforest of eastern and central Zaire.

Afrixalus lindholmi (Andersson, 1907). Jahrb. Nassau. Vereins Naturkd., 60:239.
ORIGINAL NAME: *Megalixalus lindholmi*.
TYPE(S): Holotype: NHMW 130.
TYPE LOCALITY: Bibundi, Cameroon.
DISTRIBUTION: Known only from the type locality.
COMMENT: Probably a *Leptopelis* (type is a juvenile), according to Perret, 1976, Bull. Soc. Neuchâtel. Sci. Nat., 99:24; see also Amiet, 1972, Ann. Fac. Sci. Cameroun, 9:148.

Afrixalus nigeriensis Schiøtz, 1963. Vidensk. Medd. Dansk Naturhist. Foren., 125:54.
ORIGINAL NAME: *Afrixalus congicus nigeriensis*.
TYPE(S): Holotype: ZMUC.
TYPE LOCALITY: Iperin, Nigeria.
DISTRIBUTION: Rainforest from western Nigeria to Ivory Coast.

Afrixalus orophilus (Laurent, 1947). Bull. Mus. R. Hist. Nat. Belg., 23(7):1.
ORIGINAL NAME: *Megalixalus orophilus*.
TYPE(S): RGMC.
TYPE LOCALITY: Lac Magera, Kivu, Zaire.
DISTRIBUTION: Montane savannas in Kivu (Zaire), Rwanda, and Burundi; probably also in Uganda.

Afrixalus osorioi (Ferreira, 1906). J. Sci. Math. Phys. Nat., Lisboa, (2)7:162.
ORIGINAL NAME: *Rappia osorioi*.
TYPE(S): MUP.
TYPE LOCALITY: Quilombo, Angola.
DISTRIBUTION: Zaire and Angola to Uganda.
COMMENT: Senior synonym of *Afrixalus dorsalis congicus* Laurent, according to Schiøtz, 1974, Vidensk. Medd. Dansk Naturhist. Foren., 137:10, and Perret, 1976, Bull. Soc. Neuchâtel. Sci. Nat., 99:27. See also Laurent, 1982, Ann. Mus. R. Afr. Cent., Tervuren, Ser. Octavo, Sci. Zool., 235:24.

Afrixalus paradorsalis Perret, 1960. Rev. Zool. Bot. Afr., 61:370.
ORIGINAL NAME: *Afrixalus congicus paradorsalis*.
TYPE(S): Holotype: MHNG.
TYPE LOCALITY: Foulassi, Cameroon.
DISTRIBUTION: Nigeria to Gabon.

COMMENT: See Perret, 1976, Bull. Soc. Neuchâtel. Sci. Nat., 99:28, for revalidation of species status.

Afrixalus pygmaeus (Ahl, 1931). Das Tierreich, 55:273.
ORIGINAL NAME: *Hyperolius pygmaeus.*
TYPE(S): ZMB.
TYPE LOCALITY: "Tanga", Tanzania.
DISTRIBUTION: Savannas of lowland Kenya through Tanzania to Malawi and central Mozambique, possibly to northeastern Rep. South Africa.
COMMENT: See comment under *Afrixalus spinifrons.* Mozambique and South African records probably represent a new species (JCP).

Afrixalus schneideri (Boettger, 1899). Ber. Senckenb. Naturforsch. Ges., 1899:276.
ORIGINAL NAME: *Megalixalus schneideri.*
TYPE(S): Holotype: SMF 7246.
TYPE LOCALITY: Bonamandune, Duoala, Kamerun [Cameroon].
DISTRIBUTION: Known only from the type locality.
COMMENT: Discussed by Perret, 1960, Rev. Zool. Bot. Afr., 61:371.

Afrixalus spinifrons (Cope, 1862). Proc. Acad. Nat. Sci. Philadelphia, 14:342.
ORIGINAL NAME: *Hyperolius spinifrons.*
TYPE(S): Holotype: ANSP 11320.
TYPE LOCALITY: Umvoti, Natal [Rep. South Africa].
DISTRIBUTION: Natal lowlands, Rep. South Africa.
COMMENT: Possibly conspecific with *Afrixalus pygmaeus*, according to Schiøtz, 1974, Vidensk. Medd. Dansk Naturhist. Foren., 137:15.

Afrixalus stuhlmanni (Pfeffer, 1893). Jahrb. Hamburg. Wiss. Anst., 10:31.
ORIGINAL NAME: *Megalixalus stuhlmanni.*
TYPE(S): ZMH; possibly destroyed during World War II.
TYPE LOCALITY: Zanzibar Island [Tanzania].
DISTRIBUTION: Known only from the type locality.

Afrixalus sylvaticus Schiøtz, 1974. Vidensk. Medd. Dansk Naturhist. Foren., 137:17.
TYPE(S): Holotype: ZMUC R073862.
TYPE LOCALITY: "Kwale, Kenya".
DISTRIBUTION: Forests of southern coastal Kenya.

Afrixalus uluguruensis (Barbour and Loveridge, 1928). Mem. Mus. Comp. Zool., 50:231.
ORIGINAL NAME: *Megalixalus uluguruensis.*
TYPE(S): Holotype: MCZ 13311.
TYPE LOCALITY: "Vituri, Uluguru Mountains, Tanganyika Territory [=Tanzania]".
DISTRIBUTION: Rainforests of the Usambara, Uluguru, and Uzungwe regions of Tanzania.
COMMENT: Easternmost vicariant and possibly a subspecies of *Afrixalus laevis* (RL).

Afrixalus vittiger (Peters, 1876). Monatsber. Preuss. Akad. Wiss. Berlin, 1876:22.
ORIGINAL NAME: *Hyperolius vittiger.*
TYPE(S): ZMB.
TYPE LOCALITY: Liberia.
DISTRIBUTION: Senegal to Ethiopia in savanna.
COMMENT: See comment under *Afrixalus fulvovittatus.*

Afrixalus weidholzi (Mertens, 1938). Zool. Anz., 123:244.
ORIGINAL NAME: *Megalixalus weidholzi.*
TYPE(S): Holotype: NHMW 16811.
TYPE LOCALITY: 10 km SW Diénoundialla, Senegal.
DISTRIBUTION: Gambia to northern Zaire in savannas.

Afrixalus wittei (Laurent, 1941). Rev. Zool. Bot. Afr., 35:127.
ORIGINAL NAME: *Megalixalus wittei.*
TYPE(S): Holotype: RGMC 11500.
TYPE LOCALITY: Lukafu, Katanga [=Shaba], Zaire.
DISTRIBUTION: Southern Zaire, northern Angola, adjacent Tanzania and Zambia.
COMMENT: See Perret, 1976, Arq. Mus. Bocage, (2)6:24, for Angola record.

Kassina Girard, 1853. Proc. Acad. Nat. Sci. Philadelphia, 1853:67.
TYPE SPECIES: *Cystignathus senegalensis* Duméril and Bibron, 1841, by monotypy.
DISTRIBUTION: Subsaharan Africa.
COMMENT: *Kassina* Girard, 1853, was granted priority over *Hylambates* Duméril, 1853,
    by Comm. Zool. Nomencl., 1968, Opin. 849, Bull. Zool. Nomencl., 25:20–21.
    Although Laurent and Combaz, 1950, Rev. Zool. Bot. Afr., 43:269–276, were the
    first to note the close relationship between *Hylambates* and *Kassina*, Laurent,
    1976, Ann. Mus. R. Afr. Cent., Tervuren, Ser. Octavo, Sci. Zool., 213:18–21, had
    reservations about the appropriateness of the synonymy by Van Dijk, 1966,
    Ann. Natal Mus., 18:265, and Schiøtz, 1975, Treefrogs E. Afr.:60. See also
    Dubois, 1981, Monit. Zool. Ital., N.S., Suppl., 15:225–284. Drewes, 1984, Occas.
    Pap. California Acad. Sci., 139:1–70, found "*Hylambates maculata*" to be a
    member of the genus *Kassina.*

Kassina cassinoides (Boulenger, 1903). Ann. Mag. Nat. Hist., (7)12:556.
ORIGINAL NAME: *Hylambates cassinoides.*
TYPE(S): BM.
TYPE LOCALITY: MacCarthy I., Gambia.
DISTRIBUTION: Dry savanna of West Africa from Gambia to southern Mali, northern
    Ghana, and northern Cameroon.

Kassina cochranae (Loveridge, 1941). Proc. U.S. Natl. Mus., 91:125.
ORIGINAL NAME: *Hylambates cochranae.*
TYPE(S): Syntypes: USNM 109569, MCZ 24465.
TYPE LOCALITY: "Bendaja, Liberia".
DISTRIBUTION: Forest, Sierra Leone eastward to Ivory Coast and Ghana.
COMMENT: Formerly known as *Kassina maculata* Parker, 1931, a name preoccupied
    by *Hylambates maculatus* Duméril, 1853.

Kassina decorata (Angel, 1940). Bull. Mus. Natl. Hist. Nat., Paris, 12:240.
ORIGINAL NAME: *Megalixalus decorata.*
TYPE(S): Holotype: MNHNP 1939-124.
TYPE LOCALITY: "Cameroun. Cratère de l'Eboga, Monts Manengouba".
DISTRIBUTION: Cameroon (Bamiléké Plateau and Mt. Manengouba); perhaps to
    Uele, northern Zaire.
COMMENT: This complex is in need of revision (RCD).

Kassina fusca Schiøtz, 1967. Spolia Zool. Mus. Haun., 25:79.
TYPE(S): Holotype: ZMUC R073869.
TYPE LOCALITY: "9 ml. n. [mi. N] of Walewale ('ml. 77 1/2'), Ghana".
DISTRIBUTION: Northern Ghana to southern Niger and western Nigeria in savanna.

Kassina kuvangensis (Monard, 1937). Bull. Soc. Neuchâtel. Sci. Nat., 57:13.
ORIGINAL NAME: *Cassiniopsis kuvangensis.*
TYPE(S): MHNG.
TYPE LOCALITY: Kuvangu, Angola.
DISTRIBUTION: Angola to northern Zambia.
COMMENT: *Kassina ingeri* Laurent, 1963, is a synonym according to Schiøtz, 1975,
    Treefrogs E. Afr.:61.

Kassina lamottei Schiøtz, 1967. Spolia Zool. Mus. Haun., 25:89.
TYPE(S): Holotype: ZMUC R075082.
TYPE LOCALITY: "just southwest of Zéalé, between Danané and Mt. Nimba, Côte d'Ivoire [=Ivory Coast]".
DISTRIBUTION: Western Ivory Coast in rainforest.

Kassina maculata (Duméril, 1853). Ann. Sci. Nat., Paris, (3)19:165.
ORIGINAL NAME: *Hylambates maculatus.*
TYPE(S): MNHNP.
TYPE LOCALITY: Zanzibar [Tanzania].
DISTRIBUTION: Coastal Kenya to northeastern Rep. South Africa.
COMMENT: Dubois, 1981, Monit. Zool. Ital., N.S., Suppl., 15:2633, suggested the revival of *Hylambates* as a subgenus to contain this species. See comment under *Kassina* and Schiøtz, 1975, Treefrogs E. Afr.:58.

Kassina maculosa Sternfeld, 1917. Wiss. Ergebn. Zweiten Deutsch. Zentr. Afr. Exped., 1:501.
TYPE(S): SMF 7249 designated lectotype by Mertens, 1967, Senckenb. Biol., 48:48.
TYPE LOCALITY: Duma, Ubangi, Zaire.
DISTRIBUTION: Northern Zaire to Cameroon.

Kassina mertensi Laurent, 1952. Rev. Zool. Bot. Afr., 46:272.
TYPE(S): Holotype: RGMC 117110.
TYPE LOCALITY: Kitutu, Kivu, Zaire.
DISTRIBUTION: Rainforests in Zaire.

Kassina parkeri (Scortecci, 1932). Atti Soc. Ital. Sci. Nat. Mus. Civ. Stor. Nat. Milano, 71:3.
ORIGINAL NAME: *Megalixalus parkeri.*
TYPE(S): Holotype: MSNM 673.6.
TYPE LOCALITY: Garoe, Somalia.
DISTRIBUTION: Somalia and northeastern Kenya.

Kassina senegalensis (Duméril and Bibron, 1841). Erp. Gén., 8:418.
ORIGINAL NAME: *Cystignathus senegalensis.*
TYPE(S): Syntypes: MNHNP 4507 (2 specimens).
TYPE LOCALITY: "les étangs des environ de Galam", Senegal.
DISTRIBUTION: Entire savanna region of tropical Africa from Senegal, southern Mali, and Niger to northern Cameroon, Uganda, and Kenya, thence south to Namibia, and Transvaal and Natal, Rep. South Africa.
COMMENT: Synonymy includes *Megalixalus maculifer* Ahl, 1923, according to Largen, 1975, Monit. Zool. Ital., N.S., Suppl., 6:4. Possibly composed of several cryptic species (RL).

Kassina wealii Boulenger, 1882. Cat. Batr. Sal. Brit. Mus.:131.
ORIGINAL NAME: *Cassina wealii.*
TYPE(S): Syntypes: BM.
TYPE LOCALITY: "Vleis, Kaffraria", Rep. South Africa.
DISTRIBUTION: Southern and eastern Rep. South Africa.
COMMENT: Drewes, 1984, Occas. Pap. California Acad. Sci., 139:1–70, believed that this species represents a distinct genus, more closely related to *Kassinula* and *Tornierella* than to *Kassina.*

Kassinula Laurent, 1940. Rev. Zool. Bot. Afr., 33:313.
TYPE SPECIES: *Kassinula wittei* Laurent, 1940, by original designation.
DISTRIBUTION: As for the single species.
COMMENT: *Kassinula* was resurrected from the synonymy of *Kassina* by Drewes, 1984, Occas. Pap. California Acad. Sci., 139:1–70. JLP regards this as a subgenus of *Kassina.*

Kassinula wittei Laurent, 1940. Rev. Zool. Bot. Afr., 33:314.
  TYPE(S): Holotype: RGMC 21524B.
  TYPE LOCALITY: Kansenia, Katanga [=Shaba], Zaire.
  DISTRIBUTION: Shaba Province (Zaire) and adjacent northern Zambia.

Phlyctimantis Laurent and Combaz, 1950. Rev. Zool. Bot. Afr., 43:274.
  TYPE SPECIES: *Hylambates leonardi* Boulenger, 1906, by original designation.
  DISTRIBUTION: Southern Tanzania; Liberia east to Ivory Coast and in eastern Nigeria,
    western Cameroon, and Fernando Po, and rainforest in Zaire; absent in
    apparently suitable habitats in Ghana, Togo, Benin, and western Nigeria.
  COMMENT: Schiøtz, 1967, Spolia Zool. Mus. Haun., 25:96, doubted the distinctiveness
    of this genus from *Kassina*, but Drewes, 1984, Occas. Pap. California Acad. Sci.,
    139:1–70, treated it as valid and the sister-taxon of *Kassina* + *Kassinula* +
    Tornierella.

Phlyctimantis keithae Schiøtz, 1975. Treefrogs E. Afr.:70.
  TYPE(S): Holotype: AMNH 73092.
  TYPE LOCALITY: "Dabaga forest, Iringa district", Uzungwe Mountains, Tanzania.
  DISTRIBUTION: Known only from the type locality.

Phlyctimantis leonardi (Boulenger, 1906). Ann. Mus. Civ. Stor. Nat. Genova, 3:167.
  ORIGINAL NAME: *Hylambates leonardi*.
  TYPE(S): Syntypes: MSNG and BM; MSNG 29945 designated lectotype by
    Capocaccia, 1957, Ann. Mus. Civ. Stor. Nat. Genova, 69:218.
  TYPE LOCALITY: "Punta Frailes, Fernando Po" and "Ndjalé, French Congo
    [=Gabon]"; restricted to "Punta Frailes", Fernando Po, by Mertens, 1938, Abh.
    Senckenb. Naturforsch. Ges., 442:1–52; restricted to "N'Dolè (Congo Francese
    [=Gabon])" by lectotype designation (see comment).
  DISTRIBUTION: Rainforests of West Africa from Liberia to western Zaire;
    Fernando Po.
  COMMENT: See comment under *Phlyctimantis verrucosus*. This nominal species is
    composed of at least two biological species, both of which have poorly
    understood distributions (JLP).

Phlyctimantis verrucosus (Boulenger, 1912). Ann. Mag. Nat. Hist., (8)10:141.
  ORIGINAL NAME: *Hylambates verrucosus*.
  TYPE(S): BM.
  TYPE LOCALITY: Chagwe, Mabira Forest, Uganda.
  DISTRIBUTION: Uganda west to central Zaire in forest.
  COMMENT: Schiøtz, 1975, Treefrogs E. Afr.:68, noted the possibility that
    Phlyctimantis verrucosus and *Phlyctimantis leonardi* might be conspecific.
    Laurent, 1976, Ann. Mus. R. Afr. Cent., Tervuren, Ser. Octavo, Sci. Zool., 213:
    25, believed they are distinct species, as did Drewes, 1984, Occas. Pap.
    California Acad. Sci., 139:1–70.

Tornierella Ahl, 1924. Mitt. Zool. Mus. Berlin, 11:10.
  TYPE SPECIES: *Tornierella pulchra* Ahl, 1924 (=*Rothschildia kounhiensis* Mocquard, 1905),
    by monotypy.
  DISTRIBUTION: Central Ethiopia.
  COMMENT: *Tornierella* Ahl, 1924, was synonymized with *Kassina* Girard, 1853, by
    Laurent and Combaz, 1950, Rev. Zool. Bot. Afr., 43:273, but revived by Drewes
    and Roth, 1981, Zool. J. Linn. Soc., 73:267–287. Drewes, 1984, Occas. Pap.
    California Acad. Sci., 139:39, regarded *Tornierella* as most closely related to
    Kassinula.

Tornierella kounhiensis (Mocquard, 1905). Bull. Mus. Natl. Hist. Nat., Paris, 11:288.
  ORIGINAL NAME: *Rothschildia kounhiensis*.
  TYPE(S): Holotype: MNHNP 5234-6.
  TYPE LOCALITY: Kouni Valley and Ouardji, Ethiopia.
  DISTRIBUTION: Ethiopian highlands, east of the Rift Valley.

COMMENT: Synonymy includes *Tornierella pulchra* Ahl, 1939, and *Rothschildia abyssinica* Parker, 1930, according to Drewes and Roth, 1981, Zool. J. Linn. Soc., 73:267–287. The incorrect spelling *kouniensis* has been used by several authors.

Tornierella obscura (Boulenger, 1894). Proc. Zool. Soc. London, 1894:694.
ORIGINAL NAME: *Cassina obscura*.
TYPE(S): BM.
TYPE LOCALITY: Let Marefia, Shoa, Ethiopia.
DISTRIBUTION: Ethiopian highlands, west of the Rift Valley.

SUBFAMILY: **Leptopelinae** Laurent, 1972.
CITATION: Copeia, 1972:198.
DISTRIBUTION: Subsaharan Africa.
COMMENT: As originally proposed the group name was Leptopelini, a tribe, for this group in the Hyperoliinae (=Hyperoliidae as used here). See comment under Hyperoliidae. Drewes, 1984, Occas. Pap. California Acad. Sci., 139:52, removed *Nesionixalus* (formerly in the Leptopelinae) to the synonymy of *Hyperolius* (Hyperoliinae).

Acanthixalus Laurent, 1944. Rev. Zool. Bot. Afr., 38:111.
TYPE SPECIES: *Hyperolius spinosus* Buchholz and Peters, 1875, by original designation.
DISTRIBUTION: As for the single species.
COMMENT: Drewes, 1984, Occas. Pap. California Acad. Sci., 139:1–70, regarded *Acanthixalus* as more closely related to the Hyperoliinae (as the sister-taxon of *Hyperolius*) than to the Leptopelinae. See comment under Hyperoliidae. See comment under *Hyperolius krebsi*.

Acanthixalus spinosus (Buchholz and Peters, 1875). *In* Peters, Monatsber. Preuss. Akad. Wiss. Berlin, 1875:208.
ORIGINAL NAME: *Hyperolius spinosus*.
TYPE(S): ZMB.
TYPE LOCALITY: "Cameroon".
DISTRIBUTION: Forests of southern Nigeria and Cameroon to eastern Zaire.

Leptopelis Günther, 1859 "1858". Cat. Batr. Sal. Coll. Brit. Mus.:89.
TYPE SPECIES: *Hyla aubryi* Duméril, 1856, by monotypy.
DISTRIBUTION: Subsaharan Africa south to Transkei, Rep. South Africa.
COMMENT: Taxonomic understanding of this genus in south-central Africa is far less complete than in any other genus, falling short of providing suitable data for zoogeographical treatment (JCP). See comment under *Afrixalus lindholmi*.

Leptopelis anchietae (Bocage, 1873). J. Sci. Math. Phys. Nat., Lisboa, 4:226.
ORIGINAL NAME: *Hylambates anchietae*.
TYPE(S): Syntypes: MBL T.13-233 to 236; T.13-233 recorded as holotype; destroyed in 1978 fire.
TYPE LOCALITY: Inland Mossamedes; corrected to Huila and Caconda, Mts. Chininga, Angola, by Perret, 1976, Arq. Mus. Bocage, (2)6:22–23.
DISTRIBUTION: Mount Chininga region, 1200–1700 m, Angola.
COMMENT: *Leptopelis anchietae nordequatorialis* Perret, 1966, is now considered a distinct species, as is *Leptopelis oryi* Inger, 1968. See Amiet and Schiøtz, 1974, Ann. Fac. Sci. Cameroun, 17:148–149; Schiøtz, 1975, Treefrogs E. Afr.:11–13; and Perret, 1976, Arq. Mus. Bocage, (2)6:22–23. RL thinks that both of these taxa are probably subspecies of *Leptopelis anchietae*. See comment under *Leptopelis oryi*.

Leptopelis argenteus (Pfeffer, 1893). Jahrb. Hamburg. Wiss. Anst., 10:100.
ORIGINAL NAME: *Hylambates argenteus*.
TYPE(S): Lost.
TYPE LOCALITY: Bagamoyo, Tanzania.
DISTRIBUTION: Savannas of southeastern Kenya to central Mozambique and eastern Zimbabwe.

COMMENT: Two subspecies recognized by Schiøtz, 1975, Treefrogs E. Afr.:18–24, namely *Leptopelis argenteus concolor* Ahl, 1929 (from Kenya) and *"Leptopelis argenteus meridionalis"* Schiøtz, 1975 (from Mozambique), are probably distinct species (JLP and JCP). *Meridionalis* Schiøtz, 1975, is preoccupied by *Leptopelis calcaratus meridionalis* Laurent, 1973 (from Zaire) (JLP).

Leptopelis aubryi (Duméril, 1856). Rev. Mag. Zool., Paris, (2)8:561.
ORIGINAL NAME: *Hyla aubryi.*
TYPE(S): Syntypes: MNHNP 833, 1571, 4603.
TYPE LOCALITY: Gaboon.
DISTRIBUTION: Southeastern Nigeria to lower Zaire.
COMMENT: Most of the moderately webbed species of *Leptopelis* have been confused with *Leptopelis aubryi* (RL).

Leptopelis barbouri Ahl, 1929. Sitzungsber. Ges. Naturforsch. Freunde Berlin, 1929:199.
TYPE(S): Syntypes: MCZ 13661–71; MCZ 13661 designated lectotype by Schiøtz, 1975, Treefrogs E. Afr.:48.
TYPE LOCALITY: Mt. Lutindi, Usambara Mountains, Tanzania.
DISTRIBUTION: Rainforests of Lutindi, Usambara Mountains, and Dabaga Forest, Uzungwe Mountains, Tanzania.

Leptopelis bequaerti Loveridge, 1941. Proc. U.S. Natl. Mus., 91:128.
TYPE(S): Holotype: MCZ 12000.
TYPE LOCALITY: Gbanga, Liberia.
DISTRIBUTION: Known only from the type locality.

Leptopelis bocagii (Günther, 1864). Proc. Zool. Soc. London, 1864:481.
ORIGINAL NAME: *Cystignathus bocagii.*
TYPE(S): Syntypes: including MBL T.15-232; destroyed by 1978 fire.
TYPE LOCALITY: Duque de Bragança, Angola.
DISTRIBUTION: Ethiopia to northern Namibia and Zimbabwe through eastern Rwanda and Burundi.
COMMENT: This nominal species may be composed of several species; see Largen, 1977, Monit. Zool. Ital., N.S., Suppl., 9:96. Perret, 1976, Arq. Mus. Bocage, (2)6:23–24, noted that the synonymy of *Hylambates angolensis* Bocage, 1893, was problematical since the types are of different age classes and, therefore, not easily comparable. Perret also noted that Schiøtz, 1975, Treefrogs E. Afr.: 14, and Broadley, 1971, Puku, 6:120, did not include *Hylambates angolensis* in their synonymies of *Leptopelis bocagii.*

Leptopelis boulengeri (Werner, 1898). Verh. Zool. Bot. Ges. Wien, 48:197.
ORIGINAL NAME: *Hylambates rufus* var. *boulengeri.*
TYPE(S): Syntypes: ZMB 13916 and 20049; ZMB 20049 designated lectotype by Perret, 1962, Rev. Zool. Bot. Afr., 65:240; see comment.
TYPE LOCALITY: Victoria [now Limbé], Cameroon; lectotype from Fernando Po.
DISTRIBUTION: Rainforests of Nigeria to Zaire; Fernando Po.
COMMENT: Two examples of the syntypic series of *Leptopelis boulengeri* were labeled "Typus": ZMB 20049 (from Fernando Po) and ZMB 13916 (from Victoria, Cameroon). RL regards ZMB 20049 as Werner's holotype, and therefore regards Perret's lectotype designation as invalid. Synonymy includes *Leptopelis poensis* Ahl, 1929; *Leptopelis violescens* Ahl, 1929; and *Leptopelis flaviventer* Ahl, 1929, according to Perret, 1962, Rev. Zool. Bot. Afr., 65:240. See comment under *Leptopelis occidentalis.*

Leptopelis brevipes (Boulenger, 1906). Ann. Mus. Civ. Stor. Nat. Genova, (3)2:168.
ORIGINAL NAME: *Hylambates brevipes.*
TYPE(S): Holotype: MSNG 29946.
TYPE LOCALITY: Musole, Fernando Po.
DISTRIBUTION: Fernando Po.

COMMENT: Status questioned by Mertens, 1965, Bonn. Zool. Beitr., 16:26–27. Near *Leptopelis brevirostris* (Werner) if not a synonym (JLP).

Leptopelis brevirostris (Werner, 1898). Verh. Zool. Bot. Ges. Wien, 48:199.
ORIGINAL NAME: *Hylambates brevirostris*.
TYPE(S): Syntypes: ZMB (18 specimens), NHMW 3776 and 22879; ZMB 13913 designated lectotype by Perret, 1962, Rev. Zool. Bot. Afr., 65:241.
TYPE LOCALITY: "Victoria" (now Limbé), Cameroon.
DISTRIBUTION: Rainforests of Cameroon and Gabon.
COMMENT: See comment under *Leptopelis brevipes*.

Leptopelis bufonides Schiøtz, 1967. Spolia Zool. Mus. Haun., 25:27.
TYPE(S): Holotype: ZMUC R073369.
TYPE LOCALITY: "a few miles west of Bolgatanga, Ghana, near the road to Navrongo".
DISTRIBUTION: Savannas of Senegal to northern Cameroon.
COMMENT: See Amiet, 1973, Ann. Fac. Sci. Cameroun, 12:71, and Amiet, 1974, Ann. Fac. Sci. Cameroun, 17:139, for distribution, ecology, and sonogram in Cameroon.

Leptopelis calcaratus (Boulenger, 1906). Ann. Mag. Nat. Hist., (7)17:322.
ORIGINAL NAME: *Hylambates calcaratus*.
TYPE(S): BM.
TYPE LOCALITY: Efulen, Cameroon, also Spanish [=Equatorial] Guinea.
DISTRIBUTION: Eastern Nigeria to Zaire.

Leptopelis christyi (Boulenger, 1912). Ann. Mag. Nat. Hist., (7)12:556.
ORIGINAL NAME: *Hylambates christyi*.
TYPE(S): BM.
TYPE LOCALITY: Mabira Forest, Uganda.
DISTRIBUTION: Forests of eastern Zaire and Uganda.
COMMENT: Closely related to *Leptopelis flavomaculatus* according to Schiøtz, 1975, Treefrogs E. Afr.:32.

Leptopelis cynnamomeus (Bocage, 1893). J. Sci. Math. Phys. Nat., Lisboa, (2)3:120.
ORIGINAL NAME: *Hylambates cynnamomeus*.
TYPE(S): Holotype: MBL T.16-250; destroyed by 1978 fire.
TYPE LOCALITY: Quilengues, Angola.
DISTRIBUTION: Angola to western Rwanda and Burundi through southern Zaire and Zambia.
COMMENT: Considered a subspecies of *Leptopelis viridis* by Laurent, 1973, Ann. Mus. R. Afr. Cent., Tervuren, Ser. Octavo, Sci. Zool., 202:11, but Schiøtz, 1975, Treefrogs E. Afr.:25, and Perret, 1981, Arq. Mus. Bocage, (2)6:22, considered these forms to be distinct species. Perret regarded the paratypes of *Leptopelis cynnamomeus* (from Guinea-Bissau) to be *Leptopelis viridis*. In need of revision (AC). Southern African material treated as ?*cinnamomeus* by Schiøtz appears to be composed of several undescribed cryptic species (JCP). The unjustified emendation *Leptopelis cinnamomeus* has been widely used.

Leptopelis fenestratus Laurent, 1972. Explor. Parc Natl. Virunga, (2)22:43.
TYPE(S): RGMC.
TYPE LOCALITY: Mamudiome River, north Kivu, eastern Zaire.
DISTRIBUTION: Known only from the type locality.

Leptopelis fiziensis Laurent, 1973. Ann. Mus. R. Afr. Cent., Tervuren, Ser. Octavo, Sci. Zool., 202:39.
TYPE(S): RGMC.
TYPE LOCALITY: Mokanga, Fizi Terr., south Kivu, eastern Zaire.
DISTRIBUTION: Region of Fizi, eastern Zaire and western Tanzania.

Leptopelis flavomaculatus (Günther, 1864). Proc. Zool. Soc. London, 1864:310.
ORIGINAL NAME: *Hyperolius flavomaculatus.*
TYPE(S): BM.
TYPE LOCALITY: Rovuma Bay, Tanzania.
DISTRIBUTION: Forests of coastal Kenya and Zanzibar (Tanzania) to eastern
Zimbabwe and Mozambique.
COMMENT: Closely related to *Leptopelis christyi* according to Schiøtz, 1975, Treefrogs
E. Afr.:32. Synonymy includes *Leptopelis lebeaui* (Witte, 1933), according to
Laurent, 1973, Ann. Mus. R. Afr. Cent., Tervuren, Ser. Octavo, Sci. Zool.,
202:59.

Leptopelis gramineus (Boulenger, 1898). Ann. Mus. Civ. Stor. Nat. Genova, (2)18:271.
ORIGINAL NAME: *Megalixalus gramineus.*
TYPE(S): MSNG 28564A designated lectotype by Capocaccia, 1957, Ann. Mus. Civ.
Stor. Nat. Genova, 69:217.
TYPE LOCALITY: Between Badditu and Dime, Ethiopia.
DISTRIBUTION: Ethiopian highlands, 1900–3900 m elev.
COMMENT: Synonymy includes *Leptopelis rugosus* (Ahl, 1924), according to Largen,
1977, Monit. Zool. Ital., N.S., Suppl., 9:86.

Leptopelis hyloides (Boulenger, 1906). Ann. Mus. Civ. Stor. Nat. Genova, (3)2:167.
ORIGINAL NAME: *Hylambates hyloides.*
TYPE(S): MSNG 29944A designated lectotype by Capocaccia, 1957, Ann. Mus. Civ.
Stor. Nat. Genova, 69:218.
TYPE LOCALITY: Bolama, Portuguese Guinea [=Guinea-Bissau].
DISTRIBUTION: Forests of Guinea-Bissau to Cross River in Nigeria.
COMMENT: According to Schiøtz, 1967, Spolia Zool. Mus. Haun., 25:39, this species
has been noted incorrectly in much literature as *Leptopelis aubryi*. The type of
this species appears to be *Leptopelis viridis*, in which case this species is
unnamed (AS).

Leptopelis jordani Parker, 1936. Novit. Zool., 90:12.
TYPE(S): BM.
TYPE LOCALITY: Congulu, Angola.
DISTRIBUTION: Northwestern Angola.

Leptopelis karissimbensis Ahl, 1929. Sitzungsber. Ges. Naturforsch. Freunde Berlin,
1929:195.
TYPE(S): ZMB.
TYPE LOCALITY: Mtulia Gama, Mt. Karissimbi, Rwanda.
DISTRIBUTION: Highland savannas in southwestern Uganda, western Rwanda, and
eastern Zaire.

Leptopelis kivuensis Ahl, 1929. Sitzungsber. Ges. Naturforsch. Freunde Berlin, 1929:
206.
TYPE(S): ZMB.
TYPE LOCALITY: Kisenyi, Rwanda.
DISTRIBUTION: Highland forest in eastern Zaire, Uganda, Rwanda, and Burundi.

Leptopelis macrotis Schiøtz, 1967. Spolia Zool. Mus. Haun., 25:46.
TYPE(S): Holotype: ZMUC R075568.
TYPE LOCALITY: "Gola Forest Reserve, Sierra Leone".
DISTRIBUTION: Rainforests of Sierra Leone to Ghana.

Leptopelis marginatus (Bocage, 1895). Herpetol. Angola Congo:178.
ORIGINAL NAME: *Hylambates marginatus.*
TYPE(S): Holotype: MBL T.218-241; destroyed in 1978 fire.
TYPE LOCALITY: Quissange, Angola.
DISTRIBUTION: Known only from the holotype (now lost).

COMMENT: Not discussed or considered since its description, except by Perret, 1976, Arq. Mus. Bocage, (2)6:23.

Leptopelis millsoni (Boulenger, 1894). Proc. Zool. Soc. London, 1894:644.
ORIGINAL NAME: *Hylambates millsoni*.
TYPE(S): BM.
TYPE LOCALITY: Mouth of Niger, Nigeria.
DISTRIBUTION: Rainforests of eastern Nigeria to Zaire.

Leptopelis modestus (Werner, 1898). Verh. Zool. Bot. Ges. Wien, 48:197.
ORIGINAL NAME: *Hylambates rufus* var. *modestus*.
TYPE(S): Syntypes: ZMB 114112 (2 specimens) (Cameroon), 20046 (2 specimens) (South Cameroon), 28708 (Buéa, Cameroon); ZMB 28708 designated lectotype by Perret, 1962, Rev. Zool. Bot. Afr., 65:237.
TYPE LOCALITY: Cameroon; restricted to "Buéa, Cameroun" by lectotype designation.
DISTRIBUTION: Discontinuous in transition forests from Cameroon to western Kenya through eastern Zaire.
COMMENT: Possibly composed of several cryptic species (AS).

Leptopelis moeroensis Laurent, 1973. Ann. Mus. R. Afr. Cent., Tervuren, Ser. Octavo, Sci. Zool., 202:29.
TYPE(S): Holotype. RGMC 112693.
TYPE LOCALITY: "Pweto, lac Moero, Shaba, [southeastern] Zaire".
DISTRIBUTION: Known only from the type locality.

Leptopelis natalensis (Smith, 1849). Illustr. Zool. S. Afr., Rept., App.:25.
ORIGINAL NAME: *Polypedates natalensis*.
TYPE(S): BM.
TYPE LOCALITY: A small river to the westward of Port Natal [=Durban], Rep. South Africa.
DISTRIBUTION: Transkei and Natal, Rep. South Africa.

Leptopelis nordequatorialis Perret, 1966. Zool. Jahrb., Abt. Syst., 93:434.
TYPE(S): Holotype: MHNG 1004.8.
TYPE LOCALITY: "Bangwe", Bamiléké, Cameroon.
DISTRIBUTION: Montane savanna, 1000–2000 m, West Cameroon.
COMMENT: See comments under *Leptopelis anchietae* and *Leptopelis oryi*. See Amiet, 1974, Ann. Fac. Sci. Cameroun, 17:148–149.

Leptopelis notatus (Buchholz and Peters, 1875). Monatsber. Preuss. Akad. Wiss. Berlin, 1875:205.
ORIGINAL NAME: *Hylambates notatus*.
TYPE(S): ZMB.
TYPE LOCALITY: Cameroon.
DISTRIBUTION: Forests of southeastern Nigeria to central Zaire.
COMMENT: Discussed and revalidated by Perret, 1958, Rev. Suisse Zool., 65:259, with synonymy of *cubitoalbus* Boulenger, 1906, as well as *tessmani* Nieden, 1909; the latter name having been much used before 1958. Synonymy includes *Habrahyla eiselti* according to Mertens, 1963, Senckenb. Biol., 44:175–176.

Leptopelis occidentalis Schiøtz, 1967. Spolia Zool. Mus. Haun., 25:41.
TYPE(S): Holotype: ZMUC R075598.
TYPE LOCALITY: "near Tai, Côte d'Ivoire [=Ivory Coast]".
DISTRIBUTION: Rainforests of Ghana to Liberia; possibly to Sierra Leone.
COMMENT: Possibly a subspecies of *Leptopelis boulengeri* according to Schiøtz, 1967, Spolia Zool. Mus. Haun., 25:46.

Leptopelis ocellatus (Mocquard, 1902). Bull. Mus. Natl. Hist. Nat., Paris, 8:413.
ORIGINAL NAME: *Hylambates ocellatus.*
TYPE(S): Holotype MNHNP 01-595.
TYPE LOCALITY: Gabon.
DISTRIBUTION: Cameroon, Gabon, Congo, and western Zaire.
COMMENT: Two subspecies (RL).

Leptopelis oryi Inger, 1968. Explor. Parc. Natl. Garamba, 52:118.
TYPE(S): Holotype: FMNH.
TYPE LOCALITY: Parc National Garamba, Zaire.
DISTRIBUTION: Savannas of northwestern Uganda and northeastern Zaire.
COMMENT: Considered conspecific with *Leptopelis anchietae nordequatorialis*
    (=*Leptopelis nordequatorialis* of this list) by Laurent, 1973, Ann. Mus. R. Afr.
    Cent., Tervuren, Ser. Octavo, Sci. Zool., 202:29, but provisionally retained by
    Schiøtz, 1975, Treefrogs E. Afr.:13. Unlike *Leptopelis nordequatorialis* and
    Leptopelis anchietae, *Leptopelis oryi* lacks pectoral glands (JLP); see Perret, 1976,
    Arq. Mus. Bocage, (2)6:23.

Leptopelis palmatus (Peters, 1868). Monatsber. Preuss. Akad. Wiss. Berlin, 1868:453.
ORIGINAL NAME: *Hylambates palmatus.*
TYPE(S): Holotype: ZMB 6067.
TYPE LOCALITY: Ile Principe [Gulf of Guinea].
DISTRIBUTION: Known only from the type locality.
COMMENT: Records from the mainland are now treated as *Leptopelis rufus.* See
    comment under *Leptopelis rufus.* Redefined by Perret, 1973, Ann. Fac. Sci.
    Cameroun, 15–16:81–96.

Leptopelis parkeri Barbour and Loveridge, 1928. Mem. Mus. Comp. Zool., 50:236.
TYPE(S): Holotype: MCZ 13597.
TYPE LOCALITY: "Vituru, Uluguru Mountains, Tanganyika Territory [=Tanzania]".
DISTRIBUTION: Rainforests of the Usambara and Uluguru mountains, Tanzania.

Leptopelis parvus Schmidt and Inger, 1959. Explor. Parc Natl. Upemba, 56:179.
TYPE(S): RGMC.
TYPE LOCALITY: Kanole, Upemba National Park, lower Shaba, southeastern Zaire.
DISTRIBUTION: Upemba National Park, Shaba, Zaire.

Leptopelis ragazzii (Boulenger, 1896). Ann. Mus. Civ. Stor. Nat. Genova, (2)16:554.
ORIGINAL NAME: *Hylambates ragazzii.*
TYPE(S): Holotype: MSNG 28866.
TYPE LOCALITY: Shoa Province, Ethiopia.
DISTRIBUTION: Montane forests in central Ethiopia.

Leptopelis rufus Reichenow, 1874. Arch. Naturgesch., 40:291.
TYPE(S): Holotype: ZMB, lost; MHNG 132465 designated neotype by Perret, 1973,
    Ann. Fac. Sci. Cameroun, 15–16:88.
TYPE LOCALITY: Victoria [now Limbé], Cameroon; neotype from Nkondjock,
    Cameroon.
DISTRIBUTION: Rainforests of Nigeria to lower Zaire.
COMMENT: Redefined by Perret, 1973, Ann. Fac. Sci. Cameroun, 15–16:81–90. For a
    long time before its reassessment, this species was confused with several
    others, particularly *Leptopelis palmatus.*

Leptopelis susanae Largen, 1977. Monit. Zool. Ital., N.S., Suppl., 9:122.
TYPE(S): Holotype: BM 1976.1005.
TYPE LOCALITY: 9 km N of Chencha, Gemu Gofa Province, Ethiopia.
DISTRIBUTION: Gughe Mountains between 2600 and 2700 m, southwestern Ethiopia.

Leptopelis uluguruensis Barbour and Loveridge, 1928. Mem. Mus. Comp. Zool., 50:235.
  TYPE(S): Holotype: MCZ 13586.
  TYPE LOCALITY: "Nyange, Uluguru Mountains, Tanganyika Territory [=Tanzania]".
  DISTRIBUTION: Forests of the Usambara, Uzungwe, and Uluguru mountains,
    Tanzania.

Leptopelis vannutellii (Boulenger, 1898). Ann. Mus. Civ. Stor. Nat. Genova, (2)18:722.
  ORIGINAL NAME: *Hylambates vannutellii.*
  TYPE(S): Holotype: MSNG 28565.
  TYPE LOCALITY: Between Badditu and Dime, Ethiopia.
  DISTRIBUTION: Tropical forests of southwestern Ethiopia, 1200–1500 m elev.

Leptopelis vermiculatus (Boulenger, 1909). Ann. Mag. Nat. Hist., (8)4:497.
  ORIGINAL NAME: *Hylambates vermiculatus.*
  TYPE(S): BM.
  TYPE LOCALITY: Amani, Tanzania.
  DISTRIBUTION: Forests of the Usambara and Rungwe mountains, Tanzania; probably
    also in the Uluguru and Uzungwe mountains, Tanzania.

Leptopelis viridis (Günther, 1868). Proc. Zool. Soc. London, 1868:487.
  ORIGINAL NAME: *Hylambates viridis.*
  TYPE(S): BM.
  TYPE LOCALITY: West Africa.
  DISTRIBUTION: Savanna of West Africa from Guinea and Niger to northeastern
    Zaire.
  COMMENT: See comment under *Leptopelis hyloides.*

Leptopelis xenodactylus Poynton, 1963. Ann. Natal Mus., 15:328.
  TYPE(S): NMP.
  TYPE LOCALITY: Underberg, Natal [Rep. South Africa].
  DISTRIBUTION: Highlands and Weza Forest of Natal, Rep. South Africa.

Leptopelis yaldeni Largen, 1977. Monit. Zool. Ital., N.S., Suppl., 9:113.
  TYPE(S): Holotype: BM 1976.1083.
  TYPE LOCALITY: 35 km SE of Debre Marcos, Gojjam Province, Ethiopia.
  DISTRIBUTION: Montane grassland in Gojjam Province, 2000–2700 m elev., Ethiopia.

FAMILY: **Leiopelmatidae** Mivart, 1869.
  CITATION: Proc. Zool. Soc. London, 1869:291.
  DISTRIBUTION: Northwestern USA, southwestern Canada, and New Zealand.
  COMMENT: As first formed the group name was Liopelmatina, which was proposed as a
    subfamily of the Bombinatoridae (=Discoglossidae). Kuhn, 1965, Die Amphibien:
    System und Stammesgeschichte, München:86, first employed the emended group
    name Leiopelmatidae. Fawcett and Smith, 1971, Bull. Zool. Nomencl., 28:50–52, and
    Fawcett and Smith, 1971, Great Basin Nat., 31:261–264, provided an account of the
    nomenclature including the correct spelling and use of the family name. Opinion
    on the recognition of a single family or two separate families for *Leiopelma* and
    Ascaphus differs; Savage, 1973, *In* Vial (ed.), Evol. Biol. Anurans:354, recognized
    Ascaphidae for *Ascaphus*. The association of the two genera in one family is based
    on shared primitive features which do not necessarily indicate phylogenetic
    relationship (BTC). See comment under Rhinophrynidae.
  CONTRIBUTOR: Barry T. Clarke (BTC).
  REVIEWERS: William E. Duellman (WED); Marinus S. Hoogmoed (MSH).

  Ascaphus Stejneger, 1899. Proc. U.S. Natl. Mus., 21:899.
    TYPE SPECIES: *Ascaphus truei* Stejneger, 1899.
    DISTRIBUTION: As for the single species.
    REVIEWER: Keith A. Harding (KAH).

Ascaphus truei Stejneger, 1899. Proc. U.S. Natl. Mus., 21:900.
TYPE(S): Holotype: USNM 25979.
TYPE LOCALITY: "Humptulips, [Gray's Harbor County,] Washington", USA.
DISTRIBUTION: Extreme southwestern Canada and coastal northwestern USA to northern California; western Montana and northern Idaho to northeastern Oregon and southwestern Washington, USA.
COMMENT: Reviewed by Metter, 1968, Cat. Am. Amph. Rept., 69.1–2.

Leiopelma Fitzinger, 1861. Verh. Zool. Bot. Ges. Wien, 11:218.
TYPE SPECIES: *Leiopelma hochstetteri* Fitzinger, 1861.
DISTRIBUTION: New Zealand.
COMMENT: A review of *Leiopelma* biology and literature was provided by Bell, 1982, pp. 27–89, *In* Newman (ed.), Proceeding of a Symposium Held at Victoria University of Wellington, 29–31 January 1980, Occas. Publ. No. 2, New Zealand Wildlife Service. Daugherty, Bell, Adams, and Maxson, 1981, New Zealand J. Zool., 8:543–550, discussed phylogeny and biogeography of the species. Stephenson, Robinson, and Stephenson, 1972, Canadian J. Genet. Cytol., 14:691–702, and Stephenson, Robinson, and Stephenson, 1974, Experientia, 30:1248–1250, reported on karyotypic variation.

Leiopelma archeyi Turbott, 1942. Trans. R. Soc. New Zealand, 71:248.
TYPE(S): Holotype: Auckland Mus. AMPH 2.1.
TYPE LOCALITY: Tokatea, near Coromandel, Cape Colville Range, New Zealand.
DISTRIBUTION: Cape Colville Range, Coromandel Peninsula, North Island, New Zealand.
COMMENT: Has a restricted range, but is locally abundant in suitable habitats; the total population is estimated as "probably at least in thousands", according to the IUCN Red Data Book.

Leiopelma hamiltoni McCulloch, 1919. Trans. Proc. New Zealand Inst., 51:447.
ORIGINAL NAME: *Liopelma hamiltoni*.
TYPE(S): Holotype: Dominion Mus., Wellington, New Zealand.
TYPE LOCALITY: Stephens Island, Cook Strait, New Zealand.
DISTRIBUTION: Very restricted localities on Stephens I. and Maud I., New Zealand.
COMMENT: Total population on Stephen I. is probably around 200 according to Newman, 1982, pp. 93–99, *In* Newman (ed.), Proceeding of a Symposium Held at Victoria University of Wellington, 29–31 January 1980, Occas. Publ. No. 2, New Zealand Wildlife Serv. The Maud I. population is larger, "at least several hundred" according to the IUCN Red Data Book.
PROTECTED STATUS: USA ESA—Endangered (2 Dec. 1970).

Leiopelma hochstetteri Fitzinger, 1861. Verh. Zool. Bot. Ges. Wien, 11:218.
ORIGINAL NAME: *Leiopelma Hochstetteri*.
TYPE(S): Syntypes: NHMW 16385:1, 2.
TYPE LOCALITY: Nördlichen Insel von Neu-Seeland in der Provinz Auckland und zwar in die Nähe des östlich von der Stadt Auckland gelegenen Hafens Coromandel an der Ostseite des Hauraki Golfes.
DISTRIBUTION: North and South Auckland, including Rangitoto Range, Coromandel Peninsula and Great Barrier I.; Gisborne (Huaiarau and Raukumara ranges), New Zealand.
COMMENT: Locally abundant in suitable forest creeks or water seepages according to the IUCN Red Data Book.

FAMILY: **Leptodactylidae** Werner, 1896 (1838).
CITATION: Verh. Zool. Bot. Ges. Wien, 1896:15.
DISTRIBUTION: Southern USA and the Antilles south to southern South America.
COMMENT: With the discovery that *Cystignathus* Wagler was an obligate synonym of *Leptodactylus* Fitzinger, the family-group name Cystignathidae became unavailable

according to the rules of nomenclature then in effect. The name Leptodactylidae was proposed as a replacement name by Werner (1896) and has gained nearly universal acceptance subsequently. Leptodactylidae is therefore a conserved name in zoology under the provision of Article 40 of the International Code of Zoological Nomenclature (1985) and for purposes of priority takes the date of Cystignathi Tschudi, 1838. The most recent revision is Lynch, 1971, Misc. Publ. Mus. Nat. Hist. Univ. Kansas, 53:1–238. Dowling and Duellman, 1978, Syst. Herpetol., 31.4, provided a synopsis of the literature of this family and considered it plausible that the Leptodactylidae is the stem group from which all other bufonoid frogs were derived. See comments under subfamilial headings as well as Heleophrynidae and Myobatrachidae. There is no evidence to suggest that this nominal family is monophyletic (DCC and JDL).

CONTRIBUTOR: David C. Cannatella (DCC).

REVIEWERS: Werner C. A. Bokermann (WCAB) (Brazil); Ulisses Caramaschi (UC) (Brazil); Ronald I. Crombie (RIC); William E. Duellman (WED); Eduardo Gudynas (EG) (Southern South America); W. Ronald Heyer (WRH); Marinus S. Hoogmoed (MSH); Norman J. Scott, Jr. (NJS) (Central and South America); Paulo E. Vanzolini (PEV) (Brazil).

SUBFAMILY: **Ceratophryinae** Tschudi, 1838.
  CITATION: Classif. Batr.:44.
  DISTRIBUTION: South America.
  COMMENT: As originally formed the group name was Ceratophrydes. Lynch, 1971, Misc. Publ. Mus. Nat. Hist. Univ. Kansas, 53:1–238, considered the Ceratophryinae to be the primitive subfamily from which the Telmatobiinae was derived (a view that JDL now rejects). Reig, 1972, In Blair (ed.), Evol. Genus Bufo:14–36, and Estes and Reig, 1973, In Vial (ed.), Evol. Biol. Anurans:11–63, considered the Ceratophryinae to be a distinct family, the Ceratophryidae, which gave rise directly to the Bufonidae. Also considered a distinct family by Cei, 1980, Monit. Zool. Ital., N.S., Monogr., 2:216.

Ceratophrys Wied-Neuwied, 1824. Isis von Oken, 1824:672.
  TYPE SPECIES: *Ceratophrys varius* Wied-Neuwied, 1824 (=*Bufo aurita* Raddi, 1823).
  DISTRIBUTION: South America.
  COMMENT: Lynch, 1982, Syst. Zool., 31:166–179, discussed the phylogeny and biogeography of this genus and defined the subgenera noted in the species accounts.
  REVIEWER: Enrique La Marca (ELM) (Venezuela).

Ceratophrys aurita (Raddi, 1823). Mem. Mat. Fis. Soc. Ital. Sci., Modena, 19:71.
  ORIGINAL NAME: *Bufo auritus.*
  TYPE(S): Not stated.
  TYPE LOCALITY: "Montagne d'Estrella, a due giornate circa da Rio-janeiro", Brazil.
  DISTRIBUTION: Minas Gerais and Bahia to Rio Grande do Sul, Brazil.
  COMMENT: Subgenus *Ceratophrys.*

Ceratophrys calcarata Boulenger, 1890. Proc. Zool. Soc. London, 1890:327.
  TYPE(S): BM.
  TYPE LOCALITY: "Colombia".
  DISTRIBUTION: Northeastern Colombia and Venezuela.
  COMMENT: Subgenus *Stombus.*

Ceratophrys cornuta (Linnaeus, 1758). Syst. Nat., Ed. 10, 1:212.
  ORIGINAL NAME: *Rana cornuta.*
  TYPE(S): Not traced.
  TYPE LOCALITY: "Virginia"; in error.
  DISTRIBUTION: Southern Venezuela, Brazilian Amazonia, and the Guianas.
  COMMENT: Subgenus *Stombus.* Includes *Ceratophrys testudo* Andersson, 1945, according to Cochran and Goin, 1970, Bull. U.S. Natl. Mus., 288:366.

Ceratophrys cranwelli Barrio, 1980. Physis, Buenos Aires, 39:22.
  TYPE(S): Holotype: CHINM 7195.
  TYPE LOCALITY: "Gramilla, Santiago del Estero", Argentina.
  DISTRIBUTION: Chacoan region of Argentina, Bolivia, Brazil, and Paraguay.
  COMMENT: Subgenus *Ceratophrys*. Formerly considered a synonym of *Ceratophrys ornata*, with which it is parapatric.

Ceratophrys ornata (Bell, 1843). Zool. Voy. Beagle, 5:50.
  ORIGINAL NAME: *Uperodon ornatum*.
  TYPE(S): Not traced.
  TYPE LOCALITY: Buenos Aires, Argentina.
  DISTRIBUTION: Pampean region of Argentina, Uruguay, and Rio Grande do Sul, Brazil.
  COMMENT: Subgenus *Ceratophrys*.

Ceratophrys stolzmanni Steindachner, 1882. Sitzungsber. Akad. Wiss. Wien, Math. Naturwiss. Kl., 85:188.
  TYPE(S): Syntypes: NHMW 4631.1–2 and 4632.
  TYPE LOCALITY: "Tumbez", northwestern Peru.
  DISTRIBUTION: Xeric environments in northwestern Peru and the Gulf of Guayaquil, Ecuador.
  COMMENT: Subgenus *Stombus*.

Lepidobatrachus Budgett, 1899. Q. J. Microsc. Sci., (2)42:329.
  TYPE SPECIES: *Lepidobatrachus asper* Budgett, 1899.
  DISTRIBUTION: Southern South America.
  COMMENT: Synonymies and review in Cei, 1980, Monit. Zool. Ital., N.S., Monogr., 2: 224–232. See Barrio, 1968, Physis, Buenos Aires, 28:95–106.

Lepidobatrachus asper Budgett, 1899. Q. J. Microsc. Sci., (2)42:329.
  TYPE(S): Not traced.
  TYPE LOCALITY: Paraguayan Chaco.
  DISTRIBUTION: Chaco of Paraguay and northern Argentina.
  COMMENT: Synonymy includes *Lepidobatrachus salinicola* Reig and Cei, 1963, according to Lynch, 1971, Misc. Publ. Mus. Nat. Hist. Univ. Kansas, 53:111.

Lepidobatrachus laevis Budgett, 1899. Q. J. Microsc. Sci., (2)42:329.
  TYPE(S): Not traced.
  TYPE LOCALITY: Paraguayan Chaco.
  DISTRIBUTION: Northern and eastern areas of Chacoan environments, Argentina and Paraguay.

Lepidobatrachus llanensis Reig and Cei, 1963. Physis, Buenos Aires, 24:198.
  TYPE(S): Not traced.
  TYPE LOCALITY: Punta de los Llanos, La Rioja [Argentina].
  DISTRIBUTION: La Rioja and Formosa provinces, Argentina.

SUBFAMILY: **Hylodinae** Günther, 1859 "1858".
  CITATION: Cat. Batr. Sal. Coll. Brit. Mus.:90.
  DISTRIBUTION: Southeastern Brazil.
  COMMENT: The name of this taxon has been the source of some controversy. According to Lynch, 1971, Misc. Publ. Mus. Nat. Hist. Univ. Kansas, 53:163 (following earlier, related arguments by Myers, 1962, Copeia, 1962:195–202), Hylodinae Günther, 1859 "1858", has as its type genus *Hylodes* Fitzinger, 1843, Syst. Rept.:31 (Type species: *Hylodes martinicensis* Tschudi, 1838 [=*Eleutherodactylus martinicensis*]). As such, Hylodinae Günther, 1859 "1858", is not an available name for a group based on *Hylodes* Fitzinger, 1826, Neue Classif. Rept.:38 (Type species by monotypy: *Hyla ranoides* Spix, 1824 [=*Hylodes nasus*]). Assuming the preceding to

be correct, the available name for this group is Elosiinae Miranda-Ribeiro, 1926, Arq. Mus. Nac., Rio de Janeiro, 27:27. However, Fitzinger (1843) made the statement on page 15 "Citata uncinis inclusa auctores indicant, qui genus quidem nominverunt, sed non stricte in eodem sensu proposuerunt" (=Parentheses enclose the name of the original authors of names used, but these names are not used strictly in the same sense as originally proposed). This statement makes it clear that in his use of "*Hylodes* (Fitz.)" he was not proposing a new *Hylodes*, homonymous with *Hylodes* of 1826. Rather, he was attempting to change the type species, or more likely, was simply noting a 'typical' species. *Hylodes* Fitzinger, 1843, is therefore a subsequent usage of *Hylodes* Fitzinger, 1826, that already had a type species selected by monotypy. Günther's (1859 "1858") unfortunate citation of Fitzinger (1843) notwithstanding, Hylodinae (Type genus: *Hylodes* Fitzinger, 1826) is the correct name under the International Code of Zoological Nomenclature (JMS).

Crossodactylus Duméril and Bibron, 1841. Erp. Gén., 8:635.
TYPE SPECIES: *Crossodactylus gaudichaudii* Duméril and Bibron, 1841.
DISTRIBUTION: Southern South America.
COMMENT: Features of the thigh musculature and digital pad structure in this genus were part of the rationale of Lynch, 1971, Misc. Publ. Mus. Nat. Hist. Univ. Kansas, 53:1-238, for deriving the Dendrobatidae from hylodine leptodactylids (DCC).

Crossodactylus aeneus Müller, 1924. Senckenb. Biol., 6:171.
TYPE(S): Holotype: ZSM 2/1924.
TYPE LOCALITY: "Barreira (Wasserstation der Bahn nach Therezopolis in 500 m Höhe am Südosthang der Serra dos Orgaes [=Órgãos]), Staat Rio de Janeiro", Brazil.
DISTRIBUTION: States of Rio de Janeiro and São Paulo, Brazil.

Crossodactylus dispar Lutz, 1925. C. R. Séances Soc. Biol., Paris, 93:138.
TYPE(S): Syntypes: including USNM 96738-40 (others in Brazil?).
TYPE LOCALITY: Bonito in the Serra de Bocaina, São Paulo, Brazil.
DISTRIBUTION: Southeastern Brazil and Argentina (Misiones).
COMMENT: *Crossodactylus grandis* B. Lutz, 1951, a synonym, was considered a distinct species by Lynch, 1971, Misc. Publ. Mus. Nat. Hist., 53:165, but he did not give any supporting evidence for this change. UC has examined the types and agrees with Lynch. See Cei, 1980, Monit. Zool. Ital., N.S., Monogr. 2:314-316.

Crossodactylus gaudichaudii Duméril and Bibron, 1841. Erp. Gén., 8:635.
TYPE(S): Syntypes: MNHNP 746 (2 specimens).
TYPE LOCALITY: "Brésil".
DISTRIBUTION: Southeastern Brazil.

Crossodactylus schmidti Gallardo, 1961. Neotropica, 7:34.
TYPE(S): Holotype: MACN 2943.
TYPE LOCALITY: "Yacú-poí, sobre río Uruguaí, 30 km al E de Puerto Libertad, Misiones, Argentina".
DISTRIBUTION: Misiones, Argentina; Paraná, Brazil.
COMMENT: See Cei, 1980, Monit. Zool. Ital., N.S., Monogr., 2:316-317.

Crossodactylus trachystomus (Reinhardt and Lütken, 1862). Vidensk. Medd. Dansk Naturhist. Foren., 3:177.
ORIGINAL NAME: *Tarsopterus trachystomus*.
TYPE(S): Not traced (?ZMUC).
TYPE LOCALITY: "Lagoa Santa", near Belo Horizonte, Minas Gerais, Brazil.
DISTRIBUTION: Minas Gerais, Brazil.

Hylodes Fitzinger, 1826. Neue Classif. Rept.:38.
TYPE SPECIES: *Hylodes gravenhorstii* Fitzinger, 1826 (*nomen nudum*) and *Hyla ranoides* Spix, 1824 (=*Hyla nasus* Lichtenstein, 1823); *Hyla ranoides* Spix, 1824, by monotypy.
DISTRIBUTION: Eastern South America.
COMMENT: Includes *Elosia*. Myers, 1962, Copeia, 1962:195–202, reviewed the nomenclatural history of *Hylodes*; his opinion was followed by Lynch, 1971, Misc. Publ. Mus. Nat. Hist. Univ. Kansas, 53:1–238. See Bokermann, 1966, Lista Anot. Local. Tipo Anf. Brasil.:36–38, for discussion of the type localities of the Brazilian forms under *Elosia*. Heyer, 1982, Proc. Biol. Soc. Washington, 95:377–385, defined the species groups noted in the species accounts.

Hylodes asper (Müller, 1924). Senckenb. Biol., 6:173.
ORIGINAL NAME: *Elosia aspera*.
TYPE(S): Holotype: ZSM 3/1924.
TYPE LOCALITY: "Barreira (am Südosthange der Serra dos Orgaes in 500 m Meershöhe), Staat Rio de Janeiro", Brazil.
DISTRIBUTION: Rio de Janeiro to Santa Catarina, Brazil.
COMMENT: In the *Hylodes nasus* group. The grammatically incorrect epithet *asperus* ha been used.

Hylodes babax Heyer, 1982. Proc. Biol. Soc. Washington, 95:380.
TYPE(S): Holotype: MZUSP 57949.
TYPE LOCALITY: "Brasil: Minas Gerais; Parque Nacional do Caparaó, 1200 m, 20° 26' S, 41° 47' W".
DISTRIBUTION: Caparão Mountains, Minas Gerais, Brazil.
COMMENT: In the *Hylodes lateristrigatus* group.

Hylodes glabrus (Miranda-Ribeiro, 1926). Arq. Mus. Nac., Rio de Janeiro, 27:31.
ORIGINAL NAME: *Elosia glabra*.
TYPE(S): Holotype: MN 85A.
TYPE LOCALITY: "Itatiaya", Rio de Janeiro, Brazil.
DISTRIBUTION: Known only from the type locality.
COMMENT: Cochran, 1955, Bull. U.S. Natl. Mus., 206:284, considered this species to be a synonym of *Hylodes lateristrigatus*. Heyer, 1982, Proc. Biol. Soc. Washington, 94:377–385, pointed out the difficulties in the allocation of this name to a particular population. In the *Hylodes lateristrigatus* group.

Hylodes lateristrigatus (Baumann, 1912). Zool. Jahrb., Abt. Syst., 33:89.
ORIGINAL NAME: *Elosia lateristrigata*.
TYPE(S): Syntypes: ZSM 24/1923.
TYPE LOCALITY: "Orgel-Gebirge" (=Serra dos Órgãos), Rio de Janeiro, Brazil.
DISTRIBUTION: Minas Gerais to São Paulo, Brazil.
COMMENT: Heyer, 1982, Proc. Biol. Soc. Washington, 95:377–385, noted that Bokermann, 1967, Rev. Brasil. Biol., 27:229–231, referred this name to the wrong species.

Hylodes magalhaesi (Bokermann, 1964). Neotropica, 10:102.
ORIGINAL NAME: *Elosia magalhãesi*.
TYPE(S): Holotype: WCAB 14776.
TYPE LOCALITY: "Campos do Jordão, São Paulo, Brasil, alrededores de 1550 metros de altitud".
DISTRIBUTION: São Paulo, Brazil.
COMMENT: In the *Hylodes lateristrigatus* group.

Hylodes meridionalis (Mertens, 1927). Bl. Aquar. Terrarienkd., Stuttgart, 38:2.
ORIGINAL NAME: *Elosia nasus meridionalis*.
TYPE(S): Holotype: SMF 21759.
TYPE LOCALITY: "Wasserfall in 900 m höhe, 3 km nordwestlich von Sao Francisco de Paula, Rio Grande do Sul, Brasilien".
DISTRIBUTION: Rio Grande do Sul, Brazil.

COMMENT: In the *Hylodes nasus* group.

Hylodes mertensi (Bokermann, 1956). Neotropica, 2:81.
ORIGINAL NAME: *Elosia mertensi*.
TYPE(S): Holotype: WCAB 100.
TYPE LOCALITY: "en un riacho a la altura del Km 47 de la Carretera Antigua San Pablo-Santos, Estado de San Pablo, Brasil, 700 m de altura".
DISTRIBUTION: Serra do Mar (mts.), state of São Paulo, Brazil.
COMMENT: In the *Hylodes mertensi* group.

Hylodes nasus (Lichtenstein, 1823). Verz. Doubl. Zool. Mus. K. Univ. Berlin:106.
ORIGINAL NAME: *Hyla nasus*.
TYPE(S): Not traced (?ZMB).
TYPE LOCALITY: Brazil.
DISTRIBUTION: Rio de Janeiro to Santa Catarina, Brazil.
COMMENT: In the *Hylodes nasus* group. See Hoogmoed and Gruber, 1983, Spixiana, Suppl., 9:361-362, for discussion of synonymy.

Hylodes ornatus (Bokermann, 1967). Neotropica, 13:135.
ORIGINAL NAME: *Elosia ornata*.
TYPE(S): Holotype: WCAB 19558.
TYPE LOCALITY: "la altura del km. 11 de la ruta que llega hasta el alto Itatiaia, próximo a los 2.250 m de altura, Parque Nacional do Itatiaia, Rio de Janeiro, Brasil".
DISTRIBUTION: Rio de Janeiro, Brazil.
COMMENT: In the *Hylodes lateristrigatus* group.

Hylodes otavioi Sazima and Bokermann, 1983 "1982". Rev. Brasil. Biol., 42:767.
TYPE(S): Holotype: MN 4163.
TYPE LOCALITY: "Km. 126 da estrada de Vespasiano a Conceição do Mato Dentro, Serra do Cipó, Jaboticatubas, Minas Gerais", Brazil.
DISTRIBUTION: Known only from the type locality.
COMMENT: In the *Hylodes lateristrigatus* group, according to the original description.

Hylodes perplicatus (Miranda-Ribeiro, 1926). Arq. Mus. Nac., Rio de Janeiro, 27:33.
ORIGINAL NAME: *Elosia perplicata*.
TYPE(S): Not traced.
TYPE LOCALITY: "Humboldt, Sta. Catarina", Brazil; Bokermann, 1966, Lista Anot. Local. Tipo Anf. Brasil.:38, stated the type locality as "Corupá (=Humboldt)", Santa Catarina, Brazil.
DISTRIBUTION: Known only from the type locality.
COMMENT: In the *Hylodes nasus* group.

Hylodes pulcher (Lutz, 1951). Hospital, Rio de Janeiro, 39:706.
ORIGINAL NAME: *Elosia pulchra*.
TYPE(S): Not traced.
TYPE LOCALITY: Brejo de Lapa, Itatiaia Mt., [Rio de Janeiro,] Brazil.
DISTRIBUTION: Vicinity of the type locality.
COMMENT: In the *Hylodes pulcher* group. See B. Lutz, 1952, Copeia, 1952:27-28.

Hylodes regius Gouvea, 1979. Rev. Brasil. Biol., 39:855-859.
TYPE(S): Holotype: MN 4110.
TYPE LOCALITY: "1.850 metros de altitude, no Ribeirão Brejo da Lapa, Fazenda Céu Azul, em Vargem Grande, Município de Itamonte, estado de Minas Gerais, Brasil".
DISTRIBUTION: Vicinity of the type locality (Itatiaia Mountains on the Rio Janeiro-Minas Gerais border, Brazil).

COMMENT: In the *Hylodes lateristrigatus* group.

Hylodes vanzolinii Heyer, 1982. Proc. Biol. Soc. Washington, 95:382.
TYPE(S): Holotype: MZUSP 57950.
TYPE LOCALITY: "Brasil: Minas Gerais: Parque Nacional do Caparaó, 2300 m, 20° 26′ S, 41° 47′ W".
DISTRIBUTION: Known only from the type locality.
COMMENT: In the *Hylodes lateristrigatus* group.

Megaelosia Miranda-Ribeiro, 1923. Rev. Mus. Paulista, São Paulo, 13:819.
TYPE SPECIES: *Megaelosia bufonia* Miranda-Ribeiro, 1923 (=*Hylodes goeldii* Baumann, 1912).
DISTRIBUTION: As for the single species.

Megaelosia goeldii (Baumann, 1912). Zool. Jahrb., Abt. Syst., 33:91.
ORIGINAL NAME: *Hylodes goeldii.*
TYPE(S): Originally in NHM.
TYPE LOCALITY: "Orgel Gebirge" (=Serra dos Órgãos), Rio de Janeiro, Brazil.
DISTRIBUTION: Southeastern Brazil.

SUBFAMILY: **Leptodactylinae** Werner, 1896 (1838).
CITATION: Verh. Zool. Bot. Ges. Wien, 1896:15.
DISTRIBUTION: Extreme southern Texas (USA), Sonora (Mexico), and northern Antilles, south to Brazil and southern Chile.
COMMENT: Noble, 1931, Biol. Amph.:504, was the first to recognize the subfamily. According to Lynch, 1971, Misc. Publ. Mus. Nat. Hist. Univ. Kansas, 53:1–238, the Leptodactylinae was derived from the Telmatobiinae. See comments under Telmatobiinae and *Somuncuria* (Telmatobiinae).

Adenomera Fitzinger, 1867. *In* Steindachner, Reise Freg. Novara, Amph.:37.
TYPE SPECIES: *Adenomera marmorata* Fitzinger, 1867, by monotypy.
DISTRIBUTION: South America, east of the Andes.
COMMENT: Heyer, 1974, Contrib. Sci. Nat. Hist. Mus. Los Angeles Co., 253:1–46, resurrected *Adenomera* for the *Leptodactylus marmoratus* group and Heyer, 1977, Proc. Biol. Soc. Washington, 89:581–592, compared the species phenetically.

Adenomera andreae Müller, 1923. Zool. Anz., 57:40.
TYPE(S): Holotype: ZSM 136/1911.
TYPE LOCALITY: "Peixeboi (a.d. Bragançabahn), Staat Pará, Brasilien".
DISTRIBUTION: Lowlands of northern South America east of the Andes including and limited to Amazonia to the south and east.

Adenomera bokermanni (Heyer, 1973). Contrib. Sci. Nat. Hist. Mus. Los Angeles Co., 251:31.
ORIGINAL NAME: *Leptodactylus bokermanni.*
TYPE(S): Holotype: UMMZ 104527.
TYPE LOCALITY: "Paranaguá, Estado do Paraná, Brasil. Elevation 30 m."
DISTRIBUTION: Minas Gerais, Paraná, Rio de Janeiro, Santa Catarina, and São Paulo (states), Brazil.
COMMENT: This species is composed of two cryptic species according to Heyer and Maxson, 1982, *In* Prance (ed.), Biol. Divers. Tropics:377.

Adenomera griseigularis Henle, 1981. Amphibia-Reptilia, 2:139.
TYPE(S): Holotype: ZFMK 31800.
TYPE LOCALITY: "Peru: Botanischer Garten in Tingo Maria, 641 m NN".
DISTRIBUTION: Known only from the type locality.
COMMENT: A synonym of *Leptodactylus wagneri* (WRH).

Adenomera hylaedactyla (Cope, 1868). Proc. Acad. Nat. Sci. Philadelphia, 20:115.
  ORIGINAL NAME: *Cystignathus hylaedactylus.*
  TYPE(S): Holotype: ANSP 2240.
  TYPE LOCALITY: "From the Napo or upper Maranon" River, Peru.
  DISTRIBUTION: Southeastern Colombia and Venezuela east through the Guianas and
    south into northern, eastern, and central Brazil, Paraguay, Peru, and Bolivia.
  REVIEWER: Enrique La Marca (ELM).

Adenomera lutzi Heyer, 1975. Proc. Biol. Soc. Washington, 88:315.
  TYPE(S): Holotype: BM 1905.11.1.17.
  TYPE LOCALITY: "Guyana, Chinapoon R., upper Potaro (probably Chenapown
    River)".
  DISTRIBUTION: Known only from the type locality.

Adenomera marmorata Fitzinger, 1867. *In* Steindachner, Reise Freg. Novara, Amph.:37.
  TYPE(S): Holotype: NHMW 16453.
  TYPE LOCALITY: "Brasilien"; the only Brazilian locality for the Novara is Rio de
    Janeiro and vicinity, according to Gans, 1955, Ann. Carnegie Mus., 33:275–
    285.
  DISTRIBUTION: Southeastern Brazil: states of Rio de Janeiro to Santa Catarina.

Adenomera martinezi (Bokermann, 1956). Neotropica, 2:37.
  ORIGINAL NAME: *Leptodactylus martinezi.*
  TYPE(S): Holotype: WCAB 71.
  TYPE LOCALITY: "Cachimbo, sudoeste del estado de Pará, Brasil".
  DISTRIBUTION: Pará, Mato Grosso, and Goiás states, Brazil.

Edalorhina Jiménez de la Espada, 1870. J. Sci. Math. Phys. Nat., Lisboa, 3:58.
  TYPE SPECIES: *Edalorhina perezi* Jiménez de la Espada, 1870.
  DISTRIBUTION: Colombia, Ecuador, and Peru.
  COMMENT: Heyer, 1975, Smithson. Contrib. Zool., 199:1–55, considered this genus
    most closely related to *Pseudopaludicola*. Dunn, 1949, Am. Mus. Novit., 1416:1–
    10, provided notes on the two species.

Edalorhina nasuta Boulenger, 1912. Ann. Mag. Nat. Hist., (8)10:190.
  TYPE(S): Syntypes: BM (3 specimens).
  TYPE LOCALITY: "Huancabamba, E. Peru, above 3000 ft."
  DISTRIBUTION: Departamentos of Pasco and Huanuco, Peru.
  COMMENT: Known only from a very few specimens (DCC).

Edalorhina perezi Jiménez de la Espada, 1870. J. Sci. Math. Phys. Nat., Lisboa, 3:58.
  TYPE(S): Not traced.
  TYPE LOCALITY: "Napo (Ecuador) . . . en los alrededores del pueblo de Napo,
    riberas del rio de ese nombre".
  DISTRIBUTION: Peru, Ecuador, and Colombia.

Hydrolaetare Gallardo, 1963. Neotropica, 9:42.
  TYPE SPECIES: *Limnomedusa schmidti* Cochran and Goin, 1959.
  DISTRIBUTION: As for the single species.

Hydrolaetare schmidti (Cochran and Goin, 1959). Copeia, 1959:208.
  ORIGINAL NAME: *Limnomedusa schmidti.*
  TYPE(S): Holotype: USNM 140245.
  TYPE LOCALITY: "Leticia, Amazonas Comisaria, Colombia".
  DISTRIBUTION: Amazon basin from the Madeira (Brazil) to Colombia, Peru, and
    French Guiana.
  COMMENT: Widespread, but spotty, distribution (DCC).

Leptodactylus Fitzinger, 1826. Neue Classif. Rept.:38.
TYPE SPECIES: *Rana fusca* Schneider, 1799.
DISTRIBUTION: Southern North America, South America, and the West Indies.
COMMENT: Heyer, 1969, Contrib. Sci. Nat. Hist. Mus. Los Angeles Co., 155:1–13,
   redefined the genus. Heyer, 1970, Contrib. Sci. Nat. Hist. Mus. Los Angeles Co.,
   191:1–48, discussed the relationships of the *Leptodactylus melanonotus* group. The
   Leptodactylus pentadactylus group was defined and discussed by Heyer, 1972,
   Contrib. Sci. Nat. Hist. Mus. Los Angeles Co., 231:1–8, and Heyer, 1979,
   Smithson. Contrib. Zool., 301:1–43. The *Leptodactylus marmoratus* group was
   transferred to *Adenomera* by Heyer, 1974, Contrib. Sci. Nat. Hist. Mus. Los
   Angeles Co., 253:1–46, and the *Leptodactylus fuscus* group was defined and
   discussed by Heyer, 1978, Sci. Bull. Nat. Hist. Mus. Los Angeles Co., 29:1–85.
   Relationships and biogeography of *Leptodactylus* in South America were
   discussed by Heyer and Maxson, 1982, *In* Prance (ed.), Biol. Divers. Tropics:
   375–388. Cei, 1980, Monit. Zool. Ital., N.S., Monogr., 2:320–361, discussed the
   species in Argentina.
REVIEWER: Enrique La Marca (ELM) (Venezuela).

Leptodactylus albilabris (Günther, 1859). Ann. Mag. Nat. Hist., (3)4:217.
ORIGINAL NAME: *Cystignathus albilabris*.
TYPE(S): Syntypes: BM 59.10.1.5–6, 60.5.18.61–68; BM 1947.2.1760 designated
   lectotype by Heyer, 1978, Sci. Bull. Nat. Hist. Mus. Los Angeles Co., 29:37.
TYPE LOCALITY: St. Thomas, U.S. Virgin Islands.
DISTRIBUTION: Islands of the Puerto Rico bank; virtually ubiquitous in Puerto Rico;
   northeastern Dominican Republic (Hispaniola).
COMMENT: In the *Leptodactylus fuscus* group. Includes *Leptodactylus dominicensis*
   Cochran, 1923, according to Heyer, 1978, Sci. Bull. Nat. Hist. Mus. Los
   Angeles Co., 29:37,
REVIEWERS: Albert Schwartz (AS); Richard Thomas (RT).

Leptodactylus bolivianus Boulenger, 1898. Ann. Mus. Civ. Stor. Nat. Genova, 19:131.
TYPE(S): MSNG 28875A designated lectotype by Capocaccia, 1957, Ann. Mus. Civ.
   Stor. Nat. Genova, 69:214.
TYPE LOCALITY: "Barraca", Río Madidi, and "Misiones Mosetenes", Bolivia;
   restricted to Barraca, Río Madidi, Bolivia, by lectotype designation.
DISTRIBUTION: South America south of Colombia and Venezuela, including the
   Guianas and Trinidad (see comment).
COMMENT: In the *Leptodactylus ocellatus* group. See comment under *Leptodactylus
   insularum*; distribution is provisional.

Leptodactylus bufonius Boulenger, 1894. Ann. Mag. Nat. Hist., (6)13:348.
TYPE(S): BM 1947.2.17.72 designated lectotype by Heyer, 1979, Sci. Bull. Nat. Hist.
   Mus. Los Angeles Co., 29:44.
TYPE LOCALITY: Asunción, Paraguay.
DISTRIBUTION: Southern Bolivia to northern Argentina, Paraguay, and central
   Brazil.
COMMENT: In the *Leptodactylus fuscus* group.

Leptodactylus camaquara Sazima and Bokermann, 1978. Rev. Brasil. Biol., 38:907.
TYPE(S): Holotype: WCAB 48120.
TYPE LOCALITY: "Km. 132 de Estrada Vespasiano a Conceição do Mato Dentro, Serra
   do Cipó, (1500 m) Jaboticatubas, Minas Gerais, Brasil".
DISTRIBUTION: Serra do Espinhaço, Minas Gerais, Brazil.
COMMENT: In the *Leptodactylus gracilis* group (=*Leptodactylus fuscus* group),
   according to the original description.

Leptodactylus chaquensis Cei, 1950. Acta Zool. Lilloana, 9:417.
TYPE(S): Holotype: FML 979.
TYPE LOCALITY: Simoca and Rio Colorado, Tucumán and Manantiales, Corrientes, Argentina.
DISTRIBUTION: Northern Argentina, Paraguay, northern Uruguay, and Brazil (Mato Grosso do Sul).
COMMENT: In the *Leptodactylus ocellatus* group. A sibling species of *Leptodactylus ocellatus*, according to Cei, 1950, Acta Zool. Lilloana, 9:395–423.

Leptodactylus cunicularius Sazima and Bokermann, 1978. Rev. Brasil. Biol., 38:904.
TYPE(S): Holotype: WCAB 48000.
TYPE LOCALITY: "Km 114/115 da Estrada de Vespasiano a Conceição do Mato Dentro, Serra do Cipó, Jaboticatubas, Minas Gerais, Brasil".
DISTRIBUTION: Serra do Espinhaço, Minas Gerais, Brazil.
COMMENT: In the *Leptodactylus gracilis* group (=*Leptodactylus fuscus* group), according to the original description.

Leptodactylus dantasi Bokermann, 1959. Neotropica, 5:5.
TYPE(S): Holotype: WCAB 1240.
TYPE LOCALITY: "Feijó, Territorio do Acre, Brasil".
DISTRIBUTION: Vicinity of the type locality.
COMMENT: In the *Leptodactylus melanonotus* group.

Leptodactylus elenae Heyer, 1978. Sci. Bull. Nat. Hist. Mus. Los Angeles Co., 29:45.
TYPE(S): Holotype: LACM 92096.
TYPE LOCALITY: "Argentina: Salta, Embarcación".
DISTRIBUTION: Gran Chaco of Argentina and adjacent areas to Paraguay, central Brazil, and eastern Peru.
COMMENT: In the *Leptodactylus fuscus* group.

Leptodactylus fallax Müller, 1926. Zool. Anz., 65:200.
TYPE(S): Holotype: ZSM 258/1909.
TYPE LOCALITY: Dominica [Lesser Antilles, West Indies].
DISTRIBUTION: St. Christopher, Montserrat, Guadeloupe, Dominica, and St. Lucia (now extant only on Montserrat and Dominica, Lesser Antilles).
COMMENT: *Leptodactylus fallax* is a replacement name for *Leptodactylus dominicensis* Müller, 1923, Zool. Anz., 57:49, which was preoccupied by *Leptodactylus dominicensis* Cochran, 1923. In the *Leptodactylus pentadactylus* group.
REVIEWERS: Albert Schwartz (AS); Richard Thomas (RT).

Leptodactylus flavopictus Lutz, 1926. Mem. Inst. Oswaldo Cruz, Rio de Janeiro, 1926: 144.
TYPE(S): Holotype: MN 890.
TYPE LOCALITY: Mont Serrat, Itatiaia, Rio de Janeiro, Brazil.
DISTRIBUTION: Atlantic forests of southeastern Brazil and adjacent coastal islands.
COMMENT: In the *Leptodactylus pentadactylus* group.

Leptodactylus fragilis (Brocchi, 1877). Bull. Soc. Philomath. Paris, (7)1:182.
ORIGINAL NAME: *Cystignathus fragilis*.
TYPE(S): Holotype: MNHNP 6316.
TYPE LOCALITY: "Tehuantepec (Mexique)".
DISTRIBUTION: Extreme southern Texas (USA) through eastern and southern Mexico and Central America to northern Colombia and Venezuela.
COMMENT: In the *Leptodactylus fuscus* group. Heyer, 1979, Sci. Bull. Nat. Hist. Mus. Los Angeles Co., 29:46, noted that this species was mistakenly referred to as *Leptodactylus labialis* for 30 years. Reviewed (as *Leptodactylus labialis*) by Heyer, 1971, Cat. Am. Amph. Rept., 104.1–3.
REVIEWERS: Jonathan A. Campbell (JAC); Gustavo Casas-Andreu (GCA); Oscar Flores-Villela (OFV); Jay M. Savage (JMS).

Leptodactylus furnarius Sazima and Bokermann, 1978. Rev. Brasil. Biol., 38:899.
  TYPE(S): Holotype: WCAB 47949.
  TYPE LOCALITY: "Campo Grande, (900 m) Paranapiacaba, São Paulo, Brasil".
  DISTRIBUTION: Central and southeastern Brazil.
  COMMENT: In the *Leptodactylus gracilis* (=*Leptodactylus fuscus*) group, according to
    the original description. Heyer, 1983, Proc. Biol. Soc. Washington, 96:271,
    indicated that *Leptodactylus laurae* Heyer, 1978, is a synonym.

Leptodactylus fuscus (Schneider, 1799). Hist. Amph., 1:130.
  ORIGINAL NAME: *Rana fusca*.
  TYPE(S): MNHNP 680 designated neotype by Heyer, 1978, Sci. Bull. Nat. Hist.
    Mus. Los Angeles Co., 29:50.
  TYPE LOCALITY: Not stated; neotype from "Surinam".
  DISTRIBUTION: Lowlands from Panama throughout South America, east of the
    Andes, south to southern Brazil, Bolivia, and Argentina.
  COMMENT: In the *Leptodactylus fuscus* group. Includes *Rana sibilatrix* Wied-Neuwied,
    1824; *Leptodactylus raniformis* Werner, 1899; and *Leptodactylus gualambensis*
    Gallardo, 1964, according to Heyer, 1978, Sci. Bull. Nat. Hist. Mus. Los
    Angeles Co., 29:50. See synonymy in Hoogmoed and Gruber, 1983, Spixiana,
    Suppl., 9:356.
  REVIEWERS: Jonathan A. Campbell (JAC); Jay M. Savage (JMS).

Leptodactylus geminus Barrio, 1973. Physis, Buenos Aires, 32:199.
  TYPE(S): Holotype: CHINM 5860.
  TYPE LOCALITY: "Bernardo de Irigoyen, Misiones, Argentina".
  DISTRIBUTION: Northeastern Misiones Province, Argentina, and Rio Grande do Sul
    and Santa Catarina, Brazil.
  COMMENT: In the *Leptodactylus fuscus* group. A sibling species of *Leptodactylus
    gracilis* according to the original description and Heyer, 1978, Sci. Bull. Nat.
    Hist. Mus. Los Angeles Co., 29:52. See Braun and Braun, 1979, Iheringia,
    Zool., 54:3–6, for Brazilian distribution.

Leptodactylus gracilis (Duméril and Bibron, 1841). Erp. Gén., 8:406.
  ORIGINAL NAME: *Cystignathus gracilis*.
  TYPE(S): Holotype: MNHNP 4490.
  TYPE LOCALITY: "Montévidéo", Uruguay.
  DISTRIBUTION: Southern Brazil through Uruguay to Paraguay and northern
    Argentina.
  COMMENT: In the *Leptodactylus fuscus* group. See comment under *Leptodactylus
    geminus*.

Leptodactylus hallowelli (Cope, 1862). Proc. Acad. Nat. Sci. Philadelphia, 14:153.
  ORIGINAL NAME: *Hylodes hallowelli*.
  TYPE(S): Destroyed.
  TYPE LOCALITY: Carthagena [=Cartagena], Colombia.
  DISTRIBUTION: Known only from the type locality.
  COMMENT: A *nomen dubium* (WRH).

Leptodactylus insularum Barbour, 1906. Bull. Mus. Comp. Zool., 46:228.
  TYPE(S): Syntypes: MCZ 2424, 2444, 6901–02.
  TYPE LOCALITY: San Miguel Island and Saboga Island, Bahía de Panamá.
  DISTRIBUTION: Isla San Andrés and Isla de Providencia (Colombia); San Miguel I.
    and Saboga I. (Bahía de Panamá); also Central America and northern South
    America east to Venezuela (see comment).
  COMMENT: Heyer, 1974, Contrib. Sci. Nat. Hist. Mus. Los Angeles Co., 253:43,
    included *Leptodactylus insularum* as a possible synonym of *Leptodactylus
    bolivianus*, but did not provide any evidence to support this view. Distribution
    is provisional because this species is either widely confused with, or
    conspecific with, *Leptodactylus bolivianus*.

REVIEWERS: Albert Schwartz (AS); Jonathan A. Campbell (JAC); Jay M. Savage (JMS); Richard Thomas (RT).

Leptodactylus jolyi Sazima and Bokermann, 1978. Rev. Brasil. Biol., 38:902.
TYPE(S): Holotype: WCAB 47969.
TYPE LOCALITY: "Campo Grande (900 m), Paranapicaba, São Paulo, Brasil".
DISTRIBUTION: Highlands of central and southeastern Brazil.
COMMENT: In the *Leptodactylus gracilis* group (=*Leptodactylus fuscus* group), according to the original description.

Leptodactylus knudseni Heyer, 1972. Contrib. Sci. Nat. Hist. Mus. Los Angeles Co., 231:3.
TYPE(S): Holotype: LACM 72117.
TYPE LOCALITY: Limoncocha, Napo, Ecuador.
DISTRIBUTION: Greater Amazon basin of Bolivia and Brazil north to Colombia, Venezuela, and the Guianas.
COMMENT: In the *Leptodactylus pentadactylus* group.

Leptodactylus labrosus Jiménez de la Espada, 1875. Vert. Viaj. Pacif., Batr.:36.
TYPE(S): MNCN (unnumbered) designated lectotype by Heyer, 1979, Sci. Bull. Nat. Hist. Mus. Los Angeles Co. Mus., 29:56.
TYPE LOCALITY: "Pimocha, [Guayas Province,] orillas del Rio Daule (Ecuador)".
DISTRIBUTION: Coastal central Ecuador to coastal central Peru.
COMMENT: In the *Leptodactylus fuscus* group.

Leptodactylus labyrinthicus (Spix, 1824). Spec. Nov. Testud. Ran. Brasil.:31.
ORIGINAL NAME: *Rana labyrinthica*.
TYPE(S): Holotype: ZSM 2501/0 (destroyed).
TYPE LOCALITY: Rio de Janeiro [state], Brazil.
DISTRIBUTION: Cerrados and caatingas of northern (Roraima), central, and northeastern Brazil, coastal Venezuela, eastern Paraguay, and southeastern Brazil.
COMMENT: In the *Leptodactylus pentadactylus* group. Includes *Leptodactylus wuchereri* and *Leptodactylus bufo* according to Heyer, 1979, Smithson. Contrib. Zool., 301: 15. See synonymy in Hoogmoed and Gruber, 1983, Spixiana, Suppl., 9:360.

Leptodactylus laticeps Boulenger, 1918. Ann. Mag. Nat. Hist., (9)2:431.
TYPE(S): Holotype: BM 98.11.24.7.
TYPE LOCALITY: Santa Fé, Argentina.
DISTRIBUTION: Gran Chaco of Paraguay, Bolivia, and Argentina.
COMMENT: In the *Leptodactylus pentadactylus* group.

Leptodactylus latinasus Jiménez de la Espada, 1875. Vert. Viaj. Pacif., Batr.:40.
TYPE(S): MNCN jar no. 335.
TYPE LOCALITY: Uruguay: Montevideo.
DISTRIBUTION: Gran Chaco of Argentina and Paraguay; Uruguay; northeastern and southern Brazil.
COMMENT: In the *Leptodactylus fuscus* group. Includes *Leptodactylus prognathus* Boulenger, 1868, and *Leptodactylus anceps* Gallardo, 1964, according to Heyer, 1978, Sci. Bull. Nat. Hist. Mus. Los Angeles Co., 29:56.

Leptodactylus longirostris Boulenger, 1882. Cat. Batr. Sal. Brit. Mus.:240.
TYPE(S): BM 76.5.26.4 designated lectotype by Heyer, 1978, Sci. Bull. Nat. Hist. Mus. Los Angeles Co., 29:61.
TYPE LOCALITY: "Santarem", Brazil; see Crombie and Heyer, 1983, Rev. Brasil. Biol., 43:291–296, for discussion of type locality.
DISTRIBUTION: Guianas, Venezuela, and Brazilian Amazonia.
COMMENT: In the *Leptodactylus fuscus* group.

Leptodactylus macrosternum Miranda-Ribeiro, 1926. Arq. Mus. Nac., Rio de Janeiro, 27: 147.
ORIGINAL NAME: *Leptodactylus ocellatus macrosternum.*
TYPE(S): Holotype: MZUSP 448.
TYPE LOCALITY: Bahia [Brazil].
DISTRIBUTION: Amazonian Colombia, Venezuela, and the Guianas south through Brazil to Paraguay.
COMMENT: In the *Leptodactylus ocellatus* group.

Leptodactylus marambaiae Izecksohn, 1976. Rev. Brasil. Biol., 36:528.
TYPE(S): Holotype: EI 4123.
TYPE LOCALITY: Brasil: Rio de Janeiro, Restinga da Marambaia.
DISTRIBUTION: Known only from the type locality.
COMMENT: In the *Leptodactylus fuscus* group.

Leptodactylus melanonotus (Hallowell, 1861 "1860"). Proc. Acad. Nat. Sci. Philadelphia, 12:485.
ORIGINAL NAME: *Cystignathus melanonotus.*
TYPE(S): Lost.
TYPE LOCALITY: Nicaragua.
DISTRIBUTION: Western (from Sonora south) and southern Mexico through Central America to central Ecuador.
COMMENT: In the *Leptodactylus melanonotus* group.
REVIEWERS: Jonathan A. Campbell (JAC); Gustavo Casas-Andreu (GCA); Oscar Flores-Villela (OFV); Jay M. Savage (JMS).

Leptodactylus mystaceus (Spix, 1824). Spec. Nov. Testud. Ran. Brasil.:27.
ORIGINAL NAME: *Rana mystacea.*
TYPE(S): Syntypes: ZSM 2504/0 and 2505/0 (lost); Méhelÿ, 1904, Ann. Hist. Nat. Mus. Natl. Hungarici, 2:219, designated ZSM 2504/0 lectotype.
TYPE LOCALITY: Bahia, Brazil; restricted to Solimões [Brazil] by lectotype designation of Méhelÿ, 1904, Ann. Hist. Nat. Mus. Natl. Hungarici, 2:219; restricted to "Salvador, Bahia", Brazil by Bokermann, 1966, Lista Anot. Local. Tipo Anf. Brasil.:90.
DISTRIBUTION: Amazon basin from its southern limit in Brazil to Paraguay, Bolivia, Peru, Ecuador, Colombia, Venezuela, and the Guianas.
COMMENT: In the *Leptodactylus fuscus* group. Heyer, 1983, Proc. Biol. Soc. Washington, 96:270, placed *Leptodactylus amazonicus* Heyer, 1978, in synonymy. Hoogmoed and Gruber, 1983, Spixiana, Suppl., 9:357, discussed the history of the types and provided a synonymy.

Leptodactylus mystacinus (Burmeister, 1861). Reise La-Plata-Staaten, 2:532.
ORIGINAL NAME: *Cystignathus mystacinus.*
TYPE(S): MLU unnumbered.
TYPE LOCALITY: Argentina.
DISTRIBUTION: Southeastern Bolivia and eastern Brazil to Uruguay and central Argentina.
COMMENT: In the *Leptodactylus fuscus* group.

Leptodactylus notoaktites Heyer, 1978. Sci. Bull. Nat. Hist. Mus. Los Angeles Co., 29:68.
TYPE(S): Holotype: MZUSP 25428.
TYPE LOCALITY: "Brasil: São Paulo, Iporanga".
DISTRIBUTION: Southeastern Brazil.
COMMENT: In the *Leptodactylus fuscus* group.

Leptodactylus ocellatus (Linnaeus, 1758). Syst. Nat., Ed. 10, 1:211.
ORIGINAL NAME: *Rana ocellata.*
TYPE(S): Holotype: NHRM.
TYPE LOCALITY: America.
DISTRIBUTION: South America east of the Andes.

COMMENT: In the *Leptodactylus ocellatus* group. See Hoogmoed and Gruber, 1983, Spixiana, Suppl., 9:355, for synonymy.

Leptodactylus pentadactylus (Laurenti, 1768). Synops. Rept.:32.
ORIGINAL NAME: *Rana pentadactyla.*
TYPE(S): Not traced.
TYPE LOCALITY: "Indiis"; corrected to Surinam by Müller, 1927, Abh. Senckenb. Naturforsch. Ges., 40:276.
DISTRIBUTION: Honduras south to coastal Colombia and in the Amazon Basin south to Peru and northern Brazil.
COMMENT: In the *Leptodactylus pentadactylus* group.
REVIEWERS: Jonathan A. Campbell (JAC); Jay M. Savage (JMS).

Leptodactylus podicipinus (Cope, 1862). Proc. Acad. Nat. Sci. Philadelphia, 14:156.
ORIGINAL NAME: *Cystignathus podicipinus.*
TYPE(S): Holotype: ANSP 14539.
TYPE LOCALITY: Paraguay.
DISTRIBUTION: Northern Uruguay and central Argentina north through Bolivia and southern and central Brazil.
COMMENT: In the *Leptodactylus melanonotus* group.

Leptodactylus poecilochilus (Cope, 1862). Proc. Acad. Nat. Sci. Philadelphia, 14:156.
ORIGINAL NAME: *Cystignathus poecilochilus.*
TYPE(S): Holotype: USNM 4347.
TYPE LOCALITY: Turbo, Antioquia, Colombia.
DISTRIBUTION: Lowlands of southwestern Pacific Costa Rica to northern Colombia and Venezuela.
COMMENT: In the *Leptodactylus fuscus* group.
REVIEWERS: Jonathan A. Campbell (JAC); Jay M. Savage (JMS).

Leptodactylus pustulatus (Peters, 1870). Monatsber. Preuss. Akad. Wiss. Berlin, 1870: 647.
ORIGINAL NAME: *Entomoglossus pustulatus.*
TYPE(S): Lost.
TYPE LOCALITY: Ceará, northeastern Brazil.
DISTRIBUTION: Central Brazil.
COMMENT: In the *Leptodactylus melanonotus* group.

Leptodactylus rhodomystax Boulenger, 1883. Proc. Zool. Soc. London, 1883:637.
TYPE(S): BM 1947.12.17.81 designated lectotype by Heyer, 1979, Smithson. Contrib. Zool., 301:30.
TYPE LOCALITY: "Yurimaguas", Huallaga River, Loreto, Peru.
DISTRIBUTION: Guianas and southern Venezuela through northern and central Brazil to eastern Ecuador and eastern Peru.
COMMENT: In the *Leptodactylus pentadactylus* group. See comment under *Leptodactylus riveroi.*

Leptodactylus rhodonotus (Günther, 1868). Proc. Zool. Soc. London, 1868:481.
ORIGINAL NAME: *Cystignathus rhodonotus.*
TYPE(S): Holotype: BM 1947.2.17.39.
TYPE LOCALITY: Chyavetes [=Chayavitas], eastern Peru.
DISTRIBUTION: Amazonian Peru and Bolivia.
COMMENT: In the *Leptodactylus pentadactylus* group.

Leptodactylus rhodostima Cope, 1874. Proc. Acad. Nat. Sci. Philadelphia, 26:127.
TYPE(S): Lost (RIC).
TYPE LOCALITY: "Nauta", Departamento Loreto, Peru.
DISTRIBUTION: Known only from the type locality.

COMMENT: Heyer, 1974, Contrib. Sci. Nat. Hist. Mus. Los Angeles Co., 253:44, considered this form to possibly belong in *Lithodytes*. Definitely not a *Leptodactylus* (RIC).

Leptodactylus riveroi Heyer and Pyburn, 1983. Proc. Biol. Soc. Washington, 96:560.
TYPE(S): Holotype: USNM 232400.
TYPE LOCALITY: "Colombia; Vaupés, Timbó, 01° 06' S, 70° 01' W, elevation 170 m."
DISTRIBUTION: Amazonian South America.
COMMENT: A morphological intermediate between the *Leptodactylus melanonotus* and *Leptodactylus ocellatus* groups according to the original description. Specimens allocated to *Leptodactylus rhodomystax* by Rivero, 1968, Mem. Soc. Cienc. Nat. La Salle, 28:145–150, are of this species (EG).

Leptodactylus rugosus Noble, 1923. Zoologica, New York, 3:297.
TYPE(S): Holotype: AMNH 1169.
TYPE LOCALITY: Kaieteur Falls, British Guiana [=Guyana].
DISTRIBUTION: Guiana Shield region from Colombia to French Guiana.
COMMENT: In the *Leptodactylus pentadactylus* group.

Leptodactylus silvanimbus McCranie, Wilson, and Porras, 1980. J. Herpetol., 14:361.
TYPE(S): Holotype: USNM 212046.
TYPE LOCALITY: "Belén Gualcho, Cordillera de Celaque, Depto. Ocotepeque, Depto. Ocotepeque, Honduras, elevation 1700–1900 m (14° 29' N, 88° 47' W)".
DISTRIBUTION: Departamento Ocotepeque, Honduras.
COMMENT: In the *Leptodactylus pentadactylus* group.
REVIEWERS: Jonathan A. Campbell (JAC); Jay M. Savage (JMS).

Leptodactylus spixii Heyer, 1983. Proc. Biol. Soc. Washington, 96:270.
TYPE(S): Holotype: USNM 96409.
TYPE LOCALITY: "Brazil: Rio de Janeiro; Saco de São Francisco, Niteroi".
DISTRIBUTION: East coast of Brazil.
COMMENT: This is the same species that Heyer, 1978, Sci. Bull. Nat. Hist. Mus. Los Angeles Co., 29:64, discussed as *Leptodactylus mystaceus*; see Heyer, 1983, Proc. Biol. Soc. Washington, 96:270–272, and Hoogmoed and Gruber, 1983, Spixiana, Suppl., 9:357–358, for discussion of nomenclatural problem.

Leptodactylus stenodema Jiménez de la Espada, 1875. Vert. Viaj. Pacif., Batr.:64.
TYPE(S): MNCN 190 designated lectotype by Heyer, 1979, Smithson. Contrib. Zool., 301:34–35.
TYPE LOCALITY: San José de Moti, Napo, Ecuador.
DISTRIBUTION: Central and western Amazon basin of Brazil; from Colombia south to Peru and east to the Guianas.
COMMENT: In the *Leptodactylus pentadactylus* group. Includes *Leptodactylus vilarsi* according to Heyer, 1979, Smithson. Contrib. Zool., 301:14.

Leptodactylus syphax Bokermann, 1978. Rev. Brasil. Biol., 29:13.
TYPE(S): Holotype: WCAB 16141.
TYPE LOCALITY: Cuiabá, São Vicente, Mato Grosso, Brazil.
DISTRIBUTION: Central to northeastern Brazil.
COMMENT: In the *Leptodactylus pentadactylus* group.

Leptodactylus tapiti Sazima and Bokermann, 1978. Rev. Brasil. Biol., 38:910.
TYPE(S): Holotype: WCAB 47622.
TYPE LOCALITY: "Chapada dos Veadeiros, (1800 m), Alto Paraíso de Goiás, Goiás, Brasil".
DISTRIBUTION: Known only from the type locality.
COMMENT: In the *Leptodactylus gracilis* group (=*Leptodactylus fuscus* group), according to the original description.

Leptodactylus troglodytes Lutz, 1926. Mem. Inst. Oswaldo Cruz, Rio de Janeiro, 19:149.
TYPE(S): A. Lutz coll. unnumbered (now MN?).
TYPE LOCALITY: Pernambuco, Brazil.
DISTRIBUTION: Northeastern Brazil.
COMMENT: In the *Leptodactylus fuscus* group.

Leptodactylus ventrimaculatus Boulenger, 1902. Ann. Mag. Nat. Hist., (7)9:53.
TYPE(S): BM 1947.2.17.78 designated lectotype by Heyer, 1978, Sci. Bull. Nat. Hist.
Mus. Los Angeles Co., 29:73.
TYPE LOCALITY: Bulun, northwestern Ecuador.
DISTRIBUTION: Central Ecuador to northern Peru, west of the Andes.
COMMENT: In the *Leptodactylus fuscus* group.

Leptodactylus viridis Jim and Spirandelli-Cruz, 1973. J. Cient. Fac. Cienc. Med. Biol.
Botucatu, 3:13.
TYPE(S): Holotype: MZUSP 50175.
TYPE LOCALITY: "Fazenda Pedra Branca, Município de Itajibá, Estado da Bahia",
Brazil.
DISTRIBUTION: Known only from the type locality.
COMMENT: Formal description subsequently by Jim and Spirandelli-Cruz, 1979,
Rev. Brasil. Biol., 34:707. In the *Leptodactylus ocellatus* group according to
Heyer and Maxson, 1982, *In* Prance (ed.), Biol. Divers. Tropics, but placed in
the *Leptodactylus melanonotus* group in the original description.

Leptodactylus wagneri (Peters, 1862). Monatsber. Preuss. Akad. Wiss. Berlin, 1862:232.
ORIGINAL NAME: *Plectromantis wagneri*.
TYPE(S): Probably ZSM 1080/0, no longer extant; neotype designated by Heyer,
1970, Contrib. Sci. Nat. Hist. Mus. Los Angeles Co., 191:39, as NHRM
unnumbered (holotype of *Eleutherodactylus leptodactyloides*).
TYPE LOCALITY: Originally "an den Westseite der Anden in Ecuador"; but by
neotype designation of Heyer, 1970, Contrib. Sci. Nat. Hist. Mus Los Angeles
Co., 191:39, the type locality became Pastaza, Ecuador, on the east side of the
Andes.
DISTRIBUTION: St. Vincent, the Grenadines, Grenada, Tobago, Trinidad, and South
America south to the Tropic of Capricorn.
COMMENT: In the *Leptodactylus melanonotus* group. See comment under *Adenomera
griseigularis*.
REVIEWERS: Albert Schwartz (AS); Richard Thomas (RT).

Limnomedusa Fitzinger, 1843. Syst. Rept., 1:31.
TYPE SPECIES: *Cystignathus macroglossus* Duméril and Bibron, 1841.
DISTRIBUTION: As for the single species.
COMMENT: See Lynch, 1978, Occas. Pap. Mus. Nat. Hist. Univ. Kansas, 72:39, for
comment on subfamily placement. Reviewed by Barrio, 1971, Physis, Buenos
Aires, 30:667–672.

Limnomedusa macroglossa (Duméril and Bibron, 1841). Erp. Gén., 8:405.
ORIGINAL NAME: *Cystignathus macroglossus*.
TYPE(S): Not traced.
TYPE LOCALITY: "Montévideo", Uruguay.
DISTRIBUTION: Southern Brazil (Paraná to Rio Grande do Sul), Uruguay, and
northeastern Argentina.
COMMENT: See Gudynas and Gehrau, 1981, Iheringia, Zool., 60:81–99, for
distribution and comments.

Lithodytes Fitzinger, 1843. Syst. Rept.:31.
TYPE SPECIES: *Hylodes lineatus* Duméril and Bibron, 1841.
DISTRIBUTION: As for the single species.

COMMENT: See comment under *Leptodactylus rhodostima*.
REVIEWER: Enrique La Marca (ELM).

Lithodytes lineatus (Schneider, 1799). Hist. Amph., 1:138.
   ORIGINAL NAME: *Rana lineata*.
   TYPE(S): Not traced.
   TYPE LOCALITY: British Guiana [=Guyana].
   DISTRIBUTION: Eastern Peru, Ecuador, Bolivia, and Brazil through southern
      Venezuela to the Guianas.

Paratelmatobius Lutz and Carvalho, 1958. Mem. Inst. Oswaldo Cruz, Rio de Janeiro, 56:
   241.
   TYPE SPECIES: *Paratelmatobius lutzii* Lutz and Carvalho, 1958.
   DISTRIBUTION: Brazil.

Paratelmatobius gaigeae (Cochran, 1938). Proc. Biol. Soc. Washington, 51:41.
   ORIGINAL NAME: *Leptodactylus gaigeae*.
   TYPE(S): Holotype: USNM 96759.
   TYPE LOCALITY: "Bonito in the Serra da Bocaina, near the boundary between Rio de
      Janeiro and São Paulo", Brazil.
   DISTRIBUTION: Rio de Janeiro and São Paulo, Brazil.

Paratelmatobius lutzii Lutz and Carvalho, 1958. Mem. Inst. Oswaldo Cruz, Rio de
   Janeiro, 56:241.
   TYPE(S): Not traced.
   TYPE LOCALITY: Brejo da Lapa, Alto Itatiaia, State of Rio de Janeiro, Brazil.
   DISTRIBUTION: Itatiaia Mountains, southeastern Brazil.

Physalaemus Fitzinger, 1826. Neue Classif. Rept.:39.
   TYPE SPECIES: *Physalaemus cuvieri* Fitzinger, 1826.
   DISTRIBUTION: Mexico to and including South America.
   COMMENT: Argentinian species discussed by Cei, 1980, Monit. Zool. Ital., N.S.,
      Monogr., 2. See Lynch, 1970, Copeia, 1970:488–496, for discussion of species
      groups noted in accounts. Cannatella and Duellman, 1984, Copeia, 1984:902–
      921, revised the monophyletic *Physalaemus pustulosus* group and noted that
      Physalaemus is probably paraphyletic with respect to *Pseudopaludicola*.

Physalaemus aguirrei Bokermann, 1966. Physis, Buenos Aires, 26:194.
   TYPE(S): Holotype: WCAB 19303.
   TYPE LOCALITY: "Refugio Sooretama, Linhares, Espírito Santo, Brasil".
   DISTRIBUTION: Known only from the type locality.
   COMMENT: In the *Physalaemus cuvieri* group.

Physalaemus albifrons (Spix, 1824). Spec. Nov. Testud. Ran. Brasil.:48.
   ORIGINAL NAME: *Bufo albifrons*.
   TYPE(S): Syntypes: ZSM 49/0 and 50/0 (both now lost); see Hoogmoed and Gruber,
      1983, Spixiana, Suppl., 9:374, for discussion.
   TYPE LOCALITY: "Habitat in Provincia Bahia", Brazil.
   DISTRIBUTION: Eastern Brazil to Argentina (Entre Ríos).
   COMMENT: In the *Physalaemus cuvieri* group.

Physalaemus albonotatus (Steindachner, 1864). Verh. Zool. Bot. Ges. Wien, 1864:275.
   ORIGINAL NAME: *Leiuperus albonotatus*.
   TYPE(S): Not traced.
   TYPE LOCALITY: "Caiçara, Matogrosso, Pará" (Pará, in error), Brazil.
   DISTRIBUTION: Mato Grosso and Mato Grosso do Sul (Brazil), Paraguay, and the
      Chacoan regions of Bolivia and Argentina.
   COMMENT: In the *Physalaemus cuvieri* group. *Physalaemus albonotatus* is a sibling

species of *Physalaemus cuvieri*; see Barrio, 1965, Physis, Buenos Aires, 25:421–448.

Physalaemus barrioi Bokermann, 1967. Rev. Brasil. Biol., 27:141.
TYPE(S): Holotype: WCAB 31298.
TYPE LOCALITY: "1600 m de altitude, Campo de Fruticultura da Bocaina, Serra da Bocaina, São José do Barreiro, São Paulo, Brasil".
DISTRIBUTION: Serra do Bocaina, Brazil.
COMMENT: In the *Physalaemus cuvieri* group.

Physalaemus biligonigerus (Cope, 1861 "1860"). Proc. Acad. Nat. Sci. Philadelphia, 12: 517.
ORIGINAL NAME: *Liuperus biligonigerus.*
TYPE(S): Holotype: ANSP 2265.
TYPE LOCALITY: Buenos Aires, Argentina.
DISTRIBUTION: Northern and central Argentina; adjacent Bolivia; Paraguay; Uruguay; southern Brazil.
COMMENT: In the *Physalaemus cuvieri* group. Reviewed by Barrio, 1965, Physis, Buenos Aires, 25:421–448, who noted that this is a sibling species of *Physalaemus santafecinus.*

Physalaemus centralis Bokermann, 1962. Rev. Brasil. Biol., 22:216.
TYPE(S): Holotype: WCAB 8057.
TYPE LOCALITY: "Xingu, rio Coluene, Mato Grosso, Brasil".
DISTRIBUTION: Mato Grosso and São Paulo, Brazil; northeastern Paraguay.
COMMENT: In the *Physalaemus cuvieri* group.

Physalaemus cicada Bokermann, 1966. Rev. Brasil. Biol., 26:257.
TYPE(S): Holotype: WCAB 32086.
TYPE LOCALITY: "Fazenda Cana Brava, 10 km al este de Maracás, Bahia, Brasil, 1350 m".
DISTRIBUTION: Bahia, Brazil.
COMMENT: In the *Physalaemus cuvieri* group.

Physalaemus coloradorum Cannatella and Duellman, 1984. Copeia, 1984:904.
TYPE(S): Holotype: KU 178271.
TYPE LOCALITY: "Santo Domingo de los Colorados, 580 m, Provincia Pichincha, Ecuador (0° 15′ S, 79° 90′ W)".
DISTRIBUTION: Pacific lowlands and foothills of the Andes (to 800 m) in western Ecuador, from Río Cupa south to Río Baba.
COMMENT: In the *Physalaemus pustulosus* group. See comment under *Physalaemus.*

Physalaemus cuvieri Fitzinger, 1826. Neue Classif. Rept.:65.
TYPE(S): Not traced.
TYPE LOCALITY: Brazil.
DISTRIBUTION: Northeastern, central, and southern Brazil; Misiones and Entre Ríos, Argentina; eastern Paraguay.
COMMENT: In the *Physalaemus cuvieri* group. Reviewed by Barrio, 1965, Physis, Buenos Aires, 25:421–448, who noted that this is a sibling species of *Physalaemus albonotatus* and *Physalaemus centralis.*

Physalaemus enesefae Heatwole, Solano, and Heatwole, 1965. Acta Biol. Venezuelica, 4:355.
TYPE(S): Holotype: MCZ 51770 (formerly UPRP 1947).
TYPE LOCALITY: "Kilometer 38 on Venezuela highway no. 10, between El Dorado and La Laja, Bolivar State, Venezuela. Altitude about 100 m."
DISTRIBUTION: Llanos regions of Venezuela.
COMMENT: In the *Physalaemus cuvieri* group. Probably a synonym of *Physalaemus ephippifer* (DCC).

REVIEWER: Enrique La Marca (ELM).

Physalaemus ephippifer (Steindachner, 1864). Verh. Zool. Bot. Ges. Wien, 1864:277.
ORIGINAL NAME: *Leiuperus ephippifer*.
TYPE(S): Not traced.
TYPE LOCALITY: "Parà und Caiçara [a locality in Mato Grosso, apparently in error]", Brazil.
DISTRIBUTION: Mouth of the Amazon (Brazil) and the Guianas.
COMMENT: In the *Physalaemus cuvieri* group. See comments under *Physalaemus enesefae* and *Physalaemus fischeri*.

Physalaemus evangelistai Bokermann, 1967. Rev. Brasil. Biol., 27:138.
TYPE(S): Holotype: WCAB 14708.
TYPE LOCALITY: "próximo a Palácio, Km 105 da estrada que vai de Lagoa Santa A Guanhães e Conceição do Mato Dentro, Serra do Cipó, município de Jaboticatubas, Minas Gerais, Brasil".
DISTRIBUTION: Serra do Espinhaço, Minas Gerais, Brazil.
COMMENT: In the *Physalaemus cuvieri* group.

Physalaemus fernandezae (Müller, 1926). Zool. Anz., 65:143.
ORIGINAL NAME: *Paludicola fernandezae*.
TYPE(S): Holotype: ZSM 137/1925.
TYPE LOCALITY: "Christiano Muerto (zwischen Neochaea und Bahia Blanca), Prov. Buenos Aires, Argentinien".
DISTRIBUTION: Uruguay and adjacent Argentina (Buenos Aires, Entre Ríos, and Corrientes provinces).
COMMENT: In the *Physalaemus cuvieri* group. Synonymy includes *Physalaemus barbouri* according to Cei, 1980, Monit. Zool. Ital., N.S., Monogr., 2:409. See comment under *Physalaemus henselii*. Reviewed by Barrio, 1964, Acta Zool. Lilloana, 20:285–305.

Physalaemus fischeri (Boulenger, 1890). Proc. Zool. Soc. London, 1890:327.
ORIGINAL NAME: *Paludicola fischeri*.
TYPE(S): BM.
TYPE LOCALITY: "Venezuela".
DISTRIBUTION: Venezuela.
COMMENT: Probably a synonym of *Physalaemus ephippifer* (DCC).
REVIEWER: Enrique La Marca (ELM).

Physalaemus fuscomaculatus (Steindachner, 1864). Verh. Zool. Bot. Ges. Wien, 1864: 272.
ORIGINAL NAME: *Eupemphix fuscomaculatus*.
TYPE(S): Holotype: NHMW 4316.
TYPE LOCALITY: "Caiçara", near S. Luiz de Cáceres, Mato Grosso, Brazil.
DISTRIBUTION: Mato Grosso (Brazil) to Tucumán (Argentina).
COMMENT: Milstead, 1963, Copeia, 1963:565–566, commented on the taxonomic problems associated with this species.

Physalaemus gracilis (Boulenger, 1883). Ann. Mag. Nat. Hist., (5)6:17.
ORIGINAL NAME: *Paludicola gracilis*.
TYPE(S): BM.
TYPE LOCALITY: "province of Rio Grande do Sul", Brazil.
DISTRIBUTION: Southern Brazil, Paraguay, and Uruguay to adjacent Argentina.
COMMENT: In the *Physalaemus cuvieri* group. Synonymy includes *Physalaemus bischoffi* (Boulenger, 1887), according to Milstead, 1960, Copeia, 1960:83–89.

Physalaemus henselii (Peters, 1872). Monatsber. Preuss. Akad. Wiss. Berlin, 1872:223.
ORIGINAL NAME: *Paludicola henselii*.
TYPE(S): Not traced.
TYPE LOCALITY: "aus Rio Grande", Rio Grande do Sul, Brazil.
DISTRIBUTION: Southern Brazil, Uruguay, and adjacent Argentina (Entre Ríos Province) and Paraguay.

COMMENT: In the *Physalaemus cuvieri* group. Synonymy includes *Physalaemus barbouri* Parker, 1927, according to Milstead, 1960, Copeia, 1960:83–89. See comment under *Physalaemus fernandezae*. Reviewed by Barrio, 1964, Acta Zool. Lilloana, 20:285–305.

Physalaemus jordanensis Bokermann, 1967. Rev. Brasil. Biol., 27:135.
TYPE(S): Holotype: WCAB 34353.
TYPE LOCALITY: "Lagoinha da Serra, 1900 m, Campos do Jordão, São Paulo, Brasil".
DISTRIBUTION: Serra da Mantiqueira, São Paulo, Brazil.
COMMENT: In the *Physalaemus cuvieri* group.

Physalaemus kroyeri (Reinhardt and Lütken, 1862). Vidensk. Medd. Dansk Naturhist. Foren., 1861:176.
ORIGINAL NAME: *Gomphobates kröyeri*.
TYPE(S): Not traced (? ZMUC).
TYPE LOCALITY: "Cachoeiro [=Cachoeira da São Félix] ved Floden Paraguacu, 18 portugisiske Miil Bahia", Brazil.
DISTRIBUTION: Sergipe and Bahia, Brazil.
COMMENT: In the *Physalaemus cuvieri* group. Bokermann, 1966, Rev. Brasil. Biol., 26: 253–259, commented on this species. The incorrect spelling *kroeyeri* has been used for this species; under the Rules of Zoological Nomenclature only German (not Scandinavian) umlauts are corrected by the addition of an 'e'.

Physalaemus lisei Braun and Braun, 1977. Rev. Brasil. Biol., 37:867.
TYPE(S): Holotype: MRGS 8082.
TYPE LOCALITY: "Municipio de São Francisco de Paula, Rio Grande do Sul, Brasil".
DISTRIBUTION: Rio Grande do Sul, Brazil.
COMMENT: In the *Physalaemus cuvieri* group, according to the original description.

Physalaemus maculiventris (Lutz, 1925). C. R. Séances Soc. Biol., Paris, 93:138.
ORIGINAL NAME: *Eupemphix maculiventris*.
TYPE(S): Syntypes: including UMMZ 92444 (formerly USNM 96844) and USNM 96841 (now at MN).
TYPE LOCALITY: "Montagnes, près de Santos", São Paulo, Brazil.
DISTRIBUTION: Rio de Janeiro and São Paulo to Santa Catarina, Brazil.
COMMENT: In the *Physalaemus cuvieri* group. See B. Lutz, 1951, Mem. Inst. Oswaldo Cruz, Rio de Janeiro, 49:669–683.

Physalaemus moreirae (Miranda-Ribeiro, 1937). Campo, Rio de Janeiro, 1937:68.
ORIGINAL NAME: *Engystomops moreirae*.
TYPE(S): Not traced.
TYPE LOCALITY: Sorocaba, São Paulo [Brazil].
DISTRIBUTION: Known only from the type locality.
COMMENT: Provisionally placed in the *Physalaemus pustulosus* group.

Physalaemus nanus (Boulenger, 1888). Ann. Mag. Nat. Hist., (6)1:187.
ORIGINAL NAME: *Eupemphix nana*.
TYPE(S): BM.
TYPE LOCALITY: "Lages, Santa Catharina", Brazil.
DISTRIBUTION: São Paulo to Rio Grande do Sul, Brazil.
COMMENT: In the *Physalaemus signifer* group.

Physalaemus nattereri (Steindachner, 1863). Sitzungsber. Akad. Wiss. Wien, Math. Naturwiss. Kl., 48:159.
ORIGINAL NAME: *Eupemphix nattereri*.
TYPE(S): Syntypes: NHMW 13559, 16523, 16524 (2 specimens), 16525 (3 specimens), 18500.
TYPE LOCALITY: "Cuyaba in Brasilien".
DISTRIBUTION: Central and southeastern Brazil; eastern Paraguay.

COMMENT: In the *Physalaemus biligonigerus* group.

Physalaemus obtectus Bokermann, 1966. Physis, Buenos Aires, 26:197.
  TYPE(S): Holotype: WCAB 20498.
  TYPE LOCALITY: "Refugio Sooretama, Linhares, Espírito Santo, Brasil".
  DISTRIBUTION: Known only from the type locality.
  COMMENT: In the *Physalaemus signifer* group.

Physalaemus olfersii (Lichtenstein and Martens, 1856). Nomencl. Rept. Amph. Mus.
  Zool. Berolin.:40.
  ORIGINAL NAME: *Phryniscus olfersii.*
  TYPE(S): Not traced (?ZMB).
  TYPE LOCALITY: "Brasilien".
  DISTRIBUTION: Widespread in the Atlantic forests of southeastern Brazil.
  COMMENT: In the *Physalaemus signifer* group.

Physalaemus petersi (Jiménez de la Espada, 1872). An. Soc. Esp. Hist. Nat., 1:86.
  ORIGINAL NAME: *Engystomops petersi.*
  TYPE(S): Not traced.
  TYPE LOCALITY: "Oriente en el Ecuador"; probably Napo-Pastaza [Ecuador],
    according to Peters, 1955, Rev. Ecuat. Entomol. Parasitol., 3–4:349.
  DISTRIBUTION: Amazon Basin in Brazil to the foothills of the Andes in Bolivia,
    Peru, Ecuador, and Colombia; also from the mouth of the Amazon and
    French Guiana.
  COMMENT: In the *Physalaemus pustulosus* group. Synonymy includes *Eupemphix
    freibergi* Donoso-Barros, 1969, Bol. Soc. Concepción, 41:183 (Holotype:
    Donoso-Barros 745, now at IZUC; Type locality: "Runerrabaque, Río Beni,
    Bolivia"), according to Cannatella and Duellman, 1984, Copeia, 1984:908.

Physalaemus pustulatus (Shreve, 1941). Proc. New England Zool. Club, 18:80.
  ORIGINAL NAME: *Edalorhina pustulata.*
  TYPE(S): Holotype: MCZ 7666.
  TYPE LOCALITY: "Guayaquil, Ecuador".
  DISTRIBUTION: Southwestern Ecuador and northeastern Peru.
  COMMENT: In the *Physalaemus pustulosus* group. See comment under *Physalaemus.*

Physalaemus pustulosus (Cope, 1864). Proc. Acad. Nat. Sci. Philadelphia, 16:180.
  ORIGINAL NAME: *Paludicola pustulosa.*
  TYPE(S): Holotype: No. 4339 (either ANSP or USNM); apparently lost.
  TYPE LOCALITY: "New Granada on the River Truando", Colombia.
  DISTRIBUTION: Eastern and southern Mexico through Central America to Colombia
    and Venezuela.
  COMMENT: In the *Physalaemus pustulosus* group. See comment under *Physalaemus
    pustulosus.*
  REVIEWERS: Jonathan A. Campbell (JAC); Gustavo Casas-Andreu (GCA); Oscar
    Flores-Villela (OFV); Enrique La Marca (ELM); Jay M. Savage (JMS).

Physalaemus riograndensis Milstead, 1960. Copeia, 1960:87.
  TYPE(S): Holotype: FMNH 82578.
  TYPE LOCALITY: "4 kilometers southeast of Osório, Rio Grande do Sul, Brazil".
  DISTRIBUTION: Corrientes and Entre Rios provinces (Argentina), Uruguay, southern
    Paraguay, and Rio Grande do Sul (Brazil).
  COMMENT: In the *Physalaemus cuvieri* group.

Physalaemus santafecinus Barrio, 1965. Physis, Buenos Aires, 25:430.
  TYPE(S): Holotype: CHINM 1141.
  TYPE LOCALITY: "Helvetia, Santa Fe, Argentina".
  DISTRIBUTION: Corrientes and Santa Fe provinces, Argentina; eastern Paraguay.

COMMENT: In the *Physalaemus biligonigerus* group. A sibling species of *Physalaemus biligonigerus* according to Barrio, 1965, Physis, Buenos Aires, 25:421–448.

Physalaemus signifer (Girard, 1853). Proc. Acad. Nat. Sci. Philadelphia, 6:424.
ORIGINAL NAME: *Rhinoderma signifera*.
TYPE(S): ANSP, probably lost.
TYPE LOCALITY: Rio de Janeiro [Brazil].
DISTRIBUTION: Rio de Janeiro and São Paulo, Brazil.
COMMENT: In the *Physalaemus signifer* group. Synonymy includes *Physalaemus bresslaui* according to Bokermann, 1962, An. Acad. Brasil. Cienc., 34:563–568. The incorrect epithet *signiferus* has been used.

Physalaemus soaresi Izecksohn, 1965. Rev. Brasil. Biol., 25:165.
TYPE(S): Holotype: EI 1797.
TYPE LOCALITY: "Horto Florestal de Santa Cruz, Municipio de Itaguaí, Estado do Rio de Janeiro, Brasil".
DISTRIBUTION: Known only from the type locality.
COMMENT: In the *Physalaemus cuvieri* group.

Pleurodema Tschudi, 1838. Classif. Batr.:47.
TYPE SPECIES: *Pleurodema bibroni* Tschudi, 1838, by monotypy.
DISTRIBUTION: South America.
COMMENT: Duellman and Veloso, 1977, Occas. Pap. Mus. Nat. Hist. Univ. Kansas, 64: 1–46, discussed phylogeny within the genus. Argentinian species reviewed by Cei, 1980, Monit. Zool. Ital., N.S., Monogr., 2:361–384, who arranged species groups for them.

Pleurodema bibroni Tschudi, 1838. Classif. Batr.:85.
TYPE(S): Syntypes: in MNHNP (several, not traced yet) and RMNH 2277 (a specimen of *Pleurodema thaul*), which was referred to by Tschudi, 1838, Classif. Batr.:85, as "Syn. Bombinator ocellatus Mus. Lugd." This specimen is from Valparaíso, Chile. Designation of a lectotype from the MNHNP material seems advisable (MSH).
TYPE LOCALITY: "America merid. (Monte-Video)".
DISTRIBUTION: Uruguay and Rio Grande do Sul, Brazil.
COMMENT: This species was long confused with *Pleurodema thaul*, until the work of Donoso-Barros, 1969, Bol. Soc. Biol. Concepción, 41:161. See Braun and Braun, 1973, Iheringia, Zool., 44:28–31, for Brazilian distribution. See Barrio, 1977, Physis, Buenos Aires, 37:311–331, for review, distribution, and biology.

Pleurodema borellii (Peracca, 1895). Boll. Mus. Zool. Anat. Comp. Univ. Torino, 5:26.
ORIGINAL NAME: *Paludicola borellii*.
TYPE(S): Not traced; ?MSNT.
TYPE LOCALITY: Tucumán, Argentina.
DISTRIBUTION: Northwestern Argentina, at elevations of 400 to nearly 3000 m.
COMMENT: The species was confused by Parker, 1927, Ann. Mag. Nat. Hist., (9)20: 450–478, to be a junior synonym of *Pleurodema cinerea*.

Pleurodema brachyops (Cope, 1869 "1868"). Proc. Acad. Nat. Sci. Philadelphia, 20:312.
ORIGINAL NAME: *Lystris brachyops*.
TYPE(S): Syntypes: ANSP 2260–64.
TYPE LOCALITY: "Magdalene River, New Grenada [=Colombia]".
DISTRIBUTION: Guyana and northern Brazil (Roraima) through Venezuela (including Isla Margarita) and Colombia into Panama in dry llanos and savanna areas; also Curaçao, Aruba, Bonaire, and Klein Bonaire in the Netherlands Antilles.
REVIEWER: Enrique La Marca (ELM).

Pleurodema bufonina Bell, 1843. Zool. Voy. Beagle, 5:39.
TYPE(S): Not traced.
TYPE LOCALITY: "Port Desire, in Patagonia, and high up the river Santa Cruz",
   Argentina.
DISTRIBUTION: Patagonian Argentina and southern Chile.
COMMENT: This is the southernmost frog (DCC).

Pleurodema cinerea Cope, 1877. Proc. Am. Philos. Soc., 17:40.
TYPE(S): Not traced; not in ANSP (DCC) or USNM (RIC).
TYPE LOCALITY: "Juliaca", Peru.
DISTRIBUTION: Northwestern Argentina through Bolivia to southeastern Peru.

Pleurodema diplolistris (Peters, 1870). Monatsber. Preuss. Akad. Wiss. Berlin, 1870:648.
ORIGINAL NAME: *Cystignathus diplolistris.*
TYPE(S): Not traced (?ZMB).
TYPE LOCALITY: "Céara" (=Ceará), northeastern Brazil.
DISTRIBUTION: Northeastern Brazil, caatinga region.

Pleurodema guayapae Barrio, 1964. Physis, Buenos Aires, 24:478.
TYPE(S): Holotype: CHINM 175.
TYPE LOCALITY: "Guayapa (Establecimiento Santa Rosa), próximo a Patquía, La
   Rioja, Argentina".
DISTRIBUTION: Central Argentina.
COMMENT: This species and *Pleurodema nebulosa* are sibling species (DCC).

Pleurodema kriegi (Müller, 1926). Zool. Anz., 65:194.
ORIGINAL NAME: *Paludicola kriegi.*
TYPE(S): Holotype: ZSM 138/1925.
TYPE LOCALITY: "Fuss der Sierra Grande von Cordoba, Provinz Cordoba,
   Argentinien".
DISTRIBUTION: Province of Córdoba, Argentina.
COMMENT: See Barrio, 1977, Physis, Buenos Aires, 37:311–331, for review.

Pleurodema marmorata (Duméril and Bibron, 1841). Erp. Gén., 8:421.
ORIGINAL NAME: *Leiuperus marmoratus.*
TYPE(S): Syntypes: MNHNP (not traced).
TYPE LOCALITY: "Potosi", Bolivia.
DISTRIBUTION: Central Peru to central Bolivia and northeastern Chile.

Pleurodema nebulosa (Burmeister, 1861). Reise La-Plata-Staaten, 2:532.
ORIGINAL NAME: *Leiuperus nebulosus.*
TYPE(S): Not traced; ?MLU.
TYPE LOCALITY: Mendoza, Argentina.
DISTRIBUTION: Western Argentina.
COMMENT: See comment under *Pleurodema guayapae.*

Pleurodema thaul (Lesson, 1826). *In* DuPerry (ed.), Voy. Coquille, Zool.:64.
ORIGINAL NAME: *Bufo thaul.*
TYPE(S): Not traced.
TYPE LOCALITY: Concepción, Chile.
DISTRIBUTION: Chile, Argentina, and Bolivia.
COMMENT: Duellman and Veloso, 1977, Occas. Pap. Mus. Nat. Hist. Univ. Kansas,
   64, regarded this species as a composite of three forms.

Pleurodema tucumana Parker, 1927. Ann. Mag. Nat. Hist., (9)20:468.
TYPE(S): Holotype: BM 1902.7.29.75.
TYPE LOCALITY: "Tapia, Tucuman, Argentina, 2300 feet".
DISTRIBUTION: Central Argentina.

Pseudopaludicola Miranda-Ribeiro, 1926. Arq. Mus. Nac., Rio de Janeiro, 27:152.
TYPE SPECIES: *Liuperus falcipes* Hensel, 1867.
DISTRIBUTION: South America.
COMMENT: Closely related to *Physalaemus* and *Pleurodema,* according to Cei, 1980,
Monit. Zool. Ital., N.S., Monogr., 2:410. See comment under *Physalaemus.*
CONTRIBUTOR: Eduardo Gudynas (EG).

Pseudopaludicola ameghini (Cope, 1887). Proc. Am. Philos. Soc., 24:50.
ORIGINAL NAME: *Paludicola ameghini.*
TYPE(S): Syntypes: ANSP 11262-63.
TYPE LOCALITY: Chupada [=Chapada], Mato Grosso, Brazil.
DISTRIBUTION: Southern Brazil and eastern Bolivia through Paraguay to Argentina.
COMMENT: Reviewed by Cei and Roig, 1961, Notas Biol. Fac. Cienc. Exact. Fis. Nat.,
Corr. Zool., 1:32, and Cei, 1980, Monit. Zool. Ital., N.S., Monogr., 2:412-414,
who removed it from the synonymy of *Pseudopaludicola falcipes.* See comment
under *Pseudopaludicola ternetzi.*

Pseudopaludicola bolivianus Parker, 1927. Ann. Mag. Nat. Hist., (9)20:450-478.
ORIGINAL NAME: *Pseudopaludicola boliviana.*
TYPE(S): Holotype: BM 1927.8.1.1.
TYPE LOCALITY: "Sta. Cruz, Bolivia".
DISTRIBUTION: Gran Chaco of Bolivia and Paraguay.
COMMENT: Considered a synonym of *Pseudopaludicola pusilla* by Lynch, 1971, Misc.
Publ. Mus. Nat. Hist. Univ. Kansas, 53:186, without comment.

Pseudopaludicola falcipes (Hensel, 1867). Arch. Naturgesch., 33:134.
ORIGINAL NAME: *Liuperus falcipes.*
TYPE(S): Not traced.
TYPE LOCALITY: Rio Grande do Sul [Brazil].
DISTRIBUTION: Southern Brazil through Paraguay and Uruguay to northern and
central Argentina.
COMMENT: Milstead, 1963, Copeia, 1963:565-566, who examined the types,
considered the following to be synonyms: *Paludicola mystacalis* Cope, 1887,
Proc. Am. Philos. Soc., 24:49 (Syntypes: ANSP 11238-40; Type locality:
Chupada [=Chapada dos Guimarães], Mato Grosso, Brazil); *Paludicola saltica*
Cope, 1887, Proc. Am. Philos. Soc., 24:48 (Syntypes: ANSP 11228-34 and
11236-37; Type locality: Chupada [=Chapada dos Guimarães], Mato Grosso,
Brazil). Lynch, 1971, Misc. Publ. Mus. Nat. Hist. Univ. Kansas, 53:1-238,
considered them separate species without comment. UC and EG also regard
them as separate species. See Cei, 1980, Monit. Zool. Ital., N.S., Monogr., 2:
410-411.

Pseudopaludicola pusillus (Ruthven, 1916). Occas. Pap. Mus. Zool. Univ. Michigan, 30:1.
ORIGINAL NAME: *Paludicola pusilla.*
TYPE(S): Holotype: UMMZ 48305.
TYPE LOCALITY: "Fundacion, [Sierra de Santa Marta,] Colombia".
DISTRIBUTION: Northeastern Colombia to central and southern Venezuela, Guyana,
and Surinam.
COMMENT: See comment under *Pseudopaludicola boliviana.*

Pseudopaludicola ternetzi Miranda-Ribeiro, 1937. Campo, Rio de Janeiro, 1937:68.
TYPE(S): Not traced.
TYPE LOCALITY: Goyaz [=Goiás], Brazil; restricted to Passa Três, Goiás [Brazil], by
Bokermann, 1966, Lista Anot. Local. Tipo Anf. Brasil.:88.
DISTRIBUTION: Known only from the type locality.
COMMENT: Considered a junior synonym of *Pseudopaludicola ameghini* by
Bokermann, 1966, Lista Anot. Local. Tipo Anf. Brasil.:88, without comment.

Vanzolinius Heyer, 1974. Proc. Biol. Soc. Washington, 87:88.
TYPE SPECIES: *Leptodactylus discodactylus* Boulenger, 1883, by original designation.
DISTRIBUTION: As for the single species.

COMMENT: Most closely related to *Adenomera* and *Lithodytes,* according to Heyer, 1975, Smithson. Contrib. Zool., 199.

Vanzolinius discodactylus (Boulenger, 1883). Proc. Zool. Soc. London, 1883:637.
ORIGINAL NAME: *Leptodactylus discodactylus.*
TYPE(S): Holotype: BM 84.2.18.44.
TYPE LOCALITY: "Yurimaguas, Huallaga River, northeastern Peru".
DISTRIBUTION: Amazonian Peru and Ecuador; state of Amazonas, Brazil.

SUBFAMILY: **Telmatobiinae** Fitzinger, 1843.
CITATION: Syst. Rept.:43.
DISTRIBUTION: Coextensive with the distribution of the family.
COMMENT: As first formed, the group name was Telmatobii. The first use of the spelling Telmatobiidae was by Miranda-Ribeiro, 1926, Arq. Mus. Nac., Rio de Janeiro, 27:12. The first use of the group name Telmatobiinae was by Vellard, 1951, Mem. Mus. Hist. Nat. Javier Prado, 1:21. Lynch, 1971, Misc. Publ. Mus. Nat. Hist. Univ. Kansas, 53:1–238, considered the Telmatobiinae to have been derived from the Ceratophryinae (a view JDL now rejects). The Telmatobiinae in turn gave rise to the Hylodinae and the Leptodactylinae (rendering the "Telmatobiinae" paraphyletic—JDL). See comment under *Somuncuria.* Lynch also arranged the genera of Telmatobiinae into tribes which are noted in the generic accounts. Lynch, 1978, Occas. Pap. Mus. Nat. Hist. Univ. Kansas, 72:1–57, redefined the tribes Alsodini and Telmatobiini and discussed the phylogenetic relationships of the genera.

Adelophryne Hoogmoed and Lescure, 1984. Zool. Meded., Leiden, 58:92.
TYPE SPECIES: *Adelophryne adiastola* Hoogmoed and Lescure, 1984, by original designation.
DISTRIBUTION: Northern South America east of the Andes (roughly, the Guiana Shield).
COMMENT: This genus shows variation in the number of phalanges in the 4th digit: 2 or 3. In part, this character is shared with *Euparkerella* and *Phyllonastes.* See comment under *Phyllonastes.*
CONTRIBUTOR: Marinus S. Hoogmoed (MSH).

Adelophryne adiastola Hoogmoed and Lescure, 1984. Zool. Meded., Leiden, 58:95.
TYPE(S): Holotype: UTA A-4943.
TYPE LOCALITY: "Yapima, Vaupés River, Vaupés, Colombia. (69° 28' W 1° 03' N)".
DISTRIBUTION: Known only from the type locality.
COMMENT: This species has only two phalanges in the 4th digit (MSH).

Adelophryne gutturosa Hoogmoed and Lescure, 1984. Zool. Meded., Leiden, 58:101.
TYPE(S): Holotype: BM 1983.1139.
TYPE LOCALITY: "between camp IV and V, northern slopes of Mount Roraima, Guyana (60° 46' W 5° 17' N), 3000 feet (914 m)".
DISTRIBUTION: Guiana Shield, from Mount Roraima to Serra do Veado, Amapá, Brazil.
COMMENT: This species has three phalanges in the 4th digit (MSH).

Alsodes Bell, 1843. Zool. Voy. Beagle, 5:41.
TYPE SPECIES: *Alsodes monticola* Bell, 1843.
DISTRIBUTION: Chile and Argentina.
COMMENT: Tribe Telmatobiini. See comment under *Telmatobius laevis. Alsodes monticola, Alsodes nodosus,* and *Alsodes montanus* were transferred from *Eupsophus* by Formas, 1978, Stud. Neotrop. Fauna Environ., 13:1–9. Argentinian species reviewed by Cei, 1980, Monit. Zool. Ital., N.S., Monogr., 2:286–299. Karyological relationships discussed and species groups defined by Formas and Vera, 1983, Copeia, 1983:1104–1107.

REVIEWERS: Ramón Formas (RF); Esteban O. Lavilla (EOL).

Alsodes barrioi Veloso, Díaz, Iturra, and Penna, 1981. Medio Ambiente, 51:72.
TYPE(S): Holotype: DBCUCH 022.
TYPE LOCALITY: "Cabrería, Cordillera de Nahuelbuta. 40 Km. al Este de Angol,
Provincia de Malleco, Chile. Lat. 38° S Long. 73° O".
DISTRIBUTION: Known only from the type locality.

Alsodes gargola Gallardo, 1970. Neotropica, 16:78.
TYPE(S): Holotype: MACN 18704.
TYPE LOCALITY: "Argentina, Provincia de Río Negro, Cerro Catedral, Lago
Tonchek, 1700 m".
DISTRIBUTION: Known only from the type locality.

Alsodes illotus (Barbour, 1922). Proc. Biol. Soc. Washington, 35:113.
ORIGINAL NAME: *Paludicola illotus.*
TYPE(S): Holotype: MCZ 8314.
TYPE LOCALITY: "the Cordillera west of Mendoza, about 7000 alt., Argentina".
DISTRIBUTION: Mendoza Province, Argentina.
COMMENT: Known only from 2 specimens. May be a synonym of *Alsodes nodosus*
according to Lynch, 1978, Occas. Pap. Mus. Nat. Hist. Univ. Kansas, 72:1–57.

Alsodes laevis Philippi, 1902. Supl. Batr. Chil. Descr. Hist. Fis. Polit. Chile:43.
TYPE(S): Syntypes: including FMNH 9978.
TYPE LOCALITY: "Potrero", Chile (=? Potrero Grande, near Santiago, Chile).
DISTRIBUTION: Known only from the type locality.
COMMENT: Transferred to *Alsodes* from *Telmatobius* by Lynch, 1978, Occas. Pap.
Mus. Nat. Hist. Univ. Kansas, 72:50. Not collected since description.

Alsodes montanus Lataste, 1902. *In* Philippi, Supl. Batr. Chil. Descr. Hist. Fis. Polit.
Chile:47.
TYPE(S): Syntypes: FMNH 9575 and 4 others, now lost.
TYPE LOCALITY: "Habitat in lacu quodam Andium altiorum provinciae Santiago",
Chile; corrected to near Potrero Grande, Province of Aconcagua, Chile, by
Müller, 1938, Zool. Anz., 121:313–317.
DISTRIBUTION: Known only from the type locality.
COMMENT: Transferred to *Alsodes* from *Telmatobius* by Veloso, Sallaberry, Navarro,
Iturra, Valencia, Penna, and Díaz, 1982, *In* Veloso and Bustos (eds.), Veg. Vert.
Inf. Arica–Lago Chungara:204.

Alsodes monticola Bell, 1843. Zool. Voy. Beagle, 5:41.
TYPE(S): Not traced.
TYPE LOCALITY: "in the island of Inchy, archipelago of Chonos, north part of Cape
Tres Montes, from the same great height as *Bufo chilensis* (from 500 to 2500
feet elevation)".
DISTRIBUTION: Southern Chile.
COMMENT: In the *Alsodes monticola* group.

Alsodes nodosus (Duméril and Bibron, 1841). Erp. Gén., 8:413.
ORIGINAL NAME: *Cystignathus nodosus.*
TYPE(S): Holotype: MNHNP 763.
TYPE LOCALITY: "Valparaiso", Chile.
DISTRIBUTION: Central Chile.
COMMENT: In the *Alsodes nodosus* group. See comment under *Alsodes illotus.*

Alsodes pehuenche Cei, 1976. Atti Soc. Ital. Sci. Nat. Mus. Civ. Stor. Nat. Milano, 117:
162.
TYPE(S): Holotype: IBMUNC 1646-1.
TYPE LOCALITY: Pehuenche Valley, 2500 m, Mendoza, Argentina.
DISTRIBUTION: Pehuenche Valley, in Andean Cordilleras of southern Mendoza
Province (2000–2500 m), Argentina.

COMMENT: Not assigned to species group.

Alosodes tumultuosus Veloso, Iturra, and Galleguillos, 1979. Physis, Buenos Aires, 38:95.
TYPE(S): Holotype: DBCUCH 143.
TYPE LOCALITY: "La Parva 2.600 m. Santiago de Chile (Lat. 33° 31' S, Long. 70° 20' W)".
DISTRIBUTION: Known only from the type locality.
COMMENT: In the *Alsodes monticola* group.

Alsodes vanzolinii (Donoso-Barros, 1974). Bol. Soc. Biol. Concepción, 48:226.
ORIGINAL NAME: *Eupsophus vanzolinii*.
TYPE(S): Holotype: IZUC 4938.
TYPE LOCALITY: "Macho Ramadilla, Provincia de Arauco", Chile.
DISTRIBUTION: Vicinity of the type locality.
COMMENT: In the *Alsodes monticola* group.

Alsodes verrucosus (Philippi, 1902). Supl. Batr. Chil. Descr. Hist. Fis. Polit. Chile:83.
ORIGINAL NAME: *Borborocoetes verrucosus*.
TYPE(S): Not traced.
TYPE LOCALITY: "in Andibus Provinciae Cautin", Chile.
DISTRIBUTION: Northern lakes of Neuquén Province to the slopes of Cerro Tronador, Río Negro Province, Argentina.
COMMENT: In the *Alsodes monticola* group.

Atelognathus Lynch, 1978. Occas. Pap. Mus. Nat. Hist. Univ. Kansas, 72:15.
TYPE SPECIES: *Batrachophrynus patagonicus* Gallardo, 1962, by original designation.
DISTRIBUTION: Patagonia (extreme southern Argentina and Chile).
COMMENT: Tribe Telmatobiini. See Cei, 1984, Herpetologica, 40:47–51, for comments on identification.

Atelognathus grandisonae (Lynch, 1975). Bull. S. California Acad. Sci., 74:160.
ORIGINAL NAME: *Telmatobius grandisonae*.
TYPE(S): Holotype: BM 1962.629.
TYPE LOCALITY: "the Plateau below the south peak, Puerto Eden, Wellington Island, Magallanes, Chile, 640 m."
DISTRIBUTION: Known only from the type locality.

Atelognathus nitoi (Barrio, 1973). Physis, Buenos Aires, 32:208.
ORIGINAL NAME: *Telmatobius nitoi*.
TYPE(S): Holotype: CHINM 4621.
TYPE LOCALITY: "Río Challhuaco, cerro Blanco, Parque Nacional Nahuel Huapi, Bariloche, Río Negro, Argentina".
DISTRIBUTION: Known only from the type locality.

Atelognathus patagonicus (Gallardo, 1962). Neotropica, 8(26):54.
ORIGINAL NAME: *Batrachophrynus patagonicus*.
TYPE(S): Holotype: MACN 2766.
TYPE LOCALITY: "Laguna Blanca, Zapala, Neuquén, Argentina".
DISTRIBUTION: Neuquén, Argentina.
COMMENT: Transferred to *Atelognathus* by Lynch, 1978, Occas. Pap. Mus. Nat. Hist. Univ. Kansas, 72:1–57.

Atelognathus praebasalticus (Cei and Roig, 1968). Physis, Buenos Aires, 27:275.
ORIGINAL NAME: *Telmatobius praebasalticus*.
TYPE(S): Holotype: IBMUNC 1845/6.
TYPE LOCALITY: "Laguna del Teru, Zapala, Neuquén", Argentina.
DISTRIBUTION: Neuquén, Argentina.

Atelognathus reverberii (Cei, 1969). J. Herpetol., 3:8.
ORIGINAL NAME: *Telmatobius reverberii*.
TYPE(S): Holotype: IBMUNC 1980/1.
TYPE LOCALITY: "Laguna Minuelo, 3 km north of Laguna Raimunda, Meseta of Somuncura, Río Negro, Patagonia, Argentina (1400 m)".
DISTRIBUTION: Known only from the type locality.

Atelognathus salai Cei, 1984. Herpetologica, 40:47.
TYPE(S): Holotype: KU 192116.
TYPE LOCALITY: "Andean slopes facing Mount ap Iwan, ca. 1100 m, 16 km south of Portezuelo, northern border of Lago Buenos Aires, Provincia de Santa Cruz, Argentina, 46° 08' S lat., 71° 42' W long."
DISTRIBUTION: Known only from the type locality.

Atelognathus solitarius (Cei, 1970). Herpetologica, 26:18.
ORIGINAL NAME: *Telmatobius solitarius*.
TYPE(S): Holotype: IBMUNC 2045.
TYPE LOCALITY: "Las Bayas Creek, 48 km south Pilcaniyeu, Río Negro, Patagonia, Argentina, 1200 m".
DISTRIBUTION: Known only from the type locality.

Barycholos Heyer, 1969. Contrib. Sci. Nat. Hist. Mus. Los Angeles Co., 155:6.
TYPE SPECIES: *Leptodactylus pulcher* Boulenger, 1898, by original designation.
DISTRIBUTION: Ecuador; Goiás, Brazil.
COMMENT: Lynch, 1971, Misc. Publ. Mus. Nat. Hist. Univ. Kansas, 53:1–238, and Lynch, 1973, Herpetologica, 29:232–235, considered this genus most closely related to *Adenomera*. Heyer, 1969, Contrib. Sci. Nat. Hist. Mus. Los Angeles Co., 155:6, and Heyer, 1975, Smithson. Contrib. Sci., 199:1–55, considered it closely allied with *Eleutherodactylus* (Telmatobiinae: Eleutherodactylini). Lynch, 1980, Bull. Mus. Natl. Hist. Nat. Paris, (4)2:289–302, considered *Barycholos* most closely related to the *Eleutherodactylus discoidalis* group.

Barycholos pulcher (Boulenger, 1898). Proc. Zool. Soc. London, 1898:122.
ORIGINAL NAME: *Leptodactylus pulcher*.
TYPE(S): BM 1947.2.17.38 designated lectotype by Heyer, 1969, Contrib. Sci. Nat. Hist. Mus. Los Angeles Co., 155:6.
TYPE LOCALITY: "Chimbo", Chimborazo Province, Ecuador; in the same paper as the description Boulenger noted "Chimbo" as "Puente del Chimbo, the railway terminus about 70 miles from Guayaquil, at an elevation of about 1000 ft."
DISTRIBUTION: Pacific lowlands of Ecuador.

Barycholos savagei Lynch, 1980. Bull. Mus. Natl. Hist. Nat., Paris, (4)2(A)1:290.
TYPE(S): Holotype: MNHNP 1946-328.
TYPE LOCALITY: "between the Rio Tapirapé and Conceicao [=Conceição], Estado Goiás, Brasil".
DISTRIBUTION: State of Goiás, Brazil.
COMMENT: A distance of 3200 km separates this species and its only congener (DCC).

Batrachophrynus Peters, 1873. Monatsber. Preuss. Akad. Wiss. Berlin, 1873:411.
TYPE SPECIES: *Batrachophrynus macrostomus* Peters, 1873.
DISTRIBUTION: As for the single species.
COMMENT: Tribe Telmatobiini.

Batrachophrynus macrostomus Peters, 1873. Monatsber. Preuss. Akad. Wiss. Berlin, 1873:412.
TYPE(S): Not traced (? ZMB).
TYPE LOCALITY: Peru.
DISTRIBUTION: Andes of southern Peru and Bolivia.

Batrachyla Bell, 1843. Zool. Voy. Beagle, 5:43.
TYPE SPECIES: *Batrachyla leptopus* Bell, 1843.
DISTRIBUTION: Central and southern Chile, and adjacent Argentina.
COMMENT: Tribe Batrachylini.
REVIEWER: Ramón Formas (RF).

Batrachyla antartandica Barrio, 1967. Physis, Buenos Aires, 27:102.
TYPE(S): Holotype: CHINM 1821.
TYPE LOCALITY: "Puerto Blest, Parque Nacional Nahuel Huapi, Río Negro,
República Argentina".
DISTRIBUTION: Río Negro Province (Argentina) and Puerto Montt to Valdivia
(Chile).

Batrachyla leptopus Bell, 1843. Zool. Voy. Beagle, 5:43.
TYPE(S): Holotype: BM 1947.2.16.96 (formerly 45.5.25.29).
TYPE LOCALITY: "Valdivia", Chile
DISTRIBUTION: Concepción to Strait of Magellan (Chile); in *Nothofagus* forests from
Neuquén to lower Río Negro, Argentina.

Batrachyla taeniata (Girard, 1854). Proc. Acad. Nat. Sci. Philadelphia, 7:226.
ORIGINAL NAME: *Cystignathus taeniatus.*
TYPE(S): Not traced.
TYPE LOCALITY: "neighborhoods of Santiago, Chili [=Chile]".
DISTRIBUTION: Neuquén to lower Río Negro, Argentina; central and southern Chile.

Caudiverbera Laurenti, 1768. Synops. Rept.:43.
TYPE SPECIES: *Caudiverbera peruviana* Laurenti, 1768, by tautonomy; see Myers, 1962,
Copeia, 1962:195–202, for discussion.
DISTRIBUTION: As for the single species.
COMMENT: Tribe Calyptocephalellini. The nomenclatural history of this genus is
confused; see Myers, 1962, Copeia, 1962:195–202; also see Cei, 1962, Batr.
Chile:105; Gorham, 1966, Das Tierreich, 85:35; and Lynch, 1971, Misc. Publ. Mus.
Nat. Hist. Univ. Kansas, 53:1–238, for different opinions.
REVIEWER: Ramón Formas (RF).

Caudiverbera caudiverbera (Linnaeus, 1758). Syst. Nat., Ed. 10, 1:200.
ORIGINAL NAME: *Lacerta caudiverbera.*
TYPE(S): Not traced.
TYPE LOCALITY: Peru (in error).
DISTRIBUTION: Between 30° and 42° S lat., Chile.

Crossodactylodes Cochran, 1938. Proc. Biol. Soc. Washington, 51:41.
TYPE SPECIES: *Crossodactylodes pintoi* Cochran, 1938.
DISTRIBUTION: Central Atlantic forest region of Brazil.
COMMENT: Tribe Grypiscini.

Crossodactylodes bokermanni Peixoto, 1983 "1982". Rev. Brasil. Biol., 42:619.
TYPE(S): Holotype: EI 7173.
TYPE LOCALITY: "Santa Teresa, Estado do Espírito Santo, (19° 56' S, 40° 36' W); alt.
aprox. 675 m), Brasil".
DISTRIBUTION: Vicinity of type locality.

Crossodactylodes izecksohni Peixoto, 1983 "1982". Rev. Brasil. Biol., 42:621.
TYPE(S): Holotype: EI 7192.
TYPE LOCALITY: "Santa Teresa, Estado do Espírito Santo, (19° 56' S, 40° 36' W; alt.
aprox. 675 m), Brasil".
DISTRIBUTION: Vicinity of the type locality.

Crossodactylodes pintoi Cochran, 1938. Proc. Biol. Soc. Washington, 51:42.
TYPE(S): Holotype: MZUSP 56473 (formerly USNM 102606 [formerly MZUSP 104]).
TYPE LOCALITY: "Macahé [=Serra de Macaé] in the state of Rio de Janeiro", Brazil.
DISTRIBUTION: Rio de Janeiro and Espírito Santo, Brazil.

Cycloramphus Tschudi, 1838. Classif. Batr.:81.
TYPE SPECIES: *Cycloramphus fuliginosus* Tschudi, 1838, by monotypy.
DISTRIBUTION: Southeastern Brazil.
COMMENT: Tribe Grypiscini. Heyer, 1983, Arq. Zool., São Paulo, 30:235–339, revised
and reviewed the genus. Heyer and Maxson, 1983, Arq. Zool., São Paulo, 30:
341–373, discussed relationships, zoogeography, and speciation mechanisms.

Cycloramphus asper Werner, 1899. Zool. Anz., 22:482.
TYPE(S): Not traced; presumably formerly in ZMB.
TYPE LOCALITY: "Sta. Caterina, Brasilien".
DISTRIBUTION: Serra do Mar in the state of Santa Catarina, Brazil.
COMMENT: Synonymy includes *Cycloramphus neglectus*, according to Heyer, 1983,
Arq. Zool., São Paulo, 30:261.

Cycloramphus bandeirensis Heyer, 1983. Arq. Zool., São Paulo, 30:291.
TYPE(S): Holotype: MZUSP 52924.
TYPE LOCALITY: "Brasil: Espírito Santo, Pico da Bandeira, 2450 m".
DISTRIBUTION: Known only from the type locality.

Cycloramphus bolitoglossus (Werner, 1897). Zool. Anz., 20:265.
ORIGINAL NAME: *Borborocoetes bolitoglossus*.
TYPE(S): Not located.
TYPE LOCALITY: "Blumenau, Sta. Catharina, Brasil".
DISTRIBUTION: Serra do Mar in the states of Paraná and Santa Catarina, Brazil.
COMMENT: Synonymy includes *Craspedoglossa sanctaecatherinae* Müller, according to
Heyer, 1983, Arq. Zool., São Paulo, 30:287.

Cycloramphus boraceiensis Heyer, 1983. Arq. Zool., São Paulo, 30:293.
TYPE(S): Holotype: MZUSP 3934.
TYPE LOCALITY: "Brasil: São Paulo, Boracéia".
DISTRIBUTION: Serra do Mar in the southeastern part of the state of Rio de Janeiro
and the northern half of the state of São Paulo; offshore islands of Ilha
Grande and São Sebastião.

Cycloramphus brasiliensis (Steindachner, 1864). Verh. Zool. Bot. Ges. Wien, 14:282.
ORIGINAL NAME: *Telmatobius brasiliensis*.
TYPE(S): Holotype: NHMW 22922.
TYPE LOCALITY: Region around Rio de Janeiro, Brazil.
DISTRIBUTION: Serra dos Órgãos and Serra da Mantiqueira, Brazil.

Cycloramphus carvalhoi Heyer, 1983. Arq. Zool., São Paulo, 30:297.
TYPE(S): Holotype: AL-MN 132.
TYPE LOCALITY: "Brasil; Rio de Janeiro, Brejo da Lapa, Alto Itatiaia, 2200 m".
DISTRIBUTION: Known only from the type locality.

Cycloramphus catarinensis Heyer, 1983. Arq. Zool., São Paulo, 30:298.
TYPE(S): Holotype: USNM 137675.
TYPE LOCALITY: "Brasil; Santa Catarina, Petrópolis (probably in error for
Theresópolis-Queçaba)".
DISTRIBUTION: Known only from the type locality.

Cycloramphus cedrensis Heyer, 1983. Proc. Biol. Soc. Washington, 96:533.
TYPE(S): Holotype: MZUSP 59260.
TYPE LOCALITY: "Brazil; Santa Catarina, 12 km E of Rio dos Cedros on road to Rio
São Bernardo, approx. 26 44 S, 49 20 W".
DISTRIBUTION: Known only from the type locality.

Cycloramphus diringshofeni Bokermann, 1957. Rev. Brasil. Biol., 17:249.
TYPE(S): Holotype: WCAB 548.
TYPE LOCALITY: "São Bento do Sul, Estado de Santa Catarina, Brasil".
DISTRIBUTION: Serra do Mar in the state of Santa Catarina, Brazil.

Cycloramphus dubius (Miranda-Ribeiro, 1920). Rev. Mus. Paulista, São Paulo, 19:268.
ORIGINAL NAME: *Iliodiscus dubius*.
TYPE(S): Holotype: MZUSP 647.
TYPE LOCALITY: "Alto da Serra (S. Paulo)", Brazil.
DISTRIBUTION: State of São Paulo, Brazil.

Cycloramphus duseni (Andersson, 1914). Ark. Zool., 9:1.
ORIGINAL NAME: *Telmatobius duseni*.
TYPE(S): NHRM 1606 designated lectotype by Heyer, 1983, Proc. Biol. Soc.
Washington, 96:549.
TYPE LOCALITY: "Ypiranga, Serra do Mar, Parana, Brazil".
DISTRIBUTION: Known only from the type locality.

Cycloramphus eleutherodactylus (Miranda-Ribeiro, 1920). Rev. Mus. Paulista, São Paulo,
19:270.
ORIGINAL NAME: *Iliodiscus eleutherodactylus*.
TYPE(S): Syntypes: MZUSP 20, 24, 572, 816, 835; MZUSP 24x designated lectotype
by Bokermann, 1951, Arq. Mus. Nac., Rio de Janeiro, 42:77–106.
TYPE LOCALITY: "Alto da Serra" and "Rio Grande, São Paulo", Brazil; lectotype
from "Alto da Serra".
DISTRIBUTION: Serra dos Órgãos, Serra da Mantiqueira, Serra da Bocaina, and Serra
do Mar, Brazil.

Cycloramphus fuliginosus Tschudi, 1838. Classif. Batr.:81.
TYPE(S): Syntypes: MNHNP 750 (2 specimens); MNHNP 750 designated lectotype
by Heyer, 1983, Arq. Zool., São Paulo, 30:262.
TYPE LOCALITY: "India"; corrected to "Brésil" by Duméril and Bibron, 1841, Erp.
Gén., 8:455; the collector, Delaland, collected only in the state of Rio de
Janeiro, Brazil (PEV).
DISTRIBUTION: States of Espírito Santo and Rio de Janeiro, Brazil.

Cycloramphus granulosus Lutz, 1929. Mem. Inst. Oswaldo Cruz, Rio de Janeiro, 22:13.
TYPE(S): Syntypes: including USNM 96742 and UMMZ 92446 (formerly USNM
96747); MN-AL 1537 designated lectotype by Heyer, 1983, Arq. Zool., São
Paulo, 30:307.
TYPE LOCALITY: Bonito, Serra da Bocaina, boundary of Rio de Janeiro and São Paulo
[Brazil] (according to Cochran, 1955, Bull. U.S. Natl. Mus., 206:261).
DISTRIBUTION: Portions of the Serra da Bocaina, Serra da Mantiqueira, and Serra do
Mar, Brazil.

Cycloramphus izecksohni Heyer, 1983. Proc. Biol. Soc. Washington, 96:550.
TYPE(S): Holotype: MZUSP 57775.
TYPE LOCALITY: "Brazil; Santa Catarina, 13 km W Pirabeiraba, 26 12 S, 49 07 W".
DISTRIBUTION: Serra do Mar in the states of São Paulo, Paraná, and Santa Catarina,
Brazil.

Cycloramphus jordanensis Heyer, 1983. Arq. Zool., São Paulo, 20:308.
TYPE(S): Holotype: MZUSP 4522.
TYPE LOCALITY: "Brasil; São Paulo, Campos do Jordão".
DISTRIBUTION: Known only from the type locality.

Cycloramphus lutzorum Heyer, 1983. Arq. Zool., São Paulo, 30:309.
TYPE(S): Holotype: MZUSP 57805.
TYPE LOCALITY: "Brasil: São Paulo, about 11 km W of Iporanga on road to Apiaí".
DISTRIBUTION: Serra do Mar in the states of Paraná, Rio de Janeiro, and São Paulo,
Brazil.

Cycloramphus mirandaribeiroi Heyer, 1983. Arq. Zool., São Paulo, 30:311.
   TYPE(S): Holotype: MZUSP 57809.
   TYPE LOCALITY: "Brasil; Paraná, 9 km W São João da Graciosa on PR 410 to
      Curitiba".
   DISTRIBUTION: Serra do Mar in the state of Paraná, Brazil.

Cycloramphus ohausi (Wandolleck, 1907). Abh. Ber. K. Anthro. Ethno. Mus. Dresden,
      11:10.
   ORIGINAL NAME: *Ceratophrys ohausi.*
   TYPE(S): Holotype: MTKD D2038.
   TYPE LOCALITY: Petrópolis, Rio de Janeiro [Brazil].
   DISTRIBUTION: Serra dos Órgãos, Brazil.

Cycloramphus rhyakonastes Heyer, 1983. Arq. Zool., São Paulo, 30:314.
   TYPE(S): Holotype: MZUSP 57827.
   TYPE LOCALITY: "Brasil; Paraná, 15 km W of São João da Graciosa on PR 410 to
      Curitiba".
   DISTRIBUTION: Serra do Mar in the states of Paraná and Santa Catarina, Brazil.

Cycloramphus semipalmatus (Miranda-Ribeiro, 1920). Rev. Mus. Paulista, São Paulo, 12:
      269.
   ORIGINAL NAME: *Iliodiscus semipalmatus.*
   TYPE(S): Holotype: MZUSP 737.
   TYPE LOCALITY: Campo Grande, São Paulo, Brazil.
   DISTRIBUTION: Serra do Mar in the state of São Paulo, Brazil.

Cycloramphus stejnegeri (Noble, 1924). Proc. Biol. Soc. Washington, 37:68.
   ORIGINAL NAME: *Borborocoetes stejnegeri.*
   TYPE(S): Holotype: USNM 52608.
   TYPE LOCALITY: Organ Mountains [=Serra dos Órgãos], Brazil, 1500 m.
   DISTRIBUTION: Serra dos Órgãos, Brazil.

Cycloramphus valae Heyer, 1983. Arq. Zool., São Paulo, 30:319.
   TYPE(S): Holotype: MZUSP 57860.
   TYPE LOCALITY: "Brasil; Santa Catarina, Gruta, 20 km E Bom Jardim on road to
      Lauro Müller".
   DISTRIBUTION: Southernmost extent of Serra do Mar in the state of Santa Catarina,
      Brazil.

Dischidodactylus Lynch, 1979. Am. Mus. Novit., 2680:5.
   TYPE SPECIES: *Elosia duidensis* Rivero, 1968, by original designation.
   DISTRIBUTION: As for the single species.
   COMMENT: Lynch, 1979, Am. Mus. Novit., 2680:5, placed this genus in the
      Telmatobiinae despite the similarity of its peculiar digit morphology to that of
      the Hylodinae (DCC).

Dischidodactylus duidensis (Rivero, 1968). Am. Mus. Novit., 2334:1.
   ORIGINAL NAME: *Elosia duidensis.*
   TYPE(S): Holotype: AMNH 23190.
   TYPE LOCALITY: "summit at Vegas Falls, 4600 feet, Mt. Duida, Venezuela".
   DISTRIBUTION: Cerro Duida, Venezuela.

Eleutherodactylus Duméril and Bibron, 1841. Erp. Gén., 8:620.
   TYPE SPECIES: *Hylodes martinicensis* Tschudi, 1838, by monotypy.
   DISTRIBUTION: Mexico to Argentina and Brazil; West Indies; introduced into Florida
      and Louisiana (USA).
   COMMENT: Tribe Eleutherodactylini. Synonymies for the West Indian species are
      available in Schwartz and Thomas, 1975, Carnegie Mus. Nat. Hist. Spec. Publ.,

1:14–41, and Schwartz, Thomas, and Ober, 1978, Carnegie Mus. Nat. Hist. Spec.
Publ., 5:3–8. Lesser Antillean species were reviewed by Schwartz, 1967, Stud.
Fauna Curaçao and other Caribb. Is., 91:1–62. Schwartz and Fowler, 1973, Stud.
Fauna Curaçao and other Caribb. Is., 142:50–142, reviewed the species of
Jamaica. Jamaican species groups were redefined by Crombie, 1977, Proc. Biol.
Soc. Washington, 90:194–204. Schwartz, 1969, Stud. Fauna Curaçao and other
Caribb. Is., 114:99–115, discussed the *Eleutherodactylus auriculatus* group.
Schwartz, 1965, Herpetologica, 21:27–31, discussed the phylogenetic
relationships of Cuban members of the *Eleutherodactylus auriculatus* group.
Shreve and Williams, 1963, *In* Williams, Shreve, and Humphrey, Bull. Mus.
Comp. Zool., 129:315–342, defined species groups for the Hispaniolan forms.
Schwartz, 1976, Bull. Florida State Mus., Biol. Sci., 21:1–46, reviewed, defined,
and discussed some of the phylogenetic relationships within the
Eleutherodactylus ricordii group. Schwartz, 1973, J. Herpetol., 7:249–273, discussed
the distribution and biogeography of the Hispaniolan South Island species.
Bogart, 1981, R. Ontario Mus. Life Sci. Contrib., 129:1–22, compared the
chromosomes of some species from Cuba and Puerto Rico. Joglar, 1983, Caribb.
J. Sci., 19:33–40, compared phenetically the species of Puerto Rico. According to
Savage, 1980, Proc. Biol. Soc. Washington, 93:928–942, the *Eleutherodactylus*
cruentus group is an unnatural composite. Mexican and Central American
species of the *Eleutherodactylus rugulosus* group were reviewed by Savage, 1975,
Copeia, 1975:254–306. Lynch, 1980, Am. Mus. Novit., 2696:1–24, provided a
taxonomic and distributional synopsis of the Amazonian species. Lynch, 1981,
Misc. Publ. Mus. Nat. Hist. Univ. Kansas, 72:1–46, reviewed the species of the
Andes of northern Ecuador and adjacent Colombia. Lynch and Duellman, 1980,
Misc. Publ. Mus. Nat. Hist. Univ. Kansas, 69:1–86, reviewed the species of the
Amazonian slopes of the Ecuadorian Andes. Lynch, 1979, Misc. Publ. Mus. Nat.
Hist. Univ. Kansas, 66:1–62, reviewed the species of the Andes of southern
Ecuador. Rivero and Solano, 1977, Mem. Soc. Cienc. Nat. La Salle, 37:249–263,
discussed the evolution of the species of the Andes of Venezuela. Savage and
DeWeese, 1981, Proc. Biol. Soc. Washington, 93:928–942, discussed the species
groups of Central American species, as did Ford and Savage, 1984, Occas. Pap.
Mus. Nat. Hist. Univ. Kansas, 110:1–9, who also discussed Lynch's
Eleutherodactylus unistrigatus group, from which they removed the
Eleutherodactylus omiltemanus group. Lynch, 1984, Herpetologica, 40:234–237,
discussed the *Eleutherodactylus pyrrhomerus* assembly of the *Eleutherodactylus*
unistrigatus group. Lynch, 1965, Herpetologica, 21:102–113, reviewed the
Eleutherodactylus rugulosus group. Lynch and Myers, 1983, Bull. Am. Mus. Nat.
Hist., 175:481–572, reviewed the members of the *Eleutherodactylus fitzingeri*
group found in eastern Panama and Chocoan South America, noted that all of
the features that define the *Eleutherodactylus fitzingeri* group are primitive for the
genus, and commented on the *Eleutherodactylus fitzingeri* group, *Eleutherodactylus*
gaigei group, and *Eleutherodactylus gollmeri* group of Savage. Miyamoto and
Tennant, 1984, Copeia, 1984:765–768, discussed the *Eleutherodactylus fitzingeri*
group *sensu* Savage. Lynch, 1975, Occas. Pap. Mus. Nat. Hist. Univ. Kansas, 38:
1–46, reviewed the broad-headed *Eleutherodactylus* (*Eleutherodactylus biporcatus*
group, *Eleutherodactylus sulcatus* group, and *Amblyphrynus*). Synonymy includes
Amblyphrynus, according to Lynch, 1981, Caldasia, 13:318, who provided a
cladogram of the species in the *Eleutherodactylus sulcatus* group. Lynch, 1983, *In*
Rhodin and Miyata (eds.), Adv. Herpetol. Evol. Biol.:52–57, discussed the
Eleutherodactylus devillei assembly of the *Eleutherodactylus unistrigatus* group, and
supplied a cladogram of the species. Heyer, 1984, Smithson. Contrib. Zool., 402:
1–42, discussed the systematics and zoogeography of *Eleutherodactylus guentheri*
and its closely related species, and regarded the reality of Lynch's
Eleutherodactylus binotatus group as doubtful. Synonymy includes
Microbatrachylus Taylor, 1940 "1939", according to Lynch, 1965, Nat. Hist. Misc.,
Chicago, 182:1–12. Unless otherwise noted the species group assignments in the
species accounts follow Lynch, 1976, Occas. Pap. Mus. Nat. Hist. Univ. Kansas,
61:1–24, and the assembly groups follow Lynch, 1981, Misc. Publ. Mus. Nat.
Hist. Univ. Kansas, 72:37–38.

CONTRIBUTORS: John D. Lynch (JDL); Albert Schwartz (AS) (Antilles).
REVIEWERS: Jonathan A. Campbell (JAC) (Mexico and Central America); Gustavo
Casas-Andreu (GCA) (Mexico); Oscar Flores-Villela (OFV) (Mexico); Linda
S. Ford (LSF) (Central America); Rafael Joglar (RJ) (Antilles); Juan A. Rivero
(JAR) (South America); Jay M. Savage (JMS) (Central America); Richard
Thomas (RT) (Antilles).

Eleutherodactylus aaptus Lynch and Lescure, 1980. Bull. Mus. Natl. Hist. Nat., Paris,
(4)2:304.
TYPE(S): Holotype: MNHNP 1978-2816.
TYPE LOCALITY: "Colonia, Departamento Loreto, Perú".
DISTRIBUTION: Amazonas (Colombia) and Loreto (Peru).
COMMENT: In the *Eleutherodactylus rubicundus* assembly of the *Eleutherodactylus
unistrigatus* group.

Eleutherodactylus abbotti Cochran, 1923. Proc. Biol. Soc. Washington, 36:93.
TYPE(S): Holotype: USNM 65055.
TYPE LOCALITY: "Laguna, Samaná Peninsula, [Samaná Province,] Dominican
Republic.
DISTRIBUTION: Hispaniola; widespread.
COMMENT: In the *Eleutherodactylus auriculatus* group and near *Eleutherodactylus
audanti*, according to Schwartz, 1966, Bull. Mus. Comp. Zool., 133:396, and
Schwartz, 1969, Stud. Fauna Curaçao and other Caribb. Is., 114:99–115.
Reviewed by Schwartz, 1977, Cat. Am. Amph. Rept., 191.1–2.

Eleutherodactylus acatallelus Lynch and Ruíz-Carranza, 1983. Trans. Kansas Acad. Sci.,
86:100.
TYPE(S): Holotype: ICN 7814.
TYPE LOCALITY: "Quebrada Sopladero, 33 m by road NNW Uribe, Depto. Cauca,
Colombia, 2190 m".
DISTRIBUTION: Cloud forests in the region of the type locality (Cauca, Colombia),
2190–2610 m.
COMMENT: In the *Eleutherodactylus unistrigatus* group; most similar to
Eleutherodactylus subsigillatus, according to the original description.

Eleutherodactylus acerus Lynch and Duellman, 1980. Misc. Publ. Mus. Nat. Hist. Univ.
Kansas, 69:12.
TYPE(S): Holotype: KU 165471.
TYPE LOCALITY: "11 km ESE Papallacta, Provincia Napo, Ecuador, 2660 m."
DISTRIBUTION: Known only from the type locality and vicinity between Papallacta
and Cuyujúa (Napo Province, Ecuador) in upper montane cloud forest, 2660–
2750 m.
COMMENT: In the *Eleutherodactylus unistrigatus* group; nearest to *Eleutherodactylus
glandulosus*, *Eleutherodactylus leucopus*, and *Eleutherodactylus lividus* (JDL).

Eleutherodactylus achatinus (Boulenger, 1898). Proc. Zool. Soc. London, 1898:120.
ORIGINAL NAME: *Hylodes achatinus*.
TYPE(S): Holotype: BM 1947.2.15.69 (formerly 98.4.28.106).
TYPE LOCALITY: "Cachabé [=Cachabí], a small village on the river of that name . . . ,
Prov. Esmeraldas . . . about 500 feet above the sea", Ecuador.
DISTRIBUTION: Extreme eastern Panama south through the Chocoan lowlands to El
Oro Province in southern Ecuador, 0–2330 m, also in the Cauca and
Magdalena Valleys of Colombia.
COMMENT: In the *Eleutherodactylus fitzingeri* group. Reviewed by Lynch and Myers,
1983, Bull. Am. Mus. Nat. Hist., 175:509–516, who placed *Hylodes pagmae*
Fowler, 1913, and *Eleutherodactylus brederi* Dunn, 1934, in synonymy, and
noted that this nominal species may contain undefined sibling species.

Eleutherodactylus acmonis Schwartz, 1960. Reading Public Mus. and Art Gallery Sci. Publ., 11:42.
    TYPE(S): Holotype: AMNH 63426.
    TYPE LOCALITY: West slope, El Yunque de Baracoa, Oriente [now Guantánamo] Province, Cuba.
    DISTRIBUTION: Cuba; Guantánamo Province.
    COMMENT: In the *Eleutherodactylus ricordii* group, according to the original description.

Eleutherodactylus actites Lynch, 1979. Herpetologica, 35:230.
    TYPE(S): Holotype: KU 120111.
    TYPE LOCALITY: "Pilaló, Provincia Cotopaxi, Ecuador, 2486 m".
    DISTRIBUTION: Known only from the type locality.
    COMMENT: In the *Eleutherodactylus fitzingeri* group.

Eleutherodactylus acuminatus Shreve, 1935. Occas. Pap. Boston Soc. Nat. Hist., 8:217.
    TYPE(S): Holotype: MCZ 19951.
    TYPE LOCALITY: Canelos, Oriente, [Provincia Pastaza,] Ecuador.
    DISTRIBUTION: Amazonian Ecuador, northern Peru, and adjacent Colombia.
    COMMENT: In the *Eleutherodactylus unistrigatus* group. Recent records reviewed by Lynch and Lescure, 1980, Bull. Mus. Natl. Hist. Nat., Paris, (4)2:306–307. Not considered by Lynch and Duellman, 1980, Misc. Publ. Mus. Nat. Hist. Univ. Kansas, 69:1–86.

Eleutherodactylus affinis (Werner, 1899). Verh. Zool. Bot. Ges. Wien, 49:478.
    ORIGINAL NAME: *Hylodes affinis*.
    TYPE(S): ZFMK 67 designated lectotype by Cochran and Goin, 1970, Bull. U.S. Natl. Mus., 288:414; both syntypes (and lectotype) lost, according to Böhme and Bischoff, 1984, Bonn. Zool. Monogr., 19:167.
    TYPE LOCALITY: La Unión to Chingasa, Cundinamarca, Colombia.
    DISTRIBUTION: Known only from the vicinity of the type locality in western Departamento Cundinamarca, Colombia.
    COMMENT: In the *Eleutherodactylus unistrigatus* group.

Eleutherodactylus albipes Barbour and Shreve, 1937. Bull. Mus. Comp. Zool., 80:383.
    TYPE(S): Holotype: MCZ 22045.
    TYPE LOCALITY: Pico Turquino, 5400 feet to 6000 feet, Oriente [now Santiago de Cuba] Province, Cuba.
    DISTRIBUTION: Known only from the vicinity of the type locality in the Sierra Maestra, Cuba.
    COMMENT: In the *Eleutherodactylus dimidiatus* group, according to Schwartz, 1958, Am. Mus. Novit., 1873:2, and Shreve and Williams, 1963, Bull. Mus. Comp. Zool., 129:338.

Eleutherodactylus alcoae Schwartz, 1971. Ann. Carnegie Mus., 43:26.
    TYPE(S): Holotype: CM 45889.
    TYPE LOCALITY: "22 km NE Cabo Rojo, 1500 feet (458 meters), Pedernales Province, República Dominicana".
    DISTRIBUTION: Hispaniola: the Barahona Peninsula and immediately adjacent coastal area in Haiti.
    COMMENT: In the *Eleutherodactylus ricordii* group, according to the original description. Reviewed by Schwartz, 1976, Bull. Florida State Mus., Biol. Sci., 21:20–23, and Schwartz, 1977, Cat. Am. Amph. Rept., 192.1–2.

Eleutherodactylus alfredi (Boulenger, 1898). Proc. Zool. Soc. London, 1898:480–481.
    ORIGINAL NAME: *Hylodes alfredi*.
    TYPE(S): Syntypes: BM 1947.2.15.54 (formerly 98.2.19.1) and 1947.2.14.55 (formerly 98.4.7.1); MNHNP 99-19 recorded in error as holotype by Guibé, 1950 "1948", Cat. Types Amph. Mus. Natl. Hist. Nat.:27.
    TYPE LOCALITY: "Atoyac, State of Veracruz", Mexico.
    DISTRIBUTION: Central eastern Veracruz (Mexico) to western El Petén, Guatemala.

COMMENT: In the *Eleutherodactylus alfredi* group. Shreve, 1957, Bull. Mus. Comp. Zool., 116:247, recognized two subspecies, whereas Duellman, 1960, Univ. Kansas Publ. Mus. Nat. Hist., 13:53–54, saw little justification for recognizing *Eleutherodactylus alfredi conspicuus*.

Eleutherodactylus altae Dunn, 1942. Not. Nat., Philadelphia, 104:1.
TYPE(S): Holotype: ANSP 23815.
TYPE LOCALITY: Caribbean slope of Costa Rica, on the pass between Barba and Irazú, below the divide and above the finca of Félix Delgado.
DISTRIBUTION: Volcán Poas and vicinity of the type locality, Costa Rica.
COMMENT: In the *Eleutherodactylus cruentus* group, according to Savage, 1980, Prelim. Handlist Herpetofauna Costa Rica:6, and Savage, 1982, Proc. Biol. Soc. Washington, 93:940, which is viewed as a subset of the *Eleutherodactylus unistrigatus* group of Lynch.

Eleutherodactylus altamazonicus Barbour and Dunn, 1921. Proc. Biol. Soc. Washington, 34:161.
TYPE(S): Holotype: MCZ 2028.
TYPE LOCALITY: "Upper Amazon, probably collected by the Thayer Expedition at Nauta", Departamento Loreto, Peru.
DISTRIBUTION: Eastern Peru, Ecuador, and adjacent Brazil.
COMMENT: Includes *Eleutherodactylus brevicrus* Andersson, 1945, according to Lynch, 1974, Occas. Pap. Mus. Nat. Hist. Univ. Kansas, 31:14. In the *Eleutherodactylus unistrigatus* group.

Eleutherodactylus alticola Lynn, 1937. Herpetologica, 1:89.
TYPE(S): Holotype: USNM 102524.
TYPE LOCALITY: Blue Mountain Peak, St. Thomas Parish, Jamaica.
DISTRIBUTION: Jamaica; high elevations in the Blue Mountains between Sir Johns Peak and the type locality, 3450–7420 ft.
COMMENT: In the *Eleutherodactylus gossei* group according to Goin, 1954, Ann. Carnegie Mus., 33:186; Schwartz and Fowler, 1973, Stud. Fauna Curaçao and other Caribb. Is., 43:135; and Crombie, 1977, Proc. Biol. Soc. Washington, 90: 197–204.

Eleutherodactylus anatipes Lynch and Myers, 1983. Bull. Am. Mus. Nat. Hist., 175:516.
TYPE(S): Holotype: KU 177626.
TYPE LOCALITY: "Maldonado, Prov. Carchi, Ecuador, 1410 m."
DISTRIBUTION: Drainage of the Río Mira in extreme northern Ecuador, 520–1410 m elev.
COMMENT: According to the original description *Eleutherodactylus anatipes* is probably most closely related to *Eleutherodactylus anomalus* and *Eleutherodactylus zygodactylus*. Lynch and Myers pointed out, however, that these three species may be more closely related to certain broad-headed species (*Eleutherodactylus bufoniformis* and *Eleutherodactylus necerus*) than to other member species of the *Eleutherodactylus fitzingeri* group.

Eleutherodactylus andi Savage, 1974. Herpetologica, 30:295.
TYPE(S): Holotype: LACM 76858.
TYPE LOCALITY: "Costa Rica: Provincia de San Jose: Canton de Coronado: 0.8 km N juncture Rio Claro and Rio La Hondura, 1150 m".
DISTRIBUTION: Premontane rainforests on the Atlantic slopes of the Cordillera Central and extreme northeastern Cordillera de Talamanca of Costa Rica, and extreme western Panama, 560–1360 m.
COMMENT: In the *Eleutherodactylus fitzingeri* group.

Eleutherodactylus andicola (Boettger, 1891). Zool. Anz., 14:346.
ORIGINAL NAME: *Leptodactylus andicola*.
TYPE(S): Lost, according to Heyer, 1978, Sci. Bull. Nat. Hist. Mus. Los Angeles Co.,
    29:33.
TYPE LOCALITY: Sorata, Bolivia.
DISTRIBUTION: Known only from the type locality.
COMMENT: Transferred to *Eleutherodactylus* by Heyer, 1978, Sci. Bull. Nat. Hist.
    Mus. Los Angeles Co., 29:33, who noted that the taxonomic status of this
    form is questionable.

Eleutherodactylus andrewsi Lynn, 1937. Herpetologica, 1:88.
TYPE(S): Holotype: USNM 102515.
TYPE LOCALITY: Chester Vale, St. Andrew Parish, Jamaica.
DISTRIBUTION: Jamaica; high elevations of the Blue Mountains in St. Andrew,
    Portland, and St. Thomas parishes, 2500–4250 ft.
COMMENT: In the *Eleutherodactylus gossei* group according to Goin, 1954, Ann.
    Carnegie Mus., 33:186, and Crombie, 1977, Proc. Biol. Soc. Washington, 90:
    194–204.

Eleutherodactylus angelicus Savage, 1975. Copeia, 1975:274.
TYPE(S): Holotype: LACM 76856.
TYPE LOCALITY: "Costa Rica: Provincia de Alajuela: Canton de Alajuela: Salto El
    Angel, 1380 m."
DISTRIBUTION: Cordillera de Tilarán (1200–1600 m) and north (600–1700 m) and
    eastern (900–1400 m) slopes of Volcán Poas in Costa Rica.
COMMENT: In the *Eleutherodactylus fitzingeri* group. Most closely related to
    Eleutherodactylus escoces and *Eleutherodactylus fleischmanni* according to Savage,
    1975, Copeia, 1975:299. See Savage, 1974, Rev. Biol. Tropical, 22:76, for
    discussion of type locality.

Eleutherodactylus anolirex Lynch, 1983. *In* Rhodin and Miyata (eds.), Adv. Herpetol.
    Evol. Biol.:52.
TYPE(S): Holotype: KU 168626.
TYPE LOCALITY: "18.5 km (by road) S Chitagá, Departamento de Norte de
    Santander, Colombia, 2850 m".
DISTRIBUTION: Northern Cordillera Occidental of Colombia.
COMMENT: In the *Eleutherodactylus unistrigatus* group, *Eleutherodactylus devillei*
    assembly (with *Eleutherodactylus briceni*, *Eleutherodactylus vertebralis*,
    Eleutherodactylus supernatis, and *Eleutherodactylus devillei*).

Eleutherodactylus anomalus (Boulenger, 1898). Proc. Zool. Soc. London, 1898:119.
ORIGINAL NAME: *Hylodes anomalus*.
TYPE(S): Syntypes: BM 1947.2.17.8–10 (formerly 98.4.28.98–100).
TYPE LOCALITY: "Cachabé [=Cachabí], a small village on the river of that name . . .
    Prov. Esmeraldas . . . about 500 feet above the sea", Ecuador.
DISTRIBUTION: Rainforest at elevations between 20 and 820 m, from northern
    Colombia (Serranía de Baudó) south to central-western Ecuador.
COMMENT: In the *Eleutherodactylus fitzingeri* group. Lynch and Myers, 1983, Bull.
    Am. Mus. Nat. Hist., 175:518–521, reviewed this species and discussed
    misidentifications in the literature. See comment under *Eleutherodactylus
    anatipes*.

Eleutherodactylus anonymus (A. Lutz, 1928). Mem. Inst. Oswaldo Cruz, Rio de Janeiro,
    20:40, 55.
ORIGINAL NAME: *Hylodes anonymus*.
TYPE(S): None designated; possibly MN (JDL).
TYPE LOCALITY: From the reservoir of Mamo, near La Guaira [Venezuela].
DISTRIBUTION: Known only from the holotype.

COMMENT: In the *Eleutherodactylus unistrigatus* group. Description consists solely of a figure.

Eleutherodactylus anotis Walker and Test, 1955. Occas. Pap. Mus. Zool. Univ. Michigan, 561:7.
TYPE(S): Holotype: UMMZ 109876.
TYPE LOCALITY: From a small stream at Rancho Grande, 1090 m, Estado Aragua, Venezuela.
DISTRIBUTION: Known only from the vicinity of the type locality.
COMMENT: In the *Eleutherodactylus unistrigatus* group.

Eleutherodactylus antillensis (Reinhardt and Lütken, 1863). Vidensk. Medd. Dansk Naturhist. Foren., 1862:209.
ORIGINAL NAME: *Hylodes antillensis*.
TYPE(S): Syntypes: ZMUC R1182 (St. Croix), R1183–84 (St. John), R177, R1196 (St. Thomas), R1197 (Vieques).
TYPE LOCALITY: "St. Thomas", Virgin Islands.
DISTRIBUTION: Islands of the Puerto Rico Bank; widespread in Puerto Rico at low to intermediate elevations; known from the islands of Vieques, Culebra, St. Thomas, St. John, Tortola, St. Croix, and Virgin Gorda; introduced into Panama (RIC).
COMMENT: In the *Eleutherodactylus auriculatus* group according to Schwartz, 1969, Stud. Fauna Curaçao and other Caribb. Is., 30:101.

Eleutherodactylus anzuetoi Stuart, 1941. Proc. Biol. Soc. Washington, 54:197.
TYPE(S): Holotype: UMMZ 89160.
TYPE LOCALITY: 2 km north of Nebaj, El Quiché, Guatemala.
DISTRIBUTION: Alta Verapaz, Guatemala.
COMMENT: In the *Eleutherodactylus fitzingeri* group. The holotype is a juvenile, probably of the species *Eleutherodactylus lineatus* (JMS).

Eleutherodactylus apostates Schwartz, 1973. J. Herpetol., 7:262.
TYPE(S): Holotype: CM 54093.
TYPE LOCALITY: "*Ca.* 2 km S Castillon, 3800 feet (1159 meters), Département du Sud, Haiti".
DISTRIBUTION: Hispaniola: known from Zapoti and the region of the type locality, Haiti, 3500–4800 ft. elev.
COMMENT: In the *Eleutherodactylus ricordii* group and most closely related to *Eleutherodactylus schmidti,* according to the original description. Reviewed by Schwartz, 1977, Cat. Am. Amph. Rept., 201.1.

Eleutherodactylus appendiculatus (Werner, 1894). Zool. Anz., 17:410.
ORIGINAL NAME: *Hylodes appendiculatus*.
TYPE(S): Holotype: NHMW 16507.
TYPE LOCALITY: Ecuador.
DISTRIBUTION: Cloud forests of western Ecuador (Provincia Pichincha).
COMMENT: In the *Eleutherodactylus unistrigatus* group. Redescribed by Lynch, 1970, Trans. Kansas Acad. Sci., 73:171–173.

Eleutherodactylus armstrongi Noble and Hassler, 1933. Am. Mus. Novit., 652:2.
TYPE(S): Holotype: AMNH 44554.
TYPE LOCALITY: "'El Propio Esfuerzo,' coffee finca of Luis E. Del Monte, near Barahona, [Barahona Province] D. R. [=Dominican Republic] at an altitude of 1800 feet".
DISTRIBUTION: Southern Hispaniola in the region of the La Selle–Baoruco massifs.
COMMENT: In the *Eleutherodactylus auriculatus* group according to Schwartz, 1969, Stud. Fauna Curaçao and other Caribb. Is., 114:99–115, and Schwartz, 1973, J. Herpetol., 7:269–270, or the *Eleutherodactylus ricordii* group, according to

Shreve and Williams, 1963, Bull. Mus. Comp. Zool., 129:328. Reviewed by
Schwartz, 1978, Cat. Am. Amph. Rept., 208.1–2.

Eleutherodactylus atkinsi Dunn, 1925. Occas. Pap. Boston Soc. Nat. Hist., 5:165.
TYPE(S): Holotype: MCZ 10587.
TYPE LOCALITY: Colonia Guabairo, near Cienfuegos, Las Villas [now Cienfuegos]
Province, Cuba.
DISTRIBUTION: Cuba; widespread.
COMMENT: In the *Eleutherodactylus ricordii* group, according to Schwartz, 1958, Am.
Mus. Novit., 1873:2; two subspecies recognized.

Eleutherodactylus atratus Lynch, 1979. Misc. Publ. Mus. Nat. Hist. Univ. Kansas, 66:5.
TYPE(S): Holotype: USNM 199675.
TYPE LOCALITY: "Suro Rancho, Provincia Morona-Santiago, Ecuador, 2683 m."
DISTRIBUTION: 2195–2850 m elevation on the Amazonian slopes of the eastern
Andean Cordillera in southern Ecuador.
COMMENT: In the *Eleutherodactylus unistrigatus* group.

Eleutherodactylus audanti Cochran, 1934. Occas. Pap. Boston Soc. Nat. Hist., 8:164.
TYPE(S): Holotype: MCZ 19704.
TYPE LOCALITY: "Peak la Selle", Département de l'Ouest, Haiti.
DISTRIBUTION: Hispaniola, 3800–6000 ft. elev.
COMMENT: In the *Eleutherodactylus auriculatus* group, according to Shreve and
Williams, 1963, Bull. Mus. Comp. Zool., 129:302–342; Schwartz, 1966, Bull.
Mus. Comp. Zool., 133:396 (who recognized three subspecies); and Schwartz,
1969, Stud. Fauna Curaçao and other Caribb. Is., 114:99–115; near
Eleutherodactylus abbotti. Reviewed by Schwartz, 1979, Cat. Am. Amph. Rept.,
224.1–2.

Eleutherodactylus auriculatoides Noble, 1923. Am. Mus. Novit., 61:3.
TYPE(S): Holotype: AMNH 11403.
TYPE LOCALITY: "bromeliads near Constanza–Jarabacoa Trail, Paso Bajito, [La Vega
Province,] Dominican Republic".
DISTRIBUTION: Hispaniola; the central mountains (Cordillera Central) in the
Dominican Republic.
COMMENT: In the *Eleutherodactylus auriculatus* group according to Schwartz, 1969,
Stud. Fauna Curaçao and other Caribb. Is., 30:101. Reviewed by Schwartz,
1980, Cat. Am. Amph. Rept., 246.1–2.

Eleutherodactylus auriculatus (Cope, 1862). Proc. Acad. Nat. Sci. Philadelphia, 14:152.
ORIGINAL NAME: *Hylodes auriculatus*.
TYPE(S): Formerly ANSP, now lost.
TYPE LOCALITY: Eastern Cuba.
DISTRIBUTION: Cuba and Isla de Pinos (=Isla de Juventud).
COMMENT: In the *Eleutherodactylus auriculatus* group, according to Schwartz, 1958,
Am. Mus. Novit., 1873:29, and Schwartz, 1965, Herpetologica, 21:27–31. See
also Schwartz, 1960, Reading Public Mus. and Art Gallery Sci. Publ., 11:4–5.

Eleutherodactylus azueroensis Savage, 1975. Copeia, 1975:277.
TYPE(S): Holotype: KU 114831.
TYPE LOCALITY: "Panama: Provincia de los Santos: N slope Cerro Cambutal, 480 m."
DISTRIBUTION: Peninsula de Azuero of Panama (61–940 m).
COMMENT: In the *Eleutherodactylus fitzingeri* group. Savage, 1975, Copeia, 1975:299,
suggested that *Eleutherodactylus taurus* is the nearest relative.

Eleutherodactylus bakeri Cochran, 1935. Proc. Boston Soc. Nat. Hist., 40:369.
TYPE(S): Holotype: MCZ 19837.
TYPE LOCALITY: "Mt. la Hotte [=Pic Macaya], [Département du Sud,] Haiti, 5000
feet to 7800 feet".
DISTRIBUTION: Hispaniola; the Massif de la Hotte and the Massif de la Selle, Haiti,
1900–7698 ft. elev.

COMMENT: In the *Eleutherodactylus auriculatus* group, according to Shreve and Williams, 1963, Bull. Mus. Comp. Zool., 129:302–342, and Schwartz, 1969, Stud. Fauna Curaçao and other Caribb. Is., 30:101. Reviewed by Schwartz, 1980, Cat. Am. Amph. Rept., 247.1.

Eleutherodactylus balionotus Lynch, 1979. Misc. Publ. Mus. Nat. Hist. Univ. Kansas, 66:7.
TYPE(S): Holotype: KU 142136.
TYPE LOCALITY: "13.5 km E Loja, at the crest of the cordillera (Abra de Zamora) between Provincia Loja and Zamora-Chinchipe, Ecuador, 2800 m."
DISTRIBUTION: Known only from the type locality.
COMMENT: In the *Eleutherodactylus unistrigatus* group. Forms a vicariant series with *Eleutherodactylus riveti* and *Eleutherodactylus ruidus* according to Lynch, 1979, Misc. Publ. Mus. Nat. Hist. Univ. Kansas, 66:51.

Eleutherodactylus barlagnei Lynch, 1965. Breviora, 220:2.
TYPE(S): Holotype: MCZ 35334.
TYPE LOCALITY: Matouba, *ca.* 700 meters, the Basse-Terre portion of Guadeloupe.
DISTRIBUTION: Known only from the Basse-Terre portion of Guadeloupe at elevations of 600–ca. 2100 ft.
COMMENT: In the *Eleutherodactylus auriculatus* group, according to Schwartz, 1967, Stud. Fauna Curaçao and other Caribb. Is., 90:56.

Eleutherodactylus bartonsmithi Schwartz, 1960. Reading Public Mus. and Art Gallery Sci. Publ., 11:10.
TYPE(S): Holotype: AMNH 63409.
TYPE LOCALITY: Mouth of Río Yumurí, east side, Oriente [now Guantánamo] Province, Cuba.
DISTRIBUTION: Cuba; known from the type locality and Cupeyal, Oriente (now Holguin) Province.
COMMENT: In the *Eleutherodactylus auriculatus* group, according to the original description and Schwartz, 1965, Herpetologica, 21:28–31.

Eleutherodactylus baryecuus Lynch, 1979. Misc. Publ. Mus. Nat. Hist. Univ. Kansas, 66:10.
TYPE(S): Holotype: USNM 199714.
TYPE LOCALITY: "Suro Rancho, Provincia Morona-Santiago, Ecuador, 2683 m."
DISTRIBUTION: Eastern face of the Cordillera Oriental east of Cuenca (Provincia Morono-Santiago, Ecuador) at elevations of 2195–2988 m.
COMMENT: In the *Eleutherodactylus unistrigatus* group. Forms a vicariant series with *Eleutherodactylus devillei* and *Eleutherodactylus surdus*, according to Lynch, 1976, Misc. Publ. Mus. Nat. Hist. Univ. Kansas, 66:12.

Eleutherodactylus batrachylus Taylor, 1940. Proc. New England Zool. Club, 18:13–16.
TYPE(S): Holotype: MCZ 9308.
TYPE LOCALITY: Miquihuana, Tamaulipas, Mexico.
DISTRIBUTION: Vicinity of the type locality.
COMMENT: *Eleutherodactylus batrachylus* is a replacement name for *Eleutherodactylus longipes* Barbour, 1923, Proc. New England Zool. Club, 8:81–83, which is preoccupied by *Batrachyla longipes* Baird (now = *Syrrhophus longipes*). In the *Eleutherodactylus unistrigatus* group of Lynch. Ford and Savage, 1984, Occas. Pap. Mus. Nat. Hist. Univ. Kansas, 110:7, questioned the assignment of the species to any group and regarded its inclusion in the *Eleutherodactylus unistrigatus* group as unlikely.

Eleutherodactylus berkenbuschii Peters, 1870. Monatsber. Preuss. Akad. Wiss. Berlin, 1869:879.
TYPE(S): Holotype: ZMB 6666.
TYPE LOCALITY: Mexico: Puebla: nr. Izucar de Matamoros.
DISTRIBUTION: Atlantic slopes of southern San Luis Potosí, Puebla, Veracruz, and eastern Oaxaca north of the Isthmus of Tehuantepec, Mexico.

COMMENT: In the *Eleutherodactylus fitzingeri* group. Removed from the synonymy of *Eleutherodactylus rugulosus* by Savage and De Weese, 1979, Bull. S. California Acad. Sci., 78:114, who included *Eleutherodactylus natator* Taylor, 1939, and *Eleutherodactylus vulcani* Shannon and Werler, 1955, as synonyms. Reviewed (as *Eleutherodactylus rugulosus*) by Savage, 1975, Copeia, 1975:270. See comment under *Eleutherodactylus brocchi*.

Eleutherodactylus bicolor Rueda and Lynch, 1983. Lozania, 42:2.
TYPE(S): Holotype: ICN 6190.
TYPE LOCALITY: "Cabaceras del río Luisito (afluente del río Oibita), Municipio de El Encino, Departamento de Santander, vertiente Occidental de la Cordillera Oriental de Colombia. Altura 1750 m. s. n. m."
DISTRIBUTION: Western slope of the Cordillera Oriental in Colombia at elevations of 1750–2200 m.
COMMENT: In the *Eleutherodactylus unistrigatus* group; close to *Eleutherodactylus cruentus*, according to the original description.

Eleutherodactylus bicumulus (Peters, 1863). Monatsber. Preuss. Akad. Wiss. Berlin, 1863:410.
ORIGINAL NAME: *Hylodes bicumulus*.
TYPE(S): Syntypes: ZMB 4899 (2 specimens).
TYPE LOCALITY: Caracas, Venezuela.
DISTRIBUTION: Vicinity of Caracas, Venezuela.
COMMENT: In the *Eleutherodactylus unistrigatus* group. Reviewed by Rivero, 1961, Bull. Mus. Comp. Zool., 126:70–71. See comments under *Eleutherodactylus racenisi*, *Eleutherodactylus rozei*, and *Eleutherodactylus williamsi*.

Eleutherodactylus bilineatus Bokermann, 1975 "1974". Rev. Brasil. Biol., 34:11.
TYPE(S): Holotype: WCAB 47137.
TYPE LOCALITY: "Centro de Pesquisas do Cacau, Ilhéus, Bahia, Brasil".
DISTRIBUTION: Known only from the type locality.
COMMENT: Placed in the *Eleutherodactylus fitzingeri* group by Lynch, 1976, Occas. Pap. Mus. Nat. Hist. Univ. Kansas, 61:10; subsequently not included in the group because of its obscure relationships (see Lynch and Myers, 1983, Bull. Am. Mus. Nat. Hist., 175:481–572).

Eleutherodactylus binotatus (Spix, 1824). Spec. Nov. Testud. Ran. Brasil.:31.
ORIGINAL NAME: *Rana binotata*.
TYPE(S): Holotype: ZSM 2695/0.
TYPE LOCALITY: Not stated.
DISTRIBUTION: Southeastern Brazil.
COMMENT: In the *Eleutherodactylus binotatus* group. Hoogmoed and Gruber, 1983, Spixiana, Suppl., 9:360, considered *Hyla abreviata* Spix, 1824, a synonym, and noted that this name has priority, because of the first revisor action of Wagler, 1830, Nat. Syst. Amph.:202. Hoogmoed and Gruber proposed to put the case before the International Commission of Zoological Nomenclature to conserve the current name. See comment under *Eleutherodactylus pliciferus*.

Eleutherodactylus biporcatus (Peters, 1863). Monatsber. Preuss. Akad. Wiss. Berlin, 1863:405.
ORIGINAL NAME: *Strabomantis biporcatus*.
TYPE(S): Lost.
TYPE LOCALITY: Veragoa [=Veragua], Panama.
DISTRIBUTION: Montañas del Mico, Guatemala, through low and moderate elevations (0–1000 m) to western Colombia.
COMMENT: In the *Eleutherodactylus biporcatus* group. Reviewed by Lynch, 1975, Occas. Pap. Mus. Nat. Hist. Univ. Kansas, 38:23–24.

Eleutherodactylus bockermanni Donoso-Barros, 1970. Bol. Soc. Biol. Concepción, 42:17.
TYPE(S): Holotype: Donoso-Barros 000765 (now IZUC).
TYPE LOCALITY: "Runerrabaque [=Rurrenabaque], Río Bení, Bení, Bolivia.
DISTRIBUTION: Known only from the type locality.
COMMENT: In the *Eleutherodactylus unistrigatus* group. The unjustified (but understandable) emendation of the name to *Eleutherodactylus bokermanni* was made by Lynch, 1976, Occas. Pap. Mus. Nat. Hist. Univ. Kansas, 61:1–24.

Eleutherodactylus boconoensis Rivero and Mayorga, 1973. Caribb. J. Sci., 13:75.
TYPE(S): Holotype: UPRM 04932.
TYPE LOCALITY: Páramo of Guaramacal, Boconó, Edo. Trujillo, Venezuela, 9400 ft.
DISTRIBUTION: Known only from the type locality.
COMMENT: In the *Eleutherodactylus unistrigatus* group.

Eleutherodactylus bocourti (Brocchi, 1877). Bull. Soc. Philomath. Paris, (7)1:130.
ORIGINAL NAME: *Hylodes bocourti.*
TYPE(S): Syntypes: MNHNP 6413–14, 6471 (total of 8 specimens); MNHNP 6413 designated lectotype by Guibé, 1950 "1948", Cat. Types Amph. Mus. Hist. Natl. Hist. Nat.:28.
TYPE LOCALITY: Cobán, [Alta Verapaz,] Guatemala.
DISTRIBUTION: Central Guatemala.

Eleutherodactylus bogotensis (Peters, 1863). Monatsber. Preuss. Akad. Wiss. Berlin, 1863:407.
ORIGINAL NAME: *Hylodes Bogotensis.*
TYPE(S): ZMB.
TYPE LOCALITY: Surroundings of St. Fé de Bogotá [Cundinamarca, Colombia].
DISTRIBUTION: Bogotá area, Colombia.
COMMENT: In the *Eleutherodactylus unistrigatus* assembly of the *Eleutherodactylus unistrigatus* group.

Eleutherodactylus bolbodactylus (A. Lutz, 1925). C. R. Séances Soc. Biol., Paris, 93:138.
ORIGINAL NAME: *Eupemphix bolbodactyla.*
TYPE(S): MN.
TYPE LOCALITY: Angra do Reis, Rio de Janeiro [Brazil].
DISTRIBUTION: Rio de Janeiro and São Paulo, Brazil.
COMMENT: In the *Eleutherodactylus lacteus* group.

Eleutherodactylus boulengeri Lynch, 1981. Occas. Pap. Mus. Zool. Univ. Michigan, 697:2.
TYPE(S): Holotype: UMMZ 166565.
TYPE LOCALITY: "3 km (airline) SW Cerro Munchique, Departamento de Cauca, Colombia, 2520 m."
DISTRIBUTION: Southern portions of the central Andes of Colombia (2540–2920 m) in high cloud forests; Cerro Munchique (2520 m) in the western Andes of Colombia.
COMMENT: In the *Eleutherodactylus unistrigatus* group.

Eleutherodactylus bransfordii (Cope, 1886). Proc. Am. Philos. Soc., 23:274.
ORIGINAL NAME: *Lithodytes bransfordii.*
TYPE(S): Syntypes: USNM 14179 (10 specimens); lectotype, renumbered USNM 166895, designated by Savage and Emerson, 1970, Copeia, 1970:636.
TYPE LOCALITY: Nicaragua.
DISTRIBUTION: Extreme eastern Honduras to eastern Panama, 0–1600 m; found in Costa Rica in the Atlantic lowlands and the cordilleras; found on Pacific drainages only in central Panama.
COMMENT: In the *Eleutherodactylus fitzingeri* group. Reviewed by Savage and Emerson, 1970, Copeia, 1970:623–644, who placed this species in the

Eleutherodactylus rhodopis group, and considered the following synonyms: *Hylodes polyptychus*, *Hylodes stejnegerianus*, *Hylodes underwoodi*, *Eleutherodactylus persimilis*, *Microbatrachylus rearki*, and *Microbatrachylus costaricensis*. Miyamoto, 1983, Syst. Zool., 32:43–51, studied biochemical variation, removed *Eleutherodactylus stejnegerianus* from synonymy and noted that the remaining nominal species, *Eleutherodactylus bransfordii*, was composed of two cryptic species.

Eleutherodactylus bresslerae Schwartz, 1960. Reading Public Mus. and Art Gallery Sci. Publ., 11:45.
TYPE(S): Holotype: AMNH 63432.
TYPE LOCALITY: Mouth of Río Yumurí, east side, Oriente [now Guantánamo] Province, Cuba.
DISTRIBUTION: Cuba; known from the type locality and "La Patana, Baracoa" in Guantánamo Province.
COMMENT: In the *Eleutherodactylus ricordii* group, according to Schwartz, 1976, Bull. Florida State Mus., Biol. Sci., 21:1–46.

Eleutherodactylus brevifrons Lynch, 1981 "1980". Occas. Pap. Mus. Zool. Univ. Michigan, 697:8.
TYPE(S): Holotype: UMMZ 166572.
TYPE LOCALITY: "15 km WNW Cali (=Cerro San Antonio (also known as TV tower mountain)), Departamento Valle del Cauca, Colombia, 2050 m"
DISTRIBUTION: High cloud forests (2060–2610 m) on the western slopes of the Cordillera Occidental in west-central Colombia.
COMMENT: In the *Eleutherodactylus unistrigatus* group, according to the original description.

Eleutherodactylus brevirostris Shreve, 1936. Proc. New England Zool. Club, 15:95.
TYPE(S): Holotype: MCZ 21557.
TYPE LOCALITY: "northern and eastern foothills, Massif de la Hotte, 1000–4000 ft [Département du Sud], Haiti".
DISTRIBUTION: Hispaniola; the Massif de la Hotte in Haiti, known from the type locality and south of Castillon, 3500–7698 ft.
COMMENT: In the *Eleutherodactylus ricordii* group. Reviewed by Schwartz, 1980, Cat. Am. Amph. Rept., 259.1.

Eleutherodactylus briceni (Boulenger, 1903). Ann. Mag. Nat. Hist., (7)11:481.
ORIGINAL NAME: *Hylodes briceni*.
TYPE(S): Syntypes: BM, NHMW 2287 (3 specimens), UMMZ 46471, MCZ 3888 and 7601.
TYPE LOCALITY: "Merida, Venezuela, at an altitude of 1600 metres".
DISTRIBUTION: Mérida Andes, Venezuela.
COMMENT: In the *Eleutherodactylus unistrigatus* group. Reviewed by Rivero, 1961, Bull. Mus. Comp. Zool., 126:56–57.

Eleutherodactylus brittoni Schmidt, 1920. Ann. New York Acad. Sci., 28:179.
TYPE(S): Holotype: AMNH 10318.
TYPE LOCALITY: El Yunque, near the Forester's Cabin, about 1300 feet altitude, Bosque Experimental de Luquillo, Puerto Rico.
DISTRIBUTION: Puerto Rico; known from scattered interior and upland localities, 50–2100 ft. elev.
COMMENT: In the *Eleutherodactylus auriculatus* group, according to Schwartz, 1969, Stud. Fauna Curaçao and other Caribb. Is., 30:99–115.

Eleutherodactylus brocchi (Boulenger, 1882). *In* Brocchi, Miss. Sci. Mex. Am. Cent.,
   3:60.
ORIGINAL NAME: *Hylodes brocchi.*
TYPE(S): Holotype: MHRN 2616.
TYPE LOCALITY: "Guatemala".
DISTRIBUTION: Cloud forests of Alta Verapaz and Baja Verapaz, Guatemala;
   northern highlands of Chiapas, Mexico.
COMMENT: In the *Eleutherodactylus fitzingeri* group. Reviewed by Savage, 1975,
   Copeia, 1975:279–280, who posited that *Eleutherodactylus vocalis* and
   Eleutherodactylus rugulosus (in the early sense of including *Eleutherodactylus
   berkenbuschii*) are the nearest relatives. See Johnson, Ely, and Webb, 1976,
   Trans. Kansas Acad. Sci., 79:133, for Mexican record.

Eleutherodactylus bromeliaceus Lynch, 1979. Misc. Publ. Mus. Nat. Hist. Univ. Kansas,
   66:12.
TYPE(S): Holotype: USNM 199731.
TYPE LOCALITY: "Between Sapote and Suro Rancho, Provincia Morona-Santiago,
   Ecuador, 2622 m."
DISTRIBUTION: Amazonian versant of the Cordillera de Matanga (Provincia
   Morona-Santiago, Ecuador), 1707–2622 m elev.
COMMENT: In the *Eleutherodactylus unistrigatus* group. Related to *Eleutherodactylus
   lacrimosus* and *Eleutherodactylus chalceus,* according to the original description.

Eleutherodactylus buckleyi (Boulenger, 1882). Cat. Batr. Sal. Brit. Mus.:217.
ORIGINAL NAME: *Hylodes buckleyi.*
TYPE(S): Syntypes: BM 78.1.25.40–44; BM 78.1.25.40 designated lectotype by Lynch,
   1981, Misc. Publ. Mus. Nat. Hist. Univ. Kansas, 72:4.
TYPE LOCALITY: "Intac", Provincia Imbabura, Ecuador.
DISTRIBUTION: Central Andes of Colombia south to the Nudo de Pasto; Western
   Andes in Ecuador; Eastern Andes of Ecuador south to Nevado Cayambe
   (2400–3700 m).
COMMENT: In the *Eleutherodactylus curtipes* assembly of the *Eleutherodactylus
   unistrigatus* group.

Eleutherodactylus bufoniformis (Boulenger, 1896). Ann. Mag. Nat. Hist., (6)17:19.
ORIGINAL NAME: *Hylodes bufoniformis.*
TYPE(S): Holotype: BM 1947.2.15.68 (formerly 95.11.6.54).
TYPE LOCALITY: Buenaventura, Colombia.
DISTRIBUTION: Southwestern Costa Rica to western Colombia.
COMMENT: In the *Eleutherodactylus biporcatus* group. Description amplified by
   Cochran and Goin, 1970, Bull. U.S. Natl. Mus., 288:375. Diagnosed by Lynch,
   1975, Occas. Pap. Mus. Nat. Hist. Univ. Kansas, 38:24–25.

Eleutherodactylus cabrerai Cochran and Goin, 1970. Bull. U.S. Natl. Mus., 288:399.
ORIGINAL NAME: *Eleutherodactylus surdus cabrerai.*
TYPE(S): Holotype: AMNH 14009.
TYPE LOCALITY: "Andes, Antioquia, Colombia".
DISTRIBUTION: Departamentos of Antioquia and Valle, Colombia.
COMMENT: In the *Eleutherodactylus unistrigatus* group. Elevated to species status by
   Lynch, 1976, Occas. Pap. Mus. Nat. Hist. Univ. Kansas, 61:1–24, and Lynch,
   1980, Proc. Biol. Soc. Washington, 93:327.

Eleutherodactylus cajamarcensis Barbour and Noble, 1920. Bull. Mus. Comp. Zool., 63:
   404.
TYPE(S): Holotype: MCZ 5407.
TYPE LOCALITY: Ruins near Huambos, Cajamarca, northwestern Peru.
DISTRIBUTION: Loja Basin of Ecuador, 1870–3000 m, and adjacent Peru.
COMMENT: In the *Eleutherodactylus unistrigatus* assembly of the *Eleutherodactylus
   unistrigatus* group.

Eleutherodactylus calcaratus (Boulenger, 1908). Ann. Mag. Nat. Hist., (8)2:516.
ORIGINAL NAME: *Hylodes calcaratus.*
TYPE(S): Holotype: BM 1947.2.15.53 (formerly 1909.4.30.49).
TYPE LOCALITY: San Antonio, Depto. Valle de Cauca, Colombia.
DISTRIBUTION: Cloud forests in western Colombia.
COMMENT: In the *Eleutherodactylus unistrigatus* group.

Eleutherodactylus calcarulatus Lynch, 1976. Occas. Pap. Mus. Nat. Hist. Univ. Kansas, 55:6.
TYPE(S): Holotype: KU 111218.
TYPE LOCALITY: "Tandapi, Prov. Pichincha, Ecuador, 1460 m."
DISTRIBUTION: Cloud forests of Pichincha and Imbabura provinces, Ecuador, and adjacent Nariño, Colombia.
COMMENT: In the *Eleutherodactylus unistrigatus* group. Probably most closely related to *Eleutherodactylus frater, Eleutherodactylus ockendeni,* and *Eleutherodactylus taeniatus* according to Lynch, 1976, Occas. Pap. Mus. Nat. Hist. Univ. Kansas, 55:7.

Eleutherodactylus caprifer Lynch, 1977. Copeia, 1977:282.
TYPE(S): Holotype: KU 131589.
TYPE LOCALITY: Las Palmas [=La Palma], Pichincha Province, Ecuador, 920 m.
DISTRIBUTION: Known from only four localities in southwestern Colombia and northwestern Ecuador, in an elevational range of 20–920 m.
COMMENT: In the *Eleutherodactylus fitzingeri* group. Reviewed by Lynch and Myers, 1983, Bull. Am. Mus. Nat. Hist., 175:521–523.

Eleutherodactylus carmelitae Ruthven, 1922. Misc. Publ. Mus. Zool. Univ. Michigan, 8:51.
TYPE(S): Holotype: UMMZ 54528.
TYPE LOCALITY: Quebrada Viernes Santo, 5000', San Lorenzo, Santa Marta Mts., Depto. Magdalena, Colombia.
DISTRIBUTION: Sierra Santa Marta, Colombia.
COMMENT: In the *Eleutherodactylus unistrigatus* group, according to Lynch, 1976, Occas. Pap. Mus. Nat. Hist. Univ. Kansas, 175:521–523. Subsequently placed in the *Eleutherodactylus fitzingeri* group by Lynch and Myers, 1983, Bull. Am. Mus. Nat. Hist., 175:521–523.

Eleutherodactylus carvalhoi B. Lutz, 1952. *In* Lutz and Kloss, Mem. Inst. Oswaldo Cruz, Rio de Janeiro, 50:642.
TYPE(S): MN.
TYPE LOCALITY: Itacoaí River, tributary of the Javari, Alto Solimões, Amazonas, Brazil.
DISTRIBUTION: Amazonian Brazil, Ecuador, and Peru.
COMMENT: In the *Eleutherodactylus unistrigatus* group. Distributional records and relationships discussed by Lynch and Lescure, 1980, Bull. Mus. Natl. Hist. Nat., Paris, (4)2:307.

Eleutherodactylus caryophyllaceus (Barbour, 1928). Proc. New England Zool. Club, 10:28.
ORIGINAL NAME: *Syrrhopus caryophyllaceus.*
TYPE(S): Holotype: MCZ 13039.
TYPE LOCALITY: La Loma, on the trail from Chiriquicito to Boquete, Bocas del Toro Province, Panama.
DISTRIBUTION: Southern Costa Rica to northwestern Colombia.
COMMENT: In the *Eleutherodactylus cruentus* group, according to Savage and DeWeese, 1981, Proc. Biol. Soc. Washington, 93:940, which was considered by Lynch, 1976, Occas. Pap. Mus. Nat. Hist. Univ. Kansas, 61:1–24, to be a subset of the *Eleutherodactylus unistrigatus* group.

Eleutherodactylus cavernicola Lynn, 1954. J. Washington Acad. Sci., 44:400.
TYPE(S): Holotype: USNM 135239.
TYPE LOCALITY: Portland Cave, Clarendon Parish, Jamaica.
DISTRIBUTION: Jamaica; known from the type locality and two caves near Jackson's
   Bay, Clarendon Parish.
COMMENT: In the *Eleutherodactylus ricordii* group according to Schwartz and Fowler,
   1973, Stud. Fauna Curaçao and other Caribb. Is., 43:155, and Crombie, 1977,
   Proc. Biol. Soc. Washington, 90:194–202.

Eleutherodactylus celator Lynch, 1976. Occas. Pap. Mus. Nat. Hist. Univ. Kansas, 55:22.
TYPE(S): Holotype: KU 131573.
TYPE LOCALITY: "La Delicia, Cordillera del Intac, Prov. Imbabura, Ecuador,
   2700 m."
DISTRIBUTION: High cloud forests (2500–2700 m) in northwestern Ecuador and
   southern Colombia.
COMMENT: In the *Eleutherodactylus unistrigatus* group. Most similar to
   Eleutherodactylus parvillus, according to the original description.

Eleutherodactylus cerasinus (Cope, 1876). J. Acad. Nat. Sci. Philadelphia, (2)8:112.
ORIGINAL NAME: *Hylodes cerasinus*.
TYPE(S): Holotype: USNM 32572.
TYPE LOCALITY: Eastern slope, Pico Blanco, Costa Rica.
DISTRIBUTION: Atlantic lowlands and premontane slopes of Nicaragua, Costa Rica,
   and Panama, onto both versants in western and central Panama (40–1300 m).
COMMENT: Reviewed by Savage, 1982, Proc. Biol. Soc. Washington, 94:413–420. In
   the *Eleutherodactylus cruentus* group, according to Savage, 1981, Proc. Biol. Soc.
   Washington, 93:940, which is regarded as a subset of the *Eleutherodactylus*
   unistrigatus group, by Lynch, 1976, Occas. Pap. Mus. Nat. Hist. Univ. Kansas,
   61:1–24.

Eleutherodactylus cerastes Lynch, 1975. Occas. Pap. Mus. Nat. Hist. Univ. Kansas,
   38:25.
TYPE(S): Holotype: USNM 195785.
TYPE LOCALITY: "Palma Real, Pichincha Prov., Ecuador".
DISTRIBUTION: Low to moderate elevations (500–1580 m) along the Pacific versant
   of Colombia and Ecuador.
COMMENT: In the *Eleutherodactylus biporcatus* group.

Eleutherodactylus chalceus (Peters, 1873). Monatsber. Preuss. Akad. Wiss. Berlin, 1873:
   609.
ORIGINAL NAME: *Phyllobates chalceus*.
TYPE(S): Lost, according to Lynch, 1980, Herpetologica, 36:179.
TYPE LOCALITY: Pastassa Valley, Colombia.
DISTRIBUTION: Western Colombia and Ecuador, 10–1540 m.
COMMENT: Transferred from *Syrrhophus* by Lynch, 1968, Herpetologica, 24:291.
   Synonymy includes *Syrrhopus areolatus* Boulenger, 1898, according to Lynch,
   1980, Herpetologica, 36:179. In the *Eleutherodactylus unistrigatus* group.

Eleutherodactylus chiastonotus Lynch and Hoogmoed, 1977. Proc. Biol. Soc.
   Washington, 90:425.
TYPE(S): Holotype: RMNH 17614.
TYPE LOCALITY: Brownsberg, Brokopondo District, Surinam, 500 m.
DISTRIBUTION: Low elevation forests in northeastern Brazil, French Guiana, and
   Surinam (below 700 m).
COMMENT: In the *Eleutherodactylus fitzingeri* group.

Eleutherodactylus chloronotus Lynch, 1970 "1969". J. Herpetol., 3:140.
  TYPE(S): Holotype: KU 117519.
  TYPE LOCALITY: "3 km E Papallacta, Provincia Napo, Ecuador, 2900 m."
  DISTRIBUTION: Subparamo and upper humid montane forest (2285–3350 m) along
    the eastern front of the Andes from southern Colombia (Nariño and
    Putumayo) southward to the Pastaza depression (Ecuador).
  COMMENT: In the *Eleutherodactylus unistrigatus* group. Reviewed by Lynch, 1980,
    Misc. Publ. Mus. Nat. Hist. Univ. Kansas, 69:11–18.

Eleutherodactylus chlorophenax Schwartz, 1976. Herpetologica, 32:168.
  TYPE(S): Holotype: CM 56833.
  TYPE LOCALITY: "≈ 2 km S Castillon, 1163 m, Département du Sud, Haiti".
  DISTRIBUTION: Known only from the type locality.
  COMMENT: In the *Eleutherodactylus inoptatus* group, according to the original
    description.

Eleutherodactylus cochranae Grant, 1932. J. Dep. Agr. Puerto Rico, 16:325.
  TYPE(S): Holotype: UMMZ 54528 (formerly C. Grant 5659); MCZ 18603–21
    regarded (in error) as syntypes by Barbour and Loveridge, 1946, Bull. Mus.
    Comp. Zool., 96:105.
  TYPE LOCALITY: "St. John", U.S. Virgin Islands; the putative syntypes all bear the
    datum "Hassel I., nr. St. Thomas".
  DISTRIBUTION: The Puerto Rico Bank; scattered localities in Puerto Rico as well as
    the islands of Vieques, Culebra, St. Thomas, Hassel, Bovoni Cay near St.
    Thomas, St. John, and Tortola, 0–1100 ft. elev.
  COMMENT: In the *Eleutherodactylus auriculatus* group, according to Schwartz, 1969,
    Fauna Curaçao and other Caribb. Is., 30:108. Rivero, 1963, Caribb. J. Sci., 3:81–
    85, discussed relationships with *Eleutherodactylus locustus* and distribution of
    species in Puerto Rico. See comment under *Eleutherodactylus ramosi*.

Eleutherodactylus colodactylus Lynch, 1979. Misc. Publ. Mus. Nat. Hist. Univ. Kansas,
    66:15.
  TYPE(S): Holotype: KU 142151.
  TYPE LOCALITY: "13.5 km E Loja, at the crest (Abra de Zamora) on the frontier
    between Loja and Zamora-Chinchipe provinces, Ecuador, 2800 m."
  DISTRIBUTION: High Amazonian slopes of the Andes in southern Ecuador at 2200–
    2850 m, and from the crest and Pacific versant of the Cordillera between
    Chanchaque and Huancabamba, Departamento Piurá, Peru, at 2745–3100 m.
  COMMENT: In the *Eleutherodactylus unistrigatus* group.

Eleutherodactylus colostichos La Marca and Smith, 1982. Occas. Pap. Mus. Zool. Univ.
    Michigan, 700:2.
  TYPE(S): Holotype: UMMZ 173044.
  TYPE LOCALITY: "Páramo de Los Conejos at the intersection of Quebrada Las
    Gonzales with the trail Manzano Alto–Las Gonzales, 2.5 hours on foot from
    the water pipe line known as 'Las Canalejas', Serranía del Norte, Estado
    Mérida, Venezuela".
  DISTRIBUTION: Serranía del Norte, Andes of Venezuela.
  COMMENT: In the *Eleutherodactylus unistrigatus* group.

Eleutherodactylus condor Lynch and Duellman, 1980. Misc. Publ. Mus. Nat. Hist.
    Univ. Kansas, 69:18.
  TYPE(S): Holotype: KU 146992.
  TYPE LOCALITY: "Río Piuntza, Cordillera del Condor, Provincia Morona-Santiago,
    Ecuador, 1830 m."
  DISTRIBUTION: Known only from the type locality.
  COMMENT: In the *Eleutherodactylus fitzingeri* group.

Eleutherodactylus conspicillatus (Günther, 1859 "1858"). Cat. Batr. Sal. Coll. Brit. Mus.:92.
ORIGINAL NAME: *Hylodes conspicillatus*.
TYPE(S): Holotype: BM 1947.2.16.20 (formerly 58.7.25.24).
TYPE LOCALITY: "Andes of Ecuador".
DISTRIBUTION: Colombia to Ecuador, western Brazil, and eastern Peru.
COMMENT: In the *Eleutherodactylus fitzingeri* group. See comment under *Eleutherodactylus peruvianus*. Reviewed by Lynch, 1975, Contrib. Sci. Nat. Hist. Mus. Los Angeles Co., 272:3–9. Distribution records given by Lynch and Lescure, 1980, Bull. Mus. Natl. Hist. Nat. Paris, (4)2:307.

Eleutherodactylus cooki Grant, 1932. J. Dep. Agr. Puerto Rico, 16:145.
TYPE(S): Holotype: UMMZ 73442 (formerly C. Grant 4108).
TYPE LOCALITY: Sierra de Panduras, southeastern Puerto Rico.
DISTRIBUTION: Southeastern Puerto Rico in the Sierra de Panduras region, west to the San Lorenzo–Patillas road.
COMMENT: In the *Eleutherodactylus auriculatus* group, according to Schwartz, 1969, Stud. Fauna Curaçao and other Caribb. Is., 30:101.

Eleutherodactylus coqui Thomas, 1966. Q. J. Florida Acad. Sci., 28:376.
TYPE(S): Holotype: MCZ 43208.
TYPE LOCALITY: 11.8 km S Palmer, Area Recreo La Mina, Puerto Rico.
DISTRIBUTION: Throughout Puerto Rico; introduced on St. Thomas and St. Croix, U.S. Virgin Islands, 0–3900 ft.; introduced in Florida and Louisiana, USA.
COMMENT: In the *Eleutherodactylus auriculatus* group, according to Schwartz, 1969, Stud. Fauna Curaçao and other Caribb. Is., 30:99–115. Introduced population in Miami, Florida, USA. Introduced population in Homestead, Florida, and New Orleans, Louisiana, USA, according to Rivero, 1984, J. Bromeliad Soc., 34:65.

Eleutherodactylus cornutus (Jiménez de la Espada, 1871). J. Sci. Math. Phys. Nat., Lisboa, 3:60.
ORIGINAL NAME: *Limnophys cornutus*.
TYPE(S): Not traced.
TYPE LOCALITY: "in Ecuador; ad ripas flum. Suno prope S. Jose de Moti"; rendered as Río Suno and San José de Moti, Ecuador, by Peters, 1955, Rev. Ecuat. Entomol. Parasitol., 3–4:346.
DISTRIBUTION: Moderate elevations (1150–1800 m) along the eastern face of the Andes from southern Colombia to southern Ecuador.
COMMENT: According to Lynch, 1975, Occas. Pap. Mus. Nat. Hist. Univ. Kansas, 38: 30, the name of this species has been broadly misapplied. In the *Eleutherodactylus biporcatus* group. Most closely related to *Eleutherodactylus biporcatus* and *Eleutherodactylus cerastes* according to Lynch, 1980, Misc. Publ. Mus. Nat. Hist. Univ. Kansas, 69:21.

Eleutherodactylus cosnipatae Duellman, 1978. Proc. Biol. Soc. Washington, 91:419.
TYPE(S): Holotype: KU 162298.
TYPE LOCALITY: "Río Cosñipata, 4 km SW Santa Isabel, 1,700 m, Departamento Cuzco, Perú (13° 05' S; 71° 18' W)".
DISTRIBUTION: Known only from the type locality.
COMMENT: In the *Eleutherodactylus unistrigatus* group, according to the original description.

Eleutherodactylus counouspeus Schwartz, 1964. Breviora, 208:2.
TYPE(S): Holotype: MCZ 43199.
TYPE LOCALITY: "Grotte de Counou Bois, 1 mi (1.6 km) southwest of Perrin, Dépt. du Sud, Haiti".
DISTRIBUTION: Hispaniola; Tiburon Peninsula and Massif de la Hotte, Haiti.

COMMENT: In the *Eleutherodactylus ricordii* group, according to the original
description. Reviewed by Schwartz, 1980, Cat. Am. Amph. Rept., 260.1–2.

Eleutherodactylus crassidigitus Taylor, 1952. Univ. Kansas Sci. Bull., 35:740.
TYPE(S): Holotype: KU 28369.
TYPE LOCALITY: "Isla Bonita, eastern slope Volcán Poás", Costa Rica.
DISTRIBUTION: Northern Costa Rica south and east through Panama to the
Colombian border, 10–2000 m.
COMMENT: In the *Eleutherodactylus fitzingeri* group. Reviewed by Lynch and Myers,
1983, Bull. Am. Mus. Nat. Hist., 175:523–530, who noted that this species may
be the sister-species of *Eleutherodactylus longirostris* plus *Eleutherodactylus
talamancae*, and may contain unrecognized sibling species.

Eleutherodactylus cremnobates Lynch and Duellman, 1980. Misc. Publ. Mus. Nat. Hist.
Univ. Kansas, 69:21.
TYPE(S): Holotype: KU 166036.
TYPE LOCALITY: "2 km SSW Río Reventador (Quito–Lago Agrio road), Provincia
Napo, Ecuador, 1490 m"
DISTRIBUTION: Known from three localities between 1410 and 1700 m on the
eastern face of the Cordillera Oriental drained by the Río Coca, Ecuador.
COMMENT: In the *Eleutherodactylus unistrigatus* group, according to the original
description.

Eleutherodactylus crenunguis Lynch, 1976. Occas. Pap. Mus. Nat. Hist. Univ. Kansas,
55:2.
TYPE(S): Holotype: KU 120126.
TYPE LOCALITY: "Tandapi, Prov. Pichincha, Ecuador, 1460 m."
DISTRIBUTION: Known only from the type locality.
COMMENT: In the *Eleutherodactylus rubicundus* assembly of the *Eleutherodactylus
unistrigatus* group, according to Lynch and Miyata, 1980, Breviora, 457:11.

Eleutherodactylus croceoinguinis Lynch, 1968. J. Herpetol., 2:133.
TYPE(S): Holotype: KU 110789.
TYPE LOCALITY: "Santa Cecilia, Napo, Ecuador, 340 meters".
DISTRIBUTION: Lowland Amazonian rainforests of Ecuador and adjacent Colombia
but penetrating into low cloud forest at the base of the Pastaza trench.
COMMENT: In the *Eleutherodactylus unistrigatus* group. Reviewed by Lynch, 1980,
Misc. Publ. Mus. Nat. Hist. Univ. Kansas, 69:24.

Eleutherodactylus crucifer (Boulenger, 1899). Ann. Mag. Nat. Hist., (7)4:456.
ORIGINAL NAME: *Hylodes crucifer*.
TYPE(S): Holotype: BM 1947.2.16.91 (formerly 1899.10.30.40).
TYPE LOCALITY: Porvenir, [Provincia] Bolívar, 5800 ft., Ecuador.
DISTRIBUTION: Known only from near Tandapi and the type locality, in cloud
forest habitats at 1460–1760 m.
COMMENT: In the *Eleutherodactylus unistrigatus* group.

Eleutherodactylus cruentus (Peters, 1873). Monatsber. Preuss. Akad. Wiss. Berlin, 1873:
609.
ORIGINAL NAME: *Hylodes cruentus*.
TYPE(S): Holotype: ZMB 7811.
TYPE LOCALITY: Chiriqui, Panama [see comment under *Dendrobates maculatus*].
DISTRIBUTION: Humid forest in the premontane zone on both slopes of Costa Rica
and western Panama; scattered lowland records in eastern and southwestern
Costa Rica into central Panama (40–1550 m) (according to Savage, 1981, Proc.
Biol. Soc. Washington, 94:416); to western Ecuador (according to Lynch, 1979,
In Duellman (ed.), Monogr. Mus. Nat. Hist. Univ. Kansas, 7:212).
COMMENT: Lynch, 1979, Misc. Publ. Mus. Nat. Hist. Univ. Kansas, 66:32, noted that

the frog regarded as *Eleutherodactylus cruentus* by Cochran and Goin, 1970, Bull. U.S. Natl. Mus., 288:426, was unnamed. Reviewed by Savage, 1981, Proc. Biol. Soc. Washington, 94:413–420. In the *Eleutherodactylus unistrigatus* group. In the less inclusive *Eleutherodactylus cruentus* group of Savage, 1981, Proc. Biol. Soc. Washington, 94:413, who included *Eleutherodactylus dubitus* Taylor, 1952, and *Eleutherodactylus marshae* Lynch, 1964, as synonyms.

Eleutherodactylus cruralis (Boulenger, 1902). Ann. Mag. Nat. Hist., (7)10:396.
ORIGINAL NAME: *Hylodes cruralis*.
TYPE(S): Holotype: BM 1947.2.15.70 (formerly 1901.8.2.44).
TYPE LOCALITY: "La Paz, Bolivia, 4000 m."
DISTRIBUTION: Known only from the type locality.
COMMENT: In the *Eleutherodactylus discoidalis* group.

Eleutherodactylus cryophilius Lynch, 1979. Misc. Publ. Mus. Nat. Hist. Univ. Kansas, 66:19.
TYPE(S): Holotype: USNM 199993.
TYPE LOCALITY: "6 km W San Vicente, Provincia Morona-Santiago, Ecuador, 3110 m."
DISTRIBUTION: Known from subpáramo and páramo habitats east and west of Cuenca (Morona-Santiago, Ecuador), 2835–3384 m.
COMMENT: In the *Eleutherodactylus curtipes* assembly of the *Eleutherodactylus unistrigatus* group.

Eleutherodactylus cryptomelas Lynch, 1979. Misc. Publ. Mus. Nat. Hist. Univ. Kansas, 66:21.
TYPE(S): Holotype: KU 141992.
TYPE LOCALITY: "15 km E Loja, Provincia Zamora-Chinchipe, Ecuador, 2710 m".
DISTRIBUTION: 2470–3100 m elevation on the eastern Andean Cordillera of southern Ecuador.
COMMENT: In the *Eleutherodactylus unistrigatus* group.

Eleutherodactylus cuaquero Savage, 1980. Bull. S. California Acad. Sci., 79:14.
TYPE(S): Holotype: LACM 128460.
TYPE LOCALITY: "1.75 km east southeast of Monteverde; Provincia Puntarenas, Canton de Puntarenas, Costa Rica; 1520 m".
DISTRIBUTION: Known only from the type locality in lower montane rainforest in the Cordillera de Tilarán, Puntarenas, Costa Rica.
COMMENT: In the *Eleutherodactylus fitzingeri* group. This group as envisioned by Savage, 1980, Bull. S. California Acad. Sci., 79:15, is more restricted than that by Lynch.

Eleutherodactylus cubanus Barbour, 1942. Copeia, 1942:179.
TYPE(S): Holotype: MCZ 21947.
TYPE LOCALITY: Cueva del Aura, ca. 3500 feet, Oriente [now Santiago de Cuba] Province, Cuba.
DISTRIBUTION: Known only from the type locality.
COMMENT: *Eleutherodactylus cubanus* is a replacement name for *Eleutherodactylus parvus* Barbour and Shreve, 1937, Bull. Mus. Comp. Zool. 80:386. In the *Eleutherodactylus varleyi* group, according to Shreve and Williams, 1963, Bull. Mus. Comp. Zool., 129:339. In the *Eleutherodactylus dimidiatus* group, according to Schwartz, 1958, Am. Mus. Novit., 1873:2.

Eleutherodactylus cundalli Dunn, 1926. Proc. Boston Soc. Nat. Hist., 38:121.
TYPE(S): Holotype: MCZ 11126.
TYPE LOCALITY: Spaldings, Clarendon Parish, Jamaica.
DISTRIBUTION: Jamaica; widespread.
COMMENT: In the *Eleutherodactylus ricordii* group according to Schwartz and Fowler,

1976, Stud. Fauna Curaçao and other Caribb. Is., 43:134, who considered
Eleutherodactylus lynni a synonym; see also Crombie, 1977, Proc. Biol. Soc.
Washington, 90:194–204.

Eleutherodactylus cuneatus (Cope, 1862). Proc. Acad. Nat. Sci. Philadelphia, 14:152.
ORIGINAL NAME: *Hylodes cuneatus.*
TYPE(S): Syntypes: USNM 5202 (2 specimens).
TYPE LOCALITY: Eastern Cuba.
DISTRIBUTION: Islandwide on Cuba; Isla de Pinos (=Isla de Juventud).
COMMENT: In the *Eleutherodactylus orcutti* group, but transitional to the
Eleutherodactylus ricordii group, according to Shreve and Williams, 1963, Bull.
Mus. Comp. Zool., 129:326–327. Schwartz, 1967, Stud. Fauna Curaçao and
other Caribb. Is., 91:56, and Crombie, 1977, Proc. Biol. Soc. Washington, 90:
194–204, did not recognize the *Eleutherodactylus orcutti* group. In the
Eleutherodactylus ricordii group, according to Schwartz, 1958, Am. Mus. Novit.,
1873:2.

Eleutherodactylus curtipes (Boulenger, 1882). Cat. Batr. Sal. Brit. Mus.:218.
ORIGINAL NAME: *Hylodes curtipes.*
TYPE(S): Syntypes: BM 78.1.25.29–36, of which 3 exchanged to WCAB, MSNG, and
USNM (now USNM 789); BM 78.1.25.29 designated lectotype by Lynch, 1981,
Misc. Publ. Mus. Nat. Hist. Univ. Kansas, 72:7.
TYPE LOCALITY: "Intac", Provincia Imbabura, Ecuador.
DISTRIBUTION: Elevations of 2750–4400 m in the Andes of Colombia and in the
western and eastern Andes of Ecuador south to the Desierto de Palmira.
COMMENT: Includes *Hylodes whymperi* Boulenger, 1882, and *Hyla chimboe* Fowler,
1913, according to Lynch, 1981, Misc. Publ. Mus. Nat. Hist. Univ. Kansas, 72:
7, who also described geographic variation. In the *Eleutherodactylus curtipes*
assembly of the *Eleutherodactylus unistrigatus* group.

Eleutherodactylus danae Duellman, 1978. Proc. Biol. Soc. Washington, 91:422.
TYPE(S): Holotype: KU 162307.
TYPE LOCALITY: "Río Cosñipata, 4 km (by road) SW of Santa Isabel, Departamento
Cuzco, Perú, 1,700 m (13° 05′ S; 71° 18′ W)".
DISTRIBUTION: Elevations of 1270–1700 m in the Cosñipata Valley on the lower
Andean slopes in southern Peru.
COMMENT: In the *Eleutherodactylus unistrigatus* group, according to the original
description.

Eleutherodactylus darlingtoni Cochran, 1935. Proc. Boston Soc. Nat. Hist., 40:368.
TYPE(S): Holotype: MCZ 19847.
TYPE LOCALITY: "near La Visite, La Selle Range, [Département l'Ouest,] Haiti".
DISTRIBUTION: Hispaniola; Massif de la Selle in Haiti, known from the type locality
and the ridge of the La Selle on the road to Saltrou, presumably distributed
in the Massif de la Selle; to be expected in the Dominican Republic between
Los Arroyos and El Aguacate, 5000–7000 ft.
COMMENT: In the *Eleutherodactylus ricordii* group, according to Shreve and Williams,
1963, Bull. Mus. Comp. Zool., 129:328, and Schwartz, 1973, J. Herpetol., 7:
271–272. Reviewed by Schwartz, 1982, Cat. Am. Amph. Rept., 284.1.

Eleutherodactylus daryi Ford and Savage, 1984. Occas. Pap. Mus. Nat. Hist. Univ.
Kansas, 110:1.
TYPE(S): Holotype: KU 186202.
TYPE LOCALITY: "3.8 km (by road) SE Puruhlá, Baja Verapaz, Guatemala, 1585 m".
DISTRIBUTION: Cloud forest of the Sierra Xucaneb and Sierra de las Minas, central
Guatemala.
COMMENT: In the *Eleutherodactylus omiltemanus* group; see comment under
Eleutherodactylus omiltemanus.

Eleutherodactylus decoratus Taylor, 1942. Univ. Kansas Sci. Bull., 28:299.
TYPE(S): Holotype: FMNH 100115 (formerly EHT-HMS 28720).
TYPE LOCALITY: "near Banderia [=Banderilla], 6 miles west of Jalapa, Veracruz", Mexico.
DISTRIBUTION: Southern Tamaulipas to central Veracruz, Mexico.
COMMENT: In the *Eleutherodactylus alfredi* group, with two geographic races according to Lynch, 1967, Trans. Illinois State Acad. Sci., 60:299-304.

Eleutherodactylus delicatus Ruthven, 1917. Occas. Pap. Mus. Zool. Univ. Michigan, 43:1.
TYPE(S): Holotype: UMMZ 50159.
TYPE LOCALITY: "San Lorenzo (5000 ft.), Santa Marta Mountains, Colombia".
DISTRIBUTION: Sierra Santa Marta, Colombia.
COMMENT: In the *Eleutherodactylus unistrigatus* group.

Eleutherodactylus devillei (Boulenger, 1880). Bull. Soc. Zool. France, 5:47.
ORIGINAL NAME: *Hylodes de Villei*.
TYPE(S): Holotype: MRHN 1009.
TYPE LOCALITY: "Andes of Ecuador".
DISTRIBUTION: Upper montane forests and clearings on the eastern slopes of the Andes in Napo Province, Ecuador, 2350-3155 m.
COMMENT: In the *Eleutherodactylus unistrigatus* group. Lynch, 1969, J. Herpetol., 3: 135-138, discussed the identity of this species.

Eleutherodactylus diadematus (Jiménez de la Espada, 1875). Vert. Viaj. Pacif., Batr.: pl. 3.
ORIGINAL NAME: *Hylodes diadematus*.
TYPE(S): Lost.
TYPE LOCALITY: Not stated.
DISTRIBUTION: Amazonian Ecuador and Peru.
COMMENT: In the *Eleutherodactylus unistrigatus* group. Includes *Eleutherodactylus bufonius* according to Lynch and Schwartz, 1972, J. Herpetol., 5:103-114.

Eleutherodactylus diastema (Cope, 1876). J. Acad. Nat. Sci. Philadelphia, (2)8:155.
ORIGINAL NAME: *Lithodytes diastema*.
TYPE(S): Syntypes: USNM 25170-71; USNM 25171 considered to be *Eleutherodactylus ockendeni* (=*Eleutherodactylus taeniatus*) by E. R. Dunn, according to Cochran, 1961, Bull. U.S. Natl. Mus., 220:65.
TYPE LOCALITY: Camp Mary Caretta, Panama.
DISTRIBUTION: Nicaragua south through Central America and western Colombia to Ecuador.
COMMENT: In the *Eleutherodactylus unistrigatus* group. See comment under *Eleutherodactylus moro*.

Eleutherodactylus dimidiatus (Cope, 1862). Proc. Acad. Nat. Sci. Philadelphia, 14:151.
ORIGINAL NAME: *Hylodes dimidiatus*.
TYPE(S): Holotype: USNM 5099 (?), now lost?
TYPE LOCALITY: Eastern Cuba.
DISTRIBUTION: Cuba; widespread.
COMMENT: In the *Eleutherodactylus dimidiatus* group, with two subspecies, according to Schwartz, 1958, Am. Mus. Novit., 1873:2; also see Shreve and Williams, 1963, Bull. Mus. Comp. Zool., 129:338, and Schwartz, 1973, Stud. Fauna Curaçao and other Caribb. Is., 43:135-136.

Eleutherodactylus discoidalis (Peracca, 1895). Boll. Mus. Zool. Anat. Comp. Univ. Torino, 10:124.
ORIGINAL NAME: *Hylodes discoidalis*.
TYPE(S): Syntypes: "several" in MSNT, BM 1947.2.15.63-65 (formerly 94.12.31.2-4).
TYPE LOCALITY: Tucumán, Argentina.
DISTRIBUTION: Jujuy to Tucumán (Argentina) in subtropical forest.

COMMENT: In the *Eleutherodactylus discoidalis* group. Reviewed by Cei, 1980, Monit. Zool. Ital., N.S., Monogr., 2:311–312.

Eleutherodactylus dolops Lynch and Duellman, 1980. Misc. Publ. Mus. Nat. Hist. Univ. Kansas, 69:26.
TYPE(S): Holotype: KU 143505.
TYPE LOCALITY: "Salto de Agua, 2.5 km NNE Río Reventador, Provincia Napo, Ecuador, 1660 m."
DISTRIBUTION: Elevation of 1440–1950 m on the eastern face of the Andes in Putumayo (Colombia) and Napo (Ecuador).
COMMENT: In the *Eleutherodactylus discoidalis* group.

Eleutherodactylus duellmani Lynch, 1980. Proc. Biol. Soc. Washington, 93:332.
TYPE(S): Holotype: USNM 179325.
TYPE LOCALITY: Quebrada Zapadores, 5 km ESE Chiriboga, Prov. Pichincha, Ecuador, 1920 m.
DISTRIBUTION: High cloud forests (1920–2700 m) in northwestern Ecuador and southwestern Colombia.
COMMENT: In the *Eleutherodactylus surdus* assembly of the *Eleutherodactylus unistrigatus* group, according to the original description.

Eleutherodactylus eileenae Dunn, 1926. Occas. Pap. Boston Soc. Nat. Hist., 5:212.
TYPE(S): Holotype: MCZ 11128.
TYPE LOCALITY: Mina Carlota, Las Villas [now Sancti Spíritus] Province, Cuba.
DISTRIBUTION: Cuba, from Pinar del Río Province east throughout Camagüey Province; an isolated and questionable record from Pico Turquino, Oriente (now Santiago de Cuba) Province (UMMZ 80910).
COMMENT: In the *Eleutherodactylus auriculatus* group, according to Schwartz, 1958, Am. Mus. Novit., 1873:2, and Schwartz, 1965, Herpetologica, 21:28–31.

Eleutherodactylus elassodiscus Lynch, 1973. Copeia, 1973:222.
TYPE(S): Holotype: USNM 167668.
TYPE LOCALITY: "Cuyuja, Napo Province, Ecuador, 2830 m."
DISTRIBUTION: Intermediate elevations (2300–2900 m) on the Amazonian slopes of Andes in Ecuador and southern Colombia.
COMMENT: In the *Eleutherodactylus discoidalis* group.

Eleutherodactylus elegans (Peters, 1863). Monatsber. Preuss. Akad. Wiss. Berlin, 1863: 347.
ORIGINAL NAME: *Liuperus elegans*.
TYPE(S): ZMB.
TYPE LOCALITY: Mountainous surroundings of Bogotá [Colombia].
DISTRIBUTION: Bogotá region of Colombia.
COMMENT: In the *Eleutherodactylus unistrigatus* group.

Eleutherodactylus emiliae Dunn, 1926. Occas. Pap. Boston Soc. Nat. Hist., 5:213.
TYPE(S): Holotype: MCZ 11129.
TYPE LOCALITY: Mina Carlota, Las Villas [now Sancti Spíritus] Province, Cuba.
DISTRIBUTION: Cuba; known only from the type locality in the Sierra de Trinidad.
COMMENT: In the *Eleutherodactylus dimidiatus* group, according to Schwartz, 1958, Am. Mus. Novit., 1873:2, and Shreve and Williams, 1963, Bull. Mus. Comp. Zool., 129:338.

Eleutherodactylus eneidae Rivero, 1959. Breviora, 103:4.
TYPE(S): Holotype: MCZ 30429.
TYPE LOCALITY: Doña Juana Forest, Villalba, Puerto Rico.
DISTRIBUTION: Interior uplands of Puerto Rico, from 8.5 mi. north of Sabana Grande in the west to the Bosque Experimental de Luquillo in the east, 1000–3800 ft. elev.

COMMENT: In the *Eleutherodactylus auriculatus* group, according to Schwartz, 1969, Stud. Fauna Curaçao and other Caribb. Is., 30:101.

Eleutherodactylus epipedus Heyer, 1984. Smithson. Contrib. Zool., 402:22.
TYPE(S): Holotype: MZUSP 59633.
TYPE LOCALITY: "Brazil: Espirito Santo; adjacent to Parque Nova Lombardia, near Santa Teresa".
DISTRIBUTION: Known only from Santa Teresa, Espírito Santo, Brazil.
COMMENT: In the *Eleutherodactulus guentheri* cluster of species, according to the original description. See comment under *Eleutherodactylus guentheri*.

Eleutherodactylus eremitus Lynch, 1980. Breviora, 462:2.
TYPE(S): Holotype: MCZ 92103.
TYPE LOCALITY: "La Palma–Chiriboga road (hwy. 28), 25.7 km above (NE) La Palma, Prov. Pichincha, Ecuador, 1820 m."
DISTRIBUTION: Cloud forests along the Mindo, Pilatón, and Saloya rivers in Pichincha Province, Ecuador, 1540–2100 m.
COMMENT: In the *Eleutherodactylus unistrigatus* group, *Eleutherodactylus lacrimosus* assembly, according to the original description.

Eleutherodactylus eriphus Lynch and Duellman, 1980. Misc. Publ. Mus. Nat. Hist. Univ. Kansas, 69:28.
TYPE(S): Holotype: KU 166031.
TYPE LOCALITY: "Río Jatuntinahua, 10 km SE Cuyujúa, Provincia Napo, Ecuador, 2160 m."
DISTRIBUTION: Valley of the Río Papallacta on the eastern face of the Andes in Napo Province, Ecuador, and Intendencia Putumayo, Colombia, 2160–2630 m.
COMMENT: In the *Eleutherodactylus crucifer* assembly of the *Eleutherodactylus unistrigatus* group, according to the original description.

Eleutherodactylus erythromerus Heyer, 1984. Smithson. Contrib. Zool., 402:24.
TYPE(S): Holotype: MZUSP 59640.
TYPE LOCALITY: "Brazil: Rio de Janeiro; near Teresópolis (Alto do Soberbo, 5 km NE junction BR 116 and Teresópolis bypass)".
DISTRIBUTION: Known only from the vicinity of Teresópolis, Rio de Janeiro, Brazil.
COMMENT: In the *Eleutherodactylus guentheri* cluster of species according to the original description. See comment under *Eleutherodactylus guentheri*.

Eleutherodactylus erythropleura (Boulenger, 1896). Ann. Mag. Nat. Hist., (6)17:20.
ORIGINAL NAME: *Hylodes erythropleura*.
TYPE(S): Holotype: BM 1947.2.16.95 (formerly 95.11.16.55).
TYPE LOCALITY: Cali, Colombia.
DISTRIBUTION: Cordillera Occidental and the northern half of the Cordillera Central of Colombia.
COMMENT: In the *Eleutherodactylus unistrigatus* group.

Eleutherodactylus escoces Savage, 1975. Copeia, 1975:280.
TYPE(S): Holotype: LACM 76857.
TYPE LOCALITY: "Costa Rica: Provincia de Heredia: Canton de San Rafael: south slope of Volcan Barba: E margin Alto de Roble, 0.5 km N Cerro Chompipe, nr. Rio Las Vueltas: 2030 m."
DISTRIBUTION: Premontane and lower montane evergreen forest (1100–2100 m) on the volcanos Barba, Irazú, and Turrialba, Costa Rica.
COMMENT: In the *Eleutherodactylus fitzingeri* group. See comment under *Eleutherodactylus angelicus*.

Eleutherodactylus etheridgei Schwartz, 1958. Am. Mus. Novit., 1873:16.
TYPE(S): Holotype: UMMZ 110180.
TYPE LOCALITY: United States Naval Base, Guantanamo Bay, Oriente [now Guantánamo] Province, Cuba.
DISTRIBUTION: Cuba; known from the type locality and Santiago de Cuba.

COMMENT: In the *Eleutherodactylus ricordii* group, according to Schwartz, 1958, Am. Mus. Novit., 1873:16.

Eleutherodactylus eunaster Schwartz, 1973. J. Herpetol., 7:250.
TYPE(S): Holotype: USNM 189254.
TYPE LOCALITY: "Castillon, *ca.* 2500 feet (763 m), Département de Sud, Haiti".
DISTRIBUTION: Hispaniola; known from the region of the type locality, 25 mi. north of Les Cayes on the road between Les Cayes and Jérémie, and Saint Cyr, 1900–3800 ft. elev.
COMMENT: Most closely related to *Eleutherodactylus glanduliferoides*, according to the original description, and thus associated with the *Eleutherodactylus varleyi* group of Shreve and Williams, 1963, Bull. Mus. Comp. Zool., 129:339–341. Reviewed by Schwartz, 1982, Cat. Am. Amph. Rept., 285.1.

Eleutherodactylus fenestratus (Steindachner, 1864). Verh. Zool. Bot. Ges. Wien, 14:249.
ORIGINAL NAME: *Hylodes fenestratus*.
TYPE(S): Syntypes: NHMW 19940.1 (Río Mamoré) and 19940.2 (Borba).
TYPE LOCALITY: Rio Mamoré, [Estado de Rondônia,] Brazil, and Borba, [Estado do Amazonas,] Brazil.
DISTRIBUTION: Amazon Basin of Peru and Bolivia to southern Guyana and central Brazil.
COMMENT: In the *Eleutherodactylus fitzingeri* group. Includes *Eleutherodactylus gollmeri bisignatus* Werner, 1899, and *Eleutherodactylus crepitans* Bokermann, 1965, according to Lynch, 1980, Am. Mus. Novit., 2696:6, who reviewed this species and removed it from the synonymy of *Eleutherodactylus griseus*.

Eleutherodactylus fitzingeri (Schmidt, 1858). Denkschr. Akad. Wiss. Wien, Math. Naturwiss. Kl., 14:248.
ORIGINAL NAME: *Hylodes fitzingeri*.
TYPE(S): Holotype: KM 1012/1343, lost; LACM 76859 designated neotype by Savage, 1974, Herpetologica, 30:298; Lynch and Myers, 1983, Bull. Am. Mus. Nat. Hist., 175:530, discussed reasons for rejecting the neotype designation.
TYPE LOCALITY: Mountains of New Grenada [western Panama]; neotype from "Panamá: Canal Zone: Barro Colorado Island, near the laboratory".
DISTRIBUTION: Humid lowlands and lower montane forest (0–1200 m) from eastern Nicaragua south and east throughout both Atlantic and Pacific versant of Costa Rica and Panama, and into northwestern Colombia in the inter-Andean valleys and in the Chocoan lowlands as far south as the Bay of Buenaventura.
COMMENT: In the *Eleutherodactylus fitzingeri* group. Reviewed by Savage, 1974, Herpetologica, 30:298, and Lynch and Myers, 1983, Bull. Am. Mus. Nat. Hist., 175:530–537.

Eleutherodactylus flavescens Noble, 1923. Am. Mus. Novit., 61:2.
TYPE(S): Holotype: AMNH 11402.
TYPE LOCALITY: "bushes along stream bank, La Bracita [=Los Bracitos], Prov. Pacificador [=Duarte Province], Dominican Republic".
DISTRIBUTION: Hispaniola; eastern Dominican Republic.
COMMENT: In the *Eleutherodactylus auriculatus* group, according to Schwartz, 1969, Stud. Fauna Curaçao and other Caribb. Is., 30:101. Reviewed by Schwartz, 1982, Cat. Am. Amph. Rept., 296.1–2.

Eleutherodactylus fleischmanni (Boettger, 1892). Kat. Batr. Samml. Mus. Senckenb. Naturforsch. Ges.:27.
ORIGINAL NAME: *Hylodes fleischmanni*.
TYPE(S): SMF 3778 (formerly 1200.2a) designated lectotype by Mertens, 1967, Senckenb. Biol., 48:39.
TYPE LOCALITY: San José, Costa Rica.
DISTRIBUTION: Elevations of 1050–2300 m in Costa Rica and western Panama.

COMMENT: In the *Eleutherodactylus fitzingeri* group. Reviewed by Savage, 1975, Copeia, 1975:282–284, who suggested that the nearest relatives are *Eleutherodactylus angelicus* and *Eleutherodactylus escoces*.

Eleutherodactylus fowleri Schwartz, 1973. J. Herpetol., 7:255.
TYPE(S): Holotype: USNM 189255.
TYPE LOCALITY: "1.5 mi. (2.4 km) N Los Arroyos, 4300 ft (1312 m), Pedernales Province, República Dominicana".
DISTRIBUTION: Hispaniola; known from the vicinity of the type locality (Dominican Republic) and 4.8 mi. southwest of Seguin, Département de l'Ouest, Haiti.
COMMENT: In the *Eleutherodactylus auriculatus* group, according to the original description. Reviewed by Schwartz, 1982, Cat. Am. Amph. Rept., 297.1.

Eleutherodactylus frater (Werner, 1899). Verh. Zool. Bot. Ges. Wien, 49:479.
ORIGINAL NAME: *Hylodes frater*.
TYPE(S): Holotype: ZFMK 67/235; now lost, according to Böhme and Bischoff, 1984, Bonn. Zool. Monogr., 19:168.
TYPE LOCALITY: Peperital, Departamento Meta, Colombia.
DISTRIBUTION: Eastern slopes of the Cordillera Oriental of the Departamentos of Cundinamarca and Meta and from the Serranía de la Macarena, Colombia.
COMMENT: In the *Eleutherodactylus unistrigatus* group of Lynch. In the less inclusive *Eleutherodactylus cruentus* group of Savage and DeWeese, 1980, Proc. Biol. Soc. Washington, 93:940.

Eleutherodactylus furcyensis Shreve and Williams, 1963. Bull. Mus. Comp. Zool., 129: 329.
TYPE(S): Holotype: MCZ 34307.
TYPE LOCALITY: "Furcy, [Département de l'Ouest,] Republic of Haiti".
DISTRIBUTION: Southern Hispaniola in the region of the Massif de la Selle to the western Sierra de Baoruco.
COMMENT: In the *Eleutherodactylus ricordii* group, according to the original description. Reviewed by Schwartz, 1983, Cat. Am. Amph. Rept., 309.1.

Eleutherodactylus fuscus Lynn and Dent, 1943. Copeia, 1943:235.
TYPE(S): Holotype: USNM 115976.
TYPE LOCALITY: Dolphin Head, Westmoreland Parish, Jamaica.
DISTRIBUTION: Western Jamaica; known from restricted inland portions of Hanover, Westmoreland, St. James, and St. Elizabeth parishes, 400–2250 ft. elev.
COMMENT: In the *Eleutherodactylus gossei* group according to Goin, 1954, Ann. Carnegie Mus., 33:186, and Crombie, 1977, Proc. Biol. Soc. Washington, 94: 194–204.

Eleutherodactylus gaigeae (Dunn, 1931). Occas. Pap. Boston Soc. Nat. Hist., 5:387.
ORIGINAL NAME: *Lithodytes gaigei*.
TYPE(S): Holotype: MCZ 10011.
TYPE LOCALITY: Fort Randolph, Panama Canal Zone [Panama].
DISTRIBUTION: Costa Rica to the central Chocó of western Colombia; also in the inter-Andean valleys of Colombia.
COMMENT: In the *Eleutherodactylus fitzingeri* group, but with no close relative, according to Lynch, 1980, Herpetologica, 36:178. The justified emendation of the specific epithet was made by Taylor, 1952, Univ. Kansas Sci. Bull., 35:766.

Eleutherodactylus galdi (Jiménez de la Espada, 1870). J. Sci. Math. Phys. Nat., Lisboa, 3:61.
ORIGINAL NAME: *Pristimantis galdi*.
TYPE(S): Lost.
TYPE LOCALITY: "in Ecuador; ad sylvas vicinas pagi S. Jose de Moti".
DISTRIBUTION: Eastern Ecuador.

COMMENT: Includes *Eleutherodactylus margaritifer* (Boulenger, 1912) according to Lynch, 1969, Herpetologica, 25:262–274, and Lynch, 1974, Occas. Pap. Mus. Nat. Hist. Univ. Kansas, 31:15.

Eleutherodactylus ginesi (Rivero, 1964). Caribb. J. Sci., 4:290.
ORIGINAL NAME: *Eupsophus ginesi.*
TYPE(S): Holotype: SCN 250.
TYPE LOCALITY: "Laguna Mucubaji, Edo. Mérida", Distrito Rangel, Venezuela.
DISTRIBUTION: Páramo de Mucubají, Mérida Andes of Venezuela.
COMMENT: In the *Eleutherodactylus myersi* assembly of the *Eleutherodactylus unistrigatus* group.

Eleutherodactylus gladiator Lynch, 1976. Herpetologica, 32:316.
TYPE(S): Holotype: KU 143516.
TYPE LOCALITY: "3.3 km ESE Cuyuja, Napo Province, Ecuador, elevation 2350 m."
DISTRIBUTION: Papallacta Valley near Cuyuja, Napo Province, Ecuador, at intermediate elevations (2350–2910 m) on the Amazonian slopes of the Andes.
COMMENT: Most closely related to *Eleutherodactylus leoni* and *Eleutherodactylus pyrrhomerus* according to Lynch, 1976, Herpetologica, 32:317. In the monophyletic *Eleutherodactylus pyrrhomerus* assembly of the *Eleutherodactylus unistrigatus* group, according to Lynch, 1984, Herpetologica, 40:237.

Eleutherodactylus glandulifer Cochran, 1935. Proc. Boston Soc. Nat. Hist., 40:367.
TYPE(S): Holotype: MCZ 19851.
TYPE LOCALITY: "north and east foothills of the Massif de la Hotte [=Pic Macaya], [Département du Sud,] Haiti, between 1000 feet and 4000 feet".
DISTRIBUTION: Southwestern Hispaniola; Haiti, the Massif de la Hotte, 1000–4800 ft. elev.
COMMENT: In the *Eleutherodactylus ricordii* group, according to Shreve and Williams, 1963, Bull. Mus. Comp. Zool., 129:328, and Schwartz, 1973, J. Herpetol., 7:272. Reviewed by Schwartz, 1983, Cat. Am. Amph. Rept., 310.1.

Eleutherodactylus glanduliferoides Shreve, 1936. Proc. New England Zool. Club, 15:96.
TYPE(S): Holotype: MCZ 21597.
TYPE LOCALITY: "near La Visite, La Selle Range, 5000–7000 feet, Département de l'Ouest, Haiti".
DISTRIBUTION: Known only from the vicinity of the type locality.
COMMENT: See comment under *Eleutherodactylus eunaster.* In the *Eleutherodactylus varleyi* group, according to Shreve and Williams, 1963, Bull. Mus. Comp. Zool., 129:339. Reviewed by Schwartz, 1983, Cat. Am. Amph. Rept., 322.1.

Eleutherodactylus glandulosus (Boulenger, 1880). Bull. Soc. Zool. France, 5:47.
ORIGINAL NAME: *Hylodes glandulosus.*
TYPE(S): Holotype: MRHN 1010.
TYPE LOCALITY: "Andes of Ecuador".
DISTRIBUTION: Elevations of 2105–2890 m in the upper Río Papallacta Valley on the eastern slopes of the Andes in Napo Province, Ecuador.
COMMENT: In the *Eleutherodactylus unistrigatus* group.

Eleutherodactylus glaphycompus Schwartz, 1973. J. Herpetol., 7:257.
TYPE(S): Holotype: CM 54092.
TYPE LOCALITY: "Castillon, *ca.* 2500 feet, Département du Sud, Haiti".
DISTRIBUTION: Southwestern Hispaniola; known only from the region of the type locality, 2500–3900 ft. elev.
COMMENT: In the *Eleutherodactylus ricordii* group, according to the original description, although in the same paper Schwartz suggested that *Eleutherodactylus glaphycompus* may be related to *Eleutherodactylus flavescens,* a

member of the *Eleutherodactylus auriculatus* group. Reviewed by Schwartz, 1983, Cat. Am. Amph. Rept., 323.1.

Eleutherodactylus glaucus Lynch, 1967. Trans. Kansas Acad. Sci., 70:177.
TYPE(S): Holotype: TCWC 21463.
TYPE LOCALITY: "1.6 km SW San Cristobal [de las Casas], Chiapas, México, 2100 m."
DISTRIBUTION: Known only from the type locality.
COMMENT: In the *Eleutherodactylus unistrigatus* group of Lynch. Ford and Savage, 1984, Occas. Pap. Mus. Nat. Hist. Univ. Kansas, 110:7, questioned the inclusion of this species in any species group.

Eleutherodactylus gollmeri (Peters, 1863). Monatsber. Preuss. Akad. Wiss. Berlin, 1863: 409.
ORIGINAL NAME: *Hylodes gollmeri.*
TYPE(S): Holotype: ZMB 3168.
TYPE LOCALITY: "Caracas"; in error, according to Rivero, 1961, Bull. Mus. Comp. Zool., 126:60.
DISTRIBUTION: Costa Rica and Panama.
COMMENT: In the *Eleutherodactylus fitzingeri* group.

Eleutherodactylus gossei Dunn, 1926. Proc. Boston Soc. Nat. Hist., 38:121.
TYPE(S): Holotype: MCZ 11125.
TYPE LOCALITY: Spaldings, Clarendon Parish, Jamaica.
DISTRIBUTION: Jamaica; widespread.
COMMENT: In the *Eleutherodactylus gossei* group according to Goin, 1954, Ann. Carnegie Mus., 3:186, and Crombie, 1977, Proc. Biol. Soc. Washington, 90:194–204. Schwartz and Fowler, 1973, Stud. Fauna Curaçao and other Caribb. Is., 43:91–99, recognized two subspecies.

Eleutherodactylus grabhami Dunn, 1926. Proc. Boston Soc. Nat. Hist., 38:121.
TYPE(S): Holotype: MCZ 11127.
TYPE LOCALITY: Spaldings, Clarendon Parish, Jamaica.
DISTRIBUTION: Widespread in western and central Jamaica, 500–2200 ft. elev.
COMMENT: In the *Eleutherodactylus ricordii* group according to Schwartz and Fowler, 1973, Stud. Fauna Curaçao and other Caribb. Is., 43:135, and Crombie, 1977, Proc. Biol. Soc. Washington, 90:194–204.

Eleutherodactylus grahami Schwartz, 1979. J. Herpetol., 13:200.
TYPE(S): Holotype: USNM 197337.
TYPE LOCALITY: "8.6 km W Ça Soleil, 60 m, Département de l'Artibonite, Haiti".
DISTRIBUTION: Known only from the type locality.
COMMENT: In the *Eleutherodactylus ricordii* group, according to the original description.

Eleutherodactylus grandoculis (Van Lidth de Jeude, 1904). Notes Leyden Mus., 35:93.
ORIGINAL NAME: *Hylodes grandoculis.*
TYPE(S): Holotype: RMNH 4467.
TYPE LOCALITY: Surinam.
DISTRIBUTION: Surinam.
COMMENT: In the *Eleutherodactylus unistrigatus* group. Considered a synonym of *Eleutherodactylus marmoratus* by MSH.

Eleutherodactylus granulosus (Boulenger, 1903). Ann. Mag. Nat. Hist., (7)12:553.
ORIGINAL NAME: *Hylodes granulosus.*
TYPE(S): Holotype: BM 1947.2.15.72 (formerly 1902.11.28.15).
TYPE LOCALITY: "Santo Domingo, Carabaya, S. E. Peru, 6000 feet".
DISTRIBUTION: Southeastern Peru.
COMMENT: In the *Eleutherodactylus discoidalis* group.

Eleutherodactylus greggi Bumzahem, 1955. Copeia, 1955:118.
TYPE(S): Holotype: FMNH 20876.
TYPE LOCALITY: "Volcan Tajumulco, near San Marcos, Guatemala".
DISTRIBUTION: Upper portion of the lower montane zone (2000–2700 m) in the mountains of southwestern Chiapas (Mexico) and adjacent southwestern Guatemala.
COMMENT: In the *Eleutherodactylus unistrigatus* group of Lynch. In the *Eleutherodactylus omiltemanus* group of Ford and Savage; see comment under *Eleutherodactylus omiltemanus*. *Eleutherodactylus chiquito* Lynch, 1965, is a synonym according to Savage, 1975, Copeia, 1975:270.

Eleutherodactylus greyi Dunn, 1926. Occas. Pap. Boston Soc. Nat. Hist., 5:213.
TYPE(S): Holotype: MCZ 11131.
TYPE LOCALITY: Soledad, Las Villas Province, Cuba.
DISTRIBUTION: Central Cuba.
COMMENT: In the *Eleutherodactylus ricordii* group, according to Schwartz, 1958, Am. Mus. Novit., 1873:2.

Eleutherodactylus gryllus Schmidt, 1920. Ann. New York Acad. Sci., 28:172.
TYPE(S): Holotype: AMNH 10307.
TYPE LOCALITY: El Yunque, near the Forester's Cabin, about 1300 feet altitude, Bosque Experimental de Luquillo, Puerto Rico.
DISTRIBUTION: Puerto Rico; known from a few scattered, principally upland localities from Maricao in the west to the region of the type locality in the east, 1000–3900 ft. elev.
COMMENT: In the *Eleutherodactylus auriculatus* group, according to Schwartz, 1969, Fauna Curaçao and other Caribb. Is., 30:101.

Eleutherodactylus gualteri B. Lutz, 1974. J. Herpetol., 8:293.
TYPE(S): Holotype: MN 4096.
TYPE LOCALITY: "Granja Comari, Organ Mountains at Terezopolis, Rio de Janeiro, Brazil".
DISTRIBUTION: Vicinity of the type locality and Paquequer, Rio de Janeiro, Brazil.
COMMENT: In the *Eleutherodactylus binotatus* group of Lynch. See comment under *Eleutherodactylus guentheri*. Discussed by Heyer, 1984, Smithson. Contrib. Zool., 402:25–26.

Eleutherodactylus guentheri (Steindachner, 1864). Verh. Zool. Bot. Ges. Wien, 14:246.
ORIGINAL NAME: *Hylodes Güntheri*.
TYPE(S): Holotype: NHMW 16515.
TYPE LOCALITY: "Rio dos Macacos", in the city of Rio de Janeiro, Rio de Janeiro, Brazil.
DISTRIBUTION: Southeastern Brazil.
COMMENT: In the *Eleutherodactylus binotatus* group of Lynch. Heyer, 1984, Smithson. Contrib. Zool., 402:1–42, doubted the validity of this group, but regarded the *Eleutherodactylus guentheri* cluster (*Eleutherodactylus epipedus, Eleutherodactylus erythromerus, Eleutherodactylus gualteri, Eleutherodactylus guentheri, Eleutherodactylus nasutus,* and *Eleutherodactylus oeus*) as probably monophyletic. Heyer also included *Hylodes henselii* Peters, 1871, Monatsber. Preuss. Akad. Wiss. Berlin, 1871:648 (Holotype: ZMB 6813; Type locality: Porto Alegre, Rio Grande do Sul, Brazil) in synonymy.

Eleutherodactylus guerreroensis Lynch, 1967. Proc. Biol. Soc. Washington, 80:216.
TYPE(S): Holotype: KU 86873.
TYPE LOCALITY: "3 km N Agua del Obispo, Guerrero, Mexico, 980 m".
DISTRIBUTION: Known only from the type locality.
COMMENT: In the *Eleutherodactylus alfredi* group.

Eleutherodactylus gularis (Boulenger, 1898). Proc. Zool. Soc. London, 1898:121.
ORIGINAL NAME: *Hylodes gularis.*
TYPE(S): Holotype: BM 1947.2.15.82 (formerly 98.4.28.107).
TYPE LOCALITY: "Cachabe [=Cachabí], a small village on the river of that name on
the N. W. Coast; in the Prov. Esmeraldas . . . probably about 500 feet above
the sea", Ecuador.
DISTRIBUTION: Lowlands of western Colombia and northwestern Ecuador.
COMMENT: In the *Eleutherodactylus unistrigatus* group.

Eleutherodactylus gundlachi Schmidt, 1920. Proc. Linn. Soc. New York, 33:3.
TYPE(S): Holotype: MCZ 3056.
TYPE LOCALITY: La Unión, Monte Líbano, Guantánamo, Oriente [now Guantánamo]
Province, Cuba.
DISTRIBUTION: Cuba; uplands of the Sierra Maestra, Sierra del Cobre, Sierra de la
Gran Piedra, east to the mountains north of Imías, Oriente Province.
COMMENT: *Eleutherodactylus gundlachi* is a substitute name for *Eleutherodactylus*
plicatus Barbour, 1914, Mem. Mus. Comp. Zool., 44:244, which is preoccupied
by *Hylodes plicatus* Günther, 1901 (=*Eleutherodactylus rhodopis* Cope). In the
Eleutherodactylus ricordii group, according to Schwartz, 1958, Am. Mus. Novit.,
1873:2.

Eleutherodactylus gutturalis Hoogmoed, Lynch, and Lescure, 1977. Zool. Meded.,
Leiden, 51:34.
TYPE(S): Holotype: LACM 44651.
TYPE LOCALITY: Lower Matarony River, French Guiana.
DISTRIBUTION: Northern Brazil (Amapá), southern French Guiana, and eastern
Surinam, 30–310 m.
COMMENT: In the *Eleutherodactylus fitzingeri* group.

Eleutherodactylus haitianus Barbour, 1942. Copeia, 1942:179.
TYPE(S): Holotype: USNM 107566.
TYPE LOCALITY: "Loma Rucilla of the Cordillera Central, [Santiago Province,]
Dominican Republic, 8000–10,000 feet".
DISTRIBUTION: Hispaniola; the central mountains (Cordillera Central) of the
Dominican Republic, 1550–2470 m.
COMMENT: *Eleutherodactylus haitianus* is a replacement name for *Eleutherodactylus*
intermedius Cochran, 1941, Bull. U.S. Natl. Mus., 177:70, which is preoccupied
by *Eleutherodactylus intermedius* Barbour and Shreve, 1937. In the
Eleutherodactylus auriculatus group. Reviewed by Schwartz, 1983, Cat. Am.
Amph. Rept., 335.1–2, who noted that this nominal species may be composed
of three cryptic species.

Eleutherodactylus hedricki Rivero, 1963. Breviora, 185:2.
TYPE(S): Holotype: MCZ 36903.
TYPE LOCALITY: "El Verde, west flank of El Yunque, [Bosque Experimental de
Luquillo,] Puerto Rico, 1500 feet".
DISTRIBUTION: Puerto Rico; known from the vicinity of the type locality and the
Toro Negro Forest Reserve.
COMMENT: In the *Eleutherodactylus auriculatus* group, according to Schwartz, 1969,
Stud. Fauna Curaçao and other Caribb. Is., 30:99–115.

Eleutherodactylus helonotus (Lynch, 1975). Occas. Pap. Mus. Nat. Hist. Univ. Kansas,
38:19.
ORIGINAL NAME: *Amblyphrynus helonotus.*
TYPE(S): Holotype: BM 1970.178.
TYPE LOCALITY: "Río Pitzara, Pichincha Prov., Ecuador".
DISTRIBUTION: Known only from the Pacific versant of Ecuador at low and
moderate elevations in the region of the type locality.

COMMENT: In the *Eleutherodactylus sulcatus* group, according to Lynch, 1981, Caldasia, 13:318.

Eleutherodactylus heminota Shreve and Williams, 1963. Bull. Mus. Comp. Zool., 129: 325.
ORIGINAL NAME: *Eleutherodactylus bakeri heminota.*
TYPE(S): Holotype: MCZ 31734.
TYPE LOCALITY: "Furcy, [Département de l'Ouest,] Republic of Haiti".
DISTRIBUTION: Hispaniola; the Tiburon Peninsula of Haiti and the extreme eastern Sierra de Baoruco, Barahona Province, Dominican Republic.
COMMENT: In the *Eleutherodactylus auriculatus* group, according to the original description. Schwartz, 1965, Proc. Biol. Soc. Washington, 78:167, elevated this form to species status without explanation; it has been so treated since (JDL). Reviewed by Schwartz, 1983, Cat. Am. Amph. Rept., 336.1.

Eleutherodactylus hernandezi Lynch and Ruíz-Carranza, 1983. Trans. Kansas Acad. Sci., 86:103.
TYPE(S): Holotype: ICN 7849.
TYPE LOCALITY: "vicinity of the INDERENA cabaña Chupallal de Perico, 29.4 km by road NW San Jose de Isnos, Depto. de Huila, Colombia, 2600 m".
DISTRIBUTION: Known only from the type locality.
COMMENT: In the *Eleutherodactylus unistrigatus* group, most similar to *Eleutherodactylus calcaratus, Eleutherodactylus crucifer,* and *Eleutherodactylus incanus,* according to the original description.

Eleutherodactylus heterodactylus (Miranda-Ribeiro, 1937). Campo, Rio de Janeiro, 1937:67.
ORIGINAL NAME: *Teletrema heterodactylum.*
TYPE(S): MN.
TYPE LOCALITY: Cáceres, Mato Grosso [Brazil].
DISTRIBUTION: Known only from the type locality.
COMMENT: In the *Eleutherodactylus fitzingeri* group.

Eleutherodactylus hobartsmithi Taylor, 1936. Trans. Kansas Acad. Sci., 39:355.
TYPE(S): Holotype: formerly EHT-HMS 3688 (now FMNH).
TYPE LOCALITY: "near Uruapan, Michoacan", Mexico.
DISTRIBUTION: Southwestern part of the Mexican Plateau, Mexico.
COMMENT: In the *Eleutherodactylus rhodopis* group.

Eleutherodactylus hoehnei B. Lutz, 1959 "1958". Mem. Inst. Oswaldo Cruz, Rio de Janeiro, 56:378.
TYPE(S): Holotype: IOC 2525.
TYPE LOCALITY: "Serra de Paranapiacaba, antiga Serra de Cubatão, entre a capital do Estado de São Paulo e o mar", Brazil.
DISTRIBUTION: Known only from the vicinity of the type locality in the Serra do Mar, Brazil.
COMMENT: Not assigned to species group, but possibly assignable to the *Eleutherodactylus binotatus* group according to Lynch, 1976, Occas. Pap. Mus. Nat. Hist. Univ. Kansas, 61:7.

Eleutherodactylus hylaeformis (Cope, 1875). J. Acad. Nat. Sci. Philadelphia, (2)8:107.
ORIGINAL NAME: *Phyllobates hylaeformis.*
TYPE(S): Not traced; not in ASNP or USNM.
TYPE LOCALITY: Talamanca, Pico Blanco, Costa Rica, 7000 ft.
DISTRIBUTION: Cordillera of Costa Rica.
COMMENT: See comment under *Eleutherodactylus moro.*

Eleutherodactylus hypostenor Schwartz, 1965. Bull. Mus. Comp. Zool., 132:498.
  TYPE(S): Holotype: MCZ 43187.
  TYPE LOCALITY: "10.5 mi. (16.8 km) S. Cabral, 3500 (1060 m) feet, Barahona
    Province, República Dominicana".
  DISTRIBUTION: Southwestern Hispaniola; the Tiburon Peninsula of Haiti, east into
    the Sierra de Baoruco of the Dominican Republic, 670–1070 m elev.
  COMMENT: In the *Eleutherodactylus inoptatus* group, according to Schwartz, 1965,
    Bull. Mus. Comp. Zool., 132:498. See Schwartz, 1984, Cat. Am. Amph. Rept.,
    346.1–2, for review.

Eleutherodactylus ignicolor Lynch and Duellman, 1980. Misc. Publ. Mus. Nat. Hist.
    Univ. Kansas, 69:32.
  TYPE(S): Holotype: KU 165879.
  TYPE LOCALITY: "Río Jatuntinahua, 10 km SE Cuyujúa, Provincia Napo, Ecuador".
  DISTRIBUTION: Upper humid montane forest in the upper Río Papallacta Valley
    (2160–2750 m), Napo Province, Ecuador.
  COMMENT: In the *Eleutherodactylus unistrigatus* group; most closely related to
    Eleutherodactylus prolatus, *Eleutherodactylus trachyblepharis*, and *Eleutherodactylus*
    variabilis, according to the original description.

Eleutherodactylus imitatrix Duellman, 1978. Herpetologica, 34:265.
  TYPE(S): Holotype: KU 171892.
  TYPE LOCALITY: "Finca Panguana on the Río Llullapichis, 4–5 km upstream from
    the Río Pachitea, elevation 200 m, Departamento Huánuco, Peru (08° 36' S;
    74° 57' W)".
  DISTRIBUTION: Known only from the holotype.
  COMMENT: In the *Eleutherodactylus unistrigatus* group.

Eleutherodactylus incanus Lynch and Duellman, 1980. Misc. Publ. Mus. Nat. Hist.
    Univ. Kansas, 69:34.
  TYPE(S): Holotype: KU 143465.
  TYPE LOCALITY: "Río Azuela, Provincia Napo, Ecuador, 1740 m."
  DISTRIBUTION: Cloud forest (1700–1740 m) on the eastern face of the Andes in
    Napo Province, Ecuador.
  COMMENT: In the *Eleutherodactylus unistrigatus* group.

Eleutherodactylus incomptus Lynch and Duellman, 1980. Misc. Publ. Mus. Nat. Hist.
    Univ. Kansas, 69:35.
  TYPE(S): Holotype: KU 143484.
  TYPE LOCALITY: "16.5 km NNE Santa Rosa, Provincia Napo, Ecuador, 1700 m."
  DISTRIBUTION: Elevations of 1410–1910 m on the eastern face of the Andes in Napo
    Province (Ecuador) and from 1270 m in the Pastaza Valley (Pastaza Province,
    Ecuador).
  COMMENT: In the *Eleutherodactylus unistrigatus* group; related to *Eleutherodactylus*
    carvalhoi, *Eleutherodactylus croceoinguinis*, and *Eleutherodactylus martiae*, according
    to the original description.

Eleutherodactylus ingeri (Cochran and Goin, 1961). Fieldiana: Zool., 39:543.
  ORIGINAL NAME: *Amblyphrynus ingeri*.
  TYPE(S): Holotype: FMNH 81915.
  TYPE LOCALITY: 8 km S Gachala, San Isidro, Cundinamarca, Colombia, 2350 m.
  DISTRIBUTION: Cordillera Oriental of Colombia (1750–2350 m).
  COMMENT: In the *Eleutherodactylus sulcatus* group, according to Lynch, 1981,
    Caldasia, 13:318.

Eleutherodactylus inguinalis Parker, 1940. Ann. Mag. Nat. Hist., (11)5:203.
  TYPE(S): Holotype: BM 1939.1.1.1.
  TYPE LOCALITY: New River, British Guiana. [This locality is actually in southwestern
    Surinam—MSH.]
  DISTRIBUTION: Several localities in Surinam and French Guiana.

COMMENT: In the *Eleutherodactylus unistrigatus* group.

Eleutherodactylus inoptatus (Barbour, 1914). Mem. Mus. Comp. Zool., 44:252.
ORIGINAL NAME: *Leptodactylus inoptatus*.
TYPE(S): Holotype: MCZ 3087.
TYPE LOCALITY: Diquini, Département de l'Ouest, Haiti.
DISTRIBUTION: Hispaniola; islandwide but unreported from large areas in Haiti and
the Dominican Republic; Ile de la Tortue; 0–5600 ft. elev.
COMMENT: In the *Eleutherodactylus inoptatus* group, according to Schwartz, 1965,
Bull. Mus. Comp. Zool., 132:508. Shreve and Williams, 1963, Bull. Mus. Comp.
Zool., 129:318, put this species in the more inclusive *Eleutherodactylus varians*
group (=*Eleutherodactylus auriculatus* group).

Eleutherodactylus insignitus Ruthven, 1917. Occas. Pap. Mus. Zool. Univ. Michigan,
34:1.
TYPE(S): Holotype: UMMZ 48393.
TYPE LOCALITY: Heights east of San Miguel, Santa Marta Mountains, Colombia,
6000–7000 ft.
DISTRIBUTION: Sierra Santa Marta, Colombia.
COMMENT: In the *Eleutherodactylus fitzingeri* group.

Eleutherodactylus intermedius Barbour and Shreve, 1937. Bull. Mus. Comp. Zool., 80:
384.
TYPE(S): Holotype: MCZ 21965.
TYPE LOCALITY: Near Cueva del Aura, Pico Turquino, 1500 feet to 4000 feet,
Oriente [now Santiago de Cuba] Province, Cuba.
DISTRIBUTION: Cuba; known from the mountains in Oriente (now Santiago de
Cuba) Province, 1500–6000 ft. elev.
COMMENT: In the *Eleutherodactylus dimidiatus* group, according to Schwartz, 1964,
Breviora, 108:13.

Eleutherodactylus inusitatus Lynch and Duellman, 1980. Misc. Publ. Mus. Nat. Hist.
Univ. Kansas, 69:37.
TYPE(S): Holotype: KU 166066.
TYPE LOCALITY: "Río Jatuntinahua, 10 km SE Cuyujúa, Provincia Napo, Ecuador,
2160 m."
DISTRIBUTION: Scattered localities at low to moderate elevations (1300–2160 m)
along the eastern face of the Andes in Ecuador.
COMMENT: In the *Eleutherodactylus unistrigatus* group.

Eleutherodactylus jamaicensis Barbour, 1910. Bull. Mus. Comp. Zool., 52:287.
TYPE(S): Holotype: MCZ 2512.
TYPE LOCALITY: Mandeville, Manchester Parish, Jamaica.
DISTRIBUTION: Widespread in interior areas of Jamaica, 400–4250 ft. elev.
COMMENT: Schwartz, 1969, Stud. Fauna Curaçao and other Caribb. Is., 114:99–115,
noted that this is the sole Jamaican species that might be associated with the
Eleutherodactylus auriculatus group. Placed in the *Eleutherodactylus gossei* group
by Schwartz and Fowler, 1973, Stud. Fauna Curaçao and other Caribb. Is., 43:
135; further discussed by Crombie, 1977, Proc. Biol. Soc. Washington, 90:194–
204, who removed it from the *Eleutherodactylus gossei* group and erected the
monotypic *Eleutherodactylus jamaicensis* group.

Eleutherodactylus jasperi Drewry and Jones, 1976. J. Herpetol., 10:161.
TYPE(S): Holotype: FMNH 196846.
TYPE LOCALITY: 6 km SE Cayey, Puerto Rico.
DISTRIBUTION: Puerto Rico; known only from the Sierra de Cayey, 700–850 m elev.
COMMENT: In the *Eleutherodactylus auriculatus* group, according to the original
description.

PROTECTED STATUS: USA ESA—Threatened (11 Nov. 1977) (Puerto Rico).

Eleutherodactylus johnstonei Barbour, 1914. Mem. Mus. Comp. Zool., 44:249.
TYPE(S): Syntypes: MCZ 2759 (2 specimens).
TYPE LOCALITY: St. George's, St. George Parish, Grenada.
DISTRIBUTION: Lesser Antilles; known from the islands of St. Martin, Saba, St.
Eustatius, St. Christopher, Nevis, Barbuda, Antigua, Guadeloupe, Montserrat,
Martinique, St. Lucia, St. Vincent, Barbados, and Grenada; introduced on
Jamaica, Bermuda, coastal Venezuela, Curaçao, and Georgetown, Guyana.
COMMENT: Both prior to and subsequent to the description of *Eleutherodactylus
johnstonei*, the name *Eleutherodactylus martinicensis* Tschudi has been applied to
the populations of frogs now called *Eleutherodactylus johnstonei*. Schwartz,
1967, Stud. Fauna Curaçao and other Caribb. Is., 24:18–20, discussed the
nomenclatural history of this species. In the *Eleutherodactylus auriculatus*
group, according to Schwartz, 1969, Stud. Fauna Curaçao and other Caribb.
Is., 30:101. Records of *Eleutherodactylus portoricensis* from Venezuela by Yústiz,
1977, Rev. Univ. Centroccid. Lisandro Alvarado, Tarea Común, 51:143, are
referable to *Eleutherodactylus johnstonei* (JAR).

Eleutherodactylus jota Lynch, 1980. Trans. Kansas Acad. Sci., 83:101.
TYPE(S): Holotype: KU 115212.
TYPE LOCALITY: Río Changena, Prov. Bocas del Toro, Panama, 830 m.
DISTRIBUTION: Known only from the type locality.
COMMENT: In the *Eleutherodactylus fitzingeri* group; closely allied with
Eleutherodactylus bransfordii and *Eleutherodactylus podiciferus*.

Eleutherodactylus jugans Cochran, 1937. J. Washington Acad. Sci., 27:312.
TYPE(S): Holotype: MCZ 19852.
TYPE LOCALITY: Near La Visite, Massif de la Selle, between 5000 feet and 7000 feet,
Departement de l'Ouest, Haiti.
DISTRIBUTION: Hispaniola; known from the type locality in the Massif de la Selle
in Haiti and from the same range in the Domincan Republic, 4100–7000 ft.
elev.
COMMENT: *Eleutherodactylus jugans* is a replacement name for *Leptodactylus
darlingtoni* Cochran, 1935, Proc. Boston Soc. Nat. Hist. 40:372 (not
Eleutherodactylus darlingtoni Cochran, 1935, Proc. Boston Soc. Nat. Hist., 40:368).
In the *Eleutherodactylus dimidiatus* group, according to Shreve and Williams,
1963, Bull. Mus. Comp. Zool., 169:338.

Eleutherodactylus juipoca Sazima and Cardoso, 1978. Rev. Brasil. Biol., 38:921.
TYPE(S): Holotype: MN 4013.
TYPE LOCALITY: "Souzas, Campinas, São Paulo, Brasil".
DISTRIBUTION: Vicinity of the type locality.
COMMENT: In the *Eleutherodactylus binotatus* group, according to the original
description.

Eleutherodactylus junori Dunn, 1926. Proc. Boston Soc. Nat. Hist., 38:120.
TYPE(S): Holotype: MCZ 11124.
TYPE LOCALITY: Spaldings, Clarendon Parish, Jamaica.
DISTRIBUTION: Jamaica; known only from three central localities: near Troy in
southern Trelawny Parish, the type locality, and near Kellits in Clarendon
Parish.
COMMENT: Schwartz and Fowler, 1973, Stud. Fauna Curaçao and other Caribb. Is.,
43:101, noted that without knowledge of calls or habitat this species cannot
be readily separated from *Eleutherodactylus gossei*. In the *Eleutherodactylus gossei*
group according to Crombie, 1977, Proc. Biol. Soc. Washington, 90:194–204.

Eleutherodactylus karlschmidti Grant, 1931. Copeia, 1931:55.
TYPE(S): Holotype: UMMZ 73426 (formerly C. Grant 1483).
TYPE LOCALITY: Bosque Experimental de Luquillo, Puerto Rico.
DISTRIBUTION: Puerto Rico.

COMMENT: In the *Eleutherodactylus orcutti* group, according to Shreve and Williams, 1963, Bull. Mus. Comp. Zool., 129:326–327; the *Eleutherodactylus orcutti* group was not recognized by Schwartz, 1967, Stud. Fauna Curaçao and other Caribb. Is., 91:56, or Crombie, 1977, Proc. Biol. Soc. Washington, 90:194–204. Sole member of the *Eleutherodactylus karlschmidti* group, according to Joglar, 1983, Caribb. J. Sci., 19:37.

Eleutherodactylus klinikowskii Schwartz, 1959. Herpetologica, 15:62.
TYPE(S): Holotype: AMNH 63120.
TYPE LOCALITY: Mogote de Tumbadero, 1 km E Viñales, Pinar del Río Province, Cuba.
DISTRIBUTION: Western Cuba, in the Sierra de los Organos and the Sierra del Rosario, between Guane and San Diego de los Baños.
COMMENT: In the *Eleutherodactylus ricordii* group, according to the original description.

Eleutherodactylus lacrimosus (Jiménez de la Espada, 1875). Vert. Viaj. Pacif., Batr.:pl. 3.
ORIGINAL NAME: *Cyclocephalus lacrimosus.*
TYPE(S): Lost.
TYPE LOCALITY: Unknown.
DISTRIBUTION: Northeastern Brazil west to Ecuador and northern Peru.
COMMENT: In the *Eleutherodactylus unistrigatus* group. See Lynch and Schwartz, 1972, J. Herpetol., 5:103–114, for a review.

Eleutherodactylus lacteus (Miranda-Ribeiro, 1923). Rev. Mus. Paulista, São Paulo, 13: 851.
ORIGINAL NAME: *Basanitia lactea.*
TYPE(S): Syntypes: MZUSP 504, 828; MZUSP 828 designated lectotype by Bokermann, 1966, Lista Anot. Local. Tipo Anf. Brasil.:15, by fiat.
TYPE LOCALITY: Iguape and Campo Grande, São Paulo [Brazil]; restricted to Iguape, São Paulo, Brazil, by lectotype designation.
DISTRIBUTION: Southeastern Brazil.
COMMENT: In the *Eleutherodactylus lacteus* group of Lynch. In the *Eleutherodactylus cruentus* group of Savage and DeWeese, 1980, Proc. Biol. Soc. Washington, 93: 940.

Eleutherodactylus lamprotes Schwartz, 1973. J. Herpetol., 7:253.
TYPE(S): Holotype: CM 54091.
TYPE LOCALITY: *"ca.* 2.5 km S Castillon, 3300 ft (1007 m), Département du Sud, Haiti".
DISTRIBUTION: Hispaniola; distal portion of the Tiburon Peninsula in Haiti, 2700–4800 ft. elev.
COMMENT: In the *Eleutherodactylus auriculatus* group, according to the original description.

Eleutherodactylus lancinii Donoso-Barros, 1968. Caribb. J. Sci., 8:31.
TYPE(S): Holotype: USNM 165604 (formerly Donoso-Barros 40490).
TYPE LOCALITY: "Apartaderos, Estado Mérida", Venezuela.
DISTRIBUTION: Mérida Andes of Venezuela.
COMMENT: In the *Eleutherodactylus unistrigatus* group.

Eleutherodactylus lanthanites Lynch, 1975. Contrib. Sci. Nat. Hist. Mus. Los Angeles Co., 272:10.
TYPE(S): Holotype: KU 146144.
TYPE LOCALITY: "Santa Cecilia, Provincia Napo, Ecuador, 340 m."
DISTRIBUTION: Lowland Amazonian rainforest and lower humid montane forest in Ecuador, Peru, adjacent Colombia and Amazonas, Brazil.
COMMENT: In the *Eleutherodactylus fitzingeri* group.

Eleutherodactylus laticeps (Duméril, 1853). Ann. Sci. Nat., Paris, (3)19:178.
ORIGINAL NAME: *Hylodes laticeps.*
TYPE(S): Holotype: MNHNP 509.
TYPE LOCALITY: "Yucatan", Mexico; actually probably from near Cobán, Alta
Verapaz, Guatemala (JMS).
DISTRIBUTION: Northern Guatemala, Belize, and northern Honduras.
COMMENT: In the *Eleutherodactylus fitzingeri* group. See comments under
Eleutherodactylus rostralis and *Eleutherodactylus stantoni.*

Eleutherodactylus latidiscus (Boulenger, 1898). Proc. Zool. Soc. London, 1898:121.
ORIGINAL NAME: *Hylodes latidiscus.*
TYPE(S): Syntypes: BM 1947.2.15.66–67 (formerly 98.4.28.108–109).
TYPE LOCALITY: "Cachabé [=Cachabí], a small village [about 10 miles southeast of
Concepción] on the river of that name, on the N. W. Coast, in the Prov.
Esmeraldas", Ecuador.
DISTRIBUTION: Western Ecuador and southwestern Colombia.
COMMENT: In the *Eleutherodactylus unistrigatus* group. See comment under
Eleutherodactylus tamsitti.

Eleutherodactylus leberi Schwartz, 1965. Herpetologica, 21:27.
TYPE(S): Holotype: AMNH 71968.
TYPE LOCALITY: "14.6 mi. WSW of Maffo, Oriente [now Granma] Province, Cuba".
DISTRIBUTION: Known only from the type locality in the northern foothills of the
Sierra Maestra and Los Hondones, north of Guantánamo, Cuba.
COMMENT: In the *Eleutherodactylus auriculatus* group, according to the original
description.

Eleutherodactylus lentus (Cope, 1862). Proc. Acad. Nat. Sci. Philadelphia, 14:151.
ORIGINAL NAME: *Hylodes lentus.*
TYPE(S): Syntypes: ANSP 2770–71.
TYPE LOCALITY: St. Thomas, U.S. Virgin Islands.
DISTRIBUTION: The Virgin Islands; known from St. Thomas, St. John, and St. Croix.
COMMENT: In the *Eleutherodactylus ricordii* group according to Shreve and Williams,
1963, Bull. Mus. Comp. Zool., 129:333, and Schwartz, 1976, Bull. Florida State
Mus., Biol. Sci., 21:1–46.

Eleutherodactylus leoncei Shreve and Williams, 1963. Bull. Mus. Comp. Zool., 129:335.
TYPE(S): Holotype: YPM 1167.
TYPE LOCALITY: "Forêt des Pins, near Morne La Selle, [Département de l'Ouest,]
Republic of Haiti".
DISTRIBUTION: Hispaniola; known from the Massif de la Selle in Haiti and the
Dominican Republic, 3900–7600 ft. elev.
COMMENT: In the *Eleutherodactylus ricordii* group, according to the original
description.

Eleutherodactylus leoni Lynch, 1976. Herpetologica, 32:313.
TYPE(S): Holotype: KU 130870.
TYPE LOCALITY: "on the N slope of the Nudo de Mojanda, Imbabura Province,
Ecuador, elevation 3400 m."
DISTRIBUTION: Elevations of 2710–3400 m on the Pacific slopes of the Andes and
from 2590–2700 m on the Amazonian slopes of the Andes in northern
Ecuador and southern Colombia.
COMMENT: In the *Eleutherodactylus unistrigatus* group; most closely related to
Eleutherodactylus gladiator and *Eleutherodactylus pyrrhomerus* according to
Lynch, 1976, Herpetologica, 32:317. In the monophyletic *Eleutherodactylus
pyrrhomerus* assembly, according to Lynch, 1984, Herpetologica, 40:237, who
considered *Eleutherodactylus leoni* to probably be the sister-species of
Eleutherodactylus repens.

Eleutherodactylus leptolophus Lynch, 1980. Caldasia, 13:180.
TYPE(S): Holotype: KU 169041.
TYPE LOCALITY: "26 km E Puracé, Departamento del Cauca, Colombia, 3180 m alt."
DISTRIBUTION: Known only from the type locality.
COMMENT: In the *Eleutherodactylus unistrigatus* group.

Eleutherodactylus leucopus Lynch, 1976. Proc. Biol. Soc. Washington, 88:351.
TYPE(S): Holotype: USNM 197927.
TYPE LOCALITY: "Santa Barbara, Napo Prov., Ecuador, 2590 m."
DISTRIBUTION: Intermediate elevations (2440–2700 m) in the valley of the Río
   Chingual at localities in both Colombia and Ecuador.
COMMENT: In the *Eleutherodactylus unistrigatus* group. Reviewed by Lynch and
   Duellman, 1980, Misc. Publ. Mus. Nat. Hist. Univ. Kansas, 69:41.

Eleutherodactylus lindae Duellman, 1978. Proc. Biol. Soc. Washington, 91:424.
TYPE(S): Holotype: KU 162305.
TYPE LOCALITY: "Río Cosñipata, 4 km SW Santa Isabel, 1,700 m, Departamento
   Cuzco, Perú (13° 05′ S; 71° 18′ W)".
DISTRIBUTION: Known only from the holotype.
COMMENT: In the *Eleutherodactylus unistrigatus* group.

Eleutherodactylus lineatus (Brocchi, 1879). Bull. Soc. Philomath. Paris, 3:22.
ORIGINAL NAME: *Hylodes lineatus*.
TYPE(S): Holotype: MNHNP 4885.
TYPE LOCALITY: "Attitlan (Mexique)" (locality actually in Guatemala).
DISTRIBUTION: Intermediate elevations of Guatemala and Chiapas, Mexico.
COMMENT: In the *Eleutherodactylus fitzingeri* group; in older literature often
   confounded with *Lithodytes lineatus*.

Eleutherodactylus lividus Lynch and Duellman, 1980. Misc. Publ. Mus. Nat. Hist. Univ.
   Kansas, 69:41.
TYPE(S): Holotype: KU 166005.
TYPE LOCALITY: "11 km ESE Papallacta, Provincia Napo, Ecuador, 2660 m."
DISTRIBUTION: Papallacta Valley on the eastern face of the Andes in Napo
   Province, Ecuador, 2135–2750 m.
COMMENT: In the *Eleutherodactylus unistrigatus* group.

Eleutherodactylus locustus Schmidt, 1920. Ann. New York Acad. Sci., 28:174.
TYPE(S): Holotype: AMNH 10240.
TYPE LOCALITY: El Yunque, near the Forester's Cabin, about 1300 feet altitude,
   Bosque Experimental de Luquillo, Puerto Rico.
DISTRIBUTION: Known from widely scattered interior localities in eastern Puerto
   Rico.
COMMENT: In the *Eleutherodactylus auriculatus* group, according to Schwartz, 1969,
   Stud. Fauna Curaçao and other Caribb. Is., 30:101. Derived from
   Eleutherodactylus cochranae, according to Rivero and Mayorga, 1963, Caribb. J.
   Sci., 3:81–85.

Eleutherodactylus longirostris (Boulenger, 1898). Proc. Zool. Soc. London, 1898:120.
ORIGINAL NAME: *Hylodes longirostris*.
TYPE(S): Syntypes: BM 1947.2.15.56–60 (formerly 98.4.28.101–105).
TYPE LOCALITY: "Cachabé [=Cachabí], a small village on the river of that name . . .
   Prov. Esmeraldas . . . about 500 feet above the sea", Ecuador.
DISTRIBUTION: Darién highlands of extreme eastern Panama, south throughout
   western Colombia to south Guayas Province, Ecuador, in humid forest below
   1200 m elevation; disjunct population in the middle and upper drainage of
   the Magdalena Valley, Colombia.
COMMENT: In the *Eleutherodactylus fitzingeri* group. Reviewed by Lynch and Myers,
   1983, Bull. Am. Mus. Nat. Hist., 175:537–545.

Eleutherodactylus loustes Lynch, 1979. Proc. Biol. Soc. Washington, 92:498.
TYPE(S): Holotype: KU 179234.
TYPE LOCALITY: Maldonado, Prov. Carchi, Ecuador, 1410 m.
DISTRIBUTION: Known only from the type locality.
COMMENT: In the *Eleutherodactylus unistrigatus* group; nearest *Eleutherodactylus crenunguis* and *Eleutherodactylus rubicundus*, according to the original description.

Eleutherodactylus lucioi Schwartz, 1980. Ann. Carnegie Mus., 49:105.
TYPE(S): Holotype: CM 60537.
TYPE LOCALITY: "Rivière Côtes de Fer, 11.2 km NE Môle St. Nicholas, Département du Nord Ouest, Haiti".
DISTRIBUTION: Known only from the type locality.
COMMENT: In the *Eleutherodactylus ricordii* group, according to the original description.

Eleutherodactylus luteolateralis Lynch, 1976. Occas. Pap. Mus. Nat. Hist. Univ. Kansas, 55:13.
TYPE(S): Holotype: KU 131674.
TYPE LOCALITY: "Tandapi, Prov. Pichincha, Ecuador, 1460 m."
DISTRIBUTION: Known only from the type locality.
COMMENT: In the *Eleutherodactylus unistrigatus* group.

Eleutherodactylus luteolus (Gosse, 1851). Naturalist's Sojourn in Jamaica:366.
ORIGINAL NAME: *Litoria luteola*.
TYPE(S): Holotype: BM 47.12.27.80.
TYPE LOCALITY: Content, Westmoreland Parish, Jamaica.
DISTRIBUTION: Western Jamaica.
COMMENT: In the *Eleutherodactylus gossei* group, according to Goin, 1954, Ann. Carnegie Mus., 93:186, and Crombie, 1977, Proc. Biol. Soc. Washington, 90: 194–204.

Eleutherodactylus lymani Barbour and Noble, 1920. Bull. Mus. Comp. Zool., 63:403.
TYPE(S): Holotype: MCZ 5422.
TYPE LOCALITY: Perico, Valley of the Chinchipe, [Provincia Cajamarca,] northwestern Peru.
DISTRIBUTION: Broad semiarid valleys of the Chinchipe and Huancabamba rivers in Departamento Cajamarca (Peru) and north into the semiarid and mesic valleys of the Catamayo and Zamora rivers in Loja Province (Ecuador), 690–2500 m.
COMMENT: Includes *Eleutherodactylus carrioni* Parker, 1932, according to Lynch, 1969, Herpetologica, 25:263. In the *Eleutherodactylus fitzingeri* group.

Eleutherodactylus lynchi Duellman and Simmons, 1977. Proc. Biol. Soc. Washington, 90:60.
TYPE(S): Holotype: KU 168139.
TYPE LOCALITY: "Vado Hondo (05° 26' N, 72° 44' W), 2660 m, Departmento Boyacá, Colombia".
DISTRIBUTION: Páramo de Vigajual in the Cordillera Oriental, Departamento Boyacá, Colombia, 2460–3150 m elev.
COMMENT: In the *Eleutherodactylus unistrigatus* assembly of the *Eleutherodactylus unistrigatus* group.

Eleutherodactylus lythrodes Lynch and Lescure, 1980. Bull. Mus. Natl. Hist. Nat., Paris, (4)2:308.
TYPE(S): Holotype: MNHNP 1978-2825.
TYPE LOCALITY: "Colonia, Departamento Loreto, Perú".
DISTRIBUTION: Vicinity of the type locality.

COMMENT: In the *Eleutherodactylus unistrigatus* group; most closely allied to *Eleutherodactylus variabilis* according to the original description.

Eleutherodactylus macdougalli Taylor, 1942. Univ. Kansas Sci. Bull., 28:71–73.
TYPE(S): Holotype: UIMNH 15907 (formerly EHT-HMS 27482).
TYPE LOCALITY: "above La Gloria, Oaxaca, [Mexico,] north of Niltepec, on an Atlantic exposure at an elevation of about 4,500 ft."
DISTRIBUTION: Southeastern Oaxaca, Mexico.
COMMENT: In the *Eleutherodactylus fitzingeri* group. Allied with *Eleutherodactylus lineatus* (JMS).

Eleutherodactylus malkini Lynch, 1980. Am. Mus. Novit., 2696:9.
TYPE(S): Holotype: AMNH 94228.
TYPE LOCALITY: "Estirón, Río Ampiyacu, Depto. Loreto, Peru".
DISTRIBUTION: Low elevation rainforests in the upper Amazon Basin in Brazil, Colombia, Ecuador, and Peru.
COMMENT: In the *Eleutherodactylus fitzingeri* group, according to the original description. Distribution records discussed by Lynch and Lescure, 1980, Bull. Mus. Natl. Hist. Nat. Paris, (4)2:310–311.

Eleutherodactylus mantipus (Boulenger, 1908). Ann. Mag. Nat. Hist., 8:515.
ORIGINAL NAME: *Leptodactylus mantipus*.
TYPE(S): Holotype: BM 1947.2.17.46 (formerly 1909.4.30.80).
TYPE LOCALITY: "San Antonio", Departamento del Valle, Colombia; see Lynch, 1980, Herpetologica, 29:233, for a discussion of the type locality.
DISTRIBUTION: Moderate to intermediate elevations in the Cordillera Occidental and Cordillera Central of Colombia.
COMMENT: In the *Eleutherodactylus discoidalis* group. Transferred from *Barycholos* (where it had been placed by Lynch, 1973, Herpetologica, 29:232–235) by Heyer, 1975, Smithson. Contrib. Zool., 199:32.

Eleutherodactylus marmoratus (Boulenger, 1900). Trans. Linn. Soc. London, (2)8:56.
ORIGINAL NAME: *Hylodes marmoratus*.
TYPE(S): Holotype: BM 1947.2.16.92 (formerly 99.3.25.19).
TYPE LOCALITY: "foot of Mt. Roraima, 3500 feet", Guyana.
DISTRIBUTION: Eastern Venezuela, Guyana, Surinam, and French Guiana.
COMMENT: In the *Eleutherodactylus unistrigatus* group. See comment under *Eleutherodactylus grandoculis*.

Eleutherodactylus martiae Lynch, 1974. Occas. Pap. Mus. Nat. Hist. Univ. Kansas, 31:2.
TYPE(S): Holotype: KU 152389.
TYPE LOCALITY: "Santa Cecilia, Provincia Napo, Ecuador, 340 m."
DISTRIBUTION: Amazonian slopes of the Andes of northern Ecuador (300–1300 m) and adjacent Colombia.
COMMENT: In the *Eleutherodactylus unistrigatus* group.

Eleutherodactylus martinicensis (Tschudi, 1838). Classif. Batr.:77.
ORIGINAL NAME: *Hylodes martinicensis*.
TYPE(S): Syntypes: MNHNP 4881–83, 4883A–C.
TYPE LOCALITY: Martinique (in error); Schwartz, 1967, Stud. Fauna Curaçao and other Caribb. Is., 24:34–35, has shown the syntypes to be probably from Guadeloupe.
DISTRIBUTION: Antigua, Guadeloupe, La Désirade, Iles des Saintes, Dominica, and Martinique, Lesser Antilles, West Indies.
COMMENT: In the *Eleutherodactylus auriculatus* group, according to Schwartz, 1969, Stud. Fauna Curaçao and other Caribb. Is., 30:101.

Eleutherodactylus matudai Taylor, 1941. Univ. Kansas Sci. Bull., 27:154.
TYPE(S): Holotype: USNM 110626.
TYPE LOCALITY: "Mt. Ovando, Chiapas", Mexico.
DISTRIBUTION: Lower montane zone (1500–2000 m) on the Pacific versant, from southwestern Chiapas (Mexico) to central Guatemala.
COMMENT: In the *Eleutherodactylus fitzingeri* group. Reviewed by Savage, 1975, Copeia, 1975:284–285, who suggested that the nearest relative of this species is *Eleutherodactylus milesi*.

Eleutherodactylus maussi (Boettger, 1893). Ber. Senckenb. Naturforsch. Ges., 1893:39.
ORIGINAL NAME: *Hylodes maussi*.
TYPE(S): SMF 3821 (formerly 1220.3a) was considered to be the holotype (=? lectotype) by Mertens, 1967, Senckenb. Biol., 48:39; Lynch, 1975, Occas. Pap. Mus. Nat. Hist. Univ. Kansas, 38:42, regarded MCZ 10178 as a syntype.
TYPE LOCALITY: Puerto Cabello, [Estado Carabobo,] Venezuela.
DISTRIBUTION: Coastal range of Venezuela.
COMMENT: In the *Eleutherodactylus sulcatus* group.

Eleutherodactylus megalops Ruthven, 1917. Occas. Pap. Mus. Zool. Univ. Michigan, 39:3.
TYPE(S): Holotype: UMMZ 48444.
TYPE LOCALITY: "San Lorenzo (5000'), Santa Marta Mountains, Colombia".
DISTRIBUTION: Sierra Santa Marta, Colombia.
COMMENT: In the *Eleutherodactylus unistrigatus* group.

Eleutherodactylus megalotympanum Shannon and Werler, 1955. Trans. Kansas Acad. Sci., 58:372.
TYPE(S): Holotype: formerly F. A. Shannon 4084 (now UIMNH?).
TYPE LOCALITY: Volcán San Martín, Veracruz [Mexico].
DISTRIBUTION: Sierra de los Tuxtlas, Veracruz, Mexico.
COMMENT: In the *Eleutherodactylus alfredi* group.

Eleutherodactylus melanostictus (Cope, 1876). J. Acad. Nat. Sci. Philadelphia, (2)8:109.
ORIGINAL NAME: *Lithodytes melanostictus*.
TYPE(S): Holotype: USNM 30608.
TYPE LOCALITY: Pico Blanco, eastern Costa Rica, 7000 ft.
DISTRIBUTION: Cordillera de Tilarán, Costa Rica, to Chiriquí massif of western Panama, 1128–2483 m.
COMMENT: Reviewed by Savage and DeWeese, 1981 "1980", Proc. Biol. Soc. Washington, 93:928–942, who placed it in the *Eleutherodactylus melanostictus* group, and considered *Eleutherodactylus platyrhynchus* to be a synonym. Miyamoto and Tennant, 1984, Copeia, 1984:765–768, transferred it to the *Eleutherodactylus fitzingeri* group *sensu* Savage, 1980, Prelim. Handlist Herpetofauna Costa Rica. See comment under *Eleutherodactylus monnichorum*.

Eleutherodactylus mendax Duellman, 1978. Herpetologica, 34:266.
TYPE(S): Holotype: KU 173234.
TYPE LOCALITY: "Colonia Pistipapta on the Río Umasbamba, 12 km (by road) SE of Huyro, Departamento Cuzco, Perú, elevation 1820 m (13° 03' S; 72° 30' W)".
DISTRIBUTION: Cloud forests of southern Peru.
COMMENT: In the *Eleutherodactylus unistrigatus* group.

Eleutherodactylus merendonensis Schmidt, 1933. Field Mus. Nat. Hist. Publ., Zool. Ser., 20:17.
TYPE(S): Holotype: FMNH 4672.
TYPE LOCALITY: Lower Santa Ana Canyon, west of San Pedro, Honduras.
DISTRIBUTION: Northwestern Atlantic lowlands of Honduras at Cañon Santa Ana (150–200 m).

COMMENT: In the *Eleutherodactylus fitzingeri* group. Reviewed by Savage, 1975, Copeia, 1975:285–286, who suggested a close relationship with *Eleutherodactylus punctariolus*.

Eleutherodactylus mexicanus (Brocchi, 1877). Bull. Soc. Philomath. Paris, (7)1:184.
ORIGINAL NAME: *Leiuperus mexicanus*.
TYPE(S): Holotype: MNHNP 6318.
TYPE LOCALITY: "Mexique".
DISTRIBUTION: Highlands of Oaxaca, Puebla, and adjacent Hidalgo and Veracruz, Mexico.
COMMENT: In the *Eleutherodactylus rhodopis* group.

Eleutherodactylus milesi Schmidt, 1933. Field Mus. Nat. Hist. Publ., Zool. Ser., 20:18.
TYPE(S): Holotype: FMNH 4699.
TYPE LOCALITY: Mountains west of San Pedro, Honduras.
DISTRIBUTION: Premontane and lower montane forests of the mountains (1400–1700 m) of northwestern Atlantic slope Honduras.
COMMENT: In the *Eleutherodactylus fitzingeri* group. Reviewed by Savage, 1975, Copeia, 1975:287. See comment under *Eleutherodactylus matudai*.

Eleutherodactylus mimus Taylor, 1955. Univ. Kansas Sci. Bull., 37:517.
TYPE(S): Holotype: KU 37128.
TYPE LOCALITY: "5 km NNE Tilarán, Guanacaste Province, Costa Rica".
DISTRIBUTION: Atlantic lowlands of Costa Rica and Nicaragua.
COMMENT: In the *Eleutherodactylus fitzingeri* group.

Eleutherodactylus minutus Noble, 1923. Am. Mus. Novit., 61:4.
TYPE(S): Holotype: AMNH 11404.
TYPE LOCALITY: Near Paso Bajito, Jarabacoa–Constanza Trail, La Vega Province, República Dominicana.
DISTRIBUTION: Hispaniola; Cordillera Central of the Dominican Republic between 2900–6100 ft. elev.
COMMENT: In the *Eleutherodactylus auriculatus* group, according to Schwartz, 1969, Stud. Fauna Curaçao and other Caribb. Is., 30:101.

Eleutherodactylus modipeplus Lynch, 1981. Misc. Publ. Mus. Nat. Hist. Univ. Kansas, 72:22.
TYPE(S): Holotype: KU 131283.
TYPE LOCALITY: "1 km S of the Urbina railway station, Provincia Chimborazo, Ecuador, 3650 m."
DISTRIBUTION: Known only from the edges of the Ambato–Riobamba valley in central Ecuador between 2560–3700 m elevation.
COMMENT: In the *Eleutherodactylus unistrigatus* assembly of the *Eleutherodactylus unistrigatus* group.

Eleutherodactylus monensis (Meerwarth, 1901). Mitt. Naturhist. Mus. Hamburg, 18:39.
ORIGINAL NAME: *Hylodes monensis*.
TYPE(S): Destroyed; formerly in ZMH.
TYPE LOCALITY: Isla Mona [Puerto Rico].
DISTRIBUTION: Mona I., West Indies (adjacent to Puerto Rico).
COMMENT: In the *Eleutherodactylus ricordii* group, but of uncertain affinities according to Schwartz, 1976, Bull. Florida State Mus., Biol. Sci., 21:1–46.

Eleutherodactylus monnichorum Dunn, 1940. Proc. Acad. Nat. Sci. Philadelphia, 93:107.
TYPE(S): Holotype: ANSP 21576.
TYPE LOCALITY: "Valley of the Velo, Finca Lerida, on the slope of Chiriqui volcano above Boquete, Chiriqui Province", Panama.
DISTRIBUTION: Mountains of Chiriquí, Panama.

COMMENT: In the *Eleutherodactylus fitzingeri* group of Lynch. In the less inclusive *Eleutherodactylus cruentus* group of Savage and DeWeese, 1980, Proc. Biol. Soc. Washington, 93:940. In the *Eleutherodactylus melanostictus* group *sensu* Savage (JDL).

Eleutherodactylus montanus Schmidt, 1919. Bull. Am. Mus. Nat. Hist., 41:519.
TYPE(S): Holotype: AMNH 6434.
TYPE LOCALITY: Mountainous interior of Azua Province, República Dominicana; restricted by Schwartz, 1965, Caribb. J. Sci., 4:478, to Alto Bandera, La Vega Province, República Dominicana.
DISTRIBUTION: Hispaniola; high elevations in the Cordillera Central of the Dominican Republic.
COMMENT: In the *Eleutherodactylus auriculatus* group, according to Schwartz, 1965, Caribb. J. Sci., 4:473–474.

Eleutherodactylus moro Savage, 1965. Bull. S. California Acad. Sci., 64:106.
TYPE(S): Holotype: CRE 765.
TYPE LOCALITY: "Costa Rica: Provincia de San José: Canton de Coronado: La Hondura, 1245 meters (4085 feet)".
DISTRIBUTION: Costa Rica to western Colombia.
COMMENT: In the *Eleutherodactylus unistrigatus* group of Lynch. The original description placed it in the less inclusive *Eleutherodactylus diastema* group, with *Eleutherodactylus diastema*, *Eleutherodactylus hylaeformis*, and *Eleutherodactylus vocator*. Synonymy includes *Eleutherodactylus lehmanvalenciae* Thornton, 1965, according to Savage, 1965, Copeia, 1968:878–879.

Eleutherodactylus muricatus Lynch and Miyata, 1980. Breviora, 457:2.
TYPE(S): Holotype: MCZ 94469.
TYPE LOCALITY: "Río Faisanes where it is crossed by Ecuador Highway 28 (the road from La Palma to Quito via Chiriboga), 14.4 km from the junction with Highway 30 (the Aloag to Santo Domingo de los Colorados road) at La Palma, Provincia Pichincha, Ecuador, 1380 m."
DISTRIBUTION: Spotty distribution between 800–1380 m elev. in the region of the type locality.
COMMENT: In the *Eleutherodactylus rubicundus* assembly of the *Eleutherodactylus unistrigatus* group.

Eleutherodactylus myersi (Goin and Cochran, 1963). Proc. California Acad. Sci., 31:502.
ORIGINAL NAME: *Trachyphrynus myersi*.
TYPE(S): Holotype: CAS 85177.
TYPE LOCALITY: "20 miles east of Pasto", Departamento Nariño, Colombia.
DISTRIBUTION: Páramos on the Nudo de Pasto and the southern end of the Cordillera Central in Colombia (2900–3275 m).
COMMENT: In the monophyletic *Eleutherodactylus pyrrhomerus* assembly of the *Eleutherodactylus unistrigatus* group, according to Lynch, 1984, Herpetologica, 42:237.

Eleutherodactylus nasutus (A. Lutz, 1925). C. R. Séances Soc. Biol., Paris, 93:213.
ORIGINAL NAME: *Hylodes nasutus*.
TYPE(S): Syntypes: MN 96468, USNM 96469, 96470 (lost); see comment.
TYPE LOCALITY: "Novo Friburgo, [Rio de Janeiro,] Brasil".
DISTRIBUTION: Eastern and southeastern Brazil from the states of Espírito Santo to São Paulo.
COMMENT: In the *Eleutherodactylus binotatus* group of Lynch; but see comment under *Eleutherodactylus guentheri*. Discussed by Heyer, 1984, Smithson. Contrib. Zool., 402:31–32. Cochran, 1961, Bull. U.S. Natl. Mus., 220:61, indicated that USNM 96468–70 were 'cotypes' and 96470 was exchanged with MN. Former USNM 96468 retains that number in the MN collection; USNM 96470 cannot be located (WRH).

Eleutherodactylus necerus Lynch, 1975. Occas. Pap. Mus. Nat. Hist. Univ. Kansas, 38:
  32.
  TYPE(S): Holotype: USNM 195798.
  TYPE LOCALITY: "Mindo, Pichincha Prov., Ecuador".
  DISTRIBUTION: Moderate elevations on the Pacific versant of Ecuador.
  COMMENT: In the *Eleutherodactylus biporcatus* group.

Eleutherodactylus neodreptus Schwartz, 1965. Proc. Biol. Soc. Washington, 78:165.
  TYPE(S): Holotype: MCZ 43207.
  TYPE LOCALITY: "24 km SW Barahona, 3700 feet, Barahona Province, República
    Dominicana".
  DISTRIBUTION: Known only from the type locality.
  COMMENT: Of uncertain relationship to other *Eleutherodactylus*, possibly in the
    Eleutherodactylus auriculatus group, according to the original description.

Eleutherodactylus nicefori Cochran and Goin, 1970. Bull. U.S. Natl. Mus., 288:407.
  TYPE(S): Holotype: USNM 147012.
  TYPE LOCALITY: "Páramo del Almorzadero, Santander, Colombia".
  DISTRIBUTION: Páramos of the northern Cordillera Oriental of Colombia.
  COMMENT: In the *Eleutherodactylus myersi* assembly of the *Eleutherodactylus
    unistrigatus* group.

Eleutherodactylus nigriventris (Lutz, 1925). C. R. Séances Soc. Biol., Paris, 93:139.
  ORIGINAL NAME: *Hylaplesia nigriventris*.
  TYPE(S): Not designated.
  TYPE LOCALITY: "Itatiaia et Serra de Cubatao", Brazil.
  DISTRIBUTION: Known only from Itatiaia, Brazil.
  COMMENT: In the *Eleutherodactylus lacteus* group.

Eleutherodactylus nigrogriseus (Andersson, 1945). Ark. Zool., 37A:87.
  ORIGINAL NAME: *Pseudohyla nigrogrisea*.
  TYPE(S): Syntypes: NHRM 1905 (6 specimens).
  TYPE LOCALITY: Baños, [Provincia Tungurahua,] Ecuador.
  DISTRIBUTION: Cloud forests along the eastern face of the Andes in Ecuador.
  COMMENT: In the *Eleutherodactylus unistrigatus* group. Reviewed by Lynch, 1969,
    Bull. S. California Acad. Sci., 68:219–224.

Eleutherodactylus nigrovittatus Andersson, 1945. Ark. Zool., 37A:42.
  TYPE(S): NHRM.
  TYPE LOCALITY: "Ambitagua [=Abitagua], 1200 m above the sea level", eastern
    Ecuador.
  DISTRIBUTION: Amazonian Peru, Ecuador, Colombia to 1935 m elevation.
  COMMENT: In the *Eleutherodactylus discoidalis* group. *Phyzelaphryne miriamae* Heyer,
    1977, was considered a synonym by Lynch, 1980, Bull. Mus. Natl. Hist. Nat.,
    Paris, (4)2:299–301. See comment under *Phyzelaphryne miriamae*.

Eleutherodactylus noblei Barbour and Dunn, 1926. Proc. Biol. Soc. Washington, 34:161.
  TYPE(S): Holotype: MCZ 7827.
  TYPE LOCALITY: Guápiles, Costa Rica.
  DISTRIBUTION: Eastern Honduras, Costa Rica, Nicaragua, and Panama.
  COMMENT: In the *Eleutherodactylus fitzingeri* group.

Eleutherodactylus nortoni Schwartz, 1976. Herpetologica, 32:165.
  TYPE(S): Holotype: USNM 195847.
  TYPE LOCALITY: "8.6 km SW Seguin, 1007 m, Département de l'Ouest, Haiti".
  DISTRIBUTION: Hispaniola; the southern slopes of the Massif de la Selle from
    Seguin in the west to above Cabo Rojo in the east, 1900–3850 ft. elev.
  COMMENT: In the *Eleutherodactylus inoptatus* group, according to the original
    description.

Eleutherodactylus nubicola Dunn, 1926. Proc. Boston Soc. Nat. Hist., 38:116.
TYPE(S): Holotype: MCZ 2846.
TYPE LOCALITY: Cinchona, 5100 feet elevation, St. Andrew Parish, Jamaica.
DISTRIBUTION: Jamaica; high elevations of the Blue Mountains in the conterminous parts of Portland, St. Thomas, and St. Andrew parishes.
COMMENT: In the *Eleutherodactylus gossei* group according to Goin, 1954, Ann. Carnegie Mus., 33:186, and Crombie, 1977, Proc. Biol. Soc. Washington, 90: 194–204.

Eleutherodactylus nyctophylax Lynch, 1976. Occas. Pap. Mus. Nat. Hist. Univ. Kansas, 55:16.
TYPE(S): Holotype: KU 110909.
TYPE LOCALITY: "Tandapi, Prov. Pichincha, Ecuador, 1460 m."
DISTRIBUTION: Known only from the type locality.
COMMENT: In the *Eleutherodactylus unistrigatus* group.

Eleutherodactylus obmutescens Lynch, 1980. Caldasia, 13:168.
TYPE(S): Holotype: ICN 2087.
TYPE LOCALITY: "Páramo de Puracé, alrededores de la Laguna San Rafael, Departamento del Cauca, Colombia, 3400 m."
DISTRIBUTION: Páramos between Departamentos Cauca and Huila, Colombia.
COMMENT: In the *Eleutherodactylus orcesi* assembly in the *Eleutherodactylus unistrigatus* group.

Eleutherodactylus ockendeni (Boulenger, 1912). Ann. Mag. Nat. Hist., (8)10:187.
ORIGINAL NAME: *Hylodes ockendeni*.
TYPE(S): Syntypes: BM 1947.2.16.88–90 (formerly 1907.5.7.19–21).
TYPE LOCALITY: "La Union, Rio Huacamayo, Carabaya, [Departamento Puno,] S. E. Peru, 2000 feet", southeastern Peru.
DISTRIBUTION: Amazonian Ecuador, Colombia, Brazil and Peru, 300–1200 m.
COMMENT: In the *Eleutherodactylus unistrigatus* group. Includes *Syrrhophus calcaratus* Andersson, 1945 (=*Eleutherodactylus anderssoni* Lynch, 1968) according to Lynch, 1974, Occas. Pap. Mus. Nat. Hist. Univ. Kansas, 31:16. According to Lynch, 1974, Occas. Pap. Mus. Nat. Hist. Univ. Kansas, 31:16, the Panama records of this species probably refer to *Eleutherodactylus frater*, but Lynch, 1980, Herpetologica, 36:134–185, considered the Panama records to apply to *Eleutherodactylus taeniatus*. Includes *Hylodes hylaeformis* Melin, 1941 (=*Eleutherodactylus melini* Bokermann, 1958), according to Lynch, 1980, Am. Mus. Novit., 2696:12, who provided a synonymy. Distribution records discussed by Lynch and Lescure, 1980, Bull. Mus. Natl. Hist. Nat., Paris, (4)2: 311.

Eleutherodactylus ocreatus Lynch, 1981. Misc. Publ. Mus. Nat. Hist. Univ. Kansas, 72:26.
TYPE(S): Holotype: KU 117573.
TYPE LOCALITY: "west slope of Volcán Chiles, 10 km W Tufiño, Prov. Carchi, Ecuador, 3500–3800 m."
DISTRIBUTION: Páramos del Angel (3500–4150 m) in extreme northern Ecuador.
COMMENT: In the *Eleutherodactylus myersi* assembly of the *Eleutherodactylus unistrigatus* group; most closely related to *Eleutherodactylus trepidotus*, according to the original description. In the more inclusive (and monophyletic) *Eleutherodactylus pyrrhomerus* assembly and the sister-species of *Eleutherodactylus trepidotus*, according to Lynch, 1984, Herpetologica, 40:237.

Eleutherodactylus octavioi Bokermann, 1965. Copeia, 1965:440.
TYPE(S): Holotype: WCAB 14470.
TYPE LOCALITY: "Estrada da Cascatinha, Tijuca Mountains, 350 m, Rio de Janeiro, state of Guanabara [now Rio de Janeiro], Brazil".
DISTRIBUTION: Vicinity of the type locality.

COMMENT: In the *Eleutherodactylus binotatus* group.

Eleutherodactylus oeus Heyer, 1984. Smithson. Contrib. Zool., 402:32.
   TYPE(S): Holotype: MN 1244.
   TYPE LOCALITY: "Brazil: Espirito Santo; Santa Teresa".
   DISTRIBUTION: Known only from the type locality.
   COMMENT: In the *Eleutherodactylus guentheri* cluster according to the original
      description. See comment under *Eleutherodactylus guentheri.*

Eleutherodactylus omiltemanus (Günther, 1901). Biol. Cent. Am., Rept. Batr.:216.
   ORIGINAL NAME: *Syrrhaphus omiltemanus.*
   TYPE(S): BM.
   TYPE LOCALITY: "Mexico, Omilteme in Guerrero, 8000 feet".
   DISTRIBUTION: High elevations of the Sierra Madre del Sur in Guerrero, Mexico.
   COMMENT: Lynch, 1976, Occas. Pap. Mus. Nat. Hist. Univ. Kansas, 61:1–24, placed
      the Mexican and Central American species *Eleutherodactylus greggi,*
      Eleutherodactylus glaucus, Eleutherodactylus omiltemanus, and *Eleutherodactylus*
      batrachylus in his *Eleutherodactylus unistrigatus* group. Ford and Savage, 1984,
      Occas. Pap. Mus. Nat. Hist. Univ. Kansas, 110:1–9, considered *Eleutherodactylus*
      glaucus and *Eleutherodactylus batrachylus* unassignable to species group and
      regarded the remaining species (*Eleutherodactylus greggi, Eleutherodactylus*
      omiltemanus, and a new species, *Eleutherodactylus daryi*) to form a monophyletic
      group (their *Eleutherodactylus omiltemanus* group) not associated with the
      Eleutherodactylus unistrigatus group. Synonymy includes *Eleutherodactylus*
      calcitrans, according to Lynch, 1970, Herpetologica, 26:175–176.

Eleutherodactylus orcesi Lynch, 1972. Herpetologica, 28:142.
   TYPE(S): Holotype: KU 130316.
   TYPE LOCALITY: "on the Guaranda–Ambato road on the southwest slope of Nevado
      Chimborazo, about 5 km SW of the Bolivar–Chimborazo border, Bolivar
      Province, Ecuador, 3800 m."
   DISTRIBUTION: Páramos to the north and east of Guaranda, and to the west of
      Quito, Ecuador, at elevations between 3160–3800 m.
   COMMENT: In the *Eleutherodactylus orcesi* assembly of *Eleutherodactylus unistrigatus*
      group.

Eleutherodactylus orcutti Dunn, 1928. Proc. U.S. Natl. Mus., 74:1.
   TYPE(S): Holotype: USNM 73866.
   TYPE LOCALITY: Arntully, St. Thomas Parish, Jamaica.
   DISTRIBUTION: Eastern Jamaica; inland portions of Portland, St. Andrew, and St.
      Thomas parishes, 750–4000 ft. elev.
   COMMENT: In the *Eleutherodactylus orcutti* group, according to Shreve and Williams,
      1963, Bull. Mus. Comp. Zool., 129:326–327, but placed in the *Eleutherodactylus*
      gossei group by Schwartz and Fowler, 1973, Stud. Fauna Curaçao and other
      Caribb. Is., 43:135, and Crombie, 1977, Proc. Biol. Soc. Washington, 90:194–
      204. See comment under *Eleutherodactylus semipalmatus.*

Eleutherodactylus orestes Lynch, 1979. Misc. Publ. Mus. Nat. Hist. Univ. Kansas, 66:24.
   TYPE(S): Holotype: KU 141998.
   TYPE LOCALITY: "11 km NE Urdaneta, Provincia Loja, Ecuador, 2970 m."
   DISTRIBUTION: Between 2720–3120 m on the eastern Andes from the valley of
      Cuenca to the Loja Basin, Ecuador.
   COMMENT: In the *Eleutherodactylus myersi* assembly of the *Eleutherodactylus*
      unistrigatus group.

Eleutherodactylus ornatissimus (Despax, 1911). Bull. Mus. Natl. Hist. Nat., Paris, 17:91.
   ORIGINAL NAME: *Hylodes ornatissimus.*
   TYPE(S): Holotype: MNHNP 06-264.
   TYPE LOCALITY: Ecuador.
   DISTRIBUTION: Low cloud forests in west-central Ecuador.

COMMENT: In the *Eleutherodactylus unistrigatus* group. Redescribed by Lynch, 1970, Trans. Kansas Acad. Sci., 73:173–177.

Eleutherodactylus orocostalis Rivero, 1961. Bull. Mus. Comp. Zool., 126:68.
TYPE(S): Holotype: MBUCV 2003.
TYPE LOCALITY: El Junquito, D. F. [Venezuela].
DISTRIBUTION: Vicinity of the type locality.
COMMENT: In the *Eleutherodactylus unistrigatus* group.

Eleutherodactylus orphnolaimus Lynch, 1970. Proc. Biol. Soc. Washington, 21:221.
TYPE(S): Holotype: KU 125332.
TYPE LOCALITY: "Lago Agrio, Napo, Ecuador, 330 m."
DISTRIBUTION: Eastern Ecuador.
COMMENT: In the *Eleutherodactylus unistrigatus* group.

Eleutherodactylus oxyrhyncus (Duméril and Bibron, 1841). Erp. Gén., 8:622.
ORIGINAL NAME: *Hylodes oxyrhyncus*.
TYPE(S): Holotype: MNHNP 753.
TYPE LOCALITY: Unknown.
DISTRIBUTION: Hispaniola; Massif de la Hotte and the Massif de la Selle in Haiti, 2500–4800 ft. elev.
COMMENT: In the *Eleutherodactylus ricordii* group, according to Schwartz, 1972, J. Herpetol., 5:104, who included *Eleutherodactylus femurlevis* Cochran as a synonym. Taxonomic disposition discussed by Lynch and Schwartz, 1971, J. Herpetol., 5:104–109. The unjustified (but understandable) emendation *Eleutherodactylus oxyrhynchus* has had nearly universal use (DRF).

Eleutherodactylus palmeri (Boulenger, 1912). Ann. Mag. Nat. Hist., (8)10:189.
ORIGINAL NAME: *Hylodes palmeri*.
TYPE(S): Syntypes: BM 1910.7.11.64–65.
TYPE LOCALITY: "Pueblo Rico, Choco, S.W. Colombia, 5200 feet".
DISTRIBUTION: Known only from the types.
COMMENT: In the *Eleutherodactylus unistrigatus* group.

Eleutherodactylus pantoni Dunn, 1926. Proc. Boston Soc. Nat. Hist., 38:119.
TYPE(S): Holotype: MCZ 11123.
TYPE LOCALITY: Spaldings, Clarendon Parish, Jamaica.
DISTRIBUTION: Jamaica; widespread.
COMMENT: In the *Eleutherodactylus gossei* group according to Goin, 1954, Ann. Carnegie Mus., 33:186, and Crombie, 1977, Proc. Biol. Soc. Washington, 90: 194–204. Schwartz and Fowler, 1973, Stud. Fauna Curaçao and other Caribb. Is., 43:118, suggested that *Eleutherodactylus pantoni pentasyringos* may actually be a distinct species; these authors recognized three subspecies.

Eleutherodactylus parabates Schwartz, 1964. Breviora, 208:9.
TYPE(S): Holotype: MCZ 43202.
TYPE LOCALITY: 20 km SW Hondo Valle, 5950 feet (1800 meters), Independencia Province, República Dominicana.
DISTRIBUTION: Hispaniola; Dominican Republic in the Sierra de Neiba along the Haitian border, 4800–5950 ft. elev.
COMMENT: Related to *Eleutherodactylus ventrilineatus* (a member of the *Eleutherodactylus dimidiatus* group) according to the original description.

Eleutherodactylus pardalis (Barbour, 1928). Proc. New England Zool. Club, 10:26.
ORIGINAL NAME: *Syrrhopus pardalis*.
TYPE(S): Holotype: MCZ 13057.
TYPE LOCALITY: La Loma, in the cloud forest on trail from Chiriquicito to Boquete, Bocas del Toro Province, Panama.
DISTRIBUTION: Panama; Costa Rica.

COMMENT: In the *Eleutherodactylus unistrigatus* group of Lynch and in the less inclusive *Eleutherodactylus cruentus* group of Savage, 1980, Prelim. Handlist Herpetofauna Costa Rica:6.

Eleutherodactylus parvillus Lynch, 1976. Occas. Pap. Mus. Nat. Hist. Univ. Kansas, 55:19.
TYPE(S): Holotype: KU 111345.
TYPE LOCALITY: "Tandapi, Prov. Pichincha, Ecuador, 1460 m."
DISTRIBUTION: Cloud forests in western Colombia and Ecuador, 1350–2200 m.
COMMENT: In the *Eleutherodactylus unistrigatus* group.

Eleutherodactylus parvus (Girard, 1853). Proc. Acad. Nat. Sci. Philadelphia, 6:423.
ORIGINAL NAME: *Hylodes parvus*.
TYPE(S): Not located.
TYPE LOCALITY: Rio de Janeiro [Brazil].
DISTRIBUTION: Southeastern Brazil.
COMMENT: In the *Eleutherodactylus parvus* group. Synonymy includes *Phrynanodus nanus* Ahl, 1933, according to Lynch, 1968, Copeia, 1968:875–876, and *Leptodactylus pumilio* Boulenger, 1920, according to Heyer, 1972, Contrib. Sci. Nat. Hist. Mus. Los Angeles Co., 231:2–3.

Eleutherodactylus pastazensis Andersson, 1945. Ark. Zool., (2)37A:37.
TYPE(S): Syntypes: NHRM 1918 (2 specimens); the larger specimen designated the lectotype by Lynch and Duellman, 1980, Misc. Publ. Mus. Nat. Hist. Univ. Kansas, 69:46.
TYPE LOCALITY: "Yauguilla" (=Yungilla) and "mount Tungura [=Mount Tungurahua], 1840 m above the sea level", eastern Ecuador; restricted to Yauguilla, Provincia Tungurahua, Ecuador, by lectotype designation.
DISTRIBUTION: Upper Río Pastaza Valley in the vicinity of Baños, 1800–1840 m, Ecuador.
COMMENT: In the *Eleutherodactylus unistrigatus* assembly of the *Eleutherodactylus unistrigatus* group.

Eleutherodactylus patriciae Schwartz, 1965. Caribb. J. Sci., 4:474.
TYPE(S): Holotype: MCZ 43192.
TYPE LOCALITY: 9 km NNW Valle Nuevo, about 8000 feet, on the side of Alto Bandera, La Vega Province, República Dominicana.
DISTRIBUTION: Hispaniola; Cordillera Central of the Dominican Republic, 7000–8200 ft. elev.
COMMENT: In the *Eleutherodactylus auriculatus* group, according to Schwartz, 1969, Stud. Fauna Curaçao and other Caribb. Is., 30:101.

Eleutherodactylus paulodutrai Bokermann, 1975 "1974". Rev. Brasil. Biol., 34:15.
TYPE(S): Holotype: WCAB 47227.
TYPE LOCALITY: "Centro de Pesquisas do Cacau, Ilhéus, Bahia, Brasil".
DISTRIBUTION: Atlantic forests in southern Bahia, Brazil.
COMMENT: In the *Eleutherodactylus ramagii* group.

Eleutherodactylus paulsoni Schwartz, 1964. Breviora, 208:5.
TYPE(S): Holotype: MCZ 43200.
TYPE LOCALITY: "4.5 miles (7.2 km) northwest of Les Cayes, Dépt. du Sud, Haiti".
DISTRIBUTION: Southwestern Hispaniola; the Tiburon Peninsula of Haiti.
COMMENT: In the *Eleutherodactylus ricordii* group, according to the original description.

Eleutherodactylus paululus Lynch, 1974. Occas. Pap. Mus. Nat. Hist. Univ. Kansas, 31:6.
TYPE(S): Holotype: KU 126209.
TYPE LOCALITY: "Lago Agrio, Provincia Napo, Ecuador, 330 m."
DISTRIBUTION: Base of the Amazonian slopes of the Andes in northern and central Ecuador, 300–570 m.

COMMENT: In the *Eleutherodactylus unistrigatus* group.

Eleutherodactylus peraticus Lynch, 1980. Caldasia, 13:184.
TYPE(S): Holotype: KU 168915.
TYPE LOCALITY: "7 km NE Tenerife, Departamento del Valle del Cauca, Colombia, 2850 m alt."
DISTRIBUTION: Vicinity of the type locality.
COMMENT: In the *Eleutherodactylus unistrigatus* group.

Eleutherodactylus percultus Lynch, 1979. Misc. Publ. Mus. Nat. Hist. Univ. Kansas, 66:26.
TYPE(S): Holotype: KU 166058.
TYPE LOCALITY: "Abra de Zamora, Provincia Zamora-Chinchipe, Ecuador, 2850 m."
DISTRIBUTION: Known only from the type locality.
COMMENT: In the *Eleutherodactylus unistrigatus* group.

Eleutherodactylus peruvianus (Melin, 1941). Göteborgs K. Vetensk. Vitterh. Samh. Handl., (B)1(4):43.
ORIGINAL NAME: *Hylodes peruvianus.*
TYPE(S): Holotype: NHMG 490.
TYPE LOCALITY: Roque, [Departamento San Martín,] Peru.
DISTRIBUTION: Upper Amazon Basin in western Brazil, southern Ecuador, and eastern Peru and in cloud forests on the eastern slopes of the Andes to 1910 m in Ecuador and Peru.
COMMENT: In the *Eleutherodactylus fitzingeri* group. Removed from the synonymy of *Eleutherodactylus conspicillatus* by Lynch, 1980, Am. Mus. Novit., 2696:4.

Eleutherodactylus petersi Lynch and Duellman, 1980. Misc. Publ. Mus. Nat. Hist. Univ. Kansas, 69:48.
TYPE(S): Holotype: KU 143508.
TYPE LOCALITY: "16.5 km NNE Santa Rosa, Provincia Napo, Ecuador, 1700 m."
DISTRIBUTION: In cloud forests at 1410–1950 m on the eastern face of the Andes in Departamento Putumayo (Colombia) and Provincia Napo (Ecuador).
COMMENT: In the *Eleutherodactylus unistrigatus* group.

Eleutherodactylus pezopetrus Schwartz, 1960. Reading Public Mus. and Art Gallery Sci. Publ., 11:37.
TYPE(S): Holotype: AMNH 63469.
TYPE LOCALITY: La Cantera, Miranda, Oriente [now Granma] Province, Cuba.
DISTRIBUTION: Known only from the type locality.
COMMENT: In the *Eleutherodactylus ricordii* group, according to the original description.

Eleutherodactylus pharangobates Duellman, 1978. Proc. Biol. Soc. Washington, 91:426.
TYPE(S): Holotype: KU 173236.
TYPE LOCALITY: "Buenos Aires, 2400 m, Departamento Cuzco, Perú (13° 07' S; 71° 28' W)".
DISTRIBUTION: Central Peru to northern Bolivia along the lower Amazonian slopes of the Andes.
COMMENT: In the *Eleutherodactylus unistrigatus* group.

Eleutherodactylus phoxocephalus Lynch, 1979. Misc. Publ. Mus. Nat. Hist. Univ. Kansas, 66:29.
TYPE(S): Holotype: KU 142075.
TYPE LOCALITY: "Pilaló, Provincia Cotopaxi, Ecuador, 2340 m."
DISTRIBUTION: Intermediate elevations (2030–2960 m) on the Pacific slopes of the Ecuadorian Andes from Volcán El Corazón to the Loja Basin, Ecuador.
COMMENT: In the *Eleutherodactylus unistrigatus* group.

Eleutherodactylus pictissimus Cochran, 1935. Proc. Boston Soc. Nat. Hist., 40:371.
TYPE(S): Holotype: MCZ 19846.
TYPE LOCALITY: Tardieu, Massif de la Hotte, about 3000 feet, Département du Sud, Haiti.
DISTRIBUTION: Western two-thirds of Hispaniola.
COMMENT: In the *Eleutherodactylus ricordii* group, and consisting of three geographic races, according to Schwartz, 1965, Stud. Fauna Curaçao and other Caribb. Is., 22:101–114, one of which was treated as a species (*Eleutherodactylus probolaeus*) by Schwartz and Thomas, 1975, Carnegie Mus. Nat. Hist. Spec. Publ., 1:33. Reviewed by Schwartz, 1976, Bull. Florida State Mus., Biol. Sci., 21:3–10.

Eleutherodactylus pinarensis Dunn, 1926. Occas. Pap. Boston Soc. Nat. Hist., 5:213.
TYPE(S): Holotype: MCZ 3814.
TYPE LOCALITY: Isla de Pinos [now Isla de Juventud] (Cuba); restricted by Schwartz, 1959, Herpetologica, 15:61, to Los Indios, Isla de Pinos [=Isla de Juventud], Cuba.
DISTRIBUTION: Cuba; from north-central Habana Province to northwestern Matanzas Province; isolated records from the extreme western Península de Guanahacabibes; Isla de Pinos (=Isla de Juventud).
COMMENT: In the *Eleutherodactylus ricordii* group according to Schwartz, 1958, Am. Mus. Novit., 1873:2.

Eleutherodactylus pinchoni Schwartz, 1967. Stud. Fauna Curaçao and other Caribb. Is., 24:45.
TYPE(S): Holotype: MCZ 43231.
TYPE LOCALITY: 3 km W Grand Café, 600 ft., Guadeloupe (Lesser Antilles).
DISTRIBUTION: The Basse-Terre portion of Guadeloupe, 600–2200 ft. elev.
COMMENT: In the *Eleutherodactylus auriculatus* group, according to Schwartz, 1969, Stud. Fauna Curaçao and other Caribb. Is., 30:101.

Eleutherodactylus pituinus Schwartz, 1965. Caribb. J. Sci., 4:497.
TYPE(S): Holotype: MCZ 43194.
TYPE LOCALITY: 6 mi. W Constanza, 4250 ft., La Vega Province, República Dominicana.
DISTRIBUTION: Hispaniola; Cordillera Central in the vicinity of the type locality and La Horma, 4000–5400 ft. elev., Dominican Republic.
COMMENT: In the *Eleutherodactylus auriculatus* group, according to Schwartz, 1969, Stud. Fauna Curaçao and other Caribb. Is., 30:101.

Eleutherodactylus planirostris (Cope, 1862). Proc. Acad. Nat. Sci. Philadelphia, 14:153.
ORIGINAL NAME: *Hylodes planirostris*.
TYPE(S): "Mus. Salem" (=YPM), now lost.
TYPE LOCALITY: New Providence Island, Bahama Islands.
DISTRIBUTION: Cuba, Bahamas, Cayman Is., Caicos Is.; introduced in Florida and Louisiana (USA), Jamaica, and Veracruz (Mexico).
COMMENT: In the *Eleutherodactylus ricordii* group; Schwartz, 1965, Stud. Fauna Curaçao and other Caribb. Is., 22:99–101, recognized four subspecies. Reviewed by Schwartz, 1974, Cat. Am. Amph. Rept., 154.1–4.

Eleutherodactylus platydactylus (Boulenger, 1903). Ann. Mag. Nat. Hist., (7)12:554.
ORIGINAL NAME: *Hylodes platydactylus*.
TYPE(S): Syntypes: BM 1902.11.28.11–13, 1903.6.30.8–10.
TYPE LOCALITY: "Santo Domingo, Carabaya, S.E. Peru".
DISTRIBUTION: Southeastern Peru.
COMMENT: In the *Eleutherodactylus unistrigatus* group.

Eleutherodactylus pliciferus (Boulenger, 1888). Ann. Mag. Nat. Hist., (6)2:41.
ORIGINAL NAME: *Hylodes pliciferus*.
TYPE(S): Holotype: BM 1947.2.15.98 (formerly 88.4.18.16).
TYPE LOCALITY: Iguarasse [=Igaraçu], Pernambuco, Brazil.
DISTRIBUTION: Pernambuco, Brazil.
COMMENT: In the *Eleutherodactylus binotatus* group. Doubtfully distinct from *Eleutherodactylus binotatus* (JDL).

Eleutherodactylus podiciferus (Cope, 1876). J. Acad. Nat. Sci. Philadelphia, (2)8:107.
ORIGINAL NAME: *Lithodytes podiciferus*.
TYPE(S): Syntypes: including UMMZ 92433 (formerly USNM 30664), USNM 30662, 30665-75, and MCZ (?).
TYPE LOCALITY: Pico Blanco, eastern Costa Rica.
DISTRIBUTION: Cordilleras de Tilarán, Central, and Talamanca in Costa Rica, and the Chiriquí extension of the latter range in western Panama, 100-2100 m.
COMMENT: In the *Eleutherodactylus fitzingeri* group of Lynch. In the less inclusive *Eleutherodactylus gollmeri* group of Savage, 1980, Prelim. Handlist Herpetofauna Costa Rica:7.

Eleutherodactylus poolei Cochran, 1938. Proc. Biol. Soc. Washington, 51:93.
TYPE(S): Holotype: USNM 73999.
TYPE LOCALITY: Citadel of King Christophe (=Citadelle Laferrière, Département du Nord, Haiti).
DISTRIBUTION: Known only from the type locality.
COMMENT: In the *Eleutherodactylus auriculatus* group, according to Schwartz, 1969, Stud. Fauna Curaçao and other Caribb. Is., 30:101.

Eleutherodactylus portoricensis Schmidt, 1927. Am. Mus. Novit., 279:2.
TYPE(S): Holotype: AMNH 10249.
TYPE LOCALITY: El Yunque, 2000 feet, Bosque Experimental de Luquillo, Puerto Rico.
DISTRIBUTION: Forested uplands of Puerto Rico.
COMMENT: In the *Eleutherodactylus auriculatus* group, according to Schwartz, 1969, Stud. Fauna Curaçao and other Caribb. Is., 30:101. See comment under *Eleutherodactylus johnstonei*.

Eleutherodactylus probolaeus Schwartz, 1965. Stud. Fauna Curaçao and other Caribb. Is., 22:110.
ORIGINAL NAME: *Eleutherodactylus pictissimus probolaeus*.
TYPE(S): Holotype: MCZ 43197.
TYPE LOCALITY: 0.5 mi. NW Boca de Yuma, La Altagracia Province, República Dominicana.
DISTRIBUTION: Vicinity of type locality.
COMMENT: In the *Eleutherodactylus ricordii* group. Reviewed by Schwartz, 1976, Bull. Florida State Mus., Biol. Sci., 21:23-26. See comment under *Eleutherodactylus pictissimus*.

Eleutherodactylus prolatus Lynch and Duellman, 1980. Misc. Publ. Mus. Nat. Hist. Univ. Kansas, 69:51.
TYPE(S): Holotype: KU 166008.
TYPE LOCALITY: "2 km SSW Río Reventador, Provincia Napo, Ecuador, 1490 m."
DISTRIBUTION: Lower cloud forests (1140-1490 m) on the eastern face of the Andes in Ecuador.
COMMENT: In the *Eleutherodactylus unistrigatus* group.

Eleutherodactylus prolixodiscus Lynch, 1978. Copeia, 1978:17.
TYPE(S): Holotype: KU 132726.
TYPE LOCALITY: 30 km ENE Bucaramanga, road to Cucuta, Depto. Santander, Colombia, 2485 m.
DISTRIBUTION: Northern Cordillera Oriental of Colombia and adjacent Venezuela, 2300–2485 m.
COMMENT: In the *Eleutherodactylus unistrigatus* group; the frogs from the Sierra Nevada de Santa Marta referred to this species by Lynch, 1978, Copeia, 1978: 18, are of a distinct species (JDL).

Eleutherodactylus proserpens Lynch, 1979. Misc. Publ. Mus. Nat. Hist. Univ. Kansas, 66:32.
TYPE(S): Holotype: USNM 198484.
TYPE LOCALITY: "between Sapote and Suro Rancho, Provincia Morona-Santiago, Ecuador, 2622 m."
DISTRIBUTION: Elevations between 1707–2622 m on the Amazonian slopes of the eastern Andes in southern Ecuador and the adjacent Cordillera del Condor.
COMMENT: Most closely related to *Eleutherodactylus colodactylus* according to Lynch, 1979, Misc. Publ. Mus. Nat. Hist. Univ. Kansas, 66:35. In the *Eleutherodactylus unistrigatus* group.

Eleutherodactylus pseudoacuminatus Shreve, 1935. Occas. Pap. Boston Soc. Nat. Hist., 8: 218.
TYPE(S): Holotype: MCZ 19948.
TYPE LOCALITY: Sarayacu, [Provincia Pastaza,] Ecuador.
DISTRIBUTION: Amazonian Ecuador and adjacent Colombia (330–570 m).
COMMENT: In the *Eleutherodactylus unistrigatus* group.

Eleutherodactylus pugnax Lynch, 1973. Bull. S. California Acad. Sci., 72:107.
TYPE(S): Holotype: KU 146466.
TYPE LOCALITY: "Salto de Agua, 2.5 km NNE Río Reventador, Napo Prov., Ecuador, 1660 m."
DISTRIBUTION: Cloud forest at 1660–2540 m on the eastern face of the Andes in northern Ecuador and southern Colombia.
COMMENT: In the *Eleutherodactylus unistrigatus* group. See Lynch, 1980, Proc. Biol. Soc. Washington, 93:336–337.

Eleutherodactylus pulvinatus Rivero, 1968. Breviora, 306:4.
TYPE(S): Holotype: MCZ 64741.
TYPE LOCALITY: "Paso del Danto, region of La Escalera around 1400 m, above San Isidro road from El Dorado to Sta. Elena de Uairén, Estado Bolívar, Venezuela".
DISTRIBUTION: Vicinity of the type locality.
COMMENT: In the *Eleutherodactylus unistrigatus* group.

Eleutherodactylus punctariolus (Peters, 1863). Monatsber. Preuss. Akad. Wiss. Berlin, 1863:462.
ORIGINAL NAME: *Hyla punctariola*.
TYPE(S): Holotype: ZMB 4918.
TYPE LOCALITY: Veragua, Panama.
DISTRIBUTION: Panama; Costa Rica.
COMMENT: In the *Eleutherodactylus fitzingeri* group. See Savage, 1975, Copeia, 1975: 287–288, for review, who suggested a close relationship with *Eleutherodactylus merendonensis*.

Eleutherodactylus pusillus Bokermann, 1967. Neotropica, 13:1.
TYPE(S): Holotype: WCAB 31461.
TYPE LOCALITY: "Estación de Fruticultura de Bocaina, próximo al salto del alto Río Mombucaba, 1.600 m, en el município de São José do Barreiro, Estado de São Paulo, Brasil".
DISTRIBUTION: Serra da Bocaina, São Paulo, Brazil.

COMMENT: In the *Eleutherodactylus parvus* group.

Eleutherodactylus pycnodermis Lynch, 1979. Misc. Publ. Mus. Nat. Hist. Univ. Kansas, 66:35.
TYPE(S): Holotype: USNM 199754.
TYPE LOCALITY: "San Vicente, Provincia Morona-Santiago, Ecuador, 2805–2835 m."
DISTRIBUTION: Cordillera de Matanga east of Cuenca, Provincia Morona Santiago, Ecuador, 2652–3384 m elev.
COMMENT: In the *Eleutherodactylus unistrigatus* group.

Eleutherodactylus pygmaeus Taylor, 1937 "1936". Trans. Kansas Acad. Sci., 39:352.
TYPE(S): Holotype: UIMNH 16125 (formerly EHT-HMS 3691).
TYPE LOCALITY: "1 mile north of Rodriguez Clara, Vera Cruz", Mexico.
DISTRIBUTION: Extreme southern Michoacán and México (state) in Mexico, south and east along the Pacific slope to Guatemala; Veracruz and eastern Oaxaca, Mexico, on the Atlantic slope.
COMMENT: In the *Eleutherodactylus rhodopis* group.

Eleutherodactylus pyrrhomerus Lynch, 1976. Herpetologica, 32:310.
TYPE(S): Holotype: KU 131606.
TYPE LOCALITY: "east edge of Pilalo, Cotopaxi Province, Ecuador, elevation 2580 m."
DISTRIBUTION: Vicinity of Pilalo, Cotopaxi Province, Ecuador (2660–2900 m), on the Pacific versant.
COMMENT: Most closely related to *Eleutherodactylus gladiator* and *Eleutherodactylus leoni* according to Lynch, 1976, Herpetologica, 32:311. In the monophyletic *Eleutherodactylus pyrrhomerus* assembly of the *Eleutherodactylus unistrigatus* group, according to Lynch, 1984, Herpetologica, 40:237.

Eleutherodactylus quaquaversus Lynch, 1974. Occas. Pap. Mus. Nat. Hist. Univ. Kansas, 31:9.
TYPE(S): Holotype: KU 123745.
TYPE LOCALITY: "south slope of the Cordillera del Dué above the Río Coca, Provincia Napo, Ecuador, 1150 m."
DISTRIBUTION: Lower Amazonian slopes (300–1830 m) of the Andes from northern Ecuador south to the Cordillera del Condor.
COMMENT: In the *Eleutherodactylus unistrigatus* group.

Eleutherodactylus quinquagesimus Lynch and Trueb, 1980. Copeia, 1980:392.
TYPE(S): Holotype: KU 167859.
TYPE LOCALITY: "Quebrada Zapadores, 5 km ESE Chiriboga, 2010 m, Provincia Pichincha, Ecuador (latitude 00° 17' S, longitude 78° 46' W)".
DISTRIBUTION: Cloud forests between 1920–2710 m elev. in Imbabura and Pichincha provinces in western Ecuador.
COMMENT: In the *Eleutherodactylus crucifer* assembly of the *Eleutherodactylus unistrigatus* group and most closely allied with *Eleutherodactylus calcaratus*, *Eleutherodactylus chloronotus*, *Eleutherodactylus crucifer*, and *Eleutherodactylus inusitatus*, according to the original description, and *Eleutherodactylus tenebrionis*, according to Lynch and Miyata, 1980, Breviora, 457:8.

Eleutherodactylus racemus Lynch, 1980. Caldasia, 13:172.
TYPE(S): Holotype: KU 168960.
TYPE LOCALITY: "Páramo de Las Hermosas, 18.0 km NE Tenerife, along frontier between Departamentos del Valle del Cauca and Tolima, 3570 m alt."
DISTRIBUTION: Vicinity of the type locality.
COMMENT: In the *Eleutherodactylus unistrigatus* group.

Eleutherodactylus racenisi Rivero, 1961. Bull. Mus. Comp. Zool., 126:78.
TYPE(S): Holotype: MBUCV 2014.
TYPE LOCALITY: El Junquito, D.F. [Venezuela].
DISTRIBUTION: Vicinity of the type locality.

COMMENT: Probably a synonym of *Eleutherodactylus bicumulus* (JDL).

Eleutherodactylus ramagii (Boulenger, 1888). Ann. Mag. Nat. Hist., (6)2:41.
ORIGINAL NAME: *Hylodes ramagii*.
TYPE(S): Holotype: BM 1947.2.15.97 (formerly 88.4.18.17).
TYPE LOCALITY: Iguarasse [=Igaraçu], Pernambuco, Brazil.
DISTRIBUTION: Paraíba to Bahia, Brazil.
COMMENT: In the *Eleutherodactylus ramagii* group.

Eleutherodactylus ramosi Rivero, 1959. Breviora, 103:2.
TYPE(S): Holotype: MCZ 30428.
TYPE LOCALITY: Bosque Estatal de Cambalache, northern Puerto Rico.
DISTRIBUTION: Known only from the holotype.
COMMENT: Schwartz and Thomas, 1975, Carnegie Mus. Nat. Hist. Spec. Publ., 1:34,
    cast some doubt on the validity of this species. Rivero, 1978, Amph. Rept.
    Puerto Rico, did not include this species in a review of the amphibians of
    Puerto Rico, but it has not yet been placed in any synonymy. JAR considers it
    a synonym of *Eleutherodactylus cochranae*.

Eleutherodactylus raniformis (Boulenger, 1896). Ann. Mag. Nat. Hist., (6)17:19.
ORIGINAL NAME: *Hylodes raniformis*.
TYPE(S): Syntypes: BM 1947.2.16.16–19 (formerly 95.11.16.48–51) (Buenaventura),
    1947.2.15.83–84 (formerly 95.11.16.52–53) (Cali); BM 1947.2.16.16 designated
    lectotype by Lynch and Myers, 1983, Bull. Am. Mus. Nat. Hist., 175:545.
TYPE LOCALITY: Buenaventura and Cali, [Departamento Valle del Cauca,] Colombia;
    restricted to Buenaventura, Departamento Valle del Cauca, Colombia, by
    lectotype designation.
DISTRIBUTION: South from east-central Panama to the Río San Juan de Micay in
    western Colombia, in the forested lowlands north and west of the Andes;
    possibly isolated populations in the inter-Andean valleys of the Río Cauca
    and Río Magdalena, Colombia.
COMMENT: In the *Eleutherodactylus fitzingeri* group. Reviewed by Lynch and Myers,
    1983, Bull. Am. Mus. Nat. Hist., 175:545–551.

Eleutherodactylus rayo Savage and DeWeese, 1979. Bull. S. California Acad. Sci., 78:
    107.
TYPE(S): Holotype: LACM 127669.
TYPE LOCALITY: "second sabana on the trail from Finca El Helechales to Sabanas
    Esperanza, 5 km, airline, east of Finca El Helechales, Canton de Buenos Aires,
    Provincia Puntarenas, Costa Rica, 1640 m."
DISTRIBUTION: Rainforests of the upper portion of the premontane and lower
    portion of the lower montane slope of the Pacific face of the Cordillera de
    Talamanca of southwestern Costa Rica, between 1600–1850 m.
COMMENT: In the *Eleutherodactylus fitzingeri* group.

Eleutherodactylus repens Lynch, 1984. Herpetologica, 40:234.
TYPE(S): Holotype: ICN 12323.
TYPE LOCALITY: "Volcán Galeras (between km 9–12 on the road to the television
    tower), Municipio Pasto, Depto. Nariño, Colombia, 3220–3300 m".
DISTRIBUTION: Municipio Pasto, Departamento Nariño, Colombia, 3150–3720 m
    elev.
COMMENT: In the monophyletic *Eleutherodactylus pyrrhomerus* assembly of the
    Eleutherodactylus unistrigatus group according to the original description.

Eleutherodactylus reticulatus Walker and Test, 1955. Occas. Pap. Mus. Zool. Univ.
    Michigan, 561:4.
TYPE(S): Holotype: UMMZ 109872.
TYPE LOCALITY: Slope of Pico Periquito ± 1275 m, Rancho Grande, Estado Aragua,
    Venezuela.
DISTRIBUTION: Vicinity of the type locality.

COMMENT: In the *Eleutherodactylus unistrigatus* group. Reviewed by Rivero, 1961, Bull. Mus. Comp. Zool., 126:76–78.

Eleutherodactylus rhabdolaemus Duellman, 1978. Trans. Kansas Acad. Sci., 81:65.
TYPE(s): Holotype: LSUMZ 26150.
TYPE LOCALITY: "Huanhuahayocc, 1650 m, on trail from Tambo to Valle del Apurimac, Departamento Ayacucho, Perú (12° 45′ S; 73° 50′ W)".
DISTRIBUTION: Lowland rainforest to cloud forest (300–2650 m) on the Amazonian slope of the Andes in Departamento Ayacucho, Peru.
COMMENT: In the *Eleutherodactylus unistrigatus* group.

Eleutherodactylus rhodesi Schwartz, 1980. Ann. Carnegie Mus., 49:108.
TYPE(s): Holotype: CM 60538.
TYPE LOCALITY: "Balladé, 8.8 km S Port-de-Paix, 30 m, Département du Nord Ouest, Haiti".
DISTRIBUTION: Vicinity of the type locality.
COMMENT: In the *Eleutherodactylus ricordii* group, according to the original description.

Eleutherodactylus rhodopis (Cope, 1867 "1866"). Proc. Acad. Nat. Sci. Philadelphia, 18: 323.
ORIGINAL NAME: *Lithodytes rhodopis*.
TYPE(s): USNM 16558 designated lectotype by Cochran, 1961, Bull. U.S. Natl. Mus., 220:66.
TYPE LOCALITY: Orizaba and Córdoba, Veracruz [Mexico]; restricted to vicinity of Orizaba [Veracruz, Mexico] by Smith and Taylor, 1948, Bull. U.S. Natl. Mus., 194:66, and lectotype designation.
DISTRIBUTION: Southern Mexico to El Salvador and extreme northwestern Honduras.
COMMENT: In the *Eleutherodactylus rhodopis* group. Synonymy includes *Eleutherodactylus loki* Shannon and Werler, 1955; *Eleutherodactylus dunni* Barbour, 1922; *Hylodes beatae* Boulenger, 1903; and *Hylodes venustus* Günther, 1901, according to Duellman, 1960, Univ. Kansas Publ. Mus. Nat. Hist., 15:18–23. Records of this species from elsewhere in Central America are based upon other forms, especially *Eleutherodactylus bransfordii* in Nicaragua and Costa Rica (JMS). See comment under *Eleutherodactylus sanmartinensis*.

Eleutherodactylus richmondi Stejneger, 1904. Annu. Rep. U.S. Natl. Mus. for 1902:593.
TYPE(s): Holotype: USNM 26884.
TYPE LOCALITY: Catalina Plantation, about 890 feet altitude, eastern slope of El Yunque, Bosque Experimental de Luquillo, Puerto Rico.
DISTRIBUTION: Puerto Rico; known from scattered, principally interior localities over most of island, 132–3800 ft. elev.
COMMENT: In the *Eleutherodactylus ricordii* group, according to Schwartz, 1976, Bull. Florida State Mus., Biol. Sci., 21:1–46.

Eleutherodactylus ricordii (Duméril and Bibron, 1841). Erp. Gén., 8:623.
ORIGINAL NAME: *Hylodes ricordii*.
TYPE(s): Holotype: MNHNP 754.
TYPE LOCALITY: "Cuba"; restricted to "Oriente [Province]", Cuba, by Schmidt, 1953, Check List N. Am. Rept. Amph., Ed. 6:236. [Note that Oriente Province has subsequently been partitioned.]
DISTRIBUTION: Granma, Santiago, and Guantánamo provinces, Cuba.
COMMENT: In the *Eleutherodactylus ricordii* group; see Schwartz, 1965, Stud. Fauna Curaçao and other Caribb. Is., 22:99–101.

Eleutherodactylus ridens (Cope, 1866). Proc. Acad. Nat. Sci. Philadelphia, 18:131.
ORIGINAL NAME: *Phyllobates ridens.*
TYPE(S): Lost.
TYPE LOCALITY: Río San Juan, Nicaragua.
DISTRIBUTION: Atlantic lowlands of extreme eastern Honduras, Nicaragua, Costa
    Rica, and Panama; premontane evergreen forests of Costa Rica and Panama
    on both Atlantic and Pacific versants; lowlands of southwestern Costa Rica,
    and in the Pacific versant evergreen forests of Panama, western Colombia,
    and northwestern Ecuador (15–1200 m).
COMMENT: Reviewed by Savage, 1981, Proc. Biol. Soc. Washington, 94:413–420,
    who included *Syrrhopus molinoi* Barbour as a synonym. In the *Eleutherodactylus
    cruentus* group, according to Savage, 1980, Prelim. Handlist Herpetofauna
    Costa Rica:6. Presumably in the more inclusive *Eleutherodactylus unistrigatus*
    group of Lynch.

Eleutherodactylus riveti (Despax, 1911). Bull. Mus. Natl. Hist. Nat., Paris, 17:92.
ORIGINAL NAME: *Hylodes riveti.*
TYPE(S): Holotype: MNHNP 02-357.
TYPE LOCALITY: "Equateur"; corrected to Mirador, 3800 m, [Tungurahua Province,
    Ecuador] by Despax, 1911, Miss. Geogr. Am. Sud, 9(2):41.
DISTRIBUTION: Both Andean cordilleras at elevations of 2620–3420 m surrounding
    the Cuenca basin in southern Ecuador.
COMMENT: In the *Eleutherodactylus unistrigatus* group. Synonymized with
    Eleutherodactylus curtipes by Lynch, 1969, Herpetologica, 25:266, but
    resurrected by Lynch, 1979, Misc. Publ. Mus. Nat. Hist. Univ. Kansas, 66:37,
    who considered it most closely related to *Eleutherodactylus balionotus.*

Eleutherodactylus ronaldi Schwartz, 1960. Reading Public Mus. and Art Gallery Sci.
    Publ., 11:14.
TYPE(S): Holotype: AMNH 63401.
TYPE LOCALITY: La Esperancita (=La Isabelica), 3500 feet, Gran Piedra, 1.9 mi. SE,
    thence 10 mi. NE Sevilla, Oriente [now Santiago de Cuba] Province, Cuba.
DISTRIBUTION: Santiago de Cuba Province, Cuba, 0–3500 ft. elev.
COMMENT: In the *Eleutherodactylus auriculatus* group, according to Schwartz, 1965,
    Herpetologica, 21:28–31.

Eleutherodactylus roseus (Boulenger, 1918). Ann. Mag. Nat. Hist., (9)2:429.
ORIGINAL NAME: *Hylodes roseus.*
TYPE(S): Holotype: BM 1947.2.16.94 (formerly 1916.4.25.28).
TYPE LOCALITY: "Andagoya, Choco, Colombia".
DISTRIBUTION: Lowlands of western Colombia and northwestern Ecuador.
COMMENT: In the *Eleutherodactylus unistrigatus* group.

Eleutherodactylus rostralis (Werner, 1896). Verh. Zool. Bot. Ges. Wien, 46:350.
ORIGINAL NAME: *Hylodes rostralis.*
TYPE(S): "Petersburger Museum" (? ZIL).
TYPE LOCALITY: Honduras.
DISTRIBUTION: Guatemala and Honduras.
COMMENT: In the *Eleutherodactylus fitzingeri* group. Listed with no discussion as a
    synonym of *Eleutherodactylus laticeps* by Smith and Smith, 1976, Synops.
    Herpetol. Mexico, 4:A-B-25.

Eleutherodactylus rozei Rivero, 1961. Bull. Mus. Comp. Zool., 126:73.
TYPE(S): Holotype: MBUCV 2018.
TYPE LOCALITY: Curucuruma, Edo. Aragua (approx. 1000 m) [Venezuela].
DISTRIBUTION: Vicinity of the type locality.
COMMENT: In the *Eleutherodactylus unistrigatus* group. Probably a synonym of
    Eleutherodactylus bicumulus (JDL).

Eleutherodactylus rubicundus (Jiménez de la Espada, 1875). Vert. Viaj. Pacif., Batr.: pl. 3.

ORIGINAL NAME: *Hylodes rubicundus.*

TYPE(S): Lost.

TYPE LOCALITY: Not stated.

DISTRIBUTION: Lower part of the Pastaza trench (1080–1300 m) and to the north in the Cordillera del Dué (1150 m), Ecuador.

COMMENT: In the *Eleutherodactylus unistrigatus* group. Taxonomic disposition discussed by Lynch, 1971, J. Herpetol., 5:112–113. Reviewed by Lynch, 1980, Misc. Publ. Mus. Nat. Hist. Univ. Kansas, 69:56.

Eleutherodactylus rufifemoralis Noble and Hassler, 1933. Am. Mus. Novit., 652:4.

TYPE(S): Holotype: AMNH 44556.

TYPE LOCALITY: Above 'Salvation Station' on property of Luis E. Del Monte, 3000 feet, near Barahona, Barahona Province, República Dominicana.

DISTRIBUTION: Hispaniola; extreme eastern portion of the Sierra de Baoruco, Dominican Republic, 2400–4520 ft. elev.

COMMENT: Noble and Hassler, 1933, Am. Mus. Novit., 652:4, considered *Eleutherodactylus rufifemoralis* allied to *Eleutherodactylus minutus*, which Shreve and Williams, 1963, Bull. Mus. Comp. Zool., 129:323, and Schwartz, 1966, Bull. Mus. Comp. Zool., 133:396, considered a member of the *Eleutherodactylus auriculatus* group (=*Eleutherodactylus varians* group in the nomenclature of Shreve and Williams). *Eleutherodactylus rufifemoralis* is of uncertain relationships at this point, owing to an omission of comments in the literature and its variance from the diagnostic features cited for the *Eleutherodactylus auriculatus* group (JDL).

Eleutherodactylus rugulosus (Cope, 1870 "1869"). Proc. Am. Philos. Soc., 11:160.

ORIGINAL NAME: *Liyla rugulosa.*

TYPE(S): Syntypes: USNM 29971–72.

TYPE LOCALITY: Pacific region of the Isthmus of Tehuantepec, Mexico.

DISTRIBUTION: Eastern Puebla and Oaxaca (Mexico) to Guatemala and El Salvador.

COMMENT: In the *Eleutherodactylus fitzingeri* group. See comment under *Eleutherodactylus berkenbuschii.* See Savage, 1975, Copeia, 1975:289–292, for synonymy and review. See comment under *Eleutherodactylus brocchi.*

Eleutherodactylus ruidus Lynch, 1979. Misc. Publ. Mus. Nat. Hist. Univ. Kansas, 66:40.

TYPE(S): Holotype: AMNH 17590.

TYPE LOCALITY: "Molleturo, Provincia Azuay, Ecuador, 2317 m."

DISTRIBUTION: Known only from the type locality.

COMMENT: In the *Eleutherodactylus unistrigatus* group. This species may represent a southern vicariant of *Eleutherodactylus orcesi* and *Eleutherodactylus thymelensis,* according to Lynch, 1979, Misc. Publ. Mus. Nat. Hist. Univ. Kansas, 66:43.

Eleutherodactylus ruizi Lynch, 1981. Caldasia, 13:319.

TYPE(S): Holotype: ICN 5211.

TYPE LOCALITY: Reserva Forestal de Yotoco, km 18, Buga–Loboguerrero road, Depto. Valle de Cauca, Colombia, 1590 m.

DISTRIBUTION: Cordillera Central and Cordillera Occidental of Colombia, 1580–2000 m; records for Sierra Nevada de Santa Marta and Bogotá are questionable (JDL).

COMMENT: In the *Eleutherodactylus sulcatus* group, nearest *Eleutherodactylus ingeri,* according to the original description.

Eleutherodactylus ruthae Noble, 1923. Am. Mus. Novit., 61:6.

TYPE(S): Holotype: AMNH 11406.

TYPE LOCALITY: Samaná, Samaná Province, República Dominicana.

DISTRIBUTION: Hispaniola; widespread.

COMMENT: In the *Eleutherodactylus inoptatus* group, according to Schwartz, 1965, Bull. Mus. Comp. Zool., 132:479–508, who recognized four subspecies.

Eleutherodactylus salaputium Duellman, 1978. Proc. Biol. Soc. Washington, 91:428.
TYPE(S): Holotype: KU 162292.
TYPE LOCALITY: "Río Cosñipata, 4 km SW Santa Isabel, 1,700 m, Departamento Cuzco, Perú (13° 05' S; 71° 18' W)".
DISTRIBUTION: Known only from the type locality.
COMMENT: In the *Eleutherodactylus unistrigatus* group.

Eleutherodactylus saltator Taylor, 1941. Proc. Biol. Soc. Washington, 54:89.
TYPE(S): Holotype: formerly EHT-HMS 24301 (now FMNH).
TYPE LOCALITY: "Omilteme, Guerrero, about 8,000 ft.", Mexico.
DISTRIBUTION: Sierra Madre del Sur, Guerrero, Mexico.
COMMENT: In the *Eleutherodactylus rhodopis* group.

Eleutherodactylus sanctaemartae Ruthven, 1917. Occas. Pap. Mus. Zool. Univ. Michigan, 39:1.
TYPE(S): Holotype: UMMZ 48605.
TYPE LOCALITY: San Lorenzo, Santa Marta Mts., Colombia, 5000 ft.
DISTRIBUTION: Sierra Santa Marta, Colombia.
COMMENT: In the *Eleutherodactylus unistrigatus* group.

Eleutherodactylus sanmartinensis Shannon and Werler, 1955. Trans. Kansas Acad. Sci., 58:375.
TYPE(S): Holotype: formerly F. A. Shannon 4750 (now UIMNH?).
TYPE LOCALITY: Volcán San Martín, Veracruz [Mexico].
DISTRIBUTION: Vicinity of the type locality.
COMMENT: Probably a color morph of *Eleutherodactylus rhodopis* (JDL).

Eleutherodactylus sartori Lynch, 1965. Nat. Hist. Misc., Chicago, 182:10.
TYPE(S): Holotype: USNM 115507.
TYPE LOCALITY: Mount Ovando, Chiapas, Mexico, 6000 ft.
DISTRIBUTION: Vicinity of the type locality.
COMMENT: See comment under *Eleutherodactylus greggi*. In the *Eleutherodactylus rhodopis* group. *Eleutherodactylus sartori* is a replacement name for *Microbatrachylus montanus* Taylor, 1942 (preoccupied by *Eleutherodactylus montanus* Schmidt, 1919).

Eleutherodactylus savagei Pyburn and Lynch, 1981. Proc. Biol. Soc. Washington, 94:404.
TYPE(S): Holotype: UTA A-3535.
TYPE LOCALITY: Sierra de la Macarena, ca. 35 km WSW Vistahermosa, Depto. Meta, Colombia, 1097–1128 m.
DISTRIBUTION: Vicinity of the type locality.
COMMENT: In the *Eleutherodactylus fitzingeri* group; most similar to *Eleutherodactylus fenestratus*, according to the original description.

Eleutherodactylus schmidti Noble, 1923. Am. Mus. Novit., 61:5.
TYPE(S): Holotype: AMNH 11405.
TYPE LOCALITY: Along stream bed, Los Bracitos, Duarte Province, República Dominicana.
DISTRIBUTION: Northern and central Hispaniola.
COMMENT: In the *Eleutherodactylus ricordii* group, according to Dunn, 1926, Proc. Boston Soc. Nat. Hist., 38:115. Reviewed by Schwartz, 1970, Caribb. J. Sci., 10:109–118, who recognized three subspecies.

Eleutherodactylus schwartzi Thomas, 1966. Q. J. Florida Acad. Sci., 7:259.
TYPE(S): Holotype: MCZ 43228.
TYPE LOCALITY: Rose Lodge, 750 feet elevation, Tortola, British Virgin Islands.
DISTRIBUTION: Tortola, St. John (evidently extinct), and Virgin Gorda in the Virgin Islands.
COMMENT: In the *Eleutherodactylus auriculatus* group, according to Schwartz, 1969, Stud. Fauna Curaçao and other Caribb. Is., 30:101.

Eleutherodactylus sciagraphus Schwartz, 1973. J. Herpetol., 7:259.
TYPE(S): Holotype: USNM 189256.
TYPE LOCALITY: "*ca.* 2 km (airline) S Castillon, 3500–3900 ft (1068–1190 m), Département du Sud, Haiti".
DISTRIBUTION: Known only from the type locality.
COMMENT: Not assigned to species group, but according to the original description it may be related to *Eleutherodactylus brevirostris*.

Eleutherodactylus scitulus Duellman, 1978. Trans. Kansas Acad. Sci., 81:67.
TYPE(S): Holotype: LSUMZ 26097.
TYPE LOCALITY: "Yuraccyacu on trail from Tambo to Valle del Apurimac, 2620 m, Departamento Ayacucho, Perú (12° 47' S; 73° 54' W)".
DISTRIBUTION: Known only from the type locality.
COMMENT: In the *Eleutherodactylus unistrigatus* group.

Eleutherodactylus semipalmatus Shreve, 1936. Proc. New England Zool. Club, 15:94.
TYPE(S): Holotype: MCZ 21561.
TYPE LOCALITY: Hispaniola; northern and eastern foothills, Massif de la Hotte, 1000 feet to 4000 feet, Département du Sud, Haiti.
DISTRIBUTION: Known from the type locality and the vicinity of Furcy-Peneau on the Montagne Noire above Pétionville, Haiti.
COMMENT: In the *Eleutherodactylus orcutti* group, according to Shreve and Williams, 1963, Bull. Mus. Comp. Zool., 129:326–327, who considered it annectant to the *Eleutherodactylus auriculatus* group. This group (the *Eleutherodactylus orcutti* group) was implicitly considered polyphyletic by several authors, including Crombie, 1977, Proc. Biol. Soc. Washington, 90:194–204. See comment under *Eleutherodactylus orcutti*. Schwartz, 1967, Stud. Fauna Curaçao and other Caribb. Is., 91:56, noted that this species might be a member of the *Eleutherodactylus ricordii* group.

Eleutherodactylus sierramaestrae Schmidt, 1920. Proc. Linn. Soc. New York, 33:3.
ORIGINAL NAME: *Eleutherodactylus sierra-maestrae*.
TYPE(S): Holotype: AMNH 6450.
TYPE LOCALITY: Sierra Maestra range, Oriente Province, Cuba. [Note that Oriente Province has been partitioned.]
DISTRIBUTION: Granma, Santiago de Cuba, and Guantánamo provinces, Cuba.
COMMENT: In the *Eleutherodactylus ricordii* group, and including *Eleutherodactylus brevipalmatus* as a synonym, according to Schwartz, 1960, Reading Public Mus. and Art Gallery Sci. Publ., 11:18.

Eleutherodactylus silvicola Lynch, 1967. Proc. Biol. Soc. Washington, 80:211.
TYPE(S): Holotype: LSUMZ 7557.
TYPE LOCALITY: "12 mi. NNE Zanatepec, Oaxaca, Mexico, 4900 ft. elevation".
DISTRIBUTION: Known only from the type locality.
COMMENT: In the *Eleutherodactylus alfredi* group.

Eleutherodactylus simoterus Lynch, 1980. Caldasia, 13:177.
TYPE(S): Holotype: ICN 759.
TYPE LOCALITY: "Páramo de Letras, páramo-subpáramo, vereda Albania, Municipio de Herveo, Departamento del Tolima, 3200 m alt."
DISTRIBUTION: Páramo de Letras, Caldas and Tolima, Colombia.

COMMENT: In the *Eleutherodactylus orcesi* assembly of the *Eleutherodactylus unistrigatus* group.

Eleutherodactylus sisyphodemus Crombie, 1977. Proc. Biol. Soc. Washington, 90:194.
TYPE(S): Holotype: USNM 200000.
TYPE LOCALITY: Vicinity of 'the cave' about 4 mi. WNW Quick Step, Trelawny Parish, Jamaica.
DISTRIBUTION: Known only from the Cockpit Country of southwestern Trelawny Parish, Jamaica, in the vicinity of the type locality.
COMMENT: In the *Eleutherodactylus gossei* group, according to Crombie, 1977, Proc. Biol. Soc. Washington, 90:200–201.

Eleutherodactylus sobetes Lynch, 1980. Proc. Biol. Soc. Washington, 93:334.
TYPE(S): Holotype: KU 179389.
TYPE LOCALITY: Quebrada Zapadores, 5 km ESE Chiriboga, Prov. Pichincha, Ecuador, 1920 m.
DISTRIBUTION: Known only from the type locality.
COMMENT: In the *Eleutherodactylus surdus* assembly of the *Eleutherodactylus unistrigatus* group, nearest *Eleutherodactylus duellmani*, according to the original description.

Eleutherodactylus spatulatus Smith, 1939. Proc. Biol. Soc. Washington, 52:187.
TYPE(S): Holotype: USNM 106027.
TYPE LOCALITY: Cuautlapan, Veracruz, Mexico.
DISTRIBUTION: Veracruz, Mexico.
COMMENT: In the *Eleutherodactylus alfredi* group. Includes *Eleutherodactylus bufonoides* Lynch, 1965, according to Lynch, 1970, Herpetologica, 26:173–174.

Eleutherodactylus spinosus Lynch, 1979. Misc. Publ. Mus. Nat. Hist. Univ. Kansas, 66:43.
TYPE(S): Holotype: USNM 199891.
TYPE LOCALITY: "Sapote, Provincia Morona-Santiago, Ecuador, 2470 m."
DISTRIBUTION: Amazonian slopes of the Cordillera de Matanga, Ecuador, 1707–2835 m elev.
COMMENT: In the *Eleutherodactylus unistrigatus* group.

Eleutherodactylus stantoni Schmidt, 1941. Field Mus. Nat. Hist. Publ., Zool. Ser., 22: 483.
TYPE(S): Holotype: UMMZ 80673.
TYPE LOCALITY: Valentin, British Honduras [=Belize].
DISTRIBUTION: Low and moderate elevations of southern Belize and possibly El Petén, Guatemala, south to uplands of Alta Verapaz, Guatemala.
COMMENT: In the *Eleutherodactylus fitzingeri* group. A synonym of *Eleutherodactylus laticeps* (JMS).

Eleutherodactylus stejnegerianus (Cope, 1893). Proc. Am. Philos. Soc., 31:338.
ORIGINAL NAME: *Hylodes stejnegerianus*.
TYPE(S): Holotype: "No. 295", USNM or ANSP; now lost.
TYPE LOCALITY: "Palmar", Provincia Puntarenas, Costa Rica.
DISTRIBUTION: Pacific drainages of Costa Rica and extreme western Panama (0–1170 m).
COMMENT: Removed from the synonymy of *Eleutherodactylus bransfordii* by Miyamoto, 1983, Syst. Zool., 32:43–51. See comment under *Eleutherodactylus bransfordii*.

Eleutherodactylus stenodiscus Walker and Test, 1955. Occas. Pap. Mus. Zool. Univ. Michigan, 561:2.
TYPE(S): Holotype: UMMZ 109886.
TYPE LOCALITY: Pico Periquito, Rancho Grande, Estado Aragua, Venezuela.
DISTRIBUTION: Known only from the type locality.

COMMENT: In the *Eleutherodactylus unistrigatus* group. Reviewed by Rivero, 1961, Bull. Mus. Comp. Zool., 126:66–68.

Eleutherodactylus stuarti Lynch, 1967. Trans. Kansas Acad. Sci., 70:180.
TYPE(S): Holotype: UMMZ 126738.
TYPE LOCALITY: "Aldea Paraiso, 13 km S La Mesilla (on Guatemala–Mexico border), Depto. Huehuetenango, Guatemala, 2200 m."
DISTRIBUTION: Region of the type locality (Huehuetenango, Guatemala, and adjacent Chiapas, Mexico).
COMMENT: In the *Eleutherodactylus alfredi* group.

Eleutherodactylus subsigillatus (Boulenger, 1902). Ann. Mag. Nat. Hist., (7)9:52.
ORIGINAL NAME: *Hylodes subsigillatus.*
TYPE(S): Holotype: BM 1947.2.17.1 (formerly 1901.8.3.14).
TYPE LOCALITY: "Salidero, 350 feet", Esmeraldas Province, Ecuador.
DISTRIBUTION: Lowlands in southwestern Colombia and western Ecuador, 100–670 m.
COMMENT: In the *Eleutherodactylus unistrigatus* group. See Lynch, 1980, Herpetologica, 36:182–184.

Eleutherodactylus sulcatus (Cope, 1874). Proc. Acad. Nat. Sci. Philadelphia, 26:126.
ORIGINAL NAME: *Hylodes sulcatus.*
TYPE(S): Holotype: ANSP 11385.
TYPE LOCALITY: "Nauta", Departamento Loreto, Peru.
DISTRIBUTION: Upper Amazon basin (150–950 m) in western Brazil, eastern Ecuador, and eastern Peru.
COMMENT: Includes *Eleutherodactylus koki* and *Eleutherodactylus macrocephalus* according to Lynch, 1975, Occas. Pap. Mus. Nat. Hist. Univ. Kansas, 38:34. In the *Eleutherodactylus sulcatus* group.

Eleutherodactylus supernatis Lynch, 1980 "1979". J. Herpetol., 13:415.
TYPE(S): Holotype: KU 179351.
TYPE LOCALITY: "El Carmelo, Prov. Napo, Ecuador, 2710 m".
DISTRIBUTION: Moderate elevations (2540–3200 m) in the Cordillera Central of Colombia from Departamento Antioquia south to northern Ecuador.
COMMENT: In the *Eleutherodactylus unistrigatus* group, near *Eleutherodactylus devillei* and *Eleutherodactylus vertebralis*, according to the original description.

Eleutherodactylus surdus (Boulenger, 1882). Cat. Batr. Sal. Brit. Mus.:212.
ORIGINAL NAME: *Hylodes surdus.*
TYPE(S): Syntypes: BM 1947.2.17.25 (formerly 60.6.16.106) and 1947.2.17.26 (formerly 71.4.16.46).
TYPE LOCALITY: "W. Ecuador" and "S. America".
DISTRIBUTION: High cloud forests in western Ecuador, 2500–2700 m.
COMMENT: In the *Eleutherodactylus unistrigatus* group, *Eleutherodactylus surdus* assembly, nearest *Eleutherodactylus baryecuus*, according to Lynch, 1980, Proc. Biol. Soc. Washington, 93:336–337.

Eleutherodactylus symingtoni Schwartz, 1957. Proc. Biol. Soc. Washington, 70:210.
TYPE(S): Holotype: AMNH 60801.
TYPE LOCALITY: "Cueva de Santo Tomás, 10 kilometers north of Cabezas, Pinar del Río Province, Cuba".
DISTRIBUTION: Pinar del Río and Matanzas provinces, Cuba.
COMMENT: Considered the sole member of the *Eleutherodactylus symingtoni* group, by Schwartz, 1957, Proc. Biol. Soc. Washington, 70:212.

Eleutherodactylus taeniatus (Boulenger, 1912). Ann. Mag. Nat. Hist., (8)10:188.
ORIGINAL NAME: *Hylodes taeniatus.*
TYPE(S): Holotype: BM 1947.2.16.99 (formerly 1909.10.30.41).
TYPE LOCALITY: "Noananoa [=Noanama], Rio San Juan, Choco, S. W. Colombia".
DISTRIBUTION: Central Panama to northwestern Ecuador.

COMMENT: In the *Eleutherodactylus unistrigatus* group. Records from Panama were previously misidentified as *Eleutherodactylus ockendeni*. See Lynch, 1980, Herpetologica, 36:184–185.

Eleutherodactylus talamancae Dunn, 1931. Occas. Pap. Boston Soc. Nat. Hist., 5:385.
TYPE(S): Holotype: MCZ 9879.
TYPE LOCALITY: "Almirante, Bocas del Toro, Panama".
DISTRIBUTION: Extreme eastern Panama to Nicaragua.
COMMENT: In the *Eleutherodactylus fitzingeri* group, possibly nearest to *Eleutherodactylus longirostris*, according to Lynch and Myers, 1983, Bull. Am. Mus. Nat. Hist., 175:541.

Eleutherodactylus tamsitti Cochran and Goin, 1970. Bull. U.S. Natl. Mus., 288:418.
ORIGINAL NAME: *Eleutherodactylus latidiscus tamsitti*.
TYPE(S): Holotype: FMNH 69735.
TYPE LOCALITY: "near San Adolfo, 1400 meters, on the Río Suaza, Acevedo, Huila, Colombia".
DISTRIBUTION: Known only from the holotype.
COMMENT: In the *Eleutherodactylus unistrigatus* group. Lynch, 1976, Occas. Pap. Mus. Nat. Hist. Univ. Kansas, 61:17, elevated this taxon to species status with no further comment.

Eleutherodactylus taurus Taylor, 1958. Univ. Kansas Sci. Bull., 39:17.
TYPE(S): Holotype: KU 43866 (not KU 43867 as reported by Savage, 1975, Copeia, 1975:292).
TYPE LOCALITY: "Golfito, Puntarenas Province", Costa Rica.
DISTRIBUTION: Lowland evergreen forests of the Golfo Dulce region of Pacific southwestern Costa Rica and adjacent Panama.
COMMENT: In the *Eleutherodactylus fitzingeri* group. See Savage, 1975, Copeia, 1975: 292–293, for review, who suggested that *Eleutherodactylus azueroensis* is the nearest relative.

Eleutherodactylus taylori Lynch, 1966. Trans. Kansas Acad. Sci., 69:76.
TYPE(S): Holotype: KU 58689.
TYPE LOCALITY: "México, Chiapas, 6.2 km S Rayón Mescalapa".
DISTRIBUTION: Known only from the type locality.
COMMENT: In the *Eleutherodactylus alfredi* group.

Eleutherodactylus tenebrionis Lynch and Miyata, 1980. Breviora, 457:7.
TYPE(S): Holotype: MCZ 90326.
TYPE LOCALITY: "Hotel Tinalandia, 16 km E Santo Domingo de los Colorados by road, Provincia Pichincha, Ecuador, 800 m".
DISTRIBUTION: Lowland rainforest in the vicinity of the type locality.
COMMENT: In the *Eleutherodactylus unistrigatus* group, nearest *Eleutherodactylus quinquagesimus*, according to the original description.

Eleutherodactylus terraebolivaris Rivero, 1961. Bull. Mus. Comp. Zool., 126:58.
TYPE(S): Holotype: MCZ 31062.
TYPE LOCALITY: Rancho Grande, Edo. Aragua [Venezuela].
DISTRIBUTION: Coastal range of Venezuela; Tobago I.
COMMENT: In the *Eleutherodactylus fitzingeri* group.

Eleutherodactylus thectopternus Lynch, 1965. Contrib. Sci. Nat. Hist. Mus Los Angeles Co., 272:14.
TYPE(S): Holotype: LACM 73087.
TYPE LOCALITY: 10 km W Andes, Depto. Antioquia, Colombia, 2090 m.
DISTRIBUTION: Northern half of Cordilleras Central and Occidental of Colombia at moderate elevations.

COMMENT: In the *Eleutherodactylus fitzingeri* group.

Eleutherodactylus thomasi Schwartz, 1959. Am. Mus. Novit., 1926:3.
TYPE(S): Holotype: AMNH 61054.
TYPE LOCALITY: 6.5 mi. NW Banao, Paso de la Trinchera, Sierra de Cubitas, Camagüey Province, Cuba.
DISTRIBUTION: Camagüey, Matanzas, Las Villas, Granma, and Oriente provinces, Cuba.
COMMENT: In the *Eleutherodactylus ricordii* group, according to Schwartz, 1959, Am. Mus. Novit., 1926:3, and including three subspecies according to Schwartz, 1960, Reading Public Mus. and Art Gallery Sci. Publ., 11:28–33. See also Schwartz, 1976, Bull. Florida State Mus., Biol. Sci., 21:1–46.

Eleutherodactylus thymalopsoides Lynch, 1976. Occas. Pap. Mus. Nat. Hist. Univ. Kansas, 55:25.
TYPE(S): Holotype: KU 131533.
TYPE LOCALITY: "Pilalo, Prov. Cotopaxi, Ecuador, 2460 m".
DISTRIBUTION: Known only from the type locality.
COMMENT: In the *Eleutherodactylus unistrigatus* group.

Eleutherodactylus thymelensis Lynch, 1972. Herpetologica, 28:144.
TYPE(S): Holotype: KU 117719.
TYPE LOCALITY: "Páramos del Angel, about 23 km SW Tulcan, Carchi Province, Ecuador, 3700 m".
DISTRIBUTION: Páramos in southern Colombia and northern Ecuador, 3310–4150 m elev.
COMMENT: In the *Eleutherodactylus orcesi* assembly of the *Eleutherodactylus unistrigatus* group.

Eleutherodactylus toftae Duellman, 1978. Herpetologica, 34:267.
TYPE(S): Holotype: KU 171863.
TYPE LOCALITY: "Finca Panguana, Río Llullapichis, 4–5 km upstream from Río Pachitea, Departamento Huánuco, Perú, 08° 36′ S, 74° 57′ W, elevation 200 m".
DISTRIBUTION: Amazonian Peru.
COMMENT: In the *Eleutherodactylus unistrigatus* group.

Eleutherodactylus trachyblepharis (Boulenger, 1918). Ann. Mag. Nat. Hist., (9)2:429.
ORIGINAL NAME: *Hylodes trachyblepharis*.
TYPE(S): Syntypes: BM 1947.2.17.2–4 (formerly 1912.11.1.58–60).
TYPE LOCALITY: "El Topo, Rio Pastaza, [Provincia Tungurahua,] E. Ecuador".
DISTRIBUTION: Low to moderate elevations (320–1250 m) in the valley of the Río Pastaza, Ecuador.
COMMENT: In the *Eleutherodactylus unistrigatus* group.

Eleutherodactylus trepidotus Lynch, 1968. Herpetologica, 24:295.
TYPE(S): Holotype: USNM 164399.
TYPE LOCALITY: "1 km west of Papallacta, Napo Province, Ecuador, 3155 m."
DISTRIBUTION: Páramo and subpáramo habitats from the region of Nevado Cayambe south to the Llangati mountains (north side of Pastaza valley), 2360–3650 m.
COMMENT: In the *Eleutherodactylus myersi* assembly of the *Eleutherodactylus unistrigatus* group; in the more inclusive (and monophyletic) *Eleutherodactylus pyrrhomerus* assembly, and the sister-species of *Eleutherodactylus ocreatus*, according to Lynch, 1984, Herpetologica, 40:237. Includes *Paludicola festae* Peracca, 1904 (a secondary homonym of *Hylodes festae* Peracca, 1904 [=*Eleutherodactylus galdi*]), according to Lynch, 1974, Occas. Pap. Mus. Nat. Hist. Univ. Kansas, 31:16. Reviewed by Lynch, 1980, Misc. Publ. Mus. Nat. Hist. Univ. Kansas, 69:58–59.

Eleutherodactylus turquinensis Barbour and Shreve, 1937. Bull. Mus. Comp. Zool., 80: 380.
TYPE(S): Holotype: MCZ 21975.
TYPE LOCALITY: Cueva del Aura, Pico Turquino, 1500 feet to 4000 feet, Oriente [now Santiago de Cuba] Province, Cuba.
DISTRIBUTION: Known only from the type locality.
COMMENT: In the *Eleutherodactylus ricordii* group, according to Schwartz, 1958, Am. Mus. Novit., 1873:2.

Eleutherodactylus turumiquirensis Rivero, 1961. Bull. Mus. Comp. Zool., 126:57.
TYPE(S): Holotype: AMNH 22557.
TYPE LOCALITY: La Trinidad, Mt. Turumiquire, in cave at 5500 ft. [Venezuela].
DISTRIBUTION: Vicinity of the type locality.
COMMENT: In the *Eleutherodactylus unistrigatus* group.

Eleutherodactylus unicolor Stejneger, 1904. Annu. Rep. U.S. Natl. Mus. for 1902:597.
TYPE(S): Holotype: USNM 26963.
TYPE LOCALITY: Camp on El Yunque at 2978 feet altitude, Bosque Experimental de Luquillo, Puerto Rico.
DISTRIBUTION: Known only from the region of the type locality.
COMMENT: Of uncertain relationships (JDL). Placed in the *Eleutherodactylus unicolor* group by Joglar, 1983, Caribb. J. Sci., 19:37.

Eleutherodactylus unistrigatus (Günther, 1859). Proc. Zool. Soc. London, 1859:416.
ORIGINAL NAME: *Hylodes unistrigatus*.
TYPE(S): Syntypes: BM 1947.2.17.7–9 (formerly 60.6.16.97–98, 60.6.16.105).
TYPE LOCALITY: "western Ecuador".
DISTRIBUTION: Inter-Andean valleys from southern Colombia to central Ecuador.
COMMENT: In the *Eleutherodactylus unistrigatus* assembly of the *Eleutherodactylus unistrigatus* group. Includes *Hylodes lehmanni* Boettger, 1892, and *Syrrhophus coeruleus* Andersson, 1945, according to Lynch, 1981, Misc. Publ. Mus. Nat. Hist. Univ. Kansas, 72:32.

Eleutherodactylus urichi (Boettger, 1894). J. Trinidad Field Nat. Club, 2:88.
ORIGINAL NAME: *Hylodes urichi*.
TYPE(S): SMF 3818 designated lectotype by Mertens, 1967, Senckenb. Biol., 48:39.
TYPE LOCALITY: Trinidad.
DISTRIBUTION: Trinidad, Tobago, St. Vincent, and Grenada (Lesser Antilles); records from Guyana, Surinam, and Venezuela need study (JDL).
COMMENT: In the *Eleutherodactylus auriculatus* group according to Schwartz, 1969, Stud. Fauna Curaçao and other Caribb. Is., 114:99–115. Hardy, 1982, Bull. Maryland Herpetol. Soc., 18:137–142, suggested that this nominal form is composed of at least two species. Composed of three subspecies according to Schwartz, 1967, Stud. Fauna Curaçao and other Caribb. Is., 24:5–17.

Eleutherodactylus vanadise La Marca, 1984. Herpetologica, 40:31.
TYPE(S): Holotype: UAM 2805.
TYPE LOCALITY: "stream in cloud forest above Truchicultura La Mucuy, 2350 m, Sierra Nevada de Mérida, Estado Mérida, Venezuela".
DISTRIBUTION: Cloud forests in the Sierra del Norte (=Culata) and Sierra Nevada de Mérida, western Venezuela.
COMMENT: In the *Eleutherodactylus unistrigatus* group, according to the original description.

Eleutherodactylus variabilis Lynch, 1968. J. Herpetol., 2:129.
TYPE(S): Holotype: KU 99011.
TYPE LOCALITY: "Limón Cocha, Napo, Ecuador, 300 meters".
DISTRIBUTION: 300–400 m elevation in Amazonian Ecuador and Colombia.

COMMENT: In the *Eleutherodactylus unistrigatus* group. Distribution records discussed by Lynch and Lescure, 1980, Bull. Mus. Natl. Hist. Nat., Paris, (4)2:312.

Eleutherodactylus varians (Gundlach and Peters, 1864). Monatsber. Preuss. Akad. Wiss. Berlin, 1864:390.
ORIGINAL NAME: *Hylodes varians*.
TYPE(S): Syntypes: ZMB 5108, MCZ 11621.
TYPE LOCALITY: Cuba.
DISTRIBUTION: Widespread on Cuba; Isla de Pinos (=Isla de Juventud).
COMMENT: In the *Eleutherodactylus auriculatus* group, according to Schwartz, 1969, Stud. Fauna Curaçao and other Caribb. Is., 30:100; four subspecies recognized by Schwartz, 1960, Reading Public Mus. and Art Gallery Sci. Publ., 11:5–10. See also Schwartz, 1965, Herpetologica, 21:28–31.

Eleutherodactylus varleyi Dunn, 1925. Occas. Pap. Boston Soc. Nat. Hist., 5:163.
TYPE(S): Holotype: MCZ 10601.
TYPE LOCALITY: Soledad, Las Villas [now Cienfuegos] Province, Cuba.
DISTRIBUTION: Islandwide on Cuba; Isla de Pinos (=Isla de Juventud).
COMMENT: In the *Eleutherodactylus varleyi* group, according to Schwartz, 1958, Am. Mus. Novit., 1873:2, and Shreve and Williams, 1963, Bull. Mus. Comp. Zool., 129:339. Includes *Eleutherodactylus phyzelus* Schwartz as a synonym, according to Schwartz, 1964, Breviora, 208:9.

Eleutherodactylus venancioi B. Lutz, 1959 "1958". Mem. Inst. Oswaldo Cruz, Rio de Janeiro, 56:374.
TYPE(S): Syntypes: IOC (6 specimens).
TYPE LOCALITY: Organ Mountains, Teresópolis, [Maritime Range,] southeastern Brazil.
DISTRIBUTION: Coastal mountains of Rio de Janeiro and São Paulo, Brazil.
COMMENT: In the *Eleutherodactylus lacteus* group.

Eleutherodactylus ventrilineatus (Shreve, 1936). Proc. New England Zool. Club, 15:98.
ORIGINAL NAME: *Leptodactylus ventrilineatus*.
TYPE(S): Holotype: MCZ 19857.
TYPE LOCALITY: Mt. La Hotte (=Pic Macaya), 5000 feet to summit, Département du Sud, Haiti.
DISTRIBUTION: Known only from the type locality.
COMMENT: A peripheral member of the *Eleutherodactylus dimidiatus* group, possibly annectant to the *Eleutherodactylus varleyi* group, according to Shreve and Williams, 1963, Bull. Mus. Comp. Zool., 129:338; in the *Eleutherodactylus dimidiatus* group, according to Schwartz, 1965, Proc. Biol. Soc. Washington, 78:168.

Eleutherodactylus ventrimarmoratus (Boulenger, 1912). Ann. Mag. Nat. Hist., (8)10:187.
ORIGINAL NAME: *Hylodes ventrimarmoratus*.
TYPE(S): Syntypes: BM 1947.2.15.73 (formerly 1911.12.12.77), 1947.2.15.74–76 (formerly 1911.1.1.51–53).
TYPE LOCALITY: "El Topo, R. Pastaza, [Provincia Tungurahua,] E. Ecuador, 4200 feet" and "Chanchamayo, [Departamento Junín,] Peru, 2600 feet".
DISTRIBUTION: Cloud forests of northern Ecuador and the rainforests in northern Ecuador south to southern Peru and east to western Brazil.
COMMENT: Includes *Eleutherodactylus ventrivittatus* Andersson, 1945, according to Lynch and Duellman, 1980, Misc. Publ. Mus. Nat. Hist. Univ. Kansas, 69:60–61. In the *Eleutherodactylus unistrigatus* group.

Eleutherodactylus versicolor Lynch, 1979. Misc. Publ. Mus. Nat. Hist. Univ. Kansas, 66:45.
TYPE(S): Holotype: KU 119858.
TYPE LOCALITY: "'15 km E Loja, 2800 m' (=13.5 km E Loja, 2800 m), a locality just east of the crest on the mountain range dividing Loja and Zamora-Chinchipe provinces, Ecuador".
DISTRIBUTION: Intermediate elevations (2750–3100 m) in the Andes of southern Ecuador.
COMMENT: In the *Eleutherodactylus unistrigatus* assembly of the *Eleutherodactylus unistrigatus* group.

Eleutherodactylus vertebralis (Boulenger, 1886). Proc. Zool. Soc. London, 1886:415.
ORIGINAL NAME: *Hylodes vertebralis*.
TYPE(S): Syntypes: BM 1947.2.17.5–6 (formerly 78.1.25.14–15).
TYPE LOCALITY: "Intac, [Pichincha Province,] Ecuador".
DISTRIBUTION: Cloud forests in western Ecuador, 1800–2710 m.
COMMENT: In the *Eleutherodactylus unistrigatus* group. See Lynch, 1979, J. Herpetol., 13:415.

Eleutherodactylus vicarius Lynch and Ruíz-Carranza, 1983. Trans. Kansas Acad. Sci., 86:105.
TYPE(S): Holotype: ICN 7764.
TYPE LOCALITY: "vicinity of the INDERENA cabaña 'Paletará,' 30.5 km by road E Coconuco, Depto. Cauca, Colombia, 3030 m."
DISTRIBUTION: Departments of Putumayo, Huila, and Cauca, Colombia, 2900–3275 m elev.
COMMENT: In the *Eleutherodactylus unistrigatus* group, most similar to *Eleutherodactylus chloronotus*, according to the original description.

Eleutherodactylus vidua Lynch, 1979. Misc. Publ. Mus. Nat. Hist. Univ. Kansas, 66:49.
TYPE(S): Holotype: KU 120082.
TYPE LOCALITY: "15 km E Ciudad Loja, Provincia Zamora-Chinchipe, Ecuador, 2800 m".
DISTRIBUTION: Mountain crests east and north of Loja, Ecuador, 2710–3100 m.
COMMENT: In the *Eleutherodactylus myersi* assembly of the *Eleutherodactylus unistrigatus* group.

Eleutherodactylus vilarsi (Melin, 1941). Göteborgs K. Vetensk. Vitterh. Samh. Handl., (B)1(4):45.
ORIGINAL NAME: *Hylodes vilarsi*.
TYPE(S): Syntypes: NHMG 491 (2 specimens); larger specimen designated lectotype by Lynch, 1975, Contrib. Sci. Nat. Hist. Mus. Los Angeles Co., 272:9.
TYPE LOCALITY: Taracuá, Rio Uaupés, [Estado do Amazonas,] Brazil.
DISTRIBUTION: Upper Amazonian Brazil, Colombia, Venezuela, and Peru.
COMMENT: In the *Eleutherodactylus fitzingeri* group. Reviewed by Lynch, 1980, Am. Mus. Novit., 2696:17, who provided a synonymy. Includes *Hylodes roseus* Melin, 1941; *Eleutherodactylus conspicillatus ileamazonicus* and *Eleutherodactylus brachypodius* Rivero, 1961, according to Lynch, 1975, Contrib. Sci. Nat. Hist. Mus. Los Angeles Co., 272:9.

Eleutherodactylus vinhai Bokermann, 1975 "1974". Rev. Brasil. Biol., 34:13.
TYPE(S): Holotype: WCAB 46694.
TYPE LOCALITY: "Centro de Pesquisas do Cacau, Ilheus, Bahia, Brasil".
DISTRIBUTION: Atlantic forest in southern Bahia, Brazil.
COMMENT: In the *Eleutherodactylus unistrigatus* group.

Eleutherodactylus viridicans Lynch, 1977. Occas. Pap. Mus. Zool. Univ. Michigan, 678:1.
TYPE(S): Holotype: UMMZ 143468.
TYPE LOCALITY: 2 km S Cerro Munchique, Depto. Cauca, Colombia, 2540 m.
DISTRIBUTION: Western flank of the Cordillera Occidental of Colombia, 2000–2540 m.
COMMENT: In the *Eleutherodactylus fitzingeri* group.

Eleutherodactylus vocalis Taylor, 1940. Univ. Kansas Sci. Bull., 26:401.
TYPE(S): Holotype: FMNH 100122 (formerly EHT-HMS 6390).
TYPE LOCALITY: "Hda. El Sabino, Uruapan, Michoacán", Mexico.
DISTRIBUTION: Southern Sinaloa south to Michoacán, Mexico.
COMMENT: In the *Eleutherodactylus fitzingeri* group. See Savage, 1975, Copeia, 1975: 293–294, for review. See comment under *Eleutherodactylus brocchi.*

Eleutherodactylus vocator Taylor, 1955. Univ. Kansas Sci. Bull., 37:522.
TYPE(S): Holotype: KU 37001.
TYPE LOCALITY: "Agua Buena, [Canton de Golfito,] Puntarenas Province, Costa Rica" (see comment).
DISTRIBUTION: Costa Rica to western Colombia.
COMMENT: In the *Eleutherodactylus unistrigatus* group. See comment under *Eleutherodactylus moro.* See Savage, 1974, Rev. Biol. Tropical, 22:75, for discussion of the type locality.

Eleutherodactylus w-nigrum (Boettger, 1892). Kat. Batr. Samml. Mus. Senckenb. Naturforsch. Ges.:28.
ORIGINAL NAME: *Hylodes w-nigrum.*
TYPE(S): Syntypes: SMF 1212 (2 specimens).
TYPE LOCALITY: Zurucuchu, W. Andes of Cuenca [Azuay Province, Ecuador].
DISTRIBUTION: Andean Colombia and Ecuador, 800–3200 m.
COMMENT: In the *Eleutherodactylus fitzingeri* group. Includes *Hylodes buergeri*, according to Cochran and Goin, 1970, Bull. U.S. Natl. Mus., 288:395.

Eleutherodactylus walkeri Lynch, 1974. Proc. Biol. Soc. Washington, 87:381.
TYPE(S): Holotype: KU 131652.
TYPE LOCALITY: "Las Palmas (junction of highways 28 and 30), Prov. Pichincha, Ecuador, 920 m."
DISTRIBUTION: Pacific slopes of Ecuadorian Andes (220–1270 m).
COMMENT: In the *Eleutherodactylus unistrigatus* group.

Eleutherodactylus warreni Schwartz, 1976. Bull. Florida State Mus., Biol. Sci., 21:26.
TYPE(S): Holotype: CM 54138.
TYPE LOCALITY: "vicinity of Palmiste, Ile de la Tortue, Haiti".
DISTRIBUTION: Known only from the type locality.
COMMENT: In the *Eleutherodactylus ricordii* group, according to Schwartz, 1976, Bull. Florida State Mus., Biol. Sci., 21:26.

Eleutherodactylus weinlandi Barbour, 1914. Mem. Mus. Comp. Zool., 44:246.
TYPE(S): Holotype: MCZ 2050.
TYPE LOCALITY: Puerto Plata, Puerto Plata Province, República Dominicana.
DISTRIBUTION: Eastern Hispaniola.
COMMENT: In the *Eleutherodactylus ricordii* group. Reviewed by Schwartz, 1976, Bull. Florida State Mus., Biol. Sci., 21:11–20, who recognized three subspecies.

Eleutherodactylus werleri Lynch and Fritts, 1965. Trans. Illinois State Acad. Sci., 58: 46–49.
TYPE(S): Holotype: UIMNH 42987.
TYPE LOCALITY: "east slope of Volcan San Martin Pajapan at 4,000 feet elevation, Veracruz, Mexico".
DISTRIBUTION: Known only from the type locality.

COMMENT: In the *Eleutherodactylus fitzingeri* group. Allied with *Eleutherodactylus lineatus* (JMS).

Eleutherodactylus wetmorei Cochran, 1932. Proc. Biol. Soc. Washington, 45:191.
TYPE(S): Holotype: USNM 72617.
TYPE LOCALITY: Fond des Nègres, Département du Sud, Haiti.
DISTRIBUTION: Principally southwestern Hispaniola, the Tiburon Peninsula of Haiti, east into the western Dominican Republic; also known from the Chaine de Marmelade, north-central Haiti.
COMMENT: In the *Eleutherodactylus auriculatus* group, according to Shreve and Williams, 1963, Bull. Mus. Comp. Zool., 129:302–342, and Schwartz, 1969, Stud. Fauna Curaçao and other Caribb. Is., 30:101. Reviewed by Schwartz, 1968, Breviora, 290:1–13, who recognized three subspecies. Schwartz, 1977, Herpetologica, 33:66–72, described an additional subspecies.

Eleutherodactylus wightmanae Schmidt, 1920. Ann. New York Acad. Sci., 28:181.
TYPE(S): Holotype: AMNH 10317.
TYPE LOCALITY: El Yunque, near the Forester's Cabin, about 1300 feet altitude, Bosque Experimental de Luquillo, Puerto Rico.
DISTRIBUTION: Puerto Rico; known from scattered interior upland localities.
COMMENT: In the *Eleutherodactylus auriculatus* group, according to Schwartz, 1969, Stud. Fauna Curaçao and other Caribb. Is., 30:101.

Eleutherodactylus williamsi Rivero, 1961. Bull. Mus. Comp. Zool., 126:72.
TYPE(S): Holotype: MBUCV 2012.
TYPE LOCALITY: El Junquito, D.F. [Venezuela].
DISTRIBUTION: Vicinity of the type locality.
COMMENT: Probably a synonym of *Eleutherodactylus bicumulus* (JDL). Specimens from Mérida Andes referred to this species by Durant, 1977, Herpetol. Rev., Suppl., 8:7, are probably *Eleutherodactylus vanadise* (ELM).

Eleutherodactylus xucanebi Stuart, 1941. Proc. Biol. Soc. Washington, 54:199.
TYPE(S): Holotype: UMMZ 89914.
TYPE LOCALITY: Finca Volcan, 49 km east of Coban, Alta Verapaz, Guatemala, 1300 m.
DISTRIBUTION: Alta Verapaz and Sierra de las Minas, Guatemala.
COMMENT: In the *Eleutherodactylus alfredi* group.

Eleutherodactylus yucatanensis Lynch, 1965. Herpetologica, 20:249.
TYPE(S): Holotype: KU 71094.
TYPE LOCALITY: "in a cave . . . , 1.5 km S, 1 km E Pueblo Nuevo X-Can, Quintana Roo, Mexico, at 10 meters elevation".
DISTRIBUTION: Northern part of the Yucatan Peninsula, Mexico.
COMMENT: In the *Eleutherodactylus alfredi* group.

Eleutherodactylus zeuctotylus Lynch and Hoogmoed, 1977. Proc. Biol. Soc. Washington, 90:432.
TYPE(S): Holotype: RMNH 17701.
TYPE LOCALITY: W slope, Vier Gebroeders Mountain, Sipaliwini, Nickerie District, Suriname.
DISTRIBUTION: Wet rainforests of northeastern South America from extreme southeastern Colombia through the Guianas, as well as scattered records from northwestern Brazil and southwestern Brazil.
COMMENT: In the *Eleutherodactylus fitzingeri* group.

Eleutherodactylus zeus Schwartz, 1958. Proc. Biol. Soc. Washington, 71:38.
TYPE(S): Holotype: AMNH 60791.
TYPE LOCALITY: "0.5 mi. south of San Vicente, Pinar del Río Province, Cuba".
DISTRIBUTION: Sierra de los Organos, Pinar del Río Province, Cuba.

COMMENT: In the *Eleutherodactylus auriculatus* group. Annectant between
Eleutherodactylus greyi (of the *Eleutherodactylus auriculatus* group) and
Eleutherodactylus symingtoni (monotypic group), according to Schwartz, 1958,
Proc. Biol. Soc. Washington, 71:41–42.

Eleutherodactylus zugi Schwartz, 1958. J. Washington Acad. Sci., 48:127.
    TYPE(S): Holotype: AMNH 60938.
    TYPE LOCALITY: Soroa, Pinar del Río Province, Cuba.
    DISTRIBUTION: Matanzas and Pinar del Río provinces, Cuba.
    COMMENT: In the *Eleutherodactylus ricordii* group; two subspecies recognized by
        Schwartz, 1960, Reading Public Mus. and Art Gallery Sci. Publ., 11:33–37.

Eleutherodactylus zygodactylus Lynch and Myers, 1983. Bull. Am. Mus. Nat. Hist., 175:
    551.
    TYPE(S): Holotype: KU 168518.
    TYPE LOCALITY: "Río Anchicayá, 8 km. W Danubio, 300 m., Department of Valle del
        Cauca, Colombia".
    DISTRIBUTION: Pacific lowlands of northwestern Colombia, 230–800 m.
    COMMENT: In the *Eleutherodactylus fitzingeri* group.

Euparkerella Griffiths, 1959. Proc. Zool. Soc. London, 132:477.
    TYPE SPECIES: *Sminthillus brasiliensis* Parker, 1926, by original designation.
    DISTRIBUTION: As for the single species.
    COMMENT: Tribe Eleutherodactylini.

Euparkerella brasiliensis (Parker, 1926). Ann. Mag. Nat. Hist., (9)18:201.
    ORIGINAL NAME: *Sminthillus brasiliensis*.
    TYPE(S): Holotype: BM 1902.11.25.8.
    TYPE LOCALITY: "Organ Mountains [=Serra dos Órgãos, state of Rio de Janeiro,]
        Brazil".
    DISTRIBUTION: Known only from the type locality.

Eupsophus Fitzinger, 1843. Syst. Rept.:31.
    TYPE SPECIES: *Cystignathus roseus* Duméril and Bibron, 1841.
    DISTRIBUTION: Chile and Argentina.
    COMMENT: Tribe Telmatobiini.
    REVIEWER: Ramón Formas (RF).

Eupsophus calcaratus (Günther, 1881). Proc. Zool. Soc. London, 1881:19.
    ORIGINAL NAME: *Cacotus calcaratus*.
    TYPE(S): Holotype: BM 1868.9.22.8.
    TYPE LOCALITY: Chiloé Island [Chile].
    DISTRIBUTION: Southern Chile.
    COMMENT: Discussed by Formas and Vera, 1982, Proc. Biol. Soc. Washington, 95:
        594–601.

Eupsophus insularis (Philippi, 1902). Supl. Batr. Chil. Descr. Hist. Fis. Polit. Chile:89.
    ORIGINAL NAME: *Cystignathus (Borborocoetes) insularis*.
    TYPE(S): Lost.
    TYPE LOCALITY: "Ex insula Mocha allatus" (=Mocha Island, Chile).
    DISTRIBUTION: Known only from the type locality.
    COMMENT: Elevated from subspecies status under *Eupsophus roseus* and discussed by
        Formas and Vera, 1982, Proc. Biol. Soc. Washington, 95:594–601.

Eupsophus migueli Formas, 1978. Stud. Neotrop. Fauna Environ., 13:2.
    TYPE(S): Holotype: IZUA 1747-A.
    TYPE LOCALITY: "Mehuín (60 km by road from Valdivia city), Coastal Range,
        Valdivia Province, Chile, 55 m elevation".
    DISTRIBUTION: Known only from the type locality.

Eupsophus roseus (Duméril and Bibron, 1841). Erp. Gén., 8:414.
ORIGINAL NAME: *Cystignathus roseus.*
TYPE(S): Syntypes: MNHNP 762 (2 specimens).
TYPE LOCALITY: "Chili" (=Chile).
DISTRIBUTION: Chile (as far north as Santiago de Chile and southward to Chonos Archipelago); Rio Negro region of Argentina.

Eupsophus vittatus (Philippi, 1902). Supl. Batr. Chil. Descr. Hist. Fis. Polit. Chile:103.
ORIGINAL NAME: *Cystignathus vittatus.*
TYPE(S): Holotype: IZUC.
TYPE LOCALITY: "Habitat in Araucanía" (vicinity of Concepción, Chile).
DISTRIBUTION: Santiago de Chile to Chiloé, Chile.
COMMENT: Synonymy includes *Eupsophus vertebralis* Grandison, 1961, Bull. Brit. Mus. (Nat. Hist.), Zool., 8:136 (Holotype: NHMW 4660.I; Type locality: Valdivia, Chile), according to Donoso-Barros, 1974, Arch. Biol. Med. Experim., 10:50.

Geobatrachus Ruthven, 1915. Occas. Pap. Mus. Zool. Univ. Michigan, 20:1.
TYPE SPECIES: *Geobatrachus walkeri* Ruthven, 1915.
DISTRIBUTION: As for the single species.
COMMENT: Tribe Eleutherodactylini.

Geobatrachus walkeri Ruthven, 1915. Occas. Pap. Mus. Zool. Univ. Michigan, 20:2.
TYPE(S): Holotype: UMMZ 47785.
TYPE LOCALITY: "San Lorenzo, (altitude 8000 feet) Santa Marta Mountains, Colombia".
DISTRIBUTION: Sierra Santa Marta, Colombia.

Holoaden Miranda-Ribeiro, 1920. Rev. Mus. Paulista, São Paulo, 12:319.
TYPE SPECIES: *Holoaden luederwaldti* Miranda-Ribeiro, 1920.
DISTRIBUTION: Southeastern Brazil.
COMMENT: Tribe Eleutherodactylini.

Holoaden bradei B. Lutz, 1958. Mem. Inst. Oswaldo Cruz, Rio de Janeiro, 56:383.
TYPE(S): Not traced.
TYPE LOCALITY: "Alto Itatiaia", Brazil.
DISTRIBUTION: Itatiaia Mountains, Brazil.

Holoaden luederwaldti Miranda-Ribeiro, 1920. Rev. Mus. Paulista, São Paulo, 12:319.
ORIGINAL NAME: *Holoaden lüderwaldti.*
TYPE(S): Holotype: MZUSP 87.
TYPE LOCALITY: "Campos do Jordão", Brazil.
DISTRIBUTION: Southeastern Brazil.

Hylactophryne Lynch, 1968. Univ. Kansas Publ. Mus. Nat. Hist., 17:511.
TYPE SPECIES: *Hylodes augusti* Dugès, 1879, by original designation.
DISTRIBUTION: Southwestern USA to southern Mexico.
COMMENT: Tribe Eleutherodactylini. Lynch, 1979, Am. Mus. Novit., 2680:6, regarded *Hylactophryne* and *Ischnocnema* as representing an ancestral grade from which *Eleutherodactylus* was derived.

Hylactophryne augusti (Dugès, 1879). *In* Brocchi, Bull. Soc. Philomath. Paris, (7)3:21.
ORIGINAL NAME: *Hylodes augusti.*
TYPE(S): Holotype: MDUG.
TYPE LOCALITY: Guanajuato, Guanajuato, Mexico.
DISTRIBUTION: Southeastern Arizona and southeastern New Mexico to central Texas (USA) south through central and western Mexico to the Isthmus of Tehuantepec (Oaxaca, Mexico).

COMMENT: Reviewed (as *Eleutherodactylus augusti*) by Zweifel, 1967, Cat. Am. Amph. Rept., 41.1–4.

Hylactophryne occidentalis (Taylor, 1941). Proc. Biol. Soc. Washington, 54:91.
ORIGINAL NAME: *Eleutherodactylus occidentalis*.
TYPE(S): Syntypes: BM 92.2.8.66–67.
TYPE LOCALITY: "Hacienda el Florencio, Zacatecas, Mexico".
DISTRIBUTION: Western Mexico.
COMMENT: Lynch, 1976, Herpetologica, 32:346–347, removed this species from *Eleutherodactylus* and resurrected the name *Hylactophryne mexicanus* for it. Lynch, 1976, Herpetologica, 32:444, noted that the correct name for this species was *Hylactophryne occidentalis*. *Eleutherodactylus occidentalis* is a replacement name for *Eleutherodactylus mexicanus* Boulenger, 1898, Proc. Zool. Soc. London, 1898:477, which was preoccupied by *Leuiperus mexicanus* Brocchi, 1879, when this species was included in *Eleutherodactylus*.

Hylactophryne tarahumaraensis (Taylor, 1940). Copeia, 1940:250.
ORIGINAL NAME: *Eleutherodactylus tarahumaraensis*.
TYPE(S): Holotype: UIMNH 15955 (formerly EHT-HMS 23008).
TYPE LOCALITY: "Mojárachic, Chihuahua, in the Tarahumara Mountains at an elevation of about 6900 feet", Mexico.
DISTRIBUTION: Eastern Sonora and western Chihuahua to Jalisco, Mexico, in the Sierra Madre Occidental.

Hylorina Bell, 1843. Zool. Voy. Beagle, 5:44.
TYPE SPECIES: *Hylorina sylvatica* Bell, 1843.
DISTRIBUTION: As for the single species.
COMMENT: Tribe Telmatobiini. Reviewed by Cei, 1980, Monit. Zool. Ital., N.S., Monogr., 2:285–286.
REVIEWER: Ramón Formas (RF).

Hylorina sylvatica Bell, 1843. Zool. Voy. Beagle, 5:44.
TYPE(S): Not traced.
TYPE LOCALITY: "Archipelago of Chonos (S. of Chiloe)", Chile
DISTRIBUTION: Chonos I. northward to Valdivia region, Chile; Tronador region of Argentina.

Insuetophrynus Barrio, 1970. Physis, Buenos Aires, 30:334.
TYPE SPECIES: *Insuetophrynus acarpicus* Barrio, 1970.
DISTRIBUTION: As for the single species.
COMMENT: Tribe Telmatobiini. Lynch, 1978, Occas. Pap. Mus. Nat. Hist. Univ. Kansas, 72:1–5, considered this genus to be the sister-taxon of *Atelognathus*.

Insuetophrynus acarpicus Barrio, 1970. Physis, Buenos Aires, 30:334.
TYPE(S): Holotype: CHINM 3697.
TYPE LOCALITY: "Mehuin, prov. Valdivia, Chile".
DISTRIBUTION: Vicinity of the type locality.
COMMENT: Diez, Valencia, and Sallaberry, 1983, Copeia, 1983:30–37, commented on life history, morphology, karyology, and molecular features.

Ischnocnema Reinhardt and Lütken, 1862. Vidensk. Medd. Dansk Naturhist. Foren., 1861:239.
TYPE SPECIES: *Leiuperus verrucosus* Reinhardt and Lütken, 1862, by monotypy.
DISTRIBUTION: Upper Amazon Basin and southeastern Brazil.
COMMENT: Tribe Eleutherodactylini. See comment under *Hylactophryne*.

Ischnocnema quixensis (Jiménez de la Espada, 1872). An. Soc. Esp. Hist. Nat., 1:87.
ORIGINAL NAME: *Oreobates quixensis*.
TYPE(S): Not traced (?MNCN).
TYPE LOCALITY: Quito, Pichincha Province, Ecuador, according to Peters, 1955, Rev. Ecuat. Entomol. Parasitol., 3–4:347.
DISTRIBUTION: Upper Amazon Basin in Colombia, Ecuador, and Peru, up to 1000 m.

Ischnocnema simmonsi Lynch, 1974. J. Herpetol., 8:85.
  TYPE(S): Holotype: KU 147068.
  TYPE LOCALITY: "Río Piuntza, Cordillera del Condor, Morona-Santiago Prov.,
    Ecuador, 1830 m".
  DISTRIBUTION: Known only from the type locality.

Ischnocnema verrucosa (Reinhardt and Lütken, 1862). Vidensk. Medd. Dansk
    Naturhist. Foren., 1861:171.
  ORIGINAL NAME: *Leiuperus verrucosus.*
  TYPE(S): Holotype: ZMUC 51.
  TYPE LOCALITY: "Byen [=city] Juiz de Fora i Minas Geraes", Brazil.
  DISTRIBUTION: Southeastern Brazil.

Lynchophrys Laurent, 1983. Acta Zool. Lilloana, 37:111.
  TYPE SPECIES: *Batrachophrynus brachydactylus* Peters, 1873, by original designation.
  DISTRIBUTION: As for the single species.
  COMMENT: In the Tribe Telmatobiini.

Lynchophrys brachydactyla (Peters, 1873). Monatsber. Preuss. Akad. Wiss. Berlin,
    1873:413.
  ORIGINAL NAME: *Batrachophrynus brachydactylus.*
  TYPE(S): Sole male in lot ZMB 7703 designated lectotype by Laurent, 1983, Acta
    Zool. Lilloana, 37:111.
  TYPE LOCALITY: Amable María, Montaña de Vitoe, Peru.
  DISTRIBUTION: Andes of southern Peru.

Macrogenioglottus Carvalho, 1946. Bol. Mus. Nac., Rio de Janeiro, N.S., Zool., 73:1.
  TYPE SPECIES: *Macrogenioglottus alipioi* Carvalho, 1946.
  DISTRIBUTION: As for the single species.
  COMMENT: Tribe Odontophrynini. Lynch, 1971, Misc. Publ. Mus. Nat. Hist. Univ.
    Kansas, 53, considered the genus to be a junior synonym of *Odontophrynus,* but
    later Lynch, 1973, BioScience, 23:497, reversed this decision.

Macrogenioglottus alipioi Carvalho, 1946. Bol. Mus. Nac., Rio de Janeiro, N.S., Zool.,
    73:2.
  TYPE(S): Holotype: MN A844.
  TYPE LOCALITY: "fazenda Pirataquicé, no Município de Ilhéus, Estado da Bahia",
    Brazil.
  DISTRIBUTION: Atlantic forest in southern Bahia to São Paulo, Brazil.

Odontophrynus Reinhardt and Lütken, 1862. Vidensk. Medd. Dansk Naturhist. Foren.,
    13:159.
  TYPE SPECIES: *Odontophrynus cultripes* Reinhardt and Lütken, 1862.
  DISTRIBUTION: Southern and eastern South America.
  COMMENT: Tribe Odontophrynini. Savage and Cei, 1965, Herpetologica, 21:178–195,
    reviewed the genus.

Odontophrynus americanus (Duméril and Bibron, 1841). Erp. Gén., 8:446.
  ORIGINAL NAME: *Pyxicephalus americanus.*
  TYPE(S): Holotype: MNHNP 4530.
  TYPE LOCALITY: "Buenos-Ayres", Argentina.
  DISTRIBUTION: Southern Brazil (from Minas Gerais south); Uruguay; Paraguay;
    southern Bolivia; northern and central Argentina.
  COMMENT: See Barrio, 1972, Physis, Buenos Aires, 31:281–291, for review.

Odontophrynus barrioi Cei, Ruíz, and Beçak, 1982. J. Herpetol., 16:97.
  TYPE(S): Holotype: MZUSP 57635.
  TYPE LOCALITY: Aguadita Springs, 2200 m, 30 km north of the village of Famatina,
    Sierra de Famatina, La Rioja Province, Argentina.
  DISTRIBUTION: Known only from the type locality.

Odontophrynus carvalhoi Savage and Cei, 1965. Herpetologica, 21:187.
TYPE(S): Holotype: MN 313.
TYPE LOCALITY: "Brazil: Estado de Pernambuco: Poção (1,035 m)".
DISTRIBUTION: Northeastern Brazil.

Odontophrynus cultripes Reinhardt and Lütken, 1862. Vidensk. Medd. Dansk
   Naturhist. Foren., 13:159.
TYPE(S): Syntypes: ZMUC and NHMW 16522.
TYPE LOCALITY: "Lagõa Santa" and "Taboleiro Grande", Minas Gerais, Brazil.
DISTRIBUTION: Minas Gerais to Rio Grande do Sul, Brazil; Paraguayan Chaco;
   possibly into Argentina.

Odontophrynus moratoi Jim and Caramaschi, 1980. Rev. Brasil. Biol., 40:357.
TYPE(S): Holotype: MZUSP 50180.
TYPE LOCALITY: "Rubião Júnior, Botucatu, São Paulo, (aprox. 22° 53' S e 48° 30' W)",
   Brazil.
DISTRIBUTION: Known only from the type locality.

Odontophrynus occidentalis (Berg, 1896). An. Mus. Nac. Buenos Aires, 5:168.
ORIGINAL NAME: *Ceratophrys occidentalis.*
TYPE(S): Presumably MACN.
TYPE LOCALITY: "Arroyo Agrio (Neuquén)", Argentina.
DISTRIBUTION: Western and central Argentina (eastern Andean foothills and Sierras
   de Córdoba and San Felipe).

Phyzelaphryne Heyer, 1977. Pap. Avulsos Zool., São Paulo, 31:152.
TYPE SPECIES: *Phyzelaphryne miriamae* Heyer, 1977, by monotypy.
DISTRIBUTION: As for the single species.
COMMENT: Tribe Eleutherodactylini. Considered a synonym of *Eleutherodactylus* by
   Lynch, 1980, Bull. Mus. Natl. Hist. Nat., Paris, (4)2(A)1:301. See comment under
   Phyzelaphryne miriamae.
CONTRIBUTOR: Marinus S. Hoogmoed (MSH).

Phyzelaphryne miriamae Heyer, 1977. Pap. Avulsos Zool., São Paulo, 31:153.
TYPE(S): Holotype: MZUSP 49894.
TYPE LOCALITY: "Brasil: Amazonas; Igarapé Puruzinho at Rio Madeira".
DISTRIBUTION: Southern Amazon basin in drainage of Madeira and Tapajos rivers.
COMMENT: Hoogmoed and Lescure, 1984, Zool. Meded., Leiden, 58:88–92,
   resurrected *Phyzelaphryne* and provided a map of its distribution. See
   comment under *Eleutherodactylus nigrovittatus*, with which it had been
   synonymized.

Phrynopus Peters, 1874. Monatsber. Preuss. Akad. Wiss. Berlin, 1874:416.
TYPE SPECIES: *Phrynopus peruanus* Peters, 1874, by monotypy.
DISTRIBUTION: Andean South America.
COMMENT: Tribe Eleutherodactylini. Lynch, 1975, Occas. Pap. Mus. Nat. Hist. Univ.
   Kansas, 35:1–51, provided synonymies and discussion of the relationships of
   and within this genus. Species groups noted in comments with the species
   records follow his revision. According to Lynch, *Phrynopus* is most closely
   related to some species of *Eleutherodactylus.* Cannatella, 1984, Occas. Pap. Mus.
   Nat. Hist. Univ. Kansas, 113, reinvestigated the phylogenetic reconstructions of
   Lynch. Even though differences were noted, Cannatella refrained from
   redefining species groups because of the topological instability of the
   alternative trees generated.

Phrynopus brunneus Lynch, 1975. Occas. Pap. Mus. Nat. Hist. Univ. Kansas, 35:14.
TYPE(S): Holotype: USNM 192909.
TYPE LOCALITY: "10 km WNW El Carmelo (=Pun), Carchi Prov., Ecuador, 3150 m".
DISTRIBUTION: Known only from the type locality.

COMMENT: In the *Phrynopus flavomaculatus* group.

Phrynopus columbianus (Werner, 1899). Verh. Zool. Bot. Ges. Wien, 49:480.
ORIGINAL NAME: *Borborocoetes columbianus.*
TYPE(S): Lost.
TYPE LOCALITY: "Monte Redondo, Buenavista", Depto. Cundinamarca or Meta, Colombia, 1000–1300 m.
DISTRIBUTION: Known only from the type locality.
COMMENT: In the *Phrynopus flavomaculatus* group.

Phrynopus cophites Lynch, 1975. Occas. Pap. Mus. Nat. Hist. Univ. Kansas, 35:16.
TYPE(S): Holotype: KU 138884.
TYPE LOCALITY: "S slope Abra Acanacu, 14 km NNE Paucartambo, Depto. Cuzco, Perú, 3400 m".
DISTRIBUTION: Páramo and elfin forest habitats on both north and south slopes of the Abra Acanacu, a pass in the Cadena de Paucartambo, on the northwestern end of the Cordillera Carabaya, in Departamento Cuzco, Peru, between 3400 and 3450 m elev.
COMMENT: In the *Phrynopus peruanus* group.

Phrynopus flavomaculatus (Parker, 1938). Ann. Mag. Nat. Hist., (11)2:440.
ORIGINAL NAME: *Eleutherodactylus flavomaculatus.*
TYPE(S): Holotype: BM 1947.2.16.11 (formerly 1935.11.3.16).
TYPE LOCALITY: "15 kilometres east of Loja City, [Loja Province,] Ecuador, at an altitude of approximately 3,000 metres".
DISTRIBUTION: Known from between 2215 and 3100 m elev. on the eastern Andean Cordillera in southern Ecuador.
COMMENT: In the *Phrynopus flavomaculatus* group. May include *Phrynopus parkeri* and *Phrynopus pereger* according to Lynch, 1975, Occas. Pap. Mus. Nat. Hist. Univ. Kansas, 35:34.

Phrynopus laplacai (Cei, 1968). J. Herpetol., 2:139.
ORIGINAL NAME: *Syrrhophus laplacai.*
TYPE(S): Holotype: IBMUNC 125-1.
TYPE LOCALITY: "road to Coroico (National road to Beni Valley), at 3 km west of Pongo, [Departamento La Paz,] in the transitional zone of Unduavi, at 3400 m."
DISTRIBUTION: Known only from the vicinity of the type locality.
COMMENT: In the *Phrynopus peruanus* group.

Phrynopus lucida Cannatella, 1984. Occas. Pap. Mus. Nat. Hist. Univ. Kansas, 113:6.
TYPE(S): Holotype: KU 162435.
TYPE LOCALITY: "north slope of Abra Tapuna, 7 km N Mahuayura, 3710 m, Departamento Ayacucho, Peru".
DISTRIBUTION: Andean Cordillera Oriental west of the Río Apurimac in Departamento Ayacucho, Peru, between 2970 and 3710 m.
COMMENT: In the *Phrynopus flavomaculatus* group, according to the original description.

Phrynopus montium (Shreve, 1938). J. Washington Acad. Sci., 28:406.
ORIGINAL NAME: *Syrrhopus montium.*
TYPE(S): Holotype: MCZ 22858.
TYPE LOCALITY: "Cascas, near Huasahuasi, Department of Junin, Peru".
DISTRIBUTION: Known only from the type locality.
COMMENT: In the *Phrynopus peruanus* group.

Phrynopus nanus (Goin and Cochran, 1963). Proc. California Acad Sci., (4)31:499.
ORIGINAL NAME: *Niceforonia nana.*
TYPE(S): Holotype: USNM 150643.
TYPE LOCALITY: "Colombia, Santander, Páramo de la Rusia".
DISTRIBUTION: Known only from the type locality.

COMMENT: In the *Phrynopus simonsii* group.

Phrynopus nebulanastes Cannatella, 1984. Occas. Pap. Mus. Nat. Hist. Univ. Kansas, 113:2.
TYPE(S): Holotype: KU 181407.
TYPE LOCALITY: "El Tambo, 31.5 km E Canchaque, 2770 m, Departamento Piura, Peru".
DISTRIBUTION: Known only from the type locality.
COMMENT: In the *Phrynopus flavomaculatus* group, according to the original description.

Phrynopus parkeri Lynch, 1975. Occas. Pap. Mus. Nat. Hist. Univ. Kansas, 35:21.
TYPE(S): Holotype: KU 135278.
TYPE LOCALITY: "the summit of the cordillera between Chanchaque [=Canchaque] and Huancabamba, Depto. Piura, Perú, 3100 m".
DISTRIBUTION: Known only from the type locality.
COMMENT: In the *Phrynopus flavomaculatus* group. See comment under *Phrynopus flavomaculatus*.

Phrynopus peraccai Lynch, 1975. Occas. Pap. Mus. Nat. Hist. Univ. Kansas, 35:30.
TYPE(S): Holotype: USNM 160947.
TYPE LOCALITY: "1 km W Papallacta, Napo Prov., Ecuador, 3155 m".
DISTRIBUTION: Vicinity of Papallacta, Napo Province, Ecuador, 3000–3350 m elev.
COMMENT: In the *Phrynopus flavomaculatus* group.

Phrynopus pereger Lynch, 1975. Occas. Pap. Mus. Nat. Hist. Univ. Kansas, 35:32.
TYPE(S): Holotype: LSUMZ 26101.
TYPE LOCALITY: "between Mitupucuru and Yuraccyacu, Depto. Ayacucho, Perú".
DISTRIBUTION: Eastern Andes west of the Río Apurimac and Cordillera Vilcabamba in Departamento Ayacucho, Peru, between 2460 and 2650 m.
COMMENT: In the *Phrynopus flavomaculatus* group. See comment under *Phrynopus flavomaculatus*.

Phrynopus peruanus Peters, 1874. Monatsber. Preuss. Akad. Wiss. Berlin, 1874:416.
TYPE(S): Not traced.
TYPE LOCALITY: "Maraynioc in Peru", Departamento Junín, Peru.
DISTRIBUTION: Known only from the type locality.
COMMENT: In the *Phrynopus peruanus* group.

Phrynopus peruvianus (Noble, 1921). Am. Mus. Novit., 29:1.
ORIGINAL NAME: *Sminthillus peruvianus*.
TYPE(S): Holotype: AMNH 14526.
TYPE LOCALITY: "near Juliaca, [Departamento Puno,] Peru".
DISTRIBUTION: Departamento Puno, Peru.
COMMENT: In the *Phrynopus peruvianus* group.

Phrynopus simonsii (Boulenger, 1900). Ann. Mag. Nat. Hist., (7)6:182.
ORIGINAL NAME: *Paludicola simonsii*.
TYPE(S): Syntypes: BM 1947.2.15.43–44; BM 1947.2.14.43 designated lectotype by Lynch, 1975, Occas. Pap. Mus. Nat. Hist. Univ. Kansas, 35:39.
TYPE LOCALITY: "Paramo, Cajamarca, 9000 feet", Peru; restricted to "8 km E Cajamarca, Depto. Cajamarca, Perú, 3000 m" by Lynch, 1975, Occas. Pap. Mus. Nat. Hist. Univ. Kansas, 35:39.
DISTRIBUTION: Vicinity of the type locality.
COMMENT: In the *Phrynopus simonsii* group.

Phrynopus wettsteini (Parker, 1932). Ann. Mag. Nat. Hist., (10)10:43.
ORIGINAL NAME: *Eupsophus wettsteini.*
TYPE(S): Holotype: NHMW 15845.
TYPE LOCALITY: "Untuaro or Pongo, Peru, 2000 metres", possibly Departamento Amazonas, Peru.
DISTRIBUTION: Known only from the type locality, presumably on the Amazonian slopes of one of the Andean Cordilleras, Peru.
COMMENT: In the *Phrynopus peruanus* group.

Phyllonastes Heyer, 1977. Pap. Avulsos Zool., São Paulo, 31:151.
TYPE SPECIES: *Euparkerella myrmecoides* Lynch, 1976, by original designation.
DISTRIBUTION: Amazonian basin of Peru and Cordillera del Condor, Ecuador.
COMMENT: This genus shares with *Euparkerella* and *Adelophryne adiastola* the unique trait of having only 2 phalanges in the 4th digit (DCC). See comment under *Adelophryne.*

Phyllonastes lochites (Lynch, 1976). Herpetologica, 32:49.
ORIGINAL NAME: *Euparkerella lochites.*
TYPE(S): Holotype: KU 147070.
TYPE LOCALITY: "the Río Piuntza locality on the northern end of the Cordillera del Condor, Morona-Santiago, Prov., Ecuador, 1550 m (approximately 3° 15′ S, 78° 20′ W)".
DISTRIBUTION: Morona-Santiago and Napo provinces, Ecuador.

Phyllonastes myrmecoides (Lynch, 1976). Herpetologica, 32:50.
ORIGINAL NAME: *Euparkerella myrmecoides.*
TYPE(S): Holotype: TCWC 41532.
TYPE LOCALITY: "Mishana (2½ hours by speedboat up the Río Nanay from the Navy dock 5 km NNE Iquitos), Depto. Loreto, Perú".
DISTRIBUTION: Departamento Loreto (Peru) and western Brazil.
COMMENT: See Hoogmoed and Lescure, 1984, Zool. Meded., Leiden, 58:88, for Brazilian records.

Proceratophrys Miranda-Ribeiro, 1920. Rev. Mus. Paulista, São Paulo, 12:301.
TYPE SPECIES: *Ceratophrys bigibbosa* Peters, 1872, by monotypy.
DISTRIBUTION: Brazil.
COMMENT: Tribe Odontophrynini.

Proceratophrys appendiculata (Günther, 1873). Ann. Mag. Nat. Hist., (4)11:418.
ORIGINAL NAME: *Ceratophrys appendiculata.*
TYPE(S): Not traced.
TYPE LOCALITY: Brazil.
DISTRIBUTION: Southern and southeastern Brazil; Paraguay.
COMMENT: Synonymy includes *Proceratophrys melanopogon,* according to Izecksohn and Peixoto, 1981, Rev. Brasil. Biol., 41:19–24.

Proceratophrys bigibbosa (Peters, 1872). Monatsber. Preuss. Akad. Wiss. Berlin, 1872: 204.
ORIGINAL NAME: *Ceratophrys bigibbosa.*
TYPE(S): Not traced.
TYPE LOCALITY: Rio Grande do Sul, Brazil.
DISTRIBUTION: Rio Grande do Sul, Brazil.
COMMENT: Reviewed by Cei, 1980, Monit. Zool. Ital., N.S., Monogr., 2:310–311.

Proceratophrys boiei (Wied-Neuwied, 1825). Beitr. Naturgesch. Brasil., 1:592.
ORIGINAL NAME: *Ceratophrys boiei.*
TYPE(S): AMNH?
TYPE LOCALITY: Bahia and Rio de Janeiro [Brazil].
DISTRIBUTION: Pernambuco to Santa Catarina, Brazil.

COMMENT: Synonymy includes *Proceratophrys renalis*, according to Izecksohn and Peixoto, 1981, Rev. Brasil. Biol., 41:19–24.

Proceratophrys cristiceps (Müller, 1884). Verh. Naturforsch. Ges. Basel, 7:279.
ORIGINAL NAME: *Ceratophrys cristiceps*.
TYPE(S): Not traced.
TYPE LOCALITY: Brazil.
DISTRIBUTION: Northeastern Brazil.
COMMENT: Bokermann, 1966, Lista Anot. Local. Tipo Anf. Brasil.:92, included *Proceratophrys goyanus* as a synonym but provided no evidence to support this view. This putative synonymy is in error, as the species are quite recognizable (UC).

Proceratophrys cristinae Braun, 1973. Iheringia, Zool., 43:91.
TYPE(S): Holotype: MRGS 04650.
TYPE LOCALITY: "Nova Petrópolis, RS [Rio Grande do Sul]", Brazil.
DISTRIBUTION: Known only from the type locality.

Proceratophrys fryi (Günther, 1873). Ann. Mag. Nat. Hist., (4)11:417.
ORIGINAL NAME: *Ceratophrys fryi*.
TYPE(S): Not traced.
TYPE LOCALITY: Serra da Mantiqueira, Minas Gerais [Brazil].
DISTRIBUTION: Minas Gerais and Espírito Santo, Brazil.

Proceratophrys goyana (Miranda-Ribeiro, 1937). Campo, Rio de Janeiro, 1937(24):24.
ORIGINAL NAME: *Stombus goyanus*.
TYPE(S): Not traced.
TYPE LOCALITY: Veadeiros e rio São Miguel, Goiás [Brazil].
DISTRIBUTION: Known only from the type locality.
COMMENT: See comment under *Proceratophrys cristiceps*.

Proceratophrys laticeps Izecksohn and Peixoto, 1981. Rev. Brasil. Biol., 41:20.
TYPE(S): Holotype: EI 5587.
TYPE LOCALITY: "Reserva Florestal da Companhia Vale do Rio Doce, no Município de Linhares, Estado do Espírito Santo", Brazil.
DISTRIBUTION: Bahia and Espírito Santo, Brazil.

Proceratophrys precrenulata (Miranda-Ribeiro, 1937). Campo, Rio de Janeiro, 1937(24):24.
ORIGINAL NAME: *Stombus precrenulatus*.
TYPE(S): Lost.
TYPE LOCALITY: Rio Mutum, Espírito Santo, Brazil.
DISTRIBUTION: Espírito Santo and Rio de Janeiro, Brazil.
COMMENT: See Izecksohn and Peixoto, 1980, Rev. Brasil. Biol., 40:605–609.

Proceratophrys schirchi (Miranda-Ribeiro, 1937). Campo, Rio de Janeiro, 1937(24):24.
ORIGINAL NAME: *Stombus schirchi*.
TYPE(S): Not traced.
TYPE LOCALITY: Rio Mutum, Espírito Santo [Brazil].
DISTRIBUTION: Known only from the type locality.

Scythrophrys Lynch, 1971. Misc. Publ. Mus. Nat. Hist. Univ. Kansas, 53:162.
TYPE SPECIES: *Zachaenus sawayae* Cochran, 1953, by original designation.
DISTRIBUTION: As for the single species.
COMMENT: Considered as having uncertain relationships to other genera, according to Heyer, 1983, Arq. Zool., Univ. São Paulo, 30:276.

Scythrophrys sawayae (Cochran, 1953). Herpetologica, 8:111.
ORIGINAL NAME: *Zachaenus sawayae.*
TYPE(S): Holotype: USNM 125530.
TYPE LOCALITY: "Banhado, Parana", Brazil.
DISTRIBUTION: Serra do Mar in the states of Paraná and Santa Catarina, Brazil.

Sminthillus Barbour and Noble, 1920. Bull. Mus. Comp. Zool., 63:402.
TYPE SPECIES: *Phyllobates limbatus* Cope, 1862.
DISTRIBUTION: As for the single species.
COMMENT: Tribe Eleutherodactylini. Most closely related to some West Indian
Eleutherodactylus, according to Lynch, 1971, Misc. Publ. Mus. Nat. Hist. Univ.
Kansas, 53:1–238, and Bogart, 1981, R. Ontario Mus. Life Sci. Contrib., 129:1–22.
CONTRIBUTOR: Albert Schwartz (AS).
REVIEWERS: Rafael Joglar (RJ); Richard Thomas (RT).

Sminthillus limbatus (Cope, 1862). Proc. Acad. Nat. Sci. Philadelphia, 14:154.
ORIGINAL NAME: *Phyllobates limbatus.*
TYPE(S): Syntypes: USNM 5205.
TYPE LOCALITY: "Eastern Cuba".
DISTRIBUTION: Habana, Cienfuegos, and Santiago de Cuba provinces, Cuba.

Somuncuria Lynch, 1978. Occas. Pap. Mus. Nat. Hist. Univ. Kansas, 72:16.
TYPE SPECIES: *Telmatobius somuncurensis* Cei, 1969, by monotypy.
DISTRIBUTION: As for the single species.
COMMENT: Tribe Telmatobiini. According to Lynch, 1978, Occas. Pap. Mus. Nat. Hist.
Univ. Kansas, 72:16, this genus is "intermediate" between *Atelognathus*
(Telmatobiinae) and *Pleurodema* (Leptodactylinae) and may be a remnant of the
"transition" from the Telmatobiinae to the Leptodactylinae.

Somuncuria somuncurensis (Cei, 1969). J. Herpetol., 3:14.
ORIGINAL NAME: *Telmatobius somuncurensis.*
TYPE(S): Holotype: IBMUNC 1982/1.
TYPE LOCALITY: "El Rincon stream, 60 km SSW from Valcheta, Río Negro,
Argentina, on the basaltic slopes of Somuncura plateau (700 m)".
DISTRIBUTION: Known only from the type locality.
COMMENT: Type locality (the only known range) is currently being destroyed by
goats and cattle (pers. comm., R. Etheridge to DRF). Reviewed (as *Telmatobius
somuncurensis*) by Cei, 1980, Monit. Zool. Ital., N.S., Monogr., 2:248–252.

Syrrhophus Cope, 1878. Am. Nat., 12:253.
TYPE SPECIES: *Syrrhophus marnockii* Cope, 1878, by monotypy.
DISTRIBUTION: Extreme southwestern and southern Texas (USA) and southern Sinaloa
(Mexico) to Guatemala.
COMMENT: Tribe Eleutherodactylini. Lynch, 1970, Univ. Kansas Publ. Mus. Nat. Hist.,
20:1–45, revised this genus and supplied synonymies for the species. Species
groups noted in comment under the species accounts are from this revision.
REVIEWERS: Jonathan A. Campbell (JAC); Gustavo Casas-Andreu (GCA); Oscar Flores-
Villela (OFV).

Syrrhophus cystignathoides (Cope, 1877). Proc. Am. Philos. Soc., 17:89.
ORIGINAL NAME: *Phyllobates cystignathoides.*
TYPE(S): Syntypes: USNM 32402–09, MCZ (formerly USNM 32405).
TYPE LOCALITY: Potrero, near Córdoba, Veracruz, Mexico.
DISTRIBUTION: Low to moderate elevations from the Rio Grande embayment (Texas,
USA) to central Nuevo León, Tamaulipas, eastern San Luis Potosí, and central
Veracruz (Mexico).
COMMENT: In the *Syrrhophus leprus* group.

Syrrhophus dennisi Lynch, 1970. Univ. Kansas Publ. Mus. Nat. Hist., 20:27.
   TYPE(S): Holotype: UMMZ 101121.
   TYPE LOCALITY: "a cave near El Panchón, 8 km. N Antiguo Morelos, Tamaulipas, Mexico, 250 m."
   DISTRIBUTION: Known only from the type locality.
   COMMENT: In the *Syrrhophus longipes* group.

Syrrhophus guttilatus (Cope, 1879). Proc. Am. Philos. Soc., 18:264.
   ORIGINAL NAME: *Malachylodes guttilatus.*
   TYPE(S): Holotype: USNM 9888.
   TYPE LOCALITY: "Guanajuato", Guanajuato, Mexico.
   DISTRIBUTION: Moderate to intermediate elevations (600–2000 m) along the Sierra Madre Oriental from the Big Bend region of Texas (USA) through Coahuila, Nuevo León, and San Luis Potosí to Guanajuato (Mexico).
   COMMENT: In the *Syrrhophus marnockii* group.

Syrrhophus interorbitalis Langebartel and Shannon, 1956. Herpetologica, 12:161.
   TYPE(S): Holotype: UIMNH 67061 (formerly F. A. Shannon 9378).
   TYPE LOCALITY: "rocky stream bed 36 miles north of Mazatlán (center of city), Sinaloa", Mexico.
   DISTRIBUTION: Pacific lowlands of Sinaloa (and probably adjacent Nayarit), Mexico.
   COMMENT: In the *Syrrhophus modestus* group.

Syrrhophus leprus Cope, 1879. Proc. Am. Philos. Soc., 18:268.
   TYPE(S): Holotype: USNM 10040.
   TYPE LOCALITY: "Santa Efigenia", Oaxaca, Mexico.
   DISTRIBUTION: Central Veracruz (Mexico) to Belize including the Isthmus of Tehuantepec.
   COMMENT: In the *Syrrhophus leprus* group.

Syrrhophus longipes (Baird, 1859). *In* Emory, Rep. U.S.-Mex. Bound. Surv., Zool., 2:35.
   ORIGINAL NAME: *Batrachyla longipes.*
   TYPE(S): Holotype: USNM 3237; now lost.
   TYPE LOCALITY: 40 leagues from [probably north of] Mexico City [Mexico].
   DISTRIBUTION: Moderate elevations (650–2000 m) along the Sierra Madre Oriental from central Nuevo León to northern Hidalgo, Mexico.
   COMMENT: In the *Syrrhophus longipes* group.

Syrrhophus marnockii Cope, 1878. Am. Nat., 12:253.
   TYPE(S): Syntypes: ANSP 10765–68.
   TYPE LOCALITY: "near San Antonio", Bexar County, Texas, USA.
   DISTRIBUTION: Edwards Plateau and the extreme eastern edge of the Stockton Plateau in Texas, USA.
   COMMENT: In the *Syrrhophus marnockii* group.

Syrrhophus modestus Taylor, 1942. Univ. Kansas Sci. Bull., 28:304.
   TYPE(S): Holotype: FMNH 100048 (formerly EHT-HMS 3756).
   TYPE LOCALITY: "Hacienda Paso del Río, Colima, México".
   DISTRIBUTION: Low elevations (to 700 m) in the lowlands and foothills of Colima and southwestern Jalisco, Mexico.
   COMMENT: In the *Syrrhophus modestus* group.

Syrrhophus nivicolimae Dixon and Webb, 1966. Contrib. Sci. Nat. Hist. Mus. Los Angeles Co., 102:1.
   TYPE(S): Holotype: LACM 3200.
   TYPE LOCALITY: "Nevado de Colima, six miles (airline) west of Atenquique, Jalisco, 7800 feet", Mexico.
   DISTRIBUTION: Southwestern Jalisco at moderate to high elevations (600–2400 m), Mexico.

COMMENT: In the *Syrrhophus modestus* group.

Syrrhophus pallidus Duellman, 1958. Occas. Pap. Mus. Zool. Univ. Michigan, 594:5.
ORIGINAL NAME: *Syrrhophus modestus pallidus*.
TYPE(S): Holotype: UMMZ 115452.
TYPE LOCALITY: "near sea level at San Blas, Nayarit", Mexico.
DISTRIBUTION: Low elevations in coastal Nayarit and the Tres Marias Is., Mexico.
COMMENT: In the *Syrrhophus modestus* group.

Syrrhophus pipilans Taylor, 1940. Proc. Biol. Soc. Washington, 53:95.
TYPE(S): Holotype: FMNH 100072 (formerly EHT-HMS 6843).
TYPE LOCALITY: "9 mi. south of Mazatlán, Guerrero, México (km. 337)".
DISTRIBUTION: South-central Guerrero through southern Oaxaca and southern
    Chiapas (Mexico) to southwestern Guatemala.
COMMENT: The sole member of the *Syrrhophus pipilans* group.

Syrrhophus rubrimaculatus Taylor and Smith, 1945. Proc. U.S. Natl. Mus., 95:583.
TYPE(S): Holotype: USNM 114070.
TYPE LOCALITY: "La Esperanza, [near Escuintla,] Chiapas", Mexico.
DISTRIBUTION: Low to moderate elevations on the Pacific versant of southeastern
    Chiapas, Mexico; probably extending into adjacent Guatemala.
COMMENT: In the *Syrrhophus leprus* group.

Syrrhophus teretistes Duellman, 1958. Occas. Pap. Mus. Zool. Univ. Michigan, 594:10.
TYPE(S): Holotype: UMMZ 115451.
TYPE LOCALITY: "3 miles northwest of Tepic, Nayarit (± 2950 feet)", Mexico.
DISTRIBUTION: Moderate elevations (840–1200 m) in the Sierra Madre Occidental of
    Nayarit, Sinaloa, and Durango, Mexico.
COMMENT: In the *Syrrhophus modestus* group.

Syrrhophus verrucipes Cope, 1885. Proc. Am. Philos. Soc., 22:383.
TYPE(S): Holotype: ANSP 11325.
TYPE LOCALITY: Near Zacualtipan (1800 feet lower in rocky gorge of a stream near
    its junction with the San Miguel River), Hidalgo, Mexico.
DISTRIBUTION: Moderate elevations in southeastern San Luis Potosí, Querétaro, and
    northwestern Hidalgo, Mexico.
COMMENT: In the *Syrrhophus marnockii* group.

Syrrhophus verruculatus (Peters, 1870). Monatsber. Preuss. Akad. Wiss. Berlin, 1870:
    650.
ORIGINAL NAME: *Phyllobates verruculatus*.
TYPE(S): Holotype: ZMB 6957.
TYPE LOCALITY: Huanusco, Veracruz, Mexico; corrected to Huatusco, Veracruz,
    Mexico, by Smith and Taylor, 1948, Bull. U.S. Natl. Mus., 194:52.
DISTRIBUTION: Puebla and Veracruz, Mexico.
COMMENT: Considered a *nomen dubium* by Lynch, 1970, Univ. Kansas Publ. Mus.
    Nat. Hist., 20:1–45.

Telmatobius Wiegmann, 1835. Nova Acta Acad. Caesar. Leop. Carol., Halle, 17:262.
TYPE SPECIES: *Telmatobius peruvianus* Wiegmann, 1835.
DISTRIBUTION: Andean South America, Ecuador to Chile and Argentina.
COMMENT: Tribe Telmatobiini. Macedo, 1960, Z. Wiss. Zool., Leipzig, 163:355–396,
    summarized the known subspecies. Cei, 1980, Monit. Zool. Ital., N.S., Monogr.,
    2:234–272, reviewed the Argentinian species and discussed the taxonomic
    problems. Chilean species reviewed by Veloso, Sallaberry, Navarro, Iturra,
    Valencia, Penna, and Díaz, 1982, *In* Veloso and Bustos-O. (eds.), Veg. Vert. Inf.
    Arica-Lago Chungara:133–194.
REVIEWER: Esteban O. Lavilla (EOL).

Telmatobius albiventris Parker, 1940. Trans. Linn. Soc. London, (3)1:211.
ORIGINAL NAME: *Telmatobius culeus albiventris.*
TYPE(S): Syntypes: 13 specimens (not traced).
TYPE LOCALITY: "Lago Pequeño, collected chiefly around Taquiri Island and near Taraco Point", Lake Titicaca, Peru.
DISTRIBUTION: Lake Titicaca and Laguna de Arapa, Peru and Bolivia.
COMMENT: Includes four subspecies; see Vellard, 1951, Mem. Mus. Hist. Nat. Javier Prado, 1:1–89, and Vellard, 1960, Mem. Mus. Hist. Nat. Javier Prado, 10:1–19.

Telmatobius arequipensis Vellard, 1955. Mem. Mus. Hist. Nat. Javier Prado, 4:20.
TYPE(S): Syntypes: MHNJP 63, 153, 331, 366.
TYPE LOCALITY: "Riachuela de Yura; praderas inundadas cerca del río Chili, riachuelos cerca de Arequipa", Peru.
DISTRIBUTION: Arequipa region of Peru.
COMMENT: Vellard, 1955, Mem. Mus. Hist. Nat. Javier Prado, 4:18–20, discussed variation in the two subspecies.

Telmatobius atacamensis Gallardo, 1962. Neotropica, 8:46.
TYPE(S): Holotype: MACN 2136.
TYPE LOCALITY: "San Antonio de los Cobres, Salta, Argentina".
DISTRIBUTION: Known only from the type locality.
COMMENT: Probably extinct (EOL).

Telmatobius brevipes Vellard, 1951. Mem. Mus. Hist. Nat. Javier Prado, 1:71.
TYPE(S): Holotype: MHNJP 246/3.
TYPE LOCALITY: "Huamachuco", La Libertad, Peru.
DISTRIBUTION: Known only from the type locality.

Telmatobius brevirostris Vellard, 1955. Mem. Mus. Hist. Nat. Javier Prado, 4:22.
TYPE(S): Holotype: MHNJP 424.
TYPE LOCALITY: "Chasqui, provincia of Ambo (2000 m.)".
DISTRIBUTION: Provinces of Ambo and Huánuco, Peru.
COMMENT: Vellard, 1955, Mem. Mus. Hist. Nat. Javier Prado, 4:20–23, discussed variation in the three subspecies.

Telmatobius ceiorum Laurent, 1970. Acta Zool. Lilloana, 27:214.
TYPE(S): Holotype: FML 1372.
TYPE LOCALITY: "km 51 ruta de Concepción a Andagalá, cerca de la Banderita, Prov. de Catamarca, alt. ± 1.900 metros".
DISTRIBUTION: Catamarca and Tucumán provinces, Argentina.

Telmatobius cirrhacelis Trueb, 1979. Copeia, 1979:715.
TYPE(S): Holotype: KU 165991.
TYPE LOCALITY: "13 km E Loja (Abra de Zamora), 2850 m, Provincia Loja, Ecuador (latitude 03° 59' S, longitude 79° 08' W)".
DISTRIBUTION: Vicinity of the type locality.

Telmatobius contrerasi Cei, 1977. J. Herpetol., 11:359.
TYPE(S): Holotype: IBMUNC 2420-1.
TYPE LOCALITY: "Cerro Madrid, Gualcamayo Valley, 3050 m, San Juan Province, Argentina".
DISTRIBUTION: Known only from the type locality.

Telmatobius crawfordi Parker, 1940. Trans. Linn. Soc. London, (3)1:212.
ORIGINAL NAME: *Telmatobius escomeli crawfordi.*
TYPE(S): Syntypes: 25 specimens, not traced.
TYPE LOCALITY: "Lagunilla Saracocha", Puno, Peru.
DISTRIBUTION: Northern Lake Titicaca and Lake Chajchora, Peru.

COMMENT: The three subspecies discussed by Vellard, 1953, Mem. Mus. Hist. Nat. Javier Prado, 2:1–53.

Telmatobius culeus (Garman, 1875). Bull. Mus. Comp. Zool., 3:276.
ORIGINAL NAME: *Cyclorhamphus culeus.*
TYPE(S): Syntypes: MCZ, UMMZ 48072 (formerly MCZ 1080), UMMZ 50096 (formerly MCZ 1079), NHMW 22866.
TYPE LOCALITY: Lake Titicaca, off Achacache, 11 fathoms deep.
DISTRIBUTION: Region in vicinity of Lake Titicaca, Peru and Bolivia; Lake Umayo, Peru.
COMMENT: The six subspecies discussed by Vellard, 1953, Mem. Mus. Hist. Nat. Javier Prado, 2:1–53.

Telmatobius halli Noble, 1938. Am. Mus. Novit., 963:1.
TYPE(S): Holotype: AMNH 44753.
TYPE LOCALITY: "Warm spring near Ollague, Chile, 10,000 ft. altitude".
DISTRIBUTION: Northern Chile.

Telmatobius hauthali Koslowsky, 1895. Rev. Mus. La Plata, 6:359.
TYPE(S): Not traced.
TYPE LOCALITY: "Aguas Calientes, 4000 metros altura", near Cazadero Grande, Catamarca, Argentina.
DISTRIBUTION: Catamarca Province, Argentina.
COMMENT: Laurent, 1977, Acta Zool. Lilloana, 32:191–196, described two subspecies: *Telmatobius hauthali pisanoi* and *Telmatobius hauthali laticeps* (now considered a distinct species). Specimens from Campo Arenal, between Andalgala and Santa María, Provincia Catamarca, Argentina, reported as *Telmatobius hauthali* by Laurent, 1970, Acta Zool. Lilloana, 25:207–226, are of an undescribed species (EOL).

Telmatobius ignavus Barbour and Noble, 1920. Bull. Mus. Comp. Zool., 63:414.
TYPE(S): Holotype: MCZ 4093.
TYPE LOCALITY: "Huancabamba, Piura, Peru".
DISTRIBUTION: Known only from the type locality.

Telmatobius intermedius Vellard, 1951. Mem. Mus. Hist. Nat. Javier Prado, 1:29.
TYPE(S): Holotype: MHNJP 238/3.
TYPE LOCALITY: "Allipacca cerca de Puquio, 3,300 m., sobre la vertiene Pacifica de los Andes, 14° 40′ L. S."
DISTRIBUTION: Known only from the type locality.

Telmatobius jelskii (Peters, 1873). Monatsber. Preuss. Akad. Wiss. Berlin, 1873:415.
ORIGINAL NAME: *Pseudobatrachus jelskii.*
TYPE(S): Not traced.
TYPE LOCALITY: "Acancocha, [Departamento Junín,] Peru".
DISTRIBUTION: Ayacucho region north to Junín region, Peru.
COMMENT: Vellard, 1955, Mem. Mus. Hist. Nat. Javier Prado, 4:14–16, discussed the four subspecies.

Telmatobius juninensis (Shreve, 1938). J. Washington Acad. Sci., 28:406.
ORIGINAL NAME: *Syrrhopus juninensis.*
TYPE(S): Holotype: MCZ 22851.
TYPE LOCALITY: "Cascas, Department of Junin, Peru".
DISTRIBUTION: Known only from the type locality.
COMMENT: Probably a *Phrynopus* (DCC).

Telmatobius laticeps Laurent, 1977. Acta Zool. Lilloana, 32:191.
ORIGINAL NAME: *Telmatobius hauthali laticeps.*
TYPE(S): Holotype: FML 02255.
TYPE LOCALITY: "km 78 Ruta Tafí del Valle", Tucumán Province, Argentina.
DISTRIBUTION: Known only from the type locality.

COMMENT: Elevated to species status by Laurent and Teran, 1981, Fund. Miguel Lillo, Misc., 71:7.

Telmatobius latirostris Vellard, 1951. Mem. Mus. Hist. Nat. Javier Prado, 1:68.
TYPE(S): Holotype: MHNJP 325/1.
TYPE LOCALITY: "quebrada en Cuervo [Cajamarca,] Norte de Peru".
DISTRIBUTION: Known only from the type locality.

Telmatobius marmoratus (Duméril and Bibron, 1841). Erp. Gén., 8:455.
ORIGINAL NAME: *Cycloramphus marmoratus.*
TYPE(S): Syntypes: MNHNP 4534-36.
TYPE LOCALITY: "Guasacona" and "Chili"; corrected implicitly to Guasacona, Puno, Peru, by Schmidt, 1954, Fieldiana: Zool., 34:282.
DISTRIBUTION: Lake Titicaca region of Peru and Bolivia; Cuzco region of Peru; Cochabamba, Boliva; Yungas de la Paz, Bolivia.
COMMENT: Synonymy includes *Telmatobius sanborni* Schmidt, 1954, according to Vellard, 1960, Mem. Mus. Hist. Nat. Javier Prado, 10:1-19. See Vellard, 1951, Mem. Mus. Hist. Nat. Javier Prado, 1:1-89, and Vellard, 1953, Mem. Mus. Hist. Nat. Javier Prado, 2:1-53, for discussion of the six subspecies.

Telmatobius niger Barbour and Noble, 1920. Bull. Mus. Comp. Zool., 63:413.
TYPE(S): Holotype: MCZ 3037.
TYPE LOCALITY: "Palmira desert, Ecuador"; corrected to vicinity of Palmira, Chimborazo Province [Ecuador] by Schmidt, 1954, Fieldiana: Zool., 34:282.
DISTRIBUTION: Both slopes of Ecuadorian Andes from the Cuenca Basin (Provincia Azuay) to Intac (Provincia Imbabura).
COMMENT: Reviewed by Trueb, 1979, Copeia, 1979:714-733.

Telmatobius oxycephalus Vellard, 1946. Acta Zool. Lilloana, 3:320.
TYPE(S): Holotype: FML 00225.
TYPE LOCALITY: "Cerro de Escalera, province de Salta, à 3.800 m".
DISTRIBUTION: Provinces of Jujuy and Salta, Argentina.
COMMENT: Synonymy includes *Telmatobius barrioi* Laurent, 1970, according to Laurent, 1977, Acta Zool. Lilloana, 32:189-206.

Telmatobius pefauri Veloso and Trueb, 1976. Occas. Pap. Mus. Nat. Hist. Univ. Kansas, 62:2.
TYPE(S): Holotype: KU 159836.
TYPE LOCALITY: "Murmuntani, 3200 m, Departamento de Arico, Provincia de Tarapacá, Chile".
DISTRIBUTION: Known only from the type locality.

Telmatobius peruvianus Wiegmann, 1835. Nova Acta Acad. Caesar. Leop. Carol., Halle, 17:262.
TYPE(S): Not traced.
TYPE LOCALITY: "Peru"; restricted to Cordillera de Guatilla [Chile], near Palca, two days' journey east of Tacna [Peru] by Schmidt, 1928, Rev. Chilena Hist. Nat., 32:98-105.
DISTRIBUTION: Northern Chile.

Telmatobius rimac Schmidt, 1954. Fieldiana: Zool., 34:278.
TYPE(S): Holotype: UMMZ 55596.
TYPE LOCALITY: "Rio Blanco, tributary of the Rio Rimac, Peru, at an altitude of about 10,000 feet".
DISTRIBUTION: Río Blanco and Lima region of Peru.
COMMENT: Vellard, 1955, Mem. Mus. Hist. Nat. Javier Prado, 4:16-18, discussed the two subspecies.

Telmatobius schreiteri Vellard, 1946. Acta Zool. Lilloana, 3:321.
TYPE(S): Holotype: FML 00216.
TYPE LOCALITY: "Aimogasta, province de La Rioja", Argentina.
DISTRIBUTION: Extra-Andean Sierra de Velazco, up to 2500–3000 m, La Rioja, Argentina.
COMMENT: This species was included as a subspecies of *Telmatobius hauthali* by Vellard, 1951, Mem. Mus. Hist. Nat. Javier Prado, 1:1–89, but was considered a distinct species by Laurent, 1977, Acta Zool. Lilloana, 32:189–206.

Telmatobius simonsi Parker, 1940. Trans. Linn. Soc. London, (3)1:210.
TYPE(S): Holotype: BM 1902.5.29.103.
TYPE LOCALITY: "Sucré, [Departamento Chuquisaca,] Bolivia (2800 m)".
DISTRIBUTION: Sucre and Parutani, Bolivia.

Telmatobius stephani Laurent, 1973. Acta Zool. Lilloana, 30:164.
TYPE(S): Holotype: FML 01743.
TYPE LOCALITY: "Río Encrucijada, ± 2000 m cerca de Las Juntas, prov. de Catamarca", Argentina.
DISTRIBUTION: Sierra del Manchao, Catamarca Province, Argentina.

Telmatobius vellardi Munsterman and Leviton, 1959. Occas. Pap. Nat. Hist. Mus. Stanford Univ., 7:1.
TYPE(S): Holotype: CAS-SU 18100.
TYPE LOCALITY: "Cajanuma Mountains, 15 kilometers south of Loja, Loja Province, southern Ecuador, at 2900 meters altitude".
DISTRIBUTION: Loja Province, southern Ecuador.
COMMENT: Reviewed by Trueb, 1979, Copeia, 1979:714–733.

Telmatobius verrucosus Werner, 1899. Zool. Anz., 22:482.
TYPE(S): Holotype: NHMW 22922.
TYPE LOCALITY: "Chaco, Bolivia"; corrected to Chaco, on the Unduavi River, 25 km northwest of Puente de la Via, La Paz, Bolivia, by Schmidt, 1954, Fieldiana: Zool., 34:284.
DISTRIBUTION: Vicinity of the type locality.
COMMENT: Synonymy includes *Telmatobius bolivianus* Parker, 1940, according to Vellard, 1951, Mem. Mus. Hist. Nat. Javier Prado, 1:76, although Parker, 1940, Trans. Linn. Soc. London, 1:203–216, noted differences between the two forms.

Telmatobius zapahuirensis Veloso, Sallaberry, Navarro, Iturra, Valencia, Penna, and Díaz, 1982. *In* Veloso and Bustos-O. (eds.), Veg. Vert. Inf. Arica–Lago Chungara: 170.
TYPE(S): Holotype: DBCUCH 0629.
TYPE LOCALITY: "en el Quebrada de Zapahuira, 30 km al Norte de Murmuntani, 3.270 m snm", Chile.
DISTRIBUTION: Known only from the type locality.

Telmatobufo Schmidt, 1952. Fieldiana: Zool., 34:11.
TYPE SPECIES: *Telmatobufo bullocki* Schmidt, 1952.
DISTRIBUTION: Southern Chile.
REVIEWER: Ramón Formas (RF).

Telmatobufo australis Formas, 1972. J. Herpetol., 6:1.
TYPE(S): Holotype: IZUA 934-A.
TYPE LOCALITY: "Pelada mountains", Provincia Valdivia, Chile.
DISTRIBUTION: Valdivia Province, Chile.

Telmatobufo bullocki Schmidt, 1952. Fieldiana: Zool., 34:12.
TYPE(S): Holotype: FMNH 23842.
TYPE LOCALITY: "Cerros de Nahuelbuta, Province of Malleco, Chile".
DISTRIBUTION: Arauco, Concepción, and Malleco provinces, Chile.

COMMENT: This species was resurrected from the synonymy of *Telmatobufo venustus* by Formas and Veloso, 1982, Proc. Biol. Soc. Washington, 95:688–693.

Telmatobufo venustus (Philippi, 1899). An. Mus. Nac. Hist. Nat., Chile, 104:723.
ORIGINAL NAME: *Bufo venustus.*
TYPE(S): Holotype: IZUC 205051.
TYPE LOCALITY: Cordillera de Chillán, Chillán Province, Chile, app. 1200 m.
DISTRIBUTION: Provinces of Chillán and Talca, Chile.
COMMENT: Redescribed by Formas and Veloso, 1982, Proc. Biol. Soc. Washington, 95:688–693.

Thoropa Cope, 1865. Nat. Hist. Rev., N.S., 5:110.
TYPE SPECIES: *Cystignathus missiessii* Eydoux and Souleyet, 1841 (=*Rana miliaris* Spix, 1824).
DISTRIBUTION: Eastern and southeastern Brazil.
COMMENT: Tribe Batrachylini. Most recently revised by Bokermann, 1965, An. Acad. Brasil. Cienc., 37:525–537.

Thoropa lutzi Cochran, 1938. Proc. Biol. Soc. Washington, 51:41.
TYPE(S): Holotype: USNM 97622.
TYPE LOCALITY: "Recreio dos Bandeirantes, Federal District, southwest of the city of Rio de Janeiro", Brazil.
DISTRIBUTION: Rio de Janeiro region, Brazil.

Thoropa miliaris (Spix, 1824). Spec. Nov. Testud. Ran. Brasil.:30.
ORIGINAL NAME: *Rana miliaris.*
TYPE(S): Holotype: ZSM 2493/0 (now lost).
TYPE LOCALITY: Amazon River [in error]; Bokermann, 1966, Lista Anot. Local. Tipo Anf. Brasil.:89, noted that Spix's specimens probably came from Rio de Janeiro, a view concurred with by Hoogmoed and Gruber, 1983, Spixiana, Suppl., 9:360.
DISTRIBUTION: Eastern Brazil.
COMMENT: See Hoogmoed and Gruber, 1983, Spixiana, Suppl., 9:360, for synonymy.

Thoropa petropolitana (Wandolleck, 1907). Abh. Ber. K. Zool. Anthro. Ethno. Mus. Dresden, 11:7.
ORIGINAL NAME: *Hylodes petropolitanus.*
TYPE(S): Syntypes: MKTD D 2037.
TYPE LOCALITY: Petrópolis, Rio de Janeiro [Brazil].
DISTRIBUTION: Espírito Santo and Rio de Janeiro, Brazil.

Tomodactylus Günther, 1900. Biol. Cent. Am., Rept. Batr.:219.
TYPE SPECIES: *Tomodactylus amulae* Günther, 1900 (=*Liuperus nitidus* Peters, 1869).
DISTRIBUTION: Southern Sinaloa south along the edge of the Mexican Plateau and the Oaxacan highlands, Mexico.
COMMENT: Tribe Eleutherodactylini. See Dixon, 1957, Texas J. Sci., 9:379–409, for most recent revision.
REVIEWERS: Jonathan A. Campbell (JAC); Gustavo Casas-Andreu (GCA); Oscar Flores-Villela (OFV).

Tomodactylus albolabris Taylor, 1943. Univ. Kansas Sci. Bull., 29:351.
TYPE(S): Holotype: FMNH 100082 (formerly EHT-HMS 29568).
TYPE LOCALITY: "Agua del Obispo, Guerrero, (km. 351)", Mexico.
DISTRIBUTION: Central Guerrero, Mexico.

Tomodactylus angustidigitorum Taylor, 1940 "1939". Univ. Kansas Sci. Bull., 26:494.
TYPE(S): Holotype: FMNH 100126 (formerly EHT-HMS 18640).
TYPE LOCALITY: "Quiroga (northeastern end of Lake Pátzcuaro), Michoacán, México, elevation 6,880 ft."
DISTRIBUTION: States of Michoacán and México and the D.F., Mexico.

Tomodactylus dilatus Davis and Dixon, 1955. Herpetologica, 11:155.
TYPE(S): Holotype: TCWC 11245.
TYPE LOCALITY: "four miles west of Mazatlán, 7400 feet, Guerrero", Mexico.
DISTRIBUTION: Central Guerrero, Mexico.

Tomodactylus fuscus Davis and Dixon, 1955. Herpetologica, 11:157.
TYPE(S): Holotype: TCWC 11252.
TYPE LOCALITY: "1½ miles southeast of Huitzilac, 7800 feet, Morelos, México".
DISTRIBUTION: Southeastern Michoacán to Morelos, Mexico.

Tomodactylus grandis Dixon, 1957. Texas J. Sci., 9:403.
TYPE(S): Holotype: TCWC 12628.
TYPE LOCALITY: "San Pedro (2 miles south Tlalpam), 7,800 feet, Distrito Federal, México".
DISTRIBUTION: Vicinity of the type locality.
COMMENT: Threatened by urbanization of Mexico City (OFV).

Tomodactylus nitidus (Peters, 1869). Monatsber. Preuss. Akad. Wiss. Berlin, 1869:878–879.
ORIGINAL NAME: *Liuperus nitidus*.
TYPE(S): Holotype: ZMB 6669.
TYPE LOCALITY: State of Puebla, Mexico; probably near Matamoros [Puebla, Mexico] according to Smith and Taylor, 1948, Bull. U.S. Natl. Mus., 194:49.
DISTRIBUTION: Highlands of western Veracruz, Puebla, Morelos, Guerrero, and Oaxaca, Mexico.
COMMENT: Synonymy includes *Tomodactylus amulae* Günther, 1901, according to Dixon, 1957, Texas J. Sci., 9:385.

Tomodactylus rufescens Duellman and Dixon, 1959. Texas J. Sci., 11:78.
TYPE(S): Holotype: UMMZ 118509.
TYPE LOCALITY: "Dos Aguas, Michoacán, México, 6900 feet".
DISTRIBUTION: Michoacán, Mexico.

Tomodactylus saxatilis Webb, 1962. Univ. Kansas Publ. Mus. Nat. Hist., 15:177.
TYPE(S): Holotype: KU 63326.
TYPE LOCALITY: "eight miles west of El Palmito, Sinaloa, approximately 6100 feet", Mexico.
DISTRIBUTION: Mixed boreal-tropical habitat in mountains of southern Sinaloa and adjacent Durango, Mexico.

Tomodactylus syristes Hoyt, 1965. J. Ohio Herpetol. Soc., 5:19.
TYPE(S): Holotype: UMMZ 124004.
TYPE LOCALITY: "66.7 km (by road) N of Pochutla, Oaxaca, México".
DISTRIBUTION: Pacific slopes of the Sierra de Miahuatlán, Oaxaca, Mexico.

Zachaenus Cope, 1866. J. Acad. Nat. Sci. Philadelphia, (2)6:94.
TYPE SPECIES: *Cystignathus parvulus* Girard, 1853.
DISTRIBUTION: Southeastern Brazil; doubtfully from Argentina.
COMMENT: Tribe Grypiscini.

Zachaenus carvalhoi Izecksohn, 1983 "1982". Arq. Univ. Fed. Rural Rio de Janeiro, 5(1):7.
TYPE(S): Holotype: EI 7243.
TYPE LOCALITY: "Santa Tereza, Estado do Espírito Santo, Brasil".
DISTRIBUTION: Known only from the type locality.

Zachaenus parvulus (Girard, 1853). Proc. Acad. Nat. Sci. Philadelphia, 6:422.
ORIGINAL NAME: *Cystignathus parvulus*.
TYPE(S): Not traced.
TYPE LOCALITY: Rio de Janeiro [Brazil].
DISTRIBUTION: Southeastern Brazil; doubtfully from Argentina.

Zachaenus roseus Cope, 1890. Proc. U.S. Natl. Mus., 12:142.
  TYPE(S): Holotype: USNM 15126.
  TYPE LOCALITY: Port Otway, Patagonia [Argentina].
  DISTRIBUTION: Known only from the holotype.
  COMMENT: The type and only known specimen is disintegrated; listed as "species inquirenda" by Lynch, 1970, Misc. Publ. Mus. Nat. Hist. Univ. Kansas, 53:142, but clearly not associated with the genus *Zachaenus* (WRH).

FAMILY: **Microhylidae** Günther, 1859 "1858" (1843).
  CITATION: Cat. Batr. Sal. Coll. Brit. Mus.:121.
  DISTRIBUTION: North and South America; Africa south of the Sahara; India and Korea to northern Australia.
  COMMENT: As first formed the group name was Micrhylidae (based on *Micrhyla* Duméril and Bibron, 1841, Erp. Gén., 6:613, an unjustified emendation of *Microhyla* Tschudi, 1838, Classif. Batr.:71). Noble, 1931, Biol. Amph.:537, was the first to use the emended spelling Microhylinae. Parker, 1934, Monogr. Frogs Fam. Microhylidae:9, was the first to use Microhylidae. For purposes of priority the Microhylidae takes the date 1843 from Hylaedactyli (based on *Hylaedactylus* [=*Kaloula*]) and Gastrophrynae (based on *Gastrophryne*; formerly a junior synonym of *Microhyla*) of Fitzinger, 1843, Syst. Rept.:33, under the provisions of Article 40 of the International Code of Zoological Nomenclature. Griffiths, 1963, Biol. Rev. Cambridge Philos. Soc., 38:241–292; Lynch, 1973, *In* Vial (ed.), Evol. Biol. Anurans: 133–182; and Trueb, 1973, *In* Vial (ed.), Evol. Biol. Anurans:65–132, placed the Microhylidae near the Ranidae. This view was disputed by Starrett, 1973, *In* Vial (ed.), Evol. Biol. Anurans:251–271, on the basis of larval features, and by Savage, 1973, *In* Vial (ed.), Evol. Biol. Anurans:351–445, who followed Starrett. Sokol, 1975, Copeia, 1975:1–23, also studying larvae, disagreed with Starrett and concurred with more popular views; but see Pyburn, 1980, Pap. Avulsos Zool., São Paulo, 33:231–238. Blommers-Schlösser, 1975, Beaufortia, 24(309):14, noted that the morphological intermediacy of the Scaphiophryninae supported the view that the Microhylidae was most closely related to the Ranidae. The internal taxonomy of the Microhylidae is problematical, differing numbers of subfamilies being used by different authors (Parker, 1934, Monogr. Frogs Fam. Microhylidae; Lynch, 1973, *In* Vial (ed.), Evol. Biol. Anurans:133–182; and Savage, 1973, *In* Vial (ed.), Evol. Biol. Anurans:351–445).
  REVIEWERS: William E. Duellman (WED); Marinus S. Hoogmoed (MSH).

SUBFAMILY: **Asterophryinae** Günther, 1859 "1858".
  CITATION: Cat. Batr. Sal. Coll. Brit. Mus.:37.
  DISTRIBUTION: Moluccan Is., Indonesia, throughout the island of New Guinea to the Louisiade Archipelago.
  COMMENT: As first formed the group name was Asterophrydidae. This subfamily was combined with the Sphenophryninae (Genyophryninae of this list) by Savage, 1973, *In* Vial (ed.), Evol. Biol. Anurans:351–445, on the basis of biogeography but Zweifel, 1972, Bull. Am. Mus. Nat. Hist., 148:411–546, presented morphological evidence to retain this subfamily. For review, revision, and synonymies see Zweifel, 1972, Bull. Am. Mus. Nat. Hist., 148:411–546.
  CONTRIBUTOR: Richard G. Zweifel (RGZ).
  REVIEWERS: Margaret Davies (MD); Michael J. Tyler (MJT).

Asterophrys Tschudi, 1838. Classif. Batr.:82.
  TYPE SPECIES: *Ceratophrys turpicola* Schlegel, 1837, by monotypy.
  DISTRIBUTION: As for the single species.

Asterophrys turpicola (Schlegel, 1837). Abbild. Amph.:30.
    ORIGINAL NAME: *Ceratophrys turpicola*.
    TYPE(S): Syntypes: RMNH 2153 (2 specimens).
    TYPE LOCALITY: West coast of New Guinea; defined by Brongersma, 1953, Proc. K.
        Nederland. Akad. Wetensch., (C)56:573, as "Lobo district, Triton Bay, Dutch
        New Guinea [Irian Jaya, Indonesia]".
    DISTRIBUTION: Lowland rainforest over much of New Guinea, but apparently
        absent from the eastern half of Papua New Guinea.
    COMMENT: The unjustified emendation (under Article 32.c.ii of the International
        Code of Zoological Nomenclature, 1985) of the specific epithet to *turpicula* has
        had widespread use.

Barygenys Parker, 1936. Ann. Mag. Nat. Hist., (10)17:73.
    TYPE SPECIES: *Barygenys cheesmanae* Parker, 1936, by original designation.
    DISTRIBUTION: High elevations of the western highlands of Papua New Guinea to the
        Louisiade Archipelago.
    COMMENT: See Zweifel, 1981 "1980", Pacif. Sci., 34:269–275, for a key to species.

Barygenys atra (Günther, 1896). Novit. Zool., 3:184.
    ORIGINAL NAME: *Xenorhina atra*.
    TYPE(S): Holotype: BM 1947.2.10.78 (formerly 96.7.7.3).
    TYPE LOCALITY: "Clyde [=Mambare] River within a few miles of the frontier
        between British and German New Guinea [Northern Province, Papua New
        Guinea]".
    DISTRIBUTION: Morobe and Northern provinces, Papua New Guinea.

Barygenys cheesmanae Parker, 1936. Ann. Mag. Nat. Hist., (10)17:74.
    TYPE(S): Holotype: BM 1947.2.10.84 (formerly 1935.3.9.125).
    TYPE LOCALITY: "Mt. Tafa (8500 ft.), Papua" (Central Province, Papua New Guinea).
    DISTRIBUTION: Mt. Tafa, 2070–2590 m elev., Papua New Guinea.

Barygenys exsul Zweifel, 1956. Am. Mus. Novit., 1766:3.
    TYPE(S): Holotype: AMNH 60103.
    TYPE LOCALITY: "Abaleti, Rossel Island, Louisiade Archipelago, Territory of Papua,
        New Guinea [Milne Bay Province, Papua New Guinea]".
    DISTRIBUTION: Eastern tip of New Guinea mainland and Woodlark, Rossel, and
        Tagula Is.

Barygenys flavigularis Zweifel, 1972. Bull. Am. Mus. Nat. Hist., 148:443.
    TYPE(S): Holotype: AMNH 82903.
    TYPE LOCALITY: "Mt. Kaindi, Morobe District [Morobe Province], Territory of New
        Guinea [Papua New Guinea], at an elevation of about 7500 ft. (2280 m.)".
    DISTRIBUTION: Known from mountains in the vicinity of Wau, Papua New Guinea.

Barygenys maculata Menzies and Tyler, 1977. J. Zool., London, 183:447.
    TYPE(S): Holotype: UP 5090.
    TYPE LOCALITY: "approximately three kilometers northwest of Agaun, Milne Bay
        Province, Papua New Guinea, altitude 1500 m".
    DISTRIBUTION: Vicinity of the type locality.

Barygenys nana Zweifel, 1972. Bull. Am. Mus. Nat. Hist., 148:444.
    TYPE(S): Holotype: AMNH 76471.
    TYPE LOCALITY: "Daulo Pass, Eastern Highlands District [Eastern Highlands
        Province], Territory of New Guinea [Papua New Guinea]".
    DISTRIBUTION: High elevations in Eastern Highlands and Western Highlands
        provinces, Papua New Guinea.

Barygenys parvula Zweifel, 1981 "1980". Pacif. Sci., 34:269.
TYPE(S): Holotype: BPBM 5689.
TYPE LOCALITY: "14 km north-northwest of Wanuma, Adelbert Mountains, elevation about 1500 m, Madang Province, Papua New Guinea".
DISTRIBUTION: Known only from the type locality.

Hylophorbus Macleay, 1878. Proc. Linn. Soc. New South Wales, 2:136.
TYPE SPECIES: *Hylophorbus rufescens* Macleay, 1878, by monotypy.
DISTRIBUTION: As for the single species.

Hylophorbus rufescens Macleay, 1878. Proc. Linn. Soc. New South Wales, 2:136.
TYPE(S): Holotype: AM R30826 (formerly MMUS 144).
TYPE LOCALITY: "Katow" (=Mawatta), near Daru, Western Province, Papua New Guinea.
DISTRIBUTION: New Guinea and nearby islands.
COMMENT: Zweifel, 1972, Bull. Am. Mus. Nat. Hist., 148:411–546, recognized three subspecies, two of them insular.

Pherohapsis Zweifel, 1972. Bull. Am. Mus. Nat. Hist., 148:456.
TYPE SPECIES: *Pherohapsis menziesi* Zweifel, 1972, by original designation.
DISTRIBUTION: As for the single species.

Pherohapsis menziesi Zweifel, 1972. Bull. Am. Mus. Nat. Hist., 148:458.
TYPE(S): Holotype: AMNH 84452.
TYPE LOCALITY: "Iarowari School, Sogeri, 1500 ft. (460 m.), 5 mi. N, 17 mi. E Port Moresby, Central District [Central Province], Territory of Papua [Papua New Guinea]".
DISTRIBUTION: Sogeri and Brown River, near Port Moresby, Papua New Guinea.

Phrynomantis Peters, 1867. Monatsber. Preuss. Akad. Wiss. Berlin, 1867:35.
TYPE SPECIES: *Phrynomantis fusca* Peters, 1867, by subsequent designation of Noble, 1926, Am. Mus. Novit., 212:20.
DISTRIBUTION: New Guinea region, from Moluccas to the easternmost islands of the Louisiade Archipelago.

Phrynomantis boettgeri (Méhelÿ, 1901). Termes. Füzetek, 24:181.
ORIGINAL NAME: *Gnathophryne boettgeri*.
TYPE(S): Holotype: SMF 4200.
TYPE LOCALITY: Galela, at 2200' above the sea [according to Boettger, 1900, Abh. Senckenb. Naturforsch. Ges., 35:368], North Halmahera, Moluccan Is., Indonesia.
DISTRIBUTION: Known only from the type locality.

Phrynomantis dubia (Boettger, 1895). Zool. Anz., 18:134.
ORIGINAL NAME: *Xenorhina dubia*.
TYPE(S): Syntypes: SMF (2 specimens); one of these, SMF 4201, designated lectotype by Mertens, 1967, Senckenb. Biol., 48:51.
TYPE LOCALITY: North Halmaheira, up to 2200' in elevation, Moluccan Is., Indonesia.
DISTRIBUTION: Known only from the type locality.

Phrynomantis eurydactyla Zweifel, 1972. Bull. Am. Mus. Nat. Hist., 148:465.
TYPE(S): Holotype: BPBM 1014.
TYPE LOCALITY: "Danowaria, 70 m., near Fak Fak on the Onin Peninsula, West Irian [Irian Jaya (New Guinea)]", Indonesia.
DISTRIBUTION: Onin Peninsula, Irian Jaya, Indonesia, to Western Province, Papua New Guinea.

Phrynomantis fusca Peters, 1867. Monatsber. Preuss. Akad. Wiss. Berlin, 1867:35.
TYPE(S): Syntypes: ZMB 5648 (2 specimens).
TYPE LOCALITY: "Amboina", Moluccan Is., Indonesia.
DISTRIBUTION: Amboina and Ceram Is., Moluccas, Indonesia, and Batanta I., Irian
Jaya, Indonesia.

Phrynomantis glandulosa Zweifel, 1972. Bull. Am. Mus. Nat. Hist., 148:469.
TYPE(S): Holotype: RMNH 16667.
TYPE LOCALITY: "Mt. Kerewa, 3340 m. (10,960 ft.), Southern Highlands District,
[Southern Highlands Province,] Territory of Papua [Papua New Guinea]".
DISTRIBUTION: Known only from the type locality.

Phrynomantis humicola Zweifel, 1972. Bull. Am. Mus. Nat. Hist., 148:471.
ORIGINAL NAME: *Phrynomantis humicola humicola.*
TYPE(S): Holotype: AMNH 66261.
TYPE LOCALITY: "Mt. Otto near Kotuni between 7000 and 8000 ft. (2130–2440 m.)
above sea level, Eastern Highlands District [Eastern Highlands Province],
Territory of New Guinea [Papua New Guinea]".
DISTRIBUTION: Western Highlands, Eastern Highlands, and Chimbu provinces,
Papua New Guinea.
COMMENT: Zweifel, 1972, Bull. Am. Mus. Nat. Hist., 148:411–546, recognized two
subspecies.

Phrynomantis infulata Zweifel, 1972. Bull. Am. Mus. Nat. Hist., 148:476.
TYPE(S): Holotype: AMNH 66687.
TYPE LOCALITY: "Arau, Kratke Mountains, elevation 4600 ft. (1400 m.), Eastern
Highlands District [Eastern Highlands Province], Territory of New Guinea
[Papua New Guinea]".
DISTRIBUTION: Known only from the type locality.

Phrynomantis kopsteini (Mertens, 1930). Zool. Meded., Leiden, 13:147.
ORIGINAL NAME: *Hylophorbus kopsteini.*
TYPE(S): Syntypes: RMNH 5310 (3 specimens).
TYPE LOCALITY: "Sanana, Soela-Inseln" (Sulabesi I., Sula Is., Indonesia).
DISTRIBUTION: Known only from the type locality.

Phrynomantis lateralis (Boulenger, 1897). Ann. Mag. Nat. Hist., (6)19:12.
ORIGINAL NAME: *Mantophryne lateralis.*
TYPE(S): BM 1947.2.11.2 designated lectotype by Zweifel, 1972, Bull. Am. Mus. Nat.
Hist., 148:480.
TYPE LOCALITY: "Mount Victoria, Owen Stanley Range, New Guinea" (probably in
Central Province, Papua New Guinea—RGZ).
DISTRIBUTION: North coast of Irian Jaya (Indonesia), and north and south of the
central range of Papua New Guinea.
COMMENT: See Zweifel, 1983, Am. Mus. Novit., 2759:4, for a discussion of the type
locality.

Phrynomantis louisiadensis (Parker, 1934). Monogr. Frogs Fam. Microhylidae:62.
ORIGINAL NAME: *Asterophrys louisiadensis.*
TYPE(S): Holotype: BM 1947.2.11.1 (formerly 99.4.25.22).
TYPE LOCALITY: "Rossel Island, Louisiadé Archip.", Milne Bay Province, Papua
New Guinea.
DISTRIBUTION: Rossel and Sudest Is., Milne Bay Province, Papua New Guinea.

Phrynomantis personata Zweifel, 1972. Bull. Am. Mus. Nat. Hist., 148:489.
TYPE(S): Holotype: AMNH 74903.
TYPE LOCALITY: "Maprik, elevation 800 ft. (240 m.), East Sepik District [East Sepik
Province], Territory of New Guinea [Papua New Guinea]".
DISTRIBUTION: Between the Sepik River and the summit of the north coastal
ranges, East Sepik and West Sepik provinces, Papua New Guinea.

Phrynomantis robusta (Boulenger, 1898). Proc. Zool. Soc. London, 1898:480.
ORIGINAL NAME: *Mantophryne robusta.*
TYPE(S): Syntypes: BM 1947.2.11.5–7 (formerly 98.3.31.9–11).
TYPE LOCALITY: "St. Aignan I. [=Misima I.], south of Fergusson I., British New Guinea [Milne Bay Province, Papua New Guinea]".
DISTRIBUTION: Throughout New Guinea from virtually sea level to at least 1920 m.

Phrynomantis slateri (Loveridge, 1955). Breviora, 50:1.
ORIGINAL NAME: *Asterophrys slateri.*
TYPE(S): Holotype: MCZ 28205.
TYPE LOCALITY: "Omati, near Port Moresby, Papua [Gulf Province, Papua New Guinea]" (the type locality is actually about 400 km northwest of Port Moresby—RGZ).
DISTRIBUTION: Known from only two localities in Western and Gulf provinces, Papua New Guinea.

Phrynomantis stictogaster Zweifel, 1972. Bull. Am. Mus. Nat. Hist., 148:503.
TYPE(S): Holotype: AMNH 74895.
TYPE LOCALITY: "Irumbofoie, elevation ca. 6600 ft. (2010 m.), 9 mi. S, and 10 mi. W Goroka, Eastern Highlands District [Eastern Highlands Province], Territory of New Guinea [Papua New Guinea]".
DISTRIBUTION: Central mountain ranges of Papua New Guinea, in Western Highlands, Eastern Highlands, and Morobe provinces.

Phrynomantis wilhelmana (Loveridge, 1948). Bull. Mus. Comp. Zool., 101:419.
ORIGINAL NAME: *Asterophrys pansa wilhelmana.*
TYPE(S): Holotype: MCZ 25910.
TYPE LOCALITY: "Mount Wilhelm, 8,000 feet, Bismarck Range, Madang Division, Australian New Guinea [Chimbu Province, Papua New Guinea]".
DISTRIBUTION: Central mountain ranges of Papua New Guinea in Southern Highlands, Western Highlands, Eastern Highlands, and Chimbu provinces.

Xenobatrachus Peters and Doria, 1878. Ann. Mus. Civ. Stor. Nat. Genova, 13:432.
TYPE SPECIES: *Xenobatrachus ophiodon* Peters and Doria, 1878, by monotypy.
DISTRIBUTION: Most of New Guinea; not recorded from the extreme eastern end or any satellite islands.

Xenobatrachus bidens (van Kampen, 1909). Nova Guinea, 13:39.
ORIGINAL NAME: *Xenorhina bidens.*
TYPE(S): Holotype: ZMA 5705.
TYPE LOCALITY: Digul River, Irian Jaya (New Guinea), Indonesia.
DISTRIBUTION: Scattered lowland localities in southern Irian Jaya (Indonesia) and Papua New Guinea.

Xenobatrachus giganteus (van Kampen, 1915). Nova Guinea, 13:40.
ORIGINAL NAME: *Xenorhina gigantea.*
TYPE(S): ZMA 5702 designated lectotype by Daan and Hillenius, 1966, Beaufortia, 13:126.
TYPE LOCALITY: "Bijenkorfbiwak" near the Lorentz River, 1700 m elev., Snow Mountains, Irian Jaya (New Guinea), Indonesia.
DISTRIBUTION: Known only from the type locality.

Xenobatrachus macrops (van Kampen, 1913). Nova Guinea, 9:460.
ORIGINAL NAME: *Xenorhina macrops.*
TYPE(S): ZMA 5725 designated lectotype by Daan and Hillenius, 1966, Beaufortia, 13:126.
TYPE LOCALITY: Hellwig Mountains (± 2500 m); "peak in Hellwig Mountains, West New Guinea [Irian Jaya, Indonesia], altitude 2200 m.", according to Daan and Hillenius, 1966, Beaufortia, 13:126.
DISTRIBUTION: Moderate to high elevations in the mountains of Irian Jaya (New Guinea), Indonesia.

Xenobatrachus mehelyi (Boulenger, 1898). Ann. Mus. Civ. Stor. Nat. Genova, (2)18:709.
ORIGINAL NAME: *Choanacantha mehelyi.*
TYPE(S): Holotype: MSNG 29112.
TYPE LOCALITY: "Vikaiku", Angabunga River, Central Province, Papua New
Guinea.
DISTRIBUTION: Moderately low elevations in the southeastern part of Papua New
Guinea, from near the Irian Jaya (Indonesia) border almost to Port Moresby.

Xenobatrachus obesus Zweifel, 1960. Am. Mus. Novit., 2012:1.
TYPE(S): Holotype: AMNH 64247.
TYPE LOCALITY: "Maratambu, Adelbert Mountains, Northeast New Guinea [Madang
Province, Papua New Guinea], elevation 2300 feet".
DISTRIBUTION: Northern foothills of the Nassau Mountains, Irian Jaya (Indonesia),
eastward in the north coast ranges of Papua New Guinea.

Xenobatrachus ocellatus (van Kampen, 1913). Nova Guinea, 9:461.
ORIGINAL NAME: *Xenorhina ocellata.*
TYPE(S): Syntypes: ZMA 5815 and 5816, FMNH 100100 (formerly EHT).
TYPE LOCALITY: Hellwig Mountains (± 2500 m) [Irian Jaya (New Guinea),
Indonesia].
DISTRIBUTION: High mountains of central Irian Jaya (New Guinea), Indonesia.

Xenobatrachus ophiodon Peters and Doria, 1878. Ann. Mus. Civ. Stor. Nat. Genova, 13:
432.
TYPE(S): MSNG 29129 designated lectotype by Capocaccia, 1957, Ann. Mus. Civ.
Stor. Nat. Genova, 69:219.
TYPE LOCALITY: Hatam, Arfak Mountains [Vogelkop Peninsula, Irian Jaya (New
Guinea), Indonesia].
DISTRIBUTION: Known only from the type locality.

Xenobatrachus rostratus (Méhelÿ, 1898). Termés. Füzetek, 21:175.
ORIGINAL NAME: *Choanacantha rostrata.*
TYPE(S): Syntypes: MNH 2414/6 (2 specimens); destroyed.
TYPE LOCALITY: "Erima", Astrolabe Bay, Madang Province, Papua New Guinea.
DISTRIBUTION: North coast of Irian Jaya (Indonesia) and Papua New Guinea, and
central mountains of Papua New Guinea.

Xenobatrachus subcroceus Menzies and Tyler, 1977. J. Zool., London, 183:450.
TYPE(S): Holotype: UP 4393.
TYPE LOCALITY: "approximately 11 km north of Lae, [Morobe Province,] Papua
New Guinea".
DISTRIBUTION: Vicinity of Lae, Papua New Guinea.

Xenorhina Peters, 1863. Monatsber. Preuss. Akad. Wiss. Berlin, 1863:82.
TYPE SPECIES: *Bombinator oxycephalus* Schlegel, 1858, by monotypy.
DISTRIBUTION: New Guinea, including some satellite islands.

Xenorhina bouwensi (Witte, 1930). Ann. Soc. R. Zool. Belg., 60:132.
ORIGINAL NAME: *Pseudengystoma bouwensi.*
TYPE(S): Holotype: MRHN 9223.
TYPE LOCALITY: "Arfak Mountains, Vogelkop Peninsula . . . 1,000 m. altitude", Irian
Jaya (New Guinea), Indonesia.
DISTRIBUTION: Known from widely separate localities on the Vogelkop Peninsula
and in the Star Mountains of eastern Irian Jaya (New Guinea), Indonesia.

Xenorhina doriae (Boulenger, 1888). Ann. Mag. Nat. Hist., (6)1:345.
ORIGINAL NAME: *Callulops doriae.*
TYPE(S): Holotype: BM 1947.2.10.99 (formerly 88.3.21.10).
TYPE LOCALITY: "Milne Gulf", Milne Bay Province, Papua New Guinea.
DISTRIBUTION: Eastern half of Papua New Guinea to Sudest I., Louisiade
Archipelago.

Xenorhina minima (Parker, 1934). Monogr. Frogs Fam. Microhylidae:67.
ORIGINAL NAME: *Asterophrys minima.*
TYPE(S): Holotype: ZMA 5818.
TYPE LOCALITY: "Went Mts., 1000–1360 m.", Irian Jaya (New Guinea), Indonesia.
DISTRIBUTION: Two localities at moderate to high elevations in the southern watershed of the central ranges of Irian Jaya (New Guinea), Indonesia.

Xenorhina oxycephala (Schlegel, 1858). Handl. Dierkd.:58.
ORIGINAL NAME: *Bombinator oxycephalus.*
TYPE(S): Syntypes: RMNH 2280 (2 specimens).
TYPE LOCALITY: New Guinea; refined by Zweifel, 1972, Bull. Am. Mus. Nat. Hist., 148:536, to "Triton Bay, West Irian [Irian Jaya (New Guinea), Indonesia]".
DISTRIBUTION: Western Irian Jaya (Indonesia), and the north coast ranges of Irian Jaya (Indonesia) and Papua New Guinea.

Xenorhina parkerorum Zweifel, 1972. Bull. Am. Mus. Nat. Hist., 148:539.
TYPE(S): Holotype: MCZ 81678.
TYPE LOCALITY: "Imigabip, 4200 ft. (1280 m.), *ca.* 11 mi. S, 9 mi. W. Telefomin, Western District [Western Province], Territory of Papua [Papua New Guinea]".
DISTRIBUTION: Central mountain ranges of eastern Irian Jaya (Indonesia) and western Papua New Guinea.

Xenorhina similis (Zweifel, 1956). Am. Mus. Novit., 1766:5.
ORIGINAL NAME: *Asterophrys similis.*
TYPE(S): Holotype: AMNH 43722.
TYPE LOCALITY: "9 kilometers northeast of Lake Habbema, 2800 meters, Netherlands New Guinea [Irian Jaya (New Guinea), Indonesia]".
DISTRIBUTION: Central mountain ranges of Irian Jaya (Indonesia) to western Papua New Guinea.

SUBFAMILY: **Brevicipitinae** Bonaparte, 1850.
CITATION: Conspect. Syst. Herpetol. Amphibiol., 1 p.
DISTRIBUTION: Sub-saharan Africa.
COMMENT: As first formed the group name was Brevicipina, a subfamily.
REVIEWERS: Alan Channing (RL); Kim M. Howell (KMH) (East Africa); Raymond Laurent (RL); John C. Poynton (JCP).

Breviceps Merrem, 1820. Syst. Amph.:177.
TYPE SPECIES: *Rana gibbosa* Linnaeus, 1758.
DISTRIBUTION: Southern Africa.
COMMENT: Last revised by Poynton, 1964, Ann. Natal Mus., 17:69–84. Illustrations of nearly all species in Passmore and Carruthers, 1979, S. Afr. Frogs.

Breviceps acutirostris Poynton, 1963. Ann. Natal Mus., 15:321.
TYPE(S): Holotype: AMG 5507.
TYPE LOCALITY: "Swellendam Mountains", southwestern Cape, Cape Province, Rep. South Africa.
DISTRIBUTION: Mountains of the southwestern Cape region, Rep. South Africa.

Breviceps adspersus Peters, 1882. Reise Mossambique, 3(Amph.):177.
TYPE(S): Syntypes: ZMB, MCZ 11619.
TYPE LOCALITY: Damaraland and Transvaal [Rep. South Africa].
DISTRIBUTION: Namibia, Botswana, Zimbabwe, Mozambique, and northern Rep. South Africa.
COMMENT: Hybridizes extensively with *Breviceps mossambicus* (see Poynton, 1982, S. Afr. J. Zool., 17:67–74). Complex differentiation at edge of range has led to a large synonymy, which needs more investigation (JCP).

Breviceps fuscus Hewitt, 1925. Ann. Natal Mus., 5:191.
TYPE(S): Syntypes: AMG.
TYPE LOCALITY: "Knysna", Rep. South Africa.
DISTRIBUTION: Southern Cape fold mountains, Rep. South Africa.

Breviceps gibbosus (Linnaeus, 1758). Syst. Nat., Ed. 10, 1:211.
ORIGINAL NAME: *Rana gibbosa.*
TYPE(S): Not designated; holotype in NHRM according to Andersson, 1900, Bih. K. Svenska Vetensk. Akad. Handl., 26, 49(1):20.
TYPE LOCALITY: Not stated.
DISTRIBUTION: Cape Peninsula to Stellenbosch, Cape Province, Rep. South Africa.

Breviceps macrops Boulenger, 1907. Ann. Mag. Nat. Hist., (7)20:46.
TYPE(S): Syntypes: BM (1 specimen), SAM (2 specimens).
TYPE LOCALITY: "Namaqualand", Rep. South Africa.
DISTRIBUTION: Coast of Little Namaqualand, Rep. South Africa.

Breviceps montanus Power, 1926. Ann. S. Afr. Mus., 20:466.
TYPE(S): Syntypes: AMG and SAM.
TYPE LOCALITY: Table Mountain, Cape Peninsula [Rep. South Africa].
DISTRIBUTION: Mountains of the southwestern Cape, Rep. South Africa.

Breviceps mossambicus Peters, 1854. Monatsber. Preuss. Akad. Wiss. Berlin, 1854:628.
TYPE(S): Syntypes: ZMB (Mozambique specimens only, Sena specimens lost—JCP).
TYPE LOCALITY: Island of Mozambique; Sena.
DISTRIBUTION: Tanzania south to northern Natal (Rep. South Africa) and Angola through Zimbabwe and southeastern Zaire.
COMMENT: Angolan material separated as an undescribed taxon by Poynton, 1982, S. Afr. J. Zool., 17:67–74, who reported extensive hybridization with *Breviceps adspersus.*

Breviceps namaquensis Power, 1926. Ann. S. Afr. Mus., 20:465.
TYPE(S): SAM.
TYPE LOCALITY: Port Nolloth, Namaqualand [Rep. South Africa].
DISTRIBUTION: Namaqualand coast of Namibia and Rep. South Africa.

Breviceps poweri Parker, 1934. Monogr. Frogs Fam. Microhylidae:195.
TYPE(S): Holotype: BM 1932.9.9.1.
TYPE LOCALITY: "Broken Hill, N. Rhodesia" (=Kabwe, Zambia).
DISTRIBUTION: Zambia, southern Shaba Province (Zaire), Malawi, and western Mozambique.

Breviceps rosei Power, 1926. Ann. S. Afr. Mus., 20:466.
TYPE(S): MMK.
TYPE LOCALITY: Lakeside, Cape Flats [Rep. South Africa].
DISTRIBUTION: Sandveld of the western Cape coastal foreland, Rep. South Africa.
COMMENT: Current synonymy includes *Breviceps fasciatus* FitzSimons and *Breviceps vansoni* FitzSimons; inclusion of especially the former needs investigation (JCP).

Breviceps sylvestris FitzSimons, 1930. Ann. Transvaal Mus., 14:46.
TYPE(S): Holotype: TM 6353.
TYPE LOCALITY: "Woodbush, Pietersburg District", Transvaal, Rep. South Africa.
DISTRIBUTION: Eastern and northern Transvaal, Rep. South Africa.
COMMENT: Two subspecies recognized.

Breviceps verrucosus Rapp, 1842. Arch. Naturgesch., 8:291.
TYPE(S): Not traced.
TYPE LOCALITY: Natal [Rep. South Africa].
DISTRIBUTION: Eastern Plateau slopes of Rep. South Africa and Lesotho.

COMMENT: Includes *Breviceps maculatus* FitzSimons, 1947, Ann. Natal Mus., 11:134, according to Passmore and Carruthers, 1979, S. Afr. Frogs:84, and *Breviceps tympanifer* Hewitt.

Callulina Nieden, 1910. Sitzungsber. Ges. Naturforsch. Freunde Berlin, 10:449.
TYPE SPECIES: *Callulina kreffti* Nieden, 1910, by monotypy.
DISTRIBUTION: As for the single species.

Callulina kreffti Nieden, 1910. Sitzungsber. Ges. Naturforsch. Freunde Berlin, 10:449.
TYPE(S): ZMB.
TYPE LOCALITY: "Amani" and "Tanga", Tanzania.
DISTRIBUTION: Usambara, Uluguru, Nguru, and Uzungwe mountains, Tanzania.

Probreviceps Parker, 1931. Ann. Mag. Nat. Hist., (10)8:262.
TYPE SPECIES: *Breviceps macrodactylus* Nieden, 1926, by original designation.
DISTRIBUTION: East Africa.

Probreviceps macrodactylus (Nieden, 1926). Das Tierreich, 49:6.
ORIGINAL NAME: *Breviceps macrodactylus*.
TYPE(S): Not traced.
TYPE LOCALITY: Usambara Mountains, Tanganyika Territory [Tanzania].
DISTRIBUTION: Usambara, Uluguru, and Rungwe mountains, Tanzania.
COMMENT: *Breviceps macrodactylus* is a replacement name for *Breviceps verrucosus* Tornier, 1896, Kriechth. Deutsch Ost-Afr.:160, which is preoccupied. Loveridge, 1957, Bull. Mus. Comp. Zool., 117:356–357, recognized three subspecies.

Probreviceps rhodesianus Poynton and Broadley, 1967. Arnoldia, Zimbabwe, 3(14):1.
TYPE(S): Holotype: NMZB (formerly UM) 10651.
TYPE LOCALITY: "immediately below the John Meikle Forest Research Station at 5300 feet (c. 1600 m) in the Stapleford Forest Reserve, Umtali District", Zimbabwe.
DISTRIBUTION: Eastern highlands of Zimbabwe north of Mutare.

Probreviceps uluguruensis (Loveridge, 1925). Proc. Zool. Soc. London, 1925:789.
ORIGINAL NAME: *Breviceps uluguruensis*.
TYPE(S): Holotype: MCZ 10442.
TYPE LOCALITY: "Bagilo, Uluguru Mtns., Tanganyika Territory [=Tanzania]".
DISTRIBUTION: Bagilo, and Nyingwa, Uluguru Mountains (6000–8000 ft.), Tanzania.

Spelaeophryne Ahl, 1924. Zool. Anz., 61:99.
TYPE SPECIES: *Spelaeophryne methneri* Ahl, 1924, by original designation.
DISTRIBUTION: As for the single species.

Spelaeophryne methneri Ahl, 1924. Zool. Anz., 61:99.
TYPE(S): Not traced.
TYPE LOCALITY: Nangoma Cave, Matumbi near Kilwa, East Africa [Tanzania].
DISTRIBUTION: Eastern Tanzania.

SUBFAMILY: **Cophylinae** Cope, 1889.
CITATION: Bull. U.S. Natl. Mus., 34:390.
DISTRIBUTION: Madagascar.
COMMENT: As first formed, the group name was Cophylidae; Parker, 1934, Monogr. Frogs Fam. Microhylidae:10, was the first to use Cophylinae. See Guibé, 1978, Bonn. Zool. Monogr., 11:140, for synonymies of several of the species. See Blommers-Schlösser, 1976, Genetica, 46:199–210, for karyotypes.
CONTRIBUTOR: Rose M. A. Blommers-Schlösser (RMABS).

Anodonthyla Müller, 1892. Verh. Naturforsch. Ges. Basel, 10:198.
TYPE SPECIES: *Anodonthyla boulengerii* Müller, 1892, by monotypy.
DISTRIBUTION: Madagascar.

Anodonthyla boulengerii Müller, 1892. Verh. Naturforsch. Ges. Basel, 10:198.
TYPE(S): NHMB.
TYPE LOCALITY: Madagascar.
DISTRIBUTION: Eastern Madagascar.
COMMENT: See Guibé, 1978, Bonn. Zool. Monogr., 11:102, for synonymy.

Anodonthyla montana Angel, 1925. Bull. Mus. Natl. Hist. Nat., Paris, 1:62.
ORIGINAL NAME: *Anodontohyla montana*.
TYPE(S): Syntypes: MNHNP 1924-104 to 1924-107.
TYPE LOCALITY: Andringitra Mountains, 2,600 meters, Madagascar.
DISTRIBUTION: Andringitra Mountains, Madagascar.

Anodonthyla rouxae Guibé, 1974. Bull. Mus. Natl. Hist. Nat., Paris, (3)1973(171):1185.
TYPE(S): Holotype: MNHNP 1973-666.
TYPE LOCALITY: Chaînes Anosyennes, Madagascar.
DISTRIBUTION: Known only from the type locality.

Cophyla Boettger, 1880. Zool. Anz., 1880:281.
TYPE SPECIES: *Cophyla phyllodactyla* Boettger, 1880, by monotypy.
DISTRIBUTION: Madagascar.

Cophyla phyllodactyla Boettger, 1880. Zool. Anz., 1880:281.
TYPE(S): SMF 4296 designated lectotype by Mertens, 1967, Senckenb. Biol., 48:49.
TYPE LOCALITY: Nossi Bé.
DISTRIBUTION: Northern Madagascar; Nossi Bé I.

Madecassophryne Guibé, 1974. Bull. Mus. Natl. Hist. Nat., Paris, (3)1973(171):1190.
TYPE SPECIES: *Madecassophryne truebae* Guibé, 1974, by monotypy.
DISTRIBUTION: Madagascar.

Madecassophryne truebae Guibé, 1974. Bull. Mus. Natl. Hist. Nat., Paris, (3)1973(171):
1192.
TYPE(S): Holotype: MNHNP 1973-149.
TYPE LOCALITY: Chaînes Anosyennes, Madagascar.
DISTRIBUTION: Chaînes Anosyennes, Madagascar.

Mantipus Peters, 1883. Sitzungsber. Preuss. Akad. Wiss. Berlin, 1883:165.
TYPE SPECIES: *Mantipus hildebrandti* Peters, 1883 (=*Plethodontohyla inguinalis* Boulenger, 1882), original designation.
DISTRIBUTION: Madagascar.

Mantipus angulifer (Werner, 1903). Zool. Anz., 26:251.
ORIGINAL NAME: *Plethodontohyla angulifera*.
TYPE(S): Not traced.
TYPE LOCALITY: Unknown.
DISTRIBUTION: Unknown.
COMMENT: Guibé, 1978, Bonn. Zool. Monogr., 11:102, doubted the validity of this species. The incorrectly formed epithet *anguliferus* has been used (DRF).

Mantipus bipunctatus Guibé, 1974. Bull. Mus. Natl. Hist. Nat., Paris, (3)1973(171):1180.
TYPE(S): Holotype: MNHNP 1962-916.
TYPE LOCALITY: Forest Fivahona, Andringitra Mountains, Madagascar.
DISTRIBUTION: Andringitra Mountains, Madagascar.

Mantipus guentherpetersi Guibé, 1974. Bull. Mus. Natl. Hist. Nat., Paris, (3)1973(171): 1181.
TYPE(S): Holotype: MNHNP 1953-165.
TYPE LOCALITY: Tsaratanana Mountains, 2600 m alt., Madagascar.
DISTRIBUTION: Tsaratanana Mountains, Madagascar.

Mantipus inguinalis (Boulenger, 1882). Cat. Batr. Sal. Brit. Mus.:473.
ORIGINAL NAME: *Plethodontohyla inguinalis*.
TYPE(S): Holotype: BM 1947.2.10.34.
TYPE LOCALITY: "East Betsileo", Madagascar.
DISTRIBUTION: Eastern and northeastern Madagascar.
COMMENT: See Guibé, 1978, Bonn. Zool. Monogr., 11:97, for synonymy.

Mantipus laevipes (Mocquard, 1895). Bull. Soc. Philomath. Paris, (8)7:134.
ORIGINAL NAME: *Mantiphrys laevipes*.
TYPE(S): Holotype: MNHNP 1893-285.
TYPE LOCALITY: Mt. Ambre [Madagascar].
DISTRIBUTION: Mt. Ambre, Madagascar.

Mantipus minutus Guibé, 1975. Bull. Mus. Natl. Hist. Nat., (3)1975(323):1087.
TYPE(S): Holotype: MNHNP 1975-15.
TYPE LOCALITY: Massif du Marojezy, Madagascar.
DISTRIBUTION: Marojezy Mountains, Madagascar.

Mantipus serratopalpebrosus Guibé, 1975. Bull. Mus. Natl. Hist. Nat., Paris, (3)1975(323):1088.
TYPE(S): Holotype: MNHNP 1975-24.
TYPE LOCALITY: Massif du Marojezy, Madagascar.
DISTRIBUTION: Marojezy Mountains, Madagascar.

Paracophyla Millot and Guibé, 1951. Mém. Inst. Sci. Madagascar, 5(1A):209.
TYPE SPECIES: *Paracophyla tuberculata* Millot and Guibé, 1951, by monotypy.
DISTRIBUTION: As for the single species.

Paracophyla tuberculata Millot and Guibé, 1951. Mém. Inst. Sci. Madagascar, 5(1A): 209.
TYPE(S): Holotype: MNHNP 1957-715.
TYPE LOCALITY: Analamazoatra Forest, Perinet, Madagascar.
DISTRIBUTION: Eastern Madagascar.

Platypelis Boulenger, 1882. Cat. Batr. Sal. Brit. Mus.:474.
TYPE SPECIES: *Platypelis cowanii* Boulenger, 1882, by monotypy.
DISTRIBUTION: Madagascar.
COMMENT: Synonymy includes *Platyhyla* Boulenger, 1889, according to Guibé, 1978, Bonn. Zool. Monogr., 11:115.

Platypelis alticola (Guibé, 1974). Bull. Mus. Natl. Hist. Nat., Paris, (3)1973(171):1182.
ORIGINAL NAME: *Platyhyla alticola*.
TYPE(S): Holotype: MNHNP 1973-693.
TYPE LOCALITY: Massif Tsaratanana, Madagascar.
DISTRIBUTION: Tsaratanana Mountains, Madagascar.
COMMENT: See Guibé, 1978, Bonn. Zool. Monogr., 11:117, for review.

Platypelis barbouri Noble, 1940. Proc. New England Zool. Club, 18:27.
TYPE(S): Holotype: MCZ 23848.
TYPE LOCALITY: Fanovana Forest, between Tananarive and Tamatave, Madagascar.
DISTRIBUTION: Eastern Madagascar.

Platypelis cowanii Boulenger, 1882. Cat. Batr. Sal. Brit. Mus.:474.
TYPE(S): Holotype: BM 1947.2.10.37.
TYPE LOCALITY: "East Betsileo", Madagascar.
DISTRIBUTION: East Betsileo, Madagascar.

Platypelis grandis (Boulenger, 1889). Ann. Mag. Nat. Hist., (4)6:247.
ORIGINAL NAME: *Platyhyla grandis.*
TYPE(S): Syntypes: BM 1947.2.10.54–55 and 1947.2.30.92.
TYPE LOCALITY: "Madagascar" and Sahambendrana, Madagascar.
DISTRIBUTION: Eastern Madagascar.
COMMENT: Synonymy and review in Guibé, 1978, Bonn. Zool. Monogr., 11:116.

Platypelis milloti Guibé, 1950. Bull. Mus. Natl. Hist. Nat., Paris, (2)22(2):214.
TYPE(S): Syntypes: MNHNP 1953-22.
TYPE LOCALITY: Nosy Bé, Madagascar.
DISTRIBUTION: Nossi Bé, Madagascar.

Platypelis pollicaris Boulenger, 1888. Ann. Mag. Nat. Hist., (6)1:106.
TYPE(S): Holotype: BM 1947.2.10.38.
TYPE LOCALITY: "Madagascar".
DISTRIBUTION: Northern, eastern, and central Madagascar.

Platypelis tsaratananaensis Guibé, 1974. Bull. Mus. Natl. Hist. Nat., Paris, (3)1973(171): 1184.
TYPE(S): Holotype: MNHNP A685.
TYPE LOCALITY: Massif Tsaratanana, 2600 m alt., Madagascar.
DISTRIBUTION: Tsaratanana Mountains, Madagascar.

Platypelis tuberculata (Ahl, 1929). Mitt. Zool. Mus. Berlin, 14:483.
ORIGINAL NAME: *Cophyla tuberculata.*
TYPE(S): Syntypes: ZMB 30645A and B.
TYPE LOCALITY: Northwestern Madagascar.
DISTRIBUTION: Northwestern Madagascar.

Platypelis tuberifera (Methuen, 1920 "1919"). Proc. Zool. Soc. London, 1919:354.
ORIGINAL NAME: *Plethodontohyla tuberifera.*
TYPE(S): Holotype: TM 10080.
TYPE LOCALITY: Ambatoharanana, Madagascar.
DISTRIBUTION: Central and northeastern Madagascar.

Plethodontohyla Boulenger, 1882. Cat. Batr. Sal. Brit. Mus.:473.
TYPE SPECIES: *Callula notosticta* Günther, 1877, by original designation.
DISTRIBUTION: Madagascar.

Plethodontohyla alluaudi (Mocquard, 1901). Bull. Mus. Natl. Hist. Nat., Paris, 6:254.
ORIGINAL NAME: *Dyscophus alluaudi.*
TYPE(S): Holotype: MNHNP 1901-235.
TYPE LOCALITY: Fort Dauphin [southern Madagascar].
DISTRIBUTION: Fort Dauphin, southern Madagascar.

Plethodontohyla brevipes Boulenger, 1882. Cat. Batr. Sal. Brit. Mus.:474.
TYPE(S): Holotype: BM 1947.2.10.42.
TYPE LOCALITY: "East Betsileo", Madagascar.
DISTRIBUTION: East Betsileo, Madagascar.

Plethodontohyla coudreaui Angel, 1938. Bull. Mus. Natl. Hist. Nat., Paris, 2(10)3:260.
TYPE(S): Holotype: MNHNP 1937-19.
TYPE LOCALITY: Betampona, Madagascar.
DISTRIBUTION: Madagascar.

Plethodontohyla laevis (Boettger, 1913). *In* Voeltzkow, Reise Ost-Afr., 3:282.
ORIGINAL NAME: *Phrynocara laeve*.
TYPE(S): SMF 4286 designated lectotype by Mertens, 1967, Senckenb. Biol., 48:50.
TYPE LOCALITY: Sakana, eastern Madagascar.
DISTRIBUTION: Central and eastern Madagascar.

Plethodontohyla notosticta (Günther, 1877). Ann. Mag. Nat. Hist., (4)19:316.
ORIGINAL NAME: *Callula notosticta*.
TYPE(S): Syntypes: BM 1947.2.10.39–41.
TYPE LOCALITY: Mahanoro and Anzahamara [Madagascar].
DISTRIBUTION: Eastern, central, and northern Madagascar.
COMMENT: See Guibé, 1978, Bonn. Zool. Monogr., 11:123, for synonymy.

Plethodontohyla ocellata Noble and Parker, 1926. Am. Mus. Novit., 232:14.
TYPE(S): Holotype: BM 1947.2.10.43.
TYPE LOCALITY: Antsihanaka, Madagascar.
DISTRIBUTION: Central and northeastern Madagascar.

Plethodontohyla tuberata (Peters, 1883). Sitzungsber. Preuss. Akad. Wiss. Berlin, 6:166.
ORIGINAL NAME: *Phrynocara tuberatum*.
TYPE(S): Not traced; probably ZMB.
TYPE LOCALITY: Interior of Madagascar.
DISTRIBUTION: Ankaratra and Andringitra mountains, Madagascar.
COMMENT: See Guibé, 1978, Bonn. Zool. Monogr., 11:127, for synonymy.

Rhombophryne Boettger, 1880. Zool. Anz., 3:567.
TYPE SPECIES: *Rhombophryne testudo* Boettger, 1880, by monotypy.
DISTRIBUTION: As for the single species.

Rhombophryne testudo Boettger, 1880. Zool. Anz., 3:567.
TYPE(S): SMF 4241 designated lectotype by Mertens, 1967, Senckenb. Biol., 48:51.
TYPE LOCALITY: Nossi Bé, Madagascar.
DISTRIBUTION: Nossi Bé and eastern Madagascar; Réunion I.

Stumpffia Boettger, 1881. Zool. Anz., 4:360.
TYPE SPECIES: *Stumpffia psologlossa* Boettger, 1881, by original designation.
DISTRIBUTION: Madagascar.

Stumpffia grandis Guibé, 1974 "1973". Bull. Mus. Natl. Hist. Nat., Paris, (3)1973(171):
1186.
TYPE(S): Holotype: MNHNP 1973-715.
TYPE LOCALITY: Massif Marojezy, Madagascar.
DISTRIBUTION: Marojezy Mountains, Madagascar.

Stumpffia madagascariensis Mocquard, 1895. Bull. Soc. Philomath. Paris, (8)7:132.
TYPE(S): Holotype: MNHNP 1893-286.
TYPE LOCALITY: Mt. Ambre, Madagascar.
DISTRIBUTION: Mt. Ambre and Ambongo, Madagascar.
COMMENT: Guibé, 1978, Bonn. Zool. Monogr., 11:115, considered the status of this
species dubious.

Stumpffia psologlossa Boettger, 1881. Zool. Anz., 4:360.
TYPE(S): SMF 7337 designated lectotype by Mertens, 1967, Senckenb. Biol., 48:51.
TYPE LOCALITY: Nossi Bé, Madagascar.
DISTRIBUTION: Islands of Nossi Bé and Sakatia; eastern Madagascar.

Stumpffia roseifemoralis Guibé, 1974 "1973". Bull. Mus. Natl. Hist. Nat., Paris,
(3)1973(171):1188.
TYPE(S): Holotype: MNHNP 1973-712.
TYPE LOCALITY: Massif Marojezy, 1300 m alt., Madagascar.
DISTRIBUTION: Marojezy Mountains, Madagascar.

Stumpffia tridactyla Guibé, 1975. Bull. Mus. Natl. Hist. Nat., Paris, (3)1975(323):1089.
TYPE(S): Holotype: MNHNP 1975-25.
TYPE LOCALITY: Massif Marojezy, Madagascar.
DISTRIBUTION: Marojezy Mountains, Madagascar.

SUBFAMILY: **Dyscophinae** Boulenger, 1882.
CITATION: Cat. Batr. Sal. Brit. Mus.:179.
DISTRIBUTION: Madagascar, Burma, southwestern China, Malaya, Sumatra, and Borneo.
COMMENT: As first formed the group name was Dyscophidae. Savage, 1973, *In* Vial
(ed.), Evol. Biol. Anurans:355, discussed the relationships of the Indo-Malayan
genera, and concluded that they were primitive members of the Asterophryinae
(including the Genyophryninae in his sense) and that the resemblance between
the African and Indo-Malayan genera was due solely to the retention of primitive
features. See comment under Asterophryinae. Parker, 1934, Monogr. Frogs Fam.
Microhylidae, considered the Dyscophinae to be the stem-group from which the
rest of the Microhylidae (excluding the Scaphiophryninae, by implication) was
derived. The literature of this controversy was reviewed by Blommers-Schlösser,
1975, Beaufortia, 24(309):7–26, who retained the African and Indo-Malayan genera
together in this group. See Blommers-Schlösser, 1976, Genetica, 46:199–210, for
karyotypes.

Calluella Stoliczka, 1872. Proc. Asiat. Soc. Bengal, 1872:146.
TYPE SPECIES: *Megalophrys guttulata* Blyth, 1855.
DISTRIBUTION: Southeastern Asia.
REVIEWER: Masafumi Matsui (MM).

Calluella brooksi (Boulenger, 1904). Ann. Mag. Nat. Hist., (7)13:42.
ORIGINAL NAME: *Colpoglossus brooksi*.
TYPE(S): Holotype: BM.
TYPE LOCALITY: "Bidi, Sarawak", Malaysia (Borneo).
DISTRIBUTION: Borneo.

Calluella flava Kiew, 1984. Malay. Nat. J., 37:163.
TYPE(S): Holotype: BM 1978.1599.
TYPE LOCALITY: "from the *kerangas* forest in the FEG Kerangas Plot situated at 190
m above sea level on the trail from Camp 5 to Sungai Berar Camp, Gunung
Mulu National Park, Sarawak", Malaysia (Borneo).
DISTRIBUTION: Known only from the type locality.

Calluella guttulata (Blyth, 1855). J. Asiat. Soc. Bengal, 24:717.
ORIGINAL NAME: *Megalophrys guttulata*.
TYPE(S): Not traced.
TYPE LOCALITY: Pegu, Burma.
DISTRIBUTION: Southern Burma to the northern part of the Malay Peninsula.
COMMENT: See Bourret, 1942, Batr. Indochine:481–483, for synonymy.

Calluella smithi (Barbour and Noble, 1916). Proc. New England Zool. Club, 6:20.
ORIGINAL NAME: *Calliglutus smithi*.
TYPE(S): Holotype: MCZ 3797.
TYPE LOCALITY: "Limbang River District, northern central Sarawak", Malaysia
(Borneo).
DISTRIBUTION: Known only from the type locality.

Calluella volzi (van Kampen, 1905). Zool. Jahrb., Abt. Syst., 22:708.
ORIGINAL NAME: *Dyscophina volzi*.
TYPE(S): Syntypes: including ZMA 587, the remaining extant specimen; designated
lectotype by Daan and Hillenius, 1966, Beaufortia, 158:120.
TYPE LOCALITY: Tadjong Laut, Sumatra [Indonesia].
DISTRIBUTION: Sumatra; Malaya.

COMMENT: See Berry, 1975, Amph. Fauna Peninsular Malaysia:110–111.

Calluella yunnanensis Boulenger, 1919. Ann. Mag. Nat. Hist., (9)3:549.
  ORIGINAL NAME: *Kalluella yunnanensis.*
  TYPE(S): Syntypes: BM (2 specimens).
  TYPE LOCALITY: "Yunnan Fou", Yunnan, China.
  DISTRIBUTION: Yunnan, Sichuan, and Guizhou (Yunkwei Plateau), China.
  COMMENT: Reviewed by Liu and Hu, 1961, Tailless Amph. China:283–285,
    including synonymy of *Calluella ocellata* Liu, 1950, Fieldiana: Zool. Mem., 2:
    232.
  REVIEWERS: Leo J. Borkin (LJB); Shuqin Hu (SH); Ermi Zhao (EZ).

Dyscophus Grandidier, 1872. Ann. Sci. Nat., Paris, Zool., (5)15:10.
  TYPE SPECIES: *Dyscophus insularis* Grandidier, 1872, by original designation.
  DISTRIBUTION: Madagascar.
  COMMENT: See Guibé, 1978, Bonn. Zool. Monogr., 11:92–95, for synonymies.
  CONTRIBUTOR: Rose M. A. Blommers-Schlösser (RMABS).

Dyscophus antongilii Grandidier, 1877. Bull. Soc. Philomath. Paris, (7)1:41.
  ORIGINAL NAME: *Dyscophus insularis* var. *antongilii.*
  TYPE(S): Holotype: MNHNP 1883-2.
  TYPE LOCALITY: Antongil Bay [Madagascar].
  DISTRIBUTION: Northeastern Madagascar.

Dyscophus guineti (Grandidier, 1875). Ann. Sci. Nat., Paris, Zool., (6)2:6.
  ORIGINAL NAME: *Kaloula guineti.*
  TYPE(S): Syntypes: MNHNP 1895-281 and 1895-282.
  TYPE LOCALITY: Sambava, coast of northeastern Madagascar.
  DISTRIBUTION: Eastern, northwestern, and central Madagascar.

Dyscophus insularis Grandidier, 1872. Ann. Sci. Nat., Paris, Zool., (5)15:10.
  TYPE(S): Holotype: MNHNP 1883-1.
  TYPE LOCALITY: Antsouhy, near Trabounzy [Madagascar].
  DISTRIBUTION: Southern and western Madagascar.

SUBFAMILY: **Genyophryninae** Boulenger, 1890.
  CITATION: Proc. Zool. Soc. London, 1890:326.
  DISTRIBUTION: Southern Philippines, Celebes, and Bali, eastward through the Lesser
    Sunda Is. and New Guinea region to New Britain and extreme northern Australia.
  COMMENT: As first formed, the group name was Genyophrynidae. With the transfer of
    Genyophryne from the Asterophryinae to the former Sphenophryninae (of Noble,
    1931, Biol. Amph.:531) by Zweifel, 1971, Am. Mus. Novit., 2469:1–13, the oldest
    name for this taxon became Genyophryninae. This was first noted by Dubois,
    1983, Bull. Mens. Soc. Linn. Lyon, 52:274. See comment under Asterophryinae.
    Some authors (e.g., Savage, 1973, *In* Vial (ed.), Evol. Biol. Anurans) have implied
    that the Sphenophryninae is paraphyletic with respect to the Asterophryinae;
    evidence of either monophyly or paraphyly has yet to be presented.
  CONTRIBUTOR: Richard G. Zweifel (RGZ).
  REVIEWERS: Margaret Davies (MD); Michael J. Tyler (MJT).

Choerophryne van Kampen, 1915. Zool. Jahrb., Abt. Syst., 37:376.
  TYPE SPECIES: *Choerophryne proboscidea* van Kampen, 1915 (=*Copiula rostellifer*
    Wandolleck, 1910).
  DISTRIBUTION: As for the single species.
  COMMENT: See Menzies and Tyler, 1977, J. Zool., London, 183:443, for validation of
    this genus as distinct from *Cophixalus.*

Choerophryne rostellifer (Wandolleck, 1910). Abh. Ber. K. Zool. Anthro. Ethno. Mus. Dresden, 13:11.
ORIGINAL NAME: *Copiula rostellifer*.
TYPE(S): Holotype: MTKD D2210, destroyed according to Obst, 1977, Zool. Abh. Staatl. Mus. Tierkd., Dresden, 34:173.
TYPE LOCALITY: Torricelli Mountains, West Sepik Province, Papua New Guinea.
DISTRIBUTION: The north coast ranges of Irian Jaya (Indonesia) and Papua New Guinea, and one locality in Western Province, Papua New Guinea.
COMMENT: Menzies and Tyler, 1977, J. Zool., London, 183:443–447, reviewed this poorly known species.

Cophixalus Boettger, 1892. Kat. Batr. Samml. Mus. Senckenb. Naturforsch. Ges.:24.
TYPE SPECIES: *Sphenophryne verrucosa* Boulenger, 1898, by subsequent designation of the International Commission of Zoological Nomenclature (see comment).
DISTRIBUTION: Moluccan Is.; New Guinea; northeastern Queensland, Australia.
COMMENT: Menzies et al., 1980, Bull. Zool. Nomencl., 36:231–235, showed that the type species (by monotypy) of *Cophixalus* Boettger, *Cophixalus geislerorum*, belongs to the genus *Oreophryne* as these genera currently are understood. In response to the petition of Menzies et al., the International Commission of Zoological Nomenclature, 1984, Bull. Zool. Nomencl., 41:12–14, designated *Sphenophryne verrucosa* Boulenger, 1898, as the type species of *Cophixalus* and placed *Cophixalus* on the Official List of Generic Names in Zoology. Australian species taxonomy and literature reviewed by Cogger, Cameron, and Cogger, 1983, Zool. Cat. Aust., 1(Amph. Rept.):52–53.

Cophixalus ateles (Boulenger, 1898). Ann. Mus. Civ. Stor. Nat. Genova, (2)18:708.
ORIGINAL NAME: *Sphenophryne ateles*.
TYPE(S): MSNG 29116 designated lectotype by Capocaccia, 1957, Ann. Mus. Civ. Stor. Nat. Genova, 69:219.
TYPE LOCALITY: "Moroka", Central Province, Papua New Guinea.
DISTRIBUTION: Known only from the type locality.
COMMENT: See Zweifel, 1980, Bull. Am. Mus. Nat. Hist., 165:407, for discussion of this species.

Cophixalus biroi (Méhelÿ, 1901). Termés. Füzetek, 24:197, 247.
ORIGINAL NAME: *Phrynixalus biroi*.
TYPE(S): Syntypes in MNH (destroyed); one syntype, BM 1901.3.9.2 ("juv. in egg"—Parker, 1934, Monogr. Frogs Fam. Microhylidae:175), remains.
TYPE LOCALITY: "Sattelberg", Morobe Province, Papua New Guinea.
DISTRIBUTION: Northern New Guinea.
COMMENT: See Zweifel, 1979, Am. Mus. Novit., 2678:1–14, for distribution map and other information.

Cophixalus cheesmanae Parker, 1934. Monogr. Frogs Fam. Microhylidae:175.
TYPE(S): Holotype: BM 1947.2.11.97 (formerly 1934.1.5.5).
TYPE LOCALITY: "Kokoda (1,200 ft.) [Northern Province], British New Guinea [Papua New Guinea]".
DISTRIBUTION: Eastern half of Papua New Guinea.
COMMENT: See Zweifel, 1979, Am. Mus. Novit., 2678:1–14, for distribution map and other information.

Cophixalus concinnus Tyler, 1979. Copeia, 1979:119.
TYPE(S): Holotype: QM J30743.
TYPE LOCALITY: "at an elevation of 1,250 m on Thornton Peak (16° 12'; 145° 20'), Cape York Peninsula, Queensland, Australia".
DISTRIBUTION: Rainforests in northeastern coastal Queensland, Australia.

Cophixalus cryptotympanum Zweifel, 1956. Am. Mus. Novit., 1766:36.
TYPE(s): Holotype: AMNH 56842.
TYPE LOCALITY: "at an elevation of 1370 meters on the north slope of Mt. Dayman, Maneau Range, Territory of Papua [Milne Bay Province, Papua New Guinea]".
DISTRIBUTION: Central mountainous regions of Papua New Guinea from Southern Highlands and Western Highlands provinces to the eastern end of the island.

Cophixalus darlingtoni Loveridge, 1948. Bull. Mus. Comp. Zool., 101:423.
ORIGINAL NAME: *Cophixalus biroi darlingtoni*.
TYPE(s): Holotype: MCZ 25930.
TYPE LOCALITY: "Toromanbanau, 7,500 feet, Bismarck Range, Madang Division [Chimbu Province], Australian New Guinea [Papua New Guinea]".
DISTRIBUTION: Central mountain ranges of Papua New Guinea in Southern Highlands, Eastern Highlands, Chimbu, and Western Highlands provinces.

Cophixalus daymani Zweifel, 1956. Am. Mus. Novit., 1766:39.
TYPE(s): Holotype: AMNH 56879.
TYPE LOCALITY: "at an elevation of 2330 meters (7320 feet) on the north slope of Mt. Dayman, Maneau Range, Territory of Papua [Milne Bay Province, Papua New Guinea]".
DISTRIBUTION: Known only from the type locality.

Cophixalus exiguus Zweifel and Parker, 1969. Am. Mus. Novit., 2390:2.
TYPE(s): Holotype: SAMA R10311.
TYPE LOCALITY: "between 1800 and 2000 feet on Mt. Hartley, 23 miles south and 5 miles east of Cooktown, Queensland", Australia.
DISTRIBUTION: Known only from the vicinity of the type locality in northeastern Queensland, Australia.

Cophixalus kaindiensis Zweifel, 1979. Am. Mus. Novit., 2678:2.
TYPE(s): Holotype: AMNH 82904.
TYPE LOCALITY: "near the summit of Mount Kaindi, about 2300 m., 5 km. west of Wau, Morobe Province, Papua New Guinea".
DISTRIBUTION: Mountains in the vicinity of Wau, Papua New Guinea.

Cophixalus montanus (Boettger, 1895). Zool. Anz., 18:133.
ORIGINAL NAME: *Phrynixalus montanus*.
TYPE(s): SMF 4198 (one of 2 syntypes) designated lectotype by Mertens, 1967, Senckenb. Biol., 48:50.
TYPE LOCALITY: North Halmaheira, at an elevation of 2,200–2,500', Moluccan Is., Indonesia; Mertens, 1967, Senckenb. Biol., 48:50, gave the type locality more specifically as "Galela".
DISTRIBUTION: Known only from Halmahera I. (see comment).
COMMENT: A record from New Guinea was based on a specimen subsequently reidentified as *Cophixalus variegatus* by Zweifel, 1956, Am. Mus. Novit., 1766:45.

Cophixalus neglectus Zweifel, 1962. Am. Mus. Novit., 2113:15.
TYPE(s): Holotype: MCZ 18505.
TYPE LOCALITY: "Bellenden Ker Range, Queensland", Australia.
DISTRIBUTION: Bellenden Ker Range, Queensland, Australia.

Cophixalus nubicola Zweifel, 1962. Am. Mus. Novit., 2087:8.
TYPE(s): Holotype: AMNH 66581.
TYPE LOCALITY: "at an elevation of 10,200 feet on a ridge of Mt. Michael, Territory of New Guinea [Eastern Highlands Province, Papua New Guinea].
DISTRIBUTION: Known only from the type locality.

Cophixalus ornatus (Fry, 1912). Rec. Aust. Mus., 9:91.
ORIGINAL NAME: *Austrochaperina ornata.*
TYPE(S): Holotype: AM R222.
TYPE LOCALITY: "twenty-five miles inland from Cairns", Queensland, Australia. See Zweifel, 1962, Am. Mus. Novit., 2113:6, for definition of the type locality and type specimen.
DISTRIBUTION: Rainforests of northeastern Queensland, Australia.

Cophixalus pansus (Fry, 1917 "1916"). Proc. Linn. Soc. New South Wales, 1916:772.
ORIGINAL NAME: *Aphantophryne pansa.*
TYPE(S): Holotype: AM R5238.
TYPE LOCALITY: "Mt. Scratchley, on the Owen Stanley Range, British New Guinea [Central or Northern Province, Papua New Guinea] . . . 12,200 ft."
DISTRIBUTION: High elevations in the Owen Stanley Range and disjunct to the northwest in mountains south of Wau, Morobe Province, Papua New Guinea.
COMMENT: See Zweifel and Allison, 1982, Am. Mus. Novit., 2723:1–14, for a review of this species.

Cophixalus parkeri Loveridge, 1948. Bull. Mus. Comp. Zool., 101:425.
TYPE(S): Holotype: MCZ 25940.
TYPE LOCALITY: "Mount Wilhelm, 8,000 feet, Bismarck Range, Madang Division, [Chimbu Province,] Australian New Guinea [Papua New Guinea]".
DISTRIBUTION: Central mountainous region of Papua New Guinea, from Chimbu Province to Morobe Province.
COMMENT: See Zweifel, 1962, Am. Mus. Novit., 2087:112, and Zweifel, 1979, Am. Mus. Novit., 2678:1–14, for information on this species.

Cophixalus pipilans Zweifel, 1980. Bull. Am. Mus. Nat. Hist., 165:404.
TYPE(S): Holotype: AMNH 83004.
TYPE LOCALITY: "vicinity of Sempi, 9 km. north of Alexishafen, Madang Province, Papua New Guinea, elevation between sea level and 50 m."
DISTRIBUTION: From the vicinity of Lae (Morobe Province) to the Adelbert Mountains (Madang Province), Papua New Guinea.

Cophixalus riparius Zweifel, 1962. Am. Mus. Novit., 2087:14.
TYPE(S): Holotype: AMNH 65975.
TYPE LOCALITY: "at an elevation of 9100 feet beside Pengagl Creek on the east slope of Mt. Wilhelm, Territory of New Guinea [Chimbu Province, Papua New Guinea]".
DISTRIBUTION: Central mountain ranges of Papua New Guinea from Southern Highlands and Western Highlands provinces southeastward to the vicinity of Wau, Morobe Province.

Cophixalus saxatilis Zweifel and Parker, 1977. Am. Mus. Novit., 2614:2.
TYPE(S): Holotype: MCZ 90205.
TYPE LOCALITY: "Black Mountain, 13 miles south and 2 miles west of Cooktown, Queensland, Australia".
DISTRIBUTION: Known only from the type locality.

Cophixalus shellyi Zweifel, 1956. Am. Mus. Novit., 1785:2.
TYPE(S): Holotype: AMNH 58551.
TYPE LOCALITY: "Kondiu, across the Wahgi River from Kup, elevation about 5000 feet, Northeast New Guinea [Chimbu Province, Papua New Guinea]".
DISTRIBUTION: Papua New Guinea: central mountain ranges from vicinity of Wau, Morobe Province, to Western Highlands Province; also disjunct populations in the Adelbert Mountains and on the Huon Peninsula.
COMMENT: See Zweifel, 1980, Bull. Am. Mus. Nat. Hist., 165:387–434, for a distribution map and additional information.

Cophixalus sphagnicola Zweifel and Allison, 1982. Am. Mus. Novit., 2723:6.
TYPE(S): Holotype: AMNH 83077.
TYPE LOCALITY: "at about 2300 m., near the summit of Mount Kaindi, 5 km. west of Wau, Morobe Province, Papua New Guinea".
DISTRIBUTION: Mountains in the vicinity of Wau, Morobe Province, Papua New Guinea.

Cophixalus tagulensis Zweifel, 1963. Am. Mus. Novit., 2141:6.
TYPE(S): Holotype: AMNH 60066.
TYPE LOCALITY: "west slope of Mt. Riu, Sudest (Tagula) Island, Louisiade Archipelago, Territory of Papua, New Guinea [Milne Bay Province, Papua New Guinea]".
DISTRIBUTION: Known only from the type locality.

Cophixalus variegatus (van Kampen, 1923). Amph. Indo-Aust. Arch.:138.
ORIGINAL NAME: *Hylophorbus variegatus*.
TYPE(S): Holotype: ZMA 5706.
TYPE LOCALITY: "New Guinea (Digul riv.) [Irian Jaya (New Guinea), Indonesia]".
DISTRIBUTION: Recorded widely in mountainous regions of New Guinea.

Cophixalus verrucosus (Boulenger, 1898). Ann. Mus. Civ. Stor. Nat. Genova, (2)18:707.
ORIGINAL NAME: *Sphenophryne verrucosa*.
TYPE(S): MSNG 29934 designated lectotype by Capocaccia, 1957, Ann. Mus. Civ. Stor. Nat. Genova, 69:220.
TYPE LOCALITY: "Two specimens from Moroka.—The British Museum also possesses specimens from Mt. Victoria". Lectotype is from Moroka, Central Province, Papua New Guinea.
DISTRIBUTION: Southern and eastern Papua New Guinea, including islands in the D'Entrecasteaux and Louisiade groups.

Copiula Méhelÿ, 1901. Termés. Füzetek, 24:242.
TYPE SPECIES: *Phrynixalus oxyrhinus* Boulenger, 1898.
DISTRIBUTION: New Guinea.
COMMENT: See Menzies and Tyler, 1977, J. Zool., London, 183:431–464, for revision. The systematic status of *Copiula* outside of the area covered by Menzies and Tyler, eastern Papua New Guinea, is unresolved (RGZ).

Copiula fistulans Menzies and Tyler, 1977. J. Zool., London, 183:435.
TYPE(S): Holotype: SAMA R14497.
TYPE LOCALITY: "approximately 11 km north of Lae [Morobe Province], Papua New Guinea".
DISTRIBUTION: Lowlands of Papua New Guinea from Finschhafen, Morobe Province, to Popondetta, Northern Province.
COMMENT: See comment under *Copiula*.

Copiula minor Menzies and Tyler, 1977. J. Zool., London, 183:441.
TYPE(S): Holotype: UP 5435.
TYPE LOCALITY: "at an altitude of 1600 m near Oiadamawa'a Peak, Goodenough Island, Milne Bay Province, Papua New Guinea".
DISTRIBUTION: Known only from Goodenough I.
COMMENT: See comment under *Copiula*.

Copiula oxyrhina (Boulenger, 1898). Proc. Zool. Soc. London, 1898:480.
ORIGINAL NAME: *Phrynixalus oxyrhinus*.
TYPE(S): Syntypes: BM 1947.2.12.1–5 (formerly 1898.3.3.12–16).
TYPE LOCALITY: "St. Aignan I. [Misima I.], south of Ferguson I., British New Guinea [Milne Bay Province, Papua New Guinea]".
DISTRIBUTION: Eastern Papua New Guinea, Central Province to Misima I., Milne Bay Province.

COMMENT: See comment under *Copiula*.

Genyophryne Boulenger, 1890. Proc. Zool. Soc. London, 1890:326.
TYPE SPECIES: *Genyophryne thomsoni* Boulenger, 1890.
DISTRIBUTION: As for the single species.

Genyophryne thomsoni Boulenger, 1890. Proc. Zool. Soc. London, 1890:327.
TYPE(S): Holotype: BM 1947.2.10.46 (formerly 1889.7.1.12).
TYPE LOCALITY: "Sudest Island [=Tagula I., Milne Bay Province, Papua New
   Guinea], between New Guinea and the Louisiade Archipelago" (Sudest I. is
   part of the Louisiade Archipelago—RGZ).
DISTRIBUTION: Eastern Papua New Guinea.
COMMENT: Reviewed by Zweifel, 1971, Am. Mus. Novit., 2469:1–13.

Oreophryne Boettger, 1895. Zool. Anz., 1895:135.
TYPE SPECIES: *Oreophryne senckenbergiana* Boettger, 1895 (=*Microhyla achatina* var.
   moluccensis Peters and Doria, 1878).
DISTRIBUTION: Southern Philippine Is., Celebes, and the Lesser Sunda Is. to New
   Guinea and New Britain.
COMMENT: See comment under *Cophixalus*. Placed on the Official List of Generic
   Names in Zoology by the International Commission of Zoological
   Nomenclature, 1984, Opinion 1266, Bull. Zool. Nomencl., 41:12–14.
REVIEWERS: Angel Alcala (AA) (Philippines); Walter C. Brown (WSB) (Philippines).

Oreophryne albopunctata (van Kampen, 1909). Nova Guinea, 9:42.
ORIGINAL NAME: *Sphenophryne albopunctata*.
TYPE(S): Syntypes: ZMA 5821–22.
TYPE LOCALITY: North River [Lorentz River] near Sabang, Irian Jaya (New Guinea),
   Indonesia.
DISTRIBUTION: Known only from the type locality.

Oreophryne annulata (Stejneger, 1908). Proc. U.S. Natl. Mus., 33:573.
ORIGINAL NAME: *Phrynixalus annulatus*.
TYPE(S): Holotype: USNM 35399.
TYPE LOCALITY: "Davao, Mindanao", Philippine Is. (see comment).
DISTRIBUTION: Mindanao and Biliran, Philippine Is.
COMMENT: Inger, 1954, Fieldiana: Zool., 33:447, considered the type locality open
   to doubt, as other records for the species are at higher elevations.

Oreophryne anthonyi (Boulenger, 1897). Ann. Mag. Nat. Hist., (6)19:10.
ORIGINAL NAME: *Sphenophryne anthonyi*.
TYPE(S): Syntypes: BM 1947.2.13.34–40 (formerly 1896.10.31.43–49), MCZ 2896.
TYPE LOCALITY: "Mount Victoria, Owen Stanley Range, [Papua New Guinea,
   probably Central Province,] New Guinea".
DISTRIBUTION: Southeastern Papua New Guinea: Owen Stanley Mountains, Central
   Province, to Mount Dayman, Milne Bay Province.
COMMENT: See Zweifel, 1983, Am. Mus. Novit., 2759:4, for a discussion of the type
   locality.

Oreophryne biroi (Méhelÿ, 1897). Termés. Füzetek, 20:400, 411.
ORIGINAL NAME: *Sphenophryne biroi*.
TYPE(S): Syntypes: MNH 21268/3 (2 specimens); destroyed.
TYPE LOCALITY: Near Friedrich Wilhelmshafen [=Madang], Madang Province,
   Papua New Guinea.
DISTRIBUTION: Recorded widely throughout New Guinea.
COMMENT: Zweifel, 1980, Bull. Am. Mus. Nat. Hist., 165:411, noted that this name
   may cover more than one species.

Oreophryne brachypus (Werner, 1898). Zool. Anz., 21:554.
ORIGINAL NAME: *Hylella brachypus.*
TYPE(S): Syntypes: ZMB 14666, 15473 (2 specimens); a third syntype is
  unaccounted for.
TYPE LOCALITY: "Ralum", Gazelle Peninsula, East New Britain Province, Papua
  New Guinea.
DISTRIBUTION: Extreme eastern New Britain.
COMMENT: Tyler, 1964, Mitt. Zool. Mus. Berlin, 40:1–8, and Tyler, 1967, Trans. R.
  Soc. S. Aust., 91:187–190, discussed this species.

Oreophryne brevicrus Zweifel, 1956. Am. Mus. Novit., 1766:23.
TYPE(S): Holotype: AMNH 43669.
TYPE LOCALITY: "at an elevation of 2800 meters, 9 kilometers northeast of Lake
  Habbema, Netherlands New Guinea [Irian Jaya, Indonesia]".
DISTRIBUTION: High elevations in the central mountain ranges of eastern Irian Jaya
  (Indonesia) and extreme western Papua New Guinea.

Oreophryne celebensis (F. Müller, 1894). Verh. Naturforsch. Ges. Basel, 10:841.
ORIGINAL NAME: *Sphenophryne celebensis.*
TYPE(S): NHMB 1340 designated lectotype by Forcart, 1946, Verh. Naturforsch.
  Ges. Basel, 57:134.
TYPE LOCALITY: Boelawa Mountains, *ca.* 1,200 m, [and] Totoiya Valley, 800 m,
  summit of the Gunung Sudara, North Celebes (Indonesia); which of these
  localities the lectotype came from cannot be determined (Forcart, 1946, Verh.
  Naturforsch. Ges. Basel, 57:134).
DISTRIBUTION: Celebes, Indonesia.
COMMENT: Parker, 1934, Monogr. Frogs Fam. Microhylidae:162, identified a
  specimen from 2600 m elevation in Irian Jaya (New Guinea), Indonesia, as
  this species but noted some morphological differences. It is most unlikely that
  the same species of *Oreophryne* would occur at such a high elevation in New
  Guinea and in Celebes as well (RGZ).

Oreophryne crucifera (van Kampen, 1913). Nova Guinea, 9:462.
ORIGINAL NAME: *Cophixalus crucifer.*
TYPE(S): Syntypes: ZMA 5819, 5820.
TYPE LOCALITY: Went Mountains, 800 and 1,050 m, Irian Jaya (New Guinea),
  Indonesia.
DISTRIBUTION: Known only from the type locality.

Oreophryne flava Parker, 1934. Monogr. Frogs Fam. Microhylidae:168.
TYPE(S): Holotype: ZMA 5823.
TYPE LOCALITY: "Lorentz River (Kloofbivak)", Irian Jaya (New Guinea), Indonesia.
DISTRIBUTION: Mountains of central Irian Jaya (New Guinea), Indonesia.

Oreophryne frontifasciata (Horst, 1883). Notes Leyden Mus., 5:243.
ORIGINAL NAME: *Callula frontifasciata.*
TYPE(S): RMNH 1807 designated lectotype by Brongersma, 1948, Zool. Meded.,
  Leiden, 29:307.
TYPE LOCALITY: "Salawatti, Morotai and Halmaheira" Is. in the Moluccas,
  Indonesia; syntypes from Salawatti and Halmahera Is. are lost.
DISTRIBUTION: With the loss of the syntypes the species is known with certainty
  only from Morotai I., Moluccas, Indonesia.

Oreophryne geislerorum (Boettger, 1892). Kat. Batr. Samml. Mus. Senckenb. Naturforsch. Ges.:24.
ORIGINAL NAME: *Cophixalus geislerorum.*
TYPE(S): Holotype: SMF 4197.
TYPE LOCALITY: "Kaiser-Wilhelmsland", later the Territory of New Guinea, now the northern part of Papua New Guinea.
DISTRIBUTION: No specific locality known; Menzies et al., 1980, Bull. Zool. Nomencl., 36:233, suggested the eastern part of the Huon Peninsula or Madang (Papua New Guinea).
COMMENT: See comment under *Cophixalus* for the generic placement of this species.

Oreophryne idenburgensis Zweifel, 1956. Am. Mus. Novit., 1766:27.
TYPE(S): Holotype: AMNH 49663.
TYPE LOCALITY: "18 kilometers southwest of Bernhard Camp, Idenburg River, Netherlands New Guinea, [Irian Jaya, Indonesia,] at an elevation of 2150 meters".
DISTRIBUTION: Known only from the type locality.

Oreophryne inornata Zweifel, 1956. Am. Mus. Novit., 1766:29.
TYPE(S): Holotype: AMNH 57000.
TYPE LOCALITY: "at an elevation of 1600 meters on the east slope of Goodenough Island, D'Entrecasteaux Islands, Territory of Papua [Milne Bay Province, Papua New Guinea]".
DISTRIBUTION: Known only from the type locality.

Oreophryne insulana Zweifel, 1956. Am. Mus. Novit., 1766:32.
TYPE(S): Holotype: AMNH 57267.
TYPE LOCALITY: "at an elevation of 1600 meters on the east slope of Goodenough Island, D'Entrecasteaux Islands, Territory of Papua [Milne Bay Province, Papua New Guinea]".
DISTRIBUTION: Goodenough I. and on the nearby mainland of Papua New Guinea at Milne Bay.

Oreophryne jeffersoniana Dunn, 1928. Am. Mus. Novit., 315:3.
TYPE(S): Holotype: AMNH 24530.
TYPE LOCALITY: "Komodo, 2500 feet altitude [Indonesia]".
DISTRIBUTION: Komodo, Sumbawa, Rintja, and western Flores Is., Indonesia.
COMMENT: Auffenberg, 1980, Bull. Florida State Mus., Biol. Sci., 25:56, considered *Oreophryne darewskyi* Mertens, 1965 (Type locality: Rintja I.), a synonym of *Oreophryne jeffersoniana.*

Oreophryne kampeni Parker, 1934. Monogr. Frogs Fam. Microhylidae:164.
TYPE(S): Holotype: BM 1947.2.12.14 (formerly 1894.12.10.143).
TYPE LOCALITY: "Moroka [Central Province], British New Guinea [Papua New Guinea]".
DISTRIBUTION: Known only from the type locality.

Oreophryne moluccensis (Peters and Doria, 1878). Ann. Mus. Civ. Stor. Nat. Genova, 13:428.
ORIGINAL NAME: *Microhyla achatina* var. *moluccensis.*
TYPE(S): MSNG 29132 designated lectotype by Capocaccia, 1957, Ann. Mus. Civ. Stor. Nat. Genvoa, 69:219.
TYPE LOCALITY: Acqui Conora on the Island of Ternate and . . . on the Island of Batcian [Batjan] [Moluccan Is., Indonesia].
DISTRIBUTION: Halmahera, Ternate, and Batjan Is., Indonesia.
COMMENT: Records for Salawatti and Morotai Is., based on lost syntypes of *Oreophryne frontifasciata*, require confirmation as to species (RGZ).

Oreophryne monticola (Boulenger, 1897). Ann. Mag. Nat. Hist., (6)19:508.
ORIGINAL NAME: *Sphenophryne monticola.*
TYPE(S): Syntypes: BM 1947.2.12.26–32 (formerly 97.6.21.92–98), MCZ 2897.
TYPE LOCALITY: "Lombok . . . collected at 4000 feet altitude", Indonesia.
DISTRIBUTION: Lombok and Bali, Lesser Sunda Is., Indonesia.

Oreophryne nana Brown and Alcala, 1967. Proc. Biol. Soc. Washington, 80:66.
TYPE(S): Holotype: CAS-SU 22055.
TYPE LOCALITY: "between 1800 and 3000 ft on the northwest side of Nacawa volcano, Mt. Hibok-hibok, Camiguin Island, Philippines Islands".
DISTRIBUTION: Known only from the type locality.

Oreophryne parkeri Loveridge, 1955. Breviora, 50:3.
TYPE(S): Holotype: MCZ 12964.
TYPE LOCALITY: "Matapan [=Matapau], [West Sepik Province,] Australian New Guinea [Papua New Guinea]".
DISTRIBUTION: Known only from the type locality.

Oreophryne rookmaakeri Mertens, 1927. Senckenb. Biol., 9:236.
TYPE(S): Holotype: SMF 22090.
TYPE LOCALITY: Rana Mese, 1,200 m elevation, Western Flores, Lesser Sunda Is., Indonesia.
DISTRIBUTION: Western Flores, 900–1200 m elev., Indonesia.

Oreophryne variabilis (Boulenger, 1896). Ann. Mag. Nat. Hist., (6)18:64.
ORIGINAL NAME: *Sphenophryne variabilis.*
TYPE(S): NHMB 1350 designated lectotype by Forcart, 1946, Verh. Naturforsch. Ges. Basel, 57:134.
TYPE LOCALITY: "Bonthain Peak, Celebes, 5000–6000 feet", Indonesia.
DISTRIBUTION: Mt. Bonthain, southern Celebes, Indonesia, from 1500 to 2000 m.

Oreophryne wolterstorffi (Werner, 1901). Verh. Zool. Bot. Ges. Wien, 51:613.
ORIGINAL NAME: *Hylella wolterstorffi.*
TYPE(S): Holotype: ZMB 16853.
TYPE LOCALITY: German New Guinea; later the Territory of New Guinea, now the northern part of Papua New Guinea.
DISTRIBUTION: No specific locality known.
COMMENT: See Tyler, 1964, Rec. S. Aust. Mus., 14:675–678, for generic assignment and descriptive notes.

Oreophryne zimmeri Ahl, 1933. Mitt. Zool. Mus. Berlin, 19:482.
TYPE(S): Holotype: ZMB 34321.
TYPE LOCALITY: Southeast Celebes (Tanke Salokko, Mengkoka Mountains, 2000 m) [Indonesia].
DISTRIBUTION: Known only from the type locality.

Sphenophryne Peters and Doria, 1878. Ann. Mus. Civ. Stor. Nat. Genova, 13:430.
TYPE SPECIES: *Sphenophryne cornuta* Peters and Doria, 1878, by monotypy.
DISTRIBUTION: New Guinea, New Britain, and extreme northern Australia.
COMMENT: Australian species' taxonomy and literature reviewed by Cogger, Cameron, and Cogger, 1983, Zool. Cat. Aust., 1(Amph. Rept.):53–54.

Sphenophryne brevicrus (van Kampen, 1913). Nova Guinea, 9:465.
ORIGINAL NAME: *Oxydactyla brevicrus.*
TYPE(S): ZMA 5714 designated lectotype by Daan and Hillenius, 1966, Beaufortia, 158:122.
TYPE LOCALITY: Hellwig Mountains, ± 2500 m, . . . Wichmann Mountains, ± 3000 m [Irian Jaya (New Guinea), Indonesia].
DISTRIBUTION: High elevations in the central mountain ranges of Irian Jaya (Indonesia) and Papua New Guinea.

Sphenophryne brevipes (Boulenger, 1897). Ann. Mag. Nat. Hist., (6)19:11.
   ORIGINAL NAME: *Liophryne brevipes.*
   TYPE(S): Holotype: BM 1947.2.12.50 (formerly 1896.10.31.31).
   TYPE LOCALITY: "Mount Victoria, Owen Stanley Range, New Guinea [Papua New
      Guinea, probably in Central Province]".
   DISTRIBUTION: Known only from the type locality.
   COMMENT: See Zweifel, 1983, Am. Mus. Novit., 2759:4, for a discussion of the type
      locality.

Sphenophryne cornuta Peters and Doria, 1878. Ann. Mus. Civ. Stor. Nat. Genova, 8:
   430.
   TYPE(S): Holotype: MSNG 29479.
   TYPE LOCALITY: Near the Wa Samson River in Northern New Guinea [Vogelkop
      Peninsula, Irian Jaya, Indonesia].
   DISTRIBUTION: Recorded over much of New Guinea, from Vogelkop Peninsula
      (Irian Jaya, Indonesia) to the vicinity of Port Moresby (Papua New Guinea)
      on the south coast and to the Adelbert Mountains (Papua New Guinea) in the
      north coast ranges.

Sphenophryne crassa Zweifel, 1956. Am. Mus. Novit., 1766:11.
   TYPE(S): Holotype: AMNH 56803.
   TYPE LOCALITY: "north slope of Mt. Dayman, Maneau Range, Territory of Papua
      [Milne Bay Province, Papua New Guinea], at an elevation of 2230 meters".
   DISTRIBUTION: Known only from the type locality.

Sphenophryne dentata Tyler and Menzies, 1971. Trans. R. Soc. S. Aust., 95:79.
   TYPE(S): Holotype: SAMA R12063.
   TYPE LOCALITY: "near Alotau, Milne Bay, [Milne Bay Province,] Territory of Papua
      [Papua New Guinea]".
   DISTRIBUTION: Known from the type locality and Mt. Dayman, 100 km to the
      northeast, Papua New Guinea.

Sphenophryne fryi Zweifel, 1962. Am. Mus. Novit., 2113:26.
   TYPE(S): Holotype: AM R2285.
   TYPE LOCALITY: "Bloomfield River, near Cooktown, North-eastern Queensland",
      Australia.
   DISTRIBUTION: Rainforests of northeastern Queensland, Australia.
   COMMENT: *Sphenophryne fryi* Zweifel, 1962, is a replacement name for
      Austrochaperina brevipes Fry, 1915, Proc. R. Soc. Queensland, 27:61, which is
      preoccupied.

Sphenophryne gracilipes (Fry, 1912). Rec. Aust. Mus., 9:93.
   ORIGINAL NAME: *Austrochaperina gracilipes.*
   TYPE(S): Holotype: AM 4536.
   TYPE LOCALITY: "Somerset, Cape York, North Queensland", Australia.
   DISTRIBUTION: Cape York Peninsula (Queensland, Australia) and southern Papua
      New Guinea.
   COMMENT: Zweifel, 1965, Am. Mus. Novit., 2214:2, erred in placing *Sphenophryne
      gracilipes* in the synonymy of *Sphenophryne robusta* (RGZ).

Sphenophryne hooglandi Zweifel, 1967. Am. Mus. Novit., 2309:2.
   TYPE(S): Holotype: AMNH 77597.
   TYPE LOCALITY: "Mt. Hunstein, Sepik District [East Sepik Province,] Territory of
      New Guinea [Papua New Guinea]".
   DISTRIBUTION: Known only from the type locality.

Sphenophryne macrorhyncha (van Kampen, 1906). Nova Guinea, 5:168.
ORIGINAL NAME: *Chaperina macrorhyncha.*
TYPE(S): Holotype: RMNH 4630.
TYPE LOCALITY: Manikion region [Irian Jaya (New Guinea), Indonesia].
DISTRIBUTION: Upland regions of New Guinea, over much of Irian Jaya, extending east into Papua New Guinea at least to the Torricelli Mountains on the north coast and Western Province in the central ranges.

Sphenophryne mehelyi Parker, 1934. Monogr. Frogs Fam. Microhylidae:156.
TYPE(S): Holotype: MNH 2414/11; destroyed.
TYPE LOCALITY: "Sattelberg", Morobe Province, Papua New Guinea.
DISTRIBUTION: Huon Peninsula, Morobe Province, Papua New Guinea.
COMMENT: *Sphenophryne mehelyi* is a replacement name for *Chaperina fusca* Méhelÿ, 1901, Termés. Füzetek, 24:207, which is preoccupied. The record for this species from New Britain (Tyler, 1967, Trans. R. Soc. S. Aust., 91:187–190) is thought to pertain to an undescribed species (Zweifel, 1980, Bull. Am. Mus. Nat. Hist., 165:387–434).

Sphenophryne palmipes Zweifel, 1956. Am. Mus. Novit., 1766:15.
TYPE(S): Holotype: AMNH 57331.
TYPE LOCALITY: "north slope of Mt. Dayman, Maneau Range, Territory of Papua [Milne Bay Province, Papua New Guinea], at an elevation of 700 meters".
DISTRIBUTION: Eastern Papua New Guinea: Huon Peninsula to d'Entrecasteaux Is.

Sphenophryne pluvialis Zweifel, 1965. Am. Mus. Novit., 2214:6.
TYPE(S): Holotype: AMNH 54195.
TYPE LOCALITY: "Speewah, elevation 1500 feet, Queensland", Australia.
DISTRIBUTION: Rainforests of northeastern Queensland, Australia.

Sphenophryne polysticta (Méhelÿ, 1901). Termés. Füzetek, 24:208, 258.
ORIGINAL NAME: *Chaperina polysticta.*
TYPE(S): Holotype: MNH 2414/12; destroyed.
TYPE LOCALITY: "Sattelberg", Morobe Province, Papua New Guinea.
DISTRIBUTION: Known only from the type locality.
COMMENT: Records for Australia result from misidentifications (Zweifel, 1962, Am. Mus. Novit., 2113:1–40).

Sphenophryne pusilla (Roux, 1910). Abh. Senckenb. Naturforsch. Ges., 33:228.
ORIGINAL NAME: *Microbatrachus pusillus.*
TYPE(S): Holotype: NHMB 2732.
TYPE LOCALITY: "Pobdjetur, Terangan", Aru Is., Indonesia.
DISTRIBUTION: Known only from the type locality.
COMMENT: Tyler, 1978, J. Nat. Hist., 12:457–460, transferred this problematic species to *Sphenophryne.*

Sphenophryne rhododactyla (Boulenger, 1897). Ann. Mag. Nat. Hist., (6)19:11.
ORIGINAL NAME: *Liophryne rhododactyla.*
TYPE(S): Syntypes: BM 1947.2.12.47–49 (formerly 1896.10.31.28–30).
TYPE LOCALITY: "Mount Victoria, Owen Stanley Range, New Guinea", Papua New Guinea, probably in Central Province.
DISTRIBUTION: Papua New Guinea in the Owen Stanley Range, Central Province, northwest to the vicinity of Wau, Morobe Province.
COMMENT: See Zweifel, 1983, Am. Mus. Novit., 2759:4, for discussion of the type locality.

Sphenophryne robusta (Fry, 1912). Rec. Aust. Mus., 9:89.
ORIGINAL NAME: *Austrochaperina robusta.*
TYPE(S): Holotype: AM R5295.
TYPE LOCALITY: "Russell River, North-eastern Queensland", Australia.
DISTRIBUTION: Rainforests of northeastern Queensland, Australia.

COMMENT: See comment under *Sphenophryne gracilipes*. Records of this species from Northern Territory, Australia, pertain to an undescribed species (RGZ).

Sphenophryne schlaginhaufeni Wandolleck, 1911. Abh. Ber. K. Zool. Anthro. Ethno. Mus. Dresden, 13:5.
   TYPE(S): Syntypes: MTKD D2212 (2 specimens), destroyed according to Obst, 1977, Zool. Abh. Staatl. Mus. Tierkd., Dresden, 34:175.
   TYPE LOCALITY: Upper reaches of the Rienjamur 650–700 m above the sea [Torricelli Mountains, West Sepik Province, Papua New Guinea].
   DISTRIBUTION: Upland regions of New Guinea; the central ranges of Irian Jaya (Indonesia) east to Chimbu Province (Papua New Guinea), and in the north coast ranges of Papua New Guinea.

SUBFAMILY: **Melanobatrachinae** Noble, 1931.
   CITATION: Biol. Amph.:538.
   DISTRIBUTION: Tanzania and southern India.
   COMMENT: Savage, 1973, *In* Vial (ed.), Evol. Biol. Anurans:355, considered, without discussion, the African genera to be more closely related to the Phrynomerinae and the Indian genus *Melanobatrachus* to be in the Microhylinae. The Melanobatrachinae as conceived here (that of Parker, 1934, Monogr. Frogs Fam. Microhylidae:196) includes the Hoplophryninae of Noble, 1931, Biol. Amph.: 538–539.

Hoplophryne Barbour and Loveridge, 1928. Mem. Mus. Comp. Zool., 50:253.
   TYPE SPECIES: *Hoplophryne uluguruensis* Barbour and Loveridge, 1928, by original designation.
   DISTRIBUTION: Usambara, Uluguru, and Magrotto mountains, Tanzania.
   REVIEWERS: Kim M. Howell (KMH); Raymond Laurent (RL); John C. Poynton (JCP).

Hoplophryne rogersi Barbour and Loveridge, 1928. Mem. Mus. Comp. Zool., 50:258.
   TYPE(S): Holotype: MCZ 13814.
   TYPE LOCALITY: "in wild banana in the rain-forest on [Mt.] Bomoli near the Institute of Amani, Usambara Mountains, Tanganyika Territory [Tanzania]".
   DISTRIBUTION: Usambara and Magrotto mountains, Tanzania.

Hoplophryne uluguruensis Barbour and Loveridge, 1928. Mem. Mus. Comp. Zool., 50: 254.
   TYPE(S): Holotype: MCZ 13766.
   TYPE LOCALITY: "in a wild banana at the top of Mt. Mbova (local name) above Nyange, Uluguru Mountains, Tanganyika Territory [Tanzania]".
   DISTRIBUTION: Uluguru Mountains, Tanzania.

Melanobatrachus Beddome, 1878. Proc. Zool. Soc. London, 1878:722.
   TYPE SPECIES: *Melanobatrachus indicus* Beddome, 1878.
   DISTRIBUTION: As for the single species.
   REVIEWERS: J. C. Daniel (JCD); Sushil Dutta (SD).

Melanobatrachus indicus Beddome, 1878. Proc. Zool. Soc. London, 1878:722.
   TYPE(S): Holotype: BM 78.9.3.1.
   TYPE LOCALITY: Anamallai Hills, southern India, 4,000 ft.
   DISTRIBUTION: Hills of Kerala, southwestern India.

Parhoplophryne Barbour and Loveridge, 1928. Mem. Mus. Comp. Zool., 50:260.
   TYPE SPECIES: *Parhoplophryne usambarica* Barbour and Loveridge, 1928, by original designation.
   DISTRIBUTION: As for the single species.
   REVIEWERS: Kim M. Howell (KMH); Raymond Laurent (RL); John C. Poynton (JCP).

Parhoplophryne usambarica Barbour and Loveridge, 1928. Mem. Mus. Comp. Zool., 50: 260.
TYPE(S): Holotype: MCZ 13818.
TYPE LOCALITY: "in the forested hills to the west of Amani, Usambara Mountains, Tanganyika Territory [=Tanzania]".
DISTRIBUTION: Amani, Usambara Mountains, Tanzania.

SUBFAMILY: **Microhylinae** Günther, 1859 "1858" (1843).
CITATION: Cat. Batr. Sal. Coll. Brit. Mus.:121.
DISTRIBUTION: North and South America; the Indo-Australian Archipelago; eastern Asia; Madagascar.
COMMENT: Carvalho, 1954, Occas. Pap. Mus. Zool. Univ. Michigan, 555:1–20, reviewed the New World genera. Walker, 1973, Occas. Pap. Mus. Nat. Hist. Univ. Kansas, 20:1–7, compared a number of features of the New World genera. Dunn, 1949, Am. Mus. Novit., 1429:1–21, reviewed South American species. Cochran, 1954, Bull. U.S. Natl. Mus., 206:361–372, reviewed the southeastern Brazilian species.
CONTRIBUTORS: Robert F. Inger (RFI) (Old World); Craig E. Nelson (CEN) (New World).
REVIEWERS: Angel Alcala (AA) (Philippines); Werner C. A. Bokermann (WCAB) (Brazil); Leo J. Borkin (LJB) (China); Walter C. Brown (WCB) (Philippines); Jonathan A. Campbell (JAC) (Mexico and Central America); Ulisses Caramaschi (UC) (Brazil); Ronald I. Crombie (RIC) (New World); J. C. Daniel (JCD) (India and Sri Lanka); Sushil Dutta (SD) (India and Sri Lanka); Eduardo Gudynas (EG) (Uruguay, Brazil, and Argentina); Keith A. Harding (KAH) (New World); Shuqin Hu (SH) (China); Enrique La Marca (ELM) (Venezuela); Masafumi Matsui (MM) (East Asia); William F. Pyburn (WFP) (New World); Jay M. Savage (JMS) (Central America); Norman J. Scott, Jr. (NJS) (Central and South America); Paulo E. Vanzolini (PEV) (Brazil); Ermi Zhao (EZ) (China).

Arcovomer Carvalho, 1954. Occas. Pap. Mus. Zool. Univ. Michigan, 555:8.
TYPE SPECIES: *Arcovomer passarellii* Carvalho, 1954, by original designation.
DISTRIBUTION: As for the single species.
COMMENT: Most closely related to *Hamptophryne* according to Carvalho, 1954, Occas. Pap. Mus. Zool. Univ. Michigan, 555:8.

Arcovomer passarellii Carvalho, 1954. Occas. Pap. Mus. Zool. Univ. Michigan, 555:9.
TYPE(S): Holotype: MN 1012 (cleared and stained).
TYPE LOCALITY: "Duque de Caxias, Estado do Rio de Janeiro, Brazil".
DISTRIBUTION: States of Espírito Santo and Rio de Janeiro, Brazil.

Chaperina Mocquard, 1892. Naturaliste, Paris, (2)6:35.
TYPE SPECIES: *Chaperina fusca* Mocquard, 1892.
DISTRIBUTION: As for the single species.

Chaperina fusca Mocquard, 1892. Naturaliste, Paris, (2)6:35.
TYPE(S): Holotype: MNHNP 91-49.
TYPE LOCALITY: Sintang, Borneo.
DISTRIBUTION: Malay Peninsula; Borneo; Palawan, Mindanao, and Jolo, Philippines.
COMMENT: Reviewed by Bourret, 1942, Batr. Indochine:505–507; Inger, 1954, Fieldiana: Zool., 33:414; Inger, 1966, Fieldiana: Zool., 52:140; and Berry, 1975, Amph. Fauna Peninsular Malaysia:111–112.

Chiasmocleis Méhelÿ, 1904. Ann. Hist. Nat. Mus. Natl. Hungarici, 2:210.
TYPE SPECIES: *Engystoma albopunctatum* Boettger, 1885.
DISTRIBUTION: Panama and South America, north and east of the Andes.
COMMENT: The validity of the various taxa within this genus has not been assessed by a modern review. Dunn, 1949, Am. Mus. Novit., 1419:5, included a key to the species then known. Duellman, 1978, Misc. Publ. Mus. Nat. Hist. Univ. Kansas, 65:187–190, compared three sympatric species. Walker and Duellman,

1974, Occas. Pap. Mus. Nat. Hist. Univ. Kansas, 26:5, commented on the morphological heterogeneity encompassed in this nominal genus (see comment under *Chiasmocleis anatipes*).

Chiasmocleis albopunctata (Boettger, 1885). Z. Naturwiss., Halle, 58:240.
ORIGINAL NAME: *Engystoma albopunctatum.*
TYPE(S): Not stated.
TYPE LOCALITY: "Paraguay".
DISTRIBUTION: Bolivia, Paraguay, and Brazil (Goiás, Mato Grosso, and São Paulo).
COMMENT: See comment under *Chiasmocleis centralis.*

Chiasmocleis anatipes Walker and Duellman, 1974. Occas. Pap. Mus. Nat. Hist. Univ. Kansas, 26:1.
TYPE(S): Holotype: KU 146035.
TYPE LOCALITY: "Santa Cecilia, 340 m, Provincia Napo, Ecuador".
DISTRIBUTION: Known only from the type locality.
COMMENT: *Chiasmocleis anatipes* was suggested, in the original description, to be close to *Chiasmocleis leucosticta* and divergent from other *Chiasmocleis*; Walker and Duellman also noted that *Nectodactylus* is the available name should generic distinction for these two species be warranted.

Chiasmocleis bassleri Dunn, 1949. Am. Mus. Novit., 1419:9.
TYPE(S): Holotype: AMNH 42699.
TYPE LOCALITY: "Rio Utoquinia to Rio Tapiche, Peru (near the Brazilian border)".
DISTRIBUTION: Eastern Peru and Ecuador.

Chiasmocleis bicegoi Miranda-Ribeiro, 1920. Rev. Mus. Paulista, São Paulo, 12:286.
TYPE(S): Holotype: MZUSP 924 (formerly 595).
TYPE LOCALITY: "Os Perús, S[ão] Paulo, Brazil".
DISTRIBUTION: State of São Paulo, Brazil.

Chiasmocleis centralis Bokermann, 1952. Pap. Avulsos Dep. Zool., São Paulo, 10:274.
TYPE(S): Holotype: MZUSP 7547.
TYPE LOCALITY: "Aruanã, Estado de Goiás, Brasil".
DISTRIBUTION: Known only from the type locality.
COMMENT: In the original description, Bokermann suggested that *Chiasmocleis centralis* is allied with *Chiasmocleis shudikarensis*, but Carvalho, 1954, Occas. Pap. Mus. Zool. Univ. Michigan, 555:11, suggested affinity with *Chiasmocleis albopunctata.*

Chiasmocleis hudsoni Parker, 1940. Ann. Mag. Nat. Hist., (11)5:260.
TYPE(S): Holotype: BM 1939.1.1.3.
TYPE LOCALITY: "New River, British Guiana [=Guyana] (750 feet)" (this locality is actually in southwestern Surinam—MSH).
DISTRIBUTION: Guyana and Surinam.

Chiasmocleis leucosticta (Boulenger, 1888). Ann. Mag. Nat. Hist., (6)1:416.
ORIGINAL NAME: *Engystoma leucosticta.*
TYPE(S): Not stated; BM 88.4.23.3 registered as holotype.
TYPE LOCALITY: "Sierra do Catharina, Province Santa Catharina, Brazil".
DISTRIBUTION: Santa Catarina, Brazil.

Chiasmocleis panamensis Dunn, Trapido, and Evans, 1948. Am. Mus. Novit., 1376:1.
TYPE(S): Holotype: AMNH 52741.
TYPE LOCALITY: "Old Panama, Republic of Panama".
DISTRIBUTION: Central Panama to Magdalena, Cundinamarca, and Chocó, in Colombia.
COMMENT: Reviewed by Nelson, 1972, Copeia, 1972:895–898.

Chiasmocleis schubarti Bokermann, 1952. Pap. Avulsos Dep. Zool., São Paulo, 10:275.
TYPE(S): Holotype: MZUSP 2309.
TYPE LOCALITY: "Córrego Juncado, Linhares, Estado do Espírito Santo, Brasil".
DISTRIBUTION: Known only from the type locality.
COMMENT: Bokermann, in the original description, suggested that *Chiasmocleis schubarti* is allied to *Chiasmocleis leucosticta*; Carvalho, 1954, Occas. Pap. Mus. Zool. Univ. Michigan, 555:11, suggested affinities with *Chiasmocleis bicegoi*.

Chiasmocleis shudikarensis Dunn, 1949. Am. Mus. Novit., 1419:7.
TYPE(S): Holotype: AMNH 43674.
TYPE LOCALITY: "Shudikar-wau, upper Essequibo River, British Guiana [=Guyana] (not far from Brazilian border)".
DISTRIBUTION: Guyana, Surinam, French Guiana, and Brazil (Amazonas).

Chiasmocleis urbanae Bokermann, 1952. Pap. Avulsos Dep. Zool., São Paulo, 10:277.
TYPE(S): Holotype: MZUSP 9033.
TYPE LOCALITY: "Ilha de São Sebastião, Estado de São Paulo, Brasil".
DISTRIBUTION: Known only from the type locality.
COMMENT: Close to *Chiasmocleis spinulosa* (=*Chiasmocleis leucosticta*) according to the original description and Carvalho, 1954, Occas. Pap. Mus. Zool. Univ. Michigan, 555:11.

Chiasmocleis ventrimaculata (Andersson, 1945). Ark. Zool., 37(2):2.
ORIGINAL NAME: *Engystoma ventrimaculata*.
TYPE(S): NHRM.
TYPE LOCALITY: "Rio Pastaza, Eastern Ecuador".
DISTRIBUTION: Eastern Ecuador; Amazonian Peru.

Ctenophryne Mocquard, 1904. Bull. Mus. Natl. Hist. Nat., Paris, 1904:308.
TYPE SPECIES: *Ctenophryne geayi* Mocquard, 1904.
DISTRIBUTION: As for the single species.
COMMENT: Probably derived from *Stereocyclops* according to Carvalho, 1954, Occas. Pap. Mus. Zool. Univ. Michigan, 555:4.

Ctenophryne geayi Mocquard, 1904. Bull. Mus. Natl. Hist. Nat., Paris, 1904:308.
TYPE(S): Not stated; MNHNP 03-84 registered as holotype.
TYPE LOCALITY: "la rivière Sarare en Colombie" (=Sarare River, Norte de Santander, Colombia).
DISTRIBUTION: Northern South America from Surinam, Guyana, and Brazil to Colombia, Ecuador, and Peru.

Dasypops Miranda-Ribeiro, 1924. Bol. Mus. Nac., Rio de Janeiro, 1(4):255.
TYPE SPECIES: *Dasypops schirchi* Miranda-Ribeiro, 1924, by monotypy.
DISTRIBUTION: As for the single species.
COMMENT: Probably derived from *Hypopachus* according to Carvalho, 1954, Occas. Pap. Mus. Zool. Univ. Michigan, 555:16.

Dasypops schirchi Miranda-Ribeiro, 1924. Bol. Mus. Nac., Rio de Janeiro, 1(4):255.
TYPE(S): Not stated; MN 542 registered as holotype.
TYPE LOCALITY: "Rio Mutum, E[spírito] Santo, Brazilia [=Brazil]".
DISTRIBUTION: Coastal plain of Espírito Santo and Bahia, Brazil.

Dermatonotus Méhelÿ, 1904. Ann. Nat. Hist. Mus. Natl. Hungarici, 2:208.
TYPE SPECIES: *Engystoma mülleri* Boettger, 1885, by monotypy.
DISTRIBUTION: As for the single species.
COMMENT: Most closely allied to *Hypopachus* and *Gastrophryne* but more "primitive" than either, according to Carvalho, 1954, Occas. Pap. Mus. Zool. Univ. Michigan, 555:13.

Dermatonotus muelleri (Boettger, 1885). Z. Naturwiss., Halle, 58:241.
  ORIGINAL NAME: *Engystoma Mülleri.*
  TYPE(S): Not stated; SMF 4113 registered as holotype, according to Mertens, 1967,
      Senckenb. Biol., 48:50.
  TYPE LOCALITY: Paraguay.
  DISTRIBUTION: Central and southern Chaco, and Corrientes (Argentina); eastern
      Bolivia; Paraguay; Brazil, from Maranhão to São Paulo.
  COMMENT: Synonymy and review in Cei, 1980, Monit. Zool. Ital., N.S., Monogr., 2:
      153–155; also see Arámburu, 1953, Notas Fac. Cienc. Nat. Mus. Univ. Nac. La
      Plata, 16:273–285.

Elachistocleis Parker, 1927. Occas. Pap. Mus. Zool. Univ. Michigan, 187:4.
  TYPE SPECIES: *Rana ovalis* Schneider, 1799, by original designation.
  DISTRIBUTION: Central Panama, northern and central Colombia, and much of South
      America east of the Andes and as far south as Argentina.
  COMMENT: Probably derived from *Relictivomer* and possibly ancestral to *Synapturanus*
      and *Myersiella* according to Carvalho, 1954, Occas. Pap. Mus. Zool. Univ.
      Michigan, 555:15. The nomenclature and distributions cited for the species in
      Elachistocleis and *Relictivomer* complex are extremely provisional and almost
      certainly partly in error. Three factors that contribute importantly to the
      confusion are nomenclatural uncertainty, a distribution of morphs which is
      more complex than any continental-level synthesis has proposed, and the
      absence of statistical analyses of variation within and among proposed morphs.
      All seven of the available species-level names (including *Hypopachus
      pearsei* [=*Relictivomer pearsei*]) were referred to one monotypic species
      (*Elachistocleis ovalis*) by Parker, 1934, Monogr. Frogs Fam. Microhylidae:121–122,
      who gave a lengthy synonymy (augmented by Cochran, 1955, Bull. U.S. Natl.
      Mus., 206:366, who also recognized only one species). Two other reviews,
      Dunn, 1949, Am. Mus. Novit., 1419:13–14, and Carvalho, 1954, Occas. Pap. Mus.
      Zool. Univ. Michigan, 555:13–15, each listed three species (partitioned among
      the two genera by Carvalho). Further, Parker, 1934, Monogr. Frogs Fam.
      Microhylidae:122, cited a *bicolor* morph "with a more or less profusely spotted
      lower surface and a broad femoral stripe and some light spots in the groin . . ."
      and an *ovalis* morph "with an immaculate belly, narrow white femoral stripe
      and no inguinal spots", although in 1927, in describing the genus, he had used
      identical characterizations but reversed the assignment of names. Dunn, 1949,
      Am. Mus. Novit., 1419:13–14, adopted Parker's initial assignment, perhaps
      because he knew the immaculate-ventered morph occurs at Buenos Aires, from
      whence, he suggested, "it is possible to infer, from remarks elsewhere in the
      literature" came the type of *Oxyrhynchus bicolor* (=*Elachistocleis bicolor*). However,
      no explicit argument has been advanced as to which morph should receive the
      oldest name, *Rana ovalis*, a nomenclatural ambiguity that is critical since the
      original description cites a "yellow venter" (and since the figure that
      constitutes the original description of *Oxyrhynchus bicolor* shows an immaculate
      venter). Miranda-Ribeiro, 1920, Rev. Mus. Paulista, São Paulo, 12:5–7,
      demonstrated that the variation in this group is substantially more complex
      than the dominant two-morph view, and suggested five nomenclaturally
      distinct Brazilian forms. Dunn, 1949, Am. Mus. Novit., 1419:13–14, proposed
      that the immaculate-ventered morph was confined to the southern end of the
      generic range. However, Cochran and Goin, 1970, Bull. U.S. Natl. Mus., 288:70,
      cited a specimen of this complex from Colombia with an immaculate venter and
      Kenny, 1969, Stud. Fauna Curaçao and other Caribb. Is., 29:68, assigned some
      specimens from Trinidad to *Elachistocleis ovalis*, a species which he characterized
      as having an immaculate venter. The situation is further complicated by the
      uncertain status of *Hypopachus pearsei* Ruthven (=*Relictivomer pearsei*). Ruthven's
      decision to separate this species from the one now known as *Elachistocleis ovalis*
      was based on his mistaking sympatric *Chiasmocleis panamensis* for *Elachistocleis
      ovalis* (see Nelson, 1972, Copeia, 1972:897), thus falsely making it appear that
      Relictivomer pearsei and *Elachistocleis ovalis* occur sympatrically. Carvalho, 1954,

Occas. Pap. Mus. Zool. Univ. Michigan, 555:13–15, subsequently erected *Relictivomer* for *Hypopachus pearsei*. In contrast, most other authors who have considered the relationship of this form relative to the mottled-ventered form of *Elachistocleis* (usually called *Elachistocleis ovalis*) have either stated that they are conspecific (e.g., Parker, 1934, Monogr. Frogs Fam. Microhylidae:121; Rivero, 1961, Bull. Mus. Comp. Zool., 126:178) or stated that they would consider them conspecific "save for the statement of Ruthven that the two occur together" (Dunn, 1949, Am. Mus. Novit., 1419:77; see also Cochran and Goin, 1970, Bull. U.S. Natl. Mus., 228:77). Kenny, 1969, Stud. Fauna Curaçao and other Caribb. Is., 29:66, in his analysis of frogs from Trinidad, reached the same conclusion, but used nomenclaturally *Elachistocleis ovalis* for an immaculate-ventered form and resurrected *Bufo surinamensis* explicitly as a senior synonym of *pearsei* for (northern) populations with spotted venters. Kenny's paper is especially noteworthy as it was the first to clearly demonstrate that two biologically distinct species of this complex occur at closely adjacent localities (an observation substantiated for Surinam as well, where two forms with spotted venters occur in close proximity—MSH). Parker, in describing *Elachistocleis*, noted two morphs from Bolivia but considered them as conspecific in 1934 in his monograph; see also Rivero, 1961, Bull. Mus. Comp. Zool., 126:179, for a discussion of an interesting Bolivian series. The scheme adopted here within the *Elachistocleis-Relictivomer* complex retains all of the distinction advocated in the last thirty years, thus avoiding prematurely resynonymizing any of the forms (CEN).

Elachistocleis bicolor (Valenciennes, 1838). *In* Guérin Méneville, Icon. Règne Anim., 3(Rept.):pl. 27.
ORIGINAL NAME: *Oxyrhynchus bicolor*.
TYPE(S): Not traced; originally in "Cuv. Coll. Mus." (=? MNHNP).
TYPE LOCALITY: "l'Amerique méridionale [=South America]".
DISTRIBUTION: Central Argentina and Uruguay through Paraguay to Amazonian Brazil.
COMMENT: Synonymy and review in Cei, 1980, Monit. Zool. Ital., N.S., Monogr., 2: 155. See comment under *Elachistocleis*.

Elachistocleis ovalis (Schneider, 1799). Hist. Amph., 1:131.
ORIGINAL NAME: *Rana ovalis*.
TYPE(S): Not traced.
TYPE LOCALITY: Not stated.
DISTRIBUTION: Panama and Colombia southward, east of the Andes, to Argentina; Trinidad.
COMMENT: See comment under *Elachistocleis*.

Elachistocleis piauiensis Caramaschi and Jim, 1983. Herpetologica, 39:391.
TYPE(S): Holotype: J. Jim 6024.
TYPE LOCALITY: "Picos, State of Piauí, Northeastern Brasil (ca. 07° 05' S and 41° 30' W)".
DISTRIBUTION: Known only from the type locality.
COMMENT: See comment under *Elachistocleis*.

Elachistocleis surinamensis (Daudin, 1802). Hist. Nat. Rain. Gren. Crap.:91.
ORIGINAL NAME: *Bufo surinamensis*.
TYPE(S): Not stated.
TYPE LOCALITY: "Surinam".
DISTRIBUTION: Surinam and Trinidad.
COMMENT: See comment under *Elachistocleis*.

Gastrophryne Fitzinger, 1843. Syst. Rept.:33.
TYPE SPECIES: *Engystoma rugosum* Duméril and Bibron, 1841 (=*Engystoma carolinense* Holbrook, 1836), by monotypy.
DISTRIBUTION: Southern USA to Costa Rica.

COMMENT: Reviewed by Nelson, 1972, J. Herpetol., 6:111–137; summarized by Nelson, 1973, Cat. Am. Amph. Rept., 134.1–2. Probably derived from *Hypopachus* according to Carvalho, 1954, Occas. Pap. Mus. Zool. Univ. Michigan, 555:12. A close affinity between these two genera and the lack of close relationship between *Gastrophryne* and *Microhyla* was supported by the subsequent studies summarized by Bogart and Nelson, 1976, Herpetologica, 32: 205.

REVIEWERS: Gustavo Casas-Andreu (GCA) (Mexico); Oscar Flores-Villela (OFV) (Mexico).

Gastrophryne carolinensis (Holbrook, 1836). N. Am. Herpetol., Ed. 1, 1:83.
ORIGINAL NAME: *Engystoma carolinense*.
TYPE(S): Not stated; ANSP 1455–57 recorded as syntypes.
TYPE LOCALITY: "never been found north of Charleston [South Carolina]; its exact range extending westward to the Lower Mississippi . . .", USA; data with syntypes is "South Carolina", USA.
DISTRIBUTION: Southeastern USA from southern Florida and eastern Maryland to eastern Kansas and eastern Texas to Iowa (disjunct); introduced on northwestern Puerto Rico, Grand Bahama I., and possibly on New Providence I.
COMMENT: Reviewed by Nelson, 1972, Cat. Am. Amph. Rept., 120.1–4; details of distribution in Nelson, 1972, J. Herpetol., 6:125–128.
REVIEWERS: Albert Schwartz (AS); Richard Thomas (RT).

Gastrophryne elegans (Boulenger, 1882). Cat. Batr. Sal. Brit. Mus.:162.
ORIGINAL NAME: *Engystoma elegans*.
TYPE(S): Holotype: BM 1947.2.11.86 (formerly 56.3.17.27).
TYPE LOCALITY: "Cordova" (=Córdoba), Veracruz, Mexico.
DISTRIBUTION: Southern Veracruz (Mexico) through Guatemala to northern Honduras on the Atlantic versant.
COMMENT: Reviewed by Nelson, 1972, Cat. Am. Amph. Rept., 121.1–2; details of distribution in Nelson, 1972, J. Herpetol., 6:128–129.

Gastrophryne olivacea (Hallowell, 1857 "1856"). Proc. Acad. Nat. Sci. Philadelphia, 8: 252.
ORIGINAL NAME: *Engystoma olivaceum*.
TYPE(S): Unknown; according to Nelson, 1972, Cat. Am. Amph. Rept., 122.1, ANSP 2745 is probably the holotype.
TYPE LOCALITY: "Kansas and Nebraska", USA; restricted to "Kansas, Geary Co., Fort Riley", USA, by Smith and Taylor, 1950, Univ. Kansas Sci. Bull., 23:358; restricted to "vicinity of Lawrence, [Douglas County,] Kansas", USA, by Schmidt, 1953, Check List N. Am. Amph. Rept., Ed. 6:77.
DISTRIBUTION: Southern Arizona (USA) to Nayarit (Mexico); Kansas and Missouri (USA) to Chihuahua, Durango, Tamaulipas, and San Luis Potosí (Mexico).
COMMENT: Reviewed by Nelson, 1972, Cat. Am. Amph. Rept., 122.1–4; details of distribution in Nelson, 1972, J. Herpetol., 6:129–130.

Gastrophryne pictiventris (Cope, 1886). Proc. Am. Philos. Soc., 23:272.
ORIGINAL NAME: *Engystoma pictiventris*.
TYPE(S): Holotype: USNM 14196.
TYPE LOCALITY: "Nicaragua"; restricted by Savage, 1973, J. Herpetol., 7:37, to "between El Castillo and San Juan del Norte along the Río San Juan . . . Departamento Río San Juan, Nicaragua".
DISTRIBUTION: Southeastern Nicaragua and northeastern Costa Rica.
COMMENT: Reviewed by Nelson, 1973, Cat. Am. Amph. Rept., 135.1–2.

Gastrophryne usta (Cope, 1866). Proc. Acad. Nat. Sci. Philadelphia, 18:131.
ORIGINAL NAME: *Engystoma ustum.*
TYPE(S): Holotype: USNM 24965.
TYPE LOCALITY: "Guadalaxara" (=Guadalajara), Jalisco, Mexico; apparently in error, according to Nelson, 1972, J. Herpetol., 6:119, who corrected the type locality to "Tecoman, Colima, Mexico".
DISTRIBUTION: Central Sinaloa and central Veracruz to Chiapas (Mexico) and El Salvador on the Pacific versant.
COMMENT: Reviewed by Nelson, 1972, Cat. Am. Amph. Rept., 123.1–2. Published records for elevations above 1000 m and those for the Lerma-Chapala drainage system are apparently spurious, as discussed by Nelson, 1972, J. Herpetol., 6:118–119, who also provided details of distribution. Subspecies suggested, most recently by Lynch, 1965, Trans. Kansas Acad. Sci., 68:396–400; rejected by Nelson, 1972, J. Herpetol., 6:122.

Gastrophrynoides Noble, 1926. Am. Mus. Novit., 111:22.
TYPE SPECIES: *Engystoma borneense* Boulenger, 1897.
DISTRIBUTION: As for the single species.

Gastrophrynoides borneensis (Boulenger, 1890). Ann. Mag. Nat. Hist., (6)19:108.
ORIGINAL NAME: *Engystoma borneense.*
TYPE(S): Holotype: BM 1947.2.11.57 (formerly 97.3.4.26).
TYPE LOCALITY: "Baram district, Sarawak", Malaysia (Borneo).
DISTRIBUTION: Borneo.
COMMENT: Reviewed by Inger, 1966, Fieldiana: Zool., 52:144–145.

Glossostoma Günther, 1900. Biol. Cent. Am., Rept. Batr.:210.
TYPE SPECIES: *Glossostoma aterrimum* Günther, 1900, by monotypy.
DISTRIBUTION: Costa Rica, Panama, Colombia, and Ecuador.
COMMENT: Parker, 1934, Monogr. Frogs Fam. Microhylidae:143, 146, included these species in *Microhyla*; Carvalho, 1954, Occas. Pap. Mus. Zool. Univ. Michigan, 555:11, resurrected *Glossostoma*. This action was supported by karyotypic evidence provided by Bogart and Nelson, 1976, Herpetologica, 32:204.

Glossostoma aequatoriale (Peracca, 1904). Boll. Mus. Zool. Anat. Comp. Univ. Torino, 19:23.
ORIGINAL NAME: *Engistoma aequatoriale.*
TYPE(S): Not traced (?MSNT).
TYPE LOCALITY: "Cuenca, Ecuador".
DISTRIBUTION: Azuay, Ecuador.

Glossostoma aterrimum Günther, 1900. Biol. Cent. Am., Rept. Batr.:210.
TYPE(S): Not stated; BM 1902.5.12.6 recorded as holotype.
TYPE LOCALITY: "Costa Rica".
DISTRIBUTION: Costa Rica, Panama, Colombia, and Ecuador.

Glyphoglossus Günther, 1868. Proc. Zool. Soc. London, 1868:483.
TYPE SPECIES: *Glyphoglossus molossus* Günther, 1868.
DISTRIBUTION: As for the single species.
COMMENT: See Taylor, 1962, Univ. Kansas Sci. Bull., 43:575–578.

Glyphoglossus molossus Günther, 1868. Proc. Zool. Soc. London, 1868:483.
TYPE(S): Holotype: BM.
TYPE LOCALITY: Pegu, Burma.
DISTRIBUTION: Burma and southern Vietnam to peninsular Thailand.
COMMENT: See Bourret, 1942, Batr. Indochine:493–495, for synonymy and review.

Hamptophryne Carvalho, 1954. Occas. Pap. Mus. Zool. Univ. Michigan, 555:7.
TYPE SPECIES: *Chiasmocleis boliviana* Parker, 1927, by original designation.
DISTRIBUTION: As for the single species.

COMMENT: Most closely related to *Arcovomer* and *Chiasmocleis* but more "primitive" than either according to Carvalho, 1954, Occas. Pap. Mus. Zool. Univ. Michigan, 555:8.

Hamptophryne boliviana (Parker, 1927). Occas. Pap. Mus. Zool. Univ. Michigan, 187:3.
ORIGINAL NAME: *Chiasmocleis boliviana*.
TYPE(S): Not stated; BM 1927.8.1.1 considered holotype by Parker, 1934, Monogr. Frogs Fam. Microhylidae:119.
TYPE LOCALITY: "Buena Vista, Santa Cruz, Bolivia".
DISTRIBUTION: Northern and western sides of the Amazon basin: French Guiana, Surinam, Guyana, Brazil, Ecuador, Peru, and Bolivia.

Hyophryne Carvalho, 1954. Occas. Pap. Mus. Zool. Univ. Michigan, 555:4.
TYPE SPECIES: *Hyophryne histrio* Carvalho, 1954, by original designation.
DISTRIBUTION: As for the single species.
COMMENT: Probably derived from *Stereocyclops* according to Carvalho, 1954, Occas. Pap. Mus. Zool. Univ. Michigan, 555:6.

Hyophryne histrio Carvalho, 1954. Occas. Pap. Mus. Zool. Univ. Michigan, 555:5.
TYPE(S): Holotype: MN 1010.
TYPE LOCALITY: "Fazenda Repartimento, Municipio de Ilheus, Estado da Bahia, Brazil".
DISTRIBUTION: Known only from the holotype.

Hypopachus Keferstein, 1867. Nachr. Ges. Wiss. Göttingen, 18:351.
TYPE SPECIES: *Hypopachus seebachii* Keferstein, 1867 (=*Engystoma variolosum* Cope, 1866).
DISTRIBUTION: Southern Texas (USA) and Sonora (Mexico) to Costa Rica.
COMMENT: See comments under *Dermatonotus* and *Gastrophryne*.
REVIEWERS: Gustavo Casas-Andreu (GCA); Oscar Flores-Villela (OFV).

Hypopachus barberi Schmidt, 1939. Field Mus. Nat. Hist. Publ., Zool. Ser., 24:1.
TYPE(S): Holotype: FMNH 1912.
TYPE LOCALITY: "Tecpán, Sololá [in error for Chimaltenango], Guatemala".
DISTRIBUTION: Highlands of Chiapas (Mexico), Guatemala, and El Salvador.
COMMENT: Reviewed by Nelson, 1973, Herpetologica, 29:6–17.

Hypopachus variolosus (Cope, 1866). Proc. Acad. Nat. Sci. Philadelphia, 18:131.
ORIGINAL NAME: *Engystoma variolosum*.
TYPE(S): Holotype: USNM 6488.
TYPE LOCALITY: "Arriba" (=? uplands of), Costa Rica.
DISTRIBUTION: Southern Texas (USA) and Sonora (Mexico) to Costa Rica at elevations mostly below 1500 m.
COMMENT: See Nelson, 1974, Herpetologica, 30:250–274.

Kalophrynus Tschudi, 1838. Classif. Batr.:86.
TYPE SPECIES: *Kalophrynus pleurostigma* Tschudi, 1838.
DISTRIBUTION: Southern China to Java and Philippines.
COMMENT: See Inger, 1966, Fieldiana: Zool., 52:126–140, for synonymies, key, and review of Bornean species.

Kalophrynus bunguranus (Günther, 1895). Novit. Zool., 2:501.
ORIGINAL NAME: *Diplopelma bunguranum*.
TYPE(S): Syntypes: BM 1947.2.11.38–41 (formerly 95.5.1.105–108).
TYPE LOCALITY: Great Natuna Island [Indonesia].
DISTRIBUTION: Great Natuna I., Indonesia.

Kalophrynus heterochirus Boulenger, 1900. Proc. Zool. Soc. London, 1900:186.
ORIGINAL NAME: *Calophrynus heterochirus*.
TYPE(S): Syntypes: BM 1909.8.18.6–7.
TYPE LOCALITY: "Borneo (no precise locality)".
DISTRIBUTION: Borneo.

Kalophrynus intermedius Inger, 1966. Fieldiana: Zool., 52:131.
TYPE(S): Holotype: FMNH 139348.
TYPE LOCALITY: "Nanga Tekalit, Mengiong River, Third Division, Sarawak",
Malaysia (Borneo).
DISTRIBUTION: Borneo.

Kalophrynus menglienicus Yang and Su, 1980. Zool. Res., Kunming, 1:257.
TYPE(S): Holotype: KIZ 751377.
TYPE LOCALITY: Menglien, Yunnan, altitude 1040 m, China.
DISTRIBUTION: Yunnan, China.
COMMENT: Related to *Kalophrynus punctatus*, according to the original description.

Kalophrynus nubicola Dring, 1984 "1983". Amphibia-Reptilia, 4:109.
TYPE(S): Holotype: BM 1978.99.
TYPE LOCALITY: "camp four 1800 m, Gunung Mulu, Fourth Division, Sarawak",
Malaysia (Borneo).
DISTRIBUTION: Gunung Mulu, Sarawak, Malaysia (Borneo).

Kalophrynus palmatissimus Kiew, 1984. Malay. Nat. J., 37:146.
TYPE(S): Holotype: BM 1982.1508.
TYPE LOCALITY: "lowland dipterocarp forest at about 75 m a.s.l. at the Pasoh Forest
Reserve in Negeri Sembilian", Malaysia (Malaya).
DISTRIBUTION: Known only from the type locality.

Kalophrynus pleurostigma Tschudi, 1838. Classif. Batr.:86.
TYPE(S): Holotype: RMNH 2278.
TYPE LOCALITY: Sumatra [Indonesia].
DISTRIBUTION: Southern China to Sumatra, Borneo, Java, Natuna Is., and
Philippines.
COMMENT: See Inger, 1954, Fieldiana: Zool., 33:416–420, for discussion of
Philippine populations; see also Berry, 1975, Amph. Fauna Peninsular
Malaysia:112–113. Chinese population reviewed by Liu and Hu, 1961, Tailless
Amph. China:286–287.

Kalophrynus punctatus Peters, 1871. Monatsber. Preuss. Akad. Wiss. Berlin, 1871:579.
ORIGINAL NAME: *Calophrynus punctatus*.
TYPE(S): Holotype: MSNG 29130.
TYPE LOCALITY: Sarawak [Malaysia (Borneo)].
DISTRIBUTION: Borneo, Mentawei Is.

Kalophrynus robinsoni Smith, 1922. J. Fed. Malay States Mus., 10:280.
TYPE(S): Holotype: BM 1923.5.14.29.
TYPE LOCALITY: "Wray's camp. A halting place about four hours from Kuala Teku.
Height above sea level, 3300 feet", in mountains of Pahang (Malaya),
Malaysia.
DISTRIBUTION: Gunong Tahan and Kuala Teku, Malay Peninsula.
COMMENT: See Bourret, 1942, Batr. Indochine:501, for synonymy and review.

Kalophrynus subterrestris Inger, 1966. Fieldiana: Zool., 52:137.
TYPE(S): Holotype: FMNH 150421.
TYPE LOCALITY: "Sungei Seran, Labang, Bintulu District, Fourth Division,
Sarawak", Malaysia (Borneo).
DISTRIBUTION: Borneo.

Kaloula Gray, 1831. Zool. Misc., 1:38.
TYPE SPECIES: *Kaloula pulchra* Gray, 1831.
DISTRIBUTION: Korea and northern China to Lesser Sundas and Philippines; Sri
   Lanka.
COMMENT: Inger, 1954, Fieldiana: Zool., 33:420–445, reviewed the Philippine species.
   Inger, 1966, Fieldiana: Zool., 52:121–126, reviewed the Bornean species. Bourret,
   1942, Batr. Indochine:484–493, reviewed the Indochinese species. Liu and Hu,
   1961, Tailless Amph. China:287–295, reviewed the Chinese species.

Kaloula baleata (Müller, 1836). *In* Van Oort and Müller, Verh. Batavia. Genootsch.
   Wetensch., 16:96.
ORIGINAL NAME: *Bombinator baleatus.*
TYPE(S): Possibly RMNH 2218 (MSH).
TYPE LOCALITY: Krawang and/or Lewie Gadja, Java [Indonesia].
DISTRIBUTION: Malay Peninsula to Lesser Sundas, Celebes, Borneo, and Philippines.
COMMENT: See Berry, 1975, Amph. Fauna Peninsular Malaysia:113–114.

Kaloula borealis (Barbour, 1908). Bull. Mus. Comp. Zool., 51:321.
ORIGINAL NAME: *Cacopoides borealis.*
TYPE(S): Holotype: MCZ 2436.
TYPE LOCALITY: "Antung [=Dandong, Liaoning], Manchuria", China.
DISTRIBUTION: Jiangsu and northern and northeastern China; Korea and Cheju I.
COMMENT: Reviewed by Liu and Hu, 1961, Tailless Amph. China:288–289.

Kaloula conjuncta (Peters, 1863). Monatsber. Preuss. Akad. Wiss. Berlin, 1863:455.
ORIGINAL NAME: *Hylaedactylus (Holonectes) conjunctus.*
TYPE(S): Holotype: NHMW 22888.
TYPE LOCALITY: Luzon, Philippine Islands.
DISTRIBUTION: Philippine Is. from Luzon to Mindanao.
COMMENT: See Taylor, 1962, Univ. Kansas Sci. Bull., 43:566–569.

Kaloula mediolineata (Smith, 1917). J. Nat. Hist. Soc. Siam, 2:224.
ORIGINAL NAME: *Callula mediolineata.*
TYPE(S): Syntypes: BM 1916.4.17.3, 1917.5.14.41–44.
TYPE LOCALITY: Prachuap Kirikan, southwestern Siam [Thailand].
DISTRIBUTION: Thailand, except for extreme south.

Kaloula picta (Duméril and Bibron, 1841). Erp. Gén., 8:737.
ORIGINAL NAME: *Plectropus pictus.*
TYPE(S): Holotype: MNHNP 5027.
TYPE LOCALITY: "Manille" (=Manila), Luzon, Philippines.
DISTRIBUTION: Philippine Is. from Luzon to Mindanao.

Kaloula pulchra Gray, 1831. Zool. Misc., 1:38.
TYPE(S): Not traced.
TYPE LOCALITY: "China".
DISTRIBUTION: Southern China to Singapore; Borneo; Celebes; South India; Sri
   Lanka.
COMMENT: Apparently introduced into Borneo and Celebes (RFI). Sri Lanka
   population discussed by Kirtisinghe, 1957, Amph. Ceylon:78–80. See Berry,
   1975, Amph. Fauna Peninsular Malaysia:114–116, for account of Malayan
   population. Chinese population reviewed by Liu and Hu, 1961, Tailless
   Amph. China:293–295; see also Liu et al., 1973, Acta Zool. Sinica, 19:400–401,
   for Hainan population. Thailand population discussed by Taylor, 1962, Univ.
   Kansas Sci. Bull., 43:563–566.

Kaloula rigida Taylor, 1922. Philippine J. Sci., 21:176.
TYPE(S): Holotype: CAS 61475 (formerly EHT 7681).
TYPE LOCALITY: "Balbalan, Kalinga, Mountain Province, Luzon", Philippines.
DISTRIBUTION: Mountainous regions of Luzon, Philippines.

Kaloula rugifera Stejneger, 1924. Occas. Pap. Boston Soc. Nat. Hist., 5:119.
TYPE(S): Holotype: USNM 65520.
TYPE LOCALITY: Kiating, Szechwan [Sichuan, China].
DISTRIBUTION: Chengdu Plain and mountains to the west, Sichuan, China.
COMMENT: Reviewed by Liu, 1950, Fieldiana: Zool. Mem., 2:235–241.

Kaloula verrucosa (Boulenger, 1904). Ann. Mag. Nat. Hist., (7)13:131.
ORIGINAL NAME: *Callula verrucosa*.
TYPE(S): Syntypes: BM 1904.1.26.18–20, MCZ 2476 (2 specimens).
TYPE LOCALITY: Yunnan-fu [China].
DISTRIBUTION: Yunkwei Plateau of Sichuan, Yunnan, and Guizhou, China.
COMMENT: Reviewed by Liu and Hu, 1961, Tailless Amph. China:289–291.

Metaphrynella Parker, 1934. Monogr. Frogs Fam. Microhylidae:107.
TYPE SPECIES: *Phrynella pollicaris* Boulenger, 1890, by original designation.
DISTRIBUTION: Southern Malay Peninsula and Borneo.

Metaphrynella pollicaris (Boulenger, 1890). Proc. Zool. Soc. London, 1890:37.
ORIGINAL NAME: *Phrynella pollicaris*.
TYPE(S): Holotype: BM 87.7.30.16.
TYPE LOCALITY: Perak, 3,000 ft. [Malaysia (Malaya)].
DISTRIBUTION: Malay Peninsula.
COMMENT: Reviewed by Bourret, 1942, Batr. Indochine:503–505. See account by
Berry, 1975, Amph. Fauna Peninsular Malaysia:116–117

Metaphrynella sundana (Peters, 1867). Monatsber. Preuss. Akad. Wiss. Berlin, 1867:35.
ORIGINAL NAME: *Calohyla sundana*.
TYPE(S): Holotype: ZMB 5635.
TYPE LOCALITY: Pontianak, Borneo [West Kalimantan, Indonesia].
DISTRIBUTION: Western Borneo.
COMMENT: Reviewed by Inger, 1966, Fieldiana: Zool., 52:143–144.

Microhyla Tschudi, 1838. Classif. Batr.:71.
TYPE SPECIES: "*Hylaplesia achatina* Boie" (*nom. nud.*) (=*Microhyla achatina* Tschudi,
1838).
DISTRIBUTION: Ryukyu Is. (Japan) and China south through India to Sri Lanka and
through Southeast Asia to Sumatra, Borneo, Java, and Bali; ?Madagascar.
COMMENT: Taylor, 1962, Univ. Kansas Sci. Bull., 43:539–563, reviewed the species in
Thailand. Inger, 1966, Fieldiana: Zool., 52:145–155, reviewed the Bornean
species. Bourret, 1942, Batr. Indochine:508–529, reviewed the Indochinese
species. Liu and Hu, 1961, Tailless Amph. China:295–304, reviewed the Chinese
species.

Microhyla achatina Tschudi, 1838. Classif. Batr.:71.
TYPE(S): Syntypes: RMNH 1728 (5 specimens), WCAB (1 specimen), and MRHN (1
specimen).
TYPE LOCALITY: Java [Indonesia].
DISTRIBUTION: Java, below 1600 m.

Microhyla annamensis Smith, 1923. J. Nat. Hist. Soc. Siam, 6:47.
TYPE(S): Holotype: BM 1923.5.14.10.
TYPE LOCALITY: "Sui Kat, 1000 metres altitude, Langbian plateau, S. Annam",
Vietnam.
DISTRIBUTION: Southern Vietnam; Thailand.
COMMENT: Related to *Microhyla berdmorei*, according to the original description. See
comment under *Microhyla borneensis*.

Microhyla annectens Boulenger, 1900. Ann. Mag. Nat. Hist., (7)5:188.
TYPE(S): Syntypes: BM 1947.2.11.68–69 (formerly 1900.6.14.34–35).
TYPE LOCALITY: "Larut Hills, 4,000 feet", Perak, Malaysia (Malaya).
DISTRIBUTION: Peninsular Thailand and Malaya; Borneo.

COMMENT: See Berry, 1975, Amph. Fauna Peninsular Malaysia:117–118. See comment under *Microhyla borneensis*.

Microhyla berdmorei (Blyth, 1856). J. Asiat. Soc. Bengal, 24:720.
ORIGINAL NAME: *Engystoma berdmorei*.
TYPE(S): Not traced.
TYPE LOCALITY: Pegu, Burma.
DISTRIBUTION: Burma, northern Thailand, and Yunnan (China) through Laos and Cambodia to Malaya, Sumatra, and Borneo; Meghalaya, India (SD).
COMMENT: See Berry, 1975, Amph. Fauna Peninsular Malaysia:118–119. Synonymy includes *Microhyla fowleri* Taylor, 1934, Acad. Nat. Sci. Philadelphia, 86:284 (Holotype: ANSP 19903; Type locality: Cheng Mai, Thailand), according to Taylor, 1962, Univ. Kansas Sci. Bull., 43:560. SH and EZ regard *Microhyla fowleri* as a distinct species and regard its distribution as Thailand and Menyang, Yunnan, China.

Microhyla borneensis Parker, 1926. Ann. Mag. Nat. Hist., (10)2:473.
ORIGINAL NAME: *Microhyla borneense*.
TYPE(S): Holotype: BM 1947.2.11.82 (formerly 1911.1.30.43).
TYPE LOCALITY: Bidi District, Sarawak [Malaysia (Borneo)].
DISTRIBUTION: Borneo; Malay Peninsula.
COMMENT: See Berry, 1975, Amph. Fauna Peninsular Malaysia:119–120, and Dring, 1979, Bull. Brit. Mus. (Nat. Hist.), Zool., 34:194, who noted that the closest relatives are *Microhyla annectens* and *Microhyla annamensis*.

Microhyla butleri Boulenger, 1900. Ann. Mag. Nat. Hist., (7)6:188.
TYPE(S): Not traced.
TYPE LOCALITY: "Larut Hills at 4,000 feet", Perak, Malaya (Malaysia).
DISTRIBUTION: Southwestern and eastern China; Burma; Vietnam; Thailand; Malay Peninsula.
COMMENT: See Chang, 1947, Trans. Chinese Assoc. Adv. Sci., 9:97, and Berry, 1975, Amph. Fauna Peninsular Malaysia:120–121.

Microhyla chakrapanii Pillai, 1977. Proc. Indian Acad. Sci., (B)86:135.
TYPE(S): ZSIM.
TYPE LOCALITY: Mayabunder, North Andamans [India].
DISTRIBUTION: Andaman Is., India.

Microhyla fusca Andersson, 1943. Ark. Zool., 34A:9.
TYPE(S): Holotype: either NHRM or ZIUS.
TYPE LOCALITY: "Dalat", southern Vietnam.
DISTRIBUTION: Vietnam.

Microhyla heymonsi Vogt, 1911. Sitzungsber. Ges. Naturforsch. Freunde Berlin, 1911: 181.
TYPE(S): ZMB.
TYPE LOCALITY: Kosempo, Taiwan [China].
DISTRIBUTION: Southern China (including Hainan and Taiwan) through Southeast Asia (excluding Burma) to Malay Peninsula and Sumatra.
COMMENT: See Chan, 1977, Q. J. Taiwan Mus., 30:323–327; Chang, 1947, Trans. Chinese Assoc. Adv. Sci., 9:97; and Berry, 1975, Amph. Fauna Peninsular Malaysia:121–122.

Microhyla inornata Boulenger, 1890. Proc. Zool. Soc. London, 1890:37.
TYPE(S): Syntypes: BM 89.11.12.4, 89.11.12.30.
TYPE LOCALITY: Deli, Sumatra [Indonesia].
DISTRIBUTION: Burma and China (including Taiwan) to Malaya and Sumatra.
COMMENT: See Pillai, 1977, Proc. Indian Acad. Sci., (B)86:135, and Berry, 1975,

Amph. Fauna Peninsular Malaysia:122–123. Synonymy probably includes *Rana gracilipes* (MM).

Microhyla mixtura Liu and Hu, 1966. *In* Hu, Djao, and Liu, Acta Zool. Sinica, 18(1):79.
TYPE(S): Holotype: CIB (formerly SWIBASC) 610174.
TYPE LOCALITY: "Hua-ngo Shan, Wanyuan Hsien, Szechwan [=Sichuan], alt. 1,280 m", China.
DISTRIBUTION: Shaanxi, Sichuan, Guizhou, Hubei, and Anhui, China, 670–1594 m elev.

Microhyla ornata (Duméril and Bibron, 1841). Erp. Gén., 8:745.
ORIGINAL NAME: *Engystoma ornatum.*
TYPE(S): Holotype: MNHNP 505.
TYPE LOCALITY: "Malabar", India.
DISTRIBUTION: Ryukyu Is. (Japan), southern China (including Taiwan and Hainan) to India and Sri Lanka; Southeast Asia to Malay Peninsula.
COMMENT: See Kirtisinghe, 1957, Amph. Ceylon:88–90; Chang, 1947, Trans. Chinese Assoc. Adv. Sci., 9:98; Berry, 1975, Amph. Fauna Peninsular Malaysia: 123–124; and Liu, 1950, Fieldiana: Zool. Mem., 2:248–252.

Microhyla palmata Guibé, 1974 "1973". Bull. Mus. Natl. Hist. Nat., Paris, (Zool.)116: 1188.
TYPE(S): Holotype: MNHNP 1973-1146.
TYPE LOCALITY: Malagasy Republic, Chaînes Anosyennes, Ambanja.
DISTRIBUTION: Madagascar.
REVIEWER: Rose M. A. Blommers-Schlösser (RMABS).

Microhyla palmipes Boulenger, 1897. Ann. Mag. Nat. Hist., (6)19:108.
TYPE(S): Holotype: BM 96.12.3.40.
TYPE LOCALITY: "Pengalengan, Java, 4,000 ft.", Indonesia.
DISTRIBUTION: Malay Peninsula, Sumatra, Nias, Java, and Bali.
COMMENT: See Berry, 1975, Amph. Fauna Peninsular Malaysia:124–125.

Microhyla perparva Inger and Frogner, 1979. Sarawak Mus. J., 27:318.
TYPE(S): Holotype: FMNH 147917.
TYPE LOCALITY: "Labang Forest Reserve, Bintulu District, Sarawak", Malaysia (Borneo).
DISTRIBUTION: Sarawak, Malaysia (Borneo).

Microhyla petrigena Inger and Frogner, 1979. Sarawak Mus. J., 27:315.
TYPE(S): Holotype: FMNH 207705.
TYPE LOCALITY: "Nanga Tekalit, Kapit District, Sarawak", Malaysia (Borneo).
DISTRIBUTION: Sarawak, Malaysia (Borneo).

Microhyla picta Schenkel, 1901. Verh. Naturforsch. Ges. Basel, 13:144.
TYPE(S): Holotype: NHMB 1412.
TYPE LOCALITY: Cochin-China, Vietnam.
DISTRIBUTION: Southern Vietnam.

Microhyla pulchra (Hallowell, 1861 "1860"). Proc. Acad. Nat. Sci. Philadelphia, 12: 506.
ORIGINAL NAME: *Engystoma pulchrum.*
TYPE(S): Not traced.
TYPE LOCALITY: "Between Hong Kong and Whampoa [=Huang-Pu]", Guangdong, China.
DISTRIBUTION: Southern China (including Hainan I.) to Thailand.
COMMENT: See Chang, 1947, Trans. Chinese Assoc. Adv. Sci., 9:98.

Microhyla rubra (Jerdon, 1854). J. Asiat. Soc. Bengal, 22:534.
ORIGINAL NAME: *Engystoma rubrum*.
TYPE(S): Not traced.
TYPE LOCALITY: "The Carnatic", southern India.
DISTRIBUTION: Assam, southern India, and Sri Lanka.
COMMENT: See account by Kirtisinghe, 1957, Amph. Ceylon:92–94.

Microhyla superciliaris Parker, 1928. Ann. Mag. Nat. Hist., (10)2:486.
TYPE(S): Holotype: BM 1904.7.19.31.
TYPE LOCALITY: Batu Caves, Kuala Lumpur [Malaya, Malaysia].
DISTRIBUTION: Malaya and Sumatra.
COMMENT: See Berry, 1975, Amph. Fauna Peninsular Malaysia:125.

Microhyla zeylanica Parker and Hill, 1949. Ann. Mag. Nat. Hist., (12)1:759.
TYPE(S): Holotype: BM 1948.1.1.3.
TYPE LOCALITY: Bopatalawa, Central Province, Sri Lanka.
DISTRIBUTION: Sri Lanka.
COMMENT: Reviewed by Kirtisinghe, 1957, Amph. Ceylon:90–92.

Myersiella Carvalho, 1954. Occas. Pap. Mus. Zool. Univ. Michigan, 555:16.
TYPE SPECIES: *Engystoma subnigrum* Miranda-Ribeiro, 1920 (=*Engystoma microps*
    Duméril and Bibron, 1841), by original designation.
DISTRIBUTION: As for the single species.
COMMENT: Probably derived from *Elachistocleis* according to Carvalho, 1954, Occas.
    Pap. Mus. Zool. Univ. Michigan, 555:17. See Nelson and Lescure, 1975,
    Herpetologica, 31:391, for a review of the genus and of its single species.

Myersiella microps (Duméril and Bibron, 1841). Erp. Gén., 8:744.
ORIGINAL NAME: *Engystoma microps*.
TYPE(S): Not stated; MNHNP 5034 recorded as holotype.
TYPE LOCALITY: "Brésil"; restricted to "Rio de Janeiro", Rio de Janeiro, Brazil, by
    Nelson and Lescure, 1975, Herpetologica, 31:391.
DISTRIBUTION: Low and moderate elevations in Espírito Santo and Rio de Janeiro;
    Serra do Mar in São Paulo, Brazil.
COMMENT: See generic comment.

Otophryne Boulenger, 1900. *In* Lankester, Trans. Linn. Soc. London, (2)8:55.
TYPE SPECIES: *Otophryne robusta* Boulenger, 1900, by original designation.
DISTRIBUTION: As for the single species.
COMMENT: See comment under *Otophryne robusta*.

Otophryne robusta Boulenger, 1900. *In* Lankester, Trans. Linn. Soc. London, (2)8:55.
TYPE(S): Not stated; BM 99.3.25.18 recorded as holotype.
TYPE LOCALITY: "foot of Mt. Roraima, 3,500 ft.", Guyana.
DISTRIBUTION: Northern South America: eastern Colombia through Venezuela and
    Guyana to Amapá, Brazil.
COMMENT: On the basis of karyology, Bogart, Pyburn, and Nelson, 1976,
    Herpetologica, 32:210, suggested that *Otophryne robusta* is not closely allied to
    other New World microhylines, a suggestion possibly supported by the
    toothed larva described by Pyburn, 1980, Pap. Avulsos Zool., São Paulo, 33:
    231–238. See Rivero, 1968 "1967", Caribb. J. Sci., 7:155, for subspecies.

Phrynella Boulenger, 1887. Ann. Mag. Nat. Hist., (5)19:346.
TYPE SPECIES: *Phrynella pulchra* Boulenger, 1887.
DISTRIBUTION: As for the single species.

Phrynella pulchra Boulenger, 1887. Ann. Mag. Nat. Hist., (5)19:346.
TYPE(S): Syntypes: BM 1947.2.11.36–37 (formerly 86.12.28.39–40).
TYPE LOCALITY: Malacca [Malaya, Malaysia].
DISTRIBUTION: Malay Peninsula, Sumatra, and the Mentawei Is.

COMMENT: See Bourret, 1942, Batr. Indochine:501–503, for synonymy and review.

Ramanella Rao and Ramanna, 1925. Proc. Zool. Soc. London, 1925:1445.
   TYPE SPECIES: *Ramanella symbioitica* Rao and Ramanna, 1925 (in error for *symbiotica*)
      (=*Callula variegata* Stoliczka, 1872).
   DISTRIBUTION: Southeastern India and Sri Lanka.
   COMMENT: The species described by Rao, 1937, Proc. Indian Acad. Sci., (B)6, are of
      doubtful validity and the types are probably no longer in existence. Rao's
      illustrations depict somewhat desiccated specimens (RFI).

Ramanella anamalaiensis Rao, 1937. Proc. Indian Acad. Sci., (B)6:420.
   TYPE(S): CCB; probably lost (SD).
   TYPE LOCALITY: "Base of Anamallai Hills, Coimbatore District", Tamil Nadu, South
      India.
   DISTRIBUTION: Known only from the type.

Ramanella minor Rao, 1937. Proc. Indian Acad. Sci., (B)6:417.
   TYPE(S): CCB; probably lost (SD).
   TYPE LOCALITY: "Saklespur, Hassan District", South India.
   DISTRIBUTION: Known only from the type.

Ramanella montana (Jerdon, 1854). J. Asiat. Soc. Bengal, 22:533.
   ORIGINAL NAME: *Hylaedactylus montanus*.
   TYPE(S): Not traced.
   TYPE LOCALITY: "Mountain streams in Wynaad", South India.
   DISTRIBUTION: From near Bombay to Kerala, India.

Ramanella mormorata Rao, 1937. Proc. Indian Acad. Sci., (B)6:419.
   TYPE(S): CCB; probably lost (SD).
   TYPE LOCALITY: "Saklespur, Hassan District", South India.
   DISTRIBUTION: Known only from the type.

Ramanella obscura (Günther, 1864). Rept. Brit. India:438.
   ORIGINAL NAME: *Callula obscura*.
   TYPE(S): Holotype: BM 58.11.28.42.
   TYPE LOCALITY: "Ceylon" (=Sri Lanka).
   DISTRIBUTION: Sri Lanka.
   COMMENT: Reviewed by Kirtisinghe, 1957, Amph. Ceylon:82–83.

Ramanella palmata Parker, 1934. Monogr. Frogs Fam. Microhylidae:93.
   TYPE(S): Holotype: BM 90.11.8.62.
   TYPE LOCALITY: "Newere Ellya, 7,000 ft.", Sri Lanka.
   DISTRIBUTION: Sri Lanka.
   COMMENT: Discussed by Kirtisinghe, 1957, Amph. Ceylon:81–82.

Ramanella triangularis (Günther, 1875). Proc. Zool. Soc. London, 1875:576.
   ORIGINAL NAME: *Callula triangularis*.
   TYPE(S): Syntypes: BM 74.4.29.891–900, 74.4.29.1010.
   TYPE LOCALITY: Malabar [Kerala, India].
   DISTRIBUTION: Southwestern India.

Ramanella variegata (Stoliczka, 1872). Proc. Asiat. Soc. Bengal, 1872:111.
   ORIGINAL NAME: *Callula variegata*.
   TYPE(S): Syntypes: including NHMW 4019.
   TYPE LOCALITY: Ellore [=Eluru, Andhra Pradesh, India].
   DISTRIBUTION: Southeastern India; Sri Lanka.
   COMMENT: Reviewed by Kirtisinghe, 1957, Amph. Ceylon:83–85.

Relictivomer Carvalho, 1954. Occas. Pap. Mus. Zool. Univ. Michigan, 555:13.
TYPE SPECIES: *Hypopachus pearsei* Ruthven, 1914, by original designation.
DISTRIBUTION: As for the single species.
COMMENT: See comment under *Elachistocleis*. Possibly derived from *Dermatonotus* and
ancestral to *Elachistocleis* according to Carvalho, 1954, Occas. Pap. Mus. Zool.
Univ. Michigan, 555:14.

Relictivomer pearsei (Ruthven, 1914). Proc. Biol. Soc. Washington, 27:77.
ORIGINAL NAME: *Hypopachus pearsei*.
TYPE(S): Holotype: UMMZ 45571.
TYPE LOCALITY: "Fundacion, [Sierra Santa Marta,] Colombia".
DISTRIBUTION: Colombia and Panama.

Stereocyclops Cope, 1870 "1869". Proc. Am. Philos. Soc., 11:165.
TYPE SPECIES: *Stereocyclops incrassatus* Cope, 1870, by monotypy.
DISTRIBUTION: As for the single species.
COMMENT: Most closely allied to (and morphologically more primitive than)
Hyophryne and *Ctenophryne*, according to Carvalho, 1954, Occas. Pap. Mus. Zool.
Univ. Michigan, 555:4.

Stereocyclops incrassatus Cope, 1870 "1869". Proc. Am. Philos. Soc., 11:165.
TYPE(S): Holotype: MCZ 855.
TYPE LOCALITY: "Sao Matheos, [Espírito Santo,] south of Rio de Janeiro, Brazil" (see
comment).
DISTRIBUTION: Humid coastal forests in eastern Brazil from Espírito Santo to Bahia.
COMMENT: See Cochran, 1954, Bull. U.S. Natl. Mus., 206:371–372, for synonymy
and review. Carvalho, 1948, Bol. Mus. Nac., Rio de Janeiro, N.S., Zool., 84:1–
13, showed this species to be separate from *Hypopachus mülleri* (=*Dermatonotus
muelleri*), stated that the type was collected in the littoral of Espírito Santo,
and unscrambled the synonymies of the two species. *Stereocyclops hypomelas*
(Miranda-Ribeiro, 1920) is probably a distinct species, based on unpublished
data of Albuquerque (WCAB).

Synapturanus Carvalho, 1954. Occas. Pap. Mus. Zool. Univ. Michigan, 555:17.
TYPE SPECIES: *Engystoma microps* Duméril and Bibron, 1841 (=*Synapturanus
mirandaribeiroi* Nelson and Lescure, 1975), by original designation; see comment
under *Synapturanus mirandaribeiroi*.
DISTRIBUTION: Colombia east through the Guianas to northern Brazil.
COMMENT: Closely related to *Elachistocleis* and *Myersiella* according to Carvalho, 1954,
Occas. Pap. Mus. Zool. Univ. Michigan, 555:18. See Nelson and Lescure, 1975,
Herpetologica, 31:389–397, for a discussion of the taxonomic history and
literature of this genus.

Synapturanus mirandaribeiroi Nelson and Lescure, 1975. Herpetologica, 31:394.
TYPE(S): Holotype: MZUSP 49891.
TYPE LOCALITY: "Kanashen (a Waiwai Indian village and mission) on the upper
Essequibo River, Rupununi District, Guyana".
DISTRIBUTION: Northern Brazil, Colombia, and the Guianas in humid tropical
forests at low elevations.
COMMENT: The specimens that Carvalho, 1954, Occas. Pap. Mus. Zool. Univ.
Michigan, 555:17, misidentified as *Engystoma microps* (=*Myersiella microps*)
were, in fact, an unnamed species named *Synapturanus mirandaribeiroi* by
Nelson and Lescure, 1965, Herpetologica, 31:394; the distribution they cited
has not been reviewed since the newer species have been described.

Synapturanus rabus Pyburn, 1976. Herpetologica, 32:367.
TYPE(S): Holotype: USNM 199674.
TYPE LOCALITY: "S side of the Vaupés River near the village of Yapima (long. 69°
28' W, lat. 1° 03' N), Colombia".
DISTRIBUTION: Southeastern Vaupés, Colombia.

Synapturanus salseri Pyburn, 1975. Herpetologica, 31:440.
TYPE(S): Holotype: UTA A-4011.
TYPE LOCALITY: "Timbó, Vaupés", Colombia.
DISTRIBUTION: Known only from the type locality.

Syncope Walker, 1973. Occas. Pap. Mus. Nat. Hist. Univ. Kansas, 20:1.
TYPE SPECIES: *Syncope antenori* Walker, 1973, by original designation.
DISTRIBUTION: Eastern versant of Ecuador and Peru.

Syncope antenori Walker, 1973. Occas. Pap. Mus. Nat. Hist. Univ. Kansas, 20:3.
TYPE(S): Holotype: KU 124009.
TYPE LOCALITY: "Puerto Libre, Río Aguarico, 570 m, Provincia Napo, Ecuador".
DISTRIBUTION: Napo and Pastaza, Ecuador; Loreto, Peru.

Syncope carvalhoi Nelson, 1975. J. Herpetol., 9:81.
TYPE(S): Holotype: MZUSP 36429.
TYPE LOCALITY: "Rio Ampi-Yacú [=Amphiyacú], Estirón, Loreto, Peru".
DISTRIBUTION: Known only from the type locality.

Uperodon Duméril and Bibron, 1841. Erp. Gén., 8:746.
TYPE SPECIES: *Engystoma marmoratum* Cuvier, 1829 (=*Rana systoma* Schneider, 1799).
DISTRIBUTION: India; Sri Lanka.

Uperodon globulosus (Günther, 1864). Rept. Brit. India:416.
ORIGINAL NAME: *Cacopus globulosus.*
TYPE(S): Holotype: BM 62.12.29.4.
TYPE LOCALITY: Russelconda, Orissa, India.
DISTRIBUTION: Bengal and Orissa to Gujarat, southward to Karnataka, India.

Uperodon systoma (Schneider, 1799). Hist. Amph., 1:144.
ORIGINAL NAME: *Rana systoma.*
TYPE(S): Not traced.
TYPE LOCALITY: Eastern India.
DISTRIBUTION: Southern and Eastern India as far north as the valley of the Ganges; Sri Lanka.
COMMENT: Reviewed by Kirtisinghe, 1957, Amph. Ceylon:85–87. Böhme and Bischoff, 1984, Bonn. Zool. Monogr., 19:183, removed *Pachybatrachus petersii* Keferstein, 1868, Arch. Naturgesch., 34:274 (Holotype: ZMFK 28388; Type locality: "Neu-Sud-Wales", Australia), on the basis of type locality and collector. Cogger, Cameron, and Cogger, 1983, Zool. Cat. Aust., 1(Amph. Rept.):261, listed *Pachybatrachus petersii* as a *species inquirenda* under "Microhylidae ?".

SUBFAMILY: **Phrynomerinae** Noble, 1931.
CITATION: Biol. Amph.:538.
DISTRIBUTION: Subsaharan Africa.
COMMENT: Considered by many authors to constitute a unique family, the Phrynomeridae, based on intercalary elements.
REVIEWERS: Alan Channing (AC); Kim M. Howell (KMH) (East Africa); Raymond Laurent (RL); John C. Poynton (JCP).

Phrynomerus Noble, 1926. Am. Mus. Novit., 237:20.
TYPE SPECIES: *Brachymerus bifasciatus* Smith, 1847, by monotypy.
DISTRIBUTION: Subsaharan Africa.
COMMENT: *Phrynomerus* is a replacement name for *Brachymerus* Smith, 1847, Illustr. Zool. S. Afr., Rept.:63, which is preoccupied.

Phrynomerus affinis (Boulenger, 1901). Ann. Mus. R. Congo Belge, Tervuren, Zool., (1)2:6.
   ORIGINAL NAME: *Phrynomantis affinis.*
   TYPE(S): RGMC.
   TYPE LOCALITY: Pweto, Lake Mweru, Zaire.
   DISTRIBUTION: Shaba (Zaire) to northern Namibia and Zambia.

Phrynomerus annectens (Werner, 1910). *In* Schultze, Denkschr. Med. Naturwiss. Ges. Jena, 16:294.
   ORIGINAL NAME: *Phrynomantis annectens.*
   TYPE(S): Not traced.
   TYPE LOCALITY: Aar River, Cape Province [in error, actually in Namibia].
   DISTRIBUTION: Angola to northwestern Cape Province (Rep. South Africa).

Phrynomerus bifasciatus (Smith, 1847). Illustr. Zool. S. Afr., Rept.:pl. 63.
   ORIGINAL NAME: *Brachymerus bifasciatus.*
   TYPE(S): Not traced; Smith's material in BM may be syntypes (JCP).
   TYPE LOCALITY: "country to the east and north-east of the Cape Colony", Rep. South Africa.
   DISTRIBUTION: Somalia and Shaba (Zaire) to Rep. South Africa.
   COMMENT: See comment under *Phrynomerus microps.*

Phrynomerus microps (Peters, 1875). Monatsber. Preuss. Akad. Wiss. Berlin, 1875:210.
   ORIGINAL NAME: *Phrynomantis microps.*
   TYPE(S): ZMB.
   TYPE LOCALITY: Accra [Ghana].
   DISTRIBUTION: Savannas of West and Central Africa to Zaire.
   COMMENT: Regarded by some authors (e.g., Poynton, 1964, Ann. Natal Mus., 17:86) as conspecific with *Phrynomerus bifasciatus.*

SUBFAMILY: **Scaphiophryninae** Laurent, 1946.
   CITATION: Rev. Zool. Bot. Afr., 39:337.
   DISTRIBUTION: Madagascar.
   COMMENT: Although considered a subfamily of the Ranidae by most authors, Guibé, 1956, Bull. Mus. Natl. Hist. Nat., Paris, (2)28:180–182, suggested that the Scaphiophryninae actually belonged with the Microhylidae, an arrangement followed by Dubois, 1981, Monit. Zool. Ital., N.S., Suppl., 15:225–284. Blommers-Schlösser, 1975, Beaufortia, 24(309):7–26, noted that scaphiophrynine larvae show derived features of the Microhylidae, and summarized the literature of the controversy. Wassersug, 1984, Herpetologica, 40:138–148, provided more data on tadpole morphology which supported Blommers-Schlösser's position. Savage, 1973, *In* Vial (ed.), Evol. Biol. Anurans, included this subfamily in the Hyperoliidae with no discussion.
   CONTRIBUTOR: Rose M. A. Blommers-Schlösser (RMABS).

Pseudohemisus Mocquard, 1895. Bull. Soc. Philomath. Paris, 8(7):108.
   TYPE SPECIES: *Hemisus obscurus* Grandidier, 1872, by original designation.
   DISTRIBUTION: Madagascar.
   COMMENT: See Guibé, 1978, Bonn. Zool. Monogr., 11:105, for discussion of taxonomic status and synonymies. See nomenclatural comment under *Hemisus.*

Pseudohemisus calcaratum (Mocquard, 1895). Bull. Soc. Philomath. Paris, 8(7):108.
   ORIGINAL NAME: *Calophrynus calcaratus.*
   TYPE(S): Syntypes: MNHNP 1895-294.
   TYPE LOCALITY: Madagascar.
   DISTRIBUTION: Southern and western Madagascar.

Pseudohemisus granulosum Guibé, 1952. Mem. Inst. Sci. Madagascar, 7(1A):109.
ORIGINAL NAME: *Pseudohemisus granulosus.*
TYPE(S): Holotype: MNHNP 1953-238.
TYPE LOCALITY: Grotte d'Andranoboka, Bay Mahajamba, north of Majunga, western Madagascar.
DISTRIBUTION: Western Madagascar.

Pseudohemisus madagascariense (Boulenger, 1882). Cat. Batr. Sal. Brit. Mus.:472.
ORIGINAL NAME: *Calophrynus madagascariensis.*
TYPE(S): Holotype: BM 1947.2.7.41.
TYPE LOCALITY: "East Betsileo", Madagascar.
DISTRIBUTION: Andringitra Mountains, Madagascar.

Pseudohemisus obscurum (Grandidier, 1872). Ann. Sci. Nat., Paris, 5(15):11.
ORIGINAL NAME: *Hemisus obscurus.*
TYPE(S): Holotype: MNHNP 1895-280.
TYPE LOCALITY: Northwestern Madagascar.
DISTRIBUTION: Madagascar.
COMMENT: Guibé, 1978, Bonn. Zool. Monogr., 11:110, considered the status of this species dubious.

Pseudohemisus pustulosum Angel and Guibé, 1945. Bull. Soc. Zool. France, 70:153.
ORIGINAL NAME: *Pseudohemisus pustulosus.*
TYPE(S): Holotype: MNHNP 1945-25.
TYPE LOCALITY: Madagascar.
DISTRIBUTION: Ankaratra Mountains, central Madagascar.

Pseudohemisus verrucosum Angel, 1930. Bull. Mus. Natl. Hist. Nat., Paris, (2)2:70.
ORIGINAL NAME: *Pseudohemisus verrucosus.*
TYPE(S): Syntypes: MNHNP 1929-231 to 1929-235.
TYPE LOCALITY: Lavenambato, region Tulear, Madagascar.
DISTRIBUTION: Southwestern Madagascar.
COMMENT: Guibé, 1978, Bonn. Zool. Monogr., 11:110, considered the status of this species dubious.

Scaphiophryne Boulenger, 1882. Cat. Batr. Sal. Brit. Mus.:472.
TYPE SPECIES: *Scaphiophryne marmorata* Boulenger, 1882, by original designation.
DISTRIBUTION: Madagascar.
COMMENT: See Guibé, 1978, Bonn. Zool. Monogr., 11:110, for review and synonymies.

Scaphiophryne marmorata Boulenger, 1882. Cat. Batr. Sal. Brit. Mus.:472.
TYPE(S): Holotype: BM 1947.2.30.81.
TYPE LOCALITY: "East Betsileo", Madagascar.
DISTRIBUTION: Eastern forest of Madagascar.

FAMILY: **Myobatrachidae** Schlegel, 1850.
CITATION: Proc. Zool. Soc. London, 1850:9.
DISTRIBUTION: Mainland Australia and Tasmania; New Guinea.
COMMENT: The subfamilial classification followed here was developed by Lynch, 1971, Misc. Publ. Mus. Nat. Hist. Univ. Kansas, 53:1–238; Tyler, 1972, Zool. Meded., Leiden, 47:193–201; Lynch, 1973, In Vial (ed.), Evol. Biol. Anurans:133–182; Blake, 1973, Aust. J. Zool., 21:119–149; and Tyler, Martin, and Davies, 1977, Aust. J. Zool., 27:135–150. An alternate view of subfamilial relationships was presented by Heyer and Liem, 1976, Smithson. Contrib. Zool., 233:1–29, but this view was rejected by Farris, Kluge, and Mickevich, 1982, Syst. Zool., 31:317–327. The view that the Myobatrachidae is a distinct family was developed by Lynch, 1973, In Vial (ed.), Evol. Biol. Anurans:132–182, and Heyer and Liem, 1976, Smithson. Contrib. Zool., 233:1–29. According to Lynch, 1973, the Myobatrachidae is a paraphyletic grade (see comments under Limnodynastinae and Myobatrachinae), at the base of the bufonoid-ranoid radiation. Tyler, 1979, Monogr. Mus. Nat. Hist. Univ. Kansas. 7:94–

96, argued that the case for recognition of the Myobatrachidae requires substantiation. The refusal of Tyler and Davies to recognize the Myobatrachidae as distinct from the Leptodactylidae rests on the lack of other than biogeography to diagnose the family. JDL notes that evidence for the monophyly of this nominal family has yet to be presented and regards the recognition of this family as misleading. Many Australian workers still consider the Myobatrachidae to be part of the Leptodactylidae. For synonymies see Gorham, 1966, Das Tierreich, 85:32–222, who considered this family to be part of the Leptodactylidae as did Lynch, 1971, Misc. Publ. Univ. Kansas Mus. Nat. Hist., 53:1–238, who reviewed the taxonomy and evolutionary relationships of the group. Literature reviews and synonymies for the Australian taxa can be found in Cogger, Cameron, and Cogger, 1983, Zool. Cat. Aust., 1(Amph. Rept.):12–54.

CONTRIBUTOR: Michael J. Tyler (MJT).
REVIEWERS: Margaret Davies (MD); William E. Duellman (WED); Marinus S. Hoogmoed (MSH).

SUBFAMILY: **Limnodynastinae** Lynch, 1971.
  CITATION: Misc. Publ. Mus. Nat. Hist. Univ. Kansas, 53:83.
  DISTRIBUTION: Australia and New Guinea, including Aru Is.
  COMMENT: With the removal of *Cyclorana* (see comment under *Cyclorana* [Pelodryadinae: Hylidae]), the name Cycloraninae was replaced by the Limnodynastinae. According to Lynch, 1973, *In* Vial (ed.), Evol. Biol. Anurans: 133–182, the Cycloraninae (=Limnodynastinae) plus the Heleophryninae (=Heleophrynidae of this list) are phylogenetically closer to the other bufonoid families than to the Myobatrachinae.

Adelotus Ogilby, 1907. Proc. R. Soc. Queensland, 20:32.
  TYPE SPECIES: *Cryptotis brevis* Günther, 1863, by monotypy.
  DISTRIBUTION: As for the single species.
  COMMENT: *Adelotus* is a replacement name for *Cryptotis* Günther, 1863, Ann. Mag. Nat. Hist., (3)11:27, which is preoccupied by *Cryptotis* Pommel, 1848 (Mammalia: Insectivora).

Adelotus brevis (Günther, 1863). Ann. Mag. Nat. Hist., (3)11:27.
  ORIGINAL NAME: *Cryptotis brevis*.
  TYPE(S): Holotype: BM 1947.2.20.3 (formerly 63.6.16.95).
  TYPE LOCALITY: Clarence River, New South Wales [Australia].
  DISTRIBUTION: Great Dividing Range and coast from central-eastern Queensland to southern New South Wales, Australia.

Heleioporus Gray, 1841. Ann. Mag. Nat. Hist., (1)7:91.
  TYPE SPECIES: *Heleioporus albopunctatus* Gray, 1841, by monotypy.
  DISTRIBUTION: Southern Western Australia, southwestern New South Wales, and eastern Victoria, Australia.
  COMMENT: Reviewed by Lee, 1967, Aust. J. Zool., 15:367–439.

Heleioporus albopunctatus Gray, 1841. Ann. Mag. Nat. Hist., (1)7:91.
  TYPE(S): Holotype: BM 1947.2.19.19 (formerly 41.2.211).
  TYPE LOCALITY: Western Australia.
  DISTRIBUTION: Restricted to coast and ranges of southwestern Australia from the Murchison River south to Tambellup and east to Frank Hann National Park, Australia.

Heleioporus australiacus (Shaw, 1795). Nat. Misc., 6:pl. 200.
  ORIGINAL NAME: *Rana australiaca*.
  TYPE(S): According to Lee, 1967, Aust. J. Zool., 15:389, the "original description based on drawing sent from Australia".
  TYPE LOCALITY: New Holland [Australia].
  DISTRIBUTION: Coast and ranges from central coast of New South Wales to eastern Victoria, Australia.

Heleioporus barycragus Lee, 1967. Aust. J. Zool., 15:390.
TYPE(S): Holotype: WAM R21869.
TYPE LOCALITY: "Boya", Western Australia.
DISTRIBUTION: Darling Range and foothills east of Perth, Western Australia.

Heleioporus eyrei (Gray, 1845). *In* Eyre, J. Exped. Discov. Cent. Aust., 1:407.
ORIGINAL NAME: *Perialia eyrei*.
TYPE(S): Syntypes: BM 1947.2.19.80–83 (formerly 43.5.19.71–74).
TYPE LOCALITY: "On the banks of the River Murray", Western Australia, Australia.
DISTRIBUTION: Southwestern Australia coastal plain, extending into the Darling
    Range, from just below Geraldton in the north to Esperance in the east.

Heleioporus inornatus Lee and Main, 1954. West. Aust. Nat., 4:157.
TYPE(S): Holotype: WAM R11428.
TYPE LOCALITY: Beechina, Western Australia.
DISTRIBUTION: Darling Range in southwestern Western Australia.

Heleioporus psammophilus Lee and Main, 1954. West. Aust. Nat., 4:157.
TYPE(S): Holotype: WAM R11427.
TYPE LOCALITY: Beechina, Western Australia.
DISTRIBUTION: Coast and western edge of Darling Scarp from Dongara region to
    Esperance, Western Australia.

Kyarranus Moore, 1958. Am. Mus. Novit., 1919:1.
TYPE SPECIES: *Kyarranus sphagnicolus* Moore, 1958, by original designation.
DISTRIBUTION: New South Wales and Queensland, Australia.
COMMENT: Cogger, Cameron, and Cogger, 1983, Zool. Cat. Aust., 1(Amph. Rept.):24,
    considered *Kyarranus* to be a junior synonym of *Philoria* but provided no
    evidence or discussion.

Kyarranus kundagungan Ingram and Corben, 1975. Mem. Queensland Mus., 17:335.
TYPE(S): Holotype: QM J23944.
TYPE LOCALITY: Mistake Mountains (27° 53′ S, 152° 21′ E) 83 km SW Brisbane,
    southeast Queensland [Australia].
DISTRIBUTION: Great Dividing Range from Mistake Mountains south to Teviot Falls,
    Queensland, Australia.

Kyarranus loveridgei (Parker, 1940). Novit. Zool., 42:60.
ORIGINAL NAME: *Philoria loveridgei*.
TYPE(S): Holotype: BM 1947.2.19.94 (formerly 1933.4.8.6).
TYPE LOCALITY: McPherson Range, southern Queensland [Australia].
DISTRIBUTION: North-central New South Wales and southeastern Queensland,
    Australia.

Kyarranus sphagnicolus Moore, 1958. Am. Mus. Novit., 1919:4.
TYPE(S): Holotype: AM R16005.
TYPE LOCALITY: Point Lookout, near Ebor, New South Wales [Australia].
DISTRIBUTION: Northern New South Wales, Australia.

Lechriodus Boulenger, 1882. Cat. Batr. Sal. Brit. Mus.:116.
TYPE SPECIES: *Asterophrys melanopyga* Doria, 1875, by monotypy.
DISTRIBUTION: New Guinea; eastern Australia; Aru Is.
COMMENT: Reviewed by Zweifel, 1972, Am. Mus. Novit., 2507:1–41, who also
    discussed phylogeny within the genus.
REVIEWER: Richard G. Zweifel (RGZ).

Lechriodus aganoposis Zweifel, 1972. Am. Mus. Novit., 2507:3.
TYPE(S): Holotype: AMNH 75791.
TYPE LOCALITY: "Numbut, Mt. Rawlinson, ca. 4200 ft. (ca. 1280 m.), Morobe
District, Territory of Papua-New Guinea" (Morobe Province, Papua New
Guinea).
DISTRIBUTION: Huon Peninsula and along the central mountainous spine of New
Guinea from Purosa (Eastern Highlands Province, Papua New Guinea) west
to the Sibil Valley (Irian Jaya, Indonesia).

Lechriodus fletcheri (Boulenger, 1890). Proc. Linn. Soc. New South Wales, (2)5:594.
ORIGINAL NAME: *Phanerotis fletcheri.*
TYPE(S): Holotype: BM 1947.2.18.67 (formerly 1890.7.28.1).
TYPE LOCALITY: Dunoon, Richmond River, New South Wales [Australia].
DISTRIBUTION: Eastern New South Wales to southeastern Queensland, Australia.
COMMENT: According to Zweifel, 1972, Am. Mus. Novit., 2507:20, the records of
this species from New Guinea are based on misidentified *Lechriodus
melanopyga*. McDonald and Miller, 1982, Trans. R. Soc. S. Aust., 106:220,
demonstrated that the single record from north Queensland (Australia) is
erroneous.

Lechriodus melanopyga (Doria, 1875). Ann. Mus. Civ. Stor. Nat. Genova, 6:355.
ORIGINAL NAME: *Asterophrys melanopyga.*
TYPE(S): Holotype: MSNG 29736.
TYPE LOCALITY: Wokan, Aru Islands [Indonesia].
DISTRIBUTION: Aru Is. and northern, southern, and eastern New Guinea.

Lechriodus platyceps Parker, 1940. Novit. Zool., 42:28.
TYPE(S): Holotype: BM 76.7.18.6.
TYPE LOCALITY: "Arfak, Dutch New Guinea", Irian Jaya, Indonesia.
DISTRIBUTION: Western and central New Guinea.

Limnodynastes Fitzinger, 1843. Syst. Rept.:31.
TYPE SPECIES: *Cystignathus peronii* Duméril and Bibron, 1843, by original designation.
DISTRIBUTION: Australia and southern New Guinea.
COMMENT: The most recent generic reviews are by Parker, 1940, Novit. Zool., 42:42,
and Lynch, 1971, Misc. Publ. Mus. Nat. Hist. Univ. Kansas, 53:86.

Limnodynastes convexiusculus (Macleay, 1877). Proc. Linn. Soc. New South Wales, 2:
135.
ORIGINAL NAME: *Ranaster convexiusculus.*
TYPE(S): Not traced; presumed lost by Cogger, Cameron, and Cogger, 1983, Zool.
Cat. Aust., 1(Amph. Rept.):17.
TYPE LOCALITY: Katow, British New Guinea [Papua New Guinea]; stated as
"Mawatta, Binaturi River, near Daru, Papua New Guinea (as Katow)" by
Cogger, Cameron, and Cogger, 1983, Zool. Cat. Aust., 1(Amph. Rept.):17.
DISTRIBUTION: Southern New Guinea; northern Australia from Western Australia to
Queensland, Australia.

Limnodynastes depressus Tyler, 1976. Rec. W. Aust. Mus., 4:50.
TYPE(S): Holotype: WAM R43896.
TYPE LOCALITY: Near the former site of the Argyle Down homestead, Ord River,
Western Australia.
DISTRIBUTION: Known only from the type locality now beneath Lake Argyle, Ord
River, Kimberley Division, Western Australia.

Limnodynastes dorsalis (Gray, 1841). Ann. Mag. Nat. Hist., (1)7:91.
ORIGINAL NAME: *Cystignathus dorsalis.*
TYPE(S): Holotype: BM 1947.2.19.7 (formerly 41.(2).212).
TYPE LOCALITY: Western Australia.
DISTRIBUTION: Southwestern corner of Western Australia.

COMMENT: Prior to the revision of Martin, 1972, Aust. J. Zool., 20:170, *Limnodynastes dumerilii* was included in the synonymy of this species.

Limnodynastes dumerilii Peters, 1863. Monatsber. Preuss. Akad. Wiss. Berlin, 1863:235.
ORIGINAL NAME: *Limnodynastes (Platyplectron) dumerilii.*
TYPE(S): Syntypes: AMNH 23590, ZMB 4727 (3 specimens), 4728 (3 specimens).
TYPE LOCALITY: Buchsfelde [=Loos] near Gawler, South Australia.
DISTRIBUTION: Tasmania; southeastern South Australia through Victoria and eastern New South Wales to southeastern Queensland, Australia.
COMMENT: See comment under *Limnodynastes dorsalis.*

Limnodynastes fletcheri Boulenger, 1888. Ann. Mag. Nat. Hist., (6)2:142.
TYPE(S): Syntypes: BM 1947.2.19.9–10 (formerly 88.7.3.7–8).
TYPE LOCALITY: Guntawang, near Mudgee, New South Wales [Australia].
DISTRIBUTION: Western New South Wales and southeastern Queensland, west of the Great Dividing Range, extending into Victoria and along the River Murray into South Australia, Australia.
COMMENT: Reviewed by Moore, 1961, Bull. Am. Mus. Nat. Hist., 121:208.

Limnodynastes interioris Fry, 1913. Rec. Aust. Mus., 10:33.
ORIGINAL NAME: *Limnodynastes dorsalis interioris.*
TYPE(S): Holotype: AM R5869.
TYPE LOCALITY: Merool Creek, Riverina, New South Wales [Australia].
DISTRIBUTION: Central New South Wales, west of the Great Dividing Range and south to the Murray River, Australia.
COMMENT: Considered a distinct species by Martin, 1967, Aust. J. Zool., 20:183, who also reviewed this species.

Limnodynastes ornatus (Gray, 1842). Zool. Misc.:56.
ORIGINAL NAME: *Discoglossus ornatus.*
TYPE(S): Holotype: BM 1947.2.19.11 (formerly 42.2.24.17).
TYPE LOCALITY: Port Essington [Northern Territory, Australia].
DISTRIBUTION: Throughout northern half of New South Wales (from coast of far west), Queensland, northern half of Northern Territory, and northwestern Western Australia, Australia.

Limnodynastes peronii (Duméril and Bibron, 1841). Erp. Gén., 8:409.
ORIGINAL NAME: *Cystignathus peronii.*
TYPE(S): Syntypes: MNHNP 4499 (2 specimens); MNHNP 4500 cited erroneously as holotype by Guibé, 1950 "1948", Cat. Types Amph. Mus. Natl. Hist. Nat.: 41, according to Cogger, Cameron, and Cogger, 1983, Zool. Cat. Aust., 1(Amph. Rept.):19.
TYPE LOCALITY: "Nouvelle-Hollande?" (=Australia).
DISTRIBUTION: Queensland, New South Wales, Victoria, southeastern South Australia, and Tasmania, Australia.
COMMENT: See Moore, 1961, Bull. Am. Mus. Nat. Hist., 121:197, for a review of this species.

Limnodynastes salmini Steindachner, 1867. Reise Freg. Novara, Amph.:27.
TYPE(S): Syntypes: NHMW 14849 (2 specimens).
TYPE LOCALITY: Australia; restricted to Cape York, Queensland, Australia, by Cogger, Cameron, and Cogger, 1983, Zool. Cat. Aust., 1(Amph. Rept.):19.
DISTRIBUTION: Central inland of New South Wales to coast of northern New South Wales and eastern Queensland, Australia.
COMMENT: Moore, 1961, Bull. Am. Mus. Nat. Hist., 121:197, reviewed the limited literature on this species.

Limnodynastes spenceri Parker, 1940. Novit. Zool., 42:50.
TYPE(S): Holotype: BM 1947.2.18.79 (formerly 97.10.27.68).
TYPE LOCALITY: Alice Springs, Northern Territory [Australia].
DISTRIBUTION: Arid areas of central and western Australia.

Limnodynastes tasmaniensis Günther, 1859 "1858". Cat. Batr. Sal. Coll. Brit. Mus.:33.
TYPE(S): Syntypes: BM 1947.2.19.1–3 (formerly 45.5.2.34–36); 7 syntypes according
    to Cogger, Cameron, and Cogger, 1983, Zool. Cat. Aust., 1(Amph. Rept.):20,
    who noted that original description cited only 6.
TYPE LOCALITY: "Tasmania" and "New Holland [=Australia]".
DISTRIBUTION: Tasmania, Victoria, South Australia, New South Wales, and southern
    Queensland; introduced into Western Australia and the Northern Territory,
    Australia.
COMMENT: Littlejohn and Roberts, 1975, Aust. J. Zool., 23:113, recognized the three
    'call races' within this species; their taxonomic status is uncertain. Discussed
    by Tyler, 1978, Amph. S. Aust.

Limnodynastes terraereginae Fry, 1915. Proc. R. Soc. Queensland, 37:67.
ORIGINAL NAME: *Limnodynastes dorsalis* var. *terrae-reginae*.
TYPE(S): Holotype: AM R4535.
TYPE LOCALITY: Somerset, Cape York Peninsula [Queensland, Australia].
DISTRIBUTION: Western slopes and ranges of northern New South Wales through
    eastern Queensland to Cape York Peninsula, Australia.

Megistolotis Tyler, Martin, and Davies, 1979. Aust. J. Zool., 27:136.
TYPE SPECIES: *Megistolotis lignarius* Tyler, Martin, and Davies, 1979, by original
    designation.
DISTRIBUTION: As for the single species.
COMMENT: According to Tyler, Martin, and Davies, 1979, Aust. J. Zool., 27:135, this
    genus is closely related to *Limnodynastes*.

Megistolotis lignarius Tyler, Martin, and Davies, 1979. Aust. J. Zool., 27:137.
TYPE(S): Holotype: WAM R58299.
TYPE LOCALITY: "adjacent to the Lake Argyle–Kununurra road, 6.5 km N. of Lake
    Argyle Tourist Village, Lake Argyle, Kimberley Division, Western Australia".
DISTRIBUTION: Extreme northern Western Australia from Kalumburu to the vicinity
    of Lake Argyle, and then further northeast as far as the foot of the Arnhem
    Land escarpment in the Northern Territory, Australia.

Mixophyes Günther, 1864. Proc. Zool. Soc. London, 1864:46.
TYPE SPECIES: *Mixophyes fasciolatus* Günther, 1864, by monotypy.
DISTRIBUTION: Eastern Australia.
COMMENT: See Straughan, 1968, Proc. Linn. Soc. New South Wales, 93:52–59, for a
    review and synonymies.

Mixophyes balbus Straughan, 1968. Proc. Linn. Soc. New South Wales, 93:55.
TYPE(S): Holotype: AM R25922.
TYPE LOCALITY: "Point Lookout, New England National Park, N.S.W. [New South
    Wales, Australia], between 4,250 and 4,750 feet altitude".
DISTRIBUTION: East of the Great Dividing Range from the Dorrigo Plateau south to
    Illawarra, Australia.

Mixophyes fasciolatus Günther, 1864. Proc. Zool. Soc. London, 1864:46.
TYPE(S): Syntypes: BM 1947.2.19.89–90 (formerly 62.10.26.3, 64.1.17.39).
TYPE LOCALITY: Clarence River, New South Wales [Australia].
DISTRIBUTION: East coast of Queensland and New South Wales, Australia.

Mixophyes iteratus Straughan, 1968. Proc. Linn. Soc. New South Wales, 93:54.
TYPE(S): Holotype: AM R25929.
TYPE LOCALITY: "Tweed River, Mount Warning", New South Wales, Australia.
DISTRIBUTION: Bunya Mountains and along the Queensland-New South Wales
    border east of Stanthorpe, south to the Dorrigo Plateau, Australia.

Mixophyes schevilli Loveridge, 1933. Occas. Pap. Boston Soc. Nat. Hist., 8:56.
ORIGINAL NAME: *Mixophyes fasciolatus schevilli.*
TYPE(S): Holotype: MCZ 18150.
TYPE LOCALITY: Millaa Millaa, Bellenden Ker Range, North Queensland [Australia].
DISTRIBUTION: Atherton Tablelands and coastal ranges of northern Queensland
(Australia) from Mount Finigan south to the Johnstone River.

Neobatrachus Peters, 1863. Monatsber. Preuss. Akad. Wiss. Berlin, 1863:234.
TYPE SPECIES: *Neobatrachus pictus* Peters, 1863, by monotypy.
DISTRIBUTION: Australia, excluding Tasmania.

Neobatrachus aquilonius Tyler, Davies, and Martin, 1981. Rec. W. Aust. Mus., 9:155.
TYPE(S): Holotype: WAM R71005.
TYPE LOCALITY: "22–41 km S of Derby, Kimberley Division", Western Australia.
DISTRIBUTION: Kimberley Division, Western Australia, to the Barkly Tablelands,
Northern Territory, Australia.

Neobatrachus centralis (Parker, 1940). Novit. Zool., 42:35.
ORIGINAL NAME: *Heleioporus centralis.*
TYPE(S): Holotype: BM 1947.2.19.13 (formerly 1905.10.31.47).
TYPE LOCALITY: "100 miles east of Lake Eyre", South Australia; in error, according
to Tyler and Ledo, 1973, S. Aust. Nat., 47:75, who calculated the type locality
to be on the Birdsville Track, no more than 70 miles east of Lake Eyre.
DISTRIBUTION: Western Australia, Northern Territory, and South Australia,
Australia.

Neobatrachus pelobatoides (Werner, 1914). *In* Michaelsen and Hartmeyer (eds.), Fauna
S.W. Aust., Amph., 4:418.
ORIGINAL NAME: *Heleioporus albopunctatus* var. *pelobatoides.*
TYPE(S): Not traced.
TYPE LOCALITY: Beverley and Broome Hille, Western Australia.
DISTRIBUTION: Southwestern Western Australia.

Neobatrachus pictus Peters, 1863. Monatsber. Preuss. Akad. Wiss. Berlin, 1863:235.
TYPE(S): Syntypes: ZMB 4725–26; see Cogger, Cameron, and Cogger, 1983, Zool.
Cat. Aust., 1(Amph. Rept.):22, for discussion of confusion surrounding types.
TYPE LOCALITY: "Near Adelaide"; Roberts, 1978, Trans. R. Soc. S. Aust., 102:97,
suggested the type locality to be Buchsfelde [=Loos], 4.5 km W of Gawler,
South Australia.
DISTRIBUTION: South Australia and Victoria, Australia.
COMMENT: Roberts, 1978, Trans. R. Soc. S. Aust., 102:97, redefined this species.

Neobatrachus sudelli Lamb, 1911. Ann. Queensland Mus., 10:26.
TYPE(S): Holotype: QM J78.
TYPE LOCALITY: Warwick, southeastern Queensland [Australia].
DISTRIBUTION: Southeastern Australia from southern Queensland to the lower
southeast of South Australia.
COMMENT: Resurrected from the synonymy of *Neobatrachus pictus* by Roberts, 1978,
Trans. R. Soc. S. Aust., 102:104.

Neobatrachus sutor Main, 1957. West. Aust. Nat., 6:24.
TYPE(S): Holotype: WAM R32892.
TYPE LOCALITY: Gnoolowa Hill, 18 miles north of Mingenew, Western Australia.
DISTRIBUTION: Southwestern Western Australia to the extreme northwest of South
Australia.
COMMENT: See Main, 1965, Frogs S.W. Aust.:29, for discussion.

Neobatrachus wilsmorei (Parker, 1940). Novit. Zool., 42:36.
ORIGINAL NAME: *Heleioporus wilsmorei.*
TYPE(S): Holotype: BM 1947.2.18.68 (formerly 1937.7.22.3).
TYPE LOCALITY: Wiraga, northeast of Yalgoo, Murchison, Western Australia.
DISTRIBUTION: Southwestern Western Australia.

Notaden Günther, 1873. Ann. Mag. Nat. Hist., (4)11:350.
TYPE SPECIES: *Notaden bennettii* Günther, 1873, by monotypy.
DISTRIBUTION: Australia.
COMMENT: The most recent generic review is that of Hosmer, 1962, Am. Mus. Novit., 2077:1.

Notaden bennettii Günther, 1873. Ann. Mag. Nat. Hist., (4)11:350.
TYPE(S): Holotype: BM 1947.2.18.56 (formerly 73.4.30.17).
TYPE LOCALITY: Castlereagh River, New South Wales [Australia].
DISTRIBUTION: Plains of New South Wales and southern Queensland, Australia.

Notaden melanoscaphus Hosmer, 1962. Am. Mus. Novit., 2077:2.
TYPE(S): Holotype: NMM D10144 (formerly AMNH 67161).
TYPE LOCALITY: Borroloola, lat. 16° 15' S, long. 136° 20' E, Northern Territory, Australia.
DISTRIBUTION: Kimberley Division of Western Australia, east through the northern portion of the Northern Territory and Cape York Peninsula of Queensland, Australia.

Notaden nichollsi Parker, 1940. Novit. Zool., 42:63.
TYPE(S): Holotype: BM 1947.2.18.57 (formerly 96.7.2.19).
TYPE LOCALITY: Roebuck Bay, Western Australia.
DISTRIBUTION: Northern Western Australia and Northern Territory, Australia.

Philoria Spencer, 1901. Proc. R. Soc. Victoria, (2)13:176.
TYPE SPECIES: *Philoria frosti* Spencer, 1901, by monotypy.
DISTRIBUTION: Southeastern Australia.
COMMENT: See comment under *Kyarranus.*

Philoria frosti Spencer, 1901. Proc. R. Soc. Victoria, (2)13:176.
TYPE(S): NMM D8497 designated lectotype by Coventry, 1970, Mem. Natl. Mus. Victoria, 31:115–124.
TYPE LOCALITY: Mt. Baw Baw, Victoria [Australia].
DISTRIBUTION: Higher elevations of Mt. Baw Baw, Victoria, Australia.

Rheobatrachus Liem, 1973. Mem. Queensland Mus., 16:467.
TYPE SPECIES: *Rheobatrachus silus* Liem, 1973, by original designation.
DISTRIBUTION: Queensland, Australia.
COMMENT: Placed in a distinct subfamily, the Rheobatrachinae, by Heyer and Liem, 1976, Smithson. Contrib. Zool., 233:14, and in a separate family, the Rheobatrachidae, by Laurent, 1979, Bull. Soc. Zool. France, 104:401, but a reanalysis by Farris, Kluge, and Mickevich, 1982, Syst. Zool., 31:317–327, placed *Rheobatrachus* as the sister-taxon of the Limnodynastinae and not of the entire Myobatrachidae as posited by Heyer and Liem.

Rheobatrachus silus Liem, 1973. Mem. Queensland Mus., 16:467.
TYPE(S): Holotype: QM J22489.
TYPE LOCALITY: Kondalilla, 3 km SW Montville, SE Queensland [Australia].
DISTRIBUTION: Connondale and Blackall ranges in southeastern Queensland, Australia.
COMMENT: Reviewed by Tyler (ed.), 1983, The gastric brooding frog, Croom-Helm.

Rheobatrachus vitellinus Mahony, Tyler, and Davies, 1984. Trans. R. Soc. S. Aust., 108: 155.
    TYPE(S): Holotype: QM J42529.
    TYPE LOCALITY: "Engella National Park, 148° 38' 00" E.; 21° 01' 30" S., Queensland", Australia.
    DISTRIBUTION: Known only from the type locality.

SUBFAMILY: **Myobatrachinae** Schlegel, 1850.
  CITATION: Proc. Zool. Soc. London, 1850:9.
  DISTRIBUTION: Australia; New Guinea.
  COMMENT: The first use of the spelling Myobatrachinae (as a subfamily of the Leptodactylidae) was by Parker, 1940, Novit. Zool., 42:6. According to Lynch, 1973, *In* Vial (ed.), Evol. Biol. Anurans:133–182, the Myobatrachinae plus the Sooglossidae are more closely related to the ranoid families than to the Limnodynastinae and other bufonoids. Evidence to suggest that this nominal subfamily is monophyletic has yet to be presented (JDL).

Arenophryne Tyler, 1976. Rec. W. Aust. Mus., 4:45.
  TYPE SPECIES: *Arenophryne rotunda* Tyler, 1976, by original designation.
  DISTRIBUTION: As for the single species.
  COMMENT: Tyler, 1976, Rec. W. Aust. Mus., 4:45, and Daugherty and Maxson, 1982, Herpetologica, 38:345, considered *Arenophryne* most closely related to *Myobatrachus*.

Arenophryne rotunda Tyler, 1976. Rec. W. Aust. Mus., 4:46.
  TYPE(S): Holotype: WAM R39120.
  TYPE LOCALITY: Approx. 100 m from False Entrance Well Tank, Carrarang Station, Shark Bay, Western Australia.
  DISTRIBUTION: Vicinity of the type locality.

Assa Tyler, 1972. Zool. Meded., Leiden, 47:200.
  TYPE SPECIES: *Crinia darlingtoni* Loveridge, 1933, by monotypy.
  DISTRIBUTION: As for the single species.

Assa darlingtoni (Loveridge, 1933). Occas. Pap. Boston Soc. Nat. Hist., 8:57.
  ORIGINAL NAME: *Crinia darlingtoni*.
  TYPE(S): Holotype: MCZ 18390.
  TYPE LOCALITY: Queensland National Park, MacPherson Range, Queensland [Australia].
  DISTRIBUTION: Mountainous ranges on the extreme northeastern border of New South Wales with Queensland, Australia.

Crinia Tschudi, 1838. Classif. Batr.:38.
  TYPE SPECIES: *Crinia georgiana* Tschudi, 1838, by monotypy.
  DISTRIBUTION: Australia and southern New Guinea.
  COMMENT: Heyer, Daugherty, and Maxson, 1982, Proc. Biol. Soc. Washington, 95: 423–427, reviewed the evolutionary relationship of this genus with *Paracrinia* and *Geocrinia*, and placed *Ranidella* Girard, 1853, Proc. Acad. Nat. Sci. Philadelphia, 6:421 (Type species by original designation: *Crinia signifera* Girard, 1853), in the synonymy of *Crinia*. Cogger, Cameron, and Cogger, 1983, Zool. Cat. Aust., 1(Amph. Rept.):13–31, retained the separate genera without discussion. The status of *Ranidella* is a matter of debate but it is recognized by MJT and MD.

Crinia bilingua (Martin, Tyler, and Davies, 1980). Copeia, 1980:94.
  ORIGINAL NAME: *Ranidella bilingua*.
  TYPE(S): Holotype: WAM R59775.
  TYPE LOCALITY: Swamp on the E side of Spillway Creek at Spillway Bridge (16° 01' 47" S, 128° 47' 08" E), 11.5 km by road N of Lake Argyle Tourist Village, Kimberley Division, Western Australia.
  DISTRIBUTION: Kimberley Division, Western Australia, and northern portion of Northern Territory, Australia.

COMMENT: Formerly in *Ranidella*.

Crinia deserticola (Liem and Ingram, 1977). Victorian Nat., 94:255.
ORIGINAL NAME: *Ranidella deserticola*.
TYPE(S): Holotype: QM J22654.
TYPE LOCALITY: Charleville, southwestern Queensland, Australia.
DISTRIBUTION: Queensland, Northern Territory, and northeast of South Australia, Australia.
COMMENT: Formerly in *Ranidella*.

Crinia georgiana Tschudi, 1838. Classif. Batr.:38, 78.
TYPE(S): Holotype: MNHNP 759.
TYPE LOCALITY: King George's Sound [Western Australia].
DISTRIBUTION: Southwestern Western Australia.

Crinia glauerti Loveridge, 1933. Occas. Pap. Boston Soc. Nat. Hist., 8:57.
TYPE(S): Holotype: MCZ 18420.
TYPE LOCALITY: Mundaring, 30 miles northeast of Perth, Western Australia.
DISTRIBUTION: Southwestern Western Australia.

Crinia insignifera Moore, 1954. Am. Nat., 88:71.
TYPE(S): Holotype: AM R16007.
TYPE LOCALITY: Attadale [=Armadale], Western Australia.
DISTRIBUTION: Southwestern Western Australia.

Crinia parinsignifera Main, 1957. Aust. J. Zool., 5:53.
TYPE(S): Holotype: WAM R38735.
TYPE LOCALITY: Kingston-on-Murray, South Australia.
DISTRIBUTION: Victoria, New South Wales, Queensland, and South Australia, Australia.

Crinia pseudinsignifera Main, 1957. Aust. J. Zool., 5:52.
TYPE(S): Holotype: WAM R36153.
TYPE LOCALITY: Yorkrakine Rock, 15 miles north of Tammin [Western Australia].
DISTRIBUTION: Southwestern Western Australia.

Crinia remota (Tyler and Parker, 1974). Trans. R. Soc. S. Aust., 98:74.
ORIGINAL NAME: *Ranidella remota*.
TYPE(S): Holotype: SAMA R13524.
TYPE LOCALITY: "Morehead, [Western Province,] Papua New Guinea".
DISTRIBUTION: Southern lowlands of Papua New Guinea, and northeastern Queensland, Australia.
COMMENT: Formerly in *Ranidella*.
REVIEWER: Richard G. Zweifel (RGZ).

Crinia riparia Littlejohn and Martin, 1965. Copeia, 1965:319.
TYPE(S): Holotype: AM R26161.
TYPE LOCALITY: Alligator Gorge, 8.5 miles SSW Wilmington, Flinders Ranges, South Australia.
DISTRIBUTION: Flinders Ranges, South Australia, Australia.
COMMENT: Odendaal, Bull, and Adams, 1983, Copeia, 1983:275, reported genetic divergence from the morphologically similar *Crinia signifera*. Formerly in *Ranidella*.

Crinia signifera Girard, 1853. Proc. Acad. Nat. Sci. Philadelphia, 6:422.
ORIGINAL NAME: *Crinia (Ranidella) signifera*.
TYPE(S): Not traced.
TYPE LOCALITY: New Holland [Australia].
DISTRIBUTION: Southeastern Australia.

COMMENT: Prior to the work of Main, 1957, Aust. J. Zool., 5:30, this species was considered to be widespread in Australia; Main demonstrated the existence of several sibling species. Subsequent work has demonstrated this species to be restricted to southeastern Australia. Formerly in *Ranidella*.

Crinia sloanei Littlejohn, 1958. Proc. Linn. Soc. New South Wales, 83:225.
TYPE(S): Holotype: AM R19610.
TYPE LOCALITY: River Murray, near Tocumwal, New South Wales [Australia].
DISTRIBUTION: River Murray region of Victoria and New South Wales, Australia.
COMMENT: Formerly in *Ranidella*.

Crinia subinsignifera Littlejohn, 1957. West. Aust. Nat., 6:18.
TYPE(S): Holotype: WAM R12786.
TYPE LOCALITY: Wilgarup, 7 miles north of Manjimup, Western Australia.
DISTRIBUTION: Southwestern Western Australia.
COMMENT: Formerly in *Ranidella*.

Crinia tasmaniensis (Günther, 1864). Proc. Zool. Soc. London, 1864:48.
ORIGINAL NAME: *Pterophrynus tasmaniensis*.
TYPE(S): Holotype: BM 1947.2.19.68–75 (formerly 58.11.25.63).
TYPE LOCALITY: Van Dieman's Land [Tasmania, Australia].
DISTRIBUTION: Tasmania, Australia.
COMMENT: Discussed by Martin and Littlejohn, 1982, Tasman. Amph.:34. Formerly in *Ranidella*.

Crinia tinnula Straughan and Main, 1966. Proc. R. Soc. Queensland, 78:19.
TYPE(S): Holotype: QM J13546.
TYPE LOCALITY: Rose Creek, Beerburrum, southeastern Queensland, Australia.
DISTRIBUTION: Coastal southern Queensland from the Tweed River to Tin Can Bay, Queensland, Australia.
COMMENT: Formerly in *Ranidella*.

Geocrinia Blake, 1973. Aust. J. Zool., 21:142.
TYPE SPECIES: *Pterophrynus laevis* Günther, 1864, by original designation.
DISTRIBUTION: Southeastern and southwestern Australia.

Geocrinia laevis (Günther, 1864). Proc. Zool. Soc. London, 1864:48.
ORIGINAL NAME: *Pterophrynus laevis*.
TYPE(S): Holotype: BM 1947.2.19.65 (formerly 60.11.29.25).
TYPE LOCALITY: Tasmania [Australia].
DISTRIBUTION: Tasmania, South Australia, and Victoria, Australia.
COMMENT: Discussed by Littlejohn and Martin, 1964, Aust. J. Zool., 12:72.

Geocrinia leai (Fletcher, 1898). Proc. Linn. Soc. New South Wales, (2)22:677.
TYPE(S): Syntypes: AM R8337, R10324, R49819–24.
TYPE LOCALITY: Bridgetown and Pipe Clay Creek, near Jarrahdale, Western Australia.
DISTRIBUTION: Southwestern Western Australia.

Geocrinia rosea (Harrison, 1927). Rec. Aust. Mus., 15:279.
ORIGINAL NAME: *Crinia rosea*.
TYPE(S): Syntypes: MMUS (not located by Cogger, Cameron, and Cogger, 1983, Zool. Cat. Aust., 1(Amph. Rept.):14).
TYPE LOCALITY: Pemberton, in the Karri Country, 218 miles south of Perth [Western Australia].
DISTRIBUTION: Southwestern Western Australia.
COMMENT: See Tyler, Smith, and Johnstone, 1984, Frogs W. Aust.:50, who considered *Crinia lutea* Main, 1963, West. Aust. Nat., 8:143 (Holotype: WAM

R17616; Type locality: National Park, Nonalup, Western Australia), to be a synonym.

Geocrinia victoriana (Boulenger, 1888). Ann. Mag. Nat. Hist., (6)2:142.
ORIGINAL NAME: *Crinia victoriana.*
TYPE(S): Holotype: BM 1947.2.19.66 (formerly 88.7.3.13).
TYPE LOCALITY: Warragul, Gippsland, Victoria [Australia].
DISTRIBUTION: South of the Great Dividing Range in Victoria, Australia.
COMMENT: Discussed by Littlejohn and Martin, 1964, Aust. J. Zool., 12:75.

Myobatrachus Schlegel, 1850. Proc. Zool. Soc. London, 1850:9.
TYPE SPECIES: *Myobatrachus paradoxus* Schlegel, 1850 (=*Breviceps gouldii* Gray, 1841), by monotypy.
DISTRIBUTION: As for the single species.
COMMENT: See comment under *Arenophryne.*

Myobatrachus gouldii (Gray, 1841). Ann. Mag. Nat. Hist., (1)7:89.
ORIGINAL NAME: *Breviceps gouldii.*
TYPE(S): Holotype: BM 1947.2.20.5 (formerly 41.2.216).
TYPE LOCALITY: Western Australia.
DISTRIBUTION: Southwestern Western Australia.

Paracrinia Heyer and Liem, 1976. Smithson. Contrib. Zool., 233:12.
TYPE SPECIES: *Crinia haswelli* Fletcher, 1894, by original designation.
DISTRIBUTION: As for the single species.

Paracrinia haswelli (Fletcher, 1894). Proc. Linn. Soc. New South Wales, (2)8:522.
ORIGINAL NAME: *Crinia haswelli.*
TYPE(S): Syntypes: AM R10335, R49816–18, another syntype lost, according to Cogger, Cameron, and Cogger, 1983, Zool. Cat. Aust., 1(Amph. Rept.):24.
TYPE LOCALITY: Near head of Jervis Bay, New South Wales [Australia].
DISTRIBUTION: Southeastern New South Wales and eastern Victoria, Australia.

Pseudophryne Fitzinger, 1843. Syst. Rept.:32.
TYPE SPECIES: *Phryniscus australis* Duméril and Bibron, 1841 [not of Gray, 1835] (=*Pseudophryne semimarmorata* Lucas, 1892, according to Parker, 1940, Novit. Zool., 42:101), by original designation.
DISTRIBUTION: Southern and eastern Australia.
COMMENT: Reviewed by Parker, 1940, Novit. Zool., 42:94. Synonymy includes *Metacrinia* Parker, 1940, Novit. Zool., 42:93 (Type species by original designation: *Pseudophryne nichollsi*), according to Blake, 1973, Aust. J. Zool., 21:119–149, and *Kankanophryne* Heyer and Liem, 1976, according to Tyler and Davies, 1980, Trans. R. Soc. S. Aust., 104:17–200. *Metacrinia* retained, without discussion, by Cogger, Cameron, and Cogger, 1983, Zool. Cat. Aust., 1(Amph. Rept.):20.

Pseudophryne australis (Gray, 1835). Proc. Zool. Soc. London, 1835:57.
ORIGINAL NAME: *Bombinator australis.*
TYPE(S): Holotype: BM 1947.2.20.17 (formerly 1936.12.3.132).
TYPE LOCALITY: "Swan River", Australia; Parker, 1940, Novit. Zool., 42:102, argued that the type locality is in error because the known distribution of this species is in New South Wales, whereas the Swan River is in Western Australia; see also Moore, 1961, Bull. Am. Mus. Nat. Hist., 121:239.
DISTRIBUTION: Sydney region of New South Wales, Australia.
COMMENT: See Moore, 1961, Bull. Am. Mus. Nat. Hist., 121:235.

Pseudophryne bibronii Günther, 1859 "1858". Cat. Batr. Sal. Coll. Brit. Mus.:46.
TYPE(S): Syntypes: BM 1947.2.20.20 (formerly 1936.12.3.131) (this specimen is also a cotype of *Pseudophryne guentheri*), remaining cotypes lost or destroyed, according to Parker, 1940, Novit. Zool., 42:104.
TYPE LOCALITY: Australia; van Diemen's Land [=Tasmania].
DISTRIBUTION: Southern and eastern Australia.

COMMENT: See Cogger, Cameron, and Cogger, 1983, Zool. Cat. Aust., 1(Amph. Rept.):25, for discussion of nomenclatural confusion with *Pseudophryne guentheri*.

Pseudophryne coriacea Keferstein, 1868. Arch. Naturgesch., 34:272.
    TYPE(S): Syntypes: ZFMK 28203–07 (6 specimens); Cogger, Cameron, and Cogger, 1983, Zool. Cat. Aust., 1(Amph. Rept.):26, noted that ZFMK 28204 is a *Pseudophryne corroboree*.
    TYPE LOCALITY: Clarence River, New South Wales [Australia].
    DISTRIBUTION: Northeastern New South Wales and southeastern Queensland, Australia.
    COMMENT: Reviewed by Moore, 1961, Bull. Am. Mus. Nat. Hist., 121:247.

Pseudophryne corroboree Moore, 1953. Proc. Linn. Soc. New South Wales, 78:179.
    TYPE(S): Holotype: AM R13103.
    TYPE LOCALITY: Towong Hill Station, Corryong, Victoria [Australia]; corrected to Round Mountain, New South Wales [Australia] by Colefax, 1956, Proc. Linn. Soc. New South Wales, 80:258–266.
    DISTRIBUTION: Mountains of southeastern New South Wales and Australian Capitol Territory, Australia.

Pseudophryne dendyi Lucas, 1892. Proc. R. Soc. Victoria, (2)4:61.
    TYPE(S): Lost, according to Harrison, 1927, Rec. Aust. Mus., 15:286.
    TYPE LOCALITY: Upper Wellington River, N. Gippsland [Victoria, Australia].
    DISTRIBUTION: Eastern Victoria and southeastern New South Wales, Australia.
    COMMENT: Moore, 1961, Bull. Am. Mus. Nat. Hist., 121:244, provided a detailed review.

Pseudophryne douglasi Main, 1964. West. Aust. Nat., 9:66.
    TYPE(S): Holotype: WAM R21255.
    TYPE LOCALITY: Kookhabinna Gorge (lat. 23° 10' S, 115° 58' E), Western Australia.
    DISTRIBUTION: Northwest Cape and western edge of Hammersley Ranges, Western Australia, Australia.

Pseudophryne guentheri Boulenger, 1882. Cat. Batr. Sal. Brit. Mus.:279.
    TYPE(S): Syntypes: BM 1947.2.20.18–21 (formerly 1936.12.3.131 [see *Pseudophryne bibronii*], 69.7.27.5, 58.11.25.59, 64.10.6.9).
    TYPE LOCALITY: Swan River; Western Australia.
    DISTRIBUTION: Southwestern Western Australia south of a line connecting Kalbarri to Esperance.
    COMMENT: See comment under *Pseudophryne bibronii*.

Pseudophryne major Parker, 1940. Novit. Zool., 42:98.
    TYPE(S): Holotype: BM 1947.2.20.24 (formerly 67.3.4.56).
    TYPE LOCALITY: Gayndah, southeastern Queensland [Australia].
    DISTRIBUTION: Queensland, Australia.

Pseudophryne nichollsi Harrison, 1927. Rec. Aust. Mus., 15:284.
    TYPE(S): Syntypes: MMUS; not located.
    TYPE LOCALITY: Pemberton, Western Australia.
    DISTRIBUTION: Extreme southwest of Western Australia.
    COMMENT: Retained, without discussion, in *Metacrinia* by Cogger, Cameron, and Cogger, 1983, Zool. Cat. Aust., 1(Amph. Rept.):21.

Pseudophryne occidentalis Parker, 1940. Novit. Zool., 42:97.
    TYPE(S): Holotype: BM 1947.2.20.27 (formerly 1937.7.22.42).
    TYPE LOCALITY: Bruce Rock, Western Australia.
    DISTRIBUTION: Southwestern Western Australia and adjacent arid zone 30 mi. to northwestern South Australia.

Pseudophryne semimarmorata Lucas, 1892. Proc. R. Soc. Victoria, (2)4:61.
  TYPE(S): NMM D7196 designated lectotype by Coventry, 1970, Mem. Natl. Mus.
    Victoria, 31:115–124.
  TYPE LOCALITY: Oakleigh; Heidelberg; Ringwood; Narre Warren; Waterloo;
    Grampians [Victoria, Australia]. Lectotype from Grampian Ranges, Victoria,
    Australia.
  DISTRIBUTION: Tasmania, Victoria, southern South Australia, and southern New
    South Wales, Australia.

Taudactylus Straughan and Lee, 1966. Proc. R. Soc. Queensland, 77:63.
  TYPE SPECIES: *Taudactylus diurnus* Straughan and Lee, 1966, by original designation.
  DISTRIBUTION: Eastern to northeastern Queensland, Australia.
  COMMENT: This genus was redefined by Liem and Hosmer, 1973, Mem. Queensland
    Mus., 16:437.

Taudactylus acutirostris (Andersson, 1916). K. Svenska Vetensk. Akad. Handl., (4)52:8.
  ORIGINAL NAME: *Crinia acutirostris*.
  TYPE(S): Syntypes: NHRM 1624 (2 specimens).
  TYPE LOCALITY: Malanda, Queensland [Australia].
  DISTRIBUTION: Atherton Tableland, Queensland, Australia.

Taudactylus diurnus Straughan and Lee, 1966. Proc. R. Soc. Queensland, 77:63.
  TYPE(S): Holotype: QM J13398.
  TYPE LOCALITY: "Green's Falls, Maiala National Park, Mt. Glorious, Queensland",
    Australia.
  DISTRIBUTION: Southeastern Queensland, Australia.

Taudactylus eungellensis Liem and Hosmer, 1973. Mem. Queensland Mus., 16:445.
  TYPE(S): Holotype: QM J22433.
  TYPE LOCALITY: Eungella and Finch Hatton Gorge, Queensland [Australia]; Ingram
    and Covacevich, 1981, Mem. Queensland Mus., 20:292, discussed uncertainty
    regarding the type locality.
  DISTRIBUTION: Known only from the type locality.

Taudactylus liemi Ingram, 1980. Mem. Queensland Mus., 20:111.
  TYPE(S): Holotype: QM J32625.
  TYPE LOCALITY: Crediton (21° 12' S, 148° 33' E), Queensland [Australia].
  DISTRIBUTION: From Mt. William to Crediton in the Eungella area of mid-eastern
    Queensland, Australia.

Taudactylus rheophilus Liem and Hosmer, 1973. Mem. Queensland Mus., 16:450.
  TYPE(S): Holotype: QM J22418.
  TYPE LOCALITY: "southwest slope of Mt. Lewis (1200 m), NE Queensland",
    Australia.
  DISTRIBUTION: Great Dividing Range of northeastern Queensland, Australia.

Uperoleia Gray, 1841. Ann. Mag. Nat. Hist., (1)7:90.
  TYPE SPECIES: *Uperoleia marmorata* Gray, 1841, by monotypy.
  DISTRIBUTION: Northern and eastern Australia; southern lowlands of New Guinea.
  COMMENT: The systematics and biology of some Australian species were reviewed by
    Tyler, Davies, and Martin, 1981, Aust. J. Zool., Suppl. Ser., 79:1–64, who
    effectively left all eastern Australian populations without names by not
    applying any of the available specific names in *Uperoleia* from eastern Australia
    to other than their type specimens, according to Cogger, Cameron, and Cogger,
    1983, Zool. Cat. Aust., 1(Amph. Rept.):33.

Uperoleia arenicola Tyler, Davies, and Martin, 1981. Aust. J. Zool., Suppl. Ser., 79:26.
  TYPE(S): Holotype: SAMA R16991.
  TYPE LOCALITY: "Birndu, East Alligator River Region, Northern Territory",
    Australia.
  DISTRIBUTION: Known only from the type locality.

Uperoleia aspera Tyler, Davies, and Martin, 1981. Rec. W. Aust. Mus., 9:159.
    TYPE(S): Holotype: WAM R69648.
    TYPE LOCALITY: "28 km S of Derby (123° 43' S, 17° 30' E), Kimberley Division",
        Western Australia.
    DISTRIBUTION: Vicinity of Broome to 28 km south of Derby, Kimberley Division,
        Western Australia.

Uperoleia borealis Tyler, Davies, and Martin, 1981. Aust. J. Zool., Suppl. Ser., 79:30.
    TYPE(S): Holotype: WAM R62474.
    TYPE LOCALITY: "Dead Horse Spring, 3.7 km northeast of Lake Argyle Tourist
        Village, Kimberley Division, Western Australia".
    DISTRIBUTION: Known from three areas in the Kimberley Division, Western
        Australia (3–30 km northeast of Lake Argyle; between Kununurra and
        Wyndham; 30 km northeast of Kununurra), and from Northern Territory,
        Australia.
    COMMENT: Distributional data provided by Tyler, Watson, and Davies, 1983, Trans.
        R. Soc. S. Aust., 107:243.

Uperoleia crassa Tyler, Davies, and Martin, 1981. Aust. J. Zool., Suppl. Ser., 79:34.
    TYPE(S): Holotype: WAM R59951.
    TYPE LOCALITY: "Amax Campsite, Mitchell Plateau (14° 15' S, 125° 50' E), Kimberley
        Division, Western Australia".
    DISTRIBUTION: Known only from the type locality.

Uperoleia fimbrianus (Parker, 1926). Ann. Mag. Nat. Hist., (9)17:669.
    ORIGINAL NAME: *Pseudophryne fimbrianus*.
    TYPE(S): Holotype: BM 1947.2.18.70 (formerly 1923.11.12.3).
    TYPE LOCALITY: St. George District, Queensland [Australia].
    DISTRIBUTION: Known only from the type locality.

Uperoleia inundata Tyler, Davies, and Martin, 1981. Aust. J. Zool., Suppl. Ser., 79:39.
    TYPE(S): Holotype: SAMA R17182.
    TYPE LOCALITY: "Jabiru, East Alligator River Region, Northern Territory (126° 28' S,
        132° 56' E)", Australia.
    DISTRIBUTION: Floodplains east of Darwin, Northern Territory, Australia.

Uperoleia laevigata Keferstein, 1867. Nachr. Ges. Wiss. Göttingen, 18:349.
    ORIGINAL NAME: *Uperoleia marmorata* var. *laevigata*.
    TYPE(S): Syntypes: ZFMK 26304–313; ZFMK 26309 designated lectotype by Tyler,
        Davies, and Martin, 1981, Aust. J. Zool., Suppl. Ser., 79:13, who also noted
        that ZFMK 26312 is a *Pseudophryne bibronii*.
    TYPE LOCALITY: "Raudewick" (=Randwick), New South Wales, Australia.
    DISTRIBUTION: Known only from the type locality.
    COMMENT: See comment under *Uperoleia*.

Uperoleia lithomoda Tyler, Davies, and Martin, 1981. Aust. J. Zool., Suppl. Ser., 79:43.
    TYPE(S): Holotype: WAM R61620.
    TYPE LOCALITY: "swamp at Spillway Bridge (16° 02' S, 128° 47' E), 11.5 km north-
        east of Lake Argyle Tourist Village, Kimberley Division, Western Australia".
    DISTRIBUTION: Eastern Kimberley region (Western Australia) to the floodplains
        west of Arnhem Land, Northern Territory, Australia; southern lowlands of
        Papua New Guinea.
    COMMENT: See Tyler and Davies, 1984, Trans. R. Soc. S. Aust., 108:123, for records
        from New Guinea.

Uperoleia marmorata Gray, 1841. Ann. Mag. Nat. Hist., (1)7:90.
    TYPE(S): Holotype: BM 1947.2.19.88 (formerly 1836.12.3.130).
    TYPE LOCALITY: "Western Australia"; according to Tyler, Davies, and Martin, 1981,
        Aust. J. Zool., 79:10, the actual type locality is likely south of the Prince
        Regent River within 35 km of the coast, Western Australia.
    DISTRIBUTION: Known only from the types.

COMMENT: Prior to the revision of Tyler, Davis, and Martin, 1981, Aust. J. Zool., Suppl. Ser., 79:10, *Uperoleia marmorata* was considered widespread in eastern New South Wales.

Uperoleia micromeles Tyler, Davies, and Martin, 1981. Aust. J. Zool., Suppl. Ser., 79:46.
TYPE(S): Holotype: SAMA R17175.
TYPE LOCALITY: "in the Tanami Desert (20° 38' S, 130° 25' E), Northern Territory", Australia.
DISTRIBUTION: Tanami Desert, Northern Territory, Australia.

Uperoleia minima Tyler, Davies, and Martin, 1981. Aust. J. Zool., Suppl. Ser., 79:49.
TYPE(S): Holotype: WAM R62482.
TYPE LOCALITY: "Amax Crusher Site, 5 km south-west of the Mining Camp, Mitchell Plateau, Kimberley Division, Western Australia (14° 50' S, 125° 50' E)".
DISTRIBUTION: Known only from the vicinity of the type locality.

Uperoleia mjobergi (Andersson, 1913). K. Svenska Vetensk. Akad. Handl., (4)52:19.
ORIGINAL NAME: *Pseudophryne mjöbergi*.
TYPE(S): Syntypes: NHRM 1567 (2 specimens).
TYPE LOCALITY: Noonkambah, Kimberley Division, Western Australia.
DISTRIBUTION: Widely distributed on the Fitzroy River plains and surrounding area, Western Australia.

Uperoleia orientalis (Parker, 1940). Novit. Zool., 42:67.
ORIGINAL NAME: *Glauertia orientalis*.
TYPE(S): Holotype: BM 1947.2.19.84.
TYPE LOCALITY: Alexandria Station, Barkly Tableland, Northern Territory [Australia].
DISTRIBUTION: Known only from the type locality and Groote Eylandt, Northern Territory, Australia.
COMMENT: Prior to the review by Tyler, Davies, and Martin, 1981, Aust. J. Zool., Suppl. Ser., 79:24, the name *Uperoleia orientalis* was applied to most *Uperoleia* in the Northern Territory. Tyler, Davies, and Martin, 1983, Trans. R. Soc. S. Aust., 107:240, concluded that the distribution is probably confined to coastal areas. See comment under *Uperoleia*.

Uperoleia rugosa (Andersson, 1913). K. Svenska Vetensk. Akad. Handl., (4)52:13.
ORIGINAL NAME: *Pseudophryne rugosa*.
TYPE(S): Holotype: NHRM 1630.
TYPE LOCALITY: Mt. Colosseum, Queensland [Australia].
DISTRIBUTION: Known only from the type locality in southwestern Queensland, Australia.
COMMENT: Tyler, Davies, and Martin, 1981, Aust. J. Zool., Suppl. Ser., 79:17, redefined the species and questioned the identity of literature records.

Uperoleia russelli (Loveridge, 1933). Occas. Pap. Boston Soc. Nat. Hist., 8:89.
ORIGINAL NAME: *Glauertia russelli*.
TYPE(S): Holotype: WAM R2608.
TYPE LOCALITY: Bank of Aurillia Creek flowing into Gascoyne River near Landor Station, Western Australia.
DISTRIBUTION: Pilbara region of Western Australia.

Uperoleia talpa Tyler, Davies, and Martin, 1981. Aust. J. Zool., Suppl. Ser., 79:32.
TYPE(S): Holotype: WAM R62472.
TYPE LOCALITY: "24 km south of Derby (17° 37' S, 123° 36' E)", Western Australia.
DISTRIBUTION: Known only from 24–41 km south of Derby, Western Australia.

Uperoleia trachyderma Tyler, Davies, and Martin, 1981. Trans. R. Soc. S. Aust., 105: 149.
TYPE(S): Holotype: SAMA R20374.
TYPE LOCALITY: "Newcastle Creek floodplain at the George Redman Causeway (17° 14' S; 133° 28' E), 37 km N of Elliot", Northern Territory, Australia.
DISTRIBUTION: Confined to blacksoil plains across the Northern Territory, Australia.
COMMENT: See Tyler, Davies, and Martin, 1983, Trans. R. Soc. S. Aust., 107:241, for supplementary data on distribution.

Uperoleia variegata Tyler, Davies, and Martin, 1981. Aust. J. Zool., Suppl. Ser., 79:55.
TYPE(S): Holotype: WAM R62461.
TYPE LOCALITY: "homestead garden at Gibb River Station (16° 26' S, 126° 26' E), Kimberley Division, Western Australia".
DISTRIBUTION: Known only from the type locality.

FAMILY: **Pelobatidae** Bonaparte, 1850.
CITATION: Conspect. Syst. Herpetol. Amphibiol., 1 p.
DISTRIBUTION: Pakistan east to the Indo-Australian Archipelago and the Philippines; China; Europe, western Asia, and northern Africa; southwestern Canada and eastern USA to southern Mexico.
COMMENT: As first formed, the group name was Pelobatina. The first use of the name Pelobatidae was by Lataste, 1879, C. R. Assoc. Franç. Avanc. Sci., Paris, 1878:761. Lynch, 1973, In Vial (ed.), Evol. Biol. Anurans:133–182, presented evidence that the similarity of the Pelobatidae and Pelodytidae was the result of retained primitive features. Some workers have included the Pelodytidae as a subfamily of the Pelobatidae and most workers before Griffiths, 1959, Ann. Mag. Nat. Hist., (13)2: 626–640, and Griffiths, 1963, Biol. Rev. Cambridge Philos. Soc., 38:273, considered the Sooglossidae to be included in the Pelobatidae. Dubois, 1983, Bull. Mens. Soc. Linn. Lyon, 52:271–272, arranged the Pelobatidae into four subfamilies (Pelobatinae, Scaphiopodinae, Megophryinae, and Leptobrachiinae) but provided no discussion to support his arrangement. See comment under Pelobatinae. Evidence to suggest that this nominal family is monophyletic has yet to be presented (JDL).
REVIEWERS: William E. Duellman (WED); Marinus S. Hoogmoed (MSH).

SUBFAMILY: **Megophryinae** Noble, 1931.
CITATION: Biol. Amph.:492.
DISTRIBUTION: The Oriental Region; Pakistan and western China east to the Philippines and the Greater Sundas.
COMMENT: Lynch, 1973, In Vial (ed.), Evol. Biol. Anurans:133–182, thought that the ancestor of the bufonoids was structurally close to the Megophryinae. Evidence to suggest that this nominal subfamily is monophyletic has yet to be presented (JDL). Dubois, 1980, Bull. Mens. Soc. Linn. Lyon, 49:469–482, provided a generic and subgeneric classification followed here, except for more recent changes, although it is largely unsupported by any phylogenetic rationale. SH and EZ do not agree with this arrangement and continue to follow Myers and Leviton, 1962, Copeia, 1962:287–291, in their arrangement of *Scutiger* and *Oreolalax*.
CONTRIBUTOR: Masafumi Matsui (MM).
REVIEWERS: Leo J. Borkin (LJB); Sushil Dutta (SD); Shuqin Hu (SH); Robert F. Inger (RFI); Ermi Zhao (EZ).

Atympanophrys Tian and Hu, 1983. Acta Herpetol. Sinica, 2(2):41–48.
TYPE SPECIES: *Megophrys shapingensis* Liu, 1950.
DISTRIBUTION: As for the single species.

Atympanophrys shapingensis (Liu, 1950). Fieldiana: Zool. Mem., 2:194.
ORIGINAL NAME: *Megophrys shapingensis*.
TYPE(S): Holotype: FMNH 49405.
TYPE LOCALITY: "Shaping, Opienhsien, Szechwan [=Sichuan]", China.
DISTRIBUTION: Region of the type locality.

COMMENT: Formerly in the genus *Megophrys,* subgenus *Megophrys;* see Dubois, 1980, Bull. Mens. Soc. Linn. Lyon, 49:469–482.

Brachytarsophrys Tian and Hu, 1983. Acta Herpetol. Sinica, 2(2):41–48.
TYPE SPECIES: *Leptobrachium carinensis* Boulenger, 1899.
DISTRIBUTION: As for the single species.

Brachytarsophrys carinensis (Boulenger, 1899). Ann. Mus. Civ. Stor. Nat. Genova, (2)7: 748.
ORIGINAL NAME: *Leptobrachium carinensis.*
TYPE(S): Syntypes: BM, NHMW 2291 (2 specimens), and MSNG; MSNG 29689 designated lectotype by Capocaccia, 1957, Ann. Mus. Civ. Stor. Nat. Genova, 69:211.
TYPE LOCALITY: West slope of Karin [=Karen] Hills, east of Toungoo, Burma.
DISTRIBUTION: Jiangxi, Guangxi, Guizhou, Sichuan, Hunan, and Yunnan (China); Burma; northern Thailand.
COMMENT: Formerly in the genus *Megophrys,* subgenus *Megophrys;* see Dubois, 1980, Bull. Mens. Soc. Linn. Lyon, 49:469–482.

Leptobrachella Smith, 1931. Bull. Raffles Mus., 5:12.
TYPE SPECIES: *Leptobrachella mjöbergi* Smith, 1931.
DISTRIBUTION: Borneo; Pulau Serasan, Indonesia.
COMMENT: Reviewed by Dring, 1984 "1983", Amphibia-Reptilia, 4:89–102.

Leptobrachella baluensis Smith, 1931. Bull. Raffles Mus., 5:3–32.
TYPE(S): Holotype: BM 1947.2.25.32.
TYPE LOCALITY: Kamborangah, Kinabalu, Sabah [Malaysia (Borneo)].
DISTRIBUTION: Sabah and Sarawak, Malaysia (Borneo).

Leptobrachella brevicrus Dring, 1984 "1983". Amphibia-Reptilia, 4:98.
TYPE(S): Holotype: BM 1978.34.
TYPE LOCALITY: "camp four 1800 m, Gunung Mulu, Fourth Division, Sarawak", Malaysia (Borneo).
DISTRIBUTION: Known only from the type locality.

Leptobrachella mjobergi Smith, 1925. Sarawak Mus. J., 3:13.
ORIGINAL NAME: *Leptobrachella mjöbergi.*
TYPE(S): Holotype: BM 1947.2.25.33.
TYPE LOCALITY: Mount Gadin, near Lundu, West Sarawak [Malaysia (Borneo)].
DISTRIBUTION: Borneo.
COMMENT: Reviewed, as *Nesobia mjobergi,* by Inger, 1966, Fieldiana: Zool., 52:49–52. The incorrect spelling of the specific epithet *mjoebergi* has been used.

Leptobrachella natunae (Günther, 1895). Novit. Zool., 2:501.
ORIGINAL NAME: *Leptobrachium natunae.*
TYPE(S): BM 1947.2.25.16 designated lectotype by Dring, 1984 "1983", Amphibia-Reptilia, 4:100
TYPE LOCALITY: "Great Natuna [Island]" (=Pulau Bunguran Besar), Indonesia.
DISTRIBUTION: Pulau Bunguran Besar, Indonesia.

Leptobrachella parva Dring, 1984 "1983". Amphibia-Reptilia, 4:90.
TYPE(S): Holotype: BM 1978.1500.
TYPE LOCALITY: "stream 1A, camp one 150 m, Gunung Mulu, Fourth Division, Sarawak", Malaysia (Borneo).
DISTRIBUTION: Known only from the type locality and Deramakota (Sabah, Malaysia), Borneo.

Leptobrachella serasanae Dring, 1984 "1983". Amphibia-Reptilia, 4:101.
TYPE(S): Holotype: BM 1947.2.25.16.
TYPE LOCALITY: "Sirhassen Island (=Pulau Serasan), South Bunguran Islands, Indonesia".
DISTRIBUTION: Known only from the type locality.

Leptobrachium Tschudi, 1838. Classif. Batr.:81.
TYPE SPECIES: *Leptobrachium hasseltii* Tschudi, 1838, by monotypy.
DISTRIBUTION: Southern China to the Philippines, Indochina, and the Sunda Is. to Bali.
COMMENT: Synonymy includes *Vibrissaphora* Liu, 1945, according to Dubois, 1980, Bull. Mens. Soc. Linn. Lyon, 49:475. SH does not agree with this synonymy. Liu, Hu, and Zhao, 1980, Acta Herpetol. Sinica, 3:1–9, regarded *Vibrissaphora* as a genus. See comment under *Leptolalax*.

Leptobrachium ailaonicum (Yang, Chen, and Ma, 1983). *In* Yang, Chen, and Li, Acta Zootaxon. Sinica, 8:325.
ORIGINAL NAME: *Vibrissaphora ailaonica*.
TYPE(S): Holotype: KIZ 8200490.
TYPE LOCALITY: "Xujiaba, Mt. Ailao, Jingdong County, Yunnan, altitude 2400 m", China.
DISTRIBUTION: Yunnan, China.
COMMENT: Related to *Leptobrachium boringii*, according to the original description.

Leptobrachium boringii (Liu, 1945). J. West. China Border Res. Soc., (B)15:28.
ORIGINAL NAME: *Vibrissaphora boringii*.
TYPE(S): Holotype: CIB 237.
TYPE LOCALITY: Taosze, Mount Omei, altitude 1090 m, Szechwan [=Sichuan], China.
DISTRIBUTION: Mt. Omai, Sichuan, China.
COMMENT: Reviewed (as *Vibrissaphora boringii*) by Liu, Hu, and Zhao, 1980, Acta Herpetol. Sinica, 3(1):1–15, and Liu and Hu, 1961, Tailless Amph. China:100–103.

Leptobrachium chapaense (Bourret, 1937). Annexe Bull. Gén. Instr. Publique, Hanoi, 1937(4):18.
ORIGINAL NAME: *Megophrys hasseltii chapaensis*.
TYPE(S): Syntypes: MNHNP 38-89 to 38-92, 48-117 to 48-120 (total of 8 specimens).
TYPE LOCALITY: Chapa, Tonkin [Vietnam].
DISTRIBUTION: Northern Vietnam to Hengduanshan Mountains, Yunnan, China.
COMMENT: Reviewed by Bourret, 1942, Batr. Indochine:214–215.

Leptobrachium hasseltii Tschudi, 1838. Classif. Batr.:81.
TYPE(S): Syntypes: RMNH 2014, 2015.
TYPE LOCALITY: "Java", Indonesia.
DISTRIBUTION: Hainan I. (China) and Burma south to Sumatra, Java, Bali, and Borneo; Philippines; Meghalaya, India (SD).
COMMENT: Included in *Vibrissaphora* by Liu, Hu, Fei, and Huang, 1973, Acta Zool. Sinica, 19:394–395. Reviewed by Bourret, 1942, Batr. Indochine:211–214; Inger, 1966, Fieldiana: Zool., 52:29–37; and Inger, 1954, Fieldiana: Zool., 33: 213–216. See also Pope, 1931, Bull. Am. Mus. Nat. Hist., 61:450–453, and Berry and Hendrickson, 1963, Copeia, 1963:643–648. See comment under *Leptobrachium hendricksoni*. Records from Fujian and Guangdong (China) are referable to *Leptobrachium liui* (SH).
REVIEWERS: Angel Alcala (AA); Walter C. Brown (WCB).

Leptobrachium hendricksoni Taylor, 1962. Univ. Kansas Sci. Bull., 43:308.
   TYPE(S): Holotype: FMNH 178259 (formerly EHT 34749).
   TYPE LOCALITY: "Bhetong, Yala, Thailand".
   DISTRIBUTION: Vicinity of the type locality (Yala, Thailand) and Pahang, Kuala
      Lumpur (Malaya, Malaysia).
   COMMENT: Considered a synonym of *Leptobrachium hasseltii* by Inger, 1966,
      Fieldiana: Zool., 52:29, but considered a distinct species by Dubois, 1983,
      Alytes, Paris, 2:147–153.

Leptobrachium leishanense (Liu and Hu, 1973). *In* Hu, Djao [=Zhao], and Liu, Acta
      Zool. Sinica, 19:165.
   ORIGINAL NAME: *Vibrissaphora leishanensis*.
   TYPE(S): Holotype: CIB (formerly SWIBASC) 639000.
   TYPE LOCALITY: "Ge-tou of Fang-xiang, Leishan hsien, Kweichow [=Guizhou],
      altitude 1,100 m", China.
   DISTRIBUTION: Known only from the type locality.
   COMMENT: Reviewed (as *Vibrissaphora leishanensis*) by Liu, Hu, and Zhao, 1980, Acta
      Herpetol. Sinica, 3(1):1–15.

Leptobrachium liui (Pope, 1947). Copeia, 1947:109.
   ORIGINAL NAME: *Vibrissaphora liui*.
   TYPE(S): Holotype: FMNH 24427.
   TYPE LOCALITY: "region of San Chiang, Ch'ungan Hsien, Fukien [=Fujian]
      Province, China".
   DISTRIBUTION: Fujian, Guangdong, and Guangxi, China.
   COMMENT: Reviewed (as *Vibrissaphora liui*) by Liu, Hu, and Zhao, 1980, Acta
      Herpetol. Sinica, 3(1):1–15. See Pope, 1947, Copeia, 1947:109–112 (as
      Vibrissaphora liui). See comments under *Leptobrachium hasseltii* and *Leptobrachium*
      yaoshanense.

Leptobrachium montanum Fischer, 1885. Arch. Naturgesch., 51:44.
   TYPE(S): Not traced.
   TYPE LOCALITY: Pramassan-Alai Mountains, southeastern Borneo [Indonesia].
   DISTRIBUTION: Known only from the type locality.
   COMMENT: This nominal species retained by Dubois, 1983, Alytes, Paris, 2:147–153,
      pending revision of group.

Leptobrachium nigrops Berry and Hendrickson, 1963. Copeia, 1963:644.
   TYPE(S): Holotype: FMNH 134719.
   TYPE LOCALITY: "Singapore Catchment Area near Nee Soon Pumping Station,
      altitude 10–15 meters".
   DISTRIBUTION: Singapore and southern part of Malaya; Borneo.
   COMMENT: Reviewed by Inger, 1966, Fieldiana: Zool., 52:37–39.

Leptobrachium pullus (Smith, 1921). Proc. Zool. Soc. London, 1921:440.
   ORIGINAL NAME: *Megalophrys hasseltii* var. *pullus*.
   TYPE(S): Syntypes: BM.
   TYPE LOCALITY: Arbre Broyé [Lang Biang, southern Annam, Vietnam].
   DISTRIBUTION: Known only from the type locality.
   COMMENT: Nominal species retained by Dubois, 1983, Alytes, Paris, 2:147–153,
      with no discussion. The incorrect epithet *pullum* has been used.

Leptobrachium yaoshanense (Liu and Hu, 1981). Acta Herpetol. Sinica, 5(4):114.
   ORIGINAL NAME: *Vibrissaphora yaoshanensis*.
   TYPE(S): Holotype: CIB 610001.
   TYPE LOCALITY: Yangliuchong, Jinxiu, Yaoshan, Guangxi, altitude 1200 m, China.
   DISTRIBUTION: Guangxi and Hunan, China, 1000–1600 m elev.
   COMMENT: Related to *Leptobrachium leishanense*, according to the original

description. Discussed (as *Vibrissaphora yaoshanensis*) by Liu, Hu, and Zhao, 1980, Acta Herpetol. Sinica, 3(1):1–15. Allocated to *Leptobrachium* by Dubois, 1983, Alytes, Paris, 2:148. Guangxi specimens were previously reported as *Vibrissaphora liui* by Liu and Hu, 1962, Acta Zool. Sinica, 14(Suppl.):82–87.

Leptolalax Dubois, 1980. Bull. Mens. Soc. Linn. Lyon, 49:476.
   TYPE SPECIES: *Leptobrachium gracilis* Günther, 1872, by original designation.
   DISTRIBUTION: Burma and southern China through Thailand and Vietnam to Malaya and Borneo.
   COMMENT: Elevated from subgeneric status (under *Leptobrachium*) to generic status by Dubois, 1983, Alytes, Paris, 2:147–153.

Leptolalax bourreti Dubois, 1983. Alytes, Paris, 2:150.
   TYPE(S): Holotype: MNHNP 1938.94.
   TYPE LOCALITY: "Chapa, Vietnam, latitude 22° 21′ N, longitude 103° 50′ E".
   DISTRIBUTION: Known only from the type locality.

Leptolalax gracilis (Günther, 1872). Proc. Zool. Soc. London, 1872:598.
   ORIGINAL NAME: *Leptobrachium gracilis*.
   TYPE(S): Holotype: BM.
   TYPE LOCALITY: "Matang", Sarawak, Malaysia (Borneo).
   DISTRIBUTION: Malay Peninsula; northeastern Borneo.
   COMMENT: Reviewed by Bourret, 1942, Batr. Indochine:206–207, and Inger, 1966, Fieldiana: Zool., 52:24–28.

Leptolalax heteropus (Boulenger, 1900). Ann. Mag. Nat. Hist., (7)6:186.
   ORIGINAL NAME: *Leptobrachium heteropus*.
   TYPE(S): Holotype: Selangor Mus., Kuala Lumpur (?UMKL).
   TYPE LOCALITY: "Larut Hills at an altitude of 3500 feet", Perak, Malaya, Malaysia.
   DISTRIBUTION: Malay Peninsula, Malaysia.
   COMMENT: Reviewed by Bourret, 1942, Batr. Indochine:207–208, as *Megophrys heteropus*.

Leptolalax pelodytoides (Boulenger, 1893). Ann. Mus. Civ. Stor. Nat. Genova, (2)13:345.
   ORIGINAL NAME: *Leptobrachium pelodytoides*.
   TYPE(S): Syntypes: BM, MSNG; MSNG 29845 designated lectotype by Capocaccia, 1957, Ann. Mus. Civ. Stor. Nat. Genova, 69:212.
   TYPE LOCALITY: "Thao", "Karin Bia-Po", Karin Hills, Burma; restricted to Thao, by lectotype designation.
   DISTRIBUTION: Hong Kong, Yunnan, Guangxi, and Fujian (China), Burma, Thailand, northern Vietnam, and Malaya.
   COMMENT: Reviewed by Bourret, 1942, Batr. Indochine:208–211, as *Megophrys pelodytoides*. See also Pope, 1931, Bull. Am. Mus. Nat. Hist., 61:447–450. Dubois, 1981, Bull. Mens. Soc. Linn. Lyon, 50:187–188, provided synonymy, review, and placed *Leptobrachium minimum* Taylor, 1962, in synonymy. Dubois, 1983, Alytes, Paris, 2:147–153, considered *Megophrys oshanensis* Liu, 1950, Fieldiana: Zool. Mem., 2:197, a subspecies of *Leptolalax pelodytoides*. *Leptolalax oshanensis* was placed in the monotypic genus *Carpophrys* by Szechwan Institute of Biology (now Chengdu Institute of Biology), 1977, Syst. Key Chinese Amph.:130. Because *Carpophrys* is unsupported by a diagnosis it is a *nomen nudum* (Art. 13.a.i, Int. Code Zool. Nomencl., 1985).

Megophrys Kuhl and van Hasselt, 1822. Algemeene Konst-en Letter-Bode, 7:102.
   TYPE SPECIES: *Megophrys montana* Kuhl and van Hasselt, 1822, by monotypy.
   DISTRIBUTION: Southern, eastern, and southeastern Asia.
   COMMENT: See comment under Megophryinae. SH regards *Ophryophryne* (a subgenus, following Dubois) as a distinct genus. See comment under *Megophrys montana*.

Megophrys aceras (Boulenger, 1903). Fasc. Malay., 1:131.
ORIGINAL NAME: *Megalophrys montana* var. *aceras*.
TYPE(S): Not traced.
TYPE LOCALITY: Bukit Besar Jalor, Perak, Malay Peninsula [Malaysia].
DISTRIBUTION: Peninsular Thailand and Malaya.
COMMENT: Subgenus *Megophrys*. Reviewed by Bourret, 1942, Batr. Indochine:192–
194. See also Dring, 1979, Bull. Brit. Mus. (Nat. Hist.), Zool., 34:184.

Megophrys baluensis (Boulenger, 1899). Ann. Mag. Nat. Hist., (7)4:453.
ORIGINAL NAME: *Leptobrachium baluensis*.
TYPE(S): Holotype: RM.
TYPE LOCALITY: "Mount Kina Balu, 4200 feet", Malaysia (Borneo).
DISTRIBUTION: Northeastern Borneo.
COMMENT: Subgenus *Megophrys*. Reviewed by Inger, 1966, Fieldiana: Zool., 52:
46–48.

Megophrys boettgeri (Boulenger, 1899). Proc. Zool. Soc. London, 1899:171.
ORIGINAL NAME: *Leptobrachium boettgeri*.
TYPE(S): Syntypes: BM (5 specimens), MCZ 3790.
TYPE LOCALITY: "Kuatun, a village about 270 miles from Foochow, in the
mountains at the North-west of the Province of Fokien [=Fujian], at an
altitude of 3000 to 4000 feet or more", China.
DISTRIBUTION: Fujian, Zhejiang, Jiangxi, Anhui, Gansu, Guangdong, Guangxi,
Hunan, Shanxi, Sichuan, and Hongkong, China; Assam, India.
COMMENT: Subgenus *Megophrys*. See Pope, 1931, Bull. Am. Mus. Nat. Hist., 61:438–
444; Chang, 1947, Trans. Chinese Assoc. Adv. Sci., 9:89; and Liu and Hu,
1961, Tailless Amph. China:59. See comment under *Megophrys kempii*.

Megophrys brachykolos Inger and Romer, 1961. Fieldiana: Zool., 39:533.
TYPE(S): Holotype: FMNH 69063.
TYPE LOCALITY: "The Peak, Hong Kong Island", China.
DISTRIBUTION: Hongkong, China.
COMMENT: Subgenus *Megophrys*.

Megophrys feae (Boulenger, 1887). Ann. Mus. Civ. Stor. Nat. Genova, (2)4:512.
ORIGINAL NAME: *Megalophrys feae*.
TYPE(S): Holotype: MSNG 29763.
TYPE LOCALITY: Kakhien Hills, east of Bhamo, Upper Burma.
DISTRIBUTION: Northern Burma to northern Vietnam.
COMMENT: Subgenus *Megophrys*. See Taylor, 1962, Univ. Kansas Sci. Bull., 43:296–
298, for discussion.

Megophrys gigantica Liu, Hu, and Yang, 1960. Acta Zool. Sinica, 21:172.
ORIGINAL NAME: *Megophrys giganticus*.
TYPE(S): Holotype: CIB 581539.
TYPE LOCALITY: "Hsin-ming-hsian of Chingtung, Yunnan, 2,120 m. altitude",
China.
DISTRIBUTION: Known only from the type locality.
COMMENT: Subgenus *Megophrys*. See Liu and Hu, 1961, Tailless Amph. China:
71–72.

Megophrys intermedia (Smith, 1921). Proc. Zool. Soc. London, 1921:439.
ORIGINAL NAME: *Megalophrys intermedius*.
TYPE(S): Syntypes: BM.
TYPE LOCALITY: "on the [Langbian] Plateau above 1500 meters", Annam, Vietnam.
DISTRIBUTION: Vicinity of the type locality, southern Vietnam.
COMMENT: Subgenus *Megophrys*.

Megophrys kempii (Annandale, 1912). Rec. Indian Mus., 8:20.
ORIGINAL NAME: *Megalophrys kempii.*
TYPE(S): Holotype: ZSI 17013.
TYPE LOCALITY: "Upper Rotung (2,000 ft.)", Arunachal Pradesh, India (region claimed by China).
DISTRIBUTION: Known only from the type locality.
COMMENT: Considered a synonym, without discussion, of *Megophrys boettgeri* by Gorham, 1966, Das Tierreich, 85:16.

Megophrys kuatunensis Pope, 1927. Am. Mus. Novit., 352:1.
TYPE(S): Holotype: AMNH 30126.
TYPE LOCALITY: "Kuatun Village, Ch'ungan Hsien, northwestern Fukien [=Fujian] Province, China; altitude 5500–6000 feet", China.
DISTRIBUTION: Fujian, Hunan, and Zhejiang, China.
COMMENT: Subgenus *Megophrys*. Closely allied to *Megophrys boettgeri* and *Megophrys minor*, according to Pope, 1931, Bull. Am. Mus. Nat. Hist., 61:444.

Megophrys lateralis (Anderson, 1871). Proc. Asiat. Soc. Bengal, 40:29.
ORIGINAL NAME: *Ixalus lateralis.*
TYPE(S): Not traced.
TYPE LOCALITY: Western Yunnan [China].
DISTRIBUTION: Yunnan, Guangdong, Hunan, and Hongkong, China; northeastern India; Bangladesh; Burma; northern Vietnam.
COMMENT: Subgenus *Megophrys*.

Megophrys longipes (Boulenger, 1885). Proc. Zool. Soc. London, 1885:850.
ORIGINAL NAME: *Megalophrys longipes.*
TYPE(S): Holotype: BM.
TYPE LOCALITY: "The mountains of Perak, Straits of Malacca, at a height of 3,300 feet", Malaysia (Malaya).
DISTRIBUTION: Thailand, Cambodia, and southern Vietnam, south to Malaya.
COMMENT: Subgenus *Megophrys*. Reviewed by Bourret, 1942, Batr. Indochine:197–198. See also Pope, 1931, Bull. Am. Mus. Nat. Hist., 61:437–438, and Taylor, 1962, Univ. Kansas Sci. Bull., 43:290–292.

Megophrys microstoma (Boulenger, 1903). Ann. Mag. Nat. Hist., (7)12:186.
ORIGINAL NAME: *Ophryophryne microstoma.*
TYPE(S): Syntypes: BM.
TYPE LOCALITY: "Man-Son Mountains, Tonkin, altitude 3000–4000 feet", Vietnam.
DISTRIBUTION: Northern Vietnam and adjacent Guangxi, China.
COMMENT: Subgenus *Ophryophryne*. See comment under *Megophrys*. See Liu and Hu, 1962, Acta Zool. Sinica, 14(Suppl.):80–82.

Megophrys minor Stejneger, 1926. Proc. Biol. Soc. Washington, 39:53.
TYPE(S): Holotype: USNM 68816.
TYPE LOCALITY: "On mountain, about 3000 feet altitude, above Kwanghsien, 55 kilometers northwest of Chengtu [=Chengdu], Szechwan [=Sichuan], China".
DISTRIBUTION: Guizhou, Tibet, Sichuan, Yunnan, Hubei, Hunan, and Guangxi, China.
COMMENT: Subgenus *Megophrys*. See Liu and Hu, 1961, Tailless Amph. China:68.

Megophrys montana Kuhl and Van Hasselt, 1822. Algemeene Konst-en Letter-Bode, 7: 102.
TYPE(S): Syntypes: RMNH 2212 (4 specimens).
TYPE LOCALITY: Java [Indonesia].
DISTRIBUTION: Thailand southeast to Sumatra, Java, Natuna, and Borneo; Philippines.
COMMENT: Subgenus *Megophrys*. According to Dubois, 1982, Bull. Mus. Natl. Hist.

Nat., Paris, (4)4(A):263–269, this name has priority over *Megophrys monticola* Kuhl and Van Hasselt, 1822, Isis von Oken, 1822:475. Synonymy includes *Ceratophryne nasuta* Schlegel, 1858, as a subspecies, according to Inger, 1954, Fieldiana: Zool., 33:223, and Inger, 1966, Fieldiana: Zool., 52:39–46. *Megophrys nasuta* considered a distinct species by Taylor, 1962, Univ. Kansas Sci. Bull., 43: 284–287.

REVIEWERS: Angel Alcala (AA); Walter C. Brown (WCB).

Megophrys nankiangensis Liu and Hu, 1966. *In* Hu, Djao, and Liu, Acta Zool. Sinica, 18:72.

TYPE(S): Holotype: CIB 610588.

TYPE LOCALITY: "Kuang-wu Shan of Nankiang Hsien, Szechwan [=Sichuan], alt. 1,750 m", China.

DISTRIBUTION: Known only from the type locality.

COMMENT: Subgenus *Megophrys*. Closely related to *Megophrys omeimontis* according to the original description.

Megophrys omeimontis Liu, 1950. Fieldiana: Zool. Mem., 2:191.

TYPE(S): Holoype: FMNH 49406.

TYPE LOCALITY: "Mount Omei, Szechwan [=Sichuan], altitude 3,600 feet", China.

DISTRIBUTION: Tibet, Sichuan, Guangxi, and Yunnan, China, 850–2060 m elev.

COMMENT: Subgenus *Megophrys*. Reviewed by Liu and Hu, 1961, Tailless Amph. China:63–65, and Fei, Ye, and Huang, 1983, Acta Herpetol. Sinica, 2(2):49–52, who described two new subspecies.

Megophrys pachyprocta Huang, 1981. *In* Huang and Fei, Acta Zootaxon. Sinica, 6:211.

ORIGINAL NAME: *Megophrys pachyproctus*.

TYPE(S): Holotype: NPIB 770650.

TYPE LOCALITY: "Gelin of Medoxian, Xizang [=Tibet], altitude 1,530 m", China.

DISTRIBUTION: Known only from the type locality.

COMMENT: Similar to *Megophrys minor*, according to the original description.

Megophrys palpebralespinosa Bourret, 1937. Annexe Bull. Gén. Instr. Publique, Hanoi, 1937(4):16.

TYPE(S): Syntypes: MNHNP 48-114 and 48-116.

TYPE LOCALITY: Chapa, Tonkin [Vietnam].

DISTRIBUTION: Northern Vietnam; Yunnan, China.

COMMENT: Subgenus *Megophrys*. Reviewed by Bourret, 1942, Batr. Indochine:204–205, and Liu and Hu, 1961, Tailless Amph. China:57.

Megophrys parva (Boulenger, 1893). Ann. Mus. Civ. Stor. Nat. Genova, (2)13:344.

ORIGINAL NAME: *Leptobrachium parvum*.

TYPE(S): Syntypes: BM, MSNG; MSNG 29412 designated lectotype by Capocaccia, 1957, Ann. Mus. Civ. Stor. Nat. Genova, 69:211.

TYPE LOCALITY: "District of Karin Bia-po", Burma.

DISTRIBUTION: Sikkim, Assam, and Darjeeling (India) through Bangladesh and Burma to Thailand and southern China.

COMMENT: Subgenus *Megophrys*. Reviewed by Bourret, 1942, Batr. Indochine:203–204, and Liu and Hu, 1961, Tailless Amph. China:66–67.

Megophrys poilani (Bourret, 1937). Annexe Bull. Gén. Instr. Publique, Hanoi, 1937(4):8.

ORIGINAL NAME: *Ophryophryne poilani*.

TYPE(S): Holotype: MNHNP 1948/113.

TYPE LOCALITY: Dong-Tam-Ve, Vietnam.

DISTRIBUTION: Annam, Vietnam.

COMMENT: Subgenus *Ophryophryne*.

Megophrys robusta (Boulenger, 1908). Proc. Zool. Soc. London, 1908:418.
ORIGINAL NAME: *Megalophrys robusta*.
TYPE(S): ZSI.
TYPE LOCALITY: Darjeeling [West Bengal, India].
DISTRIBUTION: Darjeeling, West Bengal, India.
COMMENT: Subgenus *Megophrys*. *Megalophrys robusta* is a replacement name for
Xenophrys gigas Jerdon, 1870, Proc. Asiat. Soc. Bengal, 1870:85, which is
preoccupied by *Megalophrys gigas* Blyth, 1854.

Megophrys spinata Liu and Hu, 1973. *In* Hu, Djao, and Liu, Acta Zool. Sinica, 19(2):
163.
ORIGINAL NAME: *Megophrys spinatus*.
TYPE(S): Holotype: CIB 63II0615.
TYPE LOCALITY: "Fang-xiang, Lei-shan Hsien, Kweichow [=Guizhou], altitude 1,100
m", China.
DISTRIBUTION: Guizhou, Sichuan, and Guangxi, China.
COMMENT: Subgenus *Megophrys*. Related closely to *Megophrys omeimontis* according
to the original description.

Scutiger Theobald, 1868. J. Asiat. Soc. Bengal, 37:83.
TYPE SPECIES: *Bombinator sikimmensis* Blyth, 1854.
DISTRIBUTION: High altitudes (1000–5300 m) of southwestern China (including
Tibet), northern Burma, Nepal, and northern India.
COMMENT: *Oreolalax* Myers and Leviton, 1962, considered a subgenus of *Scutiger* by
Dubois, 1979, Rev. Suisse Zool., 86:631–640. SH rejects this view and considers
these taxa to be distinct genera.

Scutiger adungensis Dubois, 1979. Rev. Suisse Zool., 86:631.
TYPE(S): Holotype: BM 1932.6.8.7.
TYPE LOCALITY: "la valée de l'Adung, Birmanie, a la frontière tibéto-birmane, a
l'altitude de 12000 pieds (3650 m)".
DISTRIBUTION: Known only from the type locality.
COMMENT: Subgenus *Scutiger*, according to Dubois, 1980, Bull. Mens. Soc. Linn.
Lyon, 49:478. This species is intermediate between *Scutiger* and *Oreolalax*, as
defined by Myers and Leviton, 1962, Copeia, 1962:287–291, according to the
original description.

Scutiger alticola (Procter, 1922). Ann. Mag. Nat. Hist., (9)9:583.
ORIGINAL NAME: *Cophophryne alticola*.
TYPE(S): Holotype: BM 1922.3.3.1.
TYPE LOCALITY: "Kharta Valley, Tibet; altitude 16,500 feet", China.
DISTRIBUTION: Kharta and Tumbi valleys, Tibet, China; northwestern Nepal, 3200–
5300 m.
COMMENT: Subgenus *Scutiger*. In the *Scutiger sikimmensis* group, according to
Dubois, 1978, Senckenb. Biol., 59:169.

Scutiger boulengeri (Bedriaga, 1898). Wiss. Result. Przewalski Cent. Asien Reisen,
Zool., 3:63.
ORIGINAL NAME: *Leptobrachium boulengeri*.
TYPE(S): Syntypes: ZIL 1609 (2 specimens); ZIL 1609a considered holotype by Liu,
1950, Fieldiana: Zool. Mem., 2:184; now lost (LJB).
TYPE LOCALITY: Dichu, Upper Yangtze Kiang, [Sichuan,] China.
DISTRIBUTION: Sichuan, Qinghai, and Tibet, China.
COMMENT: Subgenus *Scutiger*. Liu, 1950, Fieldiana: Zool. Mem., 2:181–185,
discussed this species (as *Megophrys boulengeri*) and included *Megophrys
weigoldi* Vogt, 1924, Zool. Anz., 60:342 (Type locality: Washan, Szechwan
[=Sichuan], China), in synonymy. SH considers this synonymy to be in error.
See comment under *Scutiger tainingensis*.

Scutiger chintingensis Liu and Hu, 1960. Scientia Sinica, 9:770.
TYPE(S): Holotype: CIB (formerly Liu) 70.
TYPE LOCALITY: "Chinting, Mt. Omei (3,050 m), Szechwan [=Sichuan]", China.
DISTRIBUTION: Sichuan, China.
COMMENT: Subgenus *Oreolalax*. See Liu and Hu, 1961, Tailless Amph. China:87–89.
Discussed (as *Scutiger boulengeri*) by Liu, 1950, Fieldiana: Zool. Mem., 2:181–185.

Scutiger chuanbeiensis (Tian, 1983). Acta Herpetol. Sinica, 2(4):59–62.
ORIGINAL NAME: *Oreolalax chuanbeiensis*.
TYPE(S): Holotype: CIB 750344.
TYPE LOCALITY: Pingwu County, Sichuan, China.
DISTRIBUTION: Known only from the type locality.

Scutiger glandulatus (Liu, 1950). Fieldiana: Zool. Mem., 2:137.
ORIGINAL NAME: *Aelurophryne glandulata*.
TYPE(S): Holotype: FMNH 49392.
TYPE LOCALITY: "Hopachai, Lifanhsien, Szechwan [=Sichuan], China, altitude 8,500 feet".
DISTRIBUTION: Sichuan and Yunnan, China.
COMMENT: Subgenus *Scutiger*. Liu and Hu, 1961, Tailless Amph. China:110, included *Aelurophryne brevipes* Liu, 1950, as a synonym.

Scutiger gongshanensis Yang and Su, 1979. *In* Yang, Su, and Li, Acta Zootaxon. Sinica, 4:185.
TYPE(S): Holotype: KIZ 730388.
TYPE LOCALITY: "12th Bridge, Gongshan Xian, Yunnan, altitude 2750 m", China.
DISTRIBUTION: Yunnan, China, 2500–3300 m elev.
COMMENT: Subgenus *Scutiger*.

Scutiger jingdongensis (Ma, Yang, and Li, 1983). Acta Zootaxon. Sinica, 8:323.
ORIGINAL NAME: *Oreolalax jingdongensis*.
TYPE(S): Holotype: KIZ 8200588.
TYPE LOCALITY: Mt. Ailao, Jingdong, Yunnan, altitude 2400 m, China.
DISTRIBUTION: Yunnan, China.
COMMENT: Subgenus *Oreolalax*. Closely related to *Scutiger rugosus*, according to the original description.

Scutiger liangbeiensis (Liu and Fei, 1979). *In* Liu, Hu, and Fei, Acta Zootaxon. Sinica, 4(1):83.
ORIGINAL NAME: *Oreolalax liangbeiensis*.
TYPE(S): Holotype: CIB 65II0345.
TYPE LOCALITY: "Puxiong of Yuexi-Xian, Sichuan, altitude 2950 m", China.
DISTRIBUTION: Sichuan, China.
COMMENT: Subgenus *Oreolalax*. Closely related to *Scutiger major*, according to the original description.

Scutiger lichuanensis (Hu and Fei, 1979). *In* Liu, Hu, and Fei, Acta Zootaxon. Sinica, 4(1):86.
ORIGINAL NAME: *Oreolalax lichuanensis*.
TYPE(S): Holotype: CIB 74I0915.
TYPE LOCALITY: "Han-chi of Lichuan-Xian, Hubei, altitude 1790 m", China.
DISTRIBUTION: South-central China (Hubei, Sichuan, and Guizhou), 1790–2300 m elev.
COMMENT: Subgenus *Oreolalax*. Related to *Scutiger popei*, according to the original description.

Scutiger maculatus (Liu, 1950). Fieldiana: Zool. Mem., 2:136.
ORIGINAL NAME: *Aelurophryne maculata.*
TYPE(S): Holotype: FMNH 55869.
TYPE LOCALITY: "Hasa, 11,000 feet altitude, Kantze, Sikang [now Sichuan], China".
DISTRIBUTION: Sichuan and Tibet, China.
COMMENT: Subgenus *Scutiger.* See Liu and Hu, 1961, Tailless Amph. China:112–113.

Scutiger major Liu and Hu, 1960. Scientia Sinica, 9:764.
TYPE(S): Holotype: CIB 570952.
TYPE LOCALITY: Mt. Omei (2000 m), Sichuan, China.
DISTRIBUTION: Sichuan, China.
COMMENT: Subgenus *Oreolalax.* Related to *Scutiger popei* according to the original description. See Liu and Hu, 1961, Tailless Amph. China:77–80.

Scutiger mammatus (Günther, 1896). Ann. Mus. Zool. Acad. Sci. Imp. St. Petersbourg, 1:208.
ORIGINAL NAME: *Bufo mammatus.*
TYPE(S): Syntypes: ZIL 1968 (2 specimens).
TYPE LOCALITY: Tungsolo, Kham Plateau, Sichuan, China.
DISTRIBUTION: Tibet, Qinghai, and Sichuan, China.
COMMENT: Subgenus *Scutiger.* Reviewed by Liu, 1950, Fieldiana: Zool. Mem., 2: 120–125, and Liu and Hu, 1961, Tailless Amph. China:106–108. Former Kashmir specimens allocated to *Scutiger occidentalis* Dubois, 1978.

Scutiger nepalensis Dubois, 1974 "1973". Bull. Soc. Zool. France, 98:496.
TYPE(S): Holotype: MNHNP 1974.1095.
TYPE LOCALITY: Small torrent, Khaptar, on the road between Doti and Chainpur, 20 km west of Sacred lake, Dah Khaptar, western Nepal (29° 25′ N, 81° 02′ E, altitude 2950 m).
DISTRIBUTION: Known only from the type locality.
COMMENT: Subgenus *Scutiger.* In the *Scutiger sikimmensis* group, according to Dubois, 1978, Senckenb. Biol., 59:169.

Scutiger nyingchiensis Fei, 1977. Acta Zool. Sinica, 23:54.
TYPE(S): Holotype: CIB 73I0400.
TYPE LOCALITY: "Nyingchi, Xizang [=Tibet], alt. 3040 m", China.
DISTRIBUTION: Southeastern Tibet, China, 2730–4560 m elev.
COMMENT: Subgenus *Scutiger.*

Scutiger occidentalis Dubois, 1978. Senckenb. Biol., 59:164.
TYPE(S): Holotype: MNHNP 1977.1069.
TYPE LOCALITY: Shukdhari, 2920–2940 m alt., Sonamarg, Kashmir [India].
DISTRIBUTION: Kashmir and Ladakh, western Himalayas, 2680–3900 m elev.
COMMENT: Subgenus *Scutiger.* In the *Scutiger sikimmensis* group, according to the original description.

Scutiger omeimontis Liu and Hu, 1960. Scientia Sinica, 9:767.
TYPE(S): Holotype: CIB 57065.
TYPE LOCALITY: Changshingkao, Mt. Omei, Sichuan, China.
DISTRIBUTION: Sichuan, Yunnan, and Tibet, China.
COMMENT: Subgenus *Oreolalax.* Related to *Scutiger schmidti,* according to the original description. See Liu and Hu, 1961, Tailless Amph. China:80–82.

Scutiger pingii Liu, 1954. J. West China Border Res. Soc., (B)14:35.
TYPE(S): Holotype: CIB 375.
TYPE LOCALITY: Yenwot'ang, Chaochiao, Szechwan [=Sichuan], China.
DISTRIBUTION: Vicinity of the type locality.
COMMENT: Subgenus *Oreolalax.* Type species of *Oreolalax* Myers and Leviton, 1962,

by original designation. See Liu and Hu, 1961, Tailless Amph. China:89–92. See comment under *Scutiger*.

Scutiger pingwuensis Liu and Tian, 1981. Acta Herpetol. Sinica, 5:5.
  TYPE(S): Holotype: CIB 750793.
  TYPE LOCALITY: "Wang-ba-chu, Pingwu, northern Sichuan, alt. 2200 m", China.
  DISTRIBUTION: Known only from the type locality.
  COMMENT: Subgenus *Oreolalax*. Related to *Scutiger chintingensis*, according to the original description.

Scutiger popei Liu, 1947. Copeia, 1947:125.
  TYPE(S): Holotype: FMNH 49404.
  TYPE LOCALITY: "Lungtung, Pao-hsing (Mupin), Sikang [=Sichuan]; altitude 3400 feet", China.
  DISTRIBUTION: Sichuan, Gansu, and ?Shaanxi, China.
  COMMENT: Subgenus *Oreolalax*. See Liu and Hu, 1961, Tailless Amph. China:82–83.

Scutiger puxiongensis (Liu and Fei, 1979). *In* Liu, Hu, and Fei, Acta Zootaxon. Sinica, 4:84.
  ORIGINAL NAME: *Oreolalax puxiongensis*.
  TYPE(S): Holotype: CIB 65II0646.
  TYPE LOCALITY: "Pu-xiong of Yuexi-Xian, Sichuan, altitude 2900 m", China.
  DISTRIBUTION: Sichuan, 2600–2900 m alt., China.
  COMMENT: Subgenus *Oreolalax*. Closely related to *Scutiger schmidti*, according to the original description.

Scutiger rhodostigmatus (Hu and Fei, 1979). *In* Liu, Hu, and Fei, Acta Zootaxon. Sinica, 4:87.
  ORIGINAL NAME: *Oreolalax rhodostigmatus*.
  TYPE(S): Holotype: CIB 71001.
  TYPE LOCALITY: "Zunyi-Xian, Guizhou, altitude 1040 m", China.
  DISTRIBUTION: Hubei, Sichuan, and Guizhou, China, 1158–1830 m elev.
  COMMENT: Subgenus *Oreolalax*.

Scutiger ruginosus Zhao and Jiang, 1982. Acta Herpetol. Sinica, 1(1):79.
  TYPE(S): Holotype: CIB 80A0079.
  TYPE LOCALITY: "Xinduqiao, Kangding, Sichuan, alt. 3400 m", China.
  DISTRIBUTION: Known only from the type locality.

Scutiger rugosus Liu, 1943. J. West China Border Res. Soc., (B)14:37.
  TYPE(S): Holotype: CIB 909.
  TYPE LOCALITY: Yenwot'ang, Chaochiao, Szechwan [=Sichuan], China.
  DISTRIBUTION: Southern Sichuan and Hengduanshan Mountains, Yunnan, China.
  COMMENT: Subgenus *Oreolalax*. See Liu and Hu, 1961, Tailless Amph. China:74–76.

Scutiger schmidti Liu, 1947. Copeia, 1947:123.
  TYPE(S): Holotype: CIB (formerly Liu Coll.) 156.
  TYPE LOCALITY: "Mt. Omei, Szechwan [=Sichuan]; 7800 feet altitude", China.
  DISTRIBUTION: Western Sichuan, China.
  COMMENT: Subgenus *Oreolalax*. See Liu and Hu, 1961, Tailless Amph. China:85–87.

Scutiger sikimmensis (Blyth, 1854). J. Asiat. Soc. Bengal, 23:300.
  ORIGINAL NAME: *Bombinator sikimmensis*.
  TYPE(S): Not traced.
  TYPE LOCALITY: Sikkim [India].
  DISTRIBUTION: Nepal east through Sikkim (India) to southern Tibet (China).
  COMMENT: Subgenus *Scutiger*. In the *Scutiger sikimmensis* group, according to Dubois, 1978, Senckenb. Biol., 59:169.

Scutiger tainingensis (Liu, 1950). Fieldiana: Zool. Mem., 2:132.
ORIGINAL NAME: *Aelurophryne tainingensis.*
TYPE(S): Holotype: FMNH 49395.
TYPE LOCALITY: Taining, 11,500 feet altitude, Sikang [now Sichuan], China.
DISTRIBUTION: Vicinity of the type locality.
COMMENT: Subgenus *Scutiger.* Reviewed by Liu and Hu, 1961, Tailless Amph.
China:111–112. A synonym of *Scutiger boulengeri* (SH).

Scutiger tuberculatus Liu and Fei, 1979. *In* Liu, Hu, and Fei, Acta Zootaxon. Sinica,
4:89.
TYPE(S): Holotype: CIB 65II0448.
TYPE LOCALITY: "Pu-xiong of Yuexi-Xian, Sichuan, altitude 3000 m", China.
DISTRIBUTION: Pu-xiong of Yuaxi-Xian, Ye-le of Mianning-Xian, and Luo-Ji-Shan of
Xichang-Xian, Sichuan, 2650–3750 m elev., China.
COMMENT: Related to *Scutiger glandulatus*, according to the original description, and
in the subgenus *Scutiger*, by implication.

Scutiger xiangchengensis (Fei and Huang, 1983). Acta Herpetol. Sinica, 2(1):71.
ORIGINAL NAME: *Oreolalax xiangchengensis.*
TYPE(S): Holotype: CIB 80I1286.
TYPE LOCALITY: "Xiangcheng County, Sichuan, altitude 2800 m", China.
DISTRIBUTION: Vicinity of the type locality, 2680–3120 m elev.
COMMENT: Subgenus *Oreolalax*. Related to *Scutiger rugosus*, according to the original
description.

SUBFAMILY: **Pelobatinae** Bonaparte, 1850.
CITATION: Conspect. Syst. Herpetol. Amphibiol., 1 p.
DISTRIBUTION: Europe, western Asia, and northwestern Africa; southern Canada and
USA south to southern Mexico.
COMMENT: The first use of the spelling Pelobatinae was by Fejérváry, 1921, Arch.
Naturgesch., (A)87:25. See comment under Pelobatidae. Roček, 1981 "1980", Acta
Univ. Carol., Prague, Biol., 1980(1–2):140–156, discussed the relationships between
the living and fossil taxa and suggested the independent evolution of the
Pelobates group and the *Scaphiopus* group, which he treated as separate families,
the Pelobatidae and Scaphiopodidae.

Pelobates Wagler, 1830. Nat. Syst. Amph.:206.
TYPE SPECIES: *Bufo fuscus* Laurenti, 1768.
DISTRIBUTION: Europe, western Asia, and northwestern Africa.
COMMENT: See Mertens and Wermuth, 1960, Amph. Rept. Europas:42–44, for
synonymies for European species.
REVIEWER: Leo J. Borkin (LJB).

Pelobates cultripes (Cuvier, 1829). Règne Animal, Ed. 2, 2:105.
ORIGINAL NAME: *Rana cultripes.*
TYPE(S): Not traced.
TYPE LOCALITY: Southern France.
DISTRIBUTION: Iberian Peninsula and southern France.

Pelobates fuscus (Laurenti, 1768). Synops. Rept.:28.
ORIGINAL NAME: *Bufo fuscus.*
TYPE(S): Not traced.
TYPE LOCALITY: Restricted to "Wien", Austria, by Mertens and Müller, 1928, Abh.
Senckenb. Naturforsch. Ges., 41:18.
DISTRIBUTION: France, Belgium, Netherlands, Denmark, southern Sweden, and
northern Italy east to southern Siberia, western Kazakhstan, and northern
Caucasus in USSR.

Pelobates syriacus Boettger, 1889. Zool. Anz., 12:145.
  TYPE(S): SMF 1722 (formerly 1437.1a) designated lectotype by Mertens, 1967, Senckenb. Biol., 48:38.
  TYPE LOCALITY: Haifa [Israel].
  DISTRIBUTION: Northern Israel; Lebanon; northern Syria; northern Iraq; Turkey; Caspian Iran; eastern Transcaucasia (USSR); Balkan Peninsula north to southern Yugoslavia and southeastern Romania.

Pelobates varaldii Pasteur and Bons, 1959. Trav. Inst. Scient. Chérifien, Rabat, Ser. Zool., 17:117.
  TYPE(S): Holotype: MNHNP.
  TYPE LOCALITY: "Merja Samora", Morocco.
  DISTRIBUTION: Northwestern Morocco.

Scaphiopus Holbrook, 1836. N. Am. Herpetol., Ed. 1, 1:85.
  TYPE SPECIES: *Scaphiopus solitarius* Holbrook, 1836 (=*Rana holbrookii* Harlan, 1835), by monotypy.
  DISTRIBUTION: South-central Canada, USA, and Mexico south to the southern edge of the Mexican Plateau.
  COMMENT: Kluge, 1966, Contrib. Sci. Nat. Hist. Mus. Los Angeles Co., 113:1–26, discussed phylogeny of this genus and its subgenera.
  REVIEWER: Jonathan A. Campbell (JAC); Gustavo Casas-Andreu (GCA) (Mexico); Ronald I. Crombie (RIC); Oscar Flores-Villela (OFV) (Mexico).

Scaphiopus bombifrons Cope, 1863. Proc. Acad. Nat. Sci. Philadelphia, 15:53.
  TYPE(S): Syntypes: USNM 3704 (Fort Union), 3520 (Platte River), and 3703 (Llano Estacado).
  TYPE LOCALITY: "Fort Union, on Missouri River, lat. 48° N"; "On Platte River, 200 miles west of Fort Kearney"; "Llano Estacado Texas". Restricted to Fort Williams [=Fort Union], North Dakota, USA, by Schmidt, 1953, Check List N. Am. Amph. Rept., Ed. 6:59.
  DISTRIBUTION: Southern Alberta and southwestern Saskatchewan (Canada) southward into Montana, North Dakota, south to eastern Arizona (USA), Chihuahua, and Tamaulipas (Mexico).
  COMMENT: Subgenus *Spea*.

Scaphiopus couchii Baird, 1854. Proc. Acad. Nat. Sci. Philadelphia, 7:62.
  TYPE(S): Syntypes: USNM 3713–14; lost according to Kellogg, 1932, Bull. U.S. Natl. Mus., 160:20.
  TYPE LOCALITY: "Coahuila and Tamaulipas", Mexico; restricted to "Matamoros, Tamaulipas", Mexico, by Smith and Taylor, 1950, Univ. Kansas Sci. Bull., 33:345.
  DISTRIBUTION: Southeastern California to southwestern Oklahoma (USA) and south to northern Nayarit, Zacatecas, San Luis Potosí, and northern Veracruz (Mexico).
  COMMENT: Subgenus *Scaphiopus*. Reviewed by Wasserman, 1970, Cat. Am. Amph. Rept., 85.1–4.

Scaphiopus hammondii Baird, 1859 "1857". Rep. Explor. Surv. R.R. Route Mississippi River–Pacific Ocean, 10(Pt. 4, no. 4):12.
  TYPE(S): Holotype: USNM 3695.
  TYPE LOCALITY: "Fort Reading", California, USA.
  DISTRIBUTION: Western California (USA) and northwestern Baja California (Mexico).
  COMMENT: Subgenus *Spea*. See comment under *Scaphiopus multiplicatus*.

Scaphiopus holbrookii (Harlan, 1835). Med. Phys. Res.:105.
ORIGINAL NAME: *Rana holbrookii*.
TYPE(S): Not known to exist.
TYPE LOCALITY: "South Carolina", USA; restricted to "Charleston", South Carolina, USA, by Schmidt, 1953, Check List N. Am. Amph. Rept., Ed. 6:58.
DISTRIBUTION: Massachusetts to Florida and west to eastern Louisiana; eastern Oklahoma and western Louisiana to extreme southern Texas, USA.
COMMENT: Reviewed by Wasserman, 1968, Cat. Am. Amph. Rept., 70.1–2. Subgenus *Scaphiopus*. Some authors regard the allopatric western subspecies *Scaphiopus holbrookii hurterii* Strecker, 1910, to be a distinct species.

Scaphiopus intermontanus Cope, 1883. Proc. Acad. Nat. Sci. Philadelphia, 35:15.
TYPE(S): Syntypes: ANSP 13787 (Salt Lake City), 13788–89 + 2 (Pyramid Lake) lost.
TYPE LOCALITY: "Salt Lake City", Salt Lake County, Utah, USA, and "Pyramid Lake, [Storey County,] Nevada", USA; restricted to "Salt Lake City", Salt Lake County, Utah, USA, by Schmidt, 1953, Check List N. Am. Amph. Rept., Ed. 6:59.
DISTRIBUTION: Great Basin of western North America, north to southern Idaho (USA) and British Columbia (Canada) south to eastern California, northern Arizona, and northeastern New Mexico east to western Colorado and southwestern Wyoming (USA).
COMMENT: Subgenus *Spea*.

Scaphiopus multiplicatus Cope, 1863. Proc. Acad. Nat. Sci. Philadelphia, 15:52.
TYPE(S): Holotype: USNM 3694.
TYPE LOCALITY: "Valley of Mexico".
DISTRIBUTION: Southwestern USA, excluding California, to the southern edge of the Mexican Plateau.
COMMENT: Considered a species distinct from *Scaphiopus hammondii* by Brown, 1976, Contrib. Sci. Nat. Hist. Mus. Los Angeles Co., 286:1–15. Subgenus *Spea*.

FAMILY: **Pelodytidae** Bonaparte, 1850.
CITATION: Conspect. Syst. Herpetol. Amphibiol., 1 p.
DISTRIBUTION: Southwestern Europe and the Caucasus.
COMMENT: Lynch, 1973, *In* Vial (ed.), Evol. Biol. Anurans:133–182, considered the Pelodytidae to be derived from the Pelobatinae (Pelobatidae), a statement not supported by his phylogenetic tree, which shows similarity due to shared primitive features. Savage, 1973, *In* Vial (ed.), Evol. Biol. Anurans:351–445, considered the Pelodytidae to be a subfamily (the Pelodytinae) of the Pelobatidae.
REVIEWERS: Steven C. Anderson (SCA); Leo J. Borkin (LJB); William E. Duellman (WED); Marinus S. Hoogmoed (MSH).

Pelodytes Bonaparte, 1838. Icon. Fauna Ital., 2, 23:[3].
TYPE SPECIES: *Rana punctata* Daudin, 1802.
DISTRIBUTION: Southwestern Europe and the Caucasus.
COMMENT: See Mertens and Wermuth, 1960, Amph. Rept. Europas:44, for synonymies.

Pelodytes caucasicus Boulenger, 1896. Ann. Mag. Nat. Hist., (6)17:406.
TYPE(S): Holotype: BM.
TYPE LOCALITY: "Mount Lomis, Caucasus, 7000 feet", near Bakuriani, Georgia, USSR.
DISTRIBUTION: Northwestern Caucasus and western Transcaucasia, USSR; adjacent Turkey.
COMMENT: See Başoğlu and Özeti, 1973, Turkiye Amph.:82–84, and Goluber, 1980, Vestn. Zool., Kiev, 3:52–55.

Pelodytes punctatus (Daudin, 1802). Hist. Nat. Rain. Gren. Crap.:51.
ORIGINAL NAME: *Rana punctata*.
TYPE(S): Not traced.
TYPE LOCALITY: Vicinity of Beauvois, Department Oise, northern France.
DISTRIBUTION: Belgium through France to Spain and extreme northwestern Italy.

FAMILY: **Pipidae** Gray, 1825.
CITATION: Ann. Philos., (2)10:213.
DISTRIBUTION: South America east of the Andes and in adjacent Panama; south of the Sahara in Africa.
COMMENT: Gray, 1825, Ann. Philos., (2)10:214, originally named this group Piprina (an implicit subfamily) based on *"Pipra* Laurenti" (an unjustified emendation of *Pipa* Laurenti). Under the provisions of Article 35.d of the International Code of Zoological Nomenclature (1985) family-group names based on improperly formed type genera must be corrected. Reig, 1973, Ameghiniana, 17:3–7; Lynch, 1973, *In* Vial (ed.), Evol. Biol. Anurans:133–182; and Starrett, 1973, *In* Vial (ed.), Evol. Biol. Anurans:252–271, placed this family phylogenetically near to the Rhinophrynidae. Sokol, 1977, J. Zool., London, 182:505, argued that pipids are not primitive. Tinsley, 1981, Monit. Zool. Ital., N.S., Suppl., 19:367, supported an early separation from other anurans.
REVIEWERS: William E. Duellman (WED); Marinus S. Hoogmoed (MSH).

SUBFAMILY: **Pipinae** Gray, 1825.
CITATION: Ann. Philos., (2)10:213.
DISTRIBUTION: Northern South America east of the Andes and in adjacent Panama.
COMMENT: The first use of the subfamilial name Pipinae was by Noble, 1931, Biol. Amph.:491.
CONTRIBUTOR: David C. Cannatella (DCC).
REVIEWERS: Werner C. A. Bokermann (WCAB) (Brazil); Ulisses Caramaschi (UC) (Brazil); Ronald I. Crombie (RIC); Keith A. Harding (KAH); Enrique La Marca (ELM) (Northern South America); Norman J. Scott, Jr. (NJS); Paulo E. Vanzolini (PEV) (Brazil).

Pipa Laurenti, 1768. Synops. Rept.:24.
TYPE SPECIES: *Pipa americana* Laurenti, 1768 (=*Rana pipa* Linnaeus, 1758).
DISTRIBUTION: Northern South America and Panama.
COMMENT: Dunn, 1948, Am. Mus. Novit., 1384, reviewed the genus.

Pipa arrabali Izecksohn, 1976. Rev. Brasil. Biol., 36:508.
TYPE(S): Holotype: EI 5311.
TYPE LOCALITY: "Vila Amazônia, Município de Parintins, Estado do Amazonas, Brasil".
DISTRIBUTION: Known only from the type locality.

Pipa aspera Müller, 1924. Zool. Anz., 58:291.
TYPE(S): Holotype: ZSM 19/1923; destroyed (DCC).
TYPE LOCALITY: "Albina (Unterlauf des Maroni), Surinam".
DISTRIBUTION: Southeastern Venezuela, Guyana, and Surinam; Amazonas and Pará, Brazil.

Pipa carvalhoi (Miranda-Ribeiro, 1937). Campo, Rio de Janeiro, 1937(4):54.
ORIGINAL NAME: *Protopipa carvalhoi*.
TYPE(S): Not traced.
TYPE LOCALITY: Riacho do Cavallo, Serra da Cachoeira, near Casinhas (590 m), municipality Surubim, State of Pernambuco, Brazil.
DISTRIBUTION: States of Pernambuco, Ceará, Espírito Santo, Bahia, Minas Gerais, and Paraíba, Brazil.

Pipa myersi Trueb, 1984. Herpetologica, 40:225.
TYPE(S): Holotype: KU 113665.
TYPE LOCALITY: "7 km above the mouth of the Río Ucurgantí, Provincia Darién, Panama, 30 m".
DISTRIBUTION: Río Chucunaque drainage of Provincia Darién, Panama; doubtfully from Río Zulia, Norte de Santander, Colombia.
COMMENT: Specimens of this species from eastern Panama were referred to *Pipa parva* by Heatwole, 1963, Copeia, 1963:436–437.

Pipa parva Ruthven and Gaige, 1923. Occas. Pap. Mus. Zool. Univ. Michigan, 136:1.
TYPE(S): Holotype: UMMZ 57443.
TYPE LOCALITY: "Sabana de Mendoza, [Estado Trujillo,] Venezuela".
DISTRIBUTION: Northeastern Colombia and northwestern Venezuela.
COMMENT: See comment under *Pipa myersi*.

Pipa pipa (Linnaeus, 1758). Syst. Nat., Ed. 10, 1:210.
ORIGINAL NAME: *Rana pipa*.
TYPE(S): Based on a plate in Seba, 1734, Loc. Nat. Thes. Desc. Icon. Exp., vol. 1.
TYPE LOCALITY: Surinam.
DISTRIBUTION: Bolivia to Colombia and the Guianas to Peru, Ecuador, and Brazil; Trinidad.

Pipa snethlageae Müller, 1914. Ann. Mag. Nat. Hist., (8)14:102.
TYPE(S): Holotype: ZSM 1/1914; destroyed (DCC).
TYPE LOCALITY: "Utinga, near Pará (Belém), state of Pará, N.E. Brazil".
DISTRIBUTION: Known only from the type locality.

SUBFAMILY: **Xenopodinae** Fitzinger, 1843.
CITATION: Syst. Rept.:33.
DISTRIBUTION: Africa south of the Sahara
COMMENT: As first formed the group name was Xenopoda. Dubois, 1983, Bull. Mens. Soc. Linn. Lyon, 52:271, regarded Dactylethrinae Hogg, 1838, as the correct name for this taxon. Dactylethrinae is based on *Dactylethra* Cuvier, 1829, a junior synonym of *Xenopus* which was synonymized prior to 1961. Under the provisions of Article 40 of the International Code of Zoological Nomenclature (1985) Dactylethrinae is not an available name. The incorrect group name Xenopinae has had widespread use. The monophyly of this group has yet to be demonstrated (JDL). See comment under *Xenopus*.
CONTRIBUTOR: R. C. Tinsley (RCT).
REVIEWERS: J.-L. Amiet (JLA) (Cameroon); David C. Cannatella (DCC); Alan Channing (AC); Kim M. Howell (KMH); Raymond Laurent (RL); John C. Poynton (JCP).

Hymenochirus Boulenger, 1896. Ann. Mag. Nat. Hist., (6)18:420.
TYPE SPECIES: *Xenopus boettgeri* Tornier, 1896, by original designation and monotypy.
DISTRIBUTION: Forested equatorial Africa from Nigeria and Cameroon south through Gabon and east throughout the Zaire River Basin.
COMMENT: The intensive techniques of biochemical and genetic analysis, which have provided comparative information on the evolution of *Xenopus* species, have not yet been applied to the other Xenopodinae, and studies of the interrelationships of *Hymenochirus* species are scanty. Sokol, 1977, J. Morphol., 154: 357, discussed intergeneric affinities. Perret, 1966, Zool. Jahrb., Abt. Syst., 93: 304, provided a key to species.

Hymenochirus boettgeri (Tornier, 1896). Kriechth. Deutsch Ost-Afr.:163.
ORIGINAL NAME: *Xenopus boettgeri*.
TYPE(S): Not traced.
TYPE LOCALITY: "Ituri-Fähre bei Wandesoma", Zaire.
DISTRIBUTION: Nigeria and Cameroon and through the Zaire Basin to eastern Zaire.

COMMENT: Perret and Mertens, 1957, Bull. Inst. Franç. Afr. Noire, (A)19:552, distinguished the subspecies *Hymenochirus boettgeri boettgeri* and *Hymenochirus boettgeri camerunensis*, closely related to *Hymenochirus feae*.

Hymenochirus boulengeri Witte, 1930. Rev. Zool. Bot. Afr., 19:240.
TYPE(S): Holotype: RGMC 3375.
TYPE LOCALITY: Mauda, Belgian Congo [Zaire].
DISTRIBUTION: Eastern Zaire.

Hymenochirus curtipes Noble, 1924. Bull. Am. Mus. Nat. Hist., 49:155.
TYPE(S): Holotype: AMNH 9453.
TYPE LOCALITY: Zambi, lower Congo [Zaire].
DISTRIBUTION: Western Zaire.

Hymenochirus feae Boulenger, 1906. Ann. Mus. Civ. Stor. Nat. Genova, (3)2:158.
TYPE(S): Not stated but BM 1947.2.24.81–82 (formerly 1906.3.30.172–173) and MSNG 29941 (4 specimens) apparent syntypes; MSNG 29941A designated lectotype by Capocaccia, 1957, Ann. Mus. Civ. Stor. Nat. Genova, 69:210.
TYPE LOCALITY: Fernand-Vaz, French Congo [Gabon].
DISTRIBUTION: Gabon.
COMMENT: Perret and Mertens, 1957, Bull. Inst. Franç. Afr. Noire, (A)19:554, regarded *Hymenochirus feae* as a subspecies of *Hymenochirus boettgeri*, but Perret, 1966, Zool. Jahrb., Abt. Syst., 93:305, recognized *Hymenochirus feae* as a distinct species.

Pseudhymenochirus Chabanaud, 1920. Bull. Com. Études Hist. Scient. Afr. Occid. Franç., 1920:494.
TYPE SPECIES: *Pseudhymenochirus merlini* Chabanaud, 1920.
DISTRIBUTION: As for the single species.
COMMENT: Lamotte, 1963, Bull. Inst. Franç. Afr. Noire, (A)25:944, and Arnoult and Lamotte, 1968, Bull. Inst. Franç. Afr. Noire, (A)30:293, considered *Pseudhymenochirus* as a subgenus of *Hymenochirus*. Sokol, 1977, J. Morphol., 154:357, concluded that these genera were very closely related but distinctive primitive characters of *Pseudhymenochirus* may justify separation "if one so desires."

Pseudhymenochirus merlini Chabanaud, 1920. Bull. Com. Études Hist. Scient. Afr. Occid. Franç., 1920:494.
TYPE(S): Holotype: MNHNP 1920-186.
TYPE LOCALITY: Dixine (near Conakry), French Guinea [Guinea].
DISTRIBUTION: Guinea, Guinea-Bissau, and Sierra Leone.
COMMENT: Sokol, 1977, J. Morphol., 154:357, considered *Pseudhymenochirus* a primitive *Hymenochirus*, rather than an intermediate between *Hymenochirus* and *Xenopus* as proposed by Dunn, 1948, Am. Mus. Novit., 1384:5. Geographically, *Pseudhymenochirus merlini* is separated by 2000 km from the westernmost *Hymenochirus* (in Nigeria) (Menzies, 1967, J. West Afr. Sci. Assoc., 12:23).

Xenopus Wagler, 1827. Isis von Oken, 20:726.
TYPE SPECIES: *Xenopus boiei* Wagler, 1827 (=*Bufo laevis* Daudin, 1802).
DISTRIBUTION: Africa south of the Sahara with an isolated record in the Ennedi (northeastern Chad).
COMMENT: Fossil evidence suggested that diversification of the genus preceded separation of African and South American continental plates according to Estes, 1975, Herpetologica, 31:263. Unfortunately, *Xenopus* is diagnosed solely on features primitive for the family; therefore, the fossil "*Xenopus*" from South America may actually be more closely related to the Pipinae than to Recent *Xenopus* (DCC). Almost all extant species have been confused with one another

for varying periods; older literature records require considerable evaluation. Recognition of series of diploid-polyploid cryptic species has produced new problems for establishing identity and distribution from museum records (Loumont, 1983, Rev. Suisse Zool., 90:169). Recent comparative techniques have provided data on interspecific relationships, including analysis of albumins (Bisbee, Baker, Wilson, Hadji-Azimi, and Fischberg, 1977, Science, Washington, D.C., 195:785), karyotypes (Tymowska and Fischberg, 1973, Chromosoma, 44: 335), mating calls (Vigny, 1979, J. Zool., London, 188:103), LDH isozymes (Vonwyl and Fischberg, 1980, J. Exp. Zool., 211:281), and hemoglobins (Muir, 1981, J. Exp. Zool., 218:327).

Xenopus amieti Kobel, du Pasquier, Fischberg, and Gloor, 1980. Rev. Suisse Zool., 87: 920.
TYPE(S): Holotype: MHNG 2030.80.
TYPE LOCALITY: "Massif du Manengouba; altitude 2000 m; 5° 03' N, 9° 49' E", Cameroon.
DISTRIBUTION: Volcanic highlands of western Cameroon.
COMMENT: Morphologically resembles *Xenopus fraseri* (2n = 36) and *Xenopus ruwenzoriensis* (2n = 108) but distinguished by its chromosome number of 2n = 72 (Kobel, Du Pasquier, Fischberg, and Gloor, 1980, Rev. Suisse Zool., 87:920).

Xenopus andrei Loumont, 1983. Rev. Suisse Zool., 90:170.
TYPE(S): Holotype: MHNG 2088.32.
TYPE LOCALITY: "Longyi (Nord de Kribi)", southern Cameroon.
DISTRIBUTION: Known only from the type locality on the Atlantic coast of Cameroon.
COMMENT: One of a group of cryptic species resembling *Xenopus fraseri* but distinguished from it by chromosome number (2n = 72) and mating call.

Xenopus borealis Parker, 1936. Ann. Mag. Nat. Hist., (10)18:596.
ORIGINAL NAME: *Xenopus laevis borealis*.
TYPE(S): Syntypes: 9 collections of specimens listed as cotypes by Parker, 1936, Ann. Mag. Nat. Hist., (10)18:601, and in BM catalogue; one collection not specified, BM 1947.2.24.71–74 (formerly 1935.12.1.53–57); others: BM 1901.1.3.34–36, 1910.10.31.26, 1909.11.15.4–7, 1929.10.13.3–6, 1913.4.24.17, 1932.5.2.36–38, 1935.11.2.11–12, 1912.11.8.4–12.
TYPE LOCALITY: Marsabit; hot spring of Lake Nakuru; Nairobi (2 collections); Lake Naivasha (3 collections); Mt. Elgon, 6000 feet; Leikipia, 7000–8000 feet [Kenya].
DISTRIBUTION: Savanna in central and northern Kenya.
COMMENT: Tymowska and Fischberg, 1973, Chromosoma, 44:336, distinguished *Xenopus borealis* from the *Xenopus laevis* group by chromosome morphology and suggested closer affinities with *Xenopus muelleri*.

Xenopus boumbaensis Loumont, 1983. Rev. Suisse Zool., 90:169.
TYPE(S): Holotype: MHNG 2088.31.
TYPE LOCALITY: "Mawa, à mi-chemin entre Yokadouma et Moloundou", southern Cameroon.
DISTRIBUTION: Known only from the type locality in equatorial forest, Cameroon.
COMMENT: One of a group of cryptic species resembling *Xenopus fraseri* but distinguished from it by chromosome number (2n = 72) and a mating call of a single note (found elsewhere within the genus only in *Xenopus borealis*; see Loumont, 1983, Rev. Suisse Zool., 90:170).

Xenopus clivii Peracca, 1898. Boll. Mus. Zool. Anat. Comp. Univ. Torino, 13(321):3.
TYPE(S): Not stated.
TYPE LOCALITY: Saganeiti and Adi Caié, Eritrea [Ethiopia].
DISTRIBUTION: Through Ethiopia and into northern Kenya.

COMMENT: Chromosome number 2n = 36 (Tymowska and Fischberg, 1973, Chromosoma, 44:337).

Xenopus epitropicalis Fischberg, Colombelli, and Picard, 1982. Alytes, Paris, 1(4):53.
TYPE(S): Holotype: BM 1982.462.
TYPE LOCALITY: "Confluent de la Funa et de la Kemi, à 8 km au sud du centre de Kinshasa (Zaire); altitude 350 m; 4° 18′ S, 15° 18′ E".
DISTRIBUTION: Cameroon south and east through the Zaire Basin (Gabon and western Zaire and eastward to Garamba).
COMMENT: *Xenopus epitropicalis* is tetraploid (2n = 40) with respect to *Xenopus tropicalis* (see Fischberg, Colombelli, and Picard, 1982, Alytes, Paris, 1(4):53); although morphologically difficult to distinguish, these species also differ in mating call characteristics (Loumont, 1983, Rev. Suisse Zool., 90:174).

Xenopus fraseri Boulenger, 1905. Proc. Zool. Soc. London, 1905:250.
TYPE(S): Not stated, but BM 1947.2.24.78–79 (formerly 1852.2.22.23–24) recorded as syntypes.
TYPE LOCALITY: "West Africa . . . therefore probably from Nigeria or Fernando Po".
DISTRIBUTION: Forested West Africa from Cameroon and Fernando Po eastward throughout the Zaire River Basin to the Zaire-Uganda border, and southward to Angola.
COMMENT: *Xenopus fraseri* forms part of a diploid-polyploid cryptic species group with chromosome numbers of 2n = 36 (*Xenopus fraseri*), 2n = 72 (*Xenopus amieti, Xenopus andrei, Xenopus boumbaensis*), and 2n = 108 (*Xenopus ruwenzoriensis*) (Kobel, Du Pasquier, Fischberg, and Gloor, 1980, Rev. Suisse Zool., 87:924; Loumont, 1983, Rev. Suisse Zool., 90:169). Existing literature records assigned to *Xenopus fraseri* therefore require re-evaluation.

Xenopus gilli Rose and Hewitt, 1927. Trans. R. Soc. S. Afr., 14:344.
TYPE(S): Not stated; AMG 5112 recorded as holotype.
TYPE LOCALITY: "Near Cape Town", Rep. South Africa, but specified as near Sylvermyn River by Rose and Hewitt, 1927, Trans. R. Soc. S. Afr., 14:343.
DISTRIBUTION: Restricted to the Cape Flats and Cape Peninsula together with isolated inland localities on the southwestern Cape, Rep. South Africa (Rau, 1978, Ann. S. Afr. Mus., 76:248).
COMMENT: Kobel, Du Pasquier, and Tinsley, 1981, J. Zool., London, 194:321, demonstrated natural hybridization and gene introgression between this species and *Xenopus laevis* (both with 2n = 36 chromosomes).

Xenopus laevis (Daudin, 1802). Hist. Nat. Rain. Gren. Crap.:85.
ORIGINAL NAME: *Bufo laevis*.
TYPE(S): No longer in existence according to Poynton, 1964, Ann. Natal Mus., 17:31.
TYPE LOCALITY: Not stated.
DISTRIBUTION: Savanna from Rep. South Africa northward to Kenya, Uganda, and northeastern Zaire and westward to Cameroon; in Rep. South Africa to top of Drakensberg Mountains; introduced in southern California, USA.
COMMENT: Range extends over 40° of latitude, occupying the cooler upland regions between the rainforests of the west and the hotter, drier savannas of the east and north (Tinsley, 1981, Monit. Zool. Ital., N.S., Suppl., 15:135). A chain of subspecies recognized (*laevis, petersi, poweri, victorianus, bunyoniensis, sudanensis*) (see Schmidt and Inger, 1959, Explor. Parc Natl. Upemba, 56:8; Perret, 1966, Zool. Jahrb., Abt. Syst., 93:301) and an unnamed subspecies from Malawi (Vonwyl and Fischberg, 1980, J. Exp. Zool., 211:282)—but *Xenopus borealis* is now considered a distinct species. Bisbee, Baker, Wilson, Hadji-Azimi, and Fischberg, 1977, Science, Washington, D.C., 195:787, suggested that the chromosome number 2n = 36, basic to several species, may reflect ancient tetraploidy and that total genome duplication occurred in an ancestor of the *Xenopus laevis* group.

Xenopus muelleri (Peters, 1844). Monatsber. Preuss. Akad. Wiss. Berlin, 1844:37.
ORIGINAL NAME: *Dactylethra mülleri.*
TYPE(S): ZMB.
TYPE LOCALITY: Angola and Mozambique; restricted to Tete, Zambezi
[Mozambique], by Loveridge, 1957, Bull. Mus. Comp. Zool., 117:308.
DISTRIBUTION: Relatively arid savanna from Upper Volta eastward across Sudan-
Guinea zone to northeastern Zaire, then south along East African coastal belt
into Rep. South Africa; isolated record in the Ennedi (northeastern Chad).
COMMENT: Chromosome number 2n = 36 (Tymowska and Kobel, 1972,
Cytogenetics, 11:271). A savanna species, like *Xenopus laevis*, but distinguished
throughout extensive range by preference for hotter, more lowland regions
(Tinsley, 1981, Monit. Zool. Ital., N.S., Suppl., 15:135).

Xenopus ruwenzoriensis Tymowska and Fischberg, 1973. Chromosoma, 44:337.
TYPE(S): Not stated.
TYPE LOCALITY: "Semliki, Uganda"; amplified by Fischberg and Kobel, 1978,
Experientia, 34:1012, to "Rain forest near Bundibugyo in the Semliki Valley at
the foot of the Ruwenzori Mountain (1° N, 30° E; altitude 700 m)".
DISTRIBUTION: Known only from the type locality, border of Uganda with Zaire.
COMMENT: Distinguished by chromosome number (2n = 108), hexaploid with
respect to *Xenopus laevis*, by Tymowska and Fischberg, 1973, Chromosoma, 44:
337. Morphology described by Fischberg and Kobel, 1978, Experientia, 34:
1012. Further karyotype description by Tymowska and Fischberg, 1980,
Cytogenet. Cell. Genet., 27:39, who cited the authorities for the name *Xenopus
ruwenzoriensis* as Fischberg and Kobel, 1978. No type material was noted in
either account.

Xenopus tropicalis (Gray, 1864). Ann. Mag. Nat. Hist., (3)14:316.
ORIGINAL NAME: *Silurana tropicalis.*
TYPE(S): Not stated, but BM 1947.2.24.83–86 (formerly 1864.9.22.1–4) recorded as
types.
TYPE LOCALITY: Lagos, West Africa [Nigeria].
DISTRIBUTION: Forested West Africa from Senegal to Cameroon and throughout the
Zaire River Basin to eastern Zaire.
COMMENT: Loumont, 1983, Rev. Suisse Zool., 90:176, restricted *Xenopus tropicalis* to
the west of tropical Africa only, and considered that records to the south and
east (including the Zaire Basin) belong to *Xenopus epitropicalis*. Synonymy
includes *Xenopus calcaratus*. Most primitive of the *Xenopus* species, set apart
from the rest of the genus by chromosome number (2n = 20) (Tymowska,
1973, Cytogenet. Cell. Genet., 12:298), osteology (Estes, 1975, Herpetologica,
31:269), serum albumins (Bisbee, Baker, Wilson, Hadji-Azimi, and Fischberg,
1977, Science, Washington, D.C., 195:785), and other characters (Tinsley, 1981,
Monit. Zool. Ital., N.S., Suppl., 15:140).

Xenopus vestitus Laurent, 1972. Explor. Parc Natl. Virunga, (2)22:9.
TYPE(S): Not stated, but RGMC 118287 recorded as holotype.
TYPE LOCALITY: "Musugereza, près de Rutshuru, ± 1250 m, Kivu, Congo [=Zaire]".
DISTRIBUTION: Highland swamps and lakes bordering the Western Rift in
southwestern Uganda, Rwanda, and eastern Zaire, and rivers draining the
Virunga volcanoes. Record suggesting southward extension to "Musosa,
Tanganyika District, Zaire" (Tinsley, 1975, J. Zool., London, 175:488)
considered doubtful by Tinsley, Kobel, and Fischberg, 1979, J. Zool., London,
188:89).
COMMENT: Synonymy includes *Xenopus kigesiensis* Tinsley, 1973, J. Zool., London,
169:3, according to Tinsley, 1975, J. Zool., London, 175:474. Chromosome
number (2n = 72) tetraploid with respect to *Xenopus laevis* (see Tymowska,
Fischberg, and Tinsley, 1977, Cytogenet. Cell. Genet., 19:346). Interactions
with three sympatric *Xenopus* species include recent invasion of lakes in
southwestern Uganda by the related *Xenopus vestitus* and *Xenopus wittei* and

their replacement of previous *Xenopus laevis bunyoniensis* populations (Tinsley, 1981, Monit. Zool. Ital., N.S., Suppl., 15:145).

Xenopus wittei Tinsley, Kobel, and Fischberg, 1979. J. Zool., London, 188:73.
TYPE(S): Holotype: BM 1977.2039.
TYPE LOCALITY: "Chelima Forest (waterhole alongside Kabale–Rutenga road), Kigezi District, S.W. Uganda; alt. 2200 m. 1° 04′ S, 29° 55′ E".
DISTRIBUTION: Highland swamps and lakes bordering the Western Rift in southwestern Uganda, Rwanda, and the Kabasha Escarpment, eastern Zaire.
COMMENT: Synonymy includes *Xenopus* (*laevis*) *bunyoniensis* Tymowska and Fischberg, 1973, Chromosoma, 44:337. Closely related to *Xenopus vestitus* with similar karyotypes (2n = 72); Tinsley, Kobel, and Fischberg, 1979, J. Zool., London, 188:95, suggested that they share an allopolyploid origin with one ancestor in common.

FAMILY: **Pseudidae** Fitzinger, 1843.
CITATION: Syst. Rept.:33.
DISTRIBUTION: Tropical lowlands east of the Andes in South America.
COMMENT: As first formed, the group name was Pseudae. Until Savage and Carvalho, 1953, Zoologica, New York, 38:193–200, resurrected the family it was placed either in the Leptodactylidae or the Hylidae. Savage and Carvalho considered the Pseudidae to be derived from the Leptodactylidae. Burger, 1954, Herpetologica, 10: 194–196, suggested that they were derived from the Hylidae. The most recent revision is that by Gallardo, 1961, Bull. Mus. Comp. Zool., 125:108–134. A checklist of the species and subspecies was provided by Duellman, 1977, Das Tierreich, 95: 197–201.
CONTRIBUTOR: William E. Duellman (WED).
REVIEWERS: Werner C. A. Bokermann (WCAB) (Brazil); Ulisses Caramaschi (UC); Eduardo Gudynas (Southeastern South America); Keith A. Harding (KAH); Marinus S. Hoogmoed (MSH); Enrique La Marca (ELM) (Northern South America); Norman J. Scott, Jr. (NJS); Paulo E. Vanzolini (PEV) (Brazil).

Lysapsus Cope, 1862. Proc. Acad. Nat. Sci. Philadelphia, 14:155.
TYPE SPECIES: *Lysapsus limellum* Cope, 1862.
DISTRIBUTION: Tropical South America east of the Andes.
COMMENT: For discussion see Savage and Carvalho, 1953, Zoologica, New York, 38: 193–200; Gallardo, 1961, Bull. Mus. Comp. Zool. 125:111–134; and Cei, 1980, Monit. Zool. Ital., N.S., Monogr., 2:422–425.

Lysapsus limellus Cope, 1862. Proc. Acad. Nat. Sci. Philadelphia, 14:155.
ORIGINAL NAME: *Lysapsus limellum*.
TYPE(S): Formerly Smithsonian Mus. (USNM) 5495; now lost.
TYPE LOCALITY: Río Curumba, Paraguay [=Corumbá, on Rio Paraguai, Mato Grosso do Sul, Brazil].
DISTRIBUTION: Guyana and northern Brazil; central and southern Brazil, Uruguay, Paraguay, northern Argentina, and eastern Bolivia.
COMMENT: For subspecies and distribution see Gallardo, 1964, Acta Zool. Lilloana, 20:193–209.

Lysapsus mantidactylus (Cope, 1862). Proc. Acad. Nat. Sci. Philadelphia, 14:352.
ORIGINAL NAME: *Pseudis mantidactyla*.
TYPE(S): Formerly in ANSP; now lost.
TYPE LOCALITY: Buenos Aires, Argentina.
DISTRIBUTION: Northeastern Argentina, Uruguay, and extreme southern Brazil (Rio Grande do Sul).
COMMENT: See comment under *Pseudis minuta*.

Pseudis Wagler, 1830. Nat. Syst. Amph.:203.
TYPE SPECIES: *Rana paradoxa* Linnaeus, 1758.
DISTRIBUTION: Guianas, northeastern Venezuela, Trinidad, and southern Brazil, Paraguay, eastern Bolivia, northeastern Argentina, and Uruguay.

COMMENT: For discussion see Savage and Carvalho, 1953, Zoologica, New York, 38: 193–200, and Gallardo, 1961, Bull. Mus. Comp. Zool., 125:111–134.

Pseudis minuta Günther, 1859 "1858". Cat. Batr. Sal. Coll. Brit. Mus.:6.
TYPE(S): Holotype: BM 1947.2.25.96.
TYPE LOCALITY: "South America".
DISTRIBUTION: Unknown.
COMMENT: Gudynas and Rudolf, 1983, C.E.D. Orione Contrib. Biol., Montevideo, 9:1–7, commented on and reviewed literature on an Uruguayan pseudid that has alternatively been allocated to *Pseudis minuta* or *Lysapsus mantidactylus* by various authors, and regarded the issue as still unresolved.

Pseudis paradoxa (Linnaeus, 1758). Syst. Nat., Ed. 10, 1:212.
ORIGINAL NAME: *Rana paradoxa*.
TYPE(S): Syntypes: NHRM 144–148.
TYPE LOCALITY: "Surinam".
DISTRIBUTION: Lower Río Magdalena Valley as well as Arauca and Meta in Colombia, Guianas, northeastern Venezuela, Trinidad, central and southern Brazil, Paraguay, eastern Bolivia, and northeastern Argentina.
COMMENT: Six subspecies were recognized by Gallardo, 1961, Bull. Mus. Comp. Zool., 125:111–134; an isolated population in lower Río Magdalena Valley, Colombia was recognized as a seventh subspecies by Cochran and Goin, 1970, Bull. U.S. Natl. Mus., 288:89. Argentinian populations discussed by Cei, 1980, Monit. Zool. Ital., N.S., Monogr., 2:415–422.

FAMILY: **Ranidae** Gray, 1825.
CITATION: Ann. Philos., (2)10:213.
DISTRIBUTION: Cosmopolitan except for southern South America and most of Australia.
COMMENT: The original spelling of the family name was Ranadae. The first use of the justified emendation Ranidae was by Bonaparte, 1831, Sagg. Distrib. Met. Degli Animal. Vert.:66. Dubois, 1981, Monit. Zool. Ital., N.S., Suppl., 15:225–284, provided generic synonymies, a review of the nomenclatural literature, and a classification, but did not supply the phylogenetic rationale for that classification. Wallace, King, and Wilson, 1973, Syst. Zool., 22:1–13, reported on albumin evolution among some ranid genera and groups of *Rana*. The Ranidae are treated in varying degrees of completeness in several regional studies: Schmidt and Inger, 1959, Explor. Parc Natl. Upemba, 56:1–264 (Zaire); Schiøtz, 1963, Vidensk. Medd. Dansk Naturhist. Foren., 125:1–92 (Nigeria); Poynton, 1964, Ann. Natal Mus., 17:1–334; Passmore and Carruthers, 1979, S. Afr. Frogs (Rep. South Africa); Perret, 1966, Zool. Jahrb., Abt. Syst., 93:289–464 (Cameroon); Guibé, 1979, Bonn. Zool. Monogr., 11 (Madagascar); Liu, 1950, Fieldiana: Zool. Mem., 2:1–396 (western China); Liu and Hu, 1961, Tailless Amph. China:137–245 (China); Bourret, 1942, Batr. Indochine (Indochina); Brown, 1952, Bull. Mus. Comp. Zool., 107:1–64 (Solomons); Inger, 1954, Fieldiana: Zool., 34:181–531 (Philippines); Taylor, 1962, Univ. Kansas Sci. Bull., 43:265–599 (Thailand); Inger, 1966, Fieldiana: Zool., 52:1–402 (Borneo); van Kampen, 1923, Amph. Indo-Aust. Arch. (Indonesia and the Papuan region); and Wright and Wright, 1949, Handbook Frogs Toads, Ed. 3 (USA and Canada). Laurent, 1951, Rev. Zool. Bot. Afr., 45:116–122, and Laurent, 1979, Bull. Soc. Zool. France, 104:347–422, included the Rhacophoridae and the Mantellinae in the Ranidae, but excluded the Arthroleptinae and Astylosterninae which he placed in the Hyperoliidae. See comments under Arthroleptidae and the subfamilies of Ranidae.
REVIEWERS: William E. Duellman (WED); Marinus S. Hoogmoed (MSH).

SUBFAMILY: **Mantellinae** Laurent, 1946.
CITATION: Rev. Zool. Bot. Afr., 39:336.
DISTRIBUTION: Madagascar; southern India and Sri Lanka.
COMMENT: Discussion and review in Blommers-Schlösser, 1979, Beaufortia, 29:1–77; including *Mantella*, *Mantidactylus*, *Laurentomantis*, and *Pseudophilautus*. Liem, 1969,

Fieldiana: Zool., 37:1–145, considered the Mantellinae to be the primitive stem-group of the Rhacophoridae. See Blommers-Schlösser, 1978, Genetica, 48:23–40, for karyotypes.
CONTRIBUTOR: Rose M. A. Blommers-Schlösser (RMABS).

Laurentomantis Dubois, 1980. Bull. Mus. Natl. Hist. Nat., Paris, (4)2(A):350.
TYPE SPECIES: *Microphryne malagasia* Methuen and Hewitt, 1913, by monotypy.
DISTRIBUTION: Madagascar.
COMMENT: *Laurentomantis* is a replacement name for *Trachymantis* Methuen and Hewitt, 1920, Proc. Zool. Soc. London, 1920:352, which is preoccupied.

Laurentomantis horrida (Boettger, 1880). Zool. Anz., 3:282.
ORIGINAL NAME: *Hemimantis horrida.*
TYPE(S): Holotype: SMF 7177.
TYPE LOCALITY: Nosy Bé, Madagascar.
DISTRIBUTION: Northern Madagascar and Nossi Bé I.

Laurentomantis malagasia (Methuen and Hewitt, 1913). Ann. Transvaal Mus., 4:55.
ORIGINAL NAME: *Microphryne malagasia.*
TYPE(S): Holotype: TM 10076.
TYPE LOCALITY: Folohy, eastern Madagascar.
DISTRIBUTION: Eastern Madagascar.

Laurentomantis ventrimaculata (Angel, 1935). Bull. Soc. Zool. France, 60:205.
ORIGINAL NAME: *Trachymantis malagasia* var. *ventrimaculatus.*
TYPE(S): Syntypes: MNHNP 1935-172 and 1935-173.
TYPE LOCALITY: Isaka Ivondro, alt. 700 m, near Fort-Dauphin, Madagascar.
DISTRIBUTION: Southern Madagascar.

Mantella Boulenger, 1882. Cat. Batr. Sal. Brit. Mus.:141.
TYPE SPECIES: *Dendrobates betsileo* Grandidier, 1872, by subsequent designation of Liem, 1970, Fieldiana: Zool., 57:100.
DISTRIBUTION: Madagascar.
COMMENT: See Guibé, 1964, Senckenb. Biol., 45:259–264, and Busse, 1981, Amphibia-Reptilia, 2:23–42, for synonymies and revision.

Mantella aurantiaca Mocquard, 1900 "1901". Bull. Soc. Philomath. Paris, 2(9):110.
TYPE(S): Syntypes: MNHNP 1899-412, 1899-413.
TYPE LOCALITY: Forest between Beforana and Moramanga, Madagascar.
DISTRIBUTION: Eastern Madagascar.

Mantella betsileo (Grandidier, 1872). Ann. Sci. Nat., Paris, (5)15:11.
ORIGINAL NAME: *Dendrobates betsileo.*
TYPE(S): Syntypes: MNHNP 1895-278, 1895-279.
TYPE LOCALITY: Betsileo [Madagascar].
DISTRIBUTION: Madagascar.

Mantella laevigata Methuen and Hewitt, 1913. Ann. Transvaal Mus., 4:57.
TYPE(S): Holotype: TM 10074.
TYPE LOCALITY: Folohy, eastern Madagascar.
DISTRIBUTION: Eastern Madagascar.

Mantella madagascariensis (Grandidier, 1872). Ann. Sci. Nat., Paris, (5)15:10.
ORIGINAL NAME: *Dendrobates madagascariensis.*
TYPE(S): Syntypes: MNHNP 1895-276, 1895-277.
TYPE LOCALITY: Forest Ambalavatou, between Mananzarine and Fianarantsoa, Madagascar.
DISTRIBUTION: Madagascar.

Mantidactylus Boulenger, 1895. Ann. Mag. Nat. Hist., (6)15:450.
TYPE SPECIES: *Rana guttulata* Boulenger, 1881, by subsequent designation of Ahl, 1931,
Das Tierreich, 55:10
DISTRIBUTION: Madagascar and nearby islands.
COMMENT: See Blommers-Schlösser, 1979, Beaufortia, 29:1–77, for definition of
species groups, synonymies, and review. Guibé, 1978, Bonn. Zool. Monogr., 11:
13–59, provided synonymies of the species.

Mantidactylus acuticeps Ahl, 1929. Mitt. Zool. Mus. Berlin, 1929:471.
TYPE(S): Lost.
TYPE LOCALITY: Central Madagascar.
DISTRIBUTION: Central Madagascar.

Mantidactylus aerumnalis (Peracca, 1893). Boll. Mus. Zool. Anat. Comp. Univ. Torino,
8(156):10.
ORIGINAL NAME: *Rana aerumnalis.*
TYPE(S): Lost.
TYPE LOCALITY: Andrangoloaka, central Madagascar.
DISTRIBUTION: Andringitra and Ankaratra mountains and central Madagascar.
COMMENT: Synonymy in Guibé, 1978, Bonn. Zool. Monogr., 11:44.

Mantidactylus aglavei (Methuen and Hewitt, 1913). Ann. Transvaal Mus., 4:54.
ORIGINAL NAME: *Rhacophorus aglavei.*
TYPE(S): Holotype: TM 10073.
TYPE LOCALITY: Anamalozoatra Forest, Madagascar.
DISTRIBUTION: Andringitra Mountains and eastern forests of Madagascar.
COMMENT: Synonymy in Guibé, 1978, Bonn. Zool. Monogr., 11:62. Review in
Blommers-Schlösser, 1979, Beaufortia, 29:25.

Mantidactylus albofrenatus (Müller, 1892). Festschr. Naturforsch. Ges. Basel, 1892:197.
ORIGINAL NAME: *Rana albofrenata.*
TYPE(S): Holotype: NHMB 792.
TYPE LOCALITY: Madagascar.
DISTRIBUTION: Eastern Madagascar.
COMMENT: See Blommers-Schlösser, 1979, Beaufortia, 29:20, for review.

Mantidactylus alutus (Peracca, 1893). Boll. Mus. Zool. Anat. Comp. Univ. Torino,
8(156):12.
ORIGINAL NAME: *Rana aluta.*
TYPE(S): Syntypes: MNHNP 1894-1 and 1894-2.
TYPE LOCALITY: Andrangoloaka, Madagascar.
DISTRIBUTION: Central Madagascar.

Mantidactylus ambohimitombi Boulenger, 1919. Proc. Zool. Soc. London, 1918:260.
TYPE(S): Syntypes: BM 1947.2.26.25–32.
TYPE LOCALITY: Ambohimitombi Forest, Madagascar.
DISTRIBUTION: Eastern and central Madagascar.

Mantidactylus argenteus Methuen, 1920 "1919". Proc. Zool. Soc. London, 1919:353.
TYPE(S): Holotype: TM 10078.
TYPE LOCALITY: Folohy, eastern Madagascar.
DISTRIBUTION: Eastern Madagascar, Andringitra Mountains.

Mantidactylus asper (Boulenger, 1882). Cat. Batr. Sal. Brit. Mus.:465.
ORIGINAL NAME: *Rana aspera.*
TYPE(S): Syntypes: including BM 82.316.80–82 (4 others not traced).
TYPE LOCALITY: "East Betsileo", Madagascar.
DISTRIBUTION: Eastern Madagascar: Marojezy, Andringitra, and Tsaratanana
mountains.

COMMENT: See Guibé, 1978, Bonn. Zool. Monogr., 11:25, for synonymy.

Mantidactylus bertini (Guibé, 1947). Bull. Mus. Natl. Hist. Nat., Paris, (2)19(2):152.
ORIGINAL NAME: *Gephyromantis bertini.*
TYPE(S): Holotype: MNHNP 1935-168.
TYPE LOCALITY: Isaka-lvondro, Madagascar.
DISTRIBUTION: Eastern Madagascar and Anosyenne Chaîne.

Mantidactylus betsileanus (Boulenger, 1882). Cat. Batr. Sal. Brit. Mus.:460.
ORIGINAL NAME: *Rana betsileana.*
TYPE(S): Syntypes: BM 1947.2.26.33–45, MCZ 15362.
TYPE LOCALITY: "East Betsileo" and "Ankafana, Betsileo", Madagascar.
DISTRIBUTION: Madagascar, except for southern part.
COMMENT: See Guibé, 1978, Bonn. Zool. Monogr., 11:41, for synonymy.

Mantidactylus bicalcaratus (Boettger, 1913). *In* Voeltzkow, Reise Ost-Afr., 3:320.
ORIGINAL NAME: *Rhacophorus bicalcaratus.*
TYPE(S): SMF 6811 designated lectotype by Mertens, 1967, Senckenb. Biol., 48:48.
TYPE LOCALITY: Island Sainte Marie, Madagascar.
DISTRIBUTION: Eastern Madagascar.
COMMENT: See Blommers-Schlösser, 1979, Beaufortia, 29:50, for synonymy and
    review.

Mantidactylus biporus (Boulenger, 1889). Ann. Mag. Nat. Hist., (6)4:246.
ORIGINAL NAME: *Rana bipora.*
TYPE(S): Syntypes: BM 1947.2.26.46–52.
TYPE LOCALITY: Madagascar.
DISTRIBUTION: Madagascar.

Mantidactylus blanci (Guibé, 1974). Bull. Mus. Natl. Hist. Nat., Paris, (3)1973(145):
    1015.
ORIGINAL NAME: *Gephyromantis blanci.*
TYPE(S): Holotype: MNHNP 1972-183.
TYPE LOCALITY: Ambalamarovandana, 1500 m alt., Andringitra Mountains,
    Madagascar.
DISTRIBUTION: Andringitra Mountains, Madagascar.

Mantidactylus blommersae (Guibé, 1975). Bull. Mus. Natl. Hist. Nat., Paris,
    (3)1975(323):1081.
ORIGINAL NAME: *Gephyromantis blommersae.*
TYPE(S): Holotype: MNHNP 1975-5.
TYPE LOCALITY: 25 km south of Moramanga, Madagascar.
DISTRIBUTION: Eastern Madagascar.
COMMENT: See Blommers-Schlösser, 1979, Beaufortia, 29:33, for review.

Mantidactylus boulengeri (Methuen, 1920 "1919"). Proc. Zool. Soc. London, 1919:351.
ORIGINAL NAME: *Gephyromantis boulengeri.*
TYPE(S): Holotype: TM 10876.
TYPE LOCALITY: Folohy, eastern Madagascar.
DISTRIBUTION: Eastern Madagascar.
COMMENT: Synonymy in Guibé, 1978, Bonn. Zool. Monogr., 11:53.

Mantidactylus bourgati Guibé, 1974. Bull. Mus. Natl. Hist. Nat., Paris, (3)1973(145):
    1009.
TYPE(S): Holotype: MNHNP 1972-437.
TYPE LOCALITY: "Ambalamarovandana", Andringitra Mountains, Madagascar.
DISTRIBUTION: Andringitra Mountains, Madagascar.

Mantidactylus brevipalmatus Ahl, 1929. Mitt. Zool. Mus. Berlin, 1929:473.
TYPE(S): Formerly in ZMB; lost.
TYPE LOCALITY: Northwestern Madagascar.
DISTRIBUTION: Northwestern Madagascar.

Mantidactylus curtus (Boulenger, 1882). Cat. Batr. Sal. Brit. Mus.:461.
ORIGINAL NAME: *Rana curta.*
TYPE(S): Syntypes: BM 1947.2.10.28–31 (and 3 others not traced).
TYPE LOCALITY: "East Betsileo" and "Ankafana, Betsileo", Madagascar.
DISTRIBUTION: Mountains and eastern part of Madagascar.

Mantidactylus decaryi (Angel, 1930). Bull. Soc. Zool. France, 55:549.
ORIGINAL NAME: *Gephyromantis decaryi.*
TYPE(S): Syntypes: MNHNP 1930-435 to 1930-438.
TYPE LOCALITY: Midongy du Sud between 500 and 600 m alt., Pic d'Ivohibe, 1100
    m alt., Prov. de Farafangano, Madagascar.
DISTRIBUTION: Mountains and eastern part of Madagascar.

Mantidactylus depressiceps (Boulenger, 1882). Cat. Batr. Sal. Brit. Mus.:467.
ORIGINAL NAME: *Rhacophorus depressiceps.*
TYPE(S): Syntypes: BM (4 specimens); BM 1947.2.27.50 designated lectotype by
    Blommers-Schlösser, 1979, Beaufortia, 29:35.
TYPE LOCALITY: "East Betsileo" and "Ankafana, Betsileo", Madagascar; restricted to
    East Betsileo by lectotype designation.
DISTRIBUTION: Eastern Madagascar.
COMMENT: See Blommers-Schlösser, 1979, Beaufortia, 29:35, for synonymy.

Mantidactylus domerguei (Guibé, 1974). Bull. Mus. Natl. Hist. Nat., Paris, (3)1973(145):
    1014.
ORIGINAL NAME: *Gephyromantis domerguei.*
TYPE(S): Holotype: MNHNP 1972-190.
TYPE LOCALITY: Ambalamarovandana, 1500 m alt., Andringitra Mountains,
    Madagascar.
DISTRIBUTION: Mountains of Madagascar.
COMMENT: See Blommers-Schlösser, 1979, Beaufortia, 29:32, for review.

Mantidactylus eiselti (Guibé, 1975). Bull. Mus. Natl. Hist. Nat., Paris, (3)1975(323):
    1083.
ORIGINAL NAME: *Gephyromantis eiselti.*
TYPE(S): Holotype: MNHNP 1975-2.
TYPE LOCALITY: Perinet, Madagascar.
DISTRIBUTION: Eastern forest of Madagascar.
COMMENT: See Blommers-Schlösser, 1979, Beaufortia, 29:29, for review.

Mantidactylus elegans (Guibé, 1974). Bull. Mus. Natl. Hist. Nat., Paris, (3)1973(145):
    1012.
ORIGINAL NAME: *Rhacophorus elegans.*
TYPE(S): Holotype: MNHNP 1953-142.
TYPE LOCALITY: Forest d'Ivohibé, Andringitra Mountains, Madagascar.
DISTRIBUTION: Andringitra and Tsaratanana mountains, Madagascar.
COMMENT: See Guibé, 1978, Bonn. Zool. Monogr., 11:30, for review. See comment
    under *Mantidactylus.*

"*Mantidactylus elegans*" (Guibé, 1974). Bull. Mus. Natl. Hist. Nat., Paris, (3)1973(171):
    1175.
ORIGINAL NAME: *Gephyromantis elegans.*
TYPE(S): Holotype: MNHNP 1972-1827.
TYPE LOCALITY: Chaînes Anosyennes, Madagascar.
DISTRIBUTION: Mountains of Madagascar.

COMMENT: This name is preoccupied (see previous account) and is being replaced by Blommers-Schlösser, In press.

Mantidactylus femoralis (Boulenger, 1882). Cat. Batr. Sal. Brit. Mus.:463.
ORIGINAL NAME: *Rana femoralis.*
TYPE(S): Syntypes: BM 1947.2.22.65–68.
TYPE LOCALITY: "East Betsileo", Madagascar.
DISTRIBUTION: Madagascar.
COMMENT: See Guibé, 1978, Bonn. Zool. Monogr., 11:26, for synonymy.

Mantidactylus flavicrus (Boulenger, 1889). Ann. Mag. Nat. Hist., (6)4:245.
ORIGINAL NAME: *Rana flavicrus.*
TYPE(S): Holotype: BM 1947.2.26.53.
TYPE LOCALITY: Madagascar.
DISTRIBUTION: Madagascar.

Mantidactylus flavobrunneus Blommers-Schlösser, 1979. Beaufortia, 29:54.
TYPE(S): Holotype: ZMA 7172.
TYPE LOCALITY: 20 km south of Moramanga, Madagascar.
DISTRIBUTION: Eastern Madagascar.

Mantidactylus glandulosus Methuen and Hewitt, 1913. Ann. Transvaal Mus., 4:60.
TYPE(S): TM; lost.
TYPE LOCALITY: Folohy; eastern Madagascar.
DISTRIBUTION: Eastern Madagascar.

Mantidactylus grandidieri Mocquard, 1895. Bull. Soc. Philomath. Paris, 8(7):105.
TYPE(S): Syntypes: MNHNP 1883-580 and 1895-255.
TYPE LOCALITY: Eastern Madagascar.
DISTRIBUTION: Eastern and central Madagascar.
COMMENT: See Blommers-Schlösser, 1979, Beaufortia, 29:7, for review.

Mantidactylus grandisonae Guibé, 1974. Bull. Mus. Natl. Hist. Nat., Paris, (3)1973(171): 1170.
TYPE(S): Holotype: MNHNP 1972-1085.
TYPE LOCALITY: Ambana, alt. 1000 m, Chaînes Anosyennes, Madagascar.
DISTRIBUTION: Madagascar.

Mantidactylus granulatus (Boettger, 1881). Zool. Anz., 4:361.
ORIGINAL NAME: *Limnodytes granulatus.*
TYPE(S): SMF 6728 designated by Mertens, 1967, Senckenb. Biol., 48:47
TYPE LOCALITY: Nosy Be, Madagascar.
DISTRIBUTION: Mayotte (Comoros Is.), Madagascar, and Nossi Bé.

Mantidactylus guttulatus (Boulenger, 1881). Ann. Mag. Nat. Hist., (5)7:360 "361".
ORIGINAL NAME: *Rana guttulata.*
TYPE(S): Syntypes: BM 1947.2.25.48–52.
TYPE LOCALITY: Southeastern Betsileo, Madagascar.
DISTRIBUTION: Eastern and central Madagascar.

Mantidactylus inaudax (Peracca, 1893). Boll. Mus. Zool. Anat. Comp. Univ. Torino, 8(156):7.
ORIGINAL NAME: *Rana inaudax.*
TYPE(S): Syntypes lost (RMABS).
TYPE LOCALITY: Andrangoloaka, Madagascar.
DISTRIBUTION: Madagascar.

Mantidactylus klemmeri (Guibé, 1974). Bull. Mus. Natl. Hist. Nat., Paris, (3)1973(171): 1175.
ORIGINAL NAME: *Gephyromantis klemmeri.*
TYPE(S): Holotype: MNHNP 1973-955.
TYPE LOCALITY: Massif du Marojezy, 600 m alt., Madagascar.
DISTRIBUTION: Marojezy Mountains, Madagascar.

Mantidactylus liber (Peracca, 1893). Boll. Mus. Zool. Anat. Comp. Univ. Torino, 8(156):14.
ORIGINAL NAME: *Rhacophorus liber.*
TYPE(S): BM 1947.2.8.63 designated lectotype by Blommers-Schlösser, 1979, Beaufortia, 29:47.
TYPE LOCALITY: Andrangoloaka, Madagascar.
DISTRIBUTION: Eastern and central Madagascar.
COMMENT: Synonymy and review in Blommers-Schlösser, 1979, Beaufortia, 29:47.

Mantidactylus lugubris (Duméril, 1853). Ann. Sci. Nat., Paris, (3)19:157.
ORIGINAL NAME: *Polypedates lugubris.*
TYPE(S): Syntypes: MNHNP 4583 and 4583A, B, and C.
TYPE LOCALITY: Madagascar.
DISTRIBUTION: Mountains of eastern and central Madagascar.
COMMENT: See Guibé, 1978, Bonn. Zool. Monogr., 11:21.

Mantidactylus luteus Methuen and Hewitt, 1913. Ann. Transvaal Mus., 4:51.
TYPE(S): Holotype: TM 10077.
TYPE LOCALITY: Folohy, Eastern Madagascar.
DISTRIBUTION: Eastern Madagascar.

Mantidactylus madecassus (Millot and Guibé, 1950). Mém. Inst. Sci. Madagascar, 4(1A): 203.
ORIGINAL NAME: *Rhacophorus (Philautus) madecassus.*
TYPE(S): Holotype: MNHNP 1953-246.
TYPE LOCALITY: Andringitra Mountains, 2520 m alt., Madagascar.
DISTRIBUTION: Andringitra Mountains, Madagascar.
COMMENT: See Guibé, 1978, Bonn. Zool. Monogr., 11:39, for review.

Mantidactylus majori Boulenger, 1896. Ann. Mag. Nat. Hist., (6)18:420.
TYPE(S): Syntypes: BM 1947.2.10.26–27.
TYPE LOCALITY: Ivohimanita, Madagascar.
DISTRIBUTION: Eastern Madagascar.

Mantidactylus microtympanum Angel, 1935. Bull. Soc. Zool. France, 60:202.
TYPE(S): Syntypes: MNHNP 1935-170 and 1935-171.
TYPE LOCALITY: Isaka-Ivondro, 700 m alt. [Madagascar].
DISTRIBUTION: Mountains and eastern part of Madagascar.

Mantidactylus opiparis (Peracca, 1893). Boll. Mus. Zool. Anat. Comp. Univ. Torino, 8(156):9.
ORIGINAL NAME: *Rana opiparis.*
TYPE(S): Syntypes lost (RMABS).
TYPE LOCALITY: Andrangoloaka, Madagascar.
DISTRIBUTION: Madagascar.
COMMENT: Review and synonymy in Blommers-Schlösser, 1979, Beaufortia, 29:21.

Mantidactylus pauliani Guibé, 1974. Bull. Mus. Natl. Hist. Nat., Paris, (3)1973(171): 1171.
TYPE(S): Holotype: MNHNP 1972-1508.
TYPE LOCALITY: Nosiarivo, Ankaratra Mountains, Madagascar.
DISTRIBUTION: Ankaratra Mountains, Madagascar.

Mantidactylus peraccae (Boulenger, 1896). Ann. Mag. Nat. Hist., (6)18:421.
ORIGINAL NAME: *Rhacophorus peraccae.*
TYPE(S): Holotype: BM 1947.2.9.70.
TYPE LOCALITY: Ivohimanita, northwestern Madagascar.
DISTRIBUTION: Western and central Madagascar.
COMMENT: See Blommers-Schlösser, 1979, Beaufortia, 29:423, for review.

Mantidactylus plicifer (Boulenger, 1882). Cat. Batr. Sal. Brit. Mus.:464.
ORIGINAL NAME: *Rana plicifera.*
TYPE(S): Syntypes: BM 82.3.16.56–59.
TYPE LOCALITY: "East Betsileo", Madagascar.
DISTRIBUTION: Mountains of Madagascar.
COMMENT: The grammatically incorrect epithet *pliciferus* has been used (DRF).

Mantidactylus pseudoasper Guibé, 1974. Bull. Mus. Natl. Hist. Nat., Paris, (3)1973(171):
   1173.
TYPE(S): Holotype: MNHNP 1973-752.
TYPE LOCALITY: Massif du Marojezy, 300 m alt., Madagascar.
DISTRIBUTION: Madagascar in the Marojezy Mountains.

Mantidactylus pulcher (Boulenger, 1882). Cat. Batr. Sal. Brit. Mus.:467.
ORIGINAL NAME: *Rhacophorus pulcher.*
TYPE(S): BM 1947.2.27.65 designated lectotype by Blommers-Schlösser, 1979,
   Beaufortia, 29:45.
TYPE LOCALITY: "Ankafana, Betsileo", Madagascar.
DISTRIBUTION: Eastern and central Madagascar.
COMMENT: See Blommers-Schlösser, 1979, Beaufortia, 29:45, for review.

Mantidactylus punctatus Blommers-Schlösser, 1979. Beaufortia, 29:51.
TYPE(S): Holotype: ZMA 7171A.
TYPE LOCALITY: Tampoketsa d'Ankazobe, alt. 1600 m, Madagascar.
DISTRIBUTION: Tampoketsa d'Ankazobe, Madagascar.

Mantidactylus redimitus (Boulenger, 1889). Ann. Mag. Nat. Hist., (6)4:245.
ORIGINAL NAME: *Rana redimita.*
TYPE(S): Holotype: BM 1947.2.26.55.
TYPE LOCALITY: Madagascar.
DISTRIBUTION: Mountains of eastern Madagascar.

Mantidactylus tornieri (Ahl, 1928). Zool. Anz., 75:316.
ORIGINAL NAME: *Rhacophorus tornieri.*
TYPE(S): Holotype: ZMB 30533.
TYPE LOCALITY: Ankoraka, Sahambendrana, central Madagascar.
DISTRIBUTION: Eastern and central Madagascar.
COMMENT: See Blommers-Schlösser, 1979, Beaufortia, 29:40, for review.

Mantidactylus tricinctus (Guibé, 1947). Bull. Mus. Natl. Hist. Nat., Paris, (2)19(2):154.
ORIGINAL NAME: *Gephyromantis tricinctus.*
TYPE(S): Syntypes: MNHNP 1931-216 and 1931-217.
TYPE LOCALITY: Befotaka and Vondroso, Madagascar.
DISTRIBUTION: Eastern mountains of Madagascar.
COMMENT: See Guibé, 1978, Bonn. Zool. Monogr., 11:34, for review.

Mantidactylus ulcerosus (Boettger, 1880). Zool. Anz., 3:282.
ORIGINAL NAME: *Limnodytes ulcerosus.*
TYPE(S): Holotype: SMF 6605.
TYPE LOCALITY: Nosy Be, Madagascar.
DISTRIBUTION: Madagascar; Nossi Bé.
COMMENT: See Guibé, 1978, Bonn. Zool. Monogr., 11:36, for synonymy.

Mantidactylus webbi (Grandison, 1953). Ann. Mag. Nat. Hist., (12)6:855.
ORIGINAL NAME: *Rhacophorus webbi.*
TYPE(S): Holotype: BM 1953.1.2.34.
TYPE LOCALITY: Nosy Mangabé, Antongil Bay, eastern Madagascar.
DISTRIBUTION: Madagascar.

Mantidactylus wittei Guibé, 1974. Bull. Mus. Natl. Hist. Nat., Paris, (3)1973(171):1169.
TYPE(S): Holotype: MNHNP 1953-60.
TYPE LOCALITY: Forest Ankarafantsika, near Ambanja and Ampijoroa, Madagascar.
DISTRIBUTION: Madagascar.

Pseudophilautus Laurent, 1943. Bull. Mus. R. Hist. Nat. Belg., 19(5):2.
TYPE SPECIES: *Ixalus temporalis* Günther, 1864, by original designation.
DISTRIBUTION: As for the single species.
REVIEWERS: J. C. Daniel (JCD); Sushil Dutta (SD); Robert F. Inger (RFI).

Pseudophilautus temporalis (Günther, 1864). Rept. Brit. India:434.
ORIGINAL NAME: *Ixalus temporalis.*
TYPE(S): Syntypes: BM 1947.2.6.8, 1947.2.6.10–11.
TYPE LOCALITY: "Ceylon" (=Sri Lanka).
DISTRIBUTION: Sri Lanka and Malabar coast of India.
COMMENT: Removed from the synonymy of *Philautus leucorhinus* (Rhacophoridae) by Laurent, 1943, Bull. Mus. R. Hist. Nat. Belg., 19:2. Treated as a junior synonym of *Philautus leucorhinus* by most subsequent authors (e.g., Kirtisinghe, 1957, Amph. Ceylon:68, without discussion. Probably a *Philautus* (RFI, WED, and SD).

SUBFAMILY: **Petropedetinae** Noble, 1931.
CITATION: Biol. Amph.:520.
DISTRIBUTION: Subsaharan Africa.
COMMENT: Laurent, 1951, Rev. Zool. Bot. Afr., 45:120, believed this group to be derived from the Raninae. Acting as first revisor, Dubois, 1982, Bull. Zool. Nomencl., 39: 136, considered Cacosterninae Noble, 1931, Biol. Amph.:540 (based on *Cacosternum* Boulenger, 1887), to be a junior synonym of Petropedetinae Noble, 1931. We use the nomenclaturally correct Petropedetinae rather than the widely used junior synonym Phrynobatrachinae Laurent, 1940, Rev. Zool. Bot. Afr., 34:79 (based on *Phrynobatrachus* Günther, 1862). Dubois, 1983, Bull. Zool. Nomencl., 134:140, petitioned the International Commission of Zoological Nomenclature to grant priority to Phrynobatrachinae. We (DRF and JDL) disagree with this petition and see the situation as identical to that with Genyophryninae Boulenger, 1890, *vs.* Sphenophryninae Noble, 1931, one of simple priority (see Dubois, 1983, Bull. Mens. Soc. Linn. Lyon, 52:275). The use of Phrynobatrachinae, although used widely, has far from universal acceptance; Laurent, 1980, Bull. Soc. Zool. France, 104:397–422, has adopted the use of Petropedetinae. Should Petropedetinae become 'universally' accepted, for purposes of priority it will take its date from Hemimantidae Hoffmann, 1878, *In* Bronn, Klass. Ordn. Thier-Reichs Wiss. Wort Bild, 6:613 (based on *Hemimantis* Peters, 1863, which was placed in the synonymy of *Phrynobatrachus* prior to 1961).
REVIEWERS: Alan Channing (AC) (Southern Africa); Kim M. Howell (KMH) (East Africa); Raymond Laurent (RL); John C. Poynton (JCP).

Anhydrophryne Hewitt, 1919. Rec. Albany Mus., 3:182.
TYPE SPECIES: *Anhydrophryne rattrayi* Hewitt, 1919, by monotypy.
DISTRIBUTION: As for the single species.
COMMENT: Closely related to *Arthroleptella* according to Poynton, 1964, Ann. Natal Mus., 17:155.

Anhydrophryne rattrayi Hewitt, 1919. Rec. Albany Mus., 3:182.
TYPE(S): AMG.
TYPE LOCALITY: Hogsback, Amatola Mountains [Cape Province, South Africa].
DISTRIBUTION: Amatola Mountains, Cape Province, Rep. South Africa.

Arthroleptella Hewitt, 1926. Ann. S. Afr. Mus., 20:426.
TYPE SPECIES: *Arthroleptis lightfooti* Boulenger, 1910, by original designation.
DISTRIBUTION: Cape Province and Natal, Rep. South Africa.

Arthroleptella hewitti FitzSimons, 1947. Ann. Natal Mus., 11:125.
TYPE(S): TM.
TYPE LOCALITY: Cathedral Peak area, Drakensberg [Rep. South Africa].
DISTRIBUTION: Natal and East Grigualand, Rep. South Africa.

Arthroleptella lightfooti (Boulenger, 1910). Ann. S. Afr. Mus., 5:538.
ORIGINAL NAME: *Arthroleptis lightfooti.*
TYPE(S): Lost.
TYPE LOCALITY: Newlands, near Cape Town [Cape Province, Rep. South Africa].
DISTRIBUTION: Mountains of southwestern Cape Province, Rep. South Africa.

Arthroleptides Nieden, 1910. Sitzungsber. Ges. Naturforsch. Freunde Berlin, 1910:445.
TYPE SPECIES: *Arthroleptides martiensseni* Nieden, 1910, by monotypy.
DISTRIBUTION: Mountains of Tanzania and Kenya.

Arthroleptides dutoiti Loveridge, 1935. Bull. Mus. Comp. Zool., 79:17.
TYPE(S): MCZ.
TYPE LOCALITY: Koitobos River, 7200 feet, Mount Elgon, Kenya.
DISTRIBUTION: Rocky montane streams of Mount Elgon, Kenya.

Arthroleptides martiensseni Nieden, 1910. Sitzungsber. Ges. Naturforsch. Freunde Berlin, 1910:445.
TYPE(S): Not traced (ZMB?).
TYPE LOCALITY: Amani, Usambara Mountains, Tanzania.
DISTRIBUTION: Rocky montane streams of Usambara, Uluguru, Uzungwe, and Magrotto mountains, Tanzania.

Cacosternum Boulenger, 1887. Ann. Mag. Nat. Hist., (5)20:51.
TYPE SPECIES: *Cacosternum nanum* Boulenger, 1887, by monotypy.
DISTRIBUTION: Southern and eastern Africa.

Cacosternum boettgeri (Boulenger, 1882). Cat. Batr. Sal. Brit. Mus.:118.
ORIGINAL NAME: *Arthroleptis boettgeri.*
TYPE(S): Syntypes: BM (4 specimens).
TYPE LOCALITY: "Kaffraria", Cape Province, Rep. South Africa.
DISTRIBUTION: Southern Africa and East Africa to Somalia.

Cacosternum capense Hewitt, 1926. Rec. Albany Mus., 3:367.
TYPE(S): SAM.
TYPE LOCALITY: Cape Flats, near Cape Town [Cape Province, Rep. Africa].
DISTRIBUTION: Cape Flats and Malmesbury District, Cape Province, Rep. South Africa.

Cacosternum leleupi Laurent, 1950. Rev. Zool. Bot. Afr., 44:138.
TYPE(S): RGMC.
TYPE LOCALITY: Kundelungu, 1750 m, Katanga [Shaba Province, Zaire].
DISTRIBUTION: Shaba Province, Zaire.
COMMENT: Reviewed by Schmidt and Inger, 1959, Explor. Parc Natl. Upemba, 56: 135.

Cacosternum namaquense Werner, 1910. *In* Schultze, Denkschr. Med. Naturwiss. Ges. Jena, 16:294.
TYPE(S): Not traced.
TYPE LOCALITY: Kamaggas and Gemsbok, near Steinkopf, Little Namaqualand [Cape Province, Rep. South Africa].
DISTRIBUTION: Namaqualand, Rep. South Africa.

Cacosternum nanum Boulenger, 1887. Ann. Mag. Nat. Hist., (5)20:52.
TYPE(S): BM.
TYPE LOCALITY: Kaffraria [Cape Province, South Africa].
DISTRIBUTION: Southern Mozambique; eastern Transvaal midlands, Natal, and eastern and southern Cape Province, Rep. South Africa.

Dimorphognathus Boulenger, 1906. Ann. Mag. Nat. Hist., (7)17:321.
TYPE SPECIES: *Heteroglossa africana* Hallowell, 1857, by monotypy.
DISTRIBUTION: As for the single species.
COMMENT: *Dimorphognathus* is a replacement name for *Heteroglossa* Hallowell, 1857, Proc. Acad. Nat. Sci. Philadelphia, 9:48–72, which is preoccupied.

Dimorphognathus africanus (Hallowell, 1857). Proc. Acad. Nat. Sci. Philadelphia, 9:64.
ORIGINAL NAME: *Heteroglossa africana*.
TYPE(S): Holotype: ANSP 3215.
TYPE LOCALITY: "Gaboon".
DISTRIBUTION: Cameroon, Gabon, and Congo.

Microbatrachella Hewitt, 1926. Ann. S. Afr. Mus., 20:420.
TYPE SPECIES: *Phrynobatrachus capensis* Boulenger, 1910, by original designation.
DISTRIBUTION: As for the single species.
COMMENT: A derivative of *Phrynobatrachus* according to Poynton, 1964, Ann. Natal Mus., 17:145. *Microbatrachella* is a replacement name for *Microbatrachus* Hewitt, 1926, Ann. S. Afr. Mus., 20:413–431, which is preoccupied by *Microbatrachus* Roux, 1910.

Microbatrachella capensis (Boulenger, 1910). Ann. S. Afr. Mus., 5:528.
ORIGINAL NAME: *Phrynobatrachus capensis*.
TYPE(S): Lost.
TYPE LOCALITY: Cape Flats, near Cape Town [Cape Province, Rep. South Africa].
DISTRIBUTION: Cape Flats, Cape Province, Rep. South Africa.

Natalobatrachus Hewitt and Methuen, 1913. Trans. R. Soc. S. Afr., 3:107.
TYPE SPECIES: *Natalobatrachus bonebergi* Hewitt and Methuen, 1913, by monotypy.
DISTRIBUTION: As for the single species.
COMMENT: Noble, 1924, Bull. Am. Mus. Nat. Hist., 49:88; Laurent, 1957, Rev. Zool. Bot. Afr., 66:274; and Loveridge, 1957, Bull. Mus. Comp. Zool., 117:346, included *Natalobatrachus* in *Phrynobatrachus*. See Poynton, 1964, Ann. Natal Mus., 17:143–144, and Poynton, 1976, Rev. Zool. Afr., 90:218–219, for discussion.

Natalobatrachus bonebergi Hewitt and Methuen, 1913. Trans. R. Soc. S. Afr., 3:107.
TYPE(S): AMG.
TYPE LOCALITY: Mariannhill, Natal [Rep. South Africa].
DISTRIBUTION: Transkei and Natal, Rep. South Africa.

Nothophryne Poynton, 1963. Ann. Natal Mus., 15:324.
TYPE SPECIES: *Nothophryne broadleyi* Poynton, 1963, by original designation.
DISTRIBUTION: As for the single species.

Nothophryne broadleyi Poynton, 1963. Ann. Natal Mus., 15:326.
TYPE(S): Holotype: NMZB (formerly UM) 4331.
TYPE LOCALITY: "Mount Mlanje, Nyasaland [=Malawi]".
DISTRIBUTION: Mt. Mulanje (Malawi) and Mt. Ribaue (Mozambique).

Petropedetes Reichenow, 1874. Arch. Naturgesch., 80:290.
TYPE SPECIES: *Petropedetes cameronensis* Reichenow, 1874, by monotypy.
DISTRIBUTION: Sierra Leone through Ivory Coast and Nigeria to Cameroon; Fernando Po.

COMMENT: Amiet, 1973, Bull. Inst. Fondam. Afr. Noire, (A)35:462–474, discussed the
Cameroon species. Perret, 1984, Bull. Soc. Neuchâtel. Sci. Nat., 107:169,
provided an identification matrix for the species.
CONTRIBUTOR: J.-L. Amiet (JLA).
REVIEWER: Jean-Luc Perret (JLP).

Petropedetes cameronensis Reichenow, 1874. Arch. Naturgesch., 80:290.
TYPE(S): Not traced.
TYPE LOCALITY: "Bimbia", near Victoria (now Limbé), Cameroon.
DISTRIBUTION: Eastern Nigeria and southwestern Cameroon.
COMMENT: Synonymy includes *Petropedetes obscurus* Ahl, 1924, according to Perret,
1984, Bull. Soc. Neuchâtel. Sci. Nat., 107:167–170.

Petropedetes johnstoni (Boulenger, 1887). Proc. Zool. Soc. London, 1887:564.
ORIGINAL NAME: *Cornufer johnstoni.*
TYPE(S): BM.
TYPE LOCALITY: "Rio del Rey", Cameroon.
DISTRIBUTION: Known only from the type locality.
COMMENT: Recognized as a *Petropedetes* by Boulenger, 1900, Proc. Zool. Soc.
London, 1900:439. See comment under *Petropedetes parkeri.*

Petropedetes natator Boulenger, 1905. Ann. Mag. Nat. Hist., (2)3:270.
TYPE(S): Syntypes: BM.
TYPE LOCALITY: "Sierra Leone".
DISTRIBUTION: Hilly forested parts of West Africa: Sierra Leone, Rep. Guinea, and
Ivory Coast.
COMMENT: Possibly generically distinct from other *Petropedetes*, according to JLA
in Perret, 1984, Bull. Soc. Neuchâtel. Sci. Nat., 107:167.

Petropedetes newtoni (Bocage, 1895). J. Sci. Math. Phys. Nat., Lisboa, (2)3:270.
ORIGINAL NAME: *Tympanoceros newtoni.*
TYPE(S): Not stated; not found in the MBL by Perret, 1976, Arq. Mus. Bocage,
(2)6:21.
TYPE LOCALITY: "Fernando Po".
DISTRIBUTION: Southern and southwestern Cameroon, Fernando Po, and Equatorial
Guinea (=Rio Muni).

Petropedetes palmipes Boulenger, 1905. Ann. Mag. Nat. Hist., (15)7:282.
TYPE(S): Syntypes: BM.
TYPE LOCALITY: "Efulen, South Cameroon".
DISTRIBUTION: Western slope of the southern Cameroon Plateau.

Petropedetes parkeri Amiet, 1983. Rev. Suisse Zool., 90:458.
TYPE(S): Holotype: BM 1936.3.4.124.
TYPE LOCALITY: "Atolo (región de Mamfe)", Cameroon.
DISTRIBUTION: Northern and southern slopes of the Adamaoua Plateau, western
and southern slopes of the Cameroon Range and Yaoundé Hills.
COMMENT: Specimens incorrectly allocated to *Petropedetes johnstoni* prior to
description of *Petropedetes parkeri.*

Petropedetes perreti Amiet, 1973. Bull. Inst. Fondam. Afr. Noire, (A)35:463.
TYPE(S): Holotype: MHNG 1253.90 (formerly JLA 71.196).
TYPE LOCALITY: "Nsoung, 1400–1500 m", Cameroon.
DISTRIBUTION: Southern and western slopes of the Cameroon Range, except Mt.
Cameroon, above 1000 m.

Phrynobatrachus Günther, 1862. Proc. Zool. Soc. London, 1862:190.
TYPE SPECIES: *Phrynobatrachus natalensis* Günther, 1862, by monotypy.
DISTRIBUTION: Africa south of the Sahara.

COMMENT: See Laurent, 1941, Rev. Zool. Bot. Afr., 34:192–210, and Poynton, 1964, Ann. Natal Mus., 17:137–144, for generic definition and discussions. Genus here considered to include *Stenorhynchus* Smith, 1849; *Hemimantis* Peters, 1863; *Hylarthroleptis* Ahl, 1923; *Pararthroleptis* Ahl, 1923 (part); and *Pseudoarthroleptis* Deckert, 1938.

CONTRIBUTOR: Alice G. C. Grandison (AGCG).

Phrynobatrachus accraensis (Ahl, 1923). Sitzungsber. Ges. Naturforsch. Freunde Berlin, 1923:98.
ORIGINAL NAME: *Hylarthroleptis accraensis.*
TYPE(S): Holotype: ZMB.
TYPE LOCALITY: "Accra", Ghana
DISTRIBUTION: West Africa.
COMMENT: Reviewed by Guibé and Lamotte, 1963, Mém. Inst. Franç. Afr. Noire, 66:601–627.

Phrynobatrachus acridoides (Cope, 1867). J. Acad. Nat. Sci. Philadelphia, (2)6:198.
ORIGINAL NAME: *Staurois acridoides.*
TYPE(S): Syntypes: ANSP 10066–71, MCZ 15026–32.
TYPE LOCALITY: "Zanzibar", Tanzania.
DISTRIBUTION: Sahel of East Africa to Natal, Rep. South Africa.
COMMENT: See Witte, 1941, Explor. Parc Natl. Albert, 33:74–80, and Poynton, 1964, Ann. Natal Mus., 17:140–141, for synonymy and review.

Phrynobatrachus acutirostris Nieden, 1912. Wiss. Ergebn. Deutsch. Zentr. Afr. Exped., 4:173.
TYPE(S): Holotype: ?ZMB.
TYPE LOCALITY: "Rugegewald", Lake Region of Central Africa.
DISTRIBUTION: Lake Region of eastern Zaire, Rwanda.
COMMENT: See Witte, 1941, Explor. Parc Natl. Albert, 33:70–73, for review.

Phrynobatrachus albomarginatus Witte, 1933. Rev. Zool. Bot. Afr., 24:98.
TYPE(S): Holotype: RGMC 3018.
TYPE LOCALITY: "Mauda (Uele)", Zaire.
DISTRIBUTION: Known only from the type locality.

Phrynobatrachus alleni Parker, 1936. Zool. Meded., Leiden, 19:91.
TYPE(S): Holotype: BM 1947.2.4.33 (formerly 1929.6.1.12).
TYPE LOCALITY: "Firestone Plantation, Du River, Liberia".
DISTRIBUTION: Sierra Leone, Guinea, Ivory Coast, Ghana, and Nigeria.
COMMENT: Reviewed by Guibé and Lamotte, 1963, Mém. Inst. Franç. Afr. Noire, 66:601–627.

Phrynobatrachus alticola Guibé and Lamotte, 1961. Bull. Mus. Natl. Hist. Nat., Paris, (2)33:574.
TYPE(S): Holotype: MNHNP 8956.
TYPE LOCALITY: "Forêt arborée, piste de Bié, region du Mont Nimba (Guinée)".
DISTRIBUTION: Guinea to Sierra Leone.
COMMENT: Reviewed by Guibé and Lamotte, 1963, Mém. Inst. Franç. Afr. Noire, 66:601–627.

Phrynobatrachus anotis Schmidt and Inger, 1959. Explor. Parc Natl. Upemba, 56:139.
TYPE(S): Holotype: Institut des Parcs Nationaux Congo Belge (Bruxelles) 1958 (now in RGMC or MRHN).
TYPE LOCALITY: "Lusinga, 1810 m, Parc National de l'Upemba, Katanga [=Shaba], Belgian Congo [=Zaire]".
DISTRIBUTION: Parc National de l'Upemba, Shaba, Zaire.

Phrynobatrachus asper Laurent, 1951. Rev. Zool. Bot. Afr., 44:364.
TYPE(S): RGMC.
TYPE LOCALITY: "Riv. Makenda, 5 km au sud de May ya Moto, 2450–2500 m, bassin de l'Elila, Territoire de Mwenga, Kivu", Zaire.
DISTRIBUTION: Itombwe Highlands, southern Kivu, eastern Zaire, above 8000 ft. in swamps and montane forest.

Phrynobatrachus auritus Boulenger, 1900. Proc. Zool. Soc. London, 1900:440.
TYPE(S): Syntypes: BM 1947.2.30.2–4 (formerly 1900.2.17.83–85).
TYPE LOCALITY: "Benito River", Rio Muni, Equatorial Guinea.
DISTRIBUTION: Forests of Nigeria, South Cameroon to Gabon, eastern Zaire, and Rwanda.
COMMENT: See Lamotte and Xavier, 1966, Bull. Inst. Franç. Afr. Noire, (A)28:1605–1619. An eastern vicariant of *Phrynobatrachus plicatus* (RL), with which it has been confused.

Phrynobatrachus batesii (Boulenger, 1906). Ann. Mag. Nat. Hist., (7)17:318.
ORIGINAL NAME: *Arthroleptis batesii*.
TYPE(S): Syntypes: BM 1947.2.6.76–80 (formerly 1906.5.28.105–107, 1902.11.12.86–87).
TYPE LOCALITY: "Efulen and Zima", South Cameroon.
DISTRIBUTION: Forests of Ghana, eastern Nigeria, and South Cameroon.

Phrynobatrachus bequaerti (Barbour and Loveridge, 1929). Proc. New England Zool. Club, 11:25.
ORIGINAL NAME: *Arthroleptis bequaerti*.
TYPE(S): Holotype: MCZ 14751.
TYPE LOCALITY: "a swamp on Mt. Vissoke, Belgian Congo [=Zaire], 8000–9000 feet altitude".
DISTRIBUTION: Eastern Zaire (region of Mt. Ruwenzori to Lake Kivu); Rwanda; Burundi.

Phrynobatrachus bottegi (Boulenger, 1894). Ann. Mus. Civ. Stor. Nat. Genova, (2)15:16.
ORIGINAL NAME: *Arthroleptis bottegi*.
TYPE(S): Holotype: MSNG 28845.
TYPE LOCALITY: "Auata" River, Bale Province, Ethiopia (05° 05' N, 39° 08' E)".
DISTRIBUTION: Ethiopia and Uganda.

Phrynobatrachus calcaratus (Peters, 1863). Monatsber. Preuss. Akad. Wiss. Berlin, 1863:451.
ORIGINAL NAME: *Hemimantis calcaratus*.
TYPE(S): Syntypes: ?ZMB.
TYPE LOCALITY: "Boutry", Ghana.
DISTRIBUTION: West Africa to eastern Zaire; Fernando Po.
COMMENT: Reviewed by Guibé and Lamotte, 1963, Mém. Inst. Franç. Afr. Noire, 66:601–627. See comment under *Phrynobatrachus rouxi*.

Phrynobatrachus congicus (Ahl, 1923). Sitzungsber. Ges. Naturforsch. Freunde Berlin, 1923:103.
ORIGINAL NAME: *Hylarthroleptis congicus*.
TYPE(S): Holotype: ?ZMB.
TYPE LOCALITY: "Congo".
DISTRIBUTION: Type locality (no explicit locality).

Phrynobatrachus cornutus (Boulenger, 1906). Ann. Mag. Nat. Hist., (7)17:318.
ORIGINAL NAME: *Arthroleptis cornutus*.
TYPE(S): Syntypes: BM 1947.2.30.49–50 (formerly 1906.5.28.103–104).
TYPE LOCALITY: "Zima", South Cameroon.
DISTRIBUTION: Cameroon; Fernando Po.

COMMENT: See Perret, 1966, Zool. Jahrb., Abt. Syst., 93:365, for subspecies.

Phrynobatrachus cricogaster Perret, 1957. Rev. Suisse Zool., 64:527.
   TYPE(S): Holotype: MHNG 923.31.
   TYPE LOCALITY: "Massif du Manengouba, 30 km de Nkongsamba, 1000 m, foret de
      montagne", Cameroon.
   DISTRIBUTION: Nigeria and Cameroon above 1000 m in the southern and western
      edges of the Cameroon Range.

Phrynobatrachus cryptotis Schmidt and Inger, 1959. Explor. Parc Natl. Upemba, 56:143.
   TYPE(S): Holotype: formerly Institut des Parcs Nationaux du Congo Belge
      (Bruxelles) 1926; now in RGMC, MRHN, or FMNH.
   TYPE LOCALITY: "upper Bwalo River (an affluent from the left of the Muye, which
      is an affluent from the right of the Lufira), 1750 m, Parc National de
      l'Upemba, Upper Katanga [=Shaba], Belgian Congo [=Zaire]".
   DISTRIBUTION: Shaba Province, Zaire.
   COMMENT: Zimbabwean and Zambian material previously allocated to this species
      is referable to *Phrynobatrachus mababiensis* as is most of the type material of
      Phrynobatrachus cryptotis (JCP).

Phrynobatrachus dalcqi Laurent, 1952. Rev. Zool. Bot. Afr., 46:25.
   TYPE(S): RGMC.
   TYPE LOCALITY: "Haute Lubitshako, 1900–2000 m, Terr. de Fizi, Kivu", Zaire.
   DISTRIBUTION: Montane region of Great Lakes, Central Africa.

Phrynobatrachus dendrobates (Boulenger, 1919). Rev. Zool. Afr., 7:8.
   ORIGINAL NAME: *Arthroleptis dendrobates.*
   TYPE(S): Holotype: BM 1947.2.4.32 (formerly 1919.8.16.30).
   TYPE LOCALITY: "Madié"; corrected to "Medje, Belgian Congo" (=Zaire) by Noble,
      1924, Bull. Am. Mus. Nat. Hist., 49:335, and to Medje, Uele, Congo [=Zaire],
      by Laurent, 1972, Explor. Parc Natl. Virunga, (2)22:108.
   DISTRIBUTION: Uganda and Upper Zaire.
   COMMENT: See Laurent, 1972, Explor. Parc Natl. Virunga, (2)22:108, for discussion
      on distinctness of species.

Phrynobatrachus dispar (Peters, 1870). Monatsber. Preuss. Akad. Wiss. Berlin, 1870:649.
   ORIGINAL NAME: *Arthroleptis dispar.*
   TYPE(S): Not traced (ZMB?).
   TYPE LOCALITY: "Ilha do Principe".
   DISTRIBUTION: Principe and São Tomé Is., Gulf of Guinea.

Phrynobatrachus elberti (Ahl, 1923). Sitzungsber. Ges. Naturforsch. Freunde Berlin,
      1923:101.
   ORIGINAL NAME: *Hylarthroleptis elberti.*
   TYPE(S): Syntypes: ZMB.
   TYPE LOCALITY: "Buala am Uam, Neu-Kamerun [=Cameroon]".
   DISTRIBUTION: Known only from the type locality.

Phrynobatrachus feae (Boulenger, 1906). Ann. Mus. Civ. Stor Nat. Genova, (3)2:161.
   ORIGINAL NAME: *Arthroleptis feae.*
   TYPE(S): Syntypes: (25 specimens) including BM 1947.2.6.88–91 (formerly
      1906.3.30.123–126).
   TYPE LOCALITY: "Prince's Island [=Principe], 100 to 300 m."
   DISTRIBUTION: Principe I., Gulf of Guinea.

Phrynobatrachus francisci Boulenger, 1912. Ann. Mag. Nat. Hist., (8)10:141.
   TYPE(S): Holotype: BM 1947.2.30.29 (formerly 1911.3.21.10).
   TYPE LOCALITY: "Zaria Province of Northern Nigeria".
   DISTRIBUTION: Senegal to Congo.

COMMENT: Reviewed by Lamotte and Xavier, 1966, Bull. Inst. Franç. Afr. Noire, (A)28:343–361. Probably a synonym of *Phrynobatrachus natalensis* (RL).

Phrynobatrachus fraterculus (Chabanaud, 1921). Bull. Com. Études Hist. Scient. Afr. Occid. Franç., 1921:456.
ORIGINAL NAME: *Arthroleptis fraterculus.*
TYPE(S): Syntypes: MNHNP 21-153 to 21-157.
TYPE LOCALITY: "Macenta", Guinea.
DISTRIBUTION: Guinea-Bissau, Liberia, and Sierra Leone.
COMMENT: Reviewed by Guibé and Lamotte, 1963, Mém. Inst. Franç. Afr. Noire, 66:601–627.

Phrynobatrachus gastoni Barbour and Loveridge, 1928. Proc. New England Zool. Club, 10:88.
TYPE(S): Holotype: MCZ 13946.
TYPE LOCALITY: "Buta, Bas-Uelé Province, Belgian Congo" (=Zaire).
DISTRIBUTION: Known only from the type locality.

Phrynobatrachus ghanensis Schiøtz, 1964. Vidensk. Medd. Dansk Naturhist. Foren., 127:10.
TYPE(S): Holotype: ZMUC R074712.
TYPE LOCALITY: "Kakum Forest Reserve, near Mansu, Ghana".
DISTRIBUTION: Known only from the type locality.

Phrynobatrachus giorgii Witte, 1921. Rev. Zool. Afr., 9:8.
TYPE(S): Syntypes: RGMC (4 specimens).
TYPE LOCALITY: "Yambata, (Bas-Congo)".
DISTRIBUTION: Cameroon to western Zaire.

Phrynobatrachus graueri (Nieden, 1910). Sitzungsber. Ges. Naturforsch. Freunde Berlin, 1910:441.
ORIGINAL NAME: *Arthroleptis graueri.*
TYPE(S): Holotype: ZMB 21782.
TYPE LOCALITY: "Rugegewald", Lake Region of Central Africa.
DISTRIBUTION: Western Kenya and Uganda to eastern Zaire and Rwanda.
COMMENT: See Witte, 1941, Explor. Parc Natl. Albert, 33:81–84, for synonymy and review.

Phrynobatrachus guineensis Guibé and Lamotte, 1961. Bull. Mus. Natl. Hist. Nat., Paris, (2)33:571.
TYPE(S): Holotype: MNHNP 8955.
TYPE LOCALITY: "Forêt dense, Mont Tonkoui (Côte d'Ivoire)".
DISTRIBUTION: Sierra Leone to Ivory Coast.
COMMENT: Reviewed by Guibé and Lamotte, 1963, Mém. Inst. Franç. Afr. Noire, 66:601–627.

Phrynobatrachus gutturosus (Chabanaud, 1921). Bull. Com. Études Hist. Scient. Afr. Occid. Franç, 1921:452.
ORIGINAL NAME: *Arthroleptis gutturosus.*
TYPE(S): Syntypes: BM 1947.2.6.49.50 (formerly 1927.2.19.1–2), 1947.2.6.51–75 (formerly 1921.6.16.8–39), MCZ 12836, MNHNP 21-137 to 21-142, 21-280 to 21-282, AMG (1 specimen), RGMC (5 specimens).
TYPE LOCALITY: Sanikolé, Liberia.
DISTRIBUTION: Guinea-Bissau to Shaba, southeastern Zaire (see comment).
COMMENT: Material from Shaba assigned to *Phrynobatrachus gutturosus* by various authors does not agree with BM syntypes in having more extensive webbing. The material agrees more closely with *Phrynobatrachus rungwensis*. Malawi material allocated to *Phrynobatrachus gutturosus* by Poynton, 1964, Senckenb.

Biol., 45:210, and by Stewart, 1967, Amph. Malawi:96, appears to be an undescribed species differing from *Phrynobatrachus gutturosus* by having more extensive webbing and lacking discs, and from *Phrynobatrachus rungwensis* in lacking discs and possessing a conical tarsal tubercle (JCP). See Schiøtz, 1963, Vidensk. Medd. Dansk Naturhist. Foren., 125:38–39. Reviewed by Guibé and Lamotte, 1963, Mém. Inst. Franç. Afr. Noire, 66:601–627, and Schmidt and Inger, 1959, Explor. Parc Natl. Upemba, 56:151–154.

Phrynobatrachus hylaios Perret, 1959. Rev. Suisse Zool., 66:711.
ORIGINAL NAME: *Phrynobatrachus werneri hylaios.*
TYPE(S): Holotype: MHNG 964.100.
TYPE LOCALITY: "Foulassi, Cameroun; alt. 710 m, forêt".
DISTRIBUTION: South Cameroon and Adamaoua Plateau.

Phrynobatrachus keniensis Barbour and Loveridge, 1928. Proc. New England Zool. Club, 10:89.
TYPE(S): Holotype: MCZ 3479.
TYPE LOCALITY: "a marsh on the northeast slope of Mt. Kenya, Kenya Colony [=Kenya]".
DISTRIBUTION: Upland meadows of Kenya and Mt. Meru, Tanzania.

Phrynobatrachus kinangopensis Angel, 1924. Bull. Mus. Natl. Hist. Nat., Paris, 30:131.
TYPE(S): Holotype: MNHNP 24-16.
TYPE LOCALITY: "Prairies alpines du Mont Kinangop (altitude 3100 m)", Aberdare Mountains, Kenya.
DISTRIBUTION: Highlands of Kenya.

Phrynobatrachus krefftii Boulenger, 1909. Ann. Mag. Nat. Hist., (8)4:496.
TYPE(S): Syntypes: BM 1947.2.30.30–31 (formerly 1909.10.19.14–15).
TYPE LOCALITY: "Amani", Usambara Mountains, Tanzania.
DISTRIBUTION: Usambara and Magrotto mountains, Tanzania.
COMMENT: Reviewed by Barbour and Loveridge, 1928, Mem. Mus. Comp. Zool., 50:201–203.

Phrynobatrachus liberiensis Barbour and Loveridge, 1927. Proc. New England Zool. Club, 10:14.
TYPE(S): Holotype: MCZ 11993.
TYPE LOCALITY: "Gbanga, Liberia".
DISTRIBUTION: Liberia and Ghana.
COMMENT: Reviewed by Guibé and Lamotte, 1963, Mém. Inst. Franç. Afr. Noire, 66:601–627.

Phrynobatrachus mababiensis FitzSimons, 1932. Ann. Transvaal Mus., 15:40.
TYPE(S): Holotype: TM 14838.
TYPE LOCALITY: "Tsotsoroga Pan, Mababe Flats", Rep. South Africa.
DISTRIBUTION: Tanzania to Shaba (Zaire), Zambia, and Zimbabwe to southern Angola and Rep. South Africa.
COMMENT: Probably a subspecies of *Phrynobatrachus ukingensis* (RL). JCP disagrees with RL and suggests that *Phrynobatrachus mababiensis* more closely resembles *Phrynobatrachus parvulus*, a taxon not distinguished from *Phrynobatrachus mababiensis* by Loveridge, 1953, Bull. Mus. Comp. Zool., 110:381.

Phrynobatrachus manengoubensis (Angel, 1940). Bull. Mus. Natl. Hist. Nat., Paris, 12:242.
ORIGINAL NAME: *Arthroleptis manengoubensis.*
TYPE(S): Syntypes: MNHNP 39-113 and 39-114.
TYPE LOCALITY: "cratère de l'Eboga, Monts Manengouba; alt. 2000 m.", Cameroon.
DISTRIBUTION: Known only from the type locality.

COMMENT: Probably a synonym of *Phrynobatrachus werneri* (AGCG).

Phrynobatrachus minutus (Boulenger, 1895). Proc. Zool. Soc. London, 1895:539.
ORIGINAL NAME: *Arthroleptis minutus*.
TYPE(S): Holotype: BM 1947.2.30.51 (formerly 95.6.11.8).
TYPE LOCALITY: "Durro" (=Duro), Ethiopia.
DISTRIBUTION: Sudan and Somalia to Zaire and Zambia.
COMMENT: The damaged holotype seems to differ from other BM material from
    Sudan and Somalia southward (JCP).

Phrynobatrachus moorii (Boulenger, 1898). Proc. Zool. Soc. London, 1898:479.
ORIGINAL NAME: *Arthroleptis moorii*.
TYPE(S): Holotype: BM 1947.2.30.52 (formerly 98.7.22.26).
TYPE LOCALITY: "Kinyamkolo, Lake Tanganyika" (=Nyamkolo, southeastern corner
    of Lake Tanganyika, northeastern Zambia).
DISTRIBUTION: Northeastern Zambia to Malawi.
COMMENT: The holotype falls within the range of variation shown by
    Phrynobatrachus natalensis from surrounding areas (JCP).

Phrynobatrachus nanus (Ahl, 1923). Sitzungsber. Ges. Naturforsch. Freunde Berlin,
    1923:103.
ORIGINAL NAME: *Pararthroleptis nanus*.
TYPE(S): Holotype: ZMB 28347.
TYPE LOCALITY: "Buala am Uam, Neu Kamerun" (Cameroon).
DISTRIBUTION: Known only from the type locality.

Phrynobatrachus natalensis (Smith, 1849). Illustr. Zool. S. Afr., Rept., App.:23.
ORIGINAL NAME: *Stereorhynchus natalensis*.
TYPE(S): Holotype: BM 1947.2.5.13 (formerly 62.3.14.20).
TYPE LOCALITY: "the country around Port Natal [=Durban]", Natal, Rep. South
    Africa.
DISTRIBUTION: Savanna areas of Africa, south of the Sahara
COMMENT: See comment under *Phrynobatrachus moorii*. Reviewed by Guibé and
    Lamotte, 1963, Mém. Inst. Franç. Afr. Noire, 66:601–627; Schmidt and Inger,
    1959, Explor. Parc Natl. Upemba, 56:155–159; Poynton, 1964, Ann. Natal Mus.,
    17:137–140; and Lamotte and Xavier, 1966, Bull. Inst. Franç. Afr. Noire, (A)28:
    343–361.

Phrynobatrachus ogoensis (Boulenger, 1906). Ann. Mus. Civ. Stor. Nat. Genova, (3)2:
    162.
ORIGINAL NAME: *Arthroleptis ogoensis*.
TYPE(S): Syntypes: (formerly 5 specimens) BM 1947.2.6.83–84 (formerly
    1906.3.30.127–128) and MSNG.
TYPE LOCALITY: "Lambarene, Ogowe", Gabon.
DISTRIBUTION: Gabon.

Phrynobatrachus pakenhami Loveridge, 1941. Proc. Biol. Soc. Washington, 54:178.
TYPE(S): Holotype: MCZ 24568.
TYPE LOCALITY: "Machengwe Swamp, near Wete, Pemba Island", Tanzania.
DISTRIBUTION: Pemba I., Tanzania.

Phrynobatrachus parkeri Witte, 1933. Rev. Zool. Bot. Afr., 24:97.
TYPE(S): Syntypes: RGMC 36504–05, 2698–2706.
TYPE LOCALITY: "Mauda" and "Kunungu (Lac Leopold II)", Zaire.
DISTRIBUTION: Type localities (west-central and northeastern Zaire).
COMMENT: Reviewed by Inger, 1968, Explor. Parc Natl. Garamba, 52:96–101.

Phrynobatrachus parvulus (Boulenger, 1905). Ann. Mag. Nat. Hist., (7)16:109.
ORIGINAL NAME: *Arthroleptis parvulus.*
TYPE(S): Syntypes: BM 1947.2.6.93–95 (formerly 1904.5.2.97–99), FMNH (1 specimen).
TYPE LOCALITY: "Banje Ngola", northeastern Loanda, Angola.
DISTRIBUTION: Angola to central Zaire, Malawi, Zimbabwe, and northeastern Namibia.
COMMENT: Reviewed by Schmidt and Inger, 1959, Explor. Parc Natl. Upemba, 56: 160–165. See comment under *Phrynobatrachus mababiensis.*

Phrynobatrachus perpalmatus Boulenger, 1898. Proc. Zool. Soc. London, 1898:479.
TYPE(S): Syntypes: BM 1947.2.4.34–35 (formerly 98.7.22.24–25).
TYPE LOCALITY: "about Lake Mwero", Zambia-Zaire boundary.
DISTRIBUTION: Cameroon, Sudan, and eastern Zaire to Mozambique, central Zaire, and Zambia.
COMMENT: Reviewed by Schmidt and Inger, 1959, Explor. Parc Natl. Upemba, 56: 165–169, and Inger, 1968, Explor. Parc Natl. Garamba, 52:106–108. Loveridge's records for Mozambique and Malawi are based on *Phrynobatrachus acridoides;* see Poynton, 1964, Ann. Natal Mus., 17:140–141.

Phrynobatrachus petropedetoides Ahl, 1924. Zool. Anz., 61:102.
TYPE(S): Syntypes: ?ZMB.
TYPE LOCALITY: "Ruwenzori, 1800 m" and "Westlich des Albert-Edward-Sees" (E. Zaire), but Ahl clearly intended restriction to Ruwenzori, 1800 m (AGCG).
DISTRIBUTION: Montane forests of eastern Zaire, southwestern Uganda, and extreme western Tanzania.
COMMENT: See Laurent, 1972, Explor. Parc Natl. Virunga, (2)22:107–109, for discussion.

Phrynobatrachus plicatus (Günther, 1859 "1858"). Cat. Batr. Sal. Coll. Brit. Mus.:88.
ORIGINAL NAME: *Hyperolius plicatus.*
TYPE(S): Holotype: BM 1947.2.29.47 (formerly 49.10.9.1).
TYPE LOCALITY: "Coast of Guinea".
DISTRIBUTION: Forests of West Africa from Guinea eastward to Nigeria.
COMMENT: See Witte, 1941, Explor. Parc Natl. Albert, 33:73–74, for synonymy and review. See Lamotte and Xavier, 1966, Bull. Inst. Franç. Afr. Noire, (A)28: 1606, for synonymy (inclusion of *Phrynobatrachus aelleni* Loveridge, 1955) and comparison to *Phrynobatrachus auritus.* See comment under *Phrynobatrachus auritus.*

Phrynobatrachus pygmaeus (Ahl, 1923). Sitzungsber. Ges. Naturforsch. Freunde Berlin, 1923:105.
ORIGINAL NAME: *Arthroleptis pygmaeus.*
TYPE(S): Holotype: ?ZMB 28346.
TYPE LOCALITY: "Buala am Uam, Neu-Kamerun" (Cameroon).
DISTRIBUTION: Known only from the type locality.

Phrynobatrachus rouxi (Nieden, 1912). Wiss. Ergebn. Deutsch. Zentr. Afr. Exped., 4: 178.
ORIGINAL NAME: *Arthroleptis rouxi.*
TYPE(S): Holotype: ZMB 23102.
TYPE LOCALITY: "NW-Budduwald", Uganda.
DISTRIBUTION: Uganda and adjacent Zaire.
COMMENT: Laurent, 1972, Explor. Parc Natl. Virunga, (2)22:16, discussed probable synonymy with *Phrynobatrachus calcaratus.*

Phrynobatrachus rungwensis (Loveridge, 1932). Bull. Mus. Comp. Zool., 72:386.
ORIGINAL NAME: *Arthroleptis rungwensis.*
TYPE(S): Holotype: MCZ 17141.
TYPE LOCALITY: "just below the Moravian Mission at Ilolo at the base of Rungwe Mountain, southwestern Tanganyika Territory [=Tanzania]".
DISTRIBUTION: Southwestern Tanzania and adjacent Zaire; Malawi.
COMMENT: See comment under *Phrynobatrachus gutturosus.*

Phrynobatrachus scapularis (Witte, 1933). Rev. Zool. Bot. Afr., 24:100.
ORIGINAL NAME: *Arthroleptis scapularis.*
TYPE(S): Holotype: RGMC 7740.
TYPE LOCALITY: "Buta (Uele)", northeastern Zaire.
DISTRIBUTION: Northeastern Zaire.
COMMENT: Discussed by Inger, 1968, Explor. Parc Nat. Garamba, 52:102–106.

Phrynobatrachus sciangallarum (Scortecci, 1943). Miss. Biol. Sagan-Omo, 7(Zool.):329.
ORIGINAL NAME: *Arthroleptis-Phrynobatrachus sciangallarum.*
TYPE(S): Not traced.
TYPE LOCALITY: "Murle", Gemu-Gofa Province, Ethiopia, 05° 10′ N, 36° 13′ E, 200 m.
DISTRIBUTION: Known only from the type locality.

Phrynobatrachus steindachneri Nieden, 1910. Arch. Naturgesch., 76:241.
TYPE(S): Syntypes: ZMB (28 specimens), MCZ 19577.
TYPE LOCALITY: "Banjo", Cameroon; corrected to 200 km ENE Bamenda, Cameroon, by Amiet, 1971, Ann. Fac. Sci. Cameroun, 5:93.
DISTRIBUTION: Nigeria and central Cameroon Range (Cameroon), West Africa.

Phrynobatrachus sulfureogularis Laurent, 1951. Rev. Zool. Bot. Afr., 44:362.
TYPE(S): Holotype: RGMC.
TYPE LOCALITY: "Massif du Nanzergwa, 2300–2500 m, Territoire de Bururi, Urundi [=Burundi]", Central Africa.
DISTRIBUTION: Known only from the type locality.

Phrynobatrachus tellinii Peracca, 1904. Boll. Mus. Zool. Anat. Comp. Univ. Torino, 19: 467.
TYPE(S): Syntypes: 2 specimens, including MSNT 504 (3095) (1 specimen).
TYPE LOCALITY: Between Massaua and Chezere, Eritrea [Ethiopia].
DISTRIBUTION: Known only from the type locality.

Phrynobatrachus tokba (Chabanaud, 1921). Bull. Com. Études Hist. Scient. Afr. Occid. Franç., 3:454.
ORIGINAL NAME: *Arthroleptis tokba.*
TYPE(S): Syntypes: MNHNP 21-144, 21-152, BM 1947.2.6.85–87 (formerly 1921.6.16.5–7).
TYPE LOCALITY: "N'Zébéla" and "N'Zérékoré, Guinée Francaise".
DISTRIBUTION: Known only from the type locality.

Phrynobatrachus ukingensis (Loveridge, 1932). Bull. Mus. Comp. Zool., 72:385.
ORIGINAL NAME: *Arthroleptis ukingensis.*
TYPE(S): Holotype: MCZ 17137.
TYPE LOCALITY: "Madehani, Ukinga Mountains, Tanganyika Territory [=Tanzania]".
DISTRIBUTION: Virgin forests of Ukinga and Rungwe mountains (southern Tanzania) and Misuku Mountains (Malawi).
COMMENT: See comment under *Phrynobatrachus mababiensis.*

Phrynobatrachus uzungwensis Grandison and Howell, 1984 "1983". Amphibia-Reptilia, 4:119.
TYPE(S): Holotype: BM 1982.553.
TYPE LOCALITY: "about 1000 m in the Mwanihana Forest Reserve, 7° 45′ S: 36° 48′ E, Uzungwe Mts., Kilombero District, Morogoro Region, Tanzania".
DISTRIBUTION: Uzungwe and Uluguru mountains of central Tanzania.

Phrynobatrachus versicolor Ahl, 1924. Zool. Anz., 61:100.
TYPE(S): Syntypes: (214 specimens) ZMB, BM 1947.2.4.26 (formerly 1935.2.8.1),
MCZ 17532–33.
TYPE LOCALITY: "Rugegewald", Rwanda.
DISTRIBUTION: Zaire to Rwanda, Burundi, and southwestern Uganda in mountain
swamps.
COMMENT: See Laurent, 1972, Explor. Parc Natl. Virunga, (2)22:106, for discussion.

Phrynobatrachus villiersi Guibé, 1959. Bull. Mus. Natl. Hist. Nat., Paris, (2)31(2):134.
TYPE(S): Holotype: MNHNP 58-485.
TYPE LOCALITY: "Yapo, (Côte d'Ivoire)".
DISTRIBUTION: Ivory Coast and Ghana.

Phrynobatrachus vogti Ahl, 1924. Zool. Anz., 61:103.
TYPE(S): Syntypes: ZMB.
TYPE LOCALITY: "Boutry", Ghana.
DISTRIBUTION: Known only from the type locality.

Phrynobatrachus werneri (Nieden, 1910). Arch. Naturgesch., 76:242.
ORIGINAL NAME: *Arthroleptis werneri.*
TYPE(S): Syntypes: ZMB 20434, 20789 (total of 5 specimens).
TYPE LOCALITY: "Banjobezirk" and "Bamenda", Cameroon.
DISTRIBUTION: Southeastern Nigeria and southwestern Cameroon, in Cameroon
Range (except for Mount Cameroon).

Phrynobatrachus zavattarii (Scortecci, 1943). Miss. Biol. Sagan-Omo, 7(Zool.):327.
ORIGINAL NAME: *Arthroleptis-Phrynobatrachus zavattarii.*
TYPE(S): Syntypes: 4 specimens, deposition unknown.
TYPE LOCALITY: "Caschei" (=Ciacche), Gemu-Gofa Province, Ethiopia, 05° 00' N, 37°
33' E, ca. 1500 m.
DISTRIBUTION: Known only from the type locality.

Phrynodon Parker, 1935. Ann. Mag. Nat. Hist., (10)16:402.
TYPE SPECIES: *Phrynodon sandersoni* Parker, 1935, by original designation.
DISTRIBUTION: As for the single species.
COMMENT: Affinities with *Petropedetes* were discussed by Amiet, 1981, Amphibia-
Reptilia, 2:1–13.
CONTRIBUTOR: J.-L. Amiet (JLA).
REVIEWER: Jean-Luc Perret (JLA).

Phrynodon sandersoni Parker, 1935. Ann. Mag. Nat. Hist., (10)16:403.
TYPE(S): Holotype: BM 1907.5.22.76.
TYPE LOCALITY: "5 miles inland from Kribi, S. Cameroon".
DISTRIBUTION: Southwestern Cameroon and Fernando Po.

SUBFAMILY: **Raninae** Gray, 1825.
CITATION: Ann. Philos., (2)10:213.
DISTRIBUTION: Coextensive with the family.
COMMENT: This group displays taxonomic confusion on a grand scale due to the size of
the group and the divergent systematic philosophies of current and past workers.
This 'group' is likely paraphyletic with respect to the Mantellinae and through
that group to the Rhacophoridae. Laurent, 1961, Rev. Zool. Bot. Afr., 43:199,
believed the Raninae to be ancestral to the Phrynobatrachinae. As here conceived
the Raninae includes the Platymantinae of Savage, 1973, *In* Vial (ed.), Evol. Biol.
Anurans:354. Lynch, 1973, *In* Vial (ed.), Evol. Biol. Anurans:133–182, and Dubois,
1981, Monit. Zool. Ital., N.S., Suppl., 15:225–283, did not consider the
Platymantinae differentiable from the Raninae; recognition requires the partition
of the subgenus *Hylarana* of *Rana*, according to Savage, 1973. The generic

definitions and boundaries within the Raninae are badly in need of revision. Unfortunately, the only attempt at phylogenetic reconstruction (Clarke, 1981, Monit. Zool. Ital., N.S., Suppl., 15:285–331) was restricted to African genera. Generic and subgeneric boundaries are so unstable that we have not attempted to follow 'the most recent literature'. Instead we have opted to recognize as many genera as are currently recognized by some segment of the working herpetological community. Dubois, 1981, Monit. Zool. Ital., N.S., Suppl., 15:225–284, discussed these problems at length and provided a gradistic system of genera and subgenera of the Raninae (including the Platymantinae as used here). He considered *Rana* to have four groups of subgenera (most of which are treated as genera in this list): (1) *Rana, Hylarana, Strongylopus, Paa, Altirana,* and *Nanorana;* (2) *Hildebrandtia, Ptychadena,* and (by implication) *Lanzarana;* (3) *Tomopterna, Euphlyctis,* and *Limnonectes;* (4) *Pyxicephalus* and *Aubria.* The gradistic nature of this arrangement (as well as the traditional one) makes the problems difficult to discuss, much less solve. Note, however, that Clarke, 1981, Monit. Zool. Ital., N.S., Suppl., 15:285–331, considered *Euphlyctis* as only distantly related to *Tomopterna* and retained it as a subgenus of *Rana.* Dubois, 1975, Bull. Mus. Natl. Hist. Nat., Paris, (3)324(Zool.)231:1093–1115, suggested that *Euphlyctis* might be polyphyletic. See generic accounts for further comments. Our taxonomy is pragmatic but we caution the use of our taxonomy (or any other current taxonomy) as a source of phylogenetic or phenetic information.

CONTRIBUTORS: Leo J. Borkin (LJB) (Palearctic Region); Sushil Dutta (SD) (Tropical Asia); Shuqin Hu (SH) (China); Masafumi Matsui (MM) (East Asia, including Greater Sundas); Jean-Luc Perret (JLP) (Africa [excluding *Strongylopus* and *Tomopterna*]).

REVIEWERS: J.-L. Amiet (JLA) (Cameroon); Steven C. Anderson (SCA) (southwestern Asia); Leo J. Borkin (LJB); Alan Channing (AC) (Southern Africa); J. C. Daniel (JCD) (India and Sri Lanka); Kim M. Howell (KMH) (East Africa); Raymond Laurent (RL) (Africa); John C. Poynton (JCP) (Africa); Ermi Zhao (EZ) (China).

Altirana Stejneger, 1927. J. Washington Acad. Sci., 17:318.
   TYPE SPECIES: *Altirana parkeri* Stejneger, 1927, by original designation.
   DISTRIBUTION: As for the single species.
   COMMENT: Considered a subgenus of *Rana* and related to the subgenus *Paa* (=*Rana liebigii* group of Boulenger, 1920, Rec. Indian Mus., 20:1–226) of *Rana* according to Dubois, 1981, Monit. Zool. Ital., N.S., Suppl., 15:234. See comment under Raninae.

Altirana parkeri Stejneger, 1927. J. Washington Acad. Sci., 17:318.
   TYPE(s): Holotype: USNM 72328.
   TYPE LOCALITY: Tingri, 15,000 feet altitude, Tibet [China].
   DISTRIBUTION: Tibet (China) and Nepal.
   COMMENT: Reviewed by Liu, 1950, Fieldiana: Zool. Mem., 2:329–330; Liu and Hu, 1961, Tailless Amph. China:217–220; and Dubois, 1974, Bull. Mus. Natl. Hist. Nat., Paris, (3)213(Zool.)143:377.

Amolops Cope, 1865. Nat. Hist. Rev., N.S., 5:117.
   TYPE SPECIES: *Polypedates afghana* Günther, 1859 "1858", by monotypy.
   DISTRIBUTION: Nepal, northeastern India, western and southern China to the Greater Sunda Is.
   COMMENT: Inger, 1966, Fieldiana: Zool., 52:256, noted that *Amolops* is distinguished from *Staurois* by possession of its tadpole of an abdominal sucker. He also noted that the type species of *Staurois, Staurois natator,* does not exhibit this trait. Thus, the definition of *Staurois* in Noble, 1931, Biol. Amph.:522, actually applies to *Amolops.* Subsequent to Inger's (1966) partition of *Staurois* (*sensu lato*) into *Staurois* and *Amolops* a number of *Amolops* species have been treated as *Staurois* by a number of authors, none of which have refuted his position. Synonymies and reviews (as *Staurois* in the sense of Noble, 1931) of Chinese species available in Liu, 1950, Fieldiana: Zool. Mem., 2:330–359, and Liu and Hu, 1961,

Tailless Amph. China:226–243. Bornean species reviewed and genus discussed by Inger, 1966, Fieldiana: Zool., 52:256–278, and Inger and Gritis, 1983, Fieldiana: Zool., N.S., 19:1–13. A number of species currently placed in other genera probably belong in this genus (MM); see *Rana longimanus* and *Rana gerbillus*. See comment under *Rana* (*Hylarana*).

Amolops afghanus (Günther, 1859 "1858"). Cat. Batr. Sal. Coll. Brit. Mus.:81.
ORIGINAL NAME: *Polypedates afghana*.
TYPE(S): Syntypes: BM (1 adult, 2 larvae).
TYPE LOCALITY: "Afghanistan" (in error; see comment).
DISTRIBUTION: Eastern Himalayan region of India and Nepal to Thailand, China (Yunnan and Tibet).
COMMENT: No *Amolops* species has subsequently been collected in Afghanistan and Boulenger, 1890, Fauna Brit. India:462–463, considered Günther's *Polypedates afghana* to be conspecific with Boulenger's *Rana latopalmata*, which he regarded as not occurring in Afghanistan. Annandale, 1912, Rec. Indian Mus., 8:7–36, also noted that this species did not occur in Afghanistan. Thus, the types are unlikely to have come from Afghanistan (SCA). See Dubois, 1974, Bull. Mus. Natl. Hist. Nat., Paris, (2)213(Zool.)143:356–357, and Taylor, 1962, Univ. Kansas Sci. Bull., 43:474–477. Also see Bourret, 1942, Batr. Indochine: 392, and Pope and Boring, 1940, Peking Nat. Hist. Bull., 15:47. See comment under *Amolops kaulbacki*.

Amolops cavitympanum (Boulenger, 1893). Proc. Zool. Soc. London, 1893:525.
ORIGINAL NAME: *Rana cavitympanum*.
TYPE(S): BM.
TYPE LOCALITY: Kina Balu, Sabah [Malaysia (Borneo)].
DISTRIBUTION: Borneo.

Amolops chunganensis (Pope, 1929). Am. Mus. Novit., 352:3.
ORIGINAL NAME: *Rana chunganensis*.
TYPE(S): Holotype: AMNH 30479.
TYPE LOCALITY: Kuatun village, northwestern Ch'ungan Hsien, Fukien [=Fujian], 4500–5000 feet altitude [China].
DISTRIBUTION: Shaanxi, Gansu, Sichuan, Guizhou, Guangxi, Hunan, and Fujian, China.
COMMENT: Reviewed (as *Staurois chunganensis*) by Liu, 1950, Fieldiana: Zool. Mem., 2:337–344.

Amolops daiyunensis (Liu and Hu, 1975). Acta Zool. Sinica, 21:268.
ORIGINAL NAME: *Staurois daiyunensis*.
TYPE(S): Holotype: CIB (formerly SWIBASC) 64II0934.
TYPE LOCALITY: Dehua, Daiyun Shan, altitude 1100 m, Fujian, China.
DISTRIBUTION: Fujian, China.
COMMENT: Related to *Amolops hainanensis* (as *Staurois hainanensis*), according to the original description.

Amolops formosus (Günther, 1875). Proc. Zool. Soc. London, 1875:570.
ORIGINAL NAME: *Polypedates formosus*.
TYPE(S): Holotype: BM 1947.2.4.18.
TYPE LOCALITY: "Khassya" (=Khasi Hills), Assam, India.
DISTRIBUTION: Northeastern India and Nepal.
COMMENT: See Dubois, 1974, Bull. Mus. Natl. Hist. Nat., Paris, (3)213(Zool.)143:357, for synonymy of *Rana himalayana* Boulenger, 1888, Ann. Mag. Nat. Hist., (6)11:567 (Syntypes: BM 1947.2.3.83–84 and 1947.2.27.94–95; Type locality: Darjiling, eastern Himalayas [India]).

Amolops granulosus (Liu and Hu, 1961). Tailless Amph. China:233.
ORIGINAL NAME: *Staurois granulosus*.
TYPE(S): Holotype: CIB (formerly SWIBASC) 55321.
TYPE LOCALITY: Mao Xian, Sichuan, altitude 1500 m, China.
DISTRIBUTION: Sichuan and Hubei, 650–1750 m elev., China.
COMMENT: Figure of tadpoles in the original description indicates that this species
is a member of *Amolops* (*sensu* Inger, 1966) and not *Staurois* (MM).

Amolops hainanensis (Boulenger, 1899). Proc. Zool. Soc. London, 1899:958.
ORIGINAL NAME: *Staurois hainanensis*.
TYPE(S): Syntypes: BM (2 specimens).
TYPE LOCALITY: "Five-finger Mountains, in the interior of the island", Hainan,
China.
DISTRIBUTION: Hainan I., China.
COMMENT: Reviewed (as *Staurois hainanensis*) by Bourret, 1942, Batr. Indochine:394–
396; Liu and Hu, 1961, Tailless Amph. China:241–242; and Liu, Hu, Fei, and
Huang, 1973, Acta Zool. Sinica, 19(4):396.

Amolops hongkongensis (Pope and Romer, 1951). Fieldiana: Zool., 31:609.
ORIGINAL NAME: *Staurois hongkongensis*.
TYPE(S): Holotype: FMNH 64157.
TYPE LOCALITY: Tai Mo Shan, New Territories, Colony of Hongkong [China].
DISTRIBUTION: Hong Kong I. and New Territories on adjacent mainland China.

Amolops jerboa (Günther, 1872). Proc. Zool. Soc. London, 1872:599.
ORIGINAL NAME: *Hylorana jerboa*.
TYPE(S): Syntypes: BM (2 specimens).
TYPE LOCALITY: "Matang", Sarawak, Malaysia (Borneo).
DISTRIBUTION: Malaya; Sumatra; Borneo; Java.
COMMENT: Reviewed (as *Staurois jerboa*) by Bourret, 1942, Batr. Indochine:382–385.
Bourret included *Rana maosonii* Boulenger, 1889, Ann. Mag. Nat. Hist., (5)13:
397 (Type locality: "Batavia", Java), in the synonymy of this species. Inger,
1966, Fieldiana: Zool., 52:263, did not include *Rana maosonii* in his synonymy
of *Amolops jerboa*, so the status of *Rana maosonii* is unclear. See comment under
Rana gerbillus.

Amolops kaulbacki (Smith, 1940). Rec. Indian Mus., 42:472.
TYPE(S): Holotype: BM 1940.6.1.1.
TYPE LOCALITY: "Pangnamdim", Upper Burma.
DISTRIBUTION: Upper Burma; northwestern Sichuan, China, 4000–7000 ft. elev.
COMMENT: Transferred to *Amolops* by Dubois, 1974, Bull. Mus. Natl. Hist. Nat.,
Paris, (3)213(Zool.)143:361, who suggested that it is probably a subspecies
of *Amolops afghanus*, and that *Staurois lifanensis* Liu, 1945, J. West China Border
Res. Soc., (B)15:33 (Holotype: CIB 1062; Type locality: Nankou, Lifan City,
Lifan, Sichuan, China) is a junior synonym.

Amolops kinabaluensis Inger, 1966. Fieldiana: Zool., 52:266.
TYPE(S): Holotype: FMNH 109798.
TYPE LOCALITY: "Kiau, Mount Kina Balu, Sabah", Malaysia (Borneo).
DISTRIBUTION: Known only from the type locality.

Amolops larutensis (Boulenger, 1899). Ann. Mag. Nat. Hist., (7)1:273.
ORIGINAL NAME: *Rana larutensis*.
TYPE(S): Syntypes: BM (3 specimens).
TYPE LOCALITY: "Larut Peak, 3000 ft.", Perak, Malaysia (Malaya).
DISTRIBUTION: Malaya.
COMMENT: Reviewed by Bourret, 1942, Batr. Indochine:393–394. See also Berry,
1975, Amph. Fauna Peninsular Malaysia:58–59, for account.

Amolops loloensis (Liu, 1950). Fieldiana: Zool. Mem., 2:353.
  ORIGINAL NAME: *Staurois loloensis.*
  TYPE(S): Holotype: FMNH 49408.
  TYPE LOCALITY: "Lolokou, Chaochiaohsien, Sikang [=Sichuan], 10000 feet altitude",
    China.
  DISTRIBUTION: Sichuan and Yunnan, altitude 1680 m, China.
  COMMENT: Reviewed (as *Staurois loloensis*) by Liu and Hu, 1961, Tailless Amph.
    China:235–237.

Amolops mantzorum (David, 1871). Nouv. Arch. Mus. Natl. Hist. Nat., Paris, 7,
    Bull.:45.
  ORIGINAL NAME: *Polypedates mantzorum.*
  TYPE(S): MNHNP?; not mentioned by Guibé, 1950 "1948", Cat. Types Amph. Mus.
    Natl. Hist. Nat.
  TYPE LOCALITY: Muping [=Baoxing], Sichuan, China.
  DISTRIBUTION: Sichuan, Gansu, and Yunnan, 3000–6000 ft. elev., China.
  COMMENT: Synonymy includes *Staurois kangtingensis* Liu, 1950, Fieldiana: Zool.
    Mem., 2:349 (Holoytpe: FMNH 49412; Type locality: "Kangting, Sikang
    [=Sichuan], 8000 feet altitude"), according to Liu and Hu, 1961, Tailless
    Amph. China:239, 249, who reviewed the species.

Amolops monticola (Anderson, 1871). J. Asiat. Soc. Bengal, 40:20.
  ORIGINAL NAME: *Hylorana monticola.*
  TYPE(S): ZSI.
  TYPE LOCALITY: "Darjeeling, 3500 feet", West Bengal, India.
  DISTRIBUTION: Darjeeling region of India and Tibet (China), 1550–2350 m elev.
  COMMENT: Herpetol. Dep. Sichuan Biol. Res. Inst., 1977, Acta Zool. Sinica, 23:56–
    57, transferred this species (as *Staurois monticola*) from *Rana* to *Staurois*
    (=*Amolops, sensu* Inger, 1966) (LJB and MM).

Amolops nasicus (Boulenger, 1903). Ann. Mag. Nat. Hist., (7)12:187.
  ORIGINAL NAME: *Rana nasica.*
  TYPE(S): Syntypes: BM (4 specimens).
  TYPE LOCALITY: "Man-Son Mountains, Tonkin, altitude 3000–4000 ft.", Vietnam.
  DISTRIBUTION: Tonkin, Vietnam; Guizhou, Hunan, Yunnan, and Hainan I., China.
  COMMENT: Transferred to *Staurois* (=*Amolops, sensu* Inger, 1966) by Liu and Hu,
    1959, Acta Zool. Sinica, 11:511. Reviewed by Bourret, 1942, Batr. Indochine:
    352–354, and by Liu and Hu, 1961, Tailless Amph. China:229–230 (as *Staurois
    nasica*).

Amolops phaeomerus Inger and Gritis, 1983. Fieldiana: Zool., N.S., 19:9.
  TYPE(S): Holotype: FMNH 136140.
  TYPE LOCALITY: "Nanga Tekalit, Kapit District, Third Division, Sarawak", Malaysia
    (Borneo).
  DISTRIBUTION: Baleh River basin, Sarawak, Malaysia (Borneo).

Amolops poecilus Inger and Gritis, 1983. Fieldiana: Zool., N.S., 19:11.
  TYPE(S): Holotype: FMNH 144532.
  TYPE LOCALITY: "Nanga Tekalit, Kapit District, Third Division, Sarawak", Malaysia
    (Borneo).
  DISTRIBUTION: Baleh River basin, Sarawak, Malaysia (Borneo).

Amolops ricketti (Boulenger, 1899). Proc. Zool. Soc. London, 1899:168.
  ORIGINAL NAME: *Rana ricketti.*
  TYPE(S): Syntypes: BM (2 specimens).
  TYPE LOCALITY: "Kuatun, a village about 270 miles from Foochow, in the [Kuatun]
    mountains at the North-west of the Province of Fokien [=Fujian], at an
    altitude of 3000 to 4000 feet or more", China.
  DISTRIBUTION: Sichuan, Guizhou, Anhui, Hubei, Hunan, Zhejiang, Guangdong,
    Jiangsi, Guangxi, and Fujian, China, 400–1300 m elev.

COMMENT: Reviewed by Pope, 1931, Bull. Am. Mus. Nat. Hist., 61:558–562, and
Bourret, 1942, Batr. Indochine:387–390, as *Staurois ricketti*. See also Liu and
Hu, 1961, Tailless Amph. China:231–232.

Amolops torrentis (Smith, 1923). J. Nat. Hist. Soc. Siam, 6:209.
ORIGINAL NAME: *Micrixalus torrentis*.
TYPE(S): Holotype: BM (formerly M. Smith 6941).
TYPE LOCALITY: "Five-Finger mountain at 1000 metres altitude", Hainan I., China.
DISTRIBUTION: Hainan I., China.
COMMENT: Reviewed by Bourret, 1942, Batr. Indochine:396–397, as *Micrixalus
torrentis*. Transferred to *Staurois* by Liu et al., 1973, Acta Zool. Sinica, 19:398,
who illustrated tadpoles that indicate that this species is a member of *Amolops*
(*sensu* Inger, 1966) (LJB and MM).

Amolops viridimaculatus (Jiang, 1983). Acta Herpetol. Sinica, 2(3):71.
ORIGINAL NAME: *Staurois viridimaculatus*.
TYPE(S): Holotype: CIB 820821.
TYPE LOCALITY: Dahaoping, Tengchung, 1980 m, Yunnan, China.
DISTRIBUTION: Yunnan, China.
COMMENT: Related to *Amolops loloensis* (as *Staurois loloensis*), according to the
original description.

Amolops whiteheadi (Boulenger, 1887). Ann. Mag. Nat. Hist., (5)20:96.
ORIGINAL NAME: *Rana whiteheadi*.
TYPE(S): Syntypes: MNHNP (3 specimens).
TYPE LOCALITY: Mt. Kina Balu, Sabah [Malaysia (Borneo)].
DISTRIBUTION: Mt. Kina Balu, Sabah, Malaysia (Borneo).
COMMENT: Removed from the synonymy of *Amolops jerboa* by Inger and Gritis,
1983, Fieldiana: Zool., N.S., 19:1–13.

Amolops wuyiensis (Liu and Hu, 1975). Acta Zool. Sinica, 21(3):266.
ORIGINAL NAME: *Staurois wuyiensis*.
TYPE(S): Holotype: CIB 64I1211.
TYPE LOCALITY: "Sanchiang, Chungan, Fuchuen [=Fukien], altitude 600 m", China.
DISTRIBUTION: Fujian, China.
COMMENT: Related to *Amolops ricketti* (as *Staurois ricketti*), according to the original
description.

Aubria Boulenger, 1917. C. R. Hebd. Séances Acad. Sci., Paris, 165:988.
TYPE SPECIES: *Rana subsigillata* Duméril, 1856, by monotypy.
DISTRIBUTION: As for the single species.
COMMENT: The sister-taxon of *Pyxicephalus*, according to Clarke, 1981, Monit. Zool.
Ital., N.S., Suppl., 15:285–331; regarded as a subgenus of *Pyxicephalus* by Dubois,
1981, Monit. Zool. Ital., N.S., Suppl., 15:225–284. See comment under
Pyxicephalus.

Aubria subsigillata (Duméril, 1856). Rev. Mag. Zool., Paris, (2)8:560.
ORIGINAL NAME: *Rana subsigillata*.
TYPE(S): Holotype: MNHNP 1566.
TYPE LOCALITY: Gabon.
DISTRIBUTION: Rainforest of South Cameroon to Zaire.
COMMENT: See Schiøtz, 1963, Vidensk. Medd. Dansk Naturhist. Foren., 125:26–27,
and Perret, 1966, Zool. Jahrb., Abt. Syst., 93:336–338.

Batrachylodes Boulenger, 1887. Proc. Zool. Soc. London, 1887:337.
TYPE SPECIES: *Batrachylodes vertebralis* Boulenger, 1887, by monotypy.
DISTRIBUTION: Solomon Is.
COMMENT: Brown and Parker, 1970, Breviora, 346:1–31, reviewed this genus and
named new species. See comment under *Platymantis*.

CONTRIBUTOR: Walter C. Brown (WCB).
REVIEWER: Richard G. Zweifel (RGZ).

Batrachylodes elegans Brown and Parker, 1970. Breviora, 346:14.
TYPE(S): Holotype: MCZ 54559.
TYPE LOCALITY: "Mutahi, between 2200 and 3200 feet elevation, on Bougainville Island, Solomon Islands".
DISTRIBUTION: Bougainville I., Solomon Is.

Batrachylodes gigas Brown and Parker, 1970. Breviora, 346:11.
TYPE(S): Holotype: MCZ 73764.
TYPE LOCALITY: "Lake Loloru area, at 4300 feet elevation, on Bougainville Island, Solomon Islands".
DISTRIBUTION: Bougainville I., Solomon Is.

Batrachylodes mediodiscus Brown and Parker, 1970. Breviora, 346:5.
TYPE(S): Holotype: MCZ 41589.
TYPE LOCALITY: "Pipekei area, 2000 feet elevation, on Bougainville Island, Solomon Islands".
DISTRIBUTION: Buka and Bougainville Is., Solomon Is.

Batrachylodes minutus Brown and Parker, 1970. Breviora, 346:3.
TYPE(S): Holotype: MCZ 41391.
TYPE LOCALITY: "Aresi area, at 2000 feet elevation, on Bougainville Island, Solomon Islands".
DISTRIBUTION: Bougainville I., Solomon Is.

Batrachylodes montanus Brown and Parker, 1970. Breviora, 346:16.
TYPE(S): Holotype: MCZ 55009.
TYPE LOCALITY: "Melilup, between 3500 and 4000 feet elevation, on Bougainville Island, Solomon Islands".
DISTRIBUTION: Bougainville I., Solomon Is.

Batrachylodes trossulus Brown and Myers, 1949. J. Washington Acad. Sci., 39:379.
TYPE(S): Holotype: USNM 119577.
TYPE LOCALITY: Torakina, Bougainville Island, Solomon Islands.
DISTRIBUTION: Bougainville I., Choiseul I. (?), Solomon Is.

Batrachylodes vertebralis Boulenger, 1887. Proc. Zool. Soc. London, 1887:337.
TYPE(S): Holotype: BM 1947.2.29.96 (formerly 87.1.24.32).
TYPE LOCALITY: Fauro Island, Solomon Islands.
DISTRIBUTION: Solomon Is.

Batrachylodes wolfi (Sternfeld, 1918). Abh. Senckenb. Naturforsch. Ges., 36:435.
ORIGINAL NAME: *Sphenophryne wolfi*.
TYPE(S): Holotype: SMF 4228 (formerly 1156.3a).
TYPE LOCALITY: Buka Island, Solomon Islands.
DISTRIBUTION: Buka and Bougainville Is., Solomon Is.

Ceratobatrachus Boulenger, 1884. Proc. Zool. Soc. London, 1884:212.
TYPE SPECIES: *Ceratobatrachus guentheri* Boulenger, 1884, by monotypy.
DISTRIBUTION: As for the single species.
COMMENT: See comment under *Platymantis*.
CONTRIBUTOR: Walter C. Brown (WCB).
REVIEWER: Richard G. Zweifel (RGZ).

Ceratobatrachus guentheri Boulenger, 1884. Proc. Zool. Soc. London, 1884:212.
TYPE(S): Syntypes: BM 1947.2.29.60–78 (formerly 84.3.24.18–37), MCZ 2207 (2 specimens).
TYPE LOCALITY: Treasury, Shortland, and Faro Is., Solomon Is.
DISTRIBUTION: Solomon Is.; Bougainville I.

Conraua Nieden, 1908. Mitt. Zool. Mus. Berlin, 3:497.
TYPE SPECIES: *Conraua robusta* Nieden, 1908, by monotypy.
DISTRIBUTION: Tropical subsaharan Africa.
COMMENT: Revised by Lamotte and Perret, 1968, Bull. Inst. Fondam. Afr. Noire, (A)30:1603–1644. Considered the sister-taxon of at least the *tigerina* and *occipitalis* sections of the subgenus *Euphlyctis* (of *Rana*) by Clarke, 1981, Monit. Zool. Ital., N.S., Suppl., 15:285–331.

Conraua alleni (Barbour and Loveridge, 1927). Proc. New England Zool. Club, 10:14.
ORIGINAL NAME: *Pseudoxenopus alleni*.
TYPE(S): Holotype: MCZ 11991.
TYPE LOCALITY: "Firestone Plantation No. 3, Du River", Liberia.
DISTRIBUTION: Sierra Leone to Togo.
COMMENT: See Schiøtz, 1964, Vidensk. Medd. Dansk Naturhist. Foren., 127:25, for synonymy.

Conraua beccarii (Boulenger, 1911). Ann. Mus. Civ. Stor. Nat. Genova, (3)5:160.
ORIGINAL NAME: *Rana beccarii*.
TYPE(S): MSNG 29434A designated lectotype by Capocaccia, 1957, Ann. Mus. Civ. Stor. Nat. Genova, 69:214.
TYPE LOCALITY: Filfil, Eritrea [Ethiopia].
DISTRIBUTION: Ethiopia.
COMMENT: Reviewed by Mertens, 1952, Aquar. Terr. Z., 2:47–50 (as *Rana beccarii*). Synonymy includes *Rana griaulei* Angel, 1934, according to Lamotte and Perret, 1968, Bull. Inst. Fondam. Afr. Noire, (A)30:1636.

Conraua crassipes (Buchholz and Peters, 1875). *In* Peters, Monatsber. Preuss. Akad. Wiss. Berlin, 1875:201.
ORIGINAL NAME: *Rana crassipes*.
TYPE(S): ZMB.
TYPE LOCALITY: Abo, Cameroon.
DISTRIBUTION: Nigeria to Zaire.

Conraua derooi Hulselmans, 1972. Rev. Zool. Bot. Afr., 84:153.
TYPE(S): RGMC.
TYPE LOCALITY: Togo, Misahöhe.
DISTRIBUTION: Known only from the type locality.

Conraua goliath (Boulenger, 1906). Ann. Mag. Nat. Hist., (7)17:317.
ORIGINAL NAME: *Rana goliath*.
TYPE(S): BM.
TYPE LOCALITY: Efulen, Cameroon.
DISTRIBUTION: Cameroon and Equatorial Guinea.
COMMENT: See Perret, 1966, Zool. Jahrb., Abt. Syst., 93:335–336.

Conraua robusta Nieden, 1908. Mitt. Zool. Mus. Berlin, 3:497.
TYPE(S): Holotype: ZMB.
TYPE LOCALITY: "Kamerun".
DISTRIBUTION: Hills and mountains of western Cameroon.
COMMENT: See Perret, 1966, Zool. Jahrb., Abt. Syst., 93:333–335.

Discodeles Boulenger, 1918. Ann. Mag. Nat. Hist., (9)1:238.
TYPE SPECIES: *Rana guppyi* Boulenger, 1884, by subsequent designation of Boulenger, 1918, Bull. Soc. Zool. France, 43:114.
DISTRIBUTION: Admiralty, Bismarck, and Solomon Is.
COMMENT: As diagnosed and discussed by Boulenger, 1920, Rec. Indian Mus., 20:1–226, *Discodeles* (then treated as a subgenus of *Rana*) included, in addition to those species listed here, several species from India: *Rana beddomii, Rana*

diplosticta, Rana leithii, Rana leptodactyla, Rana phrynoderma, and *Rana semipalmata* (see also *Rana tasanae*). Noble, 1931, Biol. Amph.:523, considered *Discodeles* a distinct genus for the Solomon Is. species, presumably because they exhibit direct development, but he did not discuss the status of the Indian species. The status of the Indian species remains unresolved. See comment under *Platymantis.*

CONTRIBUTOR: Walter C. Brown (WCB).
REVIEWER: Richard G. Zweifel (RGZ).

Discodeles bufoniformis (Boulenger, 1884). Proc. Zool. Soc. London, 1884:210.
ORIGINAL NAME: *Rana bufoniformis.*
TYPE(S): Holotype: BM 1947.2.1.85 (formerly 84.3.24.1).
TYPE LOCALITY: Treasury Island, Solomon Islands.
DISTRIBUTION: Solomon Is.

Discodeles guppyi (Boulenger, 1884). Proc. Zool. Soc. London, 1884:211.
ORIGINAL NAME: *Rana guppyi.*
TYPE(S): Holotype: BM 1947.2.1.87 (formerly 84.3.24.2).
TYPE LOCALITY: Shortland Island, Solomon Islands.
DISTRIBUTION: Solomon Is. and New Britain I.

Discodeles malukuna Brown and Webster, 1969. Breviora, 338:2.
TYPE(S): Holotype: MCZ 79462.
TYPE LOCALITY: "Malukuna area, elevation about 2500 feet, Guadalcanal Island", Solomon Is.
DISTRIBUTION: Guadalcanal I., Solomon Is.

Discodeles opisthodon (Boulenger, 1884). Proc. Zool. Soc. London, 1884:211.
ORIGINAL NAME: *Rana opisthodon.*
TYPE(S): Syntypes: BM 1947.2.28.27 (formerly 84.3.24.3), 1947.2.1.89–91 (formerly 84.3.24.4–6).
TYPE LOCALITY: Faro and Treasury Islands, Solomon Islands.
DISTRIBUTION: Solomon Is.

Discodeles ventricosus (Vogt, 1912). Sitzungsber. Ges. Naturforsch. Freunde Berlin, 1912:8.
ORIGINAL NAME: *Rana ventricosus.*
TYPE(S): Not stated (ZMB?).
TYPE LOCALITY: Lambussa (=Rambutyo) Island, Admiralty Islands.
DISTRIBUTION: Rambutyo I., Admiralty Is.
COMMENT: *Rana ventricosus* Vogt, 1912, was a primary homonym in the genus *Rana* and the new name *Rana vogti* was proposed by Heidiger, 1934, Zool. Jahrb., Abt. Syst., 65:485. *Ventricosus* is the proper epithet in the genus *Discodeles* (WCB).

Elachyglossa Andersson, 1916. K. Svenska Vetensk. Akad. Handl., (4)55:13.
TYPE SPECIES: *Elachyglossa gyldenstolpei* Andersson, 1916, by monotypy.
DISTRIBUTION: As for the single species.
COMMENT: Derived from the *Rana cyanophlyctis* group of the subgenus *Euphlyctis,* genus *Rana,* according to Dubois, 1981, Monit. Zool. Ital., N.S., Suppl., 15:225–284. See *Occidozyga.*

Elachyglossa gyldenstolpei Andersson, 1916. K. Svenska Vetensk. Akad. Handl., (4)55: 13–14.
TYPE(S): Holotype: NHRM or ZIUS.
TYPE LOCALITY: Bang Hue Pong village, southern slope Koon Tan mountains, northern Siam [Thailand].
DISTRIBUTION: Known only from the holotype.

COMMENT: Reviewed by Bourret, 1942, Batr. Indochine:404–406. See Taylor, 1962, Univ. Kansas Sci. Bull., 43:360–362, for discussion.

Hildebrandtia Nieden, 1907. Sitzungsber. Ges. Naturforsch. Freunde Berlin, 1907:229.
  TYPE SPECIES: *Pyxicephalus ornatus* Peters, 1878, by subsequent designation of Boulenger, 1919, Trans. R. Soc. S. Afr., 8:33.
  DISTRIBUTION: Tropical and subtropical Africa.
  COMMENT: Sister-taxon of *Lanzarana*; together forming the sister-taxon of *Ptychadena*, according to Clarke, 1981, Monit. Zool. Ital., N.S., Suppl., 15:285–331. Regarded as a subgenus of *Rana* by Dubois, 1981, Monit. Zool. Ital., N.S., Suppl., 15:224–284.

Hildebrandtia macrotympanum (Boulenger, 1912). Ann. Mag. Nat. Hist., (8)10:140.
  ORIGINAL NAME: *Pyxicephalus macrotympanum.*
  TYPE(S): Holotype: BM 1947.2.28.64.
  TYPE LOCALITY: West of the Juba River, Gallaland; corrected to "between El Dere (Kenya: 03° 53′ N—39° 57′ 30″ E, 3400 ft) and Garsa (Ethiopia: 04° 05′ 09″ N—39° 40′ 20″ E, 2630 ft)" by Balletto, Cherchi, and Lanza, 1980, Monit. Zool. Ital., N.S., Suppl., 13:141.
  DISTRIBUTION: Ethiopia and Somalia into Kenya.
  COMMENT: Synonymy includes *Tomopterna scortecci* Balletto, Cherchi, and Lanza, 1978, according to Balletto, Cherchi, and Lanza, 1980, Monit. Zool. Ital., N.S., Suppl., 13:141–149, who discussed this species.

Hildebrandtia ornata (Peters, 1878). Monatsber. Preuss. Akad. Wiss. Berlin, 1878:207.
  ORIGINAL NAME: *Pyxicephalus ornatus.*
  TYPE(S): ZMB.
  TYPE LOCALITY: Taita [=Teita], Kenya.
  DISTRIBUTION: Tropical and subtropical Africa south to northern Namibia and southern Mozambique.
  COMMENT: See Schmidt and Inger, 1959, Explor. Parc Natl. Upemba, 56:38–41, for review of central African populations.

Hildebrandtia ornatissima (Bocage, 1879). J. Sci. Math. Phys. Nat., Lisboa, 7:89.
  ORIGINAL NAME: *Rana ornatissima.*
  TYPE(S): Holotype: MBL T.78-160 (destroyed in 1978 fire).
  TYPE LOCALITY: Bihé, Angola.
  DISTRIBUTION: Known only from the type locality.
  COMMENT: Removed from the synonymy of *Hildebrandtia ornata*, by Perret, 1976, Arq. Mus. Bocage, (2)6:19.

Lanzarana Clarke, 1983. Bull. Brit. Mus. (Nat. Hist.), Zool., 43:179.
  TYPE SPECIES: *Hildebrandtia largeni* Lanza, 1978, by original designation.
  DISTRIBUTION: As for the single species.
  COMMENT: Sister-taxon of *Hildebrandtia* according to Clarke, 1981, Monit. Zool. Ital., N.S., Suppl., 15:285–331. By implication, regarded as a subgenus of *Rana* by Dubois, 1981, Monit. Zool. Ital., N.S., Suppl., 15:224–284.

Lanzarana largeni (Lanza, 1978). Monit. Zool. Ital., N.S., Suppl., 10:612.
  ORIGINAL NAME: *Hildebrandtia largeni.*
  TYPE(S): Holotype: MZUF 2732.
  TYPE LOCALITY: "about 10 km N Garòe (about 08° 25′ N—48° 33′ E, ca. 500 m; Nogal Valley; northern Somalia".
  DISTRIBUTION: Somalia.

Micrixalus Boulenger, 1888. Proc. Zool. Soc. London, 1888:205.
  TYPE SPECIES: *Ixalus fuscus* Boulenger, 1882, by subsequent designation of Myers, 1942, Proc. Biol. Soc. Washington, 55:74.
  DISTRIBUTION: India and Sri Lanka; Philippines; Borneo.

COMMENT: According to Noble, 1931, Biol. Amph.:521, most closely related to the subgenus *Hylarana* of *Rana*. See comment under Raninae. Pillai, 1978, Proc. Indian Acad. Sci., (B)87:173–177, supplied a key to the species of India and Sri Lanka. See comment under *Platymantis liui*.
REVIEWERS: Angel Alcala (AA) (Philippines); Walter C. Brown (WCB) (Philippines).

Micrixalus baluensis (Boulenger, 1896). Ann. Mag. Nat. Hist., (6)17:449.
ORIGINAL NAME: *Cornufer baluensis*.
TYPE(S): Holotype: BM 1947.2.29.86 (formerly 96.4.29.14).
TYPE LOCALITY: Mount Kina Balu, Sabah [Malaysia (Borneo)].
DISTRIBUTION: Borneo.
COMMENT: Reviewed by Inger, 1966, Fieldiana: Zool., 52:255–256, who placed *Rana sariba* Shelford in synonymy.

Micrixalus borealis Annandale, 1912. Rec. Indian Mus., 8:10.
TYPE(S): Holotype: ZSI 16932.
TYPE LOCALITY: "Rotung (alt. 1,300 ft.) and about 3 miles S. of Yembung", Arunachal Pradesh, India (in an area claimed by China).
DISTRIBUTION: Southern Tibet (China) and adjacent India.
COMMENT: Closely allied to *Micrixalus tenasserimensis*, according to the original description.

Micrixalus fuscus (Boulenger, 1882). Cat. Batr. Sal. Brit. Mus.:96.
ORIGINAL NAME: *Ixalus fuscus*.
TYPE(S): Syntypes: BM 72.4.12.256, 74.4.29.258–265, 74.4.29.927–930, 74.4.29.1401–1404, 74.4.29.1459–1464, 74.4.29.1506–1508.
TYPE LOCALITY: "Travancore"; "Torocata"; "Anamallays"; "Sevagherry"; "Malabar"; "N. Canara" (all localities in India).
DISTRIBUTION: Karnata (North Canara), Kerala (Travancore Hills), and Tamil Nadu (Tirunelveli Hills), India.

Micrixalus herrei Myers, 1942. Proc. Biol. Soc. Washington, 55:71.
TYPE(S): Holotype: CAS-SU 7265.
TYPE LOCALITY: "Kallar, 30 miles northeast of Trivandrum, Travancore, South India".
DISTRIBUTION: Known only from the type locality.

Micrixalus mariae Inger, 1954. Fieldiana: Zool., 33:344.
TYPE(S): Holotype: FMNH 51360.
TYPE LOCALITY: "south slope of Mount Balabag, Mantalingajan Range, Palawan", Philippines.
DISTRIBUTION: Known only from the type locality.

Micrixalus nudis Pillai, 1978. Proc. Indian Acad. Sci., (B)87:173.
TYPE(S): Holotype: ZSIM.
TYPE LOCALITY: Kurichiat Reserve Forest, Wynad [Kerala, India].
DISTRIBUTION: Kerala, India.

Micrixalus opisthorhodus (Günther, 1868). Proc. Zool. Soc. London, 1868:484.
ORIGINAL NAME: *Ixalus opisthorhodus*.
TYPE(S): Holotype: BM.
TYPE LOCALITY: "Nilgherries [=Nilgiri Hills]", South India.
DISTRIBUTION: Nilgiris and Malabar, India.

Micrixalus sarasinorum (Müller, 1887). Verh. Naturforsch. Ges. Basel, 8:256.
ORIGINAL NAME: *Ixalus sarasinorum*.
TYPE(S): NHMB 1218 designated lectotype by Forcart, 1946, Verh. Naturforsch. Ges. Basel, 57:129.
TYPE LOCALITY: "Peradenia", Sri Lanka.
DISTRIBUTION: Sri Lanka.

COMMENT: Kirtisinghe, 1957, Amph. Ceylon, regarded the report of *Micrixalus* in Ceylon as possibly in error. Not a *Micrixalus*, but a member of the Rhacophoridae, from examination of the type (SD).

Micrixalus saxicola (Jerdon, 1853). J. Asiat. Soc. Bengal, 22:533.
ORIGINAL NAME: *Polypedates saxicola*.
TYPE(S): Not traced; ZSI.
TYPE LOCALITY: "Malabar", South India.
DISTRIBUTION: Malabar and Wynaad, South India.

Micrixalus silvaticus (Boulenger, 1882). Cat. Batr. Sal. Brit. Mus.:469.
ORIGINAL NAME: *Ixalus silvaticus*.
TYPE(S): Syntypes: BM 82.2.10.52–59 and NHMW 22913.
TYPE LOCALITY: "Malabar", South India.
DISTRIBUTION: Malabar, South India.

Micrixalus tenasserimensis (Sclater, 1892). Proc. Zool. Soc. London, 1892:24.
ORIGINAL NAME: *Rana tenasserimensis*.
TYPE(S): ZSI.
TYPE LOCALITY: Tenasserim [Burma].
DISTRIBUTION: Burma to peninsular Thailand and adjacent Malaya.
COMMENT: Reviewed by Bourret, 1942, Batr. Indochine:378–379, as *Cornufer tenasserimensis*. See also account by Berry, 1975, Amph. Fauna Peninsular Malaysia:87–88. See comment under *Micrixalus borealis*. Variously regarded by some authors as a *Micrixalus* or *Platymantis*.

Micrixalus thampii Pillai, 1981. Bull. Zool. Surv. India, 3:153.
TYPE(S): Holotype: ZSIM.
TYPE LOCALITY: Silent Valley, South India.
DISTRIBUTION: Kerala, South India.

Nannobatrachus Boulenger, 1882. Cat. Batr. Sal. Brit. Mus.:470.
TYPE SPECIES: *Nannobatrachus beddomii* Boulenger, 1882, by monotypy.
DISTRIBUTION: Southern India.

Nannobatrachus anamallaiensis Myers, 1942. Proc. Biol. Soc. Washington, 55:49.
TYPE(S): Holotype: CAS.
TYPE LOCALITY: Puthutotam Estate, Valparai, Anamallai Hills [southern India].
DISTRIBUTION: Known only from the type locality.

Nannobatrachus beddomii Boulenger, 1882. Cat. Batr. Sal. Brit. Mus.:470.
TYPE(S): Syntypes: BM.
TYPE LOCALITY: "Malabar" and "Tinnevelly [=Tirunelveli]", India.
DISTRIBUTION: Tirunelveli Hills, southern India.

Nannobatrachus kempholeyensis Rao, 1937. Proc. Indian Acad. Sci., (B)6:401.
TYPE(S): CCB; now lost (SD).
TYPE LOCALITY: "Hills of Kempholey Ghats, Hassan, Mysore, S. India".
DISTRIBUTION: Known only from the type locality.

Nannophrys Günther, 1869 "1868". Proc. Zool. Soc. London, 1868:482.
TYPE SPECIES: *Nannophrys ceylonensis* Günther, 1869, by monotypy.
DISTRIBUTION: Sri Lanka.
COMMENT: Revised by Clarke, 1983, Zool. J. Linn. Soc., 79:377–398.

Nannophrys ceylonensis Günther, 1869 "1868". Proc. Zool. Soc. London, 1868:482.
TYPE(S): Syntypes: BM 68.3.17.36–39.
TYPE LOCALITY: "Ceylon [=Sri Lanka], probably from the southern parts".
DISTRIBUTION: Sabaragamuwa, Western, Central, and Southern provinces, Sri Lanka.

COMMENT: See Kirtisinghe, 1957, Amph. Ceylon:50–51.

Nannophrys guentheri Boulenger, 1882. Cat. Batr. Sal. Brit. Mus.:115.
  TYPE(S): Syntypes: BM 1947.2.5.20–21.
  TYPE LOCALITY: "Ceylon" (=Sri Lanka).
  DISTRIBUTION: Known only from the types.
  COMMENT: The Sri Lankan record of Kirtisinghe, 1957, Amph. Ceylon:50–51, is
    based on juvenile *Nannophrys ceylonensis*, according to Clarke, 1983, Zool. J.
    Linn. Soc., 79:377–398.

Nannophrys marmorata Kirtisinghe, 1946. Ceylon J. Sci., (B)23:105.
  TYPE(S): Not stated; presumed lost.
  TYPE LOCALITY: Mousakanda, Gammaduwa, Central Province, Sri Lanka.
  DISTRIBUTION: Gammaduwa and Laggala, Central Province, Sri Lanka.
  COMMENT: Kirtisinghe, 1957, Amph. Ceylon:52, considered this form to be a
    subspecies of *Nannophrys ceylonensis*; Clarke, 1983, Zool. J. Linn. Soc., 79:387,
    treated it as a full species.

Nanorana Günther, 1896. Ann. Mus. Zool. Acad. Sci. Imp. St. Petersbourg, 1:207.
  TYPE SPECIES: *Nanorana pleskei* Günther, 1896, by monotypy.
  DISTRIBUTION: As for the single species.
  COMMENT: Regarded by Dubois, 1981, Monit. Zool. Ital., N.S., Suppl., 15:234, as a
    subgenus of *Rana*, and following Boulenger, 1920, Rec. Indian Mus., 20:107, to
    be close to the subgenus *Paa* of *Rana*.

Nanorana pleskei Günther, 1896. Ann. Mus. Zool. Acad. Sci. Imp. St. Petersbourg, 1:
  207.
  TYPE(S): Syntypes: including ZIL 1958 (Sungpan) (LJB).
  TYPE LOCALITY: Sungpan and Inchuan, the Kham Mountains, Szechwan
    [=Sichuan], [China].
  DISTRIBUTION: Sichuan, Yunnan, Gansu, and Qinghai, China.
  COMMENT: Reviewed by Liu, 1950, Fieldiana: Zool. Mem., 2:323–328, and Liu and
    Hu, 1961, Tailless Amph. China:220–221. According to Dubois and Khan,
    1979, J. Herpetol., 13:409, the Kashmir specimen reported by Mertens, 1969,
    Stuttgart. Beitr. Naturkd., 197:16, is referable to *Rana vicina*.

Nyctibatrachus Boulenger, 1882. Cat. Batr. Sal. Brit. Mus.:113.
  TYPE SPECIES: *Nyctibatrachus major* Boulenger, 1882, by subsequent designation of
    Myers, 1942, Proc. Biol. Soc. Washington, 55:54.
  DISTRIBUTION: India.

Nyctibatrachus humayuni Bhaduri and Kripalani, 1955. J. Bombay Nat. Hist. Soc., 52:
  852.
  TYPE(S): Holotype: ZSI 20628.
  TYPE LOCALITY: Mahabaleswar, Satar District (Bombay), near a way side hill stream,
    India.
  DISTRIBUTION: Western Ghats (North Canara, Mahabaleswar, and Khandala) to
    Bombay, India.

Nyctibatrachus major Boulenger, 1882. Cat. Batr. Sal. Brit. Mus.:114.
  TYPE(S): Syntypes: BM.
  TYPE LOCALITY: "Malabar" and "Wynaad", South India.
  DISTRIBUTION: Malabar and Wynaad, Kerala, India.

Nyctibatrachus pygmaeus (Günther, 1875). Proc. Zool. Soc. London, 1875:568.
  ORIGINAL NAME: *Rana pygmaea*.
  TYPE(S): BM.
  TYPE LOCALITY: Anamallai Hills, South India.
  DISTRIBUTION: Anamallai Hills, South India.

Nyctibatrachus sanctipalustris Rao, 1920. J. Bombay Nat. Hist. Soc., 27:125.
ORIGINAL NAME: *Nyctibatrachus sancti-palustris*.
TYPE(S): Holotype: ZSI.
TYPE LOCALITY: "The sacred swamps of the Cauvery [River], Brahmagiri Hills, 4000 feet, Coorg", India.
DISTRIBUTION: Mysore and Karnataka, India.

Nyctibatrachus sylvaticus Rao, 1937. Proc. Indian Acad. Sci., (B)6:399.
TYPE(S): CCB; now lost (SD).
TYPE LOCALITY: Forests of Kempholey, Saklespur, Hassan [Mysore], India.
DISTRIBUTION: Known only from the type locality.

Occidozyga Kuhl and van Hasselt, 1822. Algemeene Konst-en Letter-Bode, 7:103.
TYPE SPECIES: *Rana lima* Gravenhorst, 1829, by subsequent designation of Stejneger, 1925, Proc. U.S. Natl. Mus., 66:33.
DISTRIBUTION: Southern China to India, Philippines, Greater and Lesser Sunda Is. as far as Flores.
COMMENT: The spelling *Ooeidozyga* is an unjustified emendation according to Dubois, 1981, Monit. Zool. Ital., N.S., Suppl., 15:245, and Dubois, 1982, Bull. Mus. Natl. Hist. Nat., Paris, (4)4(A):269–272, who supplied a generic synonymy. Boulenger, 1920, Rec. Indian Mus., 20:9, regarded this group as possibly derived from the *Rana cyanophlyctis* group of the subgenus *Euphlyctis* of *Rana*. See comment under *Rana*.
REVIEWERS: Angel Alcala (AA) (Philippines); Walter C. Brown (WCB) (Philippines).

Occidozyga baluensis (Boulenger, 1896). Ann. Mag. Nat. Hist., (6)17:401.
ORIGINAL NAME: *Oreobatrachus baluensis*.
TYPE(S): Not traced.
TYPE LOCALITY: Kina Balu, Sabah [Malaysia (Borneo)].
DISTRIBUTION: Borneo.
COMMENT: Reviewed by Inger, 1966, Fieldiana: Zool., 52:238–239.

Occidozyga celebensis Smith, 1927. Proc. Zool. Soc. London, 1927:204.
ORIGINAL NAME: *Ooeidozyga celebensis*.
TYPE(S): BM.
TYPE LOCALITY: Djikoro, Mt. Bonthain [Celebes, Indonesia].
DISTRIBUTION: Celebes.

Occidozyga diminutiva (Taylor, 1922). Philippine J. Sci., 21:267.
ORIGINAL NAME: *Micrixalus diminutiva*.
TYPE(S): Holotype: CAS 61842 (formerly EHT 1066).
TYPE LOCALITY: "near Pasananka, Zamboanga, Mindanao", Philippines.
DISTRIBUTION: Mindanao and Basilan (Philippines); Sulu Archipelago.
COMMENT: Reviewed by Inger, 1954, Fieldiana: Zool., 33:256–259.

Occidozyga floresiana Mertens, 1927. Senckenb. Biol., 9:234.
ORIGINAL NAME: *Oxydozyga floresiana*.
TYPE(S): Holotype: SMF 22089.
TYPE LOCALITY: "Rana Mese, 1200 m. H., West-Flores", Indonesia.
DISTRIBUTION: Known only from the type locality.

Occidozyga laevis (Günther, 1859 "1858"). Cat. Batr. Sal. Coll. Brit. Mus.:7.
ORIGINAL NAME: *Oxyglossus laevis*.
TYPE(S): Syntypes: BM (2 specimens).
TYPE LOCALITY: Philippine Islands.
DISTRIBUTION: Borneo, Java, Sumatra, Celebes, Bali, Sumbawa, Flores, Philippines, southern Thailand, and Malaya; China (SH).
COMMENT: Inger, 1954, Fieldiana: Zool., 33:249–256; Inger, 1966, Fieldiana: Zool.,

52:240–243; and Bourret, 1942, Batr. Indochine:401–404, reviewed this species. See also Berry, 1975, Amph. Fauna Peninsular Malaysia:59–60.

Occidozyga lima (Gravenhorst, 1829). Delic. Mus. Zool. Vratislav., 1:41.
ORIGINAL NAME: *Rana lima.*
TYPE(S): Breslau Mus. (probably lost).
TYPE LOCALITY: Java [Indonesia].
DISTRIBUTION: Lower Bengal (India) to southern China (including Hainan I.), Vietnam, Malaya, and Java.
COMMENT: See Taylor, 1962, Univ. Kansas Sci. Bull., 43:346–350; Bourret, 1942, Batr. Indochine:398–401; and Pope, 1931, Bull. Am. Mus. Nat. Hist., 61:481–484, for synonymy and review. See also Berry, 1975, Amph. Fauna Peninsular Malaysia:60–61.

Occidozyga magnapustulosa (Taylor and Elbel, 1958). Univ. Kansas Sci. Bull., 38:1066.
ORIGINAL NAME: *Micrixalus magnapustulosus.*
TYPE(S): Holotype: FMNH 172780 (formerly EHT-HMS 31838).
TYPE LOCALITY: Ban Na Phua, Kan Luang, Nakhon Phanom province, altitude 200 m [Thailand].
DISTRIBUTION: Nakhon Phanom, Ubon, Loei, and Chiang Mai provinces, Thailand.
COMMENT: See Matsui, 1979, Contrib. Biol. Lab. Kyoto Univ., 25:300–302 (as *Ooeidozyga magnapustulosa*).

Occidozyga martensii (Peters, 1867). Monatsber. Preuss. Akad. Wiss. Berlin, 1867:29.
ORIGINAL NAME: *Phrynoglossus martensii.*
TYPE(S): Syntypes: ZMB 4410–11.
TYPE LOCALITY: Bangkok, Siam [Thailand].
DISTRIBUTION: Peninsular Thailand, Vietnam, and southern China (Yunnan, Guangxi, and Hainan I.).
COMMENT: See Taylor, 1962, Univ. Kansas Sci. Bull., 43:358–360, for discussion. Reviewed (as *Ooeidozyga laevis martensi*) by Pope, 1931, Bull. Am. Mus. Nat. Hist., 61:480–481.

Occidozyga semipalmata Smith, 1927. Proc. Zool. Soc. London, 1927:203.
ORIGINAL NAME: *Ooeidozyga semipalmata.*
TYPE(S): BM.
TYPE LOCALITY: Lowah, near Mt. Bonthai [Celebes, Indonesia].
DISTRIBUTION: Celebes.

Palmatorappia Ahl, 1927. Sitzungsber. Ges. Naturforsch. Freunde Berlin, 1926:113.
TYPE SPECIES: *Hylella solomonis* Sternfield, 1920, by original designation.
DISTRIBUTION: As for the single species.
COMMENT: See comment under *Platymantis.*
CONTRIBUTOR: Walter C. Brown (WCB).
REVIEWER: Richard G. Zweifel (RGZ).

Palmatorappia solomonis (Sternfeld, 1920). Abh. Senckenb. Naturforsch. Ges., 36:436.
ORIGINAL NAME: *Hylella solomonis.*
TYPE(S): SMF 6601 designated lectotype by Mertens, 1967, Senckenb. Biol., 48:44.
TYPE LOCALITY: Buka Island, Solomon Islands.
DISTRIBUTION: Solomon Is.

Platymantis Günther, 1859 "1858". Cat. Batr. Sal. Coll. Brit. Mus.:93.
TYPE SPECIES: *Platymantis pliciferus* Günther, 1859 "1858" (=*Hylodes corrugatus* Duméril, 1853), by subsequent designation of Zweifel, 1967, Copeia, 1967:120.
DISTRIBUTION: New Guinea; Philippines; Fiji; Bismarck, Admiralty, Palau, and Solomon Is.; China.
COMMENT: Dubois, 1981, Monit. Zool. Ital., N.S., Suppl., 15:225–285, believed

Platymantis, Discodeles, 'and related genera' (by implication *Ceratobatrachus, Palmatorappia,* and *Batrachylodes*) were derived from the subgenus *Euphlyctis* of *Rana.* Brown, 1965, Breviora, 218:1–16, provided a key to the species of the Solomon Is. Brown and Alcala, 1974, Occas. Pap. California Acad. Sci., 113:5–8, provided a key to the Philippine species. Brown and Tyler, 1968, Proc. Biol. Soc. Washington, 81:69–86, reviewed the species from New Britain. Zweifel, 1967, Am. Mus. Novit., 2374:1–19, reviewed the New Guinea species. Gorham, 1965, Zool. Beitr., 65:381–435, provided synonymies for species to 1965. Zweifel, 1967, Copeia, 1967:117–121, discussed the name *Platymantis* in place of the name *Cornufer.*
CONTRIBUTOR: Walter C. Brown (WCB).
REVIEWERS: Angel Alcala (AA) (Philippines); Richard G. Zweifel (RGZ).

Platymantis acrochordus (Brown, 1965). Breviora, 218:10.
ORIGINAL NAME: *Cornufer acrochordus.*
TYPE(S): Holotype: MCZ 44264.
TYPE LOCALITY: "Aresi Mountain area, south of Kunua between 2000–4000 feet, Bougainville Island, Solomon Islands".
DISTRIBUTION: Bougainville I., Solomon Is.

Platymantis aculeodactylus Brown, 1952. Bull. Mus. Comp. Zool., 107:46.
TYPE(S): Holotype: USNM 119769.
TYPE LOCALITY: Torokina, Bougainville Island, Solomon Islands.
DISTRIBUTION: Bougainville and Choiseul (?) Is., Solomon Is.

Platymantis akarithymus Brown and Tyler, 1968. Proc. Biol. Soc. Washington, 81:76.
TYPE(S): Holotype: SAMA 7073.
TYPE LOCALITY: "Pomugu area about seven miles northwest of Kandrian on the south coast of New Britain Island".
DISTRIBUTION: New Britain I.

Platymantis batantae Zweifel, 1969. Am. Mus. Novit., 2374:2.
TYPE(S): Holotype: AMNH 74192.
TYPE LOCALITY: "Mt. Besar above Wailebet, elevation 1500 feet, Batanta Island, West Irian [Irian Jaya (New Guinea)], Indonesia".
DISTRIBUTION: Batanta I., Irian Jaya (New Guinea), Indonesia.

Platymantis boulengeri (Boettger, 1892). Kat. Batr. Samml. Mus. Senckenb. Naturforsch. Ges.:18.
ORIGINAL NAME: *Cornufer boulengeri.*
TYPE(S): Holotype: SMF 7054 (formerly 1107.1a).
TYPE LOCALITY: New Britain.
DISTRIBUTION: New Britain I.

Platymantis cheesmanae Parker, 1940. Ann. Mag. Nat. Hist., (11)5:257.
TYPE(S): Holotype: BM 1938.6.5.28.
TYPE LOCALITY: "Cyclops Range, Dutch New Guinea [=Irian Jaya, Indonesia], at 3000–4000 feet".
DISTRIBUTION: Cyclops Mountains, Irian Jaya (New Guinea), Indonesia.

Platymantis cornutus (Taylor, 1922). Philippine J. Sci., 21:175.
ORIGINAL NAME: *Cornufer cornutus.*
TYPE(S): Holotype: CAS 61476.
TYPE LOCALITY: "Balbalan, Kalinga, Mountain Province, Luzon", Philippines.
DISTRIBUTION: Known only from the type locality.

Platymantis corrugatus (A. Duméril, 1853). Ann. Sci. Nat., Paris, (3)19:176.
ORIGINAL NAME: *Hylodes corrugatus.*
TYPE(S): Holotype: MNHNP 4884.
TYPE LOCALITY: Java [Indonesia]; in error.
DISTRIBUTION: Philippine Is.

COMMENT: Synonymy and discussion in Inger, 1954, Fieldiana: Zool., 33:350–354.

Platymantis dorsalis (A. Duméril, 1853). Ann. Sci. Nat., Paris, (3)19:174.
ORIGINAL NAME: *Cornufer dorsalis.*
TYPE(S): Holotype: MNHNP 4880.
TYPE LOCALITY: Java [Indonesia]; in error.
DISTRIBUTION: Philippine Is.
COMMENT: See Brown and Inger, 1964, Copeia, 1964:450, for synonymy and discussion.

Platymantis gilliardi Zweifel, 1960. Am. Mus. Novit., 2023:10.
TYPE(S): Holotype: AMNH 64253.
TYPE LOCALITY: "Iambon, Gilliard Camp no. 6, elevation 1500 feet, Whiteman Mountains, New Britain".
DISTRIBUTION: New Britain and Admiralty Is.

Platymantis guentheri (Boulenger, 1882). Cat. Batr. Sal. Brit. Mus.:108.
ORIGINAL NAME: *Cornufer guentheri.*
TYPE(S): Syntypes: BM 1947.2.31–34 (formerly 77.10.9.52).
TYPE LOCALITY: "Dinagat Island", Philippines.
DISTRIBUTION: Philippine Is.
COMMENT: Closely related to *Platymantis guppyi* (as *Cornufer guppyi*) according to Inger, 1954, Fieldiana: Zool., 33:362–365, who provided a synonymy and review.

Platymantis guppyi (Boulenger, 1884). Proc. Zool. Soc. London, 1884:211.
ORIGINAL NAME: *Cornufer guppyi.*
TYPE(S): Syntypes: BM 1947.2.29.82–83 (formerly 84.3.24.7–8).
TYPE LOCALITY: Treasury Island, Solomon Islands.
DISTRIBUTION: Solomon Is.
COMMENT: See comment under *Platymantis guentheri.*

Platymantis hazelae (Taylor, 1920). Philippine J. Sci., 16:298.
ORIGINAL NAME: *Philautus hazelae.*
TYPE(S): Holotype: CM 3427.
TYPE LOCALITY: Canlaon Volcano, Negros [Philippines].
DISTRIBUTION: Philippine Is.
COMMENT: See Inger, 1954, Fieldiana: Zool., 33:367–370, for synonymy and review.

Platymantis ingeri (Brown and Alcala, 1963). Copeia, 1963:672.
ORIGINAL NAME: *Cornufer ingeri.*
TYPE(S): Holotype: CAS-SU 21214.
TYPE LOCALITY: "700 meters, Cantaub area, 14 km southeast of Sierra Bullones, Bohol Island, Philippines".
DISTRIBUTION: Bohol I. and northeastern Mindanao I., Philippine Is.

Platymantis insulatus Brown and Alcala, 1970. Occas. Pap. California Acad. Sci., 84:2.
TYPE(S): Holotype: CAS 117441.
TYPE LOCALITY: "South Gigante Island", Philippine Is.
DISTRIBUTION: South Gigante I., Philippine Is.

Platymantis lawtoni Brown and Alcala, 1974. Occas. Pap. California Acad. Sci., 113:2.
TYPE(S): Holotype: CAS 135732.
TYPE LOCALITY: "in forest at about 800 feet elevation, Dubduban, Tablas Island", Philippines.
DISTRIBUTION: Tablas I., Philippines.

Platymantis levigatus Brown and Alcala, 1974. Occas. Pap. California Acad. Sci., 113:4.
TYPE(S): Holotype: CAS 136097.
TYPE LOCALITY: "along stream in secondary forest at about 650 feet elevation,
Dubduban, San Agustin, Tablas Island", Philippines.
DISTRIBUTION: Tablas I., Philippines.

Platymantis liui Yang, 1983. Acta Herpetol. Sinica, 2:53.
ORIGINAL NAME: *Cornufer liui.*
TYPE(S): Holotype: KIZ 195.
TYPE LOCALITY: Menglun, Mengla, Yunnan, China.
DISTRIBUTION: Yunnan, China.
COMMENT: Closely related to *Cornufer tenasserimensis* (=*Micrixalus tenasserimensis* of
this list), according to the original description. See Liu and Hu, 1959, Acta
Zool. Sinica, 11(4):521–522. Probably a member of *Micrixalus* (RGZ).

Platymantis macrops (Brown, 1965). Breviora, 218:7.
ORIGINAL NAME: *Cornufer macrops.*
TYPE(S): Holotype: MCZ 41864.
TYPE LOCALITY: Aresi area south of Kunua (elev. 3000–4000 ft.), Bougainville
Island, Solomon Islands.
DISTRIBUTION: Bougainville I., Solomon Is.

Platymantis macrosceles Zweifel, 1975. Am. Mus. Novit., 2584:2.
TYPE(S): Holotype: BPBM 1005.
TYPE LOCALITY: "Ti, Nakanai Mountains, New Britain".
DISTRIBUTION: Known only from the holotype.

Platymantis magnus Brown and Menzies, 1979. Proc. Biol. Soc. Washington, 91:966.
TYPE(S): Holotype: CAS 143640.
TYPE LOCALITY: "Madina High School, 88 km southeast of Kavieng, New Ireland",
Bismarck Archipelago.
DISTRIBUTION: Northern New Ireland, Bismarck Archipelago.

Platymantis mimicus Brown and Tyler, 1968. Proc. Biol. Soc. Washington, 81:74.
TYPE(S): Holotype: SAMA 6868.
TYPE LOCALITY: "Numundo Plantation, Willaumez Peninsula on the north coast of
New Britain Island".
DISTRIBUTION: New Britain I.

Platymantis myersi Brown, 1949. Am. Mus. Novit., 1387:1.
TYPE(S): Holotype: AMNH 35348.
TYPE LOCALITY: "Bougainville Island", Solomon Is.
DISTRIBUTION: Bougainville I., Solomon Is.

Platymantis neckeri (Brown and Myers, 1949). Am. Mus. Novit., 1418:2.
ORIGINAL NAME: *Cornufer neckeri.*
TYPE(S): Holotype: AMNH 34329.
TYPE LOCALITY: "Bougainville Island", Solomon Is.
DISTRIBUTION: Bougainville I., Solomon Is.

Platymantis nexipus Zweifel, 1975. Am. Mus. Novit., 2584:4.
TYPE(S): Holotype: BPBM 1009.
TYPE LOCALITY: St. Paul's, Baining Mountains, New Britain.
DISTRIBUTION: Known only from the holotype.

Platymantis papuensis Meyer, 1875 "1874". Monatsber. Preuss. Akad. Wiss. Berlin,
1874:139.
ORIGINAL NAME: *Platymantis corrugatus papuensis.*
TYPE(S): Not stated.
TYPE LOCALITY: "Mysore" (=Biak) I., Irian Jaya (New Guinea), Indonesia.
DISTRIBUTION: New Guinea and surrounding islands; Bismarck Archipelago.

COMMENT: Menzies, 1982, Brit. J. Herpetol., 6:236–240, discussed subspecific variation.

Platymantis parkeri (Brown, 1965). Breviora, 218:3.
ORIGINAL NAME: *Cornufer parkeri parkeri.*
TYPE(S): Holotype: MCZ 36923.
TYPE LOCALITY: "Kunua area, Bougainville Island, Solomon Islands".
DISTRIBUTION: Bougainville and Buka Is.

Platymantis pelewensis Peters, 1867. Monatsber. Preuss. Akad. Wiss. Berlin, 1867:33.
ORIGINAL NAME: *Platymantis plicifera pelewensis.*
TYPE(S): Not stated.
TYPE LOCALITY: Palau Islands.
DISTRIBUTION: Palau Is., Micronesia.

Platymantis polillensis (Taylor, 1922). Philippine J. Sci., 21:171.
ORIGINAL NAME: *Philautus polillensis.*
TYPE(S): Holotype: CAS 62250 (formerly EHT 351).
TYPE LOCALITY: "near southern end of Polillo Island", Philippines.
DISTRIBUTION: Known only from the type locality.
COMMENT: See Inger, 1954, Fieldiana: Zool., 33:365–367, for synonymy, review, and discussion.

Platymantis punctata Peters and Doria, 1878. Ann. Mus. Civ. Stor. Nat. Genova, 13:420.
TYPE(S): Holotype: MSNG 29738.
TYPE LOCALITY: "Hatam", Arfak Mountains, Vogelkop Peninsula, Irian Jaya (New Guinea), Indonesia.
DISTRIBUTION: Batanta and Waigeu Is. and Arfak Mountains, New Guinea (Irian Jaya, Indonesia).

Platymantis rhipiphalcus Brown and Tyler, 1968. Proc. Biol. Soc. Washington, 81:77.
TYPE(S): Holotype: SAMA 7071.
TYPE LOCALITY: "Pomugu area about seven miles northwest of Kandrian on the south coast of New Britain Island".
DISTRIBUTION: New Britain I.

Platymantis schmidti Brown and Tyler, 1968. Proc. Biol. Soc. Washington, 81:85.
ORIGINAL NAME: *Platymantis papuensis schmidti.*
TYPE(S): Holotype: SAMA 7618.
TYPE LOCALITY: Talasea, Willaumez Peninsula, New Britain Island, Bismarcks.
DISTRIBUTION: New Britain, New Ireland, and Manus Is., Bismarck Archipelago.
COMMENT: Menzies, 1982, Brit. J. Herpetol., 6:241–245, elevated this taxon from a subspecies of *Platymantis papuensis* to species status.

Platymantis solomonis (Boulenger, 1884). Proc. Zool. Soc. London, 1884:212.
ORIGINAL NAME: *Cornufer solomonis.*
TYPE(S): Syntypes: BM 84.3.24.9–17.
TYPE LOCALITY: Shortland, Treasury, and Faro Islands, Solomon Islands.
DISTRIBUTION: Solomon Is.

Platymantis spelaeus Brown and Alcala, 1982. Proc. Biol. Soc. Washington, 95:386.
TYPE(S): Holotype: CAS 153469.
TYPE LOCALITY: Cave, Tiyabanan, Basay, southern Negros Island, Philippine Islands.
DISTRIBUTION: Region of the type locality.

Platymantis subterrestris (Taylor, 1922). Philippine J. Sci., 21:274.
ORIGINAL NAME: *Cornufer subterrestris*.
TYPE(S): Holotype: CAS 61518.
TYPE LOCALITY: "near kilometer 101, on the Mountain Trail, Mountain Province, Luzon", Philippines.
DISTRIBUTION: Luzon, Philippines.
COMMENT: See Inger, 1954, Fieldiana: Zool., 33:360–362, for synonymy and review.

Platymantis vitianus (Duméril, 1853). Ann. Sci. Nat., Paris, (3)19:177.
ORIGINAL NAME: *Cornufer vitianus*.
TYPE(S): Syntypes: MNHNP 4887A–C.
TYPE LOCALITY: Viti Island, Fiji Islands.
DISTRIBUTION: Fiji Is.
COMMENT: Gorham, 1965, Zool. Beitr., 11:381–435, provided a synonymy and discussion.

Platymantis vitiensis (Girard, 1853). Proc. Acad. Nat. Sci. Philadelphia, 6:423.
ORIGINAL NAME: *Halophila vitiensis*.
TYPE(S): Syntypes: USNM 14575–76.
TYPE LOCALITY: Levuka, Ovalau Island, Fiji Islands.
DISTRIBUTION: Fiji Is.
COMMENT: Gorham, 1965, Zool. Beitr., 11:381–435, provided a synonymy and discussion.

Platymantis weberi Schmidt, 1932. Field Mus. Nat. Hist. Publ., Zool. Ser., 181:178.
TYPE(S): Holotype: FMNH 13723.
TYPE LOCALITY: Tulagi Island, Solomon Islands.
DISTRIBUTION: Solomon Is.
COMMENT: Brown, 1952, Bull. Mus. Comp. Zool., 107:50–53, regarded this taxon as a subspecies of *Platymantis papuensis*. Menzies, 1982, Brit. J. Herpetol., 6:236–240, regarded it as a distinct species.

Platymantis xizangensis (Hu, 1977). Acta Zool. Sinica, 23:58.
ORIGINAL NAME: *Cornufer xizangensis*.
TYPE(S): Holotype: CIB (formerly SWIBASC) 73I0492.
TYPE LOCALITY: "Bomi, Yi'ong, Xizang [=Tibet], alt. 2300 m", China.
DISTRIBUTION: Tibet, China.
COMMENT: See comment under *Platymantis liui*.

Ptychadena Boulenger, 1917. C. R. Hebd. Séances Acad. Sci., Paris, 165:988.
TYPE SPECIES: *Rana mascareniensis* Duméril and Bibron, 1841, by subsequent designation of Boulenger, 1918, Bull. Soc. Zool. France, 43:114.
DISTRIBUTION: Subsaharan Africa.
COMMENT: West African species revised by Guibé and Lamotte, 1957, Bull. Inst. Franç. Afr. Noire, (A)19:937–1003. Cameroon species reviewed by Guibé and Lamotte, 1958, Bull. Inst. Franç. Afr. Noire, (A)20:1448–1463. Regarded as a subgenus of *Rana* by Dubois, 1981, Monit. Zool. Ital., N.S., Suppl., 15:225–284. Perret, 1979, Bull. Soc. Neuchâtel. Sci. Nat., 102:5–21, discussed several species with new synonyms and corrections of previous misidentifications. Perret, 1980, Monit. Zool. Ital., N.S., Suppl., 13:151–168, discussed some species of Ethiopia. Stevens, 1972, Arnoldia, Zimbabwe, 5(38):12, supplied a key to the species of southern Africa, derived from Poynton, 1970, Ann. Natal Mus., 20:365–375. See comment under *Ptychadena floweri*. The sister-taxon of *Hildebrandtia* plus *Lanzarana* according to Clarke, 1981, Monit. Zool. Ital., N.S., Suppl., 15:285–311.

Ptychadena aequiplicata (Werner, 1898). Verh. Zool. Bot. Ges. Wien, 48:192.
ORIGINAL NAME: *Rana mascareniensis* var. *aequiplicata*.
TYPE(S): Syntypes: NHMW 9784, according to Häupl and Tiedemann, 1978, Kat. Wiss. Samml. Naturhist. Mus. Wien, 2(Vert. 1):28.
TYPE LOCALITY: Victoria [now Limbé] and Buea, Cameroon.
DISTRIBUTION: Guinea and Ivory Coast to Zaire, in rainforest.

COMMENT: See Amiet, 1974, Ann. Fac. Sci. Cameroun, 18:110.

Ptychadena anchietae (Bocage, 1867). Proc. Zool. Soc. London, 1867:843.
ORIGINAL NAME: *Rana anchietae*.
TYPE(S): Syntypes: MBL T.9-134 (2 specimens); destroyed in 1978 fire.
TYPE LOCALITY: Benguella, Angola.
DISTRIBUTION: Ethiopia and Shaba (Zaire) to Natal (Rep. South Africa) and Angola.
COMMENT: Discussed by Guibé and Lamotte, 1960, Bull. Mus. Natl. Hist. Nat.,
    Paris, 32:380–391, who placed *Rana gondokorensis* Werner, *Rana aberae* Ahl, and
    Rana migiurtina Scortecci, in synonymy. Tentatively regarded as a synonym of
    Ptychadena superciliaris by Poynton, 1970, Ann. Natal Mus., 20:365–375, but
    this was disputed by Perret, 1976, Arq. Mus. Bocage, (2)6:20, and Perret, 1979,
    Bull. Soc. Neuchâtel. Sci. Nat., 102:18. See comment under *Ptychadena
    superciliaris*.

Ptychadena ansorgii (Boulenger, 1905). Ann. Mag. Nat. Hist., (7)16:107.
ORIGINAL NAME: *Rana ansorgii*.
TYPE(S): Holotype: BM.
TYPE LOCALITY: "between Benguella and Bihé", Angola.
DISTRIBUTION: Angola, Shaba (Zaire), Malawi, and Mozambique.
COMMENT: Discussed by Stewart, 1967, Amph. Malawi:83–85, and Schmidt and
    Inger, 1959, Explor. Parc Natl. Upemba, 56:61–65. JCP disputes the correctness
    of the Malawi and Mozambique records.

Ptychadena broadleyi Stevens, 1972. Arnoldia, Zimbabwe, 5(38):1.
TYPE(S): Holotype: NMZB (formerly UM) 25882.
TYPE LOCALITY: "rock face beside the Muluzi River on Mulanje Mountain, Malawi,
    at c. 930 metres above sea level".
DISTRIBUTION: Malawi.

Ptychadena bunoderma (Boulenger, 1907). Ann. Mag. Nat. Hist., (7)19:214.
ORIGINAL NAME: *Rana bunoderma*.
TYPE(S): Holotype: BM.
TYPE LOCALITY: "Caconda, [250 km inland from] Benguella", Angola.
DISTRIBUTION: Angola.
COMMENT: See Laurent, 1964, Publ. Cult. Companhia Diamantes Angola, 67:142,
    for the synonymy of *Ptychadena buneli*.

Ptychadena christyi (Boulenger, 1919). Rev. Zool. Afr., 7:5.
ORIGINAL NAME: *Rana christyi*.
TYPE(S): Syntypes: BM (4 specimens).
TYPE LOCALITY: Medje, Ituri [Zaire].
DISTRIBUTION: Eastern Zaire.
COMMENT: See Noble, 1924, Bull. Am. Mus. Nat. Hist., 49:222–224.

Ptychadena chrysogaster Laurent, 1954. Ann. Mus. R. Congo Belge, Tervuren, Ser.
    Octavo, Sci. Zool., 34:18.
TYPE(S): RGMC.
TYPE LOCALITY: "Lac Karago, 2.250 m., Terr. de Kisenyi, Ruanda".
DISTRIBUTION: Kivu (Zaire), Rwanda, and Burundi; Angola to Mozambique.
COMMENT: Zaire population reviewed by Schmidt and Inger, 1959, Explor. Parc
    Natl. Upemba, 56:65–68. Southeastern material discussed by Poynton, 1964,
    Ann. Natal Mus., 17:134–135, and Stewart, 1967, Amph. Malawi:83–85.

Ptychadena cooperi (Parker, 1930). Proc. Zool. Soc. London, 1930:3.
ORIGINAL NAME: *Rana (Ptychadena) cooperi*.
TYPE(S): Holotype: BM 1927.7.5.15.
TYPE LOCALITY: "Wouramboulchi, Ethiopia".
DISTRIBUTION: Ethiopia.

COMMENT: See Perret, 1980, Monit. Zool. Ital., N.S., Suppl., 13:167.

Ptychadena erlangeri (Ahl, 1924). Mitt. Zool. Mus. Berlin, 11:5.
ORIGINAL NAME: *Rana erlangeri.*
TYPE(S): Holotype: ZMB 26887.
TYPE LOCALITY: Lake Abaya, Ethiopia.
DISTRIBUTION: Ethiopia, east of Lake Abaya and Challa, Province Kaffa.
COMMENT: Redescribed and discussed by Perret, 1980, Monit. Zool. Ital., N.S., Suppl., 13:151–168.

Ptychadena floweri (Boulenger, 1917). Ann. Mag. Nat. Hist., (8)20:417.
ORIGINAL NAME: *Rana floweri.*
TYPE(S): BM.
TYPE LOCALITY: "Rosaires on the Blue Nile", Sudan.
DISTRIBUTION: Senegal and Egypt to Tanzania and south to Malawi and Mozambique.
COMMENT: Dubois, 1984, Alytes, Paris, 3:39–42, recognized this species as constituting the subgenus *Parkerana* (a replacement name for *Abrana* Parker, 1931), as distinct from *Ptychadena,* and regarded both groups as subgenera of *Rana;* see comment under *Rana.* Dubois cited Drewes, 1984, Occas. Pap. California Acad. Sci., 139:62, as supporting *Parkerana* (as *Abrana*) as distinct from *Ptychadena.* Pending a more thorough examination of the problem we tentatively retain this form in *Ptychadena* and regard *Parkerana* as a subgenus of *Ptychadena.* Discussed by Loveridge, 1933, Bull. Mus. Comp. Zool., 74:310, who synonymized *Abrana cotti* Parker, 1931, and *Rana barbouri* Loveridge, 1925. See Lanza, 1981, Monit. Zool. Ital., N.S., Suppl., 15:165, for synonymy. Synonymy includes *Ptychadena frontalis* Laurent, 1954, Ann. Mus. R. Congo Belge, Tervuren, Ser. Octavo, Sci. Zool., 34:26, according to Poynton, 1970, Ann. Natal Mus., 20:365–375. Schmidt and Inger, 1959, Explor. Parc Natl. Upemba, 56:68–70, reviewed *Ptychadena frontalis.* Probably a junior synonym of *Ptychadena schillukorum* (JLP).

Ptychadena gansi Laurent, 1965. Ann. Mus. R. Afr. Cent., Tervuren, Ser. Octavo, Sci. Zool., 134:282.
TYPE(S): Holotype: MCZ 36327.
TYPE LOCALITY: 2 km N of Afgoi, southern Somalia.
DISTRIBUTION: Southern Somalia.
COMMENT: Probably a synonym of *Ptychadena mossambica* according to Lanza, 1981, Monit. Zool. Ital., N.S., Suppl., 15:166.

Ptychadena grandisonae Laurent, 1954. Ann. Mus. R. Congo Belge, Tervuren, Ser. Octavo, Sci. Zool., 34:11.
TYPE(S): Holotype: MD 506.
TYPE LOCALITY: "Muita, Luembe E., Angola".
DISTRIBUTION: Northeastern Angola, Rwanda, southeastern Zaire, and northern Zambia.
COMMENT: Reviewed by Schmidt and Inger, 1959, Explor. Parc Natl. Upemba, 56:70–75. Specimens cited by Amiet, 1973, Ann. Fac. Sci. Cameroun, 13:137, and Amiet, 1978, Ann. Fac. Sci. Cameroun, 18:112, were confused with *Ptychadena straeleni,* according to Perret, 1979, Bull. Soc. Neuchâtel. Sci. Nat., 102:18.

Ptychadena keilingi (Monard, 1937). Bull. Soc. Neuchâtel. Sci. Nat., 62:53.
ORIGINAL NAME: *Rana (Ptychadena) keilingi.*
TYPE(S): Holotype: MHNG MON 9.1932.
TYPE LOCALITY: Dala, Angola.
DISTRIBUTION: Angola and western Zambia.
COMMENT: See Laurent, 1964, Publ. Cult. Companhia Diamantes Angola, 67:141.

Ptychadena longirostris (Peters, 1870). Monatsber. Preuss. Akad. Wiss. Berlin, 1870:646.
ORIGINAL NAME: *Rana longirostris.*
TYPE(S): ZMB.
TYPE LOCALITY: Keta, Ghana.
DISTRIBUTION: Sierra Leone to Ghana and Nigeria.
COMMENT: Synonyms include *Rana leonensis* Boulenger, 1917, and *Rana guerzea* Chabanaud, 1920. See Schiøtz, 1963, Vidensk. Medd. Dansk Naturhist. Foren., 125:23, and Perret, 1981, Bull. Soc. Neuchâtel. Sci. Nat., 104:56 (comparison with *Ptychadena schubotzi*).

Ptychadena maccarthyensis (Andersson, 1937). Ark. Zool., 29A(16):9.
ORIGINAL NAME: *Rana maccarthyensis.*
TYPE(S): Syntypes: ZIUS (5 specimens).
TYPE LOCALITY: "MacCarthy Island in the Gambia river about 330 km from its mouth".
DISTRIBUTION: Gambia to Zaire (Garamba).
COMMENT: See Inger, 1968, Explor. Parc Natl. Garamba, 52:63, and Perret, 1979, Bull. Soc. Neuchâtel. Sci. Nat., 102:17.

Ptychadena mascareniensis (Duméril and Bibron, 1841). Erp. Gén., 8:350.
ORIGINAL NAME: *Rana mascareniensis.*
TYPE(S): Syntypes: MNHNP 4379–81, MCZ 1044; USNM 10975 (2 specimens) considered probable cotypes by Cochran, 1961, Bull. U.S. Natl. Mus., 220:75.
TYPE LOCALITY: "Mascareignes" and "Séchelles"; recorded as Island of Réunion, Mascarene Islands, by Cochran, 1961, Bull. U.S. Natl. Mus., 220:75.
DISTRIBUTION: Egypt to Sierra Leone and Natal (Rep. South Africa); Madagascar; Seychelles Is.; Mascarene Is.
COMMENT: Reviewed by Schmidt and Inger, 1959, Explor. Parc Natl. Upemba, 56: 76–85, who described *Ptychadena mascareniensis hylaea. Hylaea* was subsequently considered a distinct species by Lamotte, 1966, Bull. Mus. Natl. Hist. Nat., Paris, 39:647–656, but Perret, 1979, Bull. Soc. Neuchâtel. Sci. Nat., 102:7–17, considered *Ptychadena bibroni* (Hallowell, 1845) to be a West African subspecies (following Boulenger, 1882, Cat. Batr. Sal. Brit. Mus.:523) and *hylaea* to be a synonym of *bibroni.*
REVIEWER: Rose M. A. Blommers-Schlösser (RMABS).

Ptychadena mossambica (Peters, 1854). Monatsber. Preuss. Akad. Wiss. Berlin, 1854: 626.
ORIGINAL NAME: *Rana mossambica.*
TYPE(S): ZMB.
TYPE LOCALITY: "Tette" (=Tete), Mozambique.
DISTRIBUTION: Kenya, Tanzania, Malawi, Zambia, Zimbabwe, Mozambique, eastern Botswana; eastern and northern Transvaal and Natal (Rep. South Africa).
COMMENT: Discussed by Poynton, 1969 "1966", Mem. Inst. Invest. Cient. Moçambique, 8:19. Revised by Poynton, 1970, Ann. Natal Mus., 20:373, who included *Rana vernayi* FitzSimons, 1932, in synonymy. See also Perret, 1979, Bull. Soc. Neuchâtel. Sci. Nat., 102:17.

Ptychadena nana Perret, 1980. Monit. Zool. Ital., N.S., Suppl., 13:160.
TYPE(S): Holotype: ZMB 26878H.
TYPE LOCALITY: "'Somaliland', Didda, Est Plateau, Arussi, Ethiopia, 2000–3000 m".
DISTRIBUTION: Known only from the type locality.
COMMENT: Holotype originally in syntypic series of *Ptychadena neumanni* (LJB).

Ptychadena neumanni (Ahl, 1924). Mitt. Zool. Mus. Berlin, 11:4.
ORIGINAL NAME: *Rana neumanni*.
TYPE(S): Syntypes: ZMB 26879 (3 specimens), MCZ 22331–32.
TYPE LOCALITY: North-east Africa; restricted to "Gadat (Gofa), Sud Ethiopia" by
Perret, 1980, Monit. Zool. Ital., N.S., Suppl., 13:157.
DISTRIBUTION: Known only from the type locality.
COMMENT: See comment under *Ptychadena nana*.

Ptychadena newtoni (Bocage, 1886). J. Sci. Math. Phys. Nat., Lisboa, 11:73.
ORIGINAL NAME: *Rana newtoni*.
TYPE(S): Syntypes: MBL T.7-115 (2 specimens); destroyed in 1978 fire.
TYPE LOCALITY: São Tomé.
DISTRIBUTION: São Tomé I., Gulf of Guinea.
COMMENT: Removed from the synonymy of *Ptychadena mascareniensis* by Perret,
1976, Arq. Mus. Bocage, (2)6:20, who noted that this species more resembled
Ptychadena oxyrhynchus.

Ptychadena obscura (Schmidt and Inger, 1959). Explor. Parc Natl. Upemba, 56:85.
ORIGINAL NAME: *Rana (Ptychadena) obscura*.
TYPE(S): Holotype: MRHN 1425.
TYPE LOCALITY: "Kaziba, Parc National de l'Upemba, Province Katanga [=Shaba],
Belgian Congo [=Zaire]".
DISTRIBUTION: Parc National Upemba, Shaba Province (Zaire) and northern
Zambia.

Ptychadena oxyrhynchus (Smith, 1849). Illustr. Zool. S. Afr., Rept.:pl. 77.
ORIGINAL NAME: *Rana oxyrhynchus*.
TYPE(S): BM.
TYPE LOCALITY: "Kaffirland and the region of Port Natal [=Durban]", Rep. South
Africa.
DISTRIBUTION: Subsaharan Africa, circum-forest savanna from Senegal to eastern
Angola, Natal (Rep. South Africa), and Mozambique.
COMMENT: Reviewed by Schmidt and Inger, 1959, Explor. Parc Natl. Upemba, 56:
91–95. See Inger, 1968, Explor. Parc Natl. Garamba, 52:72, and Poynton, 1964,
Ann. Natal Mus., 17:124.

Ptychadena perplicata Laurent, 1964. Publ. Cult. Companhia Diamantes Angola, 67:
136.
TYPE(S): Holotype: MD 5513.
TYPE LOCALITY: "Alto Chicapa, humidiherbosa des sources du Cuílo, Lunda",
Angola.
DISTRIBUTION: Known only from the type locality.

Ptychadena perreti Guibé and Lamotte, 1958. Bull. Inst. Franç. Afr. Noire, (A)20:1456.
TYPE(S): Syntypes: MNHNP 58-367 and 58-368.
TYPE LOCALITY: "Foulassi, Sangmélima (Cameroon), en forêt".
DISTRIBUTION: Cameroon and Gabon to eastern Zaire.
COMMENT: See Amiet, 1974, Ann. Fac. Sci. Cameroun, 18:118.

Ptychadena porosissima (Steindachner, 1867). Reise Freg. Novara, Amph.:18.
ORIGINAL NAME: *Rana porosissima*.
TYPE(S): Holotype: NHMW 14772, according to Häupl and Tiedemann, 1978, Kat.
Wiss. Samml. Naturhist. Mus. Wien, 2(Vert. 1):28.
TYPE LOCALITY: "Angola".
DISTRIBUTION: Angola, Zaire, East and South Africa.
COMMENT: Discussed by Poynton, 1964, Ann. Natal Mus., 17:129, who considered
Ptychadena poyntoni Guibé, 1960, a synonym. Erroneously considered a
synonym of *Ptychadena mascareniensis* by Guibé and Lamotte, 1957, Bull. Inst.

Franç. Afr. Noire, (A)19:978. Reviewed by Schmidt and Inger, 1959, Explor. Parc Natl. Upemba, 56:96–101, who included *Ptychadena loveridgei* as a synonym.

Ptychadena pumilio (Boulenger, 1920). Ann. Mag. Nat. Hist., (9)6:106.
ORIGINAL NAME: *Rana pumilio.*
TYPE(S): Syntypes: BM (2 specimens).
TYPE LOCALITY: "Medine, Senegal".
DISTRIBUTION: Senegal to Zaire (Garamba); eastern Zaire south to Mozambique, Zimbabwe, and Zambia.
COMMENT: Regarded by some authors (e.g., Lamotte, 1969, Mem. Inst. Franç. Afr. Noire, 8:422) as a subspecies of *Ptychadena mascareniensis*. Discussed by Perret, 1979, Bull. Soc. Neuchâtel. Sci. Nat., 102:15, who considered *Ptychadena taenioscelis* Laurent, 1954, Ann. Mus. R. Congo Belge, Tervuren, Ser. Octavo, Sci. Zool., 34:25 (Holotype: RGMC 13122; Type locality: "Lukula, près de Kiambi, Tanganyika [Province]", Zaire), to be a subspecies, *Ptychadena pumilio taenioscelis*. *Ptychadena taenioscelis* discussed by Poynton, 1964, Ann. Natal Mus., 17:132, who included *Ptychadena smithi* Guibé, 1960, in synonymy. Reviewed by Schmidt and Inger, 1959, Explor. Parc Natl. Upemba, 56:109–111.

Ptychadena retropunctata (Angel, 1949). Bull. Mus. Natl. Hist. Nat., Paris, (2)21:509.
ORIGINAL NAME: *Rana retropunctata.*
TYPE(S): Syntypes: MNHNP 225–228, 9673.
TYPE LOCALITY: Mont Nimba (Guinée française).
DISTRIBUTION: Sierra Leone and Guinea (far West Africa).
COMMENT: See Schiøtz, 1964, Vidensk. Medd. Dansk Naturhist. Foren., 127:23.

Ptychadena schillukorum (Werner, 1907). Sitzungsber. Akad. Wiss. Wien, Math. Naturwiss. Kl., 116:1889.
ORIGINAL NAME: *Rana schillukorum.*
TYPE(S): Syntypes: NHMW 14844.
TYPE LOCALITY: "Khor Attar", Sudan.
DISTRIBUTION: Nile Valley of Sudan.
COMMENT: Probably a senior synonym of *Ptychadena floweri* (JLP).

Ptychadena schubotzi (Sternfeld, 1917). Wiss. Ergebn. Zweit. Deutsch. Zentr. Afr. Exped., 1(Zool.):493.
ORIGINAL NAME: *Rana schubotzi.*
TYPE(S): Holotype: SMF 6242 (formerly 1051.1a).
TYPE LOCALITY: Fort Crampel, Central African Republic.
DISTRIBUTION: Sierra Leone to Chad, Central African Republic, and northern Zaire (Garamba) in savanna.
COMMENT: Discussed by Perret, 1981, Bull. Soc. Neuchâtel. Sci. Nat., 104:53–57. Includes *Ptychadena huguettae* Inger, 1928, as a synonym, according to Perret, 1979, Bull. Soc. Neuchâtel. Sci. Nat., 102:53–54. See Schiøtz, 1964, Vidensk. Medd. Dansk Naturhist. Foren., 127:5, 22, 45 (as *Ptychadena* sp. I). See Amiet, 1974, Ann. Fac. Sci. Cameroun, 18:114 (as *Ptychadena huguettae*).

Ptychadena stenocephala (Boulenger, 1901). Ann. Mag. Nat. Hist., (7)8:515.
ORIGINAL NAME: *Rana stenocephala.*
TYPE(S): Syntypes: BM 1947.2.3.50 and 1947.2.3.56, MCZ 11755.
TYPE LOCALITY: "Entebbe, 3800 feet", Uganda.
DISTRIBUTION: West Africa (Guinea and Cameroon); Uganda.
COMMENT: Reviewed by Perret, 1979, Bull. Soc. Neuchâtel. Sci. Nat., 102:10.

Ptychadena straeleni (Inger, 1968). Explor. Parc Natl. Garamba, 52:82.
ORIGINAL NAME: *Rana straeleni.*
TYPE(S): Holotype: RGMC.
TYPE LOCALITY: Nagero, Parc National Garamba, Zaire.
DISTRIBUTION: Northern Zaire (Parc National de la Garamba) and Adamaoua Plateau, central Cameroon, in savanna.
COMMENT: Discussed by Perret, 1979, Bull. Soc. Neuchâtel. Sci. Nat., 102:18. The sonogram published by Amiet, 1974, Ann. Fac. Sci. Cameroun, 18:112, as that of *Ptychadena grandisonae* is of this species (JLP).

Ptychadena submascareniensis (Guibé and Lamotte, 1953). Bull. Mus. Natl. Hist. Nat., Paris, (2)25:362.
ORIGINAL NAME: *Rana (Ptychadena) submascareniensis.*
TYPE(S): Syntypes: MNHNP 51-198, 51-205.
TYPE LOCALITY: "massif du Nimba (Haute-Guinée française)", Guinea.
DISTRIBUTION: Guinea to Ivory Coast.

Ptychadena subpunctata (Bocage, 1866). J. Sci. Math. Phys. Nat., Lisboa, 1:73.
ORIGINAL NAME: *Rana subpunctata.*
TYPE(S): Lost.
TYPE LOCALITY: Duque de Bragança [Angola].
DISTRIBUTION: Southeastern Zaire, Botswana, Zambia, Angola, and northern Namibia.
COMMENT: Reviewed by Schmidt and Inger, 1959, Explor. Parc Natl. Upemba, 56: 102–104, and Poynton, 1964, Ann. Natal Mus., 17:127–128. Synonymy includes *Rana katangae* Witte, 1921, and *Rana chobiensis* FitzSimons, 1932.

Ptychadena superciliaris (Günther, 1859 "1858"). Cat. Batr. Sal. Coll. Brit. Mus.:17.
ORIGINAL NAME: *Rana superciliaris.*
TYPE(S): Holotype: BM.
TYPE LOCALITY: Sierra Leone.
DISTRIBUTION: Forests of Sierra Leone to Ghana.
COMMENT: *Ptychadena abyssinica* (Peters, 1881) was erroneously considered a synonym by Poynton, 1970, Ann. Natal Mus., 20:365–375, following Schmidt and Inger, 1959, Explor. Parc Natl. Upemba, 56:105–109. *Ptychadena abyssinica* was transferred to the synonymy of *Ptychadena anchietae* by Perret, 1976, Arq. Mus. Bocage, (2)6:20, and Perret, 1979, Bull. Soc. Neuchâtel. Sci. Nat., 102:18.

Ptychadena tournieri (Guibé and Lamotte, 1955). Bull. Mus. Natl. Hist. Nat., Paris, (2)27:442.
ORIGINAL NAME: *Rana (Ptychadena) tournieri.*
TYPE(S): Syntypes: MNHNP 8679, 8680, 8681, 51-193 (mont Nimba); MCZ 26856 (+2 duplicates) (Bonthé); MCZ 26690 (Ibanga, Suacoco); MCZ 27720 (Kenema); MCZ 28093 (Yundum).
TYPE LOCALITY: "Mont Nimba (Guinée française [=Guinea])"; "Petoru (Sierra Leone)"; "Bonthé (Sierra Leone)"; "Ibanga, Suacoco (Liberia)"; "Kenema (Sierra Leone)"; "Yundum (Gambie)".
DISTRIBUTION: Sierra Leone, Liberia, and Ivory Coast.
COMMENT: See Lamotte, 1967, Bull. Inst. Franç. Afr. Noire, (A)29:242, and Schiøtz, 1964, Vidensk. Medd. Dansk. Naturhist. Foren., 127:49.

Ptychadena trinodis (Boettger, 1881). Abh. Senckenb. Naturforsch. Ges., 12:414.
ORIGINAL NAME: *Rana trinodis.*
TYPE(S): Syntypes: formerly SMF, now lost (not mentioned in type catalog of Mertens, 1967, Senckenb. Biol., 48:1–206).
TYPE LOCALITY: Dakar and Rufisque, Senegal.
DISTRIBUTION: Senegal to Nigeria, Cameroon, and Zaire (Garamba).
COMMENT: Studied by Schiøtz, 1963, Vidensk. Medd. Dansk. Naturhist. Foren., 125:

24; Inger, 1968, Explor. Parc Natl. Garamba, 52:91; and Amiet, 1974, Ann. Fac. Sci. Cameroun, 18:124.

Ptychadena upembae (Schmidt and Inger, 1959). Explor. Parc Nat. Upemba, 56:111.
ORIGINAL NAME: *Rana (Ptychadena) upembae*.
TYPE(S): Holotype: RGMC 1304.
TYPE LOCALITY: "Kaswabilenga, Parc National de l'Upemba, Province Katanga [=Shaba], Belgian Congo [=Zaire]".
DISTRIBUTION: Shaba (Zaire); eastern Zambia; northern Malawi; Angola.
COMMENT: Discussed by Stewart, 1967, Amph. Malawi:76–77. See Laurent, 1964, Publ. Cult. Companhia Diamantes Angola, 67:134, for a subspecies (*Ptychadena upembae machadoi*).

Ptychadena uzungwensis (Loveridge, 1932). Bull. Mus. Comp. Zool., 72:384.
ORIGINAL NAME: *Rana mascareniensis uzungwensis*.
TYPE(S): Holotype: MCZ 16626.
TYPE LOCALITY: Dabaga, Uzungwe Mountains, Tanganyika [=Tanzania].
DISTRIBUTION: East African plateau: Rwanda, Burundi, southeastern Zaire, Tanzania, Malawi, Zambia, and Zimbabwe to Mozambique uplands and eastern Angola.
COMMENT: Synonymy of *Ptychadena macrocephala* Laurent, 1952, in Laurent, 1954, Ann. Mus. R. Congo Belge, Tervuren, Ser. Octavo, Sci. Zool., 34:9. Reviewed by Schmidt and Inger, 1959, Explor. Parc Natl. Upemba, 56:117–123. See also Poynton, 1964, Ann. Natal Mus., 17:131.

Pyxicephalus Tschudi, 1838. Classif. Batr.:46.
TYPE SPECIES: *Pyxicephalus adspersus* Tschudi, 1838, by subsequent designation of Fitzinger, 1843, Syst. Rept., 1:32.
DISTRIBUTION: Subsaharan Africa.
COMMENT: See comment under *Aubria*. Regarded as a subgenus of *Rana* by Dubois, 1981, Monit. Zool. Ital., N.S., Suppl., 15:225–284, and related to the *Rana occipitalis* group of *Euphlyctis*, a view not in agreement with Clarke, 1981, Monit. Zool. Ital., N.S., Suppl., 15:285–331, who regarded *Pyxicephalus* and *Aubria* as sister-taxa and together the sister-taxon of *Conraua* + the *Rana (Euphlyctis) occipitalis* group.

Pyxicephalus adspersus Tschudi, 1838. Classif. Batr.:84.
TYPE(S): Syntypes: MNHNP 4525 and 4527 (8 specimens total), RMNH 2258 (2 specimens).
TYPE LOCALITY: "Promontorium Bonae Spei" (=Cape of Good Hope, Rep. South Africa).
DISTRIBUTION: Nigeria to Somalia, Kenya, Tanzania, Mozambique, Malawi, Zambia, Zimbabwe, Angola, and Rep. South Africa, excluding the southwestern Cape Province.
COMMENT: See Parry, 1982, Ann. Natal Mus., 25:281–292, for discussion of geographic variation in southern Africa and subspecies. Synonymy includes *Pyxicephalus flavigula* Calabresi, 1916, according to Balletto, Cherchi, and Lanza, 1978, Monit. Zool. Ital., N.S., Suppl., 11:103–110.

Pyxicephalus obbianus Calabresi, 1927. Atti Soc. Ital. Sci. Nat. Mus. Civ. Stor. Nat. Milano, 66:15.
TYPE(S): MZUF 302 designated lectotype by Balletto, Cherchi, and Lanza, 1979, Monit. Zool. Ital., N.S., Suppl., 11:225.
TYPE LOCALITY: Dolobscio, central Somalia.
DISTRIBUTION: Northeastern and central Somalia.
COMMENT: Synonymy includes *Rana (Pyxicephalus) cimmarutai* Scortecci, 1912, according to Balletto, Cherchi, and Lanza, 1978, Monit. Zool. Ital., N.S., Suppl., 11:230. See also Lanza, 1981, Monit. Zool. Ital., N.S., Suppl., 15:166–168, for synonymy and distribution.

Rana Linnaeus, 1758. Syst. Nat., Ed. 10, 1:210.

TYPE SPECIES: *Rana temporaria* Linnaeus, 1758, by subsequent designation of Fitzinger, 1843, Syst. Rept., 1:31.

DISTRIBUTION: Coextensive with the subfamily.

COMMENT: Dubois, 1981, Monit. Zool. Ital., N.S., Suppl., 15:225–284, presented a generic and subgeneric arrangement of the ranines which is only partially followed here. See comment under Raninae. The nominal subgenera used herein are:

(1) *Rana*: Ancestral to *Hylarana* according to Dubois, 1981, Monit. Zool. Ital., N.S., Suppl., 15:225–284.

(2) *Hylarana*: Possibly polyphyletic (Dubois, 1975, Bull. Mus. Natl. Hist. Nat., Paris, (3)324(Zool.)231:1093–1115); Asian group ancestral to 'platymantine' genera (*Amolops, Batrachylodes, Ceratobatrachus, Discodeles, Micrixalus, Platymantis, Palmatorappia,* and *Staurois*) according to Savage, 1973, *In* Vial (ed.), Evol. Biol. Anurans (but see opinion of Dubois under *Euphlyctis*). Synonymies of African species provided by Perret, 1977, Rev. Suisse Zool., 84:842–844. In addition, while African workers (e.g., Perret, 1977, Rev. Suisse Zool., 84:841–868) tend to recognize *Hylarana* as a distinct genus, workers in Asia (e.g., Inger, 1954, Fieldiana: Zool., 33:183–531) do not. The placement of *Hylarana* here as a subgenus of *Rana* rather than as a distinct genus is not due to casual opinion. Rather, it is in recognition of the fact that the definition of the group in Asia (where the type species, *Rana erythraea*, is found) is very poor and that allocation of species to *Hylarana* (at least in Asia) has been very spotty. Contains the *Rana gracilis, Rana erythraea, Rana luctuosa, Rana papua, Rana swinhoana,* and *Rana chalconota* (in part) groups of Boulenger, 1920, Rec. Indian Mus., 20:1–226.

(3) *Paa*: Ancestral to *Altirana* and *Nanorana* according to Dubois, 1981, Monit. Zool. Ital., N.S., Suppl., 15:224–284. Subgenus defined and discussed by Dubois, 1976, Cah. Nepal., Doc., 6:1–275.

(4) *Euphlyctis*: Includes *Dicroglossus* Günther, 1860, in synonymy. Ancestral to *Aubria, Pyxicephalus, Occidozyga, Elachyglossa, Limnonectes,* and *Discodeles, Platymantis* and 'related genera' (? platymantines of Savage, 1973) according to Dubois, 1981, Monit. Zool. Ital., N.S., Suppl., 15:224–284, who also regarded *Euphlyctis* (as well as *Limnonectes*) close to *Tomopterna*, a view rejected by Clarke, 1981, Monit. Zool. Ital., N.S., Suppl., 15:285–311. See comment under *Conraua*. Includes the *Rana hexadactyla* (now *Rana cyanophlyctis* group), *Rana tigerina*, and *Rana grunniens* groups of Boulenger, 1920, Rec. Indian Mus., 20:1–226, according to (and modified by) Dubois, 1981, Monit. Zool. Ital., N.S., Suppl., 15:240. The historical reality of this taxon is an open question (SD).

(5) *Limnonectes*: See comment under *Euphlyctis*. This subgenus of Dubois, 1981, Monit. Zool. Ital., N.S., Suppl., 15:211–284, is equivalent to the *Rana kuhlii* group of Boulenger, 1920, Rec. Indian Mus., 20:1–226.

(6) *Babina*: Considered synonymous with *Hylarana* by Dubois, 1981, Monit. Zool. Ital., N.S., Suppl., 15:211–284, but considered a distinct genus by Okada, 1966, Fauna Japon., Anura:138–143; considered a subgenus of *Rana* by Nakamura and Ueno, 1963, Japan. Rept. Amph. Color:54. Equivalent to the *Rana holsti* group of Boulenger, 1920, Rec. Indian Mus., 20:1–226.

These subgenera (and where appropriate, their constituent species groups) are indicated in the species accounts in order to indicate the state of the literature. Considerable caution should be used in interpreting their meaning, since many of these species have not been examined seriously since Boulenger's series of revisions. Species groups for New World species follow Hillis, Frost, and Wright, 1983, Syst. Zool., 32:132–143; Webb, 1978, Contrib. Sci. Nat. Hist. Mus. Los Angeles Co., 300:1–13; and Case, 1978, Syst. Zool., 27:219–311. Farris, Kluge, and Mickevich, 1982, Syst. Zool., 31:479–490, and Farris, Kluge, and Mickevich, 1979, Syst. Zool., 28:627–634, disputed the phylogenetic arrangement of North American *Rana* proposed by Case, 1978, and Post and Uzzell, 1981, Syst. Zool., 30:170–180, noting that the *Rana boylii* group was probably a paraphyletic group from which the *Rana temporaria* group was derived. Synonymies of South

African forms in Poynton, 1964, Ann. Natal Mus., 17:102–121. Pace, 1974, Misc. Publ. Mus. Zool. Univ. Michigan, 148:1140, reviewed the *Rana pipiens* complex of the eastern USA. Greding, 1977, Bull. Chicago Herpetol. Soc., 12:58–59, compared immunologically some of the Central American species. Dubois, 1977, Mem. Soc. Zool. France, 39:161–284; Hotz and Bruno, 1979–1980, Rend. Accad. Naz. Sci. XL, Mem. Sci. Fis. Natur., 4(6):49–112; Uzzell, 1982, Amphibia-Reptilia, 3:135–143; and Berger, 1983, Experientia, 39:127–130, discussed the *Rana esculenta* complex. Orlova, Bakharev, and Borkin, 1977, Trudy Zool. Inst. Akad. Nauk SSSR, Leningrad, 74:81–101, reported on karyology and taxonomy of the *Rana temporaria* group. Boulenger, 1920, Rec. Indian Mus., 20:1–223, reviewed most of the species of southern Asia to New Guinea (as well as defining species groups still in some use). Pope and Boring, 1940, Peking Nat. Hist. Bull., 15:48–63, provided a key and reviewed many of the Chinese species. Liu, 1950, Fieldiana: Zool. Mem., 2:253–322, reviewed the species of western China. Liu and Hu, 1961, Tailless Amph. China:137–217, reviewed Chinese species and indicated phylogenetic arrangement by recognizing groups. Inger, 1954, Fieldiana: Zool., 33:259–332, reviewed the Philippine species. Inger, 1966, Fieldiana: Zool., 52:160–238, reviewed the Bornean species, and Bourret, 1942, Batr. Indochine:304–377, reviewed the species found from Burma and Indochina to Malaya.

CONTRIBUTORS: David M. Hillis (DMH) (Americas); also see list of contributors under Raninae.

REVIEWERS: Jonathan A. Campbell (JAC) (Mexico and Central America); Oscar Flores-Villela (OFV) (Mexico); Jay M. Savage (JMS) (Central America); Norman J. Scott, Jr. (NJS) (Central and South America); also see list of reviewers under Raninae.

Rana adenopleura Boulenger, 1909. Ann. Mag. Nat. Hist., (8)4:492.
TYPE(S): BM.
TYPE LOCALITY: "Fuhacho Village, altitude about 4000 feet", Taiwan, China.
DISTRIBUTION: Fujian, Jiangxi, Yunnan, Sichuan, Hainan I., and Taiwan, China; Yaeyama group of Ryukyu Is., Japan.
COMMENT: In the subgenus *Hylarana*, *Rana gracilis* group. Discussed by Pope, 1931, Bull. Am. Mus. Nat. Hist., 61:534–538, and Matsui and Utunomiya, 1983, J. Herpetol., 17:32–37. Locality records in Liu et al., 1973, Acta Zool. Sinica, 19: 395; Kuramoto, 1973, Bull. Fukuoka Univ. Educ., Nat. Sci., 22:142; and Liu and Hu, 1961, Tailless Amph. China:185. See comment under *Rana dauchina*.

Rana aenea Smith, 1922. J. Nat. Hist. Soc. Siam, 4:200.
TYPE(S): Holotype: BM (formerly M. Smith 5821).
TYPE LOCALITY: "Doi Chang, N. Siam [=Thailand], at about 1500 metres altitude".
DISTRIBUTION: Known only from the type locality.
COMMENT: In the subgenus *Euphlyctis*, *Rana grunniens* group, by implication from the original description. See Taylor, 1962, Univ. Kansas Sci. Bull., 43:446–448, and Bourret, 1942, Batr. Indochine:276–278.

Rana albolabris Hallowell, 1856. Proc. Acad. Nat. Sci. Philadelphia, 1856:153.
TYPE(S): Syntypes: ANSP (4 specimens); lost (JLP).
TYPE LOCALITY: West Africa; restricted to "Gabon" by Perret, 1977, Rev. Suisse Zool., 84:843.
DISTRIBUTION: Forested West and Central Africa.
COMMENT: A *Hylarana* according to Perret, 1977, Rev. Suisse Zool., 84:846–850, who reviewed the species.

Rana altaica Kastschenko, 1899. Result. Altai Exped.:122.
TYPE(S): Not traced.
TYPE LOCALITY: Altai [USSR].
DISTRIBUTION: Northern Xinjiang (China) and southern Siberia (USSR).
COMMENT: Subgenus *Rana*, *Rana temporaria* group. See Ye, Fei, and Xiang, 1981,

Acta Herpetol. Sinica, 5:121. Regarded as a subspecies or synonym of *Rana arvalis* by some authors.

Rana alticola Boulenger, 1882. Cat. Batr. Sal. Brit. Mus.:62.
TYPE(S): Syntypes: BM.
TYPE LOCALITY: "Shillong", Assam, India and "Moulmein", Tenasserim, Burma.
DISTRIBUTION: Hills of Assam (India) to Thailand and Tonkin (Vietnam).
COMMENT: In the subgenus *Hylarana*, *Rana erythraea* group. Reviewed by Bourret, 1942, Batr. Indochine:348–350.

Rana amieti Laurent, 1976. Rev. Zool. Afr., 90:528.
TYPE(S): Holotype: RGMC 75.43.B.1.
TYPE LOCALITY: Zaire, Pangi Territory, Lubile, Maniema Forest.
DISTRIBUTION: Known only from the type locality.
COMMENT: Subgenus *Rana*.

Rana amnicola (Perret, 1977). Rev. Suisse Zool., 84:855.
ORIGINAL NAME: *Hylarana amnicola*.
TYPE(S): Holotype: MHNG 1551.43.
TYPE LOCALITY: "Ilanga, Eséka, Cameroun méridional".
DISTRIBUTION: Central and western Cameroon and Gabon.
COMMENT: A *Hylarana* according to the original description.

Rana amurensis Boulenger, 1886. Bull. Soc. Zool. France, 1886:598.
TYPE(S): Syntypes: ZMB 9864 and ZIL 5095.
TYPE LOCALITY: "Kissakawitsch [=Kasakevichevo, near Khabarovsk], Amour [=Amur]", USSR.
DISTRIBUTION: Western Siberia east to Sakhalin I., northern and eastern Mongolia, northeastern China and Korea, north to beyond the Arctic Circle (northernmost 71° N).
COMMENT: Subgenus *Rana*, *Rana temporaria* group. Often confused with *Rana asiatica* and Asian "*Rana temporaria*"; see Borkin, 1975, Tezisy Dokladov Zool. Inst. Akad. Nauk SSSR, Leningrad, 1975:6–7. Reviewed by Pope, 1931, Bull. Am. Mus. Nat. Hist., 61:520–521, and Shannon, 1956, Herpetologica, 12:38. See also Orlova, Bakharev, and Borkin, 1977, Trudy Zool. Inst. Akad. Nauk SSSR, Leningrad, 74:81–103 (who included *Rana cruenta* Pallas, 1814, as a synonym), and Liu and Hu, 1961, Tailless Amph. China:181–188, for discussion of the *Rana temporaria* group.

Rana andersonii Boulenger, 1882. Cat. Batr. Sal. Brit. Mus.:55.
TYPE(S): Syntypes: including BM (1 specimen), others not traced.
TYPE LOCALITY: "Hotha [=Husa] Valley, Yunnan", China.
DISTRIBUTION: Upper Burma to Yunnan, Guizhou, and Hainan I. (China) and Tonkin (Vietnam).
COMMENT: In the subgenus *Hylarana*, *Rana luctuosa* group. Discussed by Pope, 1931, Bull. Am. Mus. Nat. Hist., 61:550–553; Liu, 1950, Fieldiana: Zool. Mem., 2:297–303; Bourret, 1942, Batr. Indochine:354–357; and Liu and Hu, 1961, Tailless Amph. China:206–208. See comment under *Rana grahami*.

Rana angolensis Bocage, 1866. J. Sci. Math. Phys. Nat., Lisboa, 1:73.
TYPE(S): Holotype: MBL T.8-94; destroyed in 1978 fire.
TYPE LOCALITY: Duque de Bragança, Angola.
DISTRIBUTION: Angola, eastern Zaire, Rwanda, Burundi, and Kenya to Rep. South Africa.
COMMENT: Subgenus *Rana*. See Perret, 1976, Arq. Mus. Bocage, (2)6:15–34, and Channing, 1978, Ann. Natal Mus., 23:361–365, for diagnosis. See comment under *Rana fuscigula*.

Rana anlungensis Liu and Hu, 1973. *In* Hu, Djao, and Liu, Acta Zool. Sinica, 19:167.
TYPE(S): Holotype: CIB 63III1515.
TYPE LOCALITY: "Lungtou Shan, Anlung Hsien, Kwiechow [=Guizhou], altitude 1550 m", China.
DISTRIBUTION: Known only from the type locality.
COMMENT: Closely related to *Rana schmackeri* according to the original description. In the subgenus *Hylarana*, by implication.

Rana annandalii Boulenger, 1920. Rec. Indian Mus., 20:77.
TYPE(S): BM 1947.2.1.93 designated lectotype by Dubois, 1975, Bull. Mus. Natl. Hist. Nat., Paris, (3)324(Zool.)231:1110.
TYPE LOCALITY: "Sureil, Darjeeling district, 5500 ft., . . . Suchal [=Senchal] Waterworks, near Ghoom, in the same district, . . . [and] Pashok, alt. 4500 ft.", India; restricted to Suchal waterworks near Ghoom, Darjeeling, India, by lectotype designation.
DISTRIBUTION: Darjeeling region, West Bengal, India; Nepal.
COMMENT: Subgenus *Paa*, according to Dubois, 1975, Cah. Nepal., Doc., 6:83–98.

Rana arathooni Smith, 1927. Proc. Zool. Soc. London, 1927:207.
TYPE(S): BM.
TYPE LOCALITY: Djikoro, Mt. Bonthain, South Celebes [Indonesia].
DISTRIBUTION: South Celebes.

Rana areolata Baird and Girard, 1852. Proc. Acad. Nat. Sci. Philadelphia, 6:173.
TYPE(S): Holotype: USNM 3304.
TYPE LOCALITY: "Indianola", Calhoun County, Texas, USA.
DISTRIBUTION: Southern Iowa, Indiana, and Illinois south along the eastern and western borders of the Ozark Plateau to northern Mississippi, western Louisiana, and eastern Texas; southeastern Louisiana and North Carolina to peninsular Florida on the coastal plain, USA.
COMMENT: In the subgenus *Rana*, *Rana areolata* group of the *Rana pipiens* complex. The eastern populations are considered by some authors to be a distinct species, *Rana capito* (see Case, 1978, Syst. Zool., 27:219–311, who considered *Rana capito* to be more closely related to some *Rana* other than *Rana areolata*). Reviewed by Altig and Lohoefener, 1983, Cat. Am. Amph. Rept., 324.1–4.

Rana arfaki Meyer, 1874. Monatsber. Preuss. Akad. Wiss. Berlin, 1874:138.
TYPE(S): Not traced.
TYPE LOCALITY: "Arfakgebirge", Irian Jaya (New Guinea), Indonesia.
DISTRIBUTION: New Guinea; Aru Is.
COMMENT: In the subgenus *Hylarana*, *Rana luctuosa* group.
REVIEWERS: Michael J. Tyler (MJT); Margaret Davies (MD); Richard G. Zweifel (RGZ).

Rana arnoldi Dubois, 1975. Bull. Mus. Natl. Hist. Nat., Paris, (3)324(Zool.)231:1093.
TYPE(S): Holotype: BM 1940.6.2.90.
TYPE LOCALITY: "Pangnamdim, Nam Tamai Valley, Triangle, northern Burma, 27° 42' N, 97° 54' E, altitude 910 m (3000 ft.)".
DISTRIBUTION: Tibet (China) and northern Burma.
COMMENT: Subgenus *Paa*, according to the original description. See Dubois, 1980, Bull. Mens. Soc. Linn. Lyon, 49:142–147. See comment under *Rana maculosa*.

Rana arvalis Nilsson, 1842. Skand. Fauna., 3(Amph.):92.
TYPE(S): ZMLU 1 designated lectotype by Gislén, 1959, *In* Gislén and Kauri, Acta Vertebratica, 1:301.
TYPE LOCALITY: "Calmare Län", southern Sweden.
DISTRIBUTION: Northeastern France, Belgium, Netherlands, Germany, Denmark, Sweden, and Finland south to the Alps, northern Yugoslavia, northern Romania, and east to Siberia (up to Yakutia, 124° E).

COMMENT: In the subgenus *Rana*, *Rana temporaria* group. Synonymy supplied by
Mertens and Wermuth, 1960, Amph. Rept. Europas:52–54, and discussed by
Borkin, 1975, Zool. Zh., 54:1410–1411. See comment under *Rana altaica*.

Rana asiatica Bedriaga, 1898. Wiss. Result. Przewalski Cent. Asien Reisen, Zool.,
3(1):23.
ORIGINAL NAME: *Rana temporaria* var. *asiatica*.
TYPE(S): Syntypes: ZIL 928–930, 1056, 1063, 1257, and 1501 (22 specimens).
TYPE LOCALITY: Kungess and Upper Ili River, Tien-shan, and Ordos Province, and
Bagagorgi River, tributary of Upper Chuanche River [China].
DISTRIBUTION: Southern Kazakhstan (north to Lake Balkhash) and Kirghizia (USSR)
and Xinjiang (China).
COMMENT: In the subgenus *Rana*, *Rana temporaria* group. Often confused with *Rana
amurensis* and *Rana chensinensis* (LJB).

Rana asperrima (Perret, 1977). Rev. Suisse Zool., 84:857.
ORIGINAL NAME: *Hylarana asperrima*.
TYPE(S): Holotype: MHNG 1551.52.
TYPE LOCALITY: "Ndoungué, Nkongsamba, Cameroun".
DISTRIBUTION: Western Cameroon.
COMMENT: *Hylarana* according to the original description.

Rana aurantiaca Boulenger, 1904. J. Bombay Nat. Hist. Soc., 15:430.
TYPE(S): Holotype: BM 1903.9.26.1.
TYPE LOCALITY: Trivandrum, Travancore [Kerala, South India].
DISTRIBUTION: South India and Sri Lanka.
COMMENT: In the subgenus *Hylarana*, *Rana erythraea* group.

Rana aurora Baird and Girard, 1852. Proc. Acad. Nat. Sci. Philadelphia, 6:174.
TYPE(S): Syntypes: USNM 11711 (4 specimens).
TYPE LOCALITY: "Puget Sound", Washington, USA.
DISTRIBUTION: Vancouver I., British Columbia (Canada) south along the Pacific
coast of the USA to northern Baja California (Mexico), 0–8000 ft.
COMMENT: Subgenus *Rana*, *Rana boylii* group. Reviewed by Altig and Dumas, 1972,
Cat. Am. Amph. Rept., 160.1–4. Hayes and Miyamoto, 1984, Copeia, 1984:
1018–1022, suggested that *Rana aurora aurora* and *Rana aurora draytoni*
(originally *Rana draytoni* Baird and Girard, 1852, Proc. Acad. Nat. Sci.
Philadelphia, 6:174; Distribution: Central and southern California, USA, to
extreme northern Baja California, Mexico) might be distinct species.

Rana baramica Boettger, 1901. Abh. Senckenb. Naturforsch. Ges., 25:391.
TYPE(S): Syntypes: MCZ and SMF 4331 (formerly 1069.1a); SMF 4331 designated
lectotype by Mertens, 1967, Senckenb. Biol., 48:44.
TYPE LOCALITY: Baram River, Sarawak [Malaysia (Borneo)].
DISTRIBUTION: Borneo, Singapore, and Bangka I.
COMMENT: In the subgenus *Hylarana*, *Rana luctuosa* group. Reviewed by Inger,
1966, Fieldiana: Zool., 52:160–162. See also Berry, 1975, Amph. Fauna of
Peninsular Malaysia:61–62.

Rana beddomii (Günther, 1875). Proc. Zool. Soc. London, 1875:571.
ORIGINAL NAME: *Polypedates beddomii*.
TYPE(S): BM.
TYPE LOCALITY: "in Malabar and Travancore, in the Anamallays [=Anamallai] and
Sevagherry [=Sivagiri]", Kerala, India.
DISTRIBUTION: Forests of Malabar, Kerala, southern India.
COMMENT: See comment under *Discodeles*.

Rana berlandieri Baird, 1854. Rep. U.S.–Mex. Bound. Surv., 2:27.
   TYPE(S): Syntypes: USNM 3293 (9 specimens), MCZ 155 (2 specimens); USNM
      131513 recorded as syntype by Cochran, 1961, Bull. U.S. Natl. Mus., 200:72,
      who also noted that 2 specimens of USNM 3293 were exchanged to the MCZ;
      USNM 131513 designated lectotype by Pace, 1974, Misc. Publ. Mus. Zool.
      Univ. Michigan, 148:25.
   TYPE LOCALITY: "Southern Texas generally"; lectotype from "Brownsville, Texas",
      USA.
   DISTRIBUTION: Central and western Texas and southern New Mexico (USA) to
      southern Veracruz and Oaxaca (Mexico); populations farther south of are of
      questionable taxonomic status (DMH).
   COMMENT: In the subgenus *Rana*, *Rana berlandieri* group of the *Rana pipiens*
      complex.

Rana bhagmandlensis Rao, 1922. J. Bombay Nat. Hist. Soc., 28:441.
   TYPE(S): Syntypes: BM and ZSI.
   TYPE LOCALITY: Water course in the forests of Bhagamandla, Coorg, 4000 ft.
      [Mysore, India].
   DISTRIBUTION: Mysore, South India.

Rana bilineata Pillai and Chanda, 1981. Rec. Zool. Surv. India, 79:159.
   TYPE(S): Holotype: ZSIM V/ERS.914.
   TYPE LOCALITY: Dianadubi Forest, Garo Hills [Assam, India].
   DISTRIBUTION: Assam, India.

Rana blairi Mecham, Littlejohn, Oldham, Brown, and Brown, 1973. Occas. Pap. Texas
      Tech. Univ., 18:3.
   TYPE(S): Holotype: UMMZ 131690.
   TYPE LOCALITY: "1.6 km W New Deal, Lubbock Co., Texas", USA.
   DISTRIBUTION: Western Indiana west across central and southern plains to eastern
      Colorado and New Mexico and south to central Texas; isolated population in
      southeastern Arizona, USA.
   COMMENT: In the subgenus *Rana*, *Rana pipiens* group of the *Rana pipiens* complex.

Rana blanfordii Boulenger, 1882. Cat. Batr. Sal. Brit. Mus.:23.
   TYPE(S): BM 1880.11.10.105 designated lectotype by Dubois, 1975, Bull. Mus. Natl.
      Hist. Nat., Paris, (3)324(Zool.)231:1098.
   TYPE LOCALITY: "Muscat?"; corrected to "Darjeeling", West Bengal, India, by
      Boulenger, 1905, Ann. Mag. Nat. Hist., (7)16:640.
   DISTRIBUTION: Uttar Pradesh, Darjeeling (India) and eastern Nepal, 2530–2930 m
      elev.; Yadong, Tibet (China).
   COMMENT: Subgenus *Paa*. Reviewed by Dubois, 1976, Cah. Nepal., Doc., 6:113.
      Synonymy includes *Rana yadongensis* Wu, 1977, Acta Zool. Sinica, 23:51
      (Holotype: CIB 73II02138; Type locality: Yadong, Xizang [=Tibet], alt. 2900 m,
      China), according to Dubois, 1979, Bull. Mens. Soc. Linn. Lyon, 48:657–661.

Rana blythii Boulenger, 1920. Rec. Indian Mus., 20:43–45.
   ORIGINAL NAME: *Rana macrodon* var. *blythii*.
   TYPE(S): Syntypes: BM.
   TYPE LOCALITY: "Burma, Annam, Siam, Malay Peninsula, Sumatra, Borneo,
      Philippines".
   DISTRIBUTION: Burma and Philippines through Thailand to Sumatra and Borneo.
   COMMENT: Subgenus *Euphlyctis*, *Rana grunniens* group. Reviewed by Inger, 1966,
      Fieldiana: Zool., 52:162–175. See also Dring, 1979, Bull. Brit. Mus. (Nat. Hist.),
      Zool., 34:197, whose stated distribution excluded Indochina north of
      Changwat Tak, Thailand. *Rana macrodon* var. *blythii* is a replacement name for
      Rana fusca Blyth, which is preoccupied by *Rana fusca* Meyer. Considered a
      synonym of *Rana macrodon*, without discussion, by Berry, 1975, Amph. Fauna
      Peninsular Malaysia:77.

Rana boulengeri Günther, 1889. Ann. Mag. Nat. Hist., (6)4:222.
   TYPE(S): BM.
   TYPE LOCALITY: Ichang, Hupeh [=Hubei, China].
   DISTRIBUTION: Northwestern and southwestern China, including Guangxi.
   COMMENT: Subgenus *Paa*. Reviewed by Liu, 1950, Fieldiana: Zool., 2:263–272.

Rana boylii Baird, 1854. Proc. Acad. Nat. Sci. Philadelphia, 7:62.
   TYPE(S): Syntypes: USNM 3370 (2 specimens).
   TYPE LOCALITY: "California (interior)"; corrected to El Dorado, California [USA] by
      Cope, 1889, Bull. U.S. Natl. Mus., 34:447; syntypes from El Dorado County,
      California, USA, according to Cochran, 1961, Bull. U.S. Natl. Mus., 220:72.
   DISTRIBUTION: From western Oregon south through California in coastal foothills
      and mountains to Los Angeles County, USA; isolated record in northern Baja
      California, Mexico.
   COMMENT: See Zweifel, 1955, Univ. California Publ. Zool., 54:207–292, and
      Zweifel, 1968, Cat. Am. Amph. Rept., 71.1–2, for review. In the subgenus
      Rana, *Rana boylii* group.

Rana brachytarsus (Günther, 1875). Proc. Zool. Soc. London, 1875:572.
   ORIGINAL NAME: *Polypedates brachytarsus*.
   TYPE(S): Syntypes: BM 1947.2.27.1303.
   TYPE LOCALITY: Anamallais and Sivagiris [India].
   DISTRIBUTION: Kerala, India.

Rana brevipalmata Peters, 1871. Monatsber. Preuss. Akad. Wiss. Berlin, 1871:646.
   TYPE(S): ZMB.
   TYPE LOCALITY: Pegu [Burma]; in error, outside of known distribution (SD).
   DISTRIBUTION: Malabar, Nilgiri Hills, South India.
   COMMENT: In the subgenus *Euphlyctis*, *Rana tigerina* group.

Rana brevipoda Ito, 1941. Nagoya Seibutsugakkai Kiroku, 8:77.
   TYPE(S): Lost.
   TYPE LOCALITY: Nagoya [Honshu, Japan]; Shikatsumura, Nishi-kasugai-gun, Aichi
      [Honshu, Japan], according to Nakamura and Ueno, 1963, Japan. Rept. Amph.
      Color:46.
   DISTRIBUTION: Central and southwestern Honshu, Japan.
   COMMENT: See Okada, 1966, Fauna Japon., Anura:60–62, for review. Considered a
      junior synonym of *Rana porosa* (originally *Tomopterna porosa* Cope, 1868, Proc.
      Acad. Nat. Sci. Philadelphia, 1868:139) by Nakamura and Ueno, 1963, Japan.
      Rept. Amph. Color:46–47. Because *Rana porosa* (*sensu stricto*) originated by
      introgressive hybridization with *Rana nigromaculata* (see Kawamura and
      Nishioka, 1977, *In* Taylor and Guttman (eds.), The Reproductive Biology of
      Amphibians:124–125) the nomenclature of this species is not clear. *Rana
      porosa* is here retained as a "subspecies" of *Rana brevipoda*, following most
      recent authors. In the *Rana esculenta* group, subgenus *Rana*.

Rana brownorum Sanders, 1973. J. Herpetol., 7:87.
   ORIGINAL NAME: *Rana berlandieri brownorum*.
   TYPE(S): Holotype: SM 12498.
   TYPE LOCALITY: "41 mi. W of Xicalango, Campeche, Mexico".
   DISTRIBUTION: Coastal southern Veracruz, Tabasco, Campeche, and adjacent
      Chiapas, Mexico.
   COMMENT: In subgenus *Rana*, *Rana berlandieri* group of the *Rana pipiens* complex.
      Elevated from subspecific status by Hillis, 1981, Copeia, 1981:312–319.

Rana camerani Boulenger, 1886. Bull. Soc. Zool. France, 11:597.
   TYPE(S): Syntypes: ZMB 9345 (3 specimens) and 9344 (1 specimen).
   TYPE LOCALITY: Lake Tabizhuri [2500 m alt.] and Achalkalaki, Caucasus [Georgia,
      USSR].
   DISTRIBUTION: Caucasus region of USSR, Turkey, and northwestern Iran.

COMMENT: In the subgenus *Rana*, *Rana temporaria* group. See Borkin, 1977, Trudy Zool. Inst. Akad. Nauk SSSR, Leningrad, 74:24–31. See comment under *Rana macrocnemis*.

Rana cancrivora Gravenhorst, 1829. Delic. Mus. Zool. Vratislav., 1:41.
TYPE(S): Not traced.
TYPE LOCALITY: Java [Indonesia].
DISTRIBUTION: Malay Peninsula to the Philippines and the Lesser Sundas as far as Flores; Hainan I. (China); Vietnam.
COMMENT: In the subgenus *Euphlyctis*, *Rana tigerina* group. See Inger, 1954, Fieldiana: Zool., 33:260–267, and Inger, 1966, Fieldiana: Zool., 52:175–176, for synonymy and discussion. See Liu et al., 1973, Acta Zool. Sinica, 19(4):395, for comparison to closely related species. See also Berry, 1975, Amph. Fauna Peninsular Malaysia:62–63.

Rana cascadae Slater, 1939. Herpetologica, 1:145.
TYPE(S): Holotype: USNM 10868; formerly CPS 2883.
TYPE LOCALITY: "Elysian Fields, Rainier National Park, Washington", USA.
DISTRIBUTION: Montane meadows and lakes above 1000 m in the Olympic Mountains (Washington, USA) and the Cascade Mountains (Washington, Oregon, and California, USA).
COMMENT: Subgenus *Rana*, *Rana boylii* group. Reviewed by Altig and Dumas, 1971, Cat. Am. Amph. Rept., 105.1–2.

Rana catesbeiana Shaw, 1802. Gen. Zool., 3:106.
TYPE(S): Not known to exist.
TYPE LOCALITY: North America; restricted to "vicinity of Charleston, South Carolina", USA, by Schmidt, 1953, Check List N. Am. Amph. Rept., Ed. 6:79.
DISTRIBUTION: Eastern North America, except southern Florida, north to Nova Scotia, New Brunswick, southern Quebec, and southern Ontario (Canada), west to the central plains and south to Veracruz (Mexico); introduced on Cuba, Isla de Juventud (=Isla de Pinos), Puerto Rico, Hispaniola, and Jamaica in the Antilles; introduced widely in the rest of the world.
COMMENT: Subgenus *Rana*, *Rana catesbeiana* group.

Rana celebensis (Peters, 1872). Monatsber. Preuss. Akad. Wiss. Berlin, 1872:582.
ORIGINAL NAME: *Limnodytes celebensis*.
TYPE(S): Not traced.
TYPE LOCALITY: Manado [Celebes, Indonesia].
DISTRIBUTION: Celebes.
COMMENT: In the subgenus *Hylarana*, *Rana erythraea* group.

Rana chalconota (Schlegel, 1837). Abbild. Amph.:23.
ORIGINAL NAME: *Hyla chalconota*.
TYPE(S): Syntypes: RMNH 5364, 4264 (4 specimens).
TYPE LOCALITY: Java [Indonesia].
DISTRIBUTION: Southern Thailand to Sumatra, Java, Borneo, and Celebes.
COMMENT: In the subgenus *Hylarana*, *Rana chalconota* group. Several of the other members of this species group have been transferred to *Amolops*. Reviewed by Bourret, 1942, Batr. Indochine:366–369, and Inger, 1966, Fieldiana: Zool., 52: 177–183. See also Berry, 1975, Amph. Fauna of Peninsular Malaysia:63–64.

Rana chapaensis (Bourret, 1937). Annexe Bull. Gén. Instr. Publique, Hanoi, 1937(4):34.
ORIGINAL NAME: *Hylarana chapaensis*.
TYPE(S): Syntypes: MNHNP 38-58 to -65 and 48-144 to -147 (12 specimens) (formerly Lab. Sci. Nat. Univ. Hanoi).
TYPE LOCALITY: Chapa, N. Tonkin [Vietnam].
DISTRIBUTION: Known only from the type locality.

COMMENT: Reviewed by Bourret, 1942, Batr. Indochine:341–343, who considered it
to be a member of the subgenus *Hylarana*.

Rana chensinensis David, 1875. J. Trois Voy. Chinois, 1:159.
   TYPE(S): Not traced; possibly MNHNP 1347 (4 specimens) collected by David and
      labelled as *Rana temporaria* from "Mongolia".
   TYPE LOCALITY: Inkiapo, Lao-yu River, Tsinling Mountains, above 1000 m alt.,
      Shensi [=Shaanxi], China.
   DISTRIBUTION: Soviet Far East north to 63°, east to Sakhalin I. and southern Kurile
      Is.; Hokkaido I., Japan; Korea; eastern Mongolia; northeastern, central, and
      western China south to Sichuan and Hubei.
   COMMENT: Subgenus *Rana*, *Rana temporaria* group. Often confused with *Rana*
      amurensis and *Rana asiatica*. Usually treated as a subspecies of *Rana temporaria*.
      Considered a distinct species by Kawamura, 1962, J. Sci. Hiroshima Univ., (B—
      Zool.)20:181–193; Borkin, 1975, Tezisy Dokladov Zool. Inst. Akad. Nauk SSSR,
      Leningrad, 1975:6–7 (who briefly summarized the synonymy); and by Orlova,
      Bakharev, and Borkin, 1977, Trudy Zool. Inst. Akad. Nauk SSSR, Leningrad,
      74:84–85. Synonymy includes *Rana weigoldi* Vogt, 1924, Zool. Anz., 60:339,
      according to Liu, 1950, Fieldiana: Zool. Mem., 2:280–281. See also Liu and Hu,
      1961, Tailless Amph. China:183–188, for Chinese populations; Nakamura and
      Ueno, 1963, Japan. Rept. Amph. Color:43–44, for Japanese population; and
      Orlova, Bakharev, and Borkin, 1977, Trudy Zool. Inst. Akad. Nauk SSSR,
      Leningrad, 74:81–103, for Russian population, and synonymy of *Rana*
      semiplicata Nikolskii, 1918. See comment under *Rana dybowskii*.

Rana chevronta Ye, 1981. Acta Zootaxon. Sinica, 6:334.
   TYPE(S): Holotype: CIB 65I0028.
   TYPE LOCALITY: "Toudaohe, Mt. Emei [=Omei], Sichuan, altitude 1850 m", China.
   DISTRIBUTION: Known only from the type locality.
   COMMENT: Closely related to *Rana japonica*, according to the original description.
      In the *Rana temporaria* group, subgenus *Rana*, by implication.

Rana chiricahuensis Platz and Mecham, 1979. Copeia, 1979:383.
   TYPE(S): Holotype: AMNH 100372.
   TYPE LOCALITY: "Herb Martyr Lake (elev. 1768 m), 6 km W of Portal, Coronado
      National Forest, Cochise County, Arizona", USA.
   DISTRIBUTION: Central Arizona and southwestern New Mexico (USA) south in the
      Sierra Madre Occidental to western Jalisco (Mexico).
   COMMENT: Subgenus *Rana*, *Rana montezumae* group of the *Rana pipiens* complex.
      Reviewed by Platz and Mecham, 1984, Cat. Am. Amph. Rept., 347.1–2;
      however, their distribution map is highly inaccurate for Mexico, not
      including several published records (DMH).

Rana clamitans Latreille, 1801. *In* Sonnini and Latreille, Hist. Nat. Rept., 2:157.
   TYPE(S): Holotype: MNHNP 1397.
   TYPE LOCALITY: "près de Charlestown [=Charleston]", South Carolina, USA.
   DISTRIBUTION: Eastern North America from southern Ontario, Quebec, and
      Manitoba (Canada) south to central Florida and eastern Texas (USA);
      introduced in the vicinity of Victoria (British Columbia, Canada), and in the
      USA at Toad Lake (Washington), near Ogden (Utah), and Hawaii.
   COMMENT: Subgenus *Rana*, *Rana catesbeiana* group. Reviewed by Stewart, 1983, Cat.
      Am. Amph. Rept., 337.1–4.

Rana conaensis Fei and Huang, 1981. Acta Zootaxon. Sinica, 6:212.
   TYPE(S): Holotype: NPIB 770532.
   TYPE LOCALITY: "Mama at Cona Xian, Xizang [=Tibet], altitude 2900" m, China.
   DISTRIBUTION: Southern Tibet, China.
   COMMENT: Closely related to *Rana liebigii*, according to the original description. In
      the subgenus *Paa*, by implication.

Rana cordofana (Steindachner, 1867). Reise Freg. Novara, Amph.:8.
ORIGINAL NAME: *Pyxicephalus cordofanus.*
TYPE(S): NHMW?; not mentioned in NHMW type list of Häupl and Tiedemann, 1978, Kat. Wiss. Samml. Naturhist. Mus. Wien, 2(Vert. 1).
TYPE LOCALITY: "Cordofan", Egypt.
DISTRIBUTION: The Sudan.

Rana cornii Scortecci, 1929. Atti Soc. Ital. Sci. Nat. Mus. Civ. Stor. Nat. Milano, 68: 183.
TYPE(S): Syntypes: MSNM 593–594 (4 specimens); lost in World War II (JLP).
TYPE LOCALITY: "Adamó" and "Pozzi di Guarabà", Eritrea, Ethiopia.
DISTRIBUTION: Eritrea, Ethiopia.
COMMENT: In the subgenus *Euphlyctis*, *Rana cyanophlyctis* group. Related to *Rana cyanophlyctis* and *Rana hexadactyla*, according to the original description.

Rana corrugata Peters, 1863. Monatsber. Preuss. Akad. Wiss. Berlin, 1863:412.
TYPE(S): ZMB.
TYPE LOCALITY: "Rambodde auf Ceylon [Sri Lanka]".
DISTRIBUTION: Sri Lanka.
COMMENT: In the subgenus *Limnonectes*. Reviewed by Kirtisinghe, 1957, Amph. Ceylon:35–39.

Rana crassa Jerdon, 1853. J. Asiat. Soc. Bengal, 22:531.
TYPE(S): ZSI; now probably lost (SD).
TYPE LOCALITY: Carnatic [now part Tamil Nadu and Andhra Pradesh, India].
DISTRIBUTION: Southeastern India, Uttar Pradesh; Nepal; Sri Lanka.
COMMENT: In the subgenus *Euphlyctis*, *Rana tigerina* group. Discussed by Kirtisinghe, 1957, Amph. Ceylon:32–35 (as *Rana tigrina crassa*).

Rana crassiovis Boulenger, 1920. J. Fed. Malay States Mus., 8:292.
TYPE(S): BM.
TYPE LOCALITY: Korinchi, Sumatra, 4000 ft. [Indonesia].
DISTRIBUTION: Sumatra.
COMMENT: In the subgenus *Hylarana*, *Rana chalconota* group. See comment under *Rana chalconota*.

Rana cubitalis Smith, 1917. J. Nat. Hist. Soc. Siam, 2:277.
TYPE(S): Holotype: BM.
TYPE LOCALITY: "Doi Nga Chang, N. Siam . . . . Collected on the banks of a small stream, . . . at about 500 metres elevation".
DISTRIBUTION: Karen Hills of Burma into Thailand.
COMMENT: In the subgenus *Hylarana*, *Rana gracilis* group. See Taylor, 1962, Univ. Kansas Sci. Bull., 43:424–427, and Bourret, 1942, Batr. Indochine:316–317, for discussion.

Rana curtipes Jerdon, 1853. J. Asiat. Soc. Bengal, 22:532.
TYPE(S): Not traced.
TYPE LOCALITY: Malabar (South India).
DISTRIBUTION: Hills of North Canara, Karnataka, Malabar, and Travancore (Kerala, India).
COMMENT: Placed in the *Rana curtipes* group by Boulenger, 1920, Rec. Indian Mus., 20:1–226, who considered it annectant between the subgenera *Rana* and *Hylarana*.

Rana cyanophlyctis Schneider, 1799. Hist. Amph., 1:137.
TYPE(S): Not traced.
TYPE LOCALITY: "India orientalis".
DISTRIBUTION: Southern Iran, Pakistan, and India to Aghanistan, Sri Lanka, and Malaya.

COMMENT: In the subgenus *Euphlyctis*, *Rana cyanophlyctis* group. Reviewed by Bourret, 1942, Batr. Indochine:237–239, and Kirtisinghe, 1957, Amph. Ceylon: 29–32. See also Murthy, 1968, J. Univ. Poona, 34:63–71. See comment under *Rana ehrenbergi*.

Rana daemeli (Steindachner, 1868). Sitzungsber. Akad. Wiss. Wien, Math. Naturwiss. Kl., 57:532.
ORIGINAL NAME: *Hylorana daemeli*.
TYPE(S): Syntypes: NHMW 3244 (7 specimens), 16382 (2 specimens).
TYPE LOCALITY: Cape York, Queensland, Australia.
DISTRIBUTION: South coast of New Guinea and around the north coast from Milne Bay to Huon Peninsula; northeast Queensland, Australia.
COMMENT: In the subgenus *Hylarana*, *Rana papua* group. See Cogger, Cameron, and Cogger, 1983, Zool. Cat. Aust., 1(Amph. Rept.):55, for synonymy.
REVIEWERS: Margaret Davies (MD); Michael J. Tyler (MJT); Richard G. Zweifel (RGZ).

Rana dalmatina Bonaparte, 1840. Mem. Accad. Sci. Torino, Cl. Sci. Fis. Mat. Nat., (2)2: 249.
TYPE(S): Not traced.
TYPE LOCALITY: Not stated; designated as "Dalmatien" (in Yugoslavia) by Mertens and Müller, 1928, Abh. Senckenb. Naturforsch. Ges., 41:19.
DISTRIBUTION: Northern France and extreme southern Sweden to northeastern Spain, Sicily, Greece, Carpathian Ukraine (USSR) and western Turkey.
COMMENT: Subgenus *Rana*, *Rana temporaria* group. Kothbauer and Schenkel-Brunner, 1978, Z. Zool. Syst. Evolutionsforsch., 16:144–148, reported on immunological relationships.

Rana danieli Pillai and Chanda, 1977. J. Bombay Nat. Hist. Soc., 74:136.
TYPE(S): Holotype: ZSIM V/ERS.809.
TYPE LOCALITY: Mawphlang forest, Khasi Hills, Assam, India.
DISTRIBUTION: Khasi hills, Assam, India.
COMMENT: In the subgenus *Hylarana* according to Dubois, 1981, Monit. Zool. Ital., N.S., Suppl., 15:225–281.

Rana darlingi Boulenger, 1902. Proc. Zool. Soc. London, 1902:15.
TYPE(S): Syntypes: BM (2 specimens).
TYPE LOCALITY: "Mazoe" and between Umtali and Marandellas [Zimbabwe].
DISTRIBUTION: Savanna of southern Angola, Shaba (Zaire), Zambia, Zimbabwe, Malawi, and western Mozambique.
COMMENT: In *Hylarana* according to Poynton, 1964, Ann. Natal Mus., 17:119, and Perret, 1977, Rev. Suisse Zool., 84:843. See also Laurent, 1964, Publ. Cult. Companhia Diamantes Angola, 67:132.

Rana dauchina Chang, 1933. China J., 18:209.
TYPE(S): Not traced.
TYPE LOCALITY: Hungchun-ping, Mount Omei, altitude 1300 m, Sichuan, China.
DISTRIBUTION: Sichuan, China.
COMMENT: In the subgenus *Hylarana*. Very similar to *Rana adenopleura* but differs in mating calls and egg deposition (SH). *Rana dauchina* is a replacement name for *Rana musica* Chang and Hsu, 1932, Contrib. Biol. Lab. Sci. Soc. China, Zool. Ser., 8(5):157, which is preoccupied by *Rana musica* Linnaeus. See Liu, 1950, Fieldiana: Zool. Mem., 2:253–260 (as *Rana adenopleura*).

Rana debussyi van Kampen, 1910. Natuurkd. Tijdschr. Nederl. Ind., 59:23.
TYPE(S): Holotype: ZMA; now lost.
TYPE LOCALITY: Deli, Sumatra; corrected to "Bandar Baru, Battak Mountains, Deli, Sumatra, Indonesia", by Daan and Hillenius, 1966, Beaufortia, 13:123.
DISTRIBUTION: Batak Mountains, Sumatra.

COMMENT: In the subgenus *Hylarana*, *Rana luctuosa* group.

Rana delacouri Angel, 1928. Bull. Mus. Natl. Hist. Nat., Paris, (2)34:319.
TYPE(S): Holotype: MNHNP 28-19.
TYPE LOCALITY: Bac-Kan (Tonkin) [Vietnam].
DISTRIBUTION: Known only from the type locality.
COMMENT: Subgenus *Paa*.

Rana demarchii Scortecci, 1929. Atti Soc. Ital. Sci. Nat. Mus. Civ. Stor. Nat. Milano, 68:177.
TYPE(S): Syntypes: MSNM 521 (2 specimens); lost (JLP).
TYPE LOCALITY: "Eritrea", Ethiopia.
DISTRIBUTION: Ethiopia.
COMMENT: In the subgenus *Euphlyctis*, *Rana tigerina* group.

Rana desaegeri Laurent, 1972. Explor. Parc Natl. Virunga, (2)22:91.
TYPE(S): RGMC or MRHN.
TYPE LOCALITY: Zaire, R. Byangolo.
DISTRIBUTION: Rainforest of eastern Zaire.
COMMENT: Subgenus *Rana*.

Rana diplosticta (Günther, 1875). Proc. Zool. Soc. London, 1875:574.
ORIGINAL NAME: *Ixalus diplostictus*.
TYPE(S): BM.
TYPE LOCALITY: Malabar [Kerala, India].
DISTRIBUTION: Malabar (Kerala, India).
COMMENT: See comment under *Discodeles*.

Rana diuata Brown and Alcala, 1977. Proc. Biol. Soc. Washington, 90:669.
TYPE(S): Holotype: CAS 133500.
TYPE LOCALITY: "Tagibo River, south side of Mt. Hilong-hilong, altitude 1000+ meters, Diuata Mountains, Cabadbaran, Agusan del Norte Province, Mindanao Province, Philippines".
DISTRIBUTION: Known only from the type locality.
COMMENT: Related to *Rana kuhlii*, according to the original description; in the subgenus *Limnonectes* by implication.

Rana doriae Boulenger, 1887. Ann. Mus. Civ. Stor. Nat. Genova, (2)5:482.
TYPE(S): MSNG 29298 designated lectotype by Capocaccia, 1957, Ann. Mus. Civ. Stor. Nat. Genova, 69:214.
TYPE LOCALITY: "Thagatà Juwa, Kaw-ka-riet" (=Kokarit, east of Moulmein), northern Tenasserim, Burma.
DISTRIBUTION: Burma to Malaya; Andaman Is., India.
COMMENT: In the subgenus *Euphlyctis*, *Rana grunniens* group. See Taylor, 1962, Univ. Kansas Sci. Bull., 43:390–392; Bourret, 1942, Batr. Indochine:261–263; and Berry, 1975, Amph. Fauna Peninsular Malaysia:65–66, for discussion.

Rana dracomontana Channing, 1978. Ann. Natal Mus., 23:361.
TYPE(S): Holotype: NMP 6221.
TYPE LOCALITY: "Lesotho, top of Sani Pass (29° 35' S, 29° 17' E), 2872 m".
DISTRIBUTION: Lesotho Plateau.
COMMENT: Subgenus *Rana*. Closely related to *Rana angolensis* and *Rana fuscigula* according to the original description.

Rana dunni Zweifel, 1957. Copeia, 1957:78.
TYPE(S): Holotype: AMNH 58409.
TYPE LOCALITY: "Lake Pátzcuaro, Michoacán, Mexico".
DISTRIBUTION: Lake Pátzcuaro, Lake Cuitzeo, and Río de Morelia, Michoacán, Mexico.

COMMENT: Subgenus *Rana, Rana montezumae* group of the *Rana pipiens* complex.

Rana dybowskii Günther, 1876. Ann. Mag. Nat. Hist., (4)17:387.
  TYPE(S): Holotype: BM 1947.2.1.79.
  TYPE LOCALITY: Abrek Bay, near Vladivostok [USSR].
  DISTRIBUTION: Far East USSR; Korea; Tsushima Is., Japan.
  COMMENT: In the *Rana temporaria* group, subgenus *Rana*. Discussed (as *Rana temporaria*) by Shannon, 1956, Herpetologica, 12:38–39. Probably a valid taxon with a nomenclaturally uncertain name (LJB). Genetic relationships with other members of *Rana temporaria* group examined by Kawamura, Nishioka, and Uedo, 1981, Sci. Rep. Lab. Amph. Biol. Hiroshima Univ., 5:196–323. See comment under *Rana chensinensis*.

Rana ehrenbergi Peters, 1863. Monatsber. Preuss. Akad. Wiss. Berlin, 1863:79.
  TYPE(S): ZMB.
  TYPE LOCALITY: Arabia.
  DISTRIBUTION: Southern Arabian Peninsula.
  COMMENT: Subgenus *Euphlyctis, Rana cyanophlyctis* group, according to Dubois, 1981, Monit. Zool. Ital., N.S., Suppl., 15:240, who removed this species from the synonymy of *Rana cyanophlyctis*.

Rana elberti Roux, 1911. Zool. Jahrb., Abt. Syst., 30:504.
  TYPE(S): Holotype: SMF 4470 (formerly 1062.1a).
  TYPE LOCALITY: "Wetar Iliwaki", Lesser Sundas, Indonesia.
  DISTRIBUTION: Wetar I., Sundas.
  COMMENT: In the subgenus *Hylarana, Rana gracilis* group.

Rana ercepeae Dubois, 1974 "1973". Bull. Soc. Zool. France, 98:496.
  TYPE(S): Holotype: MNHNP 1974.1091.
  TYPE LOCALITY: Torrent Jiuli Gad, near village Takundara, northwest of Chainpur, western Nepal (29° 40′ N, 81° 06′ E; altitude 2280 m).
  DISTRIBUTION: Western Nepal.
  COMMENT: Subgenus *Paa*. Closely related to *Rana rostandi*, according to the original description. Reviewed by Dubois, 1976, Cah. Nepal., Doc., 6:179–189.

Rana erythraea (Schlegel, 1837). Abbild. Amph., 1837:27.
  ORIGINAL NAME: *Hyla erythraea*.
  TYPE(S): Syntypes: RMNH 1744 (4 specimens), 1746 (9 specimens), 1749 (1 specimen).
  TYPE LOCALITY: Java [Indonesia].
  DISTRIBUTION: Java, Borneo, Negros, and Panay Is. (Philippines); southern Vietnam and Thailand through Burma to West Bengal and Orissa (India).
  COMMENT: In the subgenus *Hylarana, Rana erythraea* group. Philippine population discussed by Inger, 1954, Fieldiana: Zool., 33:324–328. Taylor, 1962, Univ. Kansas Sci. Bull., 43:417–420, discussed the Thailand populations, and Inger, 1966, Fieldiana: Zool., 52:183–184, reviewed the Bornean population. Reviewed by Bourret, 1942, Batr. Indochine:329–334. See also Berry, 1975, Amph. Fauna Peninsular Malaysia:66–67. SD regards all Indian records as representing *Rana taipehensis*.

Rana esculenta Linnaeus, 1758. Syst. Nat., Ed. 10, 1:212.
  TYPE(S): Unknown.
  TYPE LOCALITY: "In Europae fontibus"; restricted to "Mitteldeutschland" (=Central Germany) by Mertens and Müller, 1928, Abh. Senckenb. Naturforsch. Ges., 41:19; restricted to "Nürnberg", F. R. Germany, by Mertens and Müller, 1940, Abh. Senckenb. Naturforsch. Ges., 451:18.
  DISTRIBUTION: Central Europe.
  COMMENT: Subgenus *Rana, Rana esculenta* group. *Rana esculenta* had a hybrid origin

from *Rana lessonae* and *Rana ridibunda*, according to Berger, 1968, Acta Zool. Cracov., 13:301–324. See Berger, 1983, Experientia, 39:127–130. Many older records apply to *Rana lessonae*.

Rana everetti Boulenger, 1882. Cat. Batr. Sal. Brit. Mus.:72.
TYPE(S): BM.
TYPE LOCALITY: "Zamboanga", Mindanao, Philippines.
DISTRIBUTION: Philippines.
COMMENT: In the subgenus *Hylarana, Rana chalconota* group. See Inger, 1954, Fieldiana: Zool., 33:304–312, for review. See *Rana chalconota*.

Rana exilispinosa Liu and Hu, 1975. Acta Zool. Sinica, 21:265.
TYPE(S): Holotype: CIB (formerly SWIBASC) 64II06414.
TYPE LOCALITY: Daiyun shan, Fujian, altitude 1100 m, China.
DISTRIBUTION: Hong Kong, Fujian and Hunan, China, up to 1400 m elev.
COMMENT: Subgenus *Paa*. Includes *Rana paraspinosa* Dubois, 1975, according to Dubois, 1979, Bull. Mens. Soc. Linn. Lyon, 48:649–656.

Rana fansipani (Bourret, 1939). Annexe Bull. Gén. Instr. Publique, Hanoi, 1939(4):31.
ORIGINAL NAME: *Chaparana fansipani*.
TYPE(S): Holotype: MNHNP 48-139 (formerly Lab. Sci. Nat. Univ. Hanoi B-259).
TYPE LOCALITY: Mount Fan-si-pan, near Chapa (Tonkin) [Vietnam].
DISTRIBUTION: Known only from the type locality.
COMMENT: Reviewed by Bourret, 1942, Batr. Indochine:374–376, and redescribed by Dubois, 1977, Bull. Mus. Natl. Hist. Nat., Paris, (3)480(Zool. 337):981–992. Dubois, 1981, Monit. Zool. Ital., N.S., Suppl., 15:246, noted that this species may be in the subgenus *Paa*, and if so, the subgeneric name carried by this species, *Chaparana*, will have priority.

Rana fasciculispina Inger, 1970. Fieldiana: Zool., 51:169.
TYPE(S): Holotype: National Center for Reference Collections of Thailand, No. 513-1385.
TYPE LOCALITY: "Koo Soi Dao, Changwat Chantaburi, Thailand".
DISTRIBUTION: Thailand.
COMMENT: Subgenus *Paa*.

Rana feae Boulenger, 1887. Ann. Mus. Civ. Stor. Nat. Genova, (2)5:418.
TYPE(S): Holotype: MSNG 29301.
TYPE LOCALITY: "Kakhien Hills", Burma.
DISTRIBUTION: Kakhien Hills, Burma; Yunnan, China.
COMMENT: Subgenus *Paa*. Reviewed by Liu, 1950, Fieldiana: Zool. Mem., 2:277–278.

Rana fisheri Stejneger, 1893. N. Am. Fauna, 7:227.
TYPE(S): Holotype: USNM 18957.
TYPE LOCALITY: "Vegas Valley, [Clark County,] Nevada", USA.
DISTRIBUTION: Springs and marshes of Las Vegas Valley, Clark County, Nevada, USA.
COMMENT: May be extinct; not seen in many years. In the *Rana pipiens* complex, subgenus *Rana*. See comment under *Rana onca*.

Rana florensis Boulenger, 1917. Ann. Mag. Nat. Hist., (6)19:508.
TYPE(S): Not traced.
TYPE LOCALITY: Flores [Indonesia].
DISTRIBUTION: Flores, Sumbawa, and Lombok Is., Indonesia.
COMMENT: In the subgenus *Hylarana, Rana erythraea* group. Considered a subspecies of *Rana papua* (in the *Rana papua* group) by Mertens, 1927, Senckenb. Biol., 9:242, but considered a distinct species by Dunn, 1928, Am. Mus. Novit., 315:6.

Rana forreri Boulenger, 1883. Ann. Mag. Nat. Hist., (5)11:343.
TYPE(S): Holotype: BM 1882.12.5.7.
TYPE LOCALITY: "Presidio", Sinaloa, Mexico.
DISTRIBUTION: Southern Sonora south along the Pacific coast to Jalisco (Mexico); populations of this same species or closely related forms occur south along the Pacific coast to northwestern Costa Rica.
COMMENT: Subgenus *Rana, Rana berlandieri* group of the *Rana pipiens* complex. Removed from the synonymy of *Rana berlandieri* by J. Frost, 1982, Syst. Zool., 31:57–67.

Rana fragilis Liu and Hu, 1973. *In* Liu, Hu, Fei, and Huang, Acta Zool. Sinica, 19(4): 390.
TYPE(S): Holotype: CIB (formerly SWIBASC) 64III3963.
TYPE LOCALITY: China, Hainan Island, Baisha Hsien, Jingko Ling, altitude 780 m.
DISTRIBUTION: Hainan I., China.
COMMENT: Similar to *Rana kuhlii*, according to the original description, and in the subgenus *Limnonectes*, by implication.

Rana fuscigula Duméril and Bibron, 1841. Erp. Gén., 8:386.
TYPE(S): Holotype: MNHNP 4471.
TYPE LOCALITY: "environs du cap de Bonne-Espérance", Rep. South Africa.
DISTRIBUTION: Cape Province to uplands of Natal and Transvaal (Rep. South Africa) and southern Namibia.
COMMENT: Subgenus *Rana*. Reviewed by Poynton, 1964, Ann. Natal Mus., 17:103–109, who clarified the *Rana angolensis–Rana fuscigula* problem. Further diagnosis in Channing, 1978, Ann. Natal Mus., 23:361–365.

Rana galamensis Duméril and Bibron, 1841. Erp. Gén., 8:367.
TYPE(S): Holotype: MNHNP 4442.
TYPE LOCALITY: "Sénégal . . . dans les étangs de Galam".
DISTRIBUTION: Subsaharan Africa in savannas from Senegal to Mozambique.
COMMENT: In *Hylarana* according to Perret, 1977, Rev. Suisse Zool., 84:845. *Rana galamensis bravana*, of Kenya and Somalia to eastern Zaire and Mozambique, may be a distinct species according to Loveridge, 1957, Bull. Mus. Comp. Zool., 117:338. See Lanza, 1981, Monit. Zool. Ital., N.S., Suppl., 15:163, and Perret, 1977, Rev. Suisse Zool., 84:843, for synonymy under *Hylarana galamensis*, including *bravana, oubanghiensis, magrotti, fiechteri,* and *somalica*.

Rana garoensis Boulenger, 1920. Rec. Indian Mus., 20:170.
TYPE(S): BM.
TYPE LOCALITY: "Garo Hills, Assam, above Tura, at an altitude of 3,500 to 3,900 feet", India.
DISTRIBUTION: Assam and Meghalaya, India.
COMMENT: In the subgenus *Hylarana, Rana erythraea* group.

Rana gerbillus Annandale, 1912. Rec. Indian Mus., 8:10.
TYPE(S): Holotype: ZSI 16926.
TYPE LOCALITY: "Yembung, Abor foot-hills at an altitude of 1,100 ft.", Arunachal Pradesh, India (in region claimed by China).
DISTRIBUTION: Meghalaya, Arunachal Pradesh (India); Tibet (China); Burma.
COMMENT: In the subgenus *Hylarana, Rana chalconota* group (note that some former members of this group have been transferred to *Amolops*). Allied to *Rana jerboa* (=*Amolops jerboa* of this list), according to the original description.

Rana glandulosa Boulenger, 1882. Cat. Batr. Sal. Brit. Mus.:73.
TYPE(S): BM.
TYPE LOCALITY: "Sarawak", Malaysia (Borneo).
DISTRIBUTION: Southern Thailand to Malaya and Borneo.

COMMENT: In the subgenus *Hylarana*, *Rana luctuosa* group. See Taylor, 1962, Univ. Kansas Sci. Bull., 43:436–440; Inger, 1966, Fieldiana: Zool., 52:184–187; and Bourret, 1942, Batr. Indochine:362–364. See also Berry, 1975, Amph. Fauna Peninsular Malaysia:67–68.

Rana gracilipes Gressitt, 1938. Proc. Biol. Soc. Washington, 51:161.
TYPE(S): Holotype: MVZ 23108.
TYPE LOCALITY: Kuraru, altitude 150 meters Koshun district, near South Cape, Formosa [=Taiwan], China.
DISTRIBUTION: Southern Taiwan, China.
COMMENT: Probably a junior synonym of *Microhyla inornata* (MM).

Rana gracilis Gravenhorst, 1829. Delic. Mus. Zool. Vratislav., 1:45.
TYPE(S): Not traced.
TYPE LOCALITY: Sri Lanka.
DISTRIBUTION: Sri Lanka.
COMMENT: In the subgenus *Hylarana*, *Rana gracilis* group. Reviewed by Kirtisinghe, 1957, Amph. Ceylon:48–49. South India records are referable to *Rana malabarica* and *Rana temporalis*; southeastern Asian records are referable to the *Rana limnocharis* complex (SD).

Rana graeca Boulenger, 1891. Ann. Mag. Nat. Hist., (6)8:346.
TYPE(S): Not traced.
TYPE LOCALITY: Parnassus, Greece.
DISTRIBUTION: Balkan peninsula from central Yugoslavia and southern Bulgaria south; Italy.
COMMENT: In the *Rana temporaria* group, subgenus *Rana*.

Rana grahami Boulenger, 1917. Ann. Mag. Nat. Hist., (8)20:415.
TYPE(S): Not traced.
TYPE LOCALITY: Yunnanfu, Yunnan, China.
DISTRIBUTION: Sichuan, Guizhou, and Yunnan, China.
COMMENT: Boring, 1940, Peking Nat. Hist. Bull., 15:49–50, considered this species a synonym of *Rana andersonii*, but Liu and Hu, 1961, Tailless Amph. China:144–147, and Liu, Hu, and Yang, 1962, Acta Zool. Sinica, 14(3):383–385, considered it a distinct species. Discussed (as *Rana schmackeri*) by Chang and Hsu, 1932, Contrib. Biol. Lab. Sci. Soc. China, Zool. Ser., 8:165–169. See comment under *Rana margaratae*.

Rana greenii Boulenger, 1904. Spolia Zeylan., 2:74.
TYPE(S): BM.
TYPE LOCALITY: Punduloya, Central Ceylon [Sri Lanka].
DISTRIBUTION: Hills of central Sri Lanka.
COMMENT: In the subgenus *Euphlyctis*, *Rana tigerina* group. Reviewed (as *Rana limnocharis greenii*) by Kirtisinghe, 1957, Amph. Ceylon:40–43.

Rana grisea van Kampen, 1913. Nova Guinea, 9:460.
TYPE(S): Holotype: ZMA 5704.
TYPE LOCALITY: Went Mountains, ± 1300 m [Irian Jaya (New Guinea), Indonesia].
DISTRIBUTION: New Guinea; Ceram I.
COMMENT: In the subgenus *Hylarana*, *Rana papua* group.
REVIEWERS: Margaret Davies (MD); Michael J. Tyler (MJT); Richard G. Zweifel (RGZ).

Rana grunniens Sonnini and Latreille, 1801. Hist. Nat. Rept., 2:155.
TYPE(S): Not stated; 2 specimens in MNHNP, regarded as 'cotypes' by Duméril and Bibron, 1841, Erp. Gén., 8:341 and 382, who also noted that they were not conspecific and designated MNHNP 4461 as lectotype; this specimen was considered holotype by Guibé, 1950 "1948", Cat. Types Amph. Mus. Natl. Hist. Nat.:37.
TYPE LOCALITY: "la Florida et . . . les côtes de la Caroline" (in error); corrected to "Amboine", Indonesia, by Duméril and Bibron, 1841, Erp. Gén., 8:382.
DISTRIBUTION: Java; Celebes; Amboina I.
COMMENT: In the subgenus *Euphlyctis*, *Rana grunniens* group. Discussed by van Kampen, 1923, Amph. Indo-Aust. Arch.:172–173. The nomenclature and type designations are complex. See Harper, 1940, Am. Midl. Nat., 23:692–723 (who regarded this as an older name for *Rana grylio*), and Stejneger, 1940, Copeia, 1940:149–151, for discussion.

Rana grylio Stejneger, 1901. Proc. U.S. Natl. Mus., 24:212.
TYPE(S): Holotype: USNM 27443.
TYPE LOCALITY: "Bay St. Louis, Hancock Co., Mississippi", USA.
DISTRIBUTION: South Carolina and eastern Texas along the coastal plain to peninsular Florida, USA; introduced on Andros I. and New Providence I., Bahamas.
COMMENT: Subgenus *Rana*, *Rana catesbeiana* group. Reviewed by Altig and Lohoefener, 1982, Cat. Am. Amph. Rept., 286:1–2. See comment under *Rana grunniens*.

Rana guentheri Boulenger, 1882. Cat. Batr. Sal., Brit. Mus.:48.
TYPE(S): Syntypes: BM.
TYPE LOCALITY: "Amoy" and "China".
DISTRIBUTION: Central Vietnam throughout southern China (north to Yangtze River), including Hainan and Taiwan.
COMMENT: In the subgenus *Hylarana*, *Rana gracilis* group. Discussed by Pope, 1931, Bull. Am. Mus. Nat. Hist., 61:529–531; Liu, 1950, Fieldiana: Zool. Mem., 2:318–321; and Bourret, 1942, Batr. Indochine:309–312. See also Liu and Hu, 1961, Tailless Amph. China:191–193. Synonymy includes *Rana elegans* Boulenger, 1882, according to Boulenger, 1907, Proc. Zool. Soc. London, 1907:481. See also Perret, 1977, Rev. Suisse Zool., 84:843.

Rana hascheana (Stoliczka, 1870). J. Asiat. Soc. Bengal, 39:147.
ORIGINAL NAME: *Polypedates hascheanus*.
TYPE(S): Syntypes (probable): ?BM.
TYPE LOCALITY: "higher forests (about 1000 feet above sea level) in the island of Penang", Malaysia.
DISTRIBUTION: India to Vietnam and Java.
COMMENT: In the subgenus *Euphlyctis*, *Rana grunniens* group. See Taylor, 1962, Univ. Kansas Sci. Bull., 43:412–417; Bourret, 1942, Batr. Indochine:274–276; and Berry, 1975, Amph. Fauna Peninsular Malaysia:68–69, for discussion.

Rana hazarensis Dubois and Khan, 1979. J. Herpetol., 13:403.
TYPE(S): Holotype: MNHNP 1978.3056.
TYPE LOCALITY: "near Datta, northern Pakistan (Manshera District, Hazera Division, 34° 15' N 73° 15' E, elevation about 1200 m)".
DISTRIBUTION: Known only from the type locality.
COMMENT: In the subgenus *Paa*, according to the original description.

Rana heckscheri Wright, 1924. Proc. Biol. Soc. Washington, 37:143.
TYPE(S): Holotype: CU 1025; apparently lost, although Figs. 5 and 6 in Plate 38 of Wright, 1932, Life Hist. Frogs Okefinokee Swamp, are of the holotype, according to Sanders, 1984, Cat. Am. Amph. Rept., 348.2.
TYPE LOCALITY: "Alligator Swamp, Callahan, [Nassau County,] Florida", USA.
DISTRIBUTION: Southern North Carolina and southern Mississippi to northern Florida on the coastal plain, USA.

COMMENT: In the *Rana catesbeiana* group, subgenus *Rana*. Reviewed by Sanders, 1984, Cat. Am. Amph. Rept., 348.1–2.

Rana heinrichi Ahl, 1933. Mitt. Zool. Mus. Berlin, 19:577.
   ORIGINAL NAME: *Rana* (*Rana*) *heinrichi*.
   TYPE(S): ZMB.
   TYPE LOCALITY: "Nord-Celebes (Ile-Ile, 500 m)", Indonesia.
   DISTRIBUTION: Celebes, Indonesia.

Rana hexadactyla Lesson, 1834. *In* Bélang, Voy. India Orient., Zool.:331.
   TYPE(S): Not traced.
   TYPE LOCALITY: South India.
   DISTRIBUTION: Southern India, Rajasthan and Bengal; Sri Lanka; Nepal.
   COMMENT: In the subgenus *Euphlyctis*, *Rana cyanophlyctis* group, according to Dubois, 1981, Monit. Zool. Ital., N.S., Suppl., 15:240. See Mondal, 1970, Sci. Cult., 36:138–143, and Kirtisinghe, 1957, Amph. Ceylon:26–29.

Rana holsti Boulenger, 1892. Ann. Mag. Nat. Hist., (6)10:302.
   TYPE(S): Holotype: BM 92.9.3.19.
   TYPE LOCALITY: Okinawa Shima, Riu Kiu [Japan].
   DISTRIBUTION: Okinawa, Ryukyu Is., Japan.
   COMMENT: In the subgenus *Babina* according to Nakamura and Ueno, 1963, Japan. Rept. Amph. Color:54, but in the more inclusive subgenus *Hylarana* by implication of Dubois, 1981, Monit. Zool. Ital., N.S., Suppl., 15:225–284. See Matsui and Utsunomiya, 1983, J. Herpetol., 17:32–37, for discussion.

Rana holtzi Werner, 1898. Zool. Anz., 21:222.
   TYPE(S): Syntypes: NHMW 15086, MCZ 8131, ZFMK 18913–14.
   TYPE LOCALITY: "an einem bisher noch unbekannten See, Maidan Göl, im cilischen Taurus, 2400 mm hoch gefangen", Turkey.
   DISTRIBUTION: Cilician Taurus, Turkey
   COMMENT: In the *Rana temporaria* group, subgenus *Rana*. See Barar, 1969, Sci. Rep. Fac. Sci. Ege Univ., Izmir, 80:1–78, and Başoğlu and Özeti, 1973, Türkiye Amph.:105–106. See comment under *Rana macrocnemis*.

Rana hosii Boulenger, 1891. Ann. Mag. Nat. Hist., (6)7:290.
   TYPE(S): BM.
   TYPE LOCALITY: Mount Dulit, Borneo.
   DISTRIBUTION: Peninsular Thailand, Malaya, and Borneo.
   COMMENT: In the subgenus *Hylarana*, *Rana chalconota* group. See comment under *Rana chalconota*. Reviewed by Bourret, 1942, Batr. Indochine:385–387 (as *Staurois hosii*), and by Inger, 1966, Fieldiana: Zool., 52:187–191. See also Berry, 1975, Amph. Fauna Peninsular Malaysia:69–70.

Rana hubeiensis Fei and Ye, 1982. Acta Zool. Sinica, 28(3):293.
   TYPE(S): Holotype: CIB 74I0570.
   TYPE LOCALITY: Lichuan Xian, Hubei, alt. 1070 [China].
   DISTRIBUTION: Hubei and Hunan, China.
   COMMENT: Related to *Rana plancyi*, according to the original description, and by implication in the *Rana esculenta* group, subgenus *Rana*.

Rana humeralis Boulenger, 1887. Ann. Mus. Civ. Stor. Nat. Genova, (2)5:420.
   TYPE(S): MSNG 29299 designated lectotype by Capocaccia, 1957, Ann. Mus. Civ. Stor. Nat. Genova, 69:215.
   TYPE LOCALITY: "Bhamo, [and] Teinzo", Burma; restricted to Bhamo, Burma, by lectotype designation.
   DISTRIBUTION: Upper Burma.
   COMMENT: In the subgenus *Hylarana*, *Rana erythraea* group. Reviewed by Bourret, 1942, Batr. Indochine:324–325.

Rana ibanorum Inger, 1964. Fieldiana: Zool., 44:151.
TYPE(S): Holotype: FMNH 76894.
TYPE LOCALITY: "a small tributary at the juncture of the Baleh and Putai Rivers (1°
    48' N, 113° 45' E), Third Division, Sarawak", Malaysia (Borneo).
DISTRIBUTION: Northern Borneo.
COMMENT: In the subgenus *Limnonectes* according to Dubois, 1981, Monit. Zool.
    Ital., N.S., Suppl., 15:225–284. Reviewed by Inger, 1966, Fieldiana: Zool., 52:
    191–196.

Rana iberica Boulenger, 1879. Bull. Soc. Zool. France, 4:177.
TYPE(S): Not traced.
TYPE LOCALITY: Coimbra [Portugal], Pontevedra [Spain]; restricted to "Coimbra,
    Portugal" by Mertens and Müller, 1928, Abh. Senckenb. Naturforsch. Ges.,
    41:20.
DISTRIBUTION: Portugal; northwestern and central Spain.
COMMENT: In the *Rana temporaria* group, subgenus *Rana*.

Rana ijimae (Stejneger, 1901). Proc. Biol. Soc. Washington, 14:190.
ORIGINAL NAME: *Buergeria ijimae*.
TYPE(S): Holotype: TIU 19(914).
TYPE LOCALITY: Okinawa Shima [Ryukyu Is., Japan].
DISTRIBUTION: Okinawa, Ryukyu Is., Japan.
COMMENT: In the subgenus *Hylarana*. Reviewed by Okada, 1966, Fauna Japon.,
    Anura:121–123. See comment under *Rana narina*. Regarded as a synonym of
    Rana narina by Inger, 1947, Fieldiana: Zool., 32:331–332, and Nakamura and
    Ueno, 1963, Japan. Rept. Amph. Color:51.

Rana ingeri Kiew, 1978. Malay. Nat. J., 31:223.
TYPE(S): Holotype: FMNH 83012.
TYPE LOCALITY: Not stated.   •
DISTRIBUTION: Java, Mentawai Island chain on Enggano, Siberut, and Nias.
COMMENT: In the subgenus *Euphlyctis*, *Rana grunniens* group, *Rana macrodon*
    complex. See comment under *Rana malesiana*.

Rana intermedia Rao, 1937. Proc. Indian Acad. Sci., (B)6:394.
ORIGINAL NAME: *Rana intermedius*.
TYPE(S): Holotype: CCB; now lost (SD).
TYPE LOCALITY: "Saklespur, Hassan District, Mysore State", India.
DISTRIBUTION: Mysore, India.
COMMENT: Subgenus *Hylarana* and related to *Rana gracilis* and *Rana temporalis*,
    according to the original description.

Rana ishikawae (Stejneger, 1901). Proc. Biol. Soc. Washington, 14:190.
ORIGINAL NAME: *Buergeria ishikawae*.
TYPE(S): Holotype: TIU 30.
TYPE LOCALITY: Okinawa Shima [Japan].
DISTRIBUTION: Amami Oshima I. and Okinawa I., Ryukyu Is., Japan.
COMMENT: In the subgenus *Hylarana*, *Rana chalconota* group. See comment under
    Rana chalconota. See Stejneger, 1907, Bull. U.S. Natl. Mus., 58:131–134, and
    Okada, 1931, Tailless Batr. Japan. Emp.:166–168, for review and discussion.
    See Kuramoto, 1979, Japan. J. Herpetol., 8:14, for geographic records.

Rana japonica Günther, 1859 "1858". Cat. Batr. Sal. Coll. Brit. Mus.:17.
ORIGINAL NAME: *Rana temporaria* var. *japonica*.
TYPE(S): Syntypes: BM 44.2.22.106A–B (Japan), 54.2.10.26 (Ningpo); Chusan
    specimens probably lost (LJB); Boulenger, 1920, Rec. Indian Mus., 20:95,
    designated as "types" 2 specimens from Japan.
TYPE LOCALITY: "Ningpo"; "Chusan" (Zhejiang, China); "Japan".
DISTRIBUTION: China (except northern part); Japan (Honshu, Kyushu, and Shikoku
    Is.).

COMMENT: In the *Rana temporaria* group, subgenus *Rana*. See Stejneger, 1907, Bull. U.S. Natl. Mus., 58:107–113; Pope, 1931, Bull. Am. Mus. Nat. Hist., 61:525–529; Nakamura and Ueno, 1963, Japan. Rept. Amph. Color:41–42; Liu, 1950, Fieldiana: Zool. Mem., 2:285–292 (as *Rana japonica* and *Rana chaochiaoensis*); and Kuramoto, 1974, Copeia, 1974:815–822. Includes *Rana chaochiaoensis* Liu, 1945, J. West China Border Res. Soc., (B)16:7, according to Liu and Hu, 1961, Tailless Amph. China:180–181. See comment under *Rana longicrus*.

Rana jimiensis Tyler, 1963. Rec. Aust. Mus., 26:126.
TYPE(S): Holotype: AM R14711.
TYPE LOCALITY: "Manjim, Ganz River", Jimi River Valley, Western Highlands Province, Papua New Guinea.
DISTRIBUTION: Jimi River Valley, Papua New Guinea.
REVIEWERS: Margaret Davies (MD); Michael J. Tyler (MJT); Richard G. Zweifel (RGZ).

Rana johni Blair, 1965. Copeia, 1965:517.
TYPE(S): Holotype: AMNH 52908.
TYPE LOCALITY: "Arroyo Sacahuite at Palictla, 6 mi. (by highway) north of Tamazunchale, San Luis Potosi, Mexico".
DISTRIBUTION: Southeastern San Luis Potosí and eastern Hidalgo, Mexico.
COMMENT: *Rana johni* is a replacement name for *Rana moorei* Blair, 1947, Am. Mus. Novit., 1353:5, which is preoccupied by *Anchylorana moorei* Taylor, 1942, Univ. Kansas Sci. Bull., 28:199–235, after the transfer of *Anchylorana* to *Rana* by Holman, 1963, Herpetologica, 19:160–168. In the *Rana tarahumarae* group, subgenus *Rana*.

Rana johnstoni Günther, 1893. Proc. Zool. Soc. London, 1893:620.
TYPE(S): Syntypes: BM.
TYPE LOCALITY: Chiromo, Nyasaland [=Malawi]; locality doubtful, according to Poynton, 1964, Senckenb. Biol., 45:203.
DISTRIBUTION: Southern Malawi (Mt. Mulanje) and mountains of eastern Zimbabwe.
COMMENT: Discussed by Stewart, 1967, Amph. Malawi:57–58, and by Poynton, 1964, Senckenb. Biol., 45:203. See Poynton, 1966, Arnoldia, Zimbabwe, 2:1–3, for subspecies (*Rana johnstoni inyangae*).

Rana kampeni Boulenger, 1920. Rec. Indian Mus., 20:213.
TYPE(S): Holotype: ZMA; now lost.
TYPE LOCALITY: Bander Baru, Battak Mountains, Deli, Sumatra, Indonesia.
DISTRIBUTION: Deli, Sumatra.
COMMENT: In the subgenus *Hylarana*, *Rana chalconota* group. See comment under *Rana chalconota*. *Rana kampeni* Boulenger, 1920, is a replacement name for *Rana pantherina* van Kampen, 1909, Natuurkd. Tijdschr. Nederl. Ind., 69:22, which is preoccupied.

Rana keralensis Dubois, 1980. Bull. Mus. Natl. Hist. Nat., Paris, (4)2A:928.
TYPE(S): BM.
TYPE LOCALITY: Malabar, Kerala [India].
DISTRIBUTION: Mountains of Kerala, India.
COMMENT: In the subgenus *Euphlyctis*, *Rana tigerina* group. *Rana keralensis* is a replacement name for *Rana (Euphlyctis) verrucosa* Günther, 1875, which is preoccupied by *Rana temporaria verrucosus* Koch, 1872.

Rana khammonensis Smith, 1929. Ann. Mag. Nat. Hist., (10)3:296.
TYPE(S): Holotype: BM 1928.6.29.14.
TYPE LOCALITY: Napé, Khammon Plateau [Laos].
DISTRIBUTION: Annam (Vietnam) and adjacent Laos.

COMMENT: Reviewed by Bourret, 1942, Batr. Indochine:260.

Rana khasiana (Anderson, 1871). J. Asiat. Soc. Bengal, 1871:23.
ORIGINAL NAME: *Pyxicephalus khasianus*.
TYPE(S): Not traced.
TYPE LOCALITY: Khasi Hills [India].
DISTRIBUTION: Khasi Hills, Assam, India.
COMMENT: In the subgenus *Limnonectes*.

Rana kohchangae Smith, 1922. J. Nat. Hist. Soc. Siam, 4:223–225.
TYPE(S): Syntypes: BM (2 specimens) (formerly M. Smith 2976 and 2985).
TYPE LOCALITY: "Koh Chang (Chang Island) In the Inner Gulf of Siam", Thailand.
DISTRIBUTION: Koh Chang, Koh Kut, Koh Mehsi, and on the mainland at Ok Yam, Thailand.
COMMENT: In the subgenus *Euphlyctis*, *Rana grunniens* group. See Taylor, 1962, Univ. Kansas Sci. Bull., 43:393–395, and Bourret, 1942, Batr. Indochine:263–265, for review.

Rana kuangwuensis Liu and Hu, 1966. *In* Hu, Djao, and Liu, Acta Zool. Sinica, 18:77.
TYPE(S): Holotype: CIB (formerly SWIBASC) 610551.
TYPE LOCALITY: "Kuang-wu Shan, Nankiang Hsien, Szechwan [=Sichuan], alt. 1650 m.", China.
DISTRIBUTION: Sichuan, China.
COMMENT: Subgenus *Hylarana*. Related to *Rana margaratae*, according to the original description.

Rana kuhlii Tschudi, 1838. Classif. Batr.:40.
TYPE(S): Syntypes: MNHNP 4469 (1 specimen), RMNH (2 specimens).
TYPE LOCALITY: "Java", Indonesia.
DISTRIBUTION: Assam (India) and Yunnan and Taiwan (China) through Indochina to the Greater Sundas as far as Celebes.
COMMENT: In the subgenus *Limnonectes*. See Taylor, 1962, Univ. Kansas Sci. Bull., 43:408–412; Okada, 1931, Tailless Batr. Japan. Emp.:160–162; Bourret, 1942, Batr. Indochine:278–282; Pope, 1931, Bull. Am. Mus. Nat. Hist., 61:495–499; and Inger, 1966, Fieldiana: Zool., 52:196–202, for discussion and review. See also Berry, 1975, Amph. Fauna Peninsular Malaysia:71–72, and Liu and Hu, 1961, Tailless Amph. China:147–149. Though usually attributed to Duméril and Bibron (1841), Tschudi (1838) had already provided a perfectly valid description. This involves a change in the status of the type material (MSH).

Rana latastei Boulenger, 1879. Bull. Soc. Zool. France, 4:180.
TYPE(S): Holotype: MNHNP 5750.
TYPE LOCALITY: Neighborhood of Milan [Italy].
DISTRIBUTION: Plains of northern Italy and adjacent Switzerland; Nova Gorica hills in western Yugoslavia.
COMMENT: In the *Rana temporaria* group, subgenus *Rana*. Reviewed by Bruno, 1977, Natura, Milano, 68:145–156.

Rana lateralis Boulenger, 1887. Ann. Mus. Civ. Stor. Nat. Genova, (2)5:483.
TYPE(S): Holotype: MSNG 29324.
TYPE LOCALITY: "Kaw-ka-riet" (=Kokarit), east of Moulmein, Tenasserim, Burma.
DISTRIBUTION: Northern, central, and eastern Thailand; southern Burma; northern Vietnam.
COMMENT: See Taylor, 1962, Univ. Kansas Sci. Bull., 43:443–446, and Bourret, 1942, Batr. Indochine:302–304, for discussion.

Rana laticeps Boulenger, 1882. Cat. Batr. Sal. Brit. Mus.:20.
TYPE(S): Syntypes: BM.
TYPE LOCALITY: "Khassya" (=Khasi Hills, Assam) and "Bengal", India.
DISTRIBUTION: Assam (India) to Thailand, Malaya, and Borneo.

COMMENT: In the subgenus *Limnonectes* according to Dubois, 1981, Monit. Zool. Ital., N.S., Suppl., 15:225–284. See Taylor, 1962, Univ. Kansas Sci. Bull., 43: 405–407; Inger, 1966, Fieldiana: Zool., 52:202–205; and Bourret, 1942, Batr. Indochine:282–284, for review. See also Berry, 1975, Amph. Fauna Peninsular Malaysia:72–73.

Rana latouchii Boulenger, 1899. Proc. Zool. Soc. London, 1899:167.
  TYPE(S): Syntypes: BM (2 specimens).
  TYPE LOCALITY: "Kuatun, a village about 270 miles from Foochow, in the mountains at the North-west of the Province of Fokien [=Fujian], at an altitude of 3000 to 4000 feet or more", China.
  DISTRIBUTION: Taiwan, Zhejiang, Fujian, Guangxi, Hunan, Jiangxi, Jiangxu, and Anhui, China.
  COMMENT: In the subgenus *Hylarana*, *Rana gracilis* group. See Pope, 1931, Bull. Am. Mus. Nat. Hist., 61:531–534, and Liu and Hu, 1961, Tailless Amph. China:188–190.

Rana leithii Boulenger, 1888. Ann. Mag. Nat. Hist., (6)2:506.
  TYPE(S): Holotype: BM.
  TYPE LOCALITY: Matheran, Bombay, India.
  DISTRIBUTION: Western Ghats from Kasara Ghats near Bombay, southward to central Kerala; Bastar District, Madhya Pradesh, India.
  COMMENT: See comment under *Discodeles*. See Daniel and Selukar, 1963, J. Bombay Nat. Hist. Soc., 60:743.

Rana lemairii Witte, 1921. Rev. Zool. Afr., 9:3.
  TYPE(S): RGMC.
  TYPE LOCALITY: Lofoi, Katanga [=Shaba Province, Zaire].
  DISTRIBUTION: Southern Zaire, western Zambia, and northeastern Angola.
  COMMENT: A *Hylarana* according to Laurent, 1964, Publ. Cult. Companhia Diamantes Angola, 67:133. Discussed (as *Rana albolabris lemairii*) by Schmidt and Inger, 1959, Explor. Parc Natl. Upemba, 56:41–48, and (as *Hylarana lemairei*) by Perret, 1977, Rev. Suisse Zool., 84:844.

Rana leptodactyla Boulenger, 1882. Cat. Batr. Sal. Brit. Mus.:57.
  TYPE(S): Syntypes: BM.
  TYPE LOCALITY: "Malabar" and "Anamallays", India.
  DISTRIBUTION: Malabar and Anamallais, Kerala India.
  COMMENT: See comment under *Discodeles*.

Rana leptoglossa (Cope, 1868). Proc. Acad. Nat. Sci. Philadelphia, 20:140.
  ORIGINAL NAME: *Hylorana leptoglossa*.
  TYPE(S): Syntypes: MCZ 1588 (3 specimens).
  TYPE LOCALITY: Assam [India].
  DISTRIBUTION: Assam (India) through Burma to southern Thailand and Annam (Vietnam).
  COMMENT: In the subgenus *Hylarana*, *Rana gracilis* group. Reviewed (as *Hylarana leptoglossa*) by Bourret, 1942, Batr. Indochine:314–316.

Rana lepus (Andersson, 1903). Verh. Zool. Bot. Wien, 53:142.
  ORIGINAL NAME: *Chiromantis lepus*.
  TYPE(S): Holotype: NHRM.
  TYPE LOCALITY: "Kamerun".
  DISTRIBUTION: Cameroon to Zaire.
  COMMENT: A *Hylarana* according to Perret, 1977, Rev. Suisse Zool., 84:853–855. See comment under *Rana occidentalis*.

Rana lessonae Camerano, 1882 "1881". C. R. Assoc. Franç. Avanc. Sci., Paris, 10:686.
ORIGINAL NAME: *Rana esculenta* var. *lessonae*.
TYPE(S): Not traced.
TYPE LOCALITY: "Piemont; . . . Lombardie, . . . France, . . . Sicile (Modica) . . .".
DISTRIBUTION: France and southern Sweden to Volga River basin (USSR), Italy, and
   northern Balkans; possibly introduced into southern England.
COMMENT: In the *Rana esculenta* group, subgenus *Rana*. Formerly often confused
   with *Rana esculenta*. Uzzell and Hotz, 1979, Mitt. Zool. Mus. Berlin, 55:13–27,
   noted that *"Rana lessonae"* from the Italian peninsula represented an
   undescribed species.

Rana leytensis Boettger, 1893. Zool. Anz., 16:365.
TYPE(S): Holotype: SMF 4931 (formerly 1017.3a).
TYPE LOCALITY: Leyte, Philippinen
DISTRIBUTION: Philippine Is. south of Mindoro and Luzon, except Palawan.
COMMENT: In the subgenus *Euphlyctis*, *Rana grunniens* group. Considered a
   subspecies of *Rana microdisca* by Mertens, 1967, Senckenb. Biol., 48:45, but
   he provided no discussion. Treated as a distinct species by Inger, 1966,
   Fieldiana: Zool., 52:214. Reviewed (as *Rana microdisca leytensis*) by Inger, 1954,
   Fieldiana: Zool., 53:291–300.

Rana liebigii Günther, 1860. Proc. Zool. Soc. London, 1860:157.
TYPE(S): BM 1947.2.1.88 designated lectotype by Dubois, 1976, Cah. Nepal., Doc.,
   6:46.
TYPE LOCALITY: Nepal.
DISTRIBUTION: Himalayan region of eastern India; Nepal; southern Tibet, China.
COMMENT: Subgenus *Paa*. See Dubois, 1976, Cah. Nepal., Doc., 6:77, and Herpetol.
   Dep. Sichuan Biol. Res. Inst., 1977, Acta Zool. Sinica, 23:56–57.

Rana limnocharis Boie, 1835. *In* Wiegmann, Nova Acta Acad. Caesar. Leop. Carol.,
   Halle, 17:225.
TYPE(S): Not traced.
TYPE LOCALITY: Java [Indonesia].
DISTRIBUTION: China (Taiwan, Sichuan, and south of Chuanche [=Yangtze] River
   and north to Shandong) to Nepal, Pakistan, India, Sri Lanka, southern Japan,
   Philippines, Greater Sunda Is., and the Lesser Sundas as far east as Flores.
COMMENT: In the subgenus *Euphlyctis*, *Rana tigerina* group. Includes *Rana vittigera*.
   SCA regards Afghanistan records as in error. Japanese population reviewed
   by Okada, 1966, Fauna Japon., Anura:112–121. Chinese population reviewed
   by Liu, 1950, Fieldiana: Zool. Mem., 2:315–318, and Pope, 1931, Bull. Am.
   Mus. Nat. Hist., 61:491–495. Philippine populations reviewed by Inger, 1954,
   Fieldiana: Zool., 33:267–274. Borneo population reviewed by Inger, 1966,
   Fieldiana: Zool., 52:205–206. Ceylon population discussed by Kirtisinghe,
   1957, Amph. Ceylon:38–40. Southeastern Asia distribution reviewed by
   Bourret, 1942, Batr. Indochine:249–255. See also Berry, 1975, Amph. Fauna
   Peninsular Malaysia:73–74. Dubois, 1975, C. R. Hebd. Séances Acad. Sci.,
   Paris, (D)281:1717–1720, regarded Nepalese *"Rana limnocharis"* as referable to
   four species, including *Rana nepalensis*, *Rana pierrei*, and *Rana syhadrensis*.

Rana livida (Blyth, 1855). J. Asiat. Soc. Bengal, 24:718.
ORIGINAL NAME: *Polypedates lividus*.
TYPE(S): Not traced.
TYPE LOCALITY: Tenasserim [Burma].
DISTRIBUTION: Darjeeling region and mountains of Assam (India) through Burma to
   Vietnam; Shaanxi, Jiangxi, Fujian, Guangdong, Anhui, Zhejiang, Hunan,
   ?Yunnan, Guizhou, and Hainan I., China.
COMMENT: In the subgenus *Hylarana*, *Rana chalconota* group. Reviewed by Bourret,
   1942, Batr. Indochine:371–374. See Taylor, 1962, Univ. Kansas Sci. Bull., 43:

468–471. See Liu and Hu, 1961, Tailless Amph. China:212, for Chinese records, and synonymy of *Rana leporipes* Werner, 1931.

Rana longicrus Stejneger, 1898. J. Coll. Sci. Imp. Univ. Japan, 12:104.
TYPE(S): Holotype: TIU 26.
TYPE LOCALITY: Taipa, Formosa [Taiwan, China].
DISTRIBUTION: Taiwan and Fujian, China.
COMMENT: In the *Rana temporaria* group; subgenus *Rana*. Reviewed by Okada, 1931, Tailless Batr. Japan. Emp.:97–100. Systematic relationships discussed by Kuramoto, 1974, Copeia, 1974:815–822, and Kawamura, Nishioka, and Uedo, 1981, Sci. Rep. Lab. Amph. Biol. Hiroshima Univ., 5:195–323. See Liu and Hu, 1961, Tailless Amph. China:177, who regarded this form as a synonym of *Rana japonica*.

Rana longimanus Andersson, 1939. Ark. Zool., 30A(23):1–24.
TYPE(S): Holotype: ZIUS.
TYPE LOCALITY: "Kambaiti", Upper Burma; elswhere in the description noted as "little village of Kambaiti situated in N. East Burma near the border of China in a highland 2,000 m above the sea level".
DISTRIBUTION: Known only from the type locality.
COMMENT: Closely related to *Amolops formosus* (as *Rana formosa*) according to original description.

"Rana longipes" (Perret, 1960). Bull. Soc. Neuchâtel. Sci. Nat., 83:97.
ORIGINAL NAME: *Hylarana acutirostris longipes*.
TYPE(S): Holotype: MHNG 986.24.
TYPE LOCALITY: Bangwa, Bamiléké, Cameroon.
DISTRIBUTION: Western and central Cameroon (Bamiléké Plateau and Adamaoua).
COMMENT: A member of *Hylarana*; reviewed by Perret, 1977, Rev. Suisse Zool., 84: 850–853. Preoccupied by *Rana fusca* var. *longipes* Müller, 1885, and *Rana longipes* Hallowell, 1859 (DRF and LJB).

Rana luctuosa (Peters, 1871). Monatsber. Preuss. Akad. Wiss. Berlin, 1871:579.
ORIGINAL NAME: *Limnodytes luctuosus*.
TYPE(S): Holotype: MSNG 29344.
TYPE LOCALITY: Mountains of Penang, Malaya; corrected to "Sarawak (Borneo)", Malaysia, by Capocaccia, 1957, Ann. Mus. Civ. Stor. Nat. Genova, 69:215.
DISTRIBUTION: Borneo; Malaya.
COMMENT: In the subgenus *Hylarana*, *Rana luctuosa* group. Reviewed by Bourret, 1942, Batr. Indochine:360–362, and Inger, 1966, Fieldiana: Zool., 52:206–207. See also account in Berry, 1975, Amph. Fauna Peninsular Malaysia:74–75.

Rana lungshengensis Liu and Hu, 1962. Acta Zool. Sinica, 14(Suppl.):91.
TYPE(S): Holotype: CIB (formerly SBRI) 603520.
TYPE LOCALITY: "San-men of Hua-ping, Lung-shen-hsien, altitude 900 m, Kwangsi [=Guangxi]", China.
DISTRIBUTION: Guangxi, Hunan, and Guizhou, China.
COMMENT: Closely related to *Rana schmackeri* according to the original description, and, by implication, in the subgenus *Hylarana*.

Rana macrocnemis Boulenger, 1885. Proc. Zool. Soc. London, 1885:22.
TYPE(S): Holotype: BM.
TYPE LOCALITY: "Brusa", Turkey
DISTRIBUTION: Asia Minor; Caucasus Mountains; Kopet-Dag (mountains between northeastern Iran and USSR); northwestern and Caspian Iran.
COMMENT: See Borkin, 1977, Trudy Zool. Inst. Akad. Nauk SSSR, Leningrad, 74: 24–31, for taxonomic discussion. In the *Rana temporaria* group, subgenus *Rana*. Possibly includes *Rana camerani* and *Rana holtzi* (LJB).

Rana macrodactyla (Günther, 1859 "1858"). Cat. Batr. Sal. Coll. Brit. Mus.:72.
ORIGINAL NAME: *Hylarana macrodactyla.*
TYPE(S): Syntypes: BM (6 specimens).
TYPE LOCALITY: "Hong Kong" and "China"; restricted to Hong Kong [China] by
     Taylor, 1962, Univ. Kansas Sci. Bull., 43:421–423.
DISTRIBUTION: Guangdong, Guangxi, and Hainan (China) and southeastern Asia to
     Burma.
COMMENT: In the subgenus *Hylarana*, *Rana erythraea* group. Discussed by Pope,
     1931, Bull. Am. Mus. Nat. Hist., 61:540–542; Bourret, 1942, Batr. Indochine:
     338–341; Berry, 1975, Amph. Fauna Peninsular Malaysia:76–77; and Liu and
     Hu, 1961, Tailless Amph. China:197–198.

Rana macrodon Duméril and Bibron, 1841. Erp. Gén., 8:382.
TYPE(S): Syntypes: MNHNP; lectotype designated by Kiew, 1978, Malay. Nat. J.,
     31:220.
TYPE LOCALITY: "Java" and "Célèbes", Indonesia; restricted to Java by lectotype
     designation.
DISTRIBUTION: Burma to Malaya; Java; Sumatra; Borneo; Rioux Archipelago.
COMMENT: In the subgenus *Euphlyctis*, *Rana grunniens* group, according to Dubois,
     1981, Monit. Zool. Ital., N.S., Suppl., 15:225–284. Reviewed by Inger, 1966,
     Fieldiana: Zool., 52:208–212, and Bourret, 1942, Batr. Indochine:255–260. See
     comment under *Rana blythii*. Possibly two species (? including *Rana malesiana*)
     under this name in Malaya, according to Berry, 1975, Amph. Fauna
     Peninsular Malaysia:77–78. See *Rana malesiana*, with which this species has
     been confused.

Rana macroglossa Brocchi, 1877. Bull. Soc. Philomath. Paris, (7)1:177.
TYPE(S): Syntypes: MNHNP 6321, 6321A, 6321B; MNHNP 6321 designated
     lectotype by Smith, Lynch, and Reese, 1966, Bull. Zool. Nomencl., 23:169–173.
TYPE LOCALITY: Plateau of Guatemala.
DISTRIBUTION: Unknown.
COMMENT: The name *Rana macroglossa* apparently applies to a member of the *Rana
     pipiens* complex through the lectotype designation (DMH).

Rana macrognathus Boulenger, 1917. Ann. Mag. Nat. Hist., (8)20:414.
TYPE(S): Syntypes: BM.
TYPE LOCALITY: "Karin Hills, Upper Burma, 1300 to 1600 feet, and from the district
     of the Karin Bia-po", Burma.
DISTRIBUTION: Burma to northern Malaya.
COMMENT: See Taylor, 1962, Univ. Kansas Sci. Bull., 43:395–398, and Bourret, 1942,
     Batr. Indochine:265–268. Presumably in the subgenus *Euphlyctis*, *Rana
     grunniens* group, since Bourret stated that this species is intermediate between
     Rana doriae and *Rana pileata*.

Rana macrops Boulenger, 1897. Proc. Zool. Soc. London, 1897:233.
TYPE(S): Syntypes: BM (8 specimens); NHMB 1022 designated lectotype by Forcart,
     1946, Verh. Naturforsch. Ges. Basel, 57:128.
TYPE LOCALITY: "Masarang Mts., Matinang Mts., 3300 feet, and Takalekadjo Mts.,
     towards Lake Posso, 3000 feet", Celebes, Indonesia; restricted to Takalekadjo
     Mts., towards Lake Possi, 3000 feet, by lectotype designation.
DISTRIBUTION: Celebes.
COMMENT: In the subgenus *Hylarana*, *Rana chalconota* group.

Rana maculata Brocchi, 1877. Bull. Soc. Philomath. Paris, (7)1:178.
TYPE(S): Syntypes: MNHNP 6412, 6412A, 6412B; MNHNP 6412A designated
     lectotype by Smith, Lynch, and Reese, 1966, Bull. Zool. Nomencl., 23:169–173.
TYPE LOCALITY: Totonicapan, Guatemala.

DISTRIBUTION: Moderate elevations of northern Nicaragua, Honduras, El Salvador, Belize, Guatemala, and southern Chiapas and eastern Oaxaca, Mexico.
COMMENT: In the *Rana palmipes* group; subgenus *Rana*.

Rana maculosa Liu, Hu, and Yang, 1960. Acta Zool. Sinica, 12(2):161.
TYPE(S): Holotype: CIB (formerly SBRI) 581250.
TYPE LOCALITY: "Hsin-ming-hsiang, Ching-tung, Yunnan, 2100 m altitude", China.
DISTRIBUTION: Yunnan, China.
COMMENT: Subgenus *Paa*, according to Dubois and Matsui, 1983, Copeia, 1983:900. Reviewed by Dubois, 1980, Bull. Mens. Soc. Linn. Lyon, 49:142–147, who placed *Rana maculosa chayuensis* Ye, 1977 (of southern Tibet, China), in the synonymy of *Rana arnoldi*. SH rejects this synonymy and notes that Dubois has not examined specimens of *Rana maculosa chayuensis*.

Rana magna Stejneger, 1909. Smithson. Misc. Collect., 52:437.
TYPE(S): Holotype: USNM 35231.
TYPE LOCALITY: Mount Apo, Mindanao, Philippine Islands, 4000–6000 ft.
DISTRIBUTION: Known only from the type locality.
COMMENT: In the subgenus *Euphlyctis*, *Rana grunniens* group.

Rana magnaocularis J. Frost and Bagnara, 1976. Copeia, 1976:332.
TYPE(S): Holotype: USNM 197512.
TYPE LOCALITY: "Rio de Choix, 2 km N Choix, Sinaloa, Mexico".
DISTRIBUTION: East-central Sonora along the western foothills of the Sierra Madre Occidental through Sinaloa and Nayarit to central Jalisco, Mexico.
COMMENT: In the *Rana berlandieri* group of the *Rana pipiens* complex, subgenus *Rana*. Most closely related to *Rana yavapaiensis*.

Rana malabarica Tschudi, 1838. Classif. Batr.:80.
TYPE(S): Syntypes: (6 specimens) MNHNP 771, 4439, and 4440.
TYPE LOCALITY: Hills of Malabar [India].
DISTRIBUTION: Hills of Malabar, Kerala, India.
COMMENT: Probably in the subgenus *Hylarana* according to Dubois, 1981, Monit. Zool. Ital., N.S., Suppl., 15:242.

Rana malesiana Kiew, 1984. Malay. Nat. J., 37:154.
TYPE(S): Syntypes: BM 96.6.25.59–65.
TYPE LOCALITY: "Bukit Timah, Singapore".
DISTRIBUTION: Malaysian subregion of the Sunda Region: Peninsular Malaysia, Singapore, Sumatra, Java, Borneo, Pualu Kundur, Palau Gallang, Great Natuna I., Sinkeo I.
COMMENT: A member of the *Rana macrodon* complex (including *Rana macrodon*, *Rana ingeri*, and *Rana blythii*) according to the original description. In the subgenus *Euphlyctis* by implication. See Dring, 1979, Bull. Brit. Mus. (Nat. Hist.), Zool., 34:203 (as *Rana macrodon*). See comment under *Rana macrodon*.

Rana maosonensis (Bourret, 1937). Annexe Bull. Gén. Instr. Publique, Hanoi, 1937(4):36.
ORIGINAL NAME: *Hylarana maosonensis*.
TYPE(S): Syntypes: MNHNP 38-46 to -53, 48-140 to -143 (formerly in Lab. Sci. Nat. Univ. Hanoi), CAS-SU 6392, FMNH (2 specimens).
TYPE LOCALITY: Mao-Son, Tonkin [Vietnam].
DISTRIBUTION: Known only from the type locality.
COMMENT: Reviewed by Bourret, 1942, Batr. Indochine:351–352, who placed this species in the subgenus *Hylarana*.

Rana margaratae Liu, 1950. Fieldiana: Zool. Mem., 2:303.
  TYPE(S): Holotype: FMNH 49418.
  TYPE LOCALITY: "Panlungshan, Kwanhsien, Szechwan [=Sichuan], 3500 feet
    altitude", China.
  DISTRIBUTION: Gansu, Sichuan, Hubei, Hunan, Guizhou, and southern Shaanxi,
    China, 390–1500 m elev.
  COMMENT: Related to *Rana andersonii*, according to the original description, and in
    the subgenus *Hylarana* by implication. See comment under *Rana grahami*.

Rana margariana (Anderson, 1879 "1878"). Anat. Zool. Res. Yunnan, 1:846.
  ORIGINAL NAME: *Hylarana margariana*.
  TYPE(S): Probably lost, according to Bourret, 1942, Batr. Indochine:335.
  TYPE LOCALITY: "In a hill stream debouching into the Irawady, in the second
    defile", Burma.
  DISTRIBUTION: Burma.
  COMMENT: Reviewed by Bourret, 1942, Batr. Indochine:334–335, who regarded this
    form as a *Hylarana*.

Rana mawphlangensis Pillai and Chanda, 1977. J. Bombay Nat. Hist. Soc., 74:138.
  TYPE(S): Holotype: ZSIM V/ERS 803.
  TYPE LOCALITY: Mawphlang, Khasi Hills [Assam, India].
  DISTRIBUTION: Meghalaya, Assam, and Manipur, India.

Rana megapoda Taylor, 1942. Univ. Kansas Sci. Bull., 28:310.
  TYPE(S): Holotype: FMNH 100025 (formerly EHT-HMS 3280).
  TYPE LOCALITY: "near Chapala, Jalisco", Mexico.
  DISTRIBUTION: Jalisco east to Guanajuato and north into San Luis Potosí, Mexico.
  COMMENT: In the *Rana montezumae* group of the *Rana pipiens* complex, subgenus
    Rana.

Rana melanomenta Taylor, 1920. Philippine J. Sci., 16:268.
  TYPE(S): Holotype: formerly Philippine Bureau of Science 1661; destroyed in
    World War II.
  TYPE LOCALITY: Papahag Island, Sulu Islands [Philippines].
  DISTRIBUTION: Papahag I., Sulu Archipelago, Philippines.
  COMMENT: Closely related to *Rana similis* (=*Rana signata*), according to the original
    description. In the subgenus *Hylarana* by implication. Reviewed by Inger,
    1954, Fieldiana: Zool., 33:324.

Rana miadis Barbour and Loveridge, 1929. Bull. Mus. Comp. Zool., 69:143.
  TYPE(S): Holotype: MCZ 14847.
  TYPE LOCALITY: "Little Corn Island fourty miles off the Nicaraguan coast",
    Nicaragua.
  DISTRIBUTION: Little Corn I., Nicaragua.
  COMMENT: In the *Rana pipiens* complex, subgenus *Rana*.

Rana micrixalus Taylor, 1923. Philippine J. Sci., 22:526.
  TYPE(S): Holotype: CAS 60143 (formerly EHT 1598).
  TYPE LOCALITY: Abungabung, Basilan Island [Philippines].
  DISTRIBUTION: Basilan I. and Mindanao I., Philippines.

Rana microdisca Boettger, 1892. Ber. Offenbacher Vereins Naturkd., 1892:137.
  TYPE(S): SMF 5418 (formerly 1017.2A) designated lectotype by Mertens, 1967,
    Senckenb. Biol., 48:45.
  TYPE LOCALITY: Tengger-Gerbirge, 1200 m H., Ost-Java [Indonesia].
  DISTRIBUTION: Java, Borneo, Palawan, and Mindanao (Philippines), and the Lesser
    Sunda Is.
  COMMENT: In the subgenus *Euphlyctis*, *Rana grunniens* group. Reviewed by Inger,
    1966, Fieldiana: Zool., 52:212–222. See comment under *Rana tweediei*.

Rana milleti Smith, 1921. Proc. Zool. Soc. London, 1921:431.
TYPE(S): Syntypes: BM.
TYPE LOCALITY: "Dalat", Langbian Plateau, southern Annam, Vietnam.
DISTRIBUTION: Annam, Vietnam.
COMMENT: Reviewed by Bourret, 1942, Batr. Indochine:312–314, who considered it
to be in the subgenus *Hylarana*.

Rana minica Dubois, 1975. Bull. Mus. Natl. Hist. Nat., Paris, (3)324(Zool.)231:1100.
TYPE(S): Holotype: MNHNP 1974.1484.
TYPE LOCALITY: Dial Bajar, south of Chainpur, River Seti, West Nepal, altitude 1000
m, 29° 26′ N, 81° 08′ E.
DISTRIBUTION: Western Nepal and Uttar Pradesh and Himanchal Pradesh (India),
1000–2000 m elev.
COMMENT: Subgenus *Paa*. Reviewed by Dubois, 1976, Cah. Nepal., Doc., 6:146–158.

Rana minima Ting and Tsai, 1979. Acta Zootaxon. Sinica, 4(3):297.
ORIGINAL NAME: *Rana minimus*.
TYPE(S): Holotype: Fujian Normal University 58001.
TYPE LOCALITY: Vicinity of Lingshi Monastery, Dongzhang, altitude 300 m, Fuqing-
Xian, Fujian, China.
DISTRIBUTION: Fujian, China, 300–500 m elev.
COMMENT: Closely related to the *Hylarana* group, according to the original
description.

Rana miopus Boulenger, 1918. J. Nat. Hist. Soc. Siam, 3:11–12.
TYPE(S): Not traced.
TYPE LOCALITY: Khao Wang Hip, Nakhon Si Thammarat [Thailand].
DISTRIBUTION: Type locality (Thailand), southern Vietnam, and Malaya.
COMMENT: In the subgenus *Hylarana*, *Rana erythraea* group. See Taylor, 1962, Univ.
Kansas Sci. Bull., 43:427–43, and Bourret, 1942, Batr. Indochine:326–327, for
review. See also Berry, 1975, The Amph. Fauna Peninsular Malaysia:79–80.

Rana modesta Boulenger, 1882. Cat. Batr. Sal. Brit. Mus.:25.
TYPE(S): Syntypes: BM.
TYPE LOCALITY: "Goronta" and "Manado", Celebes, Indonesia.
DISTRIBUTION: Celebes.
COMMENT: In the subgenus *Euphlyctis*, *Rana grunniens* group.

Rana moluccana Boettger, 1895. Zool. Anz., 18:132.
TYPE(S): Syntypes: SMF (2 specimens); SMF 6562 noted as holotype (?lectotype) by
Mertens, 1967, Senckenb. Biol., 48:45.
TYPE LOCALITY: "Halmaheira und Ternate", Moluccan Is., Indonesia; restricted to
"Ternate, Molukken" by apparent lectotype designation.
DISTRIBUTION: Moluccas, Indonesia.
COMMENT: Subgenus *Hylarana*. Regarded as a subspecies of *Rana papua*, without
comment, by Mertens, 1967, Senckenb. Biol., 48:45.
REVIEWER: Richard G. Zweifel (RGZ).

Rana montezumae Baird, 1854. Proc. Acad. Nat. Sci. Philadelphia, 7:61.
TYPE(S): Syntypes: USNM 3344, 39383–96, MCZ 2600 (formerly USNM 39397);
USNM 3344 designated lectotype by Cochran, 1961, Bull. U.S. Natl. Mus.,
220:75.
TYPE LOCALITY: City of Mexico, Distrito Federal, Mexico.
DISTRIBUTION: San Luis Potosí, Queretaro, and Jalisco south to the edge of the
Mexican Plateau, Mexico.
COMMENT: In the *Rana montezumae* group of the *Rana pipiens* complex, subgenus
Rana.

Rana montivaga Smith, 1921. Proc. Zool. Soc. London, 1921:436.
TYPE(S): Syntypes: BM.
TYPE LOCALITY: "Dalat, Langbian Plateau, at 1500 metres", Vietnam.
DISTRIBUTION: Annam, Vietnam.

COMMENT: Allied with *Rana varians*, according to the original description. Reviewed by Bourret, 1942, Batr. Indochine:346–348, who considered it to be in the subgenus *Hylarana*. See comment under *Rana narina*.

Rana mortenseni Boulenger, 1903. Ann. Mag. Nat. Hist., (7)12:219.
TYPE(S): Syntypes: ZMUC.
TYPE LOCALITY: "Koh Chang Island, in Siam [Thailand]".
DISTRIBUTION: Burma and Thailand.
COMMENT: Subgenus *Hylarana, Rana gracilis* group.

Rana murthii Pillai, 1979. Bull. Zool. Surv. India, 2:39.
TYPE(S): Holotype: ZSIM.
TYPE LOCALITY: Naduvattom, Western Ghats, South India.
DISTRIBUTION: Western Ghats, South India.

Rana muscosa Camp, 1917. Univ. California Publ. Zool., 17:118.
ORIGINAL NAME: *Rana boylii muscosa*.
TYPE(S): Holotype: MVZ 771.
TYPE LOCALITY: "Arroyo Seco Cañon, at about 1300 feet altitude, near Pasadena, [Los Angeles County,] California", USA.
DISTRIBUTION: Sierra Nevada of California and extreme western Nevada (near Lake Tahoe), 4500–1200 ft. elev.; disjunct populations in San Gabriel, San Bernardino, and San Jacinto mountains, in southern California from 1200–7500 ft. elev., USA.
COMMENT: See Zweifel, 1955, Univ. California Publ. Zool., 54:207–292, and Zweifel, 1968, Cat. Am. Amph. Rept., 65.1–2, for review. In the *Rana boylii* group, subgenus *Rana*.

Rana namiyei Stejneger, 1901. Proc. Biol. Soc. Washington, 14:1901.
TYPE(S): Holotype: TIU 31A
TYPE LOCALITY: Okinawa shima, Riu Kiu [Japan].
DISTRIBUTION: Okinawa I., Ryukyu Is., Japan.
COMMENT: In the subgenus *Limnonectes*. See Stejneger, 1907, Bull. U.S. Natl. Mus., 58:136–139, and Okada, 1966, Fauna Japon., Anura:126–130, for review.

Rana narina Stejneger, 1901. Proc. Biol. Soc. Washington, 14:189.
TYPE(S): Holotype: TIU 19A
TYPE LOCALITY: Okinawa shima, Riu Kiu [Japan].
DISTRIBUTION: Ryukyu Is., Japan; Taiwan, Fujian, and Zhejiang, China.
COMMENT: In the subgenus *Hylarana*. See Stejneger, 1907, Bull. U.S. Natl. Mus., 58:134–136; Okada, 1966, Fauna Japon., Anura:123–126; and Nakamura and Ueno, 1963, Japan. Rept. Amph. Color:51. See comment under *Rana ijimae*. Liu and Hu, 1961, Tailless Amph. China:212, considered Chinese populations of *Rana montivaga* to be referable to *Rana swinhoana* Boulenger, 1903, Ann. Mag. Nat. Hist., (7)12:556, which is treated in this list as a subspecies of *Rana narina*, following Wang and Chan, 1977, Q. J. Taiwan Mus., 30:329–339 (who also included *Rana kosempensis* Werner, 1913, as a synonym).

Rana nepalensis Dubois, 1975. C. R. Hebd. Séances Acad. Sci., Paris, (D)281:1720.
TYPE(S): Holotype: MNHNP 1975.1606.
TYPE LOCALITY: Godavari, central Nepal, alt. 1560 m".
DISTRIBUTION: Nepal.
COMMENT: See original description for discussion of confusion of this species with *Rana limnocharis*. In the subgenus *Euphlyctis, Rana tigerina* group by implication.

Rana nicobariensis (Stoliczka, 1870). J. Asiat. Soc. Bengal, 39:150.
ORIGINAL NAME: *Hylorana Nicobariensis*.
TYPE(S): Syntypes (probable): ?BM.
TYPE LOCALITY: "Nicobar" Is., India.
DISTRIBUTION: Palawan I. (Philippines); Bali to Malay Peninsula; Nicobar Is. (India); Thailand.

COMMENT: In the subgenus *Hylarana*, *Rana erythraea* group. Synonymy and discussion in Taylor, 1962, Univ. Kansas Sci. Bull., 43:430–433; Bourret, 1942, Batr. Indochine:343–346; Inger, 1954, Fieldiana: Zool., 33:331–333; Inger, 1966, Fieldiana: Zool., 52:223–228; and Berry, 1975, Amph. Fauna Peninsular Malaysia:80–81.

Rana nigrolineata Liu and Hu, 1959. Acta Zool. Sinica, 11(4):516.
TYPE(S): Holotype: CIB (formerly SWIBASC) 571085.
TYPE LOCALITY: "Meng-yang, Yunnan, 680 meters altitude", China.
DISTRIBUTION: Yunnan, China.
COMMENT: Closely related to *Rana lateralis*, according to the original description. See also Liu and Hu, 1961, Tailless Amph. China:175–177.

Rana nigromaculata Hallowell, 1861 "1860". Proc. Acad. Nat. Sci. Philadelphia, 12:500.
TYPE(S): Not traced.
TYPE LOCALITY: Japan.
DISTRIBUTION: Lower Amur and Ussuri River valleys (USSR) through northeastern to west-central China and Korea; Japan.
COMMENT: In the *Rana esculenta* group; subgenus *Rana*. Reviewed by Kawamura, 1962, J. Sci. Hiroshima Univ., (B—Zool.)20:181–193; Pope, 1931, Bull. Am. Mus. Nat. Hist., 61:515–520; Liu, 1950, Fieldiana: Zool. Mem., 2:309–313; Liu and Hu, 1961, Tailless Amph. China:169; and Kawamura and Nishioka, 1979, Mitt. Zool. Mus. Berlin, 55:171.

Rana nigrovittata (Blyth, 1855). J. Asiat. Soc. Bengal, 24:718.
ORIGINAL NAME: *Limnodytes nigrovittatus*.
TYPE(S): ZSI.
TYPE LOCALITY: Mergui, Tenasserim, Burma.
DISTRIBUTION: Assam (India) to Yunnan (China), Vietnam and south to Malaya.
COMMENT: In the subgenus *Hylarana*, *Rana gracilis* group. See Taylor, 1962, Univ. Kansas Sci. Bull., 43:440–443; Bourret, 1942, Batr. Indochine:317–320; Berry, 1975, Amph. Fauna Peninsular Malaysia:81–82; and Liu and Hu, 1961, Tailless Amph. China:195–197.

Rana nitida Smedley, 1931. Bull. Raffles Mus., 5:107.
TYPE(S): Not traced (?RM or BM).
TYPE LOCALITY: Tanah Rata, Pahang [Malaya, Malaysia].
DISTRIBUTION: Malaya.
COMMENT: In the subgenus *Limnonectes*. See Bourret, 1942, Batr. Indochine:285–286. See comment under *Rana tweediei*.

Rana oatesii Boulenger, 1892. Ann. Mag. Nat. Hist., (6)9:141.
TYPE(S): Syntypes: BM.
TYPE LOCALITY: "Toungoo", Burma.
DISTRIBUTION: Burma.
COMMENT: In the subgenus *Hylarana*, *Rana erythraea* group. Reviewed by Bourret, 1942, Batr. Indochine:327–329.

Rana occidentalis (Perret, 1960). Bull. Soc. Neuchâtel. Sci. Nat., (3)83:98.
ORIGINAL NAME: *Hylarana lepus occidentalis*.
TYPE(S): MNHNP 1970-901 designated lectotype by Perret, 1983, Bull. Soc. Neuchâtel. Sci. Nat., 106:109–113.
TYPE LOCALITY: "Guineé"; corrected to "Mont Nimba, Côte d'Ivoire, forêt Bié et Gouéla" by Perret, 1977, Rev. Suisse Zool., 74:844.
DISTRIBUTION: Forests of Guinea, Liberia, Ivory Coast, Ghana, and Nigeria.
COMMENT: A member of *Hylarana*. See Perret, 1977, Rev. Suisse Zool., 74:844. Discussed, redefined, and compared with *Rana lepus* (as *Hylarana lepus*) by Perret, 1983, Bull. Soc. Neuchâtel. Sci. Nat., 106:109–113.

Rana occipitalis Günther, 1859 "1858". Cat. Batr. Sal. Coll. Brit. Mus.:130.
   TYPE(S): Syntypes: BM (12 specimens).
   TYPE LOCALITY: "West Africa", "Africa", and "Gambia".
   DISTRIBUTION: Northern Zambia and Angola to Sudan and across to Senegal.
   COMMENT: In the subgenus *Euphlyctis*, *Rana tigerina* group, according to Dubois,
       1981, Monit. Zool. Ital., N.S., Suppl., 15:240.

Rana okinavana Boettger, 1895. Zool. Anz., 18:266.
   TYPE(S): Syntypes: SMF, Bremen Mus.; SMF 5830 (formerly SMF 1047.3a)
       designated lectotype by Mertens, 1967, Senckenb. Biol., 48:45.
   TYPE LOCALITY: "Liu kiu [Ryukyu]-Inseln, angebich von Okinawa, der mittleren
       Gruppe", Japan.
   DISTRIBUTION: Amami and Okinawa, Ryukyu Is., Japan.
   COMMENT: Kuramoto, 1972, Caryologia, 25:547–559, reported the karyotype.
       Reviewed by Okada, 1966, Fauna Japon., Anura:62–65, as *Rana macropus* (see
       comment under *Buergeria japonica*: Rhacophoridae).

Rana omiltemana Günther, 1900. Biol. Cent. Am., Rept. Batr.:200.
   TYPE(S): Syntypes: BM 1895.7.15.31–35.
   TYPE LOCALITY: Omilteme, Guerrero, Mexico.
   DISTRIBUTION: Sierra Madre del Sur in Guerrero, Mexico.
   COMMENT: In the *Rana pipiens* complex, subgenus *Rana*.

Rana onca Cope, 1875. *In* Yarrow, Rep. Geog. Geol. Explor. Surv. West 100th Merid.,
   5(Zool.):528.
   TYPE(S): Holotype: USNM 25331.
   TYPE LOCALITY: "Utah"; corrected to "probably collected in the vicinity of St.
       George, [Washington County,] Utah", USA, by Pace, 1974, Misc. Publ. Mus.
       Zool. Univ. Michigan, 148:29.
   DISTRIBUTION: Known only from the holotype.
   COMMENT: In the *Rana pipiens* complex, subgenus *Rana*. This name has been
       applied with no discussion (and apparently without examining specimens) by
       several authors to *Rana yavapaiensis* in western Arizona, USA, and to *Rana
       fisheri*, from Nevada, USA.

Rana ornativentris Werner, 1903. Abh. Bayer. Akad. Wiss., Math. Physik. Kl., 22, Abt.
   2:383.
   ORIGINAL NAME: *Rana japonica* var. *ornativentris*.
   TYPE(S): ZSM, according to Stejneger, 1907, Bull. U.S. Natl. Mus., 58:108.
   TYPE LOCALITY: Akanuma and Tadenuma, Nikko [Honshu, Japan].
   DISTRIBUTION: Honshu, Shikoku, and Kyushu Is., Japan.
   COMMENT: See Kawamura, 1962, J. Sci. Hiroshima Univ., (B—Zool.)20:181–193, and
       Okada, 1966, Fauna Japon., Anura:81–90, for review. In the *Rana temporaria*
       group, subgenus *Rana*.

Rana palmipes Spix, 1824. Spec. Nov. Testud. Ran. Brasil.:5.
   TYPE(S): Syntypes: ZSM 963/0 (2 specimens); now lost.
   TYPE LOCALITY: "Amazonenfluss [=Amazon River]", Brazil.
   DISTRIBUTION: Low elevations from Veracruz, Mexico, south through Central
       America and across northern South America, south to northeastern Brazil on
       the Atlantic coast and to northwestern Peru on the Pacific coast.
   COMMENT: In the *Rana palmipes* group, subgenus *Rana*.
   REVIEWERS: Werner C. A. Bokermann (WCAB); Ulisses Caramaschi (UC); Eduardo
       Gudynas (EG); Paulo E. Vanzolini (PEV).

Rana palustris LeConte, 1825. Ann. Lyc. Nat. Hist. New York, 1:282.
   TYPE(S): Not known to exist.
   TYPE LOCALITY: Not stated; designated as "vicinity of Philadelphia", Pennsylvania,
      USA by Schmidt, 1953, Check List N. Am. Amph. Rept., Ed. 6:83.
   DISTRIBUTION: Eastern North America, from Quebec through Ontario (Canada) to
      Minnesota, south to northern South Carolina, Georgia, Alabama, to eastern
      Texas (USA).
   COMMENT: In the *Rana areolata* group of the *Rana pipiens* complex, subgenus *Rana*.
      Reviewed by Schaaf and Smith, 1971, Cat. Am. Amph. Rept., 117.1–3.

Rana papua Lesson, 1830. Voy. Coquille, Zool., 2:59.
   TYPE(S): Syntypes: MNHNP 4575 (2 specimens).
   TYPE LOCALITY: "Ile de Waigiou" (=Waigeo I.), Irian Jaya (New Guinea), Indonesia.
   DISTRIBUTION: New Guinea.
   COMMENT: See comment under *Rana florensis*. In the subgenus *Hylarana*, *Rana papua*
      group.
   REVIEWERS: Margaret Davies (MD); Michael J. Tyler (MJT); Richard G. Zweifel
      (RGZ).

Rana paramacrodon Inger, 1966. Fieldiana: Zool., 52:228.
   TYPE(S): Holotype: FMNH 76883.
   TYPE LOCALITY: "Sungei Tawan, a small tributary of the Kalabakan River, Tawau
      District, Sabah", Malaysia (Borneo).
   DISTRIBUTION: Western and northern Borneo; Malaya.
   COMMENT: In the subgenus *Euphlyctis*, *Rana grunniens* group, according to the
      original description. See account by Berry, 1975, Amph. Fauna Peninsular
      Malaysia:83–85.

Rana parkeriana Mertens, 1938. Senckenb. Biol., 20:425.
   ORIGINAL NAME: *Rana albolabris parkeriana*.
   TYPE(S): Holotype: BM.
   TYPE LOCALITY: "Congulu" (=Congolo), western Angola.
   DISTRIBUTION: Western Angola in lowland forest and swampy areas along the
      coast.
   COMMENT: A *Hylarana* according to Perret, 1977, Rev. Suisse Zool., 84:844. *Rana
      albolabris parkeriana* is a replacement name for *Rana albolabris acutirostris* Parker,
      1936, Novit. Zool., 40:115–146, which is preoccupied.

Rana perezi Seoane, 1885. Zoologist, 1885:171.
   TYPE(S): Syntypes: including MCZ 6832.
   TYPE LOCALITY: Coruña, Spain.
   DISTRIBUTION: Southern France; Iberia; northwestern Africa; introduced on the
      Azores and Canary Is.
   COMMENT: In the *Rana esculenta* group, subgenus *Rana*. Formerly often treated as a
      subspecies of *Rana ridibunda*. The relationships with other western Palearctic
      green frogs were discussed by Uzzell, 1982, Amphibia-Reptilia, 3:135–142. See
      Rana saharica.

Rana persimilis van Kampen, 1923. Amph. Indo-Aust. Arch.:223.
   TYPE(S): Holotype: NHMB 1029.
   TYPE LOCALITY: "Sumatra (Laut tader)", Indonesia.
   DISTRIBUTION: Sumatra.
   COMMENT: Subgenus *Hylarana*, *Rana erythraea* group, by implication from the
      original description.

Rana phrynoderma Boulenger, 1882. Cat. Batr. Sal. Brit. Mus.:462.
   TYPE(S): BM.
   TYPE LOCALITY: "Anamallays", Kerala, India.
   DISTRIBUTION: Anamalai Hills, Kerala, South India.

COMMENT: See comment under *Discodeles*.

Rana phrynoides Boulenger, 1917. Ann. Mag. Nat. Hist., (8)20:413.
   TYPE(S): Syntypes: BM.
   TYPE LOCALITY: "Yunnan and Tongchuan fu", China.
   DISTRIBUTION: Yunnan, Guizhou, and Sichuan (China), 5000–8000 ft. elev., to
      northern Vietnam and Upper Burma.
   COMMENT: Subgenus *Paa*. Reviewed by Liu, 1950, Fieldiana: Zool. Mem., 2:272–
      277; Pope, 1931, Bull. Am. Mus. Nat. Hist., 61:499–500; and Bourret, 1942,
      Batr. Indochine:293–295 (as *Rana phrynoides* and *Rana yunnanensis*). See Liu
      and Hu, 1961, Tailless Amph. China:162–164, who considered *Rana*
      yunnanensis Anderson, 1879, a synonym.

Rana pierrei Dubois, 1975. C. R. Hebd. Séances Acad. Sci., Paris, (D)281:1720.
   TYPE(S): Holotype: MNHNP 1975.1680.
   TYPE LOCALITY: Birtamode, East Nepal, alt. 200 m.
   DISTRIBUTION: Central and eastern Nepal.
   COMMENT: See original description for discussion of this species being confused
      with *Rana limnocharis*. In the subgenus *Euphlyctis*, *Rana tigerina* group by
      implication.

Rana pileata Boulenger, 1916. J. Nat. Hist. Soc. Siam, 2:103.
   TYPE(S): Syntypes: BM.
   TYPE LOCALITY: "Khao Cebab, Chantabun", Chanthaburi Province, Thailand.
   DISTRIBUTION: Thailand; Chiang I.
   COMMENT: In the subgenus *Euphlyctis*, *Rana grunniens* group. See Taylor, 1962,
      Univ. Kansas Sci. Bull., 43:398–401, and Bourret, 1942, Batr. Indochine:269–
      270.

Rana pipiens Schreber, 1782. Naturforscher, Halle, 18:182.
   TYPE(S): Not designated; UMMZ 71365 designated neotype by Pace, 1974, Misc.
      Publ. Mus. Zool. Univ. Michigan, 148:16.
   TYPE LOCALITY: New York and Raccoon Landing, Gloucester County, New Jersey;
      restricted to "White Plains, New York", USA, by Schmidt, 1953, Check List
      N. Am. Amph. Rept., Ed. 6:82; neotype is from "Fall Creek, Etna, Thompkins
      County, New York", USA.
   DISTRIBUTION: Great Basin Region from northern Arizona, western Nevada, and
      Washington (USA) to southern Canada; east to southeastern Canada and New
      Jersey (USA).
   COMMENT: Synonymy and discussion in Pace, 1974, Misc. Publ. Mus. Zool. Univ.
      Michigan, 148:16–18. In the *Rana pipiens* group of the *Rana pipiens* complex,
      subgenus *Rana*.

Rana plancyi Lataste, 1880. Bull. Soc. Zool. France, 5:64.
   TYPE(S): Not traced.
   TYPE LOCALITY: Peking [=Beijing], China.
   DISTRIBUTION: Eastern China (including Taiwan); Korea.
   COMMENT: In the *Rana esculenta* group, subgenus *Rana*. See Stejneger, 1907, Bull.
      U.S. Natl. Mus., 58:101–102, and Okada, 1931, Tailless Batr. Japan. Emp.:92–95,
      for synonymy and review. See also Pope, 1931, Bull. Am. Mus. Nat. Hist., 61:
      509–510; Shannon, 1956, Herpetologica, 12:36–38; and Liu and Hu, 1961,
      Tailless Amph. China:166–167. Relationships with *Rana nigromaculata*
      discussed by Kawamura and Nishioka, 1979, Mitt. Zool. Mus. Berlin, 55:171–
      185. Kuramoto, 1983, Sci. Rep. Lab. Amph. Biol. Hiroshima Univ., 6:253–267,
      suggested that *Rana plancyi fukiensis* (of Fujian and Taiwan, China) and *Rana*
      plancyi chosenica (of southwestern China) might best be regarded as distinct
      species, *Rana fukiensis* and *Rana chosenica*.

Rana pleuraden Boulenger, 1904. Ann. Mag. Nat. Hist., (7)13:131.
TYPE(S): Not traced.
TYPE LOCALITY: "Yunnan fu (altitude about 6000 feet)", Yunnan, China.
DISTRIBUTION: Yunnan, Sichuan, and Guizhou (Yunkwei Plateau), China.
COMMENT: Subgenus *Rana*. Reviewed by Liu, 1950, Fieldiana: Zool. Mem., 2:260–
262. See Liu and Hu, 1961, Tailless Amph. China:170–171.

Rana plicatella Stoliczka, 1873. J. Asiat. Soc. Bengal, 42:116.
TYPE(S): Not traced.
TYPE LOCALITY: Penang or Province Wellesley [Malaya, Malaysia].
DISTRIBUTION: Yala Province (Thailand) and Malaya.
COMMENT: In the subgenus *Euphlyctis*, *Rana grunniens* group. See Taylor, 1962,
Univ. Kansas Sci. Bull., 43:401–405; Bourret, 1942, Batr. Indochine:270–272;
and Berry, 1975, Amph. Fauna Peninsular Malaysia:85–86, for synonymy and
discussion.

Rana polunini Smith, 1951. Ann. Mag. Nat. Hist., (12)4:727.
TYPE(S): Holotype: BM 1950.1.6.4.
TYPE LOCALITY: Langtang village, 11,000 ft., Nepal.
DISTRIBUTION: Border area of Nepal and China (Tibet), 2610–3990 m elev.
COMMENT: Subgenus *Paa*. Reviewed by Dubois, 1976, Cah. Nepal., Doc., 6:116–145.

Rana pretiosa Baird and Girard, 1853. Proc. Acad. Nat. Sci. Philadelphia, 6:378.
TYPE(S): Syntypes: USNM 11409 (5 specimens).
TYPE LOCALITY: "Oregon . . . on Puget Sound", Washington, USA.
DISTRIBUTION: Southeastern Alaska (USA), southwestern Canada and northwestern
USA south to northern California, Nevada, and Utah.
COMMENT: In the *Rana boylii* group, subgenus *Rana*. Reviewed by Turner and
Dumas, 1972, Cat. Am. Amph. Rept., 119.1–4.

Rana pueblae Zweifel, 1955. Univ. California Publ. Zool., 54:253.
TYPE(S): Holotype: UMMZ 99474.
TYPE LOCALITY: "2.8 miles northeast of Huauchinango, Río, Texcapa, Puebla,
México".
DISTRIBUTION: Known only from the type locality.
COMMENT: In the *Rana tarahumarae* group, subgenus *Rana*.

Rana pustulosa Boulenger, 1883. Ann. Mag. Nat. Hist., (5)11:343.
TYPE(S): Holotype: BM 1883.4.16.42.
TYPE LOCALITY: Ventanas, Durango, Mexico.
DISTRIBUTION: Southern Sinaloa to Jalisco and Michoacán, Mexico.
COMMENT: In the *Rana tarahumarae* group; subgenus *Rana*. Synonymy includes
Rana sinaloae Zweifel, 1954, according to Webb, 1984, *In* Seigel et al. (eds.),
Mus. Nat. Hist. Univ. Kansas Spec. Publ., 10:237, and *Rana trilobata*, according
to Hillis, Frost, and Frost, 1983, J. Herpetol., 17:73–75. See comment under
Rana zweifeli.

Rana quadrana Liu, Hu, and Yang, 1960. Acta Zool. Sinica, 12(2):286.
ORIGINAL NAME: *Rana quadranus*.
TYPE(S): Holotype: CIB (formerly SBRI) 571357.
TYPE LOCALITY: "Kwan-yang, Wushan, Szechwan [=Sichuan], 1463 m altitude",
China.
DISTRIBUTION: Shaanxi, Gansu, Sichuan, Hubei, and Anhui, China, 650–2700 m
elev.
COMMENT: Related to *Rana spinosa* according to the original description, and in the
subgenus *Paa* by implication. See Liu and Hu, 1961, Tailless Amph. China:
150–153.

Rana raja Smith, 1930. Bull. Raffles Mus., 3:96–97.
ORIGINAL NAME: *Rana cancrivora raja*.
TYPE(S): Not traced (? RM or BM).
TYPE LOCALITY: Pattani, Pattani, Thailand.
DISTRIBUTION: Pattani, Songkhla, and Phatthalung (Thailand); Kuala Lumpur
(Malaya).

COMMENT: See Taylor, 1962, Univ. Kansas Sci. Bull., 43:373–376, for discussion; in the subgenus *Euphlyctis*, *Rana tigerina* group, by implication.

Rana rara Dubois and Matsui, 1983. Copeia, 1983:895.
ORIGINAL NAME: *Rana (Paa) rara*.
TYPE(S): Holotype: MNHNP 1981.1001.
TYPE LOCALITY: "in Lake Rara (Rara Daha), Western Nepal, 29° 31′ N, 82° 05′ E, altitude 2990 m".
DISTRIBUTION: Western Nepal.
COMMENT: Subgenus *Paa*, according to the original description.

Rana ridibunda Pallas, 1771. Reise Russ. Reichs, 1:458.
TYPE(S): Unknown.
TYPE LOCALITY: Caspian Sea, Volga, and Jaico [USSR]; restricted to "Gurjew, Nord Küste des Kaspischen Meeres" by Mertens and Müller, 1928, Abh. Senckenb. Naturforsch. Ges., 41:20.
DISTRIBUTION: Central Europe east of northwestern France, north to southern shore of Baltic Sea, south to northern Italy and the Balkans; southwestern Asia, east to ca. 81° E in Asiatic USSR and Xinjiang (China), south to Afghanistan and Pakistan.
COMMENT: In the *Rana esculenta* group, subgenus *Rana*. Unnamed taxa similar to *Rana ridibunda* revealed in peninsular Italy by Uzzell and Hotz, 1979, Mitt. Zool. Mus. Berlin, 55:13–27; in Greece and Yugoslavia by Hotz and Uzzell, 1982, Proc. Acad. Nat. Sci. Philadelphia, 134:50–79, and by Tunner and Heppich, 1982, Z. Zool. Syst. Evolutionsforsch., 20:209–223. Status of North African frogs is uncertain. See *Rana saharica*. See Ma, 1979, Nat. Hist., Shanghai, 1979(1):37, for Chinese record.

Rana rostandi Dubois, 1974. Bull. Soc. Zool. France, 98:495.
TYPE(S): Holotype: MNHNP 1973.310.
TYPE LOCALITY: Lac Kutsab Terna Tal, altitude 2900 m, near village Thini, northwestern Nepal (28° 46′ N, 83° 44′ E).
DISTRIBUTION: Nepal, 2400–3500 m elev.
COMMENT: Subgenus *Paa*. Reviewed by Dubois, 1976, Cah. Nepal., Doc., 6:159–178.

Rana rugosa Temminck and Schlegel, 1838. *In* Von Siebold, Fauna Japon., Rept.:110.
TYPE(S): Syntypes: RMNH 2064 (9 specimens).
TYPE LOCALITY: Japan; probably Nagasaki, according to Stejneger, 1907, Bull. U.S. Natl. Mus., 58:123.
DISTRIBUTION: Honshu, Shikoku, and Kyushu Is., Japan; Korea; northeastern China.
COMMENT: Subgenus *Rana*. See Stejneger, 1907, Bull. U.S. Natl. Mus., 58:123–127, and Okada, 1966, Fauna Japon., Anura:104–112, for review. See comment under *Rana tientaiensis*.

Rana rugulosa Wiegmann, 1835. Nova Acta Acad. Caesar. Leop. Carol., Halle, 17:258.
ORIGINAL NAME: *Rana tigerina rugulosa*.
TYPE(S): Holotype: ZMB 3721.
TYPE LOCALITY: Cape Syng-more, Macao [China].
DISTRIBUTION: Burma and southern China (north to Yangtze River and including Taiwan) to Thailand; introduced in Borneo (Sabah, Malaysia).
COMMENT: In the subgenus *Euphlyctis*, *Rana tigerina* group. Reviewed by Okada, 1931, Tailless Batr. Japan. Emp.:147–149; Pope, 1937, Bull. Am. Mus. Nat. Hist., 61:487–491; and (as *Rana tigerina rugulosa*) by Liu, 1950, Fieldiana: Zool. Mem., 2:321–322. See Matsui, 1979, Contrib. Biol. Lab. Kyoto Univ., 25:334–336, for discussion of Bornean population.

Rana ruwenzorica Laurent, 1972. Explor. Parc Natl. Virunga, (2)22:93.
TYPE(S): RGMC or MRHN.
TYPE LOCALITY: Zaire, Kikyo, Munsenene.
DISTRIBUTION: Ruwenzori Range (Zaire and Uganda); probably other nearby mountains in Central Africa.

COMMENT: Subgenus *Rana*.

Rana saharica Boulenger, 1913. Novit. Zool., 20:84.
ORIGINAL NAME: *Rana esculenta* var. *saharica*.
TYPE(S): BM.
TYPE LOCALITY: El Golea, Tedikel oasis, Algeria.
DISTRIBUTION: Morocco to Tunisia.
COMMENT: In the *Rana esculenta* group, subgenus *Rana*. Prior to Uzzell, 1982, Amphibia-Reptilia, 3:135–143, this species was considered to be a synonym of *Rana perezi*, or, following Pasteur and Bons, 1959, Trav. Inst. Scient. Chérifien, Rabat, Ser. Zool., 17:1–240, a synonym of *Rana ridibunda*. Although northwest African members of the *Rana esculenta* complex are here tentatively regarded as *Rana saharica*, Hemmer, Konrad, and Bachmann, 1980, Amphibia-Reptilia, 1:41–48, suggested that two species were hybridizing in North Africa. Populations of the *Rana esculenta* complex of northeastern Africa and Arabia are not currently allocated to species.

Rana sanguinea Boettger, 1893. Zool. Anz., 16:364.
TYPE(S): SMF 6221 (formerly 1062.a) considered holotype by Mertens, 1967, Senckenb. Biol., 48:45; MCZ 9935–38 were considered syntypes by Barbour and Loveridge, 1929, Bull. Mus. Comp. Zool., 69:331.
TYPE LOCALITY: Culion, Calamianes [Philippines].
DISTRIBUTION: Palawan I., Philippines; Celebes; Ceram I., Moluccas, Indonesia.
COMMENT: In the subgenus *Hylarana*, *Rana erythraea* group. Most closely related to *Rana papua* (in the *Rana papua* group of Boulenger, 1920, Rec. Indian Mus., 20: 1–226) according to Inger, 1954, Fieldiana: Zool., 33:328–331, who reviewed this species.

Rana sauriceps Rao, 1937. Proc. Indian Acad. Sci., (B)6:396.
TYPE(S): CCB; now lost (SD).
TYPE LOCALITY: "Wattekole, Coorg [Mysore], S. India".
DISTRIBUTION: Mysore, India.
COMMENT: Subgenus *Hylarana*, according to the original description.

Rana sauteri Boulenger, 1909. Ann. Mag. Nat. Hist., (8)4:493.
TYPE(S): Syntypes: BM (5 specimens).
TYPE LOCALITY: "Kanshirei villege, altitude about 2000 ft.", Taiwan, China.
DISTRIBUTION: Taiwan and Guangxi, China; Indochina.
COMMENT: In the subgenus *Hylarana*, *Rana gracilis* group, according to Boulenger, 1920, Rec. Indian Mus., 20:1–226, but apparently in the *Rana temporaria* group, subgenus *Rana*, according to the original description. Reviewed by Bourret, 1942, Batr. Indochine:321–322.

Rana schmackeri Boettger, 1892. Kat. Batr. Samml. Mus. Senckenb. Naturforsch. Ges.:11.
TYPE(S): Holotype: SMF 6241 (formerly 1054.2a).
TYPE LOCALITY: "Kao-cha-hien bei Ichang, Prov. Hubei, Central-China".
DISTRIBUTION: Southeastern China north to Gansu and Shaanxi; Hainan I.
COMMENT: In the subgenus *Hylarana*, *Rana luctuosa* group. Discussed by Chang and Hsu, 1932, Contrib. Biol. Lab. Sci. Soc. China, Zool. Ser., 8:165–169, and Liu and Hu, 1961, Tailless Amph. China:208–211 (who discussed the *Rana luctuosa* group). See comment under *Rana grahami*.

Rana scutigera Andersson, 1916. K. Svenska Vetensk. Akad. Handl., (4)55:14.
TYPE(S): Not traced.
TYPE LOCALITY: Haut Sanuk [Thailand].
DISTRIBUTION: Peninsular Thailand.
COMMENT: Reviewed by Bourret, 1942, Batr. Indochine:370–371, who regarded it as a member of the subgenus *Hylarana*.

Rana semipalmata Boulenger, 1882. Cat. Batr. Sal. Brit. Mus.:56.
TYPE(S): BM.
TYPE LOCALITY: "Malabar", Kerala, South India.
DISTRIBUTION: Malabar and Anamallai hills, Kerala, South India.
COMMENT: See comment under *Discodeles*.

Rana septentrionalis Baird, 1854. Proc. Acad. Nat. Sci. Philadelphia, 7:61.
TYPE(S): Not known.
TYPE LOCALITY: "Northern Minnesota"; restricted to "Lake Itasca", Clearwater
    County, Minnesota, USA, by Schmidt, 1953, Check List N. Am. Amph. Rept.,
    Ed. 6:80.
DISTRIBUTION: Southwestern Newfoundland west to southeastern Manitoba
    (Canada), south to northern New York on the east and Wisconsin and
    northern Minnesota on the west (USA).
COMMENT: In the *Rana catesbeiana* group, subgenus *Rana*. Reviewed by Hedeen,
    1977, Cat. Am. Amph. Rept., 202:1–2.

Rana shini Ahl, 1930. Sitzungsber. Ges. Naturforsch. Freunde Berlin, 1930:315.
TYPE(S): Not traced.
TYPE LOCALITY: Yaoshan, Kwangsi [=Guangxi], China.
DISTRIBUTION: Guangxi and Guizhou, China.
COMMENT: Considered a synonym of *Rana spinosa* (subgenus *Paa*) with no
    discussion, by Gorham, 1974, Checklist World Amph.:151. See Liu and Hu,
    1962, Acta Zool. Sinica, 14(Suppl.):76.

Rana shuchinae Liu, 1950. Fieldiana: Zool. Mem., 2:313.
TYPE(S): Holotype: FMNH 55871.
TYPE LOCALITY: "Lolokou, Chaochiaohsien, Sikang [=Sichuan], 10000 feet altitude",
    China.
DISTRIBUTION: Sichuan and Yunnan, China.
COMMENT: Discussed by Liu and Hu, 1961, Tailless Amph. China:174–175.

Rana sierramadrensis Taylor, 1939 "1938". Univ. Kansas Sci. Bull., 25:397–399.
TYPE(S): Holotype: FMNH 100038 (formerly EHT-HMS 3963B).
TYPE LOCALITY: "near Agua del Obispo", Guerrero, Mexico.
DISTRIBUTION: Sierra Madre del Sur of Guerrero and Oaxaca, Mexico.
COMMENT: In the *Rana palmipes* group, subgenus *Rana*.

Rana signata (Günther, 1872). Proc. Zool. Soc. London, 1872:600.
ORIGINAL NAME: *Polypedates signatus*.
TYPE(S): Not traced.
TYPE LOCALITY: Matang [Sarawak, Malaysia (Borneo)].
DISTRIBUTION: Peninsular Thailand and Malaya; Sumatra; Borneo; Philippines.
COMMENT: In the subgenus *Hylarana*, *Rana luctuosa* group. Reviewed by Bourret,
    1942, Batr. Indochine:364–366; Inger, 1954, Fieldiana: Zool., 33:312–324; and
    Inger, 1966, Fieldiana: Zool., 52:233. See also account by Berry, 1975, Amph.
    Fauna Peninsular Malaysia:86–87.

Rana sikimensis Jerdon, 1870. Proc. Asiat. Soc. Bengal, 1870:83.
TYPE(S): Holotype: ZSI.
TYPE LOCALITY: Darjeeling [West Bengal] and Khasi Hills [Assam, India].
DISTRIBUTION: Himalayan region of West Bengal, Sikkim, and Assam (India) and
    Nepal.
COMMENT: Subgenus *Paa*. Dubois, 1974, Bull. Mus. Natl. Hist. Nat., Paris,
    (3)213(Zool. 143):365–368, discussed the species (as *Rana assamensis* Sclater,
    1892), and was the first to note that *Rana sikimensis* Jerdon, 1870, was the
    oldest name for this species. See Dubois, 1976, Cah. Nepal., Doc., 6:208, for
    additional discussion (as *Rana sikimensis*).

Rana sphenocephala Cope, 1889. Proc. Am. Philos. Soc., 23:517.

ORIGINAL NAME: *Rana halecina sphenocephala*.

TYPE(S): Not known to exist; neotype designated as UMMZ 56130 by Pace, 1974, Misc. Publ. Mus. Zool. Univ. Michigan, 148:1–140.

TYPE LOCALITY: "a sulphur spring near the St. John's River, about three hundred miles from Key West", Florida, USA; neotype from "Enterprise, Volusia County, Florida", USA.

DISTRIBUTION: Southern New York south along the Atlantic coastal plain to southern Florida, west to eastern Texas, and north to eastern Kansas, southern Illinois, and southern Ohio (excluding most of the Appalachian Mountains); introduced on Grand Bahama I., Bahamas.

COMMENT: In the *Rana pipiens* group of the *Rana pipiens* complex, subgenus *Rana*. *Rana sphenocephala* is a replacement name for *Rana oxyrhynchus* Hallowell, 1856, Proc. Acad. Nat. Sci. Philadelphia, 8:141–143, which is preoccupied by *Rana oxyrhynchus* Smith, 1849. Pace, 1974, Misc. Publ. Mus. Zool. Univ. Michigan, 148:1–140, revived the older name *Rana utricularius* Harlan, 1825, Am. J. Sci. Arts, 10:53–65 (Type: not designated but ANSP 2803 designated neotype by Pace (1974:18); Type locality: Pennsylvania and New Jersey; restricted to vicinity of Philadelphia by Schmidt, 1953, Check List N. Am. Amph. Rept., Ed. 6:82; neotype from "Philadelphia, Pennsylvania", USA), which Pace corrected to *Rana utricularia*. A petition is currently under consideration by the International Commission on Zoological Nomenclature to suppress *Rana utricularia* in favor of *Rana sphenocephala*. According to Article 80 of the International Code of Zoological Nomenclature (1963), the most commonly used name should be used until a decision has been made by the Commission. Because *Rana sphenocephala* has had considerably greater usage than has *Rana utricularia* (Brown, Smith, and Funk, 1976, Herpetol. Rev., 7:5), the former name is adopted here pending a decision by the Commission (DMH).

Rana spinidactyla Cope, 1865. Proc. Acad. Nat. Sci. Philadelphia, 17:197.

TYPE(S): Formerly ANSP, now lost.

TYPE LOCALITY: Natal [Rep. South Africa].

DISTRIBUTION: Unknown.

COMMENT: Considered a synonym of *Ptychadena mascareniensis* by Loveridge, 1957, Bull. Mus. Comp. Zool., 117:342; according to Poynton, 1964, Ann. Natal Mus., 17:93, it is impossible to match this name to any known frog from Natal.

Rana spinosa David, 1875. J. Trois Voy. Chinois, 2:253.

TYPE(S): Not traced.

TYPE LOCALITY: "Ouang-Mao-Tsae", a mountain village in Jiangsi near the Fujian boundary, China.

DISTRIBUTION: Guizhou and southern China (north to Yangtze River) to northern Vietnam.

COMMENT: Subgenus *Paa*. Discussed by Bourret, 1942, Batr. Indochine:287–291; Pope, 1931, Bull. Am. Mus. Nat. Hist., 61:500–508; and Liu and Hu, 1961, Tailless Amph. China:156–159. See also Chang, 1947, Trans. Chinese Assoc. Adv. Sci., 9:93.

Rana spinulosa Smith, 1923. J. Nat. Hist. Soc. Siam, 6:207.

ORIGINAL NAME: *Rana (Hylarana) spinulosa*.

TYPE(S): Holotype: BM (formerly M. Smith 6889).

TYPE LOCALITY: "Tun-fao, Kachek river, altitude 200 metres", Hainan I., China.

DISTRIBUTION: Hainan I., China.

COMMENT: Subgenus *Hylarana*, and closely related to *Rana nigrovittata*, according to the original description. See Bourret, 1942, Batr. Indochine:320–321.

Rana sternosignata Murray, 1885. Ann. Mag. Nat. Hist., (5)16:120.
TYPE(S): Not designated.
TYPE LOCALITY: "Mulleer [=Malir] near Kurrachee [=Karachi]; Zandra and Quetta, in South Afghanistan" (all localities actually in Pakistan).
DISTRIBUTION: Baluchistan (Pakistan) and Afghanistan to Kashmir (India).
COMMENT: Subgenus *Paa*.

Rana subaspera Barbour, 1908. Proc. Biol. Soc. Washington, 21:189.
TYPE(S): Holotype: MCZ 2440.
TYPE LOCALITY: Riu Kiu Islands [Japan].
DISTRIBUTION: Amamioshima and Tokunoshima, Ryukyu Is., Japan.
COMMENT: In the subgenus *Hylarana* according to Dubois, 1981, Monit. Zool. Ital., N.S., Suppl 15:225–284, but in a more exclusive subgenus, *Babina* (with *Rana holsti*), according to Nakamura and Ueno, 1963, Japan. Rept. Amph. Color:53. See Matsui and Utsunamiya, 1983, J. Herpetol., 17:32–37.

Rana syhadrensis Annandale, 1919. Rec. Indian Mus., 16:123.
TYPE(S): ZSI.
TYPE LOCALITY: Medha and Khandala, Bombay [India].
DISTRIBUTION: Eastern and western India; Nepal.
COMMENT: In the subgenus *Euphlyctis*, *Rana tigerina* group. Dubois, 1974, Bull. Mus. Natl. Hist. Nat., Paris, (3)213(Zool. 143):383–384, removed this species from the synonymy of *Rana limnocharis*.

Rana sylvatica LeConte, 1825. Ann. Lyc. Nat. Hist. New York, 1:282.
TYPE(S): Not known to exist.
TYPE LOCALITY: Not stated; designated as "vicinity of New York", New York, USA, by Schmidt, 1953, Check List N. Am. Amph. Rept., Ed. 6:81.
DISTRIBUTION: Alaska (USA) and Labrador (Canada) south to northern Idaho, Minnesota, northern Georgia, and Maryland (USA); isolated populations in southern Missouri and adjacent Arkansas, and northern Colorado (USA).
COMMENT: Subgenus *Rana*. Relationship of this species to other *Rana* is enigmatic; it appears not to be closely related to any of the established species groups. See Case, 1978, Syst. Zool., 27:299–311; Post and Uzzell, 1981, Syst. Zool., 30:170–180. Includes *Rana maslini* Porter, 1969, Herpetologica, 25:213, according to Bagdonas and Pettus, 1976, J. Herpetol., 10:105–112. Reviewed by Martof, 1970, Cat. Am. Amph. Rept., 86.1–4.

Rana tagoi Okada, 1928. Annot. Zool. Japon., 11:271.
TYPE(S): Holotype: TIU 2962.
TYPE LOCALITY: Mountain regions of Gifu Prefecture (Kamitakamura, Yoshikigun), altitude 300 feet [Japan].
DISTRIBUTION: Mountain regions of Honshu, Shikoku, and Kyushu Is., Japan.
COMMENT: Subgenus *Rana*, *Rana temporaria* group. See Nakamura and Ueno, 1963, Japan. Rept. Amph. Color:38–40.

Rana taipehensis Van Denburgh, 1909. Proc. California Acad. Sci., (4)3:56.
TYPE(S): Holotype: CAS 18007.
TYPE LOCALITY: "Taipeh, Formosa" (=Taipeh, Taiwan, China).
DISTRIBUTION: Southern China (west to eastern Yunnan and including Taiwan and Hainan I.) to central Vietnam; eastern India.
COMMENT: In the subgenus *Hylarana*. Discussed by Pope, 1931, Bull. Am. Mus. Nat. Hist., 61:539–540; Bourret, 1942, Batr. Indochine:335–337; and Liu and Hu, 1961, Tailless Amph. China:199–201. See comment under *Rana erythraea*.

Rana taiwaniana Otsu, 1973. Q. J. Taiwan Mus., 26:114.
TYPE(S): Holotype: Mus. Yamagata Univ., Sect. Zool., i—1,206.
TYPE LOCALITY: "Shanlin Chiti of Taiwan", north side of Mt. Ali, alt. 7600 m, Taiwan, China.
DISTRIBUTION: Known only from the type locality.

COMMENT: In the subgenus *Hylarana*.

Rana tarahumarae Boulenger, 1917. Ann. Mag. Nat. Hist., (8)20:416.
TYPE(S): Syntypes: BM 1947.2.1.63–64 (formerly 1914.1.28.148–149) and
    1947.2.28.76–79 (formerly 1911.12.12.36–39).
TYPE LOCALITY: "Ioquiro [=Yoquivo] and Barranca del Cobre, Sierra Tarahumaré,
    [Chihuahua,] N.W. Mexico"; restricted to Yoquivo, Chihuahua, Mexico, by
    Smith and Taylor, 1950, Univ. Kansas Sci. Bull., 33:327.
DISTRIBUTION: Extreme southern Arizona (USA) south through the Sierra Madre
    Occidental of Sonora, Chihuahua, Sinaloa, Nayarit, Jalisco, and
    Aguascalientes (Mexico).
COMMENT: Reviewed by Zweifel, 1965, Cat. Am. Amph. Rept., 66.1–2. The
    southern populations here referred to *Rana tarahumarae* may be a distinct
    species (DMH). In the *Rana tarahumarae* group, subgenus *Rana*. The USA
    population is effectively extinct (pers. comm., S. F. Hale and C. J. May to
    DRF).

Rana tasanae Smith, 1921. J. Nat. Hist. Soc. Siam, 4:193.
TYPE(S): BM.
TYPE LOCALITY: "Tasan, 25 miles S. W. Chumporn, Peninsular Siam [Thailand]".
DISTRIBUTION: Peninsular Thailand.
COMMENT: Closely related to *Rana beddomii* according to the original description.
    See comment under *Rana beddomii*. Reviewed by Bourret, 1942, Batr.
    Indochine:376–377. *Rana tasanae* is a replacement name for *Rana pullus* Smith,
    1921, J. Fed. Malay States Mus., 10:197, which is preoccupied by *Rana pullus*
    Stoliczka, 1870.

Rana taylori Smith, 1959. Herpetologica, 15:214.
TYPE(S): Holotype: FMNH 103210; not KU 2978 as stated in the original
    description; 2978 refers to R. C. Taylor's personal catalogue.
TYPE LOCALITY: "Peralta, Costa Rica".
DISTRIBUTION: Low elevations along the Atlantic coast of Nicaragua and Costa Rica.
COMMENT: In the *Rana pipiens* complex, subgenus *Rana*.

Rana temporalis (Günther, 1864). Rept. Brit. India:427.
ORIGINAL NAME: *Hylorana temporalis*.
TYPE(S): BM.
TYPE LOCALITY: "Ceylon" (=Sri Lanka).
DISTRIBUTION: Anamalai Hills (Kerala, India); Sri Lanka.
COMMENT: In the subgenus *Hylarana*, *Rana erythraea* group. Discussed by
    Kirtisinghe, 1957, Amph. Ceylon:45–48.

Rana temporaria Linnaeus, 1758. Syst. Nat., Ed. 10, 1:212.
TYPE(S): Unknown.
TYPE LOCALITY: Europe; restricted to "Schweden" by Mertens and Müller, 1928,
    Abh. Senckenb. Naturforsch. Ges., 41:20.
DISTRIBUTION: Throughout Europe east to the Urals, but excluding most of Iberia,
    much of Italy, and the southern Balkans.
COMMENT: In the *Rana temporaria* group, subgenus *Rana*.

Rana tenuilingua Rao, 1937. Proc. Indian Acad. Sci., (B)6:397.
TYPE(S): CCB; now lost (SD).
TYPE LOCALITY: "Kemphole Ghats, Hassan, Mysore, South India".
DISTRIBUTION: Mysore, India.

Rana tiannanensis Yang and Li, 1980. Zool. Res., Kunming, 1(2):261.
TYPE(S): Holotype: KIZ 77I0185.
TYPE LOCALITY: Hekou, Dawei Hill, altitude 1200 m, Yunnan, China.
DISTRIBUTION: Yunnan, China.

COMMENT: Related to *Rana anlungensis,* according to the original description. In the subgenus *Hylarana,* by implication.

Rana tientaiensis Chang, 1933. Peking Nat. Hist. Bull., 8:75–80.
TYPE(S): Lost.
TYPE LOCALITY: Tientai, east-central Chekiang [=Zhejiang], China.
DISTRIBUTION: Zhejiang and Anhui, China.
COMMENT: Considered a synonym of *Rana rugosa* by Liu and Hu, 1961, Tailless Amph. China:141–142, but considered a distinct species by Szechwan Biol. Res. Inst., 1977, Syst. Key Chinese Amph.:41, 82, and Zhao and Huang, 1982, Acta Herpetol. Sinica, 1(1):10.

Rana tigerina Daudin, 1802. Hist. Nat. Rain. Gren. Crap.:42.
TYPE(S): MNHNP (now lost).
TYPE LOCALITY: Bengal, India.
DISTRIBUTION: India to Malaya and southern China (north to Hubei and including Taiwan); Sri Lanka; introduced on Madagascar.
COMMENT: In the subgenus *Euphlyctis, Rana tigerina* group. Taiwan population reviewed by Okada, 1931, Tailless Batr. Japan. Emp.:149–151. Reviewed by Bourret, 1942, Batr. Indochine:240–241. See also accounts by Berry, 1975, Amph. Fauna Peninsular Malaysia:88–89, and Taylor, 1962, Univ. Kansas Sci. Bull., 43:368–371. The unjustified emendation *Rana tigrina* has had widespread use.
REVIEWER: Rose M. A. Blommers-Schlösser (RMABS).

Rana timorensis Smith, 1927. Proc. Zool. Soc. London, 1927:211.
TYPE(S): BM.
TYPE LOCALITY: Diamplong, South Timor [Indonesia].
DISTRIBUTION: Timor I., Indonesia.

Rana tormota. Wu, 1977. Acta Zool. Sinica, 23:113.
ORIGINAL NAME: *Rana tormotus.*
TYPE(S): Holotype: CIB (formerly SWIBASC) 720058.
TYPE LOCALITY: "Tau-hua-qu, Huangshan, Anhui, altitude 650 m", China.
DISTRIBUTION: Huang-Shan, Anhui, China.
COMMENT: In the subgenus *Hylarana,* according to the original description.

Rana toumanoffi Bourret, 1941. Instr. Publique, Hanoi, 1941:23.
TYPE(S): Holotype: MNHNP 48-126; formerly in Inst. Pasteur (Saigon); formerly Lab. Sci. Nat. Univ. Hanoi.
TYPE LOCALITY: Cambodge: Mimot.
DISTRIBUTION: Known only from the type locality.
COMMENT: In the subgenus *Euphlyctis, Rana grunniens* group. Reviewed by Bourret, 1942, Batr. Indochine:272–274.

Rana travancorica Annandale, 1910. Rec. Indian Mus., 5:191.
TYPE(S): ZSI.
TYPE LOCALITY: Travancore [India].
DISTRIBUTION: Kerala, India.

Rana tsushimensis Stejneger, 1907. Bull. U.S. Natl. Mus., 58:116.
TYPE(S): Holotype: USNM 17519.
TYPE LOCALITY: "Tsushima, Japan".
DISTRIBUTION: Tsushima I., Korea Strait, Japan.
COMMENT: In the *Rana temporaria* group, subgenus *Rana.* See Kuramoto, 1974, Copeia, 1974:815–822, for a discussion of relationships. Reviewed by Okada, 1966, Fauna Japon., Anura:95–99.

Rana tweediei Smith, 1935. Bull. Raffles Mus., 10:62.

TYPE(S): Holotype: BM 1934.5.21.1.

TYPE LOCALITY: "near the River Yum, Headwater Plus River, alt. 2,000 feet", Perak, Malaysia (Malaya).

DISTRIBUTION: Lowlands (up to 900 m) of Malaya.

COMMENT: Considered a synonym of *Rana nitida* by Kiew, 1975, Malay. Nat. J., 28: 107–109, but this synonymy was disputed by Dring, 1979, Bull. Brit. Mus. (Nat. Hist.), Zool., 34:204–206, who posited that this species might be more closely related to *Rana microdisca*.

Rana unculuana Liu, Hu, and Yang, 1960. Acta Zool. Sinica, 12:164.

ORIGINAL NAME: *Rana unculuanus*.

TYPE(S): Holotype: CIB (formerly SBRI) 581665.

TYPE LOCALITY: "Hsin-ming-hsiang, Ching-tung, Yunnan, 2030 m altitude", China.

DISTRIBUTION: Known only from the type locality.

COMMENT: Reviewed by Liu and Hu, 1961, Tailless Amph. China:171–174.

Rana varians Boulenger, 1894. Ann. Mag. Nat. Hist., (6)14:86.

TYPE(S): Not traced.

TYPE LOCALITY: Palawan [Philippines].

DISTRIBUTION: Philippines; Yunnan, Guangxi, and Hainan I., China.

COMMENT: In the subgenus *Hylarana*, *Rana erythraea* group. Considered a junior synonym of *Rana sanguinea* by Inger, 1954, Fieldiana: Zool., 33:328, but considered a distinct species by Liu and Hu, 1961, Tailless Amph. China:201–203.

Rana verruculosa Roux, 1911. Zool. Jahrb., Abt. Syst., 30:504.

ORIGINAL NAME: *Rana tigrina* var. *verruculosa*.

TYPE(S): SMF 6538 (formerly 1026.4a) designated lectotype by Mertens, 1967, Senckenb. Biol., 48:46.

TYPE LOCALITY: "Wetar, Iliwaki", Lesser Sundas, Indonesia.

DISTRIBUTION: Wetar I., Sundas, Indonesia.

COMMENT: In the subgenus *Euphlyctis*, *Rana tigerina* group, according to Dubois, 1981, Monit. Zool. Ital., N.S., Suppl., 15:225–284.

Rana versabilis Liu and Hu, 1962. Acta Zool. Sinica, 14(Suppl.):89.

TYPE(S): Holotype: CIB (formerly SBRI) 603803.

TYPE LOCALITY: "San-men of Hua-ping, Lung-shen-hsien, altitude 870 m, Kwangsi [=Guangxi]", China.

DISTRIBUTION: Southeastern China, including Guizhou.

COMMENT: Related to *Rana sanguinea* (and by implication, in the subgenus *Hylarana*, *Rana erythraea* group), according to the original description.

Rana vertebralis Hewitt, 1927. Rec. Albany Mus., 3:404.

TYPE(S): Holotype: AMG.

TYPE LOCALITY: Summit of Mont-aux-Sources [Lesotho].

DISTRIBUTION: Highlands of Lesotho; recorded from the Umzimkulu River below the Drakensberg Escarpment, Natal, Rep. South Africa.

COMMENT: Subgenus *Rana*. Discussed by Poynton, 1964, Ann. Natal Mus., 17:109, who included *Rana umbraculata* in synonymy. See also Channing, 1979, Ann. Natal Mus., 23:797–831.

Rana vibicaria (Cope, 1894). Proc. Am. Philos. Soc., 46:197.

ORIGINAL NAME: *Levirana vibicaria*.

TYPE(S): Not stated, but AMNH 5463 is catalogued as the type; AMNH 5463 designated lectotype by Zweifel, 1964, Copeia, 1964:300.

TYPE LOCALITY: "Rancho Redondo, on the divide of the Irazú range", Costa Rica.

DISTRIBUTION: High elevations (above 1500 m) of Costa Rica and western Panama.

COMMENT: In the *Rana palmipes* group, subgenus *Rana*. See Taylor, 1952, Univ. Kansas Sci. Bull., 35:900–903, for synonymy and discussion.

Rana vicina Stoliczka, 1872. Proc. Asiat. Soc. Bengal, 1872:130.
TYPE(S): Holotype: ZSI.
TYPE LOCALITY: Marri [=Murree], western Himalayas [northern Pakistan], at an elevation to 6000 ft.
DISTRIBUTION: Himalayas and Simla, India.
COMMENT: In the subgenus *Paa*. Reviewed by Dubois, 1980 "1978", C. R. Séances Soc. Biogeogr., 485:167–169. See comment under *Nanorana pleskei*.

Rana virgatipes Cope, 1891. Am. Nat., 25:1017.
TYPE(S): Not designated but ANSP 10759–64 are labeled as types.
TYPE LOCALITY: "cut-off of a tributary of the Great Egg Harbor River in Atlantic county, New Jersey"; revised to "Mare Run tributary of Great Egg Harbor above May's landing, Atlantic County", New Jersey, USA, by Fowler, 1907, Proc. Acad. Nat. Sci. Philadelphia, 57:122.
DISTRIBUTION: Coastal plain of Atlantic coast from southern New Jersey to Georgia; populations of questionable taxonomic status in Florida, USA.
COMMENT: In the *Rana catesbeiana* group, subgenus *Rana*. Reviewed by Gosner and Black, 1968, Cat. Am. Amph. Rept., 67.1–2.

Rana warschewitschii (Schmidt, 1857). Sitzungsber. Akad. Wiss. Wien, Math. Naturwiss. Kl., 24:11.
ORIGINAL NAME: *Ixalus warschewitschii*.
TYPE(S): Not known to exist.
TYPE LOCALITY: "Unweit des Vulcanes Chiriqui, zwischen 6000 und 7000 höhe, Panama".
DISTRIBUTION: Low and moderate elevations of eastern Honduras, Nicaragua, Costa Rica, and Panama.
COMMENT: In the *Rana palmipes* group, subgenus *Rana*. See Taylor, 1952, Univ. Kansas Sci. Bull., 35:896–899, for synonymy and discussion.

Rana weiningensis Liu, Hu, and Yang, 1962. Acta Zool. Sinica, 14(3):387.
TYPE(S): Holotype: CIB (formerly SWIBASC) 590455.
TYPE LOCALITY: "Tuo-luo-he of Long-chu, Weining, altitude 1700 m, Kweichow [=Guizhou]", China.
DISTRIBUTION: Guizhou and Sichuan, China.
COMMENT: Related to *Rana varians* (and by implication in the subgenus *Hylarana*, *Rana erythraea* group), according to the original description.

Rana wittei (Angel, 1924). Bull. Mus. Natl. Hist. Nat., Paris, 30:130.
ORIGINAL NAME: *Phrynobatrachus Wittei*.
TYPE(S): Holotype: MNHNP 24-15.
TYPE LOCALITY: Molo, Mau Escarpment, Kenya Colony [=Kenya].
DISTRIBUTION: Kenya to eastern Zaire.
COMMENT: Loveridge, 1957, Bull. Mus. Comp. Zool., 117:339, included *Rana aberdariensis* in synonymy. The species is not yet well defined (JLP).

Rana woodworthi Taylor, 1923. Philippine J. Sci., 22:519.
TYPE(S): Holotype: CAS 61000 (formerly EHT 1921).
TYPE LOCALITY: "near Los Baños, Laguna Province", Luzon, Philippines; recorded as Polillo, Philippine Islands, by Cochran, 1961, Bull. U.S. Natl. Mus., 220:77.
DISTRIBUTION: Luzon I., Philippines.
COMMENT: In the subgenus *Euphlyctis*, *Rana grunniens* group. Possibly a subspecies of *Rana microdisca* according to Inger, 1954, Fieldiana: Zool., 33:292.

Rana wuchuanensis Xu, 1983. *In* Wu, Xu, Dong, Li, and Liu, Acta Zool. Sinica, 29(1):66.
TYPE(S): Holotype: Zunyi Medical College 792238.
TYPE LOCALITY: Baicun, Wuchuan, Guizhou, altitude 720 m, China.
DISTRIBUTION: Known only from the type locality.

COMMENT: Related to *Rana kuangwuensis*, according to the original description.

Rana yavapaiensis Platz and Frost, 1984. Copeia, 1984:940.
   TYPE(S): Holotype: AMNH 117632.
   TYPE LOCALITY: "Tule Creek (elev. 670 m), 34° 00', 112° 16', Yavapai Co.,
      Arizona", USA.
   DISTRIBUTION: Low and moderate elevations in the drainage of the lower
      Colorado River and its tributaries in Nevada, California, Arizona, and New
      Mexico (USA), and northern Sonora and extreme northeastern Baja
      California del Norte (Mexico).
   COMMENT: Known for a long time as the "lowland form" of *Rana pipiens* of Platz
      and Platz, 1973, Science, Washington, D.C., 179:1334–1336. This species has
      not been collected in recent years in southern California nor along the
      lower Colorado River, though old specimens exist from both of these areas.
      The southern limit of distribution is poorly known. In the *Rana berlandieri*
      group of the *Rana pipiens* complex, subgenus *Rana*. Most closely related to
      Rana magnaocularis.

Rana zweifeli Hillis, Frost, and Webb, 1984. Copeia, 1984:399.
   TYPE(S): Holotype: KU 192466.
   TYPE LOCALITY: "12 km E (by road) of Teloloapan, Guerrero, Mexico".
   DISTRIBUTION: Southern Jalisco and Colima southeast along the escarpment of the
      Mexican Plateau in Michoacán, México (state), and Morelos, throughout low
      and moderate elevations of Guerrero, and into southern Puebla and
      northwestern Oaxaca, Mexico.
   COMMENT: In the *Rana tarahumarae* group, subgenus *Rana*, according to the original
      description. This species had been mistakenly referred to as *Rana pustulosa* in
      most literature. See comment under *Rana pustulosa*.

Staurois Cope, 1865. Nat. Hist. Rev., N.S., 5:117.
   TYPE SPECIES: *Ixalus natator* Günther, 1859, by subsequent designation of Boulenger,
      1918, Ann. Mag. Nat. Hist., (9)1:117.
   DISTRIBUTION: Borneo and the Philippines.
   COMMENT: See comment under *Amolops*. Inger, 1966, Fieldiana: Zool., 52:245–255,
      provided synonymies and reviews for the Bornean species, and redefined the
      genus. Dubois, 1981, Monit. Zool. Ital., N.S., Suppl., 15:234, regarded this genus
      as closely related to *Amolops* and Asian members of the subgenus *Hylarana* of
      Rana.

Staurois latopalmatus (Boulenger, 1887). Ann. Mag. Nat. Hist., (5)20:97.
   ORIGINAL NAME: *Ixalus latopalmata*.
   TYPE(S): BM.
   TYPE LOCALITY: Mount Kina Balu, Sabah [Malaysia (Borneo)].
   DISTRIBUTION: Northern and western Borneo.

Staurois natator (Günther, 1859 "1858"). Cat. Batr. Sal. Coll. Brit. Mus.:75.
   ORIGINAL NAME: *Ixalus natator*.
   TYPE(S): Syntypes: BM 1933.9.10.9–11.
   TYPE LOCALITY: "Philippines".
   DISTRIBUTION: Philippines; Borneo.
   COMMENT: Philippine population reviewed by Inger, 1954, Fieldiana: Zool., 33:
      335–344.

Staurois tuberilinguis Boulenger, 1918. Ann. Mag. Nat. Hist., (9)1:374.
   TYPE(S): Not traced.
   TYPE LOCALITY: "Mount Kina Balu, North Borneo, altitude 4200 feet" and "Mt.
      Batu Song, Sarawak, 1000 feet", Malaysia (Borneo).
   DISTRIBUTION: Northern Borneo.
   COMMENT: Synonymy includes *Staurois parvus* Inger and Haile, 1960, according to
      Inger, 1966, Fieldiana: Zool., 52:250–251.

Strongylopus Tschudi, 1838. Classif. Batr.:38.
    TYPE SPECIES: *Rana fasciata* Tschudi, 1838 (=*Rana fasciata* Smith, 1849) (see comment).
    DISTRIBUTION: Disjunct distribution from Rep. South Africa through uplands to
        Tanzania.
    COMMENT: Although Opinion 713, 1964, Bull. Zool. Nomencl., 21:352–354,
        suppressed for the purposes of both the Law of Priority and Law of Homonymy
        all uses of *Rana fasciata* prior to *Rana fasciata* Smith, 1849, it did not suppress
        Rana fasciata Tschudi, 1838, for purposes of identifying the type species.
        Strongylopus has a polytomous relationship with African (possibly all) *Hylarana*
        and *Rana* (as here treated, subgenera of *Rana*), according to Clarke, 1981, Monit.
        Zool. Ital., N.S., Suppl., 15:285–311; considered a distinct genus by Channing,
        1979, Ann. Natal Mus., 23:797–831.
    CONTRIBUTOR: Alan Channing (AC).

Strongylopus bonaspei (Dubois, 1980). Bull. Mus. Natl. Hist. Nat., Paris, (4)2A(3):929.
    ORIGINAL NAME: *Rana bonaspei*.
    TYPE(S): Holotype: TM.
    TYPE LOCALITY: Jonkersberg, Attaqua Mountains [Rep. South Africa].
    DISTRIBUTION: Southwestern Cape, Cape Province, Rep. South Africa.
    COMMENT: Channing, 1979, Ann. Natal Mus., 23:797–831, elevated this form to
        species status. Status of species fully discussed by Greig, Boycott, and de
        Villiers, 1979, Ann. Cape Prov. Mus. (Nat. Hist.), 13:1–30. *Rana bonaspei* is a
        replacement name for *Rana fasciata montanus* FitzSimons, 1946, Ann. Transvaal
        Mus., 20:351, which is a primary homonym of *Rana temporaria montanus* Koch,
        1872.

Strongylopus fasciatus (Smith, 1849). Illustr. Zool. S. Afr., Rept.:pl. 78, fig. 1.
    ORIGINAL NAME: *Rana fasciata*.
    TYPE(S): BM 58.11.25.127 designated neotype for *Rana fasciata* Burchell, 1824, by
        Parker and Ride, 1962, Bull. Zool. Nomencl., 19:290–292; this neotype
        regarded as lectotype of *Rana fasciata* Smith, 1849, by Opinion 713, 1964, Bull.
        Zool. Nomencl., 21:352–354 (see comment).
    TYPE LOCALITY: "cap de Bonne-Espérance" (=Cape of Good Hope), Rep. South
        Africa.
    DISTRIBUTION: Disjunct distribution from Rep. South Africa through upland to
        northern Tanzania.
    COMMENT: See Opinion 713, 1964, Bull. Zool. Nomencl., 21:352–354, in which uses
        of *Rana fasciata* (including uses by Tschudi, 1838, and Duméril and Bibron,
        1843) were suppressed for the purposes of homonymy and priority under the
        plenary powers of the Commission of Zoological Nomenclature. In addition,
        Rana fasciata Smith, 1849, was placed on the Official List of Specific Names in
        Zoology. See comment under *Strongylopus*. Subspecies reviewed by Poynton,
        1964, Senckenb. Biol., 45:203–205.

Strongylopus grayii (Smith, 1849). Illustr. Zool. S. Afr., Rept.:pl. 78.
    ORIGINAL NAME: *Rana grayii*.
    TYPE(S): BM.
    TYPE LOCALITY: "western districts of the Cape Colony", Rep. South Africa.
    DISTRIBUTION: Zimbabwe and southwestern Mozambique to Rep. South Africa;
        introduced on St. Helena I.

Strongylopus hymenopus Boulenger, 1920. Ann. Mag. Nat. Hist., (9)6:106.
    ORIGINAL NAME: *Rana hymenopus*.
    TYPE(S): BM.
    TYPE LOCALITY: "South Africa".
    DISTRIBUTION: Natal Drakensberg, Rep. South Africa.

Strongylopus wageri (Wager, 1961). Afr. Wildl., 15:151.
ORIGINAL NAME: *Rana wageri*.
TYPE(S): Holotype: NMP.
TYPE LOCALITY: Not stated; designated as Weza Forest Reserve, Natal, Rep. South Africa, by Poynton, 1963, Ann. Natal Mus., 15:329.
DISTRIBUTION: Natal uplands and Transvaal Drakensberg, Rep. South Africa.
COMMENT: Name published unintentionally by Wager. Description and designation of types is in Poynton, 1963, Ann. Natal Mus., 15:329.

Tomopterna Duméril and Bibron, 1841. Erp. Gén., 8:443.
TYPE SPECIES: *Pyxicephalus delalandii* Tschudi, 1838, by subsequent designation of Boulenger, 1918, Bull. Soc. Zool. France, 1918:113.
DISTRIBUTION: India; Madagascar; subsaharan Africa.
COMMENT: Synonymies for South African species are in Poynton, 1964, Ann. Natal Mus., 17:96–102, under *Pyxicephalus*. Dubois, 1981, Monit. Zool. Ital., N.S., Suppl., 15:225–284, considered this genus a subgenus of *Rana* closely related to *Euphlyctis* and *Limnonectes*. Clarke, 1981, Monit. Zool. Ital., N.S., Suppl., 15:285–331, noted that at least the African members of *Euphlyctis* were more closely related to *Conraua* and retained *Euphlyctis* as a subgenus of *Rana*, and *Tomopterna* as a monophyletic genus of unresolved relationship to other ranines. Dubois, 1983, Alytes, Paris, 2:163–170, noted that Asian members of the genus could be placed in two groups, the *Tomopterna rufescens* group (that approached the subgenus *Euphlyctis* of *Rana*) and the *Tomopterna breviceps* group (that approached the African and Madagascan members of the genus).
CONTRIBUTORS: Alan Channing (AC) (Africa); Sushil Dutta (SD) (India).
REVIEWER: Rose M. A. Blommers-Schlösser (RMABS) (Madagascar).

Tomopterna breviceps (Schneider, 1799). Hist. Amph., 1:140.
ORIGINAL NAME: *Rana breviceps*.
TYPE(S): Syntypes: including ZMB (2 specimens).
TYPE LOCALITY: "Indes orientales"; "probablement de Tranquebar (Tamil Nadu; 11° 02′ N, 79° 51′ E)" according to Dubois, 1983, Alytes, Paris, 2:164.
DISTRIBUTION: Punjab, Sind, and Gangetic Plain to southern India and Upper Burma; Sri Lanka.
COMMENT: In the *Tomopterna breviceps* group. Synonymy includes *Rana dobsoni* Boulenger, 1882, according to Bhati and Shukla, 1975, Ann. Zool., Agra, 11:73–75. Reviewed by Kirtisinghe, 1957, Amph. Ceylon:43–45. Dubois, 1983, Alytes, Paris, 2:163–170, discussed the species and named a subspecies from Sri Lanka, *Tomopterna breviceps rolandae*, which SD regards as a distinct species. See comment under *Tomopterna strachani*.

Tomopterna cryptotis (Boulenger, 1907). Ann. Mag. Nat. Hist., (7)20:109.
ORIGINAL NAME: *Rana cryptotis*.
TYPE(S): BM.
TYPE LOCALITY: "Catequero, Ponang Kuma (Dongwenna), and in the Kafitu Swamps", Angola.
DISTRIBUTION: Subsaharan Africa in xeric regions.
COMMENT: See Carruthers and Carruthers, 1979, J. Herpetol. Assoc. Afr., 20:3–5, for distribution records. See Lanza, 1981, Monit. Zool. Ital., N.S., Suppl., 15:168, for synonymy.

Tomopterna delalandii (Tschudi, 1838). Classif. Batr.:46.
ORIGINAL NAME: *Pyxicephalus delalandii*.
TYPE(S): Syntypes: MNHNP 721, 4521, and 4529 (5 specimens), RMNH 2261 (2 specimens).
TYPE LOCALITY: "Promontorium Bonae Spei", Rep. South Africa.
DISTRIBUTION: Southwestern Cape Province, Rep. South Africa.

Tomopterna krugerensis Passmore and Carruthers, 1975. Koedoe, 18:32.
TYPE(S): Holotype: TM.
TYPE LOCALITY: South Africa, Kruger National Park.
DISTRIBUTION: Rep. South Africa-Mozambique border area to the Namibia-Angola border area.
COMMENT: Many old records probably confused with *Tomopterna cryptotis* (AC). Probably has a wider distribution northward than indicated, but obscured by confusion with other species (JCP).

Tomopterna labrosa Cope, 1868. Proc. Acad. Nat. Sci. Philadelphia, 20:138.
TYPE(S): Syntypes: MCZ 1583, 1584 (total of 3 specimens).
TYPE LOCALITY: Madagascar.
DISTRIBUTION: Southern and western forests of Madagascar.
COMMENT: Reviewed by Guibé, 1978, Bonn. Zool. Monogr., 11:9–10.
REVIEWER: Rose M. A. Blommers-Schlösser (RMABS).

Tomopterna leucorhynchus (Rao, 1937). Proc. Indian Acad. Sci., (B)6:392.
ORIGINAL NAME: *Rana leucorhynchus*.
TYPE(S): CCB; now lost (SD).
TYPE LOCALITY: "Wattakole, Coorg, South India".
DISTRIBUTION: Known only from the type locality.
COMMENT: In the *Tomopterna rufescens* group.

Tomopterna marmorata (Peters, 1854). Monatsber. Preuss. Akad. Wiss. Berlin, 1854:627.
ORIGINAL NAME: *Pyxicephalus marmoratus*.
TYPE(S): ZMB.
TYPE LOCALITY: Boror, Mozambique.
DISTRIBUTION: Northern Natal (Rep. South Africa) and Mozambique to Botswana and Zambia.
COMMENT: Possibly has a wider distribution northward than indicated but obscured by confusion with other species (JCP).

Tomopterna natalensis (Smith, 1849). Illustr. Zool. S. Afr., Rept., App.:23.
ORIGINAL NAME: *Pyxicephalus natalensis*.
TYPE(S): BM (probable holotype).
TYPE LOCALITY: "eastward of the Cape Colony", Rep. South Africa.
DISTRIBUTION: Southern Mozambique and Transvaal, Natal, and eastern Cape Province, Rep. South Africa.

Tomopterna parambikulamana (Rao, 1937). Proc. Indian Acad. Sci., (B)6:391.
ORIGINAL NAME: *Rana parambikulamana*.
TYPE(S): Holotype: CCB; now lost (SD).
TYPE LOCALITY: "Parambikulam forests, Cochin State [now part of Kerala], S. India".
DISTRIBUTION: Known only from the type locality.
COMMENT: In the *Tomopterna rufescens* group.

Tomopterna rufescens (Jerdon, 1854). J. Asiat. Soc. Bengal, 22:534.
ORIGINAL NAME: *Pyxicephalus rufescens*.
TYPE(S): Not stated.
TYPE LOCALITY: "Malabar", India.
DISTRIBUTION: Malabar (Kerala, India).
COMMENT: In the *Tomopterna rufescens* group.

Tomopterna strachani Murray, 1884. Zool. Sind:399.
TYPE(S): Karachi Mus., probably lost.
TYPE LOCALITY: "Sind (Mulleer)" (=Malir, near Karachi), Pakistan.
DISTRIBUTION: Malir, Karachi, Sind (Pakistan).

COMMENT: In the *Tomopterna breviceps* group. Khan, 1976, Biologia, Lahore, 22:208, following Mertens, 1969, Stuttgart. Beitr. Naturkd., 197:15, noted that *Tomopterna strachani* was probably a synonym of *Tomopterna breviceps*.

Tomopterna swani (Myers and Leviton, 1956). Occas. Pap. Nat. Hist. Mus. Stanford Univ., 1956:7.
ORIGINAL NAME: *Rana swani*.
TYPE(S): Holotype: CAS-SU 15371.
TYPE LOCALITY: Dharan, eastern Nepal, at an altitude of 1000 ft.
DISTRIBUTION: Nepal.
COMMENT: Transferred to *Tomopterna* from *Rana* by Dubois, 1976, Cah. Nepal., Doc., 6:12.

Tomopterna tuberculosa (Boulenger, 1882). Cat. Batr. Sal. Brit. Mus.:30.
ORIGINAL NAME: *Rana tuberculosa*.
TYPE(S): Syntypes: BM.
TYPE LOCALITY: "Pungo Andongo", Angola, and "W. Africa".
DISTRIBUTION: Angola and Nambia to Tanzania and Zimbabwe.
COMMENT: See Laurent, 1959, Publ. Cult. Companhia Diamantes Angola, 67:133, for synonymy. See also (as *Rana tuberculosa*) Schmidt and Inger, 1959, Explor. Parc Natl. Upemba, 56:36–38.

FAMILY: **Rhacophoridae** Hoffman, 1932 (1859).
CITATION: S. Afr. J. Sci., 29:562.
DISTRIBUTION: Africa; Madagascar; southern Asia to the Indo-Australian Archipelago.
COMMENT: Under the provisions of Article 40 of the International Code of Zoological Nomenclature (1985), for purposes of priority Rhacophoridae takes the date of Polypedatidae Günther, 1859 "1858", Cat. Batr. Sal. Coll. Brit. Mus.:70. Liem, 1970, Fieldiana: Zool., 57:1–145, discussed phylogenetic relationships within the family, provided generic synonymies, and considered the Rhacophoridae (in his sense, including the mantelline ranids of other authors and this checklist) to be derived from a generalized Asiatic group of the Ranidae. Lynch, 1973, *In* Vial (ed.), Evol. Biol. Anurans:133–182, considered this group to be a subfamily of the Ranidae. The subfamilial classification employed here is that of Dubois, 1981, Monit. Zool. Ital., N.S., Suppl., 15:225–284, who also supplied generic synonymies. Dubois erected the subfamilies on the basis of Liem's preferred phylogenetic tree, which showed *Philautus* as quite derived but phylogenetically most closely related to *Rhacophorus*, *Polypedates*, *Nyctixalus*, *Theloderma*, and *Chirixalus*, to the exclusion of other rhacophorids. Wagner analysis of Liem's data set shows previously hypothesized relationships to be equivocal (DCC).
CONTRIBUTORS: Rose M. A. Blommers-Schlösser (RMABS) (Madagascar); Robert F. Inger (RFI) (Asia).
REVIEWERS: Angel Alcala (AA) (Philippines); Leo J. Borkin (LJB) (Palearctic Asia); Walter C. Brown (WCB) (Philippines); J. C. Daniel (JCD) (India and Sri Lanka); William E. Duellman (WED); Sushil Dutta (SD) (India and Sri Lanka); Marinus S. Hoogmoed (MSH); Shuqin Hu (SH) (China); Masafumi Matsui (MM) (East Asia); Ermi Zhao (EZ) (China).

SUBFAMILY: **Philautinae** Dubois, 1981.
CITATION: Monit. Zool. Ital., N.S., Suppl., 13:258.
DISTRIBUTION: India and Sri Lanka through Burma and Thailand to China, the Philippines, and the Greater Sunda Is.
COMMENT: See comment under Rhacophoridae and Rhacophorinae.

Philautus Gistel, 1848. Naturgesch. Thierr.:10.
TYPE SPECIES: *Hyla aurifasciatus* Schlegel, 1837, by monotypy.
DISTRIBUTION: India and Sri Lanka through Burma and Thailand to China, the Philippines, and the Greater Sunda Is.

COMMENT: The last generic revision (Ahl, 1931, Das Tierreich, 55) is badly out of date. Even more recent, geographically restricted reviews such as those for Sri Lanka (Kirtisinghe, 1957, Amph. Ceylon), Thailand (Taylor, 1962, Univ. Kansas Sci. Bull., 63:265–599), and Borneo (Inger, 1966, Fieldiana: Zool., 52:1–402), are severely in need of revision, both with respect to species boundaries and generic definitions. Ahl, 1931, Das Tierreich, 55, created nomenclatural mischief by treating *Philautus* as a subgenus of *Rhacophorus*, thus creating many secondary homonyms for which, not surprisingly, Ahl provided his own substitute names (RFI). However, Article 59.b of the International Code of Zoological Nomenclature (1985) requires retention of Ahl's names.

Philautus acutirostris (Peters, 1867). Monatsber. Preuss. Akad. Wiss. Berlin, 1867:32.
ORIGINAL NAME: *Ixalus acutirostris*.
TYPE(S): Not traced; probably ZMB.
TYPE LOCALITY: Eastern Mindanao, Philippines.
DISTRIBUTION: Mindanao and Basilan, Philippines.

Philautus adspersus (Günther, 1872). Ann. Mag. Nat. Hist., (4)9:87.
ORIGINAL NAME: *Ixalus adspersus*.
TYPE(S): Holotype: BM 1947.2.26.89 (formerly 71.12.14.36).
TYPE LOCALITY: Central Ceylon [Sri Lanka].
DISTRIBUTION: Sri Lanka.

Philautus albopunctatus Liu and Hu, 1962. Acta Zool. Sinica, 14(Suppl.):99.
TYPE(S): Holotype: CIB (formerly SWIBASC) 601686.
TYPE LOCALITY: "Yang-liu-chung, Yaoshan, altitude 1350 m, Kwangsi [=Guangxi]", China.
DISTRIBUTION: Guangxi and Tibet, China.

Philautus alticola Ahl, 1931. Das Tierreich, 55:95.
TYPE(S): Holotype: formerly Philippine Bureau of Science 29; destroyed in World War II.
TYPE LOCALITY: Mount Bongao, Bongao Island, Sulu Archipelago [Philippines].
DISTRIBUTION: Known only from the destroyed holotype.
COMMENT: *Philautus alticola* is a replacement name for *Philautus montanus* Taylor, 1920, Philippine J. Sci., 16:305, which is preoccupied.

Philautus amoenus Smith, 1931. Bull. Raffles Mus., 5:18.
TYPE(S): Holotype: BM 1947.2.6.6 (formerly 1929.12.22.25).
TYPE LOCALITY: Kamboranga, Mount Kina Balu, Sabah [Malaysia (Borneo)].
DISTRIBUTION: Known only from the type locality.

Philautus andersoni (Ahl, 1927). Sitzungsber. Ges. Naturforsch. Freunde Berlin, 1927:36.
ORIGINAL NAME: *Rhacophorus andersoni*.
TYPE(S): Not traced.
TYPE LOCALITY: Kakhyen Hills, Burma.
DISTRIBUTION: Assam (India), northern Burma, southern Tibet and Yunnan (China).
COMMENT: *Rhacophorus andersoni* is a replacement name for *Ixalus tuberculatus* Anderson, 1878, Anat. Zool. Res. Yunnan:85, which Ahl caused to be preoccupied by *Rhacophorus tuberculatus*. Seen in the literature (incorrectly) as *Philautus tuberculatus*.

Philautus annandalii (Boulenger, 1906). J. Asiat. Soc. Bengal, 2:385.
ORIGINAL NAME: *Ixalus annandalii*.
TYPE(S): ZSI.
TYPE LOCALITY: East Himalayas at Kurseong, altitude 5000 ft., India.
DISTRIBUTION: Eastern Himalayan region, India.

Philautus argus (Annandale, 1912). Rec. Indian Mus., 8:16.
ORIGINAL NAME: *Ixalus argus.*
TYPE(S): Holotype: ZSI 16950.
TYPE LOCALITY: "Upper Renging, Abor country", Arunachal Pradesh, India (in area claimed by China).
DISTRIBUTION: Assam region (India), adjacent Tibet (China), and probably adjacent Burma.

Philautus aurifasciatus (Schlegel, 1837). Abbild. Amph.:27.
ORIGINAL NAME: *Hyla aurifasciatus.*
TYPE(S): Syntypes: probably RMNH 4266, 5064 (6 specimens); material collected by Müller on Java, which most likely was examined by Schlegel (MSH).
TYPE LOCALITY: Java [Indonesia].
DISTRIBUTION: Thailand and Cambodia to Java and Borneo.
COMMENT: See Berry, 1975, Amph. Fauna Peninsular Malaysia:91–92. *Nyctixalus margaritifer* and *Philautus pallidipes* are possible synonyms, according to Liem, 1972, Philippine J. Sci., 100:157.

Philautus banaensis Bourret, 1939. Bull. Gén. Instr. Publique, Hanoi, 1939(4):34.
TYPE(S): Syntypes: MNHNP 48-159 to -162.
TYPE LOCALITY: Bana, Annam, Vietnam.
DISTRIBUTION: Central Vietnam.
COMMENT: Reviewed by Bourret, 1942, Batr. Indochinc:464–465.

Philautus beddomii (Günther, 1875). Proc. Zool. Soc. London, 1875:575.
ORIGINAL NAME: *Ixalus beddomii.*
TYPE(S): Syntypes: BM 1947.2.26.59–66, 1947.2.26.70–78, and 1947.2.26.80–84, NHMW 22884.
TYPE LOCALITY: Malabar [Kerala, India]; corrected to Atray Mallay, Travancore [Kerala, India], by Boulenger, 1882, Cat. Batr. Sal. Brit. Mus.:102.
DISTRIBUTION: Southwestern India.

Philautus bimaculatus (Peters, 1867). Monatsber. Preuss. Akad. Wiss. Berlin, 1867:32.
ORIGINAL NAME: *Leptomantis bimaculatus.*
TYPE(S): Syntypes: including NHMW 16091.
TYPE LOCALITY: Agusan valley, Mindanao, Philippines.
DISTRIBUTION: Thailand to Borneo and Philippines.
COMMENT: Reviewed by Bourret, 1942, Batr. Indochine:471–472; see also account by Berry, 1975, Amph. Fauna Peninsular Malaysia:92–93.

Philautus bombayensis (Annandale, 1919). Rec. Indian Mus., 16:124.
ORIGINAL NAME: *Ixalus bombayensis.*
TYPE(S): Holotype: ZSI 18782.
TYPE LOCALITY: Castle Rock, Karnataka, India.
DISTRIBUTION: Karnataka to Poona, India.

Philautus carinensis (Boulenger, 1893). Ann. Mus. Civ. Stor. Nat. Genova, (2)13:339.
ORIGINAL NAME: *Ixalus carinensis.*
TYPE(S): Syntypes: BM, MSNG.
TYPE LOCALITY: Karin Bia-po, Burma.
DISTRIBUTION: Karen Hills, Burma.
COMMENT: Reviewed by Bourret, 1942, Batr. Indochine:468–469.

Philautus chalazodes (Günther, 1875). Proc. Zool. Soc. London, 1875:574.
ORIGINAL NAME: *Ixalus chalazodes.*
TYPE(S): Holotype: BM.
TYPE LOCALITY: Travancore, South India.
DISTRIBUTION: Travancore, India.

Philautus charius Rao, 1937. Proc. Indian Acad. Sci., (B)6:405.
    TYPE(S): Holotype: CCB; now lost (SD).
    TYPE LOCALITY: Kottigehar, Karnataka, India.
    DISTRIBUTION: Southwestern India.

Philautus cherrapunjiae Roonwal and Kripalani, 1961. Rec. Indian Mus., 59:326.
    TYPE(S): Holotype: ZSI 20806.
    TYPE LOCALITY: Near Circuit house, ca. 3 km from Cherrapunji town [Khasi-Jaintia
        Hill District, Meghalaya], alt. ca. 1330 metres above mean sea level [India].
    DISTRIBUTION: Northeastern India.

Philautus cornutus (Boulenger, 1920). J. Fed. Malay States Mus., 8:295.
    ORIGINAL NAME: *Ixalus cornutus.*
    TYPE(S): Not traced.
    TYPE LOCALITY: Sungei Kring, Korinchi Peak, Sumatra [Indonesia].
    DISTRIBUTION: Sumatra.

Philautus elegans Rao, 1937. Proc. Indian Acad. Sci., (B)6:407.
    TYPE(S): Holotype: CCB; now lost (SD).
    TYPE LOCALITY: Kempholey, Karnataka, India.
    DISTRIBUTION: Southwestern India.

Philautus emembranatus (Inger, 1954). Fieldiana: Zool., 33:392.
    ORIGINAL NAME: *Rhacophorus emembranatus.*
    TYPE(S): Holotype: FMNH 50684.
    TYPE LOCALITY: "east slope of Mount McKinley, Mindanao, altitude 950 meters",
        Philippines.
    DISTRIBUTION: Mindanao, Philippines.

Philautus femoralis (Günther, 1864). Rept. Brit. India:434.
    ORIGINAL NAME: *Ixalus femoralis.*
    TYPE(S): Holotype: BM 1947.2.26.89 (formerly 58.6.15.13).
    TYPE LOCALITY: "Ceylon" (=Sri Lanka).
    DISTRIBUTION: Sri Lanka; southwestern India.

Philautus flaviventris (Boulenger, 1882). Cat. Batr. Sal. Brit. Mus.:105.
    ORIGINAL NAME: *Ixalus flaviventris.*
    TYPE(S): BM.
    TYPE LOCALITY: "Malabar", India.
    DISTRIBUTION: Southwestern India.

Philautus garo (Boulenger, 1919). Rec. Indian Mus., 16:207.
    ORIGINAL NAME: *Ixalus garo.*
    TYPE(S): Not traced.
    TYPE LOCALITY: Tura, Garo Hills, Assam [Meghalaya, India].
    DISTRIBUTION: Assam, India.

Philautus glandulosus (Jerdon, 1853). J. Asiat. Soc. Bengal, 22:532.
    ORIGINAL NAME: *Ixalus glandulosa.*
    TYPE(S): Not stated
    TYPE LOCALITY: "S. India".
    DISTRIBUTION: Southwestern India.

Philautus gracilipes Bourret, 1937. Bull. Gén. Instr. Publique, Hanoi, 1937(4):52.
    TYPE(S): Holotype: MNHNP 48-156.
    TYPE LOCALITY: Chapa, Tonkin [Vietnam].
    DISTRIBUTION: Northern Vietnam; Yunnan, China.

COMMENT: Reviewed by Bourret, 1942, Batr. Indochine:461–462, and Liu and Hu, 1961, Tailless Amph. China:274–275.

Philautus gryllus Smith, 1924. Proc. Zool. Soc. London, 1924:231.
TYPE(S): Holotype: BM (formerly M. Smith 4962).
TYPE LOCALITY: "Langbian Peaks, alt. 2000 m., Langbian Plateau, S. Annam", Vietnam.
DISTRIBUTION: Southern Annam, Vietnam.
COMMENT: Reviewed by Bourret, 1942, Batr. Indochine:459–461.

Philautus hosii (Boulenger, 1895). Ann. Mag. Nat. Hist., (6)16:169.
ORIGINAL NAME: *Rhacophorus hosii.*
TYPE(S): Holotype: BM 95.7.2.21.
TYPE LOCALITY: Patah River, Sarawak [Malaysia (Borneo)].
DISTRIBUTION: Western and northern Borneo.

Philautus jacobsoni (van Kampen, 1912). Notes Leyden Mus., 34:78.
ORIGINAL NAME: *Ixalus jacobsoni.*
TYPE(S): Holotype: ZMA 5709.
TYPE LOCALITY: Mt. Ungaran, Java [Indonesia].
DISTRIBUTION: Java.

Philautus jinxiuensis Hu and Tian, 1981. Acta Herpetol. Sinica, 5:116.
TYPE(S): Holotype: CIB 660386.
TYPE LOCALITY: Jinxiu, Yao-shan, Guangxi, China.
DISTRIBUTION: Guangxi and Hunan, China.
COMMENT: Related to *Philautus carinensis*, according to the original description.

Philautus kempiae (Boulenger, 1919). Rec. Indian Mus., 16:208.
ORIGINAL NAME: *Ixalus kempiae.*
TYPE(S): BM.
TYPE LOCALITY: Tura, Garo Hills, Meghalaya, India.
DISTRIBUTION: Northeastern India.

Philautus kottigeharensis Rao, 1937. Proc. Indian Acad. Sci., (B)6:408.
TYPE(S): Holotype: CCB; now lost (SD).
TYPE LOCALITY: Kottigehar, Karnataka, India.
DISTRIBUTION: Southwestern India.

Philautus leitensis (Boulenger, 1897). Ann. Mag. Nat. Hist., (6)19:107.
ORIGINAL NAME: *Ixalus leitensis.*
TYPE(S): Holotype: BM 96.12.11.32.
TYPE LOCALITY: "Leyte, Philippines".
DISTRIBUTION: Leyte I., Philippines.

Philautus leucorhinus (Lichtenstein and Martens, 1856). Nomencl. Rept. Amph. Mus. Zool. Berolin.:36.
ORIGINAL NAME: *Ixalus leucorhinus.*
TYPE(S): ZMB.
TYPE LOCALITY: Ceylon [=Sri Lanka].
DISTRIBUTION: Southwestern India; Sri Lanka.
COMMENT: *Ixalus temporalis* Günther, 1864, removed from synonymy of this species and placed in *Pseudophilautus* of the Mantellinae (Ranidae) by Laurent, 1943, Bull. Mus. R. Hist. Nat. Belg., 19:2. Reviewed by Kirtisinghe, 1957, Amph. Ceylon:68–71.

Philautus lissobrachius (Inger, 1954). Fieldiana: Zool., 33:390.
ORIGINAL NAME: *Rhacophorus lissobrachius.*
TYPE(S): Holotype: FMNH 50683.
TYPE LOCALITY: "east slope of Mount McKinley, Davao Province, Mindanao, altitude 1340 meters", Philippines.
DISTRIBUTION: Mindanao, Philippines.

Philautus longchuanensis Yang and Li, 1979. *In* Yang, Su, and Li, Acta Zootaxon.
    Sinica, 4(2):186.
    TYPE(S): Holotype: KIZ 74110046.
    TYPE LOCALITY: Gongdong, Longchuan Xian, altitude 1,600 m, Yunnan, China.
    DISTRIBUTION: Gaoligong Shan and Hengduanshan mountains, Yunnan, China,
        1350–1600 m elev.
    COMMENT: Closely related to *Philautus gracilipes* and *Philautus rhododiscus*, according
        to the original description.

Philautus longicrus (Boulenger, 1894). Ann. Mag. Nat. Hist., (6)14:88.
    ORIGINAL NAME: *Ixalus longicrus*.
    TYPE(S): Syntypes: BM 1947.2.6.28–30 (formerly 94.6.30.129–131).
    TYPE LOCALITY: Palawan [Philippines].
    DISTRIBUTION: Palawan I., Philippines.
    COMMENT: Rao, 1937, Proc. Indian Acad. Sci., (B)6:414, described a new species
        from India using the same trivial name.

"Philautus longicrus" Rao, 1937. Proc. Indian Acad. Sci., (B)6:414.
    TYPE(S): Holotype: CCB; now lost (SD).
    TYPE LOCALITY: Kempholey, Karnataka, India.
    DISTRIBUTION: Southwestern India.
    COMMENT: This name is preoccupied by *Philautus longicrus* (Boulenger). See
        preceding entry.

Philautus maosonensis Bourret, 1937. Bull. Gén. Instr. Publique, Hanoi, 1937(4):51.
    TYPE(S): Syntypes: MNHNP 48-157, 48-158.
    TYPE LOCALITY: Mao-son, Tonkin [Vietnam].
    DISTRIBUTION: Northern Vietnam.
    COMMENT: Reviewed by Bourret, 1942, Batr. Indochine:467–468.

Philautus melanensis Rao, 1937. Proc. Indian Acad. Sci., (B)6:411.
    TYPE(S): Holotype: CCB; now lost (SD).
    TYPE LOCALITY: Kempholey, Karnataka, India.
    DISTRIBUTION: Southwestern India.

"Philautus montanus" Rao, 1937. Proc. Indian Acad. Sci., (B)6:415.
    TYPE(S): Holotype: CCB; now lost (SD).
    TYPE LOCALITY: Kempholey, Karnataka, India.
    DISTRIBUTION: Southwestern India.
    COMMENT: This specific name is preoccupied by *Philautus montanus* Taylor, 1920
        (RFI).

Philautus narainensis Rao, 1937. Proc. Indian Acad. Sci., (B)6:413.
    TYPE(S): Holotype: CCB; now lost (SD).
    TYPE LOCALITY: Kottigehar, Karnataka, India.
    DISTRIBUTION: Southwestern India.

Philautus nasutus (Günther, 1868). Proc. Zool. Soc. London, 1868:484.
    ORIGINAL NAME: *Ixalus nasutus*.
    TYPE(S): Holotype: BM.
    TYPE LOCALITY: Ceylon [=Sri Lanka].
    DISTRIBUTION: Sri Lanka.
    COMMENT: Discussed by Kirtisinghe, 1957, Amph. Ceylon:73–74.

Philautus noblei (Ahl, 1927). Sitzungsber. Ges. Naturforsch. Freunde Berlin, 1927:40.
    ORIGINAL NAME: *Rhacophorus noblei*.
    TYPE(S): Not traced.
    TYPE LOCALITY: Malabar, Kerala, India.
    DISTRIBUTION: Southwestern India.

Philautus ocellatus Liu and Hu, 1973. *In* Liu, Fei, and Huang, Acta Zool. Sinica, 19(4): 393.
TYPE(S): Holotype: CIB (formerly SWIBASC) 64III1371.
TYPE LOCALITY: "Wuzhi Shan, Hainan, altitude 700 m", China.
DISTRIBUTION: Hainan I., China, 400–700 m elev.
COMMENT: Related to *Philautus parvus* and *Philautus hazelae*, according to the original description.

Philautus pallidipes (Barbour, 1908). Proc. Biol. Soc. Washington, 21:190.
ORIGINAL NAME: *Ixalus pallidipes.*
TYPE(S): Holotype: MCZ 2442.
TYPE LOCALITY: Pangaerango, Java [Indonesia].
DISTRIBUTION: Java.
COMMENT: See comment under *Philautus aurifasciatus.*

Philautus palpebralis Smith, 1924. Proc. Zool. Soc. London, 1924:233.
TYPE(S): Holotype: BM.
TYPE LOCALITY: Langbian Peak, S. Annam [Vietnam].
DISTRIBUTION: Southern Annam, Vietnam; Yunnan, China.
COMMENT: Reviewed (as *Chirixalus palpebralis*) by Bourret, 1942, Batr. Indochine: 474–475, and Liu and Hu, 1961, Tailless Amph. China:275–277.

Philautus parkeri (Ahl, 1927). Sitzungsber. Ges. Naturforsch. Freunde Berlin, 1927:38.
ORIGINAL NAME: *Rhacophorus parkeri.*
TYPE(S): Not traced.
TYPE LOCALITY: Malabar, India.
DISTRIBUTION: Southwestern India.

Philautus parvulus (Boulenger, 1893). Ann. Mus. Civ. Stor. Nat. Genova, (2)13:339.
ORIGINAL NAME: *Ixalus parvulus.*
TYPE(S): Syntypes: BM, MSNG, NHMW 16528; MSNG 29838 designated lectotype by Capocaccia, 1957, Ann. Mus. Civ. Stor. Nat. Genova, 69:217.
TYPE LOCALITY: Karin Hills, Burma.
DISTRIBUTION: Burma and northern Thailand.
COMMENT: Taylor, 1962, Univ. Kansas Sci. Bull., 43:523–526, discussed the Thai populations and provided a synonymy; see also Bourret, 1942, Batr. Indochine:451–452.

Philautus pulcherrimus (Ahl, 1927). Sitzungsber. Ges. Naturforsch. Freunde Berlin, 1927:41.
ORIGINAL NAME: *Rhacophorus pulcherrimus.*
TYPE(S): Syntypes: BM.
TYPE LOCALITY: "Manantoddy", South India.
DISTRIBUTION: Southern India.
COMMENT: *Rhacophorus pulcherrimus* is a replacement name for *Ixalus pulcher* Boulenger, 1882, Cat. Batr. Sal. Brit. Mus.:469, which Ahl caused to be preoccupied.

Philautus rhododiscus Liu and Hu, 1962. Acta Zool. Sinica, 14(Suppl.):98.
TYPE(S): Holotype: CIB (formerly SWIBASC) 601818.
TYPE LOCALITY: "Yang-liu-chung, Yaoshan, altitude 1350 m, Kwangsi [=Guangxi]", China.
DISTRIBUTION: Guangxi and Fujian, China.

Philautus romeri Smith, 1953. Ann. Mag. Nat. Hist., (12)6:477.
TYPE(S): Holotype: BM 1952.1.6.65.
TYPE LOCALITY: Lamma Island, Hong Kong [China].
DISTRIBUTION: Known only from the type series.

Philautus schmackeri (Boettger, 1892). Kat. Batr. Samml. Mus. Senckenb. Naturforsch. Ges.:17.
ORIGINAL NAME: *Ixalus schmackeri.*
TYPE(S): Holotype: SMF 7035.
TYPE LOCALITY: Mount Halcon, Mindoro [Philippines].
DISTRIBUTION: Mindoro I., Philippines.

Philautus shillongensis Pillai and Chanda, 1973. Proc. Indian Acad. Sci., (B)78:30.
TYPE(S): Holotype: ZSIM V/ERS 472.
TYPE LOCALITY: Malki Forest, Shillong, Meghalaya, India.
DISTRIBUTION: Northeastern India.

Philautus signatus (Boulenger, 1882). Cat. Batr. Sal. Brit. Mus.:106.
ORIGINAL NAME: *Ixalus signatus.*
TYPE(S): Syntypes: BM.
TYPE LOCALITY: "Malabar", Kerala, South India.
DISTRIBUTION: Southwestern India.

Philautus similis van Kampen, 1923. Amph. Indo-Aust. Arch.:273.
TYPE(S): Holotype: RMNH 5066.
TYPE LOCALITY: "Sumatra (Mt. Talamau, 1200 m . . .)", Indonesia.
DISTRIBUTION: Sumatra.

Philautus surdus (Peters, 1863). Monatsber. Preuss. Akad. Wiss. Berlin, 1863:459.
ORIGINAL NAME: *Polypedates surdus.*
TYPE(S): Not traced; ?ZMB.
TYPE LOCALITY: Luzon [Philippines].
DISTRIBUTION: High elevations of Luzon I., Philippines.

Philautus swamianus Rao, 1937. Proc. Indian Acad. Sci., (B)6:409.
TYPE(S): Holotype: CCB; now lost (SD).
TYPE LOCALITY: Kottigehar, Karnataka, India.
DISTRIBUTION: Southwestern India.

Philautus travancoricus (Boulenger, 1891). Ann. Mag. Nat. Hist., (6)8:291.
ORIGINAL NAME: *Ixalus travancoricus.*
TYPE(S): Holotype: BM 1947.2.6.20 (formerly 91.7.2.15).
TYPE LOCALITY: Bedaraikanur, Travancore [=Bodinaikenur, Tamil Nadu, India].
DISTRIBUTION: Southwestern India.

Philautus tytthus Smith, 1940. Rec. Indian Mus., 42:475.
TYPE(S): Holotype: BM 1940.6.1.40.
TYPE LOCALITY: Htingan, 'The Triangle', northern Burma.
DISTRIBUTION: Northern Burma.

Philautus variabilis (Günther, 1859 "1858"). Cat. Batr. Sal. Coll. Brit. Mus.:74.
ORIGINAL NAME: *Ixalus variabilis.*
TYPE(S): Syntypes: BM (8 specimens).
TYPE LOCALITY: "Ceylon" (=Sri Lanka).
DISTRIBUTION: Southern India; Sri Lanka.
COMMENT: Reviewed by Kirtisinghe, 1957, Amph. Ceylon:74–77.

Philautus vermiculatus (Boulenger, 1900). Ann. Mag. Nat. Hist., (7)6:187.
ORIGINAL NAME: *Ixalus vermiculatus.*
TYPE(S): Syntypes: BM.
TYPE LOCALITY: "Larut Hills at 4000 feet", Perak, Malaya (Malaysia).
DISTRIBUTION: Malaya.
COMMENT: Reviewed by Bourret, 1942, Batr. Indochine:458–459. See accounts in

Berry, 1975, Amph. Fauna Peninsular Malaysia:95–96, and Dring, 1979, Bull. Brit. Mus. (Nat. Hist.), Zool., 34:208–210.

Philautus williamsi Taylor, 1922. Philippine J. Sci., 21:167.
TYPE(S): Holotype: CAS 62253 (formerly EHT 356).
TYPE LOCALITY: "Polillo Island", Philippines.
DISTRIBUTION: Luzon and Polillo Is., Philippines.

SUBFAMILY: **Rhacophorinae** Hoffman, 1932 (1859).
CITATION: S. Afr. J. Sci., 29:562.
DISTRIBUTION: Coextensive with the family.
COMMENT: The first use of the group name Rhacophorinae was Laurent, 1943, Bull. Mus. R. Hist. Nat. Belg., 19:16. This subfamily is the grade-group from which the Philautinae was derived. See comment under Rhacophoridae. Evidence to support the monophyly of this subfamily has yet to be presented (JDL).

Aglyptodactylus Boulenger, 1919 "1918". Proc. Zool. Soc. London, 1918:257.
TYPE SPECIES: *Limnodytes madagascariensis* Duméril, 1853, by monotypy.
DISTRIBUTION: As for the single species.
COMMENT: Blommers-Schlösser, 1979, Beaufortia, 29:65–66, considered *Aglyptodactylus* more closely related to *Boophis* than to the Mantellinae of the Ranidae, where it had been placed by Laurent, 1943, Bull. Mus. R. Hist. Nat. Belg., 19:1–16. See Blommers-Schlösser, 1978, Genetica, 48:23–40, for karyotypes.

Aglyptodactylus madagascariensis (Duméril, 1853). Ann. Sci. Nat., Paris, (3)19:155.
ORIGINAL NAME: *Limnodytes madagascariensis*.
TYPE(S): Holotype: MNHNP 4574.
TYPE LOCALITY: Madagascar.
DISTRIBUTION: Forests of Madagascar.
COMMENT: Synonymy includes *Rana inguinalis* Günther, 1877, and *Mantidactylus purpureus* Ahl, 1929, according to Guibé, 1978, Bonn. Zool. Monogr., 11:12.

Boophis Tschudi, 1838. Classif. Batr.:36.
TYPE SPECIES: *Boophis goudotii* Tschudi, 1838, by monotypy.
DISTRIBUTION: Madagascar.
COMMENT: See Blommers-Schlösser, 1979, Bijd. Dierkd., 49:261–312, for a revision and definition of species groups, and synonymies for several species. Guibé, 1978, Bonn. Zool. Monogr., 11:59–78, provided synonymies for several species. See Blommers-Schlösser, 1978, Genetica, 48:23–40, for karyotypes.

Boophis albilabris (Boulenger, 1888). Ann. Mag. Nat. Hist., (6)1:105.
ORIGINAL NAME: *Rhacophorus albilabris*.
TYPE(S): Holotype: BM 1947.2.9.16.
TYPE LOCALITY: East Imerina, Madagascar.
DISTRIBUTION: Eastern forest of Madagascar.
COMMENT: In the *Boophis luteus* group.

Boophis brygooi (Guibé, 1974). Bull. Mus. Natl. Hist. Nat., Paris, (3)1973(145)(Zool. 109):1011.
ORIGINAL NAME: *Rhacophorus brygooi*.
TYPE(S): Holotype: MNHNP 1972-236.
TYPE LOCALITY: Cirque Boby, Andringitra Mountains, Madagascar.
DISTRIBUTION: Andringitra Mountains, Madagascar.

Boophis callichromus (Ahl, 1928). Zool. Anz., 75:314.
ORIGINAL NAME: *Rhacophorus callichromus*.
TYPE(S): Syntypes: ZMB, including ZMB 30508A–B.
TYPE LOCALITY: N.W. Madagascar.
DISTRIBUTION: Madagascar.

COMMENT: In the *Boophis goudotii* group.

Boophis difficilis (Boettger, 1892). Kat. Batr. Samml. Mus. Senckenb. Naturforsch. Ges.:14.
ORIGINAL NAME: *Rhacophorus difficilis.*
TYPE(S): Holotype: SMF 6762.
TYPE LOCALITY: Foizana, E. Madagascar.
DISTRIBUTION: Madagascar.
COMMENT: In the *Boophis rhodoscelis* group.

Boophis erythrodactylus (Guibé, 1953). Nat. Malgache, 5:102.
ORIGINAL NAME: *Hyperolius erythrodactylus.*
TYPE(S): Syntypes: MNHNP 53-171.
TYPE LOCALITY: Forest of Mahajeby, near Morafenobe, West Madagascar.
DISTRIBUTION: Forest of western and eastern Madagascar.
COMMENT: In the *Boophis rappiodes* group.

Boophis goudotii Tschudi, 1838. Classif. Batr.:77.
TYPE(S): Holotype: MNHNP 4578.
TYPE LOCALITY: Madagascar.
DISTRIBUTION: Madagascar.
COMMENT: In the *Boophis goudotii* group. Synonymy includes *Rhacophorus obscurus* Boettger, 1913; *Rhacophorus fasciolatus* Ahl, 1929; *Rhacophorus kanbergi* Ahl, 1929; and *Rhacophorus flavoguttatus* Ahl, 1929, according to Blommers-Schlösser, 1979, Bijd. Dierkd., 49:285.

Boophis granulosus (Guibé, 1975). Bull. Mus. Natl. Hist. Nat., Paris, (3)1975(323)(Zool. 230):1083.
ORIGINAL NAME: *Rhacophorus granulosus.*
TYPE(S): Holotype: MNHNP 1953-150.
TYPE LOCALITY: Forest of Moramanga [Madagascar].
DISTRIBUTION: Eastern forest of Madagascar.
COMMENT: In the *Boophis tephraeomystax* group.

Boophis hillenii Blommers-Schlösser, 1979. Bijd. Dierkd., 49:299.
TYPE(S): Holotype: ZMA 7123A
TYPE LOCALITY: "near Perinet (highroad R. N. 2 at km 142), alt. 900 m.", Madagascar.
DISTRIBUTION: Eastern forest of Madagascar.
COMMENT: In the *Boophis tephraeomystax* group.

Boophis hyloides (Ahl, 1929). Mitt. Zool. Mus. Berlin, 14:481.
ORIGINAL NAME: *Rhacophorus hyloides.*
TYPE(S): Holotype: ZMB 30495.
TYPE LOCALITY: Central Madagascar.
DISTRIBUTION: Madagascar.
COMMENT: In the *Boophis goudotii* group.

Boophis idae (Steindachner, 1867). Reise Freg. Novara, Amph.:52.
ORIGINAL NAME: *Hyperolius idae.*
TYPE(S): Holotype: NHMW 14845.
TYPE LOCALITY: Madagascar.
DISTRIBUTION: Eastern Madagascar.
COMMENT: In the *Boophis tephraeomystax* group.

Boophis laurenti Guibé, 1947. Bull. Mus. Natl. Hist. Nat., Paris, (2)19:438.
TYPE(S): Holotype: MNHNP 1924-101.
TYPE LOCALITY: Andringitra Mountains, Madagascar.
DISTRIBUTION: Andringitra Mountains, Madagascar.

COMMENT: Synonymy includes *Rhacophorus andringitraensis* Millot and Guibé, 1950, according to Guibé, 1978, Bonn. Zool. Monogr., 11:76.

Boophis leucomaculatus (Guibé, 1975). Bull. Mus. Natl. Hist. Nat., Paris, (3)1975(323)(Zool. 230):1085.
ORIGINAL NAME: *Rhacophorus leucomaculatus.*
TYPE(S): Holotype: MNHNP 1975-1.
TYPE LOCALITY: Nosy Mangabé, near Antongil Bay, Madagascar.
DISTRIBUTION: Eastern Madagascar.

Boophis luteus (Boulenger, 1882). Cat. Batr. Sal. Brit. Mus.:468.
ORIGINAL NAME: *Rhacophorus luteus.*
TYPE(S): Syntypes: BM 1947.2.9.14–15.
TYPE LOCALITY: "Ankafana, Betsileo", Madagascar.
DISTRIBUTION: Madagascar.
COMMENT: In the *Boophis luteus* group. Synonymy includes *Rhacophorus isabellinus* Boettger, 1913, and *Rhacophorus luteus longicrus* Parker, 1925, according to Guibé, 1978, Bonn. Zool. Monogr., 11:73.

Boophis madagascariensis (Peters, 1874). Monatsber. Preuss. Akad. Wiss. Berlin, 1874: 618.
ORIGINAL NAME: *Rhacophorus madagascariensis.*
TYPE(S): ZMB, not traced.
TYPE LOCALITY: Madagascar.
DISTRIBUTION: Forests of Madagascar.
COMMENT: In the *Boophis goudotii* group. Synonymy includes *Rhacophorus brachychir* Boettger, 1882, and *Rhacophorus herthae* Ahl, 1929, according to Guibé, 1978, Bonn. Zool. Monogr., 11:73.

Boophis majori (Boulenger, 1896). Ann. Mag. Nat. Hist., (6)17:402.
ORIGINAL NAME: *Rhacophorus majori.*
TYPE(S): Syntypes: BM (4 specimens); BM 1947.2.7.67 designated lectotype by Blommers-Schlösser, 1979, Bijd. Dierkd., 49:280.
TYPE LOCALITY: "Ambohimitombo forest [near Perinet], Madagascar".
DISTRIBUTION: Eastern Madagascar.
COMMENT: In the *Boophis rhodoscelis* group. Synonymy includes *Hyperolius arnoulti* Guibé, 1975.

Boophis mandraka Blommers-Schlösser, 1979. Bijd. Dierkd., 49:267.
TYPE(S): Holotype: ZMA 7119A.
TYPE LOCALITY: "Mandraka valley (highroad R. N. 2 at km 67), alt. 1200 m.", Madagascar.
DISTRIBUTION: Mandraka Valley, Madagascar.
COMMENT: In the *Boophis rappiodes* group.

Boophis microtis (Guibé, 1974). Bull. Mus. Natl. Hist. Nat., Paris, (3)1973(171)(Zool. 116):1177.
ORIGINAL NAME: *Rhacophorus microtis.*
TYPE(S): Holotype: MNHNP 1973-1080.
TYPE LOCALITY: Chaînes Anosyennes, Madagascar.
DISTRIBUTION: Chaînes Anosyennes, Madagascar.

Boophis microtympanum (Boettger, 1881). Zool. Anz., 4:47.
ORIGINAL NAME: *Hylambates microtympanum.*
TYPE(S): Bremen Mus.
TYPE LOCALITY: Imerina 47° 48' E, 19° S [Madagascar].
DISTRIBUTION: Mountains of Madagascar.
COMMENT: Not assigned to species group. Synonymy includes *Rhacophorus boettgeri*

Boulenger, 1882, and *Rhacophorus arboreus* Ahl, 1928, according to Guibé, 1978, Bonn. Zool. Monogr., 11:69.

Boophis miniatus (Mocquard, 1902). Bull. Soc. Philomath. Paris, (9)4:19.
ORIGINAL NAME: *Rhacophorus miniatus.*
TYPE(S): Holotype: MNHNP 1901-386.
TYPE LOCALITY: Forest between Isaka and valley of Ambobo, near Fort-Dauphin, S. Madagascar.
DISTRIBUTION: Eastern and southern Madagascar.
COMMENT: In the *Boophis miniatus* group.

Boophis opisthodon (Boulenger, 1888). Ann. Mag. Nat. Hist., (6)1:105.
ORIGINAL NAME: *Rhacophorus opisthodon.*
TYPE(S): Holotype: BM 1947.2.8.36.
TYPE LOCALITY: Madagascar.
DISTRIBUTION: Forests of eastern Madagascar.
COMMENT: In the *Boophis opisthodon* group.

Boophis pauliani (Guibé, 1953). Nat. Malgache, 5:101.
ORIGINAL NAME: *Hyperolius pauliani.*
TYPE(S): Syntypes: MNHNP 1953-169 and 1953-170.
TYPE LOCALITY: Forests of Moramanga and Perinet [Madagascar].
DISTRIBUTION: Eastern Madagascar.
COMMENT: In the *Boophis pauliani* group.

Boophis rappiodes (Ahl, 1928). Zool. Anz., 75:315.
ORIGINAL NAME: *Rhacophorus rappiodes.*
TYPE(S): Holotype: ZMB 30540.
TYPE LOCALITY: Ankoraka, Sahambendrana, central Madagascar.
DISTRIBUTION: Madagascar.
COMMENT: In the *Boophis rappiodes* group.

Boophis reticulatus Blommers-Schlösser, 1979. Bijd. Dierkd., 49:294.
TYPE(S): Holotype: ZMA 7101A.
TYPE LOCALITY: "near Perinet (highroad R. N. 2 at km 142), alt. 1100 m.", Madagascar.
DISTRIBUTION: Madagascar.
COMMENT: In the *Boophis goudotii* group.

Boophis rhodoscelis (Boulenger, 1882). Cat. Batr. Sal. Brit. Mus.:466.
ORIGINAL NAME: *Rhacophorus rhodoscelis.*
TYPE(S): Syntypes: BM 1947.2.9.71–76 (not 1947.2.7.66–67 as stated by Blommers-Schlösser, 1979, Bijd. Dierkd., 49:278).
TYPE LOCALITY: "East Betsileo" and "Ankafana, Betsileo", Madagascar.
DISTRIBUTION: Eastern and northwestern Madagascar.
COMMENT: In the *Boophis rhodoscelis* group. Synonymy includes *Rhacophorus andrangoloaka* Ahl, 1928, and *Rhacophorus brevirostris* Ahl, 1928, according to Guibé, 1928, Bonn. Zool. Monogr., 11:74.

Boophis tephraeomystax (Duméril, 1853). Ann. Sci. Nat., Paris, (3, Zool.)19:158.
ORIGINAL NAME: *Polypedates tephraeomystax.*
TYPE(S): Syntypes: MNHNP 1660 and 4584.
TYPE LOCALITY: Nossi Bé and Madagascar.
DISTRIBUTION: Madagascar; Nossi Bé I.
COMMENT: In the *Boophis tephraeomystax* group. Synonymy includes *Polypedates crossleyi* Peters, 1874; *Polypedates dispar* Boettger, 1879; *Rhacophorus hildebrandti* Ahl, 1925; and *Rhacophorus doulioti* Angel, 1934, according to Blommers-Schlösser, 1979, Bijd. Dierkd., 49:297.

Boophis untersteini (Ahl, 1928). Zool. Anz., 75:317.
ORIGINAL NAME: *Rhacophorus untersteini.*
TYPE(S): Holotype: ZMB 30497.
TYPE LOCALITY: Central Madagascar.
DISTRIBUTION: Madagascar.
COMMENT: In the *Boophis goudotii* group.

Boophis viridis Blommers-Schlösser, 1979. Bijd. Dierkd., 49:272.
TYPE(S): Holotype: ZMA 7100A.
TYPE LOCALITY: "near Perinet (highroad R. N. 2 at km 142), alt. 900 m.",
    Madagascar.
DISTRIBUTION: Madagascar.
COMMENT: In the *Boophis rappiodes* group.

Boophis williamsi (Guibé, 1974). Bull. Mus. Natl. Hist. Nat., Paris, (3)1973(171)(Zool.
    116):1178.
ORIGINAL NAME: *Rhacophorus williamsi.*
TYPE(S): Holotype: MNHNP 1973-1091.
TYPE LOCALITY: Ambohimirandana, Ankaratra Mountains [Madagascar].
DISTRIBUTION: Madagascar.
COMMENT: Not assigned to species group.

Buergeria Tschudi, 1838. Classif. Batr.:34.
TYPE SPECIES: *Hyla buergeri* Temminck and Schlegel, 1838, by subsequent designation
    of Stejneger, 1907, Bull. U.S. Natl. Mus., 58:143.
DISTRIBUTION: Taiwan (China); Ryukyu Is. to Honshu I. (Japan).
COMMENT: Species in this genus are referred by some recent authors to *Rhacophorus*
    or *Polypedates*, but the resurrection of *Buergeria* by Liem, 1970, Fieldiana: Zool.,
    57:67, has not been challenged directly. See Kuramoto, 1984, Bull. Fukuoka
    Univ. Educ., Nat. Sci., 30:61–64, for relationships of species.

Buergeria buergeri (Temminck and Schlegel, 1838). *In* Von Siebold, Fauna Japon.,
    Rept.:113.
ORIGINAL NAME: *Hyla bürgeri.*
TYPE(S): Syntypes: RMNH 1692 (2 specimens).
TYPE LOCALITY: Japan.
DISTRIBUTION: Honshu, Kyushu, and Shikoku, Japan.
COMMENT: Reviewed (as *Polypedates buergeri*) by Okada, 1966, Fauna Japon., Anura:
    172–178. See also Stejneger, 1907, Bull. U.S. Natl. Mus., 58:150–153.

Buergeria japonica (Hallowell, 1861 "1860"). Proc. Acad. Nat. Sci. Philadelphia, 12:501.
ORIGINAL NAME: *Ixalus japonicus.*
TYPE(S): Syntypes: MCZ 2602, USNM 7313 (5 specimens).
TYPE LOCALITY: Oshima, northern Riu Kius [Japan].
DISTRIBUTION: Taiwan, China; Ryukyu Is., Japan.
COMMENT: Reviewed (as *Polypedates japonicus*) by Okada, 1966, Fauna Japon.,
    Anura:178–182; see also Stejneger, 1907, Bull. U.S. Natl. Mus., 58:155, and (as
    Rhacophorus japonicus) Nakamura and Ueno, 1963, Japan. Rept. Amph. Color:
    63–64. Synonymy includes *Rana macropus* Boulenger, 1886, Proc. Zool. Soc.
    London, 1886:414 (Holotype: BM 1882.8.16.1; Type locality: Oho Sima, Loo
    Choo [=Ryukyu] Islands [Japan]), according to Inger, 1947, Fieldiana: Zool.,
    32:297–352, and Borkin, 1979, Zool. Zh., 58:1435 (who examined the types).

Buergeria pollicaris (Werner, 1913). Mitt. Naturhist. Mus. Hamburg, 30:50.
ORIGINAL NAME: *Rhacophorus pollicaris.*
TYPE(S): Syntypes: NHMW 22881 (2 specimens).
TYPE LOCALITY: Kanshirei (?), Taiwan [China].
DISTRIBUTION: Taiwan, China.

Buergeria robusta (Boulenger, 1909). Ann. Mag. Nat. Hist., (8)4:494.
ORIGINAL NAME: *Rhacophorus robusta*.
TYPE(S): Syntypes: BM, MCZ 15412.
TYPE LOCALITY: Kankau, Alikang, and Kosempo, Taiwan [China].
DISTRIBUTION: Taiwan, China.
COMMENT: See discussion by Kuramoto, 1977, Caryologia, 30:340–341.

Chirixalus Boulenger, 1893. Ann. Mus. Civ. Stor. Nat. Genova, (2)13:340.
TYPE SPECIES: *Chirixalus doriae* Boulenger, 1893, by monotypy.
DISTRIBUTION: Southeast Asia.
COMMENT: See generic definition and content in Liem, 1970, Fieldiana: Zool., 57:94.

Chirixalus doriae Boulenger, 1893. Ann. Mus. Civ. Stor. Nat. Genova, (2)13:341.
TYPE(S): Syntypes: MSNG, NHMW 16556, BM; MSNG 19426 designated lectotype
    by Capocaccia, 1957, Ann. Mus. Civ. Stor. Nat. Genova, 69:217.
TYPE LOCALITY: Karin Bia-po, Burma.
DISTRIBUTION: Northern Burma and Thailand; Yunnan and Hainan I., China.
COMMENT: Reviewed by Bourret, 1942, Batr. Indochine:476–477. See also Liu and
    Hu, 1961, Tailless Amph. China:279–281, and Taylor, 1962, Univ. Kansas Sci.
    Bull., 43:537–539 (as *Philautus doriae*).

Chirixalus eiffingeri (Boettger, 1895). Zool. Anz., 18:267.
ORIGINAL NAME: *Rana eiffingeri*.
TYPE(S): Holotype: SMF 6737 (formerly 1074a).
TYPE LOCALITY: "Liukiu [Ryukyu]-Inseln, entweder und wahrscheinlich von
    Okinawa, der mittleren Gruppe, oder von Ohoshima, der Nordgruppe".
DISTRIBUTION: Yaeyama group of Ryukyu Is., Japan; Taiwan, China.
COMMENT: Reviewed (as *Rhacophorus eiffingeri*) by Nakamura and Ueno, 1963,
    Japan. Rept. Amph. Color:61–62. Includes *Rhacophorus iriomotensis* Okada and
    Matsui, 1964, Acta Herpetol. Japon., 1:1, according to Kuramoto, 1973, Bull.
    Fukuoka Univ. Educ., Nat. Sci., 22:145.

Chirixalus hansenae (Cochran, 1927). Proc. Biol. Soc. Washington, 40:181.
ORIGINAL NAME: *Philautus hansenae*.
TYPE(S): Holotype: USNM 70109.
TYPE LOCALITY: Nong Khor, Thailand.
DISTRIBUTION: Thailand.
COMMENT: Reviewed by Bourret, 1942, Batr. Indochine:475–476, and (as *Philautus
    hansenae*) by Taylor, 1962, Univ. Kansas Sci. Bull., 43:526–529.

Chirixalus laevis (Smith, 1924). Proc. Zool. Soc. London, 1924:230.
ORIGINAL NAME: *Philautus laevis*.
TYPE(S): Holotype: BM (formerly M. Smith 2439).
TYPE LOCALITY: "Sui Kat, alt. 1000 m., Langbian Plateau, S. Annam", Vietnam.
DISTRIBUTION: Annam, Vietnam.
COMMENT: Reviewed (as *Philautus laevis*) by Bourret, 1942, Batr. Indochine:454–455.

Chirixalus nongkhorensis (Cochran, 1927). Proc. Biol. Soc. Washington, 40:179.
ORIGINAL NAME: *Philautus nongkhorensis*.
TYPE(S): Holotype: USNM 70108.
TYPE LOCALITY: Nongkhor, Thailand.
DISTRIBUTION: Burma; Thailand.
COMMENT: Reviewed by Bourret, 1942, Batr. Indochine:473–474, and (as *Philautus
    nongkhorensis*) by Taylor, 1962, Univ. Kansas Sci. Bull., 43:531–534.

Chirixalus simus Annandale, 1915. Rec. Indian Mus., 11:345.
TYPE(S): Holotype: ZSI 17971.
TYPE LOCALITY: Nangaldai, Assam [India].
DISTRIBUTION: Northeastern India.

Chirixalus vittatus (Boulenger, 1887). Ann. Mus. Civ. Stor. Nat. Genova, (2)5:421.
ORIGINAL NAME: *Ixalus vittatus.*
TYPE(S): Syntypes: BM, MSNG; MSNG 29397 designated lectotype by Capocaccia, 1957, Ann. Mus. Civ. Stor. Nat. Genova, 69:217.
TYPE LOCALITY: Bhamo, Burma.
DISTRIBUTION: Burma to Hainan I. and Yunnan (China), Vietnam, Thailand.
COMMENT: Reviewed by Bourret, 1942, Batr. Indochine:462–464, and (as *Philautus vittatus*) by Liu and Hu, 1961, Tailless Amph. China:277–279, and Taylor, 1962, Univ. Kansas Sci. Bull., 43:529–530.

Chiromantis Peters, 1855. Monatsber. Preuss. Akad. Wiss. Berlin, 1855:56.
TYPE SPECIES: *Chiromantis xerampelina* Peters, 1855, by monotypy.
DISTRIBUTION: African tropics.
REVIEWERS: Alan Channing (AC); Kim M. Howell (KMH); Raymond Laurent (RL); John C. Poynton (JCP); Arne Schiøtz (AS).

Chiromantis petersii Boulenger, 1882. Cat. Batr. Sal. Brit. Mus.:93.
TYPE(S): Holotype: BM.
TYPE LOCALITY: "Interior of E. Africa".
DISTRIBUTION: Savannas of lowland Ethiopia and Somalia to Tanzania.
COMMENT: See Coe, 1974, J. Zool., London, 172:13–34, for distribution records, ecology, and breeding biology.

Chiromantis rufescens (Günther, 1868). Proc. Zool. Soc. London, 1868:486.
ORIGINAL NAME: *Polypedates rufescens.*
TYPE(S): Holotype: BM.
TYPE LOCALITY: "West Africa".
DISTRIBUTION: Rainforests of Sierra Leone to Uganda.
COMMENT: For synonymy see Schiøtz, 1967, Spolia Zool. Mus. Haun., 25:21.

Chiromantis xerampelina Peters, 1854. Monatsber. Preuss. Akad. Wiss. Berlin, 1854:627.
TYPE(S): Syntypes: ZMB.
TYPE LOCALITY: Tete and Sena, Mozambique.
DISTRIBUTION: Coastal Kenya and northern Namibia south to Natal, Rep. South Africa.
COMMENT: Discussed by Poynton, 1964, Ann. Natal Mus., 17:157–158.

Nyctixalus Boulenger, 1882. Ann. Mag. Nat. Hist., (5)10:35.
TYPE SPECIES: *Nyctixalus margaritifer* Boulenger, 1882, by monotypy.
DISTRIBUTION: Philippines; India; Malaya; Sumatra; Java; Borneo.
COMMENT: Dubois, 1981, Monit. Zool. Ital., N.S., Suppl., 13:255, noted that *Nyctixalus* Boulenger, 1882, is an older name for the taxon named *Hazelia* by Taylor, 1920, Philippine J. Sci., 16:292. Therefore, the name *Edwardtayloria*, proposed by Marx, 1975, Sci. Publ. Sci. Mus. Minnesota, N.S., 2:2, to replace the preoccupied name *Hazelia* is invalid. See comment under *Theloderma moloch.*

Nyctixalus margaritifer Boulenger, 1882. Ann. Mag. Nat. Hist., (5)10:35.
TYPE(S): Not traced.
TYPE LOCALITY: "East Indies"; probably Java (RFI).
DISTRIBUTION: Java.
COMMENT: Possibly a synonym of *Philautus aurifasciatus* according to Liem, 1972, Philippine J. Sci., 100:157.

Nyctixalus pictus (Peters, 1871). Monatsber. Preuss. Akad. Wiss. Berlin, 1871:580.
ORIGINAL NAME: *Ixalus pictus.*
TYPE(S): Holotype: MSNG 10062.
TYPE LOCALITY: Sarawak [Malaysia (Borneo)].
DISTRIBUTION: Borneo; Malaya; Sumatra; Palawan I. (Philippines).

COMMENT: See Bourret, 1942, Batr. Indochine:455 (as *Philautus pictus*); Brown and Alcala, 1970, Proc. California. Acad. Sci., 38:109; and Berry, 1975, Amph. Fauna Peninsular Malaysia:94–95.

Nyctixalus spinosus (Taylor, 1920). Philippine J. Sci., 16:292.
ORIGINAL NAME: *Hazelia spinosa*.
TYPE(S): Holotype: CM 3427 (formerly EHT 406).
TYPE LOCALITY: "Bunawan, Agusan [Province], Mindanao", Philippines.
DISTRIBUTION: Mindanao I., Philippines.

Polypedates Tschudi, 1838. Classif. Batr.:34.
TYPE SPECIES: *Hyla leucomystax* Gravenhorst, 1829, by subsequent designation of Fitzinger, 1843, Syst. Rept.:31.
DISTRIBUTION: Japan and China, throughout tropical Asia to Borneo, Java, and Philippines.
COMMENT: Genus redefined by Liem, 1970, Fieldiana: Zool., 57:96–98. See comment under *Rhacophorus longinasus*.

Polypedates colletti Boulenger, 1890. Proc. Zool. Soc. London, 1890:36.
ORIGINAL NAME: *Rhacophorus colletti*.
TYPE(S): Not stated.
TYPE LOCALITY: Langkhat, Sumatra [Indonesia].
DISTRIBUTION: Peninsular Thailand to Sumatra, Borneo, and islands of the South China Sea.
COMMENT: See Berry, 1975, Amph. Fauna Peninsular Malaysia:99–100, for account (as *Rhacophorus colletti*).

Polypedates cruciger Blyth, 1852. *In* Kelaart, Prodr. Faun. Zeyl., App.:48.
TYPE(S): Not traced.
TYPE LOCALITY: Ceylon [=Sri Lanka].
DISTRIBUTION: Sri Lanka.
COMMENT: Reviewed (as *Rhacophorus cruciger*) by Kirtisinghe, 1957, Amph. Ceylon: 58–63.

Polypedates dennysii (Blanford, 1881). Proc. Zool. Soc. London, 1881:224.
ORIGINAL NAME: *Rhacophorus dennysii*.
TYPE(S): RM, according to Stejneger, 1925, Proc. U.S. Natl. Mus., 66:31.
TYPE LOCALITY: Uncertain, probably southern China.
DISTRIBUTION: Sichuan, Guizhou, and southeastern China to Burma.
COMMENT: Reviewed (as *Rhacophorus dennysii*) by Liu and Hu, 1961, Tailless Amph. China:258–261, who included *Polypedates feyi* Chen, 1929, China J., 10:198–199, in synonymy. See comment under *Rhacophorus leucofasciatus*.

Polypedates dugritei David, 1871. Nouv. Arch. Mus. Natl. Hist. Nat., Paris, 7:95.
TYPE(S): Not traced.
TYPE LOCALITY: Muping [=Baoxing], Sichuan, China.
DISTRIBUTION: Hunan and southwestern Yunkwei Plateau, China.
COMMENT: Reviewed (as *Rhacophorus dugritei*) by Liu, 1950, Fieldiana: Zool. Mem., 2:370–373. Includes *Polypedates bambusicola* Barbour, 1920, Copeia, 85:98, according to Liu and Hu, 1961, Tailless Amph. China:265–273, who placed many names in synonymy.

Polypedates eques Günther, 1859 "1858". Cat. Batr. Sal. Coll. Brit. Mus.:80.
TYPE(S): Syntypes: BM 58.6.15.9–12, 1 BM (number not known) + 1 untraced.
TYPE LOCALITY: "Ceylon" (=Sri Lanka).
DISTRIBUTION: Sri Lanka.
COMMENT: See comment under *Rhacophorus longinasus*.

Polypedates feae (Boulenger, 1893). Ann. Mus. Civ. Stor. Nat. Genova, (2)13:338.
ORIGINAL NAME: *Rhacophorus feae.*
TYPE(S): MSNG designated lectotype by Capocaccia, 1957, Ann. Mus. Civ. Stor. Nat. Genova, 69:216.
TYPE LOCALITY: Thao, northern Burma.
DISTRIBUTION: Burma through northern Thailand to Tonkin, Vietnam; Yunnan, China.
COMMENT: Reviewed by Bourret, 1942, Batr. Indochine:439–441, as *Rhacophorus nigropalmatus feae.* See Liu and Hu, 1961, Tailless Amph. China:261.

Polypedates leucomystax (Gravenhorst, 1829). Delic. Mus. Zool. Vratislav., 1:26.
ORIGINAL NAME: *Hyla leucomystax.*
TYPE(S): Breslau Mus., according to Stejneger, 1907, Bull. U.S. Natl. Mus., 58:157.
TYPE LOCALITY: Java [Indonesia].
DISTRIBUTION: Sikkim and Assam, India; southern China (including Taiwan) to Philippines; introduced on Okinawa I., Japan.
COMMENT: See Taylor, 1962, Univ. Kansas Sci. Bull., 43:496–505, for a review of the Thai populations (as *Rhacophorus leucomystax*); Okada, 1931, Tailless Batr. Japan. Emp.:184–185, for review (as *Rhacophorus leucomystax*) of Taiwan (China) population. See Bourret, 1942, Batr. Indochine:425–430, for review (also as *Rhacophorus leucomystax*) of southeastern Asia populations. See also Berry, 1975, Amph. Fauna Peninsular Malaysia:101–102, for account. See also Inger, 1954, Fieldiana: Zool., 33:376–384, for Philippine population, and Liu, 1950, Fieldiana: Zool. Mem., 2:370, and Liu and Hu, 1961, Tailless Amph. China:250–251, for Chinese population (as *Rhacophorus leucomystax*). The attribution of the name *Hyla leucomystax* to either Boie or Kuhl in Gravenhorst is wrong. Gravenhorst used the label (=manuscript) name of Boie as provided by the Curator De Haan. As Gravenhorst is responsible for the description, he is the author, under the International Code of Zoological Nomenclature (1985) (MSH).

Polypedates macrotis (Boulenger, 1891). Ann. Mag. Nat. Hist., (6)14:282.
ORIGINAL NAME: *Rhacophorus macrotis.*
TYPE(S): Holotype: BM 1947.2.8.18 (formerly 91.1.27.8).
TYPE LOCALITY: Baram district, Sarawak [Malaysia (Borneo)].
DISTRIBUTION: Sumatra and Borneo; Sulu Archipelago; Palawan I. (Philippines).
COMMENT: See Berry, 1975, Amph. Fauna Peninsular Malaysia:102–103, for account (as *Rhacophorus macrotis*).

Polypedates maculatus (Gray, 1834). Illustr. Indian Zool., 1:pl. 82.
ORIGINAL NAME: *Hyla maculata.*
TYPE(S): Not traced.
TYPE LOCALITY: "Bengal" [India and Bangladesh].
DISTRIBUTION: India; Sri Lanka.
COMMENT: Reviewed (as *Rhacophorus leucomystax maculatus*) by Kirtisinghe, 1957, Amph. Ceylon:55–58.

Polypedates mutus (Smith, 1940). Rec. Indian Mus., 42:473.
ORIGINAL NAME: *Rhacophorus mutus.*
TYPE(S): Syntypes: BM 1940.6.1.3–4.
TYPE LOCALITY: N'Chang Yang, northern Burma.
DISTRIBUTION: Northern Burma; Yunnan, Guizhou, Guangxi, and Hainan I., China.
COMMENT: Removed from the synonymy of *Polypedates leucomystax* by Liu and Hu, 1961, Tailless Amph. China:248–250, 273.

Polypedates omeimontis Stejneger, 1924. Occas. Pap. Boston Soc. Nat. Hist., 5:119.
TYPE(S): Holotype: USNM 66548.
TYPE LOCALITY: Shin-Kai-Si, Mount Omei, Szechwan [=Sichuan], China.
DISTRIBUTION: Southwestern China, including Guangxi.

COMMENT: Reviewed by Liu and Hu, 1961, Tailless Amph. China:262–264.

Polypedates otilophus (Boulenger, 1893). Proc. Zool. Soc. London, 1893:527.
ORIGINAL NAME: *Rhacophorus otilophus*.
TYPE(S): Not traced.
TYPE LOCALITY: Bongon, North Borneo [Malaysia (Borneo)].
DISTRIBUTION: Borneo and Sumatra.

Rhacophorus Kuhl and van Hasselt, 1822. Algemeene Konst-en Letter-Bode, 7:104.
TYPE SPECIES: *Rhacophorus moschatus* Kuhl and van Hasselt, 1822 (=*Hyla reinwardtii*
    Schlegel, 1840), by monotypy.
DISTRIBUTION: India, Japan, and China to Celebes.
COMMENT: Dubois, 1982, Bull. Mus. Natl. Hist. Nat., Paris, (4)4(A):271–276, discussed
    the nomenclature of the type species. Inger, 1954, Fieldiana: Zool., 33:370–393,
    reviewed the Philippine species. Taylor, 1962, Univ. Kansas Sci. Bull., 43:480–
    505, reviewed the species of Thailand. Inger, 1966, Fieldiana: Zool., 52:279–340,
    reviewed the Bornean species. Bourret, 1942, Batr. Indochine:408–449, reviewed
    the southeastern Asian species. Liu and Hu, 1961, Tailless Amph. China:272–
    273, reviewed the Chinese species.

Rhacophorus angulirostris Ahl, 1927. Sitzungsber. Ges. Naturforsch. Freunde Berlin,
    1927:45.
TYPE(S): Syntypes: MNHNP 89-250, 89-251.
TYPE LOCALITY: Kina Balu, Sabah [Malaysia (Borneo)].
DISTRIBUTION: Borneo and Sumatra.
COMMENT: *Rhacophorus angulirostris* is a replacement name for *Rhacophorus
    acutirostris* Mocquard, 1890, Nouv. Arch. Mus. Natl. Hist. Nat., Paris, (3)2:151,
    which Ahl caused to be preoccupied by *Ixalus acutirostris* Peters, 1867.

Rhacophorus annamensis Smith, 1924. Proc. Zool. Soc. London, 1924:229.
TYPE(S): Holotype: BM (formerly M. Smith 2450).
TYPE LOCALITY: "Daban, alt. 200 m., Phan Rang province, S. Annam", Vietnam.
DISTRIBUTION: Southern Vietnam.
COMMENT: Reviewed (as *Rhacophorus pardalis annamensis*) by Bourret, 1942, Batr.
    Indochine:443–444.

Rhacophorus appendiculatus (Günther, 1859 "1858"). Cat. Batr. Sal. Coll. Brit. Mus.:79.
ORIGINAL NAME: *Polypedates appendiculatus*.
TYPE(S): Syntypes: BM (22 specimens).
TYPE LOCALITY: "Philippines"; "Java"; "Singapore"; "East Indies".
DISTRIBUTION: Malaya to Sumatra, Borneo, and the Philippines.
COMMENT: Reviewed by Bourret, 1942, Batr. Indochine:416–420. See also Berry,
    1975, Amph. Fauna Peninsular Malaysia:96–98, for account. Dring, 1979, Bull.
    Brit. Mus. (Nat. Hist.), Zool., 34:211, noted that the generic status of this frog
    is uncertain.

Rhacophorus arboreus (Okada and Kawano, 1924). Zool. Mag., Tokyo, 36:140.
ORIGINAL NAME: *Polypedates schlegelii* var. *arborea*.
TYPE(S): Holotype: TZM 1338.
TYPE LOCALITY: Kinugasa, Kyoto, Honshu, Japan.
DISTRIBUTION: Honshu I., Japan.
COMMENT: See Nakamura and Ueno, 1963, Japan. Rept. Amph. Color:58–60.

Rhacophorus baluensis Inger, 1954. J. Washington Acad. Sci., 44:250.
TYPE(S): Holotype: USNM 130215.
TYPE LOCALITY: "Bundu Tuhan, Mount Kina Balu, North Borneo", Sabah, Malaysia
    (Borneo).
DISTRIBUTION: Borneo.

Rhacophorus bipunctatus Ahl, 1927. Sitzungsber. Ges. Naturforsch. Freunde Berlin, 1927:146.
TYPE(S): Syntypes: BM.
TYPE LOCALITY: "Khassya" (=Khasi Hills) and "Assam", India.
DISTRIBUTION: Eastern Himalayan region of India, adjacent Tibet (China), and Karin Hills of Burma; peninsular Thailand and Perak, Malaya.
COMMENT: See Taylor, 1962, Univ. Kansas Sci. Bull., 43:487–491. *Rhacophorus bipunctatus* is a replacement name for *Rhacophorus bimaculatus* Boulenger, 1882, Cat. Batr. Sal. Brit. Mus.:90, which Ahl caused to be a secondary homonym of *Leptomantis bimaculatus* Peters, 1827, by considering *Philautus* a junior synonym of *Rhacophorus*. See comment under *Philautus*.

Rhacophorus bisacculus Taylor, 1962. Univ. Kansas Sci. Bull., 43:494.
TYPE(S): Holotype: EHT-HMS 34960 (now FMNH?).
TYPE LOCALITY: "Phu Kading, Loei province, at an elevation of 3800 ft.", Thailand.
DISTRIBUTION: Known only from the type locality.
COMMENT: Closely related to *Rhacophorus appendiculatus* and *Rhacophorus chaseni* (=*Rhacophorus appendiculatus*), according to the original description.

Rhacophorus calcadensis Ahl, 1927. Sitzungsber. Ges. Naturforsch. Freunde Berlin, 1927:46.
TYPE(S): BM.
TYPE LOCALITY: "Calcad [=Kalakkad] Hills, Tinnevelly [=Tirunelvelly] (3000 feet)", Kerala, India.
DISTRIBUTION: South India.
COMMENT: *Rhacophorus calcadensis* is a replacement name for *Rhacophorus beddomii* Boulenger, 1882, Cat. Batr. Sal. Brit. Mus.:468, which Ahl caused to be preoccupied by *Ixalus beddomii* Günther, 1875.

Rhacophorus calcaneus Smith, 1924. Proc. Zool. Soc. London, 1924:228.
TYPE(S): BM.
TYPE LOCALITY: Langbian Peak, S. Annam, Vietnam.
DISTRIBUTION: Southern Vietnam.

Rhacophorus cavirostris (Günther, 1868). Proc. Zool. Soc. London, 1868:486.
ORIGINAL NAME: *Polypedates cavirostris*.
TYPE(S): Not traced.
TYPE LOCALITY: Ceylon [=Sri Lanka].
DISTRIBUTION: Sri Lanka; Tibet, Yunnan, Guizhou, Fujian, Hainan I., and Guangxi, China.
COMMENT: See Liu and Hu, 1961, Tailless Amph. China:247–248, who regarded this as a distinct species. SD doubts the conspecificity of the Sri Lankan and Chinese populations, and regards the form in Sri Lanka as synonymous with *Rhacophorus microtympanum*.

Rhacophorus chenfui Liu, 1945. J. West China Border Res. Soc., (B)15:35.
TYPE(S): Holotype: CIB 528.
TYPE LOCALITY: Mt. Omei, Huitingsze, Szechwan [=Sichuan], China.
DISTRIBUTION: Sichuan, Guizhou, Hubei, and Fujian, China.
COMMENT: Reviewed by Liu and Hu, 1961, Tailless Amph. China:267–269.

Rhacophorus depressus Ahl, 1927. Sitzungsber. Ges. Naturforsch. Freunde Berlin, 1926:115.
TYPE(S): Not traced.
TYPE LOCALITY: Java [Indonesia].
DISTRIBUTION: Java.

Rhacophorus dulitensis Boulenger, 1892. Proc. Zool. Soc. London, 1892:507.
TYPE(S): Holotype: BM 92.6.3.15.
TYPE LOCALITY: Mount Dulit, Sarawak [Malaysia (Borneo)].
DISTRIBUTION: Sumatra and Borneo; peninsular Thailand.

COMMENT: Reviewed by Bourret, 1942, Batr. Indochine:448–449.

Rhacophorus edentulus Müller, 1894. Verh. Naturforsch. Ges. Basel, 10:840.
TYPE(S): Syntypes: BM 94.9.28.3, NHMB 1180–82; NHMB 1180 designated lectotype by Forcart, 1946, Verh. Naturforsch. Ges. Basel, 57:131.
TYPE LOCALITY: Totoiya, Bona, and Bulawa Mountains, Celebes [Indonesia].
DISTRIBUTION: Celebes.

Rhacophorus everetti Boulenger, 1894. Ann. Mag. Nat. Hist., (6)14:87.
TYPE(S): Syntypes: BM 94.6.3.126–127.
TYPE LOCALITY: Palawan [Philippines].
DISTRIBUTION: Palawan (Philippines) and Borneo.

Rhacophorus fasciatus Boulenger, 1895. Ann. Mag. Nat. Hist., (6)16:169.
TYPE(S): Syntypes: BM 95.7.2.22–23.
TYPE LOCALITY: Akah River, Sarawak [Malaysia (Borneo)].
DISTRIBUTION: Borneo.

Rhacophorus gauni (Inger, 1966). Fieldiana: Zool., 52:346.
ORIGINAL NAME: *Philautus gauni.*
TYPE(S): Holotype: FMNH 136314.
TYPE LOCALITY: "Mengiong River, upper Baleh basin, Third Division, Sarawak", Malaysia (Borneo).
DISTRIBUTION: Sarawak, Malaysia (Borneo).

Rhacophorus georgii Roux, 1904. Verh. Naturforsch. Ges. Basel, 15:430.
TYPE(S): Holotype: NHMB 1468.
TYPE LOCALITY: "Tuwa, Paluthal, West-Centr. Celebes", Indonesia.
DISTRIBUTION: Celebes.

Rhacophorus harrissoni Inger and Haile, 1959. Sarawak Mus. J., 9:270.
TYPE(S): Holotype: FMNH 83075.
TYPE LOCALITY: Ulu Patah, Baram basin, Sarawak [Malaysia (Borneo)].
DISTRIBUTION: Borneo.

Rhacophorus hecticus (Peters, 1863). Monatsber. Preuss. Akad. Wiss. Berlin, 1863:457.
ORIGINAL NAME: *Polypedates hecticus.*
TYPE(S): Not traced.
TYPE LOCALITY: Loquilocum, Samar, Philippines.
DISTRIBUTION: Samar I., Philippines.

Rhacophorus hungfuensis Liu and Hu, 1961. Tailless Amph. China:269.
TYPE(S): Holotype: CIB (formerly SWIBASC) 570960.
TYPE LOCALITY: Hongfoshan, Guanxian, Sichuan, China.
DISTRIBUTION: Sichuan and Guangxi, China.
COMMENT: Closely related to *Rhacophorus chenfui,* according to the original description.

Rhacophorus javanus Boettger, 1893. Zool. Anz., 16:338.
TYPE(S): Holotype: SMF 6982.
TYPE LOCALITY: Vulkan Tjisurupan, Java [Indonesia].
DISTRIBUTION: Java.

Rhacophorus jerdonii (Günther, 1875). Proc. Zool. Soc. London, 1875:571.
ORIGINAL NAME: *Polypedates jerdonii.*
TYPE(S): BM.
TYPE LOCALITY: Darjeeling [West Bengal, India].
DISTRIBUTION: Northern India.

Rhacophorus kajau Dring, 1984 "1983". Amphibia-Reptilia, 4:112.
TYPE(S): Holotype: BM 1978.1757.
TYPE LOCALITY: "camp one 150 m, Gunung Mulu, Fourth Division, Sarawak", Malaysia (Borneo).
DISTRIBUTION: Known only from the type locality.

Rhacophorus leucofasciatus Liu and Hu, 1962. Acta Zool. Sinica, 14(Suppl.):95.
TYPE(S): Holotype: CIB (formerly SWIBASC) 602417.
TYPE LOCALITY: "Lo-dan, Yaoshan, altitude 800 m, Kwangsi [=Guangxi]", China.
DISTRIBUTION: Known only from the type locality.
COMMENT: Related to *Rhacophorus viridis* according to the original description. SH now regards this as a young *Polypedates dennysii*.

Rhacophorus longinasus Ahl, 1931. Sitzungsber. Ges. Naturforsch. Freunde Berlin, 1931:44.
TYPE(S): BM.
TYPE LOCALITY: "Southern Ceylon [=Sri Lanka]".
DISTRIBUTION: Sri Lanka.
COMMENT: *Rhacophorus longinasus* is a replacement name for *Polypedates nasutus* Günther, 1868, Proc. Zool. Soc. London, 1868:486, which Ahl caused to be a secondary homonym of *Ixalus nasutus* Günther, 1868, Proc. Zool. Soc. London, 1868:484 (=*Philautus nasutus*). SD regards this species as a member of *Polypedates* and notes that it has been confused with *Polypedates eques*.

Rhacophorus malabaricus Jerdon, 1870. Proc. Asiat. Soc. Bengal, 1870:84.
TYPE(S): BM.
TYPE LOCALITY: Malabar [India].
DISTRIBUTION: Southwestern India.

Rhacophorus maximus Günther, 1859 "1858". Cat. Batr. Sal. Coll. Brit. Mus.:83.
TYPE(S): Syntypes: BM (4 specimens).
TYPE LOCALITY: "Nepal" and "Afghanistan" (in error).
DISTRIBUTION: Northeastern India, northern Thailand, and southern China (Yunnan and Tibet).
COMMENT: Reviewed by Liu and Hu, 1961, Tailless Amph. China:257–258.

Rhacophorus microtympanum (Günther, 1859 "1858"). Cat. Batr. Sal. Coll. Brit. Mus.:77.
ORIGINAL NAME: *Polypedates microtympanum*.
TYPE(S): BM.
TYPE LOCALITY: "Ceylon" (=Sri Lanka) and "Madras" (apparently in error).
DISTRIBUTION: Sri Lanka.
COMMENT: Reviewed by Kirtisinghe, 1957, Amph. Ceylon:63–68. See comment under *Rhacophorus cavirostris*.

Rhacophorus modestus Boulenger, 1920. J. Feder. Malay States Mus., 8:293.
TYPE(S): BM.
TYPE LOCALITY: Sungei Kumbang, Korinchi Peak, Sumatra [Indonesia].
DISTRIBUTION: Sumatra.

Rhacophorus moltrechti Boulenger, 1908. Ann. Mag. Nat. Hist., (8)2:221.
TYPE(S): BM.
TYPE LOCALITY: "Nanto district, Lake Candidje", Taiwan, China.
DISTRIBUTION: Taiwan, China.
COMMENT: Related to *Rhacophorus owstoni*, according to Kuramoto and Utsunomiya, 1981, Japan. J. Herpetol., 9:1–6.

Rhacophorus monticola Boulenger, 1896. Ann. Mag. Nat. Hist., (6)17:395.
TYPE(S): NHMB 1188 designated lectotype by Forcart, 1946, Verh. Ges. Naturforsch. Basel, 57:131.
TYPE LOCALITY: Loka, Mt. Bonthain, Celebes [Indonesia].
DISTRIBUTION: Celebes.

Rhacophorus naso Annandale, 1912. Rec. Indian Mus., 8:12.
TYPE(S): Holotype: ZSI 16929.
TYPE LOCALITY: "Egar stream between Renging and Rotung", Arunachal Pradesh, India (in area claimed by China).
DISTRIBUTION: Region of type locality.

Rhacophorus nigropalmatus Boulenger, 1895. Ann. Mag. Nat. Hist., (6)16:170.
TYPE(S): BM.
TYPE LOCALITY: Abah River, Sarawak [Malaysia (Borneo)].
DISTRIBUTION: Peninsular Thailand through Malaya; Sumatra; Borneo.
COMMENT: Reviewed by Bourret, 1942, Batr. Indochine:435–439, and Taylor, 1962, Univ. Kansas Sci. Bull., 43:482–485; see also account by Berry, 1975, Amph. Fauna Peninsular Malaysia:104–105.

Rhacophorus nigropunctatus Liu, Hu, and Yang, 1962. Acta Zool. Sinica, 14(3):388.
TYPE(S): Holotype: CIB 590405.
TYPE LOCALITY: "Long-chu, Weining, altitude 2,134 meters", western Guizhou, China.
DISTRIBUTION: Guizhou, China.
COMMENT: Related to *Rhacophorus schlegelii* (=*Rhacophorus javanus*—MM), according to the original description.

Rhacophorus notater Smith, 1924. Proc. Zool. Soc. London, 1924:227.
TYPE(S): Holotype: BM.
TYPE LOCALITY: Daban, Phan Rang Province, Annam [Vietnam].
DISTRIBUTION: Southern Annam, Vietnam.
COMMENT: Reviewed by Bourret, 1942, Batr. Indochine:444–445.

Rhacophorus owstoni (Stejneger, 1907). Bull. U.S. Natl. Mus., 58:149.
ORIGINAL NAME: *Polypedates owstoni.*
TYPE(S): Holotype: USNM 34333.
TYPE LOCALITY: "Ishigaki shimi, Yaeyama group, Riu Kiu Archipelago", Japan.
DISTRIBUTION: Miyako, Ishigaki, and Iriomoto Is., Ryukyu Is., Japan.
COMMENT: Considered by some authors (e.g., Inger, 1947, Fieldiana: Zool., 32:345) to be conspecific with *Rhacophorus schlegelii.* See comment under *Rhacophorus viridis.* Removed from the synonymy of *Rhacophorus viridis* by Kuramoto and Utsunomiya, 1981, Japan. J. Herpetol., 9:4.

Rhacophorus oxycephalus Boulenger, 1899. Proc. Zool. Soc. London, 1899:959.
TYPE(S): Syntypes: BM (4 specimens).
TYPE LOCALITY: Five-finger Mountain, Hainan [China].
DISTRIBUTION: Hainan I., China.
COMMENT: Reviewed (as *Polypedates oxycephalus*) by Pope, 1931, Bull. Am. Mus. Nat. Hist., 61:576–581.

Rhacophorus pardalis Günther, 1859 "1858". Cat. Batr. Sal. Coll. Brit. Mus.:83.
TYPE(S): Syntypes: BM (6 specimens).
TYPE LOCALITY: "Philippines"; "Borneo"; "East Indies".
DISTRIBUTION: Malaya, Sumatra, Borneo, and Philippines.
COMMENT: See Berry, 1975, Amph. Fauna Peninsular Malaysia:105–106, for account.

Rhacophorus pleurostictus (Günther, 1864). Rept. Brit. India, 1864:430.
ORIGINAL NAME: *Polypedates pleurostictus.*
TYPE(S): BM.
TYPE LOCALITY: "Madras" (probably in error—RFI).
DISTRIBUTION: South India.

Rhacophorus poecilonotus Boulenger, 1920. J. Feder. Malay States Mus., 8:294.
TYPE(S): BM.
TYPE LOCALITY: Sungei Kumbang, Korinchi Peak, Sumatra [Indonesia].
DISTRIBUTION: Sumatra.

Rhacophorus prasinatus Mou, Risch, and Lue, 1983. Alytes, Paris, 2:155.
TYPE(S): Holotype: NTNUB 054901.
TYPE LOCALITY: "Hou-keng-tzu, Shih-ting area, Taipei Hsien, Taiwan, 24° 54' N,
121° 37' E; altitude 220 m. The Hou-keng-tzu valley brook is a tributary of
Pei-shih stream of Feitsui Valley".
DISTRIBUTION: Known only from the type locality.
COMMENT: Includes *Rhacophorus smaragdinus* Lue and Mou, 1983, Q. J. Taiwan Mus.,
36:15, which shares the same holotype as *Rhacophorus prasinatus*. Mou has
repudiated the second name in a privately circulated letter as published
without his knowledge.

Rhacophorus prominanus Smith, 1924. J. Fed. Malay States Mus., 11:185.
TYPE(S): Holotype: formerly M. Smith 6691 (? BM).
TYPE LOCALITY: "Jor, Batang Padang, Perak, altitude 600 metres", Malaysia
(Malaya).
DISTRIBUTION: Peninsular Thailand and Malaya.
COMMENT: Reviewed by Taylor, 1962, Univ. Kansas Sci. Bull., 43:491–493, as
Rhacophorus dulitensis prominanus. See Berry, 1975, Amph. Fauna Peninsular
Malaysia:106–107, for account.

Rhacophorus reinwardtii (Schlegel, 1840). Abbild. Amph.:105.
ORIGINAL NAME: *Hyla reinwardtii*.
TYPE(S): Syntypes: RMNH 1870 (2 specimens), 6517 (2 specimens), and 3899.
TYPE LOCALITY: Java [Indonesia].
DISTRIBUTION: Sumatra; Java; Malay Peninsula; Yunnan and Guangxi, China (SH).
COMMENT: See Berry, 1975, Amph. Fauna Peninsular Malaysia:107, and Liu and
Hu, 1961, Tailless Amph. China:255–257, for account. Dubois, 1982, Bull. Mus.
Natl. Hist. Nat., Paris, (4)4:261–280, noted that *Rhacophorus moschatus* Kuhl
and Van Hasselt, 1822, is the name with priority for this species, but
recommended the retention of *reinwardtii* for stability. Dubois also noted that
Hypsiboas reinwardtii Wagler, 1830, is a *nomen nudum*.

Rhacophorus rhodopus Liu and Hu, 1959. Acta Zool. Sinica, 11:525.
TYPE(S): Holotype: CIB (formerly SWIBASC) 571171.
TYPE LOCALITY: "Meng-yang, Yunnan, 680 meters altitude", China.
DISTRIBUTION: Yunnan, Hunan, Hainan, and Guangxi, China.
COMMENT: Reviewed by Liu and Hu, 1961, Tailless Amph. China:253–255.

Rhacophorus robinsoni Boulenger, 1903. Fasc. Malay., 1:136.
TYPE(S): BM.
TYPE LOCALITY: Bukit Besar, 2500 ft., Pattani, Thailand.
DISTRIBUTION: Southern Thailand and adjacent Malaya.
COMMENT: Discussed by Taylor, 1962, Univ. Kansas Sci. Bull., 43:485–487, and (as
Rhacophorus pardalis robinsoni) by Bourret, 1942, Batr. Indochine:442–443. See
also Berry, 1975, Amph. Fauna Peninsular Malaysia:109, for account.

Rhacophorus rufipes Inger, 1966. Fieldiana: Zool., 52:333.
TYPE(S): Holotype: FMNH 147699.
TYPE LOCALITY: "five miles north of Labang, Fourth Division, Sarawak", Malaysia
(Borneo).
DISTRIBUTION: Sarawak, Malaysia (Borneo).

Rhacophorus schlegelii (Günther, 1859 "1858"). Cat. Batr. Sal. Coll. Brit. Mus.:81.
ORIGINAL NAME: *Polypedates schlegelii.*
TYPE(S): Syntypes: BM.
TYPE LOCALITY: "Japan".
DISTRIBUTION: Honshu, Shikoku, Kyushu, and the Ryukyu Is., Japan.
COMMENT: Reviewed by Okada, 1966, Fauna Japon., Anura:144–159. See comments under *Rhacophorus owstoni* and *Rhacophorus viridis.* See Nakamura and Ueno, 1963, Japan. Rept. Amph. Color:57–58, for discussion.

Rhacophorus taeniatus Boulenger, 1906. J. Asiat. Soc. Bengal, 2:385.
TYPE(S): Not traced.
TYPE LOCALITY: Purneah, Bengal [Bihar, India].
DISTRIBUTION: Bengal region (India and Bangladesh).

Rhacophorus taipeianus Liang and Wang, 1978. Q. J. Taiwan Mus., 31:186.
TYPE(S): Holotype: NTUMA 0801.
TYPE LOCALITY: "Shu-lin, Taipei Hsien, about 50 m above sea level", Taiwan, China.
DISTRIBUTION: Taipei Hsien, northern Taiwan, China.
COMMENT: Closely related to *Rhacophorus moltrechti, Rhacophorus viridis,* and *Rhacophorus owstoni,* according to the original description, but comparisons of call structure by Kuramoto and Utsunomiya, 1981, Japan. J. Herpetol., 9:1–6, did not support this conclusion.

Rhacophorus taroensis Smith, 1940. Rec. Indian Mus., 42:473.
TYPE(S): Not traced.
TYPE LOCALITY: Patsarlamdam, northern Burma.
DISTRIBUTION: Northern Burma.

Rhacophorus translineatus Wu, 1977. Acta Zool. Sinica, 23:59.
TYPE(S): Holotype: CIB (formerly SWIBASC) 73II0031.
TYPE LOCALITY: "Medo, Xizang [=Tibet], alt. 1500 m", China.
DISTRIBUTION: Tibet, China.

Rhacophorus tuberculatus Anderson, 1871. J. Asiat. Soc. Bengal, 40:26.
ORIGINAL NAME: *Polypedates tuberculatus.*
TYPE(S): Not traced.
TYPE LOCALITY: Seebsanger [=Sibsagar], Assam, India.
DISTRIBUTION: Assam (India) and adjacent Tibet (China).

Rhacophorus turpes Smith, 1940. Rec. Indian Mus., 42:474.
TYPE(S): Syntypes: BM 1940.6.1.29–30.
TYPE LOCALITY: Htingnan, northern Burma.
DISTRIBUTION: Northern Burma.

Rhacophorus verrucopus Huang, 1983. Acta Herpetol. Sinica, 4(4):63–65.
TYPE(S): Holotype: NPIB 770689.
TYPE LOCALITY: Beibeng, Medo County, Xizang [=Tibet] Autonomous Region, China.
DISTRIBUTION: Known only from the type locality.

Rhacophorus viridis (Hallowell, 1861 "1860"). Proc. Acad. Nat. Sci. Philadelphia, 12: 500.
ORIGINAL NAME: *Polypedates viridis.*
TYPE(S): Holotype: USNM 25397.
TYPE LOCALITY: Okinawa, Ryu Kyu Islands [Japan].
DISTRIBUTION: Amami, Toku, and Okinawa, Ryukyu Is., Japan.
COMMENT: Reviewed by Okada, 1966, Fauna Japon., Anura:166–171. See Kuramoto,

1979, Japan. J. Herpetol., 8:11–13, for discussion of two subspecies. The inclusion of this species as a subspecies of *Rhacophorus schlegelii* by Inger, 1947, Fieldiana: Zool., 32:344–345, has not been accepted by Japanese herpetologists (MM).

Rhacophorus yaoshanensis Liu and Hu, 1962. Acta Zool. Sinica, 14(Suppl.):73–104.
TYPE(S): Holotype: CIB (formerly SWIBASC) 620016.
TYPE LOCALITY: "Ling-ban, Yaoshan, Kwangsi [=Guangxi]", China.
DISTRIBUTION: Known only from the type locality.
COMMENT: Related to *Rhacophorus chenfui* according to the original description.

Theloderma Tschudi, 1838. Classif. Batr.:32.
TYPE SPECIES: *Theloderma leporosa* Tschudi, 1838, by monotypy.
DISTRIBUTION: Burma and southern China through Indochina to Malaya and Sumatra.
COMMENT: See comment under *Nyctixalus moloch*.

Theloderma asperum (Boulenger, 1886). Proc. Zool. Soc. London, 1886:415.
ORIGINAL NAME: *Ixalus asper*.
TYPE(S): Syntypes: BM (2 specimens).
TYPE LOCALITY: "Hill Garden, Larut, Perak", Malaysia (Malaya).
DISTRIBUTION: Assam (India) through Burma and adjacent China to Vietnam and Malaya.
COMMENT: See Taylor, 1962, Univ. Kansas Sci. Bull., 43.519–522, for review and synonymy. Reviewed (as *Philautus asperrimus*) by Bourret, 1942, Batr. Indochine:465–467. Ahl, 1927, Sitzungsber. Ges. Naturforsch. Freunde Berlin, 1927:32, provided a replacement name, *Rhacophorus pulcherrimus*, for this species, whose name he (apparently mistakenly) thought to be preoccupied by *Rana aspera* Boulenger, 1882 (=*Mantidactylus aspera*).

Theloderma bicolor (Bourret, 1937). Annexe Bull. Gén. Instr. Publique, Hanoi, 1937(4):42.
ORIGINAL NAME: *Rhacophorus leporosa bicolor*.
TYPE(S): Syntypes: MNHNP 38-62, 48-152, 48-153.
TYPE LOCALITY: Chapa, Tonkin, Vietnam.
DISTRIBUTION: Northern Vietnam.
COMMENT: Reviewed (as *Rhacophorus leprosus bicolor*) by Bourret, 1942, Batr. Indochine:414–416.

Theloderma corticale (Boulenger, 1903). Ann. Mag. Nat. Hist., (7)12:188.
ORIGINAL NAME: *Rhacophorus corticalis*.
TYPE(S): Syntypes: BM (4 specimens).
TYPE LOCALITY: "Man-son Mountains, Tonkin, altitude 3000–4000 feet", northern Vietnam.
DISTRIBUTION: Tonkin, northern Vietnam.
COMMENT: Reviewed (as *Rhacophorus leprosus corticalis*) by Bourret, 1942, Batr. Indochine:412–413.

Theloderma gordoni Taylor, 1962. Univ. Kansas Sci. Bull., 43:511.
TYPE(S): Holotype: FMNH 172248 (formerly EHT 33741).
TYPE LOCALITY: "Doi Suthep, above 4000 ft., Chiang Mai, Chiang Mai province", Thailand.
DISTRIBUTION: Known only from the type locality.

Theloderma horridum (Boulenger, 1903). Fasc. Malay., 1:139.
ORIGINAL NAME: *Ixalus horridus*.
TYPE(S): BM.
TYPE LOCALITY: Bukit Besar, Pattani, Thailand.
DISTRIBUTION: Southern Thailand and Malaya.

COMMENT: Reviewed (as *Philautus horridus*) by Bourret, 1942, Batr. Indochine:469–471. See Berry, 1975, Amph. Fauna Peninsular Malaysia:93–94, for account (as *Philautus horridus*).

Theloderma leporosa Tschudi, 1838. Classif. Batr.:73.
TYPE(S): Holotype: RMNH 1754 (the only remaining specimen of the two specimens mentioned by Tschudi—MSH).
TYPE LOCALITY: Padang, Sumatra [Indonesia].
DISTRIBUTION: Malaya and Sumatra; Guangxi, China.
COMMENT: Liu and Hu, 1962, Acta Zool. Sinica, 14(Suppl.):92, described the form *Rhacophorus leprosus kwangsiensis* from Yaoshan, Guangxi, China; probably it will be accorded full specific status when it becomes better known, as has happened to other forms previously treated as subspecies of *Theloderma leporosa* (RFI). Reviewed (as *Rhacophorus leprosus leprosus*) by Bourret, 1942, Batr. Indochine:411–412. See also Berry, 1975, Amph. Fauna Peninsular Malaysia:100–101, for account.

Theloderma moloch (Annandale, 1912). Rec. Indian Mus., 8:18.
ORIGINAL NAME: *Phrynoderma moloch*.
TYPE(S): Syntypes: ZSI 16951–52.
TYPE LOCALITY: Upper Renging, Abor country, 2150 feet, Assam [Arunachal Pradesh, India (in region claimed by China)].
DISTRIBUTION: Vicinity of the type locality.
COMMENT: Possibly a member of "*Hazelia*" (=*Nyctixalus*) according to Liem, 1970, Fieldiana: Zool., 57:96, but he noted that the situation required more study.

Theloderma phrynoderma (Ahl, 1927). Sitzungsber. Ges. Naturforsch. Freunde Berlin, 1927:47.
ORIGINAL NAME: *Rhacophorus phrynoderma*.
TYPE(S): Syntypes: MSNG (1 specimen), BM (2 specimens); MSNG 29414 designated lectotype by Capocaccia, 1957, Ann. Mus. Civ. Stor. Nat. Genova, 69:217.
TYPE LOCALITY: "Thao", northern Burma.
DISTRIBUTION: Northern Burma.
COMMENT: *Rhacophorus phrynoderma* is a replacement name for *Phrynoderma asperum* Boulenger, 1893, Ann. Mus. Civ. Stor. Nat. Genova, (2)13:342, which is preoccupied by *Ixalus asper* Boulenger, 1886. Reviewed (as *Rhacophorus leprosus phrynoderma*) by Bourret, 1942, Batr. Indochine:413–414.

Theloderma schmardanum (Kelaart, 1854). Prodr. Faun. Zeylan., 2:22.
ORIGINAL NAME: *Polypedates schmardana*.
TYPE(S): Not traced.
TYPE LOCALITY: Ceylon [Sri Lanka].
DISTRIBUTION: Sri Lanka.
COMMENT: Reviewed (as *Philautus schmardanus*) by Kirtisinghe, 1957, Amph. Ceylon:71–73.

Theloderma stellatum Taylor, 1962. Univ. Kansas Sci. Bull., 43:514.
TYPE(S): Holotype: FMNH 172249 (formerly EHT 35441).
TYPE LOCALITY: "Khao Sebab (mt.), *circa* 18 km NE of Chanthaburi (town) near 'the waterfall,' Chanthaburi Prov., Thailand".
DISTRIBUTION: Eastern Thailand.

FAMILY: **Rhinodermatidae** Bonaparte, 1850.
CITATION: Conspect. Syst. Herpetol. Amphibiol., 1 p.
DISTRIBUTION: Southwestern South America in temperate forests.
COMMENT: Lynch, 1973, *In* Vial (ed.), Evol. Biol. Anurans:131–182, suggested that *Rhinoderma* is the sister-taxon of the Bufonidae, but presented no evidence for this

conjecture. Formas, Pugin, and Jorquera, 1975, Physis, Buenos Aires, 34:147–157, reviewed the literature and taxonomic status of the species. Formas, 1976, Experientia, 32:1000–1002, discussed karyology and the enigmatic relationships of this group.

CONTRIBUTOR: Ramón Formas (RF).

REVIEWERS: Ulisses Caramaschi (UC); William E. Duellman (WED); Marinus S. Hoogmoed (MSH).

Rhinoderma Duméril and Bibron, 1841. Erp. Gén., 8:659.

TYPE SPECIES: *Rhinoderma darwinii* Duméril and Bibron, 1841, by monotypy.

DISTRIBUTION: Temperate forests of southern Chile and adjacent Argentina.

Rhinoderma darwinii Duméril and Bibron, 1841. Erp. Gén., 8:659.

TYPE(S): Holotype: MNHNP 4911.

TYPE LOCALITY: "Chili" (=Chile).

DISTRIBUTION: Western slopes of the Andes, Central Valley, and coastal range, from Concepción Province to Aysén Province, Chile.

Rhinoderma rufum (Philippi, 1902). Supl. Batr. Chil. Descr. Hist. Fis. Polit. Chile:10.

ORIGINAL NAME: *Heminectes rufus.*

TYPE(S): Lost; IZUA-A 1323 (from type locality) designated neotype by Formas, Pugin, and Jorquera, 1975, Physis, Buenos Aires, 34:147–157.

TYPE LOCALITY: "Vichuquen", Curicó Province, Chile.

DISTRIBUTION: Coastal Range, from San Fernando Province to Arauco Province, Chile.

FAMILY: **Rhinophrynidae** Günther, 1859 "1858".

CITATION: Cat. Batr. Sal. Coll. Brit. Mus.:127.

DISTRIBUTION: Extreme southern Texas (USA) and Michoacán (Mexico) south to Costa Rica.

COMMENT: Fouquette, 1969, Cat. Am. Amph. Rept., 78.1–2, summarized the literature of this family. Lynch, 1973, *In* Vial (ed.), Evol. Biol. Anurans:133–182, and Starrett, 1973, *In* Vial (ed.), Evol. Biol. Anurans:252–272, presented evidence that this family is phylogenetically the sister-taxon of the Pipidae. Maxson and Daugherty, 1980, Herpetologica, 36:275–280, regarded the Rhinophrynidae, on the basis of phenetic molecular distances, as most closely related to *Ascaphus* of the Leiopelmatidae.

REVIEWERS: William E. Duellman (WED); Marinus S. Hoogmoed (MSH).

Rhinophrynus Duméril and Bibron, 1841. Erp. Gén., 8:757.

TYPE SPECIES: *Rhinophrynus dorsalis* Duméril and Bibron, 1841, by monotypy.

DISTRIBUTION: As for the only species.

Rhinophrynus dorsalis Duméril and Bibron, 1841. Erp. Gén., 8:758.

TYPE(S): Holotype: MNHNP 693.

TYPE LOCALITY: "Veracruz", Mexico.

DISTRIBUTION: Mouth of the Río Balsas (Michoacán, Mexico) and extreme southern Texas (USA) along the coastal plains to northwestern Honduras, on the Caribbean versant, and Costa Rica on the Pacific versant; also in the Río Grijalva Valley of Chiapas (Mexico).

COMMENT: Reviewed by Fouquette, 1969, Cat. Am. Amph. Rept., 78.1–2.

FAMILY: **Sooglossidae** Noble, 1931.

CITATION: Biol. Amph.:494.

DISTRIBUTION: Seychelles Is. in the Indian Ocean.

COMMENT: As first formed, the group name was Sooglossinae; the first use of Sooglossidae was by Griffiths, 1963, Biol. Rev. Cambridge Philos. Soc., 38:241–292. Lynch, 1973, *In* Vial (ed.), Evol. Biol. Anurans:133–182, suggested that the Sooglossidae was the sister-taxon of the Myobatrachinae; Savage, 1973, *In* Vial (ed.),

Evol. Biol. Anurans, considered them to have affinities with the ranoids, but since Lynch considered the Myobatrachinae and Sooglossidae to be cladistically closer to ranoids than to other bufonoids, these statements are not necessarily in conflict. See Nussbaum, 1980, Herpetologica, 36:1–5, for review of systematic literature. See comment under Pelobatidae.

CONTRIBUTOR: Ronald A. Nussbaum (RAN).

REVIEWERS: William E. Duellman (WED); Marinus S. Hoogmoed (MSH).

Nesomantis Boulenger, 1909. Trans. Linn. Soc. London, (2)12:293.
TYPE SPECIES: *Nesomantis thomasseti* Boulenger, 1909, by monotypy.
DISTRIBUTION: As for the single species.

Nesomantis thomasseti Boulenger, 1909. Trans. Linn. Soc. London, (2)12:293.
TYPE(S): Holotype: BM 1907.10.15.111.
TYPE LOCALITY: Cascade, Mahé Island, Seychelles.
DISTRIBUTION: Mahé and Silhouette Is., Seychelles, Indian Ocean.

Sooglossus Boulenger, 1906. Ann. Mag. Nat. Hist., (2)17:321.
TYPE SPECIES: *Arthroleptis sechellensis* Boettger, 1896, by original designation.
DISTRIBUTION: Mahé and Silhouette Is., Seychelles, Indian Ocean.

Sooglossus gardineri (Boulenger, 1911). Trans. Linn. Soc. London, (2)14:377.
ORIGINAL NAME: *Nectophryne gardineri*.
TYPE(S): Syntypes: BM 1910.3.18.73–79.
TYPE LOCALITY: "Mahé: Morne Pilot, 2700 ft." and "Silhouette: highest jungle".
DISTRIBUTION: Mahé and Silhouette Is., Seychelles, Indian Ocean.

Sooglossus sechellensis (Boettger, 1896). Zool. Anz., 19:350.
ORIGINAL NAME: *Arthroleptis sechellensis*.
TYPE(S): SMF 7179 designated lectotype by Mertens, 1967, Senckenb. Biol., 48:43.
TYPE LOCALITY: "Auf den Seychellen in Anzahl in alten Wäldern unter feuchtem Laub".
DISTRIBUTION: Mahé and Silhouette Is., Seychelles, Indian Ocean.

ORDER CAUDATA

ORDER: **Caudata** Oppel, 1811.
CITATION: Ordn. Fam. Gatt. Rept.:72.
DISTRIBUTION: Palearctic Eurasia, North Africa, and the Americas.
COMMENT: Phylogenetic relationships between families is not firmly resolved. Edwards, 1976, J. Morphol., 148:305–328; Hecht and Edwards, 1977, In Hecht, Goody, and Hecht (eds.), Major Patterns Vert. Evol.:3–52; Estes, 1981, Handbuch Paläoherpetol., Pt. 2:1–115; and Milner, 1983, In Sims, Price, and Whalley (eds.), Evol. Time Space:431–468, discussed possible phylogenies. The last three references are particularly useful for their literature reviews. The subordinal structure preferred by AHB, following Estes (1981), and used in this checklist is: Cryptobranchoidea (Cryptobranchidae and Hynobiidae), Proteoidea (Proteidae), Amphiumoidea (Amphiumidae), Ambystomatoidea (Ambystomatidae and Dicamptodontidae), Plethodontoidea (Plethodontidae), and Salamandroidea (Salamandridae and Sirenidae).
CONTRIBUTOR: Arden H. Brame, Jr. II (AHB).
REVIEWERS: Edmund D. Brodie, Jr. (EDB); William E. Duellman (WED); Marinus S. Hoogmoed (MSH); David B. Wake (DBW).

FAMILY: **Ambystomatidae** Hallowell, 1858.
CITATION: J. Acad. Nat. Sci. Philadelphia, (2)3:338.
DISTRIBUTION: Southern Canada and Alaska (USA) south to the southern edge of the Mexican Plateau.
COMMENT: As first formed the family-group name was Ambystomidae. This was subsequently emended to Ambystomatidae by Tihen, 1958, Bull. Florida State Mus., Biol. Sci., 3:20. Edwards, 1976, J. Morphol., 148:319, considered the ambystomatine ambystomatids to be more closely related to the Plethodontidae than to the remaining "Ambystomatidae". For this reason, the Rhyacotritoninae and Dicamptodontinae were removed from the Ambystomatidae and placed in their own family; see Dicamptodontidae. In the suborder Ambystomatoidea; see comment under Caudata.
CONTRIBUTOR: Arden H. Brame, Jr. II.
REVIEWERS: Edmund D. Brodie, Jr. (EDB); Jonathan A. Campbell (JAC) (Mexico); Gustavo Casas-Andreu (GCA) (Mexico); William E. Duellman (WED); Oscar Flores-Villela (OFV) (Mexico); Keith A. Harding (KAH); Richard Highton (RH) (USA); Marinus S. Hoogmoed (MSH); David B. Wake (DBW).

Ambystoma Tschudi, 1838. Classif. Batr.:92.
TYPE SPECIES: *Lacerta subviolacea* Barton, 1804 (=*Lacerta maculata* Shaw, 1802), by original designation.
DISTRIBUTION: From Labrador, James Bay, and extreme southeastern Alaska, southward throughout southern Canada, most of the USA, and the Sierra Madre Occidental and central plateau of Mexico; apparently absent from the Florida peninsula; also absent from Nevada, southern California, southwestern Arizona (USA), Baja California, and the tropical lowlands of Mexico.
COMMENT: The nomenclatural history of this genus is extremely complex. See Tihen, 1969, Cat. Am. Amph. Rept., 75.1–4, for a review. The erroneous spelling *Amblystoma* has been used widely.

Ambystoma amblycephalum Taylor, 1940 "1939". Univ. Kansas Sci. Bull., 26:420.
ORIGINAL NAME: *Ambystoma amblycephala*.
TYPE(S): Holotype: FMNH 100104 (formerly EHT-HMS 16443).
TYPE LOCALITY: "15 km. west of Morelia, Michoacán", Mexico.
DISTRIBUTION: Known only from the type locality area in Michoacán, Mexico.

Ambystoma andersoni Krebs and Brandon, 1984. Herpetologica, 40:238.
TYPE(S): Holotype: AMNH A100096.
TYPE LOCALITY: "Laguna de Zacapu, 2000 m elevation, Michoacan, Mexico".
DISTRIBUTION: Known only from the Laguna de Zacapú and the stream flowing from it, near Zacapú, Michoacán, Mexico.

Ambystoma annulatum Cope, 1886. Proc. Am. Philos. Soc., 23:525.
  TYPE(S): Holotype: USNM 11564.
  TYPE LOCALITY: "Unknown"; Schmidt, 1953, Check List N. Am. Amph. Rept., Ed. 6:
    18, designated it as "vicinity of Hot Springs, [Garland County,] Arkansas",
    USA.
  DISTRIBUTION: Central Missouri, western Arkansas, and eastern Oklahoma, USA.
  COMMENT: Reviewed by Anderson, 1965, Cat. Am. Amph. Rept., 19.1-2.

Ambystoma bombypellum Taylor, 1940 "1939". Univ. Kansas Sci. Bull., 26:418.
  ORIGINAL NAME: *Ambystoma bombypella.*
  TYPE(S): Holotype: FMNH 100127 (formerly EHT-HMS 3997).
  TYPE LOCALITY: "near Rancho Guadalupe, 14 km. east of San Martín (Asunción),
    México", Mexico.
  DISTRIBUTION: Known only from the area of the type locality.

Ambystoma cingulatum Cope, 1868 "1867". Proc. Acad. Nat. Sci. Philadelphia, 19:205.
  ORIGINAL NAME: *Amblystoma cingulatum.*
  TYPE(S): Holotype: USNM 3786 (now lost); USNM 129396 designated neotype by
    Goin, 1950, Ann. Carnegie Mus., 31:308.
  TYPE LOCALITY: "Grahamville, [Jasper County,] S[outh]. C[arolina].", USA.
  DISTRIBUTION: Gulf coastal plain of the Florida panhandle and Alabama, north
    through the coastal plain of Georgia and South Carolina, USA.
  COMMENT: Reviewed by Martof, 1968, Cat. Am. Amph. Rept., 57.1-2.

Ambystoma dumerilii (Dugès, 1870). Naturaleza, Mexico, 1:241.
  ORIGINAL NAME: *Siredon dumerilii.*
  TYPE(S): Syntypes: including USNM 16201-202 and ANSP 13862.
  TYPE LOCALITY: "laguna de Patzcuaro", Michoacán, Mexico.
  DISTRIBUTION: Lake Pátzcuaro (Michoacán) and questionably from San Juan del Río
    (Queretaro), Mexico.
  COMMENT: The status of *Bathysiredon dumerilii queretarensis* Maldonado-Koerdell,
    1948, Mem. Rev. Soc. Cient. Antonio Alzate, 56:185-226, is questionable.
    Smith and Smith, 1976, Synops. Herpetofauna Mexico, 4:C-A-2, noted that
    until someone examines the unique type of *queretarensis* its status will remain
    uncertain. They noted that no adequate habitat for this species exists at the
    Queretaro locality, suggested that *queretarensis* was not a subspecies or
    synonym of *Ambystoma dumerilii*, and suggested that *queretarensis* be
    considered a nominal species, *Ambystoma queretarense*, pending some
    taxonomic resolution of the problem. We regard the recognition of nominally
    new species on the basis of possibilities and not on diagnoses and/or
    specimen examination to be premature. Brandon, 1976, Herpetologica, 32:429-
    438, presented information on spontaneous and induced metamorphosis.
    Sometimes placed in the monotypic genus *Bathysiredon.*
  PROTECTED STATUS: CITES—Appendix II (1 Jul. 1975).

Ambystoma flavipiperatum Dixon, 1963. Copeia, 1963:99.
  TYPE(S): Holotype: TCWC 12779.
  TYPE LOCALITY: "one mile north of Santa Cruz, Jalisco, Mexico, 4,900 ft altitude".
  DISTRIBUTION: Known only from the area of the type locality and near Tapalpa,
    Jalisco, Mexico.

Ambystoma gracile (Baird, 1859 "1857"). Rep. Explor. Surv. R.R. Route Mississippi
    River-Pacific Ocean, 10(pt. 4, no. 4):13.
  ORIGINAL NAME: *Siredon gracilis.*
  TYPE(S): Syntypes: USNM 4080 (2 specimens).
  TYPE LOCALITY: "Cascade Mountains, near latitude 44° [N.]", Oregon, USA.
  DISTRIBUTION: Southeastern Alaska south to the mouth of the Gualala River,
    Sonoma County, California, USA.

COMMENT: Reviewed by Snyder, 1963, Cat. Am. Amph. Rept., 6.1–2.

Ambystoma granulosum Taylor, 1944. Univ. Kansas Sci. Bull., 30:57.
TYPE(S): Holotype: FMNH 100106 (formerly EHT-HMS 29805).
TYPE LOCALITY: "km. 74, about 12 miles northwest of Toluca, México, México".
DISTRIBUTION: Immediate region about the type locality.

Ambystoma jeffersonianum (Green, 1827). Contrib. Maclurean Lyc., 1(1):4.
ORIGINAL NAME: *Salamandra jeffersoniana.*
TYPE(S): Not stated; according to Uzzell, 1967, Cat. Am. Amph. Rept., 47.1, USNM
    3968 might be the type.
TYPE LOCALITY: "Near Chartier's creek in the vicinity of Jefferson College
    [formerly] at Cannonsburg", Washington County, Pennsylvania, USA.
DISTRIBUTION: Southern Labrador to southeastern Manitoba (Canada) and south to
    southern Indiana, Virginia, and Kentucky (USA).
COMMENT: Reviewed by Uzzell, 1967, Cat. Am. Amph. Rept., 47.1–2.

Ambystoma lacustris Taylor and Smith, 1945. Proc. U.S. Natl. Mus., 95:532.
TYPE(S): Holotype: USNM 117410.
TYPE LOCALITY: "Lake Zumpango, México", Mexico.
DISTRIBUTION: Known only from the type locality (see comment).
COMMENT: Because the lakes of Zumpango, Chalco, Texcoco, and Xochimilco were
    historically connected it may be supposed that this was the original
    distribution of this species (DRF). Specimens from Honey, Puebla, Mexico,
    have provisionally been allocated to this species (OFV).

Ambystoma laterale Hallowell, 1856. Proc. Acad. Nat. Sci. Philadelphia, 8:6.
TYPE(S): Holotype: ANSP 1377.
TYPE LOCALITY: "Marquette, [Marquette County, Michigan, USA] on the southern
    border of Lake Superior".
DISTRIBUTION: Northern lake plains of Indiana, also in Minnesota, Massachusetts,
    northern Illinois, southeastern Wisconsin, southern Michigan (USA) and in
    Canada from Prince Edward Island and New Brunswick west to the Manitoba
    border.
COMMENT: Reviewed by Uzzell, 1967, Cat. Am. Amph. Rept., 48.1–2.

Ambystoma lermaense (Taylor, 1940 "1939"). Univ. Kansas Sci. Bull., 26:427.
ORIGINAL NAME: *Siredon lermaensis.*
TYPE(S): Holotype: FMNH 1000029 (formerly EHT-HMS 22578).
TYPE LOCALITY: "Lake Lerma, east of Toluca, México", Mexico.
DISTRIBUTION: Remnants of Lake Lerma, México, Mexico.
PROTECTED STATUS: CITES—Appendix II (1 Jul. 1975); as *Ambystoma lermaensis.*

Ambystoma mabeei Bishop, 1928. J. Elisha Mitchell Sci. Soc., 43:157.
TYPE(S): Holotype: USNM 75058.
TYPE LOCALITY: "low grounds of the Black River near Dunn, Harnett County,
    North Carolina", USA.
DISTRIBUTION: Restricted to the coastal plain of North Carolina and South Carolina,
    USA.
COMMENT: Reviewed by Hardy, 1970, Cat. Am. Amph. Rept., 81.1–2.

Ambystoma macrodactylum Baird, 1849. J. Acad. Nat. Sci. Philadelphia, (2)1:292.
ORIGINAL NAME: *Ambystoma macrodactyla.*
TYPE(S): Syntypes: including USNM 4042 (apparently the sole survivor of the
    original syntypic series).
TYPE LOCALITY: "Astoria, [Clatsop County,] Oregon", USA.
DISTRIBUTION: Southern British Columbia and Vancouver I. (Canada), south to
    northern and central California (USA) and eastward into Alberta (Canada),
    Idaho and Montana (USA).

COMMENT: Reviewed by Ferguson, 1963, Cat. Am. Amph. Rept., 4.1–2.
PROTECTED STATUS: USA ESA—Endangered (11 Mar. 1967); as *Ambystoma macrodactylum croceum* subspecies only.

Ambystoma maculatum (Shaw, 1802). Gen. Zool., 3:304.
ORIGINAL NAME: *Lacerta maculata.*
TYPE(S): Unknown.
TYPE LOCALITY: "Carolina"; restricted to "vicinity of Charleston, South Carolina", USA, by Schmidt, 1953, Check List N. Am. Amph. Rept., Ed. 6:20.
DISTRIBUTION: Nova Scotia and Gaspe Peninsula west to central Ontario in Canada, and south through the eastern USA to southern Georgia and west to Louisiana and eastern Texas.
COMMENT: Reviewed by Anderson, 1967, Cat. Am. Amph. Rept., 51.1–4.

Ambystoma mexicanum (Shaw, 1789). Nat. Misc., 9:pls. 343 and 344.
ORIGINAL NAME: *Gyrinus mexicanus.*
TYPE(S): BM according to Smith and Taylor, 1948, Bull. U.S. Natl. Mus., 194:8, but not there now.
TYPE LOCALITY: México, Mexico.
DISTRIBUTION: Originally in Lakes Xochimilco and Chalco (and presumably in the connecting lakes Texcoco and Zumpango), Valley of Mexico; known currently only from Lake Xochimilco.
COMMENT: See Smith and Smith, 1971, Synops. Herpetofauna Mexico, 1:1–245, for a synopsis of the literature.
PROTECTED STATUS: CITES—Appendix II (1 Jul. 1975).

Ambystoma opacum (Gravenhorst, 1807). Vergl. Uebersicht Zool. Syst.:431.
ORIGINAL NAME: *Salamandra opaca.*
TYPE(S): Not known to exist.
TYPE LOCALITY: New York [USA].
DISTRIBUTION: From New Hampshire and central Massachusetts southward to northern Florida, westward through southeastern New York to the region of Lake Michigan and southward through the Mississippi basin to eastern Oklahoma and eastern Texas, USA.
COMMENT: Reviewed by Anderson, 1967, Cat. Am. Amph. Rept., 46.1–2.

Ambystoma ordinarium Taylor, 1940 "1939". Univ. Kansas Sci. Bull., 26:422.
ORIGINAL NAME: *Ambystoma ordinaria.*
TYPE(S): Holotype: FMNH 100055 (formerly EHT-HMS 16367).
TYPE LOCALITY: "small stream at an elevation of about 9,000 feet, four miles west of El Mirador, near Puerto Hondo, Michoacán, Mexico".
DISTRIBUTION: Known only from the type locality area in Michoacán, Mexico.
COMMENT: Reviewed by Anderson, 1975, Cat. Am. Amph. Rept., 164.1–2.

Ambystoma platineum (Cope, 1868 "1867"). Proc. Acad. Nat. Sci. Philadelphia, 19:198.
ORIGINAL NAME: *Amblystoma platineum.*
TYPE(S): Syntypes: USNM 3998 and 39444 (recatalogued from 3988), and ANSP 1299 ?; see Uzzell, 1964, Copeia, 1964:292, for discussion.
TYPE LOCALITY: "Cleveland, [Cuyahoga County,] Ohio", USA.
DISTRIBUTION: From central Indiana east to northern New Jersey and western Massachusetts, and near Cincinnati, Ohio, USA.
COMMENT: Reviewed by Uzzell, 1967, Cat. Am. Amph. Rept., 49.1–2, who discussed difficulties with determining types. A triploid gynogen of possibly polyphyletic origin (DBW). See comment under *Ambystoma texanum.*

Ambystoma rosaceum Taylor, 1941. Copeia, 1941:143.
TYPE(S): Holotype: FMNH 100079 (formerly EHT-HMS 23054).
TYPE LOCALITY: "Mojárachic, Chihuahua, Mexico".
DISTRIBUTION: High elevations in the Sierra Madre Occidental from the region of western Zacatecas, to northern Chihuahua and northern Sonora, Mexico.

COMMENT: Reviewed by Anderson, 1978, Cat. Am. Amph. Rept., 206.1–2. Shaffer, 1983, Copeia, 1983:67, noted that the species may be composed of two allopatric populations.

Ambystoma schmidti Taylor, 1939 "1938". Univ. Kansas Sci. Bull., 25:263.
TYPE(S): Holotype: UIMNH 25042 (formerly EHT-HMS 3999).
TYPE LOCALITY: "10 miles east of San Martín (Asuncion) at Rancho Guadalupe", México, Mexico.
DISTRIBUTION: Area of the type locality.

Ambystoma talpoideum (Holbrook, 1838). N. Am. Herpetol., Ed. 1, 3:117.
ORIGINAL NAME: *Salamandra talpoidea.*
TYPE(S): Not known to exist.
TYPE LOCALITY: "sea islands on the borders of South Carolina", USA.
DISTRIBUTION: South Carolina to northern Florida and Louisiana; disjunct colonies in southeastern Oklahoma, southern Illinois to western Tennessee and Arkansas, and in valleys of western North Carolina and adjacent Tennessee, USA.
COMMENT: Reviewed by Shoop, 1964, Cat. Am. Amph. Rept., 8.1–2.

Ambystoma taylori Brandon, Maruska, and Rumph, 1981. Bull. S. California Acad. Sci., 80:116.
TYPE(S): Holotype: FMNH 212392.
TYPE LOCALITY: Laguna Alchichica, Puebla, Mexico, ca. 24 km SW Perote.
DISTRIBUTION: Known only from Laguna Alchichica, a saline crater lake in eastern Puebla, Mexico.
COMMENT: *Ambystoma subsalsum* Taylor, 1943, Copeia, 1943:151, named from Laguna Alchichica, was based on a specimen of *Ambystoma tigrinum*, according to Brandon, Maruska, and Rumph, 1981, Bull. S. California Acad. Sci., 80:112.

Ambystoma texanum (Matthes, 1855). Allg. Deutsche Naturhist. Zeitung, N.S., 1:226.
ORIGINAL NAME: *Salamandra texana.*
TYPE(S): Syntypes: including NHMW 22920.
TYPE LOCALITY: Rio Colorado and Cumming's Creek Bottom, Fayette County, Texas [USA]; restricted to "Rio Colorado bottom land", Texas, USA, by Schmidt, 1953, Check List N. Am. Amph. Rept., Ed. 6:21.
DISTRIBUTION: From eastern Ohio west to southern Iowa and south to eastern Texas, Louisiana, Mississippi, and northwestern Alabama, USA; and from Pelee I. of Ontario, Canada.
COMMENT: Reviewed by Anderson, 1967, Cat. Am. Amph. Rept., 37.1–2. Morris and Brandon, 1984, Copeia, 1984:324–337, reported on sexual parasitism by polyploids tentatively identified as *Ambystoma platineum.*

Ambystoma tigrinum (Green, 1825). J. Acad. Nat. Sci. Philadelphia, 5:116.
ORIGINAL NAME: *Salamandra tigrina.*
TYPE(S): Not known to exist.
TYPE LOCALITY: "near Moore's town [Moorestown, Burlington County,] in New Jersey", USA.
DISTRIBUTION: From the southern limits of boreal forest in central Alberta and Saskatchewan (Canada) south to Florida (USA) and Puebla (Mexico), west to Washington and Arizona (USA) and northern Sonora (Mexico); isolated population west of the Sierra Nevada between Sonoma and Santa Barbara counties, California (USA).
COMMENT: Reviewed by Gehlbach, 1967, Cat. Am. Amph. Rept., 52.1–4. The California population is considered by many workers, including AHB, to be a distinct species, *Ambystoma californiense* (originally *Amblystoma californiense* Gray, 1853, Proc. Zool. Soc. London, 1853:11 [Type: BM; Type locality: California, Monterey, in a well; Distribution: California west of the Sierra

Nevada, from Sonoma County to Santa Barbara County]). Synonymy includes *Ambystoma subsalsum* Taylor, 1943, according to Brandon, Maruska, and Rumph, 1981, Bull. S. California Acad. Sci., 80:116. See comment under *Ambystoma taylori*. Shaffer, 1983, Copeia, 1983:67–78, noted that this nominal species may be composed of several biological species.

Ambystoma tremblayi Comeau, 1943. Ann. Assoc. Canadienne-Française Avance. Sci., 9:124.
TYPE(S): Lost, according to Brame, 1959, Herpetologica, 15:20.
TYPE LOCALITY: Not given in original description; designated as "Cap Rouge, [Quebec County,] Province of Quebec, Canada", by Brame, 1959, Herpetologica, 15:20.
DISTRIBUTION: Northern Indiana and southern Michigan (USA) east through southern Quebec (Canada) to the coastal plain of Massachusetts (USA); a single record from northwestern Wisconsin (USA).
COMMENT: Reviewed by Uzzell, 1967, Cat. Am. Amph. Rept., 50.1–2.

Rhyacosiredon Dunn, 1928. Proc. New England Zool. Club, 10:85.
TYPE SPECIES: *Amblystoma altamirani* Dugès, 1895, by monotypy.
DISTRIBUTION: High mountains of Michoacán, México (state), southern Distrito Federal, and northern Morelos, Mexico.

Rhyacosiredon altamirani (Dugès, 1895). Descr. Axolotl Mont. Las Cruces:5.
ORIGINAL NAME: *Amblystoma altamirani*.
TYPE(S): Syntypes: MDUG (6 specimens).
TYPE LOCALITY: Manantiale de los Axolotes, Serranía de las Cruces, Valle de México, Distrito Federal, Mexico.
DISTRIBUTION: High mountains of central state of México, southern Distrito Federal, and northern Morelos, Mexico.

Rhyacosiredon leorae Taylor, 1943. Univ. Kansas Sci. Bull., 29:345.
TYPE(S): Holotype: FMNH 100041 (formerly EHT-HMS 22560).
TYPE LOCALITY: "mountain stream near Rio Frío, México, either in the state of Puebla or México (Balsas River drainage system)".
DISTRIBUTION: Area of the type locality near the border of the states of México and Puebla, Mexico.

Rhyacosiredon rivularis Taylor, 1940. Herpetologica, 1:171.
TYPE(S): Holotype: FMNH 100003 (formerly EHT-HMS 16388).
TYPE LOCALITY: "about 13 km. west of Villa Victoria, México, in a small stream in pine forest", Mexico.
DISTRIBUTION: Known from the area of the type locality (México, Mexico), Nevado de Toluca, and Michoacán adjacent to the type locality.

Rhyacosiredon zempoalaensis Taylor and Smith, 1945. Proc. U.S. Natl. Mus., 95:527.
TYPE(S): Holotype: USNM 116617.
TYPE LOCALITY: "at the Lakes of Zempoala, Morelos, México, in a nearly dry lake bed, elevation about 10,000 feet".
DISTRIBUTION: Known only from the area of the type locality.
COMMENT: Possibly extinct (OFV).

FAMILY: **Amphiumidae** Gray, 1825.
CITATION: Ann. Philos., (2)10:216.
DISTRIBUTION: Southeastern USA.
COMMENT: In the suborder Amphiumoidea; see comment under Caudata.
CONTRIBUTOR: Arden H. Brame, Jr. II (AHB).
REVIEWERS: Edmund D. Brodie, Jr. (EDB); William E. Duellman (WED); Keith A. Harding (KAH); Richard Highton (RH) (USA); Marinus S. Hoogmoed (MSH); David B. Wake (DBW).

Amphiuma Garden, 1821. *In* Smith, Corresp. Linnaeus, 1:333, 599.
TYPE SPECIES: *Amphiuma means* Garden, 1821, by monotypy.
DISTRIBUTION: Southeastern USA.
COMMENT: Reviewed by Salthe, 1973, Cat. Am. Amph. Rept., 147.1–4.

Amphiuma means Garden, 1821. *In* Smith, Corresp. Linnaeus, 1:333, 599.
TYPE(S): Not known to exist.
TYPE LOCALITY: Not stated; from the context, either Charleston, South Carolina, or eastern Florida [USA]; restricted by Schmidt, 1953, Check List N. Am. Amph. Rept., Ed. 6:27, to "Charleston, South Carolina", USA.
DISTRIBUTION: Coastal plain from Virginia to the southern tip of Florida and west to southern Mississippi, USA.
COMMENT: Reviewed by Salthe, 1973, Cat. Am. Amph. Rept., 148.1–2.

Amphiuma pholeter Neill, 1964. Herpetologica, 20:62.
TYPE(S): Holotype: W. T. Neill US2675 (to be deposited in FSM).
TYPE LOCALITY: "4.5 miles NE by E Rosewood, Levy County, Florida", USA.
DISTRIBUTION: Levy, Jefferson, Calhoun, and Liberty counties, Florida, USA.

Amphiuma tridactylum Cuvier, 1827. Mém. Mus. Natl. Hist. Nat., Paris, 14:7.
TYPE(S): Holotype: MNHNP 7821.
TYPE LOCALITY: New Orleans [Louisiana, USA], according to Guibé, 1950 "1948", Cat. Types. Amph. Mus. Natl. Hist. Nat.:6.
DISTRIBUTION: Southeastern Missouri and extreme southeastern Oklahoma to Gulf of Mexico in tributaries of the Mississippi River, USA.
COMMENT: Reviewed by Salthe, 1973, Cat. Am. Amph. Rept., 149.1–3.

FAMILY: **Cryptobranchidae** Fitzinger, 1826.
CITATION: Neue Classif. Rept.:41.
DISTRIBUTION: Central China; Japan; eastern USA and southeastern Canada.
COMMENT: Although Kuhn, 1967, Amphibien und Reptilien:19, cited Cryptobranchoidea Fitzinger, 1826, as originally a suborder, in the original publication it is explicitly stated to be a family, and as such is the first use of the family-group name. Relationships of fossil and living species were discussed by Meszoely, 1966, Am. Midl. Nat., 75:495–515; Naylor, 1981, Copeia, 1981:76–86; and Čkhikvadze, 1982, Vert. Hungar., 21:63–67. In the suborder Cryptobranchoidea; see comment under Caudata.
CONTRIBUTOR: Arden H. Brame, Jr. II (AHB).
REVIEWERS: Leo J. Borkin (LJB) (Asia); Edmund D. Brodie, Jr. (EDB); William E. Duellman (WED); Richard Highton (RH) (USA); Marinus S. Hoogmoed (MSH); Shuqin Hu (SH) (Asia); Masafumi Matsui (MM) (Asia); Ermi Zhao (EM) (Asia); David B. Wake (DBW).

Andrias Tschudi, 1837. Neues Jahrb. Min. Geol. Palaeont., 5:545.
TYPE SPECIES: *Salamandra scheuchzeri* Holl, 1831 (a fossil species), by monotypy.
DISTRIBUTION: Japan and western China.
COMMENT: Naylor, 1981, Copeia, 1981:76–86, suggested that *Andrias* is a synonym of *Cryptobranchus*. Estes, 1981, Handbuch Paläoherpetol., Pt. 2:14, discussed reasons for retaining two genera. Species reviewed (as *Megalobatrachus*) by Thorn, 1968, Salamandres Eur. Asie Afr. Nord:105–111.

Andrias davidianus (Blanchard, 1871). C. R. Hebd. Séances Acad. Sci., Paris, 73:79.
ORIGINAL NAME: *Sieboldia davidiana*.
TYPE(S): Holotype: MNHNP 7613 (from 'Thibet oriental').
TYPE LOCALITY: Chungpa on the River Fowho (China) (=David's Tchong-pa).
DISTRIBUTION: The mountain streams of China, from Qinghai to Jiangsu and south to Sichuan, Guangxi, and Guangdong.
COMMENT: Synonymy and review (as *Megalobatrachus davidianus*) in Liu, 1950, Fieldiana: Zool. Mem., 2:69–77.

PROTECTED STATUS: CITES—Appendix I (1 Jul. 1975); as *Andrias* (=*Megalobatrachus*) *davidianus*. USA ESA—Endangered (14 Jun. 1976); as *Andrias davidianus davidianus*.

Andrias japonicus (Temminck, 1836). Coup-d'oeil sur la faune des iles de la Sonde et de l'empire du Japon. Discours préliminaire destiné à servir d'introduction à la Faune du Japon:xxvi.
ORIGINAL NAME: *Triton japonicus*.
TYPE(S): RMNH 2392 designated lectotype by Hoogmoed, 1978, Zool. Meded., Leiden, 54:102.
TYPE LOCALITY: Mountains of Suzuka, province of Omi, on the way from Tsuchiyama to Sukanoshita, Japan.
DISTRIBUTION: Southwestern portion of the Island of Honshu northeast to the Prefecture of Gifu, Shikoku, and on the Island of Kyushu only in the Prefecture of Oita, Japan.
COMMENT: Reviewed (as *Megalobatrachus japonicus*) by Sato, 1943, Monogr. Tailed Batr. Japan:322–346. See Hoogmoed, 1978, Zool. Meded., Leiden, 58:92, for discussion of the obscure description.
PROTECTED STATUS: CITES—Appendix I (1 Jul. 1975); as *Andrias* (=*Megalobatrachus*) *japonicus*. USA ESA—Endangered (14 Jun. 1976); as *Andrias davidianus japonicus*.

Cryptobranchus Leuckart, 1821. Isis von Oken, 1(6):260.
TYPE SPECIES: *Salamandra gigantea* Barton, 1808 (=*Salamandra alleganiensis* Daudin, 1803), by monotypy.
DISTRIBUTION: As for the single species.
COMMENT: Reviewed by Dundee, 1971, Cat. Am. Amph. Rept., 101.1. See comment under *Andrias*.

Cryptobranchus alleganiensis (Daudin, 1803). Hist. Nat. Gén. Part. Rept., 8:231.
ORIGINAL NAME: *Salamandra alleganiensis*.
TYPE(S): Originally MNHNP; now lost?
TYPE LOCALITY: "les monts Alléganis, en Virginie"; restricted to "vicinity of Davenport's Plantation", North Toe River, 1 mile south of the mouth of the Bushy Creek and 4 miles ENE of the Spruce Pine Creek, Mitchell County, North Carolina, USA, by Harper, 1940, Am. Midl. Nat., 23:721. See Dundee, 1971, Cat. Am. Amph. Rept., 101.3, for discussion of the type locality.
DISTRIBUTION: Southern New York to northern Maryland; southwestern New York to southeastern Kansas, northern Arkansas, extreme northern Mississippi, and in the Appalachian Mountains from northern Alabama to western Pennsylvania, USA.
COMMENT: Reviewed by Dundee, 1971, Cat. Am. Amph. Rept., 101.1–4.

FAMILY: **Dicamptodontidae** Tihen, 1958.
CITATION: Bull. Florida State Mus., Biol. Sci., 3:21.
DISTRIBUTION: Southwestern Canada and northwestern USA.
COMMENT: Tihen, 1958, Bull. Florida State Mus., Biol. Sci., 3:21 and 25, proposed the Dicamptodontinae and Rhyacotritoninae as subfamilies of the Ambystomatidae; Edwards, 1976, J. Morphol., 148:325, placed both subfamilies in the Dicamptodontidae, an arrangement accepted by Estes, 1981, Handbuch Paläoherpetol., Pt. 2:45, as a monophyletic family. Milner, 1983, *In* Sims, Price, and Whalley (eds.), Evol. Time Space:431–468, suggested that the Dicamptodontinae and Rhyacotritoninae might not be cladistic closest relatives. See comment under Ambystomatidae. In the suborder Ambystomatoidea; see comment under Caudata.
CONTRIBUTOR: Arden H. Brame, Jr. II (AHB).
REVIEWERS: Edmund D. Brodie, Jr. (EDB); William E. Duellman (WED); Richard Highton (RH); Marinus S. Hoogmoed (MSH); David B. Wake (DBW).

SUBFAMILY: **Dicamptodontinae** Tihen, 1958.
CITATION: Bull. Florida State Mus., Biol. Sci., 3:21.
DISTRIBUTION: Southwestern Canada and northwestern USA.

COMMENT: See comment under Dicamptodontidae.

Dicamptodon Strauch, 1870. Mém. Acad. Sci. Imp. St. Pétersbourg, (7)16:68.
TYPE SPECIES: *Triton ensatus* Eschscholtz, 1833, by monotypy.
DISTRIBUTION: The Pacific coast, from southwestern British Columbia (Canada) to Santa Cruz County, California; northern Idaho, USA.
COMMENT: Reviewed by Anderson, 1969, Cat. Am. Amph. Rept., 76.1. Nussbaum, 1976, Misc. Publ. Mus. Zool. Univ. Michigan, 149:1–94, presented information on morphology and geographic variation. Daugherty, Allendorf, Dunlap, and Knudson, 1983, Copeia, 1983:679–691, reported on biochemical evolution within the genus.

Dicamptodon aterrimus (Cope, 1868 "1867"). Proc. Acad. Nat. Sci. Philadelphia, 19:201.
ORIGINAL NAME: *Amblystoma aterrimum*.
TYPE(S): Holotype: USNM 5242.
TYPE LOCALITY: "North Rocky Mountains"; data with type are "crossing of Bitter Root River, north Rocky Mountains (Montana)", USA, according to Cochran, 1961, Bull. U.S. Natl. Mus., 220:4.
DISTRIBUTION: Northern Idaho and adjacent Montana, USA.
COMMENT: Removed from the synonymy of *Dicamptodon ensatus* by Daugherty, Allendorf, Dunlap, and Knudsen, 1983, Copeia, 1983:679, on the basis of electrophoretic distance. This taxonomic change is disputed by AHB, EDB, and DBW. Nussbaum, Brodie, and Storm, 1983, Amph. Rept. Pacific Northwest:67, rejected the specific distinctness of this form.

Dicamptodon copei Nussbaum, 1970. Copeia, 1970:506.
TYPE(S): Holotype: USNM 166784.
TYPE LOCALITY: "Mar[r]atta Creek, 85 m upstream from bridge on state highway 504, SW ¼ Sec. 3, T.9 N., R.4 E., 46° 17' N, 122° 18' W, 840 m elevation, Cowlitz County, Washington", USA; type locality buried under 33 m of volcanic sediment from 1980 eruption of Mount St. Helens, according to Nussbaum, 1983, Cat. Am. Amph. Rept., 334.1.
DISTRIBUTION: Western Washington and northwestern Oregon, USA.
COMMENT: Reviewed by Nussbaum, 1983, Cat. Am. Amph. Rept., 334.1–2.

Dicamptodon ensatus (Eschscholtz, 1833). Zool. Atlas, pt. 5:6.
ORIGINAL NAME: *Triton ensatus*.
TYPE(S): Not known to exist.
TYPE LOCALITY: Vicinity of the Bay of San Francisco, California [USA]; "probably near Fort Ross, Sonoma County", California, USA, according to Nussbaum, 1976, Misc. Publ. Mus. Zool. Univ. Michigan, 149:4.
DISTRIBUTION: The Pacific coast, from southwestern British Columbia (Canada) to the Pajaro River, California (USA).
COMMENT: Reviewed by Anderson, 1969, Cat. Am. Amph. Rept., 76.1–2 (this review written prior to the description of *Dicamptodon copei* or the resurrection of *Dicamptodon aterrimus*). See also Nussbaum, 1976, Misc. Publ. Mus. Zool. Univ. Michigan, 149:1–94.

SUBFAMILY: **Rhyacotritoninae** Tihen, 1958.
CITATION: Bull. Florida State Mus., Biol. Sci., 3:25.
DISTRIBUTION: Northwestern USA.
COMMENT: Reviewed by Anderson, 1968, Cat. Am. Amph. Rept., 68.1. See comment under Dicamptodontidae.

Rhyacotriton Dunn, 1920. Proc. New England Zool. Club, 7:56.
TYPE SPECIES: *Ranodon olympicus* Gaige, 1917, by monotypy.
DISTRIBUTION: As for the single species.
COMMENT: Reviewed by Anderson, 1968, Cat. Am. Amph. Rept., 68.1.

Rhyacotriton olympicus (Gaige, 1917). Occas. Pap. Mus. Zool. Univ. Michigan, 40:2.
   ORIGINAL NAME: *Ranodon olympicus.*
   TYPE(S): Holotype: UMMZ 48607.
   TYPE LOCALITY: "Lake Cushman, [Olympic Mountains,] Washington", USA.
   DISTRIBUTION: Pacific coastal region from the Olympic Mountains of Washington
      south through Oregon into northwestern California as far south as Albion,
      Mendocino County, USA.
   COMMENT: Reviewed by Anderson, 1968, Cat. Am. Amph. Rept., 68.1–2.

FAMILY: **Hynobiidae** Cope, 1860 "1859".
   CITATION: Proc. Acad. Nat. Sci. Philadelphia, 11:125.
   DISTRIBUTION: From Kamchatka through Siberia to eastern European USSR to Turkestan,
      Afghanistan, and Iran and eastward to Korea, Japan, and China.
   COMMENT: Dunn, 1923, Proc. Am. Acad. Arts Sci., 58:445–523, discussed phylogeny
      within the Hynobiidae. In the suborder Cryptobranchoidea; see comment under
      Caudata. See Thorn, 1968, Salamandres Eur. Asie Afr. Nord:36–104, for synonymies
      and characterizations of most of the species. Zhao and Hu, 1984, Stud. Chinese
      Tailed Amph.:3–13, discussed the Chinese genera and their phylogeny.
   CONTRIBUTOR: Arden H. Brame, Jr. II (AHB).
   REVIEWERS: Steven C. Anderson (SCA); Leo J. Borkin (LJB); Edmund D. Brodie, Jr. (EDB);
      William E. Duellman (WED); Marinus S. Hoogmoed (MSH); Shuqin Hu (SH);
      Masafumi Matsui (MM); David B. Wake (DBW); Ermi Zhao (EM).

Batrachuperus Boulenger, 1878. Bull. Soc. Zool. France, 3:71.
   TYPE SPECIES: *Salamandrella sinensis* Sauvage, 1877 (=*Dermodactylus pinchonii* David,
      1871), by monotypy.
   DISTRIBUTION: Western China (Tibet), Afghanistan, and Iran.
   COMMENT: Chinese species discussed by Fei, Ye, and Tian, 1983, Acta Zootaxon.
      Sinica, 8:209–219.

Batrachuperus longdongensis Liu and Tian, 1983. Acta Zootaxon. Sinica, 8:210.
   TYPE(S): Holotype: CIB 65I0013.
   TYPE LOCALITY: Longdong River, Mt. Emei [=Omei], Sichuan, 1300 m, China.
   DISTRIBUTION: Known only from the type locality.

Batrachuperus mustersi Smith, 1940. Ann. Mag. Nat. Hist., (11)5:382.
   TYPE(S): Holotype: BM 1946.9.6.59 (formerly 1940.3.1.1).
   TYPE LOCALITY: "mountain streams of the Paghman Range, above Paghman [=17
      mi. W Kabul], at between 9000 and 10,000 feet altitude", Afghanistan.
   DISTRIBUTION: Paghman Range above Paghman, Gardan Diwal in Koh-i-Baba
      Massif, Salang Pass to northeast of Kabul, Sanglach in Maidan Province and
      probably Dasht-i-Nawar, Afghanistan.
   COMMENT: See Reilly, 1983, J. Herpetol., 17:1–9, and Böhme, 1982, Elaphe,
      3:33–36.

Batrachuperus persicus Eiselt and Steiner, 1970. Ann. Naturhist. Mus. Wien, 74:77.
   TYPE(S): Holotype: NHMW 19435:4.
   TYPE LOCALITY: Talysch Mountains near Assalem, Province of Ghilan, Iran, small
      creek about 800 meters altitude.
   DISTRIBUTION: Hyrcanian forests of the Talysch and Elburz mountains, 800–1200 m,
      Ghilan and Mazanderan provinces, Iran.
   COMMENT: See Steiner, 1973, Salamandra, 9:1–6.

Batrachuperus pinchonii (David, 1871). Nouv. Arch. Mus. Natl. Hist. Nat., Paris, 7:95.
   ORIGINAL NAME: *Dermodactylus pinchonii.*
   TYPE(S): Syntypes: MNHNP 5060 and 5061 (8 specimens), USNM 10995.
   TYPE LOCALITY: Muping [=Baoxing], Sichuan, China.
   DISTRIBUTION: Streams of the mountain ranges in western China; northern limits
      of distribution may be at Sungpan, Sichuan, and southern limits in the
      northern Taliangshan at the south western corner of Sichuan, China, from
      5000 to 13,000 ft. elev.

COMMENT: Synonymy and review in Liu, 1950, Fieldiana: Zool. Mem., 2:82–87. Includes *Batrachuperus cochranae* Liu, 1950, Fieldiana: Zool. Mem., 2:101, according to Fei, Ye, and Tian, 1983, Acta Zootaxon. Sinica, 8:209–219.

Batrachuperus tibetanus Schmidt, 1925. Am. Mus. Novit., 157:5.
TYPE(S): Holotype: FMNH 5900.
TYPE LOCALITY: "near Tibetan border of Kansu [=Gansu], southwest of Titao, 9000 feet altitude", at about latitude 33° N, in the In Hwang Ho drainage, China.
DISTRIBUTION: Gansu, Sichuan, Tibet, and Shaanxi, China.
COMMENT: Includes *Batrachuperus karlschmidti* Liu, 1950, Fieldiana: Zool. Mem., 2: 87, according to Fei, Ye, and Tian, 1983, Acta Zootaxon. Sinica, 8:209–219. Closely related to *Batrachuperus pinchonii*, according to Schmidt, 1927, Bull. Am. Mus. Nat. Hist., 54:544.

Batrachuperus yenyuanensis Liu, 1950. Fieldiana: Zool. Mem., 2:99.
TYPE(S): Holotype: FMNH 49370.
TYPE LOCALITY: "Peilinshan, Yenyuanhsien, Sikang [now Sichuan], China, 14,500 feet altitude".
DISTRIBUTION: Known only from the type locality.
COMMENT: Reviewed by Fei, Ye, and Tian, 1983, Acta Zootaxon. Sinica, 8:209–219.

Hynobius Tschudi, 1838. Classif. Batr.:56.
TYPE SPECIES: *Salamandra nebulosa* Temminck and Schlegel, 1838, by monotypy.
DISTRIBUTION: Japan, Korea, Mongolia, China, and the Siberia west of eastern European USSR (ca. 45° E) and probably Soviet Central Asia (between Pamir Massif and Samarkand).
COMMENT: Japanese species reviewed by Sato, 1943, Monogr. Tailed Batr. Japan:1– 520.

Hynobius abei Sato, 1934. J. Sci. Hiroshima Univ., B—Zool., 3:15.
TYPE(S): Holotype: ZIHU 811; lost in World War II (MM).
TYPE LOCALITY: Surroundings of Mineyama, Nagaoka, Chozen-mura, Naka-gun, Kyoto-fu Prefecture, Honshu Island, Japan.
DISTRIBUTION: Area of the type locality, and near Miyazu, Tango Province, Honshu I., Japan.
COMMENT: Reviewed by Nakamura and Ueno, 1963, Japan. Rept. Amph. Color: 10–11.

Hynobius chinensis Günther, 1889. Ann. Mag. Nat. Hist., (6)4:222.
TYPE(S): Syntypes: BM 1946.9.6.54–55 (formerly 1889.6.25–26).
TYPE LOCALITY: Ichang, Hupeh [=Hubei] Province, China.
DISTRIBUTION: Southern China, in Hubei, Zhejiang, and Fujian provinces.
COMMENT: Reviewed by Chang, 1936, Amph. Urodeles Chine:62–65.

Hynobius dunni Tago, 1931. Newt and Salamander:130.
TYPE(S): Holotype: TIU 703.
TYPE LOCALITY: Siroyama, Sayeki Cho, [Saegimachi,] Oita Prefecture, Island of Kyushu, Japan.
DISTRIBUTION: Southwestern part of Shikoku I., and northeastern part of Kyushu I., Japan.
COMMENT: See Ueno, 1976, Nature of Hata:8–11, for population in Shikoku.

Hynobius formosanus Maki, 1922. Zool. Mag., Tokyo, 34:637.
TYPE(S): Not designated.
TYPE LOCALITY: Oiwake, Musha [=Wusche], Taichu-shu, altitude 7,000 ft, Formosa [Taiwan, China].
DISTRIBUTION: Known from 6,600 to 7,000 feet on Mt. Noko and Mt. Ari, Taiwan, China.

COMMENT: Reviewed by Sato, 1941, Trans. Nat. Hist. Soc. Formosa, 31:114–124.

Hynobius kimurae Dunn, 1923. Proc. California Acad. Sci., (4)12:27.
TYPE(S): Holotype: MCZ 8546.
TYPE LOCALITY: "Mt. Heizan, near Kyoto, Hondo", Honshu I., Omi Province, Japan.
DISTRIBUTION: Mountain regions of central and western Honshu I., Japan.
COMMENT: Nakamura and Ueno, 1963, Japan. Rept. Amph. Color:12, noted that
   subsequent emendation to *Hynobius kimurai* is incorrect. These authors
   considered *Hynobius kimurae* to be a subspecies of *Hynobius naevius*. See Matsui,
   1979, *In* Sengoku (ed.), Japanese Rept. Amph. Color:106–107.

Hynobius leechii Boulenger, 1887. Ann. Mag. Nat. Hist., (5)19:67.
TYPE(S): Holotype: BM 1946.9.6.53 (formerly 1886.12.8.14).
TYPE LOCALITY: Gensan (=Wonsan), Korea; Liaohing, China.
DISTRIBUTION: Korea and northeastern China.

Hynobius lichenatus Boulenger, 1883. Ann. Mag. Nat. Hist., (5)12:165.
TYPE(S): Holotype: BM 1946.9.6.49 (formerly 1883.8.23.1).
TYPE LOCALITY: Aomori, Honshu Island, Japan.
DISTRIBUTION: Northern part of Honshu I., Japan.
COMMENT: See Matsui and Matsui, 1980, Japan. J. Herpetol., 8:103–111, for
   discussion.

Hynobius naevius (Temminck and Schlegel, 1838). *In* Von Siebold, Fauna Japon.,
   Rept.:122.
ORIGINAL NAME: *Salamandra naevia.*
TYPE(S): Syntypes: RMNH 2305 (2 larvae), 2306 (12 adults), and NHMW 2290;
   RMNH 2306A designated lectotype by Hoogmoed, 1978, Zool. Meded.,
   Leiden, 53:96.
TYPE LOCALITY: "dans les provinces Sagami, Sinano, Tanba, Tazima et Tosa",
   Honshu and Shikoku Is., Japan.
DISTRIBUTION: Southwestern part of Honshu I., and Shikoku and Kyushu Is.,
   Japan.

Hynobius nebulosus (Temminck and Schlegel, 1838). *In* Von Siebold, Fauna Japon.,
   Rept.:127, 139.
ORIGINAL NAME: *Salamandra nebulosa.*
TYPE(S): Syntypes: RMNH 2307, 2309, BM, SMF, MNHNP; RMNH 2307A
   designated lectotype by Hoogmoed, 1978, Zool. Meded., Leiden, 53:100.
TYPE LOCALITY: "Mits jama", near Nagasaki, Kyushu I., Japan.
DISTRIBUTION: Islands of Iki-shima, Kyushu, Shikoku, and southwestern Honshu,
   Japan.
COMMENT: Discussed by Nakamura and Ueno, 1963, Japan. Rept. Amph. Color:6–7.

Hynobius nigrescens Stejneger, 1907. Bull. U.S. Natl. Mus., 58:34.
TYPE(S): Holotype: TIU 57A.
TYPE LOCALITY: "Sendai, [Rikuzen Province,] Hondo [= Honshu I.], Japan".
DISTRIBUTION: North-central to northern Honshu I., Japan.
COMMENT: Includes *Hynobius sadoensis* Sato, 1940, Bull. Biogeogr. Soc. Japan, 10:165,
   according to Nakamura and Ueno, 1963, Japan. Rept. Amph. Color:10.

Hynobius okiensis Sato, 1940. Zool. Mag., Tokyo, 52:307.
TYPE(S): Syntypes: ZIHU (apparently destroyed in World War II).
TYPE LOCALITY: Dogo, Oki Island, Japan.
DISTRIBUTION: Known only from Oki I., Japan.

Hynobius retardatus Dunn, 1923. Proc. California Acad. Sci., (4)12:27.
TYPE(S): Holotype: CAS 35928.
TYPE LOCALITY: "Noboribetsu, Iburi Province, Hokkaido [Island]", Japan.
DISTRIBUTION: Hokkaido I., Japan.

COMMENT: See Sasaki, 1924, J. Coll. Agr. Hokkaido Imp. Univ., 15:1–36, for neotenic population.

Hynobius sonani (Maki, 1922). Zool. Mag., Tokyo, 34:636.
ORIGINAL NAME: *Salamandrella sonani*.
TYPE(S): Not designated.
TYPE LOCALITY: Mt. Noko, Taichu, altitude 10,000 ft., Taiwan [China].
DISTRIBUTION: High altitudes in the mountains of Taiwan, China.
COMMENT: Reviewed by Sato, 1941, Trans. Nat. Hist. Soc. Formosa, 31:114–124.

Hynobius stejnegeri Dunn, 1923. Proc. California Acad. Sci., (4)2:28.
TYPE(S): Holotype: USNM 23901.
TYPE LOCALITY: "Kumamoto, Higo Province, Kyushu [Island]", Japan.
DISTRIBUTION: Vicinity of Mount Aso, Kumamoto Prefecture, Kyushu I., Japan.

Hynobius takedai Matsui and Miyazaki, 1984. Zool. Sci., 1:665.
TYPE(S): Holotype: TZM H-03990.
TYPE LOCALITY: "in a small pool, Chiji-machi, Hakui-shi, Ishikawa Prefecture", Honshu, Japan.
DISTRIBUTION: Lowland of Ishikawa Prefecture, on the Japan Sea side of the Chubu District, central Honshu, Japan.
COMMENT: Most closely related to *Hynobius lichenatus*, according to the original description

Hynobius tokyoensis Tago, 1931. Newt and Salamander:114.
TYPE(S): Holotype: TIU 805.
TYPE LOCALITY: Tokyo, Japan.
DISTRIBUTION: Kanto and Chubu districts of Honshu, Japan.
COMMENT: Nakamura and Ueno, 1963, Japan. Rept. Amph. Color:7, considered *Hynobius tokyoensis* to be a subspecies of *Hynobius nebulosus*, but Okouchi, 1979, *In* Sengoku (ed.), Japanese Rept. Amph. Color:98, considered it a distinct species.

Hynobius tsuensis Abé, 1922. Zool. Mag., Tokyo, 34:331.
TYPE(S): Syntypes: not designated, but including ZIHU 1016a, 2 others not traced.
TYPE LOCALITY: Tsushima, Japan.
DISTRIBUTION: North and South Is. of Tsushima, Japan.

Hynobius turkestanicus Nikolsky, 1910 "1909". Trav. Soc. Nat. Univ. Imp. Kharkow, 43 for 1909:73.
TYPE(S): Probably lost; larvae under ZIL 2404 designated lectotype by Andruschko, 1973, *In* Darevsky (ed.), The problems of herpetology, Abstr. 3rd All-Union Herpetol. Conf., Leningrad:13–15; this designation is erroneous because description was based on a single specimen (LJB).
TYPE LOCALITY: 'Between Samarkand and Pamirs' Massif, southern Central Asia, USSR.
DISTRIBUTION: Known only from the type locality.
COMMENT: Terent'ev and Chernov, 1949, Key to amphibians and reptiles [of the USSR], Engl. Transl. (1965), Jerusalem:47, and Thorn, 1968, Salamandres Eur. Asie Afr. Nord:75, considered this a synonym of *Hynobius keyserlingii* (=*Salamandrella keyserlingii* of this list). Andrushko, 1974, Vestnik Leningrad. Univ., Biol., 1974(3):157–160, regarded it as a distinct species. With the replacement of *Hynobius keyserlingii* in *Salamandrella* the generic assignment of this species becomes questionable.

Liuia Zhao and Hu, 1983. Acta Herpetol. Sinica, 2(2):30.
TYPE SPECIES: *Hynobius wushanensis* Liu, Hu, and Yang, 1960 (=*Hynobius shihi* Liu, 1950), by original designation.
DISTRIBUTION: As for the single species.

Liuia shihi (Liu, 1950). Fieldiana: Zool. Mem., 2:77.
ORIGINAL NAME: *Hynobius shihi.*
TYPE(S): Holotype: FMNH 49384.
TYPE LOCALITY: "Chihsinling, Tachangsze, eastern Szechwan [=Sichuan], China".
DISTRIBUTION: Eastern Sichuan, western Hubei, and northwestern Hunan, China.
COMMENT: Transferred to *Ranodon* from *Hynobius* by Risch and Thorn, 1982, Bull. Soc. Hist. Nat. Toulouse, 117:171, who also considered *Ranodon wushanensis* Liu, Hu, and Yang, 1960, a synonym of this species.

Onychodactylus Tschudi, 1838. Classif. Batr.:57, 92.
TYPE SPECIES: *Onychodactylus schlegeli* Tschudi, 1838 (=*Salamandra japonicus* Houttuyn, 1782), by monotypy.
DISTRIBUTION: From southern Far East USSR and nearby China to Wonsan in Korea and the mountains of Honshu and Shikoku Is., Japan.
COMMENT: Reviewed by Sato, 1943, Monogr. Tailed Batr. Japan:288–321.

Onychodactylus fischeri (Boulenger, 1886). Proc. Zool. Soc. London, 1886:416.
ORIGINAL NAME: *Geomolge fischeri.*
TYPE(S): Syntypes: BM 1947.9.7.70–71.
TYPE LOCALITY: "From Chaborowska [=Khabarovsk, USSR], on the River Ussuri, Manchuria".
DISTRIBUTION: Southern Far East USSR (Primorsky Kraj) south through extreme northeastern China to Wonsan in South Korea.
COMMENT: Reviewed by Inukai, 1933, Annot. Zool. Japon., 14:193–195.

Onychodactylus japonicus (Houttuyn, 1782). Verh. Genootsch. Wetensch. Vlissingen, 9: 329.
ORIGINAL NAME: *Salamandra japonica.*
TYPE(S): Not known to exist.
TYPE LOCALITY: Not definitely stated but evidently the "Fakoneberget" (mountains of Hakone, Izu Province, Honshu I., Japan).
DISTRIBUTION: Mountains of Honshu and Shikoku Is., Japan.
COMMENT: See Nakamura and Ueno, 1963, Japan. Rept. Amph. Color:14–15, for discussion.

Pachyhynobius Fei, Qu, and Wu, 1983. Amph. Res., Kunming:1.
TYPE SPECIES: *Pachyhynobius shangchengensis* Fei, Qu, and Wu, 1983, by monotypy.
DISTRIBUTION: As for the single species.

Pachyhynobius shangchengensis Fei, Qu, and Wu, 1983. Amph. Res., Kunming:1.
TYPE(S): Holotype: Dep. Biol., Xinxiang Normal College 00227.
TYPE LOCALITY: Shangcheng, Henan, 780 m, China.
DISTRIBUTION: Vicinity of the type locality.

Pachypalaminus Thompson, 1912. Proc. California Acad. Sci., (4)3:183.
TYPE SPECIES: *Pachypalaminus boulengeri* Thompson, 1912, by original designation.
DISTRIBUTION: As for the only species.
COMMENT: Reviewed by Sato, 1943, Monogr. Tailed Batr. Japan:252–270. Nakamura and Ueno, 1963, Japan. Rept. Amph. Color:13, considered *Pachypalaminus* to be a subgenus of *Hynobius.*

Pachypalaminus boulengeri Thompson, 1912. Proc. California Acad. Sci., (4)3:184.
TYPE(S): Holotype: CAS 33192.
TYPE LOCALITY: "Odaigahara Mt., Yamato Province, Honshu [Island], Japan".
DISTRIBUTION: Three regions of Japan: Prefectures of Nara, Mie, and Wakayama, central Honshu I.; central mountains of Shikoku I.; and Mount Sobo (Prefecture of Oita), Kyushu I.

Paradactylodon Risch, 1984. Alytes, Paris, 3:44.

TYPE SPECIES: *Batrachuperus gorganensis* Clerque-Gazeau and Thorn, 1979.

DISTRIBUTION: As for the single species.

Paradactylodon gorganensis (Clerque-Gazeau and Thorn, 1979). Bull. Soc. Hist. Nat. Toulouse, 114:455.

ORIGINAL NAME: *Batrachuperus gorganensis.*

TYPE(S): Holotype: MNHNP 1978-1982.

TYPE LOCALITY: At the edge of a cavernous stream on a clay bank 200 m inside the entrance of a cave, situated between the village of Gorgan and Ali-Abad, Elburz Mountain Range of north-central Iran, near the southeast shore of the Caspian Sea and with an elevation of 400 m above its level.

DISTRIBUTION: Known only from the holotype.

Ranodon Kessler, 1866. Bull. Soc. Imp. Nat. Moscou, 39:126.

TYPE SPECIES: *Ranodon sibiricus* Kessler, 1866, by monotypy.

DISTRIBUTION: High mountains of the USSR (Ala Tau), and China (Sichuan, southern Shaanxi, western Hubei, northwestern Hunan, and northern Xinjiang).

COMMENT: Synonymy includes *Pseudohynobius* Fei and Yang, 1983, Amph. Res., Kunming:2, according to Zhao and Hu, 1984, Stud. Chinese Tailed Amph. See comment under *Ranodon tsinpaensis.*

Ranodon sibiricus Kessler, 1866. Bull. Soc. Imp. Nat. Moscou, 39:126.

TYPE(S): Syntypes: ZMM 34 (one of two syntypes).

TYPE LOCALITY: 'Neighborhood of Semipalatinsk', USSR; in error, by being outside of known distribution (LJB).

DISTRIBUTION: High mountains of western Xinjiang, China, and nearby region of the USSR (Dzhungarian Ala Tau).

Ranodon tsinpaensis Liu and Hu, 1966. Acta Zool. Sinica, 18:65.

TYPE(S): Holotype: CIB (formerly SWIBASC) 623293.

TYPE LOCALITY: Hou-tseng-tze, Chouchih Hsien, Shensi [=Shaanxi], China, at 1830 meters altitude.

DISTRIBUTION: Southern Shaanxi and western Hubei, China.

COMMENT: Synonymy includes *Hynobius flavomaculatus* Fei and Ye, 1982, Acta Zootaxon. Sinica, 7:225 (Holotype: CIB 79I107; Type locality: Hanchi, Lichuan county, Hubei, altitude 1845 m, China), according to Zhao and Hu, 1983, Acta Herpetol. Sinica, 2(2):33.

Salamandrella Dybowski, 1870. Verh. Zool. Bot. Ges. Wien, 20:237.

TYPE SPECIES: *Salamandrella keyserlingii* Dybowski, 1870, by monotypy.

DISTRIBUTION: As for the single species.

COMMENT: Considered a genus distinct from *Hynobius* by Inukai, 1932, J. Fac. Sci. Hokkaido Imp. Univ., 1:191–217, and more recently by Fei and Ye, 1983, Acta Herpetol. Sinica, 2(4):32, and Zhao and Hu, 1984, Stud. Chinese Tailed Amph.: 1–68 (who also reported on phylogenetic relations to other hynobiids). See also Sato, 1943, Monogr. Tailed Batr. Japan:272–287, for discussion. See *Hynobius turkestanicus.*

Salamandrella keyserlingii Dybowski, 1870. Verh. Zool. Bot. Ges. Wien, 20:237.

TYPE(S): Not traced; ZIL 1482 (4 specimens), collected by Dybowski at the type locality and received from the Warsaw Museum in 1871 are probably from the type series (LJB).

TYPE LOCALITY: Meadows of the Kultushnaya and Pakhabikha river valleys, southwestern corner of Lake Baikal, southern Siberia, USSR.

DISTRIBUTION: Islands of Hokkaido (Japan) and Sakhalin (USSR); Kamchatka to eastern European USSR (up to 45° E), south to northern Mongolia and northeastern China.

COMMENT: See Mertens and Wermuth, 1960, Amph. Rept. Europas:15, for
synonymy. See Borkin, Belimov, and Sedalishchev, 1984, Trudy Zool. Inst.
Akad. Nauk SSSR, Leningrad, 124:89–101, for record north (72° N) of the
Arctic Circle.

FAMILY: **Plethodontidae** Gray, 1850.
CITATION: Cat. Spec. Amph. Coll. Brit. Mus., Batr. Grad.:31.
DISTRIBUTION: Extreme southern Alaska and Nova Scotia (Canada) south to eastern Brazil
and central Bolivia; southern Europe.
COMMENT: Wake, 1966, Mem. S. California Acad. Sci., 4:1–111, provided an evolutionary
and biogeographical discussion of the family at the tribal and generic levels. In the
suborder Plethodontoidea; see comment under Caudata.
CONTRIBUTOR: Arden H. Brame, Jr. II (AHB).
REVIEWERS: Edmund D. Brodie, Jr. (EDB); William E. Duellman (WED); Keith A. Harding
(KAH); Richard Highton (RH) (USA); Marinus S. Hoogmoed (MSH); David B. Wake
(DBW).

SUBFAMILY: **Desmognathinae** Cope, 1859.
CITATION: Proc. Acad. Nat. Sci. Philadelphia, 11:122.
DISTRIBUTION: Eastern USA and southeastern Canada.
COMMENT: See comment under Plethodontidae. As first formed by Cope, 1866, J. Acad.
Nat. Sci. Philadelphia, (2)6:103, the group name was Desmognathidae. Soler, 1950,
Univ. Kansas Sci. Bull., 33:459–480, suggested that the Desmognathinae should be
considered a distinct family, but Wake, 1966, Mem. S. California Acad. Sci., 4:1–
111, disagreed.

Desmognathus Baird, 1850. J. Acad. Nat. Sci. Philadelphia, (2)1:282.
TYPE SPECIES: *Triturus fuscus* Rafinesque, 1820 (=*Salamandra fusca* Green, 1818) by the
subsequent designation of Brown, 1908, Proc. Acad. Nat. Sci. Philadelphia, 1908:
126.
DISTRIBUTION: Eastern USA and southeastern Canada, west to eastern Oklahoma and
Texas.

Desmognathus aeneus Brown and Bishop, 1947. Copeia, 1947:163.
TYPE(S): Holotype: USNM 123977.
TYPE LOCALITY: "seepage branch 100 feet north of Peachtree Creek, ½ mile S.S.E.
of Peachtree, Cherokee County, North Carolina", USA.
DISTRIBUTION: Extreme southwestern North Carolina and northern Georgia and
north central Alabama, USA.

Desmognathus auriculatus (Holbrook, 1838). N. Am. Herpetol., Ed. 1, 3:115.
ORIGINAL NAME: *Salamandra auriculata.*
TYPE(S): Unknown; listed by Dunn, 1926, Salamanders Fam. Plethodontidae:101, as
USNM 3901, but not mentioned in USNM list of types by Cochran, 1961,
Bull. U.S. Natl. Mus., 222:1–291.
TYPE LOCALITY: "Riceborough, [Liberty County,] in Georgia", USA.
DISTRIBUTION: Southeastern South Carolina, southward to central Florida, and
westward to southeastern Mississippi, USA.

Desmognathus brimleyorum Stejneger, 1895. Proc. U.S. Natl. Mus., 17:597.
TYPE(S): Holotype: USNM 22157.
TYPE LOCALITY: "Hot Springs, [Garland County,] Ark[ansas].", USA.
DISTRIBUTION: Ouachita Mountains of Arkansas and Oklahoma, and in
northeastern Texas, USA.

Desmognathus fuscus (Green, 1818). J. Acad. Nat. Sci. Philadelphia, (1)1:357.
ORIGINAL NAME: *Salamandra fusca.*
TYPE(S): Unknown.
TYPE LOCALITY: Probably the vicinity of Princeton, New Jersey [USA], according to
Schmidt, 1953, Check List N. Am. Amph. Rept., Ed. 6:29.
DISTRIBUTION: Extreme southeastern Canada and most of the eastern USA.

Desmognathus imitator Dunn, 1927. Copeia, 164:84.
ORIGINAL NAME: *Desmognathus fuscus imitator*.
TYPE(S): Holotype: USNM 72762.
TYPE LOCALITY: Indian Pass, Great Smoky Mountains, North Carolina [USA].
DISTRIBUTION: Throughout the Great Smoky Mountains at all elevations, eastern
    North Carolina and western Tennessee, USA.
COMMENT: Tilley, Merritt, Wu, and Highton, 1978, Evolution, 32:100, showed that
    Desmognathus imitator is a distinct species and removed it from the synonymy
    of *Desmognathus ochrophaeus*.

Desmognathus monticola Dunn, 1916. Proc. Biol. Soc. Washington, 29:73.
TYPE(S): Holotype: USNM 38313.
TYPE LOCALITY: "Elk Lodge Lake, near Brevard, North Carolina; altitude about 3000
    feet", USA.
DISTRIBUTION: Southwestern Pennsylvania through the Appalachian highlands to
    northern Georgia, USA.

Desmognathus ochrophaeus Cope, 1859. Proc. Acad. Nat. Sci. Philadelphia, 11:124.
ORIGINAL NAME: *Desmognathus ochrophaea*.
TYPE(S): Destroyed.
TYPE LOCALITY: "Susquehanna County, Pennsylvania", USA.
DISTRIBUTION: Mountains from New York to Georgia, USA.
COMMENT: Reviewed by Tilley, 1973, Cat. Am. Amph. Rept., 129.1–4.

Desmognathus quadramaculatus (Holbrook, 1840). N. Am. Herpetol., Ed. 1, 4:121.
ORIGINAL NAME: *Salamandra quadra-maculata*.
TYPE(S): Holotype: ANSP 490.
TYPE LOCALITY: ". . . extended in the Atlantic states . . . common in Georgia and
    Carolina, and is an inhabitant of Pennsylvania"; restricted to "Great Smoky
    Mountains", USA, by Schmidt, 1953, Check List N. Am. Amph. Rept., Ed. 6:
    32; Valentine, 1974, Cat. Am. Amph. Rept., 153.1, noted that this should be
    construed as the North Carolina, USA, side of the Great Smoky Mountains.
DISTRIBUTION: From Monroe County, West Virginia eastward to Henry County,
    Virginia, and southward through North and South Carolina to northeastern
    Georgia, in the Appalachian Mountains, USA.
COMMENT: Reviewed by Valentine, 1974, Cat. Am. Amph. Rept., 153.1–4.

Desmognathus santeetlah Tilley, 1981. Occas. Pap. Mus. Zool. Univ. Michigan, 695:3.
TYPE(S): Holotype: USNM 214218.
TYPE LOCALITY: "from a seepage area at ca. 1219 m (4000') in the headwaters of the
    N. Fork of Citico Cr. below Cherry Log Gap, Unicoi Mtns., Monroe County",
    Tennessee, USA.
DISTRIBUTION: Restricted to the Great Smoky, Great Balsam, and Unicoi mountains
    of southwestern Blue Ridge Physiographic Province (Tennessee and North
    Carolina, USA).

Desmognathus welteri Barbour, 1950. Copeia, 1950:277.
ORIGINAL NAME: *Desmognathus fuscus welteri*.
TYPE(S): Holotype: USNM 129312.
TYPE LOCALITY: "at an elevation of 2300 feet above sea level, at Looney Creek, near
    Lynch, Harlan County, Kentucky", USA.
DISTRIBUTION: Eastern Kentucky and adjacent Virginia, USA.

Desmognathus wrighti King, 1936. Herpetologica, 1:57.
TYPE(S): Holotype: USNM 101794.
TYPE LOCALITY: "Mount Le Conte, Sevier County, Tennessee, Great Smoky
    Mountains National Park", USA.
DISTRIBUTION: The Great Smoky Mountains of eastern Tennessee and western
    North Carolina and White Top Mountain of southwestern Virginia, USA.

Leurognathus Moore, 1899. Proc. Acad. Nat. Sci. Philadelphia, 51:316.
TYPE SPECIES: *Leurognathus marmorata* Moore, 1899, by monotypy.
DISTRIBUTION: As for the single species.
COMMENT: Reviewed by Martof, 1963, Cat. Am. Amph. Rept., 3.1.

Leurognathus marmoratus Moore, 1899. Proc. Acad. Nat. Sci. Philadelphia, 51:316.
ORIGINAL NAME: *Leurognathus marmorata*.
TYPE(S): Holotype: ANSP 19610.
TYPE LOCALITY: "south flank of Grandfather Mt., N.C. [Avery County, North Carolina, USA], and at an elevation of about 3,500 feet".
DISTRIBUTION: Southwestern Virginia and southward into the Great Smoky Mountains, northeastern Georgia, and the northwestern tip of South Carolina, USA.
COMMENT: Reviewed by Martof, 1963, Cat. Am. Amph. Rept., 3.1–2.

Phaeognathus Highton, 1961. Copeia, 1961:66.
TYPE SPECIES: *Phaeognathus hubrichti* Highton, 1961, by original designation.
DISTRIBUTION: As for the single species.
COMMENT: Reviewed by Brandon, 1966, Cat. Am. Amph. Rept., 26.1.

Phaeognathus hubrichti Highton, 1961. Copeia, 1961:67.
TYPE(S): Holotype: USNM 142486.
TYPE LOCALITY: "three miles (4.8 km) northwest of McKenzie on U.S. Route 31, Butler County, Alabama", USA.
DISTRIBUTION: Wooded Alabama Coastal Plain (Butler and Conecuh counties), southern edge of the Red Hills region, USA.
COMMENT: Reviewed by Brandon, 1966, Cat. Am. Amph. Rept., 26.1–2.
PROTECTED STATUS: USA ESA—Threatened (3 Dec. 1976).

SUBFAMILY: **Plethodontinae** Gray, 1850.
CITATION: Cat. Spec. Amph. Coll. Brit. Mus., Batr. Grad.:31.
DISTRIBUTION: Coextensive with the distribution of the family Plethodontidae.
COMMENT: See comment under Plethodontidae. Tribe and supergenus assignments in generic accounts follow Wake, 1966, Mem. S. California Acad. Sci., 4:1–111. Elias and Wake, 1983, *In* Rhodin and Miyata (eds.), Adv. Herpetol. Evol. Biol.:1–12, discussed phylogeny of the bolitoglossine genera. Wake and Elias, 1983, Contrib. Sci. Nat. Hist. Mus. Los Angeles Co., 345:1–19, provided diagnoses and a discussion of phylogenetic relationships of the tropical bolitoglossines.
REVIEWERS: Jonathan A. Campbell (JAC) (Mexico and Central America); Gustavo Casas-Andreu (GCA); Oscar Flores-Villela (OFV) (Mexico); Jay M. Savage (JMS) (Central America); Norman J. Scott, Jr. (NJS) (Central and South America).

Aneides Baird, 1849. *In* Heck, Icon. Encyclop. Sci., 2:257.
TYPE SPECIES: *Salamandra lugubris* Hallowell, 1849, by monotypy.
DISTRIBUTION: Pacific Coast of the western USA (except Washington, USA, and Vancouver I. in British Columbia, Canada), northern Baja California Norte (Mexico); the Sacramento Mountains of New Mexico (USA); the eastern USA in the Appalachian Mountains.
COMMENT: Tribe Plethodontini. Reviewed by Wake, 1974, Cat. Am. Amph. Rept., 157.1–2. See comment under *Plethodon*. Larson, Wake, Maxson, and Highton, 1981, Evolution, 35:405–422, provided a cladogram of the species and a discussion.

Aneides aeneus (Cope and Packard, 1881). Am. Nat., 15:878.
ORIGINAL NAME: *Plethodon aeneus*.
TYPE(S): Holotype: ANSP 10461.
TYPE LOCALITY: "near the mouth of . . ." Nickajack Cave, Marion County, Tennessee, USA.
DISTRIBUTION: Appalachian region from southern Ohio and southwestern Pennsylvania to northern Alabama and northeastern Mississippi, USA.

COMMENT: Reviewed by Gordon, 1967, Cat. Am. Amph. Rept., 30.1–2.

Aneides ferreus Cope, 1869. Proc. Acad. Nat. Sci. Philadelphia, 21:109.
   ORIGINAL NAME: *Anaides ferreus*.
   TYPE(S): Holotype: USNM 14451 (formerly 6794).
   TYPE LOCALITY: "Fort Umpqua, [Douglas County,], Oregon", USA.
   DISTRIBUTION: Northern coastal California through coastal Oregon (absent from
      the state of Washington), USA, but present on Vancouver I., British
      Columbia, Canada.
   COMMENT: Reviewed by Wake, 1965, Cat. Am. Amph. Rept., 16.1–2.

Aneides flavipunctatus (Strauch, 1870). Mém. Acad. Sci. Imp. St. Pétersbourg, (7)16:71.
   ORIGINAL NAME: *Plethodon flavipunctatus*.
   TYPE(S): ZIL?
   TYPE LOCALITY: "New Albion" (=Albion), Mendocino County, California, USA.
   DISTRIBUTION: Coastal mountains of California (USA) from western Humboldt to
      southern Santa Cruz counties, and interiorly, in northern part of range, to
      near southern base of Mt. Shasta; headwaters of Applegate River, Jackson
      County, Oregon, USA.
   COMMENT: Reviewed by Lynch, 1974, Cat. Am. Amph. Rept., 158.1–2.

Aneides hardii (Taylor, 1941). Proc. Biol. Soc. Washington, 54:77.
   ORIGINAL NAME: *Plethodon hardii*.
   TYPE(S): Holotype: FMNH 100103 (formerly EHT-HMS 23656).
   TYPE LOCALITY: "Sacramento Mountains (9,000 ft.) at Cloudcroft, [Otero County,]
      New Mexico", USA.
   DISTRIBUTION: Sacramento, Capitan, and White mountains of southern New
      Mexico, USA.
   COMMENT: The name of this species is frequently seen (incorrectly) as *Aneides
      hardyi*. Reviewed by Wake, 1965, Cat. Am. Amph. Rept., 17.1–2; see Pope and
      Highton, 1980, J. Herpetol., 14:343–346, for study of geographic genetic
      variation and literature review.

Aneides lugubris (Hallowell, 1849). Proc. Acad. Nat. Sci. Philadelphia, 4:126.
   ORIGINAL NAME: *Salamandra lugubris*.
   TYPE(S): Holotype: ANSP 1257.
   TYPE LOCALITY: "Monterey, [Monterey County,] California", USA.
   DISTRIBUTION: Coast Ranges of California (USA) from Humboldt County to
      northern Baja California Norte (Mexico); foothills of the Sierra Nevada from
      Calaveras to Madera counties, California (USA); South Farallon, Catalina, and
      Los Coronados Is., off the coast of California and Baja California Norte,
      Mexico.
   COMMENT: Reviewed by Lynch and Wake, 1974, Cat. Am. Amph. Rept., 159.1–2.

Batrachoseps Bonaparte, 1841. Icon. Fauna Ital., 2:fasc. 26, fol. 131.
   TYPE SPECIES: *Salamandrina attenuata* Eschscholtz, 1833, by monotypy.
   DISTRIBUTION: Oregon and California (USA) to northern Baja California (Mexico).
   COMMENT: Tribe Bolitoglossini; sole member of supergenus *Batrachoseps*. See Brame
      and Murray, 1968, Sci. Bull. Nat. Hist. Mus. Los Angeles Co., 4:1–35, for key to
      most of the species.

Batrachoseps aridus Brame, 1970. Contrib. Sci. Nat. Hist. Mus. Los Angeles Co., 200:2.
   TYPE(S): Holotype: LACM 56271.
   TYPE LOCALITY: "[South Fork of] Hidden Palm Canyon, a tributary of Deep
      Canyon, elevation approximately 2800 feet, (10.5 miles by road S of the
      intersection of state Highways 111 and 74, town of Palm Desert), NW end of
      Santa Rosa Mountains, from slopes on western side of the Coachella Valley,
      Riverside County, California", USA.
   DISTRIBUTION: Known only from the type locality.

PROTECTED STATUS: USA ESA—Endangered (4 Jun. 1973).

Batrachoseps attenuatus (Eschscholtz, 1833). Zool. Atlas, 5:1.
  ORIGINAL NAME: *Salamandrina attenuata.*
  TYPE(S): Unknown.
  TYPE LOCALITY: Vicinity of the Bay of San Francisco, California [USA].
  DISTRIBUTION: Southwestern Oregon through western California southward to
    southern Santa Cruz, Santa Clara, and northern San Benito counties, and the
    slopes of the Sierra Nevada in northern California below 3000 ft., and a few
    scattered localities in the northern Sacramento Valley, USA.

Batrachoseps campi Marlow, Brode, and Wake, 1979. Contrib. Sci. Nat. Hist. Mus. Los
    Angeles Co., 308:3.
  TYPE(S): Holotype: MVZ 122993.
  TYPE LOCALITY: "Long John Canyon, W slope of the Inyo Mountains, elevation
    1695 m (5560 ft), 3.2 km (2 mi) N, 5.3 km (3.3 mi) E Lone Pine, Inyo County,
    California, USA".
  DISTRIBUTION: A number of springs and seeps on both slopes of the Inyo
    Mountains, Inyo County, California, USA.
  COMMENT: Genic differentiation and the discovery of 11 new localities of
    Batrachoseps campi was presented by Yanev and Wake, 1981, Herpetologica, 37:
    16–28.

Batrachoseps nigriventris Cope, 1869. Proc. Acad. Nat. Sci. Philadelphia, 21:98.
  TYPE(S): Syntypes: ANSP 481–482; Cope cited ANSP 1865 and Smithson. Mus.
    (USNM) 6734 in the original description.
  TYPE LOCALITY: "Fort Tejon, [Kern County,] California", USA.
  DISTRIBUTION: Coastal region of California from southeastern Monterey County
    south to O'Neill Park, southern Orange County and the lower western slopes
    of the Sierra Nevada from Mariposa County south to northern Kern County
    and on Santa Cruz I.
  COMMENT: This is a cryptic species morphologically indistinguishable from
    Batrachoseps attenuatus of northern coastal California and lower slopes of
    the northern California Sierra Nevada and from northern populations of
    Batrachoseps pacificus from Monterey County and the adjacent region. Yanev,
    1980, *In* Power (ed.), The California Islands: Proceeding of a Multidisciplinary
    Symposium, Santa Barbara Mus. Nat. Hist.:531–550, showed that though this
    species is practically indistinguishable morphologically from the above
    mentioned forms, *Batrachoseps nigriventris* is highly distinctive
    electrophoretically.

Batrachoseps pacificus (Cope, 1865). Proc. Acad. Nat. Sci. Philadelphia, 17:195.
  ORIGINAL NAME: *Hemidactylium pacificum.*
  TYPE(S): Holotype: USNM 6733.
  TYPE LOCALITY: "Santa Barbara, on the coast of southern California", USA;
    corrected to one of the northern Channel Islands by Van Denburgh, 1905,
    Proc. California Acad. Sci., (3)4:5–6.
  DISTRIBUTION: Southern California, USA, and northwestern Baja California,
    Mexico, as well as the Channel Islands (Anacapa, Santa Cruz, Santa Rosa, and
    San Miguel) off the coast of and belonging to Ventura and Santa Barbara
    counties, California, USA.
  COMMENT: Yanev, 1980, *In* Power (ed.), The California Islands: Proceeding of a
    Multidisciplinary Symposium, Santa Barbara Mus. Nat. Hist.:531–550, based
    on electrophoretic evidence, considered *Batrachoseps relictus* Brame and
    Murray, 1968, Sci. Bull. Nat. Hist. Mus. Los Angeles County, 4:5, of Kern and
    Mariposa counties, California, USA, and *Batrachoseps major* Camp, 1915, Univ.
    California Publ. Zool., 12:327, of southwestern California, USA, and
    northwestern Baja California, Mexico, to be subspecies of *Batrachoseps pacificus.*

AHB disagrees with this interpretation because of the morphological distinctiveness of these forms; see Brame and Murray, 1968, Sci. Bull. Nat. Hist. Mus. Los Angeles Co., 4:1–35.

Batrachoseps simatus Brame and Murray, 1968. Sci. Bull. Nat. Hist. Mus. Los Angeles Co., 4:15.
TYPE(S): Holotype: LACM 23427.
TYPE LOCALITY: "1 to 1.5 mi SW of Democrat Hot Springs Resort turnoff, on the steep slopes to the south side of the Kern River Canyon above State Hwy. 178 (24.7 mi NE of the intersection of Niles and Baker Streets, in Bakersfield, or about 2 mi. NE of Cow Flat Creek), Kern County, California", USA.
DISTRIBUTION: Known from the Kern River Canyon area of Kern County and possibly from near Fairview in southern Tulare County, California, USA.

Batrachoseps stebbinsi Brame and Murray, 1968. Sci. Bull. Nat. Hist. Mus. Los Angeles Co., 4:18.
TYPE(S): Holotype: MVZ 81835.
TYPE LOCALITY: "3 mi west of Paris Loraine (sometimes called Loraine), Piute Mountains, southern Sierra Nevada, Kern County, California, at 2500 ft. elevation", USA.
DISTRIBUTION: Known from the vicinity of the type locality and the Tehachapi Mountains, Kern County, California, USA.

Batrachoseps wrighti (Bishop, 1937). Herpetologica, 1:93.
ORIGINAL NAME: *Plethopsis wrighti*.
TYPE(S): Holotype: USNM 102445.
TYPE LOCALITY: "8.7 miles southeast of Sandy, Clackamas County, Oregon", USA.
DISTRIBUTION: From the Columbia River Gorge of northwestern Oregon (east of Portland) southward along the western slopes of the Cascade Mountains to Lane County, USA.

Bolitoglossa Duméril, Bibron, and Duméril, 1854. Erp. Gén., 9:88.
TYPE SPECIES: *Bolitoglossa mexicana* Duméril, Bibron, and Duméril, 1854, by subsequent designation of Taylor, 1944, Univ. Kansas Sci. Bull., 30:218.
DISTRIBUTION: Northeastern Mexico through central and southern Mexico, Central America, and in Colombia, Venezuela, Ecuador, Peru, northeastern Brazil, and to central Bolivia.
COMMENT: Tribe Bolitoglossini; supergenus *Bolitoglossa*. Species group assignments are those of Wake and Lynch, 1976, Sci. Bull. Nat. Hist. Mus. Los Angeles Co., 25:57, and Elias, 1984, Contrib. Sci. Nat. Hist. Mus. Los Angeles Co., 348:1–20. Wake and Elias, 1983, Contrib. Sci. Nat. Hist. Mus. Los Angeles Co., 345:10, commented on the alpha and beta groups proposed by Wake and Lynch (1976). Wake and Lynch, 1982, Herpetologica, 38:257–272, discussed relationships and biogeography within the *Bolitoglossa dofleini* group. Larson, 1983, Herpetologica, 39:85–99, discussed relationships of the *Bolitoglossa dunni*, *Bolitoglossa morio*, *Bolitoglossa rufescens*, *Bolitoglossa dofleini*, *Bolitoglossa franklini*, and *Bolitoglossa veracrucis* groups, and reviewed the literature of *Bolitoglossa* systematics. Papenfuss, Wake, and Adler, 1984 "1983", J. Herpetol., 17:295–307, discussed the systematics of the *Bolitoglossa macrinii* group.

Bolitoglossa adspersa (Peters, 1863). Monatsber. Preuss. Akad. Wiss Berlin, 1863:468.
ORIGINAL NAME: *Spelerpes (Oedipus) adspersus*.
TYPE(S): Holotype: ZMB 4916.
TYPE LOCALITY: Bogotá, Colombia.
DISTRIBUTION: Eastern Andes north of Bogotá to the Páramo de La Rusia and south of Bogotá to Aguadita, near Fusagasuga, Colombia.
COMMENT: In the *Bolitoglossa adspersa* group.

Bolitoglossa altamazonica (Cope, 1874). Proc. Acad. Nat. Sci. Philadelphia, 26:120.
ORIGINAL NAME: *Oedipus altamazonicus.*
TYPE(S): Syntypes: ANSP or USNM, now lost or destroyed.
TYPE LOCALITY: "Nauta", Departamento de Loreto, Peru.
DISTRIBUTION: Eastern and lower slopes of the Andes from Colombia to Bolivia;
    Amazon Valley in Brazil.
COMMENT: In the *Bolitoglossa altamazonica* group.
REVIEWERS: Werner C. A. Bokermann (WCAB); Ulisses Caramaschi (UC); Paulo E.
    Vanzolini (PEV).

Bolitoglossa alvaradoi Taylor, 1954. Univ. Kansas Sci. Bull., 36:604.
TYPE(S): Holotype: KU 30484.
TYPE LOCALITY: "Moravia de Chirripo, Limón Province, Costa Rica".
DISTRIBUTION: Known only from Moravia de Chirripo (Limón Province), Pavones
    (Cartago Province), and San Carlos (Alajuela Province), Costa Rica.
COMMENT: In the *Bolitoglossa alvaradoi* group.

Bolitoglossa arborescandens Taylor, 1954. Univ. Kansas Sci. Bull., 36:600.
TYPE(S): Holotype: KU 34925.
TYPE LOCALITY: "Moravia de Chirripo, Limón Province, Costa Rica".
DISTRIBUTION: Known only from northwestern to south-central Costa Rica, 880–
    1160 m.
COMMENT: In the *Bolitoglossa alvaradoi* group.

Bolitoglossa biseriata Tanner, 1962. Herpetologica, 18:19.
TYPE(S): Holotype: UU 3847.
TYPE LOCALITY: "Rio Tuira at mouth of Paya Tributary, Darien Province, Panama".
DISTRIBUTION: Northwestern, south-central, and eastern Panama (Departments of
    Bocas del Toro, Cocle, Panamá, San Blas, and Darién) and western Colombia
    (Departments of Valle and Cauca).
COMMENT: In the *Bolitoglossa sima* group.

Bolitoglossa borburata Trapido, 1942. Bol. Soc. Venezolana Cienc. Nat., 8:297.
TYPE(S): Holotype: USNM 115509.
TYPE LOCALITY: "Valle del Río Borburata, Estado Carabobo, Venezuela, 1200 m."
DISTRIBUTION: Type locality (State of Carabobo) and the Rancho Grande and
    Choroni area of the State of Aragua, Venezuela.
COMMENT: In the *Bolitoglossa adspersa* group.

Bolitoglossa capitana Brame and Wake, 1963. Contrib. Sci. Nat. Hist. Mus. Los Angeles
    Co., 69:47.
TYPE(S): Holotype: MLS 1a.
TYPE LOCALITY: "Hacienda La Victoria [La Granja Infantil—an orphanage, 6 km
    north of Albán on the Albán to Sasaima Road] between Albán and Sasaima,
    1780 meters (5840 feet), in the Cordillera Oriental about 50 km. NW Bogotá,
    Departamento de Cundinamarca, Colombia".
DISTRIBUTION: Known only from the forest above the orphanage at the type
    locality.
COMMENT: In the *Bolitoglossa adspersa* group.

Bolitoglossa cerroensis (Taylor, 1952). Univ. Kansas Sci. Bull., 34:724.
ORIGINAL NAME: *Magnadigita cerroensis.*
TYPE(S): Holotype: KU 29961.
TYPE LOCALITY: "Cerro de la Muerte at approximately 7000 ft. elevation, Pacific
    slope, 2 km. below Millville [=Villa Mills] on the Pan American Highway",
    Cartago Province, Costa Rica.
DISTRIBUTION: Known from near Villa Mills, Chavez, Las Cruces, La Trinidad, and
    Finca La Carmen from 8500–9500 ft. elevation, Cartago and San José
    provinces, Costa Rica.

COMMENT: In the *Bolitoglossa adspersa* group.

Bolitoglossa chica Brame and Wake, 1963. Contrib. Sci. Nat. Hist. Mus. Los Angeles Co., 69:16.
TYPE(S): Holotype: James A. Peters 4366 (now USNM?).
TYPE LOCALITY: "grounds of the Hotel Zaracay, 2 km. E of Santo Domingo, 670 meters (2200 feet), Provincia de Pichincha, Ecuador".
DISTRIBUTION: Known only from the type locality, vicinity of Santo Domingo de los Colorados, and from the lower part of the Río Bolaniguas, a southern effluent of Río Guaillabamba in the Río Esmeraldas system (250–400 m alt.), Provincia de Pichincha, Ecuador.
COMMENT: In the *Bolitoglossa sima* group.

Bolitoglossa colonnea (Dunn, 1924). Field Mus. Nat. Hist. Publ., Zool. Ser., 12:96.
ORIGINAL NAME: *Oedipus colonneus.*
TYPE(S): Holotype: MCZ 9406.
TYPE LOCALITY: "La Loma, on trail from Chiriquicito to Boquete [Atlantic side], altitude about 2000 feet, Bocas del Toro [Province], Panama".
DISTRIBUTION: Known from Bocas del Toro Province, western Panamá and Alajuela, Heredia, Limón, and Cartago provinces, Costa Rica, all on the Caribbean slopes; also in the Golfo Dulce and Las Cruces areas of Pacific slope Costa Rica (Puntarenas Province); Cerro Campana, Pacific slope Panama; Barro Colorado I., Panama.
COMMENT. In the *Bolitoglossa striatula* group.

Bolitoglossa compacta Wake, Brame, and Duellman, 1972. Contrib. Sci. Nat. Hist. Mus. Los Angeles Co., 248:12.
TYPE(S): Holotype: KU 116662.
TYPE LOCALITY: "north slope of Cerro Pando, 1920–1970 m (6298–6462 ft) elevation, Provincia de Bocas del Toro, western Panamá".
DISTRIBUTION: Known only from the north slope of Cerro Pando, Provincia de Bocas del Toro, western Panama from between 1810 and 2134 m (=5937–7000 ft.) elevation.
COMMENT: In the *Bolitoglossa subpalmata* group.

Bolitoglossa cuchumatana (Stuart, 1943). Misc. Publ. Mus. Zool. Univ. Michigan, 56:14.
ORIGINAL NAME: *Oedipus cuchumatanus.*
TYPE(S): Holotype: UMMZ 89110.
TYPE LOCALITY: "Oak forest about 2 kilometers north of Nebaj, El Quiché [Department], Guatemala".
DISTRIBUTION: Departments of El Quiché and Huehuetenango, Guatemala, 1200–2500 m elev. in cloud forest
COMMENT: In the *Bolitoglossa dunni* group. See Elias, 1984, Contrib. Sci. Nat. Hist. Mus. Los Angeles Co., 348:1–20, for discussion.

Bolitoglossa cuna Wake, Brame, and Duellman, 1973. Contrib. Sci. Nat. Hist. Mus. Los Angeles Co., 248:2.
TYPE(S): Holotype: KU 116519.
TYPE LOCALITY: "Camp Sasardi, 12 m (39 ft) elevation, Territorio de San Blas, eastern Panamá".
DISTRIBUTION: Known only from the type locality and Armila, Territorio de San Blas, eastern Panama.
COMMENT: In the *Bolitoglossa sima* group.

Bolitoglossa digitigrada Wake, Brame, and Thomas, 1982. Occas. Pap. Mus. Zool. Louisiana State Univ., 58:3.
TYPE(S): Holotype: LSUMZ 25514.
TYPE LOCALITY: "along the Río Santa Rosa a few kilometers upstream from the Río Apurímac between Pataccocha and San José (12° 44' S, 73° 46' W), Departamento de Ayacucho, Peru, at an elevation of 1000 m (3300 ft.)".
DISTRIBUTION: Known only from the type locality.

Bolitoglossa dofleini (Werner, 1903). Abh. Bayer. Akad. Wiss., Math. Physik. Kl., 22: 352.

ORIGINAL NAME: *Spelerpes dofleini.*

TYPE(S): ZSM ? (probably destroyed in World War II).

TYPE LOCALITY: Guatemala; presumably Alta Verapaz, according to Stuart, 1943, Misc. Publ. Mus. Zool. Univ. Michigan, 56:17.

DISTRIBUTION: Alta Verapaz, Guatemala, from low and moderate elevations; also in northeastern Honduras.

COMMENT: In the *Bolitoglossa dofleini* group.

Bolitoglossa dunni (Schmidt, 1933). Field Mus. Nat. Hist. Publ., Zool. Ser., 20:16.

ORIGINAL NAME: *Oedipus dunni.*

TYPE(S): Holotype: FMNH 4550.

TYPE LOCALITY: "mountains west of San Pedro, Honduras. Altitude 4500 feet".

DISTRIBUTION: Mountains of El Salvador and mountains of western Honduras.

COMMENT: In the *Bolitoglossa dunni* group.

Bolitoglossa engelhardti (Schmidt, 1936). Field Mus. Nat. Hist. Publ., Zool. Ser., 20:156.

ORIGINAL NAME: *Oedipus engelhardti.*

TYPE(S): Holotype: FMNH 21065.

TYPE LOCALITY: "Volcan Atitlan, 7,000 feet above Olas de Moca, Solola, Guatemala".

DISTRIBUTION: Volcán Atitlán, 7000 ft., and Volcán Tajumulco, 6500 ft. elev., southwestern Guatemala.

COMMENT: In the *Bolitoglossa dunni* group.

Bolitoglossa epimela Wake and Brame, 1963. Rev. Biol. Tropical, 11:63.

TYPE(S): Holotype: UMMZ 119695.

TYPE LOCALITY: "a point on the Turrialba–Peralta road 6.2 miles northeast of the Río Reventazon bridge (approximately 7 miles east-northeast of Turrialba), at about 915 meters (3,000 feet) elevation, Provincia de Cartago, Costa Rica".

DISTRIBUTION: Known only from the slopes of Volcán Atitlán, Volcán Tajumulco, Costa Rica.

COMMENT: In the *Bolitoglossa epimela* group.

Bolitoglossa equatoriana Brame and Wake, 1972. Contrib. Sci. Nat. Hist. Mus. Los Angeles Co., 219:23.

TYPE(S): Holotype: LACM 70550.

TYPE LOCALITY: "Limón Cocha, 0° 24' S, 76° 37' W, Provincia de Napo, Ecuador . . . . Elevation 260 m (850 ft.)", Ecuador.

DISTRIBUTION: Known only from the type locality.

COMMENT: In the *Bolitoglossa medemi* group.

Bolitoglossa flavimembris (Schmidt, 1936). Field Mus. Nat. Hist. Publ., Zool. Ser., 20: 158.

ORIGINAL NAME: *Oedipus flavimembris.*

TYPE(S): Holotype: FMNH 20381.

TYPE LOCALITY: "Volcan Tajumulco, at 7200 feet, on the trail above El Porvenir, San Marcos [Department], Guatemala".

DISTRIBUTION: Known only from the slopes of Volcán Atitlán, Volcán Tajumulco, and Volcán Tacaná and from the mountains along the southwestern escarpment of the Guatemalan Plateau, at elevations between 7000–8000 ft. (Guatemala); adjacent border area of Chiapas, Mexico.

COMMENT: In the *Bolitoglossa morio* group.

Bolitoglossa flaviventris (Schmidt, 1936). Field Mus. Nat. Hist. Publ., Zool. Ser., 20:148.

ORIGINAL NAME: *Oedipus flaviventris.*

TYPE(S): Holotype: USNM 46922.

TYPE LOCALITY: "Chicharras, Chiapas", Mexico.

DISTRIBUTION: Pacific region of Chiapas, Mexico, and southwestern Guatemala.

COMMENT: In the *Bolitoglossa mexicana* group. AHB considers *Spelerpes attitlanensis* Brocchi, 1883, Miss. Sci. Mex. Am. Cent., pt. 3, sect. 2, 3:115, to be the oldest name for this taxon.

Bolitoglossa franklini (Schmidt, 1936). Field Mus. Nat. Hist. Publ., Zool. Ser., 20:159.
ORIGINAL NAME: *Oedipus franklini.*
TYPE(S): Holotype: FMNH 21061.
TYPE LOCALITY: "Volcan Tajumulco, at 5600 feet altitude, on the trail above El Porvenir, [Department of] San Marcos, Guatemala".
DISTRIBUTION: Intermediate elevations along the Pacific slopes of Guatemala from Volcán Atitlán WNW to the border of Chiapas, Mexico.
COMMENT: In the *Bolitoglossa franklini* group. According to Wake and Lynch, 1967, Sci. Bull. Nat. Hist. Mus. Los Angeles Co., 25:57, Schmidt's (1936) records for *Bolitoglossa franklini* from Volcán Pacaya are based on specimens of *Bolitoglossa morio.* Synonymy includes *Bolitoglossa brevipes* Bumzahem and Smith, 1952, and *Bolitoglossa nigroflavescens* Taylor, 1941, according to Wake and Lynch, 1982, Herpetologica, 38:257–272.

Bolitoglossa hartwegi Wake and Brame, 1969. Contrib. Sci. Nat. Hist. Mus. Los Angeles Co., 175:10.
TYPE(S): Holotype: UMMZ 121557.
TYPE LOCALITY: "4.5 mi. W San Cristóbal de Las Casas, Chiapas, Mexico, . . . at about 2134 m (7000 feet) elevation".
DISTRIBUTION: Mountainous regions of east-central Chiapas, Mexico, and adjacent Guatemala, 6700–9400 ft. (2043–2865 m) elevation.
COMMENT: In the *Bolitoglossa veracrucis* group.

Bolitoglossa helmrichi (Schmidt, 1936). Field Mus. Nat. Hist. Publ., Zool. Ser., 20(17): 152.
ORIGINAL NAME: *Oedipus helmrichi.*
TYPE(S): Holotype: FMNH 21063.
TYPE LOCALITY: "mountains above Finca Samac, west of Coban, Alta Verapaz, Guatemala, at 5000 feet altitude".
DISTRIBUTION: Known only from the mountainous regions of southwestern Alta Verapaz and Baja Verapaz, Guatemala.
COMMENT: In the *Bolitoglossa dunni* group.

Bolitoglossa hermosa Papenfuss, Wake, and Adler, 1984 "1983". J. Herpetol., 17:295.
TYPE(S): Holotype: MVZ 143804.
TYPE LOCALITY: "4.2 km (by road) E of Rio Santiago, elevation 825 m, Guerrero, Mexico".
DISTRIBUTION: Río Atoyac drainage on the Pacific slope of the Sierra Madre del Sur of Guerrero, Mexico, 765–2465 m elev.
COMMENT: In the *Bolitoglossa macrinii* group.

Bolitoglossa hypacra (Brame and Wake, 1962). Proc. Biol. Soc. Washington, 75:71.
ORIGINAL NAME: *Magnadigita hypacra.*
TYPE(S): Holotype: USNM 131481.
TYPE LOCALITY: "Páramo Frontino, 11,850 ft. (3,610 meters), Departamento de Antioquia, Colombia".
DISTRIBUTION: Known from the vicinity of the type locality and Puente Largo, Antioquia, Colombia.
COMMENT: In the *Bolitoglossa adspersa* group.

Bolitoglossa jacksoni Elias, 1984. Contrib. Sci. Nat. Hist. Mus. Los Angeles Co., 348:7.
TYPE(S): Holotype: MVZ 134634.
TYPE LOCALITY: "Las Nubes sector of Finca Chiblac, approximately 12 km NNE of Santa Cruz Barillas, Depto. Huehuetenango, Guatemala, at about 1,400 m elevation".
DISTRIBUTION: Only taken within 1 km of the type locality on the Caribbean escarpment of the western Cuchumatanes, Departamento Huehuetenango, Guatemala.
COMMENT: In the *Bolitoglossa mexicana* group, according to the original description.

Bolitoglossa lignicolor (Peters, 1873). Monatsber. Preuss. Akad. Wiss. Berlin, 1873:617.
ORIGINAL NAME: *Spelerpes (Oedipus) lignicolor*.
TYPE(S): Holotype: ZMB 7736.
TYPE LOCALITY: "Chiriqui", Panama (see type locality comment under *Dendrobates maculatus*).
DISTRIBUTION: From the Península de Azuero, west-central Panama, northwest to central Pacific versant of Costa Rica.
COMMENT: In the *Bolitoglossa lignicolor* group. Specimens previously referred to this species from Atlantic slope Costa Rica probably represent an undescribed species (JMS).

Bolitoglossa lincolni (Stuart, 1943). Misc. Publ. Mus. Zool. Univ. Michigan, 56:9.
ORIGINAL NAME: *Oedipus lincolni*.
TYPE(S): Holotype: UMMZ 89107.
TYPE LOCALITY: "*monte* at Salquil Grande, El Quiché, Guatemala. Altitude 2450 meters".
DISTRIBUTION: Intermediate elevations in the eastern Sierra de los Cuchumatanes, of Guatemala; Mesa Central of Chiapas (OFV).
COMMENT: In the *Bolitoglossa franklini* group. Synonymy includes *Bolitoglossa resplendens* McCoy and Walker, 1966, according to Elias, 1984, Contrib. Sci. Nat. Hist. Mus. Los Angeles Co., 348:9; see Wake, Yang, and Papenfuss, 1980, Herpetologica, 36:335–345, and Lynch and Wake, 1982, Herpetologica, 38:257–272, who disagree.

Bolitoglossa macrinii (Lafrentz, 1930). Abh. Ber. Mus. Nat. Heimatkd. Magdeburg, 6:150.
ORIGINAL NAME: *Oedipus macrinii*.
TYPE(S): Holotype: Magdeburg Museum N.V.52/29; destroyed in World War II.
TYPE LOCALITY: "Cerro Espino, 1000 m hoch subtropischer Laubwald am Südhang der Sierra Madre del Sur bei Concordia, Staat Oaxaca, Mexiko".
DISTRIBUTION: 550–1860 m in the Sierra Madre del Sur of Oaxaca, Mexico.
COMMENT: In the *Bolitoglossa macrinii* group. Reviewed by Papenfuss, Wake, and Adler, 1984 "1983", J. Herpetol., 17:295–307.

Bolitoglossa marmorea (Tanner and Brame, 1961). Great Basin Nat., 21:23.
ORIGINAL NAME: *Magnadigita marmorea*.
TYPE(S): Holotype: BYU 17704.
TYPE LOCALITY: "Crater of Volcán Baru (Chiriquí), elevation 10,500 ft., Chiriquí Province, Panama".
DISTRIBUTION: Known from the crater and vicinity of Volcán Chiriquí, at elevations of 10,500 to 11,480 ft., Chiriquí Province and from Cerro Pando, 1920–2100 m (6298–6888 ft.) elevation, Bocas del Toro Province, western Panama, and adjacent Costa Rica.
COMMENT: In the *Bolitoglossa marmorea* group.

Bolitoglossa medemi Brame and Wake, 1972. Contrib. Sci. Nat. Hist. Mus. Los Angeles Co., 219:2.
TYPE(S): Holotype: LACM 42276.
TYPE LOCALITY: "Finca Chibiguí, approximately 76° 30' W, 6° 15' N, on the Río Arquía, Departamento de Antioquia, Colombia . . . . Elevation approximately 300 m (980 ft)".
DISTRIBUTION: The Chocó region of Colombia and the Darién region of Panama.
COMMENT: In the *Bolitoglossa medemi* group.

Bolitoglossa meliana Wake and Lynch, 1982. Herpetologica, 38:258.
TYPE(S): Holotype: MVZ 160736.
TYPE LOCALITY: "vicinity of Santa Rosa Pass, 9 km NE Santa Cruz del Quiché, El Quiché, Guatemala (elevation 2520 m)".
DISTRIBUTION: Known from several localities that span approximately 160 km along the predominantly east-west axis of the Chuacús-Minas mountain systems of central Guatemala at elevations from 1650–2725 m.
COMMENT: In the *Bolitoglossa franklini* group.

Bolitoglossa mexicana Duméril, Bibron, and Duméril, 1854. Erp. Gén., 9:95.
TYPE(S): Syntypes: MNHNP 4747 (2 specimens).
TYPE LOCALITY: "province d'Oaxaca au Mexique" and "Vera Crux".
DISTRIBUTION: Veracruz (Mexico) to Honduras on the Atlantic slopes.
COMMENT: In the *Bolitoglossa mexicana* group.

Bolitoglossa minutula Wake, Brame, and Duellman, 1973. Contrib. Sci. Nat. Hist. Mus. Los Angeles Co., 248:7.
TYPE(S): Holotype: KU 116554.
TYPE LOCALITY: "north slope of Cerro Pando, 1920 m (6298 ft) elevation, Provincia de Bocas del Toro, western Panamá".
DISTRIBUTION: Known only from the vicinity of the the type locality.
COMMENT: In the *Bolitoglossa epimela* group.

Bolitoglossa morio (Cope, 1869). Proc. Acad. Nat. Sci. Philadelphia, 21:103.
ORIGINAL NAME: *Oedipus morio*.
TYPE(S): Originally USNM 6888; now apparently lost.
TYPE LOCALITY: "Mountains of Guatemala".
DISTRIBUTION: Intermediate elevations on the southwestern and southeastern highlands of Guatemala.
COMMENT: In the *Bolitoglossa morio* group. Wake and Elias, 1983, Contrib. Sci. Nat. Hist. Mus. Los Angeles Co., 345:10, placed *Magnadigita omniumsanctorum* Stuart, 1952, in the synonymy of this species. See also Elias, 1984, Contrib. Sci. Nat. Hist. Mus. Los Angeles Co., 348:10–11.

Bolitoglossa mulleri (Brocchi, 1883). Miss. Sci. Mex. Am. Cent., (3)3:116.
ORIGINAL NAME: *Spelerpes mulleri*.
TYPE(S): Syntypes: MNHNP 6395 (4 specimens).
TYPE LOCALITY: Several localities in "haute Vera Paz"; restricted by Stuart, 1943, Misc. Publ. Mus. Zool. Univ. Michigan, 56:12, to "les montagnes qui dominent Coban", Alta Verapaz, Guatemala.
DISTRIBUTION: Mountains of Alta Verapaz and Huehuetenango, Guatemala.
COMMENT: In the *Bolitoglossa mexicana* group.

Bolitoglossa nicefori Brame and Wake, 1963. Contrib. Sci. Nat. Hist. Mus. Los Angeles Co., 69:44.
TYPE(S): Holotype: MLS 4.
TYPE LOCALITY: "14 km N. [should be northeast of] San Gil, 1500 meters (4900 feet) elevation, Departamento de Santander, Colombia".
DISTRIBUTION: Santander Department, Colombia.

COMMENT: In the *Bolitoglossa adspersa* group.

Bolitoglossa nigrescens (Taylor, 1949). Univ. Kansas Sci. Bull., 33:282.
ORIGINAL NAME: *Magnadigita nigrescens*.
TYPE(S): Holotype: KU 23816.
TYPE LOCALITY: "Boquete Camp (on highway between Millville [=Villa Mills] and San Isidro del General), [San José Province,] Costa Rica, elevation 6,000 feet".
DISTRIBUTION: Type locality on the Cordillera Central in Costa Rica and Volcán Chiriquí, western Panama.
COMMENT: Considered a valid species by Hanken and Wake, 1982, Herpetologica, 38:275. Previously *Bolitoglossa nigrescens* was thought to have been based upon a juvenile specimen of *Bolitoglossa robusta*, a view shared by JMS, who thinks that Panamanian "*nigrescens*" is a distinct species.

Bolitoglossa occidentalis Taylor, 1941. Univ. Kansas Sci. Bull., 27:145.
TYPE(S): Holotype: USNM 111085.
TYPE LOCALITY: "La Esperanza [near Escuintla], Chiapas, Mexico, elevation 500 feet".
DISTRIBUTION: Pacific slopes of southeastern Oaxaca and Chiapas, Mexico, southern Guatemala, and possibly southwestern Honduras from the Department of Coneayagua.
COMMENT: In the *Bolitoglossa rufescens* group.

Bolitoglossa odonnelli (Stuart, 1943). Misc. Publ. Mus. Zool. Univ. Michigan, 56:10.
ORIGINAL NAME: *Oedipus odonnelli*.
TYPE(S): Holotype: UMMZ 89096.
TYPE LOCALITY: "*Cafetal* just east of the hacienda at Finca Volcán, [Departamento de] Alta Verapaz, Guatemala. Altitude 1200 meters".
DISTRIBUTION: Type locality and Finca Los Alpes, Alta Verapaz, and possibly the cloud forests of eastern Alta Verapaz, Guatemala.
COMMENT: In the *Bolitoglossa mexicana* group. Wake and Elias, 1983, Contrib. Sci. Nat. Hist. Mus. Los Angeles Co., 345:1–19, elevated *Bolitoglossa odonnelli* to specific status from its former position as a subspecies of *Bolitoglossa mexicana*.

Bolitoglossa orestes Brame and Wake, 1962. Copeia, 1962:171.
TYPE(S): Holotype: BM 1905.5.31.103.
TYPE LOCALITY: "Culata, 9,810 feet (3,000 meters), Cordillera de Mérida, Estado de Mérida, Venezuela".
DISTRIBUTION: Mérida, Venezuela.
COMMENT: In the *Bolitoglossa adspersa* group.

Bolitoglossa palmata (Werner, 1897). Zool. Anz., 20:266.
ORIGINAL NAME: *Spelerpes palmatus*.
TYPE(S): ZIUW q43 designated lectotype by Brame and Wake, 1962, Copeia, 1962:173.
TYPE LOCALITY: Ecuador; restricted to "'Cordillera', Ecuador" by Brame and Wake, 1962, Copeia, 1962:174.
DISTRIBUTION: Central Ecuador (Amazon drainage).
COMMENT: In the *Bolitoglossa adspersa* group.

Bolitoglossa pandi Brame and Wake, 1963. Contrib. Sci. Nat. Hist. Mus. Los Angeles Co., 69:50.
TYPE(S): Holotype: ZMH 2858.
TYPE LOCALITY: "Pandi, 1300 meters (4260 feet) elevation, Departamento de Cundinamarca, Colombia".
DISTRIBUTION: Known only from the type.
COMMENT: In the *Bolitoglossa adspersa* group.

Bolitoglossa peruviana (Boulenger, 1883). Ann. Mag. Nat. Hist., (5)12:165.
ORIGINAL NAME: *Spelerpes peruvianus.*
TYPE(S): Holotype: BM 1946.9.6.16 (formerly 1874.8.4.103).
TYPE LOCALITY: "Moyobamba", 854 m elevation, Departamento de San Martín, Peru.
DISTRIBUTION: Amazonian slopes of northern Peru and Ecuador.
COMMENT: In the *Bolitoglossa altamazonica* group.

Bolitoglossa phalarosoma Wake and Brame, 1962. Contrib. Sci. Nat. Hist. Mus. Los Angeles Co., 49:1.
TYPE(S): Holotype: BM 97.11.12.22.
TYPE LOCALITY: "Medellín, Departamento de Antioquia, Colombia . . . . The altitude of Medellín is 5,045 feet (1538) m)".
DISTRIBUTION: Department of Antioquia, Colombia, and Darién Province, Panama.
COMMENT: In the *Bolitoglossa phalarosoma* group.

Bolitoglossa platydactyla (Gray, 1831). *In* Griffith and Pidgeon, Anim. Kingdom, Suppl., 9:107.
ORIGINAL NAME: *Salamandra platydactylus.*
TYPE(S): Syntypes: BM 1946.9.6.18 (formerly 1.111.11.1a) and 1946.9.6.16 (formerly 1848.8.16.24).
TYPE LOCALITY: Mexico.
DISTRIBUTION: San Luis Potosí south to southern Veracruz and Oaxaca, Mexico, below 3500 feet.
COMMENT: In the *Bolitoglossa mexicana* group. *Salamandra platydactylus* is a replacement name for *Salamandra variegata* Gray, 1831, *In* Griffith and Pidgeon, Anim. Kingdom, Suppl., 9:107, which was preoccupied by *Salamandra variegata* Bory, 1828 (=*Triturus marmoratus*).

Bolitoglossa ramosi Brame and Wake, 1972. Contrib. Sci. Nat. Hist. Mus. Los Angeles Co., 219:9.
TYPE(S): Holotype: LACM 64601.
TYPE LOCALITY: "near Represa de Santa Rita (=Santa Rita Dam Site), Departamento de Antioquia, Colombia. This site is between Guatapé and San Rafael at about 75° 7' W, 6° 17' N, ca. 16 km by road NE of Guatapé . . . . Elevation about 1930 m (6330 ft.)".
DISTRIBUTION: Known only from the type locality.
COMMENT: In the *Bolitoglossa medemi* group.

Bolitoglossa riletti Holman, 1964. Herpetologica, 20:49.
TYPE(S): Holotype: UIMNH 52761.
TYPE LOCALITY: "3.5 miles south of Putla de Guerrero, Oaxaca, Mexico".
DISTRIBUTION: Known only from the vicinity of Putla, Oaxaca, Mexico, 700–1030 m elev.
COMMENT: In the *Bolitoglossa macrinii* group. See Papenfuss, Wake, and Adler, 1984 "1983", J. Herpetol., 17:295–307, for discussion.

Bolitoglossa robusta (Cope, 1894). Proc. Acad. Nat. Sci. Philadelphia, 46:194.
ORIGINAL NAME: *Oedipus robustus.*
TYPE(S): Holotype: AMNH 5464.
TYPE LOCALITY: "Faldas of Volcano Irazu", Costa Rica.
DISTRIBUTION: Mountains of north-central and central Costa Rica and of Bocas del Toro Province, Panama.
COMMENT: In the *Bolitoglossa subpalmata* group.

Bolitoglossa rostrata (Brocchi, 1883). Miss. Sci. Mex. Am. Cent., (3)3:112.
ORIGINAL NAME: *Spelerpes rostratus.*
TYPE(S): ?MNHNP.
TYPE LOCALITY: "les hauteurs de Tonicapam [=Totonicapán, Department of Totonicapán] (Guatemala occidental)".
DISTRIBUTION: High mountains of southern Guatemala and central Chiapas, Mexico.
COMMENT: In the *Bolitoglossa dunni* group. See Elias, 1984, Contrib. Sci. Nat. Hist. Mus. Los Angeles Co., 348:11

Bolitoglossa rufescens (Cope, 1869). Proc. Acad. Nat. Sci. Philadelphia, 21:104.
ORIGINAL NAME: *Oedipus rufescens.*
TYPE(S): Holotype: USNM 6881; not mentioned in USNM type list by Cochran, 1961, Bull. U.S. Natl. Mus., 220:1–291.
TYPE LOCALITY: "Orizava" (=Orizaba), Veracruz, Mexico.
DISTRIBUTION: San Luis Potosí (Mexico) to northern Honduras, along the Atlantic slopes.
COMMENT: In the *Bolitoglossa rufescens* group. Populations near Catemaco, Veracruz, Mexico, were referred to this species (rather than *Bolitoglossa occidentalis*) by Larson, 1983, Herpetologica, 39:97. See also Elias, 1984, Contrib. Sci. Nat. Hist. Mus. Los Angeles Co., 348:11.

Bolitoglossa salvinii (Gray, 1868). Ann. Mag. Nat. Hist., (4)2:297.
ORIGINAL NAME: *Oedipus salvinii.*
TYPE(S): Holotype: BM 1946.9.6.26 (formerly 1865.6.10.19h).
TYPE LOCALITY: Guatemala, Pacific Coast.
DISTRIBUTION: Upper coastal plain and moderate elevations of the Pacific slopes of southern Guatemala and El Salvador.
COMMENT: In the *Bolitoglossa mexicana* group.

Bolitoglossa savagei Brame and Wake, 1963. Contrib. Sci. Nat. Hist. Mus. Los Angeles Co., 69:31.
TYPE(S): Holotype: UMMZ 54595.
TYPE LOCALITY: "Cerro San Lorenzo, 1400–2100 meters (4500–7000 feet), Sierra Nevada de Santa Marta, Departamento de Magdalena, Colombia".
DISTRIBUTION: Sierra Nevada de Santa Marta, northern Colombia, and the Cordillera de Mérida, western Venezuela.
COMMENT: In the *Bolitoglossa adspersa* group. DBW now doubts that specimens from the Cordillera de Mérida are of this species.

Bolitoglossa schizodactyla Wake and Brame, 1966. Fieldiana: Zool., 51:1.
TYPE(S): Holotype: FMNH 141241.
TYPE LOCALITY: "El Valle de Anton, 560 meters (1,837 feet), Provincia de Cocle, Panama".
DISTRIBUTION: Central and northwestern Panama.
COMMENT: In the *Bolitoglossa lignicolor* group.

Bolitoglossa schmidti (Dunn, 1924). Field Mus. Nat. Hist. Publ., Zool. Ser., 12:96.
ORIGINAL NAME: *Oedipus schmidti.*
TYPE(S): Holotype: FMNH 4538.
TYPE LOCALITY: "mountains west of San Pedro, Departamento de Cortes, Honduras, at 2000 feet, on trail".
DISTRIBUTION: Department of Cortés, Honduras.
COMMENT: In the *Bolitoglossa dofleini* group.

Bolitoglossa silverstonei Brame and Wake, 1972. Contrib. Sci. Nat. Hist. Mus. Los Angeles Co., 219:15.
TYPE(S): Holotype: LACM 42283.
TYPE LOCALITY: "Quebrada Bochoramá, Loma de Encarnación, Departamento de Chocó, Colombia, about 51 km (32 mi) SE of Quibdo at approximately 76° 23' W, 5° 20' N . . . . at about 400 m (1312 ft) elevation".
DISTRIBUTION: Known only from the type.
COMMENT: In the *Bolitoglossa sima* group.

Bolitoglossa sima (Vaillant, 1911). Miss. Geogr. Am. Sud., 9:58.
ORIGINAL NAME: *Spelerpes sima*.
TYPE(S): Holotype: MNHNP 06-284.
TYPE LOCALITY: "Equateur".
DISTRIBUTION: Northwestern Ecuador.
COMMENT: In the *Bolitoglossa sima* group.

Bolitoglossa sooyorum Vial, 1963. Rev. Biol. Tropical, 11:89.
TYPE(S): Holotype: LACM 26768 (formerly CRE 2600).
TYPE LOCALITY: Cordillera Talamanca, Cerro de la Muerte at 9,000 feet, 12 miles southeast of El Empalme, Provincia de Cartago, Costa Rica.
DISTRIBUTION: Known only from the vicinity of the type locality.
COMMENT: In the *Bolitoglossa subpalmata* group.

Bolitoglossa striatula (Noble, 1918). Bull. Am. Mus. Nat. Hist., 38:344.
ORIGINAL NAME: *Oedipus striatulus*.
TYPE(S): Holotype: AMNH 6999.
TYPE LOCALITY: "Cukra [near Bluefields], Eastern Nicaragua".
DISTRIBUTION: Northeastern Honduras through Nicaragua to central Costa Rica.
COMMENT: In the *Bolitoglossa striatula* group.

Bolitoglossa stuarti Wake and Brame, 1969. Contrib. Sci. Nat. Hist. Mus. Los Angeles Co., 175:22.
TYPE(S): Holotype: UMMZ 123203.
TYPE LOCALITY: "7.8 mi (by road) SE of Ciudad Cuauhtémoc (El Ocotal), Chiapas, Mexico, in Huehuetenango [Department], Guatemala, at about 950 m (3120 feet) elevation".
DISTRIBUTION: Eastern Chiapas (Mexico) and eastern Guatemala, elevations near 1000 m.
COMMENT: In the *Bolitoglossa veracrucis* group.

Bolitoglossa subpalmata (Boulenger, 1896). Ann. Mag. Nat. Hist., (6)18:341.
ORIGINAL NAME: *Spelerpes subpalmatus*.
TYPE(S): Holotype: BM 1946.9.6.24 (formerly 1896.10.8.85).
TYPE LOCALITY: La Palma, Costa Rica.
DISTRIBUTION: Higher elevations of Costa Rica and Chiriquí Province, Panama.
COMMENT: In the *Bolitoglossa subpalmata* group.

Bolitoglossa taylori Wake, Brame, and Myers, 1970. Am. Mus. Novit., 2430:3.
TYPE(S): Holotype: KU 116544.
TYPE LOCALITY: "south ridge of Cerro Cituro, Serranía de Pirre, at an elevation of approximately 1100 meters (3608 feet), Darién Province, Republic of Panama".
DISTRIBUTION: High elevations of Darién Province, Panama.
COMMENT: In the *Bolitoglossa adspersa* group.

Bolitoglossa vallecula Brame and Wake, 1963. Contrib. Sci. Nat. Hist. Mus. Los Angeles Co., 69:27.
TYPE(S): Holotype: MLS 8a.
TYPE LOCALITY: "Yarumal, 2300 meters (7550 feet), Departamento de Antioquia, Colombia".
DISTRIBUTION: High elevations of the central Andes (Cordillera Central) of the Department of Antioquia, Colombia.

COMMENT: In the *Bolitoglossa adspersa* group.

Bolitoglossa veracrucis Taylor, 1951. Univ. Kansas Sci. Bull., 34:189.
TYPE(S): Holotype: KU 26941.
TYPE LOCALITY: "point 35 km SE of Jesús Carranza (Santa Lucretia), elev. approx.
350 feet, Veracruz, Mexico".
DISTRIBUTION: Known only from the type locality.
COMMENT: In the *Bolitoglossa veracrucis* group.

Bolitoglossa walkeri Brame and Wake, 1972. Contrib. Sci. Nat. Hist. Mus. Los Angeles
Co., 219:18.
TYPE(S): Holotype: UMMZ 128833.
TYPE LOCALITY: "Television Tower Mountain 15 km WNW Cali and 0.9 km S El
Jordan, Departamento del Valle, Colombia . . . . in cloud forest at an elevation
of 2050 m (6724 ft)".
DISTRIBUTION: Known only from Departamento de Valle, Colombia.
COMMENT: In the *Bolitoglossa medemi* group.

Bolitoglossa yucatana (Peters, 1882). Sitzungsber. Ges. Naturforsch. Freunde Berlin,
1882:137.
ORIGINAL NAME: *Spelerpes (Oedipus) yucatanus.*
TYPE(S): Holotype: ZMB 10231.
TYPE LOCALITY: Yucatan, Mexico.
DISTRIBUTION: Yucatan Peninsula of Mexico and possibly northern Guatemala.
COMMENT: In the *Bolitoglossa dofleini* group.

Bradytriton Wake and Elias, 1983. Contrib. Sci. Nat. Hist. Mus. Los Angeles Co., 345:3.
TYPE SPECIES: *Bradytriton silus* Wake and Elias, 1983, by original designation.
DISTRIBUTION: As for the single species.
COMMENT: Tribe Bolitoglossini; supergenus *Bolitoglossa.*

Bradytriton silus Wake and Elias, 1983. Contrib. Sci. Nat. Hist. Mus. Los Angeles Co.,
345:4.
TYPE(S): Holotype: MVZ 131587.
TYPE LOCALITY: "Finca Chiblac, 15 km NE Barillas, Depto. Huehuetenango,
Guatemala, elevation 1310 m (4300 ft)".
DISTRIBUTION: Known only from the immediate vicinity of the type locality in
extreme northwestern Guatemala, on the eastern slopes of the Sierra de los
Cuchumatanes.

Chiropterotriton Taylor, 1944. Univ. Kansas Sci. Bull., 30:213.
TYPE SPECIES: *Oedipus multidentata* Taylor, 1938.
DISTRIBUTION: West-central Tamaulipas in the north to the mountains of northern
Oaxaca in the south, Mexico.
COMMENT: Tribe Bolitoglossini; supergenus *Bolitoglossa.* Species formerly placed in
the *Chiropterotriton*–beta group (see Wake and Lynch, 1976, Sci. Bull. Nat. Hist.
Mus. Los Angeles Co., 25:1–65) were transferred to *Dendrotriton* and *Nototriton*
by Wake and Elias, 1983, Contrib. Sci. Nat. Hist. Mus. Los Angeles Co., 345:11.
Species group designations for the remaining species follow Wake and Lynch,
1976, Sci. Bull. Nat. Hist. Mus. Los Angeles Co., 25:1–65.

Chiropterotriton arboreus (Taylor, 1941). Herpetologica, 2:62.
ORIGINAL NAME: *Bolitoglossa arboreus.*
TYPE(S): Holotype: FMNH 100022 (formerly EHT-HMS 16743).
TYPE LOCALITY: "near Tianguistengo, Hidalgo", Mexico.
DISTRIBUTION: Vicinity of the type locality (Tianguistengo, Hidalgo) and Mesa de
Necaxa, Puebla, Mexico.
COMMENT: In the *Chiropterotriton multidentatus* group.

Chiropterotriton chiropterus (Cope, 1863). Proc. Acad. Nat. Sci. Philadelphia, 15:54.
ORIGINAL NAME: *Spelerpes chiropterus.*
TYPE(S): Unknown.
TYPE LOCALITY: Mirador, Veracruz, Mexico.
DISTRIBUTION: High elevations of the states of México, Puebla, Veracruz, and Morelos, Mexico.
COMMENT: In the *Chiropterotriton chiropterus* group.

Chiropterotriton chondrostega (Taylor, 1941). Univ. Kansas Sci. Bull., 27:113.
ORIGINAL NAME: *Bolitoglossa chondrostega.*
TYPE(S): Holotype: FMNH 100076 (formerly EHT-HMS 17304).
TYPE LOCALITY: "Durango, Hidalgo, 5,000 to 6,000 feet elevation", Mexico.
DISTRIBUTION: Southwestern Tamaulipas to Hidalgo and Veracruz, Mexico.
COMMENT: In the *Chiropterotriton chiropterus* group.

Chiropterotriton dimidiatus (Taylor, 1939). Univ. Kansas Sci. Bull., 26:408.
ORIGINAL NAME: *Bolitoglossa dimidiata.*
TYPE(S): Holotype: FMNH 100023 (formerly EHT-HMS 17677).
TYPE LOCALITY: "Guerrero, near Mineral del Monte, Southern Hidalgo, Mexico".
DISTRIBUTION: High elevations in Hidalgo, Mexico.
COMMENT: In the *Chiropterotriton chiropterus* group.

Chiropterotriton lavae (Taylor, 1942). Univ. Kansas Sci. Bull., 28:295.
ORIGINAL NAME: *Bolitoglossa lavae.*
TYPE(S): Holotype: FMNH 100118 (formerly EHT-HMS 28937).
TYPE LOCALITY: "2 miles west of La Joya, Veracruz", Mexico.
DISTRIBUTION: Known only from Tostlacuaya and La Joya, Veracruz, Mexico.
COMMENT: In the *Chiropterotriton chiropterus* group.

Chiropterotriton magnipes Rabb, 1965. Breviora, 235:1.
TYPE(S): Holotype: MCZ 30607.
TYPE LOCALITY: Cueva de Potrerillos, about 2 km WSW Ahuacatlán, which is approximately 8 km SW of Xilitla, San Luis Potosí, Mexico.
DISTRIBUTION: High elevations of San Luis Potosí, Mexico.
COMMENT: In the *Chiropterotriton multidentatus* group.

Chiropterotriton mosaueri (Woodall, 1941). Occas. Pap. Mus. Zool. Univ. Michigan, 444:1.
ORIGINAL NAME: *Oedipus mosaueri.*
TYPE(S): Holotype: UMMZ 88839.
TYPE LOCALITY: Durango, Hidalgo, Mexico, 7200 feet elevation.
DISTRIBUTION: Known only from the type locality.
COMMENT: In the *Chiropterotriton multidentatus* group.

Chiropterotriton multidentatus (Taylor, 1938). Univ. Kansas Sci. Bull., 25:289.
ORIGINAL NAME: *Oedipus multidentata.*
TYPE(S): Holotype: MCZ 14812.
TYPE LOCALITY: "Alvarez (km 53 on Potosi and Rio Verde R.R.), San Luis Potosí, Mexico, elevation 8,000 feet".
DISTRIBUTION: San Luis Potosí and southern Tamaulipas, Mexico.
COMMENT: In the *Chiropterotriton multidentatus* group.

Chiropterotriton priscus Rabb, 1956. Fieldiana: Zool., 39:11.
TYPE(S): Holotype: FMNH 95999.
TYPE LOCALITY: Cerro Potosí, near Ojo de Agua, about eleven miles west-northwest of Galeana, Nuevo León, Mexico, elevation 8000 feet.
DISTRIBUTION: Known only from the vicinity of the type locality.
COMMENT: In the *Chiropterotriton priscus* group.

Dendrotriton Wake and Elias, 1983. Contrib. Sci. Nat. Hist. Mus. Los Angeles Co., 345:11.
TYPE SPECIES: *Oedipus bromeliacia* Schmidt, 1936, by original designation.
DISTRIBUTION: Southwestern Chiapas, Mexico, through western Guatemala.
COMMENT: Tribe Bolitoglossini; supergenus *Bolitoglossa*. Reviewed (as the *Chiropterotriton bromeliacia* group) by Lynch and Wake, 1975, Contrib. Sci. Nat. Hist. Mus. Los Angeles Co., 265:1–45.

Dendrotriton bromeliacia (Schmidt, 1936). Field Mus. Nat. Hist. Publ., Zool. Ser., 20: 161.
ORIGINAL NAME: *Oedipus bromeliacia*.
TYPE(S): Holotype: FMNH 21062.
TYPE LOCALITY: "Volcan Tajumulco, at 8,000 feet altitude, on the trail above El Porvenir, [Department of] San Marcos, Guatemala".
DISTRIBUTION: High elevations in the Department of San Marcos, Guatemala.

Dendrotriton cuchumatanus (Lynch and Wake, 1975). Contrib. Sci. Nat. Hist. Mus. Los Angeles Co., 265:6.
ORIGINAL NAME: *Chiropterotriton cuchumatanus*.
TYPE(S): Holotype: MVZ 113002.
TYPE LOCALITY: "forest along highway 9N, 8.5 km (by road) SW San Juan Ixcoy, Huehuetenago, Guatemala, at about 2860 m elev."
DISTRIBUTION: Sierra Cuchumatanes, Guatemala.

Dendrotriton megarhinus (Rabb, 1960). Copeia, 1960:304.
ORIGINAL NAME: *Chiropterotriton megarhinus*.
TYPE(S): Holotype: UIMNH 40782.
TYPE LOCALITY: Northern slopes of Cerro Tres Picos, about 19 kilometers northeast of Tonalá, Chiapas, Mexico, 7000 feet elevation.
DISTRIBUTION: Known only from the type locality.

Dendrotriton rabbi (Lynch and Wake, 1975). Contrib. Sci. Nat. Hist. Mus. Los Angeles Co., 265:2.
ORIGINAL NAME: *Chiropterotriton rabbi*.
TYPE(S): Holotype: MVZ 103839.
TYPE LOCALITY: "9.5 km W, 8.5 km S (airline) La Democracia, Huehuetenango, Guatemala, . . . between 2100 and 2500 meters".
DISTRIBUTION: Near the Chiapas (Mexico) border in Guatemala (Montañas de Cuilco) and the Sierra Cuchumatanes, central Guatemala.
COMMENT: See Elias, 1984, Contrib. Sci. Nat. Hist. Mus. Los Angeles Co., 348:13.

Dendrotriton xolocalcae (Taylor, 1941). Univ. Kansas Sci. Bull., 27:148.
ORIGINAL NAME: *Bolitoglossa xolocalcae*.
TYPE(S): Holotype: USNM 111371.
TYPE LOCALITY: "Cerro Ovando, Chiapas, Mexico, between 6,800 to 8,000 feet elevation".
DISTRIBUTION: Known only from the type locality.

Ensatina Gray, 1850. Cat. Spec. Amph. Coll. Brit. Mus., Batr. Grad.:48.
TYPE SPECIES: *Ensatina eschscholtzii* Gray, 1850, by monotypy.
DISTRIBUTION: As for the only species
COMMENT: Tribe Plethodontini. Considered the sister-taxon of *Aneides* + *Plethodon* by Larson, Wake, Maxson, and Highton, 1981, Evolution, 35:405–422.

Ensatina eschscholtzii Gray, 1850. Cat. Spec. Amph. Coll. Brit. Mus., Batr. Grad.:48.
TYPE(S): Syntypes: BM 1947.2.24.45–47.
TYPE LOCALITY: California; corrected to "Monterey", California, USA, by Boulenger, 1882, Cat. Batr. Grad. Coll. Brit. Mus.:55.
DISTRIBUTION: Pacific coastal region west of the Cascades and Sierra Nevada Crests, from southern British Columbia (Canada) to southern edge of southern California (USA).

Eurycea Rafinesque, 1822. Kentucky Gazette, Lexington, N.S., 1(9):3.
TYPE SPECIES: *Eurycea lucifuga* Rafinesque, 1822, by monotypy.
DISTRIBUTION: Eastern North America (north of Mexico).
COMMENT: Tribe Hemidactylini.

Eurycea aquatica Rose and Bush, 1963. Tulane Stud. Zool., 10:121.
TYPE(S): Holotype: USNM 147138.
TYPE LOCALITY: Small springs and permanent streams two miles west of Bessemer,
Jefferson County, Alabama, along County Highway 20 [USA].
DISTRIBUTION: Known definitely only from Jefferson County, Alabama, but may
also be present in northwestern Georgia, northeastern Mississippi, and
southwestern Tennessee, USA.
COMMENT: Reviewed by Rose, 1971, Cat. Am. Amph. Rept., 116.1–2.

Eurycea bislineata (Green, 1818). J. Acad. Nat. Sci. Philadelphia, (1)1:352.
ORIGINAL NAME: *Salamandra bislineata.*
TYPE(S): Syntypes: possibly ANSP 695–698 and/or USNM 3738; see Mittleman,
1966, Cat. Am. Amph. Rept., 45.1, for discussion.
TYPE LOCALITY: Not stated; subsequently designated as "New Jersey (probably
Princeton?)" by Fowler, 1906, Annu. Rep. New Jersey State Mus., Pt. 2:65.
DISTRIBUTION: Eastern North America from the borders of the St. Lawrence in
Canada to the Gulf of Mexico in the USA.
COMMENT: Reviewed by Mittleman, 1966, Cat. Am. Amph. Rept., 45.1–4.

Eurycea junaluska Sever, Dundee, and Sullivan, 1976. Herpetologica, 32:26.
TYPE(S): Holotype: USNM 198421.
TYPE LOCALITY: U.S. Route 129, 3.2–11.2 km SE Tapoco, Graham County, North
Carolina [USA].
DISTRIBUTION: Graham County, North Carolina, and Great Smoky Mountains of
nearby Tennessee, USA.
COMMENT: Reviewed by Sever, 1983, Cat. Am. Amph. Rept., 321.1–2.

Eurycea longicauda (Green, 1818). J. Acad. Nat. Sci. Philadelphia, (1)1:351.
ORIGINAL NAME: *Salamandra longicauda.*
TYPE(S): Not known to exist.
TYPE LOCALITY: New Jersey; restricted by Schmidt, 1953, Check List N. Am. Amph.
Rept., Ed. 6:53, to "vicinity of Princeton, New Jersey", USA.
DISTRIBUTION: Southern New York southwestward to Oklahoma and southward
through the Atlantic and Gulf states, USA.
COMMENT: Reviewed by Ireland, 1979, Cat. Am. Amph. Rept., 221.1–4.

Eurycea lucifuga Rafinesque, 1822. Kentucky Gazette, Lexington, N.S., 1(9):3.
TYPE(S): Not known to exist.
TYPE LOCALITY: "near Lexington", Fayette County, Kentucky, USA.
DISTRIBUTION: Essentially limited to limestone areas, especially in and around
limestone caves, from southern Indiana and extreme southwestern Ohio
southward to central Alabama and Georgia, and from western Virginia
westward through northeastern Oklahoma and extreme southeastern Kansas,
USA.
COMMENT: Reviewed by Hutchison, 1966, Cat. Am. Amph. Rept., 24.1–2.

Eurycea multiplicata (Cope, 1869). Proc. Acad. Nat. Sci. Philadelphia, 21:106.
ORIGINAL NAME: *Spelerpes multiplicatus.*
TYPE(S): Syntypes: USNM 4038 (5 specimens).
TYPE LOCALITY: "Red River, Arkansas", USA; restricted to "near Fort Towson,
Choctaw County, Oklahoma", USA, by Dundee, 1940, Herpetologica, 6:27–28.
DISTRIBUTION: Southern Missouri, Arkansas, southeastern Kansas, and eastern
Oklahoma, USA.

COMMENT: Reviewed by Dundee, 1965, Cat. Am. Amph. Rept., 21.1–2.

Eurycea nana Bishop, 1941. Occas. Papers Mus. Zool. Univ. Michigan, 451:6.
TYPE(S): Holotype: UMMZ 89759.
TYPE LOCALITY: Lake at the head of the San Marcos River, Hays County, Texas (at San Marcos) [USA].
DISTRIBUTION: Known only from the type locality.
COMMENT: Reviewed by Brown, 1967, Cat. Am. Amph. Rept., 35.1–2.
PROTECTED STATUS: USA ESA—Threatened (14 Jul. 1980).

Eurycea neotenes Bishop and Wright, 1937. Proc. Biol. Soc. Washington, 50:142.
TYPE(S): Holotype: USNM 103161.
TYPE LOCALITY: "Culebra Creek, 5 miles north of Helotes, Bexar County, Texas", USA.
DISTRIBUTION: Springs, streams, and cave water of the Edwards Plateau region of west central Texas, USA.
COMMENT: Reviewed by Brown, 1967, Cat. Am. Amph. Rept., 36.1–2. Synonymy includes *Eurycea troglodytes* Baker, 1957, Texas J. Sci., 9:328 (Holotype: TNHC 21791; Type locality: "a pool approximately 600 ft. from the entrance of the Valdina Farms Sinkhole, Valdina Farms", Medina County, Texas, USA), and *Eurycea latitans* Smith and Potter, 1946, Herpetologica, 3:106 (Holotype: USNM 123594; Type locality: Cascade Cavern, 4.6 m southeast of Boerne, Kendall County, Texas [USA]), according to Sweet, 1984, Copeia 1984:438, who considered them to be of hybrid origin, with *Eurycea tridentifera*, and who discussed hybridization between *Eurycea neotenes* and *Eurycea tridentifera*. Literature of *Eurycea neotenes* reviewed by Brown, 1967, Cat. Am. Amph. Rept., 36.1–2. Literature of *"Eurycea troglodytes"* reviewed by Baker, 1966, Cat. Am. Amph. Rept., 23.1–2. Literature of *"Eurycea latitans"* reviewed by Brown, 1967, Cat. Am. Amph. Rept., 34.1–2.

Eurycea quadridigitata (Holbrook, 1842). N. Am. Herpetol., Ed. 2, 5:65.
ORIGINAL NAME: *Salamandra quadridigitata*.
TYPE(S): Holotype: probably ANSP 490.
TYPE LOCALITY: ". . . middle section of our state [South Carolina] . . . to the Gulf of Mexico . . . [also] specimens from Georgia, and . . . Florida"; restricted by Schmidt, 1953, Check List N. Am. Amph. Rept., Ed. 6:56, to "vicinity of Charleston, South Carolina", USA.
DISTRIBUTION: Coastal plain of the Atlantic and Gulf states from North Carolina to eastern Texas, except southern Florida; north into southeastern Oklahoma and southwestern Arkansas, USA.
COMMENT: Reviewed by Mittleman, 1967, Cat. Am. Amph. Rept., 44.1–2, under the genus *Manculus*.

Eurycea tridentifera Mitchell and Reddell, 1965. Texas J. Sci., 17:14.
TYPE(S): Holotype: USNM 153780.
TYPE LOCALITY: Honey Creek Cave, Comal County, Texas [USA].
DISTRIBUTION: Region of the type locality in western Comal County northern Bexar County and southern Kendall County, Texas, USA.
COMMENT: Placed in the genus *Typhlomolge* by Wake, 1966, Mem. S. California Acad. Sci., 4:64–66, but replaced in *Eurycea* by Potter and Sweet, 1981, Copeia, 1981:64–75. See comment under *Eurycea neotenes*.

Eurycea tynerensis Moore and Hughes, 1939. Am. Midl. Nat., 22:697.
TYPE(S): Syntypes: USNM 108548 (12 specimens); UMMZ 85534 (5 specimens);
   MCZ 25533 (1 specimen formerly UMMZ); UO (formerly UMMZ 21325) (3
   specimens); and OSUS (6 specimens, now apparently lost).
TYPE LOCALITY: "Tyner Creek, a tributary of Barron Fork Creek near Proctor, Adair
   County, Oklahoma", USA.
DISTRIBUTION: Restricted to the drainages of the Grand (Neosho) and Illinois
   rivers of the Springfield Plateau section of the Ozark plateaus of
   southwestern Missouri, northwestern Arkansas, and northeastern Oklahoma,
   USA.
COMMENT: Reviewed by Dundee, 1965, Cat. Am. Amph. Rept., 22.1–2.

Gyrinophilus Cope, 1869. Proc. Acad. Nat. Sci. Philadelphia, 21:108–109.
TYPE SPECIES: *Salamandra porphyritica* Green, 1827, by monotypy.
DISTRIBUTION: Appalachian uplift of the eastern USA and adjacent Canada.
COMMENT: Tribe Hemidactylini. Reviewed by Brandon, 1967, Cat. Am. Amph. Rept.,
   31.1–2.

Gyrinophilus palleucus McCrady, 1954. Copeia, 1954:201.
TYPE(S): Holotype: FMNH 72585.
TYPE LOCALITY: Sinking Cove Cave, Franklin County, Tennessee, altitude 900 ft.
   [USA].
DISTRIBUTION: Southern Cumberland Plateau of southern central Tennessee and
   northeastern Alabama, in the Tennessee River Valley of Roane and McMinn
   counties, Tennessee, in the Nashville Basin southeast of Nashville, Tennessee,
   and in the Highland Rim of northwestern Alabama, USA.
COMMENT: Reviewed by Brandon, 1967, Cat. Am. Amph. Rept., 32.1–2.

Gyrinophilus porphyriticus (Green, 1827). Contrib. Maclurean Lyc., 1:3.
ORIGINAL NAME: *Salamandra porphyritica*.
TYPE(S): MCZ 35778 designated neotype by Brandon, 1966, Illinois Biol. Monogr.,
   35:1–86.
TYPE LOCALITY: "French Creek near Meadville, Crawford County, P[ennsylvani]a.",
   USA.
DISTRIBUTION: Western Maine (USA) and adjacent Canada, south along the
   Appalachian uplift to Georgia and northeastern Mississippi (USA).
COMMENT: Reviewed by Brandon, 1967, Cat. Am. Amph. Rept., 33.1–3. Includes
   Gyrinophilus subterraneus Besharse and Holsinger, 1977, Copeia, 1977:626,
   according to Blaney and Blaney, 1978, Proc. W. Virginia Acad. Sci., 50(1):23.

Haideotriton Carr, 1939. Occas. Pap. Boston Soc. Nat. Hist., 8:334.
TYPE SPECIES: *Haideotriton wallacei* Carr, 1939, by original designation.
DISTRIBUTION: As for the single species.
COMMENT: Tribe Hemidactylini. Reviewed by Brandon, 1967, Cat. Am. Amph. Rept.,
   39.1.

Haideotriton wallacei Carr, 1939. Occas. Pap. Boston Soc. Nat. Hist., 8:335.
TYPE(S): Holotype: MCZ 19875.
TYPE LOCALITY: "from a 200-ft. artesian well at Albany, Dougherty County,
   Georgia", USA.
DISTRIBUTION: Albany, Dougherty County, Georgia, and a cave in Decatur County,
   Georgia; and several caves north of Marianna, Jackson County, Florida, USA.
COMMENT: Reviewed by Brandon, 1967, Cat. Am. Amph. Rept., 39.1–2.

Hemidactylium Tschudi, 1838. Classif. Batr.:59.
TYPE SPECIES: *Salamandra scutata* Temminck and Schlegel, 1838, by monotypy.
DISTRIBUTION: As for the single species.
COMMENT: Tribe Hemidactylini. Reviewed by Neill, 1963, Cat. Am. Amph. Rept., 1.1.

Hemidactylium scutatum (Temminck and Schlegel, 1838). *In* Von Siebold, Fauna Japon., Rept.:119.

ORIGINAL NAME: *Salamandra scutata.*

TYPE(S): Holotype: RMNH 2301, according to Hoogmoed, 1978, Zool. Meded., Leiden, 53:103–104.

TYPE LOCALITY: "Nashville, [Davidson County,] Tenn[essee].", USA.

DISTRIBUTION: Fairly continuous from extreme southern Maine (USA), extreme southern Quebec (Canada), extreme southern Ontario (Canada), and northern Wisconsin (USA), southward to the Fall Line in North Carolina, South Carolina, Georgia, Alabama, and Tennessee (USA); presumably disjunct populations occur in Nova Scotia (Canada), Mississippi, Arkansas, Louisiana, Georgia, and northern Florida (USA).

COMMENT: Reviewed by Neill, 1963, Cat. Am. Amph. Rept., 2.1–2.

Hydromantes Gistel, 1848. Naturgesch. Thierr.:11.

TYPE SPECIES: *Salamandra genei* Temminck and Schlegel, 1838, by monotypy.

DISTRIBUTION: North-central and western Italy to southern France; Sardinia; northern California, USA.

COMMENT: Tribe Bolitoglossini; supergenus *Hydromantes.* Lanza and Vanni, 1981, Monit. Zool. Ital., N.S., Suppl., 15:117–121, erected a genus *Hydromantoides* (Type species: *Hydromantes platycephalus* Camp, 1916, by original designation) for the New World species, and discussed biogeography. See Mertens and Wermuth, 1960, Amph. Rept. Europas:34–35, for synonymies of the European species. European species reviewed by Thorn, 1968, Salamandres Eur. Asie Afr. Nord:302–314. Wake, Maxson, and Wurst, 1978, Evolution, 32:529–539, reported on biogeography of *Hydromantes* (including *Hydromantoides*).

Hydromantes brunus Gorman, 1954. Herpetologica, 10:153.

TYPE(S): Holotype: MVZ 59530.

TYPE LOCALITY: "base of low cliffs beside State Route 140, 0.7 miles NNE Briceburg (confluence of Bear Creek and Merced River), Mariposa County, California", USA.

DISTRIBUTION: Along Merced River and North Fork Merced River, Mariposa County, California, USA.

COMMENT: Reviewed by Gorman, 1964, Cat. Am. Amph. Rept., 11.1.

Hydromantes genei (Temminck and Schlegel, 1838). *In* Von Siebold, Fauna Japon., Rept.:115.

ORIGINAL NAME: *Salamandra genei.*

TYPE(S): RMNH 2296A designated lectotype by Hoogmoed, 1978, Zool. Meded., Leiden, 53:103.

TYPE LOCALITY: Sardinia; restricted by Mertens and Müller, 1928, Abh. Senckenb. Naturforsch. Ges., 41:15, to Mountains near Iglesias, Sardinia [Italy].

DISTRIBUTION: Island of Sardinia [Italy].

COMMENT: Lanza and Vanni, 1981, Monit. Zool. Ital., N.S., Suppl., 15:117–121, noted that this nominal species may be composed of three biological species: *Hydromantes genei* (Temminck and Schlegel, 1838); *Hydromantes imperialis* Stefani, 1969; and *Hydromantes flavus* Stefani, 1969. See also Lanza, 1983, Lav. Soc. Ital. Biogeogr., N.S., 8:730.

Hydromantes italicus Dunn, 1923. Proc. New England Zool. Club, 8:40.

TYPE(S): Not known to exist.

TYPE LOCALITY: Apuan Alps and Apennines; restricted by Mertens and Müller, 1928, Abh. Senckenb. Naturforsch. Ges., 41:15, to Bäder von Porretta, northern Italy.

DISTRIBUTION: Extreme southeastern France south to central Italy.

Hydromantes platycephalus (Camp, 1916). Univ. California Publ. Zool., 17:11.
ORIGINAL NAME: *Spelerpes platycephalus.*
TYPE(S): Holotype: MVZ 5693.
TYPE LOCALITY: "head of Lyell Cañon, 10,800 ft. altitude, Yosemite National Park, [Tuolumne County,] California", USA.
DISTRIBUTION: High elevations (above 1000 m) in the Sierra Nevada from El Dorado County south to northern Tulare County, California, USA.
COMMENT: Reviewed by Gorman, 1964, Cat. Am. Amph. Rept., 11.1.

Hydromantes shastae Gorman and Camp, 1953. Copeia, 1953:39.
TYPE(S): Holotype: MVZ 52314.
TYPE LOCALITY: "entrance to limestone caves at the edge of Flat Creek Road in the narrows of Low Pass Creek (0.7 miles east of Squaw Creek Road, 18.4 miles north and 15.3 miles east of Redding), Shasta County, California", USA.
DISTRIBUTION: Vicinity of Shasta Lake, Shasta County, California, USA.
COMMENT: Reviewed by Gorman, 1964, Cat. Am. Amph. Rept., 11.1–2.

Lineatriton Tanner, 1950. Great Basin Nat., 10:39.
TYPE SPECIES: *Spelerpes lineolus* Cope, 1865, by monotypy.
DISTRIBUTION: As for the single species.
COMMENT: Tribe Bolitoglossini, supergenus *Bolitoglossa.*

Lineatriton lineolus (Cope, 1865). Proc. Acad. Nat. Sci. Philadelphia, 17:197.
ORIGINAL NAME: *Spelerpes lineolus.*
TYPE(S): Holotype: ANSP 735.
TYPE LOCALITY: "Mexican Tableland"; probably eastern central Veracruz, Mexico, according to Smith and Taylor, 1948, Bull. U.S. Natl. Mus., 194:21.
DISTRIBUTION: East-central Veracruz, 2000–4000 ft. elev., Mexico.

Nototriton Elias and Wake, 1983. Contrib. Sci. Nat. Hist. Mus. Los Angeles Co., 345:11.
TYPE SPECIES: *Spelerpes picadoi* Stejneger, 1911, by original designation.
DISTRIBUTION: Eastern Guatemala to the Meseta Central of Costa Rica.
COMMENT: Tribe Bolitoglossini; supergenus *Bolitoglossa.* Formerly the *Chiropterotriton picadoi* group of the *Chiropterotriton*-beta section of Wake and Lynch, 1976, Sci. Bull. Nat. Hist. Mus. Los Angeles Co., 25:1–65.

Nototriton barbouri (Schmidt, 1936). Proc. Biol. Soc. Washington, 49:43.
ORIGINAL NAME: *Oedipus barbouri.*
TYPE(S): Holotype: MCZ 21247.
TYPE LOCALITY: Portillo Grande, Yoro [Department], Honduras.
DISTRIBUTION: Yoro and Cortés departments, Honduras.

Nototriton diminutus (Robinson, 1976). Proc. Biol. Soc. Washington, 89:289.
ORIGINAL NAME: *Bolitoglossa diminuta.*
TYPE(S): Holotype: UCR 5217.
TYPE LOCALITY: Quebrada Valverde, a precipitous stream 8.8 km NE by road from the bridge crossing the Río Grande de Orosi near Tapanti, Cartago Province, Costa Rica, at an elevation of approximately 1555 meters.
DISTRIBUTION: Known only from the type locality in lower montane rainforest.

Nototriton nasalis (Dunn, 1924). Field Mus. Nat. Hist. Publ., Zool. Ser., 12:97.
ORIGINAL NAME: *Oedipus nasalis.*
TYPE(S): Holotype: FMNH 4568.
TYPE LOCALITY: "mountains west of San Pedro, [Cortés Department,] Honduras, at 2000 feet on trail".
DISTRIBUTION: Known only from the type locality (Cortés, Honduras) and from Santa Barbara Mountain, Santa Barbara Department, Honduras.

Nototriton picadoi (Stejneger, 1911). Proc. U.S. Natl. Mus., 41:285.
   ORIGINAL NAME: *Spelerpes picadoi.*
   TYPE(S): Holotype: USNM 48280.
   TYPE LOCALITY: La Estrella, southeast of Cartago, [Cartago Province,] Costa Rica.
   DISTRIBUTION: Northwestern to central Costa Rica, 1200–2200 m elev.
   COMMENT: *Chiropterotriton abscondens* Taylor, 1948, Herpetologica, 2:62, was placed
      in the synonymy of this species by Wake and Lynch, 1976, Sci. Bull. Nat.
      Hist. Mus. Los Angeles Co., 25:59.

Nototriton richardi (Taylor, 1949). Univ. Kansas Sci. Bull., 33:284.
   ORIGINAL NAME: *Parvimolge richardi.*
   TYPE(S): Holotype: FMNH 178295 (formerly R. C. Taylor 1436).
   TYPE LOCALITY: "Isla Bonita (American Cinchona Plantation), Atlantic slope of
      Volcán Poas [Costa Rica] at an elevation of about 6,500 feet".
   DISTRIBUTION: Known only from the vicinity of the type locality and northern San
      José Province, Costa Rica.
   COMMENT: According to Wake and Elias, 1983, Contrib. Sci. Nat. Hist. Mus. Los
      Angeles Co., 345:12, the placement of this species in *Nototriton* is problematic.

Nototriton veraepacis (Lynch and Wake, 1978). Contrib. Sci. Nat. Hist. Mus. Los
      Angeles Co., 294:2.
   ORIGINAL NAME: *Chiropterotriton veraepacis.*
   TYPE(S): Holotype: MVZ 112499.
   TYPE LOCALITY: From 4.2 km (by road) S Purulhá, Baja Verapaz, Guatemala; at an
      elevation between 1740 and 1780 meters.
   DISTRIBUTION: Eastern Guatemala in the Sierra de las Minas and nearby mountains
      above 1200 m elevation.

Nyctanolis Elias and Wake, 1983. *In* Rhodin and Miyata (eds.), Adv. Herpetol. Evol.
      Biol.:2.
   TYPE SPECIES: *Nyctanolis pernix* Elias and Wake, 1983, by original designation.
   DISTRIBUTION: As for the single species.
   COMMENT: Tribe Bolitoglossini, supergenus *Bolitoglossa.*

Nyctanolis pernix Elias and Wake, 1983. *In* Rhodin and Miyata (eds.), Adv. Herpetol.
      Evol. Biol.:2.
   TYPE(S): Holotype: MVZ 134641.
   TYPE LOCALITY: "Finca Chiblac, 10 km (air) NE Barillas, Huehuetenango,
      Guatemala, (91° 16' W, 15° 53' N), 1370 m (4500 ft) elevation".
   DISTRIBUTION: Known only from a very limited area along the border separating
      Chiapas (Mexico) and Guatemala, on the northeastern slopes of the Sierra de
      los Cuchumatanes and in the Sierra de las Minas, east-central Guatemala.

Oedipina Keferstein, 1868. Arch. Naturgesch., 34, 1:299.
   TYPE SPECIES: *Oedipina uniformis* Keferstein, 1868, by monotypy.
   DISTRIBUTION: Chiapas, Mexico, south through Central America to western Colombia
      and south-central Ecuador.
   COMMENT: Tribe Bolitoglossini, supergenus *Bolitoglossa.* Subgeneric groupings follow
      Brame, 1968, J. Herpetol., 2:1–64, who revised the genus.

Oedipina alfaroi Dunn, 1921. Proc. Biol. Soc. Washington, 34:144.
   TYPE(S): Holotype: MCZ 6938.
   TYPE LOCALITY: Zent, [Limón Province,] Costa Rica.
   DISTRIBUTION: Known from the Caribbean drainage of Limón Province, Costa Rica
      and Bocas del Toro Province, northwestern Panama.
   COMMENT: In the *Oedipina uniformis* group, *Oedipina uniformis* subgroup.

Oedipina altura Brame, 1968. J. Herpetol., 2:28.
TYPE(S): Holotype: LACM 1739.
TYPE LOCALITY: "200 yards north of El Empalme, on the Pan American Highway south of Cartago in the northern end of the Cordillera de Talamanca, Canton de Dota, Provincia de Cartago, Costa Rica, at 2286 m (7500 ft) elevation".
DISTRIBUTION: Known only from the type locality.
COMMENT: In the *Oedipina uniformis* group, *Oedipina collaris* subgroup.

Oedipina carablanca Brame, 1968. J. Herpetol., 2:16.
TYPE(S): Holotype: LACM 1728.
TYPE LOCALITY: "west shore of the river on the eastern edge of the rubber tree finca, 0.5 km south of railroad tracks (one mile east of Guapiles), 300 m (980 ft) elevation, Los Diamantes, Canton de Pococi, Provincia de Limón, Costa Rica".
DISTRIBUTION: Known only from the type locality.
COMMENT: In the *Oedipina parvipes* group.

Oedipina collaris (Stejneger, 1907). Proc. U.S. Natl. Mus., 32:465.
ORIGINAL NAME: *Spelerpes collaris*.
TYPE(S): Holotype: USNM 37350.
TYPE LOCALITY: Topaz mine, 90 miles northwest of Bluefields, Nicaragua, and 50 miles back in direct line from the coast, elevation 400 feet (120 m).
DISTRIBUTION: Caribbean drainage of central-eastern Nicaragua, northeastern Costa Rica, and Panama.
COMMENT: In the *Oedipina uniformis* group, *Oedipina collaris* subgroup.

Oedipina complex (Dunn, 1924). Occas. Pap. Boston Soc. Nat. Hist., 5:94.
ORIGINAL NAME: *Oedipus complex*.
TYPE(S): Holotype: MCZ 9408.
TYPE LOCALITY: Las Cascadas, near Gamboa, Canal Zone [Panama].
DISTRIBUTION: Eastern edge of Pacific slope Costa Rica near the Panama border, through Panama and western Colombia to northwestern Ecuador.
COMMENT: In the *Oedipina parvipes* group.

Oedipina cyclocauda Taylor, 1952. Univ. Kansas Sci. Bull., 34:764.
TYPE(S): Holotype: KU 25066.
TYPE LOCALITY: "Los Diamantes (1 mile south of Guápiles), [Provincia de Limón,] Costa Rica".
DISTRIBUTION: Caribbean slopes of northern Honduras, southeastern Nicaragua, eastern Costa Rica south to northwestern Panama.
COMMENT: In the *Oedipina uniformis* group, *Oedipina collaris* subgroup.

Oedipina elongata (Schmidt, 1936). Field Mus. Nat. Hist. Publ., Zool. Ser., 20:165.
ORIGINAL NAME: *Oedipus elongatus*.
TYPE(S): Holotype: FMNH 20059.
TYPE LOCALITY: "Escobas, the site of the water supply for Puerto Barrios, Izabal [Department], Guatemala".
DISTRIBUTION: Central Chiapas (Mexico); near the Caribbean coast of eastern Belize across the Atlantic foothills of Guatemala to the Montañas del Mico.
COMMENT: In the *Oedipina parvipes* group.

Oedipina grandis Brame and Duellman, 1970. Contrib. Sci. Nat. Hist. Mus. Los Angeles Co., 201:1.
TYPE(S): Holotype: KU 116676.
TYPE LOCALITY: Northern slopes of Cerro Pando, between 1810 and 1930 meters elevation, Provincia de Bocas del Toro, extreme western Panama near the border with Costa Rica.
DISTRIBUTION: Known only from the vicinity of the type locality.

COMMENT: In the *Oedipina uniformis* group, *Oedipina collaris* subgroup.

Oedipina ignea Stuart, 1952. Proc. Biol. Soc. Washington, 65:1.
TYPE(S): Holotype: USNM 127959.
TYPE LOCALITY: "along the Río Las Brisas, just south of Yepocapa, Department of Chimaltenango, Guatemala. Elevation about 1450 m."
DISTRIBUTION: Southwestern Guatemala, 1000–2000 m elev.
COMMENT: In the *Oedipina uniformis* group, *Oedipina uniformis* subgroup.

Oedipina parvipes (Peters, 1879). Monatsber. Preuss. Akad. Wiss. Berlin, 1879:778.
ORIGINAL NAME: *Spelerpes (Oedipus) parvipes.*
TYPE(S): Holotype: ZMB 9518.
TYPE LOCALITY: Laceres [=Cáceres], Cenia, on the Cauca River, Provincia de Antioquia, Colombia.
DISTRIBUTION: Southwestern Costa Rica through Panama to southwestern Colombia.
COMMENT: In the *Oedipina parvipes* group. AHB considers *Oedipina alleni* Taylor, 1954, Univ. Kansas Sci. Bull., 36:607, currently in the synonymy of *Oedipina parvipes*, to be a distinct species, on the basis of a distinctive morphology.

Oedipina paucidentata Brame, 1968. J. Herpetol., 2:41.
TYPE(S): Holotype: KU 37192.
TYPE LOCALITY: "near El Empalme, (along the Pan American Highway, south of Cartago) in the northern end of the Cordillera de Talamanca, Canton de Dota, Provincia de Cartago, Costa Rica, about 2286 m (7500 ft) elevation".
DISTRIBUTION: Known only from the type locality.
COMMENT: In the *Oedipina uniformis* group, *Oedipus uniformis* subgroup.

Oedipina poelzi Brame, 1963. Contrib. Sci. Nat. Hist. Mus. Los Angeles Co., 65:7.
TYPE(S): Holotype: LACM 1772.
TYPE LOCALITY: "area of the stone quarry in the vicinity of El Angel Waterfall (former American Cinchona Plantation . . .), 3.8 miles by road south of Cariblanco, along the Vara Blanca–Puerto Viejo Road, Provincia de Heredia-Provincia de Alajuela boundary, Costa Rica; elevation 1520 m".
DISTRIBUTION: North-central Costa Rica.
COMMENT: In the *Oedipina uniformis* group, *Oedipina collaris* subgroup.

Oedipina pseudouniformis Brame, 1968. J. Herpetol., 2:25.
TYPE(S): Holotype: LACM 1729.
TYPE LOCALITY: "Cienega Colorado approximately three kilometers by road east of Juan Viñas and 6.3 km by road west of Turrialba, Canton de Turrialba, Provincia de Cartago, Costa Rica, elevation 1035 m (3400 ft)".
DISTRIBUTION: Western Nicaragua to central Costa Rica.
COMMENT: In the *Oedipina uniformis* group, *Oedipina collaris* subgroup.

Oedipina stuarti Brame, 1968. J. Herpetol., 2:47.
TYPE(S): Holotype: ZMH 1341.
TYPE LOCALITY: "Amapala, Isla Tigre, in the Golfo de Fonseca, Departamento de Valle, Honduras".
DISTRIBUTION: Known only from the type locality and Tegucigalpa, Honduras.
COMMENT: In the *Oedipina uniformis* group, *Oedipina uniformis* subgroup.

Oedipina taylori Stuart, 1952. Proc. Biol. Soc. Washington, 65:2.
TYPE(S): Holotype: UMMZ 102281.
TYPE LOCALITY: "4 kilometers east of Hacienda La Trinidad (23 air line kilometers southeast of Chiquimulilla), Department of Jutiapa, Guatemala. Elevation, about 100 meters".
DISTRIBUTION: Southeastern Guatemala to central El Salvador; Motagua Valley in the vicinity of Doña María, Guatemala.

COMMENT: In the *Oedipina uniformis* group, *Oedipina uniformis* subgroup.

Oedipina uniformis Keferstein, 1868. Nachr. Ges. Wiss. Göttingen, 15:331.
TYPE(S): Holotype: ZFMK 27833.
TYPE LOCALITY: Costa Rica.
DISTRIBUTION: Mountains and lowlands of central Costa Rica to western Panama.
COMMENT: In the *Oedipina uniformis* group, *Oedipina uniformis* subgroup.

Parvimolge Taylor, 1944. Univ. Kansas Sci. Bull., 30:223.
TYPE SPECIES: *Oedipus townsendi* Dunn, 1922, by monotypy.
DISTRIBUTION: As for the single species.
COMMENT: Tribe Bolitoglossini, supergenus *Bolitoglossa*.

Parvimolge townsendi (Dunn, 1922). Proc. Biol. Soc. Washington, 35:5.
ORIGINAL NAME: *Oedipina townsendi*.
TYPE(S): Holotype: MCZ 8017.
TYPE LOCALITY: Cerro de los Estropajos, near Jalapa, Veracruz, Mexico.
DISTRIBUTION: Central and southern Veracruz, Mexico.

Plethodon Tschudi, 1838. Classif. Batr.:92.
TYPE SPECIES: *Salamandra glutinosa* Green, 1818, by subsequent designation of
Fitzinger, 1843, Syst. Rept.:33.
DISTRIBUTION: Southeastern and southwestern Canada; western and eastern USA but
absent from the Great Plains region; one population in the southern Rocky
Mountains of New Mexico.
COMMENT: Tribe Plethodontini. Synonymies and review of most species available in
Highton, 1962, Bull. Florida State Mus., Biol. Sci., 6:235–367. Highton and
Larson, 1979, Syst. Zool., 28:579–599, discussed phylogenetic relationships of
the species and defined the species groups as used here. According to Highton
and Larson, the western species lineage contains the *Plethodon vandykei*,
Plethodon neomexicanus, *Plethodon vehiculum*, and *Plethodon elongatus* groups; the
eastern lineage contains the *Plethodon cinereus*, *Plethodon glutinosus*, *Plethodon
wehrlei*, and *Plethodon welleri* groups. Larson, Wake, Maxson, and Highton, 1981,
Evolution, 35:405–422, demonstrated that the western *Plethodon* lineage was
more closely related to *Aneides* than to the eastern *Plethodon* lineage. Duncan
and Highton, 1979, Copeia, 1979:95–110, studied the interrelationships of the
large *Plethodon* (*Plethodon ouachitae*, *Plethodon caddoensis*, and *Plethodon
fourchensis*) of the Ouachita Mountains. Larson and Highton, 1978, Syst. Zool.,
27:431–448, studied geographic protein variation and divergence in the
Plethodon welleri group.

Plethodon caddoensis Pope and Pope, 1951. Bull. Chicago Acad. Sci., 9:148.
TYPE(S): Holotype: FMNH 61959.
TYPE LOCALITY: "1200 feet on Polk Creek Mountain of the Caddo Mountains,
southwestern Montgomery County, Arkansas", USA.
DISTRIBUTION: Caddo Mountains of Montgomery and Polk counties, Arkansas,
USA, 950 to 1,200 feet altitude.
COMMENT: In the *Plethodon glutinosus* group. Reviewed by Pope, 1964, Cat. Am.
Amph. Rept., 14.1.

Plethodon cinereus (Green, 1818). J. Acad. Nat. Sci. Philadelphia, (1)1:356.
ORIGINAL NAME: *Salamandra cinerea*.
TYPE(S): Not stated, but ANSP 1232–34, 1237 considered syntypes by Highton,
1962, Bull. Florida State Mus., Biol. Sci., 6:286, who also designated ANSP
1232 lectotype.
TYPE LOCALITY: "Newjersey"; revised to "near Princeton?" by Fowler, 1906, Annu.
Rep. New Jersey State Mus., 1906:57; to "vicinity of Princeton", New Jersey,
USA, by Schmidt, 1953, Check List N. Am. Amph. Rept., Ed. 6:33.
DISTRIBUTION: Northeastern USA and southeastern Canada.

COMMENT: In the *Plethodon cinereus* group. Reviewed by Smith, 1963, Cat. Am. Amph. Rept., 5.1–3 (as including *Plethodon serratus*). See comment under *Plethodon serratus*.

Plethodon dorsalis Cope, 1889. Proc. Acad. Nat. Sci. Philadelphia, 21:138.
ORIGINAL NAME: *Plethodon cinereus dorsalis*.
TYPE(S): Syntypes: USNM 3776A–D; USNM 3776A designated lectotype by Highton, 1962, Bull. Florida State Mus., Biol. Sci., 6:277.
TYPE LOCALITY: "Louisville, [Jefferson County,] Kentucky", USA.
DISTRIBUTION: Southern Indiana, southern Illinois, and western North Carolina to Tennessee, northern Alabama, and northeastern Mississippi; also in Ozark uplift of Arkansas and Oklahoma, USA.
COMMENT: In the *Plethodon welleri* group. Reviewed by Thurow, 1966, Cat. Am. Amph. Rept., 29.1–3.

Plethodon dunni Bishop, 1934. Proc. Biol. Soc. Washington, 47:169.
TYPE(S): Holotype: USNM 95196.
TYPE LOCALITY: "just outside the city limits of Portland, Oregon, in Clackamas County", USA.
DISTRIBUTION: From extreme southwestern Washington south through western Oregon to northern Del Norte County, California, USA.
COMMENT: In the *Plethodon vehiculum* group. Reviewed by Storm and Brodie, 1970, Cat. Am. Amph. Rept., 82.1–2. Brodie, 1970, Herpetologica, 26:468–516, believed that *Plethodon gordoni* is a distinct species; see Nussbaum, Brodie, and Storm, 1983, Amph. Rept. Pacific Northwest:93–94, for discussion.

Plethodon elongatus Van Denburgh, 1916. Proc. California Acad. Sci., (4)6:216.
TYPE(S): Holotype: CAS 29096.
TYPE LOCALITY: Requa, Del Norte County, California [USA].
DISTRIBUTION: Humid coastal forest from northern side of Rogue River, Oregon, to near Orick and inland to vicinity of Willow Creek, Humboldt County, California, USA.
COMMENT: In the *Plethodon elongatus* group. Reviewed by Brodie and Storm, 1971, Cat. Am. Amph. Rept., 102.1–2.

Plethodon fourchensis Duncan and Highton, 1979. Copeia, 1979:109.
TYPE(S): Holotype: USNM 204835.
TYPE LOCALITY: From 1.5 km west, 0.3 km south of the top of Wolf Pinnacle Mountain, Polk County, Arkansas [USA].
DISTRIBUTION: Known only from Fourche Mountain and Irons Fork Mountain, Polk and Scott counties, Arkansas, USA.
COMMENT: In the *Plethodon glutinosus* group.

Plethodon glutinosus (Green, 1818). J. Acad. Nat. Sci. Philadelphia, (1)1:357.
ORIGINAL NAME: *Salamandra glutinosa*.
TYPE(S): Unknown.
TYPE LOCALITY: Not mentioned; but according to Dunn, 1926, Salamanders Fam. Plethodontidae:138, "obviously Princeton, New Jersey", USA.
DISTRIBUTION: Eastern USA, west to Texas.
COMMENT: In the *Plethodon glutinosus* group.

Plethodon hoffmani Highton, 1972 "1971". Virginia Polytech. Inst. State Univ., Res. Monogr., 4:151.
TYPE(S): Holotype: USNM 135203.
TYPE LOCALITY: Clifton Forge, Alleghany County, Virginia [USA].
DISTRIBUTION: Central and west-central Pennsylvania, northwestern Maryland, eastern West Virginia, and western Virginia south to the New River, USA.
COMMENT: In the *Plethodon cinereus* group.

Plethodon hubrichti Thurow, 1957. Herpetologica, 13:59.

TYPE(S): Holotype: USNM 139087.

TYPE LOCALITY: By the Blue Ridge Parkway at about 3100 feet, 0.9 miles south of cement milepost 80 and a sign reading 'view of Black Rock Hill' in Bedford County near the Bedford-Botecourt line and roughly 10 miles ESE of Buchanan, Virginia [USA].

DISTRIBUTION: Cool, moist ravines of Peaks of Otter region, Bedford and Rockbridge counties, northeast of Roanoke, Virginia, USA.

COMMENT: In the *Plethodon cinereus* group. Highton and Larson, 1979, Syst. Zool., 28:587, elevated this form to species status from subspecies status, under *Plethodon nettingi*.

Plethodon idahoensis Slater and Slipp, 1940. Occas. Pap. Dep. Biol. Univ. Puget Sound, 8:38.

TYPE(S): Holotype: USNM 110504.

TYPE LOCALITY: Northeast corner of Couer d'Alene Lake, Kootenai County, Idaho, elevation about 2160 feet.

DISTRIBUTION: Northern Idaho and northwestern Montana, USA.

COMMENT: In the *Plethodon vandykei* group. Highton and Larson, 1979, Syst. Zool., 28:587, elevated the form to species status from subspecific status under *Plethodon vandykei*. Most authorities from 1950 to 1979 treated this form as *Plethodon vandykei idahoensis*, as did Nussbaum, Brodie, and Storm, 1983, Amph. Rept. Pacific Northwest:107. Reviewed (as *Plethodon vandykei idahoensis*) by Brodie and Storm, 1970, Cat. Am. Amph. Rept., 91.1–2.

Plethodon jordani Blatchley, 1901. Dep. Geol. Nat. Res., Indiana, Annu. Rep., 25 for 1900:762.

TYPE(S): Originally in collection of W. S. Blatchley, now lost, according to Dunn, 1926, Salamanders Fam. Plethodontidae:145.

TYPE LOCALITY: Between 3000 and 5000 feet on the slope of Mt. Collins or Indian Pass, Sevier County, Tennessee [USA].

DISTRIBUTION: Found from western Virginia through western North Carolina and extreme eastern Tennessee to northwestern South Carolina and northeastern Georgia, USA.

COMMENT: In the *Plethodon glutinosus* group. Reviewed by Highton, 1973, Cat. Am. Amph. Rept., 130.1–4.

Plethodon kentucki Mittleman, 1951. Herpetologica, 7:105.

TYPE(S): Holotype: USNM 129937.

TYPE LOCALITY: Pine Mountain, Harlan County, Kentucky [USA], 2000 feet elevation.

DISTRIBUTION: Cumberland Plateau of eastern Kentucky, southern West Virginia, and western Virginia, USA.

COMMENT: In the *Plethodon glutinosus* group. Removed from the synonymy of *Plethodon glutinosus* by Highton and MacGregor, 1983, Herpetologica, 39:189–200. See also Maha, Maxson, and Highton, 1984 "1983", J. Herpetol., 17:398–400.

Plethodon larselli Burns, 1953. Herpetologica, 10:83.

ORIGINAL NAME: *Plethodon vandykei larselli*.

TYPE(S): Holotype: USNM 134129.

TYPE LOCALITY: "north slope of Larch Mountain, three miles from summit, on the Multnomah Falls Trail, Multnomah County, Oregon", USA.

DISTRIBUTION: Lower Columbia River Gorge of Multnomah and Hood River counties, Oregon, and Skamania County, Washington, USA.

COMMENT: In the *Plethodon neomexicanus* group. Reviewed by Burns, 1964, Cat. Am. Amph. Rept., 13.1.

Plethodon neomexicanus Stebbins and Riemer, 1950. Copeia, 1950:73.
TYPE(S): Holotype: MVZ 49033.
TYPE LOCALITY: "12 miles west and 4 miles south of Los Alamos, 8,750 feet altitude
±, Sandoval County, New Mexico", USA.
DISTRIBUTION: Known only from the Jemez Mountains of New Mexico, USA,
around 9,000 ft. elev.
COMMENT: In the *Plethodon neomexicanus* group. Reviewed by Williams, 1973, Cat.
Am. Amph. Rept., 131.1–2.

Plethodon nettingi Green, 1938. Ann. Carnegie Mus., 27:295.
TYPE(S): Holotype: CM 10279.
TYPE LOCALITY: Barton Knob near Cheat Bridge, Randolph County, West Virginia,
4,000 ft. elevation [USA].
DISTRIBUTION: From altitudes above 3600 ft. in the Cheat Mountains of West
Virginia, USA.
COMMENT: In the *Plethodon cinereus* group. Former subspecies *Plethodon hubrichti*
and *Plethodon shenandoah* were elevated to species status by Highton and
Larson, 1979, Syst. Zool., 28:587.

Plethodon ouachitae Dunn and Heinze, 1933. Copeia, 1933:121.
TYPE(S): Holotype: USNM 92484.
TYPE LOCALITY: Ouachita National Forest, Rich Mountain, Polk County, Arkansas
[USA].
DISTRIBUTION: Known from the Ouachita Mountains, Polk and Scott counties,
southwestern Arkansas, and Latimer and LeFlore counties, southeastern
Oklahoma, USA.
COMMENT: In the *Plethodon glutinosus* group. Reviewed by Blair, 1967, Cat. Am.
Amph. Rept., 40.1–2.

Plethodon punctatus Highton, 1972 "1971". Virginia Polytech. Inst. State Univ., Res.
Monogr., 4:176.
TYPE(S): Holotype: USNM 190224.
TYPE LOCALITY: Between 0.1 and 0.2 mile north-northwest of the top of Cow Knob,
Pendleton County, West Virginia [USA].
DISTRIBUTION: Higher elevations (over 3000 ft.) on Shenandoah Mountain in
Pendleton County, West Virginia, and Augusta and Rockingham counties,
Virginia, and on North Mountain (over 2800 ft.), Hardy County, West
Virginia, and Shenandoah County, Virginia, USA.
COMMENT: In the *Plethodon wehrlei* group.

Plethodon richmondi Netting and Mittleman, 1938. Ann. Carnegie Mus., 27:288.
TYPE(S): Holotype: CM 14189.
TYPE LOCALITY: Ritter Park, Huntington, Cabell County, West Virginia [USA] at an
altitude of 600–700 ft.
DISTRIBUTION: Found in western Pennsylvania to southeastern Indiana and south
to northwestern North Carolina and northeastern Tennessee, USA.
COMMENT: In the *Plethodon cinereus* group.

Plethodon serratus Grobman, 1944. Ann. New York Acad. Sci., 45:306.
ORIGINAL NAME: *Plethodon cinereus serratus*.
TYPE(S): Holotype: FMNH 39464.
TYPE SPECIES: "Rich Mountain, Polk County, Arkansas [USA], at an altitude of
2500 feet".
DISTRIBUTION: Central Louisiana, the Ouachita Mountains of Arkansas and
Oklahoma, Missouri, southeastern Tennessee, and southwestern North
Carolina, west-central Georgia and adjacent Alabama, USA.
COMMENT: In the *Plethodon cinereus* group. Elevated to species status by Highton
and Webster, 1976, Evolution, 30:40.

Plethodon shenandoah Highton and Worthington, 1967. Copeia, 1967:617.
ORIGINAL NAME: *Plethodon richmondi shenandoah*.
TYPE(S): Holotype: USNM 157379.
TYPE LOCALITY: Appalachian Trail 0.02 mi. NE of its junction with Naked Top
Mountain Trail, 0.4 air miles west of the top of Hawksbill Mountain,
Shenandoah National Park, Page County, Virginia, [USA] 3650 ft. elevation.
DISTRIBUTION: Shenandoah National Park, Page and Madison counties, Virginia,
USA.
COMMENT: In the *Plethodon cinereus* group. Considered a subspecies of *Plethodon
nettingi* by Highton, 1972 "1971", Virginia Polytech. Inst. State Univ., Res.
Monogr., 4:151. Elevated to species status by Highton and Larson, 1979, Syst.
Zool., 28:587.

Plethodon stormi Highton and Brame, 1965. Pilot Register of Zool., Card No. 20:1–2.
TYPE(S): Holotype: USNM 149964.
TYPE LOCALITY: 1.25 miles south of Copper, Jackson County, Oregon [USA].
DISTRIBUTION: Southwestern Jackson County, Oregon, and northern Siskiyou
County, California, USA.
COMMENT: In the *Plethodon elongatus* group. Reviewed by Brodie, 1971, Cat. Am.
Amph. Rept., 103.1–2.

Plethodon vandykei Van Denburgh, 1906. Proc. California Acad. Sci., (4)4:61.
TYPE(S): Holotype: CAS 6910 (destroyed); CAS 47495 designated neotype by
Slevin and Leviton, 1956, Proc. California Acad. Sci., (4)28:535 (see comment).
TYPE LOCALITY: "Paradise Valley, Mount Rainier Park, Washington", USA; neotype
from Forks, Clallam County, Washington, USA (see comment).
DISTRIBUTION: Western Washington, USA.
COMMENT: In the *Plethodon vandykei* group. Reviewed by Brodie and Storm, 1970,
Cat. Am. Amph. Rept., 91.1–2. See comment under *Plethodon idahoensis*.
Highton, 1962, Bull. Florida State Mus., Biol. Sci., 6:257, rejected the neotype
designation because its locality is 130 miles from the original type locality
and because it was unnecessary to solve any complex nomenclatural problem.

Plethodon vehiculum (Cooper, 1860). Rep. Explor. Surv. R.R. Route Mississippi–Pacific
Ocean, 12(Book 2, Pt. 3, No. 4):pl. 31.
ORIGINAL NAME: *Ambystoma vehiculum*.
TYPE(S): Not designated.
TYPE LOCALITY: "Astoria, Oregon", USA.
DISTRIBUTION: Chiefly west of Cascade Range crest from southwestern British
Columbia (Canada), including Vancouver I., to Coos County, Oregon (USA).
COMMENT: In the *Plethodon vehiculum* group. Reviewed by Storm and Brodie, 1970,
Cat. Am. Amph. Rept., 83.1–2.

Plethodon websteri Highton, 1979. Brimleyana, 1:32.
TYPE(S): Holotype: USNM 204814.
TYPE LOCALITY: From 0.6 km east, 0.9 km south of Howelton, Etowah County,
Alabama [USA].
DISTRIBUTION: Known from central Alabama and west-central Georgia; apparently
disjunct populations occur in Clarke County (Alabama), Winston County
(Mississippi), West Feliciana Parish (Louisiana), and McCormick County
(South Carolina), USA.
COMMENT: In the *Plethodon welleri* group.

Plethodon wehrlei Fowler and Dunn, 1917. Proc. Acad. Nat. Sci. Philadelphia, 69:23.
TYPE(S): Holotype: ANSP 19123.
TYPE LOCALITY: Two Lick Hills, Indiana County, Pennsylvania [USA].
DISTRIBUTION: From southwestern New York to extreme north-central North
Carolina (Stokes County), Virginia, and west to southeastern Ohio and
Letcher County, Kentucky, USA.

COMMENT: In the *Plethodon wehrlei* group.

Plethodon welleri Walker, 1931. Proc. Junior Soc. Nat. Sci. Cincinnati, 2:48.
   TYPE(S): Holotype: USNM 84135.
   TYPE LOCALITY: Grandfather Mountain, above 5,000 feet near Linville, (Avery
      County), North Carolina", USA.
   DISTRIBUTION: From Mount Rogers and White Top Mountain, Virginia, south to
      Yancey County, North Carolina, at higher elevations (USA); probably adjacent
      Tennessee.
   COMMENT: In the *Plethodon welleri* group. Reviewed by Thurow, 1964, Cat. Am.
      Amph. Rept., 12.1–2.

Plethodon yonahlossee Dunn, 1917. Bull. Am. Mus. Nat. Hist., 37:598.
   TYPE(S): Holotype: AMNH 4634.
   TYPE LOCALITY: "near the Yonahlossee Road about 1.5 miles from Linville, N.C.
      [Avery County, North Carolina], altitude 4,200 feet", USA.
   DISTRIBUTION: Blue Ridge Mountains of northwestern North Carolina,
      southwestern Virginia, and northeastern Tennessee, USA.
   COMMENT: In the *Plethodon glutinosus* group. Includes *Plethodon longicrus* according
      to Guttman, Karlin, and Labanick, 1978, J. Herpetol., 12:445–454. Reviewed
      (as *Plethodon longicrus*) by Adler, 1965, Cat. Am. Amph. Rept., 18.1, and (as
      Plethodon yonahlossee) by Pope, 1965, Cat. Am. Amph. Rept., 15.1–2. See
      Highton, 1972, Virginia Polytech. Inst. State Univ., Res. Monogr., 4:172.

Pseudoeurycea Taylor, 1944. Univ. Kansas Sci. Bull., 30:209.
   TYPE SPECIES: *Spelerpes leprosus* Cope, 1869, by original designation.
   DISTRIBUTION: Nuevo León and Sonora (Mexico) south to Guatemala.
   COMMENT: Tribe Bolitoglossini, supergenus *Bolitoglossa*. Wake and Elias, 1983,
      Contrib. Sci. Nat. Hist. Mus. Los Angeles Co., 345:13, noted that *Pseudoeurycea* is
      defined solely by retention of primitive features. The *Pseudoeurycea gadovii*,
      Pseudoeurycea rex, and *Pseudoeurycea leprosa* groups (of Wake and Lynch, 1976,
      Sci. Bull. Nat. Hist. Mus. Los Angeles Co., 25:1–65) appear to be closely related,
      according to Maxson and Wake, 1981, Herpetologica, 37:109–117. Lynch, Wake,
      and Yang, 1983, Copeia, 1983:884–894, reported on electrophoretic variation in
      Mexican forms and discussed the problems with defining species groups.

Pseudoeurycea altamontana (Taylor, 1938). Univ. Kansas Sci. Bull., 25:272.
   ORIGINAL NAME: *Oedipus altamontanus*.
   TYPE(S): Holotype: FMNH 100035 (formerly EHT-HMS 12245).
   TYPE LOCALITY: "Lake Zempoala, Morelos, Mexico, . . . ; elevation 10,500 feet".
   DISTRIBUTION: Known only from the type locality and the west slope of Mount
      Popocatapetl, Mexico.
   COMMENT: Not collected in the Zempoala region in recent years (OFV).

Pseudoeurycea anitae Bogert, 1967. Am. Mus. Novit., 2314:6.
   TYPE(S): Holotype: AMNH 76365.
   TYPE LOCALITY: 0.3 km W of San Vicente Lachixio, a village in the Distrito de Sola
      de Vega, about 2100 meters elevation, Sierra Madre del Sur, Oaxaca, Mexico.
   DISTRIBUTION: Known only from the type locality.

Pseudoeurycea bellii (Gray, 1850). Cat. Spec. Amph. Coll. Brit. Mus., Batr. Grad.:46.
   ORIGINAL NAME: *Spelerpes bellii*.
   TYPE(S): Holotype: BM 1946.9.6.23 (formerly 1.111.9.9.a).
   TYPE LOCALITY: Mexico.
   DISTRIBUTION: Mountains of east-central Sonora and southern Tamaulipas to
      Tlaxcala and to central Oaxaca, Mexico.

Pseudoeurycea brunnata Bumzahem and Smith, 1955. Herpetologica, 11:73.
TYPE(S): Holotype: UIMNH 33708.
TYPE LOCALITY: "Región de Soconusco, Chiapas, Mexico".
DISTRIBUTION: Known from the type locality in Chiapas, Mexico, and the Department of San Marcos, Guatemala.

Pseudoeurycea cephalica (Cope, 1865). Proc. Acad. Nat. Sci. Philadelphia, 17:196.
ORIGINAL NAME: *Spelerpes cephalicus.*
TYPE(S): Lost (see Dunn, 1924, Field Mus. Nat. Hist. Publ., Zool. Ser., 17:99); EHT-HMS 4372 (now FMNH?) designated neotype by Smith and Taylor, 1948, Bull. U.S. Natl. Mus., 194:30.
TYPE LOCALITY: "Mexican tableland", Mexico; neotype from "Cruz Blanca, Veracruz, Veracruz", Mexico.
DISTRIBUTION: Distrito Federal and states of Veracruz, Hidalgo, México, Puebla, and Morelos in Mexico.

Pseudoeurycea cochranae (Taylor, 1943). Univ. Kansas Sci. Bull., 29:343.
ORIGINAL NAME: *Bolitoglossa cochranae.*
TYPE(S): Holotype: FMNH 100091 (formerly EHT-HMS 24594).
TYPE LOCALITY: "Cerro San Felipe, Oaxaca, México . . . . at an elevation of about 8,800 feet".
DISTRIBUTION: Mountains of central and western Oaxaca, Mexico.

Pseudoeurycea conanti Bogert, 1967. Am. Mus. Novit., 2314:21.
TYPE(S): Holotype: AMNH 13811.
TYPE LOCALITY: Under rubbish in a cafetal at Pluma Hidalgo, Distrito de Pochutla, Oaxaca, Mexico, 900 meters elevation.
DISTRIBUTION: Known only from the type locality.
COMMENT: In the *Pseudoeurycea cephalica* group.

Pseudoeurycea exspectata Stuart, 1954. Proc. Biol. Soc. Washington, 67:159.
TYPE(S): Holotype: UMMZ 107999.
TYPE LOCALITY: About 3 km west of the aldea of Miramundo, Department of Jalapa, Guatemala, elevation of 2,525 meters.
DISTRIBUTION: Known only from the type locality.

Pseudoeurycea firscheini Shannon and Werler, 1955. Herpetologica, 11:82.
TYPE(S): Holotype: UIMNH 67055 (formerly F. A. Shannon 4714).
TYPE LOCALITY: Two miles west of Acultzingo, Veracruz, Mexico, at an elevation of 7,000 feet.
DISTRIBUTION: Known only from the type locality.

Pseudoeurycea gadovii (Dunn, 1926). Salamanders Fam. Plethodontidae:437.
ORIGINAL NAME: *Oedipus gadovii.*
TYPE(S): Holotype: BM 1946.9.6.41 (formerly 1903.9.30.312).
TYPE LOCALITY: Xometla, 8,500 feet elevation, Mount Orizaba, Veracruz, Mexico.
DISTRIBUTION: Mount Orizaba and Malinche in Puebla, Mexico.

Pseudoeurycea galeanae (Taylor, 1941). Proc. Biol. Soc. Washington, 54:83.
ORIGINAL NAME: *Bolitoglossa galaenae* [sic].
TYPE(S): Holotype: FMNH 100113 (formerly EHT-HMS 17146).
TYPE LOCALITY: "near Galeana, N[uevo]. L[eón]., [Mexico,] 7,000 ft. elevation".
DISTRIBUTION: Known only from the type locality.
COMMENT: Taylor, 1944, Univ. Kansas Sci. Bull., 30:189–232, made the justified emendation of the spelling of the specific epithet.

Pseudoeurycea goebeli (Schmidt, 1936). Field Mus. Nat. Hist. Publ., Zool. Ser., 20:163.
ORIGINAL NAME: *Oedipus goebeli.*
TYPE(S): Holotype: FMNH 21064.
TYPE LOCALITY: "Volcan Tajumulco, at 8,000 feet altitude, on the trail above El
    Porvenir, San Marcos [Department], Guatemala".
DISTRIBUTION: From the vicinity of Soconusco, Chiapas, Mexico, to the high
    mountains of western Guatemala.

Pseudoeurycea juarezi Regal, 1966. Am. Mus. Novit., 2266:1.
TYPE(S): Holotype: AMNH 74403.
TYPE LOCALITY: Ravine in cloud forest, on NE slope of the Sierra de Juárez, near
    lat. 17° 48' N., long. 96° 20' W., Oaxaca, Mexico, about 58 km S of Valle
    Nacional on road between Ixtlán de Juarez and Tuxtepec.
DISTRIBUTION: Sierra Juárez and Sierra Mixe, Oaxaca, Mexico.

Pseudoeurycea leprosa (Cope, 1869). Proc. Acad. Nat. Sci. Philadelphia, 21:105.
ORIGINAL NAME: *Spelerpes leprosus.*
TYPE(S): Syntypes: USNM 19255, 103591–92, and 6340 (2 specimens); USNM 19255
    designated lectotype by Taylor, 1938, Univ. Kansas Sci. Bull., 25:274.
TYPE LOCALITY: "Orizava" (=Orizaba), Veracruz, Mexico.
DISTRIBUTION: High mountains of Puebla, Veracruz, Morelos, Distrito Federal, and
    México, Mexico.

Pseudoeurycea longicauda Lynch, Wake, and Yang, 1983. Copeia, 1983:887.
TYPE(S): Holotype: MVZ 137880.
TYPE LOCALITY: "forested slope just South Mex. hwy. 15, 23.1 km (by rd) W. Villa
    Victoria, State of Mexico (elevation 2,850–2,970 m)", Mexico.
DISTRIBUTION: Two clusters of localities in the Cordillera Volcanica of eastern
    Michoacán and adjacent state of México, in an area termed the Sierra
    Temazcaltepec; possibly in other highland areas of the western Transverse
    Volcanic Range, Mexico.

Pseudoeurycea melanomolga (Taylor, 1941). Proc. Biol. Soc. Washington, 54:81.
ORIGINAL NAME: *Bolitoglossa melanomolga.*
TYPE(S): Holotype: UIMNH 25041 (formerly EHT-HMS 24626).
TYPE LOCALITY: "about 20 km. north of San Antonio Limón (Totalco), Veracruz",
    Mexico.
DISTRIBUTION: Known only from the type locality and Teziutlán, Puebla, Mexico.

Pseudoeurycea mystax Bogert, 1967. Am. Mus. Novit., 2314:12.
TYPE(S): Holotype: AMNH 76363.
TYPE LOCALITY: 0.9 km ENE of Ayutla, in the Distrito de Villa Alta, Oaxaca,
    Mexico, at 6400 feet elevation.
DISTRIBUTION: Known only from the type locality.

Pseudoeurycea nigromaculata (Taylor, 1941). Univ. Kansas Sci. Bull., 27:141.
ORIGINAL NAME: *Bolitoglossa nigromaculata.*
TYPE(S): Holotype: USNM 110635.
TYPE LOCALITY: "Cuautlapan, Veracruz", Mexico.
DISTRIBUTION: Known only from the region of the type locality.

Pseudoeurycea praecellens (Rabb, 1955). Breviora, 42:1.
ORIGINAL NAME: *Parvimolge praecellens.*
TYPE(S): Holotype: MCZ 24701.
TYPE LOCALITY: Hacienda El Potrero, near the city of Córdoba, Veracruz, Mexico.
DISTRIBUTION: Known only from the type.
COMMENT: Wake and Lynch, 1976, Sci. Bull. Nat. Hist. Mus. Los Angeles Co., 25:
    61, suggested that the juvenile type of *Parvimolge praecellens* might actually be

a *Pseudoeurycea*; subsequently transferred to *Pseudoeurycea* by Wake and Elias, 1983, Contrib. Sci. Nat. Hist. Mus. Los Angeles Co., 345:12.

Pseudoeurycea rex (Dunn, 1921). Proc. Biol. Soc. Washington, 34:143.
ORIGINAL NAME: *Oedipus rex*.
TYPE(S): Holotype: FMNH 1814.
TYPE LOCALITY: Sierra Santa Elena, Guatemala; altitude 9500 feet.
DISTRIBUTION: High elevations of western Guatemala.
COMMENT: See Elias, 1984, Contrib. Sci. Nat. Hist. Mus. Los Angeles Co., 348:13.

Pseudoeurycea robertsi (Taylor, 1938). Univ. Kansas Sci. Bull., 25:287.
ORIGINAL NAME: *Oedipus robertsi*.
TYPE(S): Holotype: FMNH 100002 (formerly EHT-HMS 12503).
TYPE LOCALITY: "Nevada [sic] de Toluca, [México,] elevation between 10,000 and 11,000 feet", Mexico.
DISTRIBUTION: Nevado de Toluca, México (state), and eastern Michoacán, Mexico.

Pseudoeurycea scandens Walker, 1955. Occas. Pap. Mus. Zool. Univ. Michigan, 567:1.
TYPE(S): Holotype: UMMZ 100639.
TYPE LOCALITY: Cave at Rancho del Cielo, on the forested slopes of the Sierra Madre Oriental in southern Tamaulipas, about five miles northwest of Gomez Farías, Mexico, elevation about 3500 feet.
DISTRIBUTION: Southwestern Tamaulipas, Mexico, 3500–6000 ft. elev.

Pseudoeurycea smithi (Taylor, 1938). Univ. Kansas Sci. Bull., 25:269.
ORIGINAL NAME: *Oedipus smithi*.
TYPE(S): Holotype: FMNH 100011 (formerly EHT-HMS 3966).
TYPE LOCALITY: "Cerro de San Luis, 15 mi. N.W. Oaxaca, Oaxaca", Mexico.
DISTRIBUTION: High mountains of Oaxaca, Mexico.

Pseudoeurycea unguidentis (Taylor, 1941). Herpetologica, 2:57.
ORIGINAL NAME: *Bolitoglossa unguidentis*.
TYPE(S): Holotype: FMNH 100045 (formerly EHT-HMS 17102).
TYPE LOCALITY: "Cerro San Felipe, about 15 kilometers north[east] of Oaxaca, Oaxaca, Mexico, at an elevation of 2200 m" (probably around 2800 m—AHB).
DISTRIBUTION: Cerro San Felipe and nearby Cerro San Luis, Oaxaca, Mexico.
COMMENT: Lynch, Yang, and Papenfuss, 1977, Herpetologica, 33:46–52, showed *Pseudoeurycea unguidentis* to be morphologically and biochemically distinct from *Pseudoeurycea smithi*, and therefore removed it from the synonymy of *Pseudoeurycea smithi*, where it had been placed by Bogert, 1967, Am. Mus. Novit., 2314:1–27.

Pseudoeurycea werleri Darling and Smith, 1954. Trans. Kansas Acad. Sci., 57:180.
TYPE(S): Holotype: UIMNH 33897.
TYPE LOCALITY: "Volcán San Martín, Veracruz", Mexico, between 3000 and 4500 feet elevation.
DISTRIBUTION: Known from 3000–4500 ft. elev., Volcán San Martín, Veracruz, Mexico.

Pseudotriton Tschudi, 1838. Classif. Batr.:60.
TYPE SPECIES: *Salamandra subfusca* Green, 1818 (=*Salamandra rubra* Latreille, 1801), by subsequent designation of Fitzinger, 1843, Syst. Rept.:34.
DISTRIBUTION: New York to Florida and west to southern Ohio, Kentucky, Tennessee, and to eastern Louisiana in the Gulf coastal plain, USA.
COMMENT: Tribe Hemidactylini. Reviewed by Martof, 1975, Cat. Am. Amph. Rept., 165.1–2.

Pseudotriton montanus Baird, 1849. J. Acad. Nat. Sci. Philadelphia, (2)1:293.
TYPE(S): Syntypes: USNM 3839 (3 specimens) (only two specimens noted in original description—RH).
TYPE LOCALITY: South Mountain, near Carlisle, [Cumberland County,] Pennsylvania [USA].
DISTRIBUTION: Pennsylvania to Florida, westward into Kentucky and Tennessee, and to eastern Louisiana in the Gulf coastal plain, USA.
COMMENT: Reviewed by Martof, 1975, Cat. Am. Amph. Rept., 166.1-2.

Pseudotriton ruber (Latreille, 1801). *In* Sonnini and Latreille, Hist. Nat. Rept., 4:305.
ORIGINAL NAME: *Salamandra rubra.*
TYPE(S): Not known to exist.
TYPE LOCALITY: "Les Etats Unis"; probably near Philadelphia, Pennsylvania, USA; see Dunn, 1926, Salamanders Fam. Plethodontidae:274, and Schmidt, 1953, Check List N. Am. Amph. Rept., Ed. 6:48.
DISTRIBUTION: USA from New York to northwestern Florida and west to Louisiana (not in Atlantic coastal plain).
COMMENT: Reviewed by Martof, 1975, Cat. Am. Amph. Rept., 167.1-3.

Stereochilus Cope, 1869. Proc. Acad. Nat. Sci. Philadelphia, 21:100.
TYPE SPECIES: *Pseudotriton marginatus* Hallowell, 1856, by monotypy.
DISTRIBUTION: As for the single species.
COMMENT: Tribe Hemidactylini. Reviewed by Rabb, 1966, Cat. Am. Amph. Rept., 25.1.

Stereochilus marginatus (Hallowell, 1856). Proc. Acad. Nat. Sci. Philadelphia, 8:130.
ORIGINAL NAME: *Pseudotriton marginatus.*
TYPE(S): Holotype: ANSP 514.
TYPE LOCALITY: Liberty County, Georgia [USA].
DISTRIBUTION: The Atlantic coastal plain from near Petersburg in southeastern Virginia, to extreme northern Florida, USA.
COMMENT: Reviewed by Rabb, 1966, Cat. Am. Amph. Rept., 25.1-2.

Thorius Cope, 1869. Proc. Acad. Nat. Sci. Philadelphia 21:111.
TYPE SPECIES: *Thorius pennatulus* Cope, 1869, by monotypy.
DISTRIBUTION: Southern Veracruz and Puebla to Guerrero and Oaxaca, west of the Isthmus of Tehuantepec, Mexico.
COMMENT: Tribe Bolitoglossini, supergenus *Bolitoglossa.* Hanken, 1983, Copeia, 1983: 1051-1073, discussed genetic variation and taxonomy of the genus and noted that seven additional species remained undescribed.

Thorius dubitus Taylor, 1941. Univ. Kansas Sci. Bull., 27:108.
TYPE(S): Holotype: FMNH 100039 (formerly EHT-HMS 17751).
TYPE LOCALITY: "summit of mountain about two miles south of Acultzingo, Veracruz (near Puebla line)", Mexico.
DISTRIBUTION: High mountain crests of west-central Veracruz and adjacent Puebla, Mexico.

Thorius macdougalli. Taylor, 1949. Am. Mus. Novit., 1437:8.
TYPE(S): Holotype: AMNH 52136.
TYPE LOCALITY: Cerro de Humo, Maquiltianguis, Oaxaca, Mexico.
DISTRIBUTION: Known only from the type locality and 12 mi. N of Ixtlán de Juárez, Oaxaca, Mexico.

Thorius maxillabrochus Gehlbach, 1959. Copeia, 1959:205.
TYPE(S): Holotype: USNM 140293.
TYPE LOCALITY: Four miles west of Zoquitlán, Puebla, Mexico, at 8400 ft.
DISTRIBUTION: Known only from the type locality.

COMMENT: Probably a synonym of *Thorius schmidti,* by implication of Hanken, 1983, Copeia, 1983:1051–1073.

Thorius minutissimus Taylor, 1949. Am. Mus. Novit., 1437:5.
TYPE(S): Holotype: AMNH 52673.
TYPE LOCALITY: Santo Tomás Tecpan, Oaxaca, Mexico [=49 mi. WSW Tehuantepec, Oaxaca].
DISTRIBUTION: Known only from the type locality.

Thorius narisovalis Taylor, 1939. Univ. Kansas Sci. Bull., 26:416.
TYPE(S): Holotype: FMNH 100089 (formerly EHT-HMS 17859).
TYPE LOCALITY: "elevation of about 2,600–3,00 meters on Cerro San Felipe, 15 km. north[east] of Oaxaca, Oaxaca", Mexico.
DISTRIBUTION: Known only from the vicinity of the type locality.

Thorius pennatulus Cope, 1869. Proc. Acad. Nat. Sci. Philadelphia, 21:111.
TYPE(S): Syntypes: originally USNM 6341 (7 specimens), now lost; USNM 111017 designated neotype by Taylor, 1941, Univ. Kansas Sci. Bull., 27:107; Malnate, 1971, Proc. Acad. Nat. Sci. Philadelphia, 123:348, provisionally regarded ANSP 1269 as a surviving syntype.
TYPE LOCALITY: "Orizava"; probably near the city of Orizaba, Veracruz, Mexico, according to Taylor and Smith, 1945, Proc. U.S. Natl. Mus., 95:534.
DISTRIBUTION: Known from low mountains about and below Orizaba and the slopes of Volcán San Martín, Veracruz, Mexico, 800–1200 m.
COMMENT: Two subspecies recognized by Shannon and Werler, 1955, Trans. Kansas Acad. Sci., 58:360–366.

Thorius pulmonaris Taylor, 1939. Univ. Kansas Sci. Bull., 26:411.
TYPE(S): Holotype: FMNH (formerly EHT-HMS 16684).
TYPE LOCALITY: "Cerro San Felipe, about 12 km. north[east] of Oaxaca, Oaxaca, Mexico".
DISTRIBUTION: Vicinity of the type locality and Cerro San Luis, Oaxaca, Mexico.

Thorius schmidti Gehlbach, 1959. Copeia, 1959:203.
TYPE(S): Holotype: USNM 140295.
TYPE LOCALITY: Four miles west of Zoquitlán, Puebla, Mexico, at 8400 ft.
DISTRIBUTION: Known only from the type locality.
COMMENT: See comment under *Thorius maxillabrochus.*

Thorius troglodytes Taylor, 1941. Univ. Kansas Sci. Bull., 27:110.
TYPE(S): Holotype: FMNH 100112 (formerly EHT-HMS 17791).
TYPE LOCALITY: "along old road on mountains about two miles south of Acultzingo, Veracruz", Mexico.
DISTRIBUTION: Region of the type locality.

Typhlomolge Stejneger, 1896. Proc. U.S. Natl. Mus., 18:620.
TYPE SPECIES: *Typhlomolge rathbuni* Stejneger, 1896, by monotypy.
DISTRIBUTION: Underground waters of Hays, Kendall, and Comal counties, central Texas, USA.
COMMENT: Tribe Hemidactylini. Relationships to *Eurycea* and generic status discussed by Potter and Sweet, 1981, Copeia, 1981:64–75.

Typhlomolge rathbuni Stejneger, 1897. Proc. U.S. Natl. Mus., 18:620.
TYPE(S): Holotype: USNM 22686.
TYPE LOCALITY: near San Marcos, [Hays County,] Texas [USA].
DISTRIBUTION: Underground waters in Hays, Kendall, and Comal counties, central Texas, USA.
PROTECTED STATUS: USA ESA—Endangered (11 Mar. 1967).

Typhlomolge robusta Longley, 1978. Endangered Species Report, U.S. Fish and
    Wildlife Service, Albuquerque, New Mexico, (2):1–10.
    TYPE(S): Holotype: TNHC 20255.
    TYPE LOCALITY: Beneath the Blanco River, 178 m elevation, 5 airline km NE of the
        Hays County Courthouse, San Marcos, Hays County, Texas [USA].
    DISTRIBUTION: Known only from the holotype.
    COMMENT: Potter and Sweet, 1981, Copeia, 1981:70, gave a revised description.

Typhlotriton Stejneger, 1893. Proc. U.S. Natl. Mus., 15:115.
    TYPE SPECIES: *Typhlotriton spelaeus* Stejneger, 1893, by monotypy.
    DISTRIBUTION: As for the single species.
    COMMENT: Tribe Hemidactylini. Reviewed by Brandon, 1970, Cat. Am. Amph. Rept.,
        34.1.

Typhlotriton spelaeus Stejneger, 1893. Proc. U.S. Natl. Mus., 15:116.
    TYPE(S): Holotype: USNM 17903.
    TYPE LOCALITY: "Rock House Cave, [Barry County,] Missouri", USA.
    DISTRIBUTION: Restricted to caves and springs on the Salem and Springfield
        plateaus of the Ozark region of Arkansas, Kansas, Missouri and Oklahoma,
        USA.
    COMMENT: Includes *Typhlotriton nereus* according to Brandon, 1966, Copeia, 1966:
        555–561.

FAMILY: **Proteidae** Gray, 1825.
    CITATION: Ann. Philos., (2)10:215.
    DISTRIBUTION: The eastern USA and northeastern Italy and adjacent Yugoslavia.
    COMMENT: As originally formed, the group name was Proteina. Hecht, 1957, Proc. Zool.
        Soc., Calcutta, 1957:282–292; Hecht and Edwards, 1976, Am. Nat., 110:653–667; and
        Hecht and Edwards, 1977, *In* Hecht, Goody, and Hecht (eds.), Major Patterns Vert.
        Evol.:3–51, have argued for an independent origin of *Proteus* and *Necturus*. Salthe,
        1967, Copeia, 1967:100–117, suggested on the basis of courtship behavior that *Proteus*
        was in the Salamandridae. Seto, Pomerat, and Kezer, 1964, Am. Nat., 98:71–78,
        noted the very similar karyotypes of *Proteus* and *Necturus* and suggested that this
        was due to close relationship. Estes, 1981, Handbuch der Paläoherpetol., Pt. 2:26,
        discussed the problem and tentatively retained a single family. In the suborder
        Proteoidea; see comment under Caudata.
    CONTRIBUTOR: Arden H. Brame, Jr. II (AHB).
    REVIEWERS: Edmund D. Brodie, Jr. (EDB); William E. Duellman (WED); Marinus S.
        Hoogmoed (MSH); David B. Wake (DBW).

Necturus Rafinesque, 1819. J. Phys. Chim. Hist. Nat. Blainville, 88:417.
    TYPE SPECIES: *Necturus lateralis* Wagler, 1830 (=*Sirena maculosa* Rafinesque, 1818), by
        subsequent designation of Fitzinger, 1843, Syst. Rept.:35.
    DISTRIBUTION: Eastern North America, in the Atlantic and Gulf drainages.
    COMMENT: The number of species (ranging from 2 to 5, depending on author) and
        their relationships are controversial; see Mount, 1975, Rept. Amph. Alabama:
        139–144, for discussion.
    REVIEWERS: Keith A. Harding (KAH); Richard Highton (RH).

Necturus alabamensis Viosca, 1937. Copeia, 1937:121.
    TYPE(S): Holotype: USNM 102676.
    TYPE LOCALITY: "Black Warrior River near Tuscaloosa, [Tuscaloosa County,]
        Alabama", USA.
    DISTRIBUTION: Western Georgia and the panhandle of Florida to the Pearl River
        drainage in Louisiana and Mississippi, USA.
    COMMENT: Considered by some authors to be a subspecies of *Necturus beyeri*.

Necturus beyeri Viosca, 1937. Copeia, 1937:123.
TYPE(S): Holotype: USNM 102674.
TYPE LOCALITY: "Upper Calcasieu River near Oakdale, [Allen Parish,] Louisiana", USA.
DISTRIBUTION: Eastern Texas to the Pearl River drainage of southeastern Louisiana and Mississippi, USA.

Necturus lewisi Brimley, 1924. J. Elisha Mitchell Sci. Soc., 11:167.
ORIGINAL NAME: *Necturus maculosus lewisi.*
TYPE(S): Holotype: USNM 73848.
TYPE LOCALITY: "Neuse River, near Raleigh", Wake County, North Carolina, USA.
DISTRIBUTION: Neuse and Tar river systems, North Carolina, USA.

Necturus maculosus (Rafinesque, 1818). Am. Monthly Mag. Crit. Rev., 4:41.
ORIGINAL NAME: *Sirena maculosa.*
TYPE(S): Unknown.
TYPE LOCALITY: Ohio River [USA].
DISTRIBUTION: Eastern North America, in the Atlantic and Gulf of Mexico drainages.

Necturus punctatus (Gibbes, 1850). Proc. Am. Assoc. Adv. Sci., Charleston, 1850:159.
ORIGINAL NAME: *Menobranchus punctatus.*
TYPE(S): Holotype: USNM 11813.
TYPE LOCALITY: Dr. Schoolbred's plantation on the South Santee River, a few miles from its mouth, South Carolina [USA].
DISTRIBUTION: Coastal plain from Virginia to vicinity of Mobile, Alabama, USA.

Proteus Laurenti, 1768. Synops. Rept.:35.
TYPE SPECIES: *Proteus anguinus* Laurenti, 1768, by monotypy.
DISTRIBUTION: As for the single species.
COMMENT: See Mertens and Wermuth, 1960, Amph. Rept. Europas:35–36, and Thorn, 1968, Salamandres Eur. Asie Afr. Nord:115–121.

Proteus anguinus Laurenti, 1768. Synops. Rept.:37.
TYPE(S): Unknown.
TYPE LOCALITY: "in lacu Tschirnicensi, Carniolae"; restricted by Fejervary, 1906, Ann. Hist. Nat. Mus. Natl. Hungarici, 24:231, to Magdalene Cave, near Adelsberg Cave, Yugoslavia.
DISTRIBUTION: Adriatic seaboard, as far north as Istrian region and as far south as Montenegro; isolated population in northeastern Italy.

FAMILY: **Salamandridae** Gray, 1825.
CITATION: Ann. Philos., (2)10:215.
DISTRIBUTION: From the British Isles and Scandinavia eastward to the Ural Mountains, southward into the Iberian Peninsula and Asia Minor; north-central India and China to northern Vietnam; extreme northwestern Africa; southern Canada and the USA to extreme northern Mexico.
COMMENT: Intrafamilial relationships were discussed by Wake and Özeti, 1969, Copeia, 1969:124–137. See Mertens and Wermuth, 1960, Amph. Rept. Europas:15–34, for synonymies of the European species. See Thorn, 1968, Salamandres Eur. Asie Afr. Nord:121–200, for synonymies and accounts of most species. In the suborder Salamandroidea; see comment under Caudata.
CONTRIBUTOR: Arden H. Brame, Jr. II (AHB).
REVIEWERS: Steven C. Anderson (SCA) (Southwestern Asia); Leo J. Borkin (LJB) (Europe and Asia); Edmund D. Brodie, Jr. (EDB); William E. Duellman (WED); Richard Highton (RH) (USA); Marinus S. Hoogmoed (MSH); Shuqin Hu (SH) (China); Masafumi Matsui (MM) (East Asia); David B. Wake (DBW); Ermi Zhao (EZ) (China).

Chioglossa Bocage, 1864. Proc. Zool. Soc. London, 1864:264–265.
TYPE SPECIES: *Chioglossa lusitanica* Bocage, 1864, by monotypy.
DISTRIBUTION: As for the single species.

Chioglossa lusitanica Bocage, 1864. Proc. Zool. Soc. London, 1864:264–265.
TYPE(S): MBL.
TYPE LOCALITY: Mount Bussaco near Coimbra, Portugal.
DISTRIBUTION: Northwestern Spain and northern Portugal.
COMMENT: Busack, 1976, Biol. Conserv., 10:309–319, documented this species'
decreasing range, suggested that legal protection was needed, and
discussed the citation of the description.

Cynops Tschudi, 1838. Classif. Batr.:94.
TYPE SPECIES: *Salamandra subcristatus* Schlegel, 1838 (=*Molge pyrrhogaster* Boie, 1826),
by monotypy.
DISTRIBUTION: China (southern Anhui, Jiangsu, Zhejiang, Guangxi, southern Hubei,
Henan, Hunan, Yunnan, and Guizhou provinces); Honshu, Shikoku, and
Kyushu Is., and Ryukyu Is., Japan.
COMMENT: Japanese species reviewed (as *Triturus*) by Sato, 1943, Monogr. Tailed Batr.
Japan:358–388. See also Freytag, 1962, Mitt. Zool. Mus. Berlin, 38:451–459.
Synonymy includes *Hypselotriton* Wolterstorff, 1934, Zool. Anz., 108:257 (Type
species: *Molge wolterstorffi* Boulenger, 1905, by monotypy), according to Zhao
and Hu, 1984, Stud. Chinese Tailed Amph.:21.

Cynops chenggongensis Kou and Xing, 1983. Acta Herpetol. Sinica, 2(4):51.
TYPE(S): Holotype: YU A824008.
TYPE LOCALITY: Chenggong County, Yunnan Province, China.
DISTRIBUTION: Known only from the type locality.

Cynops cyanurus Liu, Hu, and Yang, 1962. Acta Zool. Sinica, 14:385.
TYPE(S): Holotype: CIB 591200.
TYPE LOCALITY: De-wu, Shui-cheng, altitude 1,790 meters, western Kweichow
[=Guizhou], China.
DISTRIBUTION: Vicinity of the type locality.

Cynops ensicauda (Hallowell, 1861 "1860"). Proc. Acad. Nat. Sci. Philadelphia, 12:494.
ORIGINAL NAME: *Triton ensicauda*.
TYPE(S): Holotype: USNM 7410.
TYPE LOCALITY: Amakarima I. and 'Ralousima . . . the northern half of Ousima
proper' (=Amami, Ryukyu Is., Japan, according to Inger, 1947, Fieldiana:
Zool., 32:316).
DISTRIBUTION: Oshima and Okinawa groups, Ryukyu Is., Japan.
COMMENT: See Nakamura and Ueno, 1963, Japan. Rept. Amph. Color:19–20 (as
Triturus pyrrhogaster), for discussion.

Cynops orphicus Risch, 1983. Alytes, Paris, 2:46.
TYPE(S): Holotype: MVZ 22474.
TYPE LOCALITY: "Dayang (Tai-Yong), Shantou Region, Guangdong Province, China,
23° 35′ N, 115° 51′ E, altitude 640 m".
DISTRIBUTION: Known only from the type locality.
COMMENT: Related to *Cynops cyanurus*, according to the original description.

Cynops orientalis (David, 1871). J. N. China Asiat. Soc., N.S., 7:203.
ORIGINAL NAME: *Triton orientalis*.
TYPE(S): Syntypes: MNHNP 4763, 8120–21.
TYPE LOCALITY: Tche-san, near Chuchowfu, Chekiang [=Zhejiang] Province, China.
DISTRIBUTION: East-central China, including Henan, southern Anhui, Jiangsu,
Zhejiang, Guangxi, Fujian, southern Hubei, and Hunan.

Cynops pyrrhogaster (Boie, 1826). Isis von Oken, 1826:215.

ORIGINAL NAME: *Molge pyrrhogaster.*

TYPE(S): ZMA 7286 designated lectotype by Hoogmoed, 1978, Zool. Meded., Leiden, 53:99.

TYPE LOCALITY: Japan; restricted to the environs of Nagasaki by Hoogmoed, 1978, Zool. Meded., Leiden, 53:99.

DISTRIBUTION: Honshu, Shikoku, and Kyushu Is., Japan.

COMMENT: Includes *Cynops shataukokensis* Freytag and Eberhardt, 1977, Salamandra, 13:150–156 (Holotype: SMF 69000; Type locality: Surrounding north of Shau Tau Kok, Hong Kong, China), according to Risch and Romer, 1980, J. Herpetol., 14:337 (who discussed the incorrect type locality). See Sawada, 1963, J. Sci. Hiroshima Univ., B—Zool., 21:135–165, for discussion. Böhme and Bischoff, 1984, Bonn. Zool. Monogr., 19, doubted the synonymy of *Cynops shataukokensis.* MSH has examined the types of *Cynops shataukokensis* and agrees with Risch and Romer. See also Freytag, 1979, Sitzungsber. Ges. Naturforsch. Berlin, 19:70–80.

Cynops wolterstorffi (Boulenger, 1905). Proc. Zool. Soc. London, 1905:277.

ORIGINAL NAME: *Molge wolterstorffi.*

TYPE(S): Syntypes: BM 1946.9.6.30–34 (formerly 1905.30.51–59).

TYPE LOCALITY: Yunnanfu, Yunnan, China.

DISTRIBUTION: Yunnan, China, inhabiting the lake outside of Yunnanfu, and also from Oshan and Cheli in the same province.

COMMENT: Reviewed (as *Hypselotriton wolterstorffi*) by Liu, 1950, Fieldiana: Zool. Mem., 2:109–110, and by Freytag, 1962, Mitt. Zool. Mus. Berlin, 38:456.

Euproctus Gené, 1838. Mem. Accad. Sci. Torino, Cl. Sci. Fis. Mat. Nat., (2)1:281.

TYPE SPECIES: *Euproctus rusconii* Gené, 1838 (=*Molge platycephala* Gravenhorst, 1829), by monotypy.

DISTRIBUTION: Pyrenees Range of Spain and France; and also on the islands of Sardinia and Corsica.

Euproctus asper (Dugès, 1852). Ann. Sci. Nat., Paris, (3)17:266.

ORIGINAL NAME: *Hemitriton asper.*

TYPE(S): Syntypes: MNHNP 1082 (4 specimens).

TYPE LOCALITY: Eaux Bonnes, Pyrenees, Spain.

DISTRIBUTION: Pyrenees Mountains of France and Spain.

Euproctus montanus (Savi, 1838). Nuovo Giorn. Lett. Tosc., Pisa, 37:211.

ORIGINAL NAME: *Megapterna montana.*

TYPE(S): Unknown.

TYPE LOCALITY: Mountains of Corsica [France].

DISTRIBUTION: Mountains of Corsica, France.

Euproctus platycephalus (Gravenhorst, 1829). Delic. Mus. Zool. Vratislav., 1:84.

ORIGINAL NAME: *Molge platycephala.*

TYPE(S): Unknown.

TYPE LOCALITY: Restricted to Sardinia [Italy] by Mertens and Müller, 1928, Abh. Senckenb. Naturforsch. Ges., 41:9.

DISTRIBUTION: Mountains of Sardinia, Italy.

Mertensiella Wolterstorff, 1925. Abh. Ber. Mus. Nat. Heimatkd. Magdeburg, 4:168.

TYPE SPECIES: Not designated.

DISTRIBUTION: Mountains of northeastern Turkey, western Caucasus of Georgian S.S.R., USSR, and the mountains of Lycia, southeastern Anatolia, Turkey, and the Island of Karpathos, Greece.

COMMENT: *Mertensiella* is a replacement name for *Exaeretus* Waga, 1876, Rev. Mag. Zool., Paris, (3)4:327, which is a junior homonym of *Exaeretus* Fieber, 1864

(Insecta: Hemiptera). Özeti, 1967, Copeia, 1967:287–298, considered *Mertensiella* to be a subgenus of *Salamandra*.

Mertensiella caucasica (Waga, 1876). Rev. Mag. Zool., Paris, (3)4:327.
 ORIGINAL NAME: *Exaeretus caucasicus*.
 TYPE(S): Syntypes: MNHNP? and MZV.
 TYPE LOCALITY: Grass zone above the forests on the higher elevations of the Caucasus Mountains.
 DISTRIBUTION: Mountains at the southeast end of the Black Sea; known from above Trabzon in northeastern Turkey to Borzhomi in the Caucasus Mountains of Georgian S.S.R., USSR.

Mertensiella luschani (Steindachner, 1891). Sitzungsber. Akad. Wiss. Wien, Math. Naturwiss. Kl., 1891:308.
 ORIGINAL NAME: *Molge luschani*.
 TYPE(S): NHMW 15077, designated lectotype by Başoğlu and Özeti, 1973, Ege Univ. Fen Fak. Kitap. Ser., 50:39.
 TYPE LOCALITY: Tortukar (Dodurga-Assary), Lycia (southeastern Anatolia), Turkey.
 DISTRIBUTION: Mountains of Lycia, southwestern Anatolia, Turkey, and the Aegean islands of Karpathos, Saria, and Kasos.

Neurergus Cope, 1862. Proc. Acad. Nat. Sci. Philadelphia, 13:343.
 TYPE SPECIES: *Neurergus crocatus* Cope, 1862, by monotypy.
 DISTRIBUTION: Anatolian Turkey from Burdur in the west to Musch in the east; Kurdistan of northwestern Iran and northern Iraq; and the Zagros Mountains of Luristan, Iran.

Neurergus crocatus Cope, 1862. Proc. Acad. Nat. Sci. Philadelphia, 13:343.
 TYPE(S): Holotype: ANSP 25670.
 TYPE LOCALITY: Lake Urmia [Iran].
 DISTRIBUTION: Kurdistan of northwestern Iran and northern Iraq, and the Zagros Mountains of Luristan, Iran; southeastern Turkey.

Neurergus kaiseri Schmidt, 1952. Nat. Hist. Misc., Chicago, 93:1.
 TYPE(S): Holotype: ZMUC 03184.
 TYPE LOCALITY: Shah Bazan, Luristan, Iran [Zagros Mountains, 1200 meters, from 10 to 15 km south of the junction of the Ab-I-Cesar and Ab-I-Diz rivers].
 DISTRIBUTION: Vicinity of the type locality.
 COMMENT: Schmidtler and Schmidtler, 1970, Senckenb. Biol., 51:49, and Schmidtler and Schmidtler, 1975, Salamandra, 11:93, showed *Neurergus kaiseri* to be a distinct species.

Neurergus microspilotus (Nesterov, 1917). Ann. Mus. Zool. Acad. Sci. Petrograd, 21:2.
 ORIGINAL NAME: *Rithrotriton derjugini* var. *microspilotus*.
 TYPE(S): Possibly ZIL, but not seen by Nikolsky, 1918, Fauna Russia, Amph.:198.
 TYPE LOCALITY: Avroman-Dagh, Kurdistan, Iran [Balch, Iraq, and Tawale, Province Kurdistan, Iran].
 DISTRIBUTION: In addition to the type locality, four other localities: 30 km south of the type locality near Paweh, 8 km east of Paweh, 25 km southeast of Paweh, and near the Iraq-Iran border in Kurdistan, Iran.
 COMMENT: Considered a distinct species by Schmidtler and Schmidtler, 1975, Salamandra, 11:93.

Neurergus strauchii (Steindachner, 1887). Sitzungsber. Akad. Wiss. Wien, Math. Naturwiss. Kl., 96(2):69.
 ORIGINAL NAME: *Molge strauchii*.
 TYPE(S): NHMW 15079 designated lectotype by Schmidtler and Schmidtler, 1970, Senckenb. Biol., 51:41–53.
 TYPE LOCALITY: Mus (Mush) west of Lake Van, eastern Anatolia, Turkey.
 DISTRIBUTION: Known only from the area of the type locality at Mus and also from Kotum and Sürüm, in southeastern Turkey.

Notophthalmus Rafinesque, 1820. Ann. Nat., Lexington, 1(22):5.
ORIGINAL NAME: *Triturus* (*Notophthalmus*).
TYPE SPECIES: *Triturus* (*Diemictylus*) *miniatus* Rafinesque, 1820 (=*Triturus* (*Notophthalmus*) *viridescens* Rafinesque, 1820), by subsequent designation of Smith, 1953, Herpetologica, 9:95–99.
DISTRIBUTION: Eastern North America southward through eastern Texas (USA) to northern Veracruz, eastern San Luis Potosí, and Puebla, Mexico.
COMMENT: *Notophthalmus* selected over *Diemictylus* under rule of first revisor. Both *Notophthalmus* and *Diemictylus* named as subgenera of *Triturus*. See Smith, 1953, Herpetologica 9:95–99, for a summary of the nomenclatural history.

Notophthalmus meridionalis (Cope, 1880). Bull. U.S. Natl. Mus., 17:30.
ORIGINAL NAME: *Diemyctylus miniatus meridionalis*.
TYPE(S): Not designated; ANSP 1104–06 (Helotes, Texas, USA) and ANSP 15977 (San Diego, Texas, USA) catalogued as types.
TYPE LOCALITY: "Matamoros, Mexico . . . tributaries of the Medina River and southward"; restricted to "Matamoros, Tamaulipas", Mexico, by Smith and Taylor, 1948, Bull. U.S. Natl. Mus., 194:15.
DISTRIBUTION: Gulf coast of Texas from Houston to the Rio Grande and into adjacent Tamaulipas, Mexico, south to northern Veracruz, eastern San Luis Potosí, and Puebla, Mexico.
COMMENT: Reviewed by Mecham, 1968, Cat. Am. Amph. Rept., 74.1–2.
REVIEWERS: Gustavo Casas-Andreu (GCA); Oscar Flores-Villela (OFV).

Notophthalmus perstriatus (Bishop, 1941). Occas. Pap. Mus. Zool. Univ. Michigan, 451:3.
ORIGINAL NAME: *Triturus perstriatus*.
TYPE(S): Holotype: UMMZ 89761.
TYPE LOCALITY: "Dedge pond, 2 miles east of Chesser's Island, Charlton County, Georgia", USA.
DISTRIBUTION: Southern Georgia and northern Florida, USA.
COMMENT: Reviewed by Mecham, 1967, Cat. Am. Amph. Rept., 38.1–2.

Notophthalmus viridescens (Rafinesque, 1820). Ann. Nat., Lexington, 1(22):5.
ORIGINAL NAME: *Triturus* (*Diemictylus*) *viridescens*.
TYPE(S): Not designated.
TYPE LOCALITY: "in Lake George, Lake Champlain, the springs and brooks of the neighborhood".
DISTRIBUTION: Southeastern Canada and eastern USA.
COMMENT: See Mecham, 1967, Cat. Am. Amph. Rept., 53.1–4, for review and synonymy. *Triturus viridescens* was selected as the correct name for this species over *Triturus miniata* by action of first revisor. See Smith, 1953, Herpetologica, 9:95–99.

Pachytriton Boulenger, 1878. Bull. Soc. Zool. France, 3:71.
TYPE SPECIES: *Triton brevipes* Sauvage, 1877, by monotypy.
DISTRIBUTION: As for the single species.

Pachytriton brevipes (Sauvage, 1877). Bull. Soc. Philomath. Paris, (7)1:115.
ORIGINAL NAME: *Triton brevipes*.
TYPE(S): Syntypes: MNHNP 5061-2 (4 specimens), BM 1947.9.5.87 (formerly 1882.7.14.50).
TYPE LOCALITY: Tsitou, Kiangsi [=Jiangxi] Province, China.
DISTRIBUTION: Mountains of the provinces of southeastern China, including southern Anhui, Zhejiang, Guangxi, Fujian, northern Guangdong, Guangxi, southern Hunan, and Guizhou.

Paramesotriton Chang, 1935. Bull. Mus. Natl. Hist. Nat., Paris, (2)7:95.
TYPE SPECIES: *Mesotriton deloustali* Bourret, 1934, by monotypy.
DISTRIBUTION: North Vietnam and China.

COMMENT: *Paramesotriton* is a replacement name for *Mesotriton* Bourret, 1934, Bull. Instr. Gén. Publique, Hanoi, 4:83, which is preoccupied by *Mesotriton* Bolkay, 1927. See Freytag, 1962, Mitt. Zool. Mus. Berlin, 38(2):451.

Paramesotriton caudopunctatus (Liu and Hu, 1973). *In* Hu, Zhao, and Liu, Acta Zool. Sinica, 19:176.
ORIGINAL NAME: *Trituroides caudopunctatus.*
TYPE(S): Holotype: CIB (formerly SWIBASC) 63II0303.
TYPE LOCALITY: "Fang-xiang, Lei-shan Hsien, Kweichow [=Guizhou], altitude 1158 m", China.
DISTRIBUTION: Known only from the type locality.
COMMENT: Related to *Paramesotriton chinensis,* according to the original description. Bischoff and Böhme, 1980, Salamandra, 16:137–148, transferred this species to *Paramesotriton.*

Paramesotriton chinensis (Gray, 1859). Proc. Zool. Soc. London, 1859:229.
ORIGINAL NAME: *Cynops chinensis.*
TYPE(S): Syntypes: BM 1947.9.6.14–15 (formerly 59.11.18.8–9; BM 1947.9.6.15 designated lectotype by Myers and Leviton, 1962, Occas. Pap. Div. Syst. Biol. Stanford Univ., 10:1.
TYPE LOCALITY: Northeastern coast of China, inland of Ningpo.
DISTRIBUTION: Anhui, Zhejiang, Hunan, Fujian, Guangdong, and Guangxi, China.

Paramesotriton deloustali (Bourret, 1934). Bull. Gén. Instr. Publique, Hanoi, 1934(4):83.
ORIGINAL NAME: *Mesotriton deloustali.*
TYPE(S): Syntypes: Lab. Sci. Nat. Univ. Indochine (Hanoi) 226, 228, 257, and 287 (now MNHNP?); Guibé, 1950 "1948", Cat. Types Amph. Mus. Natl. Hist. Nat.: 9, reported MNHNP 35-119 as a 'paratype'.
TYPE LOCALITY: Tam-Dao, 900 meters, Tonkin (Vietnam).
DISTRIBUTION: Known from the vicinity of Tam-Dao, 60 km northwest of Hanoi, Vietnam.
COMMENT: Reviewed by Bourret, 1942, Batr. Indochine:148–150.

Paramesotriton guanxiensis (Huang, Tang, and Tang, 1983). Acta Herpetol. Sinica, 2(2):37.
ORIGINAL NAME: *Trituroides guanxiensis.*
TYPE(S): Holotype: FU 81501.
TYPE LOCALITY: Paiyang Shan, Mingjiang People's Commune, Ningming County, Guangxi Zhuang Autonomous Region, altitude 178 m, China.
DISTRIBUTION: Known only from the type locality.
COMMENT: Related to *Paramesotriton chinensis* (as *Trituroides chinensis*) according to the original description.

Paramesotriton hongkongensis (Myers and Leviton, 1962). Occas. Pap. Div. Syst. Biol. Stanford Univ., 10:1.
ORIGINAL NAME: *Trituroides hongkongensis.*
TYPE(S): Holotype: CAS-SU 6378.
TYPE LOCALITY: A mountain stream on the Peak, Hong Kong Island, China.
DISTRIBUTION: Island of Hong Kong and region of Kowloon on the continent, China.

Pleurodeles Michahelles, 1830. Isis von Oken, 23:195.
TYPE SPECIES: *Pleurodeles waltl* Michahelles, 1830, by monotypy.
DISTRIBUTION: Iberian peninsula of Spain and Portugal; Morocco, Tunisia, and Algeria.

Pleurodeles poireti (Gervais, 1835). Bull. Soc. Sci. Nat. France, 6:113.
ORIGINAL NAME: *Triton poireti.*
TYPE(S): Holotype: MNHNP 4744.
TYPE LOCALITY: Bone (Algeria).
DISTRIBUTION: Algeria and Tunisia, North Africa.

Pleurodeles waltl Michahelles, 1830. Isis von Oken, 23:195.
TYPE(S): RMNH 2379 designated lectotype by Hoogmoed, 1978, Zool. Meded., Leiden, 53:103.
TYPE LOCALITY: Chiclana near Cadiz, southern Spain.
DISTRIBUTION: Iberia, except for north and northeast; Morocco.
COMMENT: Frequently referred to incorrectly as *Pleurodeles waltli*.

Salamandra Laurenti, 1768. Synops. Rept.:41.
TYPE SPECIES: *Salamandra maculosa* Laurenti, 1768 (=*Lacerta salamandra* Linnaeus, 1758), by tautonymy.
DISTRIBUTION: Middle and southern Europe, northwest Africa, and western Asia.
COMMENT: See comment under *Mertensiella*.

Salamandra atra Laurenti, 1768. Synops. Rept.:42.
TYPE(S): Unknown.
TYPE LOCALITY: Restricted by Mertens and Müller, 1928, Abh. Senckenb. Naturforsch. Ges., 41:13, to Loibl Pass, between Kärnten and Krain (Austria).
DISTRIBUTION: Alps of southern Bavaria (F. R. Germany), Austria, France, and Switzerland; and high mountains of the western part of the Balkan peninsula, Yugoslavia, and Albania.

Salamandra salamandra (Linnaeus, 1758). Syst. Nat., Ed. 10, 1:204.
ORIGINAL NAME: *Lacerta salamandra*.
TYPE(S): ZIUU.
TYPE LOCALITY: Restricted by Mertens and Müller, 1928, Abh. Senckenb. Naturforsch. Ges., 41:14, to "Nürnberg", F. R. Germany.
DISTRIBUTION: Western, central, and southern Europe, northwest Africa, and southwestern Asia as far as the Iraq-Iran border.

Salamandrina Fitzinger, 1826. Neue Classif. Rept.:41.
TYPE SPECIES: *Salamandra perspicillata* Savi, 1821 (=*Salamandra terdigitata* Lacépède, 1788), by monotypy.
DISTRIBUTION: As for the single species.

Salamandrina terdigitata (Lacépède, 1788). Hist. Nat. Quadr. Ovip. Serp., 1:496.
ORIGINAL NAME: *Salamandra ter-digitata*.
TYPE(S): Unknown.
TYPE LOCALITY: Vesuvius [Italy].
DISTRIBUTION: Italy in the Apennines from Liguria to Campania provinces.

Taricha Gray, 1850. Cat. Spec. Amph. Coll. Brit. Mus., Batr. Grad.:25.
TYPE SPECIES: *Triton torosus* Rathke, 1833, by monotypy.
DISTRIBUTION: The Pacific coastal region from southern Alaska to southern California, USA, possibly into northern Baja California, Mexico.
COMMENT: Reviewed by Nussbaum and Brodie, 1981, Cat. Am. Amph. Rept., 271.1-2.

Taricha granulosa (Skilton, 1849). Am. J. Sci. Arts, (2)7:202.
ORIGINAL NAME: *Salamandra granulosa*.
TYPE(S): Not known to exist.
TYPE LOCALITY: "Oregon"; restricted to near Oregon City, Clackamas County, Oregon [USA], by Fitch, 1938, Copeia, 1938:149.
DISTRIBUTION: Southern Alaska to Santa Cruz and Santa Clara counties, California, USA, in the humid, coastal forests.
COMMENT: Reviewed by Nussbaum and Brodie, 1981, Cat. Am. Amph. Rept., 272.1-4.

Taricha rivularis (Twitty, 1935). Copeia, 1935:73.
ORIGINAL NAME: *Triturus rivularis*.
TYPE(S): Holotype: MVZ 18131.
TYPE LOCALITY: "Gibson Creek, 1 mile west of Ukiah, [Mendocino County,] California", USA.
DISTRIBUTION: Northern California (USA), in Sonoma, Mendocino, Humboldt, and Del Norte counties.
COMMENT: Reviewed by Twitty, 1964, Cat. Am. Amph. Rept., 9.1–2.

Taricha torosa (Rathke, 1833). *In* Eschscholtz, Zool. Atlas, (5):12.
ORIGINAL NAME: *Triton torosus*.
TYPE(S): Not known to exist.
TYPE LOCALITY: "in der Umgebung der Bai St. Francisco auf Californien" (=vicinity of San Francisco Bay, California, USA).
DISTRIBUTION: Coastal California from the vicinity of San Diego north to middle Mendocino County, north of San Francisco; and the western slopes of the Sierra Nevada Range, eastern California, USA; possibly into northern Baja California, Mexico.
COMMENT: Reviewed by Nussbaum and Brodie, 1981, Cat. Am. Amph. Rept., 273.1–4.

Triturus Rafinesque, 1815. Analyse Nat.:78.
TYPE SPECIES: *Triton cristatus* Laurenti, 1768, by subsequent designation (implied) of Dunn, 1918, Bull. Mus. Comp. Zool., 62:447.
DISTRIBUTION: England, Scandinavia, continental Europe, Asia Minor around the Black Sea and to the western portions of the Caspian Sea, eastward to the Ural Mountains of the USSR.
COMMENT: *Triturus* is a replacement name for *Triton* Laurenti, 1768, Synops. Rept.:37, which is preoccupied by a gastropod genus. Species group designations follow Bucci-Innocenti, Ragghianti, and Mancino, 1983, Copeia, 1983:662–672, who reported on karyology, discussed phylogenetic relationships within the genus, and elevated several former subspecies of *Triturus cristatus* to species status.

Triturus alpestris (Laurenti, 1768). Synops. Rept.:38.
ORIGINAL NAME: *Triton alpestris*.
TYPE(S): Unknown.
TYPE LOCALITY: Etschero Mountain [northern Alps, west of Mariazell, Austria].
DISTRIBUTION: Extreme western USSR to southern Denmark, northern and eastern France, Belgium, Netherlands, northern Italy, and central Greece; isolated population in northwestern Spain.
COMMENT: In the *Triturus vulgaris* group. See Dubois and Breuil, 1983, Alytes, Paris, 2:9–18, for subspecies.

Triturus boscai (Lataste, 1879). *In* Tourneville, Bull. Soc. Zool. France, 4:72.
ORIGINAL NAME: *Pelonectes boscai*.
TYPE(S): Syntypes: MNHNP 5840 (4 specimens); BM 1946.9.6.21–22 (formerly 1920.1.20.613).
TYPE LOCALITY: Caracollera, Province of Ciudad-Real, Spain.
DISTRIBUTION: Iberian Peninsula excluding northeastern and eastern parts, Spain and Portugal.
COMMENT: In the *Triturus vulgaris* group.

Triturus carnifex (Laurenti, 1768). Synops. Rept.:38.
ORIGINAL NAME: *Triton carnifex*.
TYPE(S): Not traced.
TYPE LOCALITY: Restricted by Mertens and Müller, 1928, Abh. Senckenb. Naturforsch. Ges., 41:11, to Vienna, Austria.
DISTRIBUTION: Alpine Austria (northward to Salzburg and to the Donau of Linz), Vienna Woods, northern Yugoslavia, Istrian Peninsula, southern Alps, and Apennine Peninsula, Italy.

COMMENT: In the *Triturus cristatus* group.

Triturus cristatus (Laurenti, 1768). Synops. Rept.:39.
ORIGINAL NAME: *Triton cristatus*.
TYPE(S): Unknown.
TYPE LOCALITY: Restricted by Mertens and Müller, 1928, Abh. Senckenb.
   Naturforsch. Ges., 41:11, to "Nürnberg", F. R. Germany.
DISTRIBUTION: Northern and middle Europe from 60° (in Scandinavia from 67°) to
   the Alps, westward to middle and eastern France, eastward to central USSR.
COMMENT: In the *Triturus cristatus* group.

Triturus dobrogicus (Kiritzescu, 1903). Bull. Soc. Sci., Bucuresti, An. XII:3–4.
ORIGINAL NAME: *Triton cristatus* var. *dobrogicus*.
TYPE(S): Syntypes: including MGAB 8 (from the restricted type locality).
TYPE LOCALITY: Restricted by Mertens and Müller, 1928, Abh. Senckenb.
   Naturforsch. Ges., 41:11, to Sulina, Danube Delta [Dobrogea Province, eastern
   Romania on the Black Sea].
DISTRIBUTION: Danube Basin, in the west from about Krems, Austria, over the
   Danube lowlands to Romania (Walachia and Dobrogea provinces, Romania).
COMMENT: In the *Triturus cristatus* group.

Triturus helveticus (Razoumowsky, 1789). Hist. Nat. Jorat., 1:111.
ORIGINAL NAME: *Lacerta helvetica*.
TYPE(S): Unknown.
TYPE LOCALITY: Vernens, Kanton Waadt, Switzerland.
DISTRIBUTION: Britain; continental western Europe from northern Germany to
   southern France and northern Iberia, and east to Poland and Czechoslovakia.
COMMENT: In the *Triturus vulgaris* group.

Triturus italicus (Peracca, 1898). Boll. Mus. Zool. Anat. Comp. Univ. Torino, 13:1.
ORIGINAL NAME: *Molge italica*.
TYPE(S): Syntypes: BM 1946.9.5.93–99 and 1946.9.6.1–7, NHMW 22877.1–2, MSNT.
TYPE LOCALITY: Potenza, Basilicata, southern Italy.
DISTRIBUTION: Middle and southern Italy.
COMMENT: In the *Triturus vulgaris* group.

Triturus karelini (Strauch, 1870). Mém. Acad. Sci. Imp. St. Petersbourg, (7)16:42.
ORIGINAL NAME: *Triton karelini*.
TYPE(S): Syntypes: ZIL 44–47.
TYPE LOCALITY: Persia [Iran], south coast of the Caspian Sea
DISTRIBUTION: Balkan Peninsula, Crimea, Caucasus Range, Asia Minor, and
   northern Iran.
COMMENT: In the *Triturus cristatus* group.

Triturus marmoratus (Latreille, 1800). Hist. Nat. Salamandr. France:29.
ORIGINAL NAME: *Salamandra marmorata*.
TYPE(S): Unknown.
TYPE LOCALITY: Restricted by Mertens and Müller, 1928, Abh. Senckenb.
   Naturforsch. Ges., 41:12, to Paris, France.
DISTRIBUTION: Iberia and southern and western France.
COMMENT: In the *Triturus cristatus* group.

Triturus montandoni (Boulenger, 1880). Bull. Soc. Zool. France, 5:38.
ORIGINAL NAME: *Triton montandoni*.
TYPE(S): Syntypes: MNHNP 6252 (2 specimens), NHMW 22901.1–2.
TYPE LOCALITY: Valley of Barnarie near Brosteni, Romania; restricted by Mertens
   and Müller, 1940, Abh. Senckenb. Naturforsch. Ges., 451:10.
DISTRIBUTION: Carpathian, Tatra, and Oder mountains, Europe.

COMMENT: In the *Triturus vulgaris* group.

Triturus vittatus (Gray, 1835). *In* Jenyns, Manual Brit. Vert. Anim.:305.
   ORIGINAL NAME: *Triton vittatus*.
   TYPE(S): Syntypes: BM 1947.9.7.8–10 (formerly 1.1.10.1A–B).
   TYPE LOCALITY: "ponds near London"; in error.
   DISTRIBUTION: Caucasus of northern Asia Minor (Turkey and USSR) and
      southeastern Turkey, northern Iraq, Syria, northern Lebanon, and Israel.
   COMMENT: In the *Triturus vulgaris* group.

Triturus vulgaris (Linnaeus, 1758). Syst. Nat., Ed. 10, 1:206.
   ORIGINAL NAME: *Lacerta vulgaris*.
   TYPE(S): Not traced.
   TYPE LOCALITY: Restricted by Mertens and Müller, 1928, Abh. Senckenb.
      Naturforsch. Ges., 41:13, to "Schweden".
   DISTRIBUTION: Nearly the whole of Europe and the western part of Asia south to
      Asia Minor.
   COMMENT: In the *Triturus vulgaris* group.

Tylototriton Anderson, 1871. Proc. Zool. Soc. London, 1871:423.
   TYPE SPECIES: *Tylototriton verrucosus* Anderson, 1871, by monotypy.
   DISTRIBUTION: China; Okinawa and Amami, Ryukyu Is., Japan; northern Vietnam,
      northern Thailand, Kachin Hills of northern Burma, Sikkim, Darjeeling area in
      north-central India, and Nepal.
   COMMENT: Zhao and Hu, 1984, Stud. Chinese Tailed Amph.:14–21, discussed
      phylogeny and considered *Echinotriton* Nussbaum and Brodie, 1982,
      Herpetologica, 38:321 (Type species: *Tylototriton andersoni* Boulenger, 1892, by
      original designation), to be a subgenus. Because Zhao's subgenera are
      monophyletic sister-taxa it is expected that some workers will continue to use
      Echinotriton as a genus. The subgenera noted in the accounts are from Zhao and
      Hu, 1984.

Tylototriton andersoni Boulenger, 1892. Ann. Mag. Nat. Hist., (6)10:304.
   TYPE(S): Holotype: BM 1947.9.5.89 (formerly 1892.7.14.50); BM 1892.9.3.30,
      according to Stejneger, 1907, Bull. U.S. Natl. Mus., 58:12.
   TYPE LOCALITY: Great Loo Choo Island [=Okinawa, Ryukyu Is.].
   DISTRIBUTION: Okinawa and Anami, Ryukyu Is., Japan; Hainan I., China.
   COMMENT: Subgenus *Echinotriton*. Reviewed by Sato, 1943, Monogr. Tailed Batr.
      Japan:349–355. See comment under *Tylototriton hainanensis*.

Tylototriton asperrimus Unterstein, 1930. Sitzungsber. Ges. Naturforsch. Freunde
      Berlin, 1930:314.
   TYPE(S): ZMB (apparently lost or destroyed in World War II).
   TYPE LOCALITY: Yaoshan, Kwangsi [=Guangxi], China.
   DISTRIBUTION: Manson Mountains of Guangxi, Guangdong, Gansu, Sichuan, Hubei,
      and Hainan I., China; Mao San area of Tonkin, Vietnam.
   COMMENT: Subgenus *Echinotriton*. Reviewed by Bourret, 1942, Batr. Indochine:146–
      148, and Fang and Chang, 1932, Sinensia, Nanking, 2:117–121. See also Liu et
      al., 1973, Acta Zool. Sinica, 19:394.

Tylototriton chinhaiensis Chang, 1932. Contrib. Biol. Lab. China Sci. Soc., Zool., 8:201.
   TYPE(S): Lost; CIB 780381 designated neotype by Cai and Fei, 1984, Acta Herpetol.
      Sinica, 3(1):71–77.
   TYPE LOCALITY: Chinhai, 20 miles northeast of Ningopo, Chekiang [=Zhejiang],
      China; neotype from Chinhai, Zhejiang, China, altitude 140 m.
   DISTRIBUTION: Known only from the type locality.
   COMMENT: Subgenus *Echinotriton*.

Tylototriton hainanensis Fei and Yang, 1984. Acta Zool. Sinica, 30(1):85–91.
TYPE(S): Holotype: CIB 64III1379.
TYPE LOCALITY: Nalong, Wuzhi Shan, altitude 770 m, Hainan, China.
DISTRIBUTION: Hainan I., China.
COMMENT: Reported as *Tylototriton andersoni* by Lab. Herpetol. Szechwan Biol. Inst.,
1977, Syst. Key Chinese Amph.:14. Probably a junior synonym of *Tylototriton asperrimus* (EZ).

Tylototriton kweichowensis Fang and Chang, 1932. Sinensia, Nanking, 2(9):112.
TYPE(S): Holotype: CIB 4664.
TYPE LOCALITY: "Kung-chi-shan, Western Kweichow [Guizhou, China] . . . ; altitude
2000 meters".
DISTRIBUTION: Yunkwei Plateau, Guizhou, China.
COMMENT: Subgenus *Tylototriton*. Reviewed by Liu, 1950, Fieldiana: Zool., 2:102–
106.

Tylototriton taliangensis Liu, 1950. Fieldiana: Zool. Mem., 2:106.
TYPE(S): Holotype: FMNH 49388.
TYPE LOCALITY: "Pusakang, Fulinhsien, Sikang [now Sichuan], 8700 feet altitude",
China.
DISTRIBUTION: Yunkwei Plateau, Sichuan, China.
COMMENT: Subgenus *Tylototriton*.

Tylototriton verrucosus Anderson, 1871. Proc. Zool. Soc. London, 1871:423.
TYPE(S): Syntypes: including BM 1874.6.1.3.
TYPE LOCALITY: Hotha, West Yunnan, China.
DISTRIBUTION: Yunnan (China), to northern Burma, hills of Arunachal Pradesh,
Sikkim, Darjeeling in India, Bhutan, and eastern Nepal; Chieng Dao,
northern Thailand; and northern Vietnam.
COMMENT: Subgenus *Tylototriton*. Reviewed by Bourret, 1942, Batr. Indochine:144–
146.
REVIEWERS: J. C. Daniel (JCD); Sushil Dutta (SD).

FAMILY: **Sirenidae** Gray, 1825.
CITATION: Ann. Philos., (2)10:215.
DISTRIBUTION: Southeastern USA and extreme northeastern Mexico.
COMMENT: As first formed the group name was Serenina. Goin and Goin, 1962, Intr.
Herpetol., Ed. 1, argued for the recognition of the Sirenidae as a distinct order,
Trachystomata (also known as the Meantes), but Estes, 1965, Am. Zool., 5:319–334,
and Wake, 1966, Mem. S. California Acad. Sci., 4:1–111, retained them in the
Caudata. In the suborder Salamandroidea; see comment under Caudata.
CONTRIBUTOR: Arden H. Brame, Jr. II (AHB).
REVIEWERS: Edmund D. Brodie, Jr. (EDB); Jonathan A. Campbell (JAC) (Mexico); Gustavo
Casas-Andreu (GCA) (Mexico); William E. Duellman (WED); Oscar Flores-Villela
(OFV) (Mexico); Keith A. Harding (KAH); Richard Highton (RH) (USA); Marinus S.
Hoogmoed (MSH); David B. Wake (DBW).

Pseudobranchus Gray, 1825. Ann. Philos., (2)10:216.
TYPE SPECIES: *Siren striata* Le Conte, 1824, by monotypy.
DISTRIBUTION: South Carolina south to Florida, USA.
COMMENT: Reviewed by Martof, 1972, Cat. Am. Amph. Rept., 118.1–2.

Pseudobranchus striatus (LeConte, 1824). Ann. Lyc. Nat. Hist. New York, 1:53.
ORIGINAL NAME: *Siren striata*.
TYPE(S): Unknown.
TYPE LOCALITY: Riceborough, Liberty County, Georgia [USA].
DISTRIBUTION: South Carolina south to Florida, USA.
COMMENT: Reviewed by Martof, 1972, Cat. Am. Amph. Rept., 118.2–4.

Siren Linnaeus, 1766. Syst. Nat., Ed. 12, 1, pt. 2, sign. Rrrr 5, Addenda (not paged).
TYPE SPECIES: *Siren lacertina* Linnaeus, 1766, by monotypy.
DISTRIBUTION: Southeastern USA from South Carolina to Florida and west to Texas; north to Illinois and Indiana; northern Tamaulipas and north-central Veracruz, Mexico.
COMMENT: Reviewed by Martof, 1974, Cat. Am. Amph. Rept., 152.1–2.

Siren intermedia Barnes, 1826. Am. J. Sci., 11:269.
TYPE(S): Unknown.
TYPE LOCALITY: "Southern states"; restricted to Liberty County, Georgia [USA], by Schmidt, 1953, Check List N. Am. Amph. Rept., Ed. 6:14.
DISTRIBUTION: Southeastern USA, from South Carolina to Texas, northward to Illinois and Indiana; and in northern Tamaulipas and north-central Veracruz, Mexico (see comment).
COMMENT: Reviewed by Martof, 1973, Cat. Am. Amph. Rept., 127.1–3. Authorships and date of publication discussed by Smith, Smith, and Sawin, 1975, Great Basin Nat., 35:100–102. Author frequently cited as Le Conte, 1827, J. Acad. Nat. Sci. Philadelphia, (1)5:322. The South Texas (USA) and Mexican populations are questionably of this species (OFV).

Siren lacertina Linnaeus, 1766. Syst. Nat., Ed. 12, 1, pt. 2, sign. Rrrr 5, Addenda (not paged).
TYPE(S): Not known to exist.
TYPE LOCALITY: In swampy Carolina; restricted to vicinity of Charleston, South Carolina [USA], by Schmidt, 1953, Check List N. Am. Amph. Rept., Ed. 6:14.
DISTRIBUTION: The coastal plain from the vicinity of Washington, D.C., south through southern Alabama to peninsular Florida, USA.
COMMENT: Reviewed by Martof, 1973, Cat. Am. Amph. Rept., 128.1–2.

ORDER GYMNOPHIONA

ORDER: **Gymnophiona** Müller, 1831.
  CITATION: Z. Physiol., 4:198.
  DISTRIBUTION: Pantropical.
  COMMENT: The Gymnophiona is frequently referred to in the literature as the Apoda. The most recent major revision is that by Taylor, 1968, Caecilians of the World. The relationship of the caecilians to the other groups of modern amphibians is problematical. Nussbaum, 1979, Occas. Pap. Mus. Zool. Univ. Michigan, 682, discussed phylogeny within the Gymnophiona. Carroll and Currie, 1972, Zool. J. Linn. Soc., 57: 229–247, suggested a lepospondyl origin of this group; see Nussbaum, 1983, J. Zool., London, 199:545–554, for more discussion of this view. Lombard, 1979, Biol. J. Linn. Soc., 11:19–76, suggested that the Gymnophiona could be the sister-taxon of the Caudata + Anura, but noted that the evidence was equivocal.
  CONTRIBUTOR: Marvalee H. Wake (MHW).
  REVIEWERS: William E. Duellman (WED); Marinus S. Hoogmoed (MSH); Ronald A. Nussbaum (RAN).

FAMILY: **Caeciliidae** Gray, 1825.
  CITATION: Ann. Philos., (2)10:217.
  DISTRIBUTION: Tropics of southern North America, South America, Africa, India, and the Seychelles Is.
  COMMENT: Taylor, 1969, Univ. Kansas Sci. Bull., 48:585–687, recognized two subfamilies within the Caeciliidae. See comment under Typhlonectidae. See comment under Dermophiinae.
  CONTRIBUTOR: Marvalee H. Wake (MHW).
  REVIEWERS: William E. Duellman (WED); Marinus S. Hoogmoed (MSH); Ronald A. Nussbaum (RAN); Norman J. Scott, Jr. (NJS).

SUBFAMILY: **Caeciliinae** Gray, 1825.
  CITATION: Ann. Philos., (2)10:217.
  DISTRIBUTION: Guatemala to Argentina.
  COMMENT: Taylor, 1969, Univ. Kansas Sci. Bull., 48:604, was the first to use the subfamilial name. Subfamily redefined by Wake and Campbell, 1983, Copeia, 1983:918–922.
  REVIEWERS: Werner C. A. Bokermann (WCAB) (Brazil); Jonathan A. Campbell (JAC) (Central America); Ulisses Caramaschi (UC) (Brazil); Eduardo Gudynas (EG) (southern South America); Jay M. Savage (JMS) (Central America); Paulo E. Vanzolini (PEV) (Brazil).

Caecilia Linnaeus, 1758. Syst. Nat., Ed. 10, 1:229.
  TYPE SPECIES: *Caecilia tentaculata* Linnaeus, 1758, by subsequent designation of Dunn, 1942, Bull. Mus. Comp. Zool., 91:494.
  DISTRIBUTION: Northern South America and adjacent Central America.

Caecilia abitaguae Dunn, 1942. Bull. Mus. Comp. Zool., 91:508.
  TYPE(S): Holotype: UMMZ 89930.
  TYPE LOCALITY: "Abitagua, Oriente, Ecuador, 1100 m. elevation".
  DISTRIBUTION: Oriente, Pastaza, and Moreno-Santiago provinces, Ecuador.

Caecilia albiventris Daudin, 1803. Hist. Nat. Gén. Part. Rept., 7:423.
  TYPE(S): Holotype: MNHNP 840.
  TYPE LOCALITY: "Surinam".
  DISTRIBUTION: Known only from the type locality.
  COMMENT: Removed from the synonymy of *Caecilia tentaculata* by Taylor, 1972, Univ. Kansas Sci. Bull., 49:1018.

Caecilia antioquiaensis Taylor, 1968. Caecilians of the World:353.
  TYPE(S): Holotype: FMNH 69680.
  TYPE LOCALITY: "Valdivia, Antioquia", Colombia.
  DISTRIBUTION: Known only from the type.

Caecilia armata Dunn, 1942. Bull. Mus. Comp. Zool., 91:511.
  TYPE(S): Holotype: MN 832.
  TYPE LOCALITY: "No data, probably Brazil".
  DISTRIBUTION: Unknown; presumably from Brazil.

Caecilia attenuata Taylor, 1968. Caecilians of the World:358.
  TYPE(S): Holotype: NHMW 9117.1.
  TYPE LOCALITY: "Perú (no definite locality)".
  DISTRIBUTION: Known from the type series (Peru) and Santa Rosa, Napo, Ecuador.

Caecilia bokermanni Taylor, 1968. Caecilians of the World:359.
  TYPE(S): Holotype: KU 200984 (formerly WCAB 234).
  TYPE LOCALITY: "Chicherota, Río Bobonaza, Napo-Pastaza, Ecuador".
  DISTRIBUTION: Known only from the type locality.

Caecilia caribea Dunn, 1942. Bull. Mus. Comp. Zool., 91:509.
  TYPE(S): Holotype: MCZ 24520.
  TYPE LOCALITY: "Pensilvania [on the Río Samaná Sur, a tributary of the Río
    Magdalena] (Cauca valley south of Medellin), Colombia".
  DISTRIBUTION: Northern Colombia.

Caecilia corpulenta Taylor, 1968. Caecilians of the World:365.
  TYPE(S): Holotype: UMMZ 65253.
  TYPE LOCALITY: "Río de Pache Porte" (an unidentified locality, probably in
    Colombia or Peru according to the original description).
  DISTRIBUTION: Known only from the type.

Caecilia crassisquama Taylor, 1968. Caecilians of the World:369.
  TYPE(S): Holotype: AMNH 23434.
  TYPE LOCALITY: "Normandia, Zuñía, Río Upana, 1400–1800 m (east slope of the
    Andes), Ecuador".
  DISTRIBUTION: Known only from the type.

Caecilia degenerata Dunn, 1942. Bull. Mus. Comp. Zool., 91:505.
  TYPE(S): Holotype: MCZ 17838; not 17384 as stated in the description, according to
    Taylor, 1968, Caecilians of the World:370.
  TYPE LOCALITY: "Garagoa, [Estado Boyacá,] eastern Colombia".
  DISTRIBUTION: Boyacá and Cundinamarca, Colombia.

Caecilia disossea Taylor, 1968. Caecilians of the World:375.
  TYPE(S): Holotype: AMNH 42832.
  TYPE LOCALITY: "mouth of the Río Santiago, Perú (arising in southern Ecuador,
    emptying into the Marañon)".
  DISTRIBUTION: Amazonian Peru and Ecuador.

Caecilia dunni Hershkovitz, 1938. Occas. Pap. Mus. Zool. Univ. Michigan, 370:1.
  TYPE(S): Holotype: UMMZ 82901.
  TYPE LOCALITY: "in the middle of the road between the settlement of Archidona
    and Tena, Prov. Napo-Pastaza [Napo Province,] Ecuador (eastern slope) at an
    altitude of about 1700 ft."
  DISTRIBUTION: Atrato River drainage of western Colombia and northwestern
    Ecuador, and Amazon drainage of Napo and Pastaza provinces, Ecuador.

Caecilia flavopunctata Roze and Solano, 1963. Acta Biol. Venezuelica, 3:294.
  TYPE(S): Holotype: MBUCV 5358.
  TYPE LOCALITY: Albarico, Yaracuy, Venezuela.
  DISTRIBUTION: Known only from the type.

Caecilia gracilis Shaw, 1802. Gen. Zool., 3:597.
TYPE(S): Mus. Adolphi Friderici?
TYPE LOCALITY: "South America".
DISTRIBUTION: Guianas; Pará, Brazil; northeastern Peru.
COMMENT: Reviewed by Nussbaum and Hoogmoed, 1979, Zool. Meded., Leiden, 54:222-223.

Caecilia guntheri Dunn, 1942. Bull. Mus. Comp. Zool., 91:510.
TYPE(S): Holotype: BM 1946.9.5.12 (formerly 1860.6.16.85).
TYPE LOCALITY: "Western Ecuador".
DISTRIBUTION: Western Ecuador to northern Colombia.
COMMENT: The nomenclature of this species is confusing; see Taylor, 1968, Caecilians of the World:395-398, for discussion.

Caecilia inca Taylor, 1973. Univ. Kansas Sci. Bull., 50:206.
TYPE(S): Holotype: USNM 119008.
TYPE LOCALITY: "Fundo Sinchona", Loreto, Peru.
DISTRIBUTION: Known only from the holotype.

Caecilia leucocephala Taylor, 1968. Caecilians of the World:404.
TYPE(S): Holotype: KU 200985 (formerly W. A. Thorton 583).
TYPE LOCALITY: "Virology Field Station, Río Raposo, Valle del Cauca, south of Buenaventura, Colombia".
DISTRIBUTION: Valle del Cauca (Colombia), Cana (Dariên, Panama), and "Central Brasil".
COMMENT: Taylor, 1973, Univ. Kansas Sci. Bull., 50:210, suggested that the locality "Central Brasil" is erroneous, and the specimen (CAS 66187) is likely from a locality on the Pacific or Caribbean drainage.

Caecilia mertensi Taylor, 1973. Univ. Kansas Sci. Bull., 50:210.
TYPE(S): Holotype: CAS 63983.
TYPE LOCALITY: "Seychelle Isle"; considered as unknown in the original description (see comment).
DISTRIBUTION: Known only from the type.
COMMENT: Taylor, 1973, Univ. Kansas Sci. Bull., 50:210, believed the unique specimen to be South American, not from the Seychelles, "Despite the attached data".

Caecilia nigricans Boulenger, 1902. Ann. Mag. Nat. Hist., (7)9:51.
TYPE(S): Holotype: BM 1946.9.5.52 (formerly 1901.3.29.88).
TYPE LOCALITY: "the Rio Lita, 3000 feet", northwestern Ecuador.
DISTRIBUTION: Pacific drainage of northern Ecuador and Colombia and the Caribbean drainage of Colombia and Panama.

Caecilia occidentalis Taylor, 1968. Caecilians of the World:413.
TYPE(S): Holotype: FMNH 189202 (formerly EHT-HMS 4665).
TYPE LOCALITY: "near Popayan, Cauca, Colombia".
DISTRIBUTION: Known only from the type locality (Cauca) and El Pablado (Antioquia), Colombia.

Caecilia orientalis Taylor, 1968. Caecilians of the World:417.
TYPE(S): Holotype: James A. Peters 4688 (now USNM?).
TYPE LOCALITY: "La Bonita, Napo-Pastaza Prov., Ecuador, elevation 6300 ft."
DISTRIBUTION: Amazonian Ecuador and possibly northwestern Colombia.

Caecilia pachynema Günther, 1859. Proc. Zool. Soc. London, 1859:417.
ORIGINAL NAME: *Coecilia pachynema*.
TYPE(S): Holotype: BM 1946.9.6.83 (formerly 60.6.16.87).
TYPE LOCALITY: Western Ecuador at an elevation of 6200 ft.
DISTRIBUTION: Pacific and Caribbean drainage systems of western Ecuador and Colombia, possibly Peru.

Caecilia perdita Taylor, 1968. Caecilians of the World:399.
  TYPE(S): Holotype: UMMZ 121036.
  TYPE LOCALITY: "Andagoya, Condoto, Choco, Colombia".
  DISTRIBUTION: Pacific slope of northwestern Colombia.

Caecilia pressula Taylor, 1968. Caecilians of the World:431.
  TYPE(S): Holotype: AMNH 49475.
  TYPE LOCALITY: "Marudi Mountains, British Guiana [=Guyana]".
  DISTRIBUTION: Known only from the type locality.

Caecilia subdermalis Taylor, 1968. Caecilians of the World:434.
  TYPE(S): Holotype: ANSP 25570.
  TYPE LOCALITY: "Moscopán, Cauca, Colombia".
  DISTRIBUTION: Known only from the type.

Caecilia subnigricans Dunn, 1942. Bull. Mus. Comp. Zool., 91:511.
  TYPE(S): Holotype: ANSP 4921; not 4821 as stated in the description, according to
    Taylor, 1968, Caecilians of the World:435.
  TYPE LOCALITY: "Magdalena River, Colombia".
  DISTRIBUTION: Known from the Magdalena Valley, Colombia, and from Falcón
    state in northern Venezuela.

Caecilia subterminalis Taylor, 1968. Caecilians of the World:437.
  TYPE(S): Holotype: FMNH 189204 (formerly EHT-HMS 1732).
  TYPE LOCALITY: "Ecuador".
  DISTRIBUTION: Known only from the type.

Caecilia tentaculata Linnaeus, 1758. Syst. Nat., Ed. 10, 1:229.
  TYPE(S): NHRM; lost, according to Nussbaum and Hoogmoed, 1979, Zool. Meded.,
    Leiden, 54:224.
  TYPE LOCALITY: America.
  DISTRIBUTION: Eastern Panama through the greater part of South America east of
    the Andes, south to central Peru.

Caecilia tenuissima Taylor, 1973. Univ. Kansas Sci. Bull., 50:219.
  TYPE(S): Holotype: USNM 12353.
  TYPE LOCALITY: "Guayaquil, [Guayas,] Ecuador".
  DISTRIBUTION: Known only from the holotype.

Caecilia thompsoni Boulenger, 1902. Ann. Mag. Nat. Hist., (7)10:152.
  TYPE(S): Holotype: BM 1946.9.5.13 (formerly 1902.5.15.26).
  TYPE LOCALITY: "Villeta [between Hondo and Bogotá,] Colombia, altitude 3500
    feet".
  DISTRIBUTION: Provinces of Tolima, Cauca, Cundinamarca, and Boyacá, Colombia.

Caecilia volcani Taylor, 1969. Univ. Kansas Sci. Bull., 48:315.
  TYPE(S): Holotype: FMNH (formerly EHT-HMS 4689).
  TYPE LOCALITY: "El Valle de Antón, Coclé, Panamá (elev. 550 m)".
  DISTRIBUTION: Known only from the type locality.

Microcaecilia Taylor, 1968. Caecilians of the World:532.
  TYPE SPECIES: *Dermophis albiceps* Boulenger, 1882, by original designation.
  DISTRIBUTION: Ecuador through southern Venezuela to the Guianas; São Paulo, Brazil.
  COMMENT: Taylor, 1970, Univ. Kansas Sci. Bull., 48:313, provided a key to the species
    in this genus.

Microcaecilia albiceps (Boulenger, 1882). Cat. Batr. Grad. Coll. Brit. Mus.:98.
  ORIGINAL NAME: *Dermophis albiceps*.
  TYPE(S): Holotype: BM 1946.9.5.32 (formerly 80.12.5.147).
  TYPE LOCALITY: "Ecuador".
  DISTRIBUTION: Amazonian Ecuador.

Microcaecilia rabei (Roze and Solano, 1963). Acta Biol. Venezuelica, 3:290.
ORIGINAL NAME: *Gymnopis rabei.*
TYPE(S): Holotype: MBUCV 5126.
TYPE LOCALITY: At the foot of Cerro Lema, Río Chicanán, Bolívar, Venezuela.
DISTRIBUTION: State of Bolívar, Venezuela, and Surinam.
COMMENT: Surinam specimens reported on by Nussbaum and Hoogmoed, 1979,
Zool. Meded., Leiden, 54:225.

Microcaecilia supernumeraria Taylor, 1969. Univ. Kansas Sci. Bull., 48:307.
TYPE(S): Holotype: ZMB 5268.
TYPE LOCALITY: "São Paulo", Brazil.
DISTRIBUTION: Known only from the type.

Microcaecilia taylori Nussbaum and Hoogmoed, 1979. Zool. Meded., Leiden, 54:225.
TYPE(S): Holotype: RMNH 15165a.
TYPE LOCALITY: "Sipaliwini; forest island on western slope Vier Gebroeders
Mountain, 2° N 55° 58′ W, 250 m, Surinam".
DISTRIBUTION: Forest in and west of Sipaliwini Savanna, Surinam.

Microcaecilia unicolor (A. Duméril, 1864). Mém. Soc. Sci. Nat. Cherbourg, 9:321.
ORIGINAL NAME: *Rhinatrema unicolor.*
TYPE(S): Syntypes: MNHNP (4 specimens); MNHNP 581 designated lectotype by
Taylor, 1968, Caecilians of the World:543.
TYPE LOCALITY: "Cayenne", French Guiana.
DISTRIBUTION: French Guiana, Surinam, and Guyana.
COMMENT: Surinam specimens reported on by Nussbaum and Hoogmoed, 1977,
Zool. Meded., Leiden, 54:229.

Minascaecilia Wake and Campbell, 1983. Copeia, 1983:857.
TYPE SPECIES: *Minascaecilia sartoria* Wake and Campbell, 1983, by original designation.
DISTRIBUTION: As for the single species.

Minascaecilia sartoria Wake and Campbell, 1983. Copeia, 1983:858.
TYPE(S): Holotype: KU 189566.
TYPE LOCALITY: "Aldea Vista Hermosa, Municipio Los Amates, Departamento de
Izabal, Guatemala, 650 m".
DISTRIBUTION: Known only from the type locality in subtropical wet forest in the
Sierra de las Minas, east-central Guatemala.

Oscaecilia Taylor, 1968. Caecilians of the World:598.
TYPE SPECIES: *Caecilia ochrocephala* Cope, 1866, by original designation.
DISTRIBUTION: Panama and northern South America; possibly southern Brazil.

Oscaecilia bassleri (Dunn, 1942). Bull. Mus. Comp. Zool., 91:518.
ORIGINAL NAME: *Caecilia bassleri.*
TYPE(S): Holotype: MCZ 19401.
TYPE LOCALITY: "Pastaza R. (Canelos to Marañón)", Ecuador.
DISTRIBUTION: Amazonian Ecuador and Peru.

Oscaecilia elongata (Dunn, 1942). Bull. Mus. Comp. Zool., 91:527.
ORIGINAL NAME: *Caecilia elongata.*
TYPE(S): Holotype: ZSM 1327/0; destroyed during World War II, according to
Taylor, 1968, Caecilians of the World:605.
TYPE LOCALITY: "Panama"; see Taylor, 1961, Caecilians of the World:605, for
discussion.
DISTRIBUTION: Known definitely only from Yavisa, Darién, Panama.

Oscaecilia equatorialis Taylor, 1973. Univ. Kansas Sci. Bull., 50:221.
   TYPE(S): Holotype: USNM 166421.
   TYPE LOCALITY: "Dyott Farm, Km 121 from Quito, 6 km E Santo Domingo de los
      Colorados, Pichincha, Ecuador".
   DISTRIBUTION: Known only from the type.

Oscaecilia hypereumeces Taylor, 1968. Caecilians of the World:607.
   TYPE(S): Holotype: NHMW 9122.
   TYPE LOCALITY: "Joinville, Santa Catarina, Brasil".
   DISTRIBUTION: Known only from the type locality.
   COMMENT: Taylor, 1968, Caecilians of the World:611, had some doubt whether the
      type had actually come from the stated type locality. A second specimen,
      locality also unknown, was reported by Taylor, 1970, Univ. Kansas Sci. Bull.,
      48:857; it is part of a Duke University numerical series of material collected
      in Brazil, so it *may* support the presence of this species in that country. Taylor
      did not comment (MHW).

Oscaecilia ochrocephala (Cope, 1866). Proc. Acad. Nat. Sci. Philadelphia, 18:132.
   ORIGINAL NAME: *Caecilia ochrocephala*.
   TYPE(S): Holotype: USNM 29764.
   TYPE LOCALITY: Atlantic side of the Isthmus of Panamá [Darién].
   DISTRIBUTION: Panama.

Oscaecilia polyzona (Fischer, 1879). *In* Peters, Monatsber. Preuss. Akad. Wiss. Berlin,
   1879:936.
   ORIGINAL NAME: *Caecilia polyzona*.
   TYPE(S): Syntypes: ZMB 9524 and AMNH 23499; ZMB 9524 designated lectotype
      by Taylor, 1969, Univ. Kansas Sci. Bull., 48:282–283.
   TYPE LOCALITY: Cacéres, Antioquia, Colombia.
   DISTRIBUTION: Valleys of the Magdalena and Cauca rivers in northern Colombia.
   COMMENT: Taylor, 1969, Univ. Kansas Sci. Bull., 48:283–285, discussed this species.

Oscaecilia zweifeli Taylor, 1968. Caecilians of the World:620.
   TYPE(S): Holotype: AMNH 20079.
   TYPE LOCALITY: "a small creek tributary to Río Mazaruni, British Guiana
      [=Guyana]".
   DISTRIBUTION: Known only from the type locality.

Parvicaecilia Taylor, 1968. Caecilians of the World:546.
   TYPE SPECIES: *Gymnophis nicefori* Barbour, 1925, by original designation.
   DISTRIBUTION: Northwestern Colombia.

Parvicaecilia nicefori (Barbour, 1925). Proc. Biol. Soc. Washington, 37:125.
   ORIGINAL NAME: *Gymnophis nicefori*.
   TYPE(S): Holotype: MCZ 9609.
   TYPE LOCALITY: Honda, Tolima, Colombia, Magdalena Valley, Caribbean drainage.
   DISTRIBUTION: Magdalena Valley of northern Colombia.

Parvicaecilia pricei (Dunn, 1944). Caldasia, 2:473.
   ORIGINAL NAME: *Gymnopis pricei*.
   TYPE(S): Holotype: MCZ 36902 (formerly in ICN).
   TYPE LOCALITY: El Centro, [Barranca Bermeja,] Departamento de Santander,
      Colombia in the Magdalena Valley, Caribbean drainage.
   DISTRIBUTION: Known only from the type locality.

SUBFAMILY: **Dermophiinae** Taylor, 1969.
   CITATION: Univ. Kansas Sci. Bull., 48:610.
   DISTRIBUTION: Southern Mexico to South America; Africa; India; Seychelles.

COMMENT: Laurent, 1984, Acta Zool. Lilloana, 37:199–200, considered the two nominal subfamilies of the Caeciliidae to be separate families. He divided his Dermophiidae into two subfamilies: the Dermophiinae (without splenial teeth, except for *Gymnopis*) for the New World species, and the Herpelinae (with splenial teeth, except for *Boulengerula*) for the Old World species.

Afrocaecilia Taylor, 1968. Caecilians of the World:321.
TYPE SPECIES: *Boulengerula taitanus* Loveridge, 1935, by original designation.
DISTRIBUTION: Tanzania and Kenya.
REVIEWERS: Kim M. Howell (KMH); Raymond Laurent (RL).

Afrocaecilia changamwensis (Loveridge, 1932). Bull. Mus. Comp. Zool., 72:381.
ORIGINAL NAME: *Boulengerula changamwensis*.
TYPE(S): Holotype: MCZ 16301.
TYPE LOCALITY: Changamwe, [Coast Province,] Kenya.
DISTRIBUTION: Known only from the lowland regions in the vicinity of the type locality in Coast Province, Kenya.

Afrocaecilia taitana (Loveridge, 1935). Bull. Mus. Comp. Zool., 79:16.
ORIGINAL NAME: *Boulengerula taitana*.
TYPE(S): Holotype: MCZ 20001.
TYPE LOCALITY: "absolute summit, 4800 ft., of Mt. Mbololo, Taita Mountains, Coast Province, Kenya Colony [=Kenya]".
DISTRIBUTION: Mt. Mbololo and Wundanyi, Taita Mountains, Coast Province, Kenya.

Afrocaecilia uluguruensis (Barbour and Loveridge, 1928). Mem. Mus. Comp. Zool., 50: 183.
ORIGINAL NAME: *Boulengerula uluguruensis*.
TYPE(S): Holotype: MCZ 12367.
TYPE LOCALITY: "Vituri, Uluguru Mountains, [Morogoro Division,] Tanganyika Territory [=Tanzania]".
DISTRIBUTION: Vicinity of the type locality.

Boulengerula Tornier, 1897 "1896". Thierwelt Ost-Afr., 4:164.
TYPE SPECIES: *Boulengerula boulengeri* Tornier, 1897, by monotypy.
DISTRIBUTION: As for the only species.
REVIEWERS: Kim M. Howell (KMH); Raymond Laurent (RL).

Boulengerula boulengeri Tornier, 1897 "1896". Thierwelt Ost-Afr., 4:164.
TYPE(S): Syntypes: ZMB (4 specimens) (now lost) and BM 1946.9.5.1 (formerly 1895.11.15.3).
TYPE LOCALITY: Usambara, [Tanga Division,] E. Africa [Tanzania].
DISTRIBUTION: Usambara and Magrotto mountains, Tanzania.

Brasilotyphlus Taylor, 1968. Caecilians of the World:342.
TYPE SPECIES: *Gymnopis braziliensis* Dunn, 1945, by original designation.
DISTRIBUTION: As for the only species.
REVIEWERS: Werner C. A. Bokermann (WCAB); Ulisses Caramaschi (UC); Eduardo Gudynas (EG); Paulo E. Vanzolini (PEV).

Brasilotyphlus braziliensis (Dunn, 1945). Am. Mus. Novit., 1278:1.
ORIGINAL NAME: *Gymnopis braziliensis*.
TYPE(S): Holotype: AMNH 51751.
TYPE LOCALITY: "Manaos, [Amazonas,] Brazil".
DISTRIBUTION: Amazonas and Amapá, Brazil.

Copeotyphlinus Taylor, 1968. Caecilians of the World:597.
TYPE SPECIES: *Siphonops syntremus* Cope, 1866, by original designation.
DISTRIBUTION: As for the only species.

COMMENT: The subfamilial assignment of this genus is uncertain, because the unique holotype of the only species is lost.
REVIEWERS: Jonathan A. Campbell (JAC); Jay M. Savage (JMS).

Copeotyphlinus syntremus (Cope, 1866). Proc. Acad. Nat. Sci. Philadelphia, 18:129.
ORIGINAL NAME: *Siphonops syntremus*.
TYPE(S): Not known to exist; lost prior to 1885.
TYPE LOCALITY: "the neighboring region of Honduras"; the northern coast of Honduras, according to Taylor, 1968, Caecilians of the World:597.
DISTRIBUTION: Presumably northern Honduras.
COMMENT: Taylor erected the genus *Copeotyphlinus* for a species based on a long-lost holotype for which only the original description remains. Savage and Wake, 1972, Copeia, 1972:691; Nussbaum, 1979, J. Herpetol., 13:121–123; and Wake and Campbell, 1983, Copeia, 1983:857–863, have reviewed this problem.

Dermophis Peters, 1879. Monatsber. Preuss. Akad. Wiss. Berlin, 1879:930.
TYPE SPECIES: *Siphonops mexicanus* Duméril and Bibron, 1841, by subsequent designation of Noble, 1924, Bull. Am. Mus. Nat. Hist., 49:305.
DISTRIBUTION: Southern Mexico to northwestern Colombia.
COMMENT: Savage and Wake, 1972, Copeia, 1972:680–695, revised this genus and considered its distribution. Wake, 1980, Herpetologica, 36:244–256, discussed variation in taxonomic characters.
REVIEWERS: Jonathan A. Campbell (JAC); Gustavo Casas-Andreu (GCA); Oscar Flores-Villela (OFV); Jay M. Savage (JMS).

Dermophis mexicanus (Duméril and Bibron, 1841). Erp. Gén., 8:284.
ORIGINAL NAME: *Siphonops mexicanus*.
TYPE(S): Holotype: MNHNP 4275.
TYPE LOCALITY: "Mexique".
DISTRIBUTION: Southern Veracruz and Oaxaca (Mexico) to Atlantic slopes of Costa Rica and Pacific western Panama; lower Motagua Valley of Guatemala.
COMMENT: Synonymy includes *Dermophis costaricense* Taylor, 1955; *Dermophis eburatus* Taylor, 1968; *Dermophis gracilior* (Günther, 1902); and *Dermophis septentrionalis* Taylor, 1968, according to Savage and Wake, 1972, Copeia, 1972: 680–695.

Dermophis oaxacae (Mertens, 1930). Abh. Ber. Mus. Nat. Heimatkd. Magdeberg, 6:153.
ORIGINAL NAME: *Gymnopis multiplicata oaxacae*.
TYPE(S): Holotype: SMF 22120.
TYPE LOCALITY: Cafetal Concordia (900 m altitude, between Puerto Angel and Salina Cruz, Oaxaca, Mexico).
DISTRIBUTION: Jalisco, Michoacán, Guerrero, Oaxaca, and Chiapas, Mexico.

Dermophis parviceps (Dunn, 1924). Occas Pap. Boston Soc. Nat. Hist., 5:93.
ORIGINAL NAME: *Siphonops parviceps*.
TYPE(S): Holotype: MCZ 9407.
TYPE LOCALITY: La Loma at an elevations of 1200 ft. on the trail from the Chiriquí Lagoon to David, Atlantic slope, Province of Boca del Toro, Panamá.
DISTRIBUTION: Southern Costa Rica, northwestern Panama, and northern Colombia.
COMMENT: Synonymy includes *Dermophis balboai* Taylor, 1968; *Dermophis glandulosus* Taylor, 1955; and *Dermophis occidentalis* Taylor, 1955, according to Savage and Wake, 1972, Copeia, 1972:680–695.

Gegeneophis Peters, 1879. Monatsber. Preuss. Akad. Wiss. Berlin, 1879:932.
TYPE SPECIES: *Epicrium carnosum* Beddome, 1870.
DISTRIBUTION: India.
COMMENT: *Gegeneophis* is a replacement name for *Gegenes* Günther, 1875, Proc. Zool. Soc. London, 1875:577, which is preoccupied by *Gegenes* Hübner, 1816 (Lepidoptera).

REVIEWERS: J. C. Daniel (JCD); Sushil Dutta (SD).

Gegeneophis carnosus (Beddome, 1870). Madras Month. J. Med. Sci., 2:176.
ORIGINAL NAME: *Epicrium carnosum.*
TYPE(S): Syntypes: BM 1946.9.5.64–65 (formerly 74.4.29.453–454).
TYPE LOCALITY: Periah Peak at about 5000 ft. elevation, Wynaad, [Kerala,] India.
DISTRIBUTION: Hills of Kerala, India.

Gegeneophis fulleri (Alcock, 1904). Ann. Mag. Nat. Hist., (7)14:271.
ORIGINAL NAME: *Herpele fulleri.*
TYPE(S): Holotype: ZSI 14759.
TYPE LOCALITY: Kuttal, 6 miles southwest of Silchar, in Cachar, Assam, India.
DISTRIBUTION: Known only from the holotype.

Gegeneophis ramaswamii Taylor, 1964. Senckenb. Biol., 45:227.
TYPE(S): Holotype: MCZ 29453.
TYPE LOCALITY: "Tenmalai forest (elevation 550 ft.), Kerala (state), southern India".
DISTRIBUTION: Known only from the type locality.

Geotrypetes Peters, 1880. Sitzungsber. Ges. Naturforsch. Freunde Berlin, 1880:55.
TYPE SPECIES: *Caecilia seraphini* A. Duméril, 1859, by monotypy.
DISTRIBUTION: Tropical West Africa; western Ethiopia.
REVIEWER: Kim M. Howell (KMH); Raymond Laurent (RL).

Geotrypetes angeli Parker, 1936. Zool. Meded., Leiden, 19:87.
TYPE(S): Holotype: BM 1946.9.5.54 (formerly 1909.2.23.10).
TYPE LOCALITY: Labé, French Guinea [=Guinea].
DISTRIBUTION: Known only from the type.

Geotrypetes grandisonae Taylor, 1970. Univ. Kansas Sci. Bull., 48:849.
TYPE(S): Holotype: BM 1969.1589.
TYPE LOCALITY: "Aleku, 12 km N Dembidollo, [Wallega Province,] Ethiopia", elev.
    1846 m (34° 37′ E; 8° 39′ N).
DISTRIBUTION: Provinces of Willega, Kaffa, and Illubabor, Ethiopia.
COMMENT: Taylor, 1970, Univ. Kansas Sci. Bull., 48:853, considered the generic
    placement of this species tentative.

Geotrypetes pseudoangeli Taylor, 1968. Caecilians of the World:718.
TYPE(S): Holotype: FMNH 189185 (formerly EHT-HMS 4679; formerly MCZ
    22414).
TYPE LOCALITY: "Liberia, Sanoqueleh near Ganta".
DISTRIBUTION: Liberia.

Geotrypetes seraphini (A. Duméril, 1859). Arch. Mus. Natl. Hist. Nat., Paris, 10:222.
ORIGINAL NAME: *Caecilia Seraphini.*
TYPE(S): Syntypes: MNHNP 1256 (3 specimens).
TYPE LOCALITY: Gaboon.
DISTRIBUTION: From the Liberian coast to extreme western Zaire.
COMMENT: Synonymy includes *Geotrypetes congoensis* Taylor, 1968, according to
    Taylor, 1973, Univ. Kansas Sci. Bull., 50:187–231. Laurent, 1974, Copeia, 1974:
    787–788, commented on the provenance of the specimens of *Geotrypetes
    congoensis.*

Grandisonia Taylor, 1968. Caecilians of the World:749.
TYPE SPECIES: *Hypogeophis alternans* Stejneger, 1893, by original designation.
DISTRIBUTION: Seychelles Is., Indian Ocean.

Grandisonia alternans (Stejneger, 1893). Proc. U.S. Natl. Mus., 16:739.
    ORIGINAL NAME: *Hypogeophis alternans.*
    TYPE(S): Holotype: USNM 20418.
    TYPE LOCALITY: "Mahé, Seychelles".
    DISTRIBUTION: Seychelles Is., Indian Ocean.

Grandisonia brevis (Boulenger, 1911). Trans. Linn. Soc. London, (2)14:374.
    ORIGINAL NAME: *Hypogeophis brevis.*
    TYPE(S): Syntypes: BM 1946.9.5.24–25 (formerly 1910.3.18.84–85); BM 1946.9.5.24
        designated lectotype by Taylor, 1968, Caecilians of the World:755.
    TYPE LOCALITY: Mahé, Seychelles Islands.
    DISTRIBUTION: Seychelles Is., Indian Ocean.

Grandisonia diminutiva Taylor, 1968. Caecilians of the World:757.
    TYPE(S): Holotype: MCZ 48928.
    TYPE LOCALITY: Praslin, Seychelles.
    DISTRIBUTION: Known only from the type locality.

Grandisonia larvata (Ahl, 1934). Zool. Anz., 106:284.
    ORIGINAL NAME: *Dermophis larvata.*
    TYPE(S): ZMB.
    TYPE LOCALITY: Seychelles.
    DISTRIBUTION: Seychelles Is., Indian Ocean.

Grandisonia sechellensis (Boulenger, 1911). Trans. Linn. Soc. London, (2)14:376.
    ORIGINAL NAME: *Dermophis sechellensis.*
    TYPE(S): Syntypes: BM 1946.1.23.5 (formerly 1910.3.18.80), 1946.9.5.26.30 (formerly
        1910.3.18.75–79), 1946.9.5.44 (formerly 1907.10.15.51), 1946.9.5.45 (formerly
        1910.3.18.74) from Mahé; BM 1946.9.5.49 (formerly 1907.10.15.152) from
        Silhouette; BM 1946.9.5.31 (formerly 1910.3.18.83) from Praslin.
    TYPE LOCALITY: Mahé, Silhouette, and Praslin, Seychelles.
    DISTRIBUTION: Seychelles Is., Indian Ocean.

Gymnopis Peters, 1874. Monatsber. Preuss. Akad. Wiss. Berlin, 1874:616.
    TYPE SPECIES: *Gymnopis multiplicata* Peters, 1874, by monotypy.
    DISTRIBUTION: Guatemala to Panama.
    COMMENT: Savage and Wake, 1972, Copeia, 1972:680–695, revised this genus and
        considered its distribution. The unjustified emendation *Gymnophis* has had some
        use.
    REVIEWERS: Jonathan A. Campbell (JAC); Jay M. Savage (JMS).

Gymnopis multiplicata Peters, 1874. Monatsber. Preuss. Akad. Wiss. Berlin, 1879:939.
    TYPE(S): Holotype: ZMB 3704.
    TYPE LOCALITY: Veragua, Panamá.
    DISTRIBUTION: Honduras to Panama.
    COMMENT: Synonymy includes *Gymnopis oligozona* (Cope, 1878); *Gymnopis proxima*
        (Cope, 1875); and *Cryptopsophis simus* (Cope, 1878), according to Savage and
        Wake, 1972, Copeia, 1972:680–695.

Herpele Peters, 1879. Monatsber. Preuss. Akad. Wiss. Berlin, 1879:930.
    TYPE SPECIES: *Caecilia squalostoma* Stutchbury, 1834, by monotypy.
    DISTRIBUTION: West Africa.
    REVIEWER: Raymond Laurent (RL).

Herpele multiplicata Nieden, 1912. Sitzungsber. Ges. Naturforsch. Freunde Berlin,
    1912:210.
    TYPE(S): Formerly in ZMB; now lost.
    TYPE LOCALITY: Victoria [now Limbé], Cameroon, West Africa.
    DISTRIBUTION: Known only from the type.

Herpele squalostoma (Stutchbury, 1834). Trans. Linn. Soc. London, (1)17:362.
ORIGINAL NAME: *Caecilia squalostoma.*
TYPE(S): Not known to exist.
TYPE LOCALITY: Gabon.
DISTRIBUTION: Cameroon, southern Nigeria, Gabon, Congo, and southwestern
Zaire; Fernando Po.

Hypogeophis Peters, 1879. Monatsber. Preuss. Akad. Wiss. Berlin, 1879:936.
TYPE SPECIES: *Hypogeophis rostratus* (Cuvier, 1829) by subsequent designation of
Parker, 1958, Copeia 1958:74.
DISTRIBUTION: As for the only species.

Hypogeophis rostratus (Cuvier, 1829). Règ. Animal, Ed. 2, 2:100.
ORIGINAL NAME: *Coecilia rostrata.*
TYPE LOCALITY: Mahé, Seychelles.
DISTRIBUTION: Seychelles Is., Indian Ocean.
COMMENT: Taylor, 1969, Univ. Kansas Sci. Bull., 48:287–290, discussed inter-island
variation.

Idiocranium Parker, 1936. Proc. Zool. Soc. London, 1936:160.
TYPE SPECIES: *Idiocranium russelli* Parker, 1936, by monotypy.
DISTRIBUTION: As for the only species.
REVIEWER: Raymond Laurent (RL).

Idiocranium russelli Parker, 1936. Proc. Zool. Soc. London, 1936:160.
TYPE(S): Holotype: BM 1946.9.5.70 (formerly 1936.3.4.29).
TYPE LOCALITY: Makamunu Assumbo, Mamfe Division, Cameroon, Africa.
DISTRIBUTION: Known only from the type locality.

Indotyphlus Taylor, 1960. Univ. Kansas Sci. Bull., 40:31.
TYPE SPECIES: *Indotyphlus battersbyi* Taylor, 1960, by original designation.
DISTRIBUTION: As for the only species.
REVIEWERS: J. C. Daniel (JCD); Sushil Dutta (SD).

Indotyphlus battersbyi Taylor, 1960. Univ. Kansas Sci. Bull., 40:31.
TYPE(S): Holotype: AMNH 49974.
TYPE LOCALITY: Khandala, Poona District, [Maharashtra,] India.
DISTRIBUTION: Known only from the region of the type locality.

Lutkenotyphlus Taylor, 1968. Caecilians of the World:588.
TYPE SPECIES: *Siphonops brasiliensis* Lütken, 1852, by original designation.
DISTRIBUTION: As for the only species.
REVIEWERS: Werner C. A. Bokermann (WCAB); Ulisses Caramaschi (UC); Eduardo
Gudynas (EG); Paulo E. Vanzolini (PEV).

Lutkenotyphlus brasiliensis (Lütken, 1852 "1851"). Vidensk. Medd. Dansk Naturhist.
Foren., 1851:52.
ORIGINAL NAME: *Siphonops brasiliensis.*
TYPE(S): Holotype: ZMUC 11 RO-237.
TYPE LOCALITY: Brasil; corrected to São Paulo, Brazil, by Taylor, 1973, Univ. Kansas
Sci. Bull., 50:226.
DISTRIBUTION: Known definitely only from the type.

Mimosiphonops Taylor, 1968. Caecilians of the World:592.
TYPE SPECIES: *Mimosiphonops vermiculatus* Taylor, 1968, by original designation.
DISTRIBUTION: As for the only species.
REVIEWERS: Werner C. A. Bokermann (WCAB); Ulisses Caramaschi (UC); Eduardo
Gudynas (EG); Paulo E. Vanzolini (PEV).

Mimosiphonops vermiculatus Taylor, 1968. Caecilians of the World:592.
TYPE(S): Holotype: KU 93271.
TYPE LOCALITY: "Teresópolis, [Estado Rio de Janeiro,] Brasil".
DISTRIBUTION: Known only from the type locality.

Praslinia Boulenger, 1909. Trans. Linn. Soc. London, (2)12:292.
TYPE SPECIES: *Praslinia cooperi* Boulenger, 1909, by monotypy.
DISTRIBUTION: As for the only species.

Praslinia cooperi Boulenger, 1909. Trans. Linn. Soc. London, (2)12:293.
TYPE(S): Syntypes: BM 1946.9.5.17–18 (formerly 1907.10.15.153–154); BM
1907.10.15.153 designated lectotype by Taylor, 1968, Caecilians of the World:
768.
TYPE LOCALITY: Praslin Island, Seychelles.
DISTRIBUTION: Mahé and Praslin Is., Seychelles, Indian Ocean.

Pseudosiphonops Taylor, 1968. Caecilians of the World:583.
TYPE SPECIES: *Pseudosiphonops ptychodermis* Taylor, 1968, by original designation.
DISTRIBUTION: As for the only species.
REVIEWERS: Werner C. A. Bokermann (WCAB); Ulisses Caramaschi (UC); Eduardo
Gudynas (EG); Paulo E. Vanzolini (PEV).

Pseudosiphonops ptychodermis Taylor, 1968. Caecilians of the World:584.
TYPE(S): Holotype: MNHNP 593.
TYPE LOCALITY: "Brasil".
DISTRIBUTION: Known only from the type.

Schistometopum Parker, 1941. Ann. Mag. Nat. Hist., (11)7:17.
TYPE SPECIES: *Dermophis gregorii* Boulenger, 1894, by original designation.
DISTRIBUTION: Kenya and Tanzania; islands in the Gulf of Guinea.
REVIEWER: Kim M. Howell (KMH); Raymond Laurent (RL).

Schistometopum brevirostre (Peters, 1874). Monatsber. Preuss. Akad. Wiss. Berlin, 1874:
617.
ORIGINAL NAME: *Siphonops brevirostre*.
TYPE(S): Holotype: formerly ZMB 4711; now lost.
TYPE LOCALITY: "Westküste Afrikas, aus Guinea"; stated by Gorham, 1962, Das
Tierreich, 78:16, as Rolas Island.
DISTRIBUTION: São Tomé Is., Gulf of Guinea.

Schistometopum ephele Taylor, 1964. Univ. Kansas Sci. Bull., 46:295.
TYPE(S): Holotype: MSNG 8773.
TYPE LOCALITY: "Agua Ize (400–700 m.), Ilha São Thomé, Gulf of Guinea".
DISTRIBUTION: São Tomé Is., Gulf of Guinea.

Schistometopum garzonheydti Taylor and Salvador, 1978. Salamandra, 14:60.
TYPE(S): Holotype: MNCN 1239.
TYPE LOCALITY: "Insel Fernando Poo", Gulf of Guinea.
DISTRIBUTION: Known only from the type.

Schistometopum gregorii (Boulenger, 1894). Proc. Zool. Soc. London, 1894:646.
ORIGINAL NAME: *Dermophis gregorii*.
TYPE(S): Holotype: BM 1946.9.5.53 (formerly 1893.11.21.89).
TYPE LOCALITY: Nagatana, Tana River, Kenya Colony [=Kenya].
DISTRIBUTION: Kenya; Tanzania.

Schistometopum thomense (Bocage, 1873). J. Sci. Math. Phys. Nat., Lisboa, 4:244.
ORIGINAL NAME: *Siphonops thomense*.
TYPE(S): Probably formerly in MBL; now lost.
TYPE LOCALITY: São Tomé island.
DISTRIBUTION: São Tomé and nearby islands, Gulf of Guinea.

Siphonops Wagler, 1830. Isis von Oken, 21:742.
TYPE SPECIES: *Caecilia annulata* Mikan, 1820.
DISTRIBUTION: South America east of the Andes, north of 30° S.
REVIEWERS: Werner C. A. Bokermann (WCAB); Ulisses Caramaschi (UC); Eduardo
Gudynas (EG); Paulo E. Vanzolini (PEV).

Siphonops annulatus (Mikan, 1820). Delect. Flor. Faun. Brasil.:pl. 11.
ORIGINAL NAME: *Caecilia annulata.*
TYPE(S): Not known to exist; MNHNP 15 was suggested by Dunn, 1942, Bull. Mus.
Comp. Zool., 91:480, but this was doubted by Taylor, 1968, Caecilians of the
World:557.
TYPE LOCALITY: "Sebastianopolis [=Rio de Janeiro]", Brazil.
DISTRIBUTION: Widely distributed from northern Colombia, Venezuela, and Guyana
to Paraguay and northern Argentina; apparently not in the Pacific drainage.

Siphonops confusionis Taylor, 1968. Caecilians of the World:560.
TYPE(S): Holotype: MCZ 2482.
TYPE LOCALITY: "Petrópolis, [Rio de Janeiro,] Brasil".
DISTRIBUTION: Southern Brazil.

Siphonops hardyi Boulenger, 1888. Ann. Mag. Nat. Hist., (6)1:189.
TYPE(S): Holotype: BM 1947.2.13.87 (formerly 1887.12.29.39).
TYPE LOCALITY: "Porto Real, province of Rio de Janeiro", Brazil.
DISTRIBUTION: Southeastern Brazil.

Siphonops insulanus Ihering, 1911. Rev. Mus. Paulista, São Paulo, 8:109.
TYPE(S): Syntypes: MZUSP 945, 946, 2119, 2120.
TYPE LOCALITY: Ilha Vitoria and Ilha de São Sebastião [Brazil].
DISTRIBUTION: Known only from the type localities.

Siphonops leucoderus Taylor, 1968. Caecilians of the World:573.
TYPE(S): Holotype: NHMW 9163.
TYPE LOCALITY: "'Bahia, Brasil' . . . presumably . . . the city Baía or Bahia, now
named Salvador on recent maps, in the state of Bahia, eastern Brasil".
DISTRIBUTION: Known definitely only from the type locality.

Siphonops paulensis Boettger, 1892. Kat. Batr. Samml. Mus. Senckenb. Naturforsch.
Ges.:62.
TYPE(S): Syntypes: SMF 21, 22, 24, NHMB 1078 (formerly SMF 21.2.1b) (the fifth
syntype apparently lost); SMF 21 designated lectotype by Mertens, 1967,
Senckenb. Biol., 48:37.
TYPE LOCALITY: São Paulo, [Estado de São Paulo,] Brasil.
DISTRIBUTION: Eastern and southeastern Brazil, northern Argentina, Paraguay, and
Bolivia.

FAMILY: **Ichthyophiidae** Taylor, 1968.
CITATION: Caecilians of the World:46.
DISTRIBUTION: India to southern China, Thailand, and the Malayan Archipelago.
COMMENT: Nussbaum, 1979, Occas. Pap. Mus. Zool. Univ. Michigan, 682:27, considered
the Ichthyophiidae transitional between the Rhinatrematidae and other caecilian
families; the Ichthyophiinae and Uraeotyphlinae were included by Nussbaum in the
Ichthyophiidae on the basis of patristic similarity, but he suggested that the
Uraeotyphlinae was the sister-group of the higher caecilians (Scolecomorphidae,
Caeciliidae, and Typhlonectidae) and that the Ichthyophiinae was the sister-taxon of
the Uraeotyphlinae + higher caecilians.
CONTRIBUTOR: Marvalee H. Wake (MHW).
REVIEWERS: Angel Alcala (AA) (Philippines); Walter C. Brown (WCB) (Philippines); J. C.
Daniel (JCD) (India and Sri Lanka); William E. Duellman (WED); Sushil Dutta (SD)

(India and Sri Lanka); Marinus S. Hoogmoed (MSH); Masafumi Matsui (MM); Ronald A. Nussbaum (RAN).

SUBFAMILY: **Ichthyophiinae** Taylor, 1968.
  CITATION: Caecilians of the World:46.
  DISTRIBUTION: India, southeast Asia, Philippines, Indo-Malaysian Archipelago.
  COMMENT: See comment under Ichthyophiidae.

Caudacaecilia Taylor, 1968. Caecilians of the World:165.
  TYPE SPECIES: *Ichthyophis nigroflavus* Taylor, 1960, by original designation.
  DISTRIBUTION: Malaya, Sumatra, Borneo, and the Philippines.

  Caudacaecilia asplenia (Taylor, 1965). Univ. Kansas Sci. Bull., 46:278.
    ORIGINAL NAME: *Ichthyophis asplenius.*
    TYPE(S): Holotype: RMNH 6912B.
    TYPE LOCALITY: "Boven Mahakkam, Borneo".
    DISTRIBUTION: Mahakkam River system and Sarawak, Borneo; Malaya and southern
      Thailand.

  Caudacaecilia larutensis (Taylor, 1960). Univ. Kansas Sci. Bull., 40:44.
    ORIGINAL NAME: *Ichthyophis larutensis.*
    TYPE(S): Holotype: BM 98.9.22.208.
    TYPE LOCALITY: "Larut Hills (near Maxwell's Bungalow), Perak, Malaya, [Malaysia,]
      elevation 3,380 ft."
    DISTRIBUTION: Known only from the type locality.

  Caudacaecilia nigroflava (Taylor, 1960). Univ. Kansas Sci. Bull., 40:101.
    ORIGINAL NAME: *Ichthyophis nigroflavus.*
    TYPE(S): Holotype: USNM 129462.
    TYPE LOCALITY: "'within 20 miles of Kuala Lumpur,' Selangor, Malaya", Malaysia.
    DISTRIBUTION: Malaya, Malaysia.

  Caudacaecilia paucidentula (Taylor, 1960). Univ. Kansas Sci. Bull., 40:49.
    ORIGINAL NAME: *Ichthyophis paucidentula.*
    TYPE(S): Holotype: USNM 70671.
    TYPE LOCALITY: "Kapahieng [sometimes spelled Kepahiang], Sumatra", Indonesia.
    DISTRIBUTION: Sumatra.

  Caudacaecilia weberi (Taylor, 1920). Philippine J. Sci., 16:227.
    ORIGINAL NAME: *Ichthyophis weberi.*
    TYPE(S): Philippine Bureau of Science (destroyed in World War II); CAS-SU 21758
      designated neotype by Taylor, 1968, Caecilians of the World:181.
    TYPE LOCALITY: Malatgan River, Palawan [Philippines]; neotype is from "Iwahig,
      Palawan", Philippines (near the original type locality).
    DISTRIBUTION: Palawan, Philippines.

Ichthyophis Fitzinger, 1826. Neue Classif. Rept.:36.
  TYPE SPECIES: *Ichthyophis Hasselti* Fitzinger, 1826 (*nomen nudum*) (=*Coecilia hypocyanea*
    F. Boie, 1827).
  DISTRIBUTION: Southeastern Asia, southern Philippines, and the western part of the
    Indo-Australian Archipelago.

  Ichthyophis acuminatus Taylor, 1960. Univ. Kansas Sci. Bull., 40:98.
    TYPE(S): Holotype: AMNH 20875.
    TYPE LOCALITY: "Me Wang Valley, [northern] Thailand".
    DISTRIBUTION: Known only from the vicinity of the type locality.

  Ichthyophis atricollaris Taylor, 1965. Univ. Kansas Sci. Bull., 46:267.
    TYPE(S): Holotype: RMNH 10684.
    TYPE LOCALITY: "Long Bloee, Boven Mahakkam, Borneo".
    DISTRIBUTION: Known only from the vicinity of the type locality.

Ichthyophis bannanicus Yang, 1984. Acta Herpetol. Sinica, 3(2):73–75.
ORIGINAL NAME: *Ichthyophis bannanica.*
TYPE(S): Holotype: KIZ 74001.
TYPE LOCALITY: Mengla County, Xishuangbanna, altitude 600 m, Yunnan, China.
DISTRIBUTION: Known only from the type locality.
COMMENT: Closely related to *Ichthyophis glutinosus,* according to the original description.
REVIEWERS: Shuqin Hu (SH); Ermi Zhao (EZ).

Ichthyophis beddomei Peters, 1879. Monatsber. Preuss. Akad. Wiss. Berlin, 1879:932.
TYPE(S): Holotype: ZMB 5545; lost.
TYPE LOCALITY: "Nilgherrie Hills, [State of Tamil Nadu,] India".
DISTRIBUTION: Southern India and near Darjeeling near Sikkim in northern India.

Ichthyophis bernisi Salvador, 1975. Bonn. Zool. Beitr., 4:367.
TYPE(S): Holotype: MNCN 1240.
TYPE LOCALITY: "Isla de Java", Indonesia.
DISTRIBUTION: Known only from the type.

Ichthyophis biangularis Taylor, 1965. Univ. Kansas Sci. Bull., 46:272.
TYPE(S): Holotype: BM 72.2.19.59A.
TYPE LOCALITY: "Matang (Mt.), Sarawak, Borneo", Malaysia.
DISTRIBUTION: Known only from the type locality.

Ichthyophis billitonensis Taylor, 1965. Univ. Kansas Sci. Bull., 46:294.
TYPE(S): Holotype: ZMA 5209.
TYPE LOCALITY: "Billiton Island [=Belitung I., southeast of Sumatra] Indo-Australian Archipelago", Indonesia.
DISTRIBUTION: Known only from the type locality.

Ichthyophis bombayensis Taylor, 1960. Univ. Kansas Sci. Bull., 40:67.
TYPE(S): Holotype: BM 1888.6.11.1.
TYPE LOCALITY: "Waghii Surrat, Bombay, India" (=Waghii, Surat Dangs, Guajarat, India).
DISTRIBUTION: Known only from the type locality.

Ichthyophis dulitensis Taylor, 1960. Univ. Kansas Sci. Bull., 40:58.
TYPE(S): Holotype: BM 92.6.3.23.
TYPE LOCALITY: "Mount Dulit, Sarawak, [Malaysia,] Borneo; elevation above 2000 feet".
DISTRIBUTION: Known only from the vicinity of the type locality.

Ichthyophis elongatus Taylor, 1965. Univ. Kansas Sci. Bull., 46:270.
TYPE(S): Holotype: NHMW 9094.
TYPE LOCALITY: "Padang, Sumatra", Indonesia.
DISTRIBUTION: Sumatra.

Ichthyophis glandulosus Taylor, 1922. Philippine J. Sci., 21:516.
TYPE(S): Holotype: CAS 60073 (formerly EHT 1595A).
TYPE LOCALITY: Abung Abung Basilan, P.I. [=Abung Abung, Basilan Island, Philippine Islands].
DISTRIBUTION: Known only from Basilan and Mindanao Is., Philippines.
COMMENT: Inger, 1954, Fieldiana: Zool., 33:208, regarded this form to be probably conspecific with *Ichthyophis monochrous.*

Ichthyophis glutinosus (Linnaeus, 1758). Syst. Nat., Ed. 10, 1:229.
ORIGINAL NAME: *Caecilia glutinosus.*
TYPE(S): Holotype: NHRM.
TYPE LOCALITY: 'Habitat in Indiis'.
DISTRIBUTION: Sri Lanka.

COMMENT: Synonymy includes *Ichthyophis forcarti* Taylor, 1965, and *Ichthyophis taprobanicensis* Taylor, 1969, according to Nussbaum and Gans, 1983 "1980", Spolia Zeylan., 35:144.

Ichthyophis humphreyi Taylor, 1973. Univ. Kansas Sci. Bull., 50:190.
TYPE(S): Holotype: formerly EHT-HMS 8378 (now FMNH).
TYPE LOCALITY: Unknown.
DISTRIBUTION: Unknown.

Ichthyophis hypocyaneus (Boie, 1827). Isis von Oken, 1827:565.
ORIGINAL NAME: *Coecilia hypocyanea*.
TYPE(S): Holotype: RMNH 2408.
TYPE LOCALITY: Wet and marshy places on the northern coast of Bantam [Province], western Java [Indonesia].
DISTRIBUTION: Java.
COMMENT: The authorship of new names published by F. Boie (1827) must be attributed to him, not to the authorities that he cited in several cases, because they (H. Boie, H. Kuhl) were not responsible for the descriptions. Thus, F. Boie, using the label and manuscript names of H. Boie and H. Kuhl inadvertently became the author under the International Code of Zoological Nomenclature (1985) (MSH).

Ichthyophis javanicus Taylor, 1960. Univ. Kansas Sci. Bull., 40:77.
TYPE(S): Holotype: BM 80.5.7.3.
TYPE LOCALITY: "Java", Indonesia.
DISTRIBUTION: Known only from the type.

Ichthyophis kohtaoensis Taylor, 1960. Univ. Kansas Sci. Bull., 40:110.
TYPE(S): Holotype: USNM 72293.
TYPE LOCALITY: "Koh Tao Island, west side, Gulf of Siam", Thailand.
DISTRIBUTION: Koh Tao I. and mainland peninsular Thailand.

Ichthyophis laosensis Taylor, 1969. Univ. Kansas Sci. Bull., 48:292.
TYPE(S): Holotype: MNHNP 1928-95.
TYPE LOCALITY: "Haut Laos" (=Upper Laos).
DISTRIBUTION: Known only from the type.

Ichthyophis malabarensis Taylor, 1960. Univ. Kansas Sci. Bull., 40:80.
TYPE(S): Holotype: BM 94.3.15.3.
TYPE LOCALITY: "Maduvangard, Travancore, [state of Kerala,]. India".
DISTRIBUTION: Known only from the type.

Ichthyophis mindanaoensis Taylor, 1960. Univ. Kansas Sci. Bull., 40:69–74.
TYPE(S): Holotype: FMNH 50958.
TYPE LOCALITY: "Todaya, Mt. Apo, Davao [Province], Mindanao, P[hilippine]. I[slands]., 2800 feet elevation".
DISTRIBUTION: Mindanao, Philippines.

Ichthyophis monochrous (Bleeker, 1858). Natuurkd. Tjidschr. Nederl. Ind., 16:188.
ORIGINAL NAME: *Epicrium monochroum*.
TYPE(S): Holotype: BM 63.12.4.5.
TYPE LOCALITY: Sinkawang, Borneo [Indonesia].
DISTRIBUTION: Western Borneo.
COMMENT: The name *Ichthyophis monochrous* has been misapplied frequently to other species according to Taylor, 1968, Caecilians of the World:115. See comment under *Ichthyophis glandulosus*.

Ichthyophis orthoplicatus Taylor, 1965. Univ. Kansas Sci. Bull., 46:290.
TYPE(S): Holotype: ZSI 17010.
TYPE LOCALITY: "Ceylon"; corrected to "Pattipola, Central Province, Ceylon [=Sri Lanka]" by Taylor, 1968, Caecilians of the World:115.
DISTRIBUTION: Sri Lanka.
COMMENT: Taylor, 1969, Univ. Kansas Sci. Bull., 48:292, presumed that this was a lowland species. Reviewed by Nussbaum and Gans, 1983 "1980", Spolia Zeylan., 35:149–151.

Ichthyophis paucisulcus Taylor, 1960. Univ. Kansas Sci. Bull., 40:103.
TYPE(S): Holotype: USNM 103565.
TYPE LOCALITY: "Siantar [also known as Pematangsiantar], Sumatra", Indonesia.
DISTRIBUTION: Northern highlands of Sumatra.

Ichthyophis peninsularis Taylor, 1960. Univ. Kansas Sci. Bull., 40:61.
TYPE(S): Holotype: BM 82.12.12.6.
TYPE LOCALITY: "Malabar, [state of Kerala,] India".
DISTRIBUTION: Known only from the vicinity of the type locality (Kerala, India) and Madras (Tamil Nadu, India).

Ichthyophis pseudangularis Taylor, 1968. Caecilians of the World:127.
TYPE(S): Holotype: NHMB 4412.
TYPE LOCALITY: "Ceylon" (=Sri Lanka).
DISTRIBUTION: Sri Lanka.
COMMENT: Reviewed by Nussbaum and Gans, 1983 "1980", Spolia Zeylan., 35:148–149.

Ichthyophis sikkimensis Taylor, 1960. Univ. Kansas Sci. Bull., 40:91–94.
TYPE(S): Holotype: CAS 64216.
TYPE LOCALITY: "Darjeeling, [West Bengal,] India".
DISTRIBUTION: Sikkim and adjacent India.

Ichthyophis singaporensis Taylor, 1960. Univ. Kansas Sci. Bull., 40:55.
TYPE(S): Holotype: BM 1959.1.2.43.
TYPE LOCALITY: "Singapore".
DISTRIBUTION: Southern Malayan Peninsula and Singapore.

Ichthyophis subterrestris Taylor, 1960. Univ. Kansas Sci. Bull., 40:65.
TYPE(S): Holotype: FMNH 73927.
TYPE LOCALITY: "Travancore, Cochin [state of Kerala], plains, India".
DISTRIBUTION: Known only from the region of the type locality.

Ichthyophis sumatranus Taylor, 1960. Univ. Kansas Sci. Bull., 40:95.
TYPE(S): Holotype: USNM 70672.
TYPE LOCALITY: "Kapahiang [=Kepahiang], Sumatra", Indonesia.
DISTRIBUTION: Sumatra.

Ichthyophis supachaii Taylor, 1960. Univ. Kansas Sci. Bull., 40:107.
TYPE(S): Holotype: FMNH 189246 (formerly EHT-HMS 35498).
TYPE LOCALITY: "10 km west Nakon Si Thamarrat [=Nakhon Si Thammarat], Nakon Si Thamarrat [=Nakhon Si Thammarat] province", Thailand.
DISTRIBUTION: Nakhon Si Thammarat and Trang provinces, Thailand.

Ichthyophis tricolor Annandale, 1909. Rec. Indian Mus., 3:286.
ORIGINAL NAME: *Ichthyophis glutinosus tricolor.*
TYPE(S): Not known to exist; possibly in the ZSI.
TYPE LOCALITY: Maddathorai, India.
DISTRIBUTION: Known from a few localities in southeastern India.

Ichthyophis youngorum Taylor, 1960. Univ. Kansas Sci. Bull., 40:84.
   TYPE(S): Holotype: FMNH 189250 (formerly EHT-HMS 35946).
   TYPE LOCALITY: "Doi Suthep (Sutep), Chiang Mai, Thailand [now within the
      grounds of the Summer Palace], at approximately 1200 m in elevation".
   DISTRIBUTION: Known only from the type locality.

SUBFAMILY: **Uraeotyphlinae** Nussbaum, 1979.
   CITATION: Occas. Pap. Mus. Zool. Univ. Michigan, 687:14.
   DISTRIBUTION: India.
   COMMENT: See comment under Ichthyophiidae.

Uraeotyphlus Peters, 1879. Monatsber. Preuss. Akad. Wiss. Berlin, 1879:930.
   TYPE SPECIES: *Coecilia oxyura* Duméril and Bibron, 1841.
   DISTRIBUTION: Southern peninsular India.
   COMMENT: Transferred from the Caeciliidae to the Ichthyophiidae by Nussbaum,
      1979, Occas. Pap. Mus. Zool. Univ. Michigan, 687:1–20.

Uraeotyphlus malabaricus (Beddome, 1870). Madras Month. J. Med. Sci., 2:175.
   ORIGINAL NAME: *Cecilia malabarica*.
   TYPE(S): Holotype: BM 1946.9.5.16 (formerly 1874.4.29.181).
   TYPE LOCALITY: Malabar [state of Kerala, India].
   DISTRIBUTION: Known only from the type locality.

Uraeotyphlus menoni Annandale, 1913. Rec. Indian Mus., 9:301.
   TYPE(S): Holotype: ZSI 16707.
   TYPE LOCALITY: Trichur, Cochin [state of Kerala, India].
   DISTRIBUTION: Known from the type locality and Kottayam (Kerala, India).

Uraeotyphlus narayani Seshachar, 1939. Proc. Indian Acad. Sci., (B)9:224–228.
   TYPE(S): Possibly a specimen in CCB, according to Taylor, 1968, Caecilians of the
      World:703; a "cotype" is BM 1946.9.5.55.
   TYPE LOCALITY: Kannan, Travancore [state of Kerala, India].
   DISTRIBUTION: Known only from the type locality.

Uraeotyphlus oxyurus (Duméril and Bibron, 1841). Erp. Gén., 8:280.
   ORIGINAL NAME: *Caecilia oxyura*.
   TYPE(S): Syntypes: MNHNP 4271 (2 specimens), RMNH 2414.
   TYPE LOCALITY: "Côte du Malabar", Kerala, India.
   DISTRIBUTION: Known only from the type locality.

FAMILY: **Rhinatrematidae** Nussbaum, 1977.
   CITATION: Occas. Pap. Mus. Zool. Univ. Michigan, 682:3.
   DISTRIBUTION: Northern South America.
   COMMENT: Considered the sister-taxon of all other caecilians by Nussbaum, 1979, Occas.
      Pap. Mus. Zool. Univ. Michigan, 687.
   CONTRIBUTOR: Marvalee H. Wake (MHW).
   REVIEWERS: William E. Duellman (WED); Marinus S. Hoogmoed (MSH); Ronald A.
      Nussbaum (RAN); Norman J. Scott, Jr. (NJS).

Epicrionops Boulenger, 1883. Ann. Mag. Nat. Hist., (5)11:202.
   TYPE SPECIES: *Epicrionops bicolor* Boulenger, 1883, by monotypy.
   DISTRIBUTION: Colombia, Ecuador, Peru, and Venezuela.

Epicrionops bicolor Boulenger, 1883. Ann. Mag. Nat. Hist., (5)11:202.
   TYPE(S): Holotype: BM 1946.9.5.66 (formerly 78.1.25.48).
   TYPE LOCALITY: "Intac, [3900 ft. elev.,] Ecuador".
   DISTRIBUTION: Pacific and Amazonian slopes of the Andes in Ecuador and Peru.

Epicrionops columbianus (Rendahl and Vestergren, 1938). Ark. Zool., 31A(3):1-5.
ORIGINAL NAME: *Rhinatrema columbianus.*
TYPE(S): Holotype: NHRM 19.
TYPE LOCALITY: El Tambo, [Cauca Province,] Colombia.
DISTRIBUTION: Known only from the type.

Epicrionops lativittatus Taylor, 1968. Caecilians of the World:199.
TYPE(S): Holotype: AMNH 46205.
TYPE LOCALITY: "eastern Peru".
DISTRIBUTION: Known only from the type.

Epicrionops marmoratus Taylor, 1968. Caecilians of the World:205.
TYPE(S): Holotype: BM 1956.1.15.87.
TYPE LOCALITY: "Santo Domingo de los Colorados, west Ecuador".
DISTRIBUTION: Known only from the type locality and from near Mindo,
    Pichincha, Ecuador.

Epicrionops niger (Dunn, 1942). Bull. Mus. Comp. Zool., 91:458-459.
ORIGINAL NAME: *Rhinatrema nigrum.*
TYPE(S): Holotype: AMNH (now lost); MBUCV 5360 designated neotype by Taylor,
    1968, Caecilians of the World:209.
TYPE LOCALITY: "Arundabara, British Guiana [=Guyana], elevation 2200 feet";
    locality of neotype is "El Dorado, Bolívar, Venezuela".
DISTRIBUTION: Guyana to northeastern Venezuela.
COMMENT: Seen incorrectly as *Epicrionops nigrus.*

Epicrionops parkeri (Dunn, 1942). Bull. Mus. Comp. Zool., 91:458.
ORIGINAL NAME: *Rhinatrema parkeri.*
TYPE(S): Holotype: BM 1946.9.5.61 (formerly 97.11.12.23).
TYPE LOCALITY: "Medellin, [Antioquia,] Colombia".
DISTRIBUTION: Known only from the type.

Epicrionops peruvianus (Boulenger, 1902). Ann. Mag. Nat. Hist., (7)10:153.
ORIGINAL NAME: *Rhinatrema peruvianum.*
TYPE(S): Holotype: BM 1946.9.6.63 (formerly 1902.5.29.207).
TYPE LOCALITY: "Marcapata Valley, E. Peru".
DISTRIBUTION: Known only from the type

Epicrionops petersi Taylor, 1968. Caecilians of the World:224.
TYPE(S): Holotype: James A. Peters 7099 (now USNM?).
TYPE LOCALITY: "Agua Rica between Limón and Gualaceo, Morona-Santiago
    Province, Ecuador".
DISTRIBUTION: Ecuador and Peru.

Rhinatrema Duméril and Bibron, 1841. Erp. Gén., 8:288.
TYPE SPECIES: *Caecilia bivittata* Cuvier, 1829 (*nomen nudum*) (=*Caecilia bivittatum* Guérin-
    Méneville, 1829).
DISTRIBUTION: As for the single species.
REVIEWERS: Werner C. A. Bokermann (WCAB); Ulisses Caramaschi (UC); Eduardo
    Gudynas (EG); Paulo E. Vanzolini (PEV).

Rhinatrema bivittatum (Guérin-Méneville, 1829). Icon Règn. Anim., 3:pl. 25.
ORIGINAL NAME: *Caecilia bivittatum.*
TYPE(S): Holotype: MNHNP 585.
TYPE LOCALITY: Guyane [=Cayenne], French Guiana
DISTRIBUTION: French Guiana, Surinam, Guyana, and Brazil.
COMMENT: Biology and nomenclature discussed by Nussbaum and Hoogmoed,
    1979, Zool. Meded., Leiden, 54:219-221.

FAMILY: **Scolecomorphidae** Taylor, 1969.
CITATION: Univ. Kansas Sci. Bull., 38:297.
DISTRIBUTION: Tropical subsaharan Africa.
COMMENT: According to Nussbaum, 1979, Occ Pap. Mus. Zool. Univ. Michigan, 687, the
    Scolecomorphidae is the sister-taxon of the Caeciliidae + Typhlonectidae.
CONTRIBUTOR: Marvalee H. Wake (MHW).
REVIEWERS: William E. Duellman (WED); Marinus S. Hoogmoed (MSH); Kim M. Howell
    (KMH) (East Africa); Raymond Laurent (RL); Ronald A. Nussbaum (RAN).

Scolecomorphus Boulenger, 1883. Ann. Mag. Nat. Hist., (5)11:48.
    TYPE SPECIES: *Scolecomorphus kirkii* Boulenger, 1883, by monotypy.
    DISTRIBUTION: Tropical subsaharan Africa.

Scolecomorphus attenuatus Barbour and Loveridge, 1928. Mem. Mus. Comp. Zool., 50:
    181.
    TYPE(S): Holotype: MCZ 12294 (not 12194 as reported in the original description).
    TYPE LOCALITY: "Nyingwa, Uluguru Mountains, [Morogoro Division,] Tanganyika
        Territory [=Tanzania]".
    DISTRIBUTION: Known only from the type locality.

Scolecomorphus bornmuelleri (Werner, 1899). Verh. Zool. Bot. Ges. Wien, 49:144.
    ORIGINAL NAME: *Herpele bornmuelleri.*
    TYPE(S): Holotype: NHMW 14859.
    TYPE LOCALITY: Victoria [now Limbé], Cameroon.
    DISTRIBUTION: Known only from the type.

Scolecomorphus convexus Taylor, 1968. Caecilians of the World:637.
    TYPE(S): Holotype: ZMH 1358.
    TYPE LOCALITY: "Uhehe, Deutsch-Ost-Afrikas, . . . a district in south central
        Tanganyika [=Tanzania] in the Southern Highlands, south of the Ruahi
        [=Ruaha] River".
    DISTRIBUTION: Known only from the type locality.

Scolecomorphus kirkii Boulenger, 1883. Ann. Mag. Nat. Hist., (5)11:48.
    TYPE(S): Holotype: BM 1946.9.5.5.58 (formerly 82.1.6.23).
    TYPE LOCALITY: Not stated; "presumably . . . the region of Lake Tanganyika",
        according to Taylor, 1968, Caecilians of the World:643.
    DISTRIBUTION: Known only from southern Malawi and Ubena highlands in
        Tanzania.

Scolecomorphus lamottei Nussbaum, 1981. Copeia, 1981:265.
    TYPE(S): Holotype: MNHNP 1979-7441.
    TYPE LOCALITY: "Mont Oku, 2300 m, Cameroon".
    DISTRIBUTION: Known only from the type locality.

Scolecomorphus uluguruensis Barbour and Loveridge, 1928. Mem. Mus. Comp. Zool.,
    50:180.
    TYPE(S): Holotype: MCZ 12193.
    TYPE LOCALITY: "Nyingwa, Uluguru Mountains, [Morogoro Division,] Tanganyika
        Territory [=Tanzania]".
    DISTRIBUTION: Uluguru Mountains of Tanzania.

Scolecomorphus vittatus (Boulenger, 1895). Proc. Zool. Soc. London, 1895:412.
    ORIGINAL NAME: *Bdellophis vittatus.*
    TYPE(S): Holotype: BM 1946.9.5.59 (formerly 1895.5.29.6).
    TYPE LOCALITY: "Usambara, [Tanga Division,] German East Africa" (=Tanzania).
    DISTRIBUTION: Usambara, Uluguru, and North Pare mountains of Tanzania.

FAMILY: **Typhlonectidae** Taylor, 1968.
CITATION: Caecilians of the World:231.
DISTRIBUTION: South America.
COMMENT: Taylor, 1969, Univ. Kansas Sci. Bull., 48:585–687, suggested that the Typhlonectidae was derived from an ancestor morphologically similar to the Ichthyophiidae. Wake, 1977, J. Herpetol., 11:379–386, suggested that the Typhlonectidae was derived from a viviparous group of the Caeciliidae, a contention not refuted by Nussbaum, 1979, Occas. Pap. Mus. Zool. Univ. Michigan, 687.
CONTRIBUTOR: Marvalee H. Wake (MHW).
REVIEWERS: Werner C. A. Bokermann (WCAB); Ulisses Caramaschi (UC); William E. Duellman (WED); Eduardo Gudynas (EG); Marinus S. Hoogmoed (MSH); Ronald A. Nussbaum (RAN); Norman J. Scott, Jr. (NJS); Paulo E. Vanzolini (PEV).

Chthonerpeton Peters, 1879. Monatsber. Preuss. Akad. Wiss. Berlin, 1879:930.
TYPE SPECIES: *Siphonops indistinctus* Reinhardt and Lütken, 1861, by monotypy.
DISTRIBUTION: Southern Brazil, Uruguay, and adjacent Argentina.

Chthonerpeton braestrupi Taylor, 1968. Caecilians of the World:283.
TYPE(S): Holotype: ZMUC 12 RO-234 (formerly a cotype of *Chthonerpeton indistinctum*).
TYPE LOCALITY: "Brasil (no other locality data)".
DISTRIBUTION: Southeastern Brazil.

Chthonerpeton corrugatum Taylor, 1968. Caecilians of the World:289.
TYPE(S): Holotype: ZMH 1930.
TYPE LOCALITY: Unknown; see original description for discussion.
DISTRIBUTION: Unknown.
COMMENT: This species is almost certainly South American. See remarks by Taylor, 1968, Caecilians of the World:292.

Chthonerpeton erugatum Taylor, 1968. Caecilians of the World:295.
TYPE(S): Holotype: ZMUC 20 RO-238.
TYPE LOCALITY: Unknown.
DISTRIBUTION: Unknown.

Chthonerpeton hellmichi Taylor, 1968. Caecilians of the World:305.
TYPE(S): Holotype: ZSM 1/1964.
TYPE LOCALITY: "Punta Lara", on the Río de La Plata coast, Buenos Aires Province, Argentina.
DISTRIBUTION: Known only from the type locality.

Chthonerpeton indistinctum (Reinhardt and Lütken, 1861). Vidensk. Medd. Dansk Naturhist. Foren., 1861:202.
ORIGINAL NAME: *Siphonops indistinctus*.
TYPE(S): ZMUC RO-235 designated lectotype by Taylor, 1968, Caecilians of the World:299; ZUMC RO-234, the former cotype, is now the holotype of *Chthonerpeton braestrupi*.
TYPE LOCALITY: "Buenos Ayres", Argentina.
DISTRIBUTION: East-central Argentina to southern Brazil and Uruguay.

Chthonerpeton viviparum Parker and Wettstein, 1929. Ann. Mag. Nat. Hist., (10)4:594.
TYPE(S): Holotype: BM 1947.2.13.84 (formerly 1907.8.28.1).
TYPE LOCALITY: Santa Catarina, Brazil.
DISTRIBUTION: Santa Catarina, Brazil.

Nectocaecilia Taylor, 1968. Caecilians of the World:268.
TYPE SPECIES: *Chthonerpeton petersii* Boulenger, 1882, by original designation.
DISTRIBUTION: Colombia and Venezuela to Buenos Aires, Argentina.

Nectocaecilia cooperi Taylor, 1970. Univ. Kansas Sci. Bull., 48:845.
TYPE(S): Holotype: AMNH 82255.
TYPE LOCALITY: "Río Magdalena at Barranquilla, [Departamento Atlantico,] Colombia".
DISTRIBUTION: Known only from the type.

Nectocaecilia fasciata Taylor, 1968. Caecilians of the World:269.
TYPE(S): Holotype: MSNT 2817.
TYPE LOCALITY: "Buenos Aires (state?)", Argentina.
DISTRIBUTION: Known only from the type.

Nectocaecilia haydee (Roze, 1963). Acta Biol. Venezuelica, 3:279–282.
ORIGINAL NAME: *Chthonerpeton haydee.*
TYPE(S): Holotype: MBUCV 5356.
TYPE LOCALITY: "Encontrados, Estado Zulia, Venezuela, en un región pantanosa".
DISTRIBUTION: Caribbean drainage of Venezuela.

Nectocaecilia ladigesi Taylor, 1968. Caecilians of the World:273.
TYPE(S): Holotype: ZMH 1925/245.
TYPE LOCALITY: "Bocco do Moju" (=Rio Moju, near mouth), Pará, Brazil.
DISTRIBUTION: Drainage of the Tocantins River, Brazil, and Utinga, Belém, Brazil.

Nectocaecilia petersii (Boulenger, 1882). Cat. Batr. Grad. Coll. Brit. Mus.:104.
ORIGINAL NAME: *Chthonerpeton petersii.*
TYPE(S): Holotype: BM 1946.9.5.68 (formerly 61.9.2.6).
TYPE LOCALITY: "Upper Amazon".
DISTRIBUTION: Known only from the type.

Potomotyphlus Taylor, 1968. Caecilians of the World:256.
TYPE SPECIES: *Caecilia kaupii* Berthold, 1859, by original designation.
DISTRIBUTION: Northern South America.
COMMENT: The unjustified (but correct Latin) emendation to *Potamotyphlus* has sometimes been used.

Potomotyphlus kaupii (Berthold, 1859). Nachr. Ges. Wiss. Göttingen, 1859:181.
ORIGINAL NAME: *Caecilia kaupii.*
TYPE(S): Possibly in ZFMK.
TYPE LOCALITY: "Angostura", Ciudad Bolívar, Venezuela.
DISTRIBUTION: Amazon and Orinoco drainage systems of South America.

Potomotyphlus melanochrus Taylor, 1968. Caecilians of the World:263.
TYPE(S): Holotype: NHMW 9147.
TYPE LOCALITY: "Brasil".
DISTRIBUTION: Known only from the type.

Typhlonectes Peters, 1879. Monatsber. Preuss. Akad. Wiss. Berlin, 1879:930.
TYPE SPECIES: *Caecilia compressicauda* Duméril and Bibron, 1841, by subsequent designation of Dunn, 1942, Bull. Mus. Comp. Zool., 91:532.
DISTRIBUTION: Northern South America.

Typhlonectes anguillaformis Taylor, 1968. Caecilians of the World:235.
TYPE(S): Holotype: AMNH 56252.
TYPE LOCALITY: Unknown.
DISTRIBUTION: Unknown.

Typlnonectes compressicauda (Duméril and Bibron, 1841). Erp. Gén., 8:278.
ORIGINAL NAME: *Caecilia compressicauda.*
TYPE(S): Not designated; MNHNP 4269 catalogued as holotype.
TYPE LOCALITY: "Cayenne", French Guiana.
DISTRIBUTION: Guyana and French Guiana to Amazon drainage of Peru and Brazil.

Typhlonectes eiselti Taylor, 1968. Caecilians of the World:244.
  TYPE(S): Holotype: NHMW 9144.
  TYPE LOCALITY: "South America".
  DISTRIBUTION: Known only from the type.

Typhlonectes natans (Fischer, 1879). *In* Peters, Monatsber. Preuss. Akad. Wiss. Berlin, 1879:941.
  ORIGINAL NAME: *Caecilia natans.*
  TYPE(S): Syntypes: ZMB (2 specimens).
  TYPE LOCALITY: Río Cauca, Colombia.
  DISTRIBUTION: Drainage system of the Magdalena and Cauca rivers in Colombia.

Typhlonectes obesus Taylor, 1968. Caecilians of the World:253.
  TYPE(S): Holotype: AMNH 71434.
  TYPE LOCALITY: "Maués (at the junction of the Camiña and the Maués Guaçu rivers, Amazonas, Brasil)"; data with specimen are "Brasil: Amazonas; Maués" (PEV).
  DISTRIBUTION: Region of the type locality, including Rio Ipixuna, Tapauá, and from Belém, Pará, Brazil.

Typhlonectes venezuelensis Fuhrmann, 1914. Mém. Soc. Neuchâtel. Sci. Nat., 5:120.
  ORIGINAL NAME: *Thyphlonectes compressicauda venezuelense.*
  TYPE(S): ZMB.
  TYPE LOCALITY: Caracas, [Distrito Federal,] Venezuela.
  DISTRIBUTION: Northern Venezuela.

Appendix I. Literature Abbreviations

Both serial and book title abbreviations used in *Amphibian Species of the World* are listed alphabetically. Journal abbreviations follow the spirit of BIOSIS abbreviations, except that geographic place names are generally spelled out. Book abbreviations follow tradition except where these traditional abbreviations were found to be misleading or overly short.

Abbild. Amph.—Schlegel, H. 1837. Abbildungen neuer oder unvollständig bekannter Amphibien, nach der Natur oder dem Leben entworfen, herausgegeben und mit einem erläuternden Texte begleitet. Part 1. Arnz & Co., Düsseldorf. 31 pp.

Abbild. Naturgesch. Brasil.—Wied-Neuwied, M. A. P., Prinz von. 1822–1831. Abbildungen zur Naturgeschichte Brasiliens. Part 5 (1824). Landes-Industrie-Comptoir, Weimar. [See Smith and Smith, 1973, Synops. Herpetofauna Mexico, 2: 281, for publication data of livraisons.]

Abh. Bayer. Akad. Wiss., Math. Physik. Kl.—Abhandlungen Bayerische Akademie der Wissenschaften, Mathematisch-Physikalische Klasse. München.

Abh. Ber. K. Zool. Anthro. Ethno. Mus. Dresden—Abhandlungen und Berichte des Königlichen Zoologischen und Anthropologisch-Ethnographischen Museums zu Dresden.

Abh. Ber. Mus. Nat. Heimatkd. Magdeburg—Abhandlungen und Berichte aus dem Museum für Natur- und Heimatkunde zu Magdeburg. [Title varies; changed in 1948 to Abhandlungen und Berichte für Naturkunde und Vorgeschichte.]

Abh. Ges. Wiss. Göttingen—Abhandlungen der Gesellschaft der Wissenschaften zu Göttingen.

Abh. Senckenb. Naturforsch. Ges.—Abhandlungen der Senckenbergischen Naturforschenden Gesellschaft. Frankfurt am Main.

Account Exped. Pittsburgh–Rocky Mts.—Long, S. H. 1823. Account of an Expedition from Pittsburgh to the Rocky Mountains Performed in the Years 1819 and '20. Vol. 2. H. C. Carey & I. Lea, Philadelphia. 442 pp.

Acta Biol. Venezuelica—Acta Biologica Venezuelica. Caracas.

Acta Herpetol. Japon.—Acta Herpetologica Japonica. Herpetological Society of Japan.

Acta Herpetol. Sinica—Acta Herpetologica Sinica. Chengdu Institute of Biology, Sichuan.

Acta Univ. Carol., Prague, Biol.—Acta Universitatis Carolinae. Biologica. Prague.

Acta Univ. Upsaliensis—Acta Universitatis Upsaliensis. Uppsala, Sweden.

Acta Vertebratica—Acta Vertebratica. Stockholm.

Acta Zool., Stockholm—Acta Zoologica. Stockholm.

Acta Zool. Cracov.—Acta Zoologica Cracoviensia. Kraków.

Acta Zool. Lilloana—Acta Zoologica Lilloana. Tucumán, Argentina.

Acta Zool. Sinica—Acta Zoologica Sinica [=Dong Wu Xue Bao]. Beijing.

Acta Zootaxon. Sinica—Acta Zootaxonomica Sinica [=Dong Wu Fen Lei Xue Bao]. Beijing.

Actas VIII Congr. Latino Am. Zool.—Salinas, P. J. (ed.). 1982. Actas VIII Congreso Latino Americano de Zoología. Zoología Neotropical. 2 vols. Mérida, Venezuela.

Adv. Herpetol. Evol. Biol.—Rhodin, A. G. J., and K. Miyata (eds.). 1983. Advances in Herpetology and Evolutionary Biology. Essays in Honor of Ernest E. Williams. Museum of Comparative Zoology, Harvard University, Cambridge, Massachusetts. 725 pp.

Afr. Wildl.—African Wildlife. Wildlife Society, Linden, South Africa.

Algemeene Konst- en Letter-Bode—Algemeene Konst- en Letter-Bode. Haarlem.

Allgem. Deutsche Naturhist. Zeitung—Allgemeine Naturhistorische Zeitung. Dresden.

Alytes, Paris—Alytes. Société Batrachologique de France, Paris.

Am. J. Sci.—American Journal of Science.

Am. J. Sci. Arts—American Journal of Science and Arts.

Am. Midl. Nat.—American Midland Naturalist.

Am. Monthly Mag. Crit. Rev.—American Monthly Magazine and Critical Review. New York.

Am. Mus. Novit.—American Museum Novitates. New York.

Am. Nat.—American Naturalist.

Am. Zool.—American Zoologist.

Ameghiniana—Ameghiniana. Asociación Paleontológica Argentina, Buenos Aires.

Amph. Ceylon—Kirtisinghe, P. 1957. The Amphibia of Ceylon. Colombo. 112 pp.

Amph. Fauna Peninsular Malaysia—Berry, P. Y. 1975. The Amphibian Fauna of Peninsular Malaysia. Tropical Press, Kuala Lumpur. 130 pp.

Amph. Indo-Aust. Arch.—Kampen, P. N. van. 1923. The Amphibia of the Indo-Australian Archipelago. Brill, Leiden. xii, 304 pp.

Amph. Malawi—Stewart, M. M. 1967. Amphibians of Malawi. State University of New York Press, Albany. 163 pp.

Amph. Rept. Europas—Mertens, R., and H. Wermuth. 1960. Die Amphibien und Reptilien Europas. W. Kramer, Frankfurt am Main. 264 pp.

Amph. Rept. Pacific Northwest—Nussbaum, R. A., E. D. Brodie, Jr., and R. M. Storm. 1983. Amphibians and Reptiles of the Pacific Northwest. The University Press of Idaho. 332 pp.

Amph. Rept. Puerto Rico—Rivero, J. A. 1978. Los Anfibios y Reptiles de Puerto Rico = The Amphibians and Reptiles of Puerto Rico. Universidad de Puerto Rico, Mayagüez. [Spanish and English versions bound in one volume.]

Amph. Res., Kunming—Amphibia Research. [In Chinese.] Kunming Institute of Zoology, Kunming, Yunnan, China.

Amph. S. Aust.—Tyler, M. J. 1978. Amphibians of South Australia. Australian Government Printer, Adelaide. 84 pp.

Amph. Urodeles Chine—Chang, M. L. Y. 1936. Contribution a l'Étude Morphologique, Biologique, et Systematique des Amphibiens Urodèles de la Chine. Picart, Paris. 156 pp.

Amphibia and Reptiles—Gadow, H. 1901. Amphibia and Reptiles. Vol. 8. In Harmer, S. F., and A. E. Shipley (eds.), The Cambridge Natural History. Macmillan and Co., London. 668 pp.

Amphibia-Reptilia—Amphibia-Reptilia. Societas Europaea Herpetologica.

Amphibien und Reptilien—Kuhn, O. 1967. Amphibien und Reptilien. Katalog der Subfamilien und höheren Taxa mit Nachweis des ersten Auftretens. Fischer, Stuttgart. vii, 124 pp.

An. Acad. Brasil. Cienc.—Anais da Academia Brasileira de Ciencias. Rio de Janeiro.

An. Mus. Argent. Cienc. Nat. Bernardino Rivadavia—Anales del Museo Argentino de Ciencias Naturales "Bernardino Rivadavia". Buenos Aires. [Continues An. Mus. Nac. Buenos Aires.]

An. Mus. Nac. Buenos Aires—Anales del Museo Nacional de Buenos Aires.

An. Mus. Nac. Hist. Nat., Chile—Anales. Museo Nacional de Historia Natural, Santiago de Chile.

An. Soc. Esp. Hist. Nat.—Anales de la Sociedad Española de Historia Natural. Madrid.

Analyse Nat.—Rafinesque, C. S. 1815. Analyse de la Nature ou Tableau de l'Univers et des Corps Organisés. J. Barravecchia, Palermo. 224 pp.

Anat. Zool. Res. Yunnan—Anderson, J. 1878. Anatomical and Zoological Researches: Comprising an Account of the Zoological Results of the Two Expeditions to Western Yunnan in 1868 and 1875; and a Monograph of the Two Cetacean Genera Platanista and Orcella. 2 vols. Quaritch, London.

Anf. Nicaragua—Villa, J. 1972. Anfibios de Nicaragua. Instituto Geográfico Nacional and Banco Central de Nicaragua, Managua. 216 pp.

Anim. Kingdom—Griffith, E., and E. Pidgeon. 1831. The Class Reptilia, Arranged by the Baron C. Cuvier, with Specific Descriptions. Vol. 9 (481 pp.). In The Animal Kingdom Arranged in Conformity with its Organization by the Baron Cuvier, with Additional Descriptions of All the Species Hitherto Named, and of Many Others. 16 vols. Whittaker, London.

Ann. Assoc. Canadienne-Française Avance. Sci.—Annales de l'Association Canadienne-Française pour l'Avancement des Sciences.

Ann. Cape Prov. Mus. (Nat. Hist.)—Annals of the Cape Provincial Museum (Natural History). Grahamstown, South Africa.

Ann. Carnegie Mus.—Annals of the Carnegie Museum. Pittsburgh.

Ann. Fac. Sci. Cameroun—Annales de la Faculté des Sciences du Cameroun. Yaoundé.

Ann. Fac. Sci. Yaoundé—Annales de la Faculté des Sciences du Yaoundé. [Continues Ann. Fac. Sci. Cameroun.]

Ann. Hist. Nat. Mus. Natl. Hungarici—Annales Historico-Naturales Musei Nationalis Hungarici. Budapest.

Ann. Lyc. Nat. Hist. New York—Annals of the Lyceum of Natural History of New York.

Ann. Mag. Nat. Hist.—Annals and Magazine of Natural History. London.

Ann. Missouri Bot. Garden—Annals of the Missouri Botanical Garden. St. Louis.

Ann. Mus. Civ. Stor. Nat. Genova—Annali dell Museo Civico di Storia Naturale di Genova. [Title varies.]

Ann. Mus. R. Afr. Cent., Tervuren, Sér. Octavo, Sci. Zool.—Annales du Musée Royal de l'Afrique Centrale. Série in Octavo, Science Zoologique. Tervuren. [Continues Ann. Mus. R. Congo Belge, Tervuren, Sér. Octavo, Sci. Zool.]

Ann. Mus. R. Congo Belge, Terveren, Sér. Octavo, Sci. Zool.—Annales du Musée Royal du Congo Belge. Série in Octavo, Science Zoologique. Tervuren.

Ann. Mus. R. Congo Belge, Tervuren, N.S. Quarto, Sci. Zool.—Annales du Musée Royal du Congo Belge. Nouvelle Série in Quarto, Science Zoologique. Tervuren.

Ann. Mus. R. Congo Belge, Tervuren, Zool.—Annales du Musée Royal du Congo Belge. Zoologie. Tervuren.

Ann. Mus. Zool. Acad. Imp. Sci. St. Pétersbourg—Annuaire du Musée Zoologique de l'Académie Impériale des Sciences de St. Pétersbourg.

Ann. Mus. Zool. Acad. Sci. Petrograd—Annuaire du Musée Zoologique de l'Académie des Sciences de Petrograd. [Continues Ann. Mus. Zool. Acad. Imp. Sci. St. Pétersbourg.]

Ann. Nat., Lexington—Annals of Nature, or Annual Synopsis of New Genera and Species of Animals and Plants Discovered in North America. [1 volume published in 1820; (22):1–16 is Rafinesque.] Lexington, Kentucky.

Ann. Natal Mus.—Annals of the Natal Museum. Pietermaritzburg.

Ann Naturhist. Mus. Wien—Annalen des Naturhistorischen Museums in Wien.

Ann. New York Acad. Sci.—Annals of the New York Academy of Sciences.

Ann. Philos.—Annals of Philosophy. London.

Ann. Queensland Mus.—Annals of the Queensland Museum. Brisbane.

Ann. S. Afr. Mus.—Annals of the South African Museum. Cape Town.

Ann. Sci. Nat., Paris—Annales des Sciences Naturelles. Paris.

Ann. Soc. R. Zool. Belg.—Annales de la Société Royal Zoologique de Belgique. Bruxelles.

Ann. Transvaal Mus.—Annals of the Transvaal Museum. Pretoria.

Ann. Zool., Agra—Annals of Zoology. Agra, India.

Annexe Bull. Gén. Instr. Publique, Hanoi—Annexe au Bulletin Général de l'Instruction Publique. Hanoi.

Annot. Zool. Japon.—Annotationes Zoologicae Japonenses [=Nippon Dobutsugaku Iho]. Tokyo.

Annu. Rep. New Jersey State Mus.—Annual Report of the New Jersey State Museum. Trenton.

Annu. Rep. U.S. Natl. Mus.—Annual Report of the United States National Museum. Washington, D.C.

Aquar. Mag.—Aquarien Magazin. Stuttgart.

Aquar. Terr. Z.—Die Aquarien- und Terrarien-Zeitschrift. Stuttgart.

Arch. Biol. Med. Experim.—Archivos de Biología y Medicina Experimentales. Santiago, Chile.

Arch. Mus. Natl. Hist. Nat., Paris—Archives du Muséum National d'Histoire Naturelle. Paris.

Arch. Naturgesch.—Archiv für Naturgeschichte. [Starting in 1912—Abtheilung A.] Berlin.

Arch. Soc. Biol. Montevideo—Archivos de la Sociedad de Biología de Montevideo.

Arch. Zool. Anat. Physiol. Wiss. Med.—Archiv für Anatomie, Physiologie und Wissenschaftliche Medizin. Berlin.

Ark. Zool.—Arkiv för Zoologi. Kongliga Svenska Vetenskaps-Akademiens, Stockholm.

Arnoldia, Zimbabwe—Arnoldia. Bulawayo, Zimbabwe.

Arq. Mus. Bocage—Arquivos do Museu Bocage. Lisboa.

Arq. Mus. Nac., Rio de Janeiro—Arquivos do Museu Nacional. [Earlier volumes as Archivos do Museu Nacional.] Rio de Janeiro.

Arq. Univ. Fed. Rural Rio de Janeiro—Arquivos de Universidade Federal Rural do Rio de Janeiro.

Arq. Zool., São Paulo—Arquivos de Zoologia. Museu de Zoologia, Universidade de São Paulo, São Paulo.

Atas Simp. Biota Amaz. Zool.—Lent, H. (ed.). 1982. Atas do Simpósio sôbre a Biota Amazônica. Vol. 5 (Zoologia). Rio de Janeiro.

Atas Soc. Biol. Rio de Janeiro—Atas da Sociedad de Biologia do Rio de Janeiro.

Atlas Reise N. Afr.—Rüppel, E. 1826–1831. Atlas zu der Reise im nördlichen Afrika. Abtheilung 1. Zoologie. Frankfurt am Main.

Atti Accad. Sci. Torino, Cl. Sci. Fis. Mat. Nat.—Atti dell'Accademia della Scienze di Torino. Classe di Scienze Fisiche, Matematiche e Naturali.

Atti Soc. Ital. Sci. Nat. Mus. Civ. Stor. Nat. Milano—Atti della Società Italiana di Scienze Naturali e del Museo Civico di Storia Naturale di Milano.

Aust. CSIRO Div. Wildl. Res. Tech. Pap.—Australia Commonwealth Scientific and Industrial Research Organization. Division of Wildlife Research Technical Paper. Melbourne.

Aust. J. Zool.—Australian Journal of Zoology. Melbourne.

Aust. Wildl. Res.—Australian Wildlife Research. Melbourne.

Aust. Zool.—Australian Zoologist. Royal Zoological Society of New South Wales, Mosman.

Batr. Chile—Cei, J. M. 1962. Batracios de Chile. Ediciones de la Universidad de Chile, Santiago de Chile. 128 pp., cviii.

Batr. Indochine—Bourret, R. 1942. Les Batraciens de l'Indochine. Institut Océanographique de l'Indochine, Hanoi. x, 547 pp.

Beaufortia—Beaufortia. Series of Miscellaneous Publications of the Zoological Museum of the University of Amsterdam.

Beitr. Naturgesch. Brasil.—Wied-Neuwied, M. A. P., Prinz von. 1825. Beiträge zur Naturgeschichte von Brasilien. Vol. 1 (Verzeichniss der Amphibien). Gr. H. S. priv. Landes-Industrie-Comptoir, Weimar. xxii, 614 pp.

Beitr. Neotrop. Fauna—Beiträge zur Neotropischen Fauna. Jena.

Ber. Offenbacher Vereins Naturkd.—Berichte des Offenbacher Vereins für Naturkunde.

Ber. Senckenb. Naturforsch. Ges.—Berichte der Senckenbergischen Naturforschenden Gesellschaft in Frankfurt am Main.

Bih. K. Svenska Vetensk. Akad. Handl.—Bihang till Kongliga Svenska Vetenskaps-Akademiens. Handlingar. Stockholm.

Bijdr. Dierkd.—Bijdragen tot de Dierkunde. Universiteit van Amsterdam.

Biol. Amph.—Noble, G. K. 1931. The Biology of the Amphibia. McGraw-Hill, New York. xii, 577 pp.

Biol. Cent. Am., Rept. Batr.—Günther, G. C. L. G. 1885–1902. Biologia Centrali-Americana. Reptilia and Batrachia. Porter, London. xx, 326 pp., 76 pls. [See Smith and Smith, 1973, Synops. Herpetofauna Mexico, 2:112, for publication data.]

Biol. Conserv.—Biological Conservation. Barking, England.

Biol. Divers. Tropics—Prance, G. T. (ed.). 1982. Biological Diversification in the Tropics. Columbia University Press, New York. 714 pp.

Biol. Gabonica—Biologia Gabonica. Paris.

Biol. J. Linn. Soc.—Biological Journal of the Linnaean Society. London.

Biol. Rev. Cambridge Philos. Soc.—Biological Reviews of the Cambridge Philosophical Society.

Biologia, Lahore—Biologia. Biological Society of Pakistan, Lahore.

BioScience—BioScience. American Institute of Biological Sciences.

Bl. Aquar. Terrarienkd., Stuttgart—Blätter für Aquarien- und Terrarienkunde. Stuttgart.

Bol. Mus. Nac., Rio de Janeiro—Boletim do Museu Nacional. [Starting in 1942—N.S., Zoologia.] Rio de Janeiro.

Bol. Soc. Biol. Concepción—Boletin de la Sociedad de Biología de Concepción. Chile.

Bol. Soc. Venezolana Cienc. Nat.—Boletin de la Sociedad Venezolana de Ciencias Naturales. Caracas.

Boll. Mus. Ist. Biol. Univ. Genova—Bolletino dei Musei e degli Istituti Biologici dell'Università di Genova.

Boll. Mus. Zool. Anat. Comp. Univ. Torino—Bolletino dei Musei di Zoologia ed Anatomia Comparata della Università di Torino.

Bonn. Zool. Beitr.—Bonner Zoologische Beiträge.

Bonn. Zool. Monogr.—Bonner Zoologische Monographien.

Brazil. Species *Hyla*—Lutz, B. 1973. Brazilian Species of *Hyla*. University of Texas Press, Austin and London. xviii, 264 pp.

Breviora—Breviora. Museum of Comparative Zoology, Harvard University, Cambridge.

Brimleyana—Brimleyana. North Carolina State Museum of Natural History, Raleigh.

Brit. J. Herpetol.—British Journal of Herpetology.

Bull. Acad. Pol. Sci., Sér. Sci. Biol.—Bulletin de l'Académie Polonaise des Sciences, Série des Sciences Biologiques. Warsaw.

Bull. Am. Mus. Nat. Hist.—Bulletin of the American Museum of Natural History. New York.

Bull. Biogeogr. Soc. Japan—Bulletin of the Biogeographical Society of Japan. National Science Museum, Tokyo.

Bull. Brit. Mus. (Nat. Hist.), Zool.—Bulletin of the British Museum (Natural History), Zoology.

Bull. Carnegie Mus. Nat. Hist.—Bulletin of the Carnegie Museum of Natural History. Pittsburgh.

Bull. Chicago Acad. Sci.—Bulletin of the Chicago Academy of Sciences.

Bull. Chicago Herpetol. Soc.—Bulletin of the Chicago Herpetological Society.

Bull. Com. Études Hist. Scient. Afr. Occid. Franç.—Bulletin. Comité d'Études Historiques et Scientifiques de l'Afrique Occidental Française. Paris.

Bull. Essex Inst.—Bulletin of the Essex Institute. Salem, Massachusetts.

Bull. Florida State Mus., Biol. Sci.—Bulletin of the Florida State Museum, Biological Sciences. Gainesville.

Bull. Fukuoka Univ. Educ., Nat. Sci.—Bulletin of the Fukuoka University of Education, Natural Science [=Fukuoka Kyoiku Daigaku Kiyo Dai-san-bu Rika Hen].

Bull. Gén. Instr. Publique, Hanoi—Bulletin Générale de l'Instruction Publique. Hanoi. [See also Annexe Bull. Gén. Instr. Publique, Hanoi.]

Bull. Inst. Fondam. Afr. Noire, (A)—Bulletin de l'Institut Fondamental d'Afrique Noire, Série A, Sciences Naturelles. [Continues Bull. Inst. Franç. Afr. Noire, (A).] Dakar, Senegal.

Bull. Inst. Franç. Afr. Noire—Bulletin de l'Institut Française d'Afrique Noire. [Starting in 1954—Série A, Sciences Naturelles.] Dakar, Senegal.

Bull. Maryland Herpetol. Soc.—Bulletin of the Maryland Herpetological Society. Baltimore.

Bull. Mens. Soc. Linn. Lyon—Bulletin Mensuel de la Société Linnéenne de Lyon.

Bull. Mus. Comp. Zool.—Bulletin of the Museum of Comparative Zoology. Harvard University, Cambridge.

Bull. Mus. Natl. Hist. Nat., Paris—Bulletin du Muséum National d'Histoire Naturelle. Paris.

Bull. Mus. R. Hist. Nat. Belg.—Bulletin du Musée Royal d'Histoire Naturelle de Belgique. Bruxelles.

Bull. Natl. Mus., Singapore—Bulletin of the National Museum. Singapore. [Continues Bull. Raffles Mus.]

Bull. Raffles Mus.—Bulletin of the Raffles Museum. Singapore.

Bull. Res. Counc. Israel, Sect. B—Bulletin of the Research Council of Israel. Section B—Biology and Geology. Jerusalem.

Bull. S. California Acad. Sci.—Bulletin of the Southern California Academy of Sciences. Los Angeles.

Bull. Soc. Hist. Nat. Toulouse—Bulletin de la Société d'Histoire Naturelle de Toulouse.

Bull. Soc. Imp. Nat. Moscou—Bulletin de la Société Impériale des Naturalistes de Moscou.

Bull. Soc. Neuchâtel. Sci. Nat.—Bulletin de la Société Neuchâteloise des Sciences Naturelles.

Bull. Soc. Philomath. Paris—Bulletin de la Société Philomathique de Paris.

Bull. Soc. Sci., Bucuresti—Bulletin de la Société des Sciences. Bucuresti, Romania.

Bull. Soc. Sci. Nat. France—Bulletin. Société des Sciences Naturelles de France, Paris.

Bull. Soc. Zool. France—Bulletin de la Société Zoologique de France. Paris.

Bull. Trim. Soc. Geol. Normandie et Amis Mus. Havre—Bulletin Trimestriel de la Société Géologique de Normandie et des Amis du Muséum de Havre.

Bull. U.S. Natl. Mus.—Bulletin of the United States National Museum. Washington, D.C.

Bull. Zool. Nomencl.—Bulletin of Zoological Nomenclature. London.

Bull. Zool. Surv. India—Bulletin of the Zoological Survey of India. Calcutta.

C. E. D. Orione Contrib. Biol., Montevideo—Centro Educativo "Don Orione", Contribuciones en Biología. Montevideo.

C. R. Assoc. Franç. Avanc. Sci., Paris—Compte Rendu de l'Association Française pour l'Avancement des Sciences. Paris.

C. R. Hebd. Séances Acad. Sci., Paris—Comptes Rendus Hebdomadaires des Séances de l'Académie des Sciences. Paris.

C. R. Séances Soc. Biogeogr.—Comptes Rendus des Séances de la Société de Biogeographie. Paris.

C. R. Séances Soc. Biol. Paris—Comptes Rendus des Séances de la Société de Biologie. Paris. [Title varies.]

Caecilians of the World—Taylor, E. H. 1968. The Caecilians of the World: A Taxonomic Review. University of Kansas Press, Lawrence. xiv, 848 pp.

Cah. Nepal., Doc.—Cahiers Nepalais. Documents. Centre National de la Recherche Scientifique, Paris.

Caldasia—Caldasia. Museo de Historia Natural, Bogotá.

Campo, Rio de Janeiro—O Campo. Sociedad Rural Brasileira, Rio de Janeiro.

Canadian J. Genet. Cytol.—Canadian Journal of Genetics and Cytology. Ottawa.

Caribb. J. Sci.—Caribbean Journal of Science. Mayagüez, Puerto Rico.

Carnegie Mus. Nat. Hist. Spec. Publ.—Carnegie Museum of Natural History Special Publication. Pittsburgh.

Caryologia—Caryologia. Università degli Studi de Firenze.

Cat. Am. Amph. Rept.—Catalogue of American Amphibians and Reptiles. Society for the Study of Amphibians and Reptiles.

Cat. Batr. Sal. Brit. Mus.—Boulenger, G. A. 1882. Catalogue of the Batrachia Salientia s. Ecaudata in the Collection of the British Museum. Ed. 2. Taylor and Francis, London. xvi, 503 pp.

Cat. Batr. Sal. Coll. Brit. Mus.—Günther, G. C. L. G. 1859 "1858". Catalogue of the Batrachia Salientia in the Collection of the British Museum. Taylor and Francis, London. 160 pp. [See Sherborn, 1934, Ann. Mag. Nat. Hist., (10)13:308–312, for publication data.]

Cat. Batr. Grad. Coll. Brit. Mus.—Boulenger, G. A. 1882. Catalogue of the Batrachia Gradientia s. Caudata and Batrachia Apoda in the Collection of the British Museum. Ed. 2. Taylor and Francis, London. 127 pp.

Cat. Spec. Amph. Coll. Brit. Mus., Batr. Grad.—Gray, J. 1850. Catalogue of the Specimens of Amphibia in the Collection of the British Museum. Part II. Batrachia Gradientia. Taylor and Francis, London. 72 pp.

Cat. Types Amph. Mus. Natl. Hist. Nat.—Guibé, J. 1950 "1948". Catalogue des Types d'Amphibiens du Muséum National d'Histoire Naturelle. Paris. 71 pp.

Ceylon J. Sci.—Ceylon Journal of Science. Colombo.

Check List N. Am. Amph. Rept.—Schmidt, K. P. 1953. A Check List of North

American Amphibians and Reptiles. Ed. 6. American Society of Ichthyologists and Herpetologists. University of Chicago Press. 280 pp.

Checklist World Amph.—Gorham, S. W. 1974. Checklist of World Amphibians up to January 1, 1970. The New Brunswick Museum, Saint John, Canada. 173 pp.

China J.—China Journal. China Society of Science and Arts, Shanghai.

Chromosoma—Chromosoma. Berlin.

Cienc. Cult., Supl.—Ciencia e Cultura. Suplemento. São Paulo.

Classif. Batr.—Tschudi, J. J. von. 1838. Classification der Batrachier mit Berücksichtigung der fossilen Thiere dieser Abtheilung der Reptilien. Petitpierre, Neuchâtel. 102 pp. [Reprinted 1839 in Mém. Soc. Neuchâtel. Sci. Nat., 2:1–102; publication data available in S.S.A.R. Facsimile Reprints in Herpetology no. 17, "Classification der Batrachier" by J. J. von Tschudi.]

Comp. Biochem. Physiol.—Comparative Biochemistry and Physiology. Oxford, England.

Comun. Zool. Mus. Hist. Nat. Montevideo—Comunicaciones Zoológicas del Museo de Historia Natural de Montevideo.

Conspect. Syst. Herpetol. Amphibiol.—Bonaparte, C. L. 1850. Conspectus Systematum. Herpetologiae et Amphibiologiae. Editio reformata. Brill, Leiden.

Contrib. Biol. Lab. Sci. Soc. China, Zool. Ser.—Contributions from the Biological Laboratory of the Science Society of China. Zoological Series. Shanghai.

Contrib. Biol. Lab. Kyoto Univ.—Contributions from the Biological Laboratory. Kyoto University.

Contrib. Maclurean Lyc.—Contributions of the Maclurean Lyceum. Philadelphia.

Contrib. Sci. Nat. Hist. Mus. Los Angeles Co.—Contributions in Science. Natural History Museum of Los Angeles County.

Copeia—Copeia. American Society of Ichthyologists and Herpetologists.

Corresp. Linnaeus—Smith, J. E. 1821. A Selection of the Correspondence of Linnaeus and Other Naturalists from the Original Manuscripts. Vol. 1. Longman, Hurst, Rees, Orme and Brown, London. 605 pp.

Cytogenet. Cell Genet.—Cytogenetics and Cell Genetics. Basel. [Continues Cytogenetics.]

Cytogenetics—Cytogenetics. Basel.

Das Tierreich—Das Tierreich. Eine Zusammenstellung und Kennzeichnung der rezenten Tierformen. Walter de Gruyter & Co., Berlin.

Delect. Flor. Faun. Brasil.—Mikan, J. C. 1820. Delectus Florae et Faunae Brasiliensis. Antonii Strauss, Wien. 54 pp., 24 pls.

Delic. Mus. Zool. Vratislav.—Gravenhorst, J. L. C. 1829. Deliciae Musei Zoologici Vratislaviensis. Fasciculus primus. Chelonia et Batrachia. Voss, Leipzig. xiv, 106 pp., 17 pls.

Denkschr. Akad. Wiss. Wien., Math. Naturwiss. Kl.—Denkschriften der Kaiserlichen Akademie der Wissenschaften in Wien. Mathematisch-Naturwissenschaftliche Klasse.

Denkschr. Med. Naturwiss. Ges. Jena—Denkschriften der Medicinisch-Naturwissenschaftlichen Gesellschaft zu Jena.

Dep. Geol. Nat. Res., Indiana, Annu. Rep.—Department of Geology and Natural Resources. Annual Report. Indianapolis, Indiana.

Descr. Axolotl Mont. Las Cruces—Dugès, A. A. D. 1895. Description d'un Axolotl des Montagnes de Las Cruces (Amblystoma altamirani A. Dugès). Imprimerie du Ministère de Fomento, Institut Medico-National, México, D.F. 6 pp., 1 pl.

Descr. Égypte—1809–1827. Description de l'Égypte, ou Recueil des Observations et des Recherches qui ont été faites en Égypte pendant l'Expedition de l'Armée Française, publie par les Ordres de sa Majesté l'Empereur Napoléon le Grand. Histoire Naturelle. Vol. 1i–1iv, 2. Paris.

Doklady Akad. Nauk Ukr. S.S.R., Ser. B—Doklady Akademii Nauk Ukrainskoi S.S.R. Seriya B, Geologischeskie, Khimichieskie i Biologischeskie Nauki. Kiev.

Doñana, Acta Vert.—Doñana. Acta Vertebratica. Sevilla.

Durban Mus. Novit.—Durban Museum Novitates.

Ege Univ. Fen Fak. Kitap. Ser.—Ege Universitesi Fen Fakaltesi Kitaplar Ser. Izmir, Turkey.

Elaphe—Elaphe (Echsen–Schlangen–Schildkröten–Panzerechsen–Lurche–Kleinsäugetiere). Aquaristisch–Terraristische Beiträge. Kulturbund der DDR, Berlin.

El Medio Ambiente Páramo—Salgado-Labouriau, M. L. (ed.). 1979. El Medio Ambiente Páramo. Ediciones Centro Estudios Avanzados, Mérida, Venezuela. 235 pp.

Epistola . . . de Rana bicolore—Boddaert, P. 1772. Brief . . . aan . . . Johannes Oosterdyk Schacht naar het leven vervaardige afbeelding, van den twee-koleurigen kikvorsch, uit des vezameling van . . . Johannes Albertus Schlosser. = Epistola ad . . . Johannem Oosterdyk Schacht . . . de Rana bicolore, descripta atque accuratissima icone illustrata ex museo . . . Johannis Alberti Schlosseri. M. Magérus, Amsterdam. 48 pp.

Erläut. Fauna Brasil.—Burmeister, H. 1856. Erläuterungen zur Fauna Brasiliens, enthaltend Abbildungen und ausführliche Beschreibungen neuer oder ungenügend bekannter Thier-Arten. G. Reimer, Berlin. viii, 115 pp., 32 pls.

Erp. Gén.—Dumeril, A. M. C., and G. Bibron. 1841. Erpetologie Général ou Histoire Naturelle complète des Reptiles. Vol. 8. Roret, Paris. 784 pp.

Evol. Biol. Anurans—Vial, J. L. (ed.). 1973. Evolutionary Biology of the Anurans. Contemporary Research on Major Problems. University of Missouri Press, Columbia. xii, 470 pp.

Evol. Genus *Bufo*—Blair, W. F. (ed.). 1973. Evolution in the Genus *Bufo*. University of Texas Press, Austin. vii, 459 pp.

Evol. Time Space—Sims, R. W., J. H. Price, and P. E. S. Whalley (eds.). 1983. Evolution, Time and Space: The Emergence of the Biosphere. Academic Press, New York.

Evolution—Evolution. Society for the Study of Evolution.

Experientia—Experientia. Basel.

Explor. Parc Natl. Albert—Exploration du Parc National Albert. Mission G. F. de Witte (1933–1945). Institut des Parcs Nationaux du Congo Belge, Bruxelles.

Explor. Parc Natl. Garamba—Exploration du Parc National de la Garamba. Mission H. De Saeger. Institut des Parcs Nationaux, Kinshasa.

Explor. Parc Natl. Upemba—Exploration du Parc National de l'Upemba. Mission G. F. de Witte (1946–1949). Institut des Parcs Nationaux du Congo Belge, Bruxelles.

Explor. Parc Natl. Virunga—Exploration du Parc National de Virunga. Institut des Parcs Nationaux, Kinshasa.

Fasc. Malay.—Annandale, N. 1903. Fasciculi Malayenses. Anthropological and Zoological Results of an Expedition to Perak and the Siamese Malay States 1901–1903 undertaken by Nelson Annandale and Herbert C. Robinson. Vol. 1. Longman, London.

Fauna Brit. India—Blanford, W. T. (ed.). 1890. The Fauna of British India, including Ceylon and Burma. Published under the Authority of the Secretary of State for India in Council. London.

Fauna Japon., Anura—Okada, Y. 1966. Fauna Japonica. Anura (Amphibia). Biogeographical Society of Japan, Tokyo. 234 pp., 24 pls.

Fauna Japon., Rept.—Temminck, C. J., and H. Schlegel. 1838. Vol. III (Chelonia, Ophidia, Sauria, Batrachia). *In* Von Siebold, P. F. Fauna Japonica sive Descriptio animalium, quae in itinere per Japonianum, jussu et auspiciis superiorum, qui summum in India Batava Imperium tenent, suscepto, annis 1823–1830 colleget, notis observationibus et adumbrationibus illustratis. J. G. Lalau, Leiden. [See Hoogmoed, 1978, Zool. Meded., Leiden, 53:91–92, for some publication data.]

Fauna Russia, Amph.—Nikolsky, A. M. 1918. Zemnovodnye i presmykayushcheesya, v serii "Fauna Rossii i sopredel'nyukh stran" [=Amphibians and Reptiles. *In* Fauna of Russia and Adjacent Countries]. Izdatel'stvo Akademii Nauk, Petrograd.

Fauna S. W. Aust.—Michaelson, W., and R. Hartmeyer (eds.). 1914. Die Fauna Südwest-Australiens. Ergebnisse der Hamburger Südwestaustralischen Forschungsreise 1905. G. Fischer, Jena.

Fauna Svec., Ed. 2—Linnaeus, C. 1761. Fauna Svecica sisten Animalia Sveciae Regni Mammalia, Aves, Amphibia, Pisces, Insecta, Vermes. Distributa per Classes & Ordines, Genera & Species, cum Differentiis Specierum, Synonymis Auctorum, Nominibus Incolarum, Locis Natalium Descriptionibus Insectorum. Editio altera, auctior. Stockholm.

Festschr. Naturforsch. Ges. Basel—Festschrift zur Feier des fünfundsiebizigjährigen Bestehens der Naturforschenden Gesellschaft in Basel. 1892.

Fieldiana: Zool.—Fieldiana: Zoology. Chicago.

Fieldiana: Zool. Mem.—Fieldiana: Zoology Memoirs. Chicago.

Field and Laboratory—Field and Laboratory. Contributions from the Science Departments. Southern Methodist University, Dallas, Texas.

Field Guide Aust. Frogs—Barker, J., and G. Grigg. 1977. A Field Guide to Australian Frogs. Rigby Ltd., Adelaide. 229 pp.

Field Mus. Nat. Hist. Publ., Zool. Ser.—Field Museum of Natural History Publications. Zoological Series. Chicago.

Forma et Functio—Forma et Functio. Brunswick.

Frogs—Tyler, M. J. 1982. Frogs. Ed. 2. Collins, Sydney. 256 pp.

Frogs S. W. Aust.—Main, A. R. 1965. Frogs of southern Western Australia. Handbook No. 8. Western Australian Naturalist's Club, Perth. 73 pp.

Frogs W. Aust.—Tyler, M. J., L. A. Smith, and R. E. Johnstone. 1984. Frogs of Western Australia. Western Australia Museum, Perth. 109 pp.

Fund. Miguel Lillo, Misc.—Fundación Miguel Lillo. Misceláneas. Tucumán, Argentina.

Gen. Zool.—Shaw, G. 1802. General Zoology or Systematic Natural History. Vol. 3. T. Davidson, London. 615 pp.

Genetica—Genetica. The Hague.

Geobios, Lyon, Mem. Spec.—Geobios. Mémoire Special. Université Claude Bernard, Lyon.

Göteborgs K. Vetensk. Vitterh. Samh. Handl.—Göteborgs Kungliga Vetenskaps och Vitter-Hets Samhalles Handlingar.

Great Basin Nat.—Great Basin Naturalist. Provo, Utah.

Handbook Frogs Toads, Ed. 1—Wright, A. H., and A. A. Wright. 1933. Handbook of Frogs and Toads of the United States and Canada. Comstock Publ. Assoc., Ithaca, New York. xi, 231 pp.

Handbook Frogs Toads, Ed. 3—Wright, A. H., and A. A. Wright. 1949. Handbook of Frogs and Toads of the United States and Canada. Ed. 3. Comstock Publ. Assoc., Ithaca, New York. xiii, 640 pp.

Handbuch Paläoherpetol., Pt. 2—Estes, R. 1981. Handbuch der Paläoherpetologie/ Encyclopedia of Paleoherpetology. Part 2. Gymnophiona, Caudata. G. Fischer, Stuttgart and New York. xv, 115 pp.

Handl. Dierkd.—Schlegel, H. 1858. Handleiding tot de Beoefening der Dierkunde. Vol. 2. Natuurkundige Leercursus ten Gebruike der Koninklijke Militaire Akademie. xx, 628 pp.

Herpetol. Angola Congo—Bocage, J. V. Barboza du, 1895. Herpétologie de l'Angola et du Congo. Ministère de la Marine et des Colonies, Lisboa.

Herpetol. Not.—Herpetological Notices. San Francisco. [Privately printed by J. C. Thompson; only 3 numbers published.]

Herpetol. Rev.—Herpetological Review. Society for the Study of Amphibians and Reptiles.

Herpetologica—Herpetologica. Herpetologist's League.

Hist. Amph.—Schneider, J. 1799. Historiae Amphibiorum Naturalis et Literariae. Fasciculus Primus. Jena. xiii, 264 pp.

Hist. Brit. Rept.—Bell, T. 1839. A History of British Reptiles. London. 142 pp.

Hist. Fis. Polit. Chile—Gay, C. 1848. Historia Física y Política de Chile. Vol. 2. Zoologia. Paris and Santiago. 372 pp.

Hist. Nat. Gén. Part. Rept.—Daudin, F. M. 1801–1803. Histoire Naturelle, Générale et Particulière des Reptiles; ouvrage faisant suit à l'Histoire naturelle générale et particulière, composée par Leclerc de Buffon; et rédigée par C. S. Sonnini, membre de plusieurs sociétés savantes. 8 vols. F. Dufart, Paris. [See Harper, 1940, Am. Midl. Nat., 23:692–723, for publication data.]

Hist. Nat. Jorat—Razoumovsky, G. 1789. Histoire naturelle du Jorat et de ses environs; et celle de trois Lacs de Neuchâtel, Moral et Bienne; précédées d'un Essai sur le climat, les productions . . . les Animaux de la partie du Pays de Vaud . . . qui entre dans le plan de cet ouvrage. Vol. 1. Lausanne.

Hist. Nat. Quadrup. Ovip.—Daudin, F. M. 1800. Histoire Naturelle des Quadrupèdes Ovipaires. Marchant, Paris. 24 unnumbered pp. [See Harper, 1940, Am. Midl. Nat., 23:692–723, for discussion of this obscure work.]

Hist. Nat. Quadrup. Ovip. Serp.—Lacépède, B. G. E. 1788–1789. Histoire Naturelle des Quadrupèdes Ovipaires et des Serpents. Vol. 1 (1788). Vol. 2 (1789). Imprimerie du Roi, Paris.

Hist. Nat. Rain. Gren. Crap.—Daudin, F. M. 1802. Histoire Naturelle des Rainettes, des Grenouilles et des Crapauds. Levrault, Paris. 71 pp. (Folio Edition); 108 pp. (Quarto Edition). [See Harper, 1940, Am. Midl. Nat., 23:692–723, for discussion of publication date.]

Hist. Nat. Rept.—Sonnini, C. S., and P. A. Latreille. 1801. Histoire Naturelle des Reptiles, avec Figures dissinées d'après Nature. 4 vols. Paris. [See Harper, 1940, Am. Midl. Nat., 23:692–723, for discussion of publication date.]

Hist. Nat. Salamandr. France—Latreille, P. A. 1800. Histoire naturelle des Salamandres de France, précédée d'un Tableau méthodique des autres Reptiles indigènes . . . . Paris. xlvii, 58 pp.

Hist. Phys. Polit. Nat. Cuba, Rept.—Sagra, R. de la. 1841–1843. Histoire Physique, Politique, et Naturelle de l'ile de Cuba. Atlas, Reptiles. A. Bertrand, Paris. xviii, 242 pp., 31 pls.

Hospital, Rio de Janeiro—O Hospital. Hospital São Francisco de Assis. Sociedad Medica, Rio de Janeiro.

Icon. Encyclop. Sci.—Heck, J. G. 1849. Iconographic Encyclopaedia of Science, Literature and Art. Vol. 2 (Zoology). R. Garrique, New York. 502 pp.

Icon. Fauna Ital.—Bonaparte, L. 1832–1841. Iconographia della Fauna Italica per le quattro Classi degli Animali Vertebrati. Vol. 2. Roma. [See Salvadori, 1888, Boll. Mus. Zool. Anat. Comp. Univ. Torino, 3(48), for publication data.]

Icon. Règne Animal—Guérin-Méneville, F. E. 1829–1844. Iconographie du Règne animal de G. Cuvier, ou Représentation d'après Nature de l'une des Espèces les plus remarquables et souvent non encore figurées, de chaque Genre d'Animaux. Avec un Texte descriptif mis au Courant de la Science. 3 vols. J. B. Ballière, Paris.

Iheringia, Zool.—Iheringia, Serie Zoologia. Museu Rio-Grandense de Ciencias Naturais, Pôrto Alegre, Brazil.

Illinois Biol. Monogr.—Illinois Biological Monographs. University of Illinois Press, Urbana.

Illustr. Indian Zool.—Gray, J. E. 1834. Illustrations of Indian Zoology chiefly selected from the collection of Major-General Hardwicke. Vol. 2. London.

Illustr. Zool. S. Afr.—Smith, A. 1838–1849. Illustrations of the Zoology of South Africa; consisting chiefly of Figures and Descriptions of the Objects of Natural History collected during an Expedition into the Interior of South Africa, in the years 1834, 1835, and 1836 . . . . Vol. III. Reptilia, Appendix. Smith, Elder, & Co., London. [See Waterhouse, 1880, Proc. Zool. Soc. London, 1880:489–491, and Jentink, 1893, Notes Leyden Mus., 15:182, for publication data.]

Instituto, Coimbra—O Instituto. Jornal Scientifico e Litterario. Coimbra.

Instr. Publique, Hanoi—Instruction Publique. Hanoi.

Intr. Herpetol., Ed. 1—Goin, C. J., and O. G. Goin. 1962. Introduction to Herpetology. Ed. 1. W. H. Freeman and Co., San Francisco. 341 pp.

Intr. Herpetol., Ed. 3—Goin, C. J., O. G. Goin, and G. R. Zug. 1978. Introduction to Herpetology. Ed. 3. W. H. Freeman and Co., San Francisco. xi, 378 pp.

Intr. Vert. Viaj. Pacif.—Savage, J. M. 1978. Introduction, pp. vii–xv. In Soc. Study Amph. Rept. Reprint of "Vertebrados del Viaje al Pacifico, Batracios" by M. Jiménez de la Espada. S.S.A.R. Misc. Publ.

Invest. Zool. Chilen.—Investigaciones Zoológicas Chilenas. Universidad de Chile, Santiago.

Isis von Oken—Isis von Oken. Jena. [Title varies.]

J. Acad. Nat. Sci. Philadelphia—Journal of the Academy of Natural Sciences of Philadelphia.

J. Assam Sci. Soc.—Journal of the Assam Science Society.

J. Asiat. Soc. Bengal—Journal of the Asiatic Society of Bengal. Calcutta.

J. Biogeogr.—Journal of Biogeography.

J. Biol. Sci., Bombay—Journal of Biological Sciences. Bombay.

J. Bombay Nat. Hist. Soc.—Journal of the Bombay Natural History Society.

J. Bromeliad Soc.—Journal. Bromeliad Society. Los Angeles.

J. Cient. Fac. Cienc. Med. Biol. Botucatu—Jornada Cientifica. Faculdade de Ciencias Medicas e Biologicas de Botucatu. Brazil.

J. Coll. Agr. Hokkaido Imp. Univ. Sapporo—Journal of the College of Agriculture. Hokkaido Imperial University, Sapporo.

J. Coll. Sci. Imp. Univ., Japan—Journal of the College of Science, Imperial University. Nagoya, Japan.

J. Dep. Agr. Puerto Rico—Journal of the Department of Agriculture of Puerto Rico [or Porto Rico, depending on volume].

J. E. Afr. Nat. Hist. Soc. Natl. Mus.—Journal of the East Africa Natural History Society and National Museum. Nairobi.

J. Elisha Mitchell Sci. Soc.—Journal of the Elisha Mitchell Scientific Society.

J. Exp. Zool.—Journal of Experimental Zoology.

J. Exped. Discov. Cent. Aust.—Eyre, E. J. 1845. Journals of Expeditions of Discovery into Central Australia and Overland from Adelaide to King George's Sound in the Years 1840–1. Vol. 1. T. & W. Boone, London.

J. Exped. Discov. W. Aust.—Grey, J. 1841. Journals of Two Expeditions of Discovery in North-West and Western Australia, during the Years 1837, 38, and 39 under the Authority of her Majesty's Government . . . . Vol. 2. London.

J. Fac. Sci. Hokkaido Imp. Univ.—Journal of the Faculty of Science. Hokkaido Imperial University. Sapporo.

J. Fed. Malay States Mus.—Journal of the Federated Malay States Museum. Kuala Lumpur.

J. Herpetol.—Journal of Herpetology. Society for the Study of Amphibians and Reptiles.

J. Herpetol. Assoc. Afr.—Journal of the Herpetological Association of Africa. Stellenbosch.

J. Morphol.—Journal of Morphology.

J. N. China Asiat. Soc., N.S.—Journal of the North China Branch of the Royal Asiatic Society, New Series. Shanghai.

J. Nat. Hist.—Journal of Natural History. London. [Continues Ann. Mag. Nat. Hist.]

J. Nat. Hist. Soc. Siam—Journal of the Natural History Society of Siam. Bangkok.

J. Ohio Herpetol. Soc.—Journal of the Ohio Herpetological Society.

J. Oman Stud., Spec. Rep.—Journal of Oman Studies. Special Report.

J. Phys. Chim. Hist. Nat. Blainville—Journal de Physique, de Chimie, d'Histoire Naturelle et des Arts, avec des Planches en Taille-Douce; par M. H. M. Ducrotay de Blainville.

J. Sci. Hiroshima Univ., B—Zool.—Journal of the Hiroshima University. Series B— Division 1 (Zoology).

J. Sci. Math. Phys. Nat., Lisboa—Jornal de Sciencias, Mathematicas, Physicas e Naturaes. Academia Real das Sciencias de Lisboa.

J. Soc. Bibliogr. Nat. Hist.—Journal of the Society for the Bibliography of Natural History. London.

J. Trinidad Field Nat. Club—Journal of the Trinidad Field Naturalist's Club.

J. Trois Voy. Chinois—David, A. 1875. Journal de mon troisième Voyage d'Exploration dans l'Empire Chinoise. 2 vols. Hachette, Paris.

J. Univ. Poona—Journal of the University of Poona. India.

J. Vert. Paleontol.—Journal of Vertebrate Paleontology.

J. Voy. New South Wales—White, J. 1790. Journal of a Voyage to New South Wales. Debrett, London. 299 pp.

J. Washington Acad. Sci.—Journal of the Washington Academy of Sciences. Washington, D.C.

J. West Afr. Sci. Assoc.—Journal of the West African Science Association. Ibadan, Nigeria.

J. West China Border Res. Soc., (B)—Journal of the West China Border Research Society. Series B—Natural Sciences.

J. Zool., London—Journal of Zoology. London.

J. Zool. Soc. India—Journal of the Zoological Society of India.

Jahr. Vereins Vaterl. Naturkd. Württemberg—Jahresheft des Vereins für Vaterländische Naturkunde in Württemberg.

Jahrb. Hamburg. Wiss. Anst.—Jahrbuch der Hamburgischen Wissenschaftlichen Anstalten. Hamburg.

Jahrb. Nassau. Vereins Naturkd.—Jahrbuch des Nassauischen Vereins für Naturkunde. Wiesbaden.

Japan J. Herpetol.—Japanese Journal of Herpetology [=Hachu-Ryoseiruigaku Zasshi]. Herpetological Society of Japan.

Japan. Rept. Amph. Color—Nakamura, K., and S. I. Ueno. 1963. Japanese Reptiles and Amphibians in Color. [In Japanese.] Hoikusha, Osaka. 214 pp.

Japanese Rept. Amph. Color—Sengoku, S. (ed.). 1979. Japanese Reptiles and Amphibians in Color [=Gensyoku Ryousei-Hachuuri]. Ie-no Hikari Kyokai, Tokyo. 206 pp.

K. Svenska Vetensk. Akad. Handl.—Kongliga Svenska Vetenskaps-Akademiens. Handlingar. Stockholm.

Kasmera—Kasmera. Universidad del Zulia, Venezuela.

Kat. Batr. Samml. Mus. Senckenb. Naturforsch. Ges.—Boettger, O. 1892. Katalog der Batrachier-Sammlung im Museum der Senckenbergischen Naturforschenden Gesellschaft in Frankfurt am Main. Knauer, Frankfurt am Main. x, 73 pp.

Kat. Wiss. Samml. Naturhist. Mus. Wien—Häupl, M., and F. Tiedemann. 1978. Typenkatalog der Herpetologischen Sammlung. Kataloge der Wissenschaftlichen Sammlung des Naturhistorischen Museums in Wien. 2(Vertebrata):7–34. Wien.

Kentucky Gazette, Lexington—Kentucky Gazette. Lexington, Kentucky. [Newspaper.]

Key Amph. Rept. USSR—Terent'ev, P. V., and S. A. Chernov. 1949. Opredelitel'presmykayushchikhya i zemnovodnykh [=Key to Amphibians and Reptiles]. Moscow. [English translation—1966, Israel Program for Scientific Translations.]

Klass. Ordn. Thier-Reichs Wiss. Wort Bild—Bronn, H. G. 1878. Die Klassen und Ordnungen des Thier-Reichs Wissenschaftlich dargestellt in Wort und Bild. Vol. 6. C. F. Winter, Leipzig and Heidelberg. 726 pp.

Koedoe—Koedoe. Pretoria.

Kriechth. Deutsch-Ost-Afr.—Tornier, G. 1896 "1897". Die Kriechthiere Deutsch-Ost-Afrikas. Beiträge zur Systematik und Descendenzlehre. Reimer, Berlin.

Lav. Soc. Ital. Biogeogr., N.S.—Lavori della Società Italiana di Biogeographia. Nuova Serie.

Lehrb. Naturgesch.—Oken, L. von. 1815–1816. Lehrbuch der Naturgeschichte. Vol. 3. Zoologie. Abtheilung 1, 2. Atlas. C. H. Reclam, Leipzig. xv, 1270 pp.

Life Hist. Frogs Okefinokee Swamp—Wright, A. H. 1922. Life Histories of the Frogs of Okefinokee Swamp, Georgia. North American Salientia (Anura) No. 2. Macmillan Co., New York. xv, 497 pp.

Lista Anot. Local. Tipo Anf. Brasil.—Bokermann, W. C. A. 1966. Lista Anotada das Localidades Tipo de Anfibios Brasileiros. Servicio de Documentacão, Universidade Rural São Paulo. 183 pp.

Loc. Nat. Thes. Desc. Icon. Exp.—Seba, A. 1734. Locupletissimi Rerum naturalium Thesauri accurata Descriptio, et Iconibus artificiosissimus Expressio, per universam Physices Historium. Opus, cui in hoc Rerum Genere, nullum par exstitit. Vol. 1. Janssonio-Waesbergios, Amsterdam.

Lozania—Lozania. Museo de Historia Natural, Bogotá.

Madras Month. J. Med. Sci.—Madras Monthly Journal of Medical Science.

Mag. Zool., Paris—Magasin de Zoologie. Paris.

Major Patterns Vert. Evol.—Hecht, M., P. C. Goody, and B. M. Hecht (eds.). 1977. Major Patterns in Vertebrate Evolution. NATO Advanced Study Institutes Series. Series A—Life Sciences. Vol. 14. Plenum Press, New York and London. 908 pp.

Malay. Nat. J.—Malayan Nature Journal. Kuala Lumpur.

Manual Brit. Vert. Anim.—Jenyns, L. 1835. A Manual of British Vertebrate Animals. Cambridge and London. xxxii, 559 pp.

Med. Phys. Res.—Harlan, R. 1835. Medical and Physical Research or Original Memoires in Medicine, Surgery, Physiology, Geology, Zoology and Comparative Anatomy. Philadelphia. xxxix, 653 pp.

Medio Ambiente—Medio Ambiente. Santiago, Chile.

Mém. Acad. Imp. Sci. St. Pétersbourg—Mémoires de l'Académie Impériale des Sciences de St. Pétersbourg.

Mem. Accad. Agric. Commerc. Arti, Verona—Memorie. Accademia d'Agricultura, Scienze, Lettere ed Arti. Verona.

Mem. Accad. Sci. Torino, Cl. Sci. Fis. Mat. Nat.—Memorie dell'Accademia di Scienze di Torino. Classe di Scienze, Fisiche, Matematiche e Naturali.

Mem. Inst. Butantan, São Paulo—Memorias do Instituto Butantan. São Paulo.

Mém. Inst. Franç. Afr. Noire—Mémoires. Institut Française d'Afrique Noire. Dakar, Senegal.

Mem. Inst. Invest. Cient. Moçambique—Memorias do Instituto de Investigacão Cientifica de Moçambique.

Mem. Inst. Oswaldo Cruz, Rio de Janeiro—Memorias do Instituto Oswaldo Cruz. Rio de Janeiro.

Mém. Inst. Sci. Madagascar—Mémoires de l'Institut Scientifique de Madagascar.

Mem. Mat. Fis. Soc. Ital. Sci., Modena—Memorie Matematica et di Fisica della Società Italiana della Scienze. Modena.

Mem. Mus. Comp. Zool.—Memoires of the Museum of Comparative Zoology. Harvard University, Cambridge.

Mem. Mus. Hist. Nat. Javier Prado—Memorias del Museo de Historia Natural "Javier Prado". Lima.

Mém. Mus. Natl. Hist. Nat., Paris—Mémoires du Muséum National d'Histoire Naturelle. Paris.

Mem. Natl. Mus. Victoria—Memoires of the National Museum of Victoria. Melbourne.

Mem. Queensland Mus.—Memoires of the Queensland Museum. Brisbane.

Mem. Rev. Soc. Cient. Antonio Alzate—Memorias y Revista de la Sociedad Científico "Antonio Alzate". México.

Mem. S. California Acad. Sci.—Memoires of the Southern California Academy of Sciences. Los Angeles.

Mem. Soc. Cienc. Nat. La Salle—Memorias de la Sociedad de Ciencias Naturales "La Salle". Caracas.

Mem. Soc. Esp. Hist. Nat.—Memorias de la Sociedad Española de Historia Natural. Madrid.

Mém. Soc. Neuchâtel. Sci. Nat.—Mémoires de la Société Neuchâteloise des Sciences Naturelles. [Title varies.]

Mém. Soc. Sci. Nat. Cherbourg—Mémoires de la Société National des Sciences Naturelles et Mathematiques de Cherbourg.

Mem. Soc. Zool. France—Mémoires de la Société Zoologique de France. Paris.

Micronesica—Micronesica. University of Guam.

Milwaukee Public Mus. Contrib. Biol. Geol.—Milwaukee Public Museum. Contributions in Biology and Geology.

Misc. Publ. Mus. Nat. Hist. Univ. Kansas—Miscellaneous Publications. Museum of Natural History, University of Kansas. Lawrence.

Misc. Publ. Mus. Zool. Univ. Michigan—Miscellaneous Publications. Museum of Zoology, University of Michigan. Ann Arbor.

Miss. Biol. Sagan-Omo—1943. Missione Biologica Sagan-Omo. Vol. 7 (Zoologie). Centro Studi per l'Africa Orientale Italiana, Reale Accademia d'Italia, Roma.

Miss. Géogr. Am. Sud.—1911. Mission du Service Géographique de l'Armée pour la Mesure d'un Arc de Meridien Equatorial en Amérique du Sud (1899–1906). Vol. 9 (Zoologie). Part 2. Paris.

Miss. Sci. Mex. Am. Cent.—Brocchi, P. 1881–1883. Mission Scientifique au Mexique et dans l'Amérique Centrale. Ouvrage publié par Ordre du Ministère de l'Instruction publique. Recherches Zoologiques. Vol. 3. Paris. [See Smith and Smith, 1973, Synops. Herpetofauna Mexico, 2:x, for dates of livraisons.]

Mitt. Naturhist. Mus. Hamburg—Mitteilungen aus dem Naturhistorischen Museum in Hamburg.

Mitt. Zool. Mus. Berlin—Mitteilungen aus dem Zoologischen Museum in Berlin.

Monatsber. Preuss. Akad. Wiss. Berlin—Monatsberichte der Preussischen Akademie der Wissenschaften zu Berlin. [Title varies.]

Mongholiya i Strana Tanghutov—Przewalski, N. M. 1876. Mongholiya i strana Tanghutov trekhyetnee puteshestvie v vostochnoi naghornoi Azii [=Mongolia and the Tangut Country: A Three Years' Journey in the Eastern Highlands of Asia]. Vol. 2. St. Pétersbourg.

Monit. Zool. Ital., N.S., Monogr.—Monitore Zoologico Italiano, N.S., Monografias. Firenze.

Monit. Zool. Ital., N.S., Suppl.—Monitore Zoologico Italiano, N.S., Supplemento. Firenze.

Monogr. Frogs Fam. Microhylidae—Parker, H. W. 1934. A Monograph of the Frogs of the Family Microhylidae. Jarrold and Sons, Ltd., Norwich. viii, 208 pp.

Monogr. Mus. Nat. Hist. Univ. Kansas—Monographs of the Museum of Natural History, University of Kansas. Lawrence.

Monogr. Tailed Batr. Japan—Sato, I. 1943. Monograph of the Tailed Batrachians of Japan [=Nippon-san yubirui sosetsu]. Nippon Publ. Co., Osaka. 520 pp.

Mus. Nat. Hist. Univ. Kansas Spec. Publ.—Museum of Natural History, University of Kansas. Special Publication. Lawrence.

Mus. Senckenb.—Museum Senckenbergianum. Frankfurt am Main.

N. Am. Fauna—North American Fauna. United States Department of the Interior, Fish and Wildlife Service, Washington, D.C.

N. Am. Herpetol., Ed. 1—Holbrook, J. E. 1836–1840. North American Herpetology. Vol. 1 (1836); Vol. 2 (1838); Vol. 3 (1838); Vol. 4 (1840). Philadelphia.

N. Am. Herpetol., Ed. 2—Holbrook, J. E. 1842. North American Herpetology. Ed. 2. 5 vols. Philadelphia. [See Worthington and Worthington, 1976, pp. xiii–xvii, and Adler, pp. xxix–xlii, In Holbrook, J. E., North American Herpetology (Ed. 2), Reprint ed., Soc. Stud. Amph. Rept., Facsimile Reprints in Herpetology Ser., for publication data.]

Nachr. Ges. Wiss. Göttingen—Nachrichten von der Gesellschaft der Wissenschaften und der Georg-Augustus-Universität zu Göttingen.

Nagoya Seibutsugakkai Kiroku—[Records of the Biological Association of Nagoya.] Japan.

Nat. Hist.—Natural History. American Museum of Natural History, New York.

Nat. Hist., Shanghai—Natural History. [In Chinese.] Shanghai.

Nat. Hist. Misc., Chicago.—Natural History Miscellanea. Chicago Academy of Sciences.

Nat. Hist. Rev.—Natural History Review. A Quarterly Journal. London.

Nat. Belges—Les Naturalistes Belges. Bruxelles.

Nat. Malgache—Naturaliste Malgache. Tananarive, Madagascar.

Nat. Misc.—Shaw, G. 1789–1813. The Naturalist's Miscellany. 24 vols. London. [F. P. Nodder, often cited as coauthor, merely drew the plates, according to Smith and Smith, 1973, Synops. Herpetofauna Mexico, 2:221; see Sherborn, 1895, Ann. Mag. Nat. Hist., (6)15:375, for publication dates.]

Nat. Syst. Amph.—Wagler, J. 1830. Natürliches System der Amphibien, mit vorangehender Classification der Säugethiere und Vögel. München, Stuttgart and Tübingen. vi, 354 pp., 9 pls.

Natura, Milano—Natura. Museo Civico di Storia Naturale, Milano.

Naturaleza, Mexico—La Naturaleza. Sociedad Mexicana de Historia Natural, México.

Naturalist's Sojourn in Jamaica—Gosse, P. H. 1851. A Naturalist's Sojourn in Jamaica. Longman, Brown, Green, and Longman, London. 508 pp.

Naturaliste, Paris—Le Naturaliste. Paris.

Nature of Hata—1976. Hata no Shizen [=Nature of Hata]. Hata no Shizen wo mamoru krai [=Society for Conservation of Hata]. Japan. 45 pp.

Naturforscher, Halle—Schreber, H. 1782. Der Naturforscher. Vol. 18. J. J. Gebauer, Halle. 268 pp.

Naturgesch. Thierr.—Gistel, J. 1848. Naturgeschichte des Thierreichs für höhere Schulen. Hoffmann, Stuttgart. xvi, 216, iv pp.

Natuurkd. Tijdschr. Nederl. Ind.—Natuurkundig Tijdschrift voor Nederlandsch Indie.

Neotropica—Neotropica. Notas Zoológicas Americana. Sociedad Zoológica de La Plata.

Neue Classif. Rept.—Fitzinger, L. J. F. J. 1826. Neue Classification der Reptilien nach ihren Natürlichen Verwandtschaften nebst einer Verwandtschafts-Tafel und einem Verzeichnisse der Reptilien-Sammlung des k. k. Zoologischen Museums zu Wien. J. G. Hübner, Wien. vii, 66 pp.

Neue Denkschr. Allgem. Schweiz. Ges. Naturwiss.—Neue Denkschriften der Allgemeinen Schweizerischen Gesellschaft für die Gesammten Naturwissenschaften. =Nouveaux Mémoires de la Société Helvétique des Sciences Naturelles. Neuchâtel.

Neues Jahrb. Min. Geol. Palaeont.—Neues Jahrbuch für Mineralogie, Geologie und Paläontologie. Stuttgart.

New Zealand J. Zool.—New Zealand Journal of Zoology.

Newt and Salamander—Tago, K. 1931. Imori to Sansyouo [=Newt and Salamander]. Maruzen, Tokyo. 210 pp.

Nomencl. Rept. Amph. Mus. Zool. Berolin.—Lichtenstein, H., and E. Martens. 1856. Nomenclator Reptilium et Amphibiorum Musei Zoologici Berolinensis. Namensverzeichniss der in der zoologischen Sammlung der Königlichen Universität zu Berlin aufgestellten Arten von Reptilien und Amphibien nach ihren Ordnungen, Familien und Gattungen. Berlin. iv, 48 pp.

Not. Nat., Philadelphia—Notulae Naturae. Academy of Natural Sciences of Philadelphia.

Notas Biol. Fac. Cienc. Exact. Fis. Nat., Corr. Zool.—Notas Biológicas de la Facultad de Ciencias Exactas, Físicas, y Naturales. Corrientes Zoología. Universidad Nacional, Corrientes, Argentina.

Notas Fac. Cienc. Nat. Mus. Univ. Nac. La Plata—Notas. Facultad de Ciencias Naturales y Museo, Universidad Nacional, La Plata.

Notes Leyden Mus.—Notes from the Leyden Museum.

Nouv. Arch. Mus. Natl. Hist. Nat., Paris—Nouvelles Archives du Muséum National d'Histoire Naturelle. Paris.

Nova Acta Acad. Caesar. Leop. Carol., Halle—Nova Acta Academiae Caesareae Leopoldino-Carolinae Germinicae Naturae Curiosorum. Halle.

Nova Guinea—Nova Guinea. [Subtitle varies by volume.] Vol. 5 (1906–1917: Résultats de l'Expedition Néerlandaise à Nouvelle-Guinée en 1903 sous les auspices de Arthur Wichmann. Zoologie); Vol. 9 (1909–1914: Résultats de l'Expedition Néerlandaise à Nouvelle-Guinée en 1907 et 1909 sous les auspices de Dr. H. A. Lorentz. Zoologie); Vol. 13 (1915–1922: Résultats de l'Expedition Néerlandaise à la Nouvelle-Guinée en 1912 et 1913 sous les auspices de A. Franssen Herderschee. Zoologie). E. J. Brill, Leiden.

Novit. Zool.—Novitates Zoologicae. A Journal of Zoology in Connection with the Tring Museum.

Nuovi Ann. Sci. Nat., Bologna—Nuovi Annali dell Scienze Naturali. Bologna.

Nuovo Giorn. Lett. Tosc., Pisa—Nuovo Giornale dei Letterati Toscana. Pisa.

Occas. Pap. Boston Soc. Nat. Hist.—Occasional Papers of the Boston Society of Natural History.

Occas. Pap. California Acad. Sci.—Occasional Papers of the California Academy of Sciences. San Francisco.

Occas. Pap. Dep. Biol. Puget Sound—Occasional Papers. Department of Biology, University of Puget Sound. Tacoma, Washington.

Occas. Pap. Div. Syst. Biol. Stanford Univ.—Occasional Papers of the Division of Systematic Biology of Stanford University. Stanford, California.

Occas. Pap. Mus. Nat. Hist. Univ. Kansas—Occasional Papers of the Museum of Natural History, University of Kansas. Lawrence.

Occas. Pap. Mus. Zool. Louisiana State Univ.—Occasional Papers. Museum of Zoology, Louisiana State University, Baton Rouge.

Occas. Pap. Mus. Zool. Univ. Michigan—Occasional Papers of the Museum of Zoology, University of Michigan. Ann Arbor.

Occas. Pap. Nat. Hist. Mus. Stanford Univ.—Occasional Papers of the Natural History Museum of Stanford University. Stanford, California.

Occas. Pap. Natl. Mus. S. Rhodesia—Occasional Papers of the National Museum of Southern Rhodesia.

Occas. Pap. Mus. Texas Tech Univ.—Occasional Papers. The Museum, Texas Tech University. Lubbock.

Oecologia, Berlin—Oecologia. Berlin.

Ordn. Fam. Gatt. Rept.—Oppel, M. 1811. Die Ordnung, Familien und Gattungen der Reptilien als Prodrom einer Naturgeschichte derselben. Lindauer, München. xii, 87 pp.

Pacif. Sci.—Pacific Science. Honolulu.

Pap. Avulsos Dep. Zool., São Paulo—Papeis Avulsos do Departamento de Zoologia. Universidade de São Paulo.

Pap. Avulsos Zool, São Paulo—Papeis Avulsos Zoologia. Universidade de São Paulo.

Pearce-Sellards Ser., Texas Mem. Mus.—Pearce-Sellards Series. Texas Memorial Museum, University of Texas, Austin.

Peking Nat. Hist. Bull.—Peking Natural History Bulletin.

Periód. Zool.—Periódico Zoológica. Sociedad Entomológica Zoológica, Buenos Aires.

Philadelphia Mus. Sci. Bull.—Philadelphia Museum's Scientific Bulletin.

Philippine J. Sci.—Philippine Journal of Science. Manila.

Physis, Buenos Aires—Physis. Buenos Aires.

Pilot Register of Zool.—Pilot Register of Zoology. New York State College of Agriculture at Cornell University, Ithaca.

Poeyana—Poeyana. Instituto de Biología la Habana, Academia de Ciencias de Cuba.

Prelim. Handlist Herpetofauna Costa Rica—Savage, J. M. 1980. A Preliminary Handlist of the Herpetofauna of Costa Rica. University Graphics, Los Angeles. 111 pp.

Proc. Acad. Nat. Sci. Philadelphia—Proceedings of the Academy of Natural Science of Philadelphia. [See Fox, 1913, Proc. Acad. Nat. Sci. Philadelphia, 65:viii–xiv, for publication data.]

Proc. Am. Acad. Arts Sci.—Proceedings of the American Academy of Arts and Sciences. Cambridge, Massachusetts.

Proc. Am. Assoc. Adv. Sci., Charleston—Proceedings of the American Association for the Advancement of Science. Charleston.

Proc. Am. Philos. Soc.—Proceedings of the American Philosophical Society. Philadelphia.

Proc. Asiat. Soc. Bengal—Proceedings of the Asiatic Society of Bengal. Calcutta.

Proc. Biol. Soc. Washington—Proceedings of the Biological Society of Washington.

Proc. Boston Soc. Nat. Hist.—Proceedings of the Boston Society of Natural History.

Proc. California Acad. Sci.—Proceedings of the California Academy of Sciences. San Francisco.

Proc. Indian Acad. Sci., (B)—Proceedings of the Indian Academy of Sciences. Section B. Bangalore.

Proc. Junior Soc. Nat. Sci. Cincinnati—Proceedings of the Junior Society of Natural History. Cincinnati.

Proc. K. Nederland. Akad. Wetensch., (C)—Proceedings of the Koninklijke Nederlandse Akademie van Wetenschappen. Ser. C, Biological and Medical Sciences.

Proc. Linn. Soc. New South Wales—Proceedings of the Linnaean Society of New South Wales. Sydney.

Proc. Linn. Soc. New York—Proceedings of the Linnaean Society of New York.

Proc. Melbourne Herpetol. Symp.—Banks, C. B., and A. A. Martin (eds.). 1981. Proceedings of the Melbourne Herpetological Symposium. Royal Melbourne Zoological Gardens, Melbourne.

Proc. New England Zool. Club—Proceedings of the New England Zoological Club. Cambridge.

Proc. R. Soc. New South Wales—Proceedings of the Royal Society of New South Wales. Mosman.

Proc. R. Soc. Queensland—Proceedings of the Royal Society of Queensland.

Proc. R. Soc. Victoria—Proceedings of the Royal Society of Victoria.

Proc. U.S. Natl. Mus.—Proceedings of the United States National Museum. Washington, D.C.

Proc. W. Virginia Acad. Sci.—Proceedings of the West Virginia Academy of Sciences.

Proc. Zool. Soc., Calcutta—Proceedings of the Zoological Society. Calcutta.

Proc. Zool. Soc. London—Proceedings of the Zoological Society of London.

Prodr. Faun. Zeylan.—Kelaart, E. F. 1852–1854. Prodromus Faunae Zeylanicae; being Contributions to the Zoology of Ceylon. Vol. 1 (1852); Vol. 2 (1854). Colombo.

Publ. Cult. Companhia Diamantes Angola—Publicaciones Culturais da Companhia de Diamantes. Dundo, Angola.

Publ. Univ. État, Elisabethville—Publication de l'Université de l'État à Elisabethville. Zaire.

Puku—Puku. Chilanga, Zambia.

Q. J. Florida Acad. Sci.—Quarterly Journal of the Florida Academy of Sciences. Gainesville.

Q. J. Microsc. Sci.—Quarterly Journal of Microscopical Science. London.

Q. J. Taiwan Mus.—Quarterly Journal of the Taiwan Museum. Taipei.

Q. Rev. Biol.—Quarterly Review of Biology. Baltimore.

R. Ontario Mus. Life Sci. Contrib.—Royal Ontario Museum Life Sciences Contributions. Ottawa.

Reading Public Mus. and Art Gallery Sci. Publ.—Reading Public Museum and Art Gallery Science Publications. Reading, Pennsylvania.

Rec. Albany Mus.—Records of the Albany Museum. Grahamstown, Rep. South Africa.

Rec. Aust. Mus.—Records of the Australian Museum. Sydney.

Rec. Indian Mus.—Records of the Indian Museum. Calcutta.

Rec. Queen Victoria Mus.—Records of the Queen Victoria Museum. Launceton, Victoria, Australia.

Rec. S. Aust. Mus.—Records of the South Australian Museum. Adelaide.

Rec. W. Aust. Mus.—Records of the Western Australian Museum. Perth.

Rec. Zool. Surv. India—Records of the Zoological Survey of India. Calcutta.

Règne Animal, Ed. 2—Cuvier, G. 1829. Le Règne animal distribué d'après son Organisation, pour servir de Base à l'Histoire naturelle des Animaux et d'Introduction à l'Anatomie comparée. Nouvelle Edition, revue et augmentée par P. A. Latreille. Vol. 2. Paris.

Reise Brasil.—Wied-Neuwied, M. A. P., Prinz von. 1820–1821. Reise nach Brasilien in den Jahren 1815 bis 1817. Vol. 1 (1820); Vol. 2 (1821). H. L. Brönner, Frankfurt am Main.

Reise Freg. Novara, Amph.—Steindachner, F. 1867. Reise der Österreichischen Fregatte Novara um die Erde in den Jahren 1857, 1858, 1859, unter den Befehlen des Commodore B. von Wüllersdorf-Urbair. Zoologischer Theil. Amphibien. Staatsdruckerei, Wien. 98 pp. [See Higgins, 1963, J. Soc. Bibliogr. Nat. Hist., 4:153–159, for publication data, and Gans, 1955, Ann. Carnegie Mus., 33:275–285, for itinerary.]

Reise La-Plata-Staaten—Burmeister, H. 1861. Reise durch die La-Plata-Staaten, mit besonderer Rücksicht auf die physische Beschaffenheit und den Culturzustand der Argentinischen Republik. Ausgeführt in den Jahren 1857, 1858, 1859 und 1860. Vol. 2. H. W. Schmidt, Halle. iv, 538 pp.

Reise Mossambique—1882. Naturwissenschaftliche Reise nach Mossambique, auf Befehl seiner Majestät des Königs Friedrich Wilhelm IV. In den Jahren 1842 bis 1848 ausgeführt. Zoologie. III. G. Reimer, Berlin.

Reise N. Am.—Wied-Neuwied, M. A. P., Prinz von. 1838–1841. Reise in das Innere

Nord-Amerika in den Jahren 1832 bis 1834. Vol. 1. J. Hoelscher, Coblenz. 653 pp. [See Smith and Smith, 1973, Synops. Herpetofauna Mexico, 2:182–183, for publication data.]

Reise Ost-Afr.—Voeltzkow, A. 1913. Reise in Ost-Afrika in den Jahren 1903–1905 mit Mitteln der Hermann und Elise geb. Heckmann-Wentzel-Stiftung. Wissenschaftliche Ergebnisse. Systematischen Arbeiten. Stuttgart.

Reise Russ. Reichs—Pallas, P. S. 1771–1776. Reise durch verschiedene Provinzen des Russischen Reichs. Theil 1–3. St. Pétersbourg.

Reisen Algier—Wagner, M. F. 1841. Reisen in der Regentschaft Algier in den Jahren 1836–1838 . . . Nebst einem naturhistorischen Anhang . . . . 3 vols., Atlas. Leipzig.

Reisen Brit. Guiana—Schomburgk, M. R. 1848. Reisen in Britisch-Guiana in den Jahren 1840–44. Im Auftrage Sr. Majestät des Königs von Preussen ausgeführt. Theil 3. Versuch einer Zusammenstellung der Fauna und Flora von Britisch-Guiana. Leipzig.

Rend. Accad. Naz. Sci. XL, Mem. Sci. Fis. Natur.—Rendiconti dell'Accademia Nazionale della Scienze, detta dei XL. Memorie Scienze Fisiche e Naturali. Roma.

Rep. Geog. Geol. Explor. Surv. West 100th Merid.—1875. Report upon Geographical and Geological Explorations and Surveys West of the One Hundredth Meridian . . . Geo. M. Wheeler. Vol. 5 (Zoology). Government Printing Office, Washington, D.C.

Rep. Explor. Surv. R.R. Route Mississippi River–Pacific Ocean—1855–1859. Reports of Explorations and Surveys to Ascertain the Most Practible . . . Route for a Railroad from the Mississippi River to the Pacific Ocean. 12 vols. Washington, D.C. [See (1915) Catalogue of the Books, Maps, Manuscripts, and Drawings in the British Museum (Natural History), 5:2176–2178, for summary of this complicated work.]

Rep. Horn Exped. Cent. Aust.—Spencer, B. 1896. Report on the Work of the Horn Scientific Expedition to Central Australia. Part 2. Zoology: Amphibia. Dulau, London.

Rep. U.S.-Mex. Bound. Surv.—Emory, W. H. (ed.). 1859. Report on the United States and Mexican Boundary Survey. Vol. 2. Zoology of the Boundary. Washington, D.C. 35 pp.

Rept. Amph. Alabama—Mount, R. H. 1975. The Reptiles and Amphibians of Alabama. Agricultural Experiment Station, Auburn University. v, 347 pp.

Rept. Brit. India—Günther, A. C. L. G. 1864. The Reptiles of British India. Ray Society, London. xxvii, 452 pp.

Result. Altai Exped.—Katschenko, N. F. 1899. Rezul'taty Altaiskoi ekspeditsii. Tomsk University. ii, 158 pp., 4 pls.

Rev. Biol. Tropical—Revista de Biologia Tropical. Universidad de Costa Rica, San José.

Rev. Brasil Biol.—Revista Brasileira de Biologia. Rio de Janeiro.

Rev. Chilena Hist. Nat.—Revista Chilena de Historia Natural. Santiago.

Rev. Ecuat. Entomol. Parasitol.—Revista Ecuatoriana de Entomología y Parasitología. Guayaquil.

Rev. Int. Sci., Paris—Revue Internationale des Sciences. Paris.

Rev. Mag. Zool., Paris—Revue et Magasin de Zoologie Pure et Appliquée. Paris.

Rev. Mus. Argent. Cienc. Nat. Bernardino Rivadavia—Revista del Museo Argentino de Ciencias Naturales "Bernardino Rivadavia". Buenos Aires.

Rev. Mus. La Plata—Revista del Museo de La Plata. La Plata, Argentina.

Rev. Mus. Paulista, São Paulo—Revista do Museu Paulista. São Paulo.

Rev. Suisse Zool.—Revue Suisse de Zoologie. Geneva.

Rev. Univ. Centroccident. Lisandro Alvarado, Tarea Común—Revista de la Universidad Centro Occidental "Lisandro Alvarado". Tarea Común. Lara, Venezuela.

Rev. Zool. Afr.—Revue de Zoologie Africaine. Tervuren.

Rev. Zool. Bot. Afr.—Revue de Zoologie et Botanique Africaine. Tervuren.

S. Afr. Frogs—Passmore, N. I., and V. C. Carruthers. 1979. South African Frogs. Witwatersrand University Press, Johannesburg. xviii, 270 pp.

S. Afr. J. Zool.—South African Journal of Zoology. South African Association for the Advancement of Science.

S. Aust. Nat.—South Australian Naturalist. Field Naturalist's Society of South Australia, Adelaide.

Sagg. Distrib. Met. Degli Animal. Vert.—Bonaparte, C. L. 1831. Saggio di una Distribuzione Metodica degli Animali Vertebrati. A. Boulzaler, Roma. 144 pp.

Salamandra—Salamandra. Deutsche Gesellschaft für Herpetologie und Terrarienkunde, Frankfurt am Main.

Salamanders Fam. Plethodontidae—Dunn, E. R. 1926. The Salamanders of the Family Plethodontidae. Smith College 50th Anniversary Publication No. 7. Northampton, Massachusetts. vii, 441 pp.

Salamandres Eur. Asie Afr. Nord—Thorn, R. 1968. Les Salamandres d'Europe, d'Asie et d'Afrique Nord. Editions Paul Lechevalier, Paris. 376 pp.

Sarawak Mus. J.—Sarawak Museum Journal. Kuching, Malaysia.

Schr. Ges. Naturforsch. Freunde Berlin—Schriften der Gesellschaft Naturforschender Freunde zu Berlin.

Sci. Bull. Nat. Hist. Mus. Los Angeles Co.—Science Bulletin. Natural History Museum of Los Angeles County.

Sci. Cult.—Science and Culture. Calcutta.

Sci. Publ. Sci. Mus. Minnesota—Scientific Publications of the Science Museum of Minnesota. St. Paul.

Sci. Rep. Fac. Sci. Ege Univ., Izmir—Scientific Reports of the Faculty of Science. Ege University, Izmir, Turkey.

Sci. Rep. Lab. Amph. Biol. Hiroshima Univ.—Scientific Report of the Laboratory for Amphibian Biology. Hiroshima University.

Science, Washington, D.C.—Science. American Association for the Advancement of Science. Washington, D.C.

Scientia Sinica—Scientia Sinica. Beijing.

Senckenb. Biol.—Senckenbergiana. Biologica. Frankfurt am Main.

Sinensia, Nanking—Sinensia. Academia Sinica, Metropolitan Museum of Natural History, Nanking.

Sitzungsber. Akad. Wiss. Wien, Math. Naturwiss. Kl.—Sitzungsberichte der Akademie der Wissenschaften in Wien. Mathematisch-Naturwissenschaftliche Klasse.

Sitzungsber. Ges. Naturforsch. Freunde Berlin—Sitzungsberichte der Gesellschaft Naturforschender Freunde zu Berlin.

Sitzungsber. Preuss. Akad. Wiss. Berlin—Sitzungsberichte der Preussischen Akademie der Wissenschaften zu Berlin.

Skand. Fauna—Nilsson, S. 1842. Skandanavisk Fauna. Vol. 3 (Anfibierna). Lund. iv, 120 pp.

Smithson. Contrib. Zool.—Smithsonian Contributions to Zoology. Washington, D.C.

Smithson. Herpetol. Inform. Serv.—Smithsonian Herpetological Information Service. Washington, D.C.

Smithson. Misc. Collect.—Smithsonian Miscellaneous Collections. Washington, D.C.

Southwest Nat.—Southwestern Naturalist.

Spec. Nov. Testud. Ran. Brasil.—Spix, J. B. 1824. Animalia nova sive Species novae Testudinum et Ranarum quas in itinere per Brasiliam annis MDCCCXVII–MDCCCXX jussu et auspiciis Maximiliani Josephi I. Bavariae Regis. F. S. Hübschmann, München. iii, 53 pp. [See Adler, 1981, pp. v–vii, *In* Spix, J. B. von, and J. G. Wagler, Herpetology of Brazil, Soc. Study Amph. Rept. Facsimile Reprints in Herpetology Ser., for publication data.]

Spixiana, Suppl.—Spixiana. Supplement. Zoologische Staatssammlung, München.

Spolia Zeylan.—Spolia Zeylanica. Colombo Museum, Colombo.

Spolia Zool. Mus. Haun.—Spolia Zoologica Musei Hauniensis. Copenhagen.

Steenstrupia—Steenstrupia. Copenhagen.

Stud. Chinese Tailed Amph.—Zhao, E., and Q. Hu. 1984. Studies on Chinese Tailed Amphibians. [In Chinese.] Sichuan Scientific and Technical Publishing House, Chengdu. 68 pp.

Stud. Fauna Curaçao and other Caribb. Is.—Studies on the Fauna of Curaçao and other Caribbean Islands. Utrecht.

Stud. Fauna Suriname and other Guyanas—Studies on the Fauna of Suriname and other Guyanas. Utrecht.

Stud. Neotrop. Fauna Environ.—Studies on Neotropical Fauna and Environment. Lisse, Netherlands.

Stuttgart. Beitr. Naturkd.—Stuttgarter Beiträge zur Naturkunde.

Supl. Batr. Chil. Descr. Hist. Fis. Polit. Chile—Philippi, R. A. 1902. Suplemento a los Batraquios Chilenos Descritos en la Historia Física y Política de Chile de Don Claudio Gay. Santiago. 161 pp.

Synops. Herpetofauna Mexico—Smith, H. M., and R. B. Smith. 1971-. Synopsis of the Herpetofauna of Mexico. Vol. 1 (1971—Literature on the Mexican Axolotl). Vol. 2 (1973—Analysis of the Literature Exclusive of the Mexican Axolotl). Vol. 4 (1976—Source Analysis and Index for Mexican Amphibians). J. Johnson, North Bennington, Vermont.

Synops. Rept.—Laurenti, J. N. 1768. Specimen medicum, exhibens Synopsin Reptilium emendatum cum Experimentis circa Venena et Antidota Reptilium Austriacorum. J. T. de Trattnern, Wien. 214 pp. [Evidence suggests that the correct name of the author is J. N. Laurent.]

Syst. Amph.—Merrem, B. 1820. Versuch eines Systems der Amphibien. Tentamen Systematis Amphibiorum. J. C. Krieger, Marburg. xv, 191 pp., 1 pl.

Syst. Herpetol.—Dowling, H. G., and W. E. Duellman. 1978. Systematic Herpetology. Herpetological Information Search Systems Publications, New York.

Syst. Key Chinese Amph.—Anon. 1977. Systematic Key of the Amphibia of China. [In Chinese.] Zoological Institute of Sichuan [now Chengdu Institute of Biology], Chengdu. 93 pp.

Syst. Nat., Ed. 10—Linnaeus, C. 1758. Systema Naturae per Regna tria Naturae secundum Classes, Ordines, Genera, Species, cum Characteribus, Differentiis, Synonymis, Locis. Vol. 1. Stockholm.

Syst. Nat., Ed. 12—Linnaeus, C. 1766. Systema Naturae per Regna tria Naturae secundum Classes, Ordines, Genera, Species, cum Characteribus, Differentiis, Synonymis, Locis. Vol. 1. Stockholm.

Syst. Rept.—Fitzinger, L. J. F. J. 1843. Systema Reptilium. Fasciculus primus. Amblyglossae. Braumüller and Seidel, Wien. 106 pp. [See Smith and Grant, 1958, Herpetologica, 14:215–222, for discussion of date of publication.]

Syst. Zool.—Systematic Zoology. Society of Systematic Zoology.

Tabl. Encycl. Méth. Trois Règ. Nat., Erp.—Bonnaterre, P. J. 1789. Erpétologie. In Tableau encyclopédique et méthodique des trois Règnes de la Nature. Panckouke, Paris. xxviii, 70 pp., 26 pls.

Tailless Amph. China—Liu, C. C., and S. Hu. 1961. Tailless Amphibians of China. [In Chinese.] Shanghai. xvi, 364 pp.

Tailless Batr. Europe—Boulenger, G. A. 1897–1898. The Tailless Batrachians of Europe. 2 vols. London.

Tailless Batr. Japan. Emp.—Okada, Y. 1931. The Tailless Batrachians of the Japanese Empire. Imperial Agricultural Experiment Station, Tokyo. iv, 215 pp.

Tasman. Amph.—Martin, A. R., and M. Littlejohn. 1982. Tasmanian Amphibians. Fauna Tasman. Handbook No. 6. Univ. Tasmania.

Termés. Füzetek—Természetrajzi Füzetek. Budapest.

Texas J. Sci.—Texas Journal of Science.

Tezisy Dokladov Zool. Inst. Akad. Nauk SSSR, Leningrad—Tezisy Dokladov. Zoologischeskogo Instituta Akademii Nauk S.S.S.R. Leningrad.

Thierwelt Ost-Afr.—Tornier, G. 1897 "1896". Deutsch-Ost-Afrika. Vol. 3. Die Thierwelt Ost-Afrikas und der Nachbargebiete. Reptilien und Amphibien. Berlin. xiii, 164 pp.

Tijdschr. Nederl. Dierkd. Ver.—Tijdschrift der Nederlandsche Dierkundige Vereeniging. Leiden.

Trans. Chinese Assoc. Adv. Sci.—Transactions of the Chinese Association for the Advancement of Science. Shanghai.

Trans. Illinois State Acad. Sci.—Transactions of the Illinois State Academy of Science.

Trans. Kansas Acad. Sci.—Transactions of the Kansas Academy of Sciences.

Trans. Linn. Soc. London—Transactions of the Linnaean Society of London.
Trans. Nat. Hist. Soc. Formosa—Transactions of the Natural History Society of Formosa. Taiwan.
Trans. Proc. New Zealand Inst.—Transactions and Proceedings of the New Zealand Institute. Wellington.
Trans. R. Soc. New Zealand—Transactions of the Royal Society of New Zealand. Wellington.
Trans. R. Soc. S. Afr.—Transactions of the Royal Society of South Africa.
Trans. R. Soc. S. Aust.—Transactions of the Royal Society of South Australia.
Trans. Zool. Soc. London—Transactions of the Zoological Society of London.
Trav. Inst. Scient. Chérifien, Rabat, Sér. Zool.—Travaux de l'Institut Scientifique Chérifien. Série Zoologique. Rabat, Morocco.
Trav. Soc. Nat. Univ. Imp. Kharkow—Travaux de la Société des Naturalistes à l'Université Impériale de Kharkow. =Trudy Obschchestva estestvoispytatelei pri Imperatorskom kazanskom universitete Kharkow.
Treefrogs E. Afr.—Schiøtz, A. 1975. The Treefrogs of Eastern Africa. Steenstrupia, Copenhagen. 232 pp.
Trop. Agric. Trinidad—Tropical Agriculture. Trinidad.
Trudy Zool. Inst. Akad. Nauk SSSR, Leningrad—Trudy Zoologicheskogo Instituta Akademii Nauk S.S.S.R. Leningrad.
Tulane Stud. Zool.—Tulane Studies in Zoology. New Orleans.
Turkiye Amph.—Başoğlu, M., and N. Özeti. 1973. Turkiye Amphibileri. Ege Universitesi Fen Fakultesi Kitaplar Ser. No. 50. Izmir. 155 pp.
Univ. California Publ. Zool.—University of California Publications in Zoology.
Univ. Kansas Publ. Mus. Nat. Hist.—University of Kansas Publications. Museum of Natural History. Lawrence.
Univ. Kansas Sci. Bull.—University of Kansas Science Bulletin. Lawrence.
Veg. Vert. Inf. Arica–Lago Chungara—Veloso-M., A., and E. Bustos-O. (eds.). 1982. El Hombre y los Ecosistemas de Montaña (El Ambiente Natural y las Poblaciones Humanas de los Andes del Norte Grande de Chile [Arica, Lat. 18° 28′ S]). Man and Biosphere (MAB)—6. Vol. 1. La Vegetación y los Vertebrados Inferiores de los Pisos Altitudinalis entre Arica y el Lago Chungara. UNESCO, Santiago de Chile.
Vergl. Uebersicht Zool. Syst.—Gravenhorst, J. L. C. 1807. Vergleichende Uebersicht des Linneischen und einiger Neueren Zoologischen Systeme . . . nebst dem Eingeschalteten Verzeichniss der Zoologischen Sammlung des Verfassers und den Beschreibungen neuer Thierarten die in Derselben Vorhanden Sind. H. Dieterich, Göttingen. xx, 476 pp.
Verh. Batavia. Genootsch. Wetensch.—Verhandelingen van het Bataviaasch Genootschap van Kunsten en Wetenschappen.
Verh. Genootsch. Wetensch. Vlissingen—Verhandelingen Zeeuwsch Genootschap der Wetenschappen te Vlissingen.
Verh. Naturforsch. Ges. Basel—Verhandlungen der Naturforschenden Gesellschaft in Basel.
Verh. Zool. Bot. Ges. Wien—Verhandlungen der Zoologisch-Botanischen Gesellschaft in Wien.
Vert. Hungar.—Vertebrata Hungarica. Budapest.
Vert. Syn. Mus. Mediolanense Extant.—Cornalia, E. 1849. Vertebratorum Synopsis in Musaeo Mediolanense extantium quae per novum Orbem Cajetanas Osculati collegit Annis 1846–47–48. Speciebus novis vel minus cognitis adjectis, nec non Descriptionibus atque Iconibus illustratis, curante Aemilio Cornalia. Mediolani. 16 pp.
Vert. Viaj. Pacif., Batr.—Jiménez de la Espada, M. 1875. Vertabrados del Viaje al Pacífico Verificado de 1862 a 1865 por una Comisión de Naturalistas Enviada por el Gobierno Español. Batracios. A. Miguel Ginesta, Madrid. 208 pp.
Vert. Zool. Sind—Murray, J. A. 1884. The Vertebrate Zoology of Sind. A Systematic Account, with Descriptions of All the Known Species . . . . Richardson & Co., London; Education Society's Press, Bombay. xvi, 424 pp.

Vestn. Leningrad. Univ., Biol.—Vestnik Leningradskogo Universiteta, Seriya Biologiya.

Vestn. Zool., Kiev—Vestnik Zoologii. Kiev.

Verz. Doubl. Zool. Mus. K. Univ. Berlin—Lichtenstein, H. 1823. Verzeichniss der Doubletten des zoologischen Museums der Königl. Universität zu Berlin nebst Beschreibung vieler bisher unbekannter Arten von Säugethieren, Vögeln, Amphibien und Fischen. T. Trautwein, Berlin. x, 118 pp.

Victorian Nat.—Victorian Naturalist.

Vidensk. Medd. Dansk Naturhist. Foren.—Videnskabelige Meddelelser fra Dansk Naturhistorisk Forening i Kjøbenhavn.

Vie Milieu—Vie et Milieu. Paris.

Virginia Polytech. Inst. State Univ., Res. Monogr.—Virginia Polytechnic Institute and State University. Research Monograph.

Voy. Coquille—Duperrey, L. I. (ed.). 1826–1838. Voyage autour du Monde, exécuté par Ordre du Roi, sur la Corvette de sa Majesté, La Coquille, pendant les années 1822, 1823, 1824, 1825. Zoologie and Atlas. Arthur Bertrand, Paris. [See Sherborn and Woodward, 1906, Ann. Mag. Nat. Hist., (7)17:335–336, for publication dates.]

Voy. India Orient.—Bélanger, I. G. S. H. (ed.). 1834. Voyage aux Indes-Orientales, par le Nord de l'Europe, les Provinces du Caucase, la Géorgie, l'Arménie, et la Perse, ... pendant les années 1825–29. Zoologie. Paris.

West. Aust. Nat.—Western Australian Naturalist. Perth.

Wiss. Ergebn. Deutsch. Gran-Chaco-Exped., Amph. Rept.—Müller, L., and W. Hellmich. 1936. Wissenschaftliche Ergebnisse der Deutschen Gran Chaco-Expedition. Amphibien und Reptilien. Vol. 1. Stuttgart. 120 pp.

Wiss. Ergebn. Deutsch. Zentr. Afr. Exped.—1912. Wissenschaftliche Ergebnisse der Deutschen Zentral Afrika-Expedition 1907–1908 unter Führung Adolf Friedrichs, Herzogs zu Mecklenburg. Leipzig.

Wiss. Ergebn. Zweiten Deutsch. Zentr. Afr. Exped.—1917. Wissenschaftliche Ergebnisse der zweiten Deutschen Zentral-Afrika Expedition 1910–11 unter Führung Adolf Friedrichs, Herzogs zu Mecklenburg. 4 vols. Leipzig.

Wiss. Result. Przewalski Cent. Asien Reisen, Zool.—1898. Wissenschaftliche Resultate der von N. M. Przewalski nach Central-Asien unternommenen Reisen. Auf Kosten ... herausgegeben von der Kaiserlichen Akademie der Wissenschaften. Zoologischer Theil (Vol. 1). St. Pétersbourg.

Wochenschr. Aquar. Terrarienkd.—Wochenschrift für Aquarien- und Terrarienkunde. Braunschweig.

Z. Naturwiss., Halle—Zeitschrift für Naturwissenschaften. Halle.

Z. Physiol.—Zeitschrift für Physiologie. Untersuchung über die Natur des Menschen, der Thiere und der Pflanzen. Heidelberg.

Z. Wiss. Zool., Leipzig—Zeitschrift für Wissenschaftliche Zoologie. Leipzig.

Z. Zool. Syst. Evolutionsforsch.—Zeitschrift für zoologische Systematik und Evolutionsforschung. Hamburg and Berlin.

Zool. Abh. Staatl. Mus. Tierkd., Dresden—Zoologische Abhandlungen. Staatliches Museum für Tierkunde, Dresden.

Zool. Afr.—Zoologica Africana. Cape Town.

Zool. Anz.—Zoolgischer Anzeiger. Leipzig.

Zool. Atlas—Eschscholtz, J. F. 1829–1833. Zoologischer Atlas, enthaltend Abbildungen und Beschreibungen neuer Thierarten, während des Flottcapitains von Kotzebue zweiter Reise um die Welt, auf Russisch-Kaiserlich Kriegsschupp Predpriaetië in den Jahren 1823–1826. 5 parts. [Part 5, 1833, edited and partly written by M. H. Rathke, viii, 28 pp., 25 pls., according to Smith and Smith, 1973, Synops. Herpetofauna Mexico, 2:88.] G. Reimer, Berlin.

Zool. Beitr.—Zoologische Beiträge.

Zool. Cat. Aust.—Cogger, H. G., E. E. Cameron, and H. M. Cogger. 1983. Zoological Catalogue of Australia. Vol. 1. Amphibia and Reptilia. Australian Government Publishing Service, Canberra. vi, 313 pp.

Zool. J. Linn. Soc.—Zoological Journal of the Linnaean Society. London.

Zool. Jahrb., Abt. Syst.—Zoologische Jahrbücher. Abteilung für Systematik, Ökologie und Geographie der Tiere. [Title varies.] Jena.

Zool. Mag., Tokyo—Zoological Magazine [=Dobutsugaku Zasshi]. Zoological Society of Tokyo.

Zool. Meded., Leiden—Zoologische Mededelingen. Rijksmuseum van Natuurlijke Historie, Leiden.

Zool. Misc.—Gray, J. E. (ed.). Zoological Miscellany. Treuttl, Würtz & Co., London.

Zool. Rec.—Zoological Record. London.

Zool. Res., Kunming—Zoological Research. Kunming Institute of Zoology, Kunming, Yunnan.

Zool. Sci.—Zoological Science. Zoological Society of Japan.

Zool. Specialis—Eichwald, C. E. von. 1831. Zoologia Specialis, quam Expositis Animalis tum Vivis, tum Fossilibus potossimum Rossiae in Universum, et Poloniae in Species, in Usum Lectionum Publicarum in Universitate Caesarea Vilnensi habendarum edidit . . . Pars Posterior Specialem Expositionem Spondylozoorum Continensis. Vilna and Leipzig.

Zool. Verh., Leiden—Zoologische Verhandelingen. Rijksmuseum van Natuurlijke Historie. Leiden.

Zool. Voy. Beagle—Bell, T. 1843. The Zoology of the Voyage of the H.M.S. Beagle, under the command of Captain Fitzroy, R.N., during the years 1832 to 1836. Part 5. Reptiles. Smith, Elder and Co., London. 51 pp.

Zool. Zh.—Zoologischeskii Zhurnal. Moscow.

Zoologica, New York—Zoologica. Scientific Contributions of the New York Zoological Society.

Zoologist—The Zoologist. A Monthly Journal of Natural History. London.

Appendix II. Museum Abbreviations

The following museum abbreviations were drawn from Leviton *et al.* (1980, Museum acronyms. Second edition, Herpetol. Rev., 11:93–102), with some corrections and additions. Where known, mailing addresses have been included to facilitate communication with curatorial personnel.

AL-MN   Adolpho Lutz collection in MN.

AM   Australian Museum, Department of Herpetology, 6–8 College Street, Sydney, New South Wales 2000, Australia.

AMG   Albany Museum, Somerset Street, Grahamstown 6140, Cape Province, South Africa.

AMNH   American Museum of Natural History, Department of Herpetology, 79th Street and Central Park West, New York, New York 10024, USA.

ANSP   Academy of Natural Sciences, Department of Herpetology, 19th and Benjamin Franklin Parkway, Philadelphia, Pennsylvania 19103, USA.

BM   British Museum (Natural History), Department of Zoology, Cromwell Road, London SW7 5BD, United Kingdom.

BNHM   Bombay Natural History Museum, Hornbill House, Shahid Bhagat Singh Road, Bombay 400 023, India.

BPBM   Bernice P. Bishop Museum, Department of Zoology, 1355 Kalihi Street, Honolulu, Hawaii 96818, USA.

CAS   California Academy of Sciences, Golden Gate Park, San Francisco, California 94118, USA.

CAS-SU   Stanford University collection. [Now housed at CAS.]

CCB   Central College, Bangalore, India. [Collection lost.]

CHINM   Instituto Nacional de Microbiología, Buenos Aires, Argentina. [Now maintained at MACN.]

CIB   Chengdu Institute of Biology, Academia Sinica, P.O. Box 416, Chengdu, Sichuan, P. R. China.

CM   Carnegie Museum, Department of Herpetology, 4400 Forbes Avenue, Pittsburgh, Pennsylvania 15213, USA.

CPS   University of Puget Sound, Museum of Natural History, 1500 N. Warner Street, Tacoma, Washington 98416, USA.

CRE   Costa Rica Expeditions. [Formerly at University of Southern California; now at University of Miami, Department of Biology, P.O. Box 249118, Coral Gables, Florida 33124, USA].

CU   Cornell University, Division of Biological Sciences, Ithaca, New York 14853, USA.

DBCUCH   Universidad de Chile, Departamento de Biología Celular y Genética, Casilla 6556, Santiago 7, Chile.

EBRG   Museo de la Estación Biología de Rancho Grande, Maracay, Edo. Aragua, Venezuela.

EHT-HMS   E. H. Taylor-Hobart M. Smith. [Now divided between FMNH and UIMNH.]

EI   Eugenio Izecksohn, Universidade Federal Rural do Rio de Janeiro, Departamento de Biologia Animal, 23460 Seropédica, Itaguai, Rio de Janeiro, Brazil.

FML   Fundación Miguel Lillo, Miguel Lillo 205, Tucumán 4000, Argentina.

FMNH   Field Museum of Natural History, Division of Amphibians and Reptiles, Roosevelt Road at Lake Shore Drive, Chicago, Illinois 60605, USA.

FSM   Florida State Museum, University of Florida, Museum Road, Gainesville, Florida 32611, USA.

FU   Fudan University, Department of Biology, Shanghai, Guangdong, P. R. China.

HUJ   Hebrew University, Department of Zoology, Jerusalem, Israel.

IBMUNC   Universidad Nacional de Cuyo, Instituto de Biología Animal, Centro Universitario, Parque General San Martín, 5500 Mendoza, Argentina.

ICN   Universidad Nacional de Colombia, Instituto de Ciencias Naturales,
               Apartado Aéreo 7495, Bogotá, Colombia.
IFAN   Instituto Fondamental d'Afrique Noire, B.P. 206, Université de Dakar,
               Dakar, Senegal.
IM   Indian Museum. [Now ZSI.]
IOC   Instituto Oswaldo Cruz, C.P. 926, Avenida Brasil, Manguinhos, 20.000 Rio
               de Janeiro, Brazil.
IZUA   Universidad Austral, Instituto de Zoología, Valdivia, Chile.
IZUC   Universidad de Concepción, Instituto de Zoología, Concepción, Chile.
IZUG   Istituto di Zoologia dell'Università, Via Balbi 5, 16126 Genova, Italy.
KIZ   Kunming Institute of Zoology, Academia Sinica, Kunming, Yunnan, P. R.
               China.
KM   Muzeum Przyrodnicze Uniwersytetu Jagiellońskiego, ul. Krupnicza 50,
               Kraków, Poland.
KU   University of Kansas, Museum of Natural History, Division of
               Herpetology, Lawrence, Kansas 66045, USA.
LACM   Natural History Museum of Los Angeles County, Section of Herpetology,
               900 Exposition Boulevard, Los Angeles, California 90007, USA.
LCFM   Musée d'Histoire Naturelle, 2300 La-Chaux-de-Fond, Switzerland.
LIHUBA   Universidad de Buenos Aires, Laboratorio de Investigaciones
               Herpetológicas, Buenos Aires, Argentina. [Now maintained at MACN.]
LSUMZ   Louisiana State University, Museum of Zoology, Baton Rouge, Louisiana
               70893, USA.
MACN   Museo Argentino de Ciencias Naturales "Bernardino Rivadavia", Sección
               Herpetología, Avenida Angel Gallardo 470, 1405 Buenos Aires,
               Argentina.
MBL   Museu Bocage, Universidade de Lisboa, Rua da Escola Politécnica, Lisboa
               2, Portugal. [Collection destroyed by fire on 18 March 1978.]
MBUCV   Universidad Central de Venezuela, Museo de Biología, Apartado 59058,
               Los Chaguaramos, Caracas, Venezuela.
MCZ   Museum of Comparative Zoology, Harvard University, Cambridge,
               Massachusetts 02138, USA.
MD   Museu Regional do Dundo, C.P. 54, Dundo, Chitato, Luanda-Norte,
               Angola.
MDUG   Universidad de Guanajuato, Museo "Alfredo Dugès", Guanajuato, Mexico.
MGAB   Muzeul de Istorie Naturala "Grigore Antipa", Soseaua Kisseleff 1, Sectorul
               1, 79744 Bucharest 63, Romania.
MHNG   Museum d'Histoire Naturelle, Route de Malagnou, C.P. 284, 1211 Geneva
               6, Switzerland.
MHNJP   Universidad Nacional Mayor de San Marcos, Museo de Historia Natural
               "Javier Prado", Avenida Arenales 11434, Lima, Peru.
MHNM   Museo de Historia Natural de Montevideo, Enc. Herpetología, Casilla de
               Correo 399, Montevideo, Uruguay.
MLS   Museo del Instituto de La Salle, Apartado Aéreo 27389, Calle 11, No. 1-69,
               Bogotá, Colombia.
MLU   Martin-Luther-Universität, Zoologisches Institut, Domplatz 4, 4020 Halle,
               German Democratic Republic.
MMK   McGregor Museum, P.O. Box 316, Kimberley 8300, Cape Province, South
               Africa.
MMUS   University of Sydney, Macleay Museum, Sydney, New South Wales 2006,
               Australia.
MN   Universidade Federal de Rio de Janeiro, Museu Nacional do Rio de
               Janeiro, Quinta da Boa Vista, s/no., 20.942 Rio de Janeiro, Brazil.
MNCN   Museo Nacional de Ciencias Naturales, Paseo de la Castellana 84, Madrid
               64, Spain.
MNH   Természettudományi Múzeum, Baross u. 13 24, P.O.B. 37, 1088 Budapest,
               Hungary. [Sometimes referred to as Musei Nacionalis Hungarici.]

MNHNP   Museum National d'Histoire Naturelle, Laboratoire des Amphibiens et Reptiles, 25 Rue Cuvier, 75005 Paris, France.

MRGS   Museu do Rio Grande do Sul, C.P. 1188, 90.000 Pôrto Alegre, Rio Grande do Sul, Brazil.

MRHN   Institut Royal des Sciences Naturelles de Belgique, 31 Rue Vautier, 1040 Bruxelles, Belgium.

MSNG   Museo Civico di Storia Naturale di Genova "Giacomo Doria", Via Brigata Liguria 9, 16121 Genova, Italy.

MSNM   Museo Civico di Storia Naturale di Milano, Corso Venezia 55, 20121 Milano, Italy.

MSNT   Museo e Istituto di Zoologia Sistematica, Università di Torino, Via Giovanni Giolitti 34, 10123 Torino, Italy.

MTKD   Staatliches Museum für Tierkunde, Augustusstrasse 2, 801 Dresden, German Democratic Republic.

MUP   Universidade do Pôrto, Museu do Historia Natural, Pôrto, Portugal.

MVZ   University of California, Museum of Vertebrate Zoology, Berkeley, California 94720, USA.

MZB   Museum Zoologicum Bogoriense, Jl. Raya Juanda 3, Bogor, Java, Indonesia.

MZUF   Università di Firenze, Museo Zoologico "La Specola", Via Romana 17, 50125 Firenze, Italy.

MZUSP   Universidade de São Paulo, Museu de Zoologia, Avenida Nazareth 481, C.P. 7172, 01000 São Paulo, São Paulo, Brazil.

MZV   Instytut Zoologii, ul. Wilcza 64, 00679 Warsaw, Poland.

NHM   Naturhistorisches Museum, Bernastrasse 15, 3005 Bern, Switzerland.

NHMB   Naturhistorisches Museum, Augustinergasse 2, 4001 Basel, Switzerland.

NHMG   Naturhistoriska Museet, Box 11049, Slottskogen, 40030 Göteborg, Sweden.

NHMW   Naturhistorisches Museum, Zoologische Abtheilung, Postfach 417, Burgring 7, 1014 Wien, Austria.

NHRM   Naturhistoriska Rijkmuseet, Section for Vertebrate Zoology, Roslagsvägen 120, Box 50007, 104 05 Stockholm 50, Sweden.

NMK   National Museum of Kenya, P.O. Box 40658, Nairobi, Kenya.

NMM   National Museum of Victoria, 285–321 Russell Street, Melbourne, Victoria 3000, Australia.

NMP   Natal Museum, Loop Street, Pietermaritzburg 3201, Natal, South Africa.

NMZB   National Museum of Zimbabwe, P.O. Box 240, Bulawayo, Zimbabwe.

NPIB   Northwest Plateau Institute of Biology, Xining, Qinghai, P. R. China.

NTNUB   National Taiwan Normal University, Department of Biology, 162 East Ho Ping Road, Sec. 1, Taipei, Taiwan 117, China.

NTUMA   National Taiwan University, 1 Roosevelt Road IV, Taipei, Taiwan 107, China.

OMNH   Osaka Museum of Natural History, Nagai Park, Higashi-sumiyoshi-ku, Osaka 546, Japan.

OSUS   Oklahoma State University, Department of Zoology, Stillwater, Oklahoma 74074, USA.

OUM   Oxford University Museum, Parks Road, Oxford, United Kingdom.

QM   Queensland Museum, Gregory Terrace, Fortitude Valley, Brisbane, Queensland 4006, Australia.

QVM   Queen Victoria Museum, Wellington Street, Launceston, Tasmania 7250, Australia.

RGMC   Musée Royal de l'Afrique Centrale, Steenweg op Leuven, 1980 Tervuren, Belgium.

RM   Zoological Reference Collection, Department of Zoology, University of Singapore, Bukit Timah Road, Singapore 10. [Formerly National Museum (formerly Raffles Museum).]

RMNH   Rijksmuseum van Natuurlijke Historie, Postbus 9517, 2300 RA Leiden, Netherlands.

SAM   South African Museum, P.O. Box 61, Cape Town 8000, Cape Province, South Africa.

SAMA   South Australia Museum, North Terrace, Adelaide, South Australia 5000, Australia.

SCN   Sociedad de Ciencias Naturales "La Salle", Apartado Postal 8150, Caracas, Venezuela.

SM   Baylor University, Strecker Museum, Waco, Texas 76703, USA.

SMF   Forschungsinstitut und Natur-Museum Senckenberg, Senckenberg-Anlage 25, 6000 Frankfurt-am-Main 1, Federal Republic of Germany.

SMK   Sarawak Museum, Jl. Tun Hj. Openg, Kuching, Sarawak, Malaysia.

SMNS   Staatliches Museum für Naturkunde, Schloss Rosenstein, 7000 Stuttgart 1, Federal Republic of Germany.

SU   Stanford University. [Now CAS-SU.]

SWIBASC   Southwest Institute of Biology. [Now CIB.]

TCWC   Texas Cooperative Wildlife Collection, Department of Wildlife Science, Texas A&M University, College Station, Texas 77843, USA.

TIU   University of Tokyo [formerly Tokyo Imperial University], Science College Museum, Hongo, Bunkyo-ku, Tokyo, Japan.

TM   Transvaal Museum, P.O. Box 413, Pretoria 0001, Transvaal, South Africa.

TNHC   Texas Memorial Museum, Texas Natural History Collection, 24th and Trinity, Austin, Texas 78705, USA.

TZM   National Science Museum [=Kokuritsu Kagaku Hakabutsukan], Hyakunin-cho, 3-23-1, Shinjuku-ku, Tokyo 160, Japan.

UAM   Universidad de los Andes, Facultad de Ciencias, Departamento de Biología, Mérida, Venezuela.

UCR   Universidad de Costa Rica, Departamento de Zoología, San José, Costa Rica.

UIMNH   University of Illinois, Museum of Natural History, Urbana, Illinois 61801, USA.

UM   Umtali Museum. [Now NMZB.]

UMKL   University of Malaya, Zoology Department, Lembah Pantai, Kuala Lumpur 22-11, Malaysia.

UMMZ   University of Michigan, Museum of Zoology, Ann Arbor, Michigan 48104, USA.

UO   University of Oklahoma, Stovall Museum, 660 Parrington, Norman, Oklahoma 73069, USA.

UP   University of Papua and New Guinea, Biology Department, University P.O. Box 4820, Port Moresby, Papua New Guinea.

UPRM   Universidad de Puerto Rico, Departamento de Biología, Mayagüez, Puerto Rico 00708, USA.

UPRP   Universidad de Puerto Rico, Departamento de Biología, Río Piedras, Puerto Rico 00931, USA.

USNM   National Museum of Natural History, Division of Amphibians and Reptiles, Washington, D.C. 20560, USA.

UTA   University of Texas at Arlington, UTA Box 19489, Department of Biological Sciences, Arlington, Texas 76019, USA.

UU   University of Utah, Department of Biology, 1400 E. 2nd South Street, Salt Lake City, Utah 84112, USA.

UZMO   Universitetet i Oslo, Zoologisk Museum, Sarsgaten 1, Oslo 5, Norway.

WAM   Western Australia Museum, Francis Street, Perth, Western Australia 6000, Australia.

WCAB   Werner C. A. Bokermann, Parque Zoológico de São Paulo, C.P. 12954, 01000 São Paulo, S.P., Brazil.

YPM   Yale University, Peabody Museum, 170 Whitney Avenue, New Haven, Connecticut 06520, USA.

YU   Yunnan University, Kunming, Yunnan, P. R. China.

ZFMK   Zoologisches Forschungsinstitut und Museum Alexander Koenig, Herpetologische Abteilung, Adenauerallee 150–164, 5300 Bonn-1, Federal Republic of Germany.

ZIHU	Hiroshima University, Zoological Institute, 1-1-89 Higashi-senda-machi, Naka-ku, Hiroshima 30, Japan.
ZIK	Ukrainian Academy of Sciences, Zoological Institute, 252.150 Kiev–30, USSR.
ZIL	Zoological Institute, USSR Academy of Sciences, Leningrad 199034, USSR.
ZIUS	Universitetes Stockholm, Zoologiska Institutionen, Box 6801, 113 86 Stockholm, Sweden.
ZIUU	Uppsala Universitet, Zoologiska Museum, Villvägen 9, Box 561, 75 122 Uppsala, Sweden.
ZIUW	Universität Wien, Zoologisches Institut, Dr.-Karl-Lueger-Ring 1, 1010 Wien, Austria.
ZMA	Universiteit van Amsterdam, Zoologisch Museum, Plantage Middenlaan 53, Amsterdam–C, Netherlands.
ZMB	Universität Humboldt, Zoologisches Museum, Invalidenstrasse 43, 1040 Berlin N-4, German Democratic Republic.
ZMH	Zoologisches Museum für Hamburg, Martin-Luther-King Platz 5, 2000 Hamburg 13, Federal Republic of Germany.
ZMLU	Lunds Universitet, Zoologiska Institutionen, Helgonavägen 3, 223 62 Lund, Sweden.
ZMM	Moscow State University, Zoological Museum, Ul. Herzena 6, 103009 Moscow K-9, USSR.
ZMUC	Universitets København, Zoologisk Museum, Universitetsparken 15, 2100 København, Denmark.
ZSI	Zoological Survey of India, 34 Chittaranjan Avenue, Calcutta 700 012, India.
ZSIM	Zoological Survey of India, Mylapore, Madras 600 004, India.
ZSM	Zoologisches Sammlung des Bayerischen Staates, Schloss Nymphenburg, 8000 München 19, Federal Republic of Germany.

Taxonomic Index

A

aaptus, Eleutherodactylus 267
abatus, Bufo 34
abbotti, Eleutherodactylus 267, 272
abditaurantius, Colostethus 87
abditus, Dendrobates 96
abei, Hynobius 563
aberae, Rana 471
aberdariensis, Rana 520
abitaguae, Caecilia 619
Abrana 472
Abrana cotti 472
abreviata, Hyla 274
abscondens, Chiropterotriton 592
abyssinica, Ptychadena 476
abyssinica, Rothschildia 227
Acanthixalus 204, 212, 227
Acanthixalus spinosus 227
acarpicus, Insuetophrynus 333
acatallelus, Eleutherodactylus 267
accraensis, Hylarthroleptis 443
accraensis, Phrynobatrachus 443
aceras, Megalophrys montana 414
aceras, Megophrys 414
acerus, Eleutherodactylus 267
achalensis, Bufo 34
achatina, Hylaplesia 385
achatina, Microhyla 368, 370, 385
achatinus, Eleutherodactylus 267
achatinus, Hylodes 267
acmonis, Eleutherodactylus 268
acreana, Hyla 123, 153
acridoides, Phrynobatrachus 443, 449
acridoides, Staurois 443
Acris 120, 157
Acris crepitans 120
Acris gryllus 120
acrochordus, Cornufer 466
acrochordus, Platymantis 466
acrolopha, Rhamphophryne 75
actites, Eleutherodactylus 268
aculeodactylus, Platymantis 466
acuminata, Hyla 158
acuminata, Ololygon 158
acuminatus, Eleutherodactylus 268
acuminatus, Ichthyophis 632
acuminatus, Phyllodytes 169
acuticeps, Hyperolius 214
acuticeps, Mantidactylus 433
acutirostris, Breviceps 355
acutirostris, Crinia 406
acutirostris, Hylarana 501
acutirostris, Hyperolius 206, 214
acutirostris, Ixalus 526, 542
acutirostris, Philautus 526
acutirostris, Phrynobatrachus 443
acutirostris, Rana albolabris 509
acutirostris, Rhacophorus 542
acutirostris, Taudactylus 406
adametzi, Hyperolius 206, 212
adelaidensis, Hyla 178
adelaidensis, Litoria 178
Adelophryne 258, 338
Adelophryne adiastola 258, 338
Adelophryne gutturosa 258

Adelotus 394
Adelotus brevis 394
adelphus, Arthroleptis 14
Adenomera 240, 242, 258, 261
Adenomera andreae 240
Adenomera bokermanni 240
Adenomera griseigularis 240, 249
Adenomera hylaedactyla 241
Adenomera lutzi 241
Adenomera marmorata 240, 241
Adenomera martinezi 241
adenopleura, Rana 479, 488
adiastola, Adelophryne 258, 338
adipoventris, Ptychohyla 172
adolfi-friderici, Arthroleptis 14
adolfifriderici, Arthroleptis 14
adspersa, Bolitoglossa 573–575, 577,
    580, 582–584
adspersus, Breviceps 355, 356
adspersus, Ixalus 526
adspersus, Philautus 526
adspersus, Pyxicephalus 477
adspersus, Spelerpes 573
adungensis, Scutiger 417
aelleni, Phrynobatrachus 449
Aelurophryne brevipes 418
Aelurophryne glandulata 418
Aelurophryne maculata 419
Aelurophryne tainingensis 421
aenea, Rana 479
aeneus, Aneides 570
aeneus, Crossodactylus 237
aeneus, Desmognathus 568
aeneus, Plethodon 570
aequatoriale, Engistoma 381
aequatoriale, Glossostoma 381
aequiplicata, Ptychadena 470
aequiplicata, Rana mascareniensis 470
aerumnalis, Mantidactylus 433
aerumnalis, Rana 433
affinis, Arthroleptis 15
affinis, Eleutherodactylus 268
affinis, Hyla 126, 166
affinis, Hylodes 268
affinis, Pelodytes 192
affinis, Phrynomantis 392
affinis, Phrynomerus 392
afghana, Polypedates 452, 453
afghanus, Amolops 453, 454
afra, Nectophryne 69
africana, Heteroglossa 441
africanus, Dimorphognathus 441
Afrixalus 204, 220
Afrixalus brachycnemis 221
Afrixalus clarkei 221
Afrixalus congicus nigeriensis 222
Afrixalus congicus paradorsalis 222
Afrixalus dorsalis 221
Afrixalus dorsalis congicus 222
Afrixalus enseticola 221
Afrixalus equatorialis 221
Afrixalus fornasinii 221
Afrixalus fulvovittatus 221, 223
Afrixalus knysnae 221
Afrixalus lacteus 222
Afrixalus laevis 222, 223

Afrixalus laevis vibekensis 222
Afrixalus leptosomus 221
Afrixalus leucostictus 222
Afrixalus lindholmi 222, 227
Afrixalus nigeriensis 222
Afrixalus orophilus 222
Afrixalus osorioi 221, 222
Afrixalus paradorsalis 222
Afrixalus pygmaeus 223
Afrixalus schneideri 223
Afrixalus spinifrons 223
Afrixalus stuhlmanni 223
Afrixalus sylvaticus 223
Afrixalus uluguruensis 222, 223
Afrixalus vittiger 221, 223
Afrixalus weidholzi 223
Afrixalus wittei 224
Afrocaecilia 625
Afrocaecilia changamwensis 625
Afrocaecilia taitana 625
Afrocaecilia uluguruensis 625
Agalychnis 197, 198
Agalychnis annae 198
Agalychnis calcarifer 198
Agalychnis callidryas 198
Agalychnis craspedopus 198
Agalychnis litodryas 198
Agalychnis moreletii 198
Agalychnis saltator 199
Agalychnis spurrelli 199
aganoposis, Lechriodus 396
agilis, Hyla 158
agilis, Ololygon 158
aglavei, Mantidactylus 433
aglavei, Rhacophorus 433
Aglyptodactylus 533
Aglyptodactylus madagascariensis 533
aguirrei, Physalaemus 250
ailaonica, Vibrissaphora 411
ailaonicum, Leptobrachium 411
akarithymus, Platymantis 466
alabamensis, Necturus 606
alagoanus, Colostethus 87
alagoanus, Phyllobates 87
albicans, Hyla 123
albiceps, Dermophis 622
albiceps, Microcaecilia 622
albifrons, Bufo 250
albifrons, Hyperolius 206
albifrons, Physalaemus 250
albilabris, Boophis 533
albilabris, Cystignathus 242
albilabris, Leptodactylus 242
albilabris, Rhacophorus 533
albipes, Eleutherodactylus 268
albiventris, Bulua 22
albiventris, Caecilia 619
albiventris, Leptodactylodon 22
albiventris, Telmatobius 343
albiventris, Telmatobius culeus 343
albofrenata, Hyla 123
albofrenata, Rana 433
albofrenatus, Hyperolius 206
albofrenatus, Mantidactylus 433
alboguttata, Hyla 123
alboguttata, Litoria 178

G

H

W

Produced in cooperation with the
World Congress of Herpetology

the
Convention on International Trade in Endangered Species
of Wild Fauna and Flora

and the
Association of Systematics Collections